New This edition is plugged in to the world of contemporary business, In other words, it features expanded coverage of and detailed attention to technology and E-business. All of the following discussions have been added to the text of *Business 6e:*

1 The Global Economy in the Twenty-First Century
Building Your Business Skills: Analyzing the Price of Doing E-Business
2 A Short History of Business in the United States: The Internet Era
5 Joseph Galli: CEO of Vertical Net
Management Skills for the Twenty-First Century: Management and Technology Skills
7 Success and Failure in Small Business: Emergence of E-Commerce
8 New Changes in the Changing Workplace: Managing Knowledge Workers
2 Identifying Products: E-Business Branding
Determining Prices: Pricing for E-Business Objectives
Pricing Strategies and Tactics: Fixed versus Dynamic Pricing for E-Business
3 Advertising Media: The Internet
Advertising Media: Virtual Advertising
Advertising to Specific Markets: Data Mining
4 The Advent of the E-Intermediary
The Boom in Electronic Retailing
A Century of Change in Retailing: Retailing to the At-Home Shopper
Customer Service Operations: Order Fulfillment and E-Customer Satisfaction
5 Focus on the Customer-Service Link: E-Commerce: The "Virtual Presence" of the Customer
6 Productivity and Quality as Competitive Tools: Investing in Innovation and Technology
7 The Expanding Scope of Information Systems
Electronic Business and Communications Technologies
New Options for Organizational Design: The Networked Enterprise
Systems for Knowledge Workers and Office Applications
Telecommunications and Networks
9 The Changing Money and Banking System: The Impact of Electronic Technologies
0 The "Old" Economy versus the "New": What's a "Blue Chip" Now?

New With this edition we introduce a brand-new video library. Each chapter now concludes with an engaging video exercise that puts concepts into real business contexts. Each exercise asks students to analyze a real-world situation and to perform specific activities through discussion questions and follow-up material. All of the following cases were developed specifically for *Business 6e:*

1 Factors to Consider: Lands' End
2 Doing Business Privately: Amy's Ice Creams
3 Entering the Global Marketplace: Lands' End and Yahoo!
4 Catering to Serious Users: Patagonia
5 The Management Picture: Quick Takes Video (I)
6 The Management Picture: Quick Takes Video (II)
7 Toying with the Internet: Computer-Friendly Stuff
8 Channeling Human Resources: Showtime
9 Setting the Gold Standard: Ritz-Carlton
0 Working Out a Package: UPS and the Teamsters
1 Niche Noshing: Terra Chips
12 Keeping the Brand Healthy: Doc Martens
13 Promoting White Moustaches: The "Got Milk?" Campaign
14 Supplying the Basic Food Groups: Hain Foods
15 Tumbling Some Processes: Whirlpool
16 Making Room for Quality: Marriott
17 Whatever Ties Us Must Converge
18 Accounting for a Few Billion Sold: McDonald's
19 The World's Lenders: The World Bank and the IMF
20 Information Pays Off: Anatomy of a Stock Trade
21 How Financial Options Stack Up: IHOP

Sixth Edition

Business

Ricky W. Griffin
Texas A&M University

Ronald J. Ebert
University of Missouri–Columbia

Prentice Hall
Upper Saddle River, New Jersey 07458

Library of Congress Catalog-in-Publication Data

Griffin, Ricky W.
Business / Ricky W. Griffin, Ronald J. Ebert.—6th ed.
p. cm.
Includes bibliographical references and index.
ISBN 0-13-090463-5
1. Industrial management—United States. 2. Business enterprises—United States. I. Ebert, Ronald J. II. Title.

HD70.U5 G73 2002
658—dc21 00-068444

VP/Editorial Director: Jim Boyd
Assistant Editor: Jennifer Surich
Editorial Assistant: Virginia Sheridan
Developmental Editor: Ron Librach
Media Project Manager: Michele Faranda
Senior Marketing Manager: Debbie Clare
Managing Editor (Production): Judy Leale
Production Editor: Cindy Spreder
Permissions Coordinator: Suzanne Grappi
Associate Director, Manufacturing: Vincent Scelta
Production Manager: Arnold Vila
Art Director: Cheryl Asherman
Interior Design: Jill Little
Cover Design: Jill Little
Cover Illustration: Blair Brown
Illustrator (Interior): Precision Graphics
Assoc. Dir., Multimedia Production: Karen Goldsmith
Manager, Multimedia Production: Christy Mahon
Page Formatter II: Ashley Scattergood
Composition: Carlisle Communications
Full-Service Project Management: Lynn Steines, Carlisle Communications
Printer/Binder: R. R. Donnelley & Sons

Credits and acknowledgments borrowed from other sources and reproduced, with permission, in this textbook begin on page N-14.

10 9 8 7 6 5
ISBN 0-13-090463-5

To Dustin

I am so proud of you.
— (R.W.G.)

For Vi

From cruelty and hatred,
the hope for new life,
the joy of love,
and the remembering
of it all.
— (R.J.E.)

Overview

Contents

From the Authors Ricky Griffin and Ron Ebert

At about the time we sat down to assemble this preface, we both kept seeing a TV ad promoting "Financial Knowledge for the New Economy" as the number-one ingredient for business success. Generally speaking, you can't argue with the premise, but we feel that, especially for introductory business students, "knowledge for the new economy" has to go beyond the "financials." Students need to know something about every aspect of business and the environment in which business prospers. And make no mistake about it: We have prosperity because—or maybe despite the fact that—the rules of the game are constantly changing throughout the business environment and across the entire range of business practices. There are new forces at work. Nowadays, companies come together on short notice for collaborative projects and then, just as quickly, return to their original shapes as separate (and often competing) entities. Employees and companies share new ideas about work—about when and where it takes place, about how it gets done, about who determines roles and activities in the workplace. With communications technologies having shattered the barriers of physical distance, tight-knit teams with members positioned around the world share information just as effectively as groups huddled together in the same room.

In nearly every aspect of business today, from relationships with customers and suppliers to employees and stockholders, there are new ways of doing things, and a lot of them are surpassing traditional business practices, with surprising speed and often with better competitive results. Along with new ways come a host of unique legal and ethical (and financial) issues to challenge the creativity and judgment of people who do business. For all of these reasons we, as authors and teachers, felt a certain urgency when it became obvious that, in revising ***Business*** for its sixth edition, we had to capture the flavor and convey the excitement of the new economy in all of its rapidly evolving practices.

Ricky Griffin
Ron Ebert

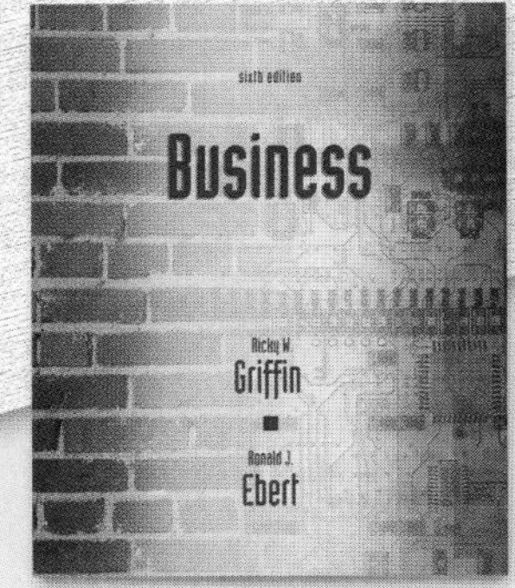

sixth edition
Business
Ricky W.
Griffin
Ronald J.
Ebert

Griffin Ebert 6e

Business 6e

6e

Rewired for E-Business & E-Commerce

Griffin/Ebert, ***Business,* Sixth Edition** explores the full range of the new economy, fron the raft of start-up dot-coms to the fleet of traditional flagship companies, with a number o innovative features.

New! It's a Wired World

Chapter 3 Understanding the Global Context of Business / 11

It's a WiredWorld

• Nokia Puts the Finishing Touches on a Telecommunications Giant

In each chapter, boxes titled **"It's a Wired World"** offer concise, concrete descriptions of the steps that established businesses are taking to keep pace with both new and old competitors in the e-business environment. Each box describes the situation faced by a real firm or industry, showing how the challenges of a business function is being met by the introduction of technology.

New! Life Cycle of an e-Business

In every chapter a box titled **"Life Cycle of an e-Business"** features Garden.com, an innovative e-business that won awards for its innovations but fell victim to the risky nature of such Internet ventures. There are some important lessons to be learned: namely, that the business world is fraught with risk, threats, and the potential for failure.

Chapter 3 Understanding the Global Context of Business / 83

Life Cycle of an e-Business

Setting Out Roots Across Borders

One of the most significant things about the Internet from a business standpoint is its amazing ability to reach and connect people no matter where they are. Some would-be web entrepreneurs envision buying and selling around the world from a single location. Unfortunately, it's not always that easy. For one thing, when a business is literally thinking in terms of shipping products across national boundaries, numerous issues must be addressed.

The managers at Garden.com quickly became all too familiar with the constraints that national boundaries can impose on any business. Agricultural products—growing plants, seeds, chemicals, and the like—are among the most highly regulated in the world. In most cases, it's actually illegal to transport them from one country to another. As a result, virtually all of Garden.com's business was conducted within the boundaries of the continental United States.

But does this mean that a firm like Garden.com is forever confined to its home country? By no means. In fact, Garden.com had every intention of entering the European market at the earliest possible opportunity. As early as 1999, there were already a few upstart e-businesses in Europe attempting to pattern themselves after Garden.com. One option the company considered, therefore, was identifying one of the most promising of these firms and buying it outright. Another option was launching its own business in Europe. Given the complexities of doing business in the European Union, however, the firm had a clear preference for buying an existing operation—if it could have found just the right one and acquired it for just the right price.

Griffin Ebert 6e

Face-to-Face Business Connections...

Like its predecessors, the sixth edition of **Business** focuses on people in business and the decisions they make on a daily basis. We have taken this commitment to new levels in an effort to provide more **personal**–and, at the same time, more **practical**–access to people who do business by letting students ask them questions about cutting-edge business issues and practices.

New! Two Part Vignettes

To engage students in real-life business situations, each chapter now opens with a vignette describing how an individual or organization has responded to an opportunity or challenge related to the topic of the chapter. The story is then revisited at the end of the chapter, where it concludes with more information and follow-up questions tailored to help students analyze the case, either on their own or in class as a group activity.

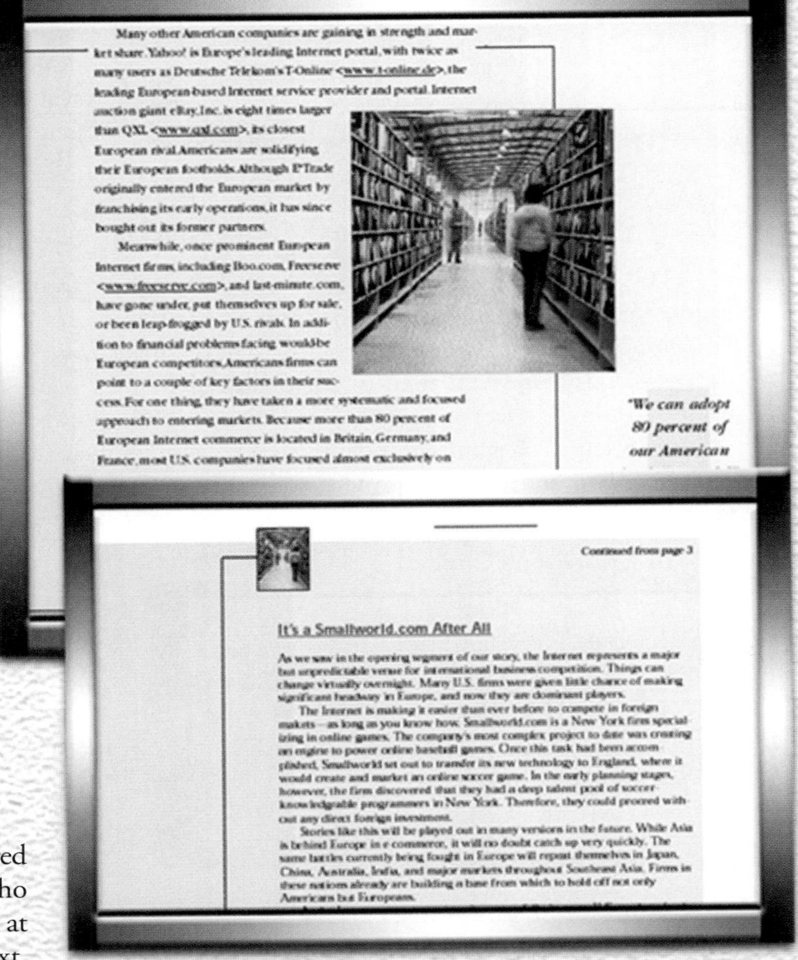

Many other American companies are gaining in strength and market share. Yahoo! is Europe's leading Internet portal, with twice as many users as Deutsche Telekom's T-Online <www.t-online.de>, the leading European-based Internet service provider and portal. Internet auction giant eBay, Inc. is eight times larger than QXL <www.qxl.com>, its closest European rival. Americans are solidifying their European footholds. Although E*Trade originally entered the European market by franchising its early operations, it has since bought out its former partners.

Meanwhile, once prominent European Internet firms, including Boo.com, Freeserve <www.freeserve.com>, and last-minute.com, have gone under, put themselves up for sale, or been leap-frogged by U.S. rivals. In addition to financial problems facing would-be European competitors, Americans firms can point to a couple of key factors in their success. For one thing, they have taken a more systematic and focused approach to entering markets. Because more than 80 percent of European Internet commerce is located in Britain, Germany, and France, most U.S. companies have focused almost exclusively on

"We can adopt 80 percent of our American

Continued from page 3

It's a Smallworld.com After All

As we saw in the opening segment of our story, the Internet represents a major but unpredictable venue for international business competition. Things can change virtually overnight. Many U.S. firms were given little chance of making significant headway in Europe, and now they are dominant players.

The Internet is making it easier than ever before to compete in foreign markets—as long as you know how. Smallworld.com is a New York firm specializing in online games. The company's most complex project to date was creating an engine to power online baseball games. Once this task had been accomplished, Smallworld set out to transfer its new technology to England, where it would create and market an online soccer game. In the early planning stages, however, the firm discovered that they had a deep talent pool of soccer-knowledgable programmers in New York. Therefore, they could proceed without any direct foreign investment.

Stories like this will be played out in many versions in the future. While Asia is behind Europe in e-commerce, it will no doubt catch up very quickly. The same battles currently being fought in Europe will repeat themselves in Japan, China, Australia, India, and major markets throughout Southeast Asia. Firms in these nations already are building a base from which to hold off not only Americans but Europeans.

New! Student Q&A's

Each chapter contains three student questions–questions that real students have asked about the facts and ideas presented in the chapter. Each question is revisited on a free student CD-ROM where it is answered by a panel of business professionals–real people who not only work in different businesses but who do so at different levels of experience. Throughout the text, questions are indicated by a CD-ROM icon.

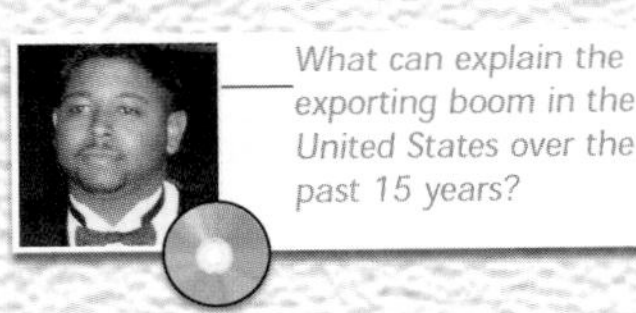
What can explain the exporting boom in the United States over the past 15 years?

Free! Student CD-ROM

This FREE student CD-ROM provides students with a first-hand look at real business issues. In each chapter, a cross section of business professionals at a variety of career stages respond to a wide-range of practical student questions. Their responses reflect their own real-life experiences and apply them to chapter content in a way that brings concepts to life and gives students a unique perspective on contemporary business.

Business 6e

Exciting End-of-Chapter Activities...

VIDEO EXERCISE

ENTERING THE GLOBAL MARKETPLACE: LANDS' END AND YAHOO!

Learning Objectives

The purpose of this video exercise is to help you

1. Understand the different reasons businesses undertake international expansion.
2. Identify the financial and marketing issues involved in selling products and services internationally.
3. Recognize the influence of culture on business decisions made by international firms.

BACKGROUND INFORMATION

- Yahoo! <www.yahoo.com> is an Internet search engine headquartered in Santa Clara, California. Its principal product is an ad-supported Internet directory that links users to millions of Web pages on demand. Yahoo! leads the field in volume of traffic (over 95 million pages viewed each day) and now has offices in Europe, Asia, and Canada, as well as a global network of 22 world properties.
- Lands' End <www.landsend.com> began in 1963 by selling sailing equipment through a catalog. Today the publicly owned firm is one of the largest apparel brands in the United States,

New! Video Exercises.

We're proud to introduce a brand-new video library for the sixth edition of ***Business!*** Each chapter now concludes with an engaging Video Exercise that puts chapter concepts into a dramatic real business context. Each video exercise asks students to analyze a real company and perform specific activities with follow-up discussion questions and assignment material.

New! Crafting Your Business Plan Exercises.

Chapter-ending exercises apply chapter material to the task of developing a business plan. Students are first encouraged to examine sample plans from a variety of businesses and then to personalize their own plans using Windows-based *Business Plan Pro* 4.0. This intuitive software offers the beginning student a step-by-step approach to understanding and building professional business plans. With version 4.0, planners can also publish to a protected Internet site, where readers can access all or part of posted plans. The educational version of the best-selling Business Plan Pro Software can be packaged with the text for $10.00.

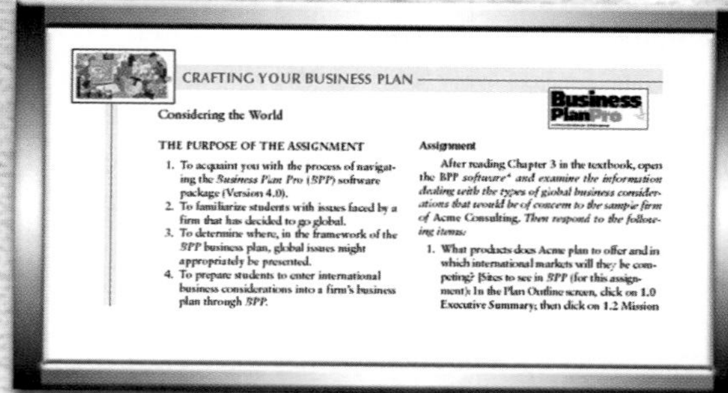

CRAFTING YOUR BUSINESS PLAN

Business Plan Pro

Considering the World

THE PURPOSE OF THE ASSIGNMENT

1. To acquaint you with the process of navigating the *Business Plan Pro* (*BPP*) software package (Version 4.0).
2. To familiarize students with issues faced by a firm that has decided to go global.
3. To determine where, in the framework of the *BPP* business plan, global issues might appropriately be presented.
4. To prepare students to enter international business considerations into a firm's business plan through *BPP*.

Assignment

After reading Chapter 3 in the textbook, open the BPP *software* and examine the information dealing with the types of global business considerations that would be of concern to the sample firm of* Acme Consulting. *Then respond to the following items:*

1. What products does Acme plan to offer and in which international markets will they be competing? [Sites to see in *BPP* (for this assignment): In the Plan Outline screen, click on 1.0 Executive Summary; then click on 1.2 Mission

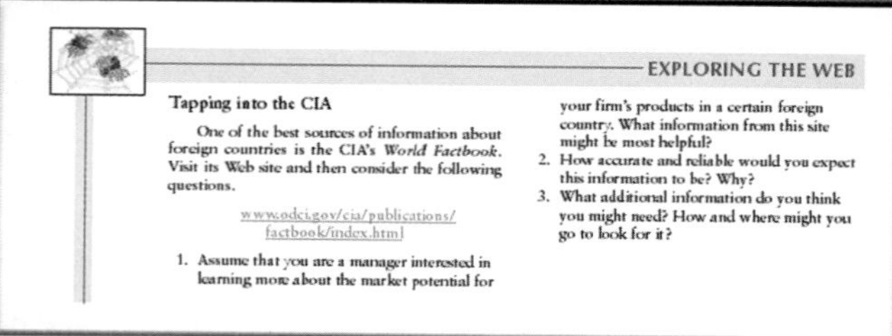

EXPLORING THE WEB

Tapping into the CIA

One of the best sources of information about foreign countries is the CIA's *World Factbook*. Visit its Web site and then consider the following questions.

www.odci.gov/cia/publications/factbook/index.html

1. Assume that you are a manager interested in learning more about the market potential for your firm's products in a certain foreign country. What information from this site might be most helpful?
2. How accurate and reliable would you expect this information to be? Why?
3. What additional information do you think you might need? How and where might you go to look for it?

New! Exploring the Web Exercises.

In these exercises, students are directed to the Internet and given hands-on activities designed to enhance their understanding of important chapter topics.

Fully *Updated!* Building Your Business Skills.

These popular end-of-chapter exercises consist of activities that allow students to apply their knowledge and critical-thinking skills to an extended problem drawn from a wide range of realistic business experiences. Each of these exercises has been specifically designed to satisfy the general criteria laid out in the Secretary of Labor's Commission of Achieving Necessary Skills (SCANS) requirements.

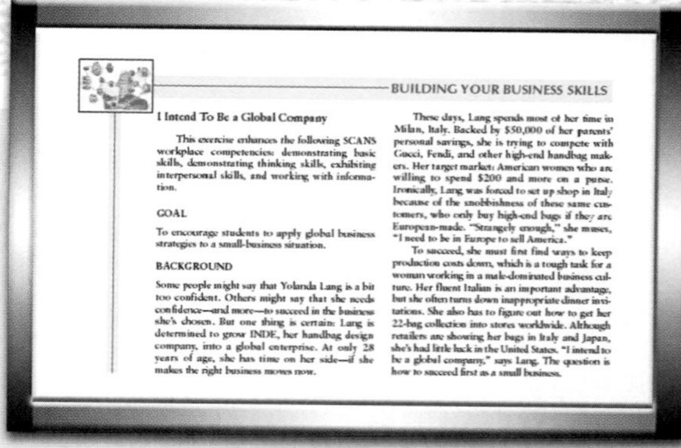

BUILDING YOUR BUSINESS SKILLS

I Intend To Be a Global Company

This exercise enhances the following SCANS workplace competencies: demonstrating basic skills, demonstrating thinking skills, exhibiting interpersonal skills, and working with information.

GOAL

To encourage students to apply global business strategies to a small-business situation.

BACKGROUND

Some people might say that Yolanda Lang is a bit too confident. Others might say that she needs confidence—and more—to succeed in the business she's chosen. But one thing is certain: Lang is determined to grow INDE, her handbag design company, into a global enterprise. At only 28 years of age, she has time on her side—if she makes the right business moves now.

These days, Lang spends most of her time in Milan, Italy. Backed by $50,000 of her parents' personal savings, she is trying to compete with Gucci, Fendi, and other high-end handbag makers. Her target market: American women who are willing to spend $200 and more on a purse. Ironically, Lang was forced to set up shop in Italy because of the snobbishness of these same customers, who only buy high-end bags if they are European-made. "Strangely enough," she muses, "I need to be in Europe to sell America."

To succeed, she must first find ways to keep production costs down, which is a tough task for a woman working in a male-dominated business culture. Her fluent Italian is an important advantage, but she often turns down inappropriate dinner invitations. She also has to figure out how to get her 22-bag collection into stores worldwide. Although retailers are showing her bags in Italy and Japan, she's had little luck in the United States. "I intend to be a global company," says Lang. The question is how to succeed first as a small business.

Griffin Ebert

Free Companion Website... myPHLIP

Prentice Hall's New myPHLIP Companion Web Site
www.prenhall.com/griffin

This powerful Prentice Hall Web site offers **chapter-specific current events, Internet exercises, and downloadable supplements**. The site also includes an **online study guide** containing true/false, multiple-choice, and essay questions.

Special Features:

- **Individual homepages** for students and faculty. These pages provide easy, one-click navigation to our vast, dynamic database of online teaching and learning resources. Faculty and students can organize online resources for all of their classes on this single, customizable homepage.
- **A powerful new point-and-click syllabus-creation tool** that faculty can use for each course and section. Teachers can also annotate and link each resource on myPHLIP to their syllabi. They can even upload their own personal resources to our site and make them available to students via personalized syllabi. Students and faculty can easily communicate with one another via e-mail, either directly or through custom homepages.
- **Faculty can post messages set to appear automatically** on every student homepage for any length of time.
- **Students can view each course syllabus** with a SmartCalendar showing the daily activities for every course that he or she is taking.
- **Students and faculty can leave notes for themselves on their own homepages**. Messages are stored in personal accounts and can be retrieved at any time.

Prentice Hall Online Courses We make it easy for you!

Now you have the freedom to personalize your own online course materials. Prentice Hall Business Publishing provides the content and support you need to create and manage your own online course materials with WebCT, Blackboard, and CourseCompass.

WebCT www.prenhall.com/webct

Gold Level Customer Support, available exclusively to adopters of Prentice Hall courses, is awarded free-of-charge upon adoption and provides you with priority assistance, training discounts, and dedicated technical support from WebCT.

Blackboard www.prenhall.com/blackboard

Take your courses to new heights in student interaction and learning. Prentice Hall's class-tested online course content is now available with Blackboard's products and easy-to-use interface.

CourseCompass www.coursecompass.com

CourseCompass ™ is a dynamic, interactive online course management tool powered by Blackboard. This exciting product allows you to teach with market-leading Pearson Education content in an easy-to-use customizable format.

6e

Unsurpassed Instructor & Student Supplements

New! Fully Integrated Instructor's Resource Manual

In the revision, we've focused our efforts on creating a new fully integrated Instructor's Resource Manual that's chock-full of time-saving resources to make prepping this course a snap. Our goal is to **simplify your life** by offering a fully comprehensive yet easy-to-use resource tool. Each chapter of the Instructor's Resource Manual contains:

- *Changes to the new edition*
- *Brief chapter outline and summaries*
- *Detailed lecture outlines customized for both PowerPoint users and acetate users, featuring traditional lecture notes and an all new feature "Hero" Notes.*
- *Sample syllabi*
- *Pop quizzes for every chapter*
- *Answers to all end-of-chapter questions, problems, and assignments*
- *A detailed Video Guide with answers to video exercise questions*
- *Suggested classroom exercises, projects, and supplemental cases*
- *Useful Web sites*

With the integrated Instructor's Resource Manual, you can get up to speed quickly and ensure that all concepts, features, and exercises hang together in your presentation of the course. This manual is **the ultimate teaching companion!**

New! Test Item File

This new **two-volume Test Item File** contains **over 4,000 questions**, all of which have been carefully checked for accuracy and quality. This comprehensive set consists of multiple-choice, true/false, and essay questions. Each test question is ranked by level of difficulty (easy, moderate, or difficult) and contains section and learning objective references to allow the instructor a quick and easy way to balance the level of their exams or quizzes. In addition, we've included a special section that contains test questions for all boxed features and vignettes in each chapter. If that's not enough, this test item file features **two pre-created sample tests** for every part plus a mid-term and final exam for immediate use or distribution—an arrangement that provides both maximum flexibility and ease of use.

New! Prentice Hall's Computerized Test Manager 4.2-ESATEST 2000 *(Windows Version)*

Our user-friendly software allows you to generate error-free tests quickly and easily by previewing questions individually on the screen and then selecting randomly, by query, or by number. The Computerized Test Manager allows you to generate random tests with our extensive bank of questions. You can also edit our questions/answers and even add some of your own. You can create an exam, administer it traditionally or online, and analyze your success with the simple click of the mouse. The newest version of our Computerized Test Manager, **ESATEST 2000**, has been improved to provide users with a vast array of new options. Enhancements now allow you to:

- *Import Test Questions from Word Processors*
- *Import/Export Tests*
- *Correlate Charts*
- *Select by Query*
- *Select by Review*
- *Select by Criteria*
- *Archive Database Capability*
- *Analyze Test Bank Items*
- *Export Grades to Excel*
- *Weight Grades*
- *Record Grades in a New Spreadsheet Format and Create a Grade Database*
- *Control Online Testing*

Telephone Test Preparation. For those instructors who prefer not to use the Computerized Test Item File, Prentice Hall provides a special 800 call-in service for ease of use. All you need to do is call the **800 Testing Help Desk** to have a customized test created. The test can then be delivered by e-mail, U.S. mail, or overnight carrier.

Griffin Ebert 6e

New! PowerPoint Slides

Enhance your classroom presentations with this well-developed PowerPoint presentation set. **More than 500 text-specific PowerPoints** highlight fundamental concepts by integrating key graphs, figures, and illustrations from the text. PowerPoint slides come **complete with lecture notes**, which are available in the Instructor's Resource Manual or on the Instructor's Resource CD. Free to adopters, PowerPoints are available on CD or can be downloaded from the Instructor's Resource Web site at **www.prenhall.com/griffin**.

New! Unique Overhead Transparencies

This extensive set of over **300 full-color overhead transparencies** is not a derivative of the PowerPoint presentation. These overheads put an additional spin on basic and important concepts by focusing on the main points of the chapter with illustrations and figures. Overhead transparencies come **complete with lecture notes**, available either in the Instructor's Resource Manual or on the Instructor's Resource CD.

New! Custom Video Library

We're proud to introduce a **brand-new video library** with ***Business,* Sixth Edition**. Each chapter now concludes with an engaging video exercise that puts concepts into real business contexts. Each exercise asks students to analyze a real-world situation and to perform specific activities through discussion questions and follow-up exercises. We provide a variety of company and business situations to simulate a diverse business climate. Exercises are designed as conversation starters to bring concepts to life and are tied to **critical-thinking exercises** and **class-activity guidelines contained in the text**. A variety of follow-up exercises are provided to further in-class discussion or furnish homework assignments.

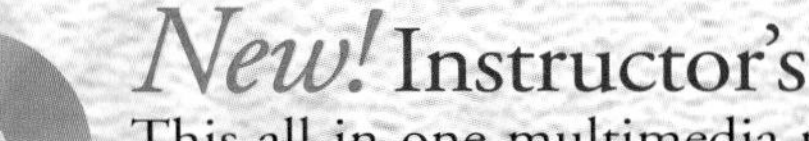

New! Instructor's Resource CD-ROM

This all-in-one multimedia product is an invaluable asset for professors who prefer to work with electronic files rather than traditional print supplements. This CD-ROM contains the Instructor's Resource Manual, PowerPoints, Test Item File, and Prentice Hall Test Manager.

New! Student Study Guide

The Student Study Guide reinforces key concepts and tests student comprehension. For each chapter, the Guide includes learning objectives, questions (true/false, multiple-choice, short-answer, essay, and critical-thinking), instructional games matching terms and definitions, word scramble, and brain teaser, plus study skills/study tips for students.

New! E-Business Online Supplement: E-Business

This **unique online supplement to** is keyed to the five parts of ***Business,* Sixth Edition** and includes learning objectives, real-world examples, discussion questions, group activities, and Internet exercises. In-depth coverage of the latest trends and concepts in e-commerce includes "Internet Privacy and Security," "Internet Davids vs. Goliaths," "Managing the Virtual Organization," "Virtual Training and Development," "Hot Online Pricing Strategies," "Internet IPOs," "IT and Communication in the Internet Age," "Emerging Legal Issues in E-Commerce," and "Preparing for a Career in E-Commerce."

New! E-Biz: Prentice Hall Guide to E-Business and E-Commerce

In the new world of business, you'll run into e-commerce no matter what direction you turn. Take your students behind the scenes to explore the dynamic world of e-business with this new value-pack supplement. This unique print supplement provides an overview of the basic concepts of e-business and e-commerce, an introduction to popular search sites, a wide range of business-related sites and addresses, and an up-to-the minute look at online job searches and career sites. The **Web component** of this supplement provides updated coverage of the latest trends, challenges, and hot concepts in e-commerce, plus additional interactive exercises. Go to **www.prenhall.com/ebiz**. This great supplement can be value-packaged with the text for free.

New! Business Plan Pro Software

Business PlanPro 4.0 (BPP) provides students with a step-by-step approach to creating a comprehensive business plan. The software is designed to stimulate student thinking about the many tasks and decisions that go into planning and running a business. Preformatted report templates, charts, and tables do the mechanics so that students can focus on the thinking. With version 4.0, planners can also publish to a protected Internet site, where readers can access all or part of posted plans. Business Plan Pro can be packaged with the textbook for a nominal fee of $10.

Beginning Your Career Search

This concise book by James S. O'Rourke IV offers some straightforward, practical advice on how to write a résumé, where and how to find company information, how to conduct yourself during an interview, and tips on the interview process. Included are copies of sample introductory, cover, follow-up, and thank-you letters. This is a free value pack item.

Self-Assessment Library

Organized according to individual, group, and organizational needs, the Self-Assessment Library features self-assessment tools designed to give students insight into their skills, abilities, and interests. The Self-Assessment Library CD is available for $5.00.

MASTERING m B BUSINESS

Introducing the Mastering Business Series and Mastering Business Essentials

What Is The *Mastering Business* Series?

It's **the most extensive cross-platform, multimedia business education resource in the world**–a "case study on steroids." *Mastering Business* is **the first fully integrated series of video–enhanced interactive exercises that span the core business education curriculum**. Modules span the business curriculum with individual episodes in each of seven disciplines-plus Business Essentials. Each episode uses a **multilayered instructional design**. Designed to supplement and extend the undergraduate business education experience, Mastering Business explores real-world situations in a way that makes key theories and concepts practical tools in the study of business.

How Does *Mastering Business* Work?

Every module of Mastering Business allows students to view each problem or decision **in a format that closely mimics actual real-world scenarios**:

- Set in an e-business called CanGo, every episode includes three separate video segments. The first clip introduces the episode topics by identifying a current problem or issue at CanGo and then proceeds to a series of multilayered exercises including multiple-choice, true/false, fill-in, matching, ranking-choices, and one- or two-sentence written-answer formats.
- Students then watch a second video clip that presents one of the possible solutions to CanGo's challenge. As in everyday business life, the resolution may be either successful or unsuccessful or even be left unresolved. Students are encouraged to respond to the situation, either individually or in teams.
- Finally, students watch the case video-a final segment followed by discussion questions. The exercise now casts episode-related topics in a new situation with questions that probe related issues.

What Is Mastering Business Essentials?

It's **a specially designed module of *Mastering Business*,** Prentice Hall's brand-new eight-discipline series of CD-ROM-based interactive exercises. Mastering Business Essentials has been **specifically developed to introduce students to the core concepts–the essentials–of the business education curriculum.**

What's Special about Mastering Business Essentials?

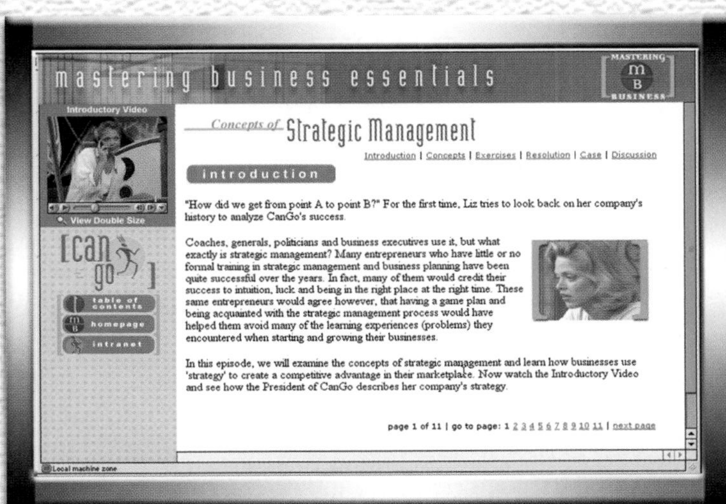

The Mastering Business Essentials module gives students an introduction to **the wide range of concerns facing businesses today**. These videos and exercises help students apply the lessons of the classroom and the textbook to **all the key areas of business.** At the fictional online entertainment company CanGo, they will encounter **the same problems as the CEO and the directors of marketing, finance, accounting, human resources, and operations.** Because all of the videos in Mastering Business Essentials visit the same team of managers and their staffs, students will see how the concerns of one department affect the efforts of the others.

The following topics are covered:

- The Goal of the Firm and Social Responsibility
- The Economic Way of Thinking
- Ethical Issues
- Concepts of Strategic Management
- Working in Groups and Teams
- Work Motivation
- Leadership
- Marketing Concepts/Strategy
- Understanding Consumer Behavior
- Strategy and Operations
- Managerial Accounting and Cost Behavior
- Raising Capital

Mastering Business Essentials can be shrinkwrapped to this textbook for an additional $5.00. The comprehensive cross-disciplinary Mastering Business Series (Strategy, Management, Accounting, Finance, Economics, Marketing, and Operations Management) can also be purchased separately. Contact your local Prentice Hall representative for details.

FINANCIAL TIMES
World business newspaper.

New Subscription offer with the *Financial Times!*

We are pleased to announce our new partnership with the Financial Times to offer a 15-week print subscription for $10 with our Introduction to Business texts. Participating professors will qualify for a complimentary one-year personal subscription to the *Financial Times.* The Prentice Hall textbook + subscription package will contain a 16-page, full-color *Financial Times* Student Guide, shrink-wrapped to the textbook. Bound inside the Student Guide will be a postcard which entitles the student to claim a pre-paid 15-week subscription to the Financial Times. The student mails in the reply card and the subscription should begin in 5 to 7 business days of receipt of the card.

Acknowledgments

Although only two names appear on the cover of this book, we could never have completed the sixth edition without the assistance of many fine individuals. Everyone who worked on the book was committed to making it the best that it could be. Quality and closeness to the customer are things that we read a lot about today. Both we and the people who worked with us took these concepts to heart in this book and made quality our watchword by listening to our users and trying to provide what they want.

First, we would like to thank all the professionals who took time from their busy schedules to review materials for *Business:*

Ed Blevins
DeVry Institute of Technology

Mary Jo Boehms
Jackson State Community College

Karen Collins
Lehigh University

Dr. Shiv Gupta
University of Findlay

James H. Kennedy
Angelina College

Robert Markus
Babson College

Bronna McNeeley
Midwestern State University

William Morrison
San Jose State

Christopher Rogers
Miami-Dade Community College

Phyllis T. Shafer
Brookdale Community College

Lynne Spellman White
Trinity Christian College

JoAnn Wiggins
Walla Walla College

A number of other professionals also made substantive contributions to the text, ranging from draft material on specialized topics to suggested resource materials to proposals for cases and examples. In particular, we are greatly indebted to Elisa Adams and Judy Block for their inventive and indefatigable contributions in their capacity as professional writers and researchers.

The supplements package for *Business,* Sixth Edition, also benefited from the able contributions of several individuals, all under the direction of Jennifer Surich at Prentice Hall. We would like to thank these people for developing the finest set of instructional and learning materials for this field.

Meanwhile, a superb team of professionals at Prentice Hall made this book a pleasure to write. Authors often get the credit when a book is successful, but the success of this book must be shared with an outstanding group of people in New Jersey. Our development editor, Ron Librach, has been a true product champion and has improved both the book and the package in more ways than we can list. Cindy Spreder, the production editor, also made many truly outstanding contributions to the project.

We also want to acknowledge the contributions of the entire team at Prentice Hall Business Publishing, including James Boyd, editorial director; Annie Todd, director of marketing; Steve Deitmer, director of development; Debbie Clare, marketing manager; Virginia Sheridan, editorial assistant; Jennifer Surich, assistant editor; Judy Leale, managing editor; Arnold Vila, production manager; Cheryl Asherman, art director; Melinda Lee Reo, photo research supervisor; Melinda Alexander, photo researcher; Kay Dellosa, image permission supervisor; and Zina Arabia, image coordinator.

Our colleagues at Texas A&M University and the University of Missouri–Columbia also deserve recognition. Each of us has the good fortune to be a part of a community of scholars who enrich our lives and challenge our ideas. Without their intellectual stimulation and support, our work would suffer greatly. Phyllis Wasburn, Dr. Griffin's staff assistant, deserves special mention of the myriad contributions she has made to this project as well.

Finally, our families. We take pride in the accomplishments of our wives, Glenda and Mary, and draw strength from the knowledge that they are there for us to lean on. And we take joy from our children, Ashley, Dustin, Matt, and Kristen. Sometimes in the late hours when we're ready for sleep but have to get one or two more pages written, looking a your pictures keeps us going. Thanks to all of you for making us what we are.

Ricky W. Griffin
Ronald J. Ebert

Chapter 1

Understanding the U.S. Business System

After reading this chapter, you should be able to:

1. ***Define*** the nature of U.S. *business* and identify its main goals.

2. ***Describe*** different types of global *economic systems* according to the means by which they control the *factors of production* through *input and output markets.*

3. ***Show*** how *demand* and *supply* affect resource distribution in the United States.

4. ***Identify*** the elements of *private enterprise* and explain the various *degrees of competition* in the U.S. economic system.

5. ***Explain*** the criteria for evaluating the success of an economic system in meeting its goals and show how the federal government attempts to manage the U.S. economy.

6. ***Discuss*** the current economic picture in the United States and summarize expert opinions about its future.

What's Hot on the Cyberspace Hit List

Electronic commerce is a major part of every industry and marketplace these days. So-called e-businesses such as Amazon.com, America Online, and eBay are all less than 10 years old but have already become household names and major players in the transformation of the United States into an information-based economy. Faced with this rapid and dynamic change, staid older businesses that want to remain vital and effective have found it necessary to refocus their own operations to encompass the Internet and electronic commerce. Some, such as IBM and Disney, have made successful transitions while others have faltered.

The music industry is an especially interesting arena for e-commerce competition—one in which both newcomers and established firms continue to struggle to find just the right approach to integrating the Internet into their operations. Giants like Universal Music Group <**www.universalmusic.com**>, Warner Music Group <**www.timewarner.com/corp/about/music/index.html**>, Sony Music <**www.sonymusic.com**>, BMG Entertainment <**www.bmgentertainment.com**>, and EMI <**www.emi.com**> have long dominated the recorded-music business. However, they are facing new and complex challenges as the Internet plays an increasingly significant role in their marketplace. New e-businesses pose both serious threats and significant opportunities for these media giants.

Consider the case of David Goldberg and Launch Media. When Goldberg, a music fanatic, was only 24 years old, he landed a plum job as director of new business development for Capitol Records. Goldberg was interested in extending the Capitol library of popular music, which ranged from Frank Sinatra to the Beatles, into new arenas. He wanted to promote Capitol's music products on CD-ROM games and to focus heavily on new and emerging forms of electronic media for both promoting and delivering music to consumers.

But senior executives at Capitol weren't interested. They listened politely, but they adopted few of his ideas and gave him little encouragement in his efforts to push into new products and product lines. They apparently believed that the old tried-and-true method of recording music on disks and tapes, advertising and promoting new recordings in magazines and on the radio, and then distributing them through traditional retailing channels was never going to change.

Finally, Goldberg left Capitol in frustration and created Launch Media <www.launchmedia.com>, which has quickly become one of the top five music-information sites on the Internet. NBC and Sony Music are two of the biggest investors in Goldberg's fledgling enterprise, and when the firm went public in April 1999, the value of his personal stake mushroomed to $12 million. But unlike some entrepreneurs in other industries and markets, Goldberg has never been interested in taking over the music business. What he wants to do is change it. And more and more industry experts are coming around to his point of view. "Our role," says one industry consultant who sees things Goldberg's way, "is to teach the industry to do things differently."

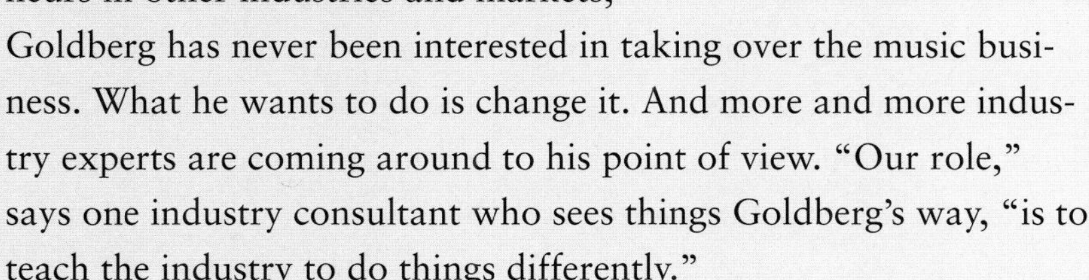

"Our role is to teach the industry to do things differently."

—Marc Schiller, CEO, Electric Artists

Some industry experts worried that Internet sites would render traditional recording companies obsolete—that consumers would simply download all the music they wanted directly from various Web sites controlled by artists or upstart Web outfits and that the recording companies would be squeezed out. But those in the know quickly realized that this isn't how things would work out. Instead, the Internet is emerging as a new catalyst for old and new music businesses alike. Web sites like launch.com are becoming platforms

Table 1.1

Plugging into Cyberspace

	Visitors in August	Revenues[1]
MTV.COM	2.2 million	$9.9 million
MP3.COM	2.0 million	$2.6 million
TUNES.COM	1.2 million	$1.4 million
UBL.COM	1.2 million	$3.7 million
LAUNCH.COM	1.1 million	$4.7 million

[1]First-half 1999, from all Web sites in the corporate family, not just the site listed.

for more and more interaction among consumers, performers, and recording labels. As you can see in Table 1.1, the five largest music-information sites on the Internet are attracting millions of visitors each month—and generating millions of dollars in revenues.

The big companies still play a vital role in all this information-related activity. For example, they still control most of the recordings, handle much of the advertising and promotion, and provide the "human contact" that remains an essential part of all entertainment enterprises. Consumers, meanwhile, can visit Web sites in the comfort of their own homes and download trial music cuts to sample music that they might want to buy. Then they can easily purchase CDs—in addition to concert tickets, posters, shirts, and other paraphernalia—directly from the same sites. Granted, performers can leverage bigger cuts of the profits, but Goldberg and others like to point out the obvious advantages of keeping everybody happy.

The challenge of building and sustaining a new business to meet changing and newly emerging customer needs is as common to small firms like Launch Media as it is to billion-dollar corporations such as Warner Music Group or Sony Music. A changing marketplace creates a need for the kind of innovative responses that have long characterized business in the United States. Such responses require vision, careful attention to quality and customer service, substantial financial commitment, internal accounting controls, and well-defined marketing strategies designed to help businesses grow over time.

These and a host of other forces provide the main themes for stories of success and failure that are told repeatedly in the annals of enterprise in the United States. As you will see in this chapter, these forces are also the key factors in the U.S. market economy. You will see, too, that although the world's economic systems differ markedly, standards for evaluating success or failure are linked to a system's capacity to achieve certain basic goals.

Our opening story continues on page 26

By focusing on the learning objectives of this chapter, you will better understand the U.S. business system and the mechanisms by which it not only pursues its goals but also permits businesses large and small to pursue theirs.

THE CONCEPT OF BUSINESS AND THE CONCEPT OF PROFIT

What do you think of when you hear the word *business*? Does your mind conjure up images of huge corporations such as General Motors and IBM? Are you reminded of smaller firms such as your local supermarket? Or do you think of even smaller one-person operations such as the dry cleaner around the corner? Each of these organizations is a **business**—an organization that provides goods or services to earn profits. Indeed, the prospect of earning **profits**—the difference between a business's revenues and its expenses—is what encourages people to open and expand businesses. After all, profits reward owners for taking the risks involved in investing their money and time.

business
An organization that provides goods or services to earn profits

profits
The difference between a business's revenues and its expenses

Today, businesses produce most of the goods and services we consume. They also employ most of the working people in the United States. Moreover, new forms of technology, service businesses, and international opportunities promise to keep production, consumption, and employment growing indefinitely. In turn, profits from businesses are paid to millions of owners and stockholders. Taxes on businesses help support governments at all levels. In many cases, businesses also support charitable causes and provide community leadership.

In this chapter, we begin our introduction to business by looking at its role in both the U.S. economy and U.S. society. There are a variety of economic systems around the world. Once you understand something about the systems of most developed countries, you will better appreciate the workings of the U.S. system. As we will see, the effects of economic forces on businesses and the effects of businesses on the economy are dynamic—and, indeed, sometimes volatile.

ECONOMIC SYSTEMS AROUND THE WORLD

A U.S. business operates differently from a business in, say, France or the People's Republic of China, and businesses in these countries vary from those in Japan or Brazil. A major factor in these differences is the economic system of a firm's home country, in which it conducts most of its business. An **economic system** is a nation's system for allocating its resources among its citizens, both individuals and organizations. In this section we show how economic systems differ according to the ownership or control of these

economic system
A nation's system for allocating its resources among its citizens

"The point is to get so much money that money's not the point anymore."

resources, which are often called factors of production. We will also describe the basic economic systems that are used in different countries.

Factors of Production

factors of production Resources used in the production of goods and services—natural resources, labor, capital, and entrepreneurs

The key difference between economic systems is the way in which they manage the **factors of production**—the basic resources that a country's businesses use to produce goods and services. Traditionally, economists have focused on four factors of production: *labor, capital, entrepreneurs,* and *natural resources.* Newer perspectives, however, tend to broaden the idea of "natural resources" to include all *physical resources.* In addition, *information resources* are now often included as well.[1] The "Life Cycle of an e-Business" box in this chapter shows how one group of entrepreneurs used the factors of production to launch an Internet-based enterprise.

labor (or **human resources**) The physical and mental capabilities of people as they contribute to economic production

Labor The people who work for businesses provide labor. Sometimes called **human resources, labor** includes both the physical and mental contributions people make as they are engaged in economic production. America Online <www.aol.com>, for example, employs over 12,000 people. The operations of a firm like AOL require a widely skilled workforce, ranging from software engineers to marketing specialists to financial analysts.

capital The funds needed to create and operate a business enterprise

Capital Obtaining and using material resources and labor requires **capital**—the funds needed to operate an enterprise. Capital is needed to start a business and to keep it operating and growing. AOL requires millions of dollars every year to run its sprawling Internet operations. A major source of capital for most smaller businesses is personal investment by owners. Personal investment can be made by the individual entrepreneurs, by partners who start businesses together, or by investors who buy stock. Revenue from the sale of products is another important ongoing source of capital.

Entrepreneurs AOL was started by James Kimsey, who possessed the technical skills to understand how the Internet works, the conceptual skills to see its enormous future potential, and the risk-taking acumen to bet his own career and capital on its promise. Many economic systems need and encourage entrepreneurs like James Kimsey, who start new businesses and who make the decisions that expand small businesses into larger ones. These people embrace the opportunities and accept the risks inherent in creating and operating businesses.

physical resources Tangible things organizations use in the conduct of their business

Physical Resources **Physical resources** are the tangible things that organizations use to conduct their business. They include natural resources and raw materials, office and production facilities, parts and supplies, computers, and other equipment. AOL, for example, requires land, buildings, and computers. The CDs that the firm uses to distribute its software are provided by other manufacturers, and forest products are used for packaging.

information resources Data and other information used by business

Information Resources While the production of tangible goods once dominated most economic systems, today **information resources** play a major role. Businesses themselves rely heavily on market forecasts, the specialized expertise and knowledge of people, and various forms of economic data for much of their work. Much of what they do results in either the creation of new information or the repackaging of existing information for new users and different audiences. AOL does not produce tangible products. Instead, it provides numerous online services for its millions of subscribers in exchange for monthly access fees. Essentially, AOL is in the information business.

Types of Economic Systems

Different types of economic systems manage these factors of production in different ways. In some systems, ownership is private; in others, the factors of production are owned or controlled by the government. Economic systems also differ in the ways decisions are

Life Cycle of an e-Business

Sowing the Seeds of a Good Idea

Cliff Sharples, Lisa Aufranc, and Jamie O'Neill became close friends in graduate school, and the bonds grew even stronger when they all went to work for Trilogy Software in Austin, Texas, in 1995. Indeed, Cliff and Lisa were married as they were making the transition to their new jobs. But all three had known from their days together in school that they wanted to start their own business, and so, only 10 weeks after moving to Austin, they left Trilogy and set out to find a niche for a new business start-up.

Interestingly, they knew immediately *how* they wanted this business to work, but not *what* they wanted to sell. The three partners were firm believers that the Internet was on the verge of becoming a major venue for business. They also had a very solid understanding of how firms market products. They wanted to combine their knowledge of marketing with the power of the Internet.

> ***"We were not scrounging around in the dark looking for cool ideas. We knew e-commerce was going to be huge. And when we hit on gardening, it felt so right."***
>
> *—Jamie O'Neill, cofounder of Garden.com*

After months of research, they settled on gardening supplies and equipment as their product base. "We were not scrounging around in the dark looking for cool ideas," says O'Neill. "We knew e-commerce was going to be huge. And when we hit on gardening, it felt so right." They named the company Garden Escape and paid $2,500 for the rights to the Web site name Garden.com. They also divided the management tasks to fit their own talents and interests. Specifically, Cliff Sharples was named President and CEO and assumed responsibility for the firm's overall strategies. As Chief Operations Officer, Jamie O'Neill took charge of the day-to-day management and administration of the company. Lisa Sharples became the Chief Marketing and Merchandising Officer, handling product mix, promotional strategies, and so forth. Finally, the three founders brought in a fourth partner, Andy Martin, as the firm's Chief Technology Officer.

By the year 2000, Garden.com was widely acclaimed as one of the premier Internet-based retail businesses in the world. The company had been featured in *Inc.* magazine and its successes acknowledged in *Forbes, Fortune,* and the *Wall Street Journal.* The firm employed over 200 people, had more standing offers of investment capital than it needed or wanted, and was already building a new corporate headquarters building.

By July 2000, however, U.S. financial markets had undergone some big changes. As investors became wary of continuing unprofitable operations, the "easy" money that had once underwritten hundreds of dot-coms dried up. Little did Garden.com anticipate the crisis that a combination of scarce capital and slowing market growth would pose during the remaining months of 2000.

You'll learn more about Cliff, Jamie, Lisa, Andy, and their associates throughout this book. Each chapter includes a boxed feature like this one that discusses some aspect of operations and activities at Garden.com as they relate to the topic of that chapter. For example, you'll learn about the firm's stance on social responsibility (Chapter 4), how it was organized (Chapter 6), how it hired new employees (Chapter 8), how and why distribution was so vital to the firm (Chapter 14), and how information technology powered the whole enterprise (Chapter 17). In the end, you'll learn how and why Garden.com failed.

Cliff Sharples

Lisa Sharples

Jamie O'Neill

planned economy
Economy that relies on a centralized government to control all or most factors of production and to make all or most production and allocation decisions

market economy
Economy in which individuals control production and allocation decisions through supply and demand

made about production and allocation. A **planned economy,** for example, relies on a centralized government to control all or most factors of production and to make all or most production and allocation decisions. In a **market economy,** individuals—producers and consumers—control production and allocation decisions through supply and demand. We will describe each of these economic types and then discuss the reality of the *mixed market economy.*

Planned Economies The two most basic forms of planned economies are *communism* (discussed here) and *socialism* (discussed as a mixed market economy). As originally proposed by nineteenth-century German economist Karl Marx, communism is a system in which the government owns and operates all sources of production. Marx envisioned a society in which individuals would ultimately contribute according to their abilities and receive economic benefits according to their needs. He also expected government ownership of production factors to be only temporary: Once society had matured, government would "wither away" and the workers would gain direct ownership.[2]

Many Eastern European countries and the former Soviet Union embraced communist systems until the latter years of the twentieth century. In the early 1990s, one country after another renounced communism as both an economic and a political system. Today, Cuba, North Korea, Vietnam, and the People's Republic of China are among the few nations with avowedly communist systems. Even in these countries, however, planned economic systems are making room for features of the free enterprise system from the lowest to the highest levels.

market
Mechanism for exchange between buyers and sellers of a particular good or service

Market Economies A **market** is a mechanism for exchange between the buyers and sellers of a particular good or service. To understand how a market economy works, consider what happens when a customer goes to a fruit market to buy apples. While one vendor is selling apples for $1 per pound, another is charging $1.50. Both vendors are free to charge what they want, and customers are free to buy what they choose. If both vendors' apples are of the same quality, the customer will buy the cheaper ones. If the $1.50 apples are fresher, though, the customer may buy them instead. In short, both buyers and sellers enjoy freedom of choice. The "Wired World" box in this chapter discusses a much more complicated and technologically sophisticated market that has been created to bring buyers and sellers together using the Internet. This market is an outgrowth of a trend in information technology called "Business to Business," or "B2B." While most early commercial Internet applications were directed toward consumers, B2B is a more recent development that some experts think might handle trillions of dollars of annual business activity in just a few years.

input market
Market in which firms buy resources from supplier households

output market
Market in which firms supply goods and services in response to demand on the part of households

Input and Output Markets Figure 1.1 provides a useful and more complete model for better understanding how the factors of production work in a pure market economy. According to this view, businesses and households interact in two different market relationships.[3] In the **input market,** firms buy resources from households, which then supply those resources. In the **output market,** firms supply goods and services in response to demand on the part of households. (We provide a more detailed discussion of supply and demand later in this chapter.)

As you can see in Figure 1.1, the activities of these two markets create a circular flow. Ford Motor Co., for example, relies on various kinds of inputs. It buys labor directly from households, which may also supply capital from accumulated savings in the form of purchases of Ford stock. Consumer buying patterns provide information when Ford must decide which models to produce and which to discontinue. In turn, Ford uses these inputs in various ways and becomes a supplier to households when it designs and produces various models of automobiles, trucks, and sports utility vehicles and offers them for sale to consumers.

Individuals, meanwhile, are free to work for Ford or an alternative employer and to invest in Ford stock or in alternative forms of saving or consumption. Similarly, Ford can create whatever vehicles it chooses and price them at whatever value it chooses. But

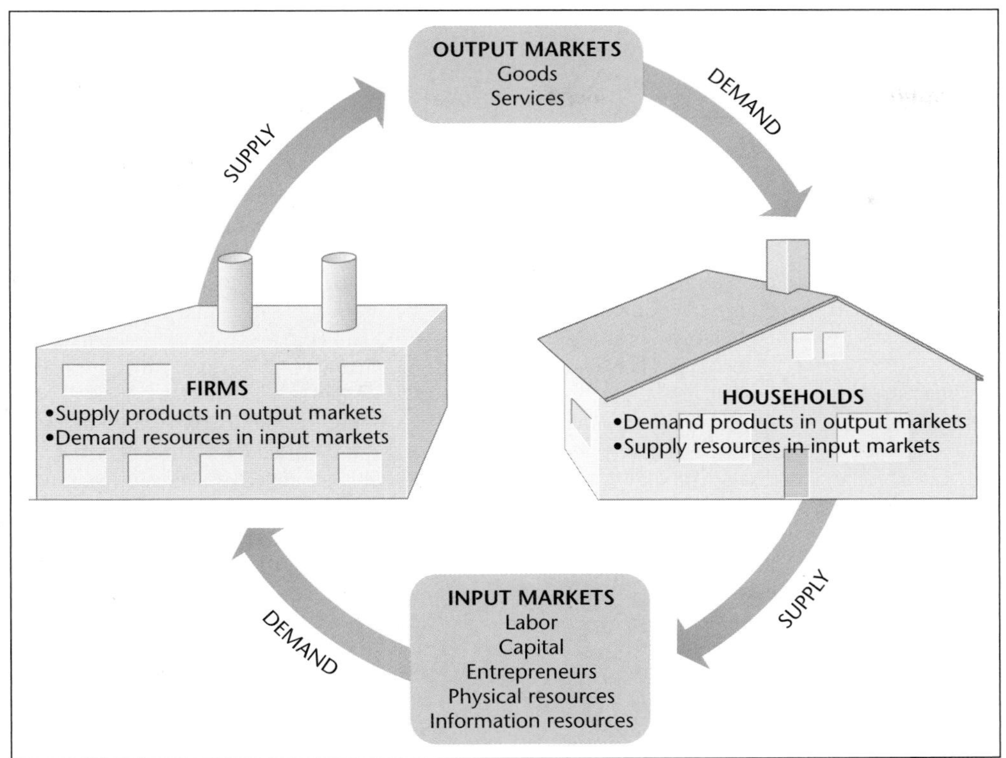

Figure 1.1
Circular Flow in a Market Economy

consumers are then free to buy their next car from Ford or Toyota or BMW. This process contrasts markedly with that of a planned economy, in which individuals may be told where they can and cannot work, companies are told what they can and cannot manufacture, and consumers may have little or no choice as to what they purchase or how much they pay. The economic basis of market processes is the laws of demand and supply; the political basis is called *capitalism*, which we discuss next.

capitalism
Market economy that provides for private ownership of production and encourages entrepreneurship by offering profits as an incentive

Capitalism **Capitalism** provides for the private ownership of the factors of production. It also encourages entrepreneurship by offering profits as an incentive. Businesses can provide whatever goods and services and charge whatever prices they choose. Similarly,

According to the model of circular flow in a market economy, this German Wal-Mart <www.walmartstores.com> *shopper plays a role in the* output market: *she demands goods that are supplied by a firm in the retailing business. Think of the German farmers from whom Wal-Mart buys the produce shown here as* households *that supply the* input market *with labor, time, skills, and investment in land.*

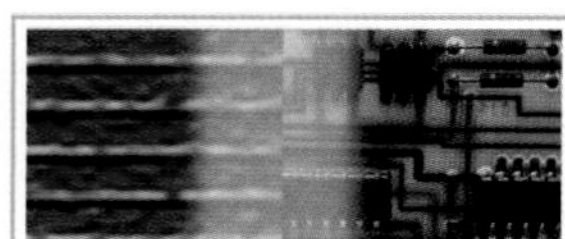

It's a WiredWorld

• Electronic B2B in the Auto Industry

As we observed in the text, a *market* is a mechanism for exchange between the buyers and sellers of a particular good or service. In earlier times, markets were actual physical settings where buyers and sellers would gather to conduct transactions. While such market settings are still used for selling things such as fish, fruits and vegetables, and antiques and collectibles, many commercial markets today differ in a fundamental respect: Buyers and sellers do not actually meet at the same place, but rather arrange their exchanges via mail orders, telephones, fax machines, and so forth. The growth of the Internet is making it even easier for some buyers and sellers to transact business at great distances.

A good example of this trend is the recently announced partnership among some of the world's largest automobile manufacturers. It all started when various individual automakers began to create their own global purchasing Web sites. Ford Motor Co., for instance, planned a site it called Auto-Xchange. The company intended to post all of its global procurement needs on the site, while also requesting that its suppliers post availability and prices for parts and equipment.

When it became apparent that other automakers were planning to do the same thing, major suppliers to the auto industry realized that they might soon be facing an unwieldy array of separate Web sites for each car company—a situation that would potentially drive up rather than reduce their own costs. Thus a coalition of the largest suppliers approached Ford and General Motors with a novel proposal: Why not team up and create a single site that could be used by both automakers and by their suppliers?

Ford and GM executives quickly saw the wisdom of this idea and then convinced DaimlerChrysler to join them. Now the Big Three plan to establish a single Web site to serve as a marketplace for all interested automobile manufacturers, suppliers, and dealers—essentially, a global virtual market including all firms in the industry. Almost immediately, France's Renault and Japan's Nissan, which is controlled by Renault, indicated a desire to join; Toyota also indicated strong interest. In addition, both Ford and GM indicated that they would encourage their foreign affiliates and strategic partners as well. The partners who are building the Web site intend to establish it as a self-contained organization that will eventually offer shares to the public.

Many experts believe that the impact of this global electronic market will be tremendous. It currently costs GM about $100 in ordering costs to buy parts or supplies the traditional way—with paper or over the telephone. However, the firm estimates that its ordering costs will drop to less than $10 under the new system. Clearly, the automakers will realize substantial cost savings. Suppliers, too, will benefit in various ways. Besides having more information about the immediate needs of different customers, they will be able to buy and sell among themselves.

customers can choose how and where to spend their money. Consider the case of Intershop <www.intershop.com>, a highly successful German start-up company. The firm, founded by three friends, buys and installs personal computers and software for individual consumers. Recently, it branched into numerous other forms of e-commerce and is fast becoming a player in the global economy. But what really sets Intershop apart is the fact that it was started in *East* Germany. Formerly part of a rigidly planned economy, this area is now blossoming under the market system of unified Germany.[4]

mixed market economy
Economic system featuring characteristics of both planned and market economies

privatization
Process of converting government enterprises into privately owned companies

Mixed Market Economies In their pure theoretical forms, planned and market economies are often seen as two extremes or opposites. In reality, however, most countries rely on some form of **mixed market economy**—a system featuring characteristics of both planned and market economies. Many of the former Eastern bloc countries are now adopting market mechanisms through a process called **privatization**—the process of converting government enterprises into privately owned companies. In recent years this practice has spread to many other countries as well. For example, the postal system in many countries is government-owned and government-managed, regardless of whether the country has a planned or market economy. The Netherlands, however, recently began the process of privatizing its TNT Post Group N.V., already among the world's most efficient post office operations. Similarly, Canada has recently privatized its air traffic control system. In each case, the new enterprise reduced its payroll, boosted efficiency and productivity, and quickly became profitable.[5]

In the partially planned system called **socialism,** the government owns and operates selected major industries. In such mixed market economies, the government may control banking, communication, transportation, and industries that produce such basic goods as oil and steel. Smaller businesses, such as clothing stores and restaurants, are privately owned. Many Western European countries, including England and France, allow free market operations in most economic areas but maintain government control in others, such as health care. Government planners in Japan give special centrally planned assistance to new industries that are expected to grow.

socialism
Planned economic system in which the government owns and operates only selected major sources of production

THE U.S. ECONOMIC SYSTEM

Understanding the complex nature of the U.S. economic system is essential to understanding the environment in which U.S. businesses operate. In this section, we describe the workings of the U.S. market economy in more detail. Specifically, we examine markets, the nature of demand and supply, private enterprise, and degrees of competition.

What are the five most important things that a businessperson should know?

Markets, Demand, and Supply

A market economy consists of many different markets. We have already noted the general nature of input and output markets. But beyond these general distinctions, virtually every input used by business and every good or service created by business has its own market. In each of these markets, businesses decide what inputs to buy, what to make and in what quantities, and what prices to charge. Likewise, customers decide what to buy and how much they are willing to pay. Literally billions of such exchanges take place every day between businesses and individuals, between different businesses, and among individuals, businesses, and governments. Moreover, exchanges conducted under conditions in one place often have an impact on exchanges elsewhere.

As the 1990s drew to a close, for example, several factors conspired to affect computer purchases in the year 2000 and beyond. For one thing, many companies had increased their computer budgets in anticipation of Y2K problems but were then able to cut those budgets after the new millennium arrived. For another, some companies began to reallocate their technology dollars, spending less on desktop computers and more on back-office equipment to run e-businesses. In addition, some firms simply started to slow down their upgrade cycles on the grounds that brand-new computers were not sufficiently superior to those they had purchased a few years earlier. Thus, rather than upgrade employee computers every two or three years, some firms started upgrading only every three or four years. As demand in the United States dropped, firms like Dell and IBM had to lower prices to keep sales from slumping too far, and lower prices meant lower profits per unit. At the same time, however, demand in other parts of the world, most notably China and India, was increasing, although not enough to fully offset domestic declines. Finally, projected lower profits induced investors to pay less for the stocks of some computer firms, causing those prices to fall as well.[6]

demand
The willingness and ability of buyers to purchase a good or service

supply
The willingness and ability of producers to offer a good or service for sale

law of demand
Principle that buyers will purchase (demand) more of a product as its price drops and less as its price increases

law of supply
Principle that producers will offer (supply) more of a product for sale as its price rises and less as its price drops

The Laws of Demand and Supply On all economic levels, decisions about what to buy and what to sell are determined primarily by the forces of demand and supply.[7] **Demand** is the willingness and ability of buyers to purchase a product (a good or a service). **Supply** is the willingness and ability of producers to offer a good or service for sale. Generally speaking, demand and supply follow basic laws:

- The **law of demand:** Buyers will purchase (demand) more of a product as its price drops and less of a product as its price increases.
- The **law of supply:** Producers will offer (supply) more of a product for sale as its price rises and less as its price drops.

The Demand and Supply Schedule To appreciate these laws in action, consider the market for pizza in your town. If everyone in town is willing to pay $25 for a pizza (a high price), the town's only pizzeria will produce a large supply. If everyone is willing to pay only $5 (a low price), however, the restaurant will make fewer pizzas. Through careful analysis we can determine how many pizzas will be sold at different prices. These results, called a **demand and supply schedule,** are obtained from marketing research and other systematic studies of the market. Properly applied, they help managers better understand the relationships among different levels of demand and supply at different price levels.

demand and supply schedule
Assessment of the relationships between different levels of demand and supply at different price levels

Demand and Supply Curves The demand and supply schedule, for example, can be used to construct demand and supply curves for pizza in your town. A **demand curve** shows how many products—in this case, pizzas—will be *demanded* (bought) at different prices. A **supply curve** shows how many pizzas will be *supplied* (baked) at different prices.

Figure 1.2 shows hypothetical demand and supply curves for pizzas. As you can see, demand increases as price decreases; supply increases as price increases. When the demand and supply curves are plotted on the same graph, the point at which they intersect is the **market price** or **equilibrium price**—the price at which the quantity of goods demanded and the quantity of goods supplied are equal. Note in Figure 1.2 that the equilibrium price for pizzas in our example is $10. At this point, the quantity of pizzas demanded and the quantity of pizzas supplied are the same: 1,000 pizzas per week.

demand curve
Graph showing how many units of a product will be demanded (bought) at different prices

supply curve
Graph showing how many units of a product will be supplied (offered for sale) at different prices

market price
(or **equilibrium price)**
Profit-maximizing price at which the quantity of goods demanded and the quantity of goods supplied are equal

Surpluses and Shortages What if the restaurant chooses to make some other number of pizzas? For example, what would happen if the owner tried to increase profits by making more pizzas to sell? Or what if the owner wanted to reduce overhead, cut back on store hours, and reduce the number of pizzas offered for sale? In either case, the result would be an inefficient use of resources and lower profits. For instance, if the restaurant supplies 1,200 pizzas and tries to sell them for $10 each, 200 pizzas will not be purchased. The demand schedule clearly shows that only 1,000 pizzas will be demanded at this price. The pizza maker will thus have a **surplus**—a situation in which the quantity supplied exceeds the quantity demanded. The restaurant will lose the money it spent making those extra 200 pizzas.

Conversely, if the pizzeria supplies only 800 pizzas, a **shortage** will result: The quantity demanded will be greater than the quantity supplied. The pizzeria will lose the extra money it could have made by producing 200 more pizzas. Even though consumers may pay more for pizzas because of the shortage, the restaurant will still earn lower profits than if it had made 1,000 pizzas. In addition, it will risk angering customers who cannot buy pizzas. To maximize profits, therefore, all businesses must constantly seek the right combination of price charged and quantity supplied. This right combination is found at the equilibrium point.

surplus
Situation in which quantity supplied exceeds quantity demanded

shortage
Situation in which quantity demanded exceeds quantity supplied

This simple example involves only one company, one product, and a few buyers. Obviously, the U.S. economy is far more complex. Thousands of companies sell hundreds of thousands of products to millions of buyers every day. In the end, however, the result is much the same: Companies try to supply the quantity and selection of goods that will earn them the largest profits.

Private Enterprise

In his book *The Wealth of Nations,* first published in 1776, Scottish economist Adam Smith argued that a society's interests are best served by **private enterprise**—a system that allows individuals to pursue their own interests without government restriction. Smith envisioned a system in which individual entrepreneurs sought their own self-interest. At the same time, the "invisible hand of competition" would lead businesses to produce the best products as efficiently as possible and to sell them at the lowest possible prices. After all, that strategy was the clearest route to successful profit making and fulfilled self-interest. In effect, each business would be working for the good of society as a whole. Society would benefit most from minimal interference with individuals' pursuit of economic self-interest.

private enterprise
Economic system that allows individuals to pursue their own interests without undue governmental restriction

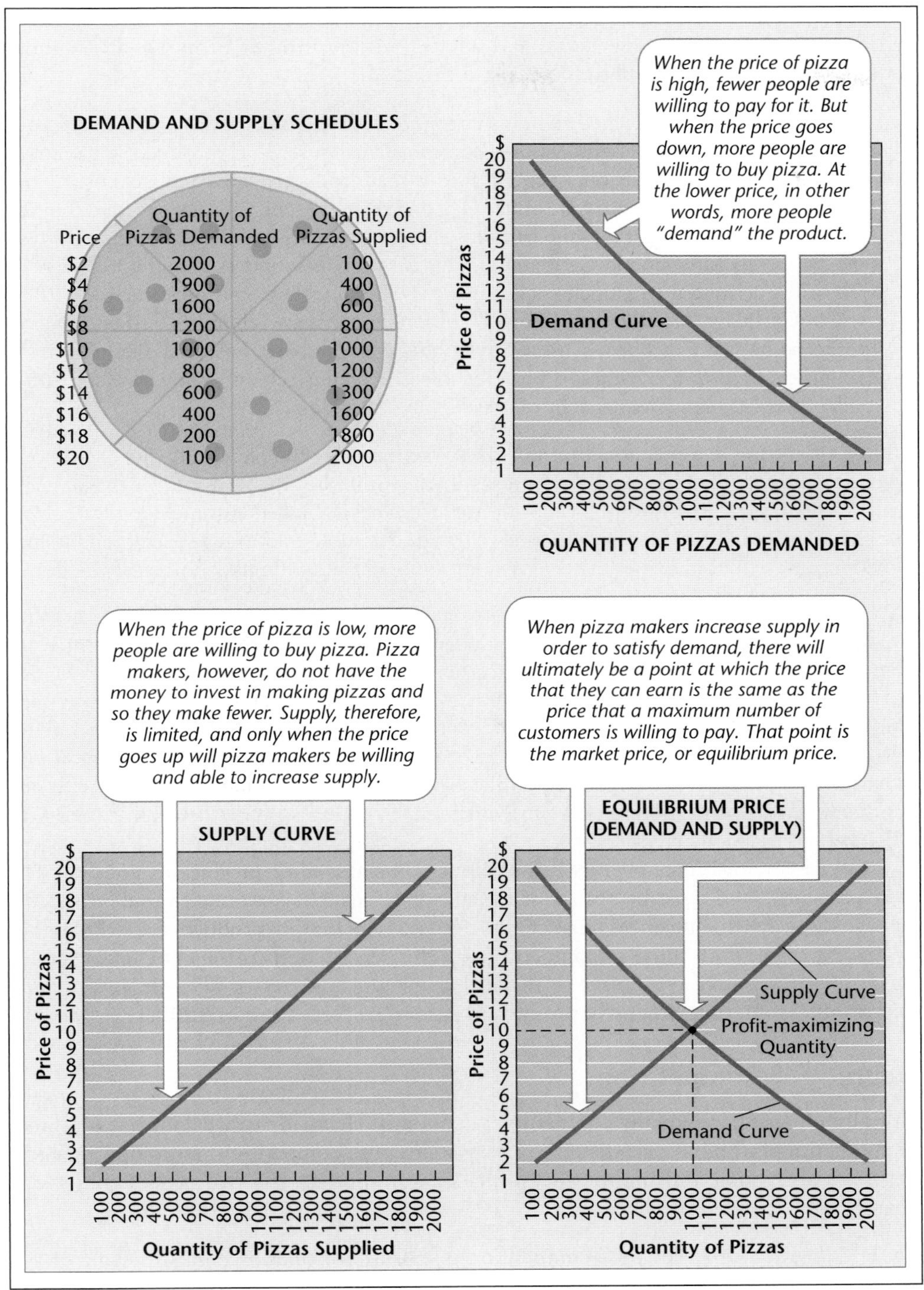

DEMAND AND SUPPLY SCHEDULES

Price	Quantity of Pizzas Demanded	Quantity of Pizzas Supplied
$2	2000	100
$4	1900	400
$6	1600	600
$8	1200	800
$10	1000	1000
$12	800	1200
$14	600	1300
$16	400	1600
$18	200	1800
$20	100	2000

Figure 1.2
Demand and Supply

Market economies are based on roughly the same concept of private enterprise. In both Smith's "pure" vision and the reality of contemporary practice, private enterprise requires the presence of four elements: *private property rights, freedom of choice, profits,* and *competition.*

Private Property Rights Smith maintained that the creation of wealth should be the concern of individuals, not the government. Thus, he argued that the ownership of the resources used to create wealth must be in the hands of individuals. Individual ownership of property is part of everyday life in the United States. No doubt you or someone

private property rights The right to buy, own, use, and sell almost any form of property

you know has bought and owned automobiles, homes, land, or stock. The right to hold **private property**—to buy, own, use, and sell almost any form of property—is a fundamental right guaranteed by the U.S. Constitution.

"I had a choice."

—*Stephan Schambach, cofounder of (East) German computer/software start-up Intershop*

Freedom of Choice A related right is *freedom of choice*. You enjoy the right to sell your labor to any employer you choose. You can also choose which products you want to buy. Finally, freedom of choice means that producers can usually choose whom to hire and what to produce. The U.S. government, for instance, does not tell Sears what it can and cannot sell. We noted earlier the success being enjoyed by Intershop in Germany. A few years ago its founders would not have been permitted to launch such a business. In fact, the communist regime of East Germany had not even allowed cofounder Stephan Schambach to study computers as he wanted. But when the Soviet bloc collapsed and East and West Germany were reunified, everything changed. "I had a choice," explains Schambach, whose start-up is now valued on Germany's equivalent of Nasdaq at $1.4 billion.[8]

Profits Naturally, a business that fails to make a profit will eventually close its doors. At least 63 percent of all small businesses in the United States fail within the first six years.[9] The lure of profits (and freedom), however, inevitably leads some people to abandon the security of working for someone else and to assume the risks of entrepreneurship. Obviously, anticipated profits also play a large part in individuals' choices of the goods or services they will produce.

competition Vying among businesses for the same resources or customers

Competition If profits motivate individuals to start businesses, competition motivates them to operate their businesses efficiently. **Competition** occurs when two or more businesses vie for the same resources or customers. For example, if you decide to buy a new pair of athletic shoes, you have a choice of several different stores in which to shop. After selecting a store, you may then choose between brands (Nike, Reebok, or Adidas). If you intend to buy only one pair of shoes, all these manufacturers are in competition with one another, as are all the shoe retailers in your area, from mass marketers such as Sears to specialty outlets such as Foot Locker.

To gain an advantage over its competitors, a business must produce its goods or services efficiently and must be able to sell them for prices that earn reasonable profits. To achieve these goals, a business must convince customers that its products are either better or less expensive than those of competitors. In this sense, competition benefits society: It forces all competitive businesses to make their products better or cheaper. A company that produces inferior, expensive products is sure to be forced out of business.

Degrees of Competition

Not all industries are equally competitive. Economists have identified four basic degrees of competition within a private enterprise system: pure competition, monopolistic competition, oligopoly, and monopoly. Table 1.2 summarizes the features of these four degrees of competition.

pure competition Market or industry characterized by numerous small firms producing an identical product

Pure Competition For **pure competition** to exist, two conditions must prevail:

1. All firms in a given industry must be small.
2. The number of firms in the industry must be large.

Under such conditions, no single firm is powerful enough to influence the price of its product or service in the marketplace.

In turn, these conditions reflect four important principles:.

1. The products offered by each firm are so similar that buyers view them as identical to those offered by other firms.
2. Both buyers and sellers know the prices that others are paying and receiving in the marketplace.

Table 1.2

Degrees of Competition

Characteristic	Pure Competition	Monopolistic Competition	Oligopoly	Monopoly
Example	Local farmer	Stationery store	Steel industry	Public utility
Number of competitors	Many	Many, but fewer than in pure competition	Few	None
Ease of entry into industry	Easy	Fairly easy	Difficult	Regulated by government
Similarity of goods or services offered by competing firms	Identical	Similar	Can be similar or different	No directly competing goods or services
Level of control over price by individual firms	None	Some	Some	Considerable

3. Because each firm is small, it is easy for any single firm to enter or leave the market.
4. Going prices are set exclusively by supply and demand and accepted by both sellers and buyers.

Agriculture is a good example of pure competition in the U.S. economy. For example, the wheat produced on one farm is essentially the same as that produced on another. Both producers and buyers are well aware of prevailing market prices. Moreover, it is relatively easy to start producing wheat and relatively easy to stop when doing so is no longer profitable.

Monopolistic Competition Fewer sellers are involved in **monopolistic competition** than in pure competition, but because there are still many buyers, sellers try to make their products at least appear to be different from those of competitors. Differentiating strategies include brand names (Tide and Cheer), design or styling (Polo and Tommy Hilfiger jeans), and advertising (Coke and Pepsi). For example, in an effort to attract health-conscious consumers, the Kraft Foods division of Philip Morris <www.kraftfoods.com/index.cgi> is actively promoting such differentiated products as low-fat Cool Whip, low-calorie Jell-O, and sugar-free Kool-Aid.

monopolistic competition
Market or industry characterized by numerous buyers and relatively numerous sellers trying to differentiate their products from those of competitors

Monopolistically competitive businesses may be large or small, but still able to easily enter or leave the market. For example, many small clothing stores compete successfully with large apparel retailers such as Liz Claiborne <www.lizclaiborne.com> and The Limited <www.limited.com>, and bebe stores, inc. (with a small *b*) <www.bebe.com> is a good case in point. The relatively small clothing chain controls its own manufacturing facilities and can respond just as quickly as firms like The Gap <www.gap.com/onlinestore.gap> to changes in fashion tastes.[10] Many single-store clothing businesses in college towns compete effectively by developing their own designs for T-shirts and caps and then copyrighting slogans and logos to prevent others from copying them. Product differentiation also gives sellers some control over the prices they charge. For instance, even though Sears shirts may have similar styling and other features, Ralph Lauren Polo shirts can be priced with little regard for the lower price of Sears shirts.

Oligopoly When an industry has only a handful of sellers, an **oligopoly** exists. As a general rule, these sellers are quite large. The entry of new competitors is difficult because large capital investment is necessary. Consequently, oligopolistic industries (the automobile, rubber, airline, and steel industries) tend to stay that way. Thus, only two

oligopoly
Market or industry characterized by a handful of (generally large) sellers with the power to influence the prices of their products

WebConnection

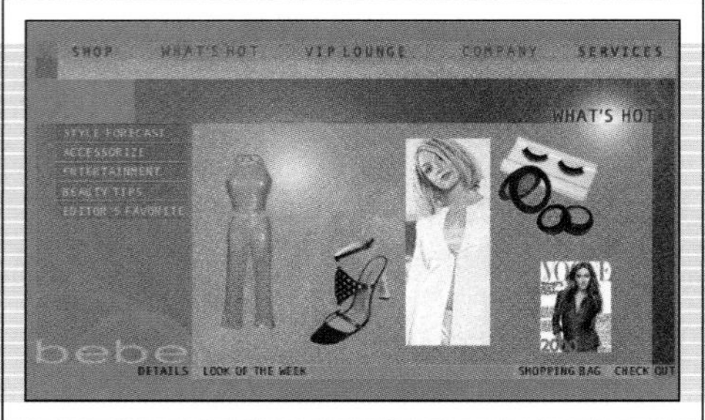

www.bebe.com

Like Gap Inc., bebe stores is a vertical retailer that manufactures and brands its own clothing. With over 100 stores nationwide (plus stores in Vancouver, Toronto, and London), bebe targets sexy, trendy clothing at mall prices to women in their 20s and 30s. To see how the company uses the Internet both to sell its products and to expand brand awareness, log on to its Web site.

"Global oligopolies are as inevitable as the sunrise."

—Business historian Louis Galambos

companies, both among the biggest in the world, manufacture large commercial aircraft: Boeing (a U.S. company) and Airbus (a European consortium). Furthermore, as the trend toward globalization continues, most experts believe that, as one forecaster puts it, "global oligopolies are as inevitable as the sunrise."[11]

Individual oligopolists have more control over their own strategies than monopolistically competitive firms. At the same time, however, the actions of any one firm can significantly affect the sales of every other firm. For example, when one firm reduces prices or offers incentives to increase sales, the others usually protect their sales by doing the same. Likewise, when one firm raises prices, the others generally follow suit. Therefore, the prices of comparable products are usually quite similar. When a major airline announces a new program of fare discounts, the others mimic this strategy almost immediately. Just as quickly, when the fare discounts end for one airline, they usually end for all the others at the same time.

monopoly
Market or industry in which there is only one producer, which can therefore set the prices of its products

natural monopoly
Industry in which one company can most efficiently supply all needed goods or services

Monopoly A **monopoly** exists when an industry or market has only one producer. Obviously, a sole supplier enjoys complete control over the prices of its products. Its only constraint is the fall of consumer demand in response to increased prices. In the United States, laws such as the Sherman Antitrust Act (1890) and the Clayton Act (1914) forbid many monopolies and regulate the prices charged by so-called **natural monopolies**

Founded in 1970 as a consortium that now includes four European companies, Airbus Industrie <www.airbus.com> *is developing the world's largest airplane. It's code-named A3XX and would carry 555 passengers on overseas routes—137 more than the 747-400 built by Boeing* <www.boeing.com>*, Airbus's only true competitor in the oligopolistic commercial jet industry. Airbus calls Boeing's 747-400 "30-year-old technology" and is climbing steadily toward its goal of gaining 50 percent of the worldwide market for over-100-seat airplanes.*

(industries in which one company can most efficiently supply all the needed goods or services). Many local electric companies are natural monopolies because they can supply all the power needed in their local area. Duplicate facilities—such as two power plants and two sets of power lines—would be wasteful.

EVALUATING ECONOMIC SYSTEMS

Figures 1.3 through 1.8 display a variety of current economic indicators that can be used to highlight some key facts about the U.S. economy. Using these data for reference points, we explain more fully the key goals of the U.S. economic system and measure the success of that system in achieving its goals. We conclude by describing government attempts to manage the U.S. economy in the interest of meeting national economic goals.

Economic Goals

Nearly every economic system has three broad goals: *stability, full employment,* and *growth*. Different systems place different emphasis on each of these goals and take different approaches to achieving them.

Stability In economic terms, **stability** is the condition in which the money available in an economy and the goods produced in that economy remain about the same. In other words, there are enough desirable products to satisfy consumer demand, and consumers have enough money, in the aggregate, to buy what they need and want. When conditions are stable, therefore, prices for consumer goods, interest rates, and wages paid to workers change very little. Stability helps maintain predictable conditions in which managers, consumers, and workers can analyze the business environment, project goals, and assess performance.

stability
Condition in which the balance between the money available in an economy and the goods produced in it are growing at about the same rate

Inflation The biggest threat to stability is **inflation**—a period of widespread price increases throughout an economic system. Typically, inflation has an impact on virtually all the goods and services that the system produces. For example, inflation explains why a pair of Levi's jeans that costs $35 today cost only $29 ten years ago and only $18 twenty years ago. For the last several years, inflation rates in the United States have been running below 3 percent. Recent annual rates have ranged from 2.6 percent to 2.9 percent. While most experts believe this trend will continue for at least the next few years, a slight surge in prices for clothing and shoes, software, and gasoline and in oil in late 1999 attracted some concern and prompted a few experts to warn that inflation might be on the upswing again.[12]

inflation
Phenomenon of widespread price increases throughout an economic system

Figure 1.3 shows inflation rates in the United States since 1960 by tracing the average annual increase in producer prices. At current levels, prices double approximately every 20 years. What does this figure mean in real terms for consumers? Among other things, if this trend remains constant, when your children enter college they will pay about twice what you are now paying for tuition, fees, textbooks, clothing, and housing.

Inflation is not necessarily or entirely bad. Stability can degenerate into stagnation and contribute to a decline in the development and marketing of new products. After all, when the marketplace has enough products to buy at reasonable prices and consumers have enough money with which to buy the products, innovation and growth in new areas are not urgent business priorities. For the same reason, the onset of inflation is often a sign of economic growth. When businesses see that they can charge higher prices, they may hire new workers, invest more money in advertising, and introduce new products. In addition, new businesses open to take advantage of perceived prosperity. At this point, a damaging inflationary trend may set in: Workers may start demanding higher wages to pay for more expensive products, and because higher wages mean lower profits, sellers may raise prices even more. Inflation can be curtailed both naturally and artificially. For example, rates of increase may slow either because of an economic slump, such as the recession that hit the United States in the late 1980s, or because of government intervention.

Figure 1.3

U.S. Producer Price Index

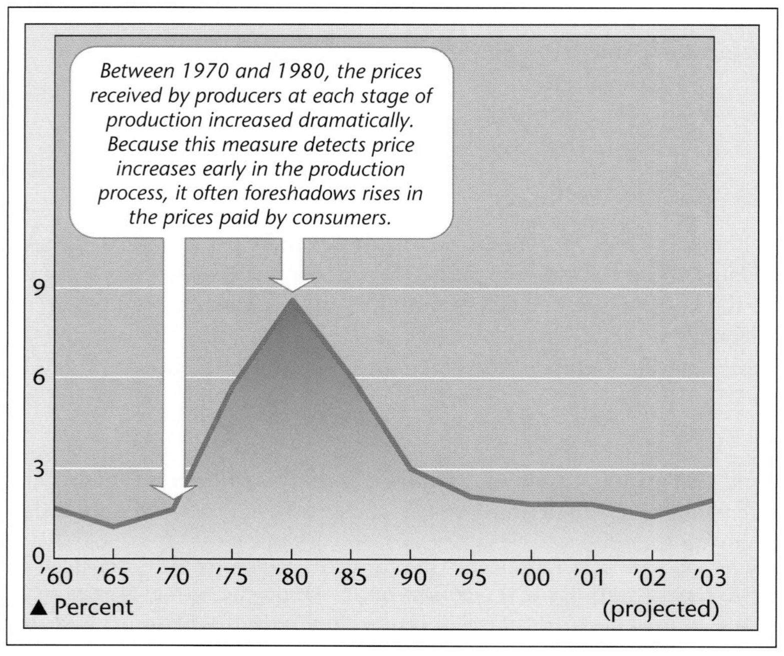
Between 1970 and 1980, the prices received by producers at each stage of production increased dramatically. Because this measure detects price increases early in the production process, it often foreshadows rises in the prices paid by consumers.
9
6
3
0
'60 '65 '70 '75 '80 '85 '90 '95 '00 '01 '02 '03
▲ Percent
(projected)

recession
Period characterized by decreases in employment, income, and production

depression
Particularly severe and long-lasting recession

unemployment
Level of joblessness among people actively seeking work

knowledge workers
Skilled employees in high-tech industries

growth
Increase in the amount of goods and services produced by a nation's resources

Recession and Depression Inflation is not the only threat to economic stability. Suppose that a major factory in your hometown closed. Hundreds or even thousands of workers would lose their jobs. If other companies in the area do not have jobs for them, these unemployed people will reduce their spending. Thus, other local businesses will suffer drops in sales and perhaps cut their own workforces. The resulting **recession,** characterized by decreases in employment, income, and production, may spread across the city, the state, or even the nation. A particularly severe and long-lasting recession, such as the one that affected much of the world in the 1930s, is called a **depression.**

Full Employment Although there is some disagreement about the meaning of the term *full employment,* the concept remains a goal of most economic systems. Strictly speaking, full employment means that everyone who wants to work has an opportunity to do so. In reality, full employment is impossible because the distributions of people and jobs do not perfectly match: There will always be people looking for work and there will always be unfilled jobs.

Unemployment The level of joblessness among people actively seeking work can define **unemployment.** Employment rates are an important element in the health of a nation's economy. For example, high unemployment suggests that businesses are performing poorly, whereas low unemployment suggests that business is better. In the years following World War II, unemployment generally varied between 5 and 10 percent.

In recent years, however, unemployment has dropped so low that many businesses have struggled to find enough qualified workers. Skilled workers have come to expect a growing array of incentives and benefits when they select employers. Signing bonuses, high salaries, and benefits ranging from on-site childcare to sand volleyball courts to rock-climbing walls are becoming commonplace as companies pull out all the stops to hire and retain talented people. This trend is especially pronounced for so-called **knowledge workers**—skilled people in high-tech industries.[13]

Growth The fundamental goal of many economic systems is **growth:** an increase in the total output—the amount of goods and services—produced by a nation's resources. In theory, we all want the whole system to expand and provide more businesses, more jobs, and more wealth for everyone. In practice, however, it is difficult to achieve growth without triggering inflation or other elements of instability. Conversely, an extended period without growth may eventually result in economic decline: business shutdowns, lost jobs, a decrease in overall wealth, and a lower standard of living for everyone.

Is continuing education more important than simply increasing your on-the-job experience? Which do you feel (education or experience) contributed the most to your job success?

Some experts have recently expressed concern about the ability of the United States to sustain the three-percent annual growth rate that it has enjoyed for the last several years. Troubling indicators include budget cuts for basic research, a decline in the number of students majoring in science and engineering, continuing debates about Internet regulation, visa quotas for high-tech workers, and encryption policies, all of which might adversely affect high-tech industries.

Assessing Economic Performance

To judge the success of an economic system in meeting its goals, economists use one or more of five measures: *gross national* and *gross domestic product, productivity, balance of trade,* and *national debt.* As we examine these data, however, it's important to keep in mind that experts continue to explore new and more accurate ways of calculating and interpreting economic information. For example, there are often differences of opinion as to how various elements should be counted and how much weight should be given to inflationary changes over time. Until 1999, the U.S. government used one formula to apply inflation rates to historical data. But after a new and more precise formula was created and applied, economic-growth statistics were subsequently altered as well. In particular, the contributions of the computer-software and banking industries have been assigned larger roles and measured more accurately. While experts had already agreed that the U.S. economy had grown significantly during the 1990s, the revised data indicated that the growth was even stronger than previously thought.[14]

Gross National Product and Gross Domestic Product If we add the total value of all the goods and services produced by an economic system in a one-year period, the sum is that country's **gross national product,** or **GNP.** GNP was historically seen as a useful indicator of economic growth because it allowed us to track an economy's performance over time. However, this measure can also be affected by inflation and other factors concerning the value of its currency. To control the effects of such factors, experts next began to compare economies according to an adjusted figure called the **real gross national product (real GNP)**—the gross national product adjusted for inflation and changes in the value of a country's currency. The recent growth in international trade, however, has also made GNP a less valid indicator of economic performance than was true in the past, mainly because GNP includes a nation's output regardless of where the factors of production are located.

gross national product (GNP)
The value of all goods and services produced by an economic system in a year regardless of where the factors of production are located

real gross national product (real GNP)
Gross national product adjusted for inflation and changes in the value of a country's currency

To get a more accurate reading of economic performance in today's global environment, many experts prefer to use **gross domestic product,** or **GDP.** Like GNP, GDP measures a nation's annual output. However, the profits earned by a U.S. company abroad are only included in GNP, not GDP, because the output is not produced domestically (in the United States). Conversely, goods and services produced by foreign workers inside the United States, as well as profits earned by foreign companies operating here, are counted in the U.S. GDP because they are produced domestically.[15] GDP per capita in the United States is $30,200. By comparison, GDP per capita in Japan is $24,500. Other countries with high GDP per capita include Canada ($21,700), Norway ($27,400), and Germany ($20,800). Currently, U.S. GDP is about $8.5 trillion, about $500 billion higher than GNP.[16]

gross domestic product (GDP)
The value of all goods and services produced in a year by a nation's economy through domestic factors of production

Productivity As a measure of economic growth, **productivity** compares what a system produces relative to the resources needed to produce it. This principle may be easier to understand if we first apply the same measure on a smaller scale: If Xerox can produce a copier for $1,000 but Canon needs $1,200 to make a comparable product, Xerox is being more productive.

productivity
Measure of economic growth that compares how much a system produces with the resources needed to produce it

This Fiat plant is the largest automotive factory in Brazil <www.fiat.com.br>. *The plant's payroll, the value of the 400,000 vehicles made here, and the profits earned by Fiat's Italian owners are produced domestically and therefore counted in the Brazilian gross domestic product. Because Brazilian labor costs are much lower than those in their home countries, DaimlerChrysler, Honda, Toyota, Volkswagen, Mercedes, and Renault also build cars in Brazil.*

U.S. workers are among the most productive in the world. Figure 1.4 shows manufacturing productivity growth since 1960 in terms of annual average percentage of increase. As you can see, that growth slowed during the 1970s but began to rise again in the late 1980s. Some experts believe that productivity both in the United States and abroad will continue to improve at even more impressive rates. Their confidence rests on the potential ability of technology to improve operations. For example, Sears, Oracle, and Carrefour (the number-one retailer in Europe and Latin America) have unveiled plans for a comprehensive purchasing network. This system will replace all of Sears' current purchasing arrangements, eliminating the need for personal contracts, paper and telephone ordering, and the like—saving millions of dollars and sharply boosting productivity in the process. Sears' managers project that this part of the business will lower Sears' costs by 10 percent to 20 percent. In turn, these reduced costs will directly serve to boost productivity.[17]

Figure 1.4

Average U.S. Productivity Growth

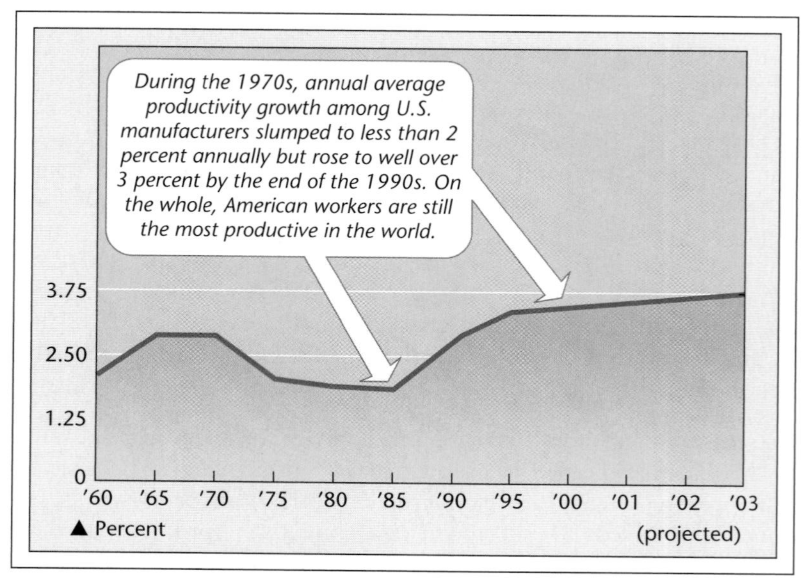
During the 1970s, annual average productivity growth among U.S. manufacturers slumped to less than 2 percent annually but rose to well over 3 percent by the end of the 1990s. On the whole, American workers are still the most productive in the world.
3.75
2.50
1.25
0
'60
'65
'70
'75
'80
'85
'90
'95
'00
'01
'02
'03
▲ Percent
(projected)

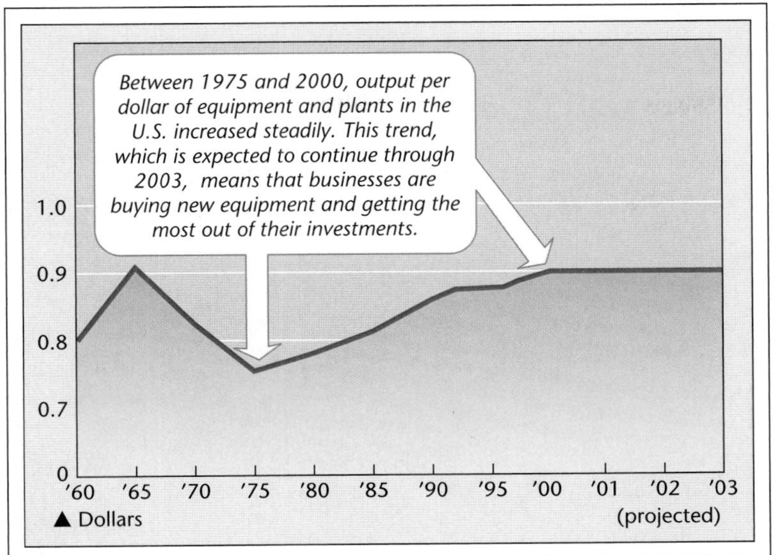

Figure 1.5 Output per Dollar of Equipment and Plants

Figure 1.5 shows another aspect of the U.S. economy that affects productivity. If we calculate output per dollar of equipment and plants, we see that U.S. businesses are investing their capital more and more efficiently; that is, they are buying new equipment and using it wisely. In 1999, for example, U.S. business spent at the rate of $1.2 trillion on capital spending—the total cost of all buildings and equipment acquired to produce goods and services or to expand operations. This figure accounted for 12.7 percent of the national economy, and most of it—$910 billion—went for equipment, especially computers and software. Telephone and cable companies and Internet firms shared significantly in the wealth. "People are convinced," explains one economist, "that Internet-based methods of distributing information and products will turn out to be much more profitable than traditional methods."[18] In theory, these investments in better manufacturing and information technology will contribute to further increases in productivity. In Chapter 16, we take a more detailed look at the importance—and specific features—of productivity.

> ***"People are convinced that Internet-based methods of distributing information and products will turn out to be much more profitable than traditional methods."***
>
> *—Kenneth J. Matheny, senior economist, Macroeconomic Advisors Inc.*

Balance of Trade *Balance of trade* is the difference between a country's *exports to* and *imports from* other countries. A *positive* balance of trade is generally considered favorable because new money flows into a country from the sales of its exports. A *negative* balance means that money is flowing out to pay for imports. During the 1980s, the United States suffered a sharply negative trend in its balance of trade. While there have been some periodic annual improvements, in general this pattern continues today. At the

WebConnection

www.exodus.com

U.S. capital spending is increasing because companies are spending money on information technology. Exodus Communications, which maintains high-tech centers (IDCs) for housing and operating corporate Web sites, is taking advantage of the trend. To find out more about IDCs, access the Exodus Web site.

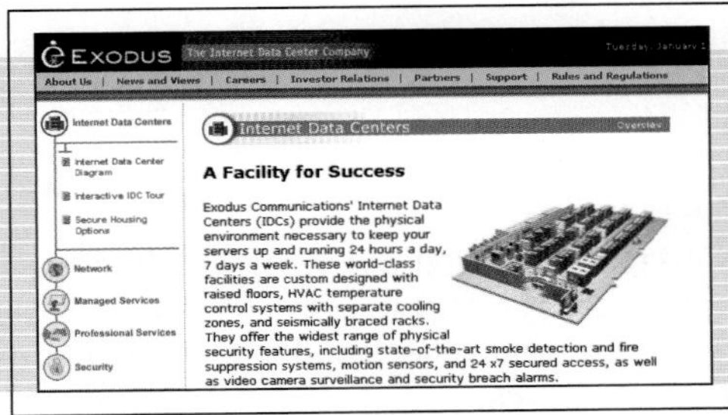

Figure 1.6
Expanding International Trade in the United States

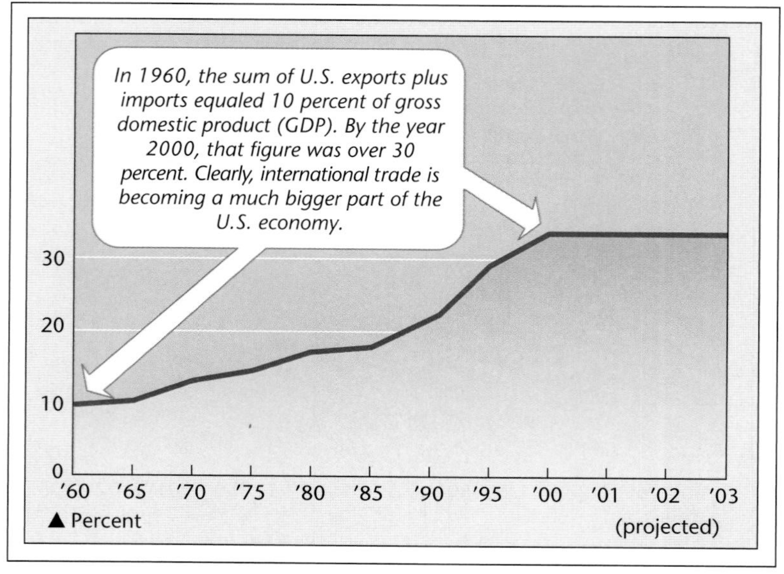
In 1960, the sum of U.S. exports plus imports equaled 10 percent of gross domestic product (GDP). By the year 2000, that figure was over 30 percent. Clearly, international trade is becoming a much bigger part of the U.S. economy.
30
20
10
0
'60 '65 '70 '75 '80 '85 '90 '95 '00 '01 '02 '03
▲ Percent
(projected)

end of 1998, for instance, the United States had a negative balance of merchandise trade of \$246.9 billion, but a positive balance of service trade of \$82.7 billion, resulting in a net negative trade balance of \$164.2 billion. As Figure 1.6 shows, international trade is becoming an increasingly important part of the U.S. economy if we measure exports plus imports as a share of GDP. Thus, makers of economic and public policy pay closer attention to such economic indicators as balance of trade.

budget deficit
Situation in which a government body spends more money than it takes in

national debt
Total amount that a nation owes its creditors

National Debt Like a business, the government takes in revenues (primarily in the form of taxes) and has expenses (military spending, social programs, and so forth). The United States ran a **budget deficit** for much of the 1970s, 1980s, and 1990s: We spent more money than we took in. This deficit created a huge **national debt**—the amount of money that the United States owes its creditors.

By the end of 1999, the national debt exceeded \$5.5 *trillion.* Because this high level of debt results in higher interest rates throughout the economy, it limits growth. Unfortunately, reducing the size of the national debt has proven to be difficult. Obviously, the only two ways to reduce any budget deficit are to increase revenues (in this case, by raising taxes) and reduce spending. Unfortunately, neither of these is a popular option: No one is happy about the prospect of paying more taxes, and the prospect of spending cuts in virtually any area (the military, social programs, environmental protection, the prison system, education, or transportation) brings outcries from so many special-interest groups that policymakers have long been reluctant to take the political risks involved.

The year 1998 saw the first U.S. budget surplus since 1969. The surplus was primarily attributable to spending cuts and tax increases implemented during the Bush and Clinton administrations. The Congressional Budget Office also forecasts continued surpluses for the next several years totaling perhaps as much as \$1.55 trillion. If, as President Bill Clinton predicted in 1999, the national debt is eliminated by the year 2014, and if everything else (GDP, inflation, productivity, and international trade) remains exactly constant, the debt reduction alone would raise the economic growth rate in the United States by 0.25% and real annual household income would grow by \$1,500.[19]

Managing the U.S. Economy

fiscal policies
Government economic policies that determine how the government collects and spends its revenues

The government also acts to manage the U.S. economic system through two sets of policies: fiscal policies and monetary policies. It manages the collection and spending of its revenues through **fiscal policies.** Tax increases, for instance, can function as fiscal policy to increase revenues. President Clinton's income tax increase in 1993 generated an estimated $50 billion in additional revenues. Similarly, budget cuts (closing military bases) function as fiscal policy when spending is decreased. Such policies can have a direct impact on inflation, growth, and employment.

Historically, an important example of a fiscal policy designed to boost employment was the Public Works Program following the Great Depression. The U.S. government employed tens of thousands of people to improve the nation's infrastructure by building roads, bridges, dams, post offices, schools, and hospitals. As a result, many people had jobs who would otherwise have had no income and the country itself benefited directly from the improvements. More recently, China announced a $1 trillion public works program to energize its own ailing economy.[20]

Monetary policies focus on controlling the size of the nation's money supply. Working primarily through the Federal Reserve System (the nation's central bank), the government can influence the ability and willingness of banks throughout the country to lend money. It can also influence the supply of money by prompting interest rates to go up or down. A primary goal in recent years has been to adjust interest rates so that inflation is held at a manageable level. For example, the Fed (as it is informally called) raised rates by 0.25 percent in early 2000 to offset a slight increase in inflation, and economists forecasted that another similar increase would be necessary by the end of the year.[21]

monetary policies Government economic policies that determine the size of a nation's money supply

THE GLOBAL ECONOMY IN THE TWENTY-FIRST CENTURY

As we leave the twentieth century behind and cross the threshold of the twenty-first century, it is useful to end our discussion of the U.S. business system with a look ahead. First, however, let's examine a variety of factors which, according to many experts, explain the booming economy that emerged in the 1990s. Table 1.3 summarizes one view of why things have gone so well for so many people in recent years.

Many of these factors are self-explanatory, but a few are worth special note. For example, financial deregulation has made it easier for banks and other lenders to compete with one another and to loan money. New methods for managing inventory by having parts and products arrive from suppliers just as they are needed has greatly reduced inventory carrying costs. The end of the Cold War has enabled the United States to cut its defense spending and direct those funds to other economic sectors.

What fields of business do today's businesspeople believe will be the most successful in the future (Internet-related, electronic, etc.)?

Three Major Forces

So, what does the future hold? First of all, most experts see three major forces driving the economy for the next decade:

- The information revolution will continue to enhance productivity across all sectors of the economy, but most notably in such information-dependent industries as finance, media, and wholesale and retail trade.

Table 1.3 *Ten Forces Driving Economic Expansion*

New breakthroughs in technology and increased productivity
Deregulation of financial markets and institutions
Increased entrepreneurial activity and investment of venture capital
New approaches to inventory management
End of the Cold War
Consumer spending boom
Budget-deficit reduction
Soaring stock market
Business-friendly federal government monetary policies
Increased international trade

Figure 1.7
Internet Users per 1,000 People

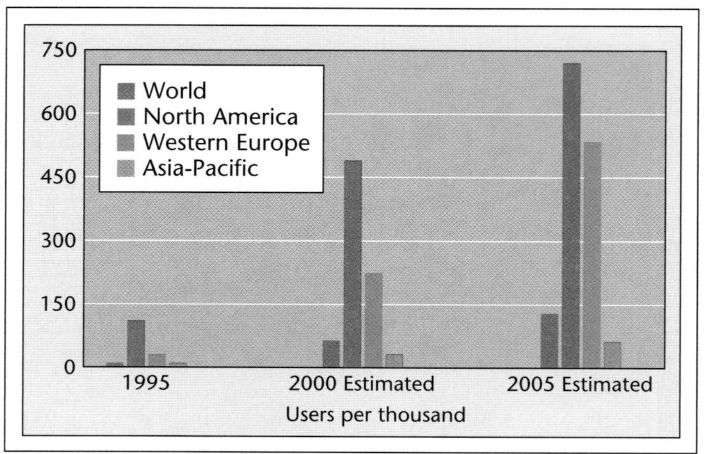

- New technological breakthroughs in such areas as biotechnology will create entirely new industries.
- Increasing globalization will create much larger markets while also fostering tougher competition among global businesses; as a result, companies will need to focus even more on innovation and cost cutting.[22]

Figures 1.7 through 1.9 clearly illustrate the significance of these forces. Figure 1.7 highlights the increased use of the Internet per 1,000 people for the entire world and for North America, Western Europe, and the Asia Pacific region for 1995 and 2000. As you can see, it also provides an estimate for 2005. The trends are clear and unambiguous: More and more people are using the Internet, and although the United States still leads the way, Western Europe is catching up and the Asia Pacific region is growing rapidly as well. Figure 1.8 amplifies these trends by isolating information-technology spending as a proportion of gross domestic product for numerous countries. Again, while the United States continues to lead the way, other countries are clearly catching up.[23]

Finally, Figure 1.9 underscores the fact that world exports are again booming. Exports grew rapidly from the late 1980s through 1997 but then flattened and subsequently declined for two years. This downward trend was primarily attributable to the currency crisis and resultant economic downturn in Asia. Between 1999 and 2000, however, exports again began increasing. Taken together, then, these data clearly reinforce the significance of information, technology, and globalization as the economic forces to be reckoned with in the twenty-first century.

Projected Trends and Patterns

As a result of these forces, economists also predict certain trends and patterns in economic indicators and competitive dynamics for at least the rest of this decade. Projected trends and patterns include the following:

- The economy will maintain strong and consistent growth rates, perhaps exceeding three percent per year.
- Inflationary surges and large budget deficits will become less likely.
- Countries that encourage free trade, innovation, and open financial systems will prosper.
- The most successful businesses will be those that are able most effectively to master new technologies and keep abreast of their competitors.[24]

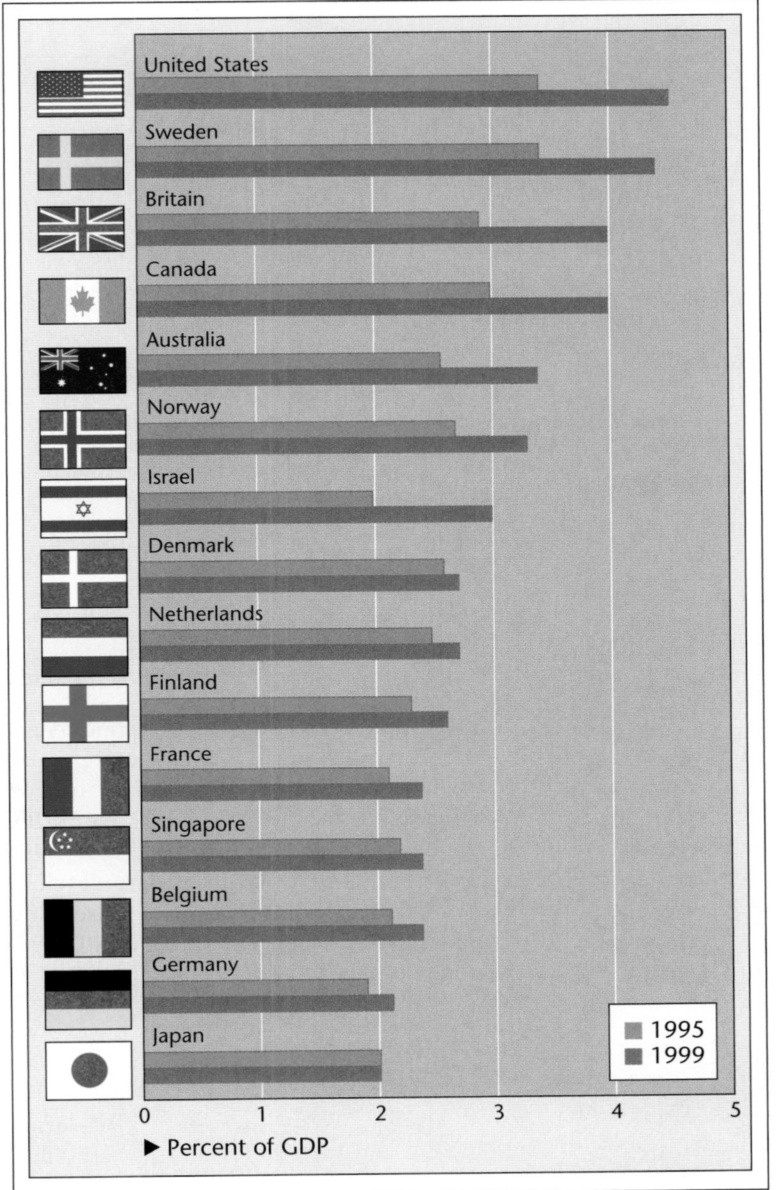

Figure 1.8
Information-Technology Spending

On the other hand, it is important to remember that the picture is not entirely rosy. The following statistics are sobering reminders that although domestic confidence in the United States is running at very high levels, some changes are still desirable:

- Because we import far more than we export, the U.S. trade deficit continues to grow, making the United States a debtor nation.
- Income inequality in the United States continues to be a problem. Although the medium household income is nearly $40,000 a year, the bottom fifth of U.S. households receives less than four percent of the national income. The top fifth, on the other hand, receives almost 50 percent of the national income.
- Consumer debt is steadily increasing. Nonbusiness bankruptcies increased 60 percent between 1991 and 1998, and many people are not saving enough to ensure themselves a comfortable retirement.
- About 44 million Americans lack health insurance.[25]

Figure 1.9
The Export Resurgence

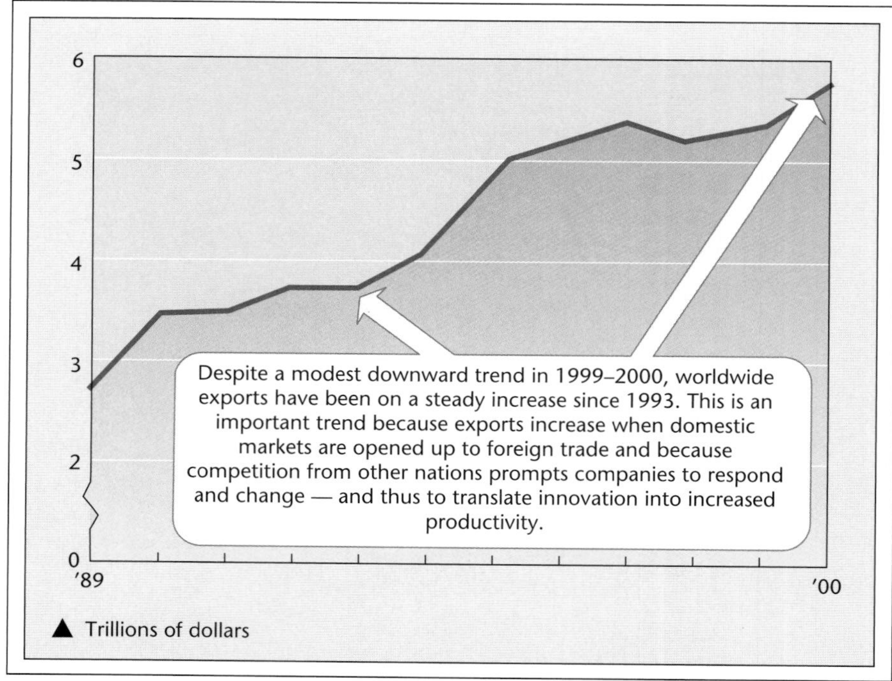

6
5
4
3
2
0
'89
'00
Despite a modest downward trend in 1999–2000, worldwide exports have been on a steady increase since 1993. This is an important trend because exports increase when domestic markets are opened up to foreign trade and because competition from other nations prompts companies to respond and change — and thus to translate innovation into increased productivity.
▲ Trillions of dollars

Still, all things considered, both the U.S. domestic economy and the global economy are in excellent shape in most respects. Businesses and entrepreneurs will enjoy tremendous opportunities for growth and expansion for at least the next several years, and managers astute enough to navigate the competitive waters will probably arrive at greater prosperity. But don't forget the old saying: If it were easy, everyone would do it. Thus, it's important for all managers—both current and future—to develop and maintain a comprehensive understanding of business so they can take more effective advantage of the opportunities and better address the challenges that they will face. This book will play a fundamental role in providing you with this understanding.

Continued from page 4

Sounding Out the Music Industry Oligopoly

The U.S. market for recorded music is an oligopoly controlled by five big firms:

- Universal/Polygram (24.5% market share)
- Warner Music (18.2% share)
- Sony Music (16.6% share)
- EMI Group PLC (12.9%)
- BMG Entertainment (12.2%)

As we noted at the outset of this chapter, there are also five major music-information sites on the Internet. What is less clear, however, is how the music business itself will change in response to the growth of the Internet.

One scenario calls for Web information sites to become a normal but separate part of the market—the recorded music giants will continue to produce music and the information sites will simply be part of the marketing process. According to a different scenario, the big music companies will eventually disappear and be replaced by Internet sites that make it easier and cheaper to get music. A third scenario sees the big music companies moving into the information business, either by initiating their own operations or by buying existing companies.

Questions for Discussion

1. Why is the recorded music market currently an oligopoly?
2. Explain how recorded-music companies and Internet-information sites use the factors of production in different ways.
3. Discuss some ways in which pricing, demand, and supply affect both recorded-music companies and Internet-information sites.
4. Which of the three scenarios posed at the end of the vignette do you regard as most likely? Why?
5. Suppose each of the five big recorded-music companies were to buy one of the Internet-information businesses. Forecast the ways in which this turn of events would affect the industry. What would you expect to happen next?

SUMMARY OF LEARNING OBJECTIVES

1 **Define the nature of U.S. *business* and identify its main goals.** *Businesses* are organizations that produce or sell goods or services to make a profit. *Profits* are the difference between a business's revenues and expenses. The prospect of earning profits encourages individuals and organizations to open and to expand businesses. The benefits of business activities also extend to wages paid to workers and to taxes that support government functions.

2 **Describe different types of global *economic systems* according to the means by which they control the *factors of production* through *input and output markets*.** An *economic system* is a nation's system for allocating its resources among its citizens. Economic systems differ in terms of who owns or controls the five basic *factors of production:* labor, capital, entrepreneurs, physical resources, and information resources. In *planned economies,* the government controls all or most factors. In *market economies,* which are based on the principles of *capitalism,* individuals and businesses control the factors of production and exchange them through *input and output markets.* Most countries today have *mixed market economies* that are dominated by one of these systems but include elements of the other. The process of *privatization* is an important means by which many of the world's planned economies are moving toward mixed market systems.

3 **Show how *demand* and *supply* affect resource distribution in the United States.** The U.S. economy is strongly influenced by markets, demand, and supply. *Demand* is the willingness and ability of buyers to purchase a good or service. *Supply* is the willingness and ability of producers to offer goods or services for sale. Demand and supply work together to set a *market* or *equilibrium price*—the price at which the quantity of goods demanded and the quantity of goods supplied are equal.

4 **Identify the elements of *private enterprise* and explain the various *degrees of competition* in the U.S. economic system.** The U.S. economy is founded on the principles of *private enterprise: private property rights, freedom of choice, profits,* and *competition.* Degrees of competition vary because not all industries are equally competitive. Under conditions of *pure competition,* numerous small firms compete in a market governed entirely by demand and supply. An *oligopoly* involves a handful of sellers only. A *monopoly* involves only one seller.

5 **Explain the criteria for evaluating the success of an economic system in meeting its goals and show how the federal government attempts to manage the U.S. economy.** The basic goals of an economic system are *stability, full employment,* and *growth.* Measures of how well an economy has accomplished these goals include *gross national product, gross domestic product, productivity, balance of trade,* and *national debt.* The U.S. government uses *fiscal policies* to manage the effects of its spending and revenue collection and *monetary policies* to control the size of the nation's money supply.

6 **Discuss the current economic picture in the United States and summarize expert opinions about its future.** The United States is riding the crest of a long-term economic boom. Growth has been strong, and unemployment and inflation remain low. Experts believe that these trends will continue for at least another few years. Important areas of the economy will include information technology, other forms of technological innovation, and globalization.

QUESTIONS AND EXERCISES

Questions for Review

1. What are the five factors of production? Is one factor more important than the others? If so, which one? Why?
2. What is GDP? Real GDP? What does each measure?
3. Explain the differences between the four degrees of competition and give an example of each. (Do not use the examples given in the text.)
4. Why is inflation both good and bad? How does the government try to control it?

Questions for Analysis

5. In recent years, many countries have moved from planned economies to market economies. Why do you think this has occurred? Can you envision a situation that would cause a resurgence of planned economies?
6. Identify a situation in which excess supply of a product led to decreased prices. Identify a situation in which a shortage led to increased prices. What eventually happened in each case? Why?
7. Explain how current economic indicators such as inflation and unemployment affect you personally. Explain how they will affect you as a manager.

Application Exercises

8. Choose a locally owned and operated business. Interview the owner to find out how the business uses the factors of production and identify its sources for acquiring them.
9. Visit a local shopping mall or shopping area. List each store that you see and determine what degree of competition it faces in the immediate environment. For example, if there is only one store in the mall that sells shoes, that store represents a monopoly. Note the businesses with direct competitors (two jewelry stores) and describe how they compete with one another.
10. Go to the library or log onto the Internet and research 10 different industries. Classify each according to degree of competition.

EXPLORING THE WEB

KNOWING THE DIFFERENCE BETWEEN RIGHT AND LEFT

Yes, Virginia, there is a central planning support group. It even has a Web page. Review the Marxism Page at:

www.anu.edu.au/polsci/marx/

and then consider the following questions:

1. Note the use of the term *Marxism* throughout the contents of the homepage. If you click to the Contemporary Marxist Material page, you'll note that the predominant term is Socialism. What do you think accounts for this difference in usage or emphasis?
2. Read *The Communist Manifesto* and play devil's advocate: Select two of the criticisms that Karl Marx and Friederich Engels leveled at capitalism in 1848 and defend the position that they are at least as applicable now as the authors believed them to be 150 years ago.

Or visit the National Center for Policy Analysis at:

www.ncpa.org/policy.html

Scroll down to and click on the "Privatization Issues" page posted by the Center, a lobbying organization that seeks to shift control of key economic resources from the public to the private sector. Although we tend to think of privatization as an issue facing former communist and socialist nations, you can explore this site to learn about different facets of the privatization issue here in the United States. Examine several sections of this site, and then consider the following questions:

1. What does the Center mean by "Privatization Innovations"? Choose one of the examples given and summarize the Center's argument for privatizing it.
2. Identify two "Privatization Deterrents" and explain the Center's reasons for characterizing each as a barrier to privatization.
3. Identify five or six of the Center's "Candidates for Privatization." Then choose one or two about which you disagree and explain why.

BUILDING YOUR BUSINESS SKILLS

ANALYZING THE PRICE OF DOING e-BUSINESS

This exercise enhances the following SCANS workplace competencies: demonstrating basic skills, demonstrating thinking skills, exhibiting interpersonal skills, and working with information.

GOAL

To encourage students to understand how the competitive environment affects a product's price.

SITUATION

Assume that you own a local business that provides Internet access to individuals and businesses in your community. Yours is one of four such businesses in the local market. Each of the four firms charges the same price: $12 per month for unlimited dial-up service. Your business also provides users with e-mail service; two of your competitors also offer e-mail service. One of these same two, plus the fourth, also provides the individual user with a free simple personal Web page. One competitor just dropped its price to $10 per month, and the other two have announced their intentions to follow suit. Your break-even price is $7 per customer. You are concerned about getting into a price war that may destroy your business.

METHOD

Divide into groups of four or five people. The assignment of each group is to develop a general strategy for handling competitors' price changes. In your discussion, take the following factors into account:

- How the demand for your product is affected by price changes
- The number of competitors selling the same or a similar product
- The methods you can use—other than price—to attract new customers and retain your current customers

ANALYSIS

Develop specific pricing strategies based on each of the following situations:

- Within a month after dropping the price to $10, one of your competitors raises the price back to $12.
- Two of your competitors drop their prices further—to $8 a month. As a result, your business falls off by 25 percent.
- One of your competitors that has provided customers with a free Web page has indicated that it will start charging an extra $2 a month for this optional service.
- Two of your competitors have announced they will charge individual users $8 a month but will charge a higher price (not yet announced) for businesses.
- All four providers (including you) are charging $8 a month. One goes out of business, and you know that another is in poor financial health.

FOLLOW-UP QUESTIONS

1. Discuss the role that various inducements other than price might play in affecting demand and supply in the market for Internet service.
2. Is it always in a company's best interest to feature the lowest prices?
3. Eventually, what form of competition is likely to characterize the market for Internet service?

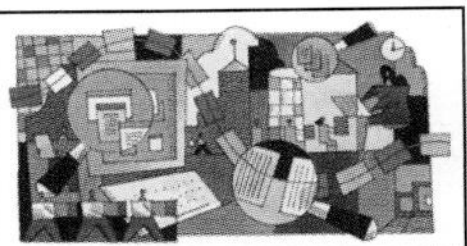

CRAFTING YOUR BUSINESS PLAN

MAKING SCENTS OF COMPETITION

THE PURPOSE OF THE ASSIGNMENT

1. To acquaint you with the process of navigating the *Business PlanPro* (BPP) software package (Version 4.0).
2. To demonstrate how two chapter topics—forms of competition and factors of production—can be integrated as components in the *BPP* planning environment.

3. To acquaint students with different forms of competition and to show how factors of production differ in importance among various companies.

ASSIGNMENT

After reading Chapter 1 in the textbook, open the BPP *software* and look around for information about types of competition and factors of production as it applies to two sample firms:* Flower Importer *(Fantastic Florals, Inc.) and* Sports Medicine Manufacturing *(Professional Athletic Equipment, Inc.). Then respond to the following items:*

1. Describe the Flower Importer's Product. [Sites to see in *BPP* (for this assignment): In the Plan Outline screen, click on **3.0 Products.** Then click on and read each of the following: **3.1 Product Description, 3.4 Sourcing,** and **3.6 Future Products.**]
2. Describe the type of competition faced by the Flower Importer. [Sites to see in *BPP:* In the Plan Outline screen, click on **3.0 Products;** then read **3.2 Competitive Comparison.** Return to the Plan Outline screen, click on and read each of the following: **4.0 Market Analysis Summary, 4.2 Industry Analysis, 4.2.3 Competition and Buying Patterns,** and **4.2.4 Main Competitors.**]
3. Repeat Steps 1 and 2 (in this assignment) for the Sports Medicine Manufacturing Company. [Sites to see in *BPP:* In the Plan Outline screen, click on **3.0 Products and Services** to identify the product. To identify the competition, in the Plan Outline screen click on **4.0 Market Analysis Summary** and **4.3 Industry Analysis.** Then read each of the following: **4.3.1 Industry Participants, 4.3.3 Competition and Buying Patterns,** and **4.3.4 Main Competitors.**]
4. Compare and contrast the kinds of competition faced by the two firms.
5. Choose one of the two companies and explore its business plan to see how many of its factors of production (labor, capital, entrepreneurs, physical resources, information resources) you can find. Try to identify at least one example of each factor for the company you have chosen. [Sites to see in *BPP:* In the Plan Outline screen, click on and explore the item categories within each of the following: **2.0 Company Summary, 3.0 Products and Services,** and **6.0 Management Summary.**]

FOR YOUR OWN BUSINESS PLAN

6. Describe in detail the competition that your business will face. Include a description of the competing firms and competing products and identify geographic locations of main competitors. What factors of production do you expect to use in your business?

*GENERAL TIPS FOR NAVIGATING IN *BPP*

1. Open the *BPP* program, examine the Welcome screen, and click on **Open a Sample Plan.**
2. From the **Open a Sample Plan** dialogue box, click on a sample company name; then click on **Open.**
3. On the Plan Manager screen, click on **Your Plan Outline;** then click on any of the lines (for example, **1.0 Executive Summary**).
4. You can always return to the Plan Outline screen by going to the bottom of the screen and clicking on the **Plan Outline** icon.
5. After finishing with one sample company, you can get to the next one by going to the top of the screen and clicking on **File** (on the menu bar). Then beneath that, select **Open Sample Plan.** This will exit you from the current company file and take you to the **Open Sample Plan** dialogue box, where you can select your next sample company.
6. When you are finished, you can close the program by going to the top of the screen and clicking on **File** (on the bar menu). Then beneath that, select **Exit.**

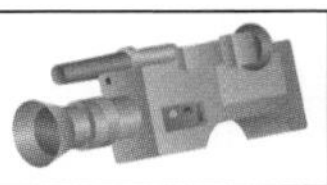

VIDEO EXERCISE

FACTORS TO CONSIDER: LANDS' END

Learning Objectives

The purpose of this video exercise is to help you

1. Understand the concept of profit.
2. Understand the nature of supply and demand.
3. Identify factors of production.

BACKGROUND INFORMATION

Lands' End began in 1963 by selling sailing equipment by catalog. By the late 1970s, its focus had shifted to clothing. In 1980, the company established a toll-free phone service that operated 24 hours a day, and by 1984 the Lands' End catalog appeared monthly. Today, the publicly owned firm, which boasts sales of $1.3 billion (for fiscal 2000), is one of the largest apparel brands in the United States, with numerous specialty catalogs and a growing international reputation.

THE VIDEO

This segment introduces Lands' End, the well-known retail-clothing catalog company, and the internal and external business environments in which it operates. You will see how the company deals with supply and demand, what kind of competition it faces, and where it goes to satisfy its production needs. The video also shows the company's employees at work and explains how the firm has grown from its entrepreneurial origins.

DISCUSSION QUESTIONS

1. How does Lands' End gauge demand for its products?
2. Where does Lands' End find labor resources?
3. Why would Lands' End's managers be concerned about making a profit?

FOLLOW-UP ASSIGNMENT

Consider a relatively small local business with which you are familiar—a favorite restaurant or independent book store. What do you think happens to the profits of this business? What would happen if the business suffered a loss in a given year?

FOR FURTHER EXPLORATION

Visit the Lands' End Web site <www.landsend.com> and locate the company's "Principles of Doing Business." Which of these relate to profit and loss? To demand and supply? To factors of production? What do you think is the purpose of publishing these principles on the company's Web site?

Chapter

2

Conducting Business in the United States

After reading this chapter, you should be able to:

1. ***Trace*** the history of business in the United States.
2. ***Identify*** the *major forms of business ownership.*
3. ***Explain*** *sole proprietorships* and *partnerships* and discuss the advantages and disadvantages of each.
4. ***Describe*** *corporations,* discuss their advantages and disadvantages, and identify different kinds of corporations.
5. ***Describe*** the basic issues involved in creating and managing a corporation.
6. ***Identify*** recent trends and issues in corporate ownership.
7. ***Discuss*** *mergers, acquisitions, divestitures,* and *spin-offs.*

Twin Pacts

Twin sisters Robin Fiddle Siegel and Mandi Fiddle Bergenfeld are pursuing a business strategy that is hard to understand. They want Twin Computer Training, Inc. <www.twincomputers.com>, their 10-year-old New York City–based consulting firm, to stay small while it grows big. A contradiction? Not to the sisters who are achieving their small-business goal through corporate alliances that, in a recent six-month period, increased the firm's revenues by 30 percent.

These alliances take shape when Twin Computer Training teams up with strategic partners, who are recognized as the best in their respective fields, to provide clients with total systems solutions. Believing that specialization is inescapable in a technologically complex business world, Twin supplements its computer-training services with the expertise of small companies in such specialties as systems integration, multimedia, Web design, and networking. "We provide our customers with a broad range of services," says Robin Fiddle Siegel, "but to succeed we have to remain focused on what we do best."

Twin's one-stop solution to serving small-business clients is catching on throughout the country. "Smart small businesses," says Daniel Nathanson, director of entrepreneurial programs at New York University's Stern School of Business, "are now creating alliances with people who offer complementary services and who have a similar client base, in order to compete against big companies." Forming alliances is so important that it is one of Twin's four stated corporate goals.

Siegel and Bergenfeld began building alliances when they started their company in 1991. Tired of working for large corporate bosses, the 27-year-old twins started working seven days a week for clients in need of computer training, specialized manuals, and around-the-clock help. They targeted corporate users in Manhattan and gave them the best service they could. By 1998, the firm was grossing $300,000 from a client roster that boasted such corporate all-stars as CBS, Chase Manhattan Bank, and Metropolitan Life.

Twin Computer's alliances take different forms, ranging from simple referrals to formal agreements involving joint bidding and revenue sharing. Each arrangement comes with risks for Twin, which will be associated with the failure of any partner. However, Siegel and Bergenfeld believe that these risks are preferable to branching into areas beyond their expertise. Rather than expanding—adding facilities, equipment, and employees—Twin calls in specialists with immediate solutions. This approach eliminates the need to keep searching for high-quality talent in a tight job market.

Granted, some companies are nervous about sharing clients, ideas, and employees with other firms in related fields. Admits Mark Voelpel, another small-business owner and alliance partner, "It's kind of a leap of faith to say that we have more to gain by opening up than we have to lose." Alliances become particularly complicated when competitors come together on a project. In these cases, the temporary partners usually sign formal legal contracts to safeguard proprietary information and guarantee confidentiality. Regardless of the internal arrangement between Twin and its partners, Siegel and Bergenfeld always present a unified front to clients. Rather than separate statements from each alliance member, clients get a single proposal, a single schedule, and one bill.

Over the years, the sisters have learned never to exchange money among alliance partners. "We don't want money to get in the way when we select our partners," explains Robin Siegel. "We are basically trading services and referrals. It's a win-win situation for us, our clients, and our partners."

"We don't want money to get in the way when we select our partners."

—Robin Siegel
cofounder, Twin Computer Training

Our opening story continues on page 58

As the owners of Twin Computer Training have learned, the structure of a business—how it organizes and relates to other companies—affects competitive and financial success. In this chapter, we examine the business structures and relationships that are open to both large and small companies. By focusing on the learning objectives of this chapter, you will better understand the options and the opportunities offered by different business structures.

A SHORT HISTORY OF BUSINESS IN THE UNITED STATES

The contemporary landscape of U.S. business ownership evolved over the course of many decades. Specifically, a look at the history of U.S. business shows a steady development from sole proprietorships to today's intricate corporate structures. We can gain a more detailed understanding of this development by tracing its history.

The Factory System and the Industrial Revolution

Industrial Revolution
Major mid-eighteenth-century change in production characterized by a shift to the factory system, mass production, and the specialization of labor

With the coming of the **Industrial Revolution** in the middle of the eighteenth century, a manufacturing revolution became possible by advances in technology and by the development of the factory system. Replacing hundreds of cottage workers who had turned out one item at a time, the factory system brought together in one place the materials and workers required to produce items in large quantities and the new machines needed for mass production.

In turn, mass production reduced duplication of equipment and allowed firms to purchase raw materials at better prices by buying in large lots. More importantly, it encouraged specialization of labor. Mass production replaced a system of highly skilled craftspeople who performed all the different tasks required to make a single item. Instead, a series of semiskilled workers, each trained to perform only one task and supported by specialized machines and tools, greatly increased output.

Laissez-Faire and the Entrepreneurial Era

Despite numerous problems during the nineteenth century, the U.S. banking system provided domestic businesses with some independence from European capital markets. In addition, improvements in transportation—the opening of the Erie Canal in the 1820s, steamboat navigation on major rivers, and the development of the railroads—made it not only possible but also economical to move products to distant markets.

Another significant feature was the rise of the entrepreneur on a grand scale. Like businesses in many other nations in the nineteenth century, U.S. business embraced the philosophy of *laissez-faire*—the principle that the government should not interfere in the

WebConnection

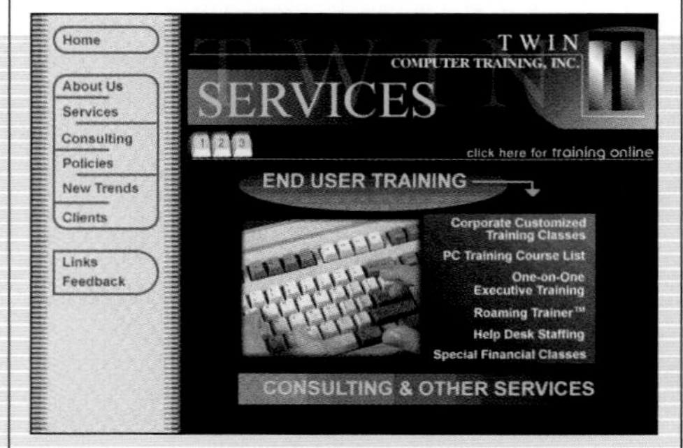

www.twincomputers.com

TWIN Computer Training, Inc. offers a wide range of custom computer training, documentation, and consulting services in the New York metropolitan area and International markets. Such training services are tailored to meet the unique business needs of customers both large and small. To understand more fully the role played by such firms as Palm Computing, Microsoft, Extensity, and Documentum and to see how TWIN can be your one-stop shop for all customized computer services and training, contact TWIN at the company's Web site.

Founders and their guests celebrate the birth of United States Steel in 1901. When it was born out of a merger of competing steel companies, U.S. Steel inherited 65% of the nation's steel-producing capacity; a little over a decade later, the firm's gross income was greater than that of the U.S. Treasury. Today it is known as USX <www.usx.com> *and is mainly in the oil business.*

economy but should instead let business function without regulation and according to its own natural laws. Risk taking and entrepreneurship became hallmarks of aggressive practices that created some of the biggest companies in the country and, ultimately, the world.

The rise of giant enterprises increased the national standard of living and made the United States a world power; but the size and economic power of such firms made it difficult, if not impossible, for competitors to enter their markets. Complete market control became a watchword in many industries, with many major corporations opting to collude rather than compete. Price fixing and other forms of market manipulation became common business practices, with captains of industry often behaving as robber barons. Reacting against unethical practices and the unregulated struggle for dominance, critics in many quarters began calling for corrective action and, ultimately, for antitrust laws and the breakup of monopolies.

Among other important laws, the Sherman Antitrust Act of 1890 and the Clayton Act of 1914 were passed specifically to limit the control a single business could gain in any given market. Other laws passed during this era sought to regulate a variety of employment and advertising practices, and still others attempted to regulate the ways in which businesses could handle their financial affairs.[1] (The appendix to this book provides more information about the legal environment of business, much of which was shaped in this era.)

The Production Era

The concepts of specialization and mass production that originated in the Industrial Revolution were further refined in the early twentieth century. At this time, many analysts of business organizations sought to focus management's attention on the production process. Especially among the theorists of so-called scientific management, increased efficiency through the "one best way" to accomplish production tasks became a major goal of management. Developed during the early 1900s, scientific management focused on maximizing output by developing the most efficient and productive ways for workers to perform carefully designed tasks.

Scientific management was given further impetus when, in 1913, Henry Ford introduced the moving assembly line and ushered in the **production era.** The focus was largely on manufacturing efficiency: By adopting fixed workstations, increasing task specialization, and moving the work to the worker, Ford increased productivity and lowered prices. In so doing, he made the automobile affordable for the average person.[2]

production era
Period during the early twentieth century in which U.S. business focused primarily on improving productivity and manufacturing efficiency

Lewis Hine, Carolina Cotton Mill, 1909. *It is estimated that children once formed about one-third of the industrial workforce in the United States. Photos like those taken by Hine were enlisted in the efforts to limit child labor—efforts that led, in 1916, to the Keating-Owens Act, which sought to discourage child labor by prohibiting interstate commerce in any goods manufactured by children under 16 years of age.*

The Concept of Countervailing Powers Both the growth of corporations and improved assembly-line output came at the expense of worker freedom. The dominance of big firms made it harder for individuals to go into business for themselves. In some cases, employer-run company towns gave people little freedom of choice, either in selecting an employer or in choosing what products to buy. If some balance were to be restored in the overall system, two elements within it had to grow in power: government and organized labor. Thus, the production era saw the rise of labor unions and the practice of collective bargaining (see Chapter 10). In addition, the Great Depression of the 1930s and World War II prompted the government to intervene in the economic system on a previously unforeseen scale. Today, business, government, and labor are often referred to by economists and politicians as the three *countervailing powers* in society: Although all are big and all are strong, not one of them completely dominates the others.

The Marketing Era

After World War II, the demand for consumer goods that had been frustrated by wartime shortages fueled the U.S. economy for some time. Despite brief periodic recessions, the 1950s and 1960s were prosperous times. Production continued to increase, technology advanced, and the standard of living rose. During this era, a new philosophy of business came of age—the marketing concept. Previously, business had been essentially production and sales oriented. Businesses tended to produce what other businesses produced, what they thought customers wanted, or simply what owners wanted to produce. Henry Ford supposedly said that his customers could buy his cars in whatever color they wanted—as long as it was black.

marketing concept
Idea that a business must focus on identifying and satisfying consumer wants in order to be profitable

According to the **marketing concept,** however, business starts with the customer. Producers of goods and services begin by determining what customers want and then providing it.[3] The most successful practitioners of the marketing concept are companies such as Procter & Gamble <www.pg.com> and Anheuser-Busch <www.anheuser-busch.com>. Such firms allow consumers to choose what best suits their needs by offering an array of products within a given market (toothpaste or beer, for example).

The Global Era

The 1980s saw the continuation of technological advances in production, computer technology, information systems, and communications capabilities. They also saw the emer-

Although no beer has yet succeeded in establishing itself as a global brand, Anheuser-Busch Companies <www.anheuser-busch.com> *is working hard to make its flagship brand, Budweiser, the first. In countries such as China (where Budweiser is called Baiwei, meaning "100 magnificents"), Anheuser aggressively targets young, upscale, better-educated beer drinkers—the counterparts of Americans who drink imported beers instead of Budweiser. Since being introduced to Bud in 1993, China has become Anheuser's fifth-largest foreign market (Canada is number one).*

gence of a truly global economy. American consumers drive cars made in Japan, wear sweaters made in Italy, and turn on CD players made in Taiwan. Elsewhere around the world, people drive Fords, drink Pepsi, wear Levi's jeans, use IBM computers, and watch Disney movies and television shows.

As we show in more detail in Chapter 3, globalization is a fact of life for most businesses today. Improved communication and transportation, in addition to more efficient international methods for financing, producing, distributing, and marketing products and services, have combined to open distant marketplaces to businesses as never before.

Admittedly, many U.S. businesses have been hurt by foreign competition. Many others, however, have profited from new foreign markets. International competition has forced many U.S. businesses to work harder than ever to cut costs, increase efficiency, and improve quality. A variety of important trends, opportunities, and challenges in the new global era are explored throughout this book.

The Internet Era

The turn of the twenty-first century has been accompanied by what many experts are calling the Internet era of business. Internet usage in North America grew from about 100 users per 1,000 people in 1995 to over 450 users per 1,000 people in 2000. Projections call for this figure to grow to nearly 750 users per 1,000 people by 2005. The growth rate in Western Europe, however, is expected to be even faster and, by 2005, will also become significant in the Pacific Asia region as well.

How does the growth of the Internet affect business? There are at least three different ways:

1. *The Internet will give a dramatic boost to trade in all sectors of the economy, especially services.* If the Internet makes it easier for all trade to grow, this is particularly true for trade in services on an international scale.
2. *The Internet will serve to level the playing field, at least to some extent, between larger and smaller enterprises regardless of what products or services they sell.* In the past, a substantial investment was needed to enter some industries and to enter foreign markets. Now, however, a small business based in central Missouri, southern

Italy, eastern Malaysia, or northern Brazil can set up a Web site and compete quite effectively with much larger businesses located around the world.

3. *The Internet also holds considerable potential as an effective and efficient networking mechanism among businesses.* So-called business-to-business networks can link firms with all of their suppliers, business customers, and strategic partners in ways that make it faster and easier for them to do business together.

TYPES OF BUSINESS ORGANIZATIONS

Whether they run small agricultural enterprises, large manufacturing concerns, or virtual e-commerce firms, all business owners must decide which form of legal organization best suits their goals: *sole proprietorship, partnership,* or *corporation.* Because this choice affects a host of managerial and financial issues, few decisions are more critical. In choosing a form of organization, entrepreneurs must consider their own preferences, their immediate and long-range needs, and the advantages and disadvantages of each form. Table 2.1 summarizes and compares the most important differences among the three major business forms.

Sole Proprietorships

sole proprietorship
Business owned and usually operated by one person who is responsible for all of its debts

The most basic legal form of business organization, the **sole proprietorship,** is owned and usually operated by one person.[4] Today, about 73 percent of all businesses in the United States are sole proprietorships; however, they account for only about 5 percent of the country's total business revenues.[5]

Although a sole proprietorship is usually small, it may be as large as a steel mill or a department store. Many of today's largest companies started out as sole proprietorships. Sears, Roebuck and Co. <www.sears.com> for example, was originally a one-man enterprise owned and operated by Richard Sears, who had started the R.W. Sears Watch Co. in 1886. (Alvah Roebuck, who had answered an advertisement for a watchmaker in 1887, joined Sears to form a partnership in 1893.)

Advantages of Sole Proprietorships Freedom is perhaps the most important benefit of sole proprietorships. Because they own their businesses completely, sole proprietors answer to no one but themselves. Moreover, they enjoy a certain degree of privacy because they need not report information about their operations to anyone (other than perhaps their banker). Finally, they alone reap the rewards of success or suffer the penalties of failure.

Furthermore, sole proprietorships are simple to form. Sometimes a proprietor can go into business simply by putting a sign on the door. The simplicity of legal setup procedures makes this form of organization appealing to self-starters and independent spirits. Sole proprietorships are also easy to dissolve. In fact, many proprietorships are organized

Table 2.1

Comparative Summary: Three Forms of Business

Business Form	Libability	Continuity	Management	Sources of Investment
Proprietorship	Personal, unlimited	Ends with death or decision of owner	Personal, unrestricted	Personal
General Partnership	Personal, unlimited	Ends with death or decision of any partner	Unrestricted or depends on partnership agreement	Personal by partner(s)
Corporation	Capital invested	As stated in charter, perpetual or for specified period of years	Under control of board of directors, which is selected by stockholders	Purchase of stock

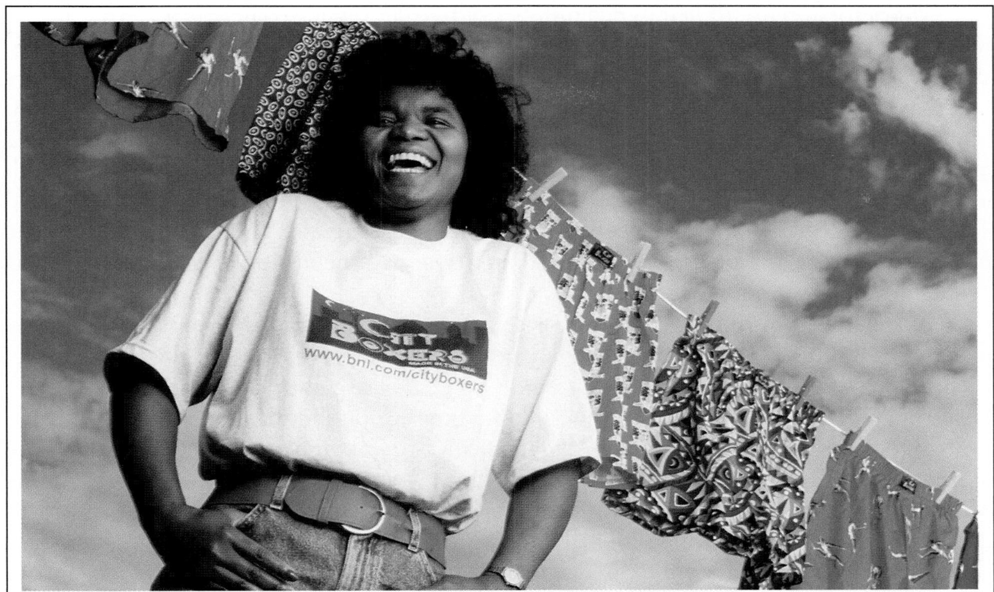

Betty Ford has set up shop online. Looking to tap into the market of men who buy in cyberspace, she's opened up City Boxers <www.cityboxers.com>, a virtual retailer that markets hand-tailored boxer shorts. In addition to the many advantages that sole proprietorships already enjoy, consider how costs are trimmed by operating online. After all, it's cheaper to build a virtual place of business than a physical storefront.

for short life spans. Rock concerts and one-time athletic events are often organized as sole proprietorships and then dissolved when the events are over.

Low start-up costs also make sole proprietorships attractive. Because some sole proprietorships must register only with state governments (to ensure that no other business bears the same name), legal fees are usually low. Some proprietorships, however, such as restaurants, beauty salons, florist shops, and pet shops must be licensed.

Finally, a particularly appealing feature of sole proprietorships is the tax benefits extended to new businesses that are likely to suffer losses in their early stages. Tax laws permit sole proprietors to treat sales revenues and operating expenses as part of their personal finances. They can thus cut their taxes by deducting business losses from income earned elsewhere (from personal sources other than the business). Because most new businesses lose money in the early stages of operation, tax incentives are quite helpful to entrepreneurs just starting out.

Disadvantages of Sole Proprietorships A major drawback of sole proprietorships, however, is **unlimited liability:** A sole proprietor is personally liable for all debts incurred by the business. If the business fails to generate enough cash, bills must be paid out of the proprietor's own pocket. If bills are not paid, creditors can claim many of the proprietor's personal possessions including personal savings, furniture, and automobiles. Another disadvantage is lack of continuity: A sole proprietorship legally dissolves when the owner dies. Although the business can be reorganized if a successor is prepared to take over, executors or heirs must otherwise sell the assets of the business.

unlimited liability
Legal principle holding owners responsible for paying off all debts of a business

Finally, a sole proprietorship depends on the resources of a single individual. If the proprietor is a skillful manager with ample resources, this limitation is not a problem. In many cases, however, owners' managerial and financial limitations put limits on their organizations. Sole proprietors often find it hard to borrow money, not only to start up but also to expand. Many commercial bankers fear that they will not be able to recover loans when sole proprietors become disabled or insolvent. Therefore, would-be proprietors must often rely on personal savings or family loans for start-up funds.

What are the pros and cons of being self-employed? Of working for a major firm?

Partnerships

The second form of legal organization is the partnership, which is frequently used by professionals.[6] The most common type of partnership, the **general partnership,** is simply a

general partnership
Business with two or more owners who share in both the operation of the firm and in financial responsibility for its debts

sole proprietorship multiplied by the number of partner-owners. There is no legal limit to the number of parties who may form a general partnership—the average number is slightly fewer than 10. Moreover, partners may invest equal or unequal sums of money and may earn profits that bear no relation to their investments. Thus, a partner with no financial investment in a two-person partnership could receive 50 percent or more of the profits. Bill Trainer and Harvey Woodman, for example, opened an automatic car wash in Houston, Texas, called Shinin' Bright. Woodman put up most of the funds, and Trainer provided the expertise needed to manage the business. They agreed to split the profits equally for the first three years. Trainer then had the option to invest some of his profits in return for a larger share.

Partnerships are often extensions of sole proprietorships. The original owner may want to expand, or the business may have grown too big for one person to handle. Richard Sears sold his watch business and, two years later, formed a mail-order catalog business. When his new business grew so large that he could no longer run it by himself, he invited former business associate Alvah Roebuck to join him as a partner. Consider the more recent example of Pentagram Design Inc. <www.pentagram.com>, a prestigious architectural design partnership formed in London by three prominent professionals who had previously been working alone. Realizing that they could attract more and larger clients by working together, the three agreed to form a partnership, which was originally called Fletcher Forbes Gill after its founders. The name was changed to Pentagram when two new partners were added in 1972, and today the firm boasts such clients as Hewlett-Packard, Anne Klein, Williams-Sonoma, and the American Museum of Natural History.[7] Like Pentagram, many professional organizations such as legal, architectural, and accounting firms are organized as partnerships.

Advantages of Partnerships The most striking advantage of general partnerships is their ability to grow with the addition of new talent and money. Because lending institutions prefer to make loans to enterprises that are not dependent on single individuals, partnerships find it easier to borrow money than sole proprietorships. Moreover, most partnerships have access to the resources of more than one individual. Thus, when they needed money to fund an expansion program, Sears and Roebuck invited new partners to join them by investing in the company. Likewise, as Pentagram's volume of work has continued to grow, the firm has kept pace by inviting new partners to join the firm and by adding various professional staff members. Most new partners invited to join Pentagram do so because it gives them greater business opportunities and a work environment that allows individuals to put their personal stamp on their work. "I look around," says

> ***"For what we want out of it as individuals, we actually have the best deal going. You can't have experience on a variety of projects when you're by yourself."***
>
> *—Lowell Williams, partner in Pentagram Design Inc.*

WebConnection

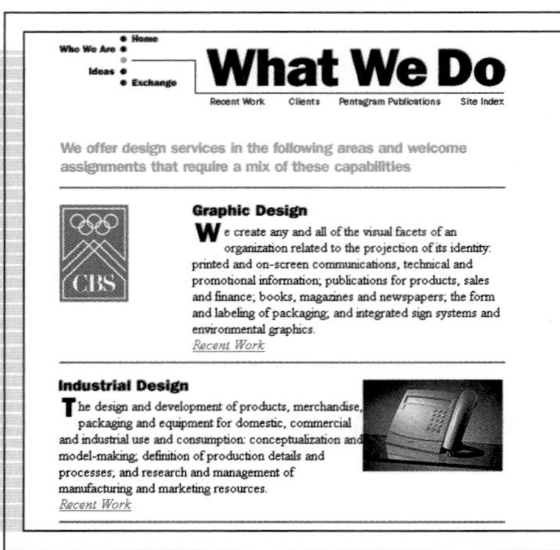

www.pentagram.com

Pentagram is a design firm with 17 full-time partners and 160 employees working out of offices in San Francisco, New York, London, and Austin, Texas. To find out how the company itself characterizes the working relationships between its "principals" and "design teams," log on to its Web site.

partner Lowell Williams, "and for what we want out of it as individuals, we actually have the best deal going. . . . You can't have experience on a variety of projects when you're by yourself." Each new partner must also buy a stake in the firm, providing an infusion of new cash to support expansion. Today, Pentagram has 17 partners, 160 employees, offices in London, New York, San Francisco, and Austin, Texas, and annual revenues in excess of $25 million.

Like a sole proprietorship, a partnership can be organized by meeting only a few legal requirements. Even so, all partnerships must begin with an agreement of some kind. All but two states subscribe to the Revised Uniform Limited Partnership Act. This statute describes a written certificate that requires the filing of specific information about the business and its partners. Partners may also agree to bind themselves in ways not specified by the certificate. In any case, a partnership agreement should answer questions such as the following:

- Who invested what sums of money?
- Who will receive what share of the profits?
- Who does what and who reports to whom?
- How may the partnership be dissolved? In the event of dissolution, how will assets be distributed?
- How will surviving partners be protected from claims made by a deceased partner's heirs?

Although it helps to clarify matters for the partners themselves, the partnership agreement is strictly a private document—no laws require partners to file their agreements with any government agency. Nor are partnerships regarded as legal entities—in the eyes of the law, a partnership is just two or more people working together. Because partnerships have no independent legal standing, the Internal Revenue Service taxes partners as individuals.

Disadvantages of Partnerships For general partnerships, as for sole proprietorships, unlimited liability is the greatest drawback: By law, each partner may be liable for all debts incurred in the name of the partnership. If any partner incurs a business debt (with or without the knowledge of the other partners), all partners may still be held liable.

For example, shortly after Trainer and Woodman's car wash opened, their equipment severely damaged a customized van. The owner sued for damages. Because the business was just getting started and had no financial reserves, Trainer and Woodman were faced with the prospect of covering the costs from their own pockets. Unfortunately, Trainer lacked the personal funds to cover his share. To keep the business afloat, Woodman agreed to lend Trainer the money for his half of the business expense.

Partnerships also share with sole proprietorships the potential lack of continuity: When one partner dies or leaves it, the original partnership dissolves, even if one or more of the other partners want it to continue. The dissolving of a partnership need not cause a loss of sales revenues. Surviving partners may form a new partnership to retain the old firm's business.

A related disadvantage is the difficulty of transferring ownership. No partner may sell out without the consent of the others. A partner who wants to retire or to transfer interest to a son or daughter must have the other partners' consent. Thus, the life of a partnership depends on the ability of retiring partners to find buyers who are compatible with current partners. Failure to do so may end a partnership. Of course, remaining partners may also buy out a retiring partner.

Finally, a partnership provides little or no guidance for resolving internal conflicts. Suppose that one partner wants to expand the business rapidly and the other wants it to grow cautiously. If the partnership agreement grants equal power, it may be difficult for the two partners to resolve the dispute. CPR MultiMedia Solutions <www.cprmms.com>, a highly successful Maryland firm specializing in big-screen projections for public events, recently went through some difficult times because of conflict between its two partners. As the business grew, it developed into two divisions: rentals and systems building. Jeff Studley took over rentals and Brett Cosor handled systems. Before long, the two partners were pulling in different directions, even competing with each other for resources. "All of a sudden," recalls Studley, "there were two moons pushing tides in different directions, and that creates a lot of turbulence." When things reached a boiling point, a trained mediator had to be called in to put the team back together again.[8]

Conflicts can involve disagreements ranging from the company smoking policy to key managerial practices. Among the events that may increase the chances of conflict among partners are a divorce by one partner, significant growth in the business, a partner bringing a spouse or relative into the business, a partner wanting to take greater profits out of the partnership, a romantic relationship between partners, a serious accident or illness affecting a partner, and unethical or questionable business practices on the part of one partner. Quite simply, it is sometimes impossible to resolve disagreements. When this impasse occurs, the partnership is usually dissolved, often in conjunction with legal battles among the former partners.

Alternatives to General Partnerships Because of these disadvantages, general partnerships are among the least popular legal forms of business. In the United States today, roughly 1.65 million partnerships generate about 6 percent of total sales revenues.[9] To resolve some of the problems inherent in general partnerships, especially unlimited liability, some partners have tried other types of agreements. The **limited partnership,** for example, allows for both limited partners and a general partner. **Limited partners** invest money without being liable for debts incurred by general partners. If the business fails, limited partners are liable only to the extent of their investments. However, limited partners cannot take active roles in business operations. By law, a limited partnership must have at least one **general** (or **active**) **partner,** mostly for liability purposes. The general partner is usually the person who runs the business and bears the responsibility for its survival and growth.

limited partnership
Type of partnership consisting of limited partners and an active or managing partner

limited partner
Partner who does not share in a firm's management and is liable for its debts only to the limit of the said partner's investment

general (or **active**) **partner**
Partner who actively manages a firm and who has unlimited liability for its debts

Figure 2.1 compares the differences in liability between general partnerships and limited partnerships. As you can see, creditors in both cases have access to the personal assets of general partners. Limited partners, however, are protected from liability incurred by the partnership.

A variation on the limited partnership, the **master limited partnership (MLP),** is growing in popularity. Under this arrangement, an organization sells shares (partnership interests) to investors on public markets such as the New York Stock Exchange <www.nyse.com>. Investors are paid back out of profits. The master partner retains at least 50-percent ownership and runs the business, while the minority partners have no management voice. (The master partner differs from a general partner, who has no such minimum ownership restriction.) The master partner must provide minority partners with detailed operating and financial data on a regular basis. The Boston Celtics Limited <www.nba.com/celtics> is among the best-known partnerships of this form. A master partnership, comprised of members of the Gaston family, owns 52 percent of the team. More than 80,000 individual investors, most with less than 10 shares each, comprise the minority partnership that owns the remaining 48 percent.

master limited partnership (MLP)
Form of organization that sells shares to investors who receive profits and pay taxes on individual income from profits

Cooperatives

Sometimes, groups of sole proprietorships or partnerships agree to work together for their common benefit by forming **cooperatives.** Although cooperatives make up only a minor segment of the U.S. economy, their role is still quite important in agriculture. A cooperative combines the freedom of the sole proprietorship with the financial power of a corporation. Cooperatives give their members greater production power, greater marketing power, or both. On the other hand, the cooperative is by nature limited to serving the specific needs of its members.

cooperative
Form of organization in which a group of sole proprietorships and/or partnerships agrees to work together for common benefits.

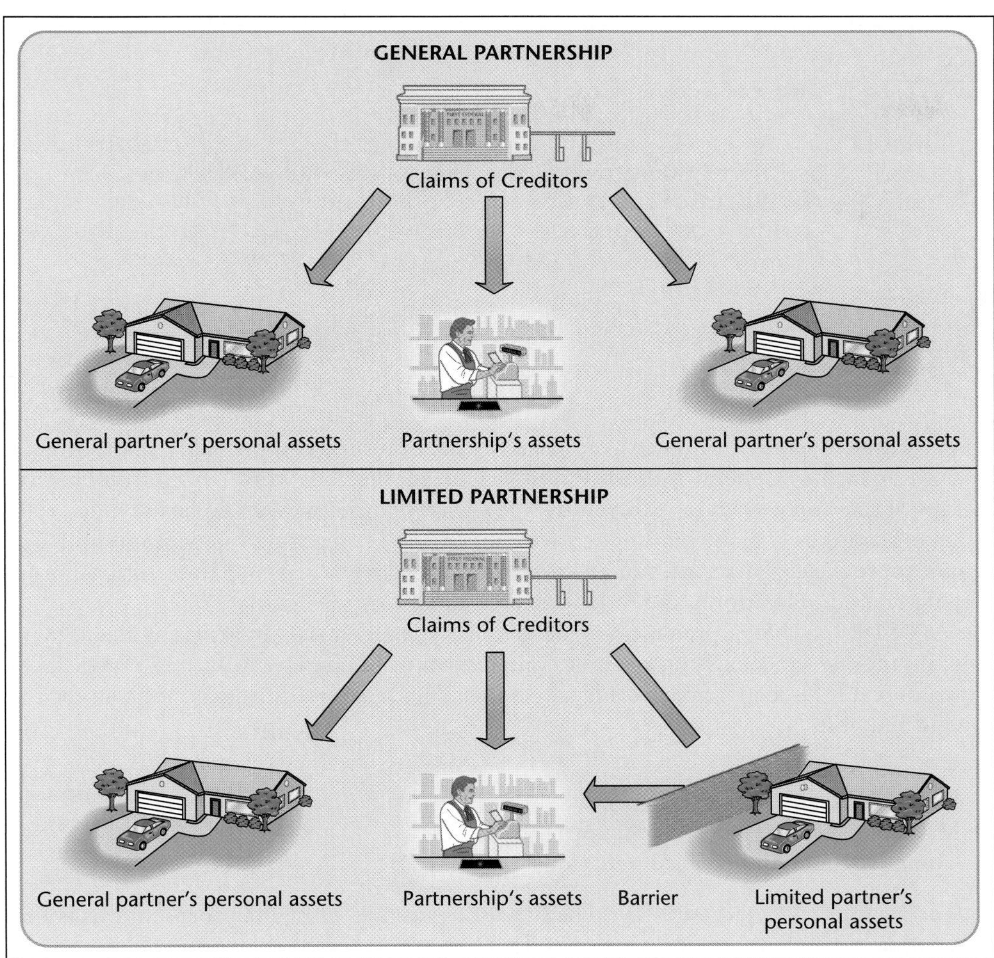

Figure 2.1
Partnership Liability

One well-known cooperative is Ocean Spray <www.oceanspray.com>, a juice producers' cooperative that includes 900 cranberry and grapefruit growers around the country and controls 75 percent of the cranberry market. The cooperative structure allows members to buy things such as fertilizer in bulk, negotiate shipping contracts, and develop a nationwide marketing campaign, just like one big company. Instead of distributing a share of the profits to stockholders, cooperatives divide all profits among their members.[10] Other big cooperatives in the United States include Riceland <www.riceland.com>, Sunkist <www.sunkist.com>, and Blue Diamond Growers <www.bluediamond.com>. Other countries also have cooperatives. Almost all Japanese farmers belong to Nokyo, one of the largest cooperatives in the world.

Corporations

There are about 4.6 million corporations in the United States. As you can see from Figure 2.2, although they account for about 20 percent of all U.S. businesses, they generate about 89 percent of all sales revenues.[11] Almost all larger businesses use this form, and corporations dominate the global business landscape. According to the most recent available data, General Motors <www.gm.com>, one of the world's largest industrial firms, posted annual revenue of over $161 billion, with total profits of almost $3 billion. Even "smaller" large corporations post huge sales figures. Ball Corporation <www.ball.com>, a Colorado-based container manufacturer that ranks 500th among U.S. corporations, posted a profit of $17 million on annual sales of $2.9 billion. Given the size and influence of this form of ownership, we will devote a great deal of attention to various aspects of corporations.

WebConnection

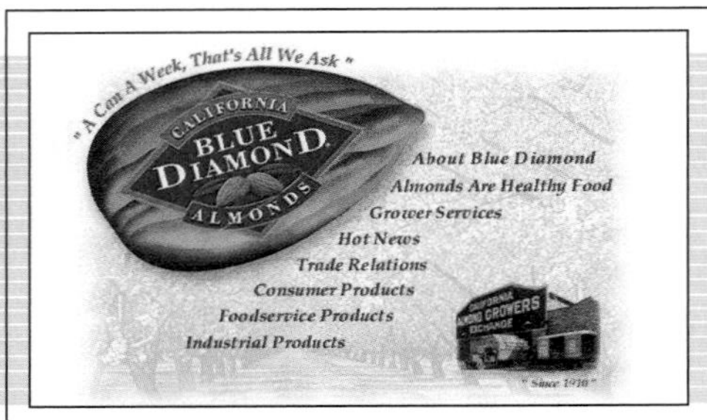

www.bluediamond.com

Boasting 4,000 growers, Blue Diamond is the world's largest tree nut processor and marketer. To find out how—and why—the company developed as a cooperative, and to find out more about the ways in which the company services its grower-members, access the firm's Web site.

The Corporate Entity When you think of corporations, you probably think of giant businesses such as General Motors and IBM. Indeed, the very word *corporation* inspires images of size and power. In reality, however, the tiny corner newsstand has as much right to incorporate as a giant automaker. Moreover, the incorporated newsstand and GM would share the characteristics of all **corporations:** legal status as separate entities, property rights and obligations, and indefinite life spans.

corporation
Business that is legally considered an entity separate from its owners and is liable for its own debts; owners' liability extends to the limits of their investments

In 1819, the U.S. Supreme Court defined a corporation as "an artificial being, invisible, intangible, and existing only in contemplation of the law." By these words, the Court defined the corporation as a legal person. Thus, corporations may perform the following activities:

- Sue and be sued
- Buy, hold, and sell property
- Make and sell products to consumers
- Commit crimes and be tried and punished for them

Advantages of Incorporation The biggest advantage of regular corporations is **limited liability:** The liability of investors is limited to their personal investments in the corporation. In the event of failure, the courts may seize and sell a corporation's assets but cannot touch the personal possessions of investors. For example, if you invest $1,000 in a corporation that goes bankrupt, you may lose your $1,000, but no more. In other words, $1,000 is the extent of your liability.

limited liability
Legal principle holding investors liable for a firm's debts only to the limits of their personal investments in it

Another corporate advantage is continuity. Because it has a legal life independent of its founders and owners, a corporation can, at least in theory, continue forever. Shares of stock

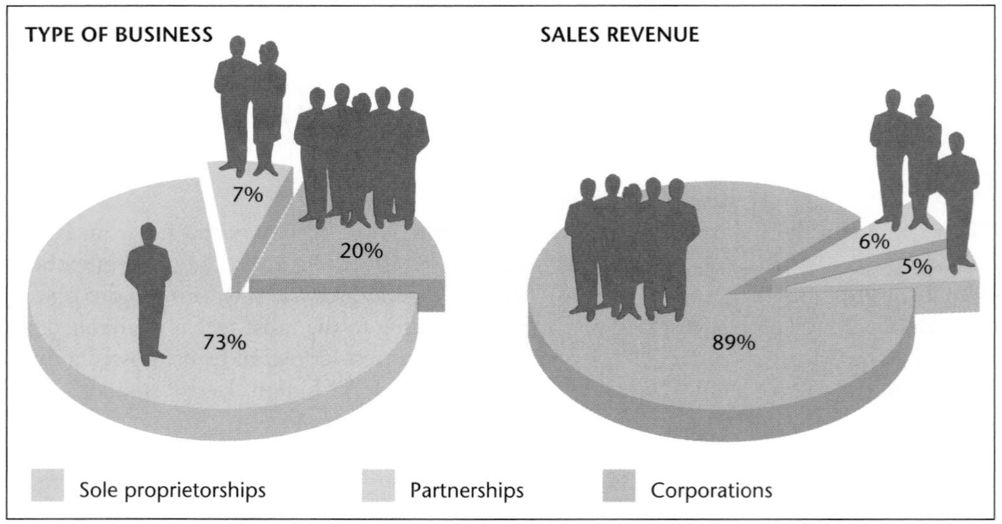

Figure 2.2
Proportions of U.S. Firms in Terms of Type of Business Organization and Sales Revenue

may be sold or passed on from generation to generation. Moreover, most corporations also benefit from the continuity provided by professional management.

Finally, corporations have advantages in raising money. By selling more stock, they can expand the number of investors and the amount of available funds. Continuity and the legal protections afforded to corporations tend to make lenders more willing to grant loans. MGM Grand, Inc. <www.mgmgrand.com> issued new stock in 2000 to help cover the costs of acquiring its major rival, Mirage Resorts, Inc. <www.mirageresorts.com>.[12]

Why do sole proprietorships and general partnerships have unlimited liabilities while other forms of business do not?

Disadvantages of Incorporation One of the corporation's chief attractions is ease of transferring ownership, however, this same feature can also complicate the lives of managers. Figure 2.3 outlines a basic **tender offer**—an offer to buy shares made by a prospective buyer directly to the target corporation's shareholders, who then make individual decisions about whether or not to sell. Now consider the recent travails of several

tender offer
Offer to buy shares made by a prospective buyer directly to a target corporation's shareholders, who then make individual decisions about whether to sell

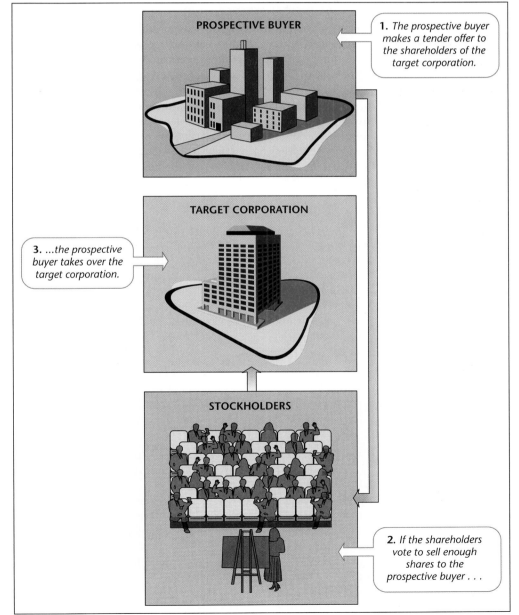

Figure 2.3
Simple Tender Offer

California-based bank corporations. First of all, one bank, First Interstate, tried to gain control of one of its largest competitors, Bank of America <www.bankofamerica.com>, by buying Bank of America shares on the open market. First Interstate was unable to acquire enough Bank of America shares to gain control and ended up having to sell its shares at a big loss. In its weakened financial state, First Interstate then became a target itself and was purchased by a third bank corporation, Wells Fargo & Company <www.wellsfargo.com>. Unfortunately, the corporate marriage paid few dividends for Wells Fargo because the cost of integrating the two companies was far greater than anticipated.

Another disadvantage of incorporation is the start-up cost. Forming a corporation is more expensive than forming a sole proprietorship or a partnership. For one thing, corporations are heavily regulated, and incorporation entails meeting the complex legal requirements of the state in which the firm is chartered. Nonetheless, some states provide much better environments in which to charter corporations than other states. For this reason, businesses often take out charters and maintain small headquarters facilities in one state while conducting most of their business in another state. With its low corporate tax rate, for instance, Delaware is home to more corporations than any other state.

double taxation
Situation in which taxes may be payable both by a corporation on its profits and by shareholders on dividend incomes

Double Taxation The greatest potential drawback to corporate organization, however, is **double taxation.** First, a regular corporation must pay income taxes on company profits. In addition, stockholders must pay taxes on income returned by their investments in the corporation. Consider the case of Dayton Hudson Corp. <www.targetcorp.com>, the large retailer who owns such chains as Target, Mervyn's, Dayton's, Hudson's, and Marshall Field's. In 1998, the firm paid corporate income taxes on profits of $935 million and also paid its shareholders a dividend of 27 cents per share. In turn, those shareholders paid personal income tax on those dividends. Thus, the profits earned by Dayton Hudson and other corporations were essentially taxed twice—once at the corporate level and again at the ownership level. In contrast, because profits are treated as owners' personal income, sole proprietorships and partnerships are taxed only once. The "Life Cycle of an e-Business" box in this chapter details some of the issues that Garden.com had to address when it made the legal transformation from partnership to corporation.

Because of the various advantages and disadvantages of the corporation as a form of business ownership, various legal statutes have led to the creation of different kinds of corporations. These laws are generally intended to help specific kinds of businesses take advantage of the benefits of the corporate model without assuming all of the attending disadvantages. We discuss these various corporate forms next.

Types of Corporations

Corporations may be broadly classified as either *public* or *private.* But within these broad categories, we can identify the specific types of corporations summarized in Table 2.2.

closely held (or **private**) **corporation**
Corporation whose stock is held by only a few people and is not available for sale to the general public

Private and Public Corporations The most common form of corporation in the United States is the **closely held corporation,** often referred to simply as a **private corporation.** The stock of a closely held corporation is held by only a few people and is not available for sale to the general public. The controlling group of stockholders may be a family, a management group, or even the firm's employees. Gallo Wine <www.gallo.com>, Levi Strauss <www.levistrauss.com>, Mars Inc. <www.mars.com>, and Hallmark <www.hallmark.com> are all private corporations.[13] Because few investors will buy unknown stocks, most new corporations start out as private corporations. As the corporation grows and investors see evidence of success, it may issue shares for sale to outside investors as a way to raise additional money.

publicly held (or **public**) **corporation**
Corporation whose stock is widely held and available for sale to the general public

When shares are publicly issued, the firm becomes a **publicly held corporation,** frequently called a **public corporation.** The stock of a public corporation is widely held and available for sale to the general public. For example, anyone who has the money can buy shares of Caterpillar, Digital Equipment, Motorola, or Silicon Graphics. In theory, anyone can buy sufficient shares in any of these firms to gain a controlling interest. In reality, of course, the large number of shares in the market and the cost per share actually make

Table 2.2

Types of Corporations

Type	Distinguishing Features	Examples
Closely Held	• Stock held by only a few people • Subject to corporate taxation	Blue Cross/Blue Shield MasterCard Primestar
Publicly Held	• Stock widely held among many investors • Subject to corporate taxation	Dell Computer Polaroid Texas Instruments
SubChapter S	• Organized much like closely held corporation • Subject to additional regulation • Subject to partnership taxation	Minglewood Associates Entech Pest Systems Frontier Bank
Limited Liability	• Organized much like a publicly held corporation • Subject to additional regulation • Subject to partnership taxation	Pacific Northwest Associates Global Ground Support Ritz Carlton
Professional	• Organized like a partnership • Subject to partnership taxation • Limited business liability • Unlimited professional liability	Norman Hui, DDS & Associates B&H Engineering Anderson, McCoy & Orta
Multinational	• Spans national boundaries • Subject to regulation in multiple countries	Toyota Nestlé General Electric

such takeovers both rare and extremely expensive. Motorola <www.motorola.com>, for instance, has issued 600 million shares of stock. With its recent share price of $100, it would thus take $30 billion to buy half the stock in the firm.

S Corporations The **S corporation,** a relatively new form of business ownership, is a hybrid of a closely held corporation and a partnership. Such a firm is organized and operates like a corporation. For tax purposes, however, it is treated as a partnership. Several stringent legal conditions must be met for a firm to qualify as an S corporation. For example, there can be no more than 35 shareholders, all shareholders must be individuals, estates, or certain kinds of trusts, and there can be only one type of stock.

S corporation
Hybrid of a closely held corporation and a partnership; organized and operated like a corporation but treated as a partnership for tax purposes

Limited Liability Corporations Another relatively new hybrid form of ownership is the **limited liability corporation, or LLC.**[14] The owners of such a business are taxed like partners, each paying personal taxes only. However, they also enjoy the benefits of limited liability accorded to corporations. LLCs have grown in popularity in recent years, partially because of IRS rulings that allow corporations, partnerships, and foreign investors to be partial owners. Myriad joint ventures and other partnerships in the wireless communications industry have made the LLC one of the fastest-growing forms of business ownership. Many local wireless services are operated as LLCs, with ownership under the control of one or more national service providers, one or more equipment suppliers, and one or more strong local partners.

limited liability corporation, or LLC
Hybrid of a publicly held corporation and a partnership in which owners are taxed as partners but enjoy the benefits of limited liability

Figure 2.4 illustrates the differences in liability among corporations, S corporations, and limited liability companies. As you can see, the personal assets of shareholders are

Life Cycle of an e-Business

Getting Off the Ground at Garden.com

When Cliff and Lisa Sharples and Jamie O'Neill left Trilogy Software <www.trilogy.com> to go into business for themselves, they initially created a three-person partnership legally named the Asbury Group—a name derived from a popular gathering place on the campus of Northwestern University they once frequented. They used this legal framework to engage in some consulting activities while they figured out what business they really wanted to launch. Why did they elect to use the partnership arrangement at first? Basically, for two reasons: It was easy to set up and they knew it would only be temporary.

After they settled on the general direction they wanted to go (that is, a Web-based retailing operation), they incorporated Asbury to take advantage of the legal benefits of corporate ownership. As part of the incorporation process, they also changed the name of the business to Garden Escape. During the early start-up period, they had plenty of capital with which to work. Indeed, so many investors wanted a piece of the new company that the founders actually turned down some of them.

Garden.com was officially launched on March 20, 1996, the first day of spring, when its Web site went live. In July of that same year, the firm opened a publishing office in Des Moines, Iowa, and announced the impending publication of an upscale magazine called *Garden Escape* <www.garden.com/cgi>. The idea was to publish a print magazine that would complement the Garden.com Web site. Garden.com also formed a strategic alliance with PRIMEDIA <www.primediainc.com> to distribute the magazine to key locations at airport and major metropolitan-area newsstands. The company hired Doug Jimerson, the editor of *Better Homes and Gardens,* to run the magazine business.

In 1998, Garden Escape entered into a partnership agreement with the leading gardening publication, *Horticulture Magazine,* to custom-design and launch its own Web site. In early 1999, the corporation officially changed its name to Garden.com to match the URL of its centerpiece Web site.

After getting all phases of their business up and running, fine-tuning their strategy, establishing Garden.com as a major Web site for garden-related products, and getting *Garden Escape* magazine off the ground, Cliff, Lisa, and Jamie finally decided in 1999 that the time was ripe for an initial public offering (IPO) of stock to raise additional capital. In September 1999, 4,100,000 shares of common stock were offered at a price of $12 a share. The IPO, therefore, generated almost $50 million in additional capital.

This cash infusion brought with it heady optimism and the means both to continue operations and to expand into new markets. By mid-2000, however, most of the new capital was gone. Unfortunately, because investors had also begun to shun dot-coms that had yet to turn a profit, another stock offering was not feasible. Senior managers, therefore, began seeking other avenues for new funding, such as additional bank credit. By November 2000, when it had become apparent that new funds were unavailable, Cliff, Lisa, and Jamie began looking for another company to assume partial or full ownership of Garden.com in exchange for the financial investment necessary to keep the business in operation.

---

similarly protected from creditors with claims on the corporation's assets. Although the LLC is unincorporated, its owners—called *members*—are liable for the company's obligations only to the extent of their capital contributions.

professional corporation Form of ownership allowing professionals to take advantage of corporate benefits while granting them limited business liability and unlimited professional liability

Professional Corporations The **professional corporation** is also a relatively fast-growing form of ownership. These corporations are most likely comprised of doctors, lawyers, accountants, and similar groups of professionals. Until recently, such firms were not allowed to incorporate and had to operate as partnerships. In recent years, however, most states have passed laws allowing them to take advantage of the health and pension plans

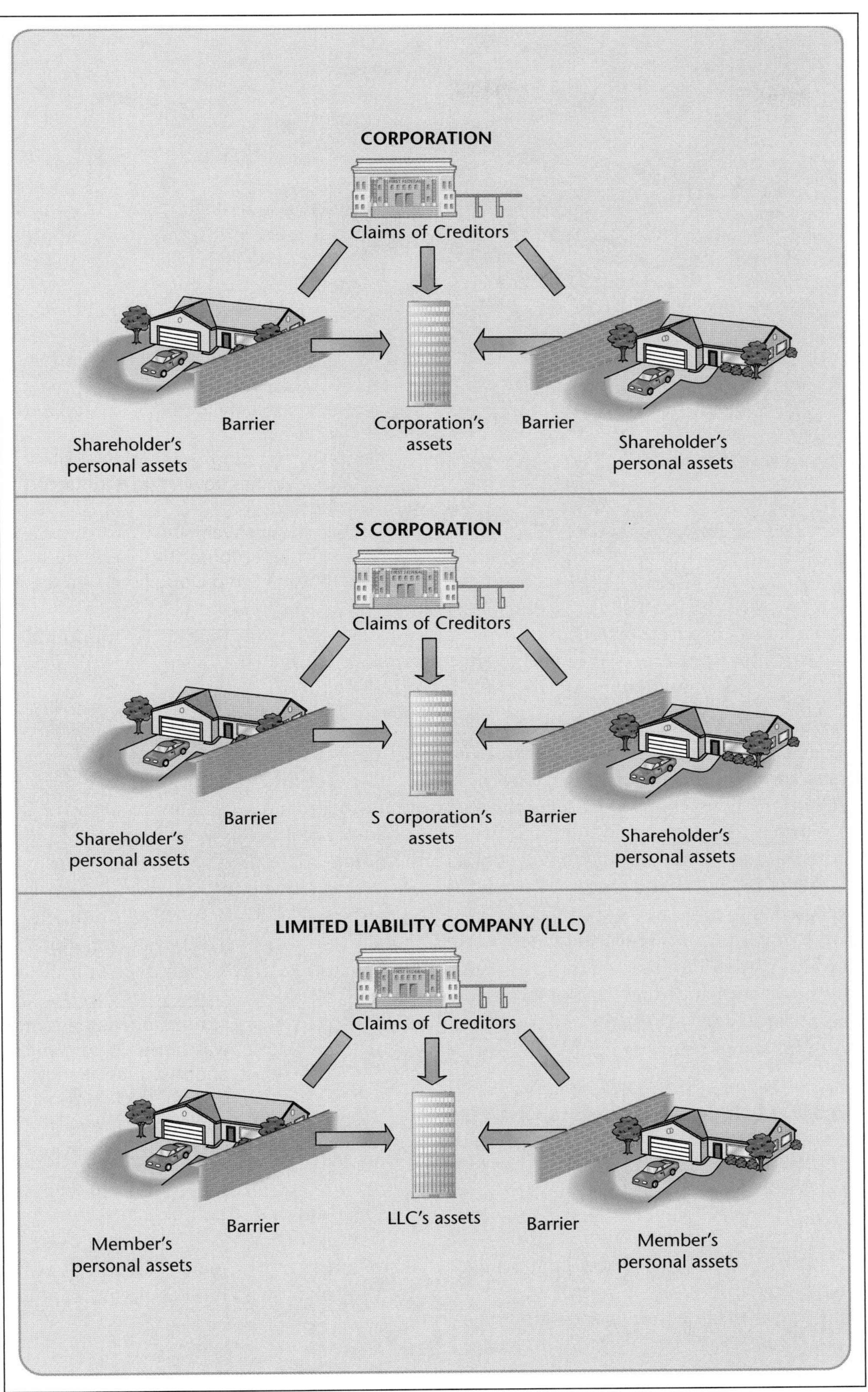

Figure 2.4
Types of Corporate Liability

Azerbaijan is on the cusp of an economic boom, fueled by, well, fuel. It is estimated that by 2005, this Caspian Sea nation, which has oil reserves of 38 billion barrels, will receive $5 billion annually from oil production—five times more than the country's 1997 budget. Azerbaijan looks to companies such as British Petroleum-Amoco <www.bpamoco.com> *to help revive its ineffective refinery equipment and help the country achieve economic independence.*

available to corporations but not to partnerships. They are not immune from unlimited liability, however: Professional negligence by a member of such a business is still accompanied by personal liability on the part of that individual.

multinational or **transnational corporation** Form of corporation spanning national boundaries

Multinational or Transnational Corporations Yet another relatively new form of corporation is the **multinational** or **transnational corporation.** As the term implies, this form of corporation spans national boundaries. Stock in such an enterprise may be traded on the exchanges of several countries, and managers are likely to be from several different countries. While such firms started as corporations headquartered in individual home countries, they have grown to the point where they see themselves as participants in a global economy rather than corporate citizens of individual countries. Nestlé S.A. <www.nestle.com>, for example, operates 522 factories in 81 countries. It has a corporate presence and incorporated subsidiaries in over 50 countries, and its stock is traded on the exchanges of eight different nations. Other examples of multinational or transnational corporations include Ford Motor Co. <www.ford.com>, Elf Aquitaine <www.totalfinaelf.com>, Hyundai Group <www.hyundai.com>, and Minolta <www.minolta.com>.

MANAGING A CORPORATION

corporate governance Roles of shareholders, directors, and other managers in corporate decision making

Creating a corporation—regardless of its type—can be complicated. In addition, once the corporate entity has come into existence, it must be managed by people who understand the complex principles of **corporate governance**—the roles of shareholders, directors, and other managers in corporate decision making.

In this section, we discuss the principles of *stock ownership* and *stockholders' rights* and describe the role of *boards of directors.* We then examine some of the most important trends in corporate ownership.

Corporate Governance

stockholder (or **shareholder**) Owner of shares of stock in a corporation

Corporate governance, which is specified for each firm by its bylaws, involves three distinct bodies. **Stockholders** (or **shareholders**) are the real owners of a corporation—investors who buy shares of ownership in the form of stock. The *board of directors* is a group of people elected by stockholders to oversee the management of the corporation. Corporate *officers* are top managers hired by the board to run the corporation on a day-to-day basis.

Stock Ownership and Stockholders' Rights Corporations sell shares in the business, which is **stock,** to investors who then become stockholders, or shareholders. Profits are distributed among stockholders in the form of dividends, and corporate managers serve at their discretion. Stockholders are the owners of a corporation. As noted earlier, in a closely held corporation, only a small number of people own the stock. In a publicly held corporation, on the other hand, large numbers of people own the stock.

stock
Share of ownership in a corporation

The IPO A common practice today is for formerly closely held corporations to sell stock to individual investors as a way of raising cash. For example, suppose the ownership of a closely held corporation is spread across 1,000,000 shares of stock valued at $100 per share, and that each of four owners has 250,000 shares. If they believe that the stock will be of value to other investors, these owners might elect to sell some of it through a process called an **initial public offering,** or **IPO.** Usually working in concert with an investment banking firm, the owners make available a specified number of shares on a certain date at a certain price.[15]

initial public offering (IPO)
First offer of shares in a closely held corporation to outside investors

Suppose that each owner sells 150,000 shares at $100. In order to make the stock attractive to potential investors, the owners must commit to plowing much of the money back into the business, rather than taking all of it in profits. As a result, 600,000 shares (150,000 × 4) are sold, reaping $60 million in new funds for the company. Moreover, because the owners still hold 40 percent of the stock, they still remain in control. Finally, because they now have new funds to invest in growth and new business opportunities for their firm, the value of the stock that they retained will—at least theoretically—become more valuable in the future.

Some analysts argue that too many firms, especially e-commerce businesses, are going public too quickly. IPOs are promoted by the investment bankers who reap percentages of sale prices but are not responsible for postsale performance. A typical firm, for instance, will spend 15 percent to 25 percent of the capital that raises through an IPO on the cost of the IPO itself.[16] Microsoft and AOL <www.aol.com> were IPOs, but so was Boston Chicken, which went public with stock valued at $10 per share, skyrocketed to a value of $36, and plummeted to under $1 before going bankrupt—all inside of five years. In truth, the typical IPO returns about one-third as much as the 500 companies on the Standard & Poor's Index <www.spglobal.com> (see Chapter 20), and about one-half of all recent IPOs are now selling below their original offering prices.[17]

In the wake of an IPO, private investors must share the company's wealth with its new public investors, but forfeit a certain amount of control: Outside investors gain voting control corresponding to their ownership shares. Occasionally, therefore, a publicly held corporation may choose to take the opposite path from an IPO—to reacquire its stock and become a closely held corporation. Levi Strauss <www.levi.com> was a publicly held company for many years. In 1985, however, the firm bought all of its own stock on the open market. Why? Levi's management reasoned that the firm could manage itself more effectively if the firm was accountable to fewer investors.

Preferred and Common Stock Corporate stock may be either preferred or common. **Preferred stock** guarantees holders fixed dividends, much like the interest paid on savings accounts. Preferred stockholders are so called because they have preference, or priority, over common stockholders when dividends are distributed and, if a business liquidates, when the value of assets is distributed. Although many major corporations issue preferred stock, few small corporations do.

preferred stock
Stock that guarantees its holders fixed dividends and priority claims over assets but no corporate voting rights

Common stock, however, must be issued by every corporation, big or small. It usually pays dividends only if the corporation makes a profit. Dividends on both common and preferred stock are paid on a per-share basis. Thus, a stockholder with 10 shares receives 10 times the dividend paid to a stockholder with 1 share. Holders of common stock have the last claims to any of the company's assets if it folds.

common stock
Stock that pays dividends and guarantees corporate voting rights, but offers last claims over assets

Another difference involves voting rights. Preferred stockholders generally have no voting rights. Common stockholders always have voting rights, with each share of stock carrying one vote. Investors who cannot attend a stockholders' meeting may delegate their voting shares to someone who will attend. This procedure, called voting by **proxy,** is the way almost all individual investors vote.

proxy
Authorization granted by shareholders for someone else to vote their shares

board of directors
Governing body of a corporation that reports to its shareholders and delegates power to run its day-to-day operations, but remains responsible for sustaining its assets

Boards of Directors By law, the governing body of a corporation is its **board of directors.** Boards communicate with stockholders and other potential investors through such channels as the annual report—a summary of the company's financial health. Directors also set policy on dividends, major spending, and executive salaries and benefits. They are legally responsible for corporate actions and are increasingly being held liable for them.

Board Makeup Although requirements differ, most states require that there be at least three directors and one board meeting per year. Large corporations tend to have as many as 20 or 30 directors. Smaller corporations often have no more than five directors. Usually, directors are people with personal or professional ties to the corporation, such as family members, lawyers, and accountants.

Many boards have both outside and inside directors. *Inside directors* are top managers who have primary responsibility for the corporation. *Outside directors* are typically attorneys, accountants, university officials, and executives from other firms. However, all directors share the same basic responsibility: to ensure that the corporation is managed in the best interests of the stockholders.

Many investors believe that outside directors should have no business ties to a firm on whose board that director sits. In theory, this practice would make the director more objective about decisions that affect the business. Recent controversies have arisen in some e-commerce firms about the preponderance of inside directors and the extent to which some outside directors actually have some business connection with those firms. The popular Web guide Yahoo! <www.yahoo.com>, for example, has a six-person board. Three of the six are current executives, and two others are affiliated with companies that do business with Yahoo! While some investors question this practice, Yahoo! executives defend it on the basis of the firm's stellar performance and by arguing that each board member remains totally objective when making decisions about the firm. Says CEO Timothy Koogle, "We are very careful about everything being at arm's length." At least one legal expert counters that "the board should not be an extension of the management team. It's like a dog chasing its own tail."[18]

"The board should not be an extension of the management team. That's like a dog chasing its own tail."

—Corporate governance expert Charles M. Elson, Stetson University College of Law

Traditionally, board members have been expected to keep a low profile, to avoid openly criticizing the firm or its executives, and to keep company activities and discussions confidential. Recently, however, some board members have begun to challenge these norms by making public statements, offering public criticisms of the firms they oversee, and openly describing what goes on at their meetings. Large stockholders and board members of the Kellogg Company <www.kelloggs.com> have been involved in an

WebConnection

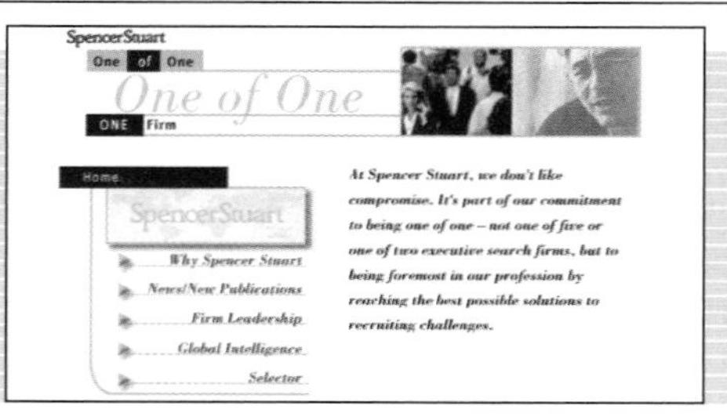

www.spencerstuart.com

The executive search firm Spencer Stuart publishes a variety of materials on the practices and problems of corporate governance. To find out what issues are addressed, visit the firm's Web site. From the company's home page, go to its "Publications" page and, from there, to the "Board Survey" page.

It's a WiredWorld

• *Profit Is No Object*

One of the most well-publicized aspects of the e-commerce explosion has been the enormous wealth created for owners of, and early investors in, such dot.com businesses as America OnLine, Amazon.com, and eBay.com. In many cases, these businesses have not yet earned any profits, and for some profitability is still years off, at best. But amid the smoke and thunder of the Internet explosion, seasoned investors and gambling speculators alike have been willing to bet big sums of money on the prospect of even bigger paydays. While there may be many beneficiaries of these investments, business founders are typically at the top of the list. But as the e-commerce craze appears to be settling down, the boards of directors of some of these firms are increasingly taking a closer look at what is going on.

Consider, for example, the case of Craig Winn and Value America, Inc. <www.valueamerica.com>. Winn is an ambitious entrepreneur whose résumé includes one business bankruptcy and virtually no experience in technology or technology management. Nevertheless, he successfully launched Value America on July 4, 1996, with a 250-page business plan and a personal investment of $150,000. The mission of Value America was to serve as a distribution pipeline between manufacturers and consumers across a wide array of product lines, effectively eliminating traditional wholesalers and retailers altogether.

Winn believed that consumers would order any of tens of thousands of products from over 1,000 different brand-name manufacturers—everything from caviar and laundry detergent to gas barbecue grills and home computers. Value America would transmit the order directly to the manufacturer, who would fill the order and send it directly to the consumer. From a business standpoint, the beauty of Winn's plan was that the firm would not carry any of its own inventory. Rather, it would simply serve as a communication conduit with little of its own capital tied up in anything but its core operation.

Almost immediately, investors began hopping onboard. When the first big investment came in ($10 million from the Union Labor Life Insurance Co.), Winn quickly paid himself back his own $150,000, claiming that it had been a business loan all along, and set his own salary at $295,000 a year. Soon, more and more money began pouring in including major investments by Paul Allen, one of the cofounders of Microsoft, and Fred Smith, founder and CEO of Fed Ex.

Winn also stocked Value America's board of directors with big-name investors and dignitaries, giving both him and his start-up instant credibility to complement his stockpile of cash. Prominent board members included Smith, former cabinet member William Bennett, former Newell-Rubbermaid vice-chairman Wolfgang Schmitt, and highly respected mutual fund manager Bill Savoy. Value America's IPO took place on April 8, 1999, and its share price went through the roof, opening at $23 a share and reaching a first-day high of $74.25 before settling at $55. This influx of investment capital gave the profitless three-year-old firm a market value of $2.4 billion and made Winn rich overnight.

Unfortunately, the hole in the roof created by the soaring stock price uncovered some fundamental flaws at Value America—problems that eventually forced the board to take serious action. For example, major cost overruns, weak financial controls, extravagant advertising, and alleged mismanagement by Winn began to undermine the firm's effectiveness even as its stock price was still rising. Winn had ordered a plush corporate jet even as the firm's losses were mounting, personally ordered the printing and mailing of a 1999 Christmas catalog despite the fact that it was weeks too late, and heavily promoted products at below-cost prices.

Finally, on November 23, 1999, the board ousted Winn as chairman and brought in a new professional management team to shore up the struggling enterprise. At that point, Winn, still a member of the board, began dumping his stock. Between November 24, 1999, and April 6, 2000, he sold almost $36 million worth of it. Combined with earlier stock sales, this brought his personal gain to a stunning $53.7 million. Meanwhile, the new management team was frantically cutting costs and laying off employees in hopes of saving the company. But another major blow came on March 30, 2000, when a team of independent auditors expressed doubts that the firm could survive as a going concern. And Winn? He was enjoying the majestic views from his new mansion on a 150-acre estate in Virginia.

increasingly public dispute about the company's performance. Some stockholders have criticized the firm's performance. While some board members have agreed, others have defended the firm's performance and future strategic plans.[19] The "Wired World" box in this chapter tells the story of a board of directors that had to intervene when a successful IPO went awry.

chief executive officer (CEO) Top manager hired by the board of directors to run a corporation

Officers Although board members oversee the corporation's operation, most of them do not participate in day-to-day management. Rather, they hire a team of managers to run the firm. As we have already seen, this team, called *officers,* is usually headed by the firm's **chief executive officer,** or **CEO,** who is responsible for the firm's overall performance. Other officers typically include a *president,* who is responsible for internal management, and *vice presidents,* who oversee various functional areas such as marketing and operations. Some officers may also be elected to serve on the board, and in some cases, a single person plays multiple roles. For example, one person might serve as board chairperson, CEO, and president. In most cases, however, a different person fills each slot.

Figure 2.5 summarizes the rights and responsibilities of each group in the corporate governance hierarchy.

Figure 2.5
Corporate Governance Hierarchy

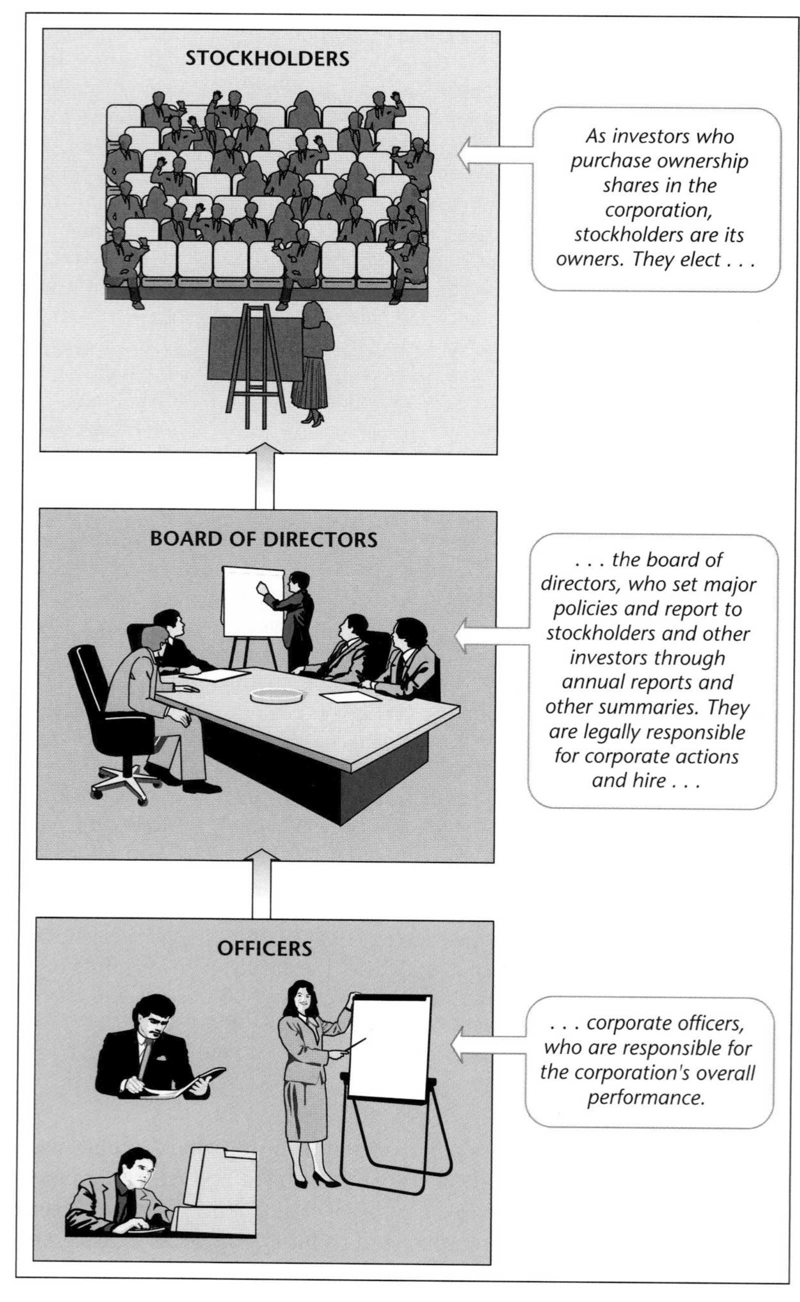

STOCKHOLDERS
As investors who purchase ownership shares in the corporation, stockholders are its owners. They elect . . .
BOARD OF DIRECTORS
. . . the board of directors, who set major policies and report to stockholders and other investors through annual reports and other summaries. They are legally responsible for corporate actions and hire . . .
OFFICERS
. . . corporate officers, who are responsible for the corporation's overall performance.

"If Anderson is C.E.O., and Wyatt is C.F.O., and you're C.O.O., then who am I, and what am I doing here?"

SPECIAL ISSUES IN CORPORATE OWNERSHIP

In recent years, several special issues have arisen or grown in importance in corporate ownership. The most important of these trends are *joint ventures* and *strategic alliances, employee stock ownership plans,* and *institutional ownership.*

Joint Ventures and Strategic Alliances

Joint ventures and strategic alliances have become increasingly popular in business today. In a **strategic alliance,** two or more organizations collaborate on a project for mutual gain. When the partners share ownership stakes in what is essentially a new enterprise, it is called a **joint venture.** The number of strategic alliances has increased rapidly in recent years on both domestic and international fronts.[20]

strategic alliance
Strategy in which two or more organizations collaborate on a project for mutual gain

joint venture
Strategic alliance in which the collaboration involves joint ownership of new venture

For example, McDonald's and Disney are partners in an innovative marketing strategic alliance. McDonald's <www.mcdonalds.com> gets exclusive rights to sell Disney-licensed merchandise tied into new movie releases and to open restaurants in certain areas of Walt Disney World <www.disney.go.com/DisneyWorld>. In return, Disney receives licensing fees from both of these activities, plus a guaranteed advertising budget from McDonald's, which jointly promotes both Disney movies and its own restaurants. Similarly, ebay.com and Wells Fargo have entered a strategic alliance that makes it easier for sellers to accept credit cards in collecting funds from buyers in online auctions. Note, however, that neither of these initiatives actually results in the creation of a new business. In contrast, recall the "Wired World" box in Chapter 1 detailing the new electronic marketplace being created by automobile manufacturers. The partners in this initiative are actually creating a new business that they will jointly own until an IPO is feasible. This initiative, therefore, represents a joint venture.

Employee Stock Ownership Programs

Still another development in corporate ownership is the **employee stock ownership plan (ESOP).** As the term suggests, this plan allows employees to own a significant share of the corporation through what are essentially trusts established on behalf of the employees. Current estimates suggest that there are now almost 10,000 ESOPs in the United States. The growth rate in new ESOPs has slowed a bit in recent years, but they still are an important part of corporate ownership patterns in the United States.[21]

employee stock ownership plan (ESOP)
Arrangement in which a corporation holds its own stock in trust for its employees, who gradually receive ownership of the stock and control its voting rights

For years, United Parcel Service (UPS) <www.ups.com>, a closely held corporation, has maintained an ESOP in which all company employees could buy stock. All told, about 66,000 hourly workers and 40,000 managers (many of whom started out as hourly workers) own stock. In late 1999, UPS made the largest initial public offering in history, selling about 10 percent of its ownership via 109 million shares of stock and raising almost $5.5 billion in a single day. The firm plans to use part of the proceeds to buy back some of its existing stock from employees and the rest to fund growth and future acquisitions. The move also dramatically boosted the value of many of its current employees' holdings.[22]

Institutional Ownership

institutional investors
Large investors, such as mutual funds and pension funds, that purchase large blocks of corporate stock

Most individual investors do not own enough stock to exert any influence on the management of big corporations. In recent years, however, more and more stock has been purchased by **institutional investors.** Because they control enormous resources, these investors—especially mutual and pension funds—can buy huge blocks of stock. For example, the national teachers' retirement system (TIAA-CREF) <www.tiaa-cref.org> has assets of over $255 billion and invests much of that amount in stocks.

Institutional investors now own almost 40 percent of all the stock in the United States. An important trend in recent years is increased involvement by such investors in the companies that they partially own. TIAA-CREF, for example, now recommends standards for the makeup of company boards: They should have a majority of independent directors, and committees should be composed entirely of unaffiliated outsiders. TIAA-CREF recently pressured Disney to add two new outside directors to its board and caused a cafeteria chain, Furr's/Bishop's (now Furr's Restaurant Group), to replace its entire board. On the whole, however, TIAA-CREF prefers to exert influence quietly and behind the scenes. Says one of the organization's executives, "I'd rather give companies the chance to make changes on their own than get their dander up with publicity."[23]

> ***"I'd rather give companies the chance to make changes on their own than get their dander up with publicity."***
>
> *—Peter Clapman, executive at institutional investor TIAA-CREF*

Mergers, Acquisitions, Divestitures, and Spin-Offs

In addition to the various special issues in corporate ownership described previously, another highly visible and important set of issues includes mergers, acquisitions, divestitures, and spin-offs. Whereas mergers and acquisitions involve the legal joining of two or more corporations, divestitures and spin-offs involve either the sale by one corporation of one or more of its business operations to another corporation or the creation of a new one.

merger
The union of two corporations to form a new corporation

acquisition
The purchase of one company by another

Mergers and Acquisitions A **merger** occurs when two firms combine to create a new company. In an **acquisition,** one firm buys another outright. Even though many such events are publicly called mergers, in reality they are acquisitions. Why? Because one of the existing firms will almost always control more than half of the ownership of the new combined firm. For example, when Daimler-Benz and Chrysler combined to create DaimlerChrysler <www.daimlerchrysler.com>, it was publicly called a merger. In truth, however, Daimler actually *acquired* Chrysler. In general, when the two firms are of roughly the same or comparable size, the combination is usually called a merger even if one firm is assuming control over the other. When the acquiring firm is substantially larger than the acquired firm, it is more likely called an acquisition.

After a merger or acquisition occurs, how can a company ensure rising stock prices?

Although mergers and acquisitions (M&As) are not new, they increased in both frequency and importance in the United States during the 1980s and 1990s. The largest and most publicized mergers in recent years include Exxon and Mobil (1998), Sprint and MCI WorldCom (1999), and America Online and Time Warner (2000).[24] Today M&As remain an important form of corporate strategy. They allow firms to increase product lines, expand operations, go international, and create new enterprises in conjunction with other organizations.

Takeover Tactics A merger or acquisition can take place in one of several different ways. The process usually starts when one firm announces that it wants to buy another for a specified price. After some negotiation, the owners or board of the second company agrees to the sale and the firm is soon taken over by the buyer. Sometimes, a firm may realize that it is a likely takeover target and cannot forestall the inevitable. It may therefore seek out a favorable buyer and, in effect, ask to be acquired. In both of these two scenarios, the acquisition is called a *friendly takeover* because the acquired company welcomes the merger.

Time Warner CEO Gerald Levin (left) and America Online CEO Stephen Case celebrate the $183 billion merger of their two companies. Even though AOL <www.aol.com> *had only one-fifth the revenue of the publishing and entertainment conglomerate, the Internet information service could afford to be the buyer because its stock was valued at twice that of Time Warner* <www.timewarner.com>. *The new company hopes to be the first to succeed in combining entertainment, communications, and online services.*

Sometimes, however, takeover targets resist. In such a case, a firm may wish to remain independent, or it may regard a purchase offer as too low or a potential buyer as a poor match. The would-be buyer, however, may persist. It may offer to buy the target firm's stock on the open market, usually at a premium price. If it can acquire a sufficient quantity of stock, it will gain control of the target company despite the resistance of the target firm's management. In this case, the acquisition is called a *hostile takeover.*

Divestitures and Spin-Offs Sometimes a corporation adopts the opposite strategy: It decides to take a part of its existing business operations and either sell it to another corporation or set it up as a new independent corporation. Several reasons might motivate such a step.

For example, a firm might decide that it needs to focus more specifically on its core businesses and thus sell off unrelated and/or underperforming businesses. Such a sale is called a **divestiture.** Consider the decision of Unilever <www.unilever.com>, a large European consumer-products company. The maker of such well-known products as Close-Up toothpaste, Dove soap, Vaseline lotions, and Q-tips, Unilever also owned several specialty chemical businesses that had been set up to make ingredients for its consumer products. When the firm decided that it needed to focus more closely on the consumer products themselves, it sold its chemical businesses to ICI <www.ici.com>, a European chemical giant. Likewise, Daewoo <www.daewoo.com>, a huge Korean concern, has been systematically selling off six of its 25 subsidiaries to reduce its debt and improve its operations and profitability.[25]

divestiture
Strategy whereby a firm sells one or more of its business units

In other cases a firm might decide to sell part of itself to raise capital. Such a sale is known as a **spin-off.** Kmart <www.kmart.com> has resorted to this strategy, selling its profitable bookstore operations, including Borders and Waldenbooks, to raise money to expand its discount chain. The actual sale was a new stock offering in a newly created corporation comprising the bookstore chains. Sometimes, a firm spins off a part of itself not because it necessarily needs the capital, but because it determines that one or more of its business units may actually be more valuable as a separate company. The Limited <www.limited.com>, for example, spun off three of its subsidiaries, Victoria's Secret, Bath & Body Works, and White Barn Candle Co., to create a new firm called Intimate Brands, Inc. <www.intimatebrands.com>, which it then offered through an IPO. The Limited retained an 84-percent ownership in Intimate Brands but also enjoyed an infusion of new capital through the spin-off. In addition, The Limited can still raise new capital anytime it wants simply by selling more Intimate Brands stock on the open market.

spin-off
Strategy of setting up one or more corporate units as new, independent corporations

Continued from page 33

Alliance by Location

While the co-owners of Twin Computer Training search New York City for alliances and client projects, the companies located in the Greenpoint Manufacturing and Design Center (GMDC) <www.gmdconline.com> need to look no further than the neighbors in their own facility. Much as proximity—being physically close—affects our personal relationships, it also affects business alliances.

That is what Frank Lionti found after he moved his three-person operation, Distinction in Woods Ltd., into GMDC, which is located in Brooklyn, New York. Lionti was hired almost immediately by a larger woodworking company to do finishing work on its custom cabinetry jobs. "They don't have to do the finishing, and I don't have to do the woodworking," says Lionti. "It's much more to their advantage and much more to my advantage."

Business alliances are common among the 40 small woodworking companies located in GMDC. First created in 1992 by a government agency charged with keeping small woodworking companies in the local area, GMDC has a communal culture that stresses cooperation. Alliances breed because custom woodworking is a specialized business: Wood finishers need wood-carvers who need cabinet designers and cabinetmakers. With the advantage of a shared $350,000 wood shop, smaller tenants can take on bigger jobs. Working together, every firm thus adds capacity without adding to their fixed costs. "I'd like to say that's something that we brilliantly engineered," says GMDC CEO David Sweeney. "But this segment of the industry just seems to easily digest cooperation and competition in the same bite."

Questions for Discussion

1. What are the advantages of business alliances for small companies like Twin Computer Training?
2. Why are companies that offer complementary services more likely to join together than those with competing services? Do you think it is smart for potential competitors to join on a project basis?
3. Why is specialization so important in today's economy, and how do alliances help companies maintain their focus?
4. If you were a small-business owner, would you accept a loose arrangement (i.e., a handshake) to finalize the terms of the alliance, or would you be likely to seal the deal with signatures on legal contracts?
5. Why do you think it is smart for Twin Computer Training to present a unified front to its clients?
6. Why is the Greenpoint Manufacturing and Design Center a breeding ground for small-business alliances?

SUMMARY OF LEARNING OBJECTIVES

1 **Trace the history of business in the United States.** Modern U.S. business structures reflect a pattern of development over centuries. Throughout much of the colonial period, sole proprietors supplied raw materials to English manufacturers. The rise of the factory system during the Industrial Revolution brought with it *mass production* and *specialization of labor.* During the *entrepreneurial era* in the nineteenth century, huge corporations—and monopolies—emerged. During the *production era* of the early twentieth century, companies grew by emphasizing output and production. During the *marketing era* of the 1950s and 1960s, businesses began focusing on sales staff, advertising, and the need to produce what consumers wanted. The *global perspective* of business emerged in the 1980s and continues today. The most recent developments are pointing toward an *Internet era* as perhaps the next big period in the evolution of business.

2 **Identify the *major forms of business ownership*.** The most common forms of business ownership are the *sole proprietorship*, the *partnership*, the *cooperative*, and the regular *corporation*. Each form has several advantages and disadvantages. The form under which a business chooses to organize is crucial because it affects both long-term strategy and day-to-day decision making. In addition to advantages and disadvantages, entrepreneurs must consider their preferences and long-range requirements.

3 **Explain *sole proprietorships* and *partnerships* and discuss the advantages and disadvantages of each.** *Sole proprietorships*, the most common form of business, consist of one person doing business. Although sole proprietorships offer freedom and privacy and are easy to form, they lack continuity and present certain financial risks. For one thing, they feature *unlimited liability:* The sole proprietor is liable for all debts incurred by the business. *General partnerships* are proprietorships with multiple owners. *Limited partnerships* allow for limited partners who can invest without being liable for debts incurred by general or active partners. In *master limited partnerships*, master partners can sell shares and pay profits to investors. Partnerships have access to a larger talent pool and more investment money than sole proprietorships, but they may be dissolved if conflicts between partners cannot be settled.

4 **Describe *corporations*, discuss their advantages and disadvantages, and identify different kinds of corporations.** *Corporations* are independent legal entities that are usually run by professional managers. The corporate form is used by most large businesses because it offers continuity and opportunities for raising money. It also features financial protection through *limited liability:* The liability of investors is limited to their personal investments. However, the corporation is a complex legal entity subject to *double taxation:* In addition to taxes paid on corporate profits, investors must pay taxes on earned income. The most common types are *closely held corporations* (also called *private corporations*), *publicly held corporations* (also called *public corporations*), *S corporations, limited liability corporations (LLCs), professional corporations*, and *multinational* or *transnational corporations.*

5 **Describe the basic issues involved in creating and managing a corporation.** Creating a corporation generally requires legal assistance to file *articles of incorporation,* to establish corporate *bylaws*, and to comply with government regulations. Corporations issue *stock* that is controlled by their owners. A closely held corporation can raise capital and become a publicly traded corporation through an *initial public offering,* or *IPO*, of stock to outside investors. Managers must understand stockholders' rights as well as the rights and duties of the *board of directors.*

6 **Identify recent trends and issues in corporate ownership.** Recent trends in corporate ownership include *joint ventures* or *strategic alliances* (in which two or more organizations collaborate on an enterprise), *employee stock ownership plans (ESOPs)* (by which employees buy large shares of their employer companies), and *institutional ownership* of corporations (by groups such as mutual and pension funds).

7 **Discuss *mergers, acquisitions, divestitures,* and *spin-offs*.** Mergers and acquisitions (M&As) are becoming increasingly popular strategies for firms today. Firms sometimes engage in *divestitures* to improve profitability and may create *spin-offs* to raise new capital.

QUESTIONS AND EXERCISES

Questions for Review

1. Why is it important to understand the history of U.S. business?
2. Compare the advantages and disadvantages of the major forms of business ownership.
3. What are the primary benefits and drawbacks to serving as a general partner in a limited partnership?
4. Why might a closely held corporation choose to remain private? Why might a closely held corporation choose to become a publicly traded corporation?

5. Why have strategic alliances become more common in recent years?

Questions for Analysis

6. How can you, as a prospective manager, better prepare yourself now for the challenges that you will face in the next 20 years?
7. What basic steps must be taken to incorporate a business in your state?
8. Go to the library or to the Internet and research a recent merger or acquisition. What factors led to the arrangement? What circumstances characterized the process of completing the arrangement? Were they friendly or unfriendly?

Application Exercises

9. Interview the owner-manager of a sole proprietorship or a general partnership. What characteristics of that business form led the owner to choose it? Does the owner ever contemplate changing the form of the business?
10. Interview the owner of or principal stockholder in a corporation. What characteristics of that business form led the individual to choose it?

EXPLORING THE WEB

STRIKING IT RICH OR STRIKING OUT?

Initial public offerings, or IPOs, are all the rage now. It seems as if the media is constantly discussing how this firm or that firm has just made its owners rich through an IPO. Investment bankers everywhere seem to be pointing their clients toward the latest IPO. There is an abundance of Internet sites now available to help observers and investors alike better navigate the IPO currents. With this in mind, begin this exercise by visiting and exploring each of the following Web sites:

- <www.ipo.com>
- <www.ipocentral.com>
- <www.ipomaven.com>
- <www.ipospotlight.com>
- <www.ipomonitor.com>

Now, respond to the following questions:

1. Who is the target audience for each of these sites?
2. What are the strengths and weaknesses of each site?
3. As a potential investor, which site would you find most useful? Why?
4. Select one recent IPO discussed on all or most of these sites. Compare and contrast what you learn about the firm from the various sites. Explain any differences that you observe.

BUILDING YOUR BUSINESS SKILLS

THE UPS AND DOWNS OF WIDGET OWNERSHIP

This exercise is designed to enhance the following SCANS workplace competencies: demonstrating basic skills, demonstrating thinking skills, exhibiting interpersonal skills, and working with information.

GOAL

To help students analyze the implications of corporate acquisitions and mergers for individual stockholders.

SITUATION

You own 500 shares of Widget International (WI). Although you like the company's products, you are disappointed with the current stock price. Analysts agree with you and warn that the company must drastically cut expenses or risk a takeover. Management begins to trim budgets, but its efforts are seen as too little too late. With the stock price continuing to drop, XYZ Corp. offers to buy WI. After successful negotiations, XYZ is set to acquire WI on January 1. When this happens, your 500 shares of WI will be converted into XYZ Corp. stock.

METHOD

Working in groups of four or five, analyze the ways in which this acquisition may affect your stock holdings. Research a similar corporate merger that took place in the past year as you consider the following factors:

- The nature of the acquiring company
- The fit between the products or services offered by the two companies
- The fiscal health of the acquiring company, as reflected in its own stock price
- The stock market's long-term reaction to the acquisition. Does the market think it is a good move?
- Changes in corporate leadership as a result of the acquisition
- Changes in the way the acquired company's products are produced and marketed
- Announced budgetary changes

FOLLOW-UP QUESTIONS

1. After one company acquires another, what factors are likely to push up the stock price of the acquired firm?
2. After one company acquires another, what factors are likely to push down the stock price of the acquired firm?
3. Did your research identify any factors that are likely to trigger a corporate takeover?
4. In an acquisition, who is likely to be named CEO (the person in charge of the acquired or acquiring company)? Who is likely to be named CEO in a merger of equals? What factors are likely to influence this decision?
5. How is the board of directors likely to change as a result of an acquisition? Of a merger?

CRAFTING YOUR BUSINESS PLAN

DEMONSTRATING GOOD BUSINESS FORM

THE PURPOSE OF THE ASSIGNMENT

1. To acquaint students with the process of navigating the *Business PlanPro* (BPP) software package (Version 4.0).
2. To locate **Form of Ownership** and its information contents in *BPP.*
3. To introduce students to various forms of ownership for different companies.
4. To prepare students to enter a firm's form of ownership into *BPP.*

ASSIGNMENT

After reading Chapter 2 in the textbook, open the BPP software* *and search for information about forms of company ownership as it applies to these sample firms:* Boulder Stop Gear (The Boulder Stop), Flower Importer (Fantastic Florals, Inc.), JavaNet Internet Café, *and* Ice Dreams Shaved Ice. *Also select a sample company of your own choice. Then respond to the following items:*

1. Describe the steps that must be taken to find **Form of Ownership** information inside *BPP.* (Where in the *BPP* menu is that information located?)
2. When observing the sample companies' business plans, did you find any ownership information that was not covered in the textbook? If so, describe it.
3. Compare and contrast the different forms of ownership among the sample firms.
4. After exploring the form of ownership for one of the sample companies, go to the top of the screen and select **Instructions.** What information is given there? Next, select **Examples.** What information is given there?

FOR YOUR OWN BUSINESS PLAN

5. Describe your intended form of ownership. Explain your choice and indicate where in the *BPP* document (that is, in which section of the planning document) you will present your choice of ownership form and the rationale for your choice.

*GENERAL TIPS FOR NAVIGATING IN *BPP*

1. Open the *BPP* program, examine the Welcome screen, and click on **Open a Sample Plan.**

2. From the **Open a Sample Plan** dialogue box, click on a sample company name; then click on **Open.**
3. On the Plan Manager screen, click on **Your Plan Outline**; then click on any of the lines (for example, **6.0 Management Summary**).
4. You can always return to the Plan Outline screen by going to the bottom of the screen and clicking on the **Plan Outline** icon.
5. After finishing with one sample company, you can get to the next one by going to the top of the screen and clicking on **File** (on the menu bar). Then beneath that, select **Open Sample Plan.** This will exit you from the current company file and take you to the **Open Sample Plan** dialogue box, where you can select your next sample company.
6. When you are finished, you can close the program by going to the top of the screen and clicking on **File** (on the bar menu). Then beneath that, select **Exit.**

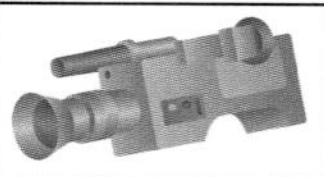

VIDEO EXERCISE

DOING BUSINESS PRIVATELY: AMY'S ICE CREAMS

Learning Objectives

The purpose of this video exercise is to help you

1. Recognize the factors that motivate people to open businesses.
2. Understand the advantages and disadvantages of incorporation.
3. Appreciate the role of corporations as employers.

BACKGROUND INFORMATION

Amy's Ice Creams is a privately held corporation formed in 1984 by Amy Miller and owned by Miller and a small group of family members and friends. Based in Austin, Texas, Amy's continues to evolve and now boasts nine stores earning close to $3.5 million. Customers' suggestions for new flavors are welcomed, and quality is never compromised. It is also famous for the zany antics of its behind-the-counter scoopers (just applying for a job is an adventure in creativity).

THE VIDEO

Amy Miller talks about some of the basic issues involved in starting up and running her business, including her philosophy and the marketing and financial savvy that she brings to the task. You'll hear about the advantages and disadvantages of incorporating, and you'll discover some of the ways in which Amy's keeps both employees and customers on their toes.

DISCUSSION QUESTIONS

1. How do Amy's organization and principles differ from those of a publicly held corporation?
2. What are some of the particular advantages of corporate ownership for a firm like Amy's? Are there any disadvantages?
3. How well do you think Amy's is working to ensure its continued survival and success? Looking into the future, what marketing, financial, or other suggestions would you offer the company?

FOLLOW-UP ASSIGNMENT

How do you think a company like Amy's can compete with national ice cream chains like Baskin-Robbins or Carvel? What does Amy's offer its customers that these firms do not? What does it offer its employees? How important are these elements in ensuring any company's continued success? (To find out more about the company, you can visit Amy's Web site at <www.amysicecream.com>.)

FOR FURTHER EXPLORATION

Find out the requirements for incorporating a business in your state. You might begin by typing *incorporation* into the search box at <www.toolkit.cch.com>. If you were going to start a small business yourself, is a corporation the form of business ownership you would choose? Why or why not? Make a list of the pros and cons that incorporation presents for the type of business that you have in mind.

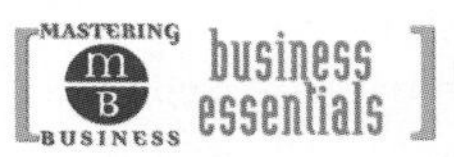

MASTERING BUSINESS ESSENTIALS

Go to the "Economic Way of Thinking" episode on the Mastering Business Essentials CD-ROM for an interactive, video-enhanced exercise on the efforts of managers at CanGo, an e-business start-up, to deal with the dilemmas of expanding and competing in the current U.S. business climate.

Chapter 3

Understanding the Global Context of Business

After reading this chapter, you should be able to:

1. **Describe** the rise of international business, identify the major world marketplaces, and discuss the United States' major trading partners.

2. **Explain** how different forms of *competitive advantage, import-export balances, exchange rates,* and *foreign competition* determine the ways in which countries and businesses respond to the international environment.

3. **Discuss** the factors involved in deciding to do business internationally and in selecting the appropriate *levels of international involvement* and *international organizational structure.*

4. **Describe** some of the ways in which *social, cultural, economic, legal,* and *political differences* among nations affect international business.

The New ETO (European Theater of Operations)

First they secured their domestic battlefields. Now they're moving into foreign territory ready to face stiff opposition from local forces. We're not talking about military conflicts. The battles we are referring to are the head-to-head confrontations awaiting U.S. Internet enterprises as they set their sights on new markets in other countries, especially Europe.

Companies such as Amazon.com, Yahoo! <www.yahoo.com>, eBay <www.ebay.com>, America Online <www.aol.com>, and E*Trade <www.etrade.com> have emerged as the key players among Internet upstarts. Although some of these firms have yet to earn a profit, each is well managed, financially solvent, and firmly entrenched in its chosen niche. As the 1990s drew to a close, each was ready to extend its reach to foreign markets, starting with Europe.

At first, both emerging European Internet enterprises and industry observers thought that U.S. companies would have a tough go of it. They argued that locals had a better understanding of European consumers and local market conditions, which would put the U.S. companies at a significant disadvantage. U.S. companies, however, proved to be more globally savvy than many people had predicted. A stock market adjustment to tech stocks in early 2000 undermined the financing options of the

European start-ups, giving the Americans just the opportunity they needed to move ahead.

Amazon.com has found it relatively easy to transport its entire operating system to European locations. "We can adopt about 80percent of our American business model," says the company's managing director in Britain. Although Amazon.com's British Web site features books and CDs by English writers and performers, the back office, distribution, and marketing functions are replicas of their U.S. counterparts. Amazon.com's European sales are five times larger than those of its nearest competitor, Bertelsmann's BOL Ltd <www.bol.de>.

Many other American companies are gaining in strength and market share. Yahoo! is Europe's leading Internet portal, with twice as many users as Deutsche Telekom's T-Online <www.t-online.de>, the leading European-based Internet service provider and portal. Internet auction giant eBay, Inc. is eight times larger than QXL <www.qxl.com>, its closest European rival. Americans are solidifying their European footholds. Although E*Trade originally entered the European market by franchising its early operations, it has since bought out its former partners.

Meanwhile, once prominent European Internet firms, including Boo.com, Freeserve <www.freeserve.com>, and lastminute.com, have gone under, put themselves up for sale, or been leap-frogged by U.S. rivals. In addition to financial problems facing would-be European competitors, American firms can point to a couple of key factors in their success. For one thing, they have taken a more systematic and focused approach to entering markets. Because more than 80 percent of European Internet commerce is located in Britain, Germany, and France, most U.S. companies have focused almost exclusively on these countries. This strategy has allowed them to concentrate their resources and generate strong market penetration where it matters most. In contrast, most European firms have tried to set up shop across the continent, spreading themselves too thin and rendering themselves vulnerable to domestic-market upheavals.

"We can adopt 80 percent of our American business model."

—Steve Frazier, director of Amazon.com's British operations

Our opening story continues on page 86

In today's climate of growing international business activity, the study and practice of basic business management has in many ways become the study and practice of international business management. The rapid emergence of e-commerce promises to reinforce this trend. A glance at the sweeping changes in the Internet markets of Europe make it easy to see how pervasive—and how important—the global environment has become for all businesses. By focusing on the learning objectives of this chapter, you will better understand the dynamics of international business management.

THE RISE OF INTERNATIONAL BUSINESS

globalization
Process by which the world economy is becoming a single interdependent system

import
Product made or grown abroad but sold domestically

export
Product made or grown domestically but shipped and sold abroad

The total volume of world trade today is immense—over $8 trillion in merchandise trade alone each year. Foreign investment in the United States and U.S. investment abroad have each passed the $1 trillion mark.[1] As more and more firms engage in international business, the world economy is fast becoming a vast and complex interdependent system—a process called **globalization.** Indeed, we often take for granted the diversity of goods and services available today as a result of international trade. Your television set, your shoes, and even your morning cup of coffee may be U.S. **imports**—products made or grown abroad and sold in the United States. At the same time, the success of many U.S. firms depends in large part on **exports**—products made or grown here and shipped for sale abroad.

The Contemporary Global Economy

International trade is becoming increasingly central to the fortunes of most nations of the world, as well as to their largest businesses. Whereas in the past many nations followed strict policies to protect domestic business, today more countries are aggressively encouraging international trade. They are continuing to open their borders to foreign business, offering incentives for their own domestic businesses to expand internationally, and making it easier for foreign firms to partner with local firms through various alliances. Similarly, as more and more industries and markets become global, firms that compete in them are also becoming global.

Several forces combined to spark and sustain globalization. For one thing, governments and businesses became more aware of the benefits of globalization to their countries and shareholders. For another, new technologies make international travel, communication, and commerce increasingly easier, faster, and cheaper than ever before. Figure 3.1, for example, shows the downward trend in the cost of a three-minute phone call from New York to London and of seaborne shipping costs per ton over the last several decades. Likewise, transatlantic travel once required several days aboard a ship. Today, travelers can easily fly between most major cities in the United States and Europe in less than a day. Finally, there are competitive pressures: Sometimes, a firm simply must enter foreign markets to keep up with its competitors.

In this section, we examine some key factors that shaped—and are shaping—today's global business environment. First, we identify and describe the *major world marketplaces*. Then we discuss some important factors that determine the ways in which both nations and their businesses respond to the international environment: the roles of different forms of *competitive advantage, import-export balances*, and *exchange rates*.

The Major World Marketplaces

The contemporary world economy revolves around three major marketplaces: North America, Europe, and Asia. This is not to say that other regions are unimportant, nor is it to suggest that all countries in these three regions are equally important. However, these three geographic regions are home to most of the world's largest economies, biggest multinational corporations, most influential financial markets, and highest-income consumers.

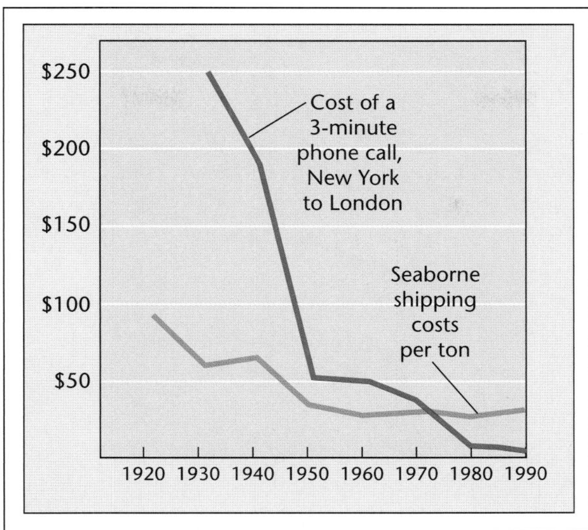

Figure 3.1
The Price of Global Communication

The World Bank, an agency of the United Nations <www.worldbank.org>, uses **per capita income**—the average income per person—as a measure to divide countries into one of three groups:[2]

per capita income
Average income per person in a country

- *High-income countries* are those with per capita income greater than $9,386. These include the United States, Canada, most of the countries in Europe, Australia, New Zealand, Japan, South Korea, Kuwait, the United Arab Emirates, Israel, Singapore, and Taiwan. Hong Kong, while technically no longer an independent nation, also falls into this category.
- *Middle-income countries* are those with per capita income of less than $9,386 but more than $765. Some of the countries in this group are the Czech Republic, Greece, Hungary, Poland, most of the countries comprising the former Soviet Bloc, Turkey, Mexico, Argentina, and Uruguay. Some of these nations, most notably Poland, Argentina, and Uruguay, are undergoing successful industrialization and economic development and are expected to move into the high-income category soon.
- *Low-income countries,* also called *developing countries,* are those with per capita income of less than $765. Some of these countries, such as China and India, have huge

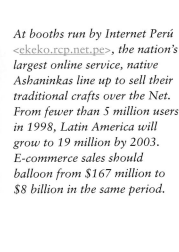

At booths run by Internet Perú <ekeko.rcp.net.pe>, the nation's largest online service, native Ashaninkas line up to sell their traditional crafts over the Net. From fewer than 5 million users in 1998, Latin America will grow to 19 million by 2003. E-commerce sales should balloon from $167 million to $8 billion in the same period.

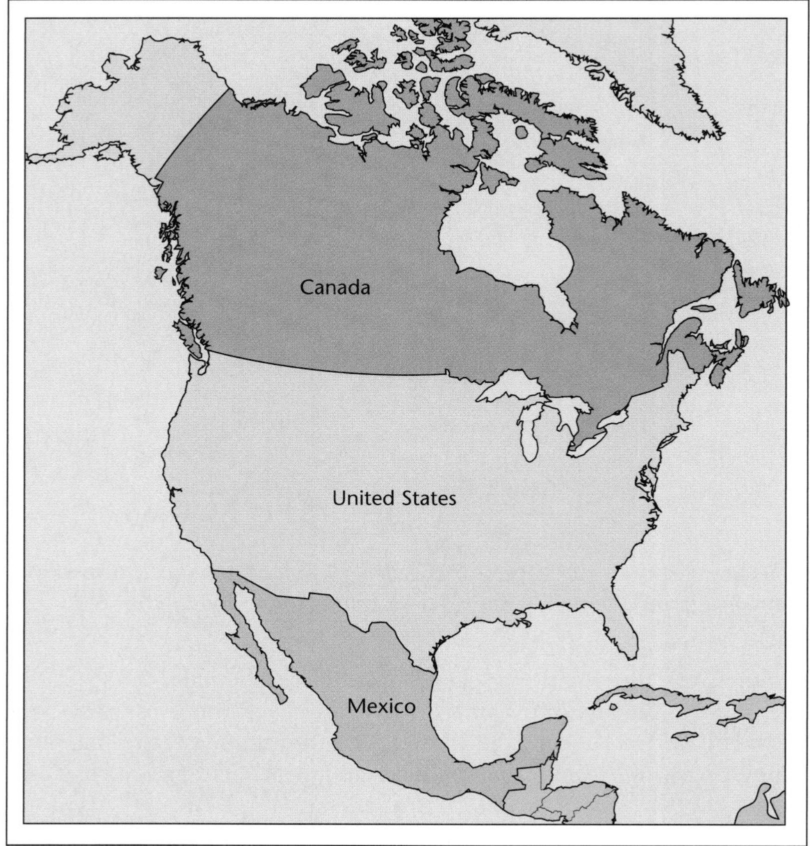

Figure 3.2
The North American Marketplace and the Nations of NAFTA

populations and are seen as potentially attractive markets for international business. Due to low literacy rates, weak infrastructures, unstable governments, and related problems, other countries in this group are less attractive to international business. For example, the East African nation of Somalia, plagued by drought, civil war, and starvation, plays virtually no role in the world economy.

North America The United States dominates the North American business region. It is the single largest marketplace and enjoys the most stable economy in the world. Canada also plays a major role in the international economy. Moreover, the United States and Canada are each other's largest trading partner. Many U.S. firms, such as General Motors <www.gmcanada.com> and Procter & Gamble <www.pg.com/canada>, have maintained successful Canadian operations for years, and many Canadian firms, such as Northern Telecom <www.nt.com> and Alcan Aluminum <www.alcan.com>, are also major international competitors.

Mexico has also become a major manufacturing center, especially along the U.S. border, where cheap labor and low transportation costs have encouraged many firms, from the United States and other countries, to build manufacturing plants. The auto industry has been especially active. For example, DaimlerChrysler <www.daimlerchrysler.com>, General Motors <www.gm.com>, Volkswagen <www.vw.com>, Nissan <www.nissandriven.com>, and Ford <www.ford.com> have large assembly plants in this region. Moreover, several of their major suppliers also built facilities in the area. From 1993 to 1999, exports of automobiles and automobile parts from Mexico increased from only $7.2 billion to $20.4 billion, and the auto industry in Mexico employs 380,000 workers.

All three of these nations, shown in Figure 3.2, enjoyed the benefits of the North American Free Trade Agreement (NAFTA). According to this agreement, over a 15-year

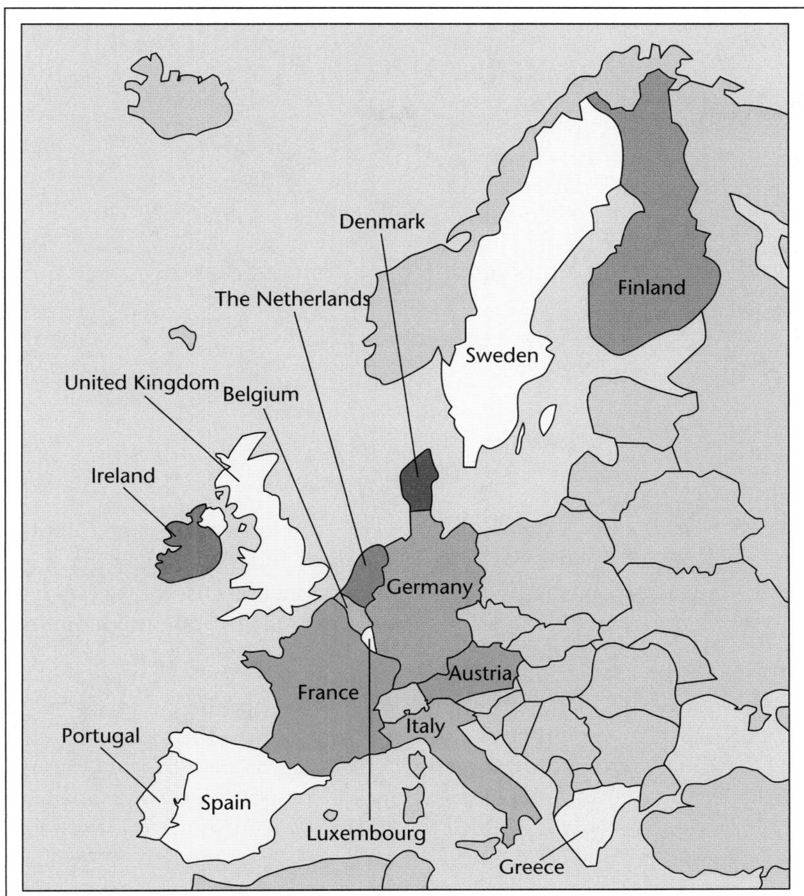

Figure 3.3
Europe and the Nations of the European Union

period, the three nations will eliminate tariffs and other major trade barriers. Since its ratification in 1994, NAFTA created several million new jobs in all three countries and substantially boosted mutual trade. Moreover, there is speculation that NAFTA will eventually expand to include other Latin American countries, with Chile seen as the most likely new member.

Europe Europe is often regarded as two regions—Western and Eastern Europe. Western Europe—dominated by Germany, the United Kingdom, France, and Italy—has long been a mature but fragmented marketplace. But the transformation of the European Union (EU) in 1992 into a unified marketplace increased the region's importance (see Figure 3.3). Major international firms such as Unilever <www.unilver.com>, Renault <www.renault.com>, Royal Dutch/Shell <www.shell.com>, Michelin <www.michelin.com>, Siemens <www.siemens.de>, and Nestlé <www.nestle.com> are all headquartered in Western Europe.

E-commerce and technology have also become increasingly important in this region.[3] There has been a surge in Internet start-ups in Southeast England, the Netherlands, and the Scandinavian countries, and Ireland is now the world's number-two exporter of software (after the United States).[4] Strasbourg, France, is a major center for biotech start-ups. Barcelona, Spain, has many flourishing software and Internet companies, and the Frankfurt region of Germany is dotted with both software and biotech start-ups.[5]

Eastern Europe, which used to be primarily communist, has also gained in importance, both as a marketplace and as a producer. For example, such multinational corporations as Daewoo <www.daewoo.com>, Nestlé, General Motors, and ABB Asea

WebConnection

www.letsbuyit.com

Letsbuyit.com is an Internet retailer founded and headquartered in Sweden. It targets European customers with a retailing concept called "co-buying." To learn more about the idea of "the power of consumers joining in numbers"—and to find out more about the company's products and distribution process—visit its Web site.*

*You'll want the United Kingdom site if you're an English-speaking browser.

Brown Boveri <www.abb.com> have set up operations in Poland. Similarly, Ford, General Motors, Suzuki <www.suzuki.com>, and Volkswagen have all built new factories in Hungary. On the other hand, governmental instability has hampered economic development in Russia, Bulgaria, Albania, Romania, and other countries in this region.

Pacific Asia Pacific Asia consists of Japan, China, Thailand, Malaysia, Singapore, Indonesia, South Korea, Taiwan, the Philippines, and Australia. Some experts still identify Hong Kong as a separate part of the region, although the former city-state is now actually part of China. Vietnam is sometimes included as part of the region. Fueled by strong entries in the automobile, electronics, and banking industries, the economies of these countries grew rapidly in the 1970s and 1980s. Unfortunately, however, a currency crisis in the late 1990s slowed growth in virtually every country of the region.

The currency crisis aside, however, Pacific Asia is an important force in the world economy and a major source of competition for North American firms. Led by firms such as Toyota <www.toyota.com>, Toshiba <www.toshiba.com>, and Nippon Steel <www.nsc.co.jp/english>, Japan dominates the region. In addition, South Korea (with such firms as

Egis is a Hungarian pharmaceutical company that has developed a number of new hypertension drugs. Because it hopes to sell these drugs in the United States and Europe, Hungarian membership in the European Union would be a plus for Egis, as well as for numerous start-ups and privatized companies in Eastern Europe.

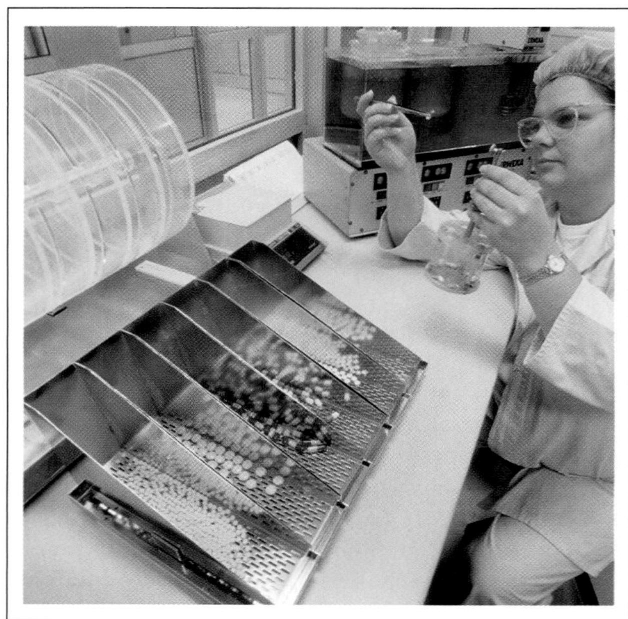

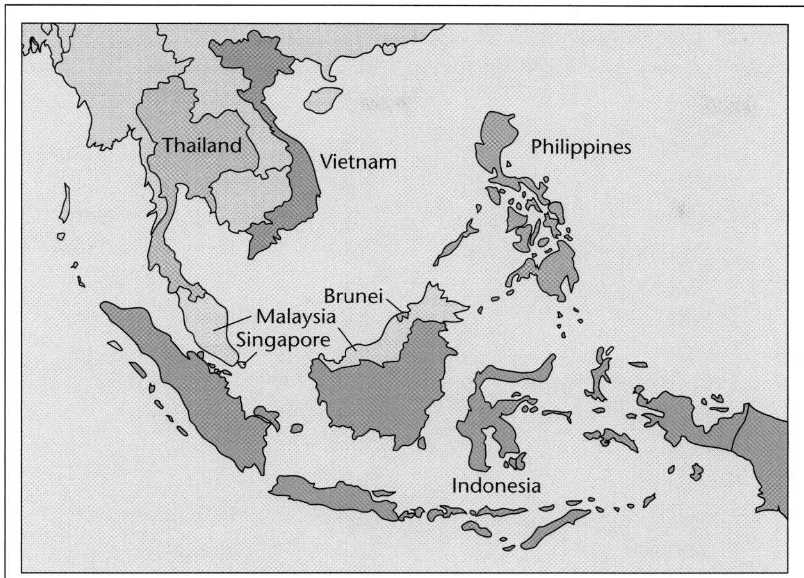

Figure 3.4
The Nations of ASEAN

Samsung <www.samsung.com> and Hyundai <www.hyundai.com>), Taiwan (owner of Chinese Petroleum <www.cpc.com.tw/english> and manufacturing home of many foreign firms), and Hong Kong (a major financial center) are also successful players in the international economy. China, the most densely populated country in the world, continues to emerge as an important market in its own right. In fact, the Chinese economy is now the world's third-largest economy behind the United States and only slightly behind Japan.

As in North America and Western Europe, technology promises to play an increasingly important role in the future of this region. In Asia, however, the emergence of technology firms has been hampered by a poorly developed electronic infrastructure, slower adoption of computers and information technology, a higher percentage of lower-income consumers, and the aforementioned currency crisis. Thus, while the future looks promising, technology companies in this region are facing several obstacles as they work to keep pace with foreign competitors.[6]

Figure 3.4 is a map of the Association of Southeast Asian Nations (ASEAN) countries of Pacific Asia. ASEAN (pronounced *OZZIE-on*) was founded in 1967 as an organization for economic, political, social, and cultural cooperation. In 1995, Vietnam became the group's first communist member. Today, the ASEAN group has a population of over 400 million and a GNP of approximately $350 billion.

Table 3.1 lists the major trading partners of the United States. As we noted earlier, these partners come from all over the world and include high-, middle-, and low-income countries. The left side of the table identifies the 25 countries from which the United States buys the most goods and services. China, for example, is our fourth-biggest supplier, Italy the tenth, and Brazil the sixteenth. The right side of the table identifies the 25 largest export markets for U.S. businesses. As you can see, the United Kingdom is our fourth-biggest export market, Singapore the tenth, and Saudi Arabia the sixteenth. Note that many countries are on both lists (indeed, Canada is at the top of both), while others appear on only one list.

Forms of Competitive Advantage

Why are there such high levels of importing, exporting, and other forms of international business activity? Because no country can produce all the goods and services that its people need. Thus, countries tend to export products that they can produce better or less expensively than other countries, using the proceeds to import products that they cannot produce as effectively.

Table 3.1

The Major Trading Partners of the United States

TOP 25 U.S. SUPPLIER COUNTRIES Rank/Country		1998 Imports ($ bil.)	TOP 25 U.S. EXPORT MARKETS Rank/Country		1998 Exports ($ bil.)
1	Canada	173.3	1	Canada	156.6
2	Japan	121.8	2	Mexico	78.8
3	Mexico	94.6	3	Japan	57.8
4	China	71.2	4	United Kingdom	39.1
5	Federal Republic of Germany	49.8	5	Federal Republic of Germany	26.7
6	United Kingdom	34.8	6	Netherlands	19.0
7	Taiwan	33.1	7	Taiwan	18.2
8	France	24.0	8	France	17.7
9	South Korea	23.9	9	Korea, South	16.5
10	Italy	21.0	10	Singapore	15.7
11	Malaysia	19.0	11	Brazil	15.1
12	Singapore	18.4	12	China	14.2
13	Thailand	13.4	13	Belgium	13.9
14	Philippines	11.9	14	Hong Kong	12.9
15	Hong Kong	10.5	15	Australia	11.9
16	Brazil	10.1	16	Saudi Arabia	10.5
17	Indonesia	9.3	17	Italy	9.0
18	Venezuela	9.2	18	Malaysia	9.0
19	Switzerland	8.7	19	Switzerland	7.2
20	Israel	8.6	20	Israel	7.0
21	Belgium	8.4	21	Philippines	6.7
22	Ireland	8.4	22	Venezuela	6.5
23	India	8.2	23	Argentina	5.9
24	Sweden	7.8	24	Ireland	5.6
25	Netherlands	7.6	25	Spain	5.5

Of course, this principle does not fully explain why various nations export and import *what* they do. Such decisions hinge partly on the advantages a particular country may enjoy regarding its abilities to create and/or sell various products and resources.[7] Traditionally, economists focused on *absolute* and *comparative advantage* to explain international trade. But because this approach focuses narrowly on such factors as natural resources and labor costs, a perspective has emerged that focuses on a more complex view of *national competitive advantage.*

absolute advantage
The ability to produce something more efficiently than any other country can

Absolute Advantage An **absolute advantage** exists when a country can produce something cheaper and/or of higher quality than any other country. Saudi oil, Brazilian coffee beans, and Canadian timber approximate absolute advantage, but examples of true absolute advantage are rare. In reality, "absolute" advantages are always relative. For example, most experts say that the vineyards of France produce the finest wines in the world. But the burgeoning wine business in California attests to the fact that producers there can also produce very good wine—wines which are almost as good as French wines and which also come in more varieties and at lower prices.

comparative advantage
The ability to produce some products more efficiently than others

Comparative Advantage A country has a **comparative advantage** in goods that it can produce more efficiently or better than other goods. For example, if businesses in a given country can make computers more efficiently than they can make automobiles, then that nation's firms have a comparative advantage in computer manufacturing. The United States has comparative advantages in the computer industry (because of technological sophistication) and in farming (because of fertile land and a temperate climate). South

It's a WiredWorld

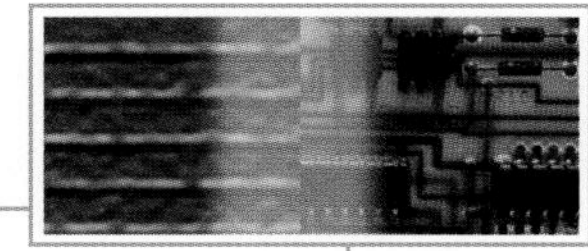

• *Nokia Puts the Finishing Touches on a Telecommunications Giant*

On the surface, one would assume that the major industrialized countries—the United States, Germany, and Japan—would be leading the way in information technology. But while this is generally true, a surprising upstart (Nokia Corp.) in a relatively remote part of the world (Finland) is at the forefront of today's emerging global communication network.

Ironically, conditions in Finland actually provide a unique catalyst for the Nokia success story. Many parts of the Finnish landscape are heavily forested, and vast regions of the country are sparsely populated. Creating, maintaining, and updating wired land-based communication networks is difficult and extremely expensive. But wireless digital systems are a relative bargain. As a result, conditions were perfect for an astute, forward-looking company like Nokia <www.nokiausa.com> to strike gold.

Nokia was formed in 1865 by Fredrik Idestam, a Finnish engineer. The company's early success is quite consistent with the theory of comparative advantage. Idestam's young company set up shop on the Nokia River in Finland to manufacture pulp and paper, using the area's lush forests as raw material. Nokia flourished in anonymity for about a century, focusing almost exclusively on its domestic market.

In the 1960s, however, management decided to expand regionally. In 1967, with the government's encouragement, Nokia took over two state-owned firms, Finnish Rubber Works and Finnish Cable Works. But it was in 1981 that a seminal event dramatically altered Nokia's destiny: Because it had done so well with the Rubber and Cable operations, the Finnish government offered to sell Nokia 51-percent ownership of the state-owned Finnish Telecommunications Co.

Because Nokia had already been developing competencies in digital technologies, the firm seized the opportunity and started pushing aggressively into a variety of telecommunications businesses. For example, Nokia created Europe's first digital telephone network in 1982. A series of other acquisitions and partnerships subsequently propelled Nokia into the number-one position in the global market for mobile telephones. Today, the firm commands a 27-percent market share in cellular telephones, comfortably ahead of second-place Motorola's 17 percent.

But Nokia hasn't been content to rest on its laurels. To the contrary, the company continues to expand into new and emerging markets. Foremost among these is technology for providing cellular phones with reliable and affordable Web content. Nokia was first out of the gate in this area and quickly established its own innovation, WAP (an acronym for *wireless application protocol*), as the likely standard that other firms will have little choice but to license for their own use.

Korea has a comparative advantage in electronics manufacturing because of efficient operations and cheap labor. As a result, U.S. firms export computers and grain to South Korea and import VCRs and stereos from South Korea. The "Wired World" box in this chapter describes how comparative advantage played a key role in the historical development of Finland's Nokia Corp.

National Competitive Advantage In recent years, a theory of national competitive advantage has become a widely accepted model of why nations engage in international trade.[8] Basically, **national competitive advantage** derives from four conditions:

national competitive advantage
International competitive advantage stemming from a combination of factor conditions, demand conditions, related and supporting industries, and firm strategies, structures, and rivalries

1. *Factor conditions* are the factors of production that we identified in Chapter 1.
2. *Demand conditions* reflect a large domestic consumer base that promotes strong demand for innovative products.
3. *Related and supporting industries* include strong local or regional suppliers and/or industrial customers.
4. *Strategies, structures, and rivalries* refer to firms and industries that stress cost reduction, product quality, higher productivity, and innovative new products.

When all of these conditions exist, a nation will be inclined to engage in international business. Japan, for instance, has an abundance of natural resources and strong domestic demand for automobiles. Its automobile producers have well-oiled supplier networks, and domestic firms have competed intensely with each other for decades. This set of circumstances explains why Japanese automobile companies like Toyota

<www.toyota.com>, Honda <www.hondacorporate.com>, Nissan <www.nissandriven.com>, and Mazda <www.mazda.com> are generally successful in foreign markets.

Import-Export Balances

Although international trade involves many advantages, trading with other nations can pose problems if a country's imports and exports do not strike an acceptable balance. In deciding whether an overall balance exists, economists use two measures: *balance of trade* and *balance of payments.*

balance of trade
Economic value of all products a country imports minus the economic value of all products it exports

Balance of Trade A nation's **balance of trade** is the total economic value of all products that it imports minus the total economic value of all products that it exports. Relatively small trade imbalances are common and are generally unimportant. Large imbalances, however, are another matter. In 1998, for example, the United States had a negative balance of *merchandise trade* of $246.9 billion and a positive balance of *service trade* of $82.7 billion. The result: an overall negative trade balance of $164.2 billion. This large negative balance continues to be a concern for U.S. business and political leaders.

trade deficit
Situation in which a country's imports exceed its exports, creating a negative balance of trade

trade surplus
Situation in which a country's exports exceed its imports, creating a positive balance of trade

Trade Deficits and Surpluses When a country's imports exceed its exports—that is, when it has a negative balance of trade—it suffers a **trade deficit.** In short, more money is flowing out of the country than flowing in. A positive balance of trade occurs when a country's exports exceed its imports and it enjoys a **trade surplus:** More money is flowing into the country than flowing out. Trade deficits and surpluses are influenced by an array of factors such as the absolute, comparative, or national competitive advantages enjoyed by the relevant trading partners, the general economic conditions prevailing in various countries, and the effect of trade agreements. For example, higher domestic costs, greater international competition, and continuing economic problems of some of its regional trading partners have slowed Japan's exports from the tremendous growth it enjoyed several years ago. But rising prosperity in both China and India have resulted in strong increases in both exports from and imports to those countries.

In general, the United States suffers from fairly large trade deficits with Japan ($64 billion), China ($56.9 billion), Germany ($23.2 billion), Canada ($16.7 billion), Mexico ($15.9 billion), and Taiwan ($15 billion). In any given year, the United States may also have smaller deficits with other countries. Our present trade deficit with Switzerland is only $1.4 billion.

Conversely, the United States enjoys healthy trade surpluses with many countries. For example, the most current figures report an $11.4 billion trade surplus with the Netherlands, $6.5 billion with Australia, $5.5 billion with Belgium-Luxembourg, and $2.4 billion with Egypt. At the lower end of the spectrum, U.S. trade surpluses with Jordan and Uruguay are $300 million each.[9]

balance of payments
Flow of all money into or out of a country

Balance of Payments The **balance of payments** refers to the flow of money into or out of a country. The money that a nation pays for imports and receives for exports—its balance of trade—comprises much of its balance of payments. Other financial exchanges are also factors. For example, money spent by tourists, money spent on foreign-aid programs, and money spent and received in the buying and selling of currency on international money markets all affect the balance of payments.

For many years, the United States enjoyed a positive balance of payments (more inflows than outflows). Recently, the balance has been negative. That trend, however, is gradually reversing itself, and many economists soon expect a positive balance of payments. Some U.S. industries have positive balances, whereas others have negative balances. U.S. firms such as Dow Chemical <www.dow.com> and Monsanto <www.pharmacia.com> are among the world leaders in chemical exports. The cigarette, truck, and industrial machinery industries also enjoy positive balances. Conversely, the metalworking-machinery, electrical-generation, airplane-parts, and auto industries suffer negative balances because the United States imports more than it exports.

Exchange Rates

The balance of imports and exports between two countries is affected by the rate of exchange between their currencies. An **exchange rate** is the rate at which the currency of one nation can be exchanged for that of another.[10] The actual exchange rate between U.S. dollars and French francs has recently been about 6.8 to 1. But let's simplify things by supposing an exchange rate between U.S. dollars and French francs is 5 to 1. This means that it costs one dollar to "buy" 5 francs; alternatively, it costs 5 francs to "buy" one dollar. This exchange rate means that one dollar or 5 francs have exactly the same purchasing power.

exchange rate
Rate at which the currency of one nation can be exchanged for the currency of another country

At the end of World War II, the major nations of the world agreed to establish fixed exchange rates. Under *fixed exchange rates,* the value of any country's currency relative to that of another country remains constant. Today, however, *floating exchange rates* are the norm, and the value of one country's currency relative to that of another varies with market conditions. For example, when many French citizens want to spend francs to buy U.S. dollars (or goods), the value of the dollar relative to the franc increases, or gets stronger; *demand* for the dollar is high. A currency is said to be strong when demand for it is high. It is also strong when there is high demand for the goods that are manufactured at the expense of that currency. Thus the value of the dollar rises with the demand for U.S. goods. On a daily basis, exchange rates fluctuate by very small degrees. Significant variations usually occur over greater spans of time.

Fluctuation in exchange rates can have an important impact on the balance of trade. Suppose, for example, that you want to buy some French wines priced at 50 francs per bottle. At an exchange rate of 5 francs to the dollar, a bottle will cost you \$10 ($50 \div 5 = 10$). But what if the franc is weaker? At an exchange rate of 10 francs to the dollar, that same bottle of wine would cost you only \$5 ($50 \div 10 = 5$).

If the dollar were stronger in relation to the franc, the prices of all American-made products would rise in France and the prices of all French-made products would fall in the United States. As a result, the French would buy fewer American-made products, and Americans would be prompted to spend more on French-made products. The result could conceivably be a U.S. trade deficit with France.

Exchange Rates and Competition Companies conducting international operations must watch exchange-rate fluctuations closely because changes affect overseas demand for their products and can be a major factor in international competition. In general, when the value of a country's domestic currency rises—becomes stronger—companies based there find it harder to export products to foreign markets and easier for foreign companies to enter local markets. It also makes it more cost-efficient for domestic companies to move production operations to lower-cost sites in foreign countries. When the value of a country's currency declines—becomes weaker—just the opposite occurs. Thus, as the value of a country's currency falls, its balance of trade should improve because domestic companies should experience a boost in exports. There should also be a corresponding decrease in the incentives for foreign companies to ship products into the domestic market.

A good case-in-point is the recent decline of the Canadian dollar relative to the U.S. dollar. In the mid-1990s, the Canadian dollar was relatively strong compared to the U.S. dollar. As a result, Canadian consumers frequently shopped for bargains on U.S. soil. But a global currency crisis in 1997 brought with it longer-lasting effects in Canada than in the United States. For the last several years, the Canadian dollar has been somewhat weaker than the U.S. dollar. It is now cheaper, therefore, for U.S. consumers to do just what their Canadian counterparts used to do—drive across the border to shop. Table 3.2 illustrates the effects of this trend. For example, the same hamburger costing \$2.39 in Niagara Falls, NY, sells for only \$2.18 (in U.S. currency) just across the border in Ontario, Canada. Likewise, a cafe latte in Seattle costs \$2.70 but only \$2.29 (again, in U.S. currency) in Vancouver. As one Vancouver store owner puts it, "There has been an exact switch. Five years ago, we would go down to Seattle to get good deals. Now the Americans come here for shopping."[11]

"Five years ago, we would go down to Seattle to get good deals. Now the Americans come here."

—Store owner in Vancouver, Canada

Table 3.2

Canadian vs. U.S. Prices

	Niagara Falls, N.Y.	Niagara Falls, Ontario
Saturday stay at Days Inn, with Jacuzzi	$260	$165
Whopper with cheese at Burger King	$2.39	$2.18
	Seattle	**Vancouver, British Columbia**
Lauryn Hill CD	$17.99	$12.60
Nintendo 64 game system	$130	$119
Grande latte at Starbucks	$2.70	$2.29
Levi's 501 jeans at the Original Levi's Store	$50	$45

The U.S. Economy and Foreign Trade Figures 3.5 and 3.6 highlight (1) recent trends in U.S. exports and imports and (2) the trade deficit that has resulted. As Figure 3.5 shows, both imports into the United States from other countries and exports from the United States to other countries have increased steadily over the last 10 years—a trend that is projected to continue. In 1999, the United States exported $965,242 billion in goods and services. In the same year, the United States imported $1,221,213 billion in goods and services. Because imports were greater than exports, the United States had a trade deficit of $255,971 billion (the difference between imports and exports). The trade deficits for the last 10 years are shown in Figure 3.6. The difference in exports and imports in this case is a *deficit* because more money flowed out of the country to pay for imports than flowed into the country from the sale of exports. Had exports been greater than imports, the difference would have been a *surplus*.

Figure 3.5

U.S. Imports and Exports

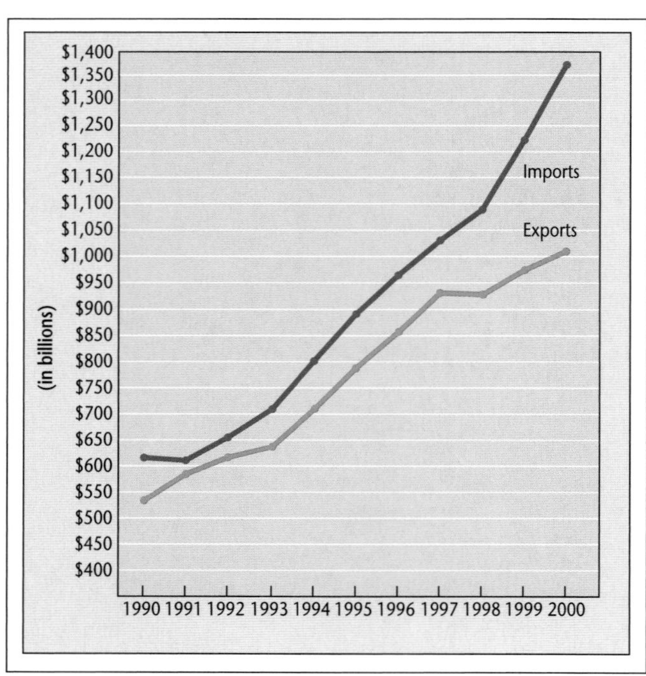

Figure 3.6

U.S. Trade Deficit

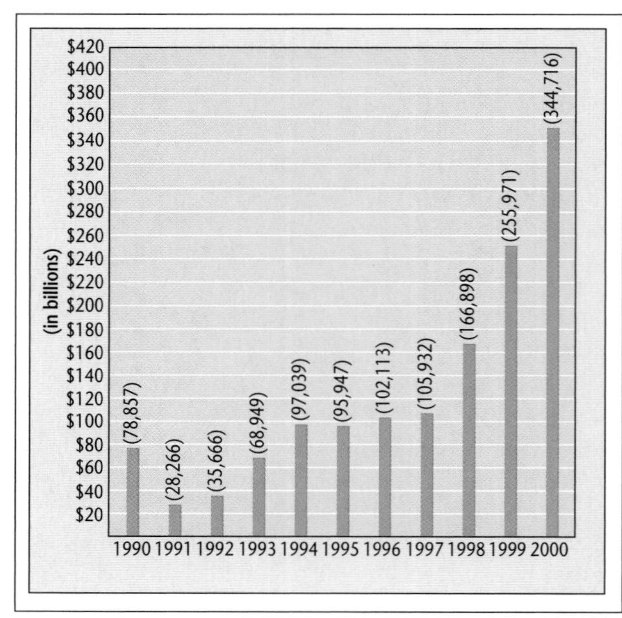

INTERNATIONAL BUSINESS MANAGEMENT

Wherever a firm is located, its success depends largely on how well it is managed. International business is so challenging because the basic management responsibilities—planning, organizing, directing, and controlling—are much more difficult to carry out when a business operates in several markets scattered around the globe.

Managing means making decisions. In this section, we examine the three most basic decisions that a company's management must make when faced with the prospect of globalization. The first decision is whether to go international at all. Once that decision has been made, managers must decide on the company's level of international involvement and on the organizational structure that will best meet its global needs.

Going International

As the world economy becomes globalized, more and more firms are conducting international operations. Wal-Mart <www.walmart.com>, for example, was once the quintessential U.S. growth company; but as managers perceived both fewer opportunities for expansion inside the United States and stronger competition from domestic competitors, they decided that foreign expansion was the key to future growth. By aggressively opening new stores and buying existing retail chains in other countries, Wal-Mart quadrupled its foreign sales to $14 billion between 1995 and 1999. Because this total represents only about 10 percent of the firm's total revenues, Wal-Mart managers have made international expansion and sales growth their primary goal for the future. Today the firm has stores in Mexico, Canada, Germany, Brazil, Argentina, China, and South Korea and has ambitious plans for continued international expansion.[12] When asked to explain why his firm set up shop in Germany, the Wal-Mart executive in charge simply noted that "Germany, being the third-largest economy in the world, is very important to us and one obviously that we can't ignore."

"Germany, being the third-largest economy in the world, is very important to us and one obviously that we can't ignore."

—Ron Tiarks,
Wal-Mart executive in Germany

This route, however, is not appropriate for every company. Companies that buy and sell fresh produce and fish may find it more profitable to confine their activities to limited geographic areas: Storage and transport costs may be too high to make international operations worthwhile. As Figure 3.7 shows, several factors enter into the decision to go international. One overriding factor is the business climate in other nations. Even experienced firms have encountered cultural, legal, and economic roadblocks (these problems are discussed in more detail later in this chapter).

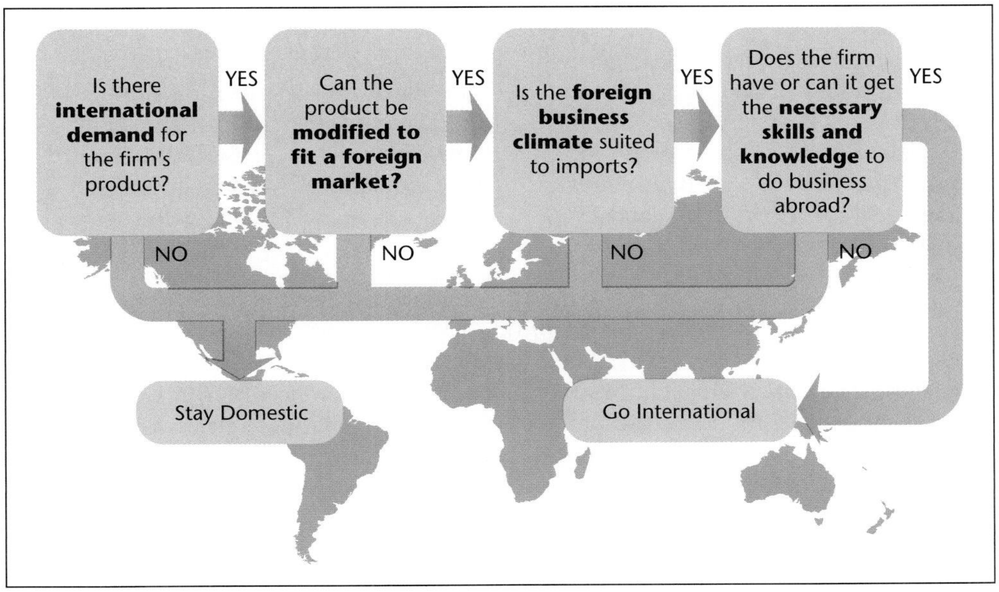

Figure 3.7
Going International

In Vietnam, the domestic film industry is short of funds and produces movies of such poor quality that audiences prefer American-made films. They don't even have to be recent. On July 10, 2000, a theater in the capital of Hanoi was showing the 1996 Tom Cruise hit Mission Impossible. *Other imported films and TV shows come from South Korea, Japan, and China.*

Gauging International Demand In considering international expansion, a company should also consider at least two other questions:

1. Is there a demand for this company's products abroad?
2. If so, must those products be adapted for international consumption?

Products that are successful in one country may be useless in another. Snowmobiles, for example, are popular for transportation and recreation in Canada and the northern United States and actually revolutionized reindeer herding in Lapland. However, there is no demand for snowmobiles in Central America. Although this is an extreme example, the point is basic to the decision to go international: Foreign demand for a company's product may be greater than, the same as, or weaker than domestic demand. Market research and/or the prior market entry of competitors may indicate whether there is an international demand for a firm's products.

One very large category of U.S. products that travels well is American popular culture. Many U.S. movies, for example, earn as much or more abroad than in their domestic release. While *Star Wars: Episode 1—The Phantom Menace* took in over $431 million in U.S. box office revenues, it garnered another $492 million at international box offices.[13] Billions of dollars are also involved in popular music, television shows, books, and even street fashions. Teenagers in Rome and Beirut sport American baseball caps as part of their popular street dress. Super Mario Brothers is advertised on billboards in Bangkok, Thailand, and Bart Simpson piñatas are sold at bazaars in Mexico City. Vintage Levi's from the 1950s and 1960s sell for as much as $3,000 in countries such as Finland and Australia.

Adapting to Customer Needs If there is international demand for its product, a firm must consider whether and how to adapt that product to meet the special demands and expectations of foreign customers. Movies, for example, have to be dubbed into foreign languages. Likewise, McDonald's restaurants sell wine in France, beer in Germany, and meatless sandwiches in India to accommodate local tastes and preferences. Ford products must have their steering wheels mounted on the right if they are to be sold in England and Japan. When Toyota launches upscale cars at home, it retains the Toyota nameplate; but those same cars are sold under the Lexus nameplate <www.lexus.com> in the United States because the firm has concluded that American consumers will not pay a premium price for a Toyota. Similarly, the firm even designed its new full-scale pick-up truck solely

"How can I sleep when people in other time zones are already up and making money?"

for the American market because Ford and General Motors sell so many big trucks in the United States; there is no domestic market in Japan for those same trucks.

Levels of Involvement

After a firm decides to go international, it must decide on the level of its international involvement. Several different levels of involvement are possible. At the most basic level, a firm may act as an *exporter* or *importer,* organize as an *international firm,* or operate as a *multinational firm.* Most of the world's largest industrial firms are multinationals.

Exporters and Importers An **exporter** is a firm that makes products in one country and then distributes and sells them in others. An **importer** buys products in foreign markets and then imports them for resale in its home country. Exporters and importers tend to conduct most of their business in their home nations. Both enterprises entail the lowest level of involvement in international operations and are excellent ways to learn the fine points of global business. Many large firms began international operations as exporters. IBM <www.ibm/planetwide/europe> and Coca-Cola <www.thecoca-colacompany.com/world>, among others, exported to Europe for several years before building manufacturing facilities there.

exporter
Firm that distributes and sells products to one or more foreign countries

importer
Firm that buys products in foreign markets and then imports them for resale in its home country

Exporting and importing have steadily increased over the last several decades. For example, exports from the United States totaled $344 billion in 1980, $708 billion in 1990, and exceeded $1.3 trillion in 2000. Conversely, imports into the United States have risen from $335 billion in 1980 to $1 trillion in 1990 to $1.4 trillion in 2000.[14] While big business was responsible for much of this growth, many smaller firms have also become very successful exporters.[15] For example, San Antonio's Pace Foods <www.pacefoods.com>, a maker of Tex-Mex products, began actively exporting to Mexico after discovering that Mexican consumers enjoyed its picante sauce as much as U.S. consumers.

What can explain the exporting boom in the United States over the past 15 years?

International Firms As firms gain experience and success as exporters and importers, they may move to the next level of involvement. An **international firm** conducts a significant portion of its business abroad. International firms also maintain manufacturing facilities overseas. Wal-Mart, for instance, is an international firm. Most of the retailer's stores are in the United States, but as we noted earlier, the company is rapidly expanding into various foreign markets.

international firm
Firm that conducts a significant portion of its business in foreign countries

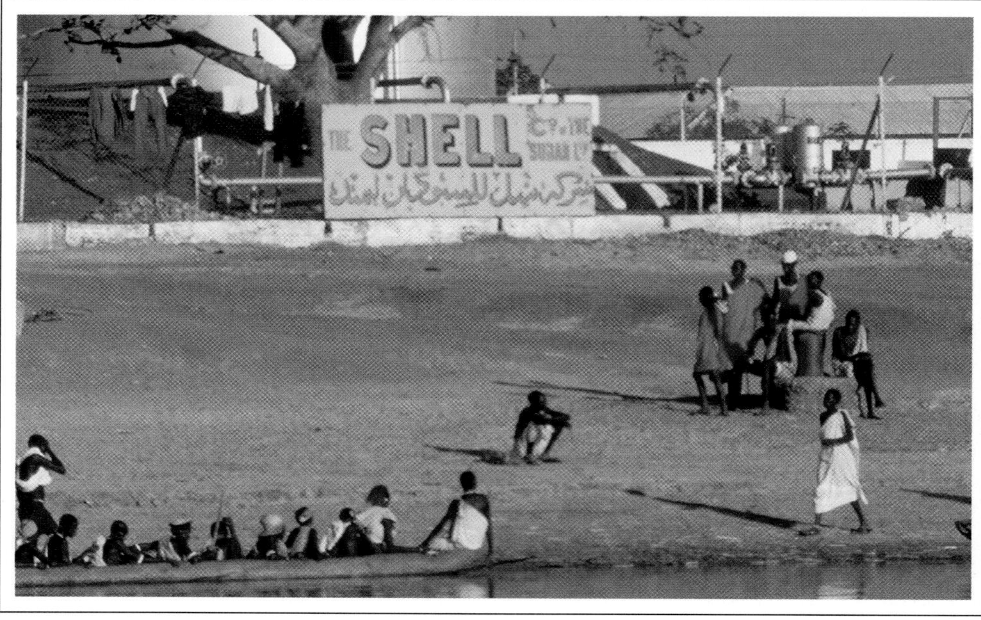

No global company enjoys greater profits than Royal Dutch/Shell <www.shell.com>. *The giant multinational oil-and-gas business operates in 130 countries, with headquarters in both London and The Hague, Netherlands. This Shell sign stands next to a park in the Sudan.*

Although an international firm may be large and influential in the global economy, it remains basically a domestic firm with international operations: Its central concern is its own domestic market. Wal-Mart, for example, still earns 90 percent of its revenues from U.S. sales. Product and manufacturing decisions typically reflect this concern. Burlington Industries <www.burlington.com>, Toys "R" Us <www.toysrus.com>, and BMW <www.bmw.com> are also international firms.

multinational firm
Firm that designs, produces, and markets products in many nations

Multinational Firms Most **multinational firms** do not ordinarily think of themselves as having domestic and international divisions. Instead, planning and decision making are geared to international markets. Headquarters locations are almost irrelevant. Royal Dutch/Shell, Nestlé, IBM, and Ford are well-known multinationals.

The economic importance of multinationals cannot be underestimated. Consider the economic impact of the 500 largest multinational corporations. In 1998, these 500 firms generated $11,463.4 billion in revenues and $440.3 billion in owner profits. They owned $38,989.3 billion in assets, and they employed 39,685,624 people. In addition, they bought supplies, materials, parts, equipment, and materials from literally thousands of other firms and paid billions of dollars in taxes. Moreover, their products affected the lives of hundreds of millions of consumers, competitors, and investors, and even protestors.[16] "Wealth," says Jürgen Schrempp, CEO of DaimlerChrysler, "is to add something to society materially and, ideally, over the long term. That's how I see my responsibility."

"Wealth is to add something to society materially and, ideally, over the long term. That's how I see my responsibility."

—Jürgen Schrempp, CEO of DaimlerChrysler

International Organizational Structures

Different levels of involvement in international business require different kinds of organizational structure. For example, a structure that would help coordinate an exporter's activities would be inadequate for the activities of a multinational firm. In this section, we consider the spectrum of international organizational strategies, including *independent agents, licensing arrangements, branch offices, strategic alliances,* and foreign *direct investment.*

independent agent
Foreign individual or organization that agrees to represent an exporter's interests

Independent Agents An **independent agent** is a foreign individual or organization that agrees to represent an exporter's interests in foreign markets. Independent agents often act as sales representatives: They sell the exporter's products, collect payment, and make sure that customers are satisfied. Independent agents often represent several firms at once and usually do not specialize in a particular product or market. Levi Strauss <www.levi.com> uses agents to market clothing products in many small countries in Africa, Asia, and South America.

Licensing Arrangements Companies seeking more substantial involvement in international business may opt for **licensing arrangements.** Firms give individuals or companies in a foreign country exclusive rights to manufacture or market their products in that market. In return, the exporter typically receives a fee plus ongoing payments called **royalties.** Royalties are usually calculated as a percentage of the license holder's sales.

Franchising is a special form of licensing that is also growing in popularity. McDonald's <www.macdonalds.com/corporate/franchise/outside> and Pizza Hut <www.pizzahut.com> franchise around the world. Similarly, Accor SA <www.accor.com/sf>, a French hotel chain, is franchising its Ibis, Sofitel, and Novotel hotels in the United States.

licensing arrangement
Arrangement in which firms choose foreign individuals or organizations to manufacture or market their products in another country

royalty
Payment made to a license holder in return for the right to market the licenser's product

Branch Offices Instead of developing relationships with foreign companies or independent agents, a firm may send some of its own managers to overseas **branch offices**. A company has more direct control over branch managers than over agents or license holders. Branch offices also give a company a more visible public presence in foreign countries. Potential customers tend to feel more secure when a business has branch offices in their country.

branch office
Foreign office set up by an international or multinational firm

Strategic Alliances In a **strategic alliance,** a company finds a partner in the country in which it would like to conduct business. Each party agrees to invest resources and capital into a new business or else to cooperate in some way for mutual benefit. This new business—the alliance—is then owned by the partners, who divide its profits. Such alliances are sometimes called joint ventures. As we saw in Chapter 2, however, the term *strategic alliance* has arisen because of the increasingly important role that such partnerships play in the larger organizational strategies of many major companies.

strategic alliance (or joint venture)
Arrangement in which a company finds a foreign partner to contribute approximately half of the resources needed to establish and operate a new business in the partner's country

The number of strategic alliances among major companies has increased significantly over the last decade and is likely to grow even more. In many countries, including Mexico, India, and China, laws make alliances virtually the only way to do international business within their borders. Mexico, for example, requires that all foreign firms investing there have local partners. Similarly, Disney's new theme park currently under construction near Hong Kong is a joint venture with local partners.

In addition to easing the way into new markets, alliances give firms greater control over their foreign activities than independent agents and licensing arrangements. At the same time, all partners in an alliance retain some say in its decisions. Perhaps most important, alliances allow firms to benefit from the knowledge and expertise of their foreign partners. Microsoft, for example, relies heavily on strategic alliances as it expands into new international markets. This approach has successfully enabled the firm to learn the intricacies of doing business in China and India, two of the hardest emerging markets to crack.

Foreign Direct Investment The term **foreign direct investment (FDI)** means buying or establishing tangible assets in another country.[17] Dell Computer, for example, is building a new assembly plant in Europe. As we noted, Disney is building a new theme park in Hong Kong; Volkswagen is building a new factory in Brazil. Each of these activities represents foreign direct investment by a firm in another country. Likewise, Ford's purchase of Land Rover from BMW and Unilever's acquisition of both Ben & Jerry's and Slim-Fast also represent major examples of FDI.[18] FDI in the United States by foreign firms in 1998 totaled $210 billion, up from only $70 billion the year before. U.S. firms invested $980 billion in other countries in 1998, up from $866 billion in 1997.[19]

foreign direct investment (FDI)
Arrangement in which a firm buys or establishes tangible assets in another country

WebConnection

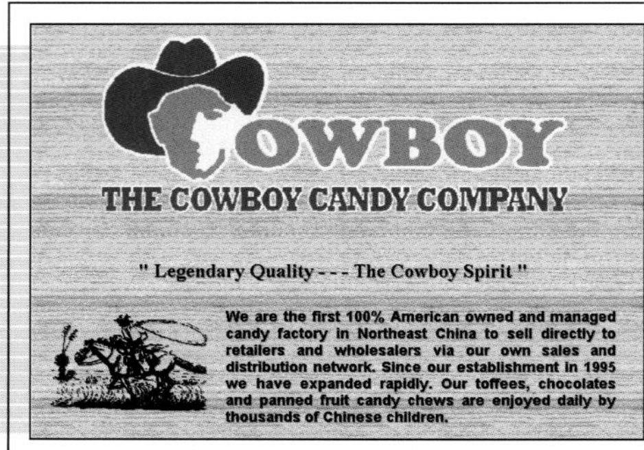

www.cowboycandy.com

Founded by two young entrepreneurs—one from Pennsylvania and one from Bulgaria—the Shenyang Shawnee Cowboy Food Co. sells candy directly to Chinese wholesalers and retailers. To find out more about the company's factory operations, which are located in the city of Shenyang, and its 32-city distribution network, log onto its Web site.

BARRIERS TO INTERNATIONAL TRADE

Whether a business is truly multinational or sells to only a few foreign markets, several factors will affect its international operations. Its success in foreign markets is largely determined by the ways in which it responds to social, economic, and political barriers to international trade. The "Life Cycle of an e-Business" box in this chapter discusses some of the barriers to international trade faced by Garden.com, as well as the firm's anticipated response to those barriers.

Social and Cultural Differences

Any firm planning to conduct business in another country must understand the social and cultural differences between the host country and the home country. Some differences, of course, are fairly obvious. Companies must, for example, take language factors into account when making adjustments in packaging, signs, and logos. Pepsi-Cola <www.pepsico.com> is exactly the same product whether it is sold in Seattle or Moscow—except for the lettering on the bottle. Less universal products, however, face a variety of conditions that require them to adjust their practices. In Thailand, for example, Kentucky Fried Chicken <www.kfc.com> has adjusted its menus, ingredients, and hours of operation to suit Thai culture. Similarly, when Bob's Big Boy <www.bobs.net> launched new restaurants in that same country, they had to add deep-fried shrimp to the menu.

As an international business major, do you think being female will help or hurt me in dealing with other cultures?

A wide range of subtle value differences can also affect international operations. For example, many Europeans shop daily. To U.S. consumers accustomed to weekly supermarket trips, the European pattern may seem like a waste of time. For many Europeans, however, shopping not only involves buying food but is also an outlet for meeting friends and exchanging political views. Consider the implications of this cultural difference for U.S. firms selling food products in European markets. First, large American supermarkets are not the norm in many parts of Europe. Second, people who shop daily do not need large refrigerators and freezers.

Economic Differences

Although cultural differences are often subtle, economic differences can be fairly pronounced. In dealing with mixed economies like those of France and Sweden, firms must be aware of when, and to what extent, the government is involved in a given industry. The French government, for instance, is heavily involved in all aspects of airplane design and manufacturing. The impact of economic differences can be even greater in planned economies like China and Vietnam.[20]

Life Cycle of an e-Business

Setting Out Roots Across Borders

One of the most significant things about the Internet from a business standpoint is its amazing ability to reach and connect people no matter where they are. Some would-be web entrepreneurs envision buying and selling around the world from a single location. Unfortunately, it's not always that easy. For one thing, when a business is literally thinking in terms of shipping products across national boundaries, numerous issues must be addressed.

The managers at Garden.com quickly became all too familiar with the constraints that national boundaries can impose on any business. Agricultural products—growing plants, seeds, chemicals, and the like—are among the most highly regulated in the world. In most cases, it's actually illegal to transport them from one country to another. As a result, virtually all of Garden.com's business was conducted within the boundaries of the continental United States.

But does this mean that a firm like Garden.com is forever confined to its home country? By no means. In fact, Garden.com had every intention of entering the European market at the earliest possible opportunity. As early as 1999, there were already a few upstart e-businesses in Europe attempting to pattern themselves after Garden.com. One option the company considered, therefore, was identifying one of the most promising of these firms and buying it outright. Another option was launching its own business in Europe. Given the complexities of doing business in the European Union, however, the firm had a clear preference for buying an existing operation—if it could have found just the right one and acquired it for just the right price.

Legal and Political Differences

Governments can affect international business activities in many ways. They can set conditions for doing business within their borders or even prohibit doing business altogether. They can control the flow of capital and use tax legislation to either discourage or encourage international activity in a given industry. In the extreme, they can even confiscate the property of foreign-owned companies. In this section, we discuss some of the more common legal and political issues in international business: *quotas, tariffs,* and *subsidies; local content laws;* and *business practice laws.*

Quotas, Tariffs, and Subsidies Even free market economies establish some system of quotas and/or tariffs. Both quotas and tariffs affect the prices and quantities of foreign-made products. A **quota** restricts the number of products of a certain type that can be imported into a country. By reducing supply, the quota raises the prices of those imports. For example, Belgian ice cream makers can ship no more than 922,315 kilograms of ice cream to the United States each year. Similarly, Canada can ship no more than 14.7 billion board feet of softwood timber per year to the United States. Quotas are often determined by treaties. Moreover, better terms are often given to friendly trading partners, and quotas are typically adjusted to protect domestic producers.

quota
Restriction on the number of products of a certain type that can be imported into a country

The ultimate form of quota is an **embargo**: a government order forbidding exportation and/or importation of a particular product—or even all the products—from a particular country. Many nations control bacteria and disease by banning certain agricultural products. The United States has embargoes against Cuba, Iraq, Libya, and Iran. Consequently, U.S. firms are forbidden from investing in these countries, and products from these countries cannot legally be sold on American markets.

embargo
Government order banning exportation and/or importation of a particular product or all products from a particular country

A **tariff** is a tax on imported products. Tariffs directly affect prices by raising the price of imports. Consumers pay not only for the products but also for tariff fees. Tariffs take two forms. *Revenue tariffs* are imposed strictly to raise money for governments. Most tariffs, however, are *protectionist tariffs,* meant to discourage the import of particular products. For example, firms that import ironing-board covers into the United States

tariff
Tax levied on imported products

WebConnection

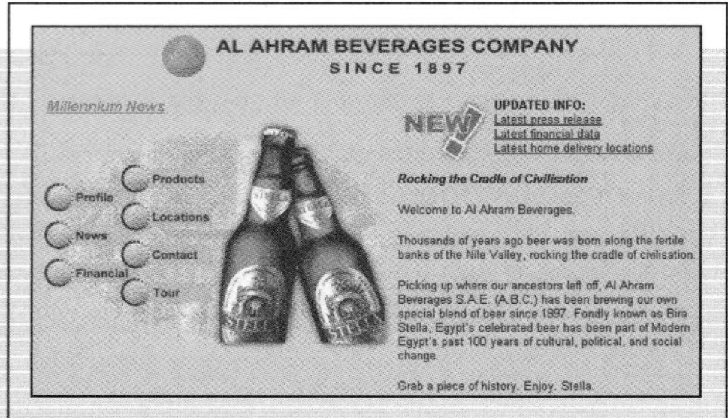

www.alahrambeverages.com

When entrepreneur Ahmed Zayat bought the Egyptian national beer company in 1997, the quality of its flagship brand, Stella, was not very dependable. Moreover, drinking alcohol is considered a sin among Muslims. But Al Ahram has now introduced a line of nonalcoholic beers that it hopes to market throughout the Muslim world. To find out more about the company—and about business in the Middle East—contact the brewery's Web site.

Considering the legal and political differences in the world, what are some of the ways in which a new corporation could benefit by manipulating the system?

pay a tariff of seven percent of the price of the product. Firms that import women's athletic shoes pay a flat rate of 90 cents per pair plus 20 percent of the price of the shoes. Each of these figures is set through a complicated process designed to put foreign and domestic firms on reasonably even competitive ground.

subsidy
Government payment to help a domestic business compete with foreign firms

A **subsidy** is a government payment to help a domestic business compete with foreign firms. Subsidies are actually indirect tariffs: They lower prices of domestic goods rather than raise prices of foreign goods. Many European governments subsidize farmers to help them compete with U.S. grain imports.

Quotas and tariffs are imposed for a variety of reasons. The U.S. government aids domestic automakers by restricting the number of Japanese cars that can be imported into this country. National security concerns have prompted the United States to limit the extent to which certain forms of technology can be *exported* to other countries (for example, computer and nuclear technology to China). The recent relaxation of controls on the licensing of technology has contributed to the export boom that we described earlier in this chapter. The United States is not the only country that uses tariffs and quotas. Italy imposes high tariffs on imported electronic goods to protect domestic firms. A Sony Walkman costs almost $150 in Italy, and CD players are prohibitively expensive.

protectionism
Practice of protecting domestic business against foreign competition

The Protectionism Debate In the United States, **protectionism**—the practice of protecting domestic business at the expense of free market competition—has long been controversial. Supporters argue that tariffs and quotas protect domestic firms and jobs, therefore, sheltering new industries until they are able to compete internationally. They argue that the United States needs such measures to counter measures imposed by other nations. Other advocates justify protectionism in the name of national security. A nation, they argue, must be able to produce the goods needed for its survival in the event of war. Thus, the U.S. government requires the U.S. Air Force to buy all its planes from U.S. manufacturers.

Critics cite protectionism as a source of friction between nations. They also charge that it drives up prices by reducing competition. They maintain that although jobs in some industries would be lost as a result of free trade, jobs in other industries (for example, electronics and automobiles) would be created if all nations abandoned protectionist tactics.

Protectionism can sometimes take on almost comic proportions. Neither Europe nor the United States grows bananas, however, both European and U.S. firms buy and sell bananas in numerous foreign markets. A disagreement flared up when the EU imposed a quota on bananas imported from Latin America—a market dominated by two large U.S. firms, Chiquita <www.chiquita.com> and Dole <www.dole.com>—in order to help firms based in current and former European colonies in the Caribbean. To retaliate, the United States imposed a 100-percent tariff on certain luxury products imported from Europe, including Louis Vuitton handbags <www.vuitton.com>, Scottish cashmere sweaters, and Parma ham.[21]

In July 1999, the United States, responding to European insistence on importing bananas from its own former colonies (as opposed to those in which U.S. companies are heavily invested), imposed a 100-percent tariff on $520 million worth of European exports, including Roquefort and foie gras. French farmers retaliated by attacking the domestic facilities of American multinationals.

Local Content Laws Many countries, including the United States, have **local content laws**—requirements that products sold in a particular country be at least partly made there. Typically, firms seeking to do business in a country must either invest there directly or take on a domestic partner. In this way, some of the profits from doing business in a foreign country stay there rather than flowing out to another nation. In some cases, the partnership arrangement is optional but wise. In Mexico, for instance, Radio Shack de Mexico is a joint venture owned by Tandy Corporation <www.radioshackunlimited.com> (49 percent) and Mexico's Grupo Gigante <www.gigante.com.mx> (51 percent). Both China and India currently require that a foreign firm wishing to establish a joint venture with a local firm must hold less than 50 percent ownership in the partnership, with the local partner having the controlling ownership stake.

local content law
Law requiring that products sold in a particular country be at least partly made there

Business Practice Laws Many businesses that enter new markets encounter a host of problems in complying with stringent, and often changing, regulations and other bureaucratic obstacles. Such practices fall under the heading of the host country's **business practice laws.** For example, as part of its entry strategy into Germany, Wal-Mart has had to buy existing retailers rather than open new ones. Why? Because the German government is not currently issuing new licenses to sell food products. Likewise, the firm had to discontinue its standard practice of promising to refund the price difference on any item sold for less elsewhere: in Germany, the practice is illegal. Finally, Wal-Mart must comply with local business-hour restrictions: stores cannot open before 7 A.M., must close by 8 P.M. on weeknights and 4 P.M. on Saturday, and must remain closed on Sunday.

business practice laws
Laws or regulations governing business practices in given countries

Sometimes, a legal—even an accepted—business practice in one country is illegal in another. In some South American countries, for example, it is sometimes legal to bribe business and government officials. The formation of **cartels**—associations of producers who control supply and prices—has given tremendous power to some nations, such as those belonging to the Organization of Petroleum Exporting Countries (OPEC). U.S. law forbids both bribery and cartels.

cartel
Association of producers whose purpose is to control supply and prices

Finally, many (but not all) countries forbid **dumping**—selling a product abroad for less than the cost of production.[22] U.S. antidumping legislation is contained in the Trade Agreements Act of 1979. This statute sets tests for determining two conditions:

dumping
Practice of selling a product abroad for less than the cost of production

1. If products are being priced at "less than fair value."
2. If the result unfairly harms domestic industry.

In 1999, for example, the United States charged Japan and Brazil with illegally dumping steel at prices as much as 70 percent below normal value. The government then imposed a significant tariff on steel imported from those countries in order to protect local manufacturers.[23]

Continued from page 65

It's a Smallworld.com After All

As we saw in the opening segment of our story, the Internet represents a major but unpredictable venue for international business competition. Things can change virtually overnight. Many U.S. firms were given little chance of making significant headway in Europe, and now they are dominant players.

The Internet is making it easier than ever before to compete in foreign markets—as long as you know how. Smallworld.com is a New York firm specializing in online games. The company's most complex project to date was creating an engine to power online baseball games. Once this task had been accomplished, Smallworld set out to transfer its new technology to England, where it would create and market an online soccer game. In the early planning stages, however, the firm discovered that they had a deep talent pool of soccer-knowledgeable programmers in New York. Therefore, they could proceed without any direct foreign investment.

Stories like this will be played out in many versions in the future. While Asia is behind Europe in e-commerce, it will no doubt catch up very quickly. The same battles currently being fought in Europe will repeat themselves in Japan, China, Australia, India, and major markets throughout Southeast Asia. Firms in these nations already are building a base from which to hold off not only Americans but Europeans.

As the Japanese now compete quite successfully in many U.S. markets (such as automobiles) and dominate certain others (such as consumer electronics), e-commerce companies being launched in Asia today will be formidable competition, not only in their homelands but in Europe and the United States. E-commerce firms from every corner of the globe will no doubt be waiting for just the right opportunities. As many European companies discovered, one misstep in the domestic market may allow firms from around the world to establish beachheads. Because so many of the traditional barriers to international expansion simply don't apply to e-commerce, no one can afford to get too comfortable.

Questions for Discussion

1. How might an e-businesses define the geographic boundaries of its markets differently from other firms?
2. How do the various forms of competitive advantage relate to e-businesses engaged in international commerce?
3. How do exchange rates affect e-commerce firms?
4. At what level of international involvement are such firms as Amazon.com, eBay, and Yahoo! currently operating?
5. What are some of the barriers to international trade that might be most relevant to e-commerce firms?

SUMMARY OF LEARNING OBJECTIVES

1 **Describe the rise of international business, identify the major world marketplaces, and discuss the United States' major trading partners.** More and more firms are engaged in international business. The term *globalization* refers to the process by which the world economy is fast becoming a single interdependent system. The three major marketplaces for international business are *North America* (the United States, Canada, and Mexico), *Western Europe* (which is dominated by Germany, the United Kingdom, France, and Italy), and the *Pacific Rim* (where the dominant country, Japan, is surrounded by such rapidly advancing nations as South Korea, Taiwan, Hong Kong, and China). The United States' major trading partners include Canada, Mexico, Japan, the United Kingdom, Taiwan, and Germany.

2 **Explain how different forms of *competitive advantage, import-export balances, exchange rates,* and *foreign competition* determine the ways in which countries and businesses respond to the international environment.** The different forms of competitive advantage are critical to international business. With an *absolute advantage,* a country engages in international trade because it can produce a product more efficiently than any other nation. *Comparative advantages* exist when they can produce some items more efficiently than they can produce other items. *National competitive advantage* stems from a combination of factor conditions, demand conditions, related and supporting industries, and firm strategies, structures, and rivalries. The *import-export balance,* including the *balance of trade* and the *balance of payments,* and *exchange rate differences* in national currencies affect the international economic environment and are important elements of international business.

3 **Discuss the factors involved in deciding to do business internationally and in selecting the appropriate *levels of international involvement* and *international organizational structure.*** In deciding whether to do business internationally, a firm must determine whether a market for its product exists abroad and, if so, whether it has the skills and knowledge to manage such a business. It must also assess the business climates of other nations to make sure that they are conducive to international operations.

A firm must also decide on its level of international involvement. It can choose to be an *exporter* or *importer,* to organize as an *international firm,* or to operate as a *multinational firm.* The choice will influence the organizational structure of its international operations, specifically, its use of *independent agents, licensing arrangements* (including *franchising*), *branch offices, strategic alliances,* and *direct investment.*

4 **Describe some of the ways in which *social, cultural, economic, legal,* and *political differences* among nations affect international business.** *Social* and *cultural differences* that can serve as barriers to trade include language, social values, and traditional buying patterns. Differences in economic systems may force businesses to establish close relationships with foreign governments before they are permitted to do business abroad. *Quotas, tariffs, subsidies,* and *local content laws* offer protection to local industries. Differences in *business practice laws* can make standard business practices in one nation illegal in another.

QUESTIONS AND EXERCISES

Questions for Review

1. How does the balance of trade differ from the balance of payments?
2. What are the three possible levels of involvement in international business? Give examples of each.
3. How does the economic system of a country affect the decisions of outside firms interested in doing business there?
4. What aspects of the culture in your state or region would be of particular interest to a foreign firm considering doing business there?

Questions for Analysis

5. Make a list of all the major items in your bedroom, including furnishings. Try to identify the country in which each item was made. Offer possible reasons why a given nation might have a comparative advantage in producing a given good.
6. Suppose that you are the manager of a small firm seeking to enter the international arena. What basic information would you need about the market that you are thinking of entering?
7. Do you support protectionist tariffs for the United States? If so, in what instances and for what reasons? If not, why not?
8. Do you think that a firm operating internationally is better advised to adopt a single standard of ethical conduct or to adapt to local conditions? Under what kinds of conditions might each approach be preferable?

Application Exercises

9. Interview the manager of a local firm that does at least some business internationally. Why did the company decide to go international? Describe the level of the firm's international involvement and the organizational structure(s) it uses for international operations.
10. Select a product familiar to you. Using library reference works to gain some insight into the culture of India, identify the problems that might arise in trying to market this product to Indian consumers.

EXPLORING THE WEB

TAPPING INTO THE CIA

One of the best sources of information about foreign countries is the CIA's *World Factbook*. Visit its Web site and then consider the following questions.

www.odci.gov/cia/publications/factbook/index.html

1. Assume that you are a manager interested in learning more about the market potential for your firm's products in a certain foreign country. What information from this site might be most helpful?
2. How accurate and reliable would you expect this information to be? Why?
3. What additional information do you think you might need? How and where might you go to look for it?

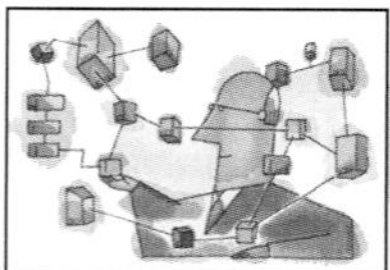

BUILDING YOUR BUSINESS SKILLS

I INTEND TO BE A GLOBAL COMPANY

This exercise enhances the following SCANS workplace competencies: demonstrating basic skills, demonstrating thinking skills, exhibiting interpersonal skills, and working with information.

GOAL

To encourage students to apply global business strategies to a small-business situation.

BACKGROUND

Some people might say that Yolanda Lang is a bit too confident. Others might say that she needs confidence—and more—to succeed in the business she's chosen. But one thing is certain: Lang is determined to grow INDE, her handbag design company, into a global enterprise. At only 28 years of age, she has time on her side—if she makes the right business moves now.

These days, Lang spends most of her time in Milan, Italy. Backed by $50,000 of her parents' personal savings, she is trying to compete with Gucci, Fendi, and other high-end handbag makers. Her target market: American women who are willing to spend $200 and more on a purse. Ironically, Lang was forced to set up shop in Italy because of the snobbishness of these same customers, who only buy high-end bags if they are European-made. "Strangely enough," she muses, "I need to be in Europe to sell America."

To succeed, she must first find ways to keep production costs down, which is a tough task for a woman working in a male-dominated business culture. Her fluent Italian is an important advantage, but she often turns down inappropriate dinner invitations. She also has to figure out how to get her 22-bag collection into stores worldwide. Although retailers are showing her bags in Italy and Japan, she's had little luck in the United States. "I intend to be a global company," says Lang. The question is how to succeed first as a small business.

METHOD

Step 1

Join together with three or four other students to discuss the steps that Lang has taken so far to break into the U.S. retail market. These steps include:

- Buying a mailing list of 5,000 shoppers from Neiman Marcus, a high-end department store and selling directly to these customers.
- Linking with a manufacturer's representative to sell her line in major U.S. cities while she herself concentrates on Europe.

Step 2

Based on what you learned in this chapter, suggest other strategies that might help Lang grow her business. Working with group members, consider whether the following options would help or hurt Lang's business. Explain why a strategy would be likely to work or why it would be likely to fail.

- Lang could relocate to the United States and sell her goods abroad through an independent agent.
- Lang could relocate to the United States and set up a branch office in Italy.
- Lang could find a partner in Italy and form a strategic alliance that would allow her to build her business on both continents.

Step 3

Working alone, create a written marketing plan for INDE. What steps would you recommend Lang take to reach her goal of becoming a global company? Compare your written response with those of other group members.

FOLLOW-UP QUESTIONS

1. What are the most promising steps that Lang can take to grow her business? What are the least promising?
2. Lang thinks that her trouble breaking into the U.S. retail market stems from the fact that her company is unknown. How would this circumstance affect the strategies suggested in Steps 1 and 2?
3. When Lang deals with Italian manufacturers, she is a young, attractive woman in a man's world. Often, she must convince men that her purpose is business and nothing else. How should Lang handle personal invitations that get in the way of business? How can she say no while still maintaining business relationships? Why is it often difficult for American women to do business in male-dominated cultures?
4. The American consulate has given Lang little business help because her products are made in Italy. Do you think the consulate's treatment of an American businessperson is fair or unfair? Explain your answer.
5. Do you think Lang's relocation to Italy will pay off? Why or why not?
6. With Lang's goals of creating a global company, can INDE continue to be a one-person operation?

CRAFTING YOUR BUSINESS PLAN

CONSIDERING THE WORLD

THE PURPOSE OF THE ASSIGNMENT

1. To acquaint you with the process of navigating the *Business Plan Pro* (*BPP*) software package (Version 4.0).
2. To familiarize students with issues faced by a firm that has decided to go global.
3. To determine where, in the framework of the *BPP* business plan, global issues might appropriately be presented.
4. To prepare students to enter international business considerations into a firm's business plan through *BPP*.

ASSIGNMENT

After reading Chapter 3 in the textbook, open the BPP *software* and examine the information dealing with the types of global business considerations that would be of concern to the sample firm of* Acme Consulting. *Then respond to the following items:*

1. What products does Acme plan to offer and in which international markets will they be competing? [Sites to see in *BPP* (for this assignment): In the Plan Outline screen, click on **1.0 Executive Summary**; then click on **1.2 Mission**

and then **4.0 Market Analysis Summary** and **4.1 Market Segmentation.** Next, while still in the Plan Outline screen, click on **2.0 Company Summary.** Finally, in the Plan Outline screen, click on **5.2 Strategic Alliances.**]

2. In Acme's business plan, see if you can find any discussion of the international organizational structures used by Acme's competitors. Assess the adequacy of the available information. [Sites to see in *BPP:* In the Plan Outline screen, click on **4.3.2 Distribution Service** and **4.3.4 Main Competitors.**]
3. What is the planned organization structure for Acme's international activities? Would you categorize Acme's relationship to its Paris partner as that of a branch office or that of a strategic alliance? [Sites to see in *BPP:* In the Plan Outline screen, click on **6.1 Organization Structure** and then on **6.2 Management Team.**]
4. Figure 3.7 (p. 77) in the textbook indicates that going international requires "necessary skills and knowledge." Does Acme's business plan indicate that the company possesses the skills and knowledge to succeed internationally? [Sites to see in *BPP*: In the Plan Outline screen, click on **6.0 Management Summary** and then on **6.2 Management Team.** Next, in the Plan Outline screen, click on **3.1 Service Description** and then click on **3.2 Competitive Comparison.**]

FOR YOUR OWN BUSINESS PLAN

5. In what ways will international considerations affect your business—say, competing companies or products from other countries, foreign sources of supply, customers in other countries, international laws, international finance, and so forth? If such considerations are not relevant now, might they become so in the future? Where in your business planning document would you include international factors?

*GENERAL TIPS FOR NAVIGATING IN BPP

1. Open the *BPP* program, examine the Welcome screen, and click on **Open a Sample Plan.**
2. From the **Open a Sample Plan** dialogue box, click on a sample company name; then click on **Open.**
3. On the Plan Manager screen, click on **Your Plan Outline;** then click on any of the lines (for example, **6.0 Management Summary**).
4. You can always return to the Plan Outline screen by going to the bottom of the screen and clicking on the **Plan Outline** icon.
5. After finishing with one sample company, you can get to the next one by going to the top of the screen and clicking on **File** (on the menu bar). Then beneath that, select **Open Sample Plan.** This will exit you from the current company file and take you to the **Open Sample Plan** dialogue box, where you can select your next sample company.
6. When you are finished, you can close the program by going to the top of the screen and clicking on **File** (on the bar menu). Then beneath that, select **Exit.**

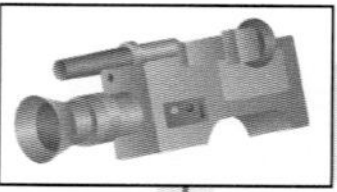

VIDEO EXERCISE

ENTERING THE GLOBAL MARKETPLACE: LANDS' END AND YAHOO!

Learning Objectives

The purpose of this video exercise is to help you

1. Understand the different reasons businesses undertake international expansion.
2. Identify the financial and marketing issues involved in selling products and services internationally.
3. Recognize the influence of culture on business decisions made by international firms.

BACKGROUND INFORMATION

- Yahoo! <www.yahoo.com> is an Internet search engine headquartered in Santa Clara, California. Its principal product is an ad-supported Internet directory that links users to millions of Web pages on demand. Yahoo! leads the field in volume of traffic (over 95 million pages viewed each day) and now has offices in Europe, Asia, and Canada, as well as a global network of 22 world properties.
- Lands' End <www.landsend.com> began in 1963 by selling sailing equipment through a catalog. Today the publicly owned firm is one of the largest apparel brands in the United States,

with a regular monthly catalog, numerous specialty catalogs, and a growing international reputation. In 1991, Lands' End sent catalogs to customers in the United Kingdom for the first time, and in 1993, it opened a warehouse and phone center there. In the following year, Lands' End started operations in Japan, and in 1995, it launched its interactive retail Web site. Lands' End opened a phone center in Germany in 1996.

THE VIDEO

This video segment shows how two very different companies have approached the same goal—expansion into international business. You will see how each copes with cultural, financial, monetary, and marketing differences as well as differences in language and methods of payment. See whether you can identify the areas in which each firm chose to adapt to the needs and expectations of the international marketplace. Distinguish these areas from the areas in which each company maintained its original product or policy.

DISCUSSION QUESTIONS

1. Compare the different reasons why Lands' End and Yahoo! decided to expand internationally.
2. How did Lands' End succeed in establishing itself in the United Kingdom and Japan?
3. How did Yahoo! succeed in France and China?
4. What international issues have provided the greatest challenges for each company?

FOLLOW-UP ASSIGNMENT

Obtain a mail-order catalog from any major U.S. clothing company and assess its product offerings and customer policies. Which of these, if any, do you think would need to be altered if the company wanted to sell overseas? How can the company customize these aspects of its business? Do you think it is likely that this company would be successful in international business? Why or why not?

FOR FURTHER EXPLORATION

Visit Yahoo!'s Web site <www.yahoo.com>. Explore some of the features and functions that appeal to you. Then, select one of the international sites listed at the bottom of the home page and compare it to the U.S. site. Identify the changes that have been made to suit the target country's language and customs. What elements of the site have *not* been changed? What do you think motivated the design and content choices that Yahoo! made in the overseas site?

Chapter

Conducting Business Ethically and Responsibly

After reading this chapter, you should be able to:

1. ***Explain*** how individuals develop their personal *codes of ethics* and why ethics are important in the workplace.
2. ***Distinguish*** *social responsibility* from *ethics,* identify *organizational stakeholders,* and trace the evolution of social responsibility in U.S. business.
3. ***Show*** how the concept of social responsibility applies both to environmental issues and to a firm's relationships with customers, employees, and investors.
4. ***Identify*** four general *approaches to social responsibility* and describe the four steps that a firm must take to implement a *social responsibility program.*
5. ***Explain*** how issues of social responsibility and ethics affect small business.

A Tale of Two Companies

As Charles Dickens once said, "It was the best of times, it was the worst of times." From an environmental perspective, the same might be said of the social performance of different companies. Businesses exist for one fundamental purpose—to earn profits for their owners. However, the manner in which they work to fulfill this purpose—and the lengths to which they are willing to go to earn even greater profits—can vary dramatically. Consider the quite different cases of Patagonia, Inc., a small privately held outdoor-apparel business, and IBP, Inc., a publicly held corporation and the world's largest processor of fresh beef.

Patagonia <**www.patagonia.com**> was founded in 1973 by a group of surfers in Ventura, California, led by Yvon Chouinard. Chouinard still runs the business today. The founders enjoyed spending part of their time hiking and mountain climbing, but they felt that the equipment available for such activities was often of poor quality, overpriced, or both. Their objective, then, was to become a provider of high-quality, reasonably priced outdoor equipment. They expressed this objective in the form of an unusual goal—to do the right thing. "Business[people] who focus on profits," says Chouinard, "wind up in the hole. For me, profit is what happens when you do everything else right."

At first, "doing the right thing" meant making the most useful, durable, and environmentally friendly products possible. For instance, mountain climbers had for years embedded steel chocks into rocks for attaching ropes and creating hand- and footholds. But Patagonia began selling aluminum chocks because they were less damaging to the natural rock face. Once the firm started making outdoor adult clothing, it quickly added a line of children's clothing as well—not because there was a known market for such products but because they wanted to find a use for the scraps of leftover fabric. Patagonia also markets one line of shirts made of fibers from recycled plastic bottles and another line of shirts made from hemp, which is easy to grow organically.

As the firm grew, its environmental concerns also became more tangible. In 1996, Patagonia decided to use only organic cotton—cotton that satisfies two criteria: (1) it is grown without fertilizers and (2) it is grown without chemical insecticides. This decision created a problem, however, because most cotton grown and sold in the United States fails to meet one or the other of the two requirements for being organic. Thus, Patagonia started dealing directly with farmers, instructing them as to what the company wanted to buy and guaranteeing them competitive prices to reduce their risk. In a few cases, Patagonia even had to co-sign loans so that some farmers could buy new equipment and technology to meet the company's stringent requirements.

"Businesspeople who focus on profits wind up in the hole. For me, profit is what happens when you do everything else right."

—Yvon Chouinard, founder and CEO of Patagonia, Inc.

Perhaps Patagonia's boldest step took place when Chouinard mandated that one percent of Patagonia's revenues would be given to environmental groups each year. (Because the firm is private, its financial records are not disclosed. Estimates suggest that the firm generates about $180 million in revenues each year.) Chouinard himself is actively involved in efforts aimed at removing dams from rivers and returning the rivers to their natural state.

Needless to say, not every company has such a strong social orientation. Iowa Beef Packers <**www.ibpinc.com**> was founded by A. D. Anderson and Currier Holman. They felt that the meat-processing industry needed modernization and new technology and saw a significant business opportunity. Anderson and Holman began setting up meat-processing plants in rural areas, starting with Denison, Iowa, in 1960. They chose rural locations in part to be closer to cattle raisers and in part because they thought rural workers would be unlikely to unionize. Today the firm (called IBP, Inc.) has plants in small towns in Iowa, Texas, Idaho, Washington, Kansas, and Illinois. It also has a pork-processing plant in China and sales offices in Canada, Japan, Korea, Mexico, Russia, Taiwan, and the United Kingdom, in addition to those in the United States. In 1999, it reported profits of $313 million from revenues of $14.1 billion.

The company grew rapidly by using highly automated and efficient plants and kept costs low by paying low wages and providing few worker benefits. But low wages and difficult working conditions led to sour labor relations, and workers did in fact unionize. In 1965, the workers struck IBP over low wages. Another major strike occurred in 1969, this one accompanied by vandalism, death threats, and 56 bombings.

Aside from its labor problems, IBP also has a checkered history in other areas of social concern as well. In the early 1970s, for example, Holman was found guilty of paying a mob-related broker $1 million to ensure that unions wouldn't interfere with the firm's New York City distribution plans. Later in the decade, IBP was investigated for anticompetitive practices, although the inquiry was subsequently dropped. In the 1980s, IBP was fined $2.6 million and penalized by OSHA for not reporting hand injuries caused by meat-cutting equipment. Another major strike over wages and working conditions crippled the firm in 1999. IBP is currently under investigation by numerous state and federal investigators for alleged environmental misconduct.

Our opening story continues on page 115

Issues of fairness, ethics, and social responsibility are becoming increasingly important as companies around the world enter an era of intense competition, not only for public and consumer support, but also for the support of employees and stockholders. By focusing on the learning objectives of this chapter, you will see that many firms establish policies on business ethics and social responsibility to stipulate exactly how managers and employees should act with regard to the environment, customers, fellow employees, and investors.

In this chapter, we look at the issues of individual ethics in business and the social responsibility of business as a whole. Remember that these issues were not always considered important in business philosophy or practice. Today, however, the ethical implications of business practices are very much in the spotlight. Managers must confront a variety of ethical problems, and companies must address many issues of social responsibility.

ETHICS IN THE WORKPLACE

Just what is *ethical behavior?* **Ethics** are beliefs about what is right and wrong or good and bad. An individual's personal values and morals and the social context in which it occurs determine whether a particular behavior is seen as being ethical or unethical. In other words, **ethical behavior** is behavior that conforms to individual beliefs and social norms about what is right and good. **Unethical behavior** is behavior that individual beliefs and social norms define as wrong and bad. **Business ethics** is a term often used to refer to ethical or unethical behaviors by a manager or employee of an organization.

Because ethics are based on both individual beliefs and social concepts, they vary from person to person, from situation to situation, and from culture to culture. Social standards, for example, tend to be broad enough to support certain differences in beliefs. Without violating the general standards of the culture, therefore, individuals may develop personal codes of ethics that reflect a fairly wide range of attitudes and beliefs. Thus, what constitutes ethical and unethical behavior is determined partly by the individual and partly by culture.

ethics
Beliefs about what is right and wrong or good and bad in actions that affect others

ethical behavior
Behavior conforming to generally accepted social norms concerning beneficial and harmful actions

unethical behavior
Behavior that does not conform to generally accepted social norms concerning beneficial and harmful actions

business ethics
Ethical or unethical behaviors by a manager or employer of an organization

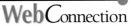

Assessing Ethical Behavior

By definition, what distinguishes ethical from unethical behavior is often subjective and subject to differences of opinion.[1] So how does one go about deciding whether or not a particular action or decision is ethical? Figure 4.1 presents a simplified three-step model for applying ethical judgments to situations that may arise during the course of business activities:

1. Gather the relevant factual information.
2. Analyze the facts to determine the most appropriate moral values.
3. Make an ethical judgment based on the rightness or wrongness of the proposed activity or policy.

WebConnection

www.patagonia.com

Founded by three young Californians who were into surfing and rock climbing, Patagonia started out in 1973 as a seller of high-quality outdoor wear. The company is also quite particular about the impact of its materials and processes on the environment and actively enforces environmentally friendly practices on the part of its suppliers. Visit its Web site to find out more about Patagonia's environmental policies.

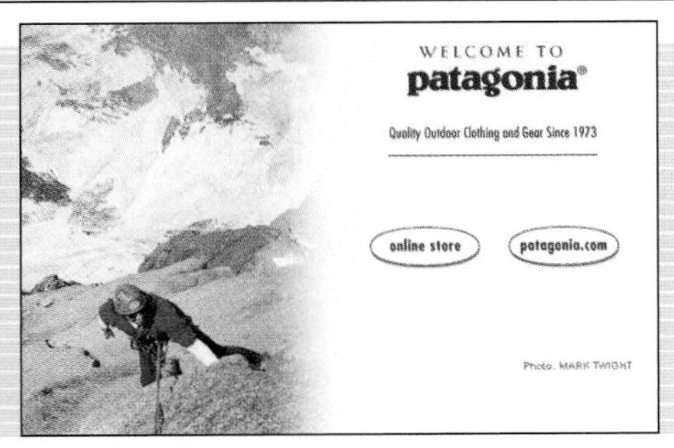

Figure 4.1
Steps in Making Ethical Judgments

Gather the relevant factual information
Analyze the facts to determine the most appropriate moral values
Make an ethical judgment based on the rightness or wrongness of the proposed activity or policy

Unfortunately, the process does not always work as smoothly as the scheme in Figure 4.1 suggests. What if the facts are not clear-cut? What if there are no agreed-upon moral values? Nevertheless, a judgment and a decision must be made. Experts point out that, otherwise, trust is impossible; and trust, they add, is indispensable to any business transaction.

In order to assess more fully the ethics of a particular behavior, we need a more complex perspective. To illustrate this perspective, let's consider a common dilemma faced by managers involving their *expense accounts*. Companies routinely provide managers with accounts to cover work-related expenses when they are traveling on company business or entertaining clients for business purposes. Common examples of such expenses include hotel bills, meals, and rental cars or taxis. Employees are expected to claim only those expenses that are accurate and work-related. For example, if a manager takes a client out to dinner while traveling on business and spends $100 for dinner, submitting a receipt for that dinner to be reimbursed for $100 is clearly accurate and appropriate. Suppose, however, that the manager then has a $100 dinner the next night in that same city with a good friend for purely social purposes. Submitting that receipt for full reimbursement would be unethical. A few managers, however, will rationalize that it is okay to submit a receipt for dinner with a friend. They will argue, perhaps, that they are underpaid and are just increasing the income due them.

Other principles that come into play in a case like this include various *ethical norms*. Consider four such norms and the issues that they entail:

- *Utility:* Does a particular act optimize what is best for those who are affected by it?
- *Rights:* Does it respect the rights of the individuals involved?
- *Justice:* Is it consistent with what we regard as fair?
- *Caring:* Is it consistent with people's responsibilities to each other?

Figure 4.2 is an expanded version of Figure 4.1 that incorporates the consideration of these ethical norms.

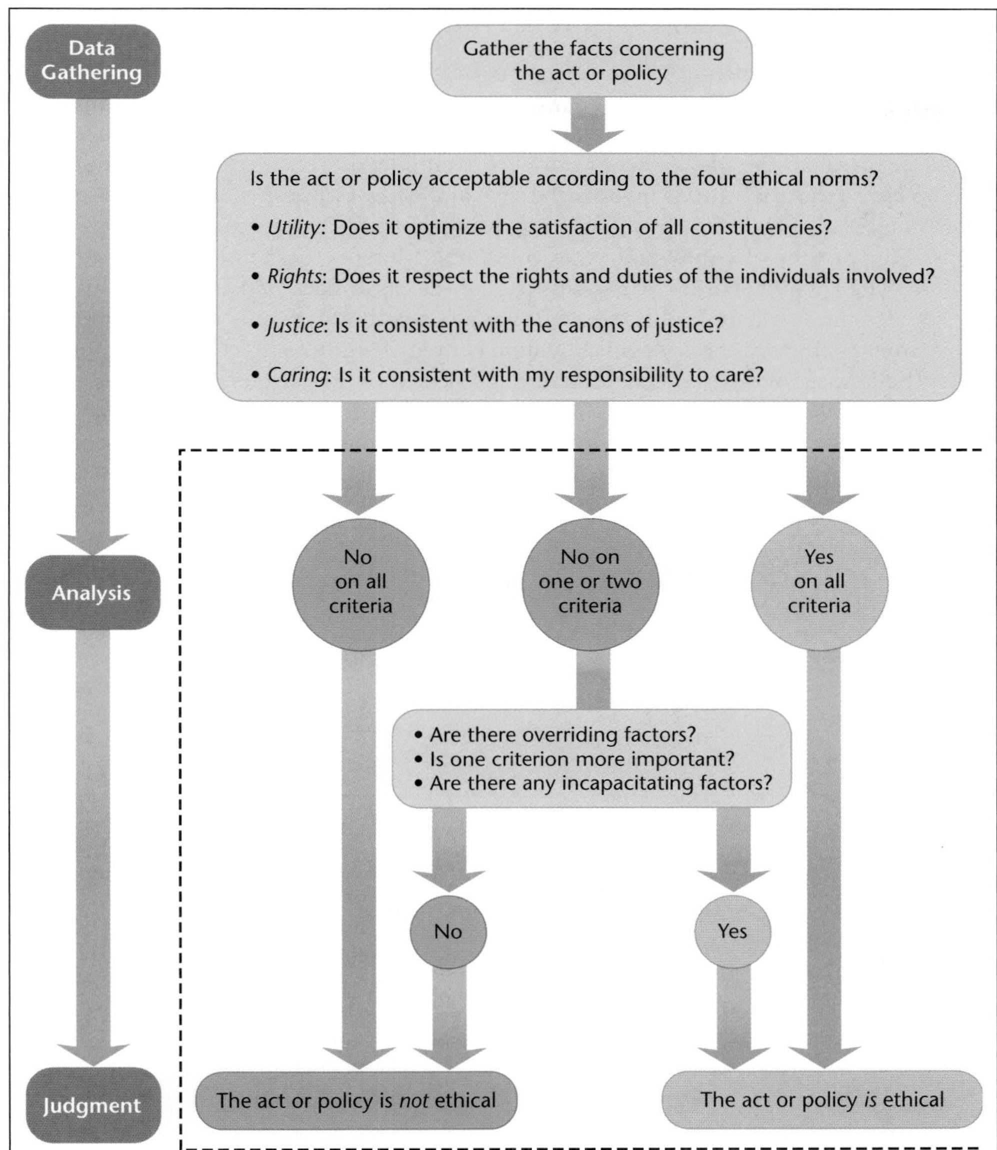

Figure 4.2
Expanded Model of Ethical Judgment Making

Now let's return to the case of the inflated expense account. While the utility norm would acknowledge that the manager benefits from padding an expense account, others, such as coworkers and owners, do not. Likewise, most experts would agree that it does not respect the rights of others. Moreover, it is clearly unfair and compromises the manager's responsibilities to others. This particular act, then, appears to be clearly unethical.

Figure 4.2, however, also provides mechanisms for considering unique circumstances—those that apply only in certain limited situations. Suppose, for example, the manager loses the receipt for the legitimate dinner but retains the receipt for the social dinner. Some people will now argue that it is okay to submit the illegitimate receipt because our manager is only doing so to get full reimbursement. Others, however, will continue to argue that submitting the wrong receipt is wrong under any circumstances. We won't pretend to arbitrate the case. For our purposes, we will simply make the following point: Changes in the situation can make issues more or less clear-cut.

Company Practices and Business Ethics

Organizations try to promote ethical behavior and discourage unethical behavior in numerous ways. As unethical and even illegal activities by both managers and employees plague more and more companies, many firms have taken additional steps to encourage ethical behavior in the workplace. Many, for example, establish codes of conduct and develop clear ethical positions on how the firm and its employees will conduct their business. An increasingly controversial area regarding business ethics and company practices involves the privacy of e-mail and other communications that take place inside an organization. The "Wired World" box in this chapter discusses these issues more fully.

Perhaps the single most effective step that a company can take is to demonstrate top management support. For instance, when United Technologies <www.utc.com>, a Connecticut-based industrial conglomerate, published its 21-page code of ethics, it also named a vice president for business practices. In contrast, recall the story of IBP in our opening vignette. One of the firm's founders, Currier Holman, was found guilty of bribing a mobster to influence organized labor in New York City. Such actions by senior managers often set the tone in organizations (namely, that it's okay to do whatever is necessary in order to boost profits).

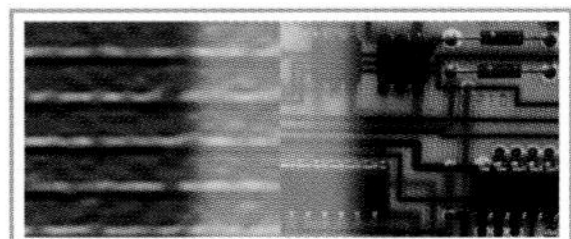

It's a WiredWorld

• *When It Comes to Privacy, It's a Small World After All*

As just about everyone today knows, e-mail has virtually become the standard method of communication in the business world. Most people enjoy its speed, ease, and casual nature. But e-mail also has its share of problems and pitfalls. One challenge, of course, is privacy. Many people assume the contents of their e-mail is private, but there may in fact be any number of people authorized to see it. Some experts have even likened e-mail to postcards sent through the U.S. mail: They pass through a lot of hands and before a lot of eyes, and, theoretically, many different people can read them.

The courts have held that e-mail messages sent or received during working hours and on company equipment are the property of the business. Compaq Computer has one full-time employee who does nothing but randomly scan e-mail messages that pass through the company's servers and monitor improper Internet usage among employees. Although less than half of all U.S. businesses have formal electronic communication policies, they do have the power of the law behind them when they do establish policies or procedures.

Aside from organizational scrutiny, people also face the threat of hackers breaking into and wreaking havoc with the company's computer network, including its e-mail system. Indeed, e-mail is one of the easiest routes for hackers to gain access to other parts of a firm's computer system. Once inside, they can read sensitive e-mail messages, destroy them, or send them to other people.

Finally, many users have good reason to regard themselves as the worst enemies to their own privacy. A surprisingly common error is inadvertently sending e-mail to the wrong address—even to a large group of people. More than one starry-eyed e-mailer has dispatched a love note to the wrong person. Even worse, a simple inadvertent click of the mouse can send a sensitive or inflammable message intended for a single recipient to everyone in the company.

But e-mail is actually only part of the privacy issue. Other concerns have arisen regarding general privacy over the Internet and cellular telephones. For consumers, Internet privacy is an especially important issue. Companies, for instance, have the capacity to monitor which Web sites individuals visit, how long they stay there, what they buy, and how frequently they return. They can use this information to make referrals to other companies who might then want to target new advertising to those individuals. Cellular and cordless telephones are not nearly as private as hard-wired phones—indeed, tapping into or eavesdropping on a cellular conversation is amazingly easy. Not surprisingly, then, concerns about the shrinking world in which we can enjoy privacy are beginning to take on an increasingly higher profile with each passing day.

WebConnection

www.privada.net

Privada offers "the infrastructure to secure privacy in a digital world." To find out how to send private electronic mail (via "Messaging Incognito"™) and conduct private Web browsing (via "Web Incognito"™), contact the company at its Web site.

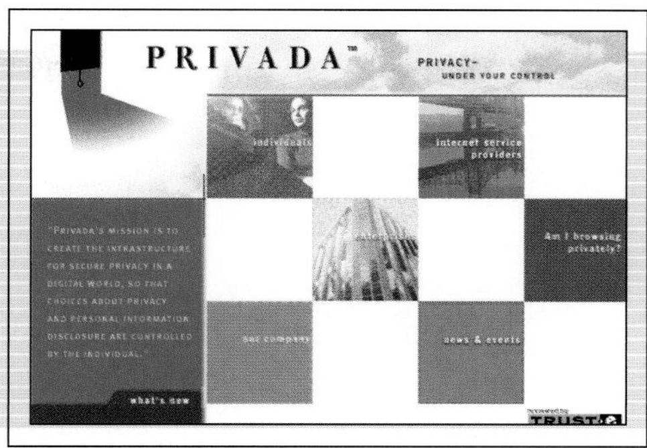

Case: The Tylenol Scare An excellent, and now classic, illustration of the power of ethical commitment involves Johnson & Johnson <www.jnj.com>. In 1982, capsules of the company's Tylenol pain reliever were found laced with cyanide. Managers at J&J quickly recalled all Tylenol bottles still on retailers' shelves and then went public with candid information throughout the crisis. Its ethical choices proved to be a crucial factor in J&J's campaign to rescue its product: Both the firm and the brand bounced back much more quickly than most observers had thought possible.

"My apologies to the consumers of Belgium."

—Former Coca-Cola CEO Douglas Ivester, when Belgian schoolchildren got sick from a bad batch of Coke

Case: The Coca-Cola Scare A more recent example involves the operations of Coca-Cola in Europe <www.thecoca-colacompany.com/world>. First, some Belgian schoolchildren suffered minor illnesses after drinking Coke made from a bad batch of carbon dioxide. Then Coke cans shipped from the company's plant in Dunkirk, France, contained some fungicide on the bottom. Neither problem was serious, but, together, the two events created a public relations problem. Douglas Ivester, who was Coke CEO at the time, flew directly to Brussels and made a straightforward public apology: "My apologies to the consumers of Belgium." The furor died down almost immediately, primarily as a result of the top manager's quick, forthright response.[2]

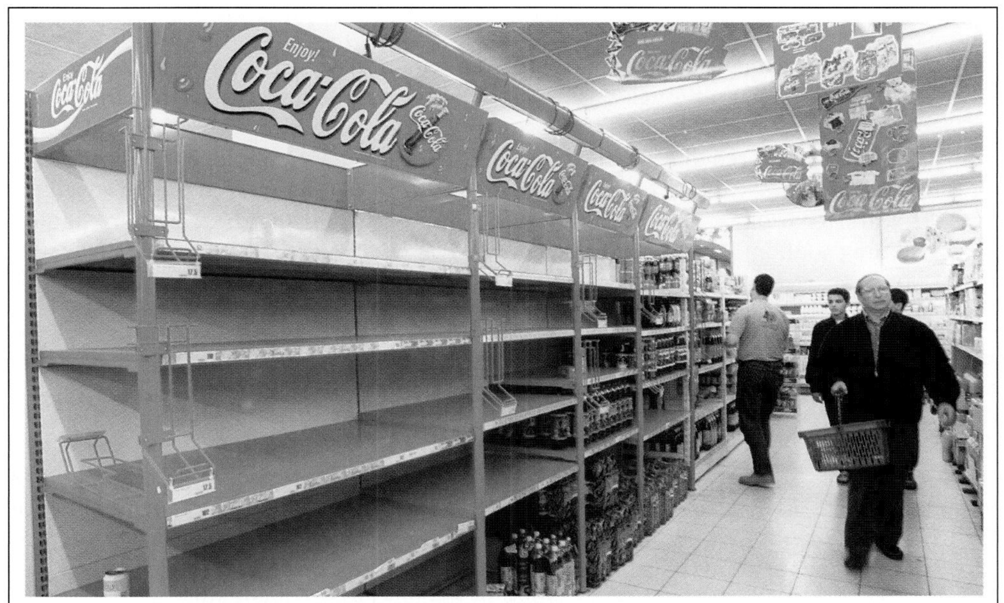

In 1999, some Belgian schoolchildren got sick after drinking Coke. The problem was a bad batch of carbon dioxide, and there was no health hazard. At first, Coke saw no reason to take action. But then the company got caught in the middle of Belgian political infighting over the incident, and Coke was removed from retail shelves for several days. Finally, former Coke CEO Douglas Ivester apologized to Belgian consumers in a series of full-page newspaper ads, adding contritely, "I should have spoken with you earlier."

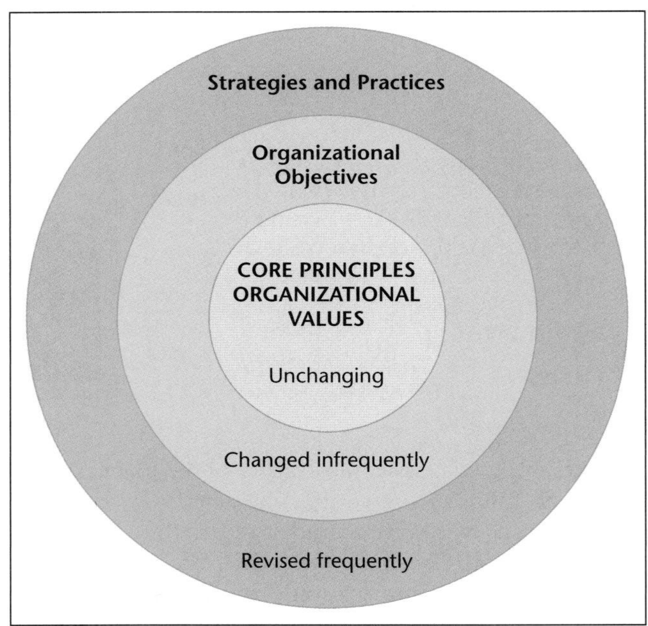

Figure 4.3
Core Principles and Organizational Values

In addition to demonstrating an attitude of honesty and openness, as in the case of Coca-Cola, firms can also take specific and concrete steps to formalize their commitment to ethical business practices. Two of the most common approaches to formalizing commitment are *adopting written codes* and *instituting ethics programs.*

Adopting Written Codes Many companies, including Johnson & Johnson, Texas Instruments <www.ti.com/corp/docs/company/ethics>, McDonald's <www.macspotlight.org/company/publications>, Starbucks <www.starbucks.com>, and Dell Computer <www.dell.com>, have adopted written codes of ethics that formally acknowledge their intent to do business in an ethical manner. The number of such companies has risen dramatically in the last three decades, and today virtually all major corporations have written codes of ethics.

"No one would say this company doesn't have a shining soul."

—Hewlett-Packard CEO Carly Fiorina, on the long-lasting impact of the firm's written code of ethics

Figure 4.3 illustrates the essential role that corporate ethics and values should play in corporate policy. You can use it to see how ethics statements might be structured most effectively. Basically, the figure suggests that although business strategies and practices can change frequently and business objectives occasionally, an organization's core principles and values should remain steadfast. Hewlett-Packard, for example, has had the same written code of ethics, called *The HP Way,* since 1957, and it has served the firm well for over 40 years. "No one," claims CEO Carly Fiorina, "would say this company doesn't have a shining soul."[3] The essential elements of *The HP Way* are as follows:

- We have trust and respect for individuals.
- We focus on a high level of achievement and contribution.
- We conduct our business with uncompromising integrity.
- We achieve our common objectives through teamwork.
- We encourage flexibility and innovation.

Instituting Ethics Programs Instances such as the Tylenol case suggest that ethical responses can be learned through experience. But can business ethics be taught, either in the workplace or in schools? Not surprisingly, business schools have become important players in the debate about ethics education. Most analysts agree that even though business schools must address the issue of ethics in the workplace, companies must take the chief responsibility for educating employees. In fact, more and more firms are doing so.

For example, both Exxon <www.exxon.com/overview/guiding_principles> and Boeing <www.boeing.com/companyoffices/aboutus/ethics> have major ethics programs. All managers must go through periodic ethics training to remind them of the importance of ethical decision making and to update them on the most current laws and regulations that might be particularly relevant to their firms. Others, such as Texas Instruments, have ethical "hot lines"—numbers that an employee can call, either to discuss the ethics of a particular problem or situation or to report unethical behavior or activities by others.

SOCIAL RESPONSIBILITY

Ethics affect individual behavior in the workplace. **Social responsibility,** however, refers to the way in which a business tries to balance its commitments to certain groups and individuals in its social environment. These groups and individuals are often called **organizational stakeholders:** those groups, individuals, and organizations that are directly affected by the practices of an organization and, therefore, have a stake in its performance.[4] Major stakeholders are identified in Figure 4.4.

social responsibility
The attempt of a business to balance its commitments to groups and individuals in its environment, including customers, other businesses, employees, and investors

organizational stakeholders
Those groups, individuals, and organizations that are directly affected by the practices of an organization and, therefore, have a stake in its performance

The Stakeholder Model of Responsibility

Many companies that strive to be responsible to their stakeholders concentrate first and foremost on five main groups: *customers, employees, investors, suppliers,* and the *local communities* where they do business. They may then select other stakeholders that are particularly relevant or important to the organization and try to address their needs and expectations as well.

Customers Businesses that are responsible to their customers strive to treat them fairly and honestly. They also seek to charge fair prices, honor warranties, meet delivery commitments, and stand behind the quality of the products they sell. L.L. Bean <www.llbean.com>, Land's End <www.landsend.com>, Dell Computer, and Johnson & Johnson are among companies with excellent reputations in this area.

Employees Businesses that are socially responsible in their dealings with employees treat workers fairly, make them a part of the team, and respect their dignity and basic human needs. Organizations such as MBNA <www.mbna.com/about_careers>, Continental Airlines <www.continental.com>, 3M Corporation <www.3m.com>, Hoecsht Celanese <www.hoecsht.com>, and Southwest Airlines <www.southwest.com> have all established strong reputations in this area. In addition, many of the same firms also go to great lengths to find, hire, train, and promote qualified minorities.

Investors To maintain a socially responsible stance toward investors, managers should follow proper accounting procedures, provide appropriate information to shareholders

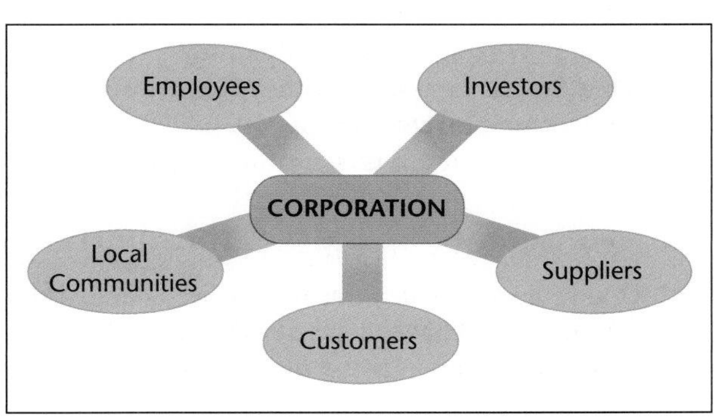

Figure 4.4
Major Corporate Stakeholders

"The employees have to assume a share of the blame for allowing the pension fund to become so big and tempting."

about financial performance, and manage the organization to protect shareholder rights and investments. They should be accurate and candid in assessing future growth and profitability and avoid even the appearance of impropriety in such sensitive areas as insider trading, stock-price manipulation, and the withholding of financial data. Some relatively new Internet businesses have recently been accused of distorting—and in some cases outright falsifying—their earnings reports to boost the price of their stocks.[5]

Suppliers Relations with suppliers should also be managed with care. For example, it might be easy for a large corporation to take advantage of suppliers by imposing unrealistic delivery schedules and reducing profits margins by constantly pushing for lower and lower prices. Many firms now recognize the importance of mutually beneficial partnership arrangements with suppliers. Thus, they keep them informed about future plans, negotiate delivery schedules and prices that are acceptable to both firms, and so forth. Ford <www.ford.com> and Wal-Mart <www.walmart.com> are among the firms acknowledged to have excellent relationships with their suppliers.

Local Communities Finally, most businesses try to be socially responsible to their local communities. They may contribute to local programs like Little League baseball, get actively involved in charitable programs like the United Way, and strive to simply be a good corporate citizen by minimizing their negative impact on the community. Target Stores <www.targetcorp.com>, for example, donate a percentage of sales to the local communities where they do business.

The stakeholder model can also provide some helpful insights on the conduct of managers in international business. In particular, to the extent that an organization acknowledges its commitments to its stakeholders, it should also recognize that it has multiple sets of stakeholders in each country where it does business. DaimlerChrysler <www.daimlerchrysler.com>, for example, has investors not only in Germany but also in the United States, Japan, and other countries where its shares are publicly traded. It also has suppliers, employees, and customers in multiple countries, and its actions affect many different communities in dozens of different countries.

The Evolution of Social Responsibility

Both U.S. society and U.S. business have changed dramatically in the last two centuries. Not surprisingly, so have views about social responsibility. Many scholars identify at least three different phases in the evolution of social responsibility.

The Entrepreneurial Era The first phase corresponds to the era in the late nineteenth century that was characterized by the entrepreneurial spirit and the *laissez-faire* philosophy. The enormous empires of men such as John D. Rockefeller, J. P. Morgan, and Cornelius Vanderbilt exercised tremendous economic power, but abuses of power inevitably led to public backlash. During this era of labor strife and predatory business practices, both individual citizens and the government first became concerned about unbridled business activity. This concern was translated into the nation's first laws regulating basic business practices.

The Great Depression The second major phase in the evolution of social responsibility occurred during the Great Depression. In the 1930s, many people blamed the failure of businesses and banks and the widespread loss of jobs on a general climate of business greed and lack of restraint. Out of the economic turmoil emerged new laws that described an expanded role for business in protecting and enhancing the general welfare of society.

The Era of Social Activism The third major phase began with the social unrest of the 1960s and 1970s, when business was often characterized as a negative social force. Some critics even charged that defense contractors had promoted the Vietnam War to spur profits. Eventually, increased activism prompted increased government regulation in a variety of areas: Health warnings were placed on cigarettes, and stricter environmental protection laws were enacted.

Contemporary Social Consciousness

Social consciousness and views toward social responsibility continue to evolve. Today's attitudes seem to be moving toward an enlightened view stressing the need for a greater social role for business. Some observers suggest that an increased awareness of the global economy and heightened campaigning on the part of environmentalists and other activists have combined to make many businesses more sensitive to their social responsibilities.

For example, retailers such as Sears <www.sears.com> and Target <www.targetcorp.com> have policies against selling handguns and other weapons. Likewise, national toy retailers KayBee and Toys "R" Us <www.toysrus.com> refuse to sell toy guns that look too realistic. Firms in numerous other industries have also integrated socially conscious thinking into their production plans and marketing efforts. The production of environmentally safe products has become a potential boom area, as many companies introduce products designed to be "environmentally friendly."

Electrolux, a Swedish appliance maker <www.electrolux.com>, has developed a line of water-efficient washing machines, a solar-powered lawn mower, and, for Brazil, the first refrigerators that are free of ozone-depleting refrigerants. Herman Miller, a Michigan-based office-furniture business <www.hermanmiller.com>, uses recycled materials and focuses on products that are simple in design, more durable, and recyclable. Ford <www.ford.com> has set up an independent brand called Think to develop and market low-pollution, electric-powered vehicles.[6] Our opening vignette described how Patagonia uses organic cotton, and the "Life Cycle of an e-Business" box in this chapter describes socially conscious policies at Garden.com.

AREAS OF SOCIAL RESPONSIBILITY

When defining its sense of social responsibility, a firm typically confronts four areas of concern: responsibilities toward the *environment,* its *customers,* its *employees,* and its *investors.*

Responsibility Toward the Environment

Figure 4.5 tells a troubling story. The chart shows atmospheric carbon dioxide (CO_2) levels for the period between 1750 and 2000 and offers three possible scenarios for future

Figure 4.5

CO_2 Emissions, Past and Future

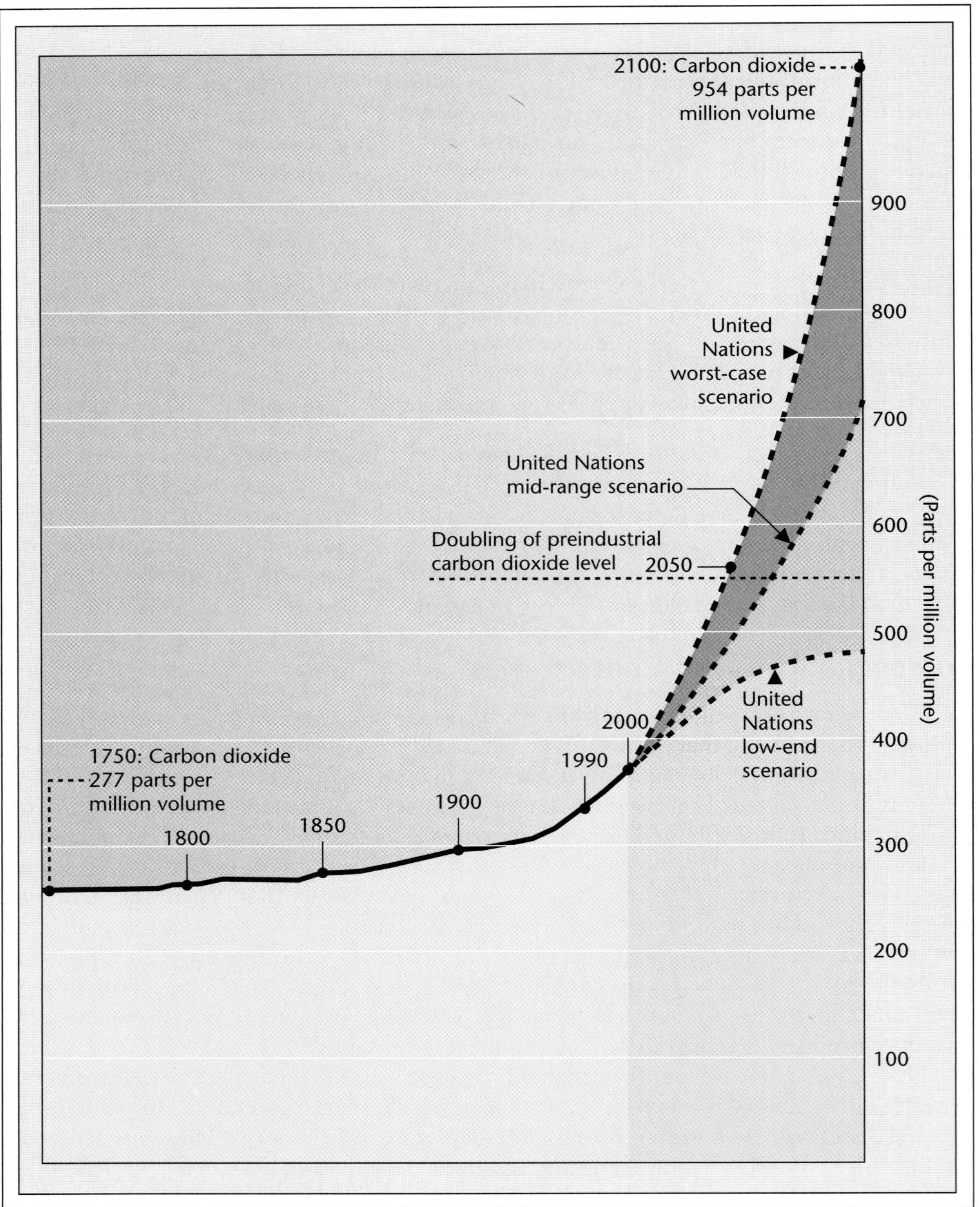

levels under different sets of conditions. The three projections—lowest, middle, highest—were developed by the Intergovernmental Panel on Climate Change <www.ipcc.ch>, which calculated likely changes in the atmosphere during this century if no efforts were made to reduce so-called *greenhouse emissions*—waste industrial gases that trap heat in the atmosphere. The criteria for estimating changes are population, economic growth, energy supplies, and technologies: The less pressure exerted by these conditions, the less the increase in CO_2 levels. Energy supplies are measured in *exajoules*—roughly the annual energy consumption of the New York Metropolitan area.

Under the lowest, or best-case, scenario, the population would only grow to 6.4 billion people, economic growth would be no more than 1.2 to 2.0 percent a year, and energy supplies would require only 8,000 exajoules of conventional oil. However, under the highest, or worst-case, scenario, the population would increase to 11.3 billion people, annual economic growth would be between 3.0 and 3.5 percent, and energy supplies would require as much as 18,400 exajoules of conventional oil.

Life Cycle of an e-Business

Putting Down Good Roots at Garden.com

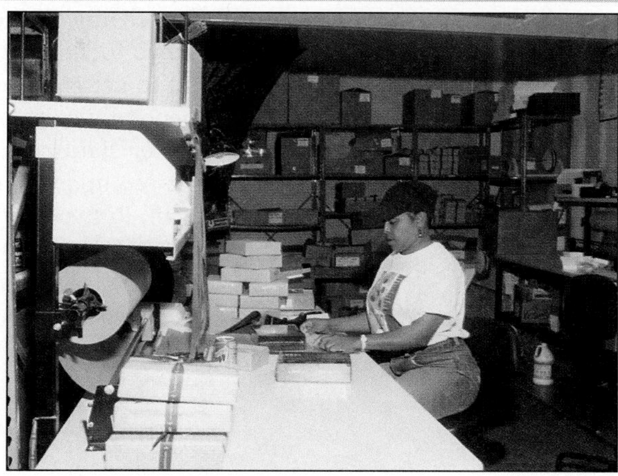

Ethics and social responsibility were fundamental underpinnings at Garden.com from its beginning. Indeed, founders Cliff and Lisa Sharples and Jamie O'Neill left their former employer, Trilogy Software, in part over a disagreement about company values. While each was careful not to be too critical of Trilogy, they nevertheless acknowledged that they were a bit uncomfortable with some of the software firm's practices and were less interested in aggressive growth and expansion than were some managers at Trilogy.

It's not surprising, then, that when they set up shop at Garden.com, they consciously worked to embed specific ethical standards and a commitment to social responsibility into their own corporate culture. For example, they provided ethical training for all employees and were quick to support ethical initiatives and decisions taken by the people who worked for them. The firm also matched all cash contributions made by employees to the Salvation Army during the holiday season each year. They also extended their commitment to social responsibility to their relationships with suppliers. In particular, they insisted that suppliers use only the most environmentally friendly insecticides, fertilizers, and packaging materials.

Lisa Sharples also made a personal project out of selecting Garden.com's own shipping and packaging materials. All products were packed in wood chips rather than Styrofoam or other synthetic materials. Inside every box there was also a set of suggestions as to how the wood chips could be either recycled or disposed of in an environmentally sound way. At first glance, gift-wrapped products might have looked a bit overpackaged. Each came in a corrugated green box tied with a ribbon and sealed with a chain. The boxes, however, were multifunctional and could readily be reused. The ribbons could be used as bookmarks or to keep the boxes sealed, and the chains made great key chains.

In addition, Garden.com was active in external causes. All three founders were active participants in local community work, such as the Austin Network, a group of business leaders committed to helping maintain the area's quality of life in the face of tremendous growth. They were also involved in various efforts designed to make information technology accessible to economically challenged groups. Perhaps their biggest commitment was to American Forests, the oldest not-for-profit organization in the United States <www.americanforests.org>, which is dedicated to preserving the world's forests. Garden.com not only helped design but also maintained the American Forests Web site and sold selected products from the organization's Famous and Historic Trees <www.oldtrees.com> product line. Occasionally, Garden.com sponsored promotions in which a percentage of certain purchase prices was donated directly to American Forests.

The resulting changes in climate would be relatively mild; we would hardly experience any day-to-day changes in the weather. We would, however, increase the likelihood of having troublesome weather around the globe: droughts, hurricanes, winter sieges, and so forth. The charges leveled against greenhouse emissions are disputed, but as one researcher puts it, "The only way to prove them for sure is hang around 10, 20, or 30 more years, when the evidence would be overwhelming. But in the meantime, we're conducting a global experiment. And we're all in the test tube."[7]

> ***"We're conducting a global experiment. And we're all in the test tube."***
>
> *—Researcher on greenhouse emissions*

Controlling *pollution*—the injection of harmful substances into the environment—is a significant challenge to contemporary business. Although noise pollution is now attracting increased concern, air, water, and land pollution remain the greatest problems in need of solutions from governments and businesses alike. In the following sections, we focus on the nature of the problems in these areas and on some of the current efforts to address them.[8]

Air Pollution Air pollution results when several factors combine to lower air quality. Carbon monoxide emitted by automobiles contributes to air pollution, as do smoke and other chemicals from manufacturing plants. Air quality is usually worst in certain geographic locations, such as the Denver area and the Los Angeles basin, where pollutants tend to get trapped in the atmosphere. For this very reason, the air around Mexico City is generally considered to be the most polluted in the entire world.

Legislation has gone a long way toward controlling air pollution. Under new laws, many companies must now install special devices to limit the pollutants they expel into the air. But such efforts are costly. Air pollution is compounded by such problems as *acid rain,* which occurs when sulfur is pumped into the atmosphere, mixes with natural moisture, and falls to the ground as rain. Much of the damage to forests and streams in the eastern United States and Canada has been attributed to acid rain originating in sulfur from manufacturing and power plants in the midwestern United States.

Water Pollution Water becomes polluted primarily from chemical and waste dumping. For years, businesses and cities dumped waste into rivers, streams, and lakes with little regard for the consequences. Cleveland's Cuyahoga River was once so polluted that it literally burst into flames one hot summer day. After an oil spill in 1994, a Houston ship channel burned for days.

Thanks to new legislation and increased awareness, water quality in many areas of the United States is improving. The Cuyahoga River now boasts fish and is even used for recreation. Laws forbidding phosphates (an ingredient found in many detergents) in New York and Florida have helped to make Lake Erie and other major waters safe for fishing and swimming again. Both the Passaic River in New Jersey and the Hudson River in New York are much cleaner now than they were just a few years ago.

Land Pollution There are two key issues in land pollution. The first is how to restore the quality of land that has already been damaged. Land and water damaged by toxic waste, for example, must be cleaned up for the simple reason that people still need to use

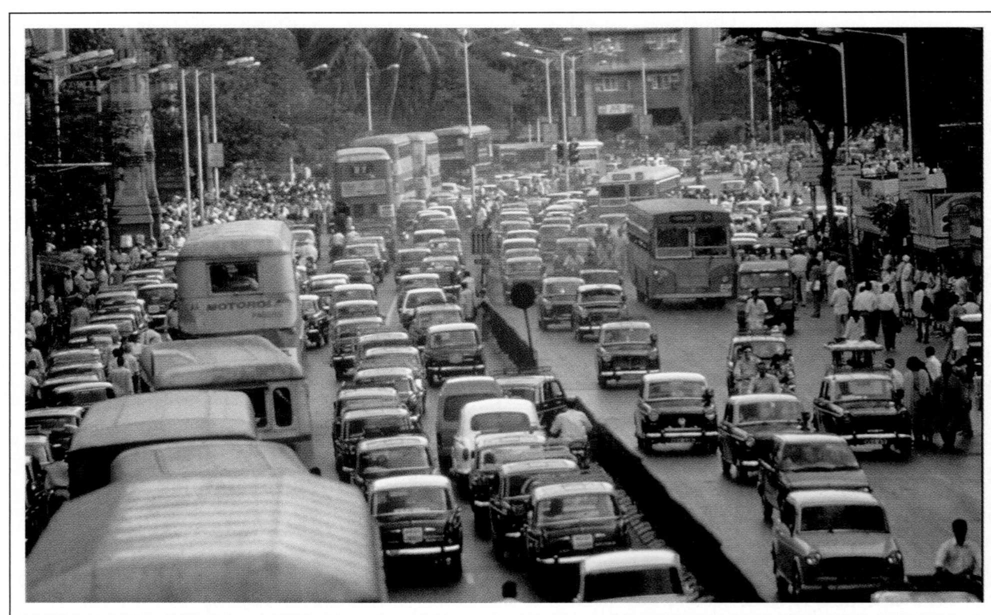

With India's population growing by 20 million people every year and city traffic doubling every five years, Indian cities are facing increasingly high levels of air pollution. As bad as urban air is in New Delhi, Bombay, and Calcutta, five countries actually produce more carbon gases. From the top down, they are the United States, the former Soviet Union, China, Japan, and Germany.

them. The second problem, of course, is the prevention of future contamination. New forms of solid-waste disposal constitute one response to these problems. Combustible wastes can be separated and used as fuels in industrial boilers, and decomposition can be accelerated by exposing waste matter to certain microorganisms.

Toxic Waste Disposal An especially controversial problem in land pollution is toxic waste disposal. Toxic wastes are dangerous chemical or radioactive by-products of manufacturing processes. U.S. manufacturers produce between 40 and 60 *million tons* of such material each year. As a rule, toxic waste must be stored; it cannot be destroyed or processed into harmless material. Few people, however, want toxic waste storage sites in their backyards. American Airlines <www.im.aa.com> recently pled guilty—and became the first major airline to gain a criminal record—to a felony charge that it had mishandled some hazardous materials packed as cargo in passenger airplanes.[9] While fully acknowledging the firm's guilt, Anne McNamara, American's general counsel, argued that "This is an incredibly complicated area with many layers of regulation. It's very easy to inadvertently step over the line."

Recycling Recycling is another controversial area in land pollution. *Recycling*—the reconversion of waste materials into useful products—has become an issue not only for municipal and state governments but also for many companies engaged in high-waste activities. Certain products, such as aluminum beverage cans and glass, can be very efficiently recycled. Others, such as plastics, are more troublesome. For example, brightly colored plastics like detergent and juice bottles must be recycled separately from clear plastics like milk jugs. Most plastic bottle caps, meanwhile, contain a vinyl lining that can spoil a normal recycling batch. Amber plastic beer containers, currently being test-marketed by Philip Morris's Miller Brewing Co. <www.millerbrewing.com>, cannot be mixed for recycling with clear soda bottles.[10] Nevertheless, many local communities actively support various recycling programs including curbside pickup of aluminum, plastics, glass, and pulp paper. Unfortunately, consumer awareness and interest in this area—and thus the policy priorities of business—are more acute at some times than at others.

"Handling hazardous waste is an incredibly complicated area with many layers of regulation. It's very easy to inadvertently step over the line."

—Anne McNamara, General counsel for American Airlines

Responsibility Toward Customers

A company that does not act responsibly toward its customers will ultimately lose their trust and thus their business. Moreover, the government controls or regulates many aspects of what businesses can and cannot do regarding consumers. The Federal Trade Commission (FTC) <www.ftc.gov> regulates advertising and pricing practices. The Food and Drug Administration (FDA) <www.fda.gov> enforces guidelines for labeling food products.

Should customers be obligated to act responsibly toward companies?

Unethical and irresponsible business practices toward customers can result in government-imposed penalties and expensive civil litigation. For example, Abbott Laboratories <www.abbott.com> recently agreed to pay $100 million to settle accusations that the firm failed to meet federal quality standards when it made hundreds of different medical test kits. The FDA indicated that it was the largest fine the agency had ever levied.[11]

Social responsibility toward customers generally falls into two categories: providing quality products and pricing products fairly. Naturally, firms differ as much in their level of concern about customer responsibility as in their approaches to environmental responsibility. Yet unlike environmental problems, many customer problems do not require expensive solutions. In fact, most problems can be avoided if companies simply adhere to regulated practices and heed laws regarding consumer rights.

Consumer Rights Much of the current interest in business responsibility toward customers can be traced to the rise of **consumerism:** social activism dedicated to protecting

consumerism
Form of social activism dedicated to protecting the rights of consumers in their dealings with businesses

To consumer-rights advocates like these protestors, foods that have undergone genetic modification (GM) to make them resistant to herbicides and pests are "frankenfoods." Such crops, they charge, make people sick and cause damage to the environment. They also contend that the policies of the World Trade Organization (WTO) <www.wto.org>*, which promotes international trade, encourage the production of frankenfoods as exportable commodities.*

the rights of consumers in their dealings with businesses. The first formal declaration of consumer rights protection came in the early 1960s when President John F. Kennedy identified four basic consumer rights. These rights are now backed by numerous federal and state laws:

1. Consumers have a right to safe products.
2. Consumers have a right to be informed about all relevant aspects of a product.
3. Consumers have a right to be heard.
4. Consumers have a right to choose what they buy.

American Home Products <www.ahp.com> provides an instructive example of what can happen to a firm that violates one or more of these consumer rights. Throughout the early 1990s, the firm aggressively marketed a drug called Pondimin, its brand name for a diet pill containing fenfluramine. In 1996 alone, doctors wrote 18 million prescriptions for Pondimin and other medications containing fenfluramine. However in 1997, the FDA reported a linkage between the pills and heart-valve disease. A class action lawsuit against the firm charged that the drug was unsafe and that users had not been provided with complete information about possible side effects. American Home eventually agreed to pay $3.75 billion to individuals who had used the drug.[12]

collusion
Illegal agreement between two or more companies to commit a wrongful act

Unfair Pricing Interfering with competition can take the form of illegal pricing practices. **Collusion** occurs when two or more firms agree to collaborate on such wrongful acts as *price fixing*. For example, a few years ago the FTC investigated pricing-related business practices at Toys "R" Us, the largest toy retailer in the country. Investigators charged that Toys "R" Us routinely pressured major suppliers to limit quantities or delay shipments of hot-selling toys to warehouse clubs such as Sam's Club or Costco. This practice would have given Toys "R" Us a head start on selling the toys at higher prices than those charged by the warehouse clubs. Although Toys "R" Us denied the charges, the firm contended that it had the right to tell suppliers that it may choose to not stock toys that are sold to warehouse clubs.

More recently, the U.S. Justice Department <www.usdoj.gov> charged three international pharmaceutical firms with illegally controlling worldwide supplies and prices of vitamins. France's Rhone-Poulenc <www.aventis.com> cooperated with the investigation, helped break the case several months earlier than expected, and was not fined. Switzerland's F. Hoffmann-LaRoche <www.laroche-sa/fr> was fined $500 million and one of its senior executives was sentenced to four months in a U.S. prison. Germany's BASF <www.basf.com> was fined $225 million.[13]

Under some circumstances, firms can also come under attack for *price gouging*—responding to increased demand with overly steep (and often unwarranted) price increases. For example, when BMW <www.bmw.com> launched its Z3 Roadsters, demand for the car was so strong that some dealers sold Z3s only to customers willing to pay thousands of dollars over sticker prices. A similar practice was adopted by Volkswagen <www.vw.com> dealers when the new Beetle was launched.

Ethics in Advertising In recent years, increased attention has been given to ethics in advertising and product information. Because of controversies surrounding the potential misinterpretation of words and phrases such as *light, reduced calorie, diet,* and *low fat,* food producers are now required to use a standardized format for listing ingredients on product packages. Similarly, controversy arose over a commercial aired during the 2000 Super Bowl game. The ad featured Christopher Reeve, a quadriplegic actor, apparently standing up from his wheelchair and walking to a podium. In reality, the images were computer altered and were intended to convey a message of hope and optimism for a foundation supporting spinal cord research. Many viewers were confused by the ads, and the day after the game, dozens of quadriplegics began calling their doctors and hospitals to inquire about the procedure that had evidently cured the actor. The ad was quickly pulled after widespread media criticism.

Another issue concerns advertising that some consumers consider morally objectionable. Benetton <www.benetton.com>, for example, aired a series of commercials featuring North Carolina inmates on death row. The ads, dubbed "We, on Death Row," prompted such an emotional outcry that several states either sued the company or threatened legal action, and Sears dropped the Benetton USA clothing line.[14] Other ads receiving criticism include Victoria's Secret <www.victoriassecret.com> models in skimpy underwear and campaigns by tobacco and alcohol companies that apparently target young people. For instance, although R. J. Reynolds <www.rjr.com> was forced to retire its longtime "spokesperson" Joe Camel, many beer commercials still feature animated frogs and lizards and other child-friendly characters.

Responsibility Toward Employees

In Chapter 8, we will see how a number of human resource management activities are essential to a smoothly functioning business. These activities—recruiting, hiring, training, promoting, and compensating—are also the basis for social responsibility toward employees.

www.esomar.nl

Headquartered in the Netherlands, ESOMAR, the World Association of Opinion and Marketing Research Professionals, is composed of more than 4,000 members—ad and media agencies, public and government institutions—in over 100 countries. ESOMAR publishes ethical "Guidelines" on a variety of marketing-research–oriented activities, ranging from "Interviewing Children" to "Conducting Marketing and Opinion Research Using the Internet."

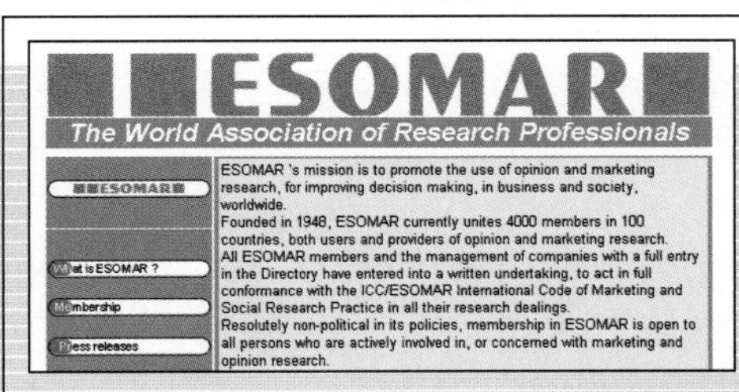

Legal and Social Commitments Socially responsible behavior toward employees has both legal and social components. By law, businesses cannot practice numerous forms of illegal discrimination against people in any facet of the employment relationship. For example, a company cannot refuse to hire someone because of ethnicity or pay someone a lower salary than someone else on the basis of gender. Such actions must be taken for job-related purposes only. A company that provides its employees with equal opportunities for rewards and advancement without regard to race, sex, or other irrelevant factors is meeting both its legal and its social responsibilities. Firms that ignore these responsibilities run the risk of losing productive, highly motivated employees. They also leave themselves open to lawsuits.

In the opinion of many people, social responsibility toward employees goes beyond equal opportunity. According to popular opinion, an organization should strive to ensure that the workplace is physically and socially safe. It should also recognize its obligations to help protect the health of its employees by providing opportunities to balance work and life pressures and preferences. From this point of view, social responsibility toward workers would also include helping them maintain proper job skills and, when terminations or layoffs are necessary, treating them with respect and compassion.

Ethical Commitments: The Special Case of Whistle-Blowers Respecting employees as people also means respecting their behavior as ethically responsible individuals. Suppose, for instance, an employee discovers that a business has been engaging in practices that are illegal, unethical, or socially irresponsible. Ideally, this employee should be able to report the problem to higher-level management, confident that managers will stop the questionable practices. Too often, however, individuals who try to act ethically on the job find themselves in trouble with their employers. If no one in the organization will take action, the employee might elect to drop the matter. Occasionally, however, the individual will inform a regulatory agency or perhaps the media. At this point, the person becomes what is popularly known as a **whistle-blower**—an employee who discovers and tries to put an end to a company's unethical, illegal, or socially irresponsible actions by publicizing them.[15] The Al Pacino–Russell Crowe movie *The Insider* featured the story of a tobacco-industry whistle-blower named Jeffrey Wigand.

whistle-blower
Employee who detects and tries to put an end to a company's unethical, illegal, or socially irresponsible actions by publicizing them

Unfortunately, whistle-blowers are sometimes demoted, and even fired, when they take their accusations public. Jeffrey Wigand was fired. "I went from making $300,000 a year," he reports, "plus stock options, plus, plus, plus—to making $30,000. Yes, there is a price I've paid."[16] Even if they retain their jobs, they may still be treated as outsiders and suffer resentment or hostility from coworkers. Many coworkers see whistle-blowers as people who simply can't be trusted.

"I went from making $300,000 a year—plus stock options, plus, plus, plus—to making $30,000."

—Whistle-blower Jeffrey Wigand

The law does offer some recourse to employees who take action. The current whistle-blower law stems from the False Claims Act of 1863, which was designed to prevent contractors from selling defective supplies to the Union Army during the Civil War. With 1986 revisions to the law, the government can recover triple damages from fraudulent contractors. If the Justice Department does not intervene, a whistle-blower can proceed with a civil suit. In that case, the whistle-blower receives 25 to 30 percent of any money recovered.

When Phillip Adams worked in the computer industry, he discovered a flaw in the chip-making process which, under certain circumstances, could lead to data being randomly deleted or altered. He reported the flaw to manufacturers, but several years later found that one company, Toshiba <www.toshiba.com>, had ignored the problem and continued to make flawed chips for 12 years. He went on to report the problem and became actively involved in a class action lawsuit based heavily on his research. Toshiba eventually agreed to a $2.1 billion settlement. Adams's share was kept confidential, but he did receive a substantial reward for his efforts.[17] The prospect of large cash rewards has also generated a spate of false or questionable accusations.[18]

Responsibility Toward Investors

Because shareholders are the owners of a company, it may sound odd to say that a firm can act irresponsibly toward its investors. Managers can abuse their responsibilities to investors in several ways. As a rule, irresponsible behavior toward shareholders means abuse of a firm's financial resources. In such cases, the ultimate losers are indeed the shareholder-owners who do not receive their due earnings or dividends. Companies can also act irresponsibly toward shareholder-owners by misrepresenting company resources.

What are some of the major legal responsibilities that pose problems for businesses today?

Improper Financial Management Occasionally, organizations or their officers are guilty of blatant financial mismanagement—offenses that are unethical but not necessarily illegal. Some firms, for example, have been accused of paying excessive salaries to senior managers, of sending them on extravagant "retreats" to exotic and expensive resorts, and of providing frivolous "perks," including ready access to corporate jets, lavish expense accounts, and memberships at plush country clubs.

In such situations, creditors can often do little, and stockholders have few options. Trying to force a management changeover is a difficult process that can drive down stock prices—a penalty that shareholders are usually unwilling to impose on themselves.

check kiting
Illegal practice of writing checks against money that has not yet been credited at the bank on which the checks are drawn

Check Kiting Certain unethical practices are illegal. **Check kiting,** for instance, involves writing a check against money that has not yet arrived at the bank on which it is drawn. In a typical scheme, managers deposit customer checks totaling, say, $1 million into the company account. Knowing that the bank will not collect all of the total deposit for several days, they proceed to write checks against the total amount deposited, knowing that their account is so important to the bank that the checks will be covered until the full deposits have been collected.

Insider Trading When someone uses confidential information to gain from the purchase or sale of stocks, that person is practicing *insider trading.* Suppose, for example, that a small firm's stock is currently trading at $50 a share. If a larger firm is going to buy the smaller one, it might have to pay as much as $75 a share for a controlling interest. Individuals who are aware of the impending acquisition before it is publicly announced might, therefore, be able to gain by buying the stock at $50 in anticipation of selling it for $75 after the proposed acquisition is announced.[19]

Individuals in a position to take advantage of such a situation generally include managers of the two firms and key individuals at banking firms working on the financial arrangements. For example, a former junior analyst with Salomon Smith Barney <www.smithbarney.com> was charged with insider trading in conjunction with a proposed merger between Washington Gas Light and Consolidated Natural Gas. Another banker with the same firm and three associates were charged with insider trading that resulted in $1.8 million in illegal profits ahead of six pending mergers, including WorldCom's bid for MCI. A compliance officer at BT Securities <www.bt.com> pled guilty to charges that he passed insider information about BT clients to his brother and two other individuals, who reaped $275,000 in illegal profits.[20]

Misrepresentation of Finances Certain behavior regarding financial representation is also illegal. In maintaining and reporting its financial status, every corporation must conform to *generally accepted accounting principles (GAAP)* (see Chapter 18). Sometimes, however, managers project profits far in excess of what they actually expect to earn. When the truth comes out, investors are disappointed.

IMPLEMENTING SOCIAL RESPONSIBILITY PROGRAMS

Thus far, we have discussed social responsibility as if there were some agreement on how organizations should behave. In fact, there are dramatic differences of opinion concerning the role of social responsibility as a business goal. Some people oppose any business activity that threatens profits. Others argue that social responsibility must take precedence over profits.

Even businesspeople who agree on the importance of social responsibility will cite different reasons for their views. Some skeptics of business-sponsored social projects fear that if businesses become too active, they will gain too much control over the ways in which those projects are addressed by society as a whole. These critics point to the influence that many businesses have been able to exert on the government agencies that are supposed to regulate their industries. Other critics claim that business organizations lack the expertise needed to address social issues. They argue, for instance, that technical experts, not businesses, should decide how to clean up polluted rivers.

Proponents of socially responsible business believe that corporations are citizens and should, therefore, help to improve the lives of fellow citizens. Still others point to the vast resources controlled by businesses and note that they help to create many of the problems social programs are designed to alleviate.

Approaches to Social Responsibility

Given these differences of opinion, it is little wonder that corporations have adopted a variety of approaches to social responsibility. Not surprisingly, organizations themselves adopt a wide range of positions on social responsibility. As Figure 4.6 illustrates, the four stances that an organization can take concerning its obligations to society fall along a continuum ranging from the lowest to the highest degree of socially responsible practices.

obstructionist stance
Approach to social responsibility that involves doing as little as possible and may involve attempts to deny or cover up violations

Obstructionist Stance The few organizations that take what might be called an **obstructionist stance** to social responsibility usually do as little as possible to solve social or environmental problems. When they cross the ethical or legal line that separates acceptable from unacceptable practices, their typical response is to deny or cover up their actions. For example, IBP, which we profiled at the outset of this chapter, may take this stance. Firms that adopt this position have little regard for ethical conduct and will generally go to great lengths to hide wrongdoing.

defensive stance
Approach to social responsibility by which a company meets only minimum legal requirements in its commitments to groups and individuals in its social environment

Defensive Stance One step removed from the obstructionist stance is the **defensive stance,** whereby the organization will do everything that is required of it legally but nothing more. This approach is most consistent with arguments against corporate social responsibility. Managers who take a defensive stance insist that their job is to generate profits. Such a firm, for example, would install pollution-control equipment dictated by law, but would not install higher-quality equipment even though it might further limit pollution.

Tobacco companies generally take this position in their marketing efforts. In the United States, they are legally required to include warnings to smokers on their products and to limit advertising to prescribed media. Domestically, they follow these rules to the letter of the law but use more aggressive marketing methods in countries that have no such rules. In many Asian and African countries, cigarettes are heavily promoted, contain higher levels of tar and nicotine than those sold in the United States, and carry few or no

Figure 4.6
Spectrum of Approaches to Corporate Social Responsibility

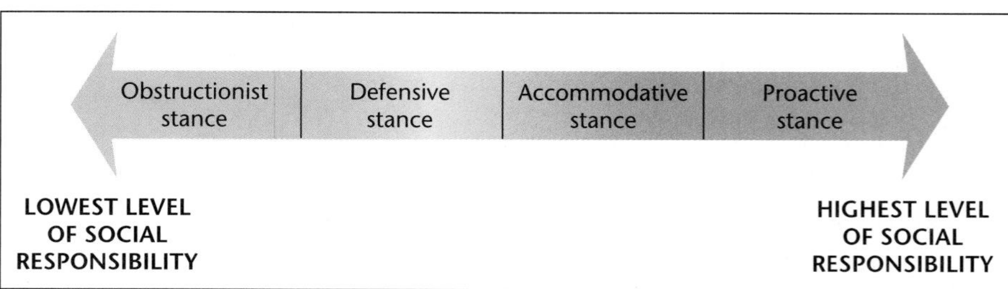

health warning labels. Firms that take this position are also unlikely to cover up wrongdoing, will generally admit to mistakes, and will take appropriate corrective actions.

Accommodative Stance A firm that adopts an **accommodative stance** meets its legal and ethical requirements but will also go further in certain cases. Such firms voluntarily agree to participate in social programs, but solicitors must convince them that given programs are worthy of their support. Both Exxon and IBM, for example, will match contributions made by their employees to selected charitable causes. Many organizations respond to requests for donations to Little League, Girl Scouts, youth soccer programs, and so forth. The point, however, is that someone has to knock on the door and ask: Accommodative organizations do not necessarily or proactively seek avenues for contributing.

accommodative stance
Approach to social responsibility by which a company, if specifically asked to do so, exceeds legal minimums in its commitments to groups and individuals in its social environment

Proactive Stance The highest degree of social responsibility that a firm can exhibit is the **proactive stance.** Firms that adopt this approach take to heart the arguments in favor of social responsibility. They view themselves as citizens in a society and proactively seek opportunities to contribute. The most common—and direct—way to implement this stance is by setting up a foundation through which to provide direct financial support for various social programs. Table 4.1 lists the top 15 largest corporate foundations based on total giving to social programs.

proactive stance
Approach to social responsibility by which a company actively seeks opportunities to contribute to the well-being of groups and individuals in its social environment

An excellent example of a different kind of proactive stance is the Ronald McDonald House <www.mcdonalds.com> program undertaken by McDonald's Corporation. These houses, located close to major medical centers, can be used by families for minimal cost while sick children are receiving medical treatment nearby. Similarly, some firms, such as UPS <www.ups.com>, Home Depot <www.homedepot.com>, and US West <www.uswest.com>, employ individuals who hope to compete in the Olympics and support them in various ways. UPS, for instance, underwrites the training and travel costs of four employees competing for Olympic berths and allows them to maintain flexible work schedules.[21] These and related programs exceed the accommodative stance—they indicate a sincere commitment to improving the general social welfare and thus represent a proactive stance to social responsibility.

Table 4.1

Top 15 Corporate Foundations

Rank	Name/(state)	Total Grants	As of Fiscal Year End Data
1.	Wal-Mart Foundation (AR)	$65,533,778	01/31/99
2.	Bank of America Foundation, Inc. (NC)	53,200,397	12/31/98
3.	AT&T Foundation (NY)	45,678,097	12/31/98
4.	The UPS Foundation (GA)	42,723,327	12/31/98
5.	GE Fund (CT)	35,516,086	12/31/98
6.	Ford Motor Company Fund (MI)	35,337,490	12/31/98
7.	Fannie Mae Foundation (DC)	32,738,878	12/31/98
8.	The Procter & Gamble Fund (OH)	32,035,814	06/30/99
9.	The Chase Manhattan Foundation (NY)	31,839,139	12/31/98
10.	SBC Foundation (TX)	31,390,284	12/31/98
11.	The Prudential Foundation (NJ)	27,854,000	12/31/99
12.	General Motors Foundation, Inc. (MI)	27,823,631	12/31/98
13.	U S WEST Foundation, Inc. (MI)	27,349,520	12/31/98
14.	First Union Regional Foundation (PA)	26,394,084	12/31/98
15.	GTE Foundation (TX)	26,252,923	12/31/98

Remember, however, that these categories are not sharply distinct: They merely label stages along a continuum of approach. Organizations do not always fit neatly into one category or another. The Ronald McDonald House program has been widely applauded, but McDonald's has also come under fire for allegedly misleading consumers about the nutritional value of its food products. Likewise, while UPS has sincere motives for helping Olympic athletes, the company will also benefit by featuring the athletes' photos on its envelopes and otherwise promoting its own benevolence. Even though IBP may take an obstructionist stance in some cases, many individual employees and managers at this firm have no doubt made substantial contributions to society in a number of different ways.

What steps should a newly formed business take to foster a socially responsible atmosphere for itself?

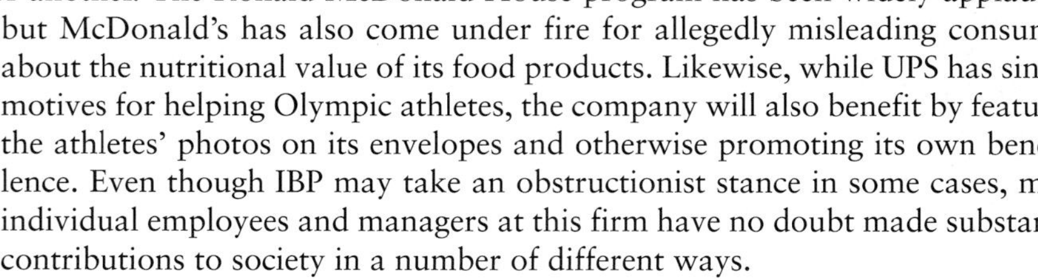

Managing Social Responsibility Programs

Making a company socially responsible in the full sense of the social response approach takes a carefully organized and managed program. In particular, managers must take steps to foster a companywide sense of social responsibility. Figure 4.7 summarizes those steps.[22]

1. *Social responsibility must start at the top.* Without the support of top management, no program can succeed. Thus, top management must embrace a strong stand on social responsibility and develop a policy statement outlining that commitment.
2. *A committee of top managers must develop a plan detailing the level of management support.* Some companies set aside percentages of profits for social programs. Levi Strauss, for example, earmarks 2.4 percent of pretax earnings for worthy projects. Managers must also set specific priorities. For instance, should the firm train the hard-core unemployed or support the arts?
3. *One executive must be put in charge of the firm's agenda.* Whether the role is created as a separate job or added to an existing one, the selected individual must monitor the program and ensure that its implementation is consistent with the firm's policy statement and strategic plan.
4. *The organization must conduct occasional* ***social audits:*** *systematic analyses of its success in using funds earmarked for its social responsibility goals.*[23] Consider the case of a company whose strategic plan calls for spending $100,000 to train 200 hard-core unemployed people and to place 180 of them in jobs. If at the end of a year the firm has spent $98,000, trained 210 people, and filled 175 jobs, a social audit will confirm the program's success. But if the program has cost $150,000, trained only 90 people, and placed only 10 of them, the audit will reveal the program's failure. Such failure should prompt a rethinking of the program's implementation and its priorities.

social audit
Systematic analysis of a firm's success in using funds earmarked for meeting its social responsibility goals

Figure 4.7
Establishing a Social Responsibility Program

The owners of Hermitage Artists salvage boxes and shipping crates from supermarkets, which would otherwise compact them and dump them in landfills. From such raw materials Hermitage makes artifacts ranging from small wooden boxes and frames to religious statues and elaborate desks. This small business in Troy, NY, combines environmentalism and the spirit of so-called "tramp art" by making salable objects of art out of discarded materials and is a collaborative operation run by men who were once homeless.

Social Responsibility and the Small Business

As the owner of a garden supply store, how would you respond to a building inspector's suggestion that a cash payment will speed your application for a building permit? As the manager of a liquor store, would you call the police, refuse to sell, or sell to a customer whose identification card looks forged? As the owner of a small laboratory, would you call the state board of health to make sure that it has licensed the company with whom you want to contract to dispose of medical waste? Who will really be harmed if a small firm pads its income statement to help it get a much-needed bank loan?

Many of the examples in this chapter illustrate big-business responses to ethical and social responsibility issues. Such examples, however, show quite clearly that small businesses must answer many of the same questions. Differences are primarily differences of scale.

At the same time, these are largely questions of *individual* ethics. What about questions of *social* responsibility? Can a small business, for example, afford a social agenda? Should it sponsor Little League baseball teams, make donations to the United Fund, and buy lightbulbs from the Lion's Club? Do joining the Chamber of Commerce and supporting the Better Business Bureau cost too much? Clearly, ethics and social responsibility are decisions faced by all managers in all organizations, regardless of rank or size. One key to business success is to decide in advance how to respond to the issues that underlie all questions of ethical and social responsibility.

Continued from page 94

Some Ethical Rants and Raves

Managers at Patagonia and IBP apparently take quite different approaches to the idea of social responsibility. Patagonia always puts its social agenda at the forefront of everything it does. In early 2000, for example, the firm set up a major new Internet operation to sell more efficiently to consumers. There's nothing particularly socially conscious about doing that, but one of the site's more interesting features is a section called "Rants & Raves." Here customers can post online reviews and comments about Patagonia products—both positive and negative. Even a firm as socially active as Patagonia is not always above criticism. Some people, for instance, criticize the company for donating money to such radical groups as Earth First.

IBP, meanwhile, continues to face a raft of problems. On January 12, 2000, the U.S. Justice Department, acting on behalf of the Environmental Protection Agency **<www.epa.gov>**, filed a lawsuit accusing IBP of violating numerous federal air, water, and hazardous-waste laws at the company's flagship plant and former headquarters in Dakota City, Nebraska. The government charges that IBP emitted up to 1,800 pounds of hydrogen sulfide per day from the Dakota City plant without informing federal regulators (disclosure is required if total emissions exceed 100 pounds per day) and that IBP violated the federal Clean Water Act by dumping excessive ammonia into the Missouri River. The suit charges IBP with either failing to file or else filing incorrectly federal toxic air reports at several plants in Iowa, Nebraska, and Kansas.

In addition, various agencies in states where IBP has operations are investigating numerous allegations about pollution. Idaho's State Division of Environmental Quality has charged IBP with exceeding state wastewater guidelines by as much as 1,200 percent. The Illinois state attorney general is seeking fines against IBP for violating the state's odor law. Officials in Nebraska are watching the federal investigation to see if there have been violations of state regulations.

Questions for Discussion

1. Compare and contrast the concept of social responsibility at Patagonia and IBP.
2. Characterize each company's approach to its customers, employees, and other stakeholders.
3. Which approach to social responsibility is each firm taking?
4. At which firm would you rather work? Why? Which firm's stock would you prefer to own (assume that Patagonia is publicly traded)? Why?
5. Using the Internet, research recent developments in the cases against IBP.

SUMMARY OF LEARNING OBJECTIVES

1 **Explain how individuals develop their personal *codes of ethics* and why ethics are important in the workplace.** Individual *codes of ethics* are derived from social standards of right and wrong. *Ethical behavior* is behavior that conforms to generally accepted social norms concerning beneficial and harmful actions. Because ethics affect the behavior of individuals on behalf of the companies that employ them, many firms are adopting formal statements of ethics. Unethical behavior can result in loss of business, fines, and even imprisonment.

2 **Distinguish *social responsibility* from ethics and trace the evolution of social responsibility in U.S. business.** *Social responsibility* refers to an organization's response to social needs. One way to understand social responsibility is to view it in terms of *stakeholders*—those groups, individuals, and organizations that are directly affected by the practices of an organization and, therefore, have a stake in its performance. Until the second half of the nineteenth century, businesses often paid little attention to stakeholders. Since then, however, both public pressure and government regulation,

especially as a result of the Great Depression of the 1930s and the social activism of the 1960s and 1970s, have forced businesses to consider the public welfare, at least to some degree. A trend toward increased social consciousness, including a heightened sense of environmental activism, has recently emerged.

3 **Show how the concept of social responsibility applies both to environmental issues and to a firm's relationships with customers, employees, and investors.** Social responsibility toward the environment requires firms to minimize pollution of air, water, and land. Social responsibility toward customers requires firms to provide products of acceptable quality, to price products fairly, and to respect consumers' rights. Social responsibility toward employees requires firms to respect workers both as resources and as people who are more productive when their needs are met. Social responsibility toward investors requires firms to manage their resources and to represent their financial status honestly.

4 **Identify four general *approaches to social responsibility* and describe the four steps a firm must take to implement a *social responsibility program*.** An *obstructionist stance* on social responsibility is taken by a firm that does as little as possible to address social or environmental problems and which may deny or attempt to cover up problems that may occur. The *defensive stance* emphasizes compliance with legal minimum requirements. Companies adopting the *accommodative stance* go beyond minimum activities, if asked. The *proactive stance* commits a company to actively seek to contribute to social projects. Implementing a social responsibility program entails four steps: (1) drafting a policy statement with the support of top management, (2) developing a detailed plan, (3) appointing a director to implement the plan, and (4) conducting *social audits* to monitor results.

5 **Explain how issues of social responsibility and ethics affect small businesses.** Managers and employees of small businesses face many of the same ethical questions as their counterparts at larger firms. Small businesses face the same issues of social responsibility and the same need to decide on an approach to social responsibility. The differences are primarily differences of scale.

QUESTIONS AND EXERCISES

Questions for Review

1. What basic factors should be considered in any ethical decision?
2. Who are an organization's stakeholders? Who are the major stakeholders with which most businesses must be concerned?
3. What are the major areas of social responsibility with which businesses should be concerned?
4. What are the four basic approaches to social responsibility?
5. In what ways do you think your personal code of ethics might clash with the operations of some companies? How might you try to resolve these differences?

Questions for Analysis

6. What kind of wrongdoing would most likely prompt you to be a whistle-blower? What kind of wrongdoing would be least likely? Why?
7. In your opinion, which area of social responsibility is most important? Why? Are there areas other than those noted in the chapter that you consider important?
8. Identify some specific ethical or social responsibility issues that might be faced by small-business managers and employees in each of the following areas: environment, customers, employees, and investors.

Application Exercises

9. Develop a list of the major stakeholders of your college or university. As a class, discuss the ways in which you think the school prioritizes these stakeholders. Do you agree or disagree with this prioritization?
10. Using newspapers, magazines, and other business references, identify and describe at least three companies that take a defensive stance to social responsibility, three that take an accommodative stance, and three that take a proactive stance.

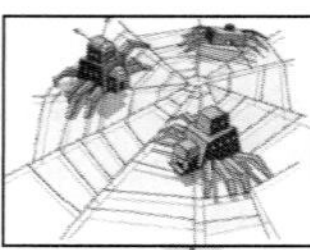

EXPLORING THE WEB

SETTING SITES ON ETHICS

Texas Instruments (TI) was a pioneer in the area of business ethics. TI was one of the very first corporations in the United States to create and publish a code of ethics for managers and employees. To learn more about ethics at TI, visit the company Web site and then answer the questions that follow:

www.ti.com/corp/docs/ethics/home.htm

1. Overall, how beneficial do you think this Web site would be for a Texas Instruments employee interested in corporate ethics?
2. Visit the area in the Web site and review the information dealing with ethics across the organization. How useful do you find this information to be?
3. Visit the area in the site about ethics in the global market. What are the strengths and weaknesses of this area?
4. One area of the Web site features an ethics quiz designed to help employees get a sense of the ethics of a particular action. How practical is this section?
5. If you were developing an ethics Web site for another company, would you pattern it after the TI site? Why or why not?
6. Why don't more companies have Web sites like this one?

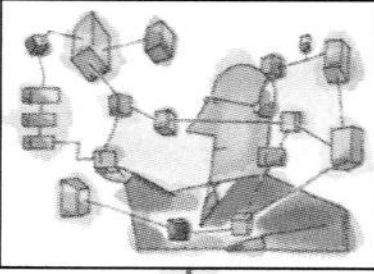

BUILDING YOUR BUSINESS SKILLS

TO LIE OR NOT TO LIE: THAT IS THE QUESTION

This exercise enhances the following SCANS workplace competencies: demonstrating basic skills, demonstrating thinking skills, exhibiting interpersonal skills, and working with information.

GOAL

To encourage students to apply general concepts of business ethics to specific situations.

BACKGROUND

Even before President Bill Clinton's public acknowledgment of an inappropriate relationship with White House intern Monica S. Lewinsky, and well before his secretary was forced to testify about the affair before a federal grand jury, the issue of workplace lying was front-page news.

Why? Perhaps because lying is so common. According to one survey, one-quarter of working American adults said that they had been asked to do something illegal or unethical on the job. Four in 10 did what they were told. Another survey of more than 2,000 secretaries showed that many employees face ethical dilemmas in their day-to-day work.

METHOD

Step 1

Working with four other students, discuss ways in which you would respond to the following ethical dilemmas. When there is a difference of opinion among group members, try to determine the specific factors that influence different responses:

- Would you lie about your supervisor's whereabouts to someone on the phone?
- Would you lie about who was responsible for a business decision that cost your company thousands of dollars to protect your own or your supervisor's job?
- Would you inflate sales and revenue data on official company accounting statements to increase stock value?
- Would you say that you witnessed a signature when you did not if you were acting in the role of a notary?
- Would you keep silent if you knew that the official minutes of a corporate meeting had been changed?

- Would you destroy or remove information that could hurt your company if it fell into the wrong hands?

Step 2

Research the commitment to business ethics at Johnson & Johnson <www.jnj.com> and Texas Instruments <www.ti.com/corp/docs/ethics/home.htm> by clicking on their respective Web sites. As a group, discuss ways in which these statements are likely to affect the specific behaviors mentioned in Step 1.

Step 3

Working with group members, draft a corporate code of ethics that would discourage the specific behaviors mentioned in Step 1. Limit your code to a single, typewritten page, but make it sufficiently broad to cover different ethical dilemmas.

FOLLOW-UP

1. What personal, social, and cultural factors do you think contribute to lying in the workplace?
2. Do you agree or disagree with the following statement? The term business ethics is an oxymoron. Support your answer with examples from your own work experience or that of a family member.
3. If you were your company's director of human resources, how would you make your code of ethics a "living document"?
4. If you were faced with any of the ethical dilemmas described in Step 1, how would you handle them? How far would you go to maintain your personal ethical standards?

CRAFTING YOUR BUSINESS PLAN

GOING IN THE ETHICAL DIRECTION

THE PURPOSE OF THE ASSIGNMENT

1. To acquaint students with the process of navigating the *Business PlanPro* (*BPP*) software package (Version 4.0).
2. To familiarize students with some of the ethical and social responsibility considerations faced by businesses and to show where the topic can be found in different sections of the *BPP* business plan.
3. To prepare students for entering social responsibility considerations into a firm's business plan through *BPP.*

ASSIGNMENT

After reading Chapter 4 in the textbook, open the BPP *software* and look around for information about the types of ethical considerations and social responsibility factors that would be of concern to the sample firm of* Southeast Health Services *(Southeast Health Plans, Inc.),* Flower Importer *(Fantastic Florals, Inc.),* JavaNet Internet Café, *and* Ice Dreams Shaved Ice. *Also select a sample company yourself. Then respond to the following items:*

1. Do you think a company in Southeast's line of business should have a code of ethics? Call up Southeast's Business Plan Outline. [Click on **Plan Outline** on the Plan Manager screen]. In which sections of Southeast's business plan would you expect to find their code of ethics? Go into those sections from the Plan Manager screen and identify information about their code of ethics. What did you find?
2. The textbook states that a firm's social responsibility includes providing quality products for its customers. Explore Southeast's business plan and describe its position on providing quality products. [Sites to see in *BPP* (for this assignment): In the Plan Outline screen, click on **1.0 Executive Summary.** Then click on and read each of **1.1 Objectives, 1.2 Mission,** and **1.3 Keys to Success.**]
3. Another dimension of social responsibility is pricing products fairly. Search through Southeast's plan to identify information about the fairness of pricing for services they

offer. Does Southeast's planned gross margin reflect "fair pricing"? Why or why not? [Sites to see in *BPP:* In the Plan Outline screen, click on **3.1 Competitive Comparison** and then on **3.3 Sourcing.** After returning to the Plan Outline screen, click on **5.1.1 Pricing Strategy** and then **1.0 Executive Summary.**]

FOR YOUR OWN BUSINESS PLAN

4. To what extent will your business plan deal with your business's social responsibilities to customers? To the local community? To employees? In what section(s) of the *BPP* document should social responsibility matters be presented? What purpose do you think they would serve?

*GENERAL TIPS FOR NAVIGATING IN BPP

1. Open the *BPP* program, examine the Welcome screen, and click on **Open a Sample Plan.**
2. From the **Open a Sample Plan** dialogue box, click on a sample company name; then click on **Open.**
3. On the Plan Manager screen, click on **Your Plan Outline**; then click on any of the lines (for example, **6.0 Management Summary**).
4. You can always return to the Plan Outline screen by going to the bottom of the screen and clicking on the **Plan Outline** icon.
5. After finishing with one sample company, you can get to the next one by going to the top of the screen and clicking on **File** (on the menu bar). Then beneath that, select **Open Sample Plan.** This will exit you from the current company file and take you to the Open Sample Plan dialogue box, where you can select your next sample company.
6. When you are finished with a sample company, you can close the program by going to the top of the screen and clicking on **File** (on the bar menu). Then beneath that, select **Exit.**

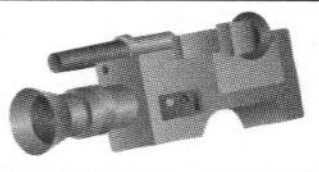

VIDEO EXERCISE

CATERING TO SERIOUS USERS: PATAGONIA

Learning Objectives

The purpose of this video exercise is to help you

1. Recognize the ethical challenges facing businesses today.
2. Understand the ways in which firms can act responsibly.
3. Understand the relationship between ethics and quality.

BACKGROUND INFORMATION

Yvon Chouinard founded Patagonia over 20 years ago, making climbing gear by hand for his friends. Today, the company makes clothing for a wide variety of activities with a focus on function, durability, and innovation. Its rigorously field-tested products are available worldwide, and it has offices in North America, Europe, and Japan, with a headquarters in Ventura, California. In addition to its commitment to customers—"serious users who rely on the product in extreme conditions"—the firm is responsible to its employees by providing a family-friendly workplace, and to the environment by donating millions of dollars to environmentalist groups in the United States and abroad.

THE VIDEO

The video segment describes the founding of Patagonia and its commitment to high-quality products. It details the company's recent struggle to maintain financial stability while avoiding the runaway growth that its managers fear would have a damaging effect on the natural environment.

DISCUSSION QUESTIONS

1. In what ways does Patagonia demonstrate its ethical commitment to employees?
2. What is the relationship between ethics and quality that Patagonia strives to maintain?
3. How would you reconcile Patagonia's highly developed sense of social responsibility with its decision to lay off 20 percent of its workforce?

FOLLOW-UP ASSIGNMENT

Choose a company in the service sector that claims to be socially responsible. In what ways are its stated ethical objectives confirmed or contradicted by its approach to employees, customers, investors, and the natural environment?

FOR FURTHER EXPLORATION

Visit the Patagonia Web site <www.patagonia.com> and explore the page "About Us." Of special interest are the "Selected Essays" in which various writers and employees, including founder Yvon Chouinard, talk about the company's history and philosophy. Read Chouinard's essay, "Patagonia: The Next 100 Years," and scan two or three of the other articles. Do these essays express a consistent viewpoint about the company's mission? Try to put the firm's philosophy in your own words. Do you think it is a sustainable business strategy? Why or why not?

MASTERING BUSINESS ESSENTIALS

Go to the "Ethics" episode on the Mastering Business Essentials CD-ROM for an interactive, video-enhanced exercise on the efforts of a manager at CanGo, an e-business start-up, to deal with a complex dilemma in business ethics.

The episode titled "Resource and Investment and Company Reputation" explores the problem of balancing a company's reputation with the demands of its market.

Chapter

5 Managing the Business Enterprise

After reading this chapter, you should be able to:

1. **Explain** the importance of setting *goals* and formulating *strategies* as the starting points of effective management.
2. **Describe** the four activities that constitute the *management process.*
3. **Identify** *types of managers* by level and area.
4. **Describe** the five basic *management skills.*
5. **Describe** the development and explain the importance of *corporate culture.*

Grounds for the Defense

Starbucks Corp. <www.starbucks.com>, the fastest-growing and, arguably, the highest-profile food and beverage company in the United States, is clearly a business Goliath. Starbucks was started in Seattle in 1971 by three coffee aficionados. Their primary business at the time was buying premium coffee beans, roasting them, and then selling the coffee by the pound. The business performed modestly well and soon grew to nine stores, all in the Seattle area. When they thought their business growth had stalled in 1987, the three partners sold Starbucks to a former employee named Howard Schultz. Schultz promptly reoriented, trading in bulk coffee sales for retail coffee sales through the firm's coffee bars.

Today, Starbucks is not only the country's largest coffee importer and roaster of specialty beans, but also the largest specialty coffee bean retailer in the United States. There are more than 2,100 Starbucks locations in the United States. The firm has revenues of over $1.3 billion a year, annual profits of almost $70 million, and a workforce of more than 26,000 employees.

What is the key to Starbucks' phenomenal growth and success? One important ingredient is its well-conceived and implemented strategy. Starbucks is on a phenomenal growth pace, opening a new coffee shop somewhere almost every day. This growth is planned and coordinated at each step of the way through careful site selection. In addition, through its astute promotional campaigns and commitment to quality, the firm has elevated the coffee-drinking taste of millions of Americans and fueled a significant increase in demand.

Its phenomenal growth rate notwithstanding, Starbucks is also continually on the alert for new business opportunities. One area of growth is the international market. In 1996, the firm opened two shops in Japan and another in Singapore. Another growth area is brand extension through ventures with other companies. Dreyer's <www.dreyers.com>, for example, distributes five flavors of Starbucks coffee ice cream to grocery freezers across the country. Capital Records <www.hollywoodandvine.com> has produced two special jazz CDs that are available only in Starbucks stores. Redhook Brewery <www.redhook.com> uses Starbucks coffee extract in its double black stout beer.

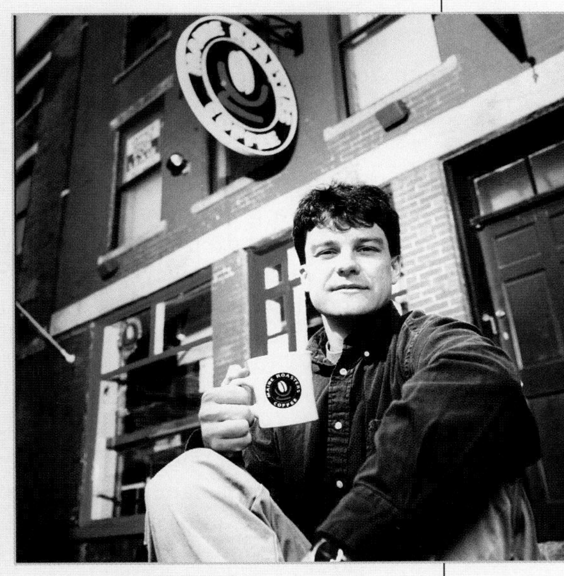

Given the enormous marketing and financial muscle that a company like Starbucks brings to the table, imagine how Rand Smith, the owner of Maine Roasters <www.maineroasters.qpg.com>, a small coffee shop in Portland, Maine, reacted when he heard that the coffee Goliath was coming to town. "It's Maine versus the national giant," said Smith, who decided to load whatever slingshot he could find.

Smith's strategy was grounded in the passion and loyalty that exist among Maine residents for the sanctity of their home state. He has mounted a finely tuned plan for portraying Starbucks as a big bully from the "outside" and his own upstart operation as the homespun underdog. To promote this image, every morning he dispatches a team of his employees to stand outside the Starbucks restaurant closest to his own store to pass out chocolate drops and to encourage Starbucks customers to "Support a Maine-owned-and-operated company." So far, his efforts are paying off. The local paper, for example, has editorialized against corporate heavyweights, community groups have picketed Starbucks, and there has even been a spate of vandalism against Starbucks, usually involving broken store windows. Smith does not condone such tactics, but he no doubt privately sees each stone being thrown through a Starbucks window as a metaphor for the stone with which David felled Goliath in an earlier time.

"It's Maine versus the national giant."

—Rand Smith, owner of Maine Roasters, upon hearing that Starbucks was coming to town

Our opening story continues on page 142

All corporations depend on effective management. Whether managers are involved in running a big international corporation like Starbucks or a small local or regional business like Maine Roasters Coffee, they perform many of the same functions, are responsible for many of the same tasks, and have many of the same responsibilities. The work of all managers involves developing strategic and tactical plans. Along with numerous other things, they must analyze their competitive environments and plan, organize, direct, and control day-to-day operations.

By focusing on the learning objectives of this chapter, you will better understand the nature of managing and the range of skills that managers like Howard Schultz and Rand Smith need if they are to compete effectively, and the importance of corporate culture.

Although our focus is on managers in *business* settings, remember that the principles of *management* apply to all kinds of organizations. Managers work in charities, churches, social organizations, educational institutions, and government agencies. The prime minister of Canada, curators at the Museum of Modern Art, the dean of your college, and the chief administrator of your local hospital are all managers. Remember, too, that managers bring to small organizations much the same kinds of skills—the ability to make decisions and respond to a variety of challenges—as they bring to large ones.

Regardless of the nature and size of an organization, managers are among its most important resources. Consider the profiles of the following three managers:

- Jenny Ming is president of Old Navy <www.oldnavy.com>, a division of The Gap Inc. <www.gapinc.com> and one of the fastest-growing retail chains around. After earning her college degree in fashion merchandising at San Jose State, she went to work for Mervyn's, a division of Dayton Hudson Corporation, first as a management trainee and then as a buyer. After he heard a supplier singing Ming's praises, Gap CEO Mickey Drexler lured her away and put her in charge of buying T-shirts for Gap stores. She continued to excel and was named to her present job in early 1999. For some time now, Old Navy has outperformed most of the other retailers including The Gap. Much of the credit goes to Ming and the relatively rare combination of skills that enables her to understand and spot the newest fashion trends, instill loyalty and dedication in those who work for her, and run a tightly controlled and focused business enterprise.[1]
- Lloyd Ward was once CEO of Maytag <www.maytagcorp.com>, one of the world's largest appliance manufacturers. He studied to be an engineer but went into marketing instead. During stints at Procter & Gamble, Ford, and PepsiCo, he honed his management skills and developed a reputation as an exemplary manager. However, he made his biggest marks at Maytag. Along with his other accomplishments, Ward convinced other executives that sweeping changes were needed at the staid old-line manufacturing business if it was to succeed in today's business environment. He overhauled the way new products are developed, solidified important strategic alliances with firms such as Sears, and developed an effective strategy for international expansion. Many experts thought the best was yet to come for Ward and Maytag. Many also thought that he was the victim of unlucky timing when Maytag profits for the third quarter dropped by 27 percent. In November 2000, the board of directors demanded and received Ward's resignation. He had been CEO for 15 months.[2]
- Joseph Galli Jr. is one of the many managers navigating the uncharted waters of e-commerce. He had a comfortable position as the number-two executive at Black and Decker before being lured away to help run Amazon.com. He recently left that company to head up Vertical Net <www.vertical.net>, a developer of online business-to-business stores and marketplaces. From his first day at work, Galli has been learning the industry, visiting the dozens of businesses that Vertical Net has bought or sold, and figuring out how to integrate all of them into one smoothly running enterprise. Unlike many dot.coms, Vertical Net is already turning a profit, and its managers have a clear plan for keeping the firm comfortably in the black. Meanwhile, Galli continues to excel in a pressure-cooker environment as different from his former environment as e-mail from snail mail.[3]

Although Jenny Ming, Lloyd Ward, and Joseph Galli are clearly different people, work in different kinds of organizations, and have different approaches to what they do, they also share one fundamental commonality with other high-level managers: responsibility for the performance and effectiveness of business enterprises and are thus accountable to shareholders, employees, customers, and other key constituents. In this chapter, we describe the management process and the skills that managers must develop to perform their functions in organizations. Perhaps you will then have a better feel for the reasons why organizations value good managers so highly.

SETTING GOALS AND FORMULATING STRATEGY

The starting point in effective management is setting **goals**—objectives that a business hopes (and plans) to achieve. Every business needs goals. We begin, therefore, by discussing the basic aspects of organizational goal setting. Remember, however, that deciding what it *intends* to do is only the first step for an organization. Managers must also make decisions about *actions* that will and will not achieve company goals. Decisions cannot be made on a problem-by-problem basis or merely to meet needs as they arise. In most companies, a broad program underlies those decisions. That program is called a *strategy*, and we will complete this section by detailing the basic steps in strategy formulation.

goal
Objective that a business hopes and plans to achieve

Setting Business Goals

Goals are performance targets—the means by which organizations and their managers measure success or failure at every level. For example, Jenny Ming's goals at Old Navy are largely tied to sales increases, profitability, and new store openings. Because her business is a subsidiary of a larger corporation, she has no goals for the stock price of her own operation. However, because Maytag is a publicly traded corporation, in addition to goals for sales and profit margins, Lloyd Ward had to focus a lot of attention on stock price. Unfortunately, by November 2000, Maytag stock was down 60 percent from its peak under Ward's predecessor. Joseph Galli's goals, meanwhile, focus generally on building an organization that can continue to grow rapidly while maintaining profitability.

Purposes of Goal Setting An organization functions systematically because it sets goals and plans accordingly. An organization commits its resources on all levels to achieving its goals. Specifically, we can identify four main purposes in organizational goal setting:

1. *Goal setting provides direction and guidance for managers at all levels.* If managers know precisely where the company is headed, there is less potential for error in the different units of the company. Starbucks, for example, has a goal of increasing capital spending by 15 percent, with all additional expenditures devoted to opening new stores. This goal clearly informs everyone in the firm that expansion into new territories is a high priority for the firm.
2. *Goal setting helps firms allocate resources.* Areas that are expected to grow will get first priority. The company allocates more resources to new projects with large sales potential than it allocates to mature products with established but stagnant sales potential. Thus, Starbucks is primarily emphasizing new store expansion, while its e-commerce initiatives are currently given a lower priority. "Our management team," says CEO Howard Schultz, "is 100% focused on growing our core business without distraction . . . from any other initiative."
3. *Goal setting helps to define corporate culture.* For years, the goal at General Electric <www.ge.com> has been to push each of its divisions to first or second in its industry. The result is a competitive (and often stressful) environment and a culture that rewards success and has little tolerance for failure. At the same time, however, GE's appliance business, television network (NBC), aircraft engine unit, and financial services business are each among the very best in their respective industries. Recently,

CEO Jack Welch set an even higher standard—to make the firm the most valuable in the world.[4]

4. *Goal setting helps managers assess performance.* If a unit sets a goal of increasing sales by 10 percent in a given year, managers in that unit who attain or exceed the goal can be rewarded. Units failing to reach the goal will also be compensated accordingly. GE has a long-standing reputation for stringently evaluating managerial performance, richly rewarding those who excel, and getting rid of those who do not. Each year the lower 10 percent of GE's managerial force are informed that either they make dramatic improvements in performance or consider alternative directions for their careers.

Kinds of Goals Goals differ from company to company, depending on the firm's purpose and mission. Every enterprise has a *purpose,* or a reason for being. Businesses seek profits, universities seek to discover and transmit new knowledge, and government agencies seek to set and enforce public policy. Many enterprises also have missions and **mission statements**—statements of how they will achieve their purposes in the environments in which they conduct their business.

mission statement
Organization's statement of how it will achieve its purpose in the environment in which it conducts its business

A company's mission is usually easy to identify, at least at a basic level of understanding. Garden.com, for example, is trying to make a profit by selling garden products and supplies on the Internet. Dell Computer <www.dell.com> has the same purpose in selling personal computers directly to consumers. Jeremy's MicroBatch Ice Creams, a Philadelphia start-up, is attempting to make a profit by transferring the microbrewery strategy to ice cream—making small quantities and selling it in limited editions.

"Our management team is 100% focused on growing our core business without distraction from any other initiative."

—Howard Schultz, CEO of Starbucks

Businesses often have to rethink their missions as the competitive environment changes. In 1999, for example, Starbucks announced that Internet marketing and sales were going to become core business initiatives. Managers subsequently realized, however, that this initiative did not fit the firm as well as they first thought. As a result, they scaled back this effort and, as we noted, made a clear recommitment to their existing retail business. The demands of change force many companies to rethink their missions and thus to revise their statements of what they are and what they do. (We discuss more fully the problems in managing change—as well as some solutions—later in this chapter.)

At many companies, top management drafts and circulates detailed mission statements. Because such a statement reflects a company's understanding of its activities as a *marketer,* it is not easily described. Consider the similarities and differences between Timex and Rolex. Although both firms share a common purpose—to sell watches at a profit—they have very different missions. Timex <www.timex.com> sells low-cost, reliable watches in outlets ranging from department stores to corner drugstores. Rolex <www.rolex.com> sells high-quality, high-priced watches through selected jewelry stores.

When a computer system can become obsolete only months after it has been designed, how does your firm deal with the exponentially increasing rate of technological advances?

WebConnection

www.microbatch.com

While still an undergraduate at the University of Pennsylvania, Jeremy Kraus came up with the idea for MicroBatch Ice Creams. His goal: to manufacture and sell ice cream according to the principles by which microbrew beers are made (high-quality ingredients, patient processing) and sell it in limited editions.

Regardless of a company's purpose and mission, however, every firm has long-term, intermediate, and short-term goals:

- **Long-term goals** relate to extended periods of time, typically five years or more. For example, American Express might set a long-term goal of doubling the number of participating merchants during the next 10 years. Kodak might adopt a long-term goal of increasing its share of the 35mm film market by 10 percent during the next eight years.
- **Intermediate goals** are set for a period of one to five years. Companies usually set intermediate goals in several areas. For example, the marketing department's goal might be to increase sales by 3 percent in two years. The production department might want to reduce expenses by 6 percent in four years. Human resources might seek to cut turnover by 10 percent in two years. Finance might aim for a 3-percent increase in return on investment in three years.
- **Short-term goals** are set for perhaps one year and are developed for several different areas. Increasing sales by 2 percent this year, cutting costs by 1 percent next quarter, and reducing turnover by 4 percent over the next six months are examples of short-term goals.

long-term goals
Goals set for an extended time, typically five years or more into the future

intermediate goals
Goals set for a period of one to five years into the future

short-term goals
Goals set for the very near future, typically less than one year

Formulating Strategy

Planning is often concerned with the nuts and bolts of setting goals, choosing tactics, and establishing schedules. In contrast, strategy tends to have a wider scope. It is by definition a "broad program" that describes an organization's intentions. A business strategy outlines how the business intends to meet its goals, and includes the organization's responsiveness to new challenges and new needs.

What does "managing strategically" mean? How can it enhance an organization's performance?

Because a well-formulated strategy is so vital to a business's success, most top managers devote much attention (and creativity) to this process. **Strategy formulation** involves three basic steps summarized in Figure 5.1.

It is interesting to note at least one change in contemporary thinking about the role of strategy. Once the responsibility of top management, strategy made its way into the everyday world of setting and implementing goals (planning) by means of a fairly rigid top-down process. Today, however, strategy formulation is often a much more democratic process.

strategy formulation
Creation of a broad program for defining and meeting an organization's goals

Setting Strategic Goals Described as long-term goals, **strategic goals** are derived directly from a firm's mission statement.

For example, Ferdinand Piëch, CEO of Volkswagen <www.vw.com>, has clear strategic goals for the European carmaker. When he took over in 1993, Volkswagen was only marginally profitable, regarded as an also-ran in the industry, and thinking about pulling out of the U.S. market altogether because its sales were so poor. Over the next few

strategic goals
Long-term goals derived directly from a firm's mission statement

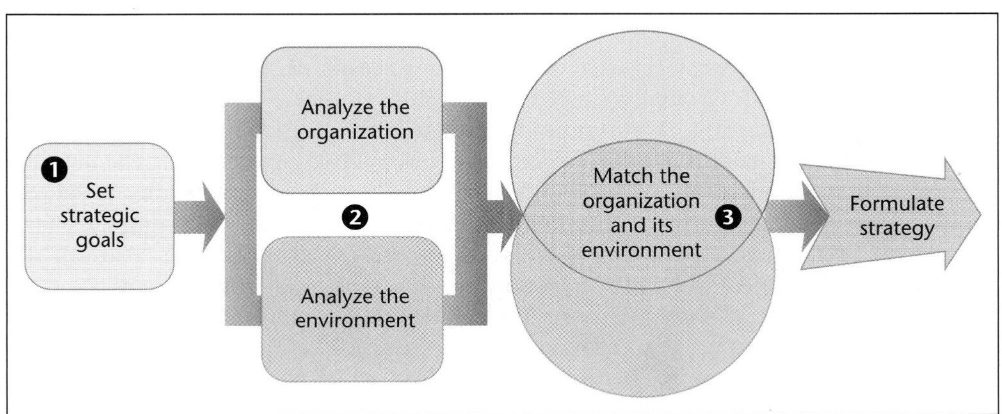

Figure 5.1
Strategy Formulation

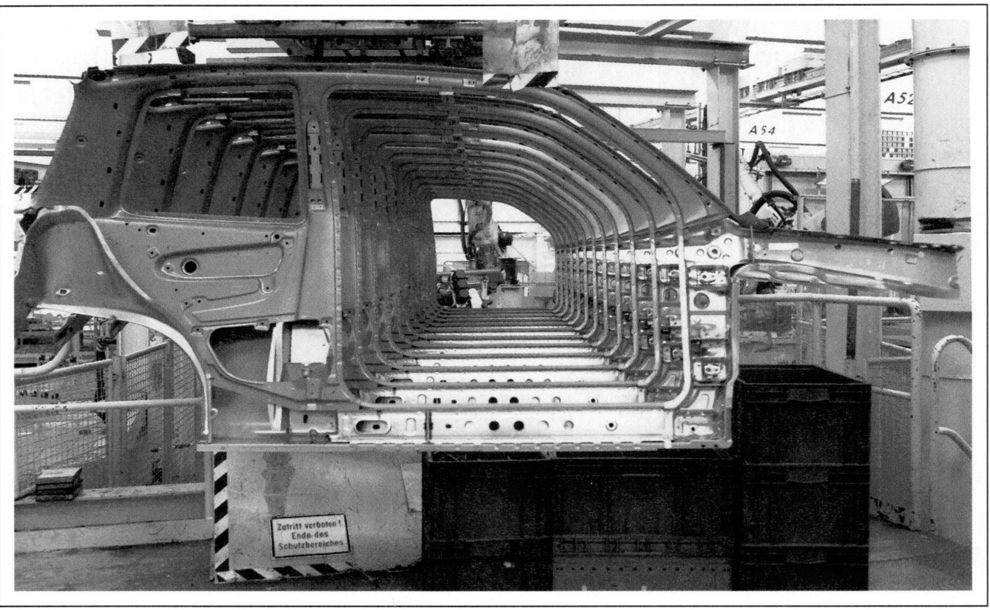

Since Ferdinand Piëch became chairman of Volkswagen <www.vw.com> in 1993, productivity at plants like this one in Wolfsburg, Germany, have increased sales to 4.7 million vehicles per year and enabled VW to catch Toyota as the world's third-largest carmaker. Piëch (who calls his management style "democratic dictatorship") requires all new projects to be self-financing and gives designers free rein to create new models only as long as they buy parts off a preset purchasing list. Current long-term goals call for matching Audi in quality and marketing high-end VWs against both Audi and Mercedes models.

years, however, Piëch totally revamped the firm and now has it making big profits. Volkswagen is now a much more formidable force in the global automobile industry. It competes with Toyota for the number-three spot in the industry (behind only General Motors and Ford), but Piëch is clearly not finished. "For the moment," he reports, "we are happy with the bronze medal. But we want to step up the stairway."[5]

> ***"For the moment we are happy with the bronze medal. But we want to step up the stairway."***
>
> *—Ferdinand Piëch, CEO of Volkswagen, on plans for improving the company's number-three standing in the industry*

Analyzing the Organization and Its Environment The term **environmental analysis** involves scanning the environment for threats and opportunities. Changing consumer tastes and hostile takeover offers are *threats,* as are new government regulations. Even more important threats come from new products and new competitors. *Opportunities,* meanwhile, are areas in which the firm can potentially expand, grow, or take advantage of existing strengths.

environmental analysis
Process of scanning the business environment for threats and opportunities

Consider the case of British entrepreneur Richard Branson and his company, Virgin Group Ltd. <www.virgin.com> . Branson started the firm in 1968, when he was 17, naming it in acknowledgment of his own lack of experience in the business world. Over the years, he has built Virgin into one of the world's best-known brands, comprising a conglomeration of over 200 entertainment, media, and travel companies worldwide. Among the best known of his enterprises are Virgin Atlantic (an international airline), Virgin Megastores (retailing), and V2 Music (record labels). Branson sees potential threats in the form of other competitors such as British Airways <www.britishairways.com> and KLM <nederland.klm.com> for Virgin Atlantic, Tower Records <www.towerrecords.com> (retailing), and the EMI Group <www.emi.fr> (recorded music).

He also sees significant opportunities because of his firm's strong brand name (especially in Europe). One of his most recent ventures is a new e-commerce firm. The business is called Virgin Mobile <www.virginmobile.com> and operates like a cellular telephone company. But in addition to providing conventional cellular service, the Virgin telephone permits the user to press a red button to go directly to a Virgin operator who can sell products, make airline and hotel reservations, and provide numerous other services. A companion Web site also complements the cellular service and its related programs. Virgin Mobile is signing up new customers at the rate of 100,000 per month.[6]

organizational analysis
Process of analyzing a firm's strengths and weaknesses

In addition to performing environmental analysis, which is analysis of *external* factors, managers must also examine *internal* factors. The purpose of **organizational analysis**

WebConnection

www.virgin.com

British-based Virgin operates businesses ranging from an airline to a chain of megamedia stores to a financial services company. Only recently, however, has its strategy included the expansion of its Web site into an international e-commerce portal. While some critics say the move is too late, Virgin counters that because it already has so many of its own products, it's well-suited to make the entrepreneurial move. To find out more about Virgin's diverse product line, contact the company's Web site.

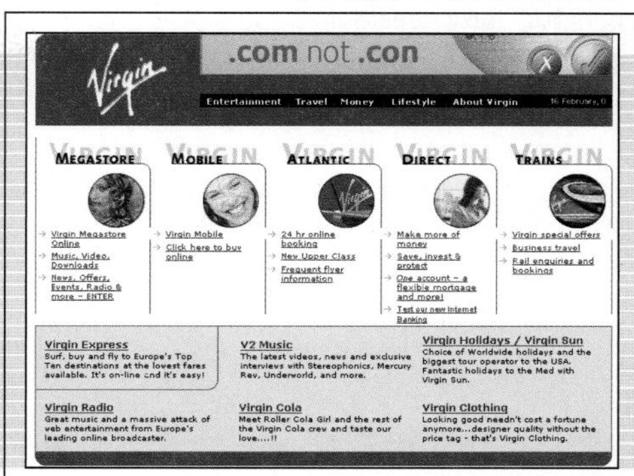

is to better understand a company's strengths and weaknesses. Strengths might include surplus cash, a dedicated workforce, an ample supply of managerial talent, technical expertise, or little competition. The absence of any of these strengths could represent an important weakness.

Branson, for example, started Virgin Mobile in part because he saw so many of his current operations as old-line traditional businesses that might be at future risk from new forms of business and competition. One strength he employs is the widespread name recognition his businesses enjoy. Another relates to finances. He sold 49 percent of Virgin Atlantic to Singapore Airlines <www.singaporeair.com> for almost $1 billion in cash, retaining ownership control but raising all of the funds he needed to launch his new venture. On the other hand, he also admits that neither he nor many of his senior managers have much experience in or knowledge about e-commerce, which may be a significant weakness.

Matching the Organization and Its Environment The final step in strategy formulation is matching environmental threats and opportunities against corporate strengths and weaknesses. The matching process is the heart of strategy formulation. More than any other facet of strategy, matching companies with their environments lays the foundation for successfully planning and conducting business.

Over the long term, this process may also determine whether a firm typically takes risks or behaves more conservatively. Either strategy can be successful. Blue Bell <www.bluebell.com>, for example, is one of the most profitable ice cream makers in the world, even though it sells its products in only five states. Based in Brenham, Texas, Blue Bell controls more than 50 percent of the market in each state in which it does business. The firm has resisted the temptation to expand too quickly. Its success is based on product freshness and frequent deliveries—strengths that may suffer if the company grows too large.

A Hierarchy of Plans Plans can be viewed on three levels: strategic, tactical, and operational. Managerial responsibilities are defined at each level. The levels constitute a hierarchy because implementing plans is practical only when there is a logical flow from one level to the next.

- **Strategic plans** reflect decisions about resource allocations, company priorities, and the steps needed to meet strategic goals. They are usually determined by the board of directors and top management. General Electric's decision that viable businesses must rank first or second within their respective markets is a matter of strategic planning.
- **Tactical plans** are shorter-range plans for implementing specific aspects of the company's strategic plans. They typically involve upper and middle management. Coca-Cola's decision to increase sales in Europe by building European bottling facilities is an example of tactical planning.

strategic plans
Plans reflecting decisions about resource allocations, company priorities, and steps needed to meet strategic goals

tactical plans
Generally short-range plans concerned with implementing specific aspects of a company's strategic plans

operational plans
Plans setting short-term targets for daily, weekly, or monthly performance

- **Operational plans,** which are developed by mid-level and lower-level managers, set short-term targets for daily, weekly, or monthly performance. McDonald's, for example, establishes operational plans when it explains to franchisees precisely how Big Macs are to be cooked, warmed, and served.

Contingency Planning and Crisis Management

Because business environments are often difficult to predict, and because the unexpected can create major problems, most managers recognize that even the best-laid plans sometimes become impractical. For instance, when the Walt Disney Co. <www.disney.go.com> announced plans to launch a cruise line replete with familiar Disney characters and themes, managers also began aggressively developing and marketing packages linking three- and four-day cruises with visits to Disney World <www.disney.go.com/DisneyWorld> in Florida. The first sailing was scheduled for early 1998, and the company began to book reservations a year in advance. However, the shipyard constructing Disney's first ship (the *Disney Magic*) notified the company in October 1997 that it was behind schedule and that the ship would be delivered several weeks late. When similar problems befall other cruise lines, they can offer to rebook passengers on alternative itineraries. Because Disney had no other ship, it had no choice but to refund the money it had collected as prebooking deposits for its first 15 cruises.

The 20,000 displaced customers were offered big discounts if they rebooked on a later cruise. Many of them, however, could not rearrange their schedules and requested full refunds. Moreover, quite a few blamed Disney, and a few expressed outrage at what they saw as poor planning by the entertainment giant. Fortunately for Disney, however, the *Disney Magic* was eventually launched and has now become very popular and very profitable.[7]

Because managers know such things can happen, they often develop alternative plans in case things go awry. Two common methods of dealing with the unknown and unforeseen are *contingency planning* and *crisis management.*

contingency planning
Identifying aspects of a business or its environment that might entail changes in strategy

Contingency Planning

Contingency planning recognizes the need to find solutions to specific aspects of a problem. By its very nature, a contingency plan is a hedge against changes that might occur. **Contingency planning,** then, is planning for change: It seeks to identify in advance important aspects of a business or its market that might change. It also identifies the ways in which a company will respond to changes. Today, many companies use computer programs for contingency planning.

Suppose, for example, that a company develops a plan to create a new division. It expects sales to increase at an annual rate of 10 percent for the next five years and develops a marketing strategy for maintaining that level. But suppose that sales have increased by only 5 percent by the end of the first year. Does the firm abandon the venture, invest more in advertising, or wait to see what happens in the second year? Any of these alternatives is possible. Regardless of the firm's choice, however, its efforts will be more efficient if managers decide in advance what to do in case sales fall below planned levels. Contingency planning helps them do exactly that. Disney learned from its mistake with its first ship, and when the second (the *Disney Wonder*) was launched a year later, managers did several things differently. For one thing, they allowed for an extra two weeks between when the ship was supposed to be ready for sailing and its first scheduled cruise. They also held open a few cabins on the *Disney Magic* as a backup for any especially disgruntled customers who might need accommodations if there were unexpected delays launching the *Disney Wonder.* The "Life Cycle of an e-Business" box in this chapter discusses various contingency plans relevant to operations at Garden.com.

crisis management
An organization's methods for dealing with emergencies

Crisis Management

A crisis is an unexpected emergency requiring immediate response. **Crisis management** involves an organization's methods for dealing with emergencies. In May 2000, for example, millions of computers around the world were hit by

Life Cycle of an e-Business

Preparing for Plan B at Garden.com

As at any firm, the management team at Garden.com had to identify potential problems, contingencies, and crises that might conceivably affect its operations. They also needed at least a basic idea about how to respond if one of those problems, contingencies, or crises actually occurred. Three major sets of concerns were especially relevant to a firm like Garden.com: technology, shipping arrangements, and weather.

Garden.com's ability to function was almost totally dependent on technology. Most customer contacts took place via e-mail, and most customer orders were generated by the company's Web page. Naturally, employees also used e-mail to communicate among themselves, but more importantly, they used both e-mail and business-to-business software to communicate with suppliers and with Federal Express <www.fedex.com>, the company's preferred shipper. Obviously, a major power failure, computer virus, or hacker attack—not to mention a major information-systems failure—would have had a significant impact on the company's ability to function.

The company used several methods to guard against these potential problems. For one thing, it maintained backup power supplies that could continue to operate its basic network in the event of a power failure. Like most information networks, the one in place at Garden.com used what is popularly called a "firewall"—an electronic barrier through which only approved users can move—to protect its system. Approved users, in turn, were those with appropriate passwords, user IDs, and so forth. Built into the firewall were special barriers that automatically guarded against common forms of viruses and hacking.

Another potential problem derived from Garden.com's reliance on a primary shipper (in this case, Federal Express). Under normal circumstances, the agreement between the two companies was a competitive advantage for Garden.com. When it placed an order to a supplier, the order information was automatically sent to FedEx as well. In turn, FedEx then knew when to pick up the order from the supplier and where to deliver it. But Garden.com could have suffered if FedEx had been shut down for some reason. What if labor disruptions had affected FedEx? What if the Federal Aviation Administration (FAA) had found major safety problems with FedEx aircraft? The carrier might have been forced to shut down. Garden.com would have been forced to turn to United Parcel Service (UPS), Airborne Express, or the U.S. Postal system. Because its systems were tightly linked to FedEx, any of these options would have created major short-term problems for the firm.

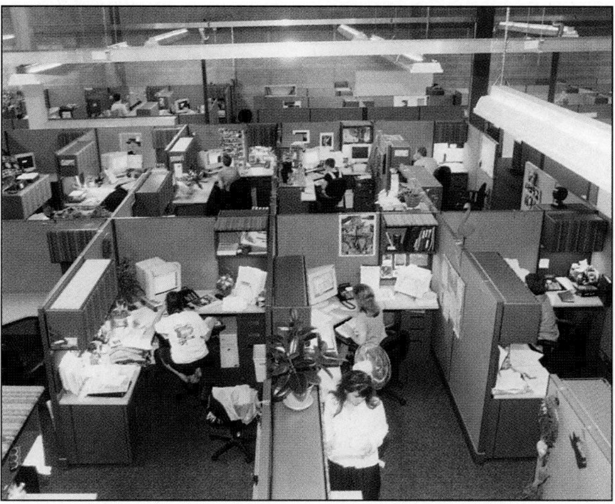

Finally, there was the weather. Weather can create a variety of problems, such as icy roads and downed power lines. More importantly, while many growers today use climate-controlled greenhouses, some still plant outdoors. An unexpected freeze or other form of severe weather could have seriously disrupted Garden.com's supplier network. In most instances, the firm had backup suppliers to whom it might have turned, but as is the case with shippers, having to resort to backups would, at a minimum, have created short-term complications.

---

a virus that was quickly dubbed the "Love Bug." The virus came disguised as an e-mail attachment with a tag line indicating that the receiver should open it to see a love note. But once opened, the virus-laden file began damaging files on the receiver's computer and transmitting itself to others via e-mail and the Internet. Among the many organizations seriously affected were not only Ford Motor Co. <www.ford.com>, Bear Stearns <www.bearstearns.com>, and Japan's Nomura Securities <www.nomura.co.jp>, but also the Pentagon <www.defenselink.mil/pubs/pentagon>, the U.S. Congress, the British Parliament, and the whole Danish government. These organizations and numerous others literally had to shut down their electronic communications networks for hours in order to set up new and more effective security procedures. Some organizations were able to get back up and running very quickly, but others took much longer. Warns Steve White, a computer-virus expert at IBM: "Everybody now needs e-mail. Somebody shuts it down and we are significantly out of business."[8]

"Everybody now needs e-mail. Somebody shuts it down and we are significantly out of business."

—Steve White, IBM computer-virus scientist, on the attack of the "Love Bug"

Designed to help employees cope under extreme or unpredictable circumstances, good crisis plans typically outline who will be in charge in different kinds of situations, how the organization will respond, and so forth. In addition, they usually lay out plans for assembling and deploying crisis management teams. Current estimates suggest that most larger firms and many midsize and smaller firms in the United States have crisis management plans. However, as many organizations learned from the "Love Bug," it is difficult to anticipate every eventuality.

THE MANAGEMENT PROCESS

management
Process of planning, organizing, directing, and controlling an organization's resources to achieve its goals

Management is the process of planning, organizing, directing, and controlling an organization's financial, physical, human, and information resources to achieve its goals. Managers oversee the use of all these resources in their respective firms. All aspects of a manager's job are interrelated. In fact, any given manager is likely to be engaged in each of these activities during the course of any given day.

Planning

planning
Management process of determining what an organization needs to do and how best to get it done

Determining what the organization needs to do and how best to get it done requires planning. **Planning** has three main components. As we have seen, it begins when managers determine the firm's goals. Next, they develop a comprehensive strategy for achieving those goals. After a strategy is developed, they design tactical and operational plans for implementing the strategy.

When Yahoo! <www.yahoo.com> was created, for example, the firm's top managers set a strategic goal of becoming a top firm in the then-emerging market for Internet search engines. But then came the hard part—figuring out how to do it. They started by assessing the ways in which people actually use the Web and concluded that users wanted to be able to satisfy a wide array of needs, preferences, and priorities by going to as few sites as possible to find what they were looking for. Thus one key component of Yahoo!'s strategy was to foster partnerships and relationships with other companies so that potential Web surfers could draw upon several sources through a single portal—which would be Yahoo!. Thus, the goal of partnering emerged as one set of tactical plans for moving forward. Yahoo! managers then began fashioning alliances with such diverse partners as Reuters <www.reuters.com>, Standard & Poor's <www.standardpoor.com>, and the Associated Press <www.ap.org> (for news coverage), RE/Max <www.remax.com> (for real estate information), and a wide array of information providers specializing in sports, weather, entertainment, shopping, and travel. The creation of individual partnership agreements with each of these partners represents a form of operational planning.

Organizing

Once one of the leading-edge high-technology firms in the world, Hewlett-Packard <www.hewlett-packard.com> began to lose some of its luster in the mid-1990s. Ironically, one of the major reasons for its slide could be traced back to what had once been a major strength. Specifically, HP had long prided itself on being little more than a corporate confederation of individual businesses. Sometimes, these businesses even ended up competing among themselves. This approach had been beneficial for much of the firm's history: It was easier for each business to make its own decisions quickly and efficiently, and the competition kept each unit on its toes. By 1998, however, problems had become apparent, and no one could quite figure out what was going on.

Enter Ann Livermore, then head of the firm's software and services business. Livermore realized that the structure that had served so well in the past was now holding the firm back. To regain its competitive edge, HP needed an integrated, organization-wide Internet strategy. Unfortunately, the company's highly decentralized organization made that impossible. Livermore led the charge to create one organization to drive a single Internet plan. "I felt we could be the most powerful company in the industry," she says, "if we could get our hardware, software, and services aligned." In fact, a reorganized HP has bounced back and is quickly regaining its competitive strength.[9]

This process—determining the best way to arrange a business's resources and activities into a coherent structure—is called **organizing.** (We explore this topic further in Chapter 6.)

organizing
Management process of determining how best to arrange an organization's resources and activities into a coherent structure

Directing

Managers have the power to give orders and demand results. Directing, however, involves more complex activities. When **directing,** a manager works to guide and motivate employees to meet the firm's objectives. Gordon Bethune, CEO of Continental Airlines <www.continental.com>, is an excellent example of a manager who excels at motivating his employees. When he took the helm of the troubled carrier in 1994, morale was dismal, most employees hated their jobs, and the company's performance was among the worst in the industry.

directing
Management process of guiding and motivating employees to meet an organization's objectives

Almost immediately, Bethune started listening to his employees to learn about their problems and hear how they thought the company could be improved. He also began to reward everyone when things went well and continued communicating with all Continental employees on a regular basis. Today, the firm is ranked among the best in the industry and is regularly identified as one of the best places to work in the United States. In May 2000, Continental was named the highest-quality airline in the United States, based on the J.D. Powers Survey of Customer Satisfaction.[10]

Controlling

controlling
Management process of monitoring an organization's performance to ensure that it is meeting its goals

Controlling is the process of monitoring a firm's performance to make sure that the firm is meeting its goals. All CEOs must pay close attention to costs and performance. Indeed, skillful controlling, like innovative directing, is one reason that Gordon Bethune has been so successful at Continental. For example, the firm focuses almost relentlessly on numerous

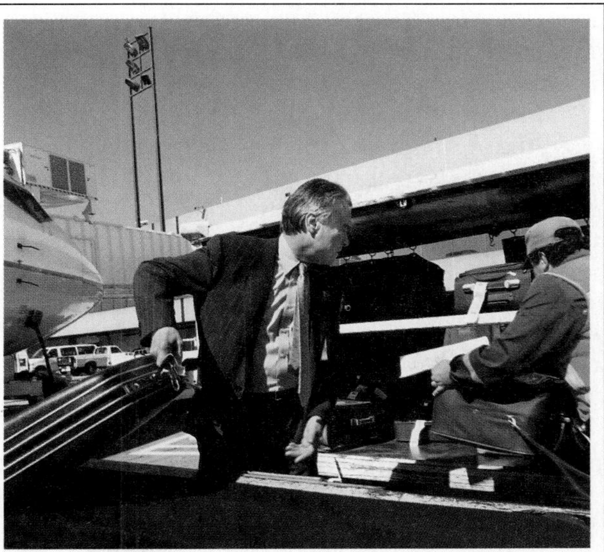

Gordon Bethune became CEO of Continental Airlines <www.continental.com> in late 1994, a year in which the company lost $619 million. In the next four years, Continental showed profits of $215 million, $319 million, $383 million, and $385 million. Bethune's specialty is directing people, and he practices one of his own key managerial principles almost religiously: "Working Together." In Bethune's scheme of things, teamwork leads to better morale, better morale to better service, and better service to greater productivity.

Figure 5.2
The Control Process

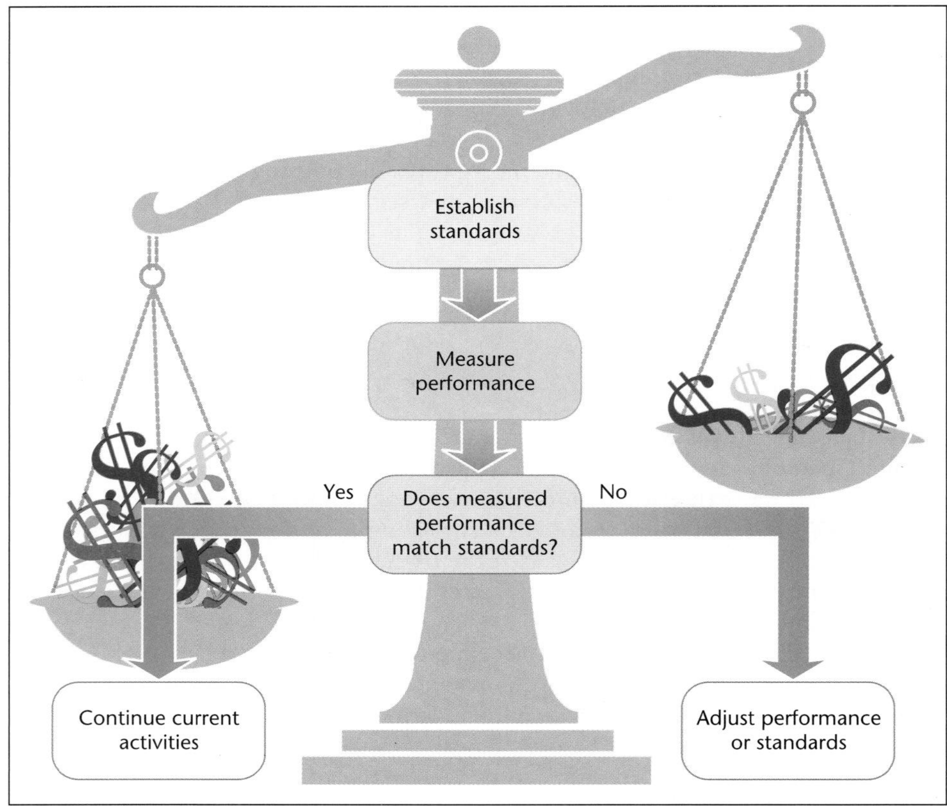

indicators of performance that can be constantly measured and adjusted. Everything from on-time arrivals to baggage-handling errors to the number of empty seats on an airplane to surveys of employee and customer satisfaction are regularly and routinely monitored. If on-time arrivals start to slip, Bethune focuses on the problem and gets it fixed. If a manager's subordinates provide less-than-glowing reviews, that manager loses part of his or her bonus. As a result, no single element of the firm's performance can slip too far before it's noticed and fixed.

Figure 5.2 illustrates the control process that begins when management establishes standards, often for financial performance. If, for example, a company wants to increase sales by 20 percent over the next 10 years, then an appropriate standard might be an increase of about 2 percent a year.

Managers then measure actual performance against standards. If the two amounts agree, the organization continues along its present course. If they vary significantly, however, one or the other needs adjustment. If sales have increased 2.1 percent by the end of the first year, things are probably fine. If sales have dropped 1 percent, some revision in plans may be needed. Perhaps the original goal should be lowered or more money should be spent on advertising. Control can also show where performance is running better than expected and thus serve as a basis for providing rewards or reducing costs. For example, when Ford recently introduced the new Explorer SportsTrac (an SUV with a pickup bed), initial sales were so strong the firm was able to delay a major advertising campaign for three months because it was selling all of the vehicles it could make anyway.

TYPES OF MANAGERS

Although all managers plan, organize, direct, and control, not all managers have the same degree of responsibility for these activities. Thus, it is helpful to classify managers according to levels and areas of responsibility.

Levels of Management

The three basic levels of management are *top, middle,* and *first-line management.* Most firms have more middle managers than top managers, and more first-line managers than middle managers. Both the power of managers and the complexity of their duties increase as they move up the ladder.

Top Managers

Like Jenny Ming, Lloyd Ward, and Joseph Galli, the fairly small number of executives who get the chance to guide the fortunes of most companies are **top managers.** Common titles for top managers include *president, vice president, treasurer, chief executive officer (CEO),* and *chief financial officer (CFO).* Top managers are responsible for the overall performance and effectiveness of the firm. They set general policies, formulate strategies, approve all significant decisions, and represent the company in dealings with other firms and with government bodies.

top managers
Managers responsible to the board of directors and stockholders for a firm's overall performance and effectiveness

Middle Managers

Just below the ranks of top managers is another group of managers who also occupy positions of considerable autonomy and importance and who are called **middle managers.** Titles such as *plant manager, operations manager,* and *division manager* designate middle-management slots. In general, middle managers are responsible for implementing the strategies, policies, and decisions made by top managers. For example, if top management decides to introduce a new product in 12 months or to cut costs by 5 percent in the next quarter, middle management must decide how to meet these goals. The manager of a Maytag washing machine factory, an Old Navy distribution center, or a Continental hub operation will likely be a middle manager.

middle managers
Managers responsible for implementing the strategies, policies, and decisions made by top managers

First-Line Managers

Those who hold such titles as *supervisor, office manager,* and *group leader* are **first-line managers.** Although they spend most of their time working with and supervising the employees who report to them, first-line managers' activities are not limited to that arena. At a building site, for example, the *project manager* not only ensures that workers are carrying out construction as specified by the architect, but also interacts extensively with materials suppliers, community officials, and middle- and upper-level managers at the home office. The manager of an Old Navy store and the flight-services manager for a specific Continental Airlines flight would also be considered first-line managers.

first-line managers
Managers responsible for supervising the work of employees

Areas of Management

In any large company, top, middle, and first-line managers work in a variety of areas including *human resources, operations, marketing, information,* and *finance.* For the most part, these areas correspond to the types of managerial skills described later in this chapter and to the wide range of business principles and activities discussed in the rest of this book.

Human Resource Managers

Most companies have *human resource managers* who hire and train employees, who evaluate performance, and who determine compensation. At large firms, separate departments deal with recruiting and hiring, wage and salary levels, and labor relations. A smaller firm may have a single department—or a single person—responsible for all human resource activities. (Some key issues in human resource management are discussed in Part 3.)

Operations Managers

As we will see in Chapter 15, the term *operations* refers to the systems by which a firm produces goods and services. Among other duties, operations managers are responsible for production, inventory, and quality control. Manufacturing companies such as Texas Instruments, Ford, and Caterpillar have a strong need for operations managers at many levels. Such firms typically have a *vice president for operations* (top), *plant managers* (middle), and *production supervisors* (first-line managers). In recent years, sound operations management practices have become increasingly important to a variety of service organizations. (Operations management is examined more fully in Part 5.)

Operations managers organize work, design jobs, measure performance, control quality, and schedule work. At Boeing <www.boeing.com>, the result is a tangible product, such as a 777 jet aircraft. This 14,000-pound section is the result of coordinated operations processes being carried out in more than a dozen countries.

Marketing Managers As we will see in Chapter 11, marketing encompasses the development, pricing, promotion, and distribution of goods and services. Marketing managers are responsible for getting products from producers to consumers. Marketing is especially important for firms that manufacture consumer products, such as Procter & Gamble, Coca-Cola, and Levi Strauss. Such firms often have large numbers of marketing managers at several levels. For example, a large consumer products firm is likely to have a *vice president for marketing* (top), several *regional marketing managers* (middle), and several *district sales managers* (first-line managers). (The different areas of marketing are discussed in Part 4.)

Information Managers Occupying a fairly new managerial position in many firms, information managers design and implement systems to gather, organize, and distribute information. Huge increases in both the sheer volume of information and the ability to manage it have led to the emergence of this important function.

Although relatively few in number, the ranks of *information managers* are growing at all levels. Some firms have a top-management position called a *chief information officer.* Middle managers help design information systems for divisions or plants. Computer systems managers within smaller businesses are usually first-line managers. (Information management is discussed in more detail in Chapter 17.)

Financial Managers Nearly every company has *financial managers* to plan and oversee its accounting functions and financial resources. Levels of financial management may include *chief financial officer (CFO)* or *vice president for finance* (top), *a division controller* (middle), and an *accounting supervisor* (first-line manager). Some institutions—NationsBank <www.nationsbank.com> and Prudential <www.prudential.com>, for example—have even made effective financial management the company's reason for being. (Financial management is treated in more detail in Part 6.)

Other Managers Some firms also employ other specialized managers. Many companies, for example, have public relations managers. Chemical and pharmaceutical companies such as Monsanto <www.pharmacia.com> and Merck <www.merck.com> have research and development managers. The range of possibilities is wide, and the areas of management are limited only by the needs and imagination of the firm.

BASIC MANAGEMENT SKILLS

Although the range of managerial positions is almost limitless, the success that people enjoy in those positions is often limited by their skills and abilities. Effective managers must develop *technical, human relations, conceptual, decision-making,* and *time management skills.* Unfortunately, these skills are quite complex, and it is the rare manager who excels in every area.

Technical Skills

The skills needed to perform specialized tasks are called **technical skills.** A programmer's ability to write code, an animator's ability to draw, and an accountant's ability to audit a company's records are all examples of technical skills. People develop technical skills through a combination of education and experience. Technical skills are especially important for first-line managers. Many of these managers spend considerable time helping employees solve work-related problems, training them in more efficient procedures, and monitoring performance.

technical skills
Skills needed to perform specialized tasks

Human Relations Skills

Effective managers also generally have good **human relations skills**—specifically, skills in understanding and getting along with other people. A manager with poor human relations skills may have trouble getting along with subordinates, cause valuable employees to quit or transfer, and contribute to poor morale. Joseph Galli, for example, works well with people, has fun when he works, and makes everyone feel excited about the work. He also genuinely cares about the welfare of his employees. So, too, does Gordon Bethune, who routinely visits his employees throughout the company. Reports one baggage manager at Continental's Newark, New Jersey, hub: "Anybody who's worked here longer than two months can recognize Gordon."

Although human relations skills are important at all levels, they are probably most important for middle managers, who must often act as bridges between top managers, first-line managers, and managers from other areas of the organization. Managers should possess good communication skills. Many managers have found that being able to understand others, and to get them to understand you, can go far toward maintaining good relations in an organization.

human relations skills
Skills in understanding and getting along with people

"Anybody who's worked here longer than two months can recognize Gordon."

—Baggage manager at Continental's Newark, New Jersey, hub, on the airline's CEO, Gordon Bethune

Conceptual Skills

Conceptual skills refer to a person's ability to think in the abstract, to diagnose and analyze different situations, and to see beyond the present situation. Conceptual skills help managers recognize new market opportunities (and threats). They can also help managers analyze the probable outcomes of their decisions. The need for conceptual skills differs at various management levels: Top managers depend most on conceptual skills, first-line managers least. Although the purposes and everyday needs of various jobs differ, conceptual skills are needed in almost any job-related activity.

In many ways, conceptual skills may be the most important ingredient in the success of executives in e-commerce businesses. For example, the ability to foresee how a particular business application will be affected by or can be translated to the Internet is clearly conceptual in nature. The "Wired World" box in this chapter discusses this idea in more detail.

conceptual skills
Abilities to think in the abstract, diagnose and analyze different situations, and see beyond the present situation

Decision-Making Skills

Decision-making skills include the ability to define problems and select the best course of action. Figure 5.3 illustrates the following basic steps in decision making:

decision-making skills
Skills in defining problems and selecting the best courses of action

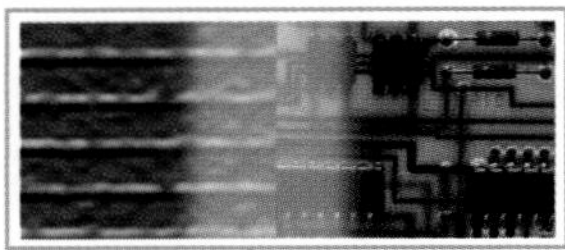

It's a WiredWorld

• *How To Spot the e-CEO*

Top managers, especially CEOs, have always moved in a fast-paced, stress-filled work environment. But the job of CEO for an e-commerce company seems to be setting new standards for pace, complexity, and stress. CEOs in traditional businesses are generally accustomed to dealing with either tangible products (such as automobiles, shoes, or computer hardware) or relatively well-defined services (accounting, transportation, or retailing operations). Moreover, the rules of the game, established over a period of decades, are relatively clear: Businesses are supposed to make profits, stock price is based on earnings, and so forth.

But the world of electronic commerce has put a few bumps in this well-worn road. Managers in this environment clearly believe that the pace of their work is faster, more complex, and more ambiguous than that of their traditional counterparts. They attribute some of these conditions to the nature of their business (which is based almost solely on information), some to the pace of change in their industries (it occurs very quickly), and some to a new set of business rules (for example, market valuation based more on intuition rather than reality). But all agree on one fundamental thing: they operate at breakneck speed with little or no margin for error. Table 5.1 highlights some of the more fundamental differences between the work of a traditional CEO and an e-CEO.

Traditional CEOs are generally expected to be encouraging, cordial, and fast moving with a dislike for ambiguity. They might also have some anxiety about confronting technology-related issues, and their average age is 57. e-CEOs, on the other hand, are more prone to evangelizing, often brutally frank, and apparently thrive on ambiguity. Furthermore, e-CEOs exhibit more anxiety when they are deprived of technology, and their average age is 38. Finally, while all CEOs are presumed to be rich, well-to-do, or comfortable, successful e-CEOs are likely to be rolling in money.

Table 5.1

Traditional CEOs versus e-CEOs

Traditional CEO	e-CEO
Encouraging	Evangelizing
Alert	Paranoid
Cordial	Brutally frank
Infotech semiliterate (at best)	Infotech literate (at least)
Clearly focused	Intensely focused
Fast moving	Faster moving
Antiambiguity	Proambiguity
Technology-confrontation-anxiety sufferer	Bandwidth-separation-anxiety sufferer
Paragon of good judgment	Paragon of good judgment
Age: 57	Age: 38
Rich	Really rich

1. *Define the problem, gather facts, and identify alternative solutions.* Current managers at bicycle maker Schwinn <www.schwinn.com>, for instance, realized that their predecessors had made some serious errors in assuming that mountain bikes were just a fad. The opposite had proved to be true, and Schwinn's share of the bicycle market had dropped dramatically.
2. *Evaluate each alternative and select the best one.* Managers at Schwinn acknowledged that they had to take corrective action. They discussed such alternatives as buying a company that made mountain bikes, launching their own line of mountain bikes, or refocusing on other product lines. They chose to develop their own line of mountain bikes and did so in 1994.
3. *Implement the chosen alternative, periodically following up and evaluating the effectiveness of that choice.* Schwinn's actions turned out to be right on track: The firm's revenues began to increase steadily after its first mountain bikes went on the market.

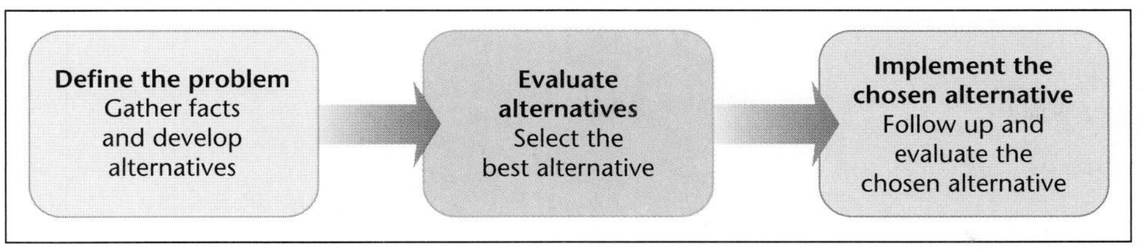

Figure 5.3
The Decision-Making Process

At first, true mountain bike enthusiasts were wary of the new products because they still associated Schwinn with recreational bicycles for casual or occasional riders. After a few professional mountain bike racers started using Schwinns, these concerns evaporated. Today, Schwinn is once again preeminent in every market in which it competes.

Time Management Skills

time management skills Skills associated with the productive use of time

Time management skills refer to the productive use that managers make of their time. In 1999, for example, General Electric CEO Jack Welch was paid $13,325,000 in salary. Assuming that he worked 50 hours a week and took 2 weeks' vacation, Welch earned $5,330 an hour—about $89 per minute. Any amount of time that Welch wastes clearly represents a large cost to GE and its stockholders. Most managers, of course, receive much smaller salaries than Welch. Their time, however, is valuable, and poor use of it still translates into costs and wasted productivity. (Actually, this example substantially underestimates Welch's earnings; he also received another $79 million in 1999 in deferred compensation such as stock options and retirement benefits.)[11]

To manage time effectively, managers must address four leading causes of wasted time:

- *Paperwork.* Some managers spend too much time deciding what to do with letters and reports. Most documents of this sort are routine and can be handled quickly. Managers must learn to recognize those documents that require more attention.
- *The telephone.* Experts estimate that managers get interrupted by the telephone every five minutes. To manage this time more effectively, they suggest having a secretary screen all calls and setting aside a certain block of time each day to return the important ones.
- *Meetings.* Many managers spend as much as four hours a day in meetings. To help keep this time productive, the person handling the meeting should specify a clear agenda, start on time, keep everyone focused on the agenda, and end on time.
- *E-mail.* Increasingly, more and more managers are also relying heavily on e-mail and other forms of electronic communication. Like memos and telephone calls, many e-mail messages are not particularly important—some are even trivial. As a result, time is wasted when managers have to sort through a variety of electronic folders, in baskets, and archives. As the average number of electronic messages grows, the potential time wasted also increases.

Management Skills for the Twenty-First Century

Although the skills discussed in this chapter have long been an important part of every successful manager's career, new skill requirements continue to emerge. As we enter the twenty-first century, most experts point to the growing importance of skills involving *global management* and *technology.*

Global Management Skills Tomorrow's managers must equip themselves with the special tools, techniques, and skills necessary to compete in a global environment. They will need to understand foreign markets, cultural differences, and the motives and practices of foreign rivals.

On a more practical level, businesses will need managers who are capable of understanding international operations. In the past, most U.S. businesses hired local managers

WebConnection

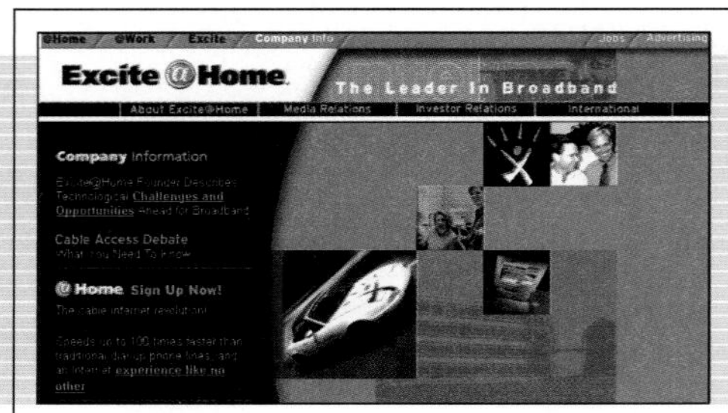

www.home.net

Tom Jermoluk left Silicon Graphics to become an e-CEO—head of an e-commerce company called @Home Network, which provides Internet services via cable TV connections. According to experts, among the skills that e-CEOs need is the ability to make real-time decisions. To find out more about "Speed" and other managerial priorities at @Home Network, contact the company.

to run their operations in the various countries in which they operated. More recently, however, the trend has been to transfer U.S. managers to foreign locations. This practice helps firms better transfer their corporate cultures to foreign operations. In addition, foreign assignments help managers become better prepared for international competition as they advance within the organization. General Motors <www.gm.com> now has almost 500 U.S. managers in foreign posts.

Management and Technology Skills Another significant issue facing tomorrow's managers is technology, especially as it relates to communication. Managers have always had to deal with information. In today's world, however, the amount of information has reached staggering proportions. In the United States alone, people exchange hundreds of millions of e-mail messages every day. New forms of technology have added to a manager's ability to process information while simultaneously making it even more important to organize and interpret an ever-increasing wealth of input.

Technology has also begun to change the way the interaction of managers shapes corporate structures. Computer networking, for example, exists because it is no longer too expensive to put a computer on virtually every desk in the company. In turn, this elaborate network controls the flow of the firm's lifeblood—information. This information no longer flows strictly up and down through hierarchies. It now flows to everyone simultaneously. As a result, decisions are made more quickly, and more people are directly involved. With e-mail, teleconferencing, and other forms of communication, neither time nor distance—nor such corporate "boundaries" as departments and divisions—can prevent people from working more closely together. More than ever, bureaucracies are breaking down, while planning, decision making, and other activities are beginning to benefit from group building and teamwork.

"E-mail is a major cultural event—it changes the way you run the organization."

—Bill Raduchel,
Chief Information Officer,
Sun Microsystems

Bill Raduchel, chief information officer of Sun Microsystems <www.sun.com>, goes so far as to say that "e-mail is a major cultural event—it changes the way you run the organization." But of course, as noted earlier, managers must also work to use information technology wisely and efficiently.

MANAGEMENT AND THE CORPORATE CULTURE

Every organization—big or small, more successful or less successful—has an unmistakable "feel" to it. Just as every individual has a unique personality, so every company has a unique identity, called **corporate culture:** the shared experiences, stories, beliefs, and norms that characterize an organization. This culture helps define the work and business climate that exists in an organization.

corporate culture
The shared experiences, stories, beliefs, and norms that characterize an organization

A strong corporate culture serves several purposes. For one thing, it directs employees' efforts and helps everyone work toward the same goals. Some cultures, for example, stress financial success to the extreme, while others focus more on quality of life. In addition, corporate culture helps newcomers learn accepted behaviors. If financial success is the key to a culture, newcomers quickly learn that they are expected to work long, hard

"I don't know how it started, either. All I know is that it's part of our corporate culture."

hours and that the "winner" is the one who brings in the most revenue. But if quality of life is more fundamental, newcomers learn that it's more acceptable to spend less time at work and that balancing work and nonwork is encouraged.

What is the significance of corporate culture in the business environment today?

Where does a business's culture come from? In some cases it emanates from the days of an organization's founder. Firms such as the Walt Disney Co., Hewlett-Packard, Wal-Mart <www.walmart.com>, and JC Penney <www.jcpenney.com>, for example, still bear the imprint of their founders. In other cases, an organization's culture is forged over a long period of time by a constant and focused business strategy. PepsiCo <www.pepsico.com>, for example, has an achievement-oriented culture tied to its long-standing goal of catching its biggest competitor, Coca-Cola <www.cokecce.com>. Similarly, Apple Computer <www.apple.com> has a sort of "counterculture" culture stemming from its self-styled image as the alternative to the staid IBM <www.ibm.com> corporate model for computer makers.

Communicating the Culture and Managing Change

Corporate culture influences management philosophy, style, and behavior. Managers, therefore, must carefully consider the kind of culture they want for their organization, then work to nourish that culture by communicating with everyone who works there. Wal-Mart, for example, is acutely conscious of the need to spread the message of its culture as it opens new stores in new areas. One of the company's methods is to regularly assign veteran managers to lead employees in new territories. Gordon Bethune delivers weekly messages for all Continental employees to update them on what's going on in the firm; the employees can either listen to it on a closed-circuit broadcast or else call into an 800 telephone number and hear a recorded version at their own convenience.

Communicating the Culture To use a firm's culture to its advantage, managers must accomplish several tasks, all of which hinge on effective communication. First, managers themselves must have a clear understanding of the culture. Second, they must transmit the culture to others in the organization. Thus, communication is one aim in training and orienting newcomers. A clear and meaningful statement of the organization's mission is also a valuable communication tool. Finally, managers can maintain the culture by rewarding and promoting those who understand it and work toward maintaining it.

Managing Change Organizations must sometimes change their cultures. In such cases, they must also communicate the nature of the change to both employees and customers. According to the CEOs of several companies that have undergone radical change in the last decade or so, the process usually goes through three stages:

1. *At the highest level, analysis of the company's environment highlights extensive change as the most effective response to its problems.* This period is typically characterized by conflict and resistance.

Procter & Gamble <www.pg.com> *has been a bastion of conformity for so long that it's been called the home of the "Proctoids"—a place where entrepreneurs and other creative types are systematically squelched. As a result, the Cincinnati-based home-products firm has for several years watched revenues flatten out and famous brands lose market share. Now P&G is betting on bold ideas and new products. A new prototype lab now spends $200 million a year on such projects as testing bandages, cosmetics, and other products on molded body parts.*

2. *Top management begins to formulate a vision of a new company.* Whatever that vision, it must include renewed focus on the activities of competitors and the needs of customers.
3. *The firm sets up new systems for appraising and compensating employees who enforce the firm's new values.* The purpose is to give the new culture solid shape from within the firm.

While some firms like to build on their legacies, others know better. When Gordon Bethune announced his rebuilding plans at Continental, he dubbed it the "Go Forward" program. He stressed that the firm had little to look back on with pride and he wanted everyone to look only to the future. Likewise, Procter & Gamble <www.pg.com> is in the midst of a major overhaul designed to remake its corporate culture into one more suited to today's competitive global business environment. Because its brands have been dominant for such a long time, managers at P&G have been criticized for having tunnel vision—focusing only on the ways they've done things in the past and then trying to repeat them. Procter & Gamble's popular Tide laundry detergent, for example, has been through more than 60 formula upgrades since it was first introduced. A new top-management team, however, is working to shake things up by advocating new approaches, new ways of thinking, and new models of product development.[12]

Continued from page 123

Down East Showdown

Starbucks has become almost synonymous with coffee—people sometimes talk about stopping for some "Starbucks" rather than stopping for coffee. There are currently more than 2,100 Starbucks locations in the United States alone, and the firm plans to open 500 stores in Europe and Asia by the end of 2003. Starbucks also plans to partner with Kraft Foods <www.kraftfoods.com> to distribute its coffee in some 25,000 U.S. grocery stores. To maintain high levels of quality control, Starbucks also refuses to franchise—it owns and operates every one of its stores.

However, a firm like Starbucks is not above reproach. It has been the target of protests at some sites because it buys most of its beans from coffee corporations and plantations in less-developed countries instead of from small independent growers. Other critics take issue with the extra "packaging" that Starbucks uses for a hot cup of coffee—double cups or corrugated bands, large plastic lids, plastic stirring sticks, and so forth. Still others lump Starbucks with other megaretailers, such as Barnes & Noble and Wal-Mart, criticizing them all for overwhelming independent family-owned businesses. Businesses like Maine Roasters Coffee.

So far, Maine Roasters is holding its own in its hometown of Portland, Maine. Rand Smith's strategy of pitching his small company as a David to Starbucks' Goliath has attracted considerable local sympathy. But Smith faces some other problems, too. For one thing, even as he pitches his business as a local, down-home operation, his original business plan called for more than 30 stores spread throughout New England. (As of yet, only a handful have been opened.) Smith openly acknowledges the inherent contradiction in his portrayal of Starbucks and his own vision. He also sees the day when he might very well be interested in selling his company—and thinks Starbucks might be the most logical buyer. In an especially ironic twist, he actually credits Starbucks with boosting sales at his coffee shops by educating consumers about specialty coffees and thus broadening the local market.

Questions for Discussion

1. Describe the management process at a big international company like Starbucks.
2. Describe the management process at a small local business like Maine Roasters Coffee.
3. Compare and contrast goals and strategies at Starbucks and Maine Roasters.
4. What are the types of managers and areas of management that exist in a firm like Starbucks? How about Maine Roasters?
5. What differences, if any, are likely to exist among the key management skills needed at Starbucks and Maine Roasters?
6. What role does corporate culture play in the operations and activities of these two firms?

SUMMARY OF LEARNING OBJECTIVES

1 **Explain the importance of setting *goals* and formulating *strategies* as the starting points of effective management.** *Goals*—the performance targets of an organization—can be *long term, intermediate,* or *short term.* They provide direction for managers, help managers decide how to allocate limited resources, define the corporate culture, and help managers assess performance. *Strategies*—the methods that a company uses to meet its stated goals—involve three major activities: *setting strategic goals, analyzing the organization and its environment,* and *matching the organization and its environment.* These strategies are translated into *strategic, tactical,* and *operational plans.*

2 **Describe the four activities that constitute the *management process.*** *Management* is the process of planning, organizing, directing, and controlling an organization's financial, physical, human, and information resources to achieve the organization's goals. *Planning* means determining what the company needs to do and how best to get it done. *Organizing* means determining how best to arrange a business's resources and the necessary jobs into an overall structure. *Directing* means guiding and motivating employees to meet the firm's objectives. *Controlling* means monitoring the firm's performance to ensure that it is meeting its goals.

3 **Identify *types of managers* by level and area.** Managers can be differentiated in two ways: by level and by area. By level, *top managers* set policies, formulate strategies, and approve decisions. *Middle managers* implement strategies, policies, and decisions. *First-line managers* usually work with and directly supervise employees. Areas of management include human resources, operations, marketing, information, and finance. Managers at all levels may be found in every area of a company.

4 **Describe the five basic *management skills*.** Most managers agree that five basic management skills are necessary for success. *Technical skills* are associated with performing specialized tasks. *Human relations skills* are associated with understanding and getting along with other people. *Conceptual skills* are the abilities to think in the abstract, to diagnose and analyze different situations, and to see beyond present circumstances. *Decision-making skills* allow managers to define problems and to select the best course of action. *Time management skills* refer to the productive use that managers make of their time.

5 **Describe the development and explain the importance of *corporate culture*.** A strong, well-defined culture can help a business reach its goals and can influence management styles. In addition to having a clear understanding of *corporate culture,* managers must be able to communicate it effectively to others. Communication is especially important when organizations find it necessary to make changes in the culture. Top management must establish new values that reflect a vision of a new company, and these values must play a role in appraising and compensating employee performance.

QUESTIONS AND EXERCISES

Questions for Review

1. What are the four main purposes of setting goals in an organization?
2. Identify and explain the three basic steps in strategy formulation.
3. Relate the five basic management skills to the four activities in the management process. For example, which skills are most important in directing?
4. What is corporate culture? How is it formed? How is it sustained?

Questions for Analysis

5. Select any group of which you are a member (your company, your family, or a club or organization, for example). Explain how planning, organizing, directing, and controlling are practiced in that group.
6. Identify managers by level and area at your school, college, or university.
7. In what kind of company would the technical skills of top managers be more important than human relations or conceptual skills? Are there organizations in which conceptual skills are not important?
8. What differences might you expect to find in the corporate cultures of a 100-year-old manufacturing firm based in the Northeast and a 1-year-old e-commerce firm set in Silicon Valley?

Application Exercises

9. Interview the manager at any level of a local company. Identify that manager's job according to level and area. Show how planning, organizing, directing, and controlling are part of this person's job. Inquire about the manager's education and work experience. Which management skills are most important for this manager's job?
10. Compare and contrast the corporate cultures of two companies that do business in most communities. Be sure to choose two companies in the same industry—for example, a Sears department store and a Wal-Mart discount store.

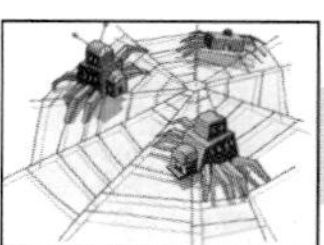

EXPLORING THE WEB

THERE'S COFFEE, AND THEN THERE'S COFFEE

This chapter's opening case profiles Starbucks and a small, locally owned competitor named Maine Roasters Coffee. Start this exercise by visiting and exploring each firm's Web site and then consider the following questions:

www.starbucks.com
www.maineroasters.qpg.com

1. Judging from the two Web sites, what differences in corporate strategies can you determine?
2. List all the things you can learn about each company from its Web site. Precisely, how do the two companies differ? How do you account for the major differences?
3. Does Maine Roasters Coffee's Web site make any reference to Starbucks? Do you think this tactic should change?

4. Again, judging from the Web sites, can you make any conjectures about the corporate cultures at the two firms?
5. What advice, if any, would you give to these two firms to enhance or improve their respective Web sites?

BUILDING YOUR BUSINESS SKILLS

SKILLFUL TALKING

This exercise enhances the following SCANS workplace competencies: demonstrating basic skills, demonstrating thinking skills, exhibiting interpersonal skills, and working with information.

GOAL

To encourage students to appreciate effective speaking as a critical human relations skill.

BACKGROUND

A manager's ability to understand and get along with supervisors, peers, and subordinates is a critical human relations skill. At the heart of this skill, says Harvard University professor of education Sarah McGinty, is the ability to speak with power and control. McGinty defines "powerful speech" in terms of the following characteristics:

- The ability to speak at length and in complete sentences
- The ability to set a conversational agenda
- The ability to deter interruptions
- The ability to argue openly and to express strong opinions about ideas, not people
- The ability to make statements that offer solutions rather than pose questions
- The ability to express humor

Taken together, says McGinty, "all this creates a sense of confidence in listeners."

METHOD

Step 1

Working alone, compare your own personal speaking style with McGinty's description of powerful speech by taping yourself as you speak during a meeting with classmates or during a phone conversation. (Tape both sides of the conversation only if the person to whom you are speaking gives permission.) Listen for the following problems:

- Unfinished sentences
- An absence of solutions
- Too many disclaimers ("I'm not sure I have enough information to say this, but . . .")
- The habit of seeking support from others instead of making definitive statements of personal conviction (saying, "I recommend consolidating the medical and fitness functions," instead of, "As Emily stated in her report, I recommend consolidating the medical and fitness functions")
- Language fillers (saying, "you know," "like," and "um" when you are unsure of your facts or uneasy about expressing your opinion)

Step 2

Join with three or four other classmates to evaluate each other's speaking styles. Finally:

- Have a 10-minute group discussion on the importance of human relations skills in business.
- Listen to other group members and take notes on the "power" content of what you hear.
- Offer constructive criticism by focusing on what speakers say rather than on personal characteristics (say, "Bob, you sympathized with Paul's position, but I still don't know what you think," instead of, "Bob, you sounded like a weakling").

FOLLOW-UP QUESTIONS

1. How do you think the power content of speech affects a manager's ability to communicate? Evaluate some of the ways in which effects may differ among supervisors, peers, and subordinates.
2. How do you evaluate yourself and group members in terms of powerful and powerless speech? List the strengths and weaknesses of the group.
3. Do you agree or disagree with McGinty that business success depends on gaining insight into your own language habits? Explain your answer.

4. In our age of computers and e-mail, why do you think personal presentation continues to be important in management?
5. McGinty believes that power language differs from company to company and that it is linked to the corporate culture. Do you agree, or do you believe that people express themselves in similar ways no matter where they are?

CRAFTING YOUR BUSINESS PLAN

FURNISHING YOURSELF WITH MANAGEMENT SKILLS

THE PURPOSE OF THE ASSIGNMENT

1. To acquaint students with the process of navigating the *Business PlanPro* (*BPP*) software package (Version 4.0).
2. To familiarize students with management-related issues that a firm must address in developing its business plan.
3. To demonstrate how three chapter topics—business goals, business strategies, and management skills—can be integrated as components in the *BPP* planning environment.

ASSIGNMENT

After reading Chapter 5 in the textbook, open the BPP *software* and look around for information about business goals, business strategies, and management skills as they apply to a sample firm:* Furniture Manufacturer *(Willamette Furniture). Then respond to the following questions:*

1. Evaluate Willamette's business objectives. Are they clearly stated? Are they measurable? [Sites to see in *BPP* (for this assignment): In the Plan Outline screen, click on **1.1 Objectives.**]
2. Evaluate Willamette's mission and strategy statements. Do they clearly state how Willamette intends to achieve its purposes? [Sites to see in *BPP:* In the Plan Outline screen, click on **1.0 Executive Summary.** Then click on **1.2 Mission.** Next click on **5.0 Strategy and Implementation** and **5.1 Strategy Pyramids.**]
3. In what areas of the business does each of Willamette's top managers work? [Sites to see in *BPP:* In the Plan Outline screen, click on **6.0 Management Summary.** Now click on **6.1 Organization Structure** and then on **6.2 Management Team.**]
4. What management skills areas are lacking in Willamette's management team? Would you classify the missing skills as technical, human resources, conceptual, or decision-making skills? [Sites to see in *BPP:* In the Plan Outline screen, click on **6.2 Management Team Gaps.**]

FOR YOUR OWN BUSINESS PLAN

5. Suppose you are ready to develop a "statement of mission" for your firm and to formulate its objectives and strategy. To what extent do you first need a clear picture of your firm's products and customers? In developing your business plan, which will you clarify first—mission/objectives/strategy or products/customers? Explain how your answer will affect your business planning process.

*GENERAL TIPS FOR NAVIGATING IN *BPP*

1. Open the *BPP* program, examine the Welcome screen, and click on **Open a Sample Plan.**
2. From the **Open a Sample Plan** dialogue box, click on a sample company name; then click on **Open.**
3. On the Plan Manager screen, click on **Your Plan Outline;** then click on any of the lines (for example, **6.0 Management Summary**).
4. You can always return to the Plan Outline screen by going to the bottom of the screen and clicking on the **Plan Outline** icon.
5. After finishing with one sample company, you can get to the next one by going to the top of the screen and clicking on **File** (on the menu bar). Then beneath that, select **Open Sample Plan.** This will exit you from the current company file and take you to the **Open Sample Plan** dialogue box, where you can select your next sample company.
6. When you are finished, you can close the program by going to the top of the screen and clicking on **File** (on the bar menu). Then beneath that, select **Exit.**

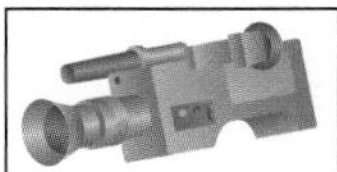

VIDEO EXERCISE

THE MANAGEMENT PICTURE: QUICK TAKES VIDEO (I)

Learning Objectives

The purpose of this video exercise is to help you

1. Appreciate the goal-setting process.
2. Understand the management process.
3. Observe some of the ways in which corporate culture is shaped and communicated.

BACKGROUND INFORMATION

Based on a real company in the same line of business, Quick Takes Video is a fictitious firm that produces corporate, industrial, and training videos and video news releases. It was founded by Hal Boylston and Karen Jarvis, and the management team includes a production coordinator, who oversees the producers responsible for the actual filming and editing of the firm's products. The production coordinator forecasts staff and equipment needs for each shoot, coordinates the use of the company's physical resources, manages producers, and keeps the shoots on schedule and on budget. Planning, organizing, leading, and controlling are all part of the production coordinator's job.

THE VIDEO

John Switzer has just been hired as Quick Takes' new production coordinator, and it is his first day on the job. After settling into his new office, he meets with Boylston and Jarvis to discuss their views of the company's future and to bring up a few questions and suggestions of his own. By attending this meeting, you'll see how the four management functions apply to Switzer's new job.

DISCUSSION QUESTIONS

1. What information about the Quick Takes culture does John receive on his first day? How does he receive it?
2. How does Quick Takes set goals? Could its managers do a better job of goal setting?
3. Which of John's questions most clearly reflect one (or more) of the four management functions?

FOLLOW-UP ASSIGNMENT

Select one of the following managers and determine, in as much detail as you can, the specific tasks that make up the four management activities (planning, organizing, directing, controlling) for each:

- The president of your college or university
- The supervisor of online software support for Dell Computer Corp.
- The manager of a Gap clothing store
- The vice president of manufacturing for Virgin Records
- An entrepreneur setting up an online retail business

FOR FURTHER EXPLORATION

Select a media firm, such as a filmmaker, a recording company, an ad agency, a newspaper, or a magazine. Visit the company's Web site and try to draw some conclusions about its corporate culture. (*Hint:* Find the page for employment opportunities.) What do you notice about the firm's culture? How would you describe it? Is the image here consistent with the impression you get about the company from its products? Is it a culture in which you would like to work? Why or why not?

MASTERING BUSINESS ESSENTIALS

Go to the "Concept of Strategic Management" episode on the Mastering Business Essentials CD-ROM for an interactive, video-enhanced exercise on the efforts of managers at CanGo, an e-business start-up, to draw up a strategic plan for marketing the company's product online.

C h a p t e r

6

Organizing the Business Enterprise

After reading this chapter, you should be able to:

1. ***Discuss*** the elements that influence a firm's *organizational structure.*

2. ***Explain*** *specialization* and *departmentalization* as the building blocks of organizational structure.

3. ***Distinguish*** between *responsibility, authority, delegation,* and *accountability,* and explain the differences between decision making in *centralized* and *decentralized organizations.*

4. ***Explain*** the differences between *functional, divisional, matrix,* and *international organizational structures.*

5. ***Describe*** the *informal organization* and discuss *intrapreneuring.*

Forging e-Connections

Construction is one of the world's oldest jobs. Ever since they lived in caves, people have been continually crafting newer, bigger, safer, and more functional places to live, work, and play. But if any industry seems tailor-made for the Internet, it just might be construction.

Construction has always been a job that encourages specialization. Very different kinds of skills and expertise are needed to create a foundation from concrete, erect walls from brick, wood, or steel, fabricate networks of pipes for plumbing and wire for electricity, construct a weatherproof roof, and finish off an interior with a high-quality appearance. There are even craft specialists within specialties—building a wall from steel, for example, or a roof from shingles is far different from building a wooden wall or a metal roof.

Putting all these pieces together, then, can be a big and complicated job. Consider just a few of the complexities in building a simple wood-frame house. Shortly after the concrete foundation has been poured and set, a supplier should deliver a load of wooden studs for constructing the frame. If the wood is delivered too early, it may get damaged, scattered, or even stolen. If it comes too late, delays will result. Quantity is also important: Too much wood means needless cost overruns, and too little wood means more delays. The contractor faces the same issues when it comes to the framing crew: They need to arrive on a certain day and finish on a certain day. Complicating things even further is the homeowner. As the project takes shape, the homeowner may decide to move a wall, add a door, or change the color of the walls.

In short, someone has to organize the overall process, ensuring—to some extent—that the right materials in the right quantities and the right people are at the job site at the right time. This individual is generally called the *contractor.* Each one of the specialists hired to perform certain specific tasks required by the overall project—roofers, plumbers, electricians, painters, and so forth—is called a *subcontractor.* Construction, says Kent Allen, a Boston e-commerce consultant, "has always been a very fragmented industry because it's so local."

"Construction has always been a very fragmented industry because it's so local."

—e-commerce consultant Kent Allen

All told, a house like the one we just described will probably require a dozen or more subcontractors. But what about a major construction project—a high-rise building or an office complex? These projects will call for hundreds of separate subcontractors working at different times over periods spanning several months or even years. The complexities of organizing such a massive project are significant indeed. A well-organized project can make the difference between profit and a loss for the contractor.

Until recently, organizing most building projects relied on paper—architects drew up blueprints, contractors drew up schedules, and paperwork flowed freely between contractors and subcontractors as materials were requested and ordered and work completed and billed. But a simple change—a redesigned doorway—or one delay—one late order of materials—could have a domino effect on dozens of other subcontractors. On top of everything else, someone had to monitor the project continually, make scheduling and delivery adjustments as needed, and then notify suppliers and subcontractors.

Slowly but surely, however, Internet technology is creeping into the construction industry. As it does, it's revolutionizing the way contractors and subcontractors work and interact with one another. It's also showing signs of enormous potential for lowering costs, shortening schedules, and improving overall efficiency. Big construction firms like the Turner Corp. <**www.turnerconstruction.com**> and the Bechtel Group <**www.bechtel.com**> have started partnering with such e-commerce companies as Bidcom <**www.bidcom.com**> and Cephren <**www.cephren.com**> to use Web technology to communicate with suppliers and subcontractors.

Now blueprints can be posted online, and suppliers and subcontractors can review their respective parts of the project online, including scheduling details. e-mail can be sent to everyone involved, work schedules issued, and bid requests sent to potential suppliers, all with the push of a button or click of a mouse. The advent of newer handheld computers is also accelerating change because they allow contractors, subcontractors, supervisors, and workers to access information at the construction project.

Our opening story continues on page 169

For companies in the construction industry, the issues involved in organizing projects and creating networks can affect operations and profits in dramatic ways. Whether a contractor or subcontractor employs five people or 50,000, a number of fundamental organizational issues determine how well a business will function. In this chapter, we consider the elements of business organization and the basic structures that firms typically use.

By focusing on the learning objectives of this chapter, you will better understand the importance of business organization and the ways in which both formal and informal aspects of its structure affect the decisions that a business makes.

WHAT IS ORGANIZATIONAL STRUCTURE?

What do we mean by the term *organizational structure?* Consider a simple analogy. In some ways, a business is like an automobile. All cars have engines, four wheels, fenders, and other structural components. They all have passenger compartments, storage areas, and various operating systems (fuel, braking, climate control). Although each component has a distinct purpose, it must also work in accord with the others. In addition, although the ways they look and fit may vary widely, all automobiles have the same basic components. Similarly, all businesses have common structural and operating components, each composed of a series of *jobs to be done* and each with a *specific overall purpose.* From company to company these components look different and fit together differently, but in every organization components have the same fundamental purpose—each must perform its own function while working in concert with the others.

Although all organizations feature the same basic elements, each must develop the structure that is most appropriate for it. What works for Texas Instruments will not work for Shell Oil, Amazon.com, or the U.S. Department of Justice. The structure of the American Red Cross will probably not work for Union Carbide or the University of Minnesota. We define **organizational structure** as the specification of the jobs to be done within an organization and the ways in which those jobs relate to one another.

organizational structure Specification of the jobs to be done within an organization and the ways in which they relate to one another

Determinants of Organization

How is an organization's structure determined? Does it happen by chance, or is there some logic that managers use to create structure? Does it develop by some combination of circumstance and strategy? Ideally, managers carefully assess a variety of important factors as they plan for and then create a structure that will allow their organization to function efficiently.

Many elements work together to determine an organization's structure. Chief among these are the organization's *purpose, mission,* and *strategy.* A dynamic and rapidly growing enterprise, for example, achieved that position because of its purpose and successful strategies for achieving it. Such a firm will need a structure that contributes to flexibility and growth. A stable organization with only modest growth will function best with a different structure.

Size, technology, and changes in environmental circumstances also affect structure. A large manufacturer operating in a strongly competitive environment—say, Boeing or Hewlett-Packard—requires a different structure than a local barbershop or video store. Moreover, even after a structure has been created, it is rarely free from tinkering—or even outright re-creation. Most organizations change their structures on an almost continuing basis.

As we saw in Chapter 5, organizing is a function of managerial planning. As such, it is conducted with an equal awareness of both a firm's external and internal environments. Since it was first incorporated in 1903, Ford Motor Co. <www.ford.com> has undergone literally dozens of major structural changes, hundreds of moderate changes, and thousands of minor changes. In the last 10 years alone, Ford has initiated several

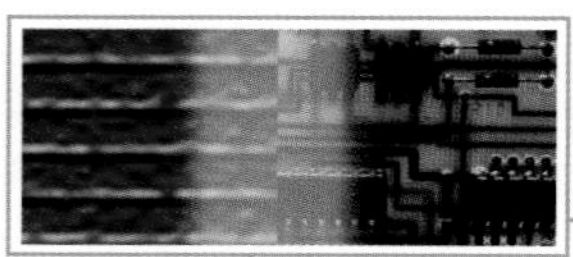

It's a WiredWorld

• Hot-Wiring Ford

Imagine going to a Web page to buy a new car. You specify the car online just as you want it—color, engine size, options—and electronically negotiate the price. Then you click "ok." Your simple action transmits a slew of information directly to a local dealer, to a financial broker, to your insurance agent, to the factory that will build your car, to the suppliers who provide the components, and to the Ford designers working on next year's models. A few days later, your new car is delivered to your driveway.

Fantasy? Not if Ford CEO Jacques Nasser has his way. Nasser and his managers at Ford are rushing headlong toward his vision of the automobile-buying future. To get there, Nasser is convinced that Ford must systematically absorb the Internet into every element of its organization. Experts agree that Ford stands at the forefront of old-line manufacturers who are working to absorb Web technology. Recall, for instance, our "Wired World" box in Chapter 1, where we described Ford's participation in an electronic marketplace for auto parts and supplies.

Another major initiative at Ford rests on its comprehensive and integrated corporate intranet. One official goes so far as to describe it as the backbone of Ford's business today. To weave one major strand in the Ford intranet, managers are strongly encouraged to create all reports on line. Nasser wants to deliver a clear message: namely, Ford manages itself on the intranet and interacts with stakeholders on the Internet.

Nasser also believes that if Ford is to embrace the Internet fully, each and every one of its employees must "think Internet." Toward that end, Ford announced in early 2000 that it would provide all of its 350,000 global employees with a home computer, a printer, and $5 a month for Internet access.

Ford is also working to integrate Web technology into its cars. Designers are trying to figure out the best way to wire cars for e-mail and news, voice-recognition systems, and satellite phone services. Nasser and Ford are clearly gambling on the future. If they're right, they may well become the car of choice for the Internet generation.

major structural changes. In 1994, the firm announced a major restructuring plan called *Ford 2000,* which was intended to integrate all of Ford's vast international operations into a single, unified structure by the year 2000. By 1998, however, midway through implementation of the grand plan, top Ford executives announced major modifications indicating that (1) additional changes would be made, (2) some previously planned changes would not be made, and (3) some recently realigned operations would be changed again. In early 1999, managers announced yet another sweeping set of changes intended to eliminate corporate bureaucracy, speed decision making, and improve communication and working relationships among people at different levels of the organization.[1] The "Wired World" box in this chapter shows how Ford's e-commerce initiatives are affecting its structure in still other ways.

Chain of Command

organization chart
Diagram depicting a company's structure and showing employees where they fit into its operations

chain of command
Reporting relationships within a company

Most businesses prepare **organization charts** to clarify structure and to show employees where they fit into a firm's operations. Figure 6.1 is an organization chart for Contemporary Landscape Services, Inc. <www2.cy-net/~clsinc/cls>, a small but thriving business in Bryan, Texas. Each box in the chart represents a job. The solid lines define the **chain of command,** or *reporting relationships,* within the company. For example, the retail shop, nursery, and landscape operations managers all report to the owner and president, Mark Ferguson. Within the landscape operation is one manager for residential accounts and another for commercial accounts. Similarly, there are other managers in the retail shop and the nursery.

The organization charts of large firms are far more complex and include individuals at many more levels than those shown in Figure 6.1. Size prevents many large firms from drawing charts that include all their managers. Typically, they create one organization chart showing overall corporate structure and separate charts for each division.

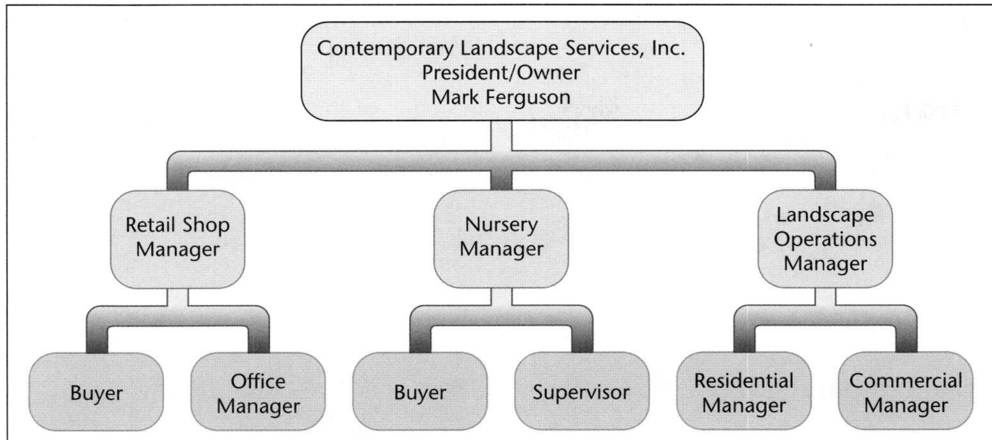

Figure 6.1
The Organization Chart

THE BUILDING BLOCKS OF ORGANIZATIONAL STRUCTURE

The first step in developing the structure of any business, large or small, involves two activities:

- *Specialization:* determining who will do what
- *Departmentalization:* determining how people performing certain tasks can best be grouped together

These two activities are the building blocks of all business organizations.[2]

Specialization

The process of identifying the specific jobs that need to be done and designating the people who will perform them leads to **job specialization.** In a sense, all organizations have only one major job, such as making cars (Ford), selling finished goods to consumers (Wal-Mart), or providing telecommunications services (AT&T). Usually, the job is more complex in nature. For example, the job of Chaparral Steel <www.txi.com/steel> is converting scrap steel, such as wrecked automobiles, into finished steel products such as beams and reinforcement bars.

job specialization
The process of identifying the specific jobs that need to be done and designating the people who will perform them

To perform this one overall job, managers actually break it down, or specialize it, into several smaller jobs. Thus, some workers transport the scrap steel to the company's mill in Midlothian, Texas. Others operate shredding equipment before turning raw materials over to the workers who then melt them into liquid form. Other specialists oversee the flow of the liquid into molding equipment in which it is transformed into new products. Finally, other workers are responsible for moving finished products to a holding area before they are shipped out to customers. When the overall job of the organization is thus broken down, workers can develop real expertise in their jobs, and employees can better coordinate their work with that done by others.

Specialization and Growth In a very small organization the owner may perform every job. As the firm grows, however, so does the need to specialize jobs so that others can perform them. To see how specialization can evolve in an organization, consider the case of the Walt Disney Co. <www.disney.go.com>. When Walt Disney first opened his studio, he and his brother Roy did everything. For example, when they created the very first animated feature, *Steamboat Willy,* they wrote the story, drew the pictures, transferred the pictures to film, provided the voices, and then went out and sold the cartoon to theater operators. Today, by sharp contrast, a Disney animated feature is made possible only through the efforts of hundreds of creators. The job of one cartoonist may be to draw the face of a single character throughout an entire feature. Another artist may be charged with erasing stray pencil marks inadvertently made by other illustrators. People other than artists are responsible for the subsequent operations that turn individual animated cells into a moving picture or for the marketing of the finished product.

Job specialization is a natural part of organizational growth. It also has certain advantages. For example, specialized jobs are learned more easily and can be performed more efficiently than nonspecialized jobs, and it is also easier to replace people who leave an organization. However, jobs at lower levels of the organization are especially susceptible to overspecialization. If such jobs become too narrowly defined, employees may become bored and careless, derive less satisfaction from their jobs, and lose sight of their roles in the organization.

Departmentalization

departmentalization
Process of grouping jobs into logical units

profit center
Separate company unit responsible for its own costs and profits

After jobs are specialized, they must be grouped into logical units, which is the process of **departmentalization.** Departmentalized companies benefit from the division of activities. Control and coordination are narrowed and made easier, and top managers can see more easily how various units are performing.

Departmentalization allows the firm to treat a department as a **profit center**—a separate unit responsible for its own costs and profits. Thus, Sears <www.sears.com> can calculate the profits it generates from men's clothing, appliances, home furnishings, and every other department within a given store. Managers can then use this information in making decisions about advertising and promotional events, space allocation, and so forth.

In an effort to improve competitiveness, Lucent Technologies <www.lucent.com>, the world's largest telephone equipment maker, recently created four new departments. These departments represent activities that have grown so large within existing departmental arrangements that they now warrant separate units. One department will focus on optical networking; another on wireless communications; a third will be responsible for semiconductor operations; and a fourth will address Lucent's e-business initiatives. Lucent managers believe that these new departments will sharpen the company's focus on these four high-growth areas.[3] "This new organization," explains one Lucent executive, "will allow Lucent to move forward in a more aggressive and flexible way as we continue to expand into new markets."

Obviously, managers do not departmentalize jobs randomly. They group them logically, according to some common thread or purpose. In general, departmentalization may occur along *customer, product, process, geographic,* or *functional lines* (or any combination of these).

customer departmentalization
Departmentalization according to types of customers likely to buy a given product

Customer Departmentalization

Stores such as Sears and Macy's <www.macys.com> are divided into departments—a men's department, a women's department, a luggage department, and so on. Each department targets a specific customer category (men, women, people who want to buy luggage). **Customer departmentalization** makes shopping easier by providing identifiable store segments. Thus, a customer shopping for a baby's playpen can bypass Lawn and Garden Supplies and head straight for Children's Furniture. Stores can also group products in locations designated for deliveries, special sales, and other service-oriented purposes. In general, the store is more efficient and customers get better service because salespeople tend to specialize and gain expertise in their departments.

product departmentalization
Departmentalization according to specific products being created

Product Departmentalization

Manufacturers and service providers often opt for **product departmentalization**—dividing an organization according to the specific product or service being created. This approach is consistent with what Lucent Technologies has done. For example, the wireless communications department will focus on cellular telephones and services, while the optical networking department will focus on fiber optical and other cable and communications technologies. Because each of these represents a defined group of products or services, Lucent managers hope that each department will be able to focus on its product line in a clear and defined way.

WebConnection

www.ibm.com/services/e-business/

IBM's Global Services unit provides a wide range of Internet-related services, including business-consulting, systems-management, and outsourcing services. Recent additions to the product line include privacy consulting and an online service specially designed for small and midsize businesses. IBM still builds and sells computers and software, but the growth of such units as Global Services reflects some dramatic changes in the company's approach to functional organization.

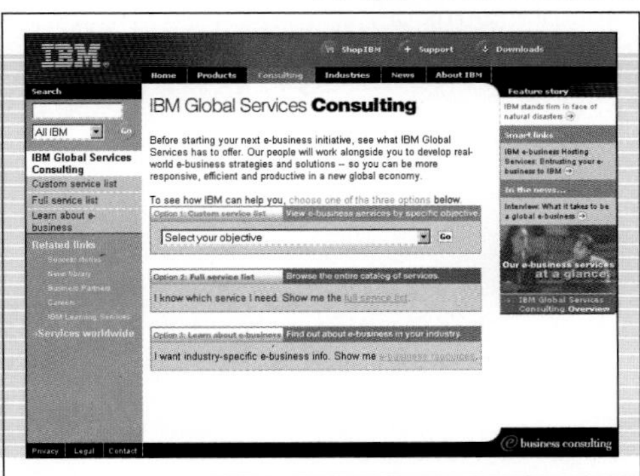

Process Departmentalization Other manufacturers favor **process departmentalization,** in which the organization is divided according to production processes. This principle is logical for the pickle maker Vlasic <www.vlasic.com>, which has separate departments to transform cucumbers into fresh-packed pickles, pickles cured in brine, and relishes. Cucumbers destined to become fresh-packed pickles must be packed into jars immediately, covered with a solution of water and vinegar, and prepared for sale. Those slated for brined pickles must be aged in brine solution before packing. Relish cucumbers must be minced and combined with a host of other ingredients. Each process requires different equipment and worker skills.

process departmentalization Departmentalization according to production processes used to create a good or service

Geographic Departmentalization Some firms are divided according to the areas of the country, or the world, that they serve. Levi Strauss, for instance, has one division for the United States <www.levi.com>, one for Europe <www.eu.levi.com>, one for the Asia Pacific region <www.levi.co.kr>, and one for Latin America <www.levi.com/lar>. Within the United States, **geographic departmentalization** is common among utilities. Pacific Power and Light is organized as four geographic departments—Southwestern, Columbia Basin, Mid-Oregon, and Wyoming.

geographic departmentalization Departmentalization according to areas served by a business

Functional Departmentalization Many service and manufacturing companies, especially smaller ones, develop departments according to a group's functions or activities—a form of organization known as **functional departmentalization.** Such firms typically have production, marketing and sales, human resources, and accounting and finance departments. Departments may be further subdivided. For example, the marketing department might be divided geographically or into separate staffs for market research and advertising.

functional departmentalization Departmentalization according to groups' functions or activities

Because different forms of departmentalization have different advantages, larger companies tend to adopt different types of departmentalization for various levels. The company illustrated in Figure 6.2 uses functional departmentalization at the top level. At the middle level, production is divided along geographic lines. At a lower level, marketing is departmentalized by product group.

ESTABLISHING THE DECISION-MAKING HIERARCHY

After jobs have been appropriately specialized and grouped into manageable departments, the next step in organizing is to establish the decision-making hierarchy. That is, managers must explicitly define reporting relationships among positions so everyone will know who has responsibility for various decisions and operations. The goal is to figure out how to structure and stabilize the organizational framework so that everyone works together to achieve common goals. Companies vary greatly in the ways in which they handle the delegation of tasks, responsibility, and authority.

Figure 6.2
Multiple Forms of Departmentalization

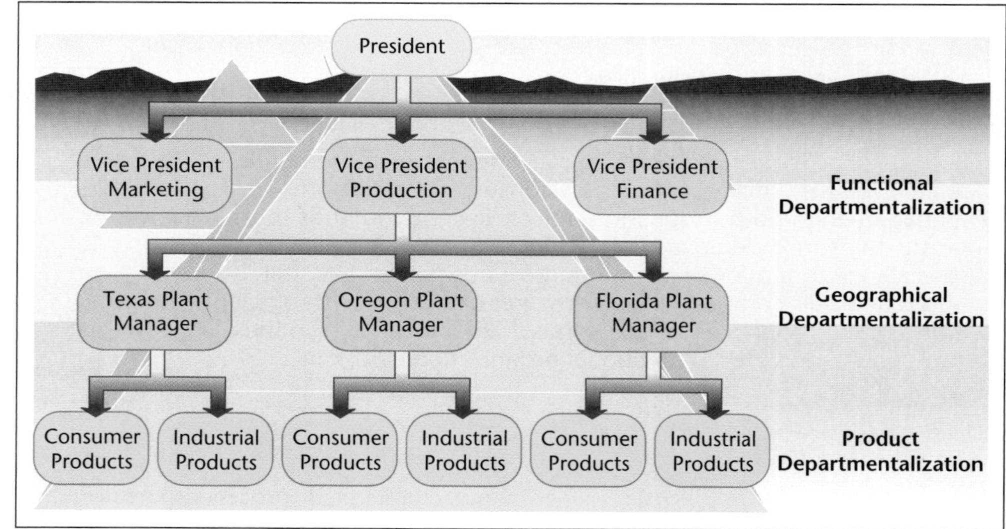

A major question that must be asked about any organization is: *Who makes which decisions?* The answer almost never focuses on an individual or even on a small group. The more accurate answer usually refers to the decision-making hierarchy. Generally speaking, the development of this hierarchy results from a three-step process:

1. *Assigning tasks:* determining who can make decisions and specifying how they should be made
2. *Performing tasks:* implementing decisions that have been made
3. *Distributing authority:* determining whether the organization is to be centralized or decentralized

For example, when Jack Greenberg took over as CEO of McDonald's <www.mcdonalds.com>, he immediately implemented several changes in the firm's decision-making hierarchy. McDonald's has always been, and continues to be, highly centralized. But Greenberg restructured both the company's decision-making process and its operations. He reduced staff at corporate headquarters in Oak Brook, Illinois, and established five regional offices throughout the United States. Now many decisions are made at the regional level. Greenberg also clamped a lid on domestic growth and increased international expansion. In addition, he purchased stakes in three new restaurant chains with an eye on expansion: Donatos Pizza <www.donatos.com>, Chipotle Mexican Grill <www.chipotle.com>, and Aroma, a British coffee chain. Greenberg then installed four new managers, one to head up international operations and the others to oversee the three new restaurant partner groups. All four of these executives report directly to Greenberg.[4] Why the changes? "Maybe it was arrogance," says Greenberg. "For 40 years, all we did was open restaurants. That's not enough anymore."

> ***"For 40 years, all we did was open restaurants. That's not enough anymore."***
> —*McDonald's CEO Jack Greenberg*

Assigning Tasks: Responsibility and Authority

The question of who is *supposed* to do what and who is entitled to do what in an organization is complex. In any company with more than one person, individuals must work out agreements about responsibilities and authority. **Responsibility** is the duty to perform an assigned task. **Authority** is the power to make the decisions necessary to complete the task.

responsibility
Duty to perform an assigned task

authority
Power to make the decisions necessary to complete a task

For example, imagine a midlevel buyer for Macy's department store who encounters an unexpected opportunity to make a large purchase at an extremely good price. Assume that an immediate decision is absolutely necessary—a decision that this buyer has no authority to make without confirmation from above. The company's policies on delegation and authority are inconsistent because the buyer is *responsible* for purchasing the clothes that will be sold in the upcoming season, but lacks the *authority* to make the needed purchases.

Performing Tasks: Delegation and Accountability

Trouble occurs when appropriate levels of responsibility and authority are not clearly delineated in the working relationships between managers and subordinates. Here, the issues become delegation and accountability. **Delegation** begins when a manager assigns a task to a subordinate. **Accountability** falls to the subordinate, who must then complete the task. If tasks are effectively delegated and performed, the organization will function smoothly. But if the subordinate does not perform the assigned task as assigned—perhaps doing a poor job or getting the work done too late—problems can arise. The work unit may suffer and the employee's performance abilities or motivation called into question.

delegation
Assignment of a task, responsibility, or authority by a manager to a subordinate

accountability
Liability of subordinates for accomplishing tasks assigned by managers

Fear of Delegating Unfortunately, many managers actually have trouble delegating tasks to others. This is especially true in small businesses where the owner-manager started out doing everything. Delegating responsibility has been especially difficult for Rene Reiser, owner of Paradise Candles, a three-employee candle manufacturer in Idaho. Reiser believes that it was her personal creative style that built her company. It took her years to develop a specialized production process, and she has found it hard to let others take charge of it. "Eventually," she concedes, "I'll have to teach someone else to do it. It makes me nervous, and I wonder, 'Will they do it in my style?' "[5]

Experts pinpoint certain reasons why some small-business managers may have trouble delegating effectively:

- The feeling that employees can never do anything as well as you can
- The fear that something will go wrong if someone else takes over a job
- The lack of time for long-range planning because you are bogged down in day-to-day operations
- The sense of being in the dark about industry trends and competitive products because of the time you devote to day-to-day operations

To overcome these tendencies, small-business owners must begin by admitting that they can never go back to running the entire show and that they can in fact prosper—with the help of their employees—if they learn to let go. This problem, however, isn't always confined to small businesses. Some managers in big companies also don't delegate as much or as well as they should. There are also several reasons for this problem:

- The fear that subordinates don't really know how to do the job
- The fear that a subordinate might "show the manager up" in front of others by doing a superb job
- The desire to keep as much control as possible over how things are done
- A simple lack of ability as to how to effectively delegate to others

The remedies in these instances are a bit different. First, all managers should recognize that they can't do everything themselves. Second, if subordinates can't do a job, they should be trained so that they can assume more responsibility in the future. Third, managers should actually recognize that if a subordinate performs well it also reflects favorably on the manager. Finally, a manager who simply doesn't know how to delegate might need specialized training in how to divide up and assign tasks to others.

Distributing Authority: Centralization and Decentralization

Delegation involves a specific relationship between managers and subordinates. Most businesses must also make decisions about general patterns of authority throughout the company. This pattern may be largely centralized or decentralized (or, usually, somewhere in between).

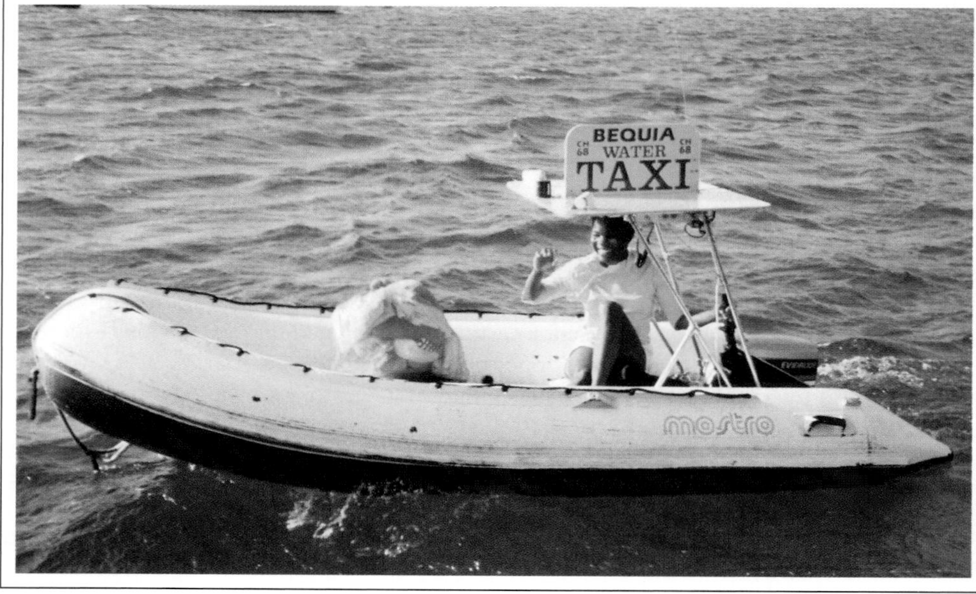

Daffodil Harris's first business required only a dinghy and a washing machine: She ran a laundry business out of an open boat, picking up and returning soggy clothes from yachts moored at the Caribbean island of Bequia. Eight years later, she was also operating Daffodil's Marine Service (to rent and repair equipment), a grocery store, a Chinese take-out restaurant, and Bequia Water Taxi. She now has 23 employees, but the multidivisional enterprise, like many small businesses, remains highly centralized, with Harris personally overseeing all of her service operations.

centralized organization Organization in which most decision-making authority is held by upper-level management

decentralized organization Organization in which a great deal of decision-making authority is delegated to levels of management at points below the top

flat organizational structure Characteristic of decentralized companies with relatively few layers of management and relatively wide spans of control

tall organizational structure Characteristic of centralized companies with multiple layers of management and relatively narrow spans of control

In a **centralized organization,** most decision-making authority is held by upper-level managers. Most lower-level decisions must be approved by upper management before they can be implemented. As we noted earlier, McDonald's practices centralization as a way to maintain standardization. All restaurants must follow precise steps in buying products and making and packaging burgers and other menu items. Most advertising is handled at the corporate level, and any local advertising must be approved by a regional manager. Restaurants even have to follow prescribed schedules for facilities' maintenance and upgrades like floor polishing and parking lot cleaning.[6] Centralized authority is also typical of small businesses.

As a company gets larger, increasingly more decisions must be made; thus, the company tends to adopt a more decentralized pattern. In a **decentralized organization,** much decision-making authority is delegated to levels of management at various points below the top. The purpose of decentralization is to make a company more responsive to its environment by breaking the company into more manageable units, ranging from product lines to independent businesses. Reducing top-heavy bureaucracies is also a common goal. Jack Welch, CEO of General Electric <www.ge.com/businesses>, is a longtime proponent of decentralized management. As he puts it, "If you don't let managers make their own decisions, you're never going to be anything more than a one-person business."

Tall and Flat Organizations Related to the concept of centralized or decentralized authority are the concepts of tall and flat organizational structures. With relatively fewer layers of management, decentralized firms tend to reflect a **flat organizational structure** like that of the hypothetical law firm described in Figure 6.3(a). In contrast, companies with centralized authority systems typically require multiple layers of management and thus **tall organizational structures.** As you can see from Figure 6.3(b), the United States Army is a good example. Because information, whether upward or downward bound, must pass through so many organizational layers, tall structures are prone to delays in information flow.

"If you don't let managers make their own decisions, you're never going to be anything more than a one-person business."

—Jack Welch, CEO of General Electric

As organizations grow in size it is both normal and necessary that they become at least somewhat taller. For instance, a small firm with only an owner-manager and a few employees is likely to have two layers—the owner-manager and the employees who report to that person. But as the firm grows, more layers will be needed. Born Information Services <www.born.com>, for instance, is a small consulting firm created and run by

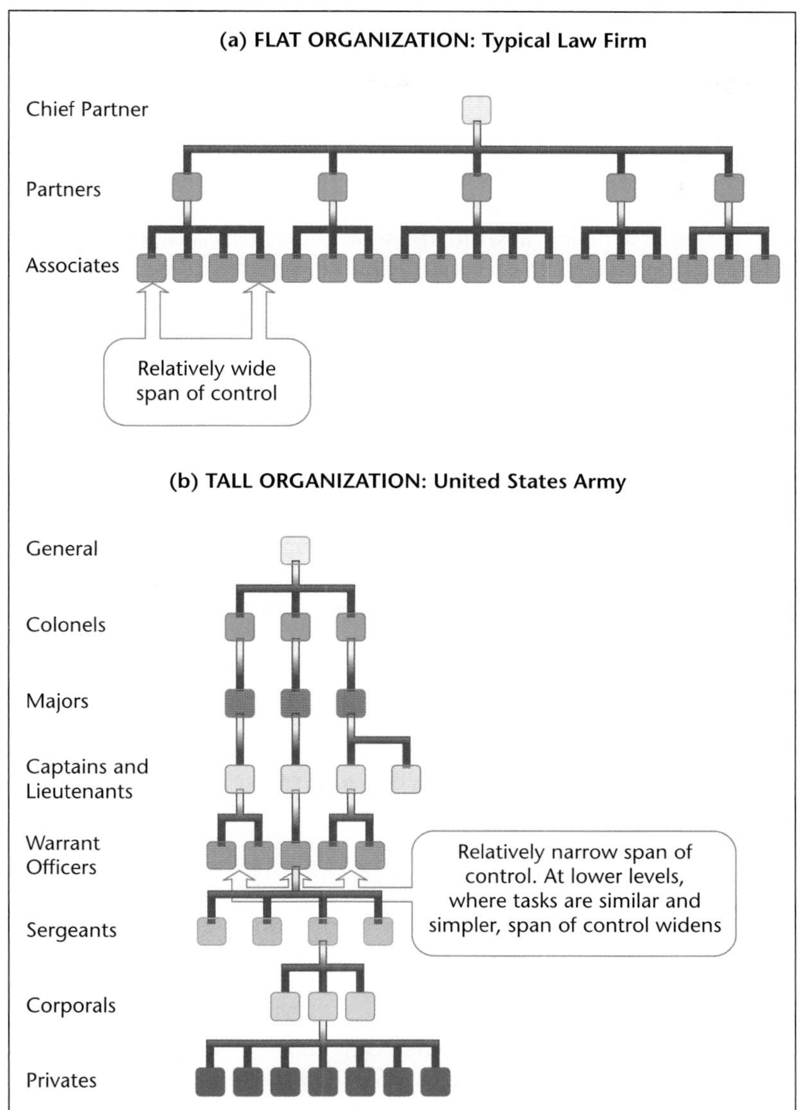

Figure 6.3
Organizational Structure and Span of Control

Rick Born. At first, all his employees reported to him. But when the size of his firm had grown to more than 20 people, Born knew that he needed help in supervising and coordinating projects. As a result, he added a layer of management consisting of what he termed "staff managers" to serve as project coordinators. This move freed up time for Born to seek new business clients.[7] Like other managers, however, Born must ensure that he has only the number of layers his firm needs. Too few layers can create chaos and inefficiency, while too many layers can create rigidity and bureaucracy.

Span of Control As you can see from Figure 6.3, the distribution of authority in an organization also affects the number of people who work for any individual manager. In a flat organizational structure, the number of people managed by one supervisor—the manager's **span of control**—is usually wide. In tall organizations, span of control tends to be relatively narrower. Span of control, however, depends on many factors. Employees' abilities and the supervisor's managerial skills help determine whether span of control is wide or narrow, as do the similarity and simplicity of tasks performed under the manager's supervision and the extent to which they are interrelated.

span of control
Number of people supervised by one manager

If lower-level managers are given more decision-making authority, their supervisors will thus have less work to do because some of the decisions they previously made will be transferred to their subordinates. By the same token, these managers may then be able to oversee and coordinate the work of more subordinates, resulting in an increased span of control. We have already seen that at McDonald's, the creation of five regional offices freed up time for the CEO, Jack Greenberg. In turn, reorganization allowed him to then create four new executive positions, one to oversee international expansion and the others to work with new restaurant partners.

Similarly, when several employees perform either the same simple task or a group of interrelated tasks, a wide span of control is possible and often desirable. For instance, because all the jobs are routine, one supervisor may well control an entire assembly line. Moreover, each task depends on another. If one station stops, everyone stops. Having one supervisor ensures that all stations receive equal attention and function equally well.

In contrast, when jobs are more diversified or prone to change, a narrow span of control is preferable. In Racine, Wisconsin, for example, the Case Corp. <www.casecorp.com> factory makes farm tractors exclusively to order in five to six weeks. Farmers can select from among a wide array of options, including engines, tires, power trains, and even a CD player. A wide assortment of machines and processes are used to construct each tractor. Although workers are highly skilled operators of their assigned machines, each machine is different. In this kind of setup, the complexities of each machine and the advanced skills needed by each operator mean that one supervisor can oversee only a small number of employees.[8]

Three Forms of Authority

Whatever type of structure a company develops it must decide who will have authority over whom. As individuals are delegated responsibility and authority in a firm, a complex web of interactions develops. These interactions may take one of three forms of authority: *line, staff,* or *committee and team.* Like departmentalization, all three forms may be found in a given company, especially a large one.

line authority
Organizational structure in which authority flows in a direct chain of command from the top of the company to the bottom

line department
Department directly linked to the production and sales of a specific product

staff authority
Authority based on expertise that usually involves advising line managers

staff members
Advisors and counselors who aid line departments in making decisions but do not have the authority to make final decisions

Line Authority The type of authority that flows up and down the chain of command is **line authority.** Most companies rely heavily on **line departments**—those directly linked to the production and sales of specific products. For example, Clark Equipment Corporation has a division that produces forklifts and small earthmovers. In this division, line departments include purchasing, materials handling, fabrication, painting, and assembly (all of which are directly linked to production) along with sales and distribution (both of which are directly linked to sales).

Each line department is essential to an organization's success. Line employees are the doers and producers in a company. If any line department fails to complete its task, the company cannot sell and deliver finished goods. Thus, the authority delegated to line departments is important. A bad decision by the manager in one department can hold up production for an entire plant. Say, for example, that the painting department manager at Clark Equipment changes a paint application on a batch of forklifts, which then show signs of peeling paint. The batch will have to be repainted (and perhaps partially reassembled) before the machines can be shipped.

Staff Authority Most companies also rely on **staff authority,** which is based on special expertise and usually involves counseling and advising line managers. Common **staff members** include specialists in areas such as law, accounting, and human resource management. A corporate attorney, for example, may be asked to advise the marketing department as it prepares a new contract with the firm's advertising agency. Legal staff, however, do not actually make decisions that affect how the marketing department does its job. Staff members, therefore, aid line departments in making decisions but do not have the authority to make final decisions.

Typically, the separation between line authority and staff responsibility is clearly delineated. As Figure 6.4 shows, this separation is usually shown in organization charts by

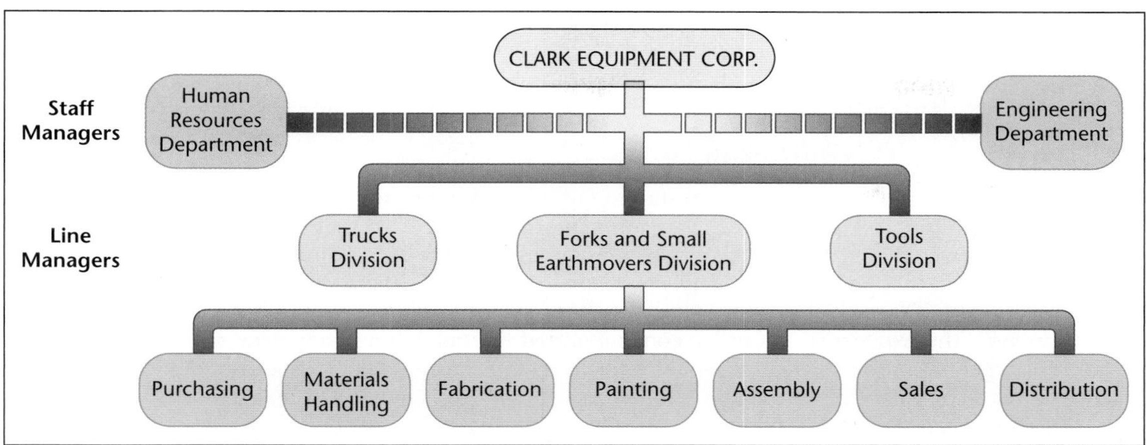

Figure 6.4
Line and Staff Organization

solid lines (line authority) and dotted lines (staff responsibility). It may help to understand this separation by remembering that whereas staff members generally provide services to management, line managers are directly involved in producing the firm's products.

Committee and Team Authority Recently, more and more organizations have started to use **committee and team authority**—authority granted to committees or work teams that play central roles in the firm's daily operations. A committee, for example, may consist of top managers from several major areas. If the work of the committee is especially important, and if the committee will be working together for an extended time, the organization may even grant it special authority as a decision-making body that goes beyond the individual authority possessed by each of its members.

committee and team authority
Authority granted to committees or work teams involved in a firm's daily operations

At the operating level, many firms today are also using work teams—groups of operating employees who are empowered to plan and organize their own work and to perform that work with a minimum of supervision. As with permanent committees, the organization will usually find it beneficial to grant special authority to work teams so that they may function more effectively.

BASIC FORMS OF ORGANIZATIONAL STRUCTURE

Organizations can structure themselves in almost an infinite number of ways—according to specialization, for example, or departmentalization or the decision-making hierarchy. Nevertheless, it is possible to identify four basic forms of organizational structure that reflect the general trends followed by most firms: *functional, divisional, matrix,* and *international.*

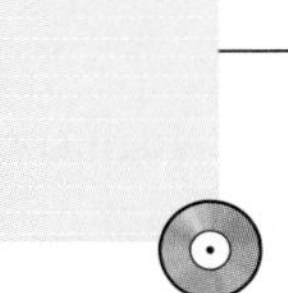

What do you feel is the best field to enter today for job success? Which field offers the best chance of employment and rapid advancement?

Functional Organization

Functional organization is the approach to organizational structure used by most small to medium-size firms. Such organizations are usually structured around basic business functions (marketing, operations, finance). Thus, within the company there is a marketing department, an operations department, and a finance department. The benefits of this approach include specialization within functional areas and smoother coordination among them. Experts with specialized training, for example, are hired to work in the marketing department, which handles all marketing for the firm. The organization structure at Garden.com is shown and discussed in this chapter's "Life Cycle of an e-Business" box.

functional organization
Form of business organization in which authority is determined by the relationships between group functions and activities

Life Cycle of an e-Business

Structuring Garden.com

Like most small businesses, Garden.com started out with a functional structure. Based on their own individual strengths and preferences, the three founding partners decided that Jamie O'Neill would head up operations as Chief Operating Officer and Lisa Sharples would take responsibility for marketing as Chief Marketing Officer. Cliff Sharples, meanwhile, assumed the role of Chief Executive Officer. They also hired Jana Wilson as CFO, or Chief Financial Officer, to head up the firm's finance function (which also included accounting). The experience of Garden.com supported the opinion of many experts that the functional form of organization offers clear advantages for most small firms, including both traditional companies and newer e-commerce businesses.

But as you can see in the accompanying organization chart, Garden.com eventually changed its organizational structure as it grew. Specifically, the firm retained its basic functional organization while adding three new divisions. One division, which was responsible for magazine and catalog publishing, was run by Doug Jimerson (Editor in Chief and Vice President, Publishing). A second division focused on business issues involving other media and was headed by Joel Toner (Vice President, Media Business Development). Brad Clark (Vice President, Enterprise Development) was in charge of the enterprise development division, a unit devoted to developing new business initiatives. This approach allowed the firm to maintain its functional focus while simultaneously branching out into new areas via self-contained divisions. Moreover, while there were other hierarchical layers within each function and division, the firm remained relatively flat and decentralized.

The informal organization also played a major role at Garden.com. For example, Andy Martin (Chief Technology Officer), who was responsible for the firm's IT systems, processes, and infrastructure, is not shown on the organization chart at all. Why? Because his work was completely integrated with every other function and division, and to distinguish Martin's activities from those of other officers would have painted an inaccurate picture of the way the company's activities were integrally interrelated. In addition, given that two of the senior managers were married and a third was their best friend, it is very likely that the informal organization would have continued to play a powerful role at Garden.com.

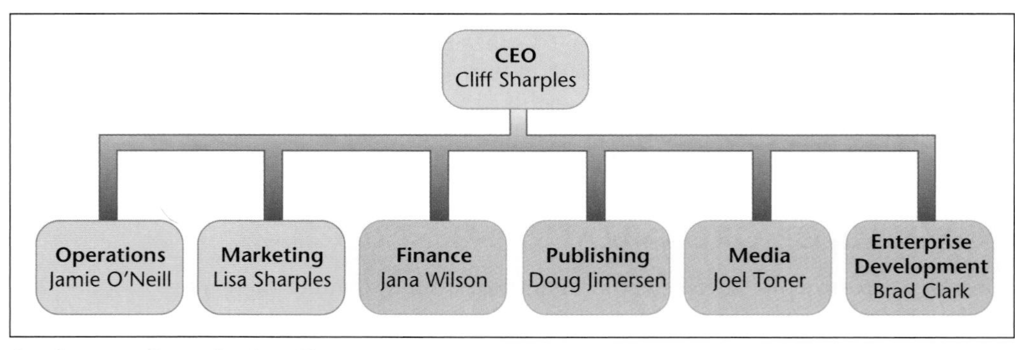

Garden.com Organization Chart

In large firms, coordination across functional departments becomes more complicated. Functional organization also fosters centralization (which may possibly be desirable) and makes accountability more difficult. As organizations grow, therefore, they tend to shed this form and move toward one of the other three structures.

divisional organization Organizational structure in which corporate divisions operate as autonomous businesses under the larger corporate umbrella

Divisional Organization

A **divisional organization** relies on product departmentalization. The firm creates product-based divisions, each of which may then be managed as a separate enterprise.

Organizations using this approach are typically structured around several **divisions**—departments that resemble separate businesses in that they produce and market their own products. The head of each division may be a corporate vice president or, if the organization is large, a divisional president. In addition, each division usually has its own identity and operates as a relatively autonomous business under the larger corporate umbrella.

division
Department that resembles a separate business in producing and marketing its own products

H. J. Heinz <www.heinz.com>, for example, is one of the world's largest food-processing companies. Heinz makes literally thousands of different products and markets them around the world. The firm is organized into seven basic divisions: food service (selling small packaged products such as mustard and relish to restaurants), infant foods, condiments (Heinz ketchup, steak sauce, and tomato sauce), Star-Kist tuna, pet foods, frozen-foods division, and one division that handles miscellaneous products including new lines being test-marketed and soups, beans, and pasta products. Because of its divisional structure, Heinz can evaluate the performance of each division independently. Until recently, Heinz also had a division for its Weight Watchers business. But because this business was performing poorly, the company sold the Weight Watchers classroom program and folded its line of frozen foods into its existing frozen-foods division.[9] Because divisions are relatively autonomous, a firm can take such action with minimal disruption to its remaining business operations.

Like Heinz, other divisionalized companies are free to buy, sell, create, and disband divisions without disrupting the rest of their operations. Divisions can maintain healthy competition among themselves by sponsoring separate advertising campaigns, fostering different corporate identities, and so forth. They can also share certain corporate-level resources (such as market research data). Of course, if too much control is delegated to divisional managers, corporate managers may lose touch with daily operations. Competition between divisions can also become disruptive, and efforts in one division may be duplicated by those of another.

Matrix Organization

In a **matrix structure,** teams are formed in which individuals report to two or more managers. One manager usually has functional expertise, while the other has more of a product or project orientation. This structure was pioneered by the National Aeronautics and Space Administration (NASA) <www.nasa.gov> for use in developing specific programs. It is a highly flexible form that is readily adaptable to changing circumstances. Matrix structures rely heavily on committee and team authority.

matrix structure
Organizational structure in which teams are formed and team members report to two or more managers

In some companies, the matrix organization is a temporary measure, installed to complete a specific project and affecting only one part of the firm. In these firms, the end of the project usually means the end of the matrix—either a breakup of the team or a

"Hey, can I get back to you? I think the restructuring has begun."

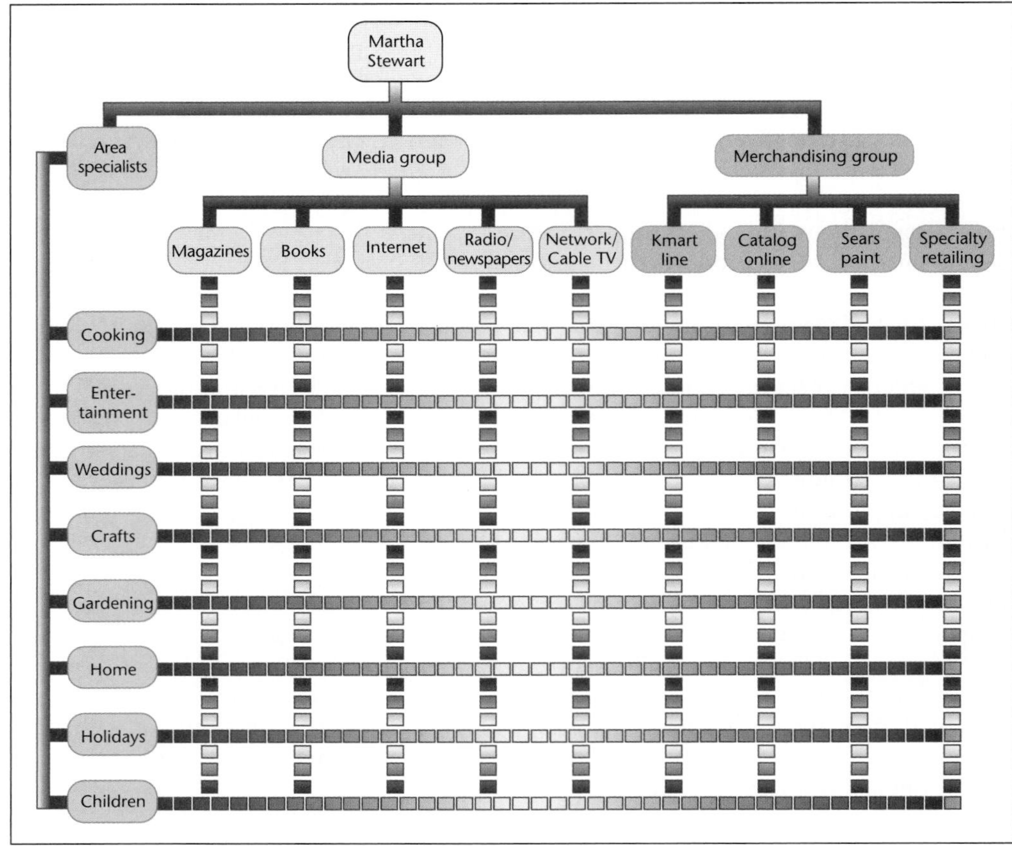

Figure 6.5
Matrix Organization at Martha Stewart

restructuring to fit it into the company's existing line-and-staff structure. Ford, for example, uses a matrix organization to design new models such as the Ford Thunderbird to be launched in 2001. A design team comprised of people from engineering, marketing, operations, and finance is created to design the new car. After its work is done, the team members move back to their permanent functional jobs. In other settings the matrix organization is a semipermanent fixture.

Figure 6.5 shows how Martha Stewart Living Omnimedia, Inc. <www.marthastewart.com> has created a matrix organization for her burgeoning lifestyle business. As you can see, the company is organized broadly into media and merchandising groups, each of which has specific product and product groups. Layered on top of this structure are teams of lifestyle experts organized into groups such as cooking, crafts, weddings, and so forth. Although each group targets specific customer needs, they all work, as necessary, across all product groups. A wedding expert, for example, might contribute to an article on wedding planning for a *Martha Stewart* magazine, contribute a story idea for a Martha Stewart cable television program, and supply content for a Martha Stewart Web site. This same individual might also help select fabrics suitable for wedding gowns to be retailed.[10]

International Organization

international organizational structures
Approaches to organizational structure developed in response to the need to manufacture, purchase, and sell in global markets

As we saw in Chapter 3, many businesses today manufacture, purchase, and sell in the world market. Thus, several different **international organizational structures** have emerged. Moreover, as competition on a global scale becomes more complex, companies often find that they must experiment with the ways in which they respond.

For example, when Wal-Mart <www.walmart.com> opened its first store outside the United States in 1992, it set up a special projects team to handle the logistics. As more stores were opened abroad in the mid-1990s, the firm created a small international department to

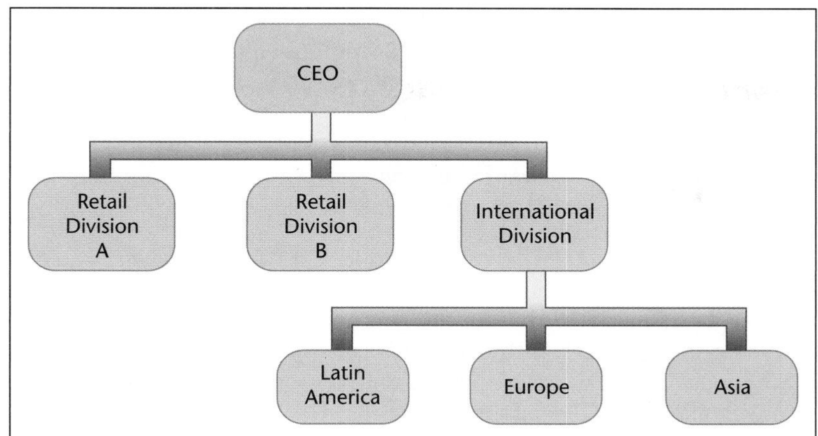

Figure 6.6
International Division Structure

handle overseas expansion. By 1999, however, international sales and expansion had become such a major part of Wal-Mart's operations that the firm created a separate international division headed up by a senior vice president. Interestingly, Wal-Mart now envisions the day when this separate division may no longer be needed, simply because international operations will have become so thoroughly integrated in the firm's overall business.

Wal-Mart typifies the form of organization outlined in Figure 6.6. Other firms have also developed a wide range of approaches to international organizational structure. The French food giant Danone Group <www.danonegroup.com>, for instance, has three major product groups: dairy products (Danone yogurts), bottled water (Evian), and cookies (Pim's). Danone's structure does not differentiate internationally, but rather integrates global operations within each product group.[11] In contrast, U.S. entertainment companies are finding it advantageous to create more local identity when they enter foreign markets. For instance, Columbia TriStar <www.columbiatristarfilms.com>, known for such U.S. television programs as *Seinfeld* and *Mad About You,* recently launched *Chinese Restaurant,* a sitcom filmed and shown only in China. "We thought the Chinese could use a few laughs," says William Pfeiffer, head of TriStar's Asian operation. Universal <www.universalpictures.com> and HBO <www.hbo.com> are also getting in on the act by setting up new television-production businesses in Germany and Japan.[12]

Finally, some companies adopt a truly global structure in which they acquire resources (including capital), produce goods and services, engage in research and development, and sell products in whatever local market is appropriate, without any consideration of national boundaries. Until a few years ago, General Electric kept its international business operations as separate divisions. Now, however, the company functions as one integrated global organization. GE businesses around the world connect and interact with each other constantly, and managers freely move back and forth among them. This integration is also reflected in the top management team: The head of GE's audit team is French, the head of quality control is Dutch, and a German runs one of GE's core business groups.[13]

Organizational Design for the Twenty-First Century

As the world grows increasingly complex and fast-paced, organizations also continue to seek new forms of organization that permit them to compete effectively. Among the most popular of these new forms are the *boundaryless organization,* the *team organization,* the *virtual organization,* and the *learning organization.*

Boundaryless Organization The *boundaryless organization* is one in which traditional boundaries and structures are minimized or eliminated altogether. For example, General Electric's fluid organization structure, in which people, ideas, and information flow freely between businesses and business groups, approximates this concept. Similarly, as firms partner with their suppliers in more efficient ways, external boundaries disappear. Some of Wal-Mart's key suppliers are tied directly into the retailer's vaunted information system. As a result, when Wal-Mart distribution centers start running low on Wrangler blue jeans, the manufacturer gets the information as soon as the retailer. Wrangler proceeds to manufacture new inventory and restock the distribution center without Wal-Mart's having to place a new order.

Team Organization *Team organization* relies almost exclusively on project-type teams, with little or no underlying functional hierarchy. People "float" from project to project as dictated by their skills and the demands of those projects. At Cypress Semiconductor <www.cypress.com>, T. J. Rodgers refuses to allow the organization to grow so large that it can't function this way. Whenever a unit or group starts getting too large, he simply splits it into smaller units. Therefore, the organization is composed entirely of small units. This strategy allows each unit to change direction, explore new ideas, and try new methods without having to deal with a rigid bureaucratic superstructure. Although few large organizations have actually reached this level of adaptability, Apple Computer <www.apple.com> and Xerox <www.xerox.com> are among those moving toward it.

Virtual Organization Closely related to the team organization is the virtual organization. A *virtual organization* has little or no formal structure. Typically, it has only a handful of permanent employees, a very small staff, and a modest administrative facility. As the needs of the organization change, its managers bring in temporary workers, lease facilities, and outsource basic support services to meet the demands of each unique situation. As the situation changes, the temporary workforce changes in parallel, with some people leaving the organization and others entering. Facilities and the subcontracted services also change. In other words, the virtual organization exists only in response to its own needs.

Global Research Consortium (GRC) is a virtual organization. GRC offers research and consulting services to firms doing business in Asia. As clients request various services, GRC's staff of three permanent employees subcontracts the work to an appropriate set of several dozen independent consultants and researchers with whom it has relationships. At any given time, therefore, GRC may have several projects under way with 20 or 30 people working on various projects. As the projects change, so too does the composition of the organization. In a sense, Garden.com was also a virtual organization. Most of its products were bought from suppliers and then distributed via Federal Express. Figure 6.7 illustrates a hypothetical virtual organization.

Gerald Ritthaler's Ritz Foods International, Inc. <www.ritzfoods.com> is an exception to many of today's organizational rules. The 68-year-old Ritthaler, a former financial officer at Gulf & Western, founded Ritz to make snack chips out of yuca, a tropical root, and it is anything but a low-overhead, "virtual" outfit. The 5,000-acre farm in Venezuela is real, as is the processing and packaging plant. As a result, Ritthaler must price his product—a healthful premium snack food—at about twice the retail price of potato chips though considerably below that of gourmet chips.

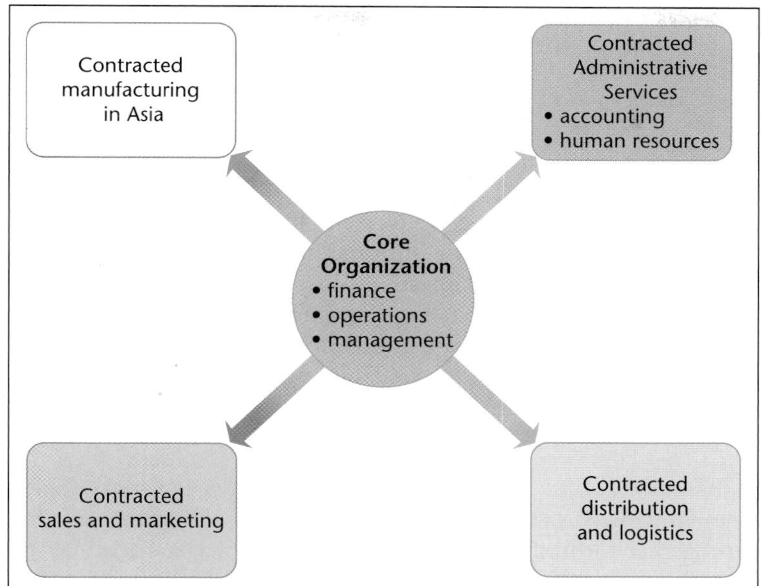

Figure 6.7
The Virtual Organization

Learning Organization The so-called *learning organization* works to integrate continuous improvement with continuous employee learning and development. Specifically, a learning organization works to facilitate the lifelong learning and personal development of all of its employees while continually transforming itself to respond to changing demands and needs.

While managers might approach the concept of a learning organization from a variety of perspectives, the most frequent goals are improved quality, continuous improvement, and performance measurement. The idea is that the most consistent and logical strategy for achieving continuous improvement is constantly upgrading employee talent, skill, and knowledge. For example, if each employee in an organization learns one new thing each day and can translate that knowledge into work-related practice, continuous improvement will logically follow. Indeed, organizations that wholeheartedly embrace this approach believe that only through constant employee learning can continuous improvement really occur.

In recent years, many different organizations have implemented this approach on various levels. Shell Oil Company <www.countonshell.com>, for example, recently purchased an executive conference center north of its headquarters in Houston. Called the Shell Learning Center, the facility boasts state-of-the-art classrooms and instructional technology, lodging facilities, a restaurant, and recreational amenities, such as a golf course, swimming pool, and tennis courts. Line managers at the firm rotate through the Center and serve as teaching faculty. Teaching assignments last anywhere from a few days to several months. At the same time, all Shell employees routinely attend training programs, seminars, and related activities, all the while gathering the latest information they need to contribute more effectively to the firm. Recent seminar topics have included time management, implications of the Americans with Disabilities Act, balancing work and family demands, and international trade theory.

INFORMAL ORGANIZATION

Much of our discussion has focused on the organization's *formal* structure—its official arrangement of jobs and job relationships. In reality, however, all organizations also have another dimension—an *informal* organization within which people do their jobs in different ways and interact with other people in ways that do not follow formal lines of communication.

How would a company that has been in operation for many years go about changing its organizational structure?

Formal Versus Informal Organizational Systems

informal organization
Network, unrelated to the firm's formal authority structure, of everyday social interactions among company employees

The formal organization of a business is the part that can be seen and represented in chart form. The structure of a company, however, is by no means limited to the organization chart and the formal assignment of authority. Frequently, the **informal organization**—everyday social interactions among employees that transcend formal jobs and job interrelationships—effectively alters a company's formal structure. Indeed, this level of organization is sometimes just as powerful, if not more powerful, than the formal structure.

On the negative side, the informal organization can reinforce office politics that put the interests of individuals ahead of those of the firm. Likewise, a great deal of harm can be caused by distorted or inaccurate information communicated without management input or review. For example, if the informal organization is highlighting false information about impending layoffs, valuable employees may act quickly (and unnecessarily) to seek other employment. Among the more important elements of the informal organization are *informal groups* and the *organizational grapevine.*

Informal Groups *Informal groups* are simply groups of people who decide to interact among themselves. They may be people who work together in a formal sense or who just get together for lunch, during breaks, or after work. They may talk about business, the boss, or nonwork-related topics like families, movies, or sports. Their impact on the organization may be positive (if they work together to support the organization), negative (if they work together in ways that run counter to the organization's interests), or irrelevant (if what they do is unrelated to the organization).

grapevine
Informal communication network that runs through an organization

Organizational Grapevine The **grapevine** is an informal communication network that can run through an entire organization.[14] Grapevines are found in all organizations except the very smallest, but they do not always follow the same patterns as formal channels of authority and communication, nor do they necessarily coincide with them. Moreover, because the grapevine typically passes information orally, it often becomes distorted in the process. Attempts to eliminate the grapevine are fruitless, but, fortunately, managers do have some control over it. By maintaining open channels of communication and responding vigorously to inaccurate information, they can minimize the damage the grapevine can do. In fact, the grapevine can actually be an asset. By getting to know the key people in the grapevine, for example, the manager can partially control the information they receive and use the grapevine to sound out employee reactions to new ideas (a change in human resource policies or benefit packages). The manager can also get valuable information from the grapevine and use it to improve decision making.

Intrapreneuring

Sometimes organizations actually take steps to encourage the informal organization. They do so for a variety of reasons, two of which we have already discussed. First, most experienced managers recognize that the informal organization exists whether they want it or not. Second, many managers know how to use the informal organization to reinforce the formal organization. Perhaps more important, however, the energy of the informal organization can be harnessed to improve productivity.

intrapreneuring
Process of creating and maintaining the innovation and flexibility of a small-business environment within the confines of a large organization

Many firms, including Compaq Computer, Rubbermaid, 3M, and Xerox, are supporting a process called **intrapreneuring:** creating and maintaining the innovation and flexibility of a small-business environment within the confines of a large, bureaucratic structure. The concept is basically sound. Historically, most innovations have come from individuals in small businesses (see Chapter 7). As businesses increase in size, however, innovation and creativity tend to become casualties in the battle for more sales and profits. In some large companies, new ideas are even discouraged, and champions of innovation have been stalled in midcareer.

Compaq <www.compaq.com> is an excellent example of how intrapreneuring works to counteract this trend. The firm has one major division called the New Business Group.

When a manager or engineer has an idea for a new product or product application, the individual takes it to the New Business Group and "sells" it. The managers in the group itself are then encouraged to help the innovator develop the idea for field testing. If the product takes off and does well, it is then spun off into its own new business group or division. If it doesn't do as well as hoped, it may still be maintained as part of the New Business Group or may be phased out.

Continued from page 150

Building on Cybersites

As we noted at the beginning of this story, Cephren and Bidcom are at the forefront in applying Web technology to construction projects. Cephren, for example, has created a software network that serves as a communications system for the contractors and subcontractors who are working together on a project. Clients pay a start-up fee of $750 and a monthly fee of $1,250 to use the Cephren system, plus an initial $1,500 training fee. Each member of the construction team receives a password that allows access to the facet of the project that is relevant to the respective team member's work. Thus, a middle manager working at the construction site might need access to blueprints but not to the minutes of the senior management team's last meeting.

Bidcom is another emerging player in this new construction model. While Cephren focuses primarily on organizing construction projects more efficiently, Bidcom focuses more tightly on the job of linking contractors and suppliers. Using the Bidcom system, for example, a contractor can put out a call for bids on 100 steel doors or 500 windows, with corresponding specifications and delivery details. Suppliers, meanwhile, can review the call and submit bids directly to the contractor. This overall improvement in efficiency can potentially save thousands of dollars on a big construction project.

Of course, not everyone is rushing to this new way of doing business. But all the major companies are at least taking steps in this direction. Experts forecast that by the year 2004, at least 10 percent of all construction-industry business will be conducted online. One major construction firm, WebCor <www.webcor.com>, indicates that in two years it will do business only with subcontractors and suppliers who are able to work online. We may never live and work in virtual buildings, but, increasingly, the construction of old-fashioned brick-and-mortar facilities is taking place in cyberspace.

Questions for Discussion

1. What elements of organizational structure are most relevant to the construction industry?
2. Why do you think some firms are so eager and some reluctant to adopt this new technology?
3. What new pitfalls might exist for a construction project being managed totally online?
4. Are the organizational effects of new technology more likely to be felt within a given construction company or in the way that construction companies relate to one another? Why?
5. In what ways, if any, might new technology affect the informal organization that exists at a construction site?

SUMMARY OF LEARNING OBJECTIVES

1 **Discuss the elements that influence a firm's *organizational structure*.** Every business needs structure to operate. *Organizational structure* varies according to a firm's mission, purpose, and strategy. Size, technology, and changes in environmental circumstances also influence structure. In general, although all organizations have the same basic elements, each develops the structure that contributes to the most efficient operations.

2 **Explain *specialization* and *departmentalization* as the building blocks of organizational structure.** The building blocks of organizational structure are *job specialization* and *departmentalization*. As a firm grows, it usually has a greater need for people to perform specialized tasks (specialization). It also has a greater need to group types of work into logical units (departmentalization). Common forms of departmentalization are *customer, product, process, geographic,* and *functional*. Large businesses often use more than one form of departmentalization.

3 **Distinguish between *responsibility, authority, delegation,* and *accountability,* and explain the differences between decision making in *centralized* and *decentralized organizations*.** *Responsibility* is the duty to perform a task; *authority* is the power to make the decisions necessary to complete tasks. *Delegation* begins when a manager assigns a task to a subordinate; *accountability* means that the subordinate must complete the task. *Span of control* refers to the number of people who work for any individual manager. The more people supervised, the wider the span of control. Wide spans are usually desirable when employees perform simple or unrelated tasks. When jobs are diversified or prone to change, a narrower span is generally preferable.

In a *centralized organization,* only a few individuals in top management have real decision-making authority. In a *decentralized organization,* much authority is delegated to lower-level management. When both *line* and *line-and-staff systems* are involved, *line departments* generally have authority to make decisions, whereas *staff departments* have a responsibility to advise. A relatively new concept, *committee and team authority,* empowers committees or work teams involved in a firm's daily operations.

4 **Explain the differences between *functional, divisional, matrix,* and *international organizational structures*.** In a *functional organization,* authority is usually distributed among such basic functions as marketing and finance. In a *divisional organization,* the various divisions of a larger company, which may be related or unrelated, operate in a relatively autonomous fashion. In a *matrix organization,* in which individuals report to more than one manager, a company creates teams to address specific problems or to conduct specific projects. A company that has divisions in many countries may require an additional level of *international organization* to coordinate those operations.

5 **Describe the *informal organization* and discuss *intrapreneuring*.** The *informal organization* consists of the everyday social interactions among employees that transcend formal jobs and job interrelationships. To foster the innovation and flexibility of a small business within the big-business environment, some large companies encourage *intrapreneuring*—creating and maintaining the innovation and flexibility of a small-business environment within the confines of a large bureaucratic structure.

QUESTIONS AND EXERCISES

Questions for Review

1. What is an organization chart? What purpose does it serve?
2. Explain the significance of size as it relates to organizational structure. Describe the changes that are likely to occur as an organization grows.
3. What is the difference between responsibility and authority?
4. Why do some managers have difficulties in delegating authority? Why does this problem tend to plague smaller businesses?
5. Why is a company's informal organization important?

Questions for Analysis

6. Draw up an organization chart for your college or university.
7. Describe a hypothetical organizational structure for a small printing firm. Describe changes that might be necessary as the business grows.
8. Compare and contrast the matrix and divisional approaches to organizational structure. How would you feel personally about working in a matrix organization in which you were assigned simultaneously to multiple units or groups?

Application Exercises

9. Interview the manager of a local service business—a fast-food restaurant. What types of tasks does this manager typically delegate? Is the appropriate authority also delegated in each case?
10. Using books, magazines, or personal interviews, identify a person who has succeeded as an intrapreneur. In what ways did the structure of the intrapreneur's company help this individual succeed? In what ways did the structure pose problems?

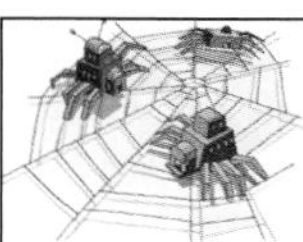

EXPLORING THE WEB

HOW TO ORGANIZE A MAGIC KINGDOM

This chapter alludes to the years when Walt Disney and his brother Roy first opened their studio. To introduce the concept of job specialization, we describe the opposite practice—a few people doing just about everything. As their jobs grew more complex, the Disney brothers found it increasingly necessary to assign facets of their jobs to other people. Today, the Walt Disney Company is a multinational entertainment empire. The company's Web site can be found at:

www.disney.go.com

Browse this Web site and then consider the following questions and activities:

1. Using the Disney Web site as a guide, diagram an organization structure that might make sense for the firm. Make your diagram as detailed as possible.
2. What base of departmentalization does Disney apparently use?
3. Disney has a history of being relatively centralized. What impact would this practice likely have on the firm's current structure?
4. Can you draw any implications from your diagram about the firm's span of control?
5. Disney employs people it calls "Imagineers." See what you can learn about the jobs performed by these people, and compare them with the various roles played by intrapreneurs.
6. Research Disney's "real" organizational structure. Compare and contrast it with the one you diagrammed. What basic factors might account for major differences?

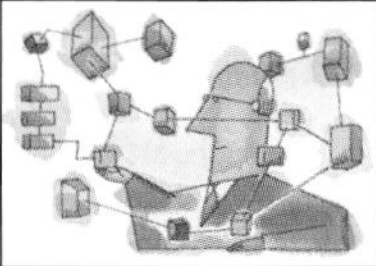

BUILDING YOUR BUSINESS SKILLS

GETTING WITH THE PROGRAM

This exercise enhances the following SCANS workplace competencies: demonstrating basic skills, demonstrating thinking skills, exhibiting interpersonal skills, and working with information.

GOAL

To encourage students to understand the relationship between organizational structure and a company's ability to attract and keep valued employees.

SITUATION

You are the founder of a small but growing high-technology company that develops new computer software. With your current workload and new contracts in the pipeline, your business is thriving except for one problem: You cannot find computer programmers for product development. Worse yet, current staff members are being lured away by other high-tech firms. After suffering a particularly discouraging personnel raid in which competitors captured three of your most valued employees, you schedule a meeting with your director of human resources to plan organizational changes designed to encourage worker loyalty. You already pay top dollar, but the continuing exodus tells you that programmers are looking for something more.

METHOD

Working with three or four classmates, identify some ways in which specific organizational changes might improve the working environment and encourage employee loyalty. As you analyze the following factors, ask yourself the obvious question: If I were a programmer, what organizational changes would encourage me to stay?

- *Level of job specialization.* With many programmers describing their jobs as tedious because of the focus on detail in a narrow work area, what changes, if any, would you make in job specialization? Right now, for instance, few of your programmers have any say in product design.
- *Decision-making hierarchy.* What decision-making authority would encourage people to stay? Is expanding worker authority likely to work better in a centralized or decentralized organization?

- *Team authority.* Can team empowerment make a difference? Taking the point of view of the worker, describe the ideal team.
- *Intrapreneuring.* What can your company do to encourage and reward innovation?

FOLLOW-UP QUESTIONS

1. With the average computer programmer earning nearly $70,000, and with all competitive firms paying top dollar, why might organizational issues be critical in determining employee loyalty?
2. If you were a programmer, what organizational factors would make a difference to you? Why?
3. As the company founder, how willing would you be to make major organizational changes in light of the shortage of qualified programmers?

CRAFTING YOUR BUSINESS PLAN

DOCTORING THE ORGANIZATION

THE PURPOSE OF THE ASSIGNMENT

1. To acquaint students with the process of navigating the *Business PlanPro* (*BPP*) software package (Version 4.0).
2. To provide an example that illustrates ways in which organizational options can be presented in a business plan.
3. To demonstrate how three chapter topics—organization structure, departmentalization, and authority and responsibility—can be integrated as components in the *BPP* planning environment.

ASSIGNMENT

After reading Chapter 6 in the textbook, open the BPP *software* and look around for information about organizational structure, departmentalization, and authority and responsibility as they apply to a sample firm:* Medical Equipment Development *(Medquip, Inc.). Then respond to the following items:*

1. Construct an organization chart for Medquip, Inc. [Sites to see in *BPP* (for this assignment): In the Plan Outline screen, click on each of the following: **6.0 Management Summary; 6.1 Organization Structure; 6.2 Management Team;** and **Table: Personnel** (located beneath **6.4 Personnel Plan.**]
2. Explain how Medquip's organizational structure is set up to take advantage of its competitor's weakness in product innovation. [Sites to see in *BPP:* In the Plan Outline screen, click on **4.2.4 Main Competitors.**]
3. Which type of departmentalization—customer, product, functional, or process—does Medquip use? Give examples from Medquip's business plan to support your answer.
4. For each job position at Medquip, how clearly are its authority and responsibility delineated in the business plan?

FOR YOUR OWN BUSINESS PLAN

5. Describe the composition of your firm's management team. Explain the responsibilities of each position in the firm and identify its organizational structure. Do you plan to modify that organizational structure as the firm and its managers gain experience? Explain in your plan why you expect the company's structure either to remain constant or to change.

*GENERAL TIPS FOR NAVIGATING IN BPP

1. Open the *BPP* program, examine the Welcome screen, and click on **Open a Sample Plan.**
2. From the **Open a Sample Plan** dialogue box, click on a sample company name; then click on **Open.**
3. On the Plan Manager screen, click on **Your Plan Outline**; then click on any of the lines (for example, **6.0 Management Summary**).
4. You can always return to the Plan Outline screen by going to the bottom of the screen and clicking on the **Plan Outline** icon.

5. After finishing with one sample company, you can get to the next one by going to the top of the screen and clicking on **File** (on the menu bar). Then beneath that, select **Open Sample Plan.** This will exit you from the current company file and take you to the **Open Sample Plan** dialogue box, where you can select your next sample company.
6. When you are finished, you can close the program by going to the top of the screen and clicking on **File** (on the bar menu). Then beneath that, select **Exit.**

VIDEO EXERCISE

THE MANAGEMENT PICTURE: QUICK TAKES VIDEO (II)

Learning Objectives

The purpose of this video exercise is to help you

1. Recognize the difference between responsibility and authority.
2. Understand the decision-making process.
3. Understand the three forms of authority.

BACKGROUND INFORMATION

Based on a real company in the same line of business, Quick Takes Video is a fictitious firm that produces corporate, industrial, and training videos and video news releases. It was founded by Hal Boylston and Karen Jarvis, and the management team includes a production coordinator, who oversees the producers responsible for the actual filming and editing of the firm's products. The production coordinator forecasts staff and equipment needs for each shoot, coordinates the use of the company's physical resources, manages producers, and keeps the shoots on schedule and on budget. The new production coordinator, John Switzer, reports to Hal Boylston.

THE VIDEO

In this segment, Switzer runs into trouble with a producer named Susan, who reports to him. She disagrees with his decision to give her a freelance crew instead of a staff crew for a shoot that she considers very important. Switzer discusses the problem with Boylston, to whom Susan used to report, and wonders whether Susan will make a habit of taking her complaints to Boylston or will get used to reporting to Switzer, her new supervisor.

DISCUSSION QUESTIONS

1. In what ways might Switzer have contributed to the disagreement with Susan? How could Susan have helped to avoid the confrontation?
2. What kind of authority does Switzer have (line, staff, or committee)? What does that kind of authority imply about his working relationship with Susan?
3. Bolyston advises Switzer to give Susan time to get used to a new manager and to accept the fact that she is somewhat spoiled. What do you think of this advice?

FOLLOW-UP ASSIGNMENT

Have you ever disagreed with the decision of a boss (or perhaps an instructor or other supervisor)? How did you deal with the problem? Did you consult others in the organization? What kinds of reporting hierarchy existed in the organization, and how did that hierarchy affect the outcome of the disagreement? Would you take the same action if you had it to do over? Why or why not?

FOR FURTHER EXPLORATION

Choose a formal organization with which you are familiar, such as your college, your employer, or a club or other organization to which you belong. Draw an organization chart for this entity, including appropriate lines of authority. Decide whether it closely resembles a functional, divisional, matrix, or perhaps even an international organization. Determine whether relationships of responsibility and authority are consistent in this organization.

Chapter

7

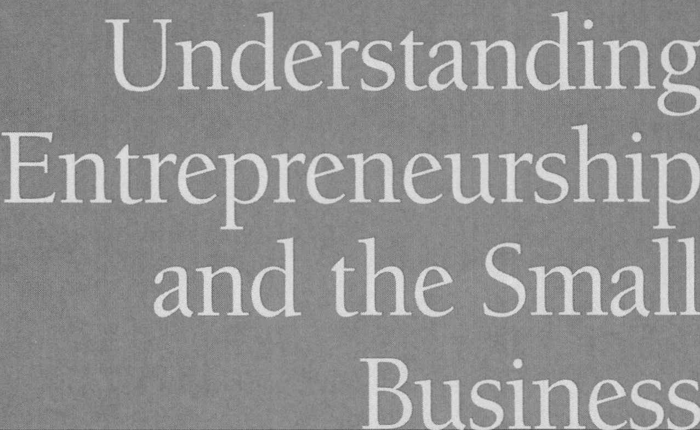

Understanding Entrepreneurship and the Small Business

After reading this chapter, you should be able to:

Define *small business* and explain its importance to the U.S. economy.

Explain which *types of small business* best lend themselves to success.

Define *entrepreneurship* and describe some basic *entrepreneurial characteristics.*

Describe the *start-up decisions* made by small businesses and identify sources of *financial aid* and *management advice* available to such enterprises.

Identify the advantages and disadvantages of *franchising.*

Please Turn to Chapter 11

Few small-business retailers have the nerve to go head-to-head with giant megastores. As the record shows, even fewer know the secret of emerging with a profit (or even intact). But competing with Goliaths is exactly what Barbara Babbit Kaufman is doing with the small chain of Atlanta-based independent bookstores that she calls Chapter 11 <**www.chapter11books.com**>. Moreover, Kaufman is succeeding as a small-business owner because of entrepreneurial drive, market savvy, and strategic acumen that have grown the chain from 1 to 13 locations and pushed annual revenues to over $10 million in just eight years. Granted, Kaufman is not a typical small bookstore owner. "A lot of people," she explains, "open bookstores because books are their passion. Retail is my passion."

Kaufman helped start Chapter 11 in 1990 with a $200,000 investment from family and friends. Rather than try to compete with the likes of Borders <**www.borders.com**> and Barnes & Noble <**www.barnesandnoble.com**> through superior service, wide selection, or literary allure, Kaufman chose the brash, aggressive style of a David fighting Goliath on the battlefield of price. The company's slogan says it all: "Prices So Low, You'd Think We Were Going Bankrupt," which is a playful reference to both the chain's name and the federal bankruptcy code.

Chapter 11 offers a 30 percent discount on a typical best-seller (the same as the superstores) and discounts all books at least 11 percent—a slightly better deal than that offered by the superstores. What Chapter 11 does a *lot* better is promote its *image* as a rock-bottom pricer. In 2000, for example, Chapter 11 not only advertised John Grisham's novel *The Brethren* at $15.99 but focused its message on the difference between that price and those being charged elsewhere (the highest price was $27.95). Not only is the price good, but, more importantly, the strategy has also convinced consumers that Chapter 11 prices can't be beat. "I assume I get the best price here," says a typically loyal Atlanta customer.

How does Kaufman manage to offer the prices that back up her strategy? Basically, she keeps overhead low. Each Chapter 11 store has only 3,000 to 6,000 square feet, compared with at least 20,000 square feet for a Barnes & Noble or Borders store. Relying on her instincts rather than research to choose sites, Kaufman also locates her stores in low-cost strip malls that offer the kind of fast access that customers want. Of her second location, Kaufman recalls, "I lived nearby, and I knew it was a power center with great traffic and that spaces didn't come available often. Even though I wasn't ready to open a second store, I knew I had to. . . . When you've lived in a market all your life, you know the habits of its shoppers." Admittedly, Kaufman often follows the lead of Wolf Camera <**www.wolf camera.com**>, another Atlanta-based small business, in choosing store sites. "Out of our 13 locations," she acknowledges, "all but three are close to Wolf. Our customer demographics are the same. Why do market research twice?"

Although Kaufman takes a mass-market approach to bookselling, aiming for the majority of readers rather than specialty markets, she gives managers the freedom to customize the look and feel of each store for its neighborhood. Managers order, display, and promote books according to what they think will sell. With limited space, Chapter 11 stores lack the amenities and ambiance of the superstores, and customers looking for coffee bars and couches won't find them. To customers who know exactly what they want, who want to shop quickly, and who have little interest in the superstore experience, smallness is an advantage.

So far, Kaufman's personal drive and good business sense have created one of the few independent booksellers in the nation that competes successfully with the megastores. She plans to build on Chapter 11's accomplishments, but like many small-business owners, she first must find the capital to move ahead.

"A lot of people open bookstores because books are their passion. Retail is my passion."

—Barbara Babbit Kaufman,
small bookstore owner

Our opening story continues on page 200

In many ways, Chapter 11 is no different from thousands of small companies trying to succeed in a competitive marketplace. Like Chapter 11, small companies face the challenge of defining a market niche and developing strategies to survive and thrive, often in the face of daunting competition. They also face obstacles that threaten their very existence and are responsible for the failure of millions of small businesses every year. Nevertheless, small-business ownership remains a prominent feature of the American dream. In this chapter, we consider what small businesses are and why they are so important to the U.S. economy.

WHAT IS A SMALL BUSINESS?

The term *small business* defies easy definition. Clearly, locally owned and operated restaurants, hair salons, and accounting firms are small businesses, and giant corporations such as Sony, Caterpillar, and Eastman Kodak are big businesses. Between these two extremes fall thousands of companies that cannot be easily categorized.

Small Business Administration (SBA) Federal agency charged with assisting small businesses

The U.S. Department of Commerce <www.osec.doc.gov> considers a business "small" if it has fewer than 500 employees; but the U.S. **Small Business Administration (SBA)** <www.sba.gov>, a government assistance agency for small businesses, regards some companies with 1,500 employees as small. The SBA bases its definition on two factors: *number of employees* and *total annual sales.* For example, manufacturers are defined as "small" according to the first criterion and grocery stores according to the second. Thus, although an independent grocery store with $13 million in sales may sound large, the SBA still sees it as a small business when its revenues are compared with those of truly large food retailers.

small business Independently owned and managed business that does not dominate its market

Because it is sometimes difficult to define a small business in strict numerical terms, we define a **small business** as one that is independently owned and managed and does not dominate its market. A small business, then, cannot be part of another business: Operators must be their own bosses, free to run their businesses as they please. In addition, to be considered small, a business must have relatively little influence in its market. For example, although Compaq Computer <www.compaq.com> and Dell Computer <www.dell.com> were both certainly small businesses when they were founded by entrepreneurs in 1984, they are now among the dominant companies in the personal computer market.

The Importance of Small Business in the U.S. Economy

As Figure 7.1 shows, most U.S. businesses employ fewer than 100 people, and most U.S. workers are employed by small firms. For example, Figure 7.1(a) shows that 86.09 percent of all U.S. businesses employ 20 or fewer people; another 11 percent employ between 20 and 99 people. In contrast, only about one-tenth of 1 percent employ 1,000 or more workers. Figure 7.1(b) shows that 25.60 percent of all U.S. workers are employed by firms with fewer than 20 people; another 29.10 percent work in firms that employ between 20 and 99 people. The vast majority of these companies are owner operated.[1] Figure 7.1(b) also shows that 12.70 percent of U.S. workers are employed by firms with 1,000 or more total employees.

On the basis of numbers alone, then, small business is a strong presence in the economy, which is true in virtually all the world's mature economies. In Germany, for example, companies with fewer than 500 employees produce two-thirds of the nation's gross national product, train nine of 10 apprentices, and employ four of every five workers. Small businesses also play major roles in the economies of Italy, France, and Brazil. In addition, experts agree that small businesses will be quite important in the emerging economies of countries such as Russia and Vietnam. The contribution of small business

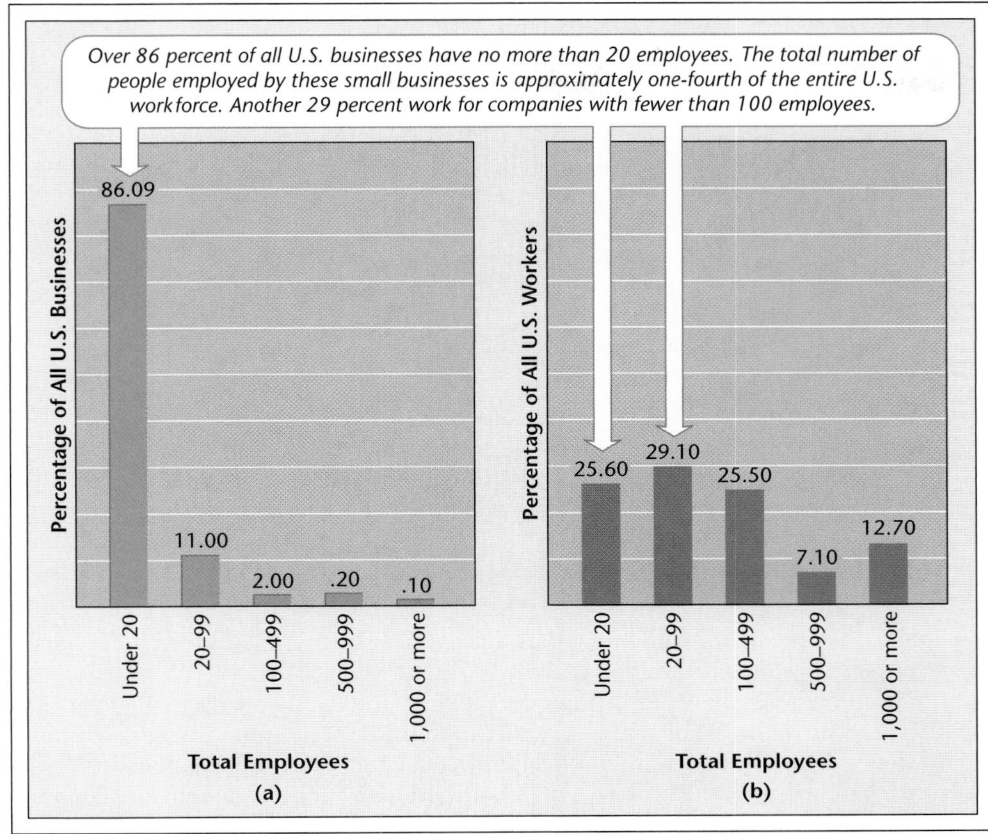

Figure 7.1

The Importance of Small Business in the United States

can be measured in terms of its effects on key aspects of an economic system. In the United States, these aspects include *job creation, innovation,* and *importance to big business.*

Job Creation In the early 1980s, a widely circulated study proposed that small businesses create eight of every 10 new jobs in the United States. This contention touched off considerable interest in the fostering of small business as a matter of public policy. As we will see, relative job growth among businesses of different sizes is not easy to determine. It is clear, however, that small business—especially in certain industries—is an important source of new (and often well-paid) jobs in this country. According to the SBA, seven of the 10 industries that added the most new jobs in 1998 were in sectors dominated by small businesses. Moreover, small businesses currently account for 38 percent of all jobs in high-technology sectors of the economy.[2]

Note that new jobs are also being created by small firms specializing in international business. For example, Bob Knosp operates a small business in Bellevue, Washington, that makes computerized sign-making systems. Knosp gets over half his sales from abroad and has dedicated almost 75 percent of his workforce to handling international sales. According to the SBA, small businesses account for 96 percent of all U.S. exporters.[3]

Although small businesses certainly create many new jobs each year, the importance of big businesses in job creation should also not be overlooked. While big businesses cut thousands of jobs in the late 1980s and early 1990s, the booming U.S. economy resulted in large-scale job creation in many larger businesses beginning in the mid-1990s. Figure 7.2 details the changes in the number of jobs at 16 large U.S. companies during the 10-year period between 1990 and 1999. As you can see, General Motors <www.gm.com> eliminated 181,100 jobs and General Mills <www.generalmills.com> and Kmart <www.kmart.com> eliminated over 86,000 jobs each. Wal-Mart <www.walmart.com>

Figure 7.2
Big Business: Jobs Created and Lost

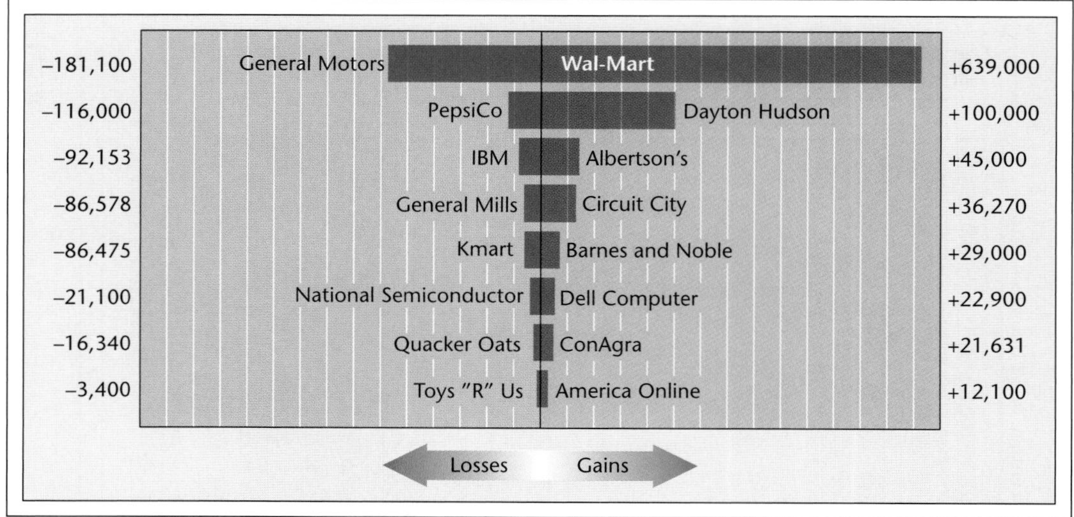

alone, however, created 639,000 new jobs during the same period and Dayton Hudson <www.targetcorp.com> an additional 100,000.

But even these data have to be interpreted with care. PepsiCo <www.pepsico.com>, for example, "officially" eliminated 116,000 jobs. However, most of those losses came in 1997, when the firm sold its restaurant chains (KFC, Pizza Hut, and Taco Bell) to Tricon <www.triconglobal.com>. Therefore, many of the jobs weren't actually eliminated but simply "transferred" to another employer. Likewise, while most of Wal-Mart's 639,000 new jobs are indeed "new," some came when the company acquired other businesses and were thus not net new jobs.

At least one message is clear: Business success, more than business size, accounts for most new job creation. Whereas successful retailers such as Wal-Mart and Dayton Hudson have been adding thousands of new jobs, struggling chains such as Kmart have been eliminating thousands. At the same time, flourishing high-tech giants such as Dell, Intel, and Microsoft continue to add jobs at a constant pace. It is also essential to take a long-term view when analyzing job growth. Figure 7.2 shows that IBM <www.ibm.com> has eliminated 92,153 jobs. But the firm actually cut a total of 163,381 jobs between 1990 and 1994. Since 1995, it has created 71,228 new jobs as the company has recovered from the economic slump that made the original job cuts so severe.

The reality, then, is that jobs are created by companies of all sizes, all of which hire workers and all of which lay them off. Although small firms often hire at a faster rate than large ones, they are also likely to eliminate jobs at a far higher rate. Small firms are also the first to hire in times of economic recovery, large firms the last. Conversely, however, big companies are also the last to lay off workers during economic downswings. Figure 7.3 shows that in 1999 almost 35 percent of all small businesses had job openings, and almost 20 percent were planning to hire new employees.

Innovation History has shown that major innovations are as likely to come from small businesses (or individuals) as from big businesses. For example, small firms and individuals invented the personal computer and the stainless-steel razor blade, the transistor radio and the photocopying machine, the jet engine and the self-developing photograph. They also gave us the helicopter and power steering, automatic transmissions and air conditioning, cellophane, and the 19-cent ballpoint pen. Today, says the SBA, small businesses supply 55 percent of all "innovations" introduced into the American marketplace.[4]

History is repeating itself infinitely more rapidly in the age of computers and high-tech communication. For example, much of today's most innovative software is being

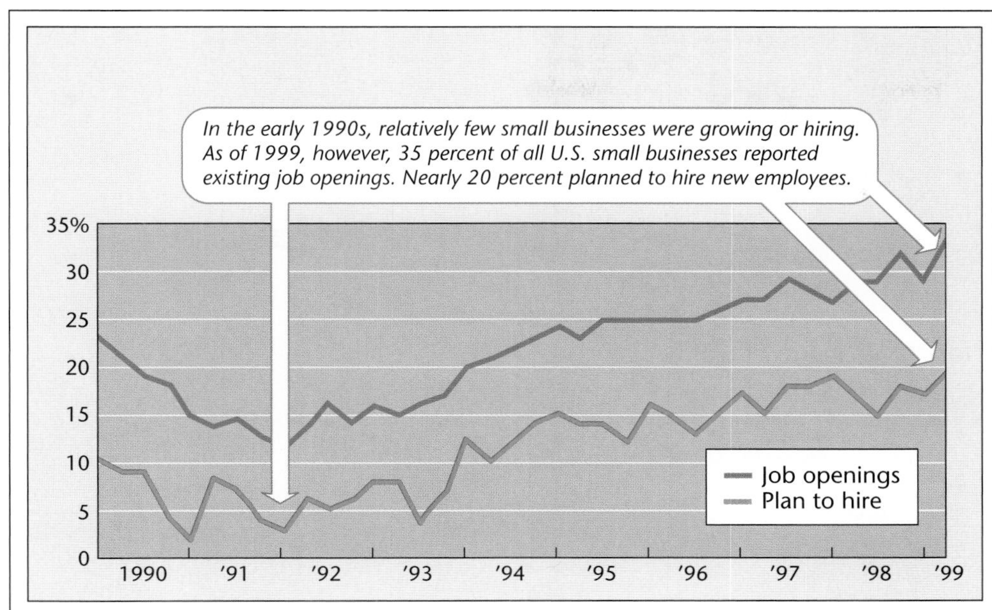

Figure 7.3

Job Openings and Hiring Plans for Small Business, 1990–1999

written at new start-up companies such as Trilogy Software, Inc. <www.trilogy.com>, an Austin, Texas–based company started by Stanford dropout Joe Liemandt. Trilogy's products help optimize and streamline complicated sales and marketing processes for big-business customers such as IBM and Whirlpool.[5] Yahoo! and Netscape brought the Internet into the average American living room, and online companies such as Amazon.com are using it to redefine our shopping habits. Each of these firms started out as a small business. So did Alain Rossmann's Phone.com, a new but growing enterprise that helps big companies provide wireless access to the Internet. Similarly, eToys Inc., another dot.com start-up, is also making major inroads in the toy retailing business. Garden.com, of course, also fell into this category.

Importance to Big Business Most of the products made by big manufacturers are sold to consumers by small businesses. For example, the majority of dealerships selling Fords, Chevrolets, Toyotas, and Volvos are independently owned and operated. Moreover, small businesses provide big businesses with many of the services, supplies, and raw materials they need. As we previously noted, Trilogy Software has become an important supplier to big businesses. Likewise, Microsoft <www.microsoft.com> relies heavily on small businesses in the course of its routine business operations. For example, the software giant outsources much of its routine code-writing functions to hundreds of sole proprietorships and other small firms. It also outsources much of its packaging, delivery, and distribution to smaller companies. Dell Computer <www.dell.com> uses this same strategy, buying most of the parts and components used in its computers from small suppliers around the world.

Popular Forms of Small-Business Enterprise

Not surprisingly, small businesses are more common in some industries than in others. The major small-business industry groups are *services, retailing, construction, financial and insurance, wholesaling, transportation,* and *manufacturing*. Obviously, each group differs in its requirements for employees, money, materials, and machines. Remember: The more resources an industry requires, the harder it is to start a business and the less likely that the industry is dominated by small firms. Remember, too, that "small" is a relative term: The criteria

If you were a young entrepreneur with significant start-up capital and could create any type of company you wanted, what would it be? Who would be your target market?

Figure 7.4
Small Business by Industry

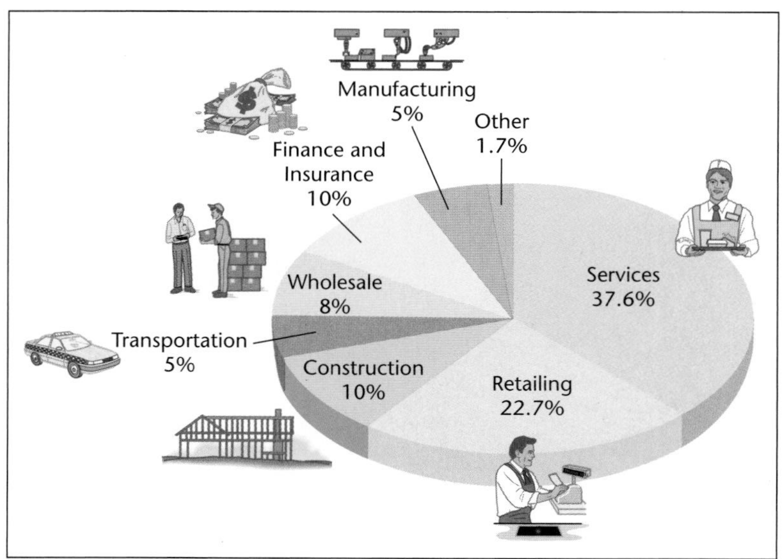

(number of employees and total annual sales) differ from industry to industry and are often meaningful only when compared with businesses that are truly large. Figure 7.4 shows the distribution of all U.S. businesses employing fewer than 20 people across industry groups.

Services Partly because they require few resources, service businesses are the fastest-growing segment of small-business enterprise. In addition, no other industry group offers a higher return on time invested. Finally, services appeal to the talent for innovation typified by many small enterprises. As Figure 7.4 shows, 37.6 percent of all businesses with fewer than 20 employees are services.

Small-business services range from shoeshine parlors to car rental agencies, from marriage counseling to computer software, from accounting and management consulting to professional dog walking. In Dallas, for example, Jani-King <www.janiking.com> has prospered by selling commercial cleaning services to local companies. In Virginia Beach, Virginia, Jackson Hewitt Tax Service <www.jacksonhewitt.com> has found a profitable niche in providing computerized tax preparation and electronic tax-filing services. Great Clips Inc. <www.greatclips.com> is a fast-growing family-run chain of hair salons headquartered in Minneapolis.

Retailing A retail business sells directly to consumers products manufactured by other firms. There are hundreds of different kinds of retailers, ranging from wig shops and frozen yogurt stands to automobile dealerships and department stores. Usually, however, people who start small businesses favor specialty shops—for example, big men's clothing or gourmet coffees—that let them focus limited resources on narrow market segments. Retailing accounts for 22.7 percent of all businesses with fewer than 20 employees.

John Mackey, for example, launched Whole Foods <www.wholefoodsmarket.com> out of his own frustration at being unable to find a full range of natural foods at other stores. He soon found, however, that he had tapped a lucrative market and started an ambitious expansion program. Today, with 90 outlets in 20 states and Washington, DC, Whole Foods is the largest natural-foods retailer in the United States, three times larger than its biggest competitor.[6] Likewise, when Olga Tereshko found it difficult to locate just the right cloth diapers and breast-feeding supplies for her newborn son, she decided to start selling them herself. Instead of taking the conventional retailing route, however, Tereshko set up shop on the Internet. Her business, called Little Koala <www.littlekoala.com>, has continued to expand at a rate of about 10 percent a month, and she has established a customer base of 8,000 to 9,000 loyal customers.[7]

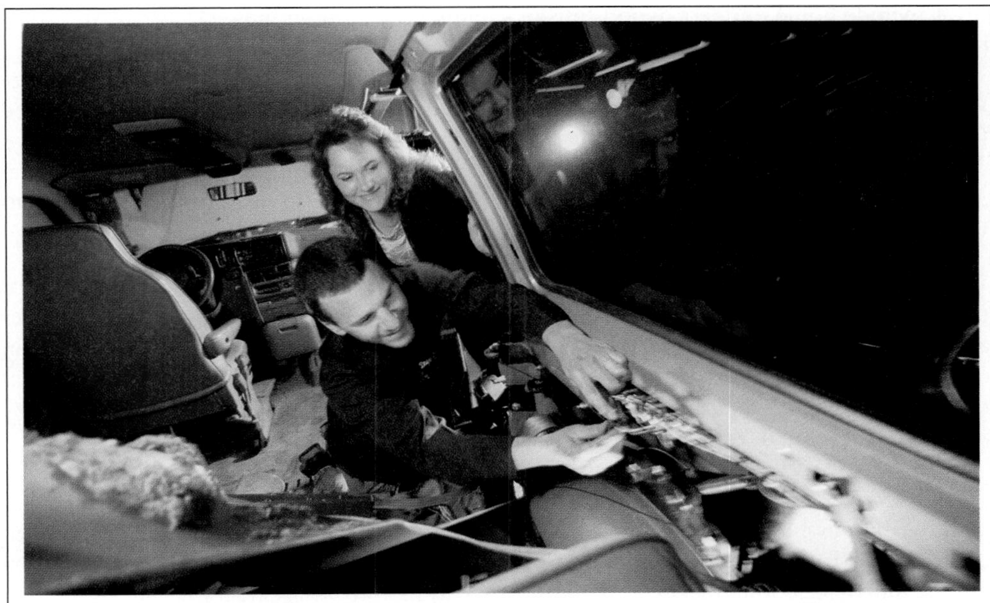

Peter and Christina Ruprecht operate a small business in the service sector. Located in Fairfield, New Jersey, Drive-Master Co., Inc. <www.drivemaster.net> makes driving systems for the physically challenged and adapts vans so that they can be driven by disabled persons from wheelchairs. The company was started by Ruprecht's father, who lost the use of both legs to polio in 1952, and today, it distributes through 400 dealerships nationwide.

"The online business," says Tereshko, "is growing each month. More people are getting used to computers and going online. The Web increases your visibility, and business grows faster." Jeff Levy, an Atlanta-based consultant who tracks Web usage, agrees but cautions that "very few brands . . . have been built solely on the Web. You can market solely on the Web if you are only trying to reach people online."[8]

"Very few brands have been built solely on the Web. You can market solely on the Web if you are only trying to reach people online."

—Jeff Levy, e-commerce consultant

Construction About 10 percent of businesses with fewer than 20 employees are involved in construction. Because many construction jobs are relatively small local projects, local construction firms are often ideally suited as contractors. Many such firms are begun by skilled craftspeople who start out working for someone else and subsequently decide to work for themselves. Common examples of small construction

WebConnection

www.justballs.com

The name pretty much sums it up: This Princeton, New Jersey, company sells balls and just balls. "It isn't a niche market," says Josh Worby, a founding vice president. "It's a niche product category that represents a $6 billion market worldwide. Demand penetrates every demographic category." To buy any kind of ball, or to find the history or rules for any ball game, log on to the company's Web site.

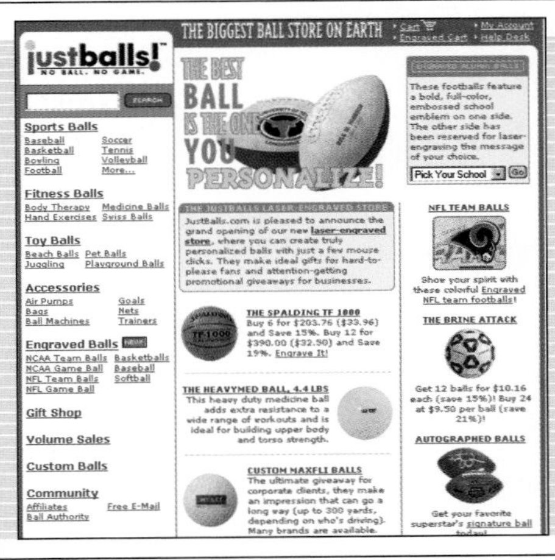

firms include home builders, wood finishers, painters, and plumbing, electrical, and roofing contractors.

For example, Marek Brothers Construction <www.marekbros.com> in College Station, Texas, was started by two brothers, Pat and Joe Marek. They originally worked for other contractors but started their own partnership in 1980. Their only employee is a receptionist. They manage various construction projects, including new-home construction and remodeling, by subcontracting out the actual work to other businesses or individual craftspersons. Marek Brothers has annual gross income of about $5 million.

Finance and Insurance Financial and insurance businesses also comprise about 10 percent of all firms with less than 20 employees. In most cases, these businesses are either affiliates of or sell products provided by larger national firms. Although the deregulation of the banking industry has reduced the number of small local banks, other businesses in this sector are still doing quite well.

Typically, local State Farm Mutual offices are small businesses. State Farm <www.statefarm.com> itself is a major insurance company, but its local offices are run by 16,500 independent agents. In turn, agents hire their own staffs and run their own offices as independent businesses. They sell various State Farm insurance products and earn commissions from the premiums paid by their clients. Some local savings and loan operations, mortgage companies, and pawn shops also fall into this category.

Wholesaling Small-business owners often do very well in wholesaling, too—about 8 percent of businesses with fewer than 20 employees are wholesalers. A wholesale business buys products from manufacturers or other producers and then sells them to retailers. Wholesalers usually buy goods in bulk and store them in quantities at locations that are convenient for retailers. For a given volume of business, therefore, they need fewer employees than manufacturers, retailers, or service providers.

They also serve fewer customers than other providers—usually those who repeatedly order large volumes of goods. Wholesalers in the grocery industry, for instance, buy packaged food in bulk from companies such as Del Monte and Campbell's and then sell it to both large grocery chains and smaller independent grocers. Luis Espinoza has found a promising niche for Inca Quality Foods, a Midwestern wholesaler that imports and distributes Hispanic foods for consumers from Mexico, the Caribbean, and Central America. Partnered with the large grocery-store chain Kroger, Espinoza's firm continues to grow steadily.[9]

Transportation Some small firms—about 5 percent of all companies with fewer than 20 employees—do well in transportation and transportation-related businesses. Such firms include local taxi and limousine companies, charter airplane services, and tour operators. In addition, in many smaller markets, bus companies and regional airlines subcontract local equipment maintenance to small businesses.

Consider some of the transportation-related small businesses at a ski resort like Steamboat Springs, Colorado. Most visitors fly to the town of Hayden, about 15 miles from Steamboat. While some visitors rent vehicles, many others use the services of Alpine Taxi, a small local operation, to transport them to their destinations in Steamboat. While on vacation, they also rely on the local bus service, which is subcontracted by the town to another small business, to get to and from the ski slopes each day. Other small businesses offer van tours of the region, hot-air balloon rides, and helicopter lifts to remote areas for extreme skiers. Still others provide maintenance support at Hayden for Continental, American, and United aircraft that serve the area during ski season.

Manufacturing More than any other industry, manufacturing lends itself to big business—and for good reason. Because of the investment normally required in equipment, energy, and raw materials, a good deal of money is usually needed to start a manufacturing business. Automobile manufacturing, for example, calls for billions of dollars of investment and thousands of workers before the first automobile rolls off the assembly

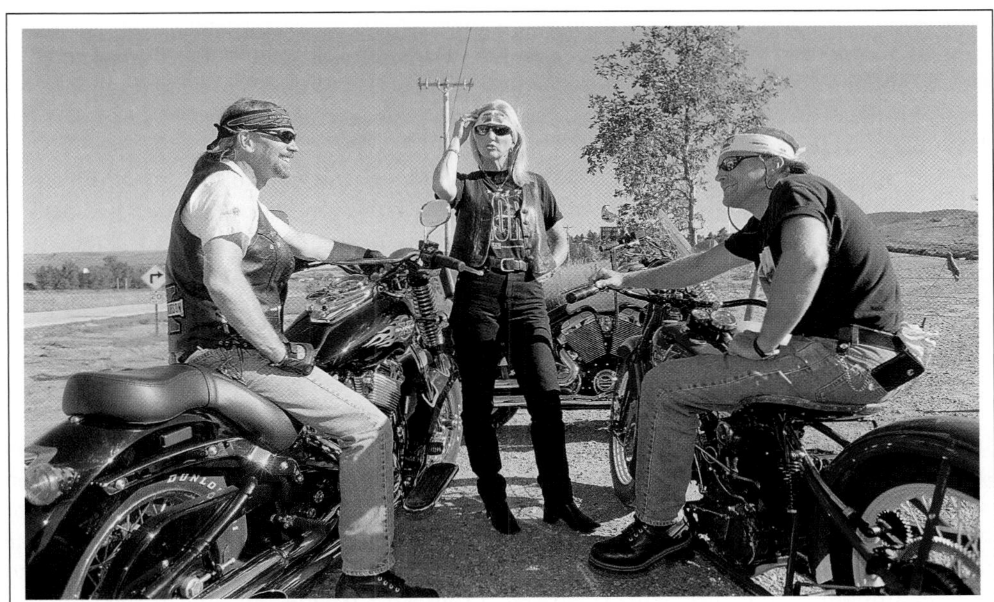

Excelsior-Henderson Motorcycle Manufacturing Co. <www.excelsior-henderson.com> *is proof that small businesses can be built in the manufacturing sector. Based in Belle Plaine, Minnesota, the company was founded by brothers Dave (left) and Dan Hanlon and Dave's wife Jennie in 1993. They started with money from 400 investors and then went public, raising nearly $100 million. Only then did they actually start constructing a factory, designing motorcycles, and hiring experts in manufacturing, sales, marketing, and engineering.*

line. Obviously, such requirements shut out most individuals. Although Henry Ford began with $28,000, it has been a long time since anyone started a new U.S. car company from scratch.

This is not to say that there are no small-business owners who do well in manufacturing—about 5 percent of businesses with fewer than 20 employees are involved in some aspect of manufacturing. Indeed, it is not uncommon for small manufacturers to outperform big business in such innovation-driven industries as chemistry, electronics, toys, and computer software. Some small manufacturers prosper by locating profitable niches. For example, brothers Dave and Dan Hanlon and Dave's wife Jennie recently started a new motorcycle manufacturing business called Excelsior-Henderson. (Excelsior and Henderson are actually names of classic motorcycles from the early years of the twentieth century; the Hanlons acquired the rights to these brand names because of the images they evoke among motorcycle enthusiasts.) The Hanlons started by building 4,000 bikes in 1999 and expect to increase slowly to annual production of 20,000 per year. So far, Excelsior-Henderson motorcycles have been well received (the top-end Excelsior-Henderson Super X sells for about $18,000), and many Harley-Davidson dealers have started to sell them as a means of diversifying their product lines.[10]

ENTREPRENEURSHIP

In the previous section, we discussed several popular forms of small business. We also described a couple of firms that started small and grew larger (sometimes much larger). In each of these cases, growth was spurred by the imagination and skill of the entrepreneurs who operated those companies. Although the concepts of *entrepreneurship* and *small business* are closely related, in this section we begin by discussing some important, though often subtle, differences between them. Then we describe some key characteristics of entrepreneurial personalities and activities.

The Distinction between Entrepreneurship and Small Business

entrepreneur
Businessperson who accepts both the risks and the opportunities involved in creating and operating a new business venture

Many small-business owners like to think of themselves as **entrepreneurs**—people who assume the risk of business ownership with a primary goal of growth and expansion.

However, a person may be a small-business owner only, an entrepreneur only, or both. Consider a person who starts a small pizza parlor with no plans other than to earn enough money from the restaurant to lead a comfortable life. That person is clearly a small-business owner. With no plans to grow and expand, however, that person is not really an entrepreneur.

Conversely, an entrepreneur starts with one pizza parlor and fulfills the ambition of turning it into a national chain to rival Domino's or Little Caesar's. Although this person may have started as a small-business owner, the growth of the firm resulted from entrepreneurial vision and activity. Thus, the basic distinction between small-business ownership and entrepreneurship is aspiration—the former wants to remain small and support a lifestyle whereas the latter is motivated to grow, expand, and build.

Entrepreneurial Characteristics

In general, most successful entrepreneurs have characteristics that set them apart from most other business owners—for example, resourcefulness and a concern for good, often personal, customer relations. Most successful entrepreneurs also have a strong desire to be their own bosses. Many express a need to "gain control over my life" or "build for the family" and believe that building successful businesses will help them do it. They can also handle ambiguity and deal with surprises. Table 7.1 provides an interesting contrast between some of the characteristics and stereotypes that typified entrepreneurs in the past and those that describe many of today's most successful entrepreneurs.

Yesterday's entrepreneur was stereotyped as "the boss"—someone who was self-reliant and male and who made snap, seat-of-the-pants decisions. In contrast, today's entrepreneur is seen more as an inquisitive, open-minded leader who relies on networks, business plans, and consensus. While today's entrepreneur may be male, there is an

Table 7.1

Entrepreneurs: Past and Present

Then	Now
Small business founder	**True entrepreneur**
Boss	Leader
Lone Ranger	Networker
Secretive	Open
Self-reliant	Inquisitive
Seat-of-the-pants	Letter of the business plan
Snap decisions	Consensus decisions
Male ownership	Mixed ownership
Idea	**Execution**
In 1982, 80% of *Inc.* 500 CEO's believed their companies' success was based on novel, unique or proprietary ideas	1992, 80% of *Inc.* 500 CEOs said that the ideas for their companies were ordinary and that they owed their success of superior execution
Knows the Trade	**Knows the Business**
Eastern, one of the first airlines in the United States, was founded by pilot Eddie Rickenbacker	Federal Express, an overnight delivery service utilizing airplanes, was developed from a business plan written by Fred Smith while he was studying for his M.B.A.
Automation	**Innovation**
Technology lets business automate the work that people had always done	Technology lets people do things that they've never done before

almost equal likelihood that she will be female. Past and present entrepreneurs also have fundamentally different views as to why they succeeded, the role of automation in business, and the importance of trade versus business knowledge.[11]

Consider, for instance, Patrick Byrne. Byrne runs Overstock.com, an e-commerce firm that buys excess inventory from manufacturers of clothing, electronics products, and other products, which it then resells at deeply discounted prices on the Internet. Byrne started out in the business world by creating a personal-investment fund called High Plains. Over a period of years, he amassed a $100 million portfolio, a portion of which he then used to buy Overstock.com. Along the way, he also found time to earn a Ph.D. in philosophy from Stanford and a black belt in *tae kwon do*. He also bicycled across the United States three times, studied philosophy at Cambridge, and learned five new languages, including Mandarin Chinese. He learned about Overstock.com when its owners came to High Plains seeking capital. "The financials," admits Byrne, "were a joke. But buried in all that was this billion-dollar idea." Instead of simply investing in the business, Byrne bought it. Many investors now see Overstock.com as perhaps the next big Internet success story.[12]

> ***"The financials were a joke. But buried in all that was this billion-dollar idea."***
>
> *—CEO Patrick Byrne of Overstock.com, on why he bought the company rather than investing in it*

Among other things, Patrick Byrne's story clearly illustrates the role of *risk* in entrepreneurship. Assuming risk is almost always a central element of entrepreneurship. Interestingly, however, most successful entrepreneurs seldom see what they do as risky. While others may see numerous possibilities for failure and balk at gambling everything on a new venture, most entrepreneurs are so passionate about their ideas and feel so strongly about their plans that they see little or no likelihood of failure. Byrne, for example, saw major problems with the financial outlook for Overstock.com but believed so strongly in the underlying value of what the firm was all about that he was willing to take an enormous personal gamble on its prospects for success.[13]

SUCCESS AND FAILURE IN SMALL BUSINESS

For every Henry Ford, Walt Disney, Mary Kay Ash, or Bill Gates—people who transformed small businesses into major corporations—there are many small-business owners and entrepreneurs who fail. Figure 7.5 illustrates recent trends in new business start-ups and failures. As you can see, over the last 10 years new business start-ups have numbered between 150,000 and 190,000 per year, with 155,141 new businesses being launched in 1998. Over this same period, business failures have run between 50,000 and 100,000, with a total of 71,857 failing in 1998. In this section, we look first at a few key trends in small-business start-ups. Then we examine some of the main reasons for success and failure in small-business undertakings.

Trends in Small-Business Start-Ups

Thousands of new businesses are started in the United States every year. Several factors account for this trend, and in this section we focus on five of them:

- The emergence of e-commerce
- Entrepreneurs who cross over from big business
- Increased opportunities for minorities and women
- New opportunities in global enterprise
- Improved rates of survival among small businesses

Emergence of e-Commerce Clearly, the most significant recent trend in small-business start-ups is the rapid emergence of electronic commerce. Because the Internet has provided fundamentally new ways of doing business, savvy entrepreneurs have been able to create and expand new businesses faster and easier than ever before. Such leading-edge firms as America Online, Amazon.com, E*Trade, and eBay, for example, owe their

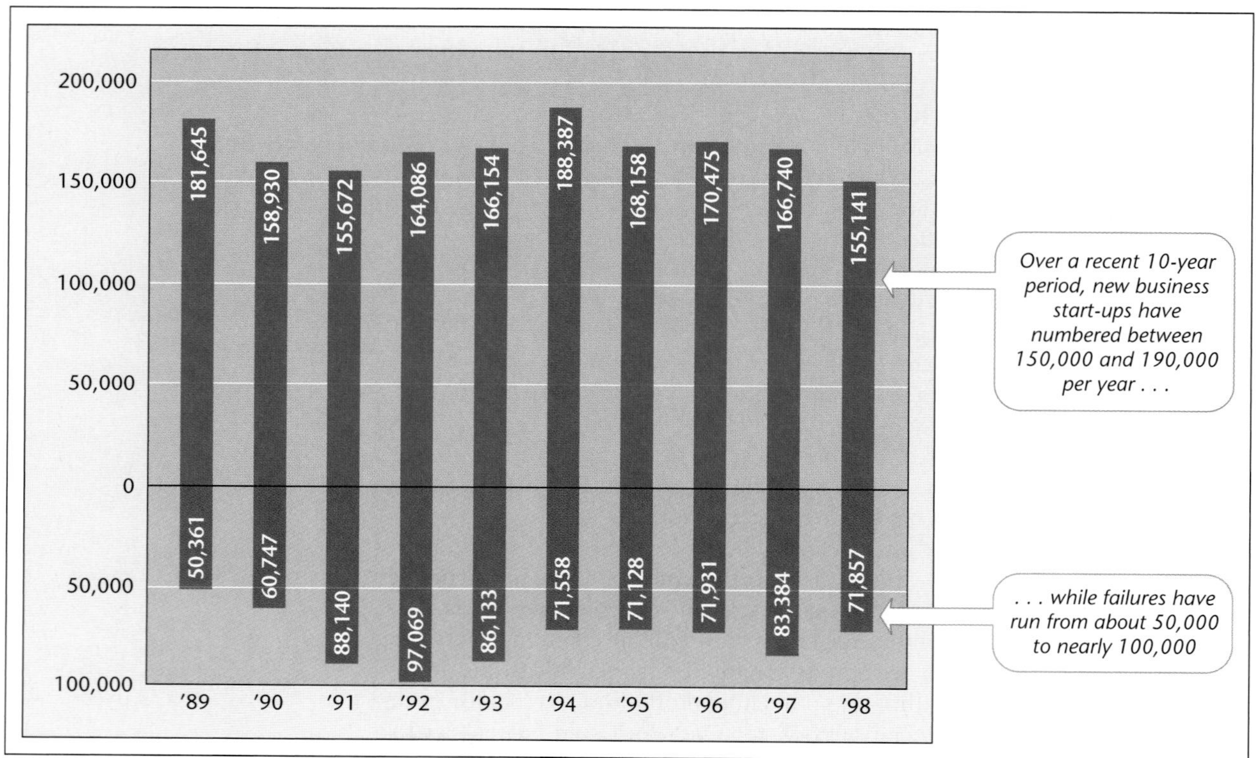

Figure 7.5
Start-Ups: Success and Failure

very existence to the Internet. Figure 7.6 amplifies this point by summarizing the tremendous growth in online commerce from 1997 through 2001. In addition, one recent study reported that in 1999, the Internet economy grew overall by 62 percent over the previous year and provided jobs for 2.5 million people.[14]

It seems as if new ideas emerge virtually every day. Andrew Beebe, for example, is scoring big with BigStep.com, a Web business that essentially creates, hosts, and maintains Web sites for other small businesses. So far, BigStep.com has signed up 75,000 small-business clients. Beebe actually provides his basic services for free but earns money by charging for so-called premium services such as customer billing. Karl Jacob's Keen.com is a Web business that matches people looking for advice with experts who have the answers. Keen got the idea when he and his father were struggling to fix a boat motor and didn't know where to turn for help. Keen.com attracted 100,000 subscribers in just three months.[15]

Crossovers from Big Business It is interesting to note that increasingly more businesses are being started by people who have opted to leave big corporations and put their experience and know-how to work for themselves. In some cases, these individuals see great new ideas they want to develop. Often, they get burned out working for a big corporation. Sometimes, they have lost their jobs, only to discover that working for themselves was a better idea anyway.

Cisco Systems CEO John Chambers is acknowledged as one of the best entrepreneurs around. But he spent several years working first at IBM and then at Wang Laboratories <www.wang.com/GLOBAL> before he set out on his own. Under his leadership, Cisco <www.cisco.com> has become one of the largest and most important technology companies in the world. For a few days in March 2000, Cisco had the world's highest market capitalization, and it remains one of the world's most valuable companies.[16] In a more unusual case, Gilman Louie recently left an executive position at

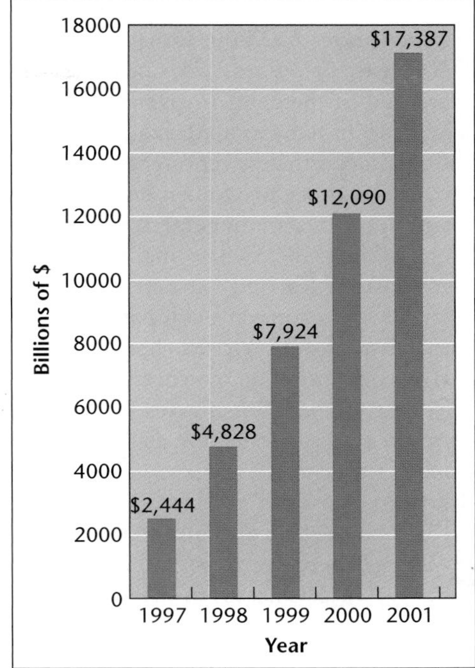

Figure 7.6
Growth of Online Commerce

Hasbro toy company's online group <www.hasbro.com> to head up a CIA-backed venture capital firm called In-Q-It. The firm's mission is to help nurture high-tech companies making products of interest to the nation's spies.[17]

Opportunities for Minorities and Women In addition to big-business expatriates, more small businesses are being started by minorities and women. For example, the number of Black-owned businesses has increased by 46 percent during the most recent five-year period for which data are available and now totals about 620,000. Chicago's Gardner family is just one of thousands of examples illustrating this trend. The Gardners are the founders of Soft Sheen Products, Inc., a firm specializing in ethnic hair products. Soft Sheen attained sales of $80 million in the year before the Gardners sold it to France's L'Oréal S.A. <www.lorealparisusa.com> for more than $160 million. The emergence of such opportunities is hardly surprising, either to Black entrepreneurs or to the corporate marketers who have taken an interest in their companies. Black purchasing power topped $530 billion in 1999. Up from just over $300 billion in 1990, that increase of 73 percent far outstrips the 57 percent increase experienced by all Americans.[18]

www.fuxito.com

Cofounded by a 20-year-old Jamaican soccer star/Harvard economics major, Fúxito (which combines the Spanish words for *soccer* and *success*) strives to be the new media site for everything soccer, including news, discussion boards, athlete interviews, a recruiting database for coaches, Web site-building technology, and e-commerce.

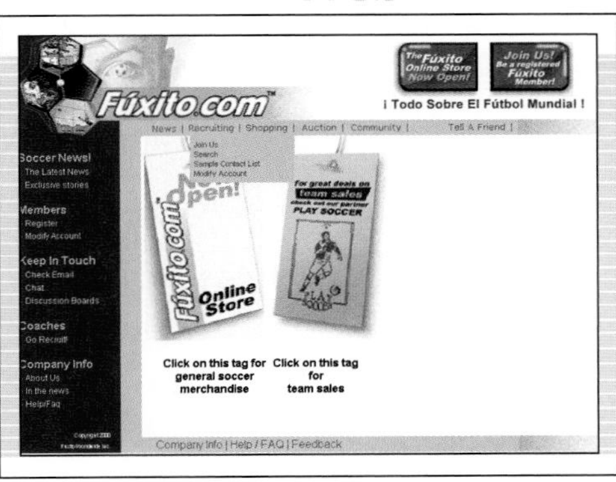

Hispanic-owned businesses have grown at an even faster rate of 76 percent and now number about 862,000. Other ethnic groups are also making their presence felt among U.S. business owners. Business ownership among Asians and Pacific Islanders has increased 56 percent, to over 600,000. Although the number of businesses owned by American Indians and Alaska Natives is still somewhat small, at slightly over 100,000, the total nevertheless represents a five-year increase of 93 percent.[19]

The number of women entrepreneurs is also growing rapidly. Celeste Johnson, for example, left a management position at Pitney Bowes <www.pitneybowes.com> to launch Obex, Inc., which makes gardening and landscaping products from mixed recycled plastics. Katrina Garnett gave up a lucrative job at Oracle <www.oracle.com> to start her own software company, Crossworlds Software, Inc. <www.crossworlds.com>. Laila Rubenstein closed her management-consulting practice to create Greeting Cards.com, Inc., an Internet-based business selling customizable electronic greetings. "Women-owned businesses," says Teresa Cavanaugh, director of the Women Entrepreneur's Connection at BankBoston, "is the largest emerging segment of the small-business market. Women-owned businesses are an economic force that no bank can afford to overlook."[20]

"Women-owned businesses are an economic force that no bank can afford to overlook."

—Teresa Cavanaugh, Director, Women Entrepreneur's Connection, BankBoston

Likewise, the number of women-owned businesses is also growing rapidly. There are now 9.1 million businesses owned by women—38 percent of all businesses in the United States. Combined, they generate nearly $4 trillion in revenue a year—an increase of 132 percent since 1992. The number of people employed nationwide at women-owned businesses since 1992 has grown to around 27.5 million—an increase of 108 percent.[21] Figure 7.7 summarizes the corporate backgrounds of women entrepreneurs and provides some insight into what they like about running their own businesses. Corporate positions in general management (25 percent), sales (21 percent), and accounting and finance (18 percent) account for almost two-thirds of the women who start their own businesses. Once in charge of their own businesses, women also report that they like being their own bosses, setting their own hours, controlling their own destinies, relating to customers, making decisions, and achieving goals.

Global Opportunities Many entrepreneurs today are also finding new opportunities in foreign markets. Doug Mellinger, for example, is founder and CEO of PRT Group, Inc., a software development company. One of Mellinger's biggest problems was finding enough trained programmers: There are not enough American programmers to go around, and foreign-born programmers face strict immigration quotas. So Mellinger set up shop on Barbados, a Caribbean island eager for economic development. The local government helps him attract foreign programmers and has gone to great lengths to make it easy for him to do business. Today, PRT, which is a part of enherent Corp. <www.enherent.com>, has both customers and suppliers from dozens of nations around the world.[22]

Better Survival Rates Finally, more people are encouraged to test their skills as entrepreneurs because the failure rate among small businesses has been declining in recent years. During the 1960s and 1970s, less than half of all new start-ups survived more than 18 months—only one in five lasted 10 years. Now, however, new businesses have a better chance of surviving. Of new businesses started in the 1980s, for instance, over 77 percent remained in operation for at least three years. Today, the SBA estimates that at least 40 percent of all new businesses can expect to survive for six years. As you can see from Figure 7.8, which shows the small-business survival rate over a 10-year period, the key is longevity. For the reasons discussed in the next section, small businesses suffer a higher mortality rate than larger concerns. Among those, however, that manage to stay in business for six to 10 years, the survival rate levels off.

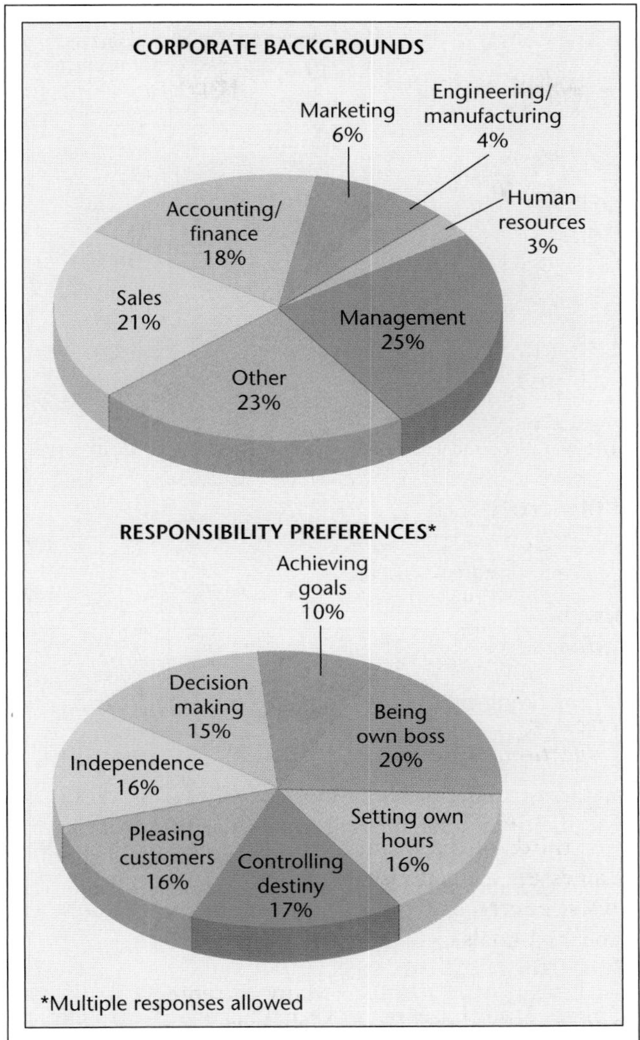

Figure 7.7
Profiles of Women Entrepreneurs

Reasons for Failure

What do you consider to be the greatest risk factors that entrepreneurs and small business owners face today and in the immediate future?

Unfortunately, 63 percent of all new businesses will not celebrate a sixth anniversary. Why do some succeed and others fail? Although no set pattern has been established, four general factors contribute to small-business failure:

- *Managerial incompetence or inexperience.* Some would-be entrepreneurs assume that they can succeed through common sense, overestimate their own managerial acumen, or think that hard work alone will lead to success. If managers do not know how to make basic business decisions or understand the basic concepts and principles of management, they are unlikely to be successful in the long run.
- *Neglect.* Some entrepreneurs try either to launch their ventures in their spare time or to devote only a limited amount of time to a new business. But starting a small business requires an overwhelming time commitment. Entrepreneurs who are not willing to put in the time and effort that a business requires are unlikely to survive.
- *Weak control systems.* Effective control systems are needed to keep a business on track and to help alert entrepreneurs to potential trouble. If control systems do not signal

Figure 7.8
Small-Business Survival Rate

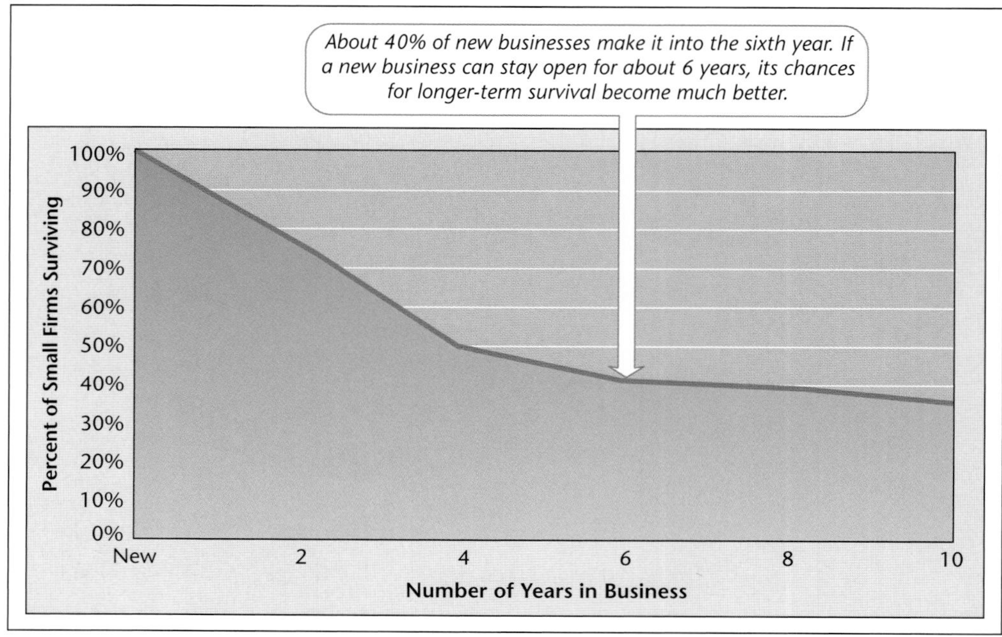
About 40% of new businesses make it into the sixth year. If a new business can stay open for about 6 years, its chances for longer-term survival become much better.
Percent of Small Firms Surviving
100%
90%
80%
70%
60%
50%
40%
30%
20%
10%
0%
New
2
4
6
8
10
Number of Years in Business

impending problems, managers may be in serious trouble before more visible difficulties alert them.

- *Insufficient capital.* Some entrepreneurs are overly optimistic about how soon they will start earning profits. In most cases, however, it takes months or years before a business is likely to start turning a profit. Amazon.com, for example, has still not earned a profit. Most experts say that a new business should have enough capital to operate at least six months without earning a profit—some recommend enough to last a year.[23]

Reasons for Success

Similarly, four basic factors are typically cited to explain small-business success:

- *Hard work, drive, and dedication.* Small-business owners must be committed to succeeding and be willing to put in the time and effort to make it happen. Gladys

"Won't all these new rules impact adversely on the viability of small businesses with fewer than fifty employees?"

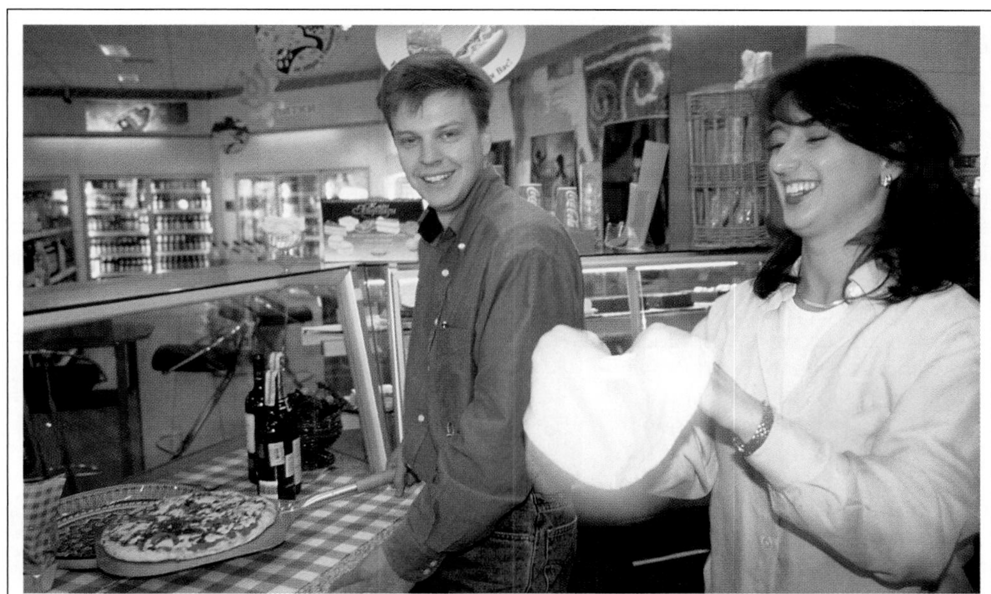

Rick and Stacy Komendera went straight out of college to Russia in the early 1990s. In June 1999, they opened their first Pizza Picazzo outlet in Moscow, where the number of cafés and fast-food restaurants grew by 30 percent between May 1998 and May 1999. They also found a powerful ally in their first franchisee—BP Amoco, which has refitted several of its 24-hour gas stations in the Russian capital in order to make room for Pizza Picazzos.

Edmunds, a single teenage mother in Pittsburgh, washed laundry, made chicken dinners to sell to cab drivers, and sold fire extinguishers and Bibles door-to-door to earn money to launch her own business. Today, Edmunds Travel Consultants employs eight people and earns about $6 million in annual revenue.[24]

- *Market demand for the products or services being provided.* Careful analysis of market conditions can help small-business owners assess the probable reception of their products in the marketplace. Whereas attempts to expand local restaurants specializing in baked potatoes, muffins, and gelato have been largely unsuccessful, hamburger and pizza chains continue to have an easier time expanding into new markets.
- *Managerial competence.* Successful small-business owners may acquire competence through training or experience or by using the expertise of others. Few successful entrepreneurs succeed alone or straight out of college. Most spend time working in successful companies or partner with others in order to bring more expertise to a new business.
- *Luck.* Lady Luck also plays a role in the success of some firms. For example, after Alan McKim started Clean Harbors <www.cleanharbors.com>, an environmental cleanup firm based in New England, he struggled to keep his business afloat. Then the U.S. government committed $1.6 billion to toxic waste cleanup—McKim's specialty. He was able to get several large government contracts and put his business on solid financial footing. Had the government fund not been created at just the right time, McKim may well have failed.

The "Life Cycle of an e-Business" box in this chapter discusses the means by which Garden.com initially capitalized on the factors that improve a start-up's chances for success but eventually succumbed to other factors that doomed it to failure.

STARTING AND OPERATING THE SMALL BUSINESS

The Internet, of course, is rewriting virtually all of the rules for starting and operating a small business. Getting into business is easier and faster than ever before, there are many more potential opportunities than at any time in history, and the ability to gather and assimilate information is at an all-time high. Even so, however, would-be entrepreneurs must still make the right decisions when they start. They must decide precisely *how* to get into business. Should they buy an existing business or build from the ground up? In

Life Cycle of an e-Business

Sprouting the Entrepreneurial Spirit at Garden.com

Throughout this book, we have been tracing the life cycle of Garden.com. At several points, for example, we have indicated various reasons for the firm's initial success and alluded to some of the reasons for its eventual failure. It will be instructive to look again at some of the specific reasons for new business success (and failure) that we have itemized in this chapter and show how they apply to the Garden.com story. First, let's examine the general reasons for new business success and their relevance to Garden.com.

In part, new business success is a product of hard work, drive, and dedication. From the very beginning, Jamie O'Neill and Lisa and Cliff Sharples shared the same vision and passion for business success and committed most of their waking hours to achieving it. Indeed, they collectively poured their hearts and souls into their venture. Of course, they were helped by strong demand for their products and services. Their own managerial competence was also a key factor—first, in determining just the right business and, second, in knowing just how to meet the demand that made it feasible.

Luck, too, played at least a small role in their initial success. For one thing, their timing seemed impeccable: They launched Garden.com just as the Internet was exploding as a business model and secured their venture capital just as investors were lining up to fund Internet start-ups. They also avoided tough competition in the initial stages because no one else was setting up shop in the same market.

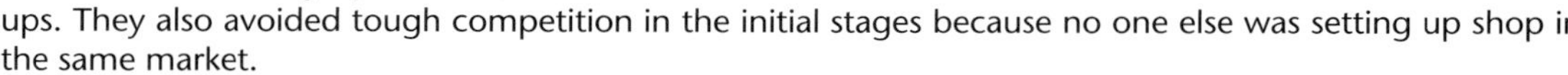

So why did Garden.com eventually go under? The overriding reason was insufficient capital. During the late 1990s, investors seemed willing to pour an unending stream of capital into virtually any promising dot-com business. Like most such firms, Garden.com had secured a substantial amount of financing. By 2000, however, the business climate had changed considerably, as investors became increasingly wary of firms that had yet to show a profit.

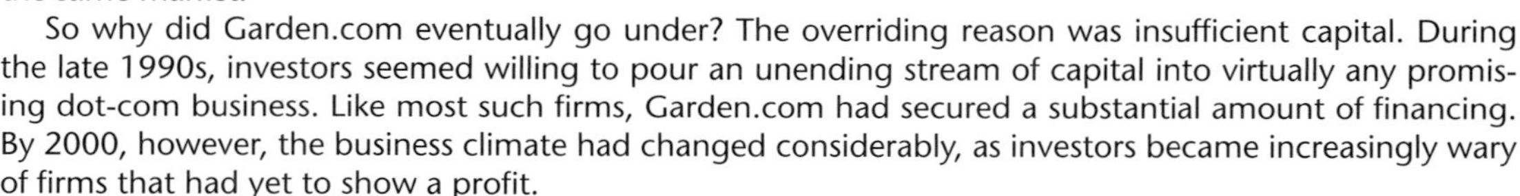

As its cash began to dry up in the summer of 2000, Garden.com was simply unable to secure the additional funding it needed to remain afloat. The firm may also have had flawed control systems that failed to alert senior managers to the impending cash shortage. In particular, it is conceivable that if they had known earlier of the impending shortfall, they could have cut costs more quickly, secured additional financing before the investment community backed away the dot-com sector, or both.

Regardless of the specific reasons for the eventual failure that followed upon Garden.com's initial success, both current and would-be entrepreneurs can learn some valuable lessons from its story. For one thing, a business can never have too much money. For another, while investors may tolerate periodic losses, they can quickly become impatient if losses mount too quickly and profits remain elusive. Finally, business owners and managers must never let their guard down: No matter how promising things look, a cash shortage, especially when combined with shifts in the financial and investment environment, can spell trouble for any business.

addition, would-be entrepreneurs must find appropriate sources of financing and decide when and how to seek the advice of experts.

Starting the Small Business

An old Chinese proverb suggests that a journey of a thousand miles begins with a single step. This is also true of a new business. The first step is the individual's commitment to becoming a business owner. Next comes choosing the goods or services to be offered—a process that means investigating one's chosen industry and market. Making this choice also requires would-be entrepreneurs to assess not only industry trends but also their own skills. Like the managers of big businesses, small-business owners must also be sure that they understand the true nature of the enterprises in which they are engaged.

Buying Out an Existing Business After choosing a product and making sure that the choice fits their own skills and interests, entrepreneurs must decide whether to buy an existing business or to start from scratch. Consultants often recommend the first approach. Quite simply, the odds are better: If successful, an existing business has already proved its ability to draw customers at a profit. It has also established working relationships with lenders, suppliers, and the community. Moreover, the track record of an existing business gives potential buyers a much clearer picture of what to expect than any estimate of a new business's prospects. Around 30 percent of the new businesses started in the past decade were bought from someone else. The McDonald's empire <www.mcdonalds.com>, for example, was started when Ray Kroc bought an existing hamburger business and then turned it into a global phenomenon. Likewise, Starbucks <www.starbucks.com> was a struggling mail-order business when Howard Schultz bought it and turned his attention to retail expansion.

Starting from Scratch Some people seek the satisfaction that comes from planting an idea, nurturing it, and making it grow into a strong and sturdy business. There are also practical reasons to start a business from scratch. A new business does not suffer the ill effects of a prior owner's errors. The start-up owner is also free to choose lenders, equipment, inventories, locations, suppliers, and workers, unbound by a predecessor's commitments and policies. Of the new businesses begun in the past decade, 64 percent were started from scratch. Garden.com was among these.

The risks of starting a business from scratch are greater than those of buying an existing firm. Founders of new businesses can only make predictions and projections about their prospects. Success or failure thus depends heavily on identifying a genuine business opportunity—a product for which many customers will pay well but that is currently unavailable to them. To find openings, entrepreneurs must study markets and answer the following questions:

- Who are my customers?
- Where are they?
- At what price will they buy my product?
- In what quantities will they buy?
- Who are my competitors?
- How will my product differ from those of my competitors?

Finding answers to these questions is a difficult task even for large, well-established firms. But where can the small-business owner get the necessary information? Other sources of assistance are discussed later in this chapter, but we briefly describe three of the most accessible here:

- The best way to gain knowledge about a market is to work in it before going into business in it. For example, if you once worked in a bookstore and now plan to open one of your own, you probably already have some idea about the kinds of books people request and buy.
- A quick scan of the local Yellow Pages or an Internet search will reveal many potential competitors, as will advertisements in trade journals. Personal visits to these establishments and Web sites can give you insights into their strengths and weaknesses.
- Studying magazines, books, and Web sites aimed specifically at small businesses can also be of help, as can hiring professionals to survey the market for you.

Financing the Small Business

Although the choice of how to start is obviously important, it is meaningless unless a small-business owner can obtain the money to set up shop. Among the more common sources for funding are family and friends, personal savings, banks and similar lending institutions, investors, and governmental agencies. Lending institutions are more likely to help finance the purchase of an existing business than a new business because the risks are better understood. Individuals starting up new businesses, on the other hand, are more likely to have to rely on their personal resources.

According to a study by the National Federation of Independent Business <www.nfibonline.com>, an owner's personal resources, not loans, are the most important source of money. Including money borrowed from friends and relatives, personal resources account for over two-thirds of all money invested in new small businesses and one-half of that invested in the purchase of existing businesses. When Michael Dorf and his friends decided to launch a New York nightclub dubbed the Knitting Factory <www.knittingfactory.com>, he started with $30,000 of his own money. Within four months of opening, Dorf asked his father to co-sign the first of four consecutive Milwaukee bank loans (for $70,000, $200,000, $300,000, and, to move to a new facility, $500,000, respectively). Dorf and his partners also engaged in creative bartering, such as putting a sound system company's logo on all its advertising in exchange for free equipment. Finally, because the Knitting Factory has become so successful, other investors are now stepping forward to provide funds—$650,000 from one investor and $4.2 million from another.[25]

Strategic alliances are also becoming a popular method for financing business growth. When Steven and Andrew Grundy decided to launch a CD-exchange Internet business called Spun.com, they had very little capital and so made extensive use of alliances with other firms. They partnered, for example, with wholesaler Alliance Entertainment Corp. <www. aent.com> as a CD supplier. Orders to Spun.com actually go to Alliance, which ships products to customers and bills Spun.com directly. This setup has allowed Spun.com to promote a vast inventory of labels without actually having to buy inventory. All told, the firm has created an alliance network that has provided the equivalent of $40 million in capital.[26]

New York's Knitting Factory <www.knittingfactory.com> has been host to hundreds of progressive rock and jazz bands since 1987, when CEO Michael Dorf opened it on a $30,000 investment. Within four months, Dorf was able to get over a $1 million in bank loans. Once the club became known to local musicians and music followers, he was able to attract venture capital, including $4.2 million from a New York City investment firm. Between 1994 and 1998, revenues skyrocketed from $270,000 to $6 million (an increase of 2,134 percent).

Although banks, independent investors, and government loans all provide much smaller portions of start-up funds than the personal resources of owners, they are important in many cases. Getting money from these sources, however, requires some extra effort. Banks and private investors usually want to see formal **business plans**—detailed outlines of proposed businesses and markets, owners' backgrounds, and other sources of funding. Government loans have strict eligibility guidelines.

business plan
Document that tells potential lenders why money is needed, how it will be used, and when it will be repaid

Other Sources of Investment Two other sources of start-up funds are venture capital companies and small-business investment companies.

Venture Capital Companies **Venture capital companies** are groups of small investors seeking to make profits on companies with rapid growth potential. Most of these firms do not lend money: they invest it, supplying capital in return for stock. The venture capital company may also demand a representative on the board of directors. In some cases, managers may even need approval from the venture capital company before making major decisions. Of all venture capital currently committed in the United States, 29 percent comes from true venture capital firms.[27]

venture capital company
Group of small investors that invest money in companies with rapid growth potential

For example, Dr. Drew Pinsky, cohost of MTV's *Loveline,* recently got venture capital funding to extend his program to the Internet from a group of investors collectively known as Garage.com. Garage.com is comprised of several individuals and other investors who specialize in financing Internet start-ups.[28] Similarly, Softbank Inc. <www.softbank> is a venture capital firm that has provided funds to over 300 Web companies including Yahoo! and E*trade. As founder Masayoshi Son puts it, "We're a strategic holding company, investing in companies that are very important in the digital information industry—in e-commerce, financial services, and media."

small-business investment company (SBIC)
A government-regulated investment company that borrows money from the SBA to invest in or lend to a small business

Small-Business Investment Companies Taking a more balanced approach in their choices than venture capital companies, **small-business investment companies (SBICs)** seek profits by investing in companies with potential for rapid growth. Created by the Small Business Investment Act of 1958, SBICs are federally licensed to borrow money from the SBA and to invest it in or lend it to small businesses. They are themselves investments for their shareholders. Past beneficiaries of SBIC capital include Apple Computer, Intel, and Federal Express. In addition, the government has recently begun to sponsor **minority enterprise small-business investment companies (MESBICs)**. As the name suggests, MESBICs specialize in financing businesses that are owned and operated by minorities.

minority enterprise small-business investment company (MESBIC)
Federally sponsored company that specializes in financing businesses that are owned and operated by minorities

WebConnection

www.garage.com

Garage.com uses the resources of the Internet to help entrepreneurs find venture capital. The online firm screens business plans, "narrowcasts" them to those prospects who are most likely to be interested, and coordinates e-mail discussions between business owners and prospective investors. To find out more about what venture capitalism can offer the small business—and what online networking can do for the venture-capitalist process—go to the Garage.com Web site.

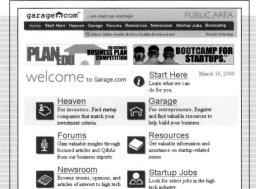

SBA Financial Programs Since its founding in 1953, the SBA has offered more than 20 financing programs to small businesses that meet standards in size and independence. Eligible firms must also be unable to get private financing at reasonable terms. Because of these and other restrictions, SBA loans have never been a major source of small-business financing. In addition, budget cutbacks at the SBA have reduced the number of firms benefiting from loans. Nevertheless, several SBA programs currently offer funds to qualified applicants:

guaranteed loans program Program in which the SBA guarantees to repay 75 to 85 percent of small-business commercial loans up to $750,000

immediate participation loans program Program in which small businesses are loaned funds put up jointly by banks and the SBA

local development companies (LDCs) program Program in which the SBA works with local for-profit or not-for-profit organizations seeking to boost a community's economy

- Under the SBA's **guaranteed loans program,** small businesses can borrow from commercial lenders. The SBA guarantees to repay 75 to 85 percent of the loan amount, not to exceed $750,000. Under a related program, companies engaged in international trade can borrow up to $1.25 million. Such loans may be made for as long as 15 years. Most SBA lending activity flows through this program.
- Sometimes both the desired bank and SBA-guaranteed loans are unavailable (perhaps because the business cannot meet stringent requirements). In such cases, the SBA may help finance the entrepreneur through its **immediate participation loans program.** Under this arrangement, the SBA and the bank each put up a share of the money, with the SBA's share not to exceed $150,000.
- Under the **local development companies (LDCs) program,** the SBA works with a corporation (either for-profit or not-for-profit) founded by local citizens who want to boost the local economy. The SBA can lend up to $500,000 for each small business to be helped by an LDC.

Spurred in large part by the boom in Internet businesses, both venture capital and loans are becoming easier to get. As Figure 7.9 shows, most small businesses report that it has generally gotten increasingly easier to obtain loans over the last 10 years. The "Wired World" box in this chapter discusses an even more extreme situation: Some technology companies are being offered so much venture capital that they are turning down part of it to keep from diluting their ownership unnecessarily.

Sources of Management Advice

Financing is not the only area in which small businesses need help. Until World War II, the business world involved few regulations, few taxes, few records, few big competitors, and no computers. Since then, simplicity has given way to complexity: Today, few entrepreneurs are equipped with all the business skills they need to survive. Small-business owners can no longer be their own troubleshooters, lawyers, bookkeepers, financiers, and tax experts. For these jobs, they rely on professional help. To survive and grow, however, small businesses also need advice regarding management. This advice is usually available from four sources: *advisory boards, management consultants, the SBA,* and a process called *networking.*

WebConnection

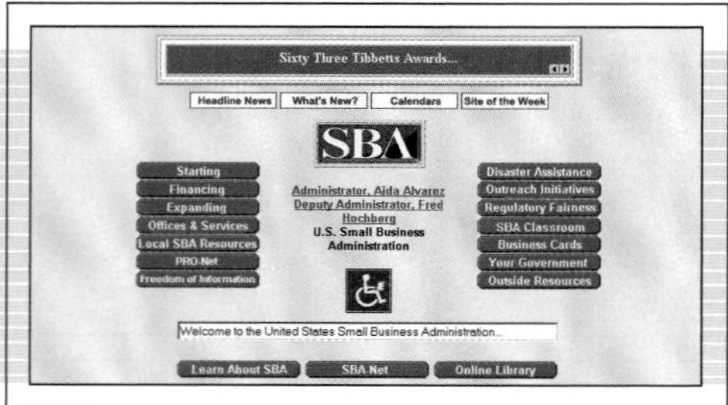

www.sba.gov

The SBA Web site is a virtual gold mine of information on starting, financing, and expanding small businesses, as well as disaster assistance and pertinent legislation and regulation. It also offers links to a wide variety of additional sites.

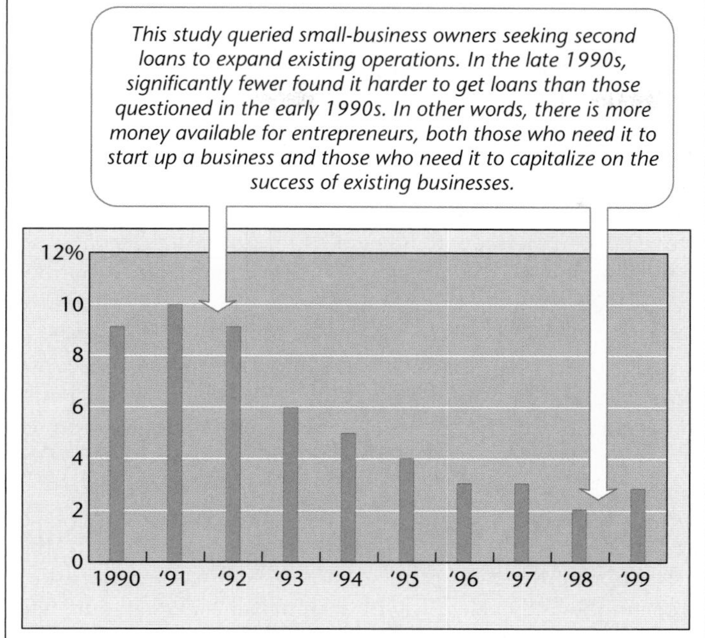

This study queried small-business owners seeking second loans to expand existing operations. In the late 1990s, significantly fewer found it harder to get loans than those questioned in the early 1990s. In other words, there is more money available for entrepreneurs, both those who need it to start up a business and those who need it to capitalize on the success of existing businesses.
12%
10
8
6
4
2
0
1990 '91 '92 '93 '94 '95 '96 '97 '98 '99

Figure 7.9

Firms Finding Money Easier to Find

It's a WiredWorld

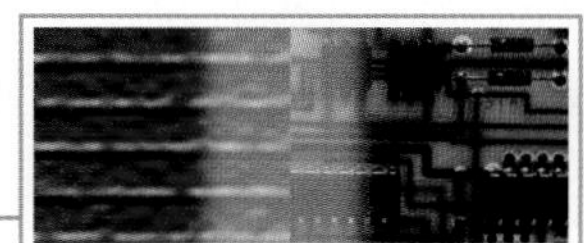

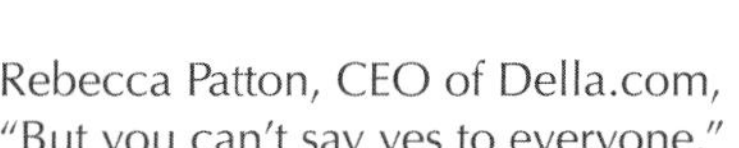

• *A Wealth of Investors for Picky Start-Ups*

Most people wouldn't dream of passing up $30 million, but in Silicon Valley, giving up cash is *de rigueur* for a growing number of tech start-ups.

The reason: With so much cash available and banks and venture capital firms clamoring for a piece of the next big thing, start-ups want to ensure they don't give away too much and dilute the company's value.

Competition among investment firms has never been tougher as businesses pick and choose who will supply their seed money. Even companies with no-name CEOs and untested business models are turning away investors.

• I-drive.com, which allows users to store, organize and share information on the Web, took $17 million but was offered almost $50 million. It refused the extra.

• Linuxcare <www.linuxcare.com>, which provides technical support for companies using Linux, took $32.5 million in investments but spurned offers that totaled nearly $300 million.

• Della.com, an online aggregator of wedding registry sites, and Yodlee.com, which aggregates personalized Web sites, have refused several million dollars in financing.

The access to cash is being fueled by the growth in venture capital firms, which shot up from about 250 in 1992 to al least 850 today, says Todd Carter, an investment banker with Banc Boston Robertson Stephens. "We see a heightened level of competition."

Entrepreneurs say the piles of cash are a mixed blessing. "There are great people out there who have money, and you want to have them involved in the company," says Rebecca Patton, CEO of Della.com, "But you can't say yes to everyone."

More companies choose to stick it out until they can go public. An initial public offering is generally a cheaper way to raise funds and keep control of the company. For example, a venture capitalist might offer to give a company $20 million in exchange for 20% of the company. But in the public market, the company could likely sell 20% of its firm for $200 million.

Jeff Bonforte, CEO of I-drive.com, says picking the right investors is as important as accepting the right amount of cash. "You pick a VC like you pick a girlfriend or a wife," says Bonforte, whose company is funded by Draper Fisher Jurvetson. "You're locked in with these people. . . . A lead investor will make your life hell if you don't go along with what they want."

Advisory Boards All companies, even those that do not legally need boards of directors, can benefit from the problem-solving abilities of advisory boards. Thus, some small businesses create boards to provide advice and assistance. For example, an advisory board might help an entrepreneur determine the best way to finance a plant expansion or to start exporting products to foreign markets.

management consultant
Independent outside specialist hired to help managers solve business problems

Management Consultants Opinions vary widely about the value of **management consultants**—experts who charge fees to help managers solve business problems. They often specialize in one area, such as international business, small business, or manufacturing. Thus, they can bring an objective and trained outlook to problems and provide logical recommendations. They can be quite expensive, however, as some consultants charge $1,000 or more for a day of assistance.

Like other professionals, consultants should be chosen with care. They can be found through major corporations that have used their services and that can provide references and reports on their work. Management consultants are most effective when the client helps (for instance, by providing schedules and written proposals for work to be done).

The Small Business Administration Even more important than its financing role is the SBA's role in helping small-business owners improve their management skills. It is easy for entrepreneurs to spend money—SBA programs are designed to show them how to spend it wisely. The SBA offers small businesses four major management counseling programs at virtually no cost:

Service Corps of Retired Executives (SCORE)
SBA program in which retired executives work with small businesses on a volunteer basis

Active Corps of Executives (ACE)
SBA program in which currently employed executives work with small businesses on a volunteer basis

Small Business Institute (SBI)
SBA program in which college and university students and instructors work with small-business owners to help solve specific problems

Small Business Development Center (SBDC)
SBA program designed to consolidate information from various disciplines and make it available to small businesses

- A small-business owner who needs help in starting a new business can get it free through the **Service Corps of Retired Executives** (**SCORE**) <www.score.org>. All SCORE members are retired executives, and all are volunteers. Under this program, the SBA tries to match the expert to the need. For example, if a small-business owner needs help putting together a marketing plan, the SBA will send a SCORE counselor with marketing expertise.
- Like SCORE, the **Active Corps of Executives** (**ACE**) program is designed to help small businesses that cannot afford consultants. The SBA recruits ACE volunteers from virtually every industry. All ACE volunteers are currently involved in successful activities, mostly as small-business owners themselves. Together, SCORE and ACE have more than 12,000 counselors working out of 350 chapters throughout the United States. They provide assistance to some 140,000 small businesses each year.
- The talents and skills of students and instructors at colleges and universities are fundamental to the **Small Business Institute** (**SBI**) <www.smallbizinst.com>. Under the guidance of seasoned professors of business administration, students seeking advanced degrees work closely with small-business owners to help solve specific problems, such as sagging sales or rising costs. Students earn credit toward their degrees, with their grades depending on how well they handle a client's problems. Several hundred colleges and universities counsel thousands of small-business owners through this program every year.
- The newest of the SBA's management counseling projects is its **Small Business Development Center** (**SBDC**) program <www.sba.gov/sbdc>. Begun in 1976, SBDCs are designed to consolidate information from various disciplines and institutions, including technical and professional schools. Then they make this knowledge available to new and existing small businesses. In 1995, universities in 45 states took part in the program.

networking
Interactions among businesspeople for the purpose of discussing mutual problems and opportunities and perhaps pooling resources

Networking Increasingly, small-business owners are discovering the value of **networking**—meeting regularly with one another to discuss common problems and opportunities and, perhaps most important, pool resources. Businesspeople have long joined organizations such as the local chamber of commerce and the National Federation of Independent Businesses (NFIB) to make such contacts.

Today, organizations are springing up all over the United States to facilitate small-business networking. In particular, women and minorities have found networking to be an effective problem-solving tool. The National Association of Women Business Owners (NAWBO) <www.nawbo.org>, for example, provides a variety of networking forums. The NAWBO also has chapters in most major cities where its members can meet regularly. Increasingly, women are relying more on other women to help locate venture capital, establish relationships with customers, and provide such essential services as accounting and legal advice. According to Patty Abramson of the Women's Growth Capital Fund <www.womensgrowthcapital.com>, all of these tasks have traditionally been harder for women because, until now, they've never had friends in the right places. "I wouldn't say this is about discrimination," adds Abramson. "It's about not having the relationships, and business is about relationships."

"I wouldn't say this is about discrimination. It's about not having the relationships, and business is about relationships."

—*Patty Abramson, Women's Growth Capital Fund, on the growth of networking among women in business*

FRANCHISING

The next time you drive or walk around town, be on the alert for a McDonald's, Taco Bell, Subway, Denny's, or KFC restaurant, a 7-Eleven or Circle K convenience store, a RE/Max or Coldwell Banker real estate office, a Super 8 or Ramada motel, a Blockbuster Video store, a Sylvan Learning Center educational center, an Express Oil Change or Precision Auto Wash car-service center, or a Supercuts hair salon. What do these businesses have in common? In most cases, they will be franchised operations, operating under licenses issued by parent companies to local entrepreneurs who own and manage them.

As many would-be businesspeople have discovered, franchising agreements are an accessible doorway to entrepreneurship. A **franchise** is an arrangement that permits the *franchisee* (buyer) to sell the product of the *franchiser* (seller, or parent company). Franchisees can thus benefit from the selling corporation's experience and expertise. They can also consult the franchiser for managerial and financial help.

franchise
Arrangement in which a buyer (franchisee) purchases the right to sell the good or service of the seller (franchiser)

For example, the franchiser may supply financing. It may pick the store location, negotiate the lease, design the store, and purchase necessary equipment. It may train the first set of employees and managers and provide standardized policies and procedures. Once the business is open, the franchiser may offer savings by allowing the franchisee to purchase from a central location. Marketing strategy (especially advertising) may also be handled by the franchiser. Finally, franchisees may benefit from continued management counseling. In short, franchisees receive—that is, invest in—not only their own ready-made businesses but also expert help in running them.

Advantages and Disadvantages of Franchising

Compare and contrast the advantages of franchising a company to those of starting your own.

Franchises offer many advantages to both sellers and buyers. For example, franchisers benefit from the ability to grow rapidly by using the investment money provided by franchisees. This strategy has enabled giant franchisers such as McDonald's and Baskin-Robbins to mushroom into billion-dollar concerns in a brief time.

For the franchisee, the arrangement combines the incentive of owning a business with the advantage of access to big-business management skills. Unlike the person who starts from scratch, the franchisee does not have to build a business step-by-step. Instead, the business is established virtually overnight. Moreover, because each franchise outlet is probably a carbon copy of every other outlet, the chances of failure are reduced. McDonald's, for example, is a model of consistency—Big Macs taste the same everywhere.

Of course owning a franchise also involves certain disadvantages. Perhaps the most significant is the start-up cost. Franchise prices vary widely. Fantastic Sam's <www.fantasticsams.com> hair salon franchise fees are $30,000, but a Gingiss Formalwear <www.gingiss.com> franchise can run as high as $125,000. Extremely

WebConnection

www.ifa.org

The IFA is dedicated to promoting the business environment for franchising. Pages organize information on such areas of interest as "Government Regulations" and "U.S. Emerging Markets," and in addition to news and activities, the site includes a "Virtual Franchise Opportunities Mall" for prospective franchisees.

profitable or hard-to-get franchises are even more expensive. A McDonald's franchise costs at least $650,000 to $750,000, and a professional sports team can cost several hundred million dollars. Franchisees may also have continued obligations to contribute percentages of sales to parent corporations.

Buying a franchise also entails less tangible costs. For one thing, the small-business owner sacrifices some independence. A McDonald's franchisee cannot change the way hamburgers or milkshakes are made. Nor can franchisees create individual identities in their communities—for all practical purposes, the McDonald's owner is anonymous. In addition, many franchise agreements are difficult to terminate.

Finally, although franchises minimize risks, they do not guarantee success. Many franchisees have seen their investments—and their dreams—disappear because of poor locations, rising costs, or lack of continued franchiser commitment. Moreover, figures on failure rates are artificially low because they do not include failing franchisees bought out by their franchising parent companies. An additional risk is that the chain itself could collapse. In any given year, dozens—sometimes hundreds—of franchisers close shop or stop selling franchises.

Continued from page 175

The Next Installment

Barbara Babbit Kaufman is not likely to rest on the success of Chapter 11. Having carved out a retailing niche that emphasizes discount prices and shopping convenience, she has already expanded beyond familiar business territory by acquiring Onyx Entertainment, a book and music store based in Gainesville, Georgia. The acquisition not only moves Chapter 11 into the music business but also widens its geographic reach as a bookseller.

Kaufman, however, has just started to put her expansion plans into action. For one thing, she is planning to open another 15 stores in the Atlanta area. She is also trying to attract outside funding for expansion into another Southeastern city. Kaufman has also developed a Web site for Chapter 11. So far, it lacks the comprehensiveness of Amazon.com. But also unlike Amazon.com, Kaufman is focusing entirely on books, and some visitors say that her site is easier to use because of its simplicity and focus on a single product category.

Kaufman's ultimate goal is to go national. But big obstacles—namely, Barnes & Noble and Borders—stand in her way. If she can obtain the kind of financing she needs, though, some observers think she has a real fighting chance to succeed.

Questions for Discussion

1. Do you consider Barbara Babbit Kaufman a successful entrepreneur? Why?
2. Why is it important for a small company to find a marketing niche? Why is this particularly important when small companies compete directly with big businesses for the same customers?
3. Why was choosing locations in low-cost strip malls a smart business strategy? Would it be feasible for Borders or Barnes & Noble to use the same strategy?
4. What risks does Kaufman run in acquiring Onyx Entertainment? What are the risks of expanding to another city? What are the risks of becoming a national chain? Why do you think that many small businesses fail when they expand too rapidly or with too little capital?

SUMMARY OF LEARNING OBJECTIVES

1 **Define *small business* and explain its importance to the U.S. economy.** A *small business* is independently owned and managed and does not dominate its market. Small businesses are crucial to the economy because they create new jobs, foster *entrepreneurship* and *innovation,* and supply goods and services needed by larger businesses.

2 **Explain which *types of small business* best lend themselves to success.** Services are the easiest operations for small-business owners to start because they require low levels of resources. They also offer high returns on investment and tend to foster innovation. Retailing and wholesaling are more difficult because they usually require some experience, but they are still attractive to many entrepreneurs. Construction and financial and insurance operations are also common sectors for small business. As the most resource-intensive areas of the economy, transportation and manufacturing are the areas least populated by small firms.

3 **Define *entrepreneurship* and describe some basic *entrepreneurial characteristics.*** *Entrepreneurs* are small business owners who assume the risk of business ownership. Unlike small business owners, they seek growth and expansion as their primary goal. Most successful entrepreneurs share a strong desire to be their own bosses and believe that building businesses will help them gain control over their lives and build for their families. Many also enjoy taking risks and committing themselves to the necessary time and work. Finally, most report that freedom and creative expression are important factors in the decision to own and operate their own businesses.

4 **Describe the *start-up decisions* made by small businesses and identify sources of *financial aid* and *management advice* available to such enterprises.** The Internet is rewriting the rules of business start-up. In deciding to go into business, the entrepreneur must still first choose between buying an existing business and starting from scratch. Both approaches involve practical advantages and disadvantages. A successful existing business has working relationships with other businesses and has already proved its ability to make a profit. New businesses, on the other hand, allow owners to plan and work with clean slates, but it is hard to make projections about the business's prospects.

Although small-business owners generally draw heavily on their own resources for financing, they can get financial aid from venture capital firms, which seek profits from investments in companies with rapid growth potential. The *Small Business Administration (SBA)* also sponsors a variety of loan programs, including *small-business investment companies.* Finally, foreign firms and other nonbank lenders make funds available under various circumstances. Management advice is available from *advisory boards, management consultants, the SBA,* and the practice of *networking* (meeting regularly with people in related businesses to discuss problems and opportunities).

5 **Identify the advantages and disadvantages of *franchising*.** *Franchising* has become a popular form of small-business ownership because the *franchiser* (parent company) supplies financial, managerial, and marketing assistance to the *franchisee*, who buys the right to sell the franchiser's product. Franchising also enables small businesses to grow rapidly. Finally, the risks in franchising are lower than those in starting a new business from scratch. The costs of purchasing a franchise can be quite high, however, and the franchisee sacrifices independence and creativity. In addition, owning franchises provides no guarantee of success.

QUESTIONS AND EXERCISES

Questions for Review

1. Why are small businesses important to the U.S. economy?
2. What key factors typically contribute to the success and failure of small businesses?
3. What industries are easiest for small businesses to enter? What industries are hardest? Why?
4. From the standpoint of the franchisee, what are the primary advantages and disadvantages of most franchise arrangements?

Questions for Analysis

5. If you were going to open a small business, what type would it be? Why?
6. Do you think you would be a successful entrepreneur? Why or why not?
7. Would you prefer to buy an existing business or start your own business from scratch? Why?
8. Under what circumstances might it be wise for an entrepreneur to turn down venture capital? Under what circumstances might it be advisable to take more venture capital than the entrepreneur actually needs?

Application Exercises

9. Select a small local firm that has gone out of business recently. Identify as many factors as you can that led to the company's failure.
10. Using the Internet, research the role of small business in another country.

EXPLORING THE WEB

TAKING A FIELD TRIP TO THE SBA

One of the most important contacts for most small-business owners is the Small Business Administration (SBA). You can reach the SBA's Web site at the following address:

www.sbaonline.sba.gov/textonly/

Begin by examining the sections on "Starting Your Business," "Financing Your Business," and "Expanding Your Business." After you have examined these features, consider the following questions:

1. Assume that you are planning to purchase an existing small business. In the previous areas, what was the most important information that you could find? Identify other sections of the SBA site that might be relevant to you. What useful information did you find by browsing a few of these additional areas?
2. Assume that you are planning to start a new small business from scratch. Again, review the sections of the SBA site that might be most relevant, and report on the available information.
3. Assume that you are already operating a small business but are concerned about increasing competition. In what sections of its Web site does the SBA offer material that might be helpful to you?
4. Use the SBA links to visit the Web sites maintained by your U.S. representative and senator. What specific information on these sites, if any, might be most helpful to a small-business owner?
5. Overall, do you think the SBA site is likely to be more helpful for an existing business or for a new business just starting out? Why?

BUILDING YOUR BUSINESS SKILLS

WORKING THE INTERNET

This exercise enhances the following SCANS workplace competencies: demonstrating basic skills, demonstrating thinking skills, exhibiting interpersonal skills, and working with information.

GOAL

To encourage students to define the opportunities and problems for small companies doing business on the Internet.

SITUATION

Suppose you and two partners own a gift basket store, specializing in special occasion baskets for individual and corporate clients. Your business is doing well in your community, but you believe there may be opportunity for growth through a virtual storefront on the Internet.

METHOD

Step 1

Join with two other students and assume the role of business partners. Start by researching Internet businesses. Look at books and articles at the library and contact the following Web sites for help:

- Small Business Administration <www.sba.gov>
- IBM Small Business Center <www.business center.ibm.com>
- Apple Small Business Home Page <www.smallbusiness.apple.com>

These sites may lead you to other sites, so keep an open mind.

Step 2

Based on your research, determine the importance of the following small-business issues:

- An analysis of changing company finances as a result of expansion onto the Internet
- An analysis of your new competitive marketplace (the world) and how it affects your current marketing approach, which focuses on your local community
- Identification of sources of management advice as the expansion proceeds
- The role of technology consultants in launching and maintaining the Web site
- Customer service policies in your virtual environment

FOLLOW-UP QUESTIONS

1. Do you think your business would be successful on the Internet? Why or why not?
2. Based on your analysis, how will Internet expansion affect your current business practices? What specific changes are you likely to make?
3. Do you think that operating a virtual storefront will be harder or easier than doing business in your local community? Explain your answer.

CRAFTING YOUR BUSINESS PLAN

FITTING IN TO THE ENTREPRENEURIAL MOLD

THE PURPOSE OF THE ASSIGNMENT

1. To acquaint students with the process of navigating the *Business PlanPro* (*BPP*) software package (Version 4.0).
2. To familiarize students with the ways in which entrepreneurship and small business considerations enter into the business planning framework of *BPP.*

3. To encourage students to apply their textbook information on entrepreneurship to the preparation of their *BPP* small business plans.

ASSIGNMENT

After reading Chapter 7 in the textbook, open the BPP *software* and look around for information about planning a new start-up company called* Corporate Fitness. *In the Plan Outline screen, click on **1.0 Executive Summary** to familiarize yourself with an overview of this firm. Then respond to the following questions:*

1. Which industry category for small businesses—wholesaling, retailing, services, or manufacturing—best describes Corporate Fitness's line of business?
2. The textbook identifies several characteristics of successful entrepreneurs. Judging by its business plan, do you think the management team of Corporate Fitness has an entrepreneurial orientation? [Sites to see in *BPP* (for this assignment): In the Plan Outline screen, click on each of the following: **6.0 Management Summary, 6.2 Management Team, 6.3 Management Team Gaps.**]
3. Look at Corporate Fitness's planned sales growth and the firm's plans for promoting its business during the coming year. Do you have confidence in the projected growth figures? Why or why not? [Sites to see in *BPP:* In the Plan Outline screen, click on **7.0 Financial Plan.** Then click on **7.4 Projected Profit and Loss,** and beneath that, click on **Table: Profit and Loss.** In the Plan Outline screen, click on each of the following in turn: **5.1 Marketing Strategy, 5.1.2 Promotion Strategy, 5.2.1 Sales Forecast,** and **Table: Sales Forecast** (located beneath **5.2.1 Sales Forecast.**]
4. Your textbook identifies several sources of advice for starting and running small businesses. Judging from its business plan, do you think that Corporate Fitness is planning to seek advice from any of those sources in getting started? Do you think it is a good idea to discuss the planned use of such sources in the business plan? Explain why or why not.

FOR YOUR OWN BUSINESS PLAN

5. What sources of advice and assistance do you plan to tap in getting your firm off the ground? What kinds of advice—that is, in which areas and for what kinds of activities—will you need most at specific stages in the future development of your firm? Identify in your business plan your plans for seeking advice, the specific value that you expect to gain from each of your sources, and the points in time when you expect to tap different sources.

*GENERAL TIPS FOR NAVIGATING IN *BPP*

1. Open the *BPP* program, examine the Welcome screen, and click on **Open a Sample Plan.**
2. From the **Open a Sample Plan** dialogue box, click on a sample company name; then click on **Open.**
3. On the Plan Manager screen, click on **Your Plan Outline**; then click on any of the lines (for example, **6.0 Management Summary**).
4. You can always return to the Plan Outline screen by going to the bottom of the screen and clicking on the **Plan Outline** icon.
5. After finishing with one sample company, you can get to the next one by going to the top of the screen and clicking on **File** (on the menu bar). Then beneath that, select **Open Sample Plan.** This will exit you from the current company file and take you to the **Open Sample Plan** dialogue box, where you can select your next sample company.
6. When you are finished, you can close the program by going to the top of the screen and clicking on **File** (on the bar menu). Then beneath that, select **Exit.**

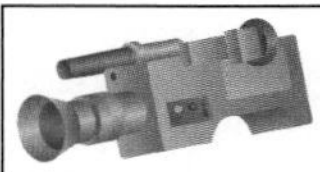

VIDEO EXERCISE

TOYING WITH THE INTERNET: COMPUTER FRIENDLY STUFF

Learning Objectives

The purpose of this video exercise is to help you

1. Understand what motivates an entrepreneur.
2. Appreciate the reasons for success and failure in an entrepreneurial or small business enterprise.
3. Recognize the importance of filling a specific market need.

BACKGROUND INFORMATION

Computer Friendly Stuff (CFS) is a small toy and software company started in Chicago by entrepreneur Chris Cole and a few of his friends. The firm's early financing was obtained by selling 50-percent ownership to a small group of fellow entrepreneurs whom Cole could trust and who were not averse to taking risks. After a somewhat shaky start, the firm has grown into a healthy operation with sales all over the world.

THE VIDEO

In this segment, CFS President Cole talks about the firm's first attempts to market its products, which include such accessories and software as screensavers designed to make computers more fun. Cole describes some of the company's early marketing efforts, which were not initially successful, and the sales and marketing lessons it learned by experience.

DISCUSSION QUESTIONS

1. What was wrong with CFS's initial marketing strategy of "starting at the top"?
2. Some small-business owners might feel that international sales require a major effort that won't pay for itself in terms of sales. How do you think Cole would respond?
3. At the end of the video, CFS is more poised to try to crack the U.S. market. Do you think it can succeed this time?

FOLLOW-UP ASSIGNMENT

Visit the local branch of a major toy chain, such as Toys "R" Us or Noodle Kidoodle. Choose a product category—dolls, crafts, electronic games and software, or educational toys like science kits. How many of the items in your category are made by well-known national brands? How many brands are new to you? How many are imports? Compare the way different products are displayed and promoted. Suppose you were the president of a small firm like CFS. What would you do to make sure your products sell better in this store?

FOR FURTHER EXPLORATION

Visit the CFS Web site <www.computerbug.com> and assess the variety of products offered there. Has the company continued to grow? Who appear to be its primary customers (describe by age, gender, etc.)? How well does CFS appear to be reaching this group or groups? What suggestions would you make to Cole about using his Web site as a marketing tool?

Chapter 8

Managing Human Resources

After reading this chapter, you should be able to:

1 ***Define*** *human resource management,* discuss its strategic significance, and explain how managers plan for human resources.

2 ***Identify*** the issues involved in *staffing* a company, including *internal* and *external recruiting* and *selection.*

3 ***Discuss*** different ways in which organizations go about developing the capabilities of employees and managers.

4 ***Explain*** ways in which organizations evaluate employee performance.

5 ***Discuss*** the importance of *wages and salaries, incentives,* and *benefit programs* in attracting and keeping skilled workers.

6 ***Describe*** some of the key legal issues involved in hiring, compensating, and managing workers in today's workplace.

7 ***Discuss*** *workforce diversity,* the management of *knowledge workers,* and the use of *contingent and temporary workers* as important changes in the contemporary workplace.

And All the M&Ms You Can Eat . . .

Imagine working for a company with its own on-site cafeteria and medical and day care facilities. Imagine working for a company that provides free on-site dental care and massage therapy. Imagine working for a company that has a lavish on-site exercise facility. How about one that launders your dirty exercise clothes after your workout session? Imagine working for a company that offers unlimited sick days. Imagine working for a company that provides free soda, coffee, tea, and juice. Imagine working for a company that actually encourages you to go home at the end of the day. If that's not enough, imagine working for a company that gives everyone free M&Ms every Wednesday of the year. Nirvana? No, it's a real company—SAS Institute, Inc.

Based in rural North Carolina, SAS Institute <www.sas.com> is perhaps the least well-known major software company in the world today. SAS got its start in 1976 when two North Carolina State University professors, James Goodnight and John Sall, created a unique software package to analyze agricultural data around the state. They called their software the Statistical Analysis System, or SAS for short. Goodnight and Sall quickly found numerous new applications for their product and left NC State to start their own business, which eventually became known simply as SAS Institute.

SAS designs complex statistical software that helps big companies better manage, analyze, and interpret especially large quantities of data and information. Marriott Hotels, for example, uses SAS software to manage its frequent-visitor program and to track occupancy rates and patterns in all its hotels. The U.S. government uses SAS software to compute the Consumer Price Index and other complex economic measures. Giant pharmaceutical companies such as Pfizer and Merck use SAS software to compare near-infinite combinations of elements as they develop new drugs.

Because SAS is a private firm, the general public knows little about its revenues and profits. A few details are illuminating, however. For one thing, Jim Goodnight, who owns two-thirds of the company and serves as CEO, is listed by *Forbes* magazine as the 43rd richest individual in the United States, with a personal net worth of $3 billion. Senior vice president John Sall owns the other third and he still spends much of his time writing code. SAS also hires several hundred new employees each year—a clear indicator that it's consistently growing at a strong pace. The firm also continues to invest in impressive—and clearly expensive—buildings and related facilities.

But SAS is even more interesting beneath the surface. Even though it pays salaries that are merely competitive for the industry, the firm's employees are almost fanatical in their devotion to SAS in general and to Jim Goodnight in particular. As a result, annual turnover at SAS is less than four percent—far below that of other firms in the industry—and employees are constantly coming up with new and better ways of doing things. Both insiders and outside experts agree that the key to all this loyalty and creativity is the way Goodnight treats his employees. Says human resources head David Russo: "Jim's idea is that if you hire adults and treat them like adults, then they'll behave like adults."

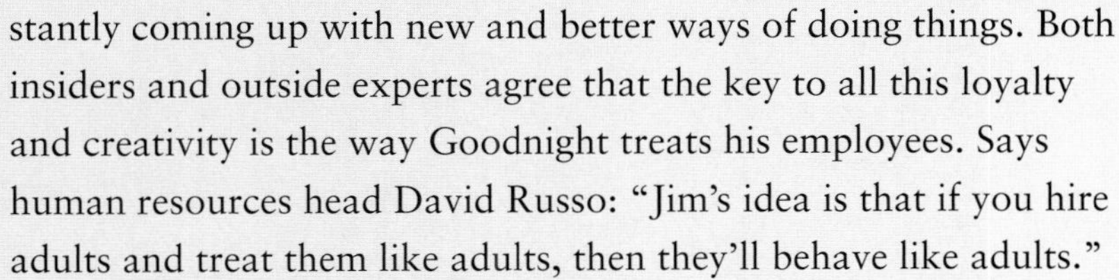

"The idea is that if you hire adults and treat them like adults, then they'll behave like adults."

—David Russo, head of human resources at SAS Institute

All SAS employees get unlimited sick days—which they can use to stay home and care for a sick family member. To keep work from interfering with employees' family lives, SAS also operates the largest childcare facility in the state. Company cafeterias stock baby seats and highchairs so that employees can eat with their children. SAS has also adopted a seven-hour workday—the switchboard shuts down at 5:00 P.M., and the front gate is locked at 6:00 P.M.

Unlike executives at many high-tech firms in other parts of the country, Goodnight doesn't want his employees working late or coming back to the office on weekends. He himself never checks his e-mail or voice messages in the evenings or on weekends.

If they want, however, employees can come in early—to work out in a lavish 36,000-square-foot gym and health center. The center also offers massages several times a week, as well as classes in golf, tennis, tai chi, and African dance. The staff even launders dirty workout clothes at the end of the day and returns them clean and neatly folded. SAS provides unlimited free soda, coffee, tea, and juice, and has live piano music in the cafeteria. The company shuts down for the week between Christmas and New Year's Day each year, but everyone still gets paid. An on-site health clinic has two full-time physicians and six nurses, and health insurance is free for everyone. Every Wednesday, bowls of free M&Ms are set out all over the company. All told, SAS buys 22.5 tons of M&Ms each year.

All this issues from Jim Goodnight's most fundamental philosophic principle: If you treat people with dignity and respect and reward them for their contributions, they will treat you the same way in return. When this relationship can be established and maintained within the context of a business, everyone wins.

Our opening story continues on page 232

The ability to attract and retain talented and motivated employees often marks the difference between success and failure in today's competitive business environment. Enlightened managers are coming to recognize—like Jim Goodnight—that motivated and committed employees, combined with an effective strategy and efficient operations, make a formidable combination. This chapter discusses ways in which organizations strive to achieve a competitive advantage by attracting and retaining the best employees and by developing their capabilities. By focusing on the learning objectives, you will better understand some of the formal systems and processes that companies use in human resource management.

THE FOUNDATIONS OF HUMAN RESOURCE MANAGEMENT

Human resource management (HRM) is the set of organizational activities directed at attracting, developing, and maintaining an effective workforce. Human resource management takes place within a complex and ever-changing environmental context and is increasingly being recognized for its strategic importance.[1]

human resource management (HRM)
Set of organizational activities directed at attracting, developing, and maintaining an effective workforce

The Strategic Importance of HRM

Human resources are critical for effective organizational functioning. HRM (or *personnel,* as it is sometimes called) was once relegated to second-class status in many organizations, but its importance has grown dramatically in the last two decades. This new importance stems from increased legal complexities, the recognition that human resources are a valuable means for improving productivity, and the awareness today of the costs associated with poor human resource management.

Indeed, managers now realize that the effectiveness of their HR function has a substantial impact on a firm's bottom-line performance. Poor human resource planning can result in spurts of hiring followed by layoffs—costly in terms of unemployment compensation payments, training expenses, and morale. Haphazard compensation systems do not attract, keep, and motivate good employees, and outmoded recruitment practices can expose the firm to expensive and embarrassing legal action. Consequently, the chief human resource executive of most large businesses is a vice president directly accountable to the CEO, and many firms are developing strategic HR plans that are integrated with other strategic planning activities.

Human Resource Planning

As you can see in Figure 8.1, the starting point in attracting qualified human resources is planning. In turn, HR planning involves *job analysis* and *forecasting* the demand for and supply of labor.

job analysis
Systematic analysis of jobs in an organization

Job Analysis **Job analysis** is a systematic analysis of jobs within an organization. A job analysis is made up of two parts:

- The **job description** lists the duties of a job, its working conditions, and the tools, materials, and equipment used to perform it.
- The **job specification** lists the skills, abilities, and other credentials needed to do the job.

job description
Systematic evaluation of the duties, working conditions, tools, materials, and equipment related to the performance of a job

job specification
Description of the skills, abilities, and other credentials required by a job

Job analysis information is used in many HR activities. For instance, knowing about job content and job requirements is necessary to develop appropriate selection methods and job-relevant performance appraisal systems and to set equitable compensation rates.

Forecasting HR Demand and Supply After managers fully understand the jobs to be performed within an organization, they can start planning for the organization's

Figure 8.1

The Human Resource Planning Process

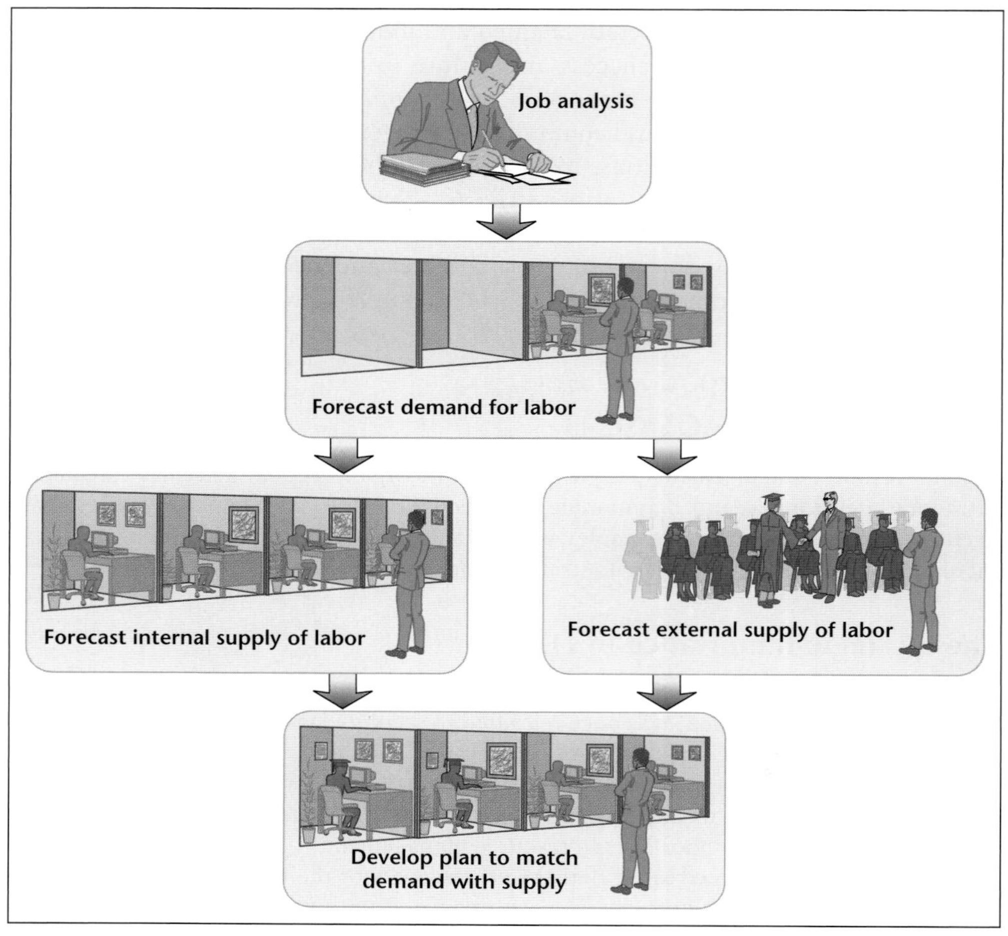

future HR needs. The manager starts by assessing trends in past HR usage, future organizational plans, and general economic trends. A good sales forecast is often the foundation, especially for smaller organizations. Historical ratios can then be used to predict demand for types of employees, such as operating employees and sales representatives. Large organizations use much more complicated models to predict HR needs.

Forecasting the supply of labor is really two tasks:

- Forecasting *internal supply*—the number and type of employees who will be in the firm at some future date.
- Forecasting *external supply*—the number and type of people who will be available for hiring from the labor market at large.

The simplest approach merely adjusts present staffing levels for anticipated turnover and promotions. Again, however, large organizations use extremely sophisticated models to make these forecasts.

replacement chart Listing of each managerial position, who occupies it, how long that person will likely stay in the job, and who is qualified as a replacement

Replacement Charts At higher levels of the organization, managers plan for specific people and positions. The technique most commonly used is the **replacement chart,** which lists each important managerial position, who occupies it, how long that person will probably stay in it before moving on, and who (by name) is now qualified or soon will be qualified to move into it. This technique allows ample time to plan developmental experiences for people identified as potential successors to critical managerial jobs. Charles Knight, CEO of Emerson Electric Co. <www.emersonelectric.com>, maintains an entire room for posting the credentials of his top 700 executives.

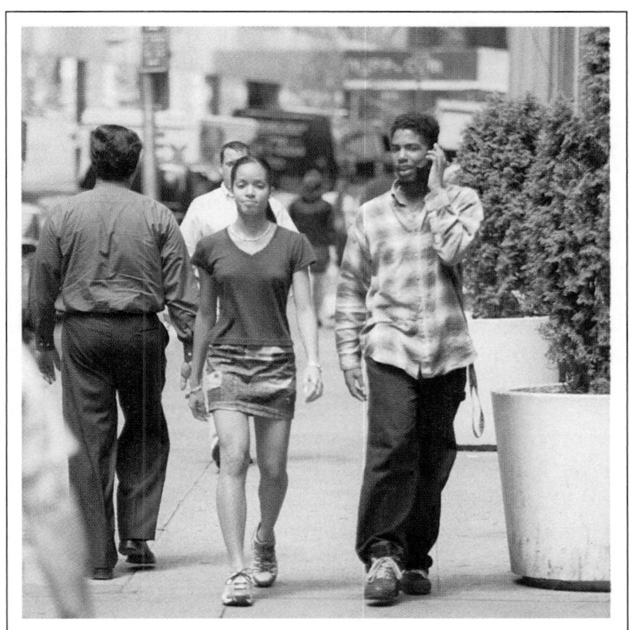

It's no secret that Internet start-ups have proliferated, and both software and hardware companies continue to grow. One result is rapidly growing demand for computer-savvy young people, and many companies have realized that focusing only on college juniors and seniors means ignoring too much talent. Interns Shamarrah Broadus, 18, and Henry Fabian, 16, have Wall Street offices at Market Technologies Group <www.mtgny.com>, *a small software-training company in New York. And they don't make minimum wage: such internships pay from $4,000 to $10,000 for a summer.*

Skills Inventories To facilitate both planning and identifying people for transfer or promotion, some organizations also have **employee information systems,** or **skills inventories.** These systems are usually computerized and contain information on each employee's education, skills, work experience, and career aspirations. Such a system can quickly locate every employee who is qualified to fill a position requiring, for example, a degree in chemical engineering, three years of experience in an oil refinery, and fluency in Spanish.

employee information system (or **skills inventory)** Computerized system containing information on each employee's education, skills, work experiences, and career aspirations

Forecasting the external supply of labor is a different problem altogether. How does a manager, for example, predict how many electrical engineers will be seeking work in California or Florida three years from now? To get an idea of the future availability of labor, planners must rely on information from outside sources such as state employment commissions, government reports, and figures supplied by colleges on the number of students in major fields.

Matching HR Supply and Demand After comparing future demand and internal supply, managers can make plans to manage predicted shortfalls or overstaffing. If a shortfall is predicted, new employees can be hired, present employees can be retrained and transferred into understaffed areas, individuals approaching retirement can be convinced to stay on, or labor-saving or productivity-enhancing systems can be installed.

If the organization needs to hire, the external labor-supply forecast helps managers plan how to recruit according to whether the type of person needed is readily available or scarce in the labor market. The use of temporary workers also helps managers in staffing by giving them extra flexibility. If overstaffing is expected to be a problem, the main options are transferring the extra employees, not replacing individuals who quit, encouraging early retirement, and laying people off.

STAFFING THE ORGANIZATION

When managers have determined that new employees are needed, they must then turn their attention to recruiting and hiring the right mix of people. Staffing the organization is one of the most complex and important tasks of good HR management. In this section, we will describe both the process of acquiring staff from outside the company (*external staffing*) and the process of promoting staff from within (*internal staffing*). Both external and internal staffing, however, start with effective recruiting.

recruiting
Process of attracting qualified persons to apply for open jobs

Recruiting Human Resources Once an organization has an idea of its future HR needs, the next phase is usually recruiting new employees. **Recruiting** is the process of attracting qualified persons to apply for the jobs that are open. Where do recruits come from? Some recruits are found internally while others come from outside of the organization.

internal recruiting
Practice of considering present employees as candidates for job openings

Internal Recruiting **Internal recruiting** means considering present employees as candidates for openings. Promotion from within can help build morale and keep high-quality employees from leaving. In unionized firms, the procedures for notifying employees of internal job-change opportunities are usually spelled out in the union contract. For higher-level positions, a skills inventory system may be used to identify internal candidates or managers may be asked to recommend individuals who should be considered.

external recruiting
Practice of attracting people outside an organization to apply for jobs

External Recruiting **External recruiting** involves attracting people outside the organization to apply for jobs. External recruiting methods include advertising, campus interviews, employment agencies or executive search firms, union hiring halls, referrals by present employees, and hiring "walk-ins" or "gate-hires" (people who show up without being solicited). A manager must select the most appropriate method for each job. The manager might, for instance, use the state employment service to find a maintenance worker but not a nuclear physicist. Private employment agencies can be a good source of clerical and technical employees, and executive search firms specialize in locating top-management talent. Newspaper ads are often used because they reach a wide audience and thus allow minorities equal opportunity to find out about and apply for job openings.

Recruiters have faced a difficult job in recent years as unemployment has continued to drop. By early 1998, unemployment had dropped to a 23-year low of 4.6 percent. As a result, recruiters at firms such as Sprint, PeopleSoft, and Cognex had started to stress how much "fun" it is to work for them, reinforcing this message with ice cream socials, karaoke contests, softball leagues, and free movie nights. The "Wired World" box in this chapter shows how some companies are also using the Internet to recruit prospective employees.

Selecting Human Resources

Once the recruiting process has attracted a pool of applicants, the next step is to select someone to hire. The intent of the selection process is to gather from applicants informa-

Michael Pehl, CEO of i-Cube <www.icube.com>, an IT-consulting-services company, needs employees—good employees—in the worst way. He's willing to pay $15,000 for billboards touting i-Cube as "An Incredible Place to Work," and he has launched a variety of incentives to motivate current employees as recruiters. Anyone making a successful referral may get $2,000, a 32-inch TV, and a VCR. Eight successful referrals in a calendar year can be worth as much as a Jeep Wrangler.

It's a WiredWorld

• *Companies Put Web To Work as Recruiter*

At DVCi Technologies' office in New York, employees never know who's looking over their shoulders. Their moves are broadcast live to the world via a Webcam, part of the company's effort to attract new hires by giving them a glimpse behind the scenes.

The video show is the latest example of how companies are using Web sites as an increasingly creative recruiting tool. It's no longer enough to post jobs on the Internet. Employers today are attracting candidates with such tactics as downloaded video and audio feeds, online employment tests and real-time chats with recruiters.

"We had to differentiate ourselves," says Haim Ariav at DVCi Technologies <www.dvci-muffinhead.com>, a provider of Internet solutions. His movements—a wave, pen chewing, typing—are broadcast online at www.recruitcam.com. "It's been phenomenal. We've hired a lot of people through it, and we're still getting e-mail."

How others are using Web sites:

• **Giving visitors a behind-the-scenes look.** The U.S. Army's Web site <www.army.mil> includes a virtual tour of barracks. Visitors can click and drag their computer mouse to see sweeping views of bedrooms, laundry rooms and court yard. Visitors can also chat with online cyber-recruiters or download a video of an Abrams M1A2 tank.

• **Letting job candidates "meet" current employees.** Visitors to Chicago-based Andersen Consulting's Web site <www.arthurandersen.com> can view pictures of employees and read messages. Entries range from "I love water skiing" to "my job gives me satisfaction and balance."

And at San Jose, California-based Cisco Systems <www.cisco.com>, visitors can join in an online program called "Make Friends At Cisco." Job candidates can ask to get in touch with current workers to grill them about what it's like to work there.

• **Staying in touch with potential hires.** At Sprint's site <www.sprint.com>, jobseekers can send e-mail about their ideal job. The company will send automatic e-mail if future job postings match the criteria.

"There are a lot of ways to establish long-term relationships with this tool," says Sonja Ambur, national staffing director in Kansas City, Missouri. "Every company is looking at ways to maximize the Internet as a recruiting tool."

Some jobseekers say the tactics work. Marta Sant, 28, took a job with DVCi Technologies after viewing the company through its Webcam.

"I looked at the pictures and thought it was fun," says Sant, senior art director. "I e-mail my friends and family, and they can see me."

tion that will predict their job success and then to hire the candidates likely to be most successful. Of course, the organization can only gather information about factors that are predictive of future performance. The process of determining the predictive value of information is called **validation.**

validation
Process of determining the predictive value of information

Application Forms The first step in selection is usually asking the candidate to fill out an application blank. An application form is an efficient method of gathering information about the applicant's previous work history, educational background, and other job-related demographic data. It should not contain questions about areas unrelated to the job such as gender, religion, or national origin. Application form data are generally used informally to decide whether a candidate merits further evaluation, and interviewers use application forms to familiarize themselves with candidates before interviewing them.

Tests Tests of ability, skill, aptitude, or knowledge that is relevant to a particular job are usually the best predictors of job success, although tests of general intelligence or personality are occasionally useful as well. In addition to being validated, tests should be administered and scored consistently. All candidates should be given the same directions, allowed the same amount of time, and offered the same testing environment (temperature, lighting, distractions).

Interviews Although a popular selection device, the interview is sometimes a poor predictor of job success. For example, biases inherent in the way people perceive and judge others on first meeting affect subsequent evaluations. Interview validity can be improved by training interviewers to be aware of potential biases and by increasing the

WebConnection

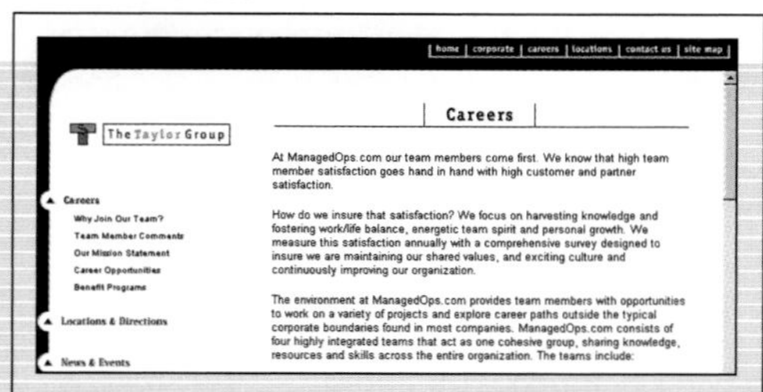

www.managedops.com

At Managed Ops, a systems integrator located in Bedford, New Hampshire, hiring new employees is serious business. It's also a methodical—indeed, intensive—process designed to make just the right person-job fit. To find out more about Taylor—and to hear from some employees who were hired after as many as eight interviews—log on to the company's Web site.

When you interview somebody for a job, what do you look for in his or her personality, appearance, and job skills?

structure of the interview. In a structured interview, questions are written in advance and all interviewers follow the same question list with each candidate. Such structure introduces consistency into the interview procedure and allows the organization to validate the content of the questions. For interviewing managerial or professional candidates, a somewhat less structured approach can be used. Although question areas and information-gathering objectives are still planned in advance, specific questions vary with the candidates' backgrounds.

Other Techniques Organizations also use other selection techniques that vary with circumstances. Polygraph tests, once popular, are declining in popularity. On the other hand, organizations occasionally require that applicants take physical exams (being careful that their practices are consistent with the Americans with Disabilities Act, which is discussed later in this chapter). More organizations are using drug tests, especially in situations in which drug-related performance problems could create serious safety hazards. Applicants at a nuclear power plant, for example, will probably be tested for drugs. Some organizations also run credit checks on prospective employees.

DEVELOPING HUMAN RESOURCES

Regardless of how effective a selection system is, most employees need additional training if they are to grow and develop in their jobs. This process begins with *orientation* and then proceeds to the selection of the best *training techniques and methods.*

New Employee Orientation

orientation
Process of introducing new employees to the organization so that they can more quickly become effective contributors

An important part of an organization's training and development program is new employee orientation. **Orientation** is the process of introducing new employees to the organization so that they can more quickly become effective contributors. Poor orientation can result in disenchantment, dissatisfaction, anxiety, turnover, and other employee problems. But effective orientation can play a key role in job satisfaction, performance, retention, and similar areas. An effective orientation program will help newcomers feel like part of a team, introduce them quickly to coworkers, supervisors, and other new employees, and in a variety of other ways ease the transition from outsider to an insider.

Training and Development Techniques and Methods

Depending upon both the content of the program and the instructor(s) selected to present it, a number of techniques and methods can be used for the actual delivery of information. We examine some of the more popular techniques and methods in this section.

work-based program
Training technique that ties training and development activities directly to task performance

on-the-job training
Work-based training, sometimes informal, conducted while an employee is in an actual work situation

Work-Based Programs One major family of techniques and methods consists of various **work-based programs** that tie training and development activities directly to task performance. The most common method of work-based training is **on-the-job training.** Some experts suggest that as much as 60 percent of training in the United States occurs on the job. In this situation, the employee works in the actual work situation and is shown how to perform a task more effectively by a supervisor or experienced employee.

Another work-based program is **vestibule training,** which involves a work simulation situation in which the job is performed under conditions closely simulating the real work environment. American Airlines <www.aa.com>, for example, requires that pilots regularly undergo training and assessment in a flight simulator that resembles as closely as possible the actual cockpit of a jetliner. Likewise, machine operators might be trained on simulated equipment that is comparable to that which they would use in the actual job setting.

vestibule training
Worked-based training conducted in a simulated environment away from the work site

Another method of work-based training program is **systematic job rotations and transfers.** This method is most likely used for lower level managers or for operating employees being groomed for promotions to supervisory management positions. As the term suggests, the employee is systematically rotated or transferred from one job to another. The employee thus learns a wider array of tasks and acquires more abilities and develops a more comprehensive view of the work of an organization or a particular subunit.

systematic job rotation and transfer
Work-based training in which employees are systematically moved from one job to another so that they can learn a wider array of tasks and skills

Instructional-Based Programs A second family of techniques and methods involves **instructional-based programs.** The most commonly used of these programs is the **lecture or discussion approach.** In these situations, a trainer presents the material in a descriptive fashion to those attending a trainee program. Just as a college professor lectures to students on a particular subject matter, an organizational trainer "lectures" trainees. Depending on the situation and the size of the training class, the instructor may opt for a pure lecture method or may include discussion with trainees. Sometimes lectures are video- or audiotaped so that various individuals in the organization can receive the same training at different points and time and at different locations.

instructional-based program
Training designed to impart new knowledge and information

lecture or **discussion approach**
Instructional-based training in which knowledge and information are descriptively presented

Southwest Airlines <www.southwest.com> uses lecture and discussion programs to teach reservations specialists to cope with new federal guidelines regarding food allergies and airlines. The U.S. Department of Transportation <www.dot.gov> has been pressuring airlines to better accommodate passengers with certain food-related allergies, especially allergies involving peanuts. Although such allergies are rare, they are also very dangerous. Southwest decided to use lecture and discussion training programs because they were the most cost effective.[2]

Another instructional-based program is **computer-assisted instruction.** A trainee sits at a personal computer and operates software that has been specifically developed to impart certain material. The actual training materials are stored on the computer's hard drive, a CD-ROM, or a Web site. One major advantage of this method is that it allows self-paced learning and immediate feedback.

computer-assisted instruction
Instruction-based training in which knowledge and information are presented via computer

Training Technology In recent years, the technology used for training has changed dramatically. Just a few years ago, virtually all training involved paper and pencil, individual instruction, and mechanical reproduction of tasks. More recently, however, new technology has reshaped the way many companies deliver training. As we already noted, computer-assisted instruction has become more popular. Obviously, computer-assisted instruction was impossible before the advent of computers, and it has only been within the last few years with the widespread adoption of personal computers that computer-assisted instruction has become widely used.

Video Teleconferencing Video teleconferencing is also being used increasingly as a training tool. Companies find that when trainers in centralized locations deliver material live by satellite hookup to remote sites, training can be delivered just as effectively as transporting people to common training sites while saving travel costs. In the early days of video teleconferencing, communication tended to be one way: Both the trainer and trainees simply saw the material as it was presented on a monitor. Now, however, there is considerably more interaction. Trainees usually have the ability to interact verbally or electronically.

Interactive Video Yet another new method is interactive video, which is essentially a combination of standard video and computer-based instruction. The material is presented

WebConnection

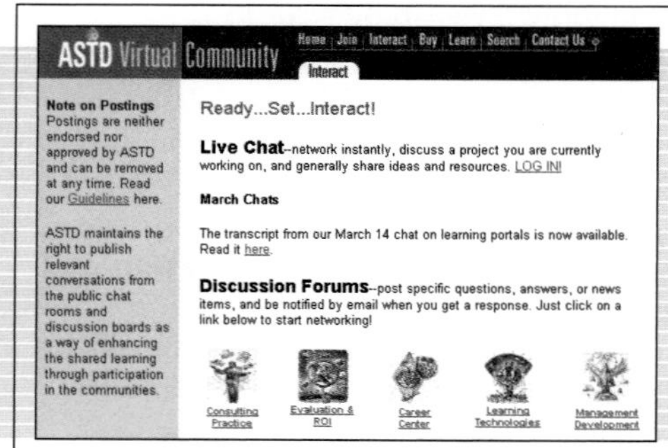

www.astd.org/virtual_community/

Founded in 1944, ASTD is a professional association specializing in workplace learning and performance. It offers expertise in the competitive advantage of efficient training and performance by researching and providing information on such areas as intellectual capital, training and performance measurement, and educational practices in other countries.

via videotechnology on a monitor from a central serving mechanism, a video disk, CD-ROM, or Web site. The trainee interacts with the system by a mouse or keyboard. Feedback can be provided when inadequate responses or improper answers are given and the trainee can also skip over material that has already been learned.

Team-Building and Group-Based Training Also increasingly popular in recent years are various team-building and group-based methods of training. As more and more organizations are using teams as a basis for doing their jobs, it should not be surprising that many of the same companies are developing training programs specifically designed to facilitate intragroup cooperation among members of teams.

One popular method involves various outdoor training exercises. Some programs, for example, involve a group going through a physical obstacle course that requires climbing, crawling, and other physical activities. Outward Bound <www.outwardbound.org> and several other independent companies specialize in offering these kinds of programs, and their clients include such firms as General Foods, Xerox, and Burger King. Participants must see the relevance of such programs if they are to be successful. Firms don't want employees returning from team-building programs to report merely that the experience "was childlike and fun and fairly inoffensive."[3]

> ***"It was childlike and fun and fairly inoffensive."***
>
> *—Employee returning from team-building training program*

EVALUATING EMPLOYEE PERFORMANCE

performance appraisal Formal evaluation of an employee's job performance in order to determine the degree to which the employee is performing effectively

Another important part of human resource management is **performance appraisal:** the specific and formal evaluation of an employee in order to determine the degree to which the employee is performing effectively. Appraisals are important because they provide a benchmark to better assess the extent to which recruiting and selection processes are adequate: Performance appraisals help managers assess the extent to which they are recruiting and selecting the best employees. They also contribute to effective training and development and compensation.

The Performance Appraisal Process

Several questions must be answered as part of the performance appraisal process. These questions generally relate to who conducts the performance appraisal and provides feedback to the individual whose performance was evaluated.

Conducting the Performance Appraisal The individual's supervisor is the most likely person to conduct a performance appraisal. Naturally, supervisors usually have the most knowledge of the job requirements and the most opportunity to observe employees performing their jobs. In addition, supervisors are usually responsible for the performance of their subordinates. Thus, the individual supervisor is responsible for employees' high performance and accountable for their inadequate performance.

Providing Performance Feedback After the performance appraisal, the next major activity is providing feedback, coaching, and counseling. Many managers do a poor job in this area, in part because they don't understand how to do it properly and in part because they don't enjoy it. Almost by definition, "performance appraisal" in many organizations tends to focus on negatives. As a result, managers may have a tendency to avoid giving feedback because they know an employee who gets negative feedback may be angry, hurt, discouraged, or argumentative. But clearly, if employees are not told about their shortcomings, they will have no concrete reason for trying to improve and no guidance as to *how* to improve. It is critical, therefore, that a rater follow-up on the appraisal by providing feedback.

Methods for Appraising Performance

Because of the nature of many jobs today, especially managerial work, most methods for appraising performance rely on judgments and ratings. Therefore, a great deal of effort has been spent in trying to make relatively subjective evaluations as meaningful and useful as they can be. While some of the methods are based on relative rankings, others are based on ratings. In this section, we examine a few of the more popular methods, which we have categorized as either *ranking* or *rating methods.*

Ranking Methods The **simple ranking method** requires the manager to rank in order from top to bottom or best to worst each member of a particular work group or department. The individual ranked first is presumed to be the top performer, the individual ranked second is presumed to be the second-best performer, and so forth. The basis for the ranking is generally global or overall performance.

simple ranking method Performance appraisal method that ranks employees from best to worst

Another ranking method that has been in use for many years, the **forced distribution method,** involves grouping employees into predefined frequencies of performance ratings. Those frequencies are determined in advance and are imposed upon the rater. A decision might be made, for instance, that 10 percent of the employees in a work group will be grouped as "outstanding," 20 percent as "very good," 40 percent as "average," and 20 percent as "below average." The remaining 10 percent will be grouped as "poor." The forced distribution method is familiar to many students because it is the principle used by professors who grade on a so-called bell or normal curve.

forced distribution method Performance appraisal method that classifies employees into different performance categories based on a predetermined distribution

Rating Methods One of the most popular and widely used methods is the **graphic rating scale,** which consists simply of a statement or question about some aspect of an individual's job performance. Following the statement or question is a series of answers or possible responses from which the rater must select the one that best fits. For example, one common set of responses to a graphic rating scale with five possible alternatives is *strongly agree, agree, neither agree nor disagree, disagree,* and *strongly disagree.* These responses, or "descriptors," are usually arrayed along a bar, line, or similar visual representation marked with numbers or letters corresponding to each descriptor. Figure 8.2 shows a sample graphic rating scale.

graphic rating scale Performance rating method using a numerical scale to rate performance along a set of dimensions

Graphic rating scales are appealing because they are relatively easy to develop. A manager simply brainstorms or otherwise develops a list of statements or questions that are presumably related to relevant indicators of performance. Moreover, a wide array of performance dimensions can be tapped with various rating scales on the same form. As we noted, each descriptor on the rating form is accompanied by a number or a letter. Most rating scales have ranges of one to five or one to seven, although occasionally a scale may use only one to three or perhaps as many as one to nine alternatives. To develop a performance measure, the manager simply adds up the points for a particular employee's responses to obtain an overall index of performance.

Somewhat different is the **critical incident method.** A *critical incident* is simply an example of especially good or poor performance on the part of the employee. Organizations that rely upon this method often require raters to recall such instances and then describe what the employee did (or did not do) that led to success or failure. This

critical incident method Performance rating method based on stated examples that reflect especially good or poor performance

Figure 8.2

Performance Rating Scale

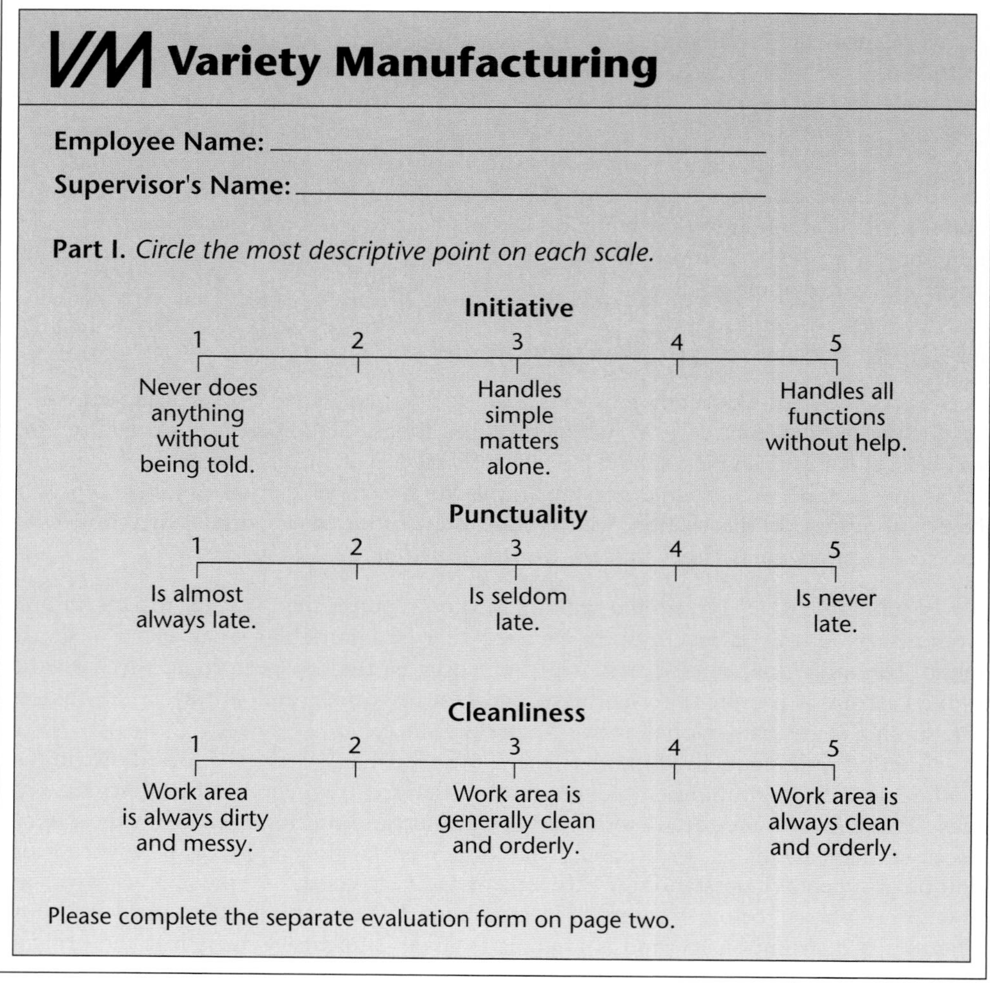

VM Variety Manufacturing

Employee Name: ______________________

Supervisor's Name: ______________________

Part I. *Circle the most descriptive point on each scale.*

Initiative

1	2	3	4	5
Never does anything without being told.		Handles simple matters alone.		Handles all functions without help.

Punctuality

1	2	3	4	5
Is almost always late.		Is seldom late.		Is never late.

Cleanliness

1	2	3	4	5
Work area is always dirty and messy.		Work area is generally clean and orderly.		Work area is always clean and orderly.

Please complete the separate evaluation form on page two.

technique not only provides information for feedback but defines performance in fairly clear, behavioral terms. In other cases, managers keep logs or diaries in which they record examples or critical incidents.

PROVIDING COMPENSATION AND BENEFITS

compensation
Set of rewards that organizations provide to individuals in return for their willingness to perform various jobs and tasks

Employees do not work for free—they expect to be compensated for the time, talent, and effort they devote to their jobs and to helping the organization achieve its goals. In this section, we explore basic compensation, incentives and performance-based rewards, and employee benefits and services. **Compensation** is the set of rewards that organizations provide to individuals in return for their willingness to perform various jobs and tasks within the organization. As we shall see, compensation involves a number of different elements including base salary, incentives, bonuses, benefits, and other rewards. Compensation should never be a random decision, but rather the result of a careful and systematic strategic process.

Determining Basic Compensation

wages
Compensation in the form of money paid for time worked

Basic compensation means the base level of wages or salary paid to an employee. **Wages** generally refer to hourly compensation paid to operating employees. Most of the jobs that are paid on an hourly-wage basis are lower-level or operating-level jobs. Rather than expressing compensation on an hourly basis, the organization may instead describe compensation on an annual or monthly basis. Many college graduates, for example, compare job offers on the basis of annual **salary,** such as $36,000 versus $38,000 a year.

salary
Compensation in the form of money paid for discharging the responsibilities of a job

Pay Surveys in Compensation One common source of information that many organizations use in determining base compensation is **pay surveys**—surveys of compensation paid to employees by other employers in a particular geographic area, an industry, or an occupational group. Pay surveys provide the information that an organization needs to avoid problems of an imbalance between its own pay scale and those of comparable organizations. Some pay surveys are conducted by professional associations. This is especially true for managerial and professional jobs.

pay survey
Method used to obtain information about compensation paid to employees by other employers

In general, then, the wage and salary survey simply asks other organizations what they pay people to perform various jobs. Most organizations participate in such surveys because they will get access to the resulting data. There is, for example, a consortium of eight large electronic companies in the United States that routinely survey one another to determine what each pays new engineers and other professional employees who are hired directly out of college. They alternate the responsibility for conducting surveys from year to year, with the responsible organization sharing its results with the other members.

Job Evaluation Another means of determining basic compensation is *job evaluation,* which should not be confused with *job analysis.* Recall that managers use job analysis to better understand the requirements and nature of a job and its performance so that appropriate individuals can be recruited and selected. **Job evaluation** is a method for determining the relative value or worth of a job to the organization so individuals who perform the job can be appropriately compensated. In other words, it is mostly concerned with establishing internal pay equity. A number of job evaluation techniques and methods have been established.

job evaluation
Methods for determining the relative worth of jobs in order to set compensation levels

Establishing a Pay Structure A third method for determining basic compensation is establishing a *pay structure.* Compensation for different jobs is based on the organization's assessment of the relative value to the organization of each job class. Thus, there should be a logical rank ordering of compensation levels from the most to the least valuable jobs throughout the organization. The organization may also find it necessary to group certain jobs together: Two or more jobs that are valued relatively equally will be compensated at approximately the same level. In addition, the organization decides on minimum and maximum pay ranges for each job or job class. Managers might use performance, *seniority* (a system giving priority in promotions to employees with greater length of service), or a combination of the two to determine how much a person can be paid for doing a particular job.

> ***"The information age is real time, and employees keep an eye on where everyone is."***
>
> *—Mike Caggiano, compensation executive for FutureNext*

Because of today's tight labor market, many job seekers are finding it possible to demand higher salaries than ever before. The Internet is also playing a key role in this trend, because job seekers and current employees can more easily get a sense of what their true market value is. If they can document the claim that their value is higher than what their current employer now pays or is offering, they are in a position to demand higher salaries. Consider the case of one compensation executive who met recently with a subordinate to discuss a raise. The executive was surprised when the subordinate produced data from five different Web sites backing up a claim for a bigger raise than the executive had intended to offer. "The information age," the executive now realizes, "is real time, and [employees] keep an eye on where everyone is."[4]

Performance-Based Compensation

Besides basic compensation, many organizations also try to offer some form of performance-based rewards as well. The reason is obvious: When rewards are associated

After four years at Monster.com, an Internet career and recruitment site, Colleen McGrath (right) felt that she was growing stale in her job. She soon found a position (and a $5,000 raise) with another Internet company, but when she was about to leave, Monster.com founder and CEO Jeff Taylor (left) made a counteroffer: promotion to special projects manager and a $4,000 raise (with more to come). Taylor understands that the competition among dot-coms for skilled workers is fierce and often makes use of such counteroffers, which human resource specialists refer to as "battlefield promotions."

with higher levels of performance, employees will presumably be motivated to work harder in order to reap those awards.

merit pay plan
Performance-based pay plan basing part of compensation on employee merit

Merit Pay Plans *Merit pay* refers to pay awarded to employees according to the relative value of their contributions. Employees who make greater contributions get higher pay than those who make lesser contributions. **Merit pay plans,** then, are compensation plans that formally base at least some meaningful portion of compensation on merit. The most general form of merit pay plan is the *raise*—an annual salary increase granted to employees because of their relative merit. In such plans, merit is usually determined or defined according to individual performance and overall contribution to the organization.

skill-based or **knowledge-based pay**
Performance-based pay plan rewarding employees for acquiring new skills or knowledge

Skill- and Knowledge-Based Pay Systems Although these systems are usually not strictly viewed as merit systems, it is worth noting how **skill-based pay** or **knowledge-based pay** systems focus employee attention on different areas but still rely on similar motivational processes. Instead of rewarding employees for increased performance, such systems reward them for the acquisition of more skills or knowledge. Skill-based pay systems reward employees not for any specific level of performance, but for the acquisition of job-related skills. Knowledge-based pay systems reward employees for learning: Presumably, as they acquire more and more skills and knowledge, employees become more valuable to the organization.

piece-rate incentive plan
Incentive-based pay plan that provides payment for each unit produced

Incentive Compensation Systems Incentive compensation systems are among the oldest forms of performance-based rewards. Indeed, some companies were using individual piece-rate incentive plans over a hundred years ago. Under a **piece-rate incentive plan,** the organization pays an employee a certain amount of money for every unit produced. An employee might, for example, be paid one dollar for every dozen units of a product successfully completed. But such simplistic systems fail to account for such factors as minimum wage levels and rely on two questionable assumptions: (1) that performance is totally under an individual's control and that (2) the individual employee does a single task continuously during the course of the employee's work time. Today, therefore, incentive compensation systems tend to be much more sophisticated.

individual incentive plan
Incentive-based pay plan that rewards individual performance on a real-time basis

Incentive Pay Plans Generally speaking, **individual incentive plans** reward individual performance on a real-time basis. That is, rather than increasing a person's base salary at the end of the year, an employer gives an individual a salary increase or some other financial reward for outstanding performance immediately or shortly after the performance occurred. Individual incentive systems are most common when performance can be objectively assessed—in terms of number of units of output or similar measures—rather than on a subjective assessment by a superior. Perhaps the most common form of individual incentive is the **sales commission** paid to people engaged in sales work.

sales commission
Individual incentive plan rewarding employees with a percentage of sales volume that they generate

Other Forms of Incentive Occasionally organizations use other forms of incentives. For example, a non-monetary incentive, such as additional time off or a special perk, might be a useful incentive. Thus a company might sponsor a sales contest in which the sales group that attains the highest level of increase over a specified period will receive an extra week of paid vacation, perhaps even at a prearranged place, such as a tropical resort or a ski lodge. Continental Airlines <www.continental.com> gives away six Ford Explorers every six months as an incentive for attendance: Only employees with perfect attendance for the previous six months are eligible for a lottery drawing that determines the winners.

Team and Group Incentive Systems The merit compensation and incentive compensation systems described in the preceding section deal primarily with reward plans for individuals. There are also performance-based reward programs for teams and groups. Given today's increasing trends toward team- and group-based methods of work, such programs are growing in importance.

Gainsharing Many organizations use **gainsharing programs,** which are designed to share with employees the cost savings from productivity improvements. The underlying assumption is that employees and the employer have the same goals and should, therefore, share in incremental economic gains. In general, organizations start by measuring team- or group-level productivity. The team or work group itself is then charged with lowering costs and otherwise improving productivity through any measures that members develop and their manager approves. Any resulting cost savings or productivity gains are then quantified and translated into dollar values. According to a predetermined formula, these dollar savings are then allocated to both employer and employees.

gainsharing program
Group-based incentive plan that gives rewards for productivity improvements

Performance Increases Gainsharing-type plans are among the most popular group incentive-reward systems. Other organizations, however, have developed different systems. Some companies, for example, use true incentives at the team or group level. Just like individual incentives, some team or group incentives tie rewards directly to performance increases. Also like individual incentives, team or group incentives are paid as they are earned rather than added to base salaries. They are distributed at the team or group level rather than at the individual level.

Profit Sharing Other team- or group-level incentives go beyond the contributions of a specific work group. These are generally organization-wide incentives. One long-standing type of plan is called **profit sharing:** At the end of the year, some portion of the company's profits is paid into a profit-sharing pool that is then distributed to all employees. Continental Airlines uses two organization-wide incentive programs: In addition to a generous profit-sharing program, Continental gives every employee a $65 check for each month that the airline is ranked in the top three in the United States for on-time arrivals.

profit sharing
Group-based incentive plan in which employees are paid a share of company profits

Indirect Compensation and Benefits

In addition to financial compensation, most organizations provide employees with an array of other indirect compensation and benefits. **Benefits** generally refer to various rewards, incentives, and other things of value that an organization gives employees in addition to wages, salaries, and other forms of direct financial compensation. Because these benefits have tangible value, they represent a meaningful form of compensation even though they are not generally expressed in financial terms. Typically, they are regarded as indirect compensation. The "Life Cycle of an e-Business" box in this chapter describes several of the benefits that Garden.com provided for employees.

benefits
Compensation other than wages and salaries

Life Cycle of an e-Business

Massage Breaks and Pet Accommodations

Any organization that wants to be competitive when it comes to attracting and retaining the best employees must provide a solid package of indirect compensation and benefits. In high-tech markets, where firms often face shortages of talent, benefit packages can be a key factor in effective HR management. Garden.com was no exception to this rule.

First of all, Garden.com offered employees what most people would consider the "standard" benefits. They all got health insurance, vacation time, and several paid holidays each year. They got free parking adjacent to the building, and the firm maintained a very casual work environment. Garden.com also offered an attractive stock-purchase plan to all employees.

In addition, Garden.com offered several unusual benefits. For one thing, all employees had access to a company kitchen stocked with free coffee, tea, soda, bottled water, and snacks. The company also sponsored regularly scheduled visits by massage professionals and car repair technicians. Employees could sign up for these services in advance and, for a token fee, get a massage or have their oil changed while they worked. A neighborhood dry-cleaning establishment picked up and dropped off twice a week. The company even offered yoga and stress-management classes.

But perhaps most unusual of all, Garden.com was a "pet-friendly" work site: Employees could bring their pets to work. A few people tried bringing cats to work, and one employee brought her bird. But dogs were far and away the most common beneficiary of the policy. On any given day, more than 100 Garden.com employees brought their dogs to work. Those who regularly brought their pets were grouped together in one part of the building, where they used "baby gates" to keep pets confined to their own work areas. To deal with noise, there was a "three barks and you're out" policy. Once out, a rambunctious canine could get back in the door only with an obedience school certificate.

protection plan Mandated coverage protecting employees whose income is threatened or reduced by illness, disability, death, or retirement

unemployment insurance Mandated coverage protecting employees who are laid off

social security Mandated federal retirement program

Mandated Protection Plans **Protection plans** protect employees when their income is threatened or reduced by illness, disability, death, unemployment, or retirement. A number of these plans are required by law but others are optional. One mandated benefit is **unemployment insurance,** which provides a basic subsistence payment to employees who are between jobs. It is intended for people who have stopped working for one organization but who are assumed to be actively seeking employment with another. Employers pay premiums to an unemployment insurance fund.

Also mandated is **social security** (officially the Old Age Survivors and Disability Insurance Program). The original purpose of this program was to provide some limited income to retired individuals to supplement personal savings, private pensions, and part-time work. It is funded through employee and employer taxes withheld on a payroll basis.

Workers' compensation is mandated insurance that covers individuals who suffer a job-related illness or accident. Employers bear the cost of workers' compensation insurance. The exact premium is related to each employer's past experience with job-related accidents and illnesses. Almost 90 million workers in the United States are protected under the Workers' Compensation Insurance Program.

Optional Protection Plans Another major category of employee benefits consists of various optional protection plans. These plans provide protection in many of the same areas as those discussed previously, except that organizations can choose whether or not to provide them. Perhaps the most common optional protection plan is insurance coverage. Health insurance is probably the most important type of coverage. In recent years, it has been expanded by many organizations to include such things as special programs for prescription drugs, vision care products, mental health services, and dental care. Other kinds of coverage include life insurance, long-term disability insurance, and so forth.

workers' compensation insurance
Legally required insurance covering workers who are injured or become ill on the job

In addition to pension benefits guaranteed under the Social Security Act, many companies establish **private pension plans** for employees. These are prearranged plans administered by the organization to provide income to employees upon their retirement.

private pension plan
Prearranged company pensions provided to retired employees

Paid Time Off Many organizations provide employees with a certain amount of time off with pay. Although no U.S. laws mandate paid time off, it has come to be expected by most employees. A major type of this benefit is the *paid holiday.* Most full-time employees receive about 10 paid holidays per year. In part to boost flagging morale, Coca-Cola <www.coca-cola.com> recently added May 8—the day the first Coke hit the market in 1886—as a new paid holiday every year.[5]

Paid vacations are usually for periods of one, two, or more weeks during which an employee can take time off from work and continue to be paid. Most organizations vary the amount of paid vacation with an individual's seniority. Another common paid time off plan is *sick leave.* This benefit is provided when individuals are sick or otherwise physically unable to perform their job. Most organizations allow an individual to accumulate sick time according to some schedule, such as one sick day per month.

Sometimes an organization will allow an employee to take off a small number of days simply for personal business. This benefit is usually called *personal leave.* Occasions might include funerals, religious observances, weddings, birthdays, or simply personal-choice holidays. Finally, organizations are usually required by law to allow employees to miss work if they are called for jury duty.

Other Types of Benefits In addition to protection plans and paid time off, many organizations offer a growing array of other benefit programs. **Wellness programs,** for example, concentrate on keeping employees from becoming sick rather than simply paying their expenses when they get sick. In some organizations these programs are simple, involving little more than organized jogging or walking during lunch breaks. More elaborate programs include smoking cessation, blood pressure and cholesterol screening, and stress management. Some organizations maintain full-fledged health clubs on site and provide counseling and programs for fitness and weight loss.

wellness program
Benefit in the form of programs designed to help employees from becoming sick

Childcare benefits are also becoming extremely popular. In fact, any organization that wants to be considered "family-friendly" must have some type of childcare benefits, and a valid claim to being "family-friendly" is increasingly becoming a competitive advantage. These plans might include scheduling help, referrals to various types of services, or reimbursement accounts for childcare expenses. In many cases, they actually include company-paid day care. Amgen Inc. <wwwext.amgen.com>, the world's largest biotechnology company, recently opened the nation's largest corporate childcare center. The facility can provide daylong care for as many as 430 children between the ages of 6 weeks and 5 years. Employees clearly see the facility as a major benefit. "It offers peace of mind," says one. "You know where your child is—she's 10 minutes away. It's nice to stop by and visit if you have the chance."[6]

"It offers peace of mind. You know where your child is—she's 10 minutes away."

—Amgen employee on the benefits of the company's childcare facilities

Cafeteria Benefit Plans Most benefit programs are designed for all the employees in an organization. Although the exact benefits may vary according to the employee's level in the organization, within those levels plans are generally "one size fits all." In contrast, **cafeteria-style benefit plans** allow employees to choose those benefits that they really want. Under these plans, the organization typically establishes a budget indicating how

cafeteria benefit plan
Benefit plan that sets limits on benefits per employee, each of whom may choose from a variety of alternative benefits

much it is willing to spend, per employee, on benefits. Employees are then presented with a list of possible benefits and the cost of each. They are then free to put them together in any combination they wish.

THE LEGAL CONTEXT OF HR MANAGEMENT

As much or more than any area of business, HR management is heavily influenced by federal law and judicial review. In this section, we summarize some of the most important and far-reaching areas of HR regulation.

Equal Employment Opportunity

equal employment opportunity Legally mandated nondiscrimination in employment on the basis of race, creed, sex, or national origin

illegal discrimination Discrimination against protected classes that causes them to be unfairly differentiated from others

protected class Set of individuals who by nature of one or more common characteristics are protected by law from discrimination on the basis of any of those characteristics

The basic goal of all **equal employment opportunity** regulation is to protect people from unfair or inappropriate discrimination in the workplace. Let's begin by noting that discrimination in itself is not illegal. Whenever one person is given a pay raise and another is not, for example, the organization has made a decision to distinguish one person from another. As long as the basis for this discrimination is purely job-related (made, for instance, on the basis of performance or seniority) and is applied objectively and consistently, the action is legal and appropriate. Problems arise when distinctions among people are not job-related. In such cases, the resulting discrimination is illegal. Various court decisions, coupled with interpretations of the language of various laws, suggest that **illegal discrimination** actions by an organization or its managers cause members of a "protected class" to be unfairly differentiated from other members of the organization.

Protected Classes in the Workplace Illegal discrimination is based on a stereotype, belief, or prejudice about *classes* of individuals. At one time, for example, common stereotypes regarded Black employees as less dependable than White employees, women as less suited to certain types of work than men, and disabled individuals as unproductive employees. Based on these stereotypes, some organizations routinely discriminated against Blacks, women, and the disabled. To combat discrimination, various laws have been passed to protect various classes of individuals. A **protected class** consists of all individuals who share one or more common characteristics as indicated by a given law. The most common criteria for defining protected classes include race, color, religion, gender, age, national origin, disability status, and status as a military veteran.

Do you think that the increased numbers of businesses on the Internet will make racial and gender issues obsolete? If so, what other social issues do you think will arise?

Equal Employment Opportunity Legislation A large body of legal regulation has been enacted to ensure equal employment opportunity for various protected classes. We discuss the major laws and related regulations in the following section.

Title VII of the Civil Rights Act of 1964 Federal law forbidding employment discrimination on the basis of race, color, religious beliefs, sex, or national origin

Title VII of the Civil Rights Act of 1964 To date, the most significant single piece of legislation affecting the legal context to HR management has been **Title VII of the Civil Rights Act of 1964.** This law protects classes of people regardless of race, color, religious belief, sex, or national origin. It makes it illegal for an employer to do any of the following on any of these grounds:

- Fail or refuse to hire or to discharge any individual
- Discriminate against any individual in any aspect of the employment relationship
- Segregate, limit, or classify employees or applicants in any way that could deprive an individual of employment opportunities

Equal Pay Act of 1963 Federal law requiring organizations to pay men and women the same pay for doing equal work

Equal Pay Act of 1963 The **Equal Pay Act of 1963** requires that organizations provide the same pay for men and women who do equal work. The law defines equality in terms of skill, responsibility, effort, and working conditions. Thus an organization cannot pay a man more than it pays a woman for the same job on the grounds that, say, "he needs more money because he has a bigger family to support." This principle rests on the con-

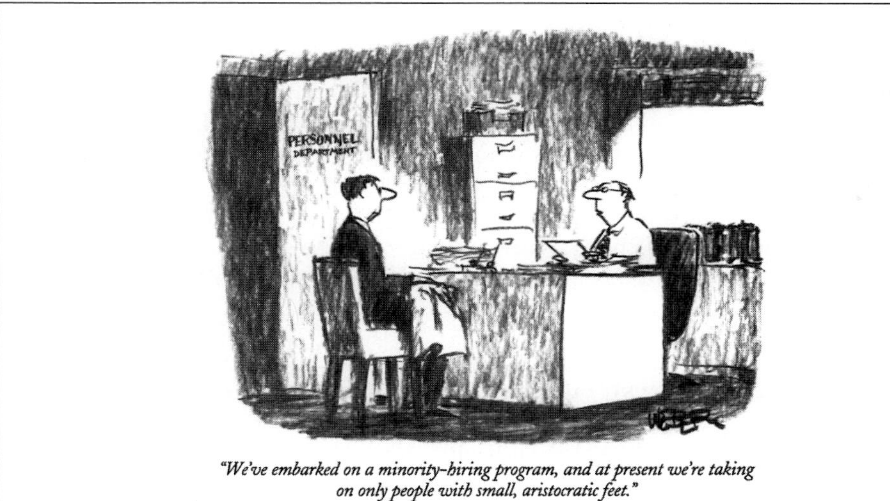

"We've embarked on a minority-hiring program, and at present we're taking on only people with small, aristocratic feet."

cept of **comparable worth:** the principle that jobs that are worth the same to an organization should be compensated at the same level regardless of who performs them. Thus, even if a man and a woman have different job titles, gender cannot play a role in their compensation if both jobs are equally valuable to the firm.

comparable worth
Principle that jobs which are worth the same should be compensated at the same level regardless of who performs them

Age Discrimination and Employment Act The **Age Discrimination and Employment Act (ADEA)** was first passed in 1967 and later amended in 1986. It prohibits discrimination against employees over the age of 40. The ADEA is similar to Title VII of the 1964 Civil Rights Act in terms of both its major provisions and the procedures that are followed when discrimination is alleged. The University of Notre Dame, for example, recently lost an age discrimination lawsuit after its head football coach implied that one of his assistants was too old to be effective and subsequently fired him.

Age Discrimination and Employment Act (ADEA)
Federal law prohibiting discrimination against people over 40 on the basis of age

Pregnancy Discrimination Act of 1979 As its name suggests, the **Pregnancy Discrimination Act of 1979** was passed to protect pregnant women from discrimination in the workplace. The law requires that a pregnant woman be treated like any other employee. It specifies that a woman cannot be refused a job or promotion, be fired, or otherwise discriminated against simply because she is pregnant (or has had an abortion). She also cannot be forced to leave her employment as long as she is physically able to work. Finally, the law also specifies that if other employees have the right to receive their jobs back after leaves of absence, then the same benefit must be extended to pregnant women. In one recent case, actress Hunter Tylo won a $5 million judgment against the producers of the television series *Melrose Place* when they used her pregnancy as a basis for writing her out of the show.[7]

Pregnancy Discrimination Act of 1979
Federal law forbidding discrimination against women who are pregnant

Civil Rights Act of 1991 The **Civil Rights Act of 1991** amends Title VII of the Civil Rights Act of 1964. This law makes it easier for individuals who feel they have been discriminated against to take legal action. It also provides, for the first time, for the potential payment of compensatory and punitive damages in cases of discrimination covered by Title VII.

Civil Rights Act of 1991
Amendment that extends Title VII of the Civil Rights Act of 1964 and provides for compensatory and punitive damages

Americans with Disabilities Act of 1990 The **Americans with Disabilities Act of 1990 (ADA)** is one of the most recent pieces of equal employment opportunity legislation. The ADA was passed in response to growing concerns about employment opportunities denied to people with various disabilities. Specifically, the ADA prohibits discrimination based on disability in all aspects of the employment relationship, such as job application procedures, hiring, firing, promotion, compensation, and training. It also covers other employment activities, such as advertising, recruiting, tenure, layoffs, leave, and benefits.

Americans with Disabilities Act of 1990 (ADA)
Federal law prohibiting discrimination on the basis of disability and requiring employers to make reasonable accommodation for disabled applicants and employees

In addition, the ADA requires that organizations make reasonable accommodations for disabled employees as long as the accommodations themselves do not pose an undue burden on the organization.

Family and Medical Leave Act of 1993
Federal law requiring employers to provide unpaid leave for specified family and medical reasons

Family and Medical Leave Act of 1993 The **Family and Medical Leave Act of 1993** was passed in part to remedy weaknesses in the Pregnancy Discrimination Act of 1979. It requires employers with more than 50 employees to provide up to 12 weeks unpaid leave for employees after the birth or adoption of a child. It also covers employees who must leave to care for a seriously ill child, spouse, or parent, or to get treatment for a serious illness of their own. The organization must provide the returning employee with the same or comparable job.

Equal Employment Opportunity Commission (EEOC)
Agency created by Title VII to enforce discrimination-related laws

Enforcing Equal Employment Opportunity The enforcement of equal opportunity legislation is handled by two agencies. The **Equal Employment Opportunity Commission,** or **EEOC** <www.eeoc.gov>, is a division of the Department of Justice. It was created by Title VII of the 1964 Civil Rights Act and has specific responsibility for enforcing Title VII, the Equal Pay Act, and the Americans with Disabilities Act.

The other agency charged with monitoring equal employment opportunity legislation is the Office of Federal Contract Compliance Programs, or OFCCP <www.dol.gov/dol/esa/public/of_org.htm>. The OFCCP is responsible for enforcing executive orders that apply to companies doing business with the federal government. A business with government contracts must have on file a written **affirmative action plan:** that is, a written statement of how the organization intends to actively recruit, hire, and develop members of relevant protected classes.

affirmative action plan
Practice of recruiting qualified employees belonging to racial, gender, or ethnic groups who are underrepresented in an organization

Organizations other than those under OFCCP jurisdiction may also draw up affirmative action plans. In fact, courts have often demanded that those found guilty of discrimination institute such plans to remedy past discrimination. There have even been cases in which the courts imposed hiring quotas on offending organizations. In those instances, companies were forced to hire specific numbers of protected-class members over specified periods of time. Remember, however, that these cases are rare and have clearly specified time limits. In general, affirmative action does *not* mean that an organization must hire a certain number of employees from protected classes. In fact, such quota systems, where not imposed by a court order, are considered a form of **reverse discrimination** and are themselves illegal.

reverse discrimination
Practice of discriminating against well-represented groups by overhiring members of underrepresented groups

Legal Issues in Compensation

As we noted earlier, most employment regulations are designed to provide equal employment opportunity. Some legislation, however, goes beyond equal employment opportunity and really deals more substantively with other issues. One such area is legislation covering compensation.

Fair Labor Standards Act
Federal law setting minimum-wage and overtime pay requirements

Laws Affecting Total Compensation Over the years, the federal government has passed several laws dealing with total compensation. The most far-reaching law was the **Fair Labor Standards Act** of 1938, which established a minimum hourly wage. The purpose of the law was to ensure that everyone who works would receive an income sufficient to meet basic needs. The first minimum wage of 25 cents an hour has been revised many times and is now $5.15 per hour. The 1938 law also formally defined the workweek in the United States as 40 hours per week. It further specified that all full-time employees must be paid at a rate of one and a half times their normal hourly rate for each hour of overtime work beyond 40 hours in a week.

Employee Retirement Income Security Act of 1974 (ERISA)
Federal law regulating private pension plans

Laws Affecting Other Forms of Compensation Another important piece of legislation that affects compensation is the **Employee Retirement Income Security Act of 1974,** or **ERISA.** This law guarantees a basic minimum benefit that employees can expect to be paid upon retirement. Specifically, ERISA guarantees a basic benefit as opposed to a complete pension replacement for employees who are eligible for pensions at the time when they are terminated by an organization. ERISA was passed in part because of abuses on the part of organizations that manipulated pension plans in order to control costs or to channel money to other uses.

Contemporary Legal Issues in HR Management

In addition to these established areas of HR legal regulation, there are several emerging legal issues that will likely become more and more important with the passage of time. These include employee safety and health, various emerging areas of discrimination law, employee rights, employment-at-will, and ethics and human resource management.

Employee Safety and Health The **Occupational Safety and Health Act of 1970,** or **OSHA** <www.osha.gov>, is the single most comprehensive piece of legislation ever passed regarding worker safety and health. OSHA holds that every employer has an obligation to furnish each employee with a place of employment that is free from hazards that cause or are likely to cause death or physical harm. It is generally enforced through inspections of the workplace by OSHA inspectors. If an OSHA compliance officer believes that a violation has occurred, a citation is issued. Nonserious violations may result in fines of up to $1,000 for each incident. Serious or willful and repeated violations may incur fines of up to $10,000 per incident.

Occupational Safety and Health Act of 1970 (OSHA) Federal law setting and enforcing guidelines for protecting workers from unsafe conditions and potential health hazards in the workplace

Emerging Areas of Discrimination Law There are also several emerging areas of discrimination law that managers must also be familiar with. In this section, we will discuss some of the most important.

AIDS in the Workplace Although AIDS is considered a disability under the ADA, the AIDS situation itself is sufficiently severe enough that it warrants special attention. Employers cannot legally require an AIDS or any other medical examination as a condition for making an offer of employment. After an offer has been extended, however, the organization can make its offer contingent upon the individual's taking a physical examination. If an individual is found to be HIV positive, an employer cannot discriminate against the job applicant in its hiring decision. But many health insurance plans exclude "pre-existing conditions" from coverage, and if such a clause exists in the employer's health insurance plan, a new employee with AIDS may not be covered by the employer's plan.

Essentially, organizations must follow a certain set of guidelines and employ common sense when dealing with AIDS-related issues. They must, for example, treat AIDS like any other disease covered by law. They must maintain the confidentiality of all medical records. They cannot discriminate against a person with AIDS, and they should try to educate coworkers about AIDS. They cannot discriminate against AIDS victims in training or in consideration for promotion, and they must accommodate or make a good-faith effort to accommodate AIDS victims.

Sexual Harassment Sexual harassment has been a problem in organizations for a long time and is a violation of Title VII of the Civil Rights Act of 1964. **Sexual harassment** is defined by the EEOC as unwelcome sexual advances in the work environment. If the conduct is indeed unwelcome and occurs with sufficient frequency to create an abusive work environment, the employer is responsible for changing the environment by warning, reprimanding, or perhaps firing the harasser.

The courts have ruled and defined that there are two types of sexual harassment:

- In cases of **quid pro quo harassment,** the harasser offers to exchange something of value for sexual favors. A male supervisor, for example, might tell or suggest to a female subordinate that he will recommend her for promotion or give her a raise in exchange for sexual favors.
- The creation of a **hostile work environment** is a subtler form of sexual harassment. A group of male employees who continually make off-color jokes and lewd comments and perhaps decorate the work environment with inappropriate photographs may create a

sexual harassment Practice or instance of making unwelcome sexual advances in the workplace

quid pro quo harassment Form of sexual harassment in which sexual favors are requested in return for job-related benefits

hostile work environment Form of sexual harassment, deriving from off-color jokes, lewd comments, and so forth, that makes the work environment uncomfortable for some employees hostile work environment for a female colleague, who becomes uncomfortable working in that environment. As we noted earlier, it is the organization's responsibility for dealing with this sort of problem.

Although most cases involve men harassing women, there are many other situations in which sexual harassment can be identified. Sometimes women harass men, and same-sex harassment also occurs. Regardless of the pattern, however, the same bottom-line rules apply: Sexual harassment is illegal and the organization is responsible for controlling it.

employment-at-will
Principle, increasingly modified by legislation and judicial decision, that organizations should be able to retain or dismiss employees at their discretion

Employment-at-Will The concept of **employment-at-will** holds that both employer and employee have the mutual right to terminate an employment relationship anytime for any reason and with or without advance notice to the other. Specifically, it holds that an organization employs an individual at its own will and can therefore terminate that employment at any time for any reason. Over the last two decades, however, terminated employees have challenged the employment-at-will doctrine by filing lawsuits against former employers on the grounds of wrongful discharge.[8]

The legal basis of these lawsuits ranges from the various pieces of civil rights legislation discussed earlier to specific clauses in union contracts. Union contracts, for example, frequently specify the steps that must be followed before an organization can terminate any individual. Some lawsuits argue that the same process must be accorded to all employees, whether union members or not. Numerous lawsuits in the last several years have put limits on employment-at-will provisions in certain circumstances. In the past, for example, organizations were guilty of firing employees who filed worker compensation claims or took excessive time off to serve on jury duty. More recently, however, the courts have ruled that employees may not be fired for exercising rights protected by law.

NEW CHALLENGES IN THE CHANGING WORKPLACE

As we have seen throughout this chapter, human resource managers face several ongoing challenges in their efforts to keep their organizations staffed with effective workforces. To complicate matters, new challenges arise as the economic and social environments of business change. We conclude this chapter with a look at several of the most important human resource management issues facing business today.

Managing Workforce Diversity

workforce diversity
Range of workers' attitudes, values, and behaviors that differ by gender, race, and ethnicity

One extremely important set of human resource challenges centers on **workforce diversity**—the range of workers' attitudes, values, beliefs, and behaviors that differ by gender, race, age, ethnicity, physical ability, and other relevant characteristics. In the past, organizations tended to work toward homogenizing their workforces, getting everyone to think and behave in similar ways. Partly as a result of affirmative action efforts, however, many U.S. organizations are now creating more diverse workforces, embracing more women, ethnic minorities, and foreign-born employees than ever before.

Figure 8.3 helps put the changing U.S. workforce into perspective by illustrating changes in the percentages of different groups of workers—males and females, whites, blacks, Hispanics, Asians, and others—in the total workforce in the years 1986, 1996, and (as projected) 2006. The picture is clearly one of increasing diversity. By 2006, say experts, almost half of all workers in the labor force will be women and almost one-third will be Blacks, Hispanics, Asian Americans, and others.

What are some general guidelines for a successful workforce diversity program?

Today, organizations are recognizing not only that they should treat everyone equitably, but also that they should acknowledge the individuality of each person they employ. They are also recognizing that diversity can be a competitive advantage. For example, by hiring the best people available from every single group rather than hiring from just one or a few groups, a firm can develop a higher-quality labor force. Similarly, a diverse workforce can bring a wider array of information to bear on problems and can provide insights on marketing products to a wider range of

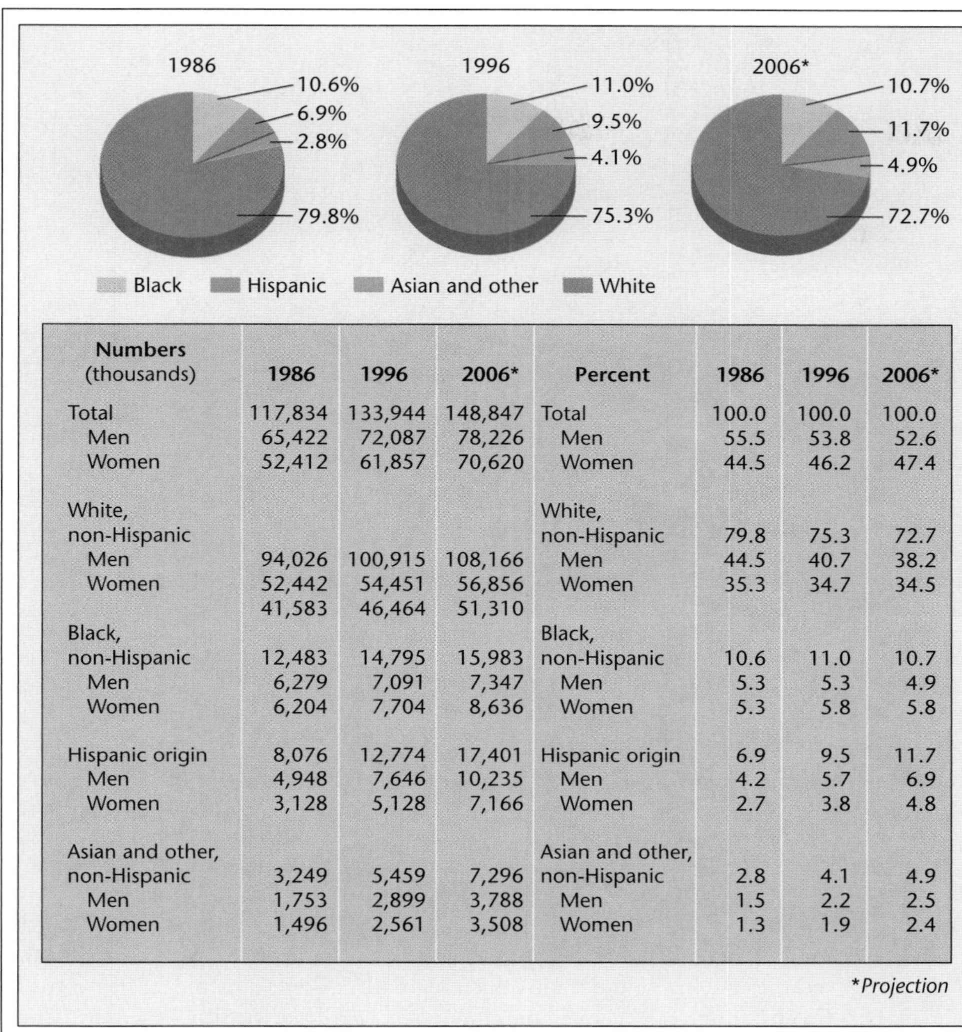

Numbers (thousands)	1986	1996	2006*	Percent	1986	1996	2006*
Total	117,834	133,944	148,847	Total	100.0	100.0	100.0
Men	65,422	72,087	78,226	Men	55.5	53.8	52.6
Women	52,412	61,857	70,620	Women	44.5	46.2	47.4
White,				White,			
non-Hispanic				non-Hispanic	79.8	75.3	72.7
Men	94,026	100,915	108,166	Men	44.5	40.7	38.2
Women	52,442	54,451	56,856	Women	35.3	34.7	34.5
	41,583	46,464	51,310				
Black,				Black,			
non-Hispanic	12,483	14,795	15,983	non-Hispanic	10.6	11.0	10.7
Men	6,279	7,091	7,347	Men	5.3	5.3	4.9
Women	6,204	7,704	8,636	Women	5.3	5.8	5.8
Hispanic origin	8,076	12,774	17,401	Hispanic origin	6.9	9.5	11.7
Men	4,948	7,646	10,235	Men	4.2	5.7	6.9
Women	3,128	5,128	7,166	Women	2.7	3.8	4.8
Asian and other,				Asian and other,			
non-Hispanic	3,249	5,459	7,296	non-Hispanic	2.8	4.1	4.9
Men	1,753	2,899	3,788	Men	1.5	2.2	2.5
Women	1,496	2,561	3,508	Women	1.3	1.9	2.4

*Projection

Figure 8.3
Changing Composition of the U.S. Workforce

consumers. Says the head of workforce diversity at IBM: "We think it is important for our customers to look inside and see people like them. If they can't . . . the prospect of them becoming or staying our customers declines."

"We think it is important for our customers to look inside and see people like them. If they can't, the prospect of them becoming or staying our customers declines."

—Head of workforce diversity at IBM

Managing Knowledge Workers

Traditionally, employees added value to organizations because of what they did or because of their experience. In the "information age," however, many employees add value because of what they know.[9]

The Nature of Knowledge Work These employees are usually called **knowledge workers,** and the skill with which they are managed is a major factor in determining which firms will be successful in the future. Knowledge workers, including computer scientists, engineers, and physical scientists, provide special challenges for the HR manager. They tend to work in high-technology firms and are usually experts in some abstract knowledge base. They often like to work independently and tend to identify more strongly with their professions than with any organization—even to the extent of defining performance in terms recognized by other members of their professions.

knowledge worker
Employee who is of value because of the knowledge that the employee possesses

As the importance of information-driven jobs grows, the need for knowledge workers continues to grow as well. But these employees require extensive and highly specialized

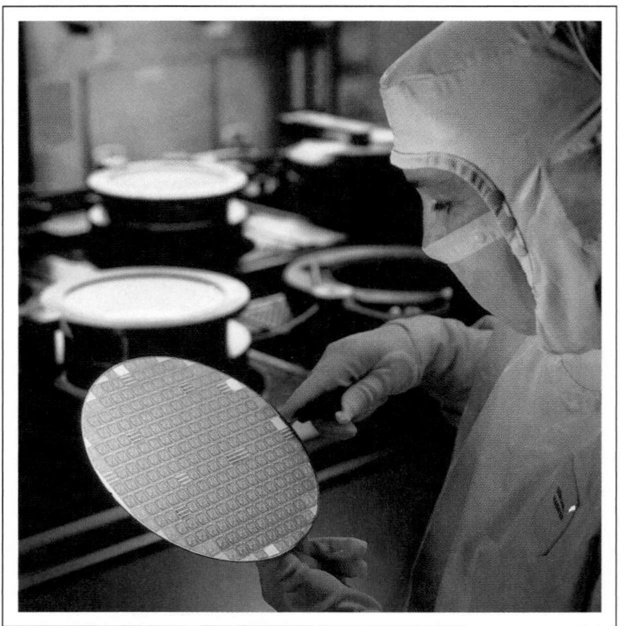

Every year the toy industry sells about 10 million scientific toys, such as chemistry sets. It also sells about 30 million electronic toys. These discrepancies help account for the fact that more and more science-minded college students—like this Power PC chip builder at Intel Corp. <www.intel.com>—are opting for computer-industry jobs instead of jobs in the traditional hard sciences, such as chemistry. Many experts predict that the current lure of quick financial solvency will result in a future shortage of science researchers and teachers.

training, and not every organization is willing to make the human capital investments necessary to take advantage of these jobs. In fact, even after knowledge workers are on the job, retraining and training updates are critical to prevent their skills from becoming obsolete. It has been suggested, for example, that the "half-life" of a technical education in engineering is about three years. The failure to update such skills will not only result in the loss of competitive advantage but will also increase the likelihood that the knowledge worker will go to another firm that is more committed to updating the worker's skills.

Knowledge Worker Management and Labor Markets In recent years, the demand for knowledge workers has been growing at a dramatic rate. As a result, organizations that need these workers must introduce regular market adjustments (upward) in order to pay them enough to keep them. This is especially critical in areas in which demand is growing, since even entry-level salaries for these employees are skyrocketing. Once an employee accepts a job with a firm, the employer faces yet another dilemma. Once hired, workers are more subject to the company's internal labor market, which is not likely to be growing as quickly as the external market for knowledge workers as a whole. Consequently, the longer employees remain with a firm, the further behind the market their pay falls—unless it is regularly adjusted upward.

The growing demand for these workers has inspired some fairly extreme measures for attracting them in the first place.[10] High starting salaries and sign-on bonuses are common. British Petroleum Exploration <www.bpamoco.com> was recently paying starting petroleum engineers with undersea platform-drilling knowledge—not experience, just knowledge—salaries in the six figures, plus sign-on bonuses of over $50,000 and immediate profit sharing. Even with these incentives, HR managers complain that in the Gulf Coast region, they cannot retain specialists because young engineers soon leave to accept sign-on bonuses with competitors. Laments one HR executive: "We wind up six months after we hire an engineer having to fight off offers for that same engineer for more money."[11]

"We wind up six months after we hire an engineer having to fight off offers for that same engineer for more money."

—Eric Campbell, HR executive at Docent Inc.

Contingent and Temporary Workers

A final contemporary HR issue of note involves the use of contingent and temporary workers. Indeed, recent years have seen an explosion in the use of such workers by organizations.

This young woman is one of 1,500 temporary workers at Sola Optical <www.sola.com>, one of the country's biggest makers of eyeglasses. Sola keeps at least 100 temps working at all times, because human resources managers like both the scheduling flexibility and the opportunity to try out potential permanent employees. On the other hand, of course, temps earn about one-third less than full-timers and usually get no benefits, such as health care.

Trends in Contingent and Temporary Employment In recent years, the number of contingent workers in the workforce has increased dramatically. A **contingent worker** is a person who works for an organization on something other than a permanent or full-time basis. Categories of contingent workers include independent contractors, on-call workers, temporary employees (usually hired through outside agencies), and contract and leased employees. Another category is part-time workers. The financial services giant Citigroup <www.citigroup.com>, for example, makes extensive use of part-time sales agents to pursue new clients. About 10 percent of the U.S. workforce currently uses one of these alternative forms of employment relationships. Experts suggest, however, that this percentage is increasing at a consistent pace.

contingent worker
Employee hired on something other than a full-time basis to supplement an organization's permanent workforce

Managing Contingent and Temporary Workers Given the widespread use of contingent and temporary workers, HR managers must understand how to use such employees most effectively. That is, they need to understand how to manage contingent and temporary workers.

One key is careful planning. Even though one of the presumed benefits of using contingent workers is flexibility, it still is important to integrate such workers in a coordinated fashion. Rather than having to call in workers sporadically and with no prior notice, organizations try to bring in specified numbers of workers for well-defined periods of time. The ability to do so comes from careful planning.

A second key is understanding contingent workers and acknowledging their advantages and disadvantages. That is, the organization must recognize what it can and can't achieve from the use of contingent and temporary workers. Expecting too much from such workers, for example, is a mistake that managers should avoid.

Third, managers must carefully assess the real cost of using contingent workers. We noted previously that many firms adopt this course of action to save labor costs. The organization should be able to document precisely its labor–cost savings. How much would it be paying people in wages and benefits if they were on permanent staff? How does this cost compare with the amount spent on contingent workers? This difference, however, could be misleading. We also noted, for instance, that contingent workers might be less effective performers than permanent and full-time employees. Comparing employee for employee on a direct-cost basis, therefore, is not necessarily valid. Organizations must learn to adjust the direct differences in labor costs to account for differences in productivity and performance.

Finally, managers must fully understand their own strategies and decide in advance how they intend to manage temporary workers, specifically focusing on how to integrate them into the organization. On a very simplistic level, for example, an organization with a large contingent workforce must make some decisions about the treatment of contingent workers relative to the treatment of permanent full-time workers. Should contingent workers be invited to the company holiday party? Should they have the same access to such employee benefits as counseling services and child care? There are no right or wrong answers to such questions. Managers must understand that they need to develop a strategy for integrating contingent workers according to some sound logic and then follow that strategy consistently over time.[12]

Continued from page 208

How Paternal Is Too Paternal?

Jim Goodnight's HR strategy has paid major dividends for SAS Institute. The firm has a loyal and dedicated workforce and phenomenally low turnover for a firm in its industry. It continues to receive accolades for being one of the very best employers in the United States.

But SAS and Jim Goodnight do have their critics. For one thing, some observers feel that the place is almost *too* perfect. They say that it conjures up images of Stepford, the fictional town created by novelist Ira Levin in *The Stepford Wives* where "disobedient" or "nonconformist" spouses were replaced by androids. This criticism resurfaced when Goodnight developed a housing subdivision adjacent to the SAS campus so that employees could buy discounted homes with mortgages financed through the company.

Critics also allege that SAS's lavish benefit packages smack of paternalism—that the company treats employees as if they can't take care of their own lives without the company's help. They also point to one glaring omission in SAS's reward system—stock and stock options for employees. While most growing high-tech companies give their employees a chance to prosper along with the company through stock ownership, Jim Goodnight and John Sall retain full ownership of SAS.

Even though these may be legitimate reservations, most observers and employees feel that the criticism is unwarranted. After all, no company can provide everything for its employees, and no one is "forced" to accept the benefits that SAS does provide. Perhaps more importantly, most observers and employees continue to view SAS as a model employer.

Questions for Discussion

1. Evaluate SAS Institute's employment practices from a strict business perspective.
2. How does the history of the firm affect its employment practices?
3. Which SAS benefits appeal most to you personally? Which appeal least to you?
4. Would you have an interest in working for SAS? Why or why not?
5. Are there potential pitfalls or problems with the firm's approach to HR management that might arise in the future?
6. How would you respond to the critics of SAS?

SUMMARY OF LEARNING OBJECTIVES

1 **Define *human resource management,* discuss its strategic significance, and explain how managers plan for human resources.** *Human resource management,* or *HRM,* is the set of organizational activities directed at attracting, developing, and maintaining an effective workforce. HRM plays a key strategic role in organizational performance. Planning for human resource needs entails several steps. Conducting a *job analysis* enables managers to create detailed, accurate job descriptions and specifications. After analysis is complete, managers must *forecast* demand and supply for both the numbers and types of workers they will need. Then they consider steps to match supply with demand.

2 **Identify the issues involved in *staffing* a company, including *internal* and *external recruiting* and *selection.*** *Recruiting* is the process of attracting qualified persons to apply for jobs that an organization has open. *Internal recruiting* involves considering present employees for new jobs. This approach helps build morale and rewards an organization's best employees. *External recruiting* means attracting people from outside the organization to apply for openings. When organizations are actually selecting people for jobs, they generally use such selection techniques as *application blanks, tests, interviews,* and other techniques. Regardless of what selection techniques are used, they must be valid predictors of an individual's expected performance in the job.

3 **Discuss different ways in which organizations go about developing the capabilities of employees and managers.** If a company is to get the most out of its workers, it must develop both those workers and their skills. Nearly all employees undergo some initial *orientation process* that introduces them to the company and to their new jobs. Many employees are given the opportunity to acquire new skills through various *work-based* and *instructional-based programs.*

4 **Explain ways in which organizations evaluate employee performance.** *Performance appraisals* help managers decide who needs training and who should be promoted. Appraisals also tell employees how well they are meeting expectations. Although a variety of alternatives are available for appraising performance, employee supervisors are most commonly used. No matter who does the evaluation, however, feedback to the employee is very important. Managers can select from a variety of ranking and rating methods for use in performance appraisal.

5 **Discuss the importance of *wages and salaries, incentives,* and *benefit programs* in attracting and keeping skilled workers.** *Wages and salaries, incentives,* and *benefit packages* may all be parts of a company's *compensation program.* By paying its workers as well as or better than competitors, a business can attract and keep qualified personnel. Incentive programs can also motivate people to work more productively. *Indirect compensation* also plays a major role in effective and well-designed compensation systems.

6 **Describe some of the key legal issues involved in hiring, compensating, and managing workers in today's workplace.** In hiring, compensating, and managing workers, managers must obey a variety of federal laws. *Equal employment opportunity* and *equal pay* laws forbid discrimination other than action based on legitimate job requirements. The concept of *comparable worth* holds that different jobs requiring equal levels of training and skill should pay the same. Firms are also required to provide employees with safe working environments, as set down by the guidelines of the *Occupational Safety and Health Administration.* Managers must consider *employment-at-will* issues (that is, limitations on their rights to hire and fire at their own discretion). AIDS and *sexual harassment* are other key contemporary legal issues in business.

7 **Discuss *workforce diversity,* the management of *knowledge workers,* and the use of *contingent and temporary workers* as important changes in the contemporary workplace.** *Workforce diversity* refers to the range of workers' attitudes, values, beliefs, and behaviors that differ by gender, race, ethnicity, age, and physical ability. Today, many U.S. businesses are working to create workforces that reflect the growing diversity of the population as it enters the labor pool. Although many firms see the diverse workforce as a competitive advantage, not all are equally successful in or eager about implementing diversity programs.

Many firms today also face challenges in managing *knowledge workers.* The recent boom in high-technology companies has led to rapidly increasing salaries and high turnover among the workers who are best prepared to work in those companies. *Contingent workers* are temporary and part-time employees hired to supplement an organization's permanent workforce. Their numbers have grown significantly since the early 1980s and are expected to rise further. The practice of hiring contingent workers is gaining in popularity because it gives managers more flexibility and because temps are usually not covered by employers' benefit programs.

QUESTIONS AND EXERCISES

Questions for Review

1. What are the advantages and disadvantages of internal and external recruiting? Under what circumstances is each more appropriate?
2. Why is the formal training of workers so important to most employers? Why don't employers simply let people learn about their jobs as they perform them?
3. What different forms of compensation do firms typically use to attract and keep productive workers?
4. What are some of the most significant laws affecting human resource management?

Questions for Analysis

5. What are your views on drug testing in the workplace? What would you do if your employer asked you to submit to a drug test?
6. Have you or anyone you know ever suffered discrimination in a hiring decision? Did either of you do anything about it?
7. What training do you think you are most likely to need when you finish school and start your career?
8. How much will benefit considerations affect your choice of an employer after graduation?

Application Exercises

9. Interview an HR manager at a local company. Focus on a position for which the firm is currently recruiting applicants and identify the steps in the selection process.
10. Identify some journals in your library that might be useful to an HR manager. What topics have been covered in recent features and cover stories?

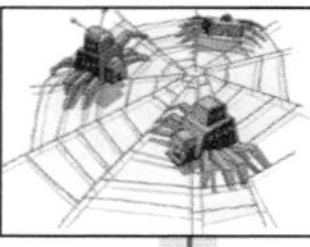

EXPLORING THE WEB

KEEPING THE INTERNET ON RETAINER

One of the most important issues facing managers today is compliance with various legal regulations. The following Web site summarizes many employment cases that were resolved by arbitration:

www.lawmemo.com/emp/sum/subjects/arbitration/bytopic.htm

Visit the site and review some of the cases. Choose two or three that seem interesting to you and write a brief description of each. Describe the potential implications for HR managers and respond to the following questions:

1. How useful is the Internet in keeping human resource managers informed about legal actions that may affect them?
2. Does relying on the Internet for legal information pose any risks?
3. What other legal information about HRM might be useful to have on the Internet?

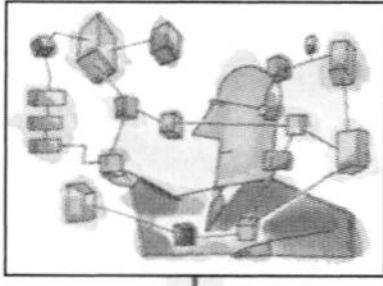

BUILDING YOUR BUSINESS SKILLS

GETTING ONLINE FOR A JOB

This exercise enhances the following SCANS workplace competencies: demonstrating basic skills, demonstrating thinking skills, exhibiting interpersonal skills, working with information, applying systems knowledge, and using technology.

GOAL

To introduce students to career-search resources available on the Internet.

BACKGROUND

If companies are on one side of the external staffing process, people looking for work are on the other. Companies need qualified candidates to fill job openings and candidates need jobs that are right for them. The challenge, of course, is to make successful matches. Increasingly, this matchmaking is being conducted on the Internet. Companies are posting jobs in cyberspace, and job seekers are posting résumés in response.

The number of job postings has grown dramatically in recent years. On a typical Sunday, you might find as many as 50,000 postings on the Monster Board, a leading job site. That's about five times the number that you'd find in the national edition of the *New York Times.* With so many companies looking for qualified candidates online, it makes good business sense to learn how to use the system.

METHOD

Using Internet career resources means locating job databases and preparing and posting a résumé. (You will therefore need access to the Internet to complete this exercise.)

Step 1

Team up with three classmates to investigate and analyze specific job databases. In each case, write a short report describing the database (which you and other group members may use during an actual job search). Summarize the site and its features as well as advantages, disadvantages, and costs.

Start with the following sites and add others that you find on your own:

- The Monster Board: <www.monster.com>
- CareerMosaic: <www.careermosaic.com>
- College Grad Job Hunter: <www.collegegrad.com>
- HRS Federal Job Search: <www.hrsjobs.com>
- America's Job Bank: <www.ajb.dni.us/>

Step 2

Investigate the job opportunities listed on the home pages of various companies. Among the companies you can try, consider the following:

- AT&T: <www.att.com>
- IBM: <www.ibm.com>
- Chase Manhattan Bank: <www.chasemanhattan.com>
- JC Penney: <www.jcpenney.com>
- McDonald's: <www.mcdonalds.com>
- General Electric: <www.ge.com>

Write a summary of the specific career-related information you find on each site.

Step 3

Working with group members, research strategies for composing effective cyberspace résumés. The following Web sites provide some helpful information on formats and personal and job-related information that should be included in your résumé. They also offer hints on the art of creating a scannable résumé:

- E-Span: <www.espan.com>
- JobSource: <www.jobsource.com>
- Career Magazine: <www.careermag.com>

Two books by Joyce Lain Kennedy, *Electronic Job Search Revolution* and *Electronic Résumé Revolution,* also contain valuable information.

Step 4

Working as a group, create an effective electronic résumé for a fictitious college graduate looking for a first job. Pay attention to format, language, style, and the effective communication of background and goals.

Step 5

Working as a group, learn how to post your résumé online. (Do not submit the résumé that you created for this exercise, which is, after all, fictitious.) The databases provided will guide you in this process.

FOLLOW-UP QUESTIONS

1. Why is it necessary to learn how to conduct an electronic job search? Do you think it will be more or less necessary in the years ahead?
2. Why do you think more computer-related jobs than nontechnical jobs are posted online? Do you think this situation will change?
3. Why is it a waste of time to stylize your résumé with different fonts, point sizes, and centered headings?
4. What is the advantage of e-mailing your résumé directly to a company rather than applying for the same job through an online databank?

CRAFTING YOUR BUSINESS PLAN

MAINTAINING HEALTHY HUMAN RESOURCES

THE PURPOSE OF THE ASSIGNMENT

1. To acquaint you with the process of navigating the *Business PlanPro* (*BPP*) software package (Version 4.0).
2. To familiarize students with the HR issues faced by a sample firm as it develops its business plan.
3. To demonstrate how four chapter topics—legal and ethical issues in managing people, hiring and training employees, financial incentives programs, and external versus internal staffing—can be integrated as components in the *BPP* planning environment.

ASSIGNMENT

After reading Chapter 8 in the textbook, open the BPP *software* and look around for information about HRM as it applies to a sample firm:* Southeast Health Service *(Southeast Health Plans, Inc.). Then respond to the following items:*

1. Explore Southeast's business plan, paying special attention to the management team, the types of employees the company has, and the clients that will be buying its products. In doing so, identify legal and ethical issues you expect Southeast to experience in managing its people. [Sites to see in *BPP* (for this assignment): In the Plan Outline screen, click on each of **1.0 Executive Summary, 1.1 Objectives,** and **1.2 Mission.** After returning to the Plan Outline screen, examine each of the following: **Table: Startup** (located beneath **2.2 Startup Summary**), **3.3 Sourcing, 3.4 Future Products, 6.2 Management Team,** and **6.5 Other Management Considerations.**]
2. Judging from both the company's growth expectations and the contents of its business plan, describe Southeast's plans for hiring and training its sales staff. [Sites to see in *BPP:* In the Plan Outline screen, click on **1.1 Objectives.** Then click on each of the following: **1.2 Mission** and **1.3 Keys to Success.**]
3. Considering Southeast's growth projections, what type of incentives program would you recommend for its sales staff? Individual merit pay? Individual bonuses? Companywide profit sharing? Explain the reasons for your recommendations. [Sites to see in *BPP:* In the Plan Outline screen, click on **4.0 Market Analysis Summary.** After returning to the Plan Outline screen, click on **Table: Sales Forecast** (located beneath **5.2.1 Sales Forecast**). From there, click on **5.1.1 Pricing Strategy.**]
4. Judging from the contents of its business plan, do you think Southeast intends to rely on external or on internal staffing for future management personnel? In what ways might the choice between external and internal options affect Southeast's performance? [Sites to see in *BPP:* In the Plan Outline screen, click on each of the following: **6.0 Management Summary, 6.2 Management Team,** and **Table: Personnel** (located beneath **6.4 Personnel Plan** in the Plan Outline screen).]

FOR YOUR OWN BUSINESS PLAN

5. In analyzing your own plan, would you consider Southeast Health Plans, Inc. to administer your firm's benefits package? Identify the services that Southeast would provide and which ones you would otherwise have to provide yourself. How would you estimate the costs of obtaining these services? [Sites to see in *BPP:* To learn about Southeast's experience with benefits planning, go to the Plan Outline screen and click on each of the following: **6.2 Management Team** and **Table: Personnel** (located beneath **6.4 Personnel Plan** in the Plan Outline screen).]

*GENERAL TIPS FOR NAVIGATING IN *BPP*

1. Open the *BPP* program, examine the Welcome screen, and click on **Open a Sample Plan.**
2. From the **Open a Sample Plan** dialogue box, click on a sample company name; then click on **Open.**
3. On the Plan Manager screen, click on **Your Plan Outline**; then click on any of the lines (for example, **6.0 Management Summary**).
4. You can always return to the Plan Outline screen by going to the bottom of the screen and clicking on the **Plan Outline** icon.
5. After finishing with one sample company, you can get to the next one by going to the top of the screen and clicking on **File** (on the menu bar). Then beneath that, select **Open**

Sample Plan. This will exit you from the current company file and take you to the **Open Sample Plan** dialogue box, where you can select your next sample company.

6. When you are finished, you can close the program by going to the top of the screen and clicking on **File** (on the bar menu). Then beneath that, select **Exit.**

VIDEO EXERCISE

CHANNELING HUMAN RESOURCES: SHOWTIME

Learning Objectives

The purpose of this video exercise is to help you

1. Identify the many ways in which HR managers can actively develop human resources.
2. Appreciate the role of mentoring in employee development.
3. Understand how a performance appraisal system can be designed and administered.

BACKGROUND INFORMATION

Showtime Networks Inc. (SNI) <www.showtime.com> is a wholly owned subsidiary of Viacom, Inc. <www.viacom.com>, a giant media conglomerate, and operates the premium television networks Showtime, The Movie Channel (TMC), Flix, and Showtime Event Television. It also operates the premium network Sundance Channel <www.sundancechannel.com>, a joint venture with Robert Redford and PolyGram Filmed Entertainment. One of the biggest challenges at SNI is attracting, retaining, and motivating a committed workforce. Demographic changes, work and family issues, and increasing diversities of age, race, and lifestyle tax the creativity of the company's HR staff.

THE VIDEO

This segment introduces various SNI executives who discuss the company's HR policies and challenges. The firm is a leader in creating a broad training and career-development program that serves a wide range of employee needs. It also uses a performance appraisal system that employees helped design and sponsors a formal program for encouraging mentoring.

DISCUSSION QUESTIONS

1. Among the organizational changes recently made at SNI are the combining of the legal and the human resource departments and the appointment of an HR manager to each SNI division. What are the pros and cons of these changes?
2. How good a job do you think SNI is doing to offer employees a chance to develop and improve their skills? Can you suggest additional programs that the company could undertake to achieve this goal?
3. Do you think the performance appraisal system at SNI is effective? Why or why not?

FOLLOW-UP ASSIGNMENT

Consider a small business such as a restaurant or consulting firm. What particular human resource challenges does this firm face in acknowledging diversity and in planning career-development programs? Sketch a plan for overcoming common obstacles, making your recommendations as specific as you can. Include any benefits that the business will enjoy from diversity and career development.

FOR FURTHER EXPLORATION

Visit the Web site of the Occupational Safety and Health Administration <www.osha.gov> and use the "News Room" or the search function to research the current status of OSHA initiatives on any of the following: indoor air pollution, asbestos removal, workplace violence. Where does OSHA stand on the issue, and what future action, if any, is it planning to take?

MASTERING BUSINESS ESSENTIALS

Go to the "Individual Behavior: Causal Attributions" episode on the Mastering Business Essentials CD-ROM for an interactive, video-enhanced exercise on the efforts of a manager at CanGo, an e-business start-up, to apply professional judgment to a staffing decision.

C h a p t e r

Understanding Employee Motivation and Leadership

After reading this chapter, you should be able to:

1. ***Describe*** the nature and importance of *psychological contracts* in the workplace.
2. ***Discuss*** the importance of *job satisfaction* and *employee morale* and summarize their roles in human relations in the workplace.
3. ***Identify*** and summarize the most important *theories of employee motivation.*
4. ***Describe*** some of the strategies used by organizations to improve *job satisfaction* and *employee motivation.*
5. ***Discuss*** different managerial styles of *leadership* and their impact on human relations in the workplace.

A New Deal in the Workplace

Back in the "good old days," businesses and workers operated according to a fairly well-defined and clearly understood set of agreements about what each offered to the other in the employment deal. For their part, businesses provided employees with a comfortable salary and benefit package and a secure job that they could expect to keep as long as they worked hard and stayed out of trouble. Employees, meanwhile, contributed their time, talent, and energy, along with steadfastness. Many people worked for the same company for 30 or 40 years or longer. Losing your job bordered on disgrace and changing jobs to work for a competitor was almost on a par with treason. This relationship was even immortalized in a classic 1950s book simply called *The Organization Man,* a phrase that quickly embedded itself in the vernacular of popular culture.

Over the last decade or so, all this has changed radically. Most experts agree that the revolution in employment relationships started in the late 1980s, when major U.S. corporations all across the United States laid off longtime and dedicated employees by the thousands. For their part, workers contributed to the trend by embracing a philosophy that extolled job-hopping as the best way to get ahead. As a consequence of these trends, the old employment contract has fundamentally changed in business after business.

Consider the case of BMC Software <**www.bmc.com**>, a Houston-based high-tech company with annual revenues of about $1.2 billion. BMC is a fast-growing enterprise with about 4,500 employees, many of them just recently out of school. BMC employees routinely work 10- to 12-hour days—most work several nights a week, and many report that vacations just never seem to happen. "This place isn't for wimps," reports one employee. Surprisingly, however, BMC is ranked number 56 on *Fortune*'s list of the "100 Best Companies to Work For."

"This place isn't for wimps."

—BMC Software employee

Why the apparent contradiction? Maybe it has something to do with BMC's lavish benefits package. The list seems to go on forever—hammocks stretched between trees in a beautifully landscaped office park, an on-site gym, a putting green, a basketball court, a horseshoe pit, and a beach volleyball court. An herb garden to supply the kitchen with fresh ingredients for each day's free gourmet lunch. Free snack areas with big-screen televisions, comfortable seating areas, and free sodas, coffee, tea, and popcorn. On-site massage therapy. A bank, a sundries store, a dry cleaner, a hair salon, and a nail salon. A piano player greeting workers each morning on the company Steinway. Says 30-year-old Christine Choi: "You never have to leave the place."

BMC employees also make above-average salaries, and most have generous stock options or stock-purchase plans. They also describe their work as fun and their employer as the next best thing to a member of the family. Have "the good old days" returned? Quite the contrary. BMC still has a problem keeping its best employees (there's a 14-percent turnover per year) and makes it clear to people that although they enjoy job security right now, there's no guarantee about the future. Instead of resurrecting bygone ways of doing things, BMC reflects a "new deal" between organizations and their employees.

Our opening story continues on page 261

As you will see in this chapter, people work for reasons other than money. They want interesting work that makes them feel part of a team and that satisfies their intellectual, social, and emotional needs. They also want to be well rewarded for their talents and their contributions to the success of a business. Organizations also want certain things from their employees—things like hard work and dedication. All these mutual—and sometimes conflicting—needs affect psychological contracts, attitudes and morale, employee motivation, and leadership in the workplace. By focusing on the learning objectives of this chapter, you will better understand why employee behavior, attitudes, and motivation are important to all types of businesses. You will also understand the role of leadership in motivating employees—or team members—to high levels of achievement.

human relations
Interactions between employers and employees and their attitudes toward one another

The foundation of good **human relations**—the interactions between employers and employees and their attitudes toward one another—is a satisfied and motivated workforce. But satisfaction and motivation usually are based on what some people call the "psychological contract" that exists between organizations and employees. Thus, we begin our discussion by examining the nature and meaning of *psychological contracts.*

PSYCHOLOGICAL CONTRACTS IN ORGANIZATIONS

psychological contract
Set of expectations held by employees concerning what they will contribute to an organization (referred to as *contributions*) and what the organization will in return provide the employees (referred to as *inducements*)

Whenever we buy a car or sell a house, both buyer and seller sign a contract that specifies the terms of the agreement—who pays what to whom, when it's paid, and so forth. In some ways, a psychological contract resembles a legal contract. On the whole, however, it's less formal and less rigidly defined. A **psychological contract** is the set of expectations held by employees concerning what they will contribute to an organization (referred to as *contributions*) and what the organization will provide the employees (referred to as *inducements*) in return.

BMC Software's Christine Choi contributes her education, skills, effort, time, and energy. In return for these contributions, BMC provides inducements for her to remain with the firm. As we saw in our opening story, BMC's inducement package includes a good place to work, lavish benefits, and a nice salary. Both BMC and Choi seem to be satisfied with the relationship and are thus likely to maintain it, at least for the time being.

In other situations, however, things might not work out as well. If either party perceives an inequity in the contract, that party may seek a change. The employee, for example, might ask for a pay raise, promotion, or a bigger office. Also, the employee might put forth less effort or look for a better job elsewhere. The organization can also initiate change by training workers to improve their skills, transferring them to new jobs, or terminating them.

Does downsizing improve quality in the workforce?

All organizations face the basic challenge of managing psychological contracts. They want value from their employees, and they must give employees the right inducements. Valuable but underpaid employees may perform below their capabilities or leave for better jobs. Conversely, overpaying employees who contribute little incurs unnecessary costs.

The massive wave of downsizing and cutbacks that swept the U.S. economy in the 1980s and early 1990s has complicated the process of managing psychological contracts. Many organizations used to offer at least reasonable assurances of job permanence as a fundamental inducement to employees. Now, however, because job permanence is less likely, alternative inducements—such as lavish benefits packages—may be needed instead.

If psychological contracts are created, maintained, and managed effectively, the result is likely to be workers who are satisfied and motivated. On the other hand, poorly managed psychological contracts may result in dissatisfied, unmotivated workers. Although most people have a general idea of what job satisfaction is, both job satisfaction and high morale can be elusive in the workplace. Because they are critical to an organization's success, we now turn our attention to discussing their importance.

THE IMPORTANCE OF SATISFACTION AND MORALE

Broadly speaking, **job satisfaction** is the degree of enjoyment that people derive from performing their jobs. If people enjoy their work, they are relatively satisfied; if they do not enjoy their work, they are relatively dissatisfied. In turn, satisfied employees are likely to have high **morale**—the overall attitude that employees have toward their workplace. Morale reflects the degree to which they perceive that their needs are being met by their jobs. It is determined by a variety of factors, including job satisfaction and satisfaction with such things as pay, benefits, coworkers, and promotion opportunities.[1] The "Life Cycle of an e-Business" box in this chapter shows how satisfaction and morale were key considerations in managing the workplace at Garden.com.

job satisfaction
Degree of enjoyment that people derive from performing their jobs

morale
Overall attitude that employees have toward their workplace

Life Cycle of an e-Business

Cultivating Morale and Motivation at Garden.com

One of the many ingredients in the initial success enjoyed by Garden.com was the morale and motivation of its workforce. Morale, for example, was almost uniformly high. Because the company had a relatively flat, decentralized organization, people at all levels could get involved in making decisions and having a real impact on the business. This situation was reinforced by a conscious effort on the part of the firm's leaders to make freedom, flexibility, and autonomy consistent factors in everyday work life.

Beyond decision making, Garden.com also provided flexible work-scheduling opportunities for everyone. In effect, people were free to come and go as they chose. The only thing that really mattered was that they got their jobs done effectively. Under such conditions, the firm enjoyed a very low rate of turnover and had such a good reputation that it could take its pick of high-quality applicants whenever it needed to hire. The firm also benefited from the motivational intensity that employees brought to work. Because many of them owned Garden.com stock, they were keenly interested in lowering costs, increasing revenues, avoiding inefficiencies, and developing new market opportunities.

A good case in point is Carson Fustes. Ms. Fustes had previously lived and worked in Boulder, Colorado, and first came to know Garden.com as a customer after browsing its Web site. The more she interacted with the company as a customer, the more impressed she became both with the way the organization was managed and the way it treated employees. Eventually, Fustes did enough research on the company to decide that she wanted to work there. So she applied for a position at the firm's Austin headquarters and was hired as a Supplier Analyst. She truly loved both the job and the company, where her responsibilities included reviewing the qualifications of potential new suppliers and monitoring the performance of existing ones.

Unfortunately, Garden.com's problems eventually led to layoffs, and the value of the stock options held by employees dropped dramatically. Fustes and her colleagues have now moved on to other opportunities, but most will always remember fondly the heady days at Garden.com when they thought the world was their oyster.

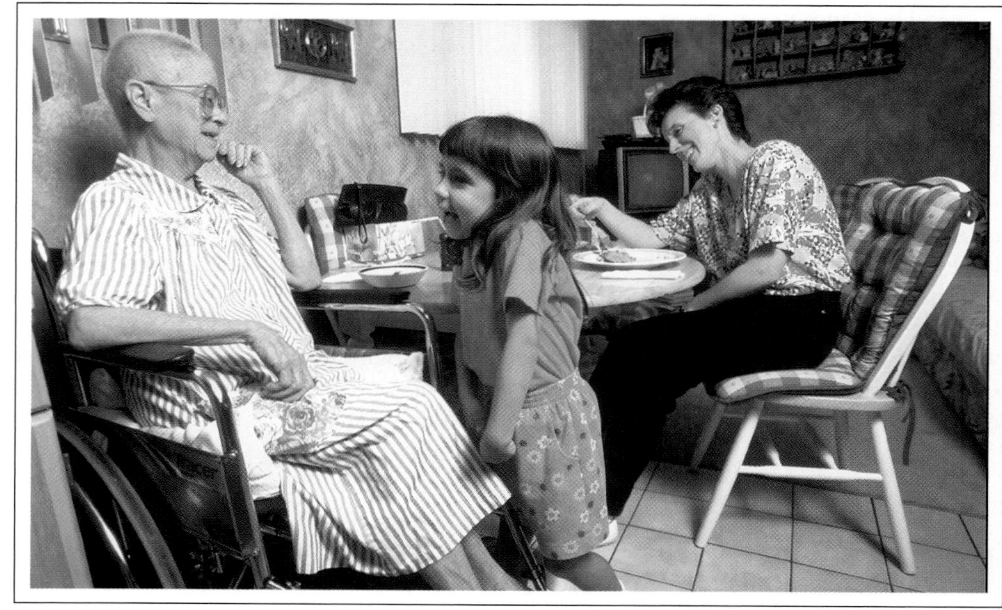

Jackie Demo works at health care products maker Baxter Export Corp. <www.baxter.com>, *where she enjoys flexible hours and at least one day a week of telecommuting. Demo starts her day at 6:30 in the morning, which gets her home in time to pick her daughter up from day care and look in on her terminally ill mother-in-law. In return for its flexibility—30% of Baxter employees telecommute, work part-time, or share jobs—the company gets greater commitment from its employees.*

Companies can improve morale and job satisfaction in a variety of ways. Some large firms, for example, have instituted companywide programs designed specifically to address employees' needs. The numerous benefits provided by BMC Software clearly fit into this category. Forty-six of *Fortune*'s "100 Best Companies to Work For" offer take-home meals for employees who don't have time to cook. Another 26 provide personal concierge services to help harried employees with everything from buying birthday gifts and organizing social events to planning vacations and maintaining cars.[2] Managers at Hyatt Hotels <www.hyatt.com> report that conducting frequent surveys of employee attitudes, soliciting employee input, and—most important—acting on that input give the company an edge in recruiting and retaining productive workers. Managers of smaller businesses realize that the personal touch can reap big benefits in employee morale. For example, First Tennessee <www.ftb.com>, a midsize regional bank, believes that work and family are so closely related that family considerations should enter into job design. Thus, it offers such benefits as on-site child care.

When workers are satisfied and morale is high, the organization benefits in many ways. Compared with dissatisfied workers, for example, satisfied employees are more committed and loyal. Such employees are more likely to work hard and to make useful contributions. In addition, they tend to have fewer grievances and engage in fewer negative behaviors (complaining, deliberately slowing their work pace, and so forth) than dissatisfied counterparts. Finally, satisfied workers tend not only to come to work every day but also to remain with the organization. By promoting satisfaction and morale, then, management is working to ensure more efficient operations.

Conversely, the costs of dissatisfaction and poor morale are high. Dissatisfied workers are far more likely to be absent for minor illnesses, personal reasons, or a general disinclination to go to work. Low morale may also result in high *turnover*—the percentage of an organization's workforce who quit and must be replaced. High levels of turnover have many negative consequences including the disruption of production schedules, high retraining costs, and decreased productivity.

In fact, evidence suggests that job satisfaction and employee morale may directly affect a company's performance. The results of one study, highlighted in Figure 9.1, focused on the businesses that made *Fortune*'s list of the "100 Best Companies to Work For." The study compared the average annual return to shareholders (a major indicator of company

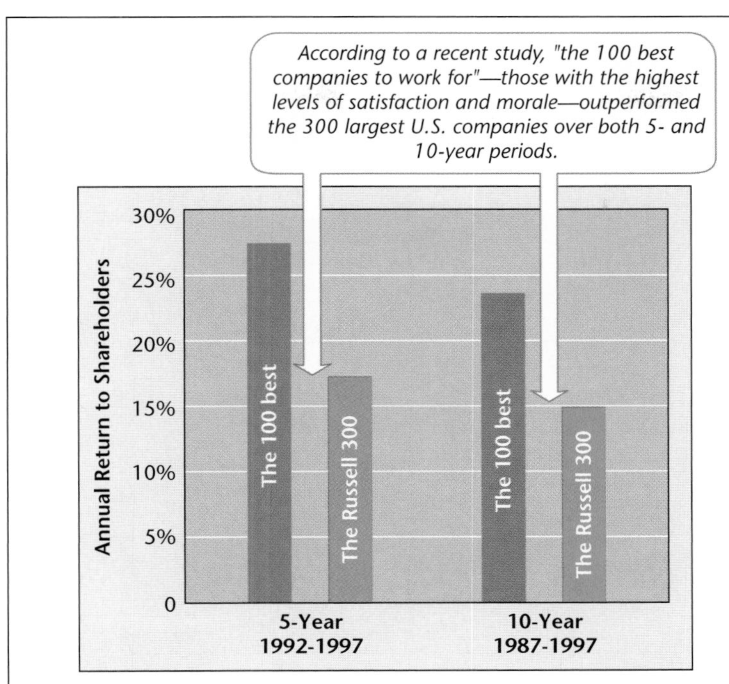

Figure 9.1

Satisfaction and Return to Shareholders

performance) for periods of five and 10 years for those firms against the 300 largest U.S. companies. As you can see, the sample of 100 companies with the highest levels of satisfaction and morale significantly outperformed the larger sample over both time periods. Of course, many other factors contributed to the performance of both sets of companies, but these differences nevertheless underscore the significance of a satisfied workforce.[3]

Recent Trends in Managing Satisfaction and Morale

Achieving high levels of job satisfaction and morale seems like a reasonable organizational goal, especially in light of findings such as those summarized in Figure 9.1. From the late 1980s through the mid-1990s, many major companies went through periods of massive

www.containerstore.com

According to Kip Tindell, president of The Container Store, "A funny thing happens when you take the time to educate your employees, pay them well, and treat them as equals. You end up with extremely motivated and enthusiastic people."

The Container Store, the nation's leading retailer of storage and organization products, was selected by *Fortune* magazine as the "Best Company to Work For in America" in the magazine's third annual survey. In addition to paying its employees 50 to 100 percent higher than industry average, the company provides all first year, full-time employees with more than 235 hours of formal training.

Figure 9.2
Expansion of Benefits

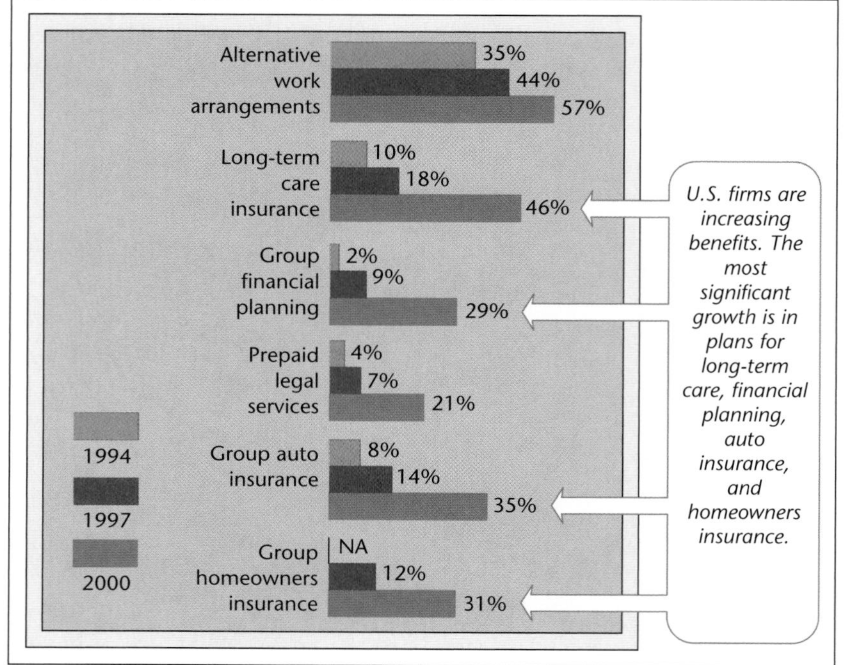

layoffs and cutbacks. AT&T <www.att.com>, for example, eliminated 40,000 jobs. Although this case is extreme, such firms as Nabisco <www.nabisco.com>, Apple Computer <www.apple.com>, ConAgra <www.conagra.com>, Exxon <www.exxon.com>, and Delta Airlines <www.delta-air.com> also cut thousands of jobs. Even in more recent—and prosperous—times, Chubb Corporation <www.chubb.com>, Eastman Kodak <www.kodak.com>, and Entergy Corporation <www.entergy.com> have cut jobs. Not surprisingly, then, satisfaction and morale plummeted in many companies. Workers feared for their job security, and even those who kept their jobs were unhappy about their less fortunate colleagues and friends.

In the late 1990s, however, things changed dramatically. A booming economy and the creation of thousands of new jobs led to low unemployment in most industries and regions. As a result, companies suddenly found themselves having to work harder not only to retain current employees who were being courted by other employers, but also to offer creative incentives to secure new employees, many of whom had multiple job opportunities to consider.

In the process, many leading firms came up with innovative benefits and "perks" designed to keep employees happy, boost satisfaction, and enhance morale. Figure 9.2 shows some recent trends in the area of benefits. In 1994, for example, no major employer reported offering employees group homeowner's insurance. By 1997, 12 percent had such plans; and by 2000, about one-third were offering this benefit. Virtually all of this expansion in benefits and perks results from the desire of businesses to make themselves more attractive workplaces by maintaining job satisfaction and employee morale.[4]

MOTIVATION IN THE WORKPLACE

motivation
The set of forces that cause people to behave in certain ways

Although job satisfaction and morale are important, employee motivation is even more critical to a firm's success. As we saw in Chapter 5, motivation is one part of the managerial function of directing. Broadly defined, **motivation** is the set of forces that cause people to behave in certain ways. One worker may be motivated to work hard to produce as much as possible, whereas another may be motivated to do just enough to survive. Managers must understand these differences in behavior and the reasons for them.

Over the years, a steady progression of theories and studies has attempted to address these issues. In this section, we survey the major studies and theories of employee motivation. In particular, we focus on three approaches to human relations in the workplace that reflect a basic chronology of thinking in the area: *classical theory* and *scientific management, behavior theory,* and *contemporary motivational theories.*[5]

Classical Theory

According to the so-called **classical theory of motivation,** workers are motivated solely by money. In his seminal book, *The Principles of Scientific Management,* industrial engineer Frederick Taylor (1911) proposed a way for both companies and workers to benefit from this widely accepted view of life in the workplace. If workers are motivated by money, Taylor reasoned, then paying them more should prompt them to produce more. Meanwhile, the firm that analyzed jobs and found better ways to perform them would be able to produce goods more cheaply, make higher profits, and thus pay and motivate workers better than its competitors.

classical theory of motivation
Theory holding that workers are motivated solely by money

Taylor's approach is known as *scientific management.* His ideas captured the imagination of many managers in the early twentieth century. Soon, plants across the United States were hiring experts to perform *time-and-motion studies:* Industrial-engineering techniques were applied to each facet of a job in order to determine how to perform it most efficiently. These studies were the first scientific attempts to break down jobs into easily repeated components and to devise more efficient tools and machines for performing them.

Behavior Theory: The Hawthorne Studies

In 1925, a group of Harvard researchers began a study at the Hawthorne Works of Western Electric outside Chicago. With an eye to increasing productivity, they wanted to examine the relationship between changes in the physical environment and worker output.

The results of the experiment were unexpected, even confusing. For example, increased lighting levels improved productivity. For some reason, however, so did lower lighting levels. Moreover, against all expectations, increased pay *failed* to increase productivity. Gradually, the researchers pieced together the puzzle. The explanation lay in the workers' response to the *attention* that they were receiving. The researchers concluded that productivity rose in response to almost any management action that workers interpreted as special attention. This finding, known widely today as the **Hawthorne effect,** had a major influence on human relations theory, although in many cases it amounted simply to convincing managers that they should pay more attention to employees.

Hawthorne effect
Tendency for productivity to increase when workers believe they are receiving special attention from management

Contemporary Motivational Theories

Following the Hawthorne studies, managers and researchers alike focused more attention on the importance of good human relations in motivating employee performance. Stressing the factors that cause, focus, and sustain workers' behavior, most motivation theorists are concerned with the ways in which management thinks about and treats employees. The major motivation theories include the *human resources model, the hierarchy of needs model, two-factor theory, expectancy theory, equity theory,* and *goal-setting theory.*

Human Resources Model: Theories X and Y

In an important study, behavioral scientist Douglas McGregor concluded that managers had radically different beliefs about how best to use the human resources employed by a firm. He classified these beliefs into sets of assumptions that he labeled "Theory X" and "Theory Y." The basic differences between these two theories are highlighted in Table 9.1.

Table 9.1

Theory X and Theory Y

Theory X	Theory Y
People are lazy.	People are energetic.
People lack ambition and dislike responsibility.	People are ambitious and seek responsibility.
People are self-centered.	People can be selfless.
People resist change.	People want to contribute to business growth and change.
People are gullible and not very bright.	People are intelligent.

Theory X
Theory of motivation holding that people are naturally irresponsible and uncooperative

Theory Y
Theory of motivation holding that people are naturally responsible, growth oriented, self-motivated, and interested in being productive

hierarchy of human needs model
Theory of motivation describing five levels of human needs and arguing that basic needs must be fulfilled before people work to satisfy higher-level needs

Managers who subscribe to **Theory X** tend to believe that people are naturally lazy and uncooperative and must therefore be either punished or rewarded to be made productive. Managers who are inclined to accept **Theory Y** tend to believe that people are naturally energetic, growth oriented, self-motivated, and interested in being productive.

McGregor generally favored Theory Y beliefs. Thus, he argued that Theory Y managers are more likely to have satisfied and motivated employees. Of course, Theory X and Y distinctions are somewhat simplistic and offer little concrete basis for action. Their value lies primarily in their ability to highlight and classify the behavior of managers in light of their attitudes toward employees.

Maslow's Hierarchy of Needs Model Psychologist Abraham Maslow's **hierarchy of human needs model** proposed that people have several different needs that they attempt to satisfy in their work. He classified these needs into five basic types and suggested that they be arranged in the hierarchy of importance as shown in Figure 9.3. According to Maslow, needs are hierarchical because lower-level needs must be met before a person will try to satisfy higher-level needs.

Once a set of needs has been satisfied, it ceases to motivate behavior. This is the sense in which the hierarchical nature of lower- and higher-level needs affects employee motivation and satisfaction. For example, if you feel secure in your job, a new pension plan will probably be less important to you than the chance to make new friends and join an informal network among your coworkers. If, however, a lower-level need suddenly becomes unfulfilled, most people immediately refocus on that lower level. Suppose, for example, that you are seeking to meet your self-esteem needs by working as a divisional manager at a major company. If you learn that your division, and consequently your job,

Figure 9.3

Maslow's Hierarchy of Needs

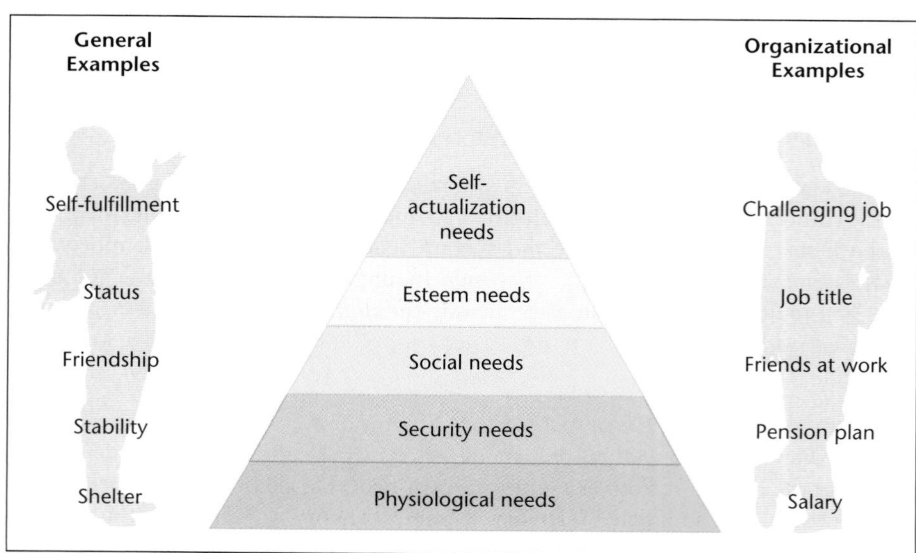

may be eliminated, you might very well find the promise of job security at a new firm as motivating as a promotion once would have been at your old company.

Maslow's theory recognizes that because different people have different needs, they are motivated by different things. Unfortunately, it provides few specific guidelines for action in the workplace. Furthermore, research has found that the hierarchy varies widely, not only for different people but across different cultures.

Two-Factor Theory After studying a group of accountants and engineers, psychologist Frederick Herzberg concluded that job satisfaction and dissatisfaction depend on two factors: *hygiene factors,* such as working conditions, and *motivation factors,* such as recognition for a job well done.

According to the **two-factor theory,** hygiene factors affect motivation and satisfaction only if they are absent or fail to meet expectations. For example, workers will be dissatisfied if they believe that they have poor working conditions. If working conditions are improved, however, they will not necessarily become satisfied; they will simply be not dissatisfied. If workers receive no recognition for successful work, they may be neither dissatisfied nor satisfied. If recognition is provided, they will likely become more satisfied.

two-factor theory
Theory of motivation holding that job satisfaction depends on two types of factors, hygiene and motivation

Figure 9.4 illustrates the two-factor theory. Note that motivation factors lie along a continuum from *satisfaction* to *no satisfaction.* Hygiene factors, in contrast, are likely to produce feelings that lie on a continuum from *dissatisfaction* to *no dissatisfaction.* Whereas motivation factors are directly related to the work that employees actually perform, hygiene factors refer to the environment in which they perform it.

This theory thus suggests that managers should follow a two-step approach to enhancing motivation. First, they must ensure that hygiene factors—working conditions, clearly stated policies—are acceptable. This practice will result in an absence of dissatisfaction. Then they must offer motivation factors—recognition, added responsibility—as means of improving satisfaction and motivation.

Research suggests that although two-factor theory works in some professional settings, it is less effective in clerical and manufacturing settings. (Herzberg's research was limited to

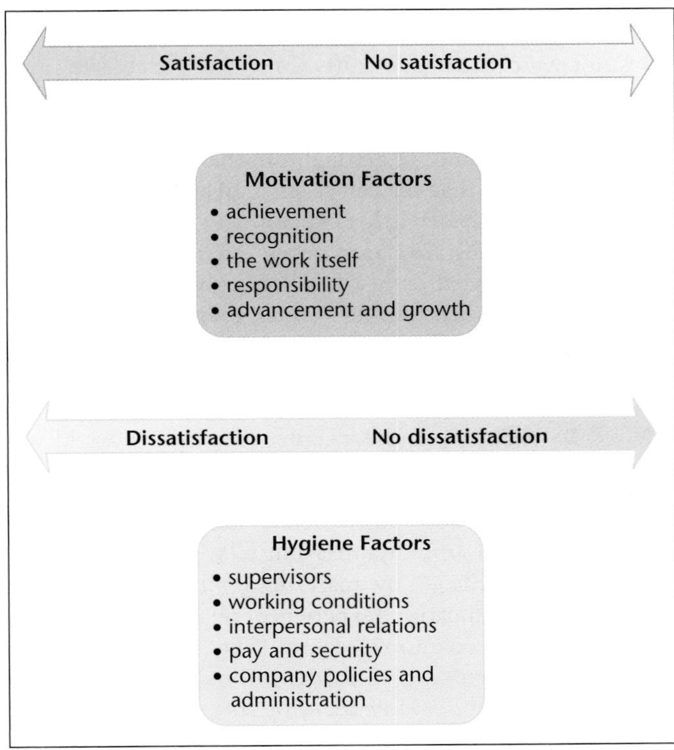

Figure 9.4
Two-Factor Theory of Motivation

Figure 9.5
Expectancy Theory Model

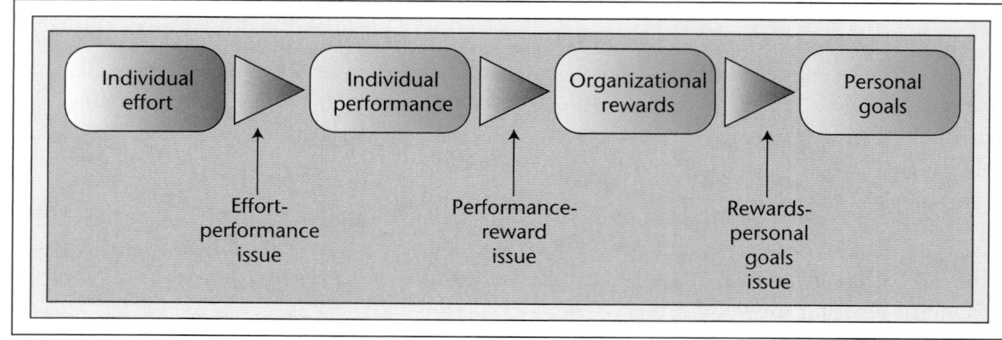

accountants and engineers.) In addition, one person's hygiene factor may be another person's motivation factor. For example, if money represents nothing more than pay for time worked, it may be a hygiene factor for one person. For another person, however, money may be a motivation factor because it represents recognition and achievement.

expectancy theory
Theory of motivation holding that people are motivated to work toward rewards that they want and that they believe they have a reasonable chance of obtaining

Expectancy Theory The **expectancy theory** suggests that people are motivated to work toward rewards that they want *and* that they believe they have a reasonable chance—or expectancy—of obtaining. A reward that seems out of reach is likely to be undesirable even if it is intrinsically positive. Figure 9.5 illustrates expectancy theory in terms of issues that are likely to be considered by an individual employee. Consider the case of an assistant department manager who learns that her firm needs to replace a retiring division manager two levels above her in the organization. Even though she wants the job, she does not apply because she doubts that she will be selected. In this case, she raises the *performance-reward issue:* for some reason, she believes that her performance will not get her the position. Note that she may think that her performance merits the new job but that performance alone will not be enough; perhaps she expects the reward to go to someone with more seniority.

Assume that our employee also learns that the firm is looking for a production manager on a later shift. She thinks that she could get this job but does not apply because she does not want to change shifts. In this instance, she raises the *rewards-personal goals issue.* Finally, she learns of an opening one level higher—department manager—in her own division. She may well apply for this job because she both wants it and thinks that she has a good chance of getting it. In this case, her consideration of all the issues has led to an expectancy that she can reach a given goal.

Expectancy theory helps explain why some people do not work as hard as they can when their salaries are based purely on seniority. Paying employees the same whether they work very hard or just hard enough to get by removes the financial incentive for them to work harder. In other words, they ask themselves, "If I work harder, will I get a pay raise?" and conclude that the answer is no. Similarly, if hard work will result in one or more *undesirable* outcomes—say, a transfer to another location or a promotion to a job that requires unpleasant travel—employees will not be motivated to work hard. The "Wired World" box in this chapter examines ways in which the expectancy theory of motivation has been instrumental at a dot.com business called TixToGo.

equity theory
Theory of motivation holding that people evaluate their treatment by employers relative to the treatment of others

Equity Theory The **equity theory** focuses on social comparisons—people evaluating their treatment by the organization relative to the treatment of others. This approach holds that people begin by analyzing *inputs* (what they contribute to their jobs in terms of time, effort, education, experience) relative to *outputs* (what they receive in return—salary, benefits, recognition, security). The result is a ratio of contribution to return. Then they compare their own ratios with those of other employees: They ask whether their ratios are *equal to, greater than,* or *less than* those of the people with whom they are

It's a WiredWorld

• The Future of Compensation?

What would it take to get someone to work for free? Let's rephrase the question in more realistic terms: What would it take to get someone to work for no income today but with the potential for a big payoff in the future? That's the question that a Silicon Valley start-up company recently asked. The answers that it got may be surprising. The company found that the right people would actually be quite enthusiastic about this prospect—as long as the potential rewards were substantial and the probability of getting them within reason.

The company in question is TixToGo <www.tixtogo.com>, which sells events and activities, such as tours and programs, for other vendors. The firm was actually a fledgling Internet site when its founder approached Lu Cordova, head of a consulting company and acting director of another Internet start-up firm, with an offer to become CEO. He wanted Cordova to run the firm while he devoted more time to looking for new funding. The only problem was that TixToGo only had $12,000 in the bank and, with four other full-time employees, had no money to pay Cordova. Although she was intrigued with the firm's prospects, Cordova wasn't excited about working for free. So, she devised her own compensation plan, which revolved around the promise that she would be given an attractive salary retroactive to her start date, payable in cash or equity, if the firm was successful in obtaining new funding.

Now, just because Cordova was willing to buy into this plan, it did not follow that anyone else at TixToGo was interested. The skeptics were quickly proven wrong, however, when Cordova was able to attract six full-time employees, two part-timers, and eight outside consultants and contractors—all for deferred pay. Moreover, each individual was given the option of taking his or her deferred pay in cash or stock. Actually, however, "deferred pay" might have been a misnomer. After all, if TixToGo never gets the funding it needs, no one, starting with Cordova, will ever be paid a cent, deferred or otherwise.

Why would someone accept this deal? One major reason is the potential payoff. Many of the new TixToGo employees have taken their future compensation in stock. The number of shares received by each is determined by dividing the dollar amount of the employee's salary by the per-share valuation used in determining the venture capitalists' stake ($11 per share). As a result, an individual could end up with several thousand shares of stock. If the firm then subsequently goes public, a truly big payoff would be in the offing.

Outside consultants and contractors also bought in. They took part of their fees in cash, generally just enough to cover costs, and the rest in stock based on the same per-share valuation estimate offered to employees. One contractor, for example, put together a television ad for TixToGo. The normal fee would have been $250,000. In this instance, however, the contractor took $70,000 in cash and $20,000 in stock. Like employees, contractors stand to make a bundle if the stock price takes off.

At this point, we are left with one significant question: How realistic is it for employees and contractors to expect a big payday in the future? Given the recent spate of successful high-technology public offerings and the initial interest shown by investors, TixToGo appears to have a promising future. One investor, for instance, wrote Cordova a check for $50,000 on the basis of its compensation system alone—without even seeing a business plan. Because TixToGo also seems to be attracting the attention of several other big-time investment groups, the prospects for success seem to be quite promising.

comparing themselves. Depending on their assessments, they experience feelings of equity or inequity. Figure 9.6 illustrates the three possible results of such an assessment.

For example, suppose a new college graduate gets a starting job at a large manufacturing firm. His starting salary is $25,000 a year, he gets a compact company car, and he shares an office with another new employee. If he later learns that another new employee has received the same salary, car, and office arrangement, he will feel equitably treated. If the other newcomer, however, has received $30,000, a full-size company car, and a private office, he may feel inequitably treated (see Result 2 in Figure 9.6).

Note, however, that for an individual to feel equitably treated, the two ratios do not have to be the same, only *fair.* Assume, for instance, that our new employee has a bachelor's degree and two years of work experience. Perhaps he learns subsequently that the

Figure 9.6
Equity Theory: Possible Assessments

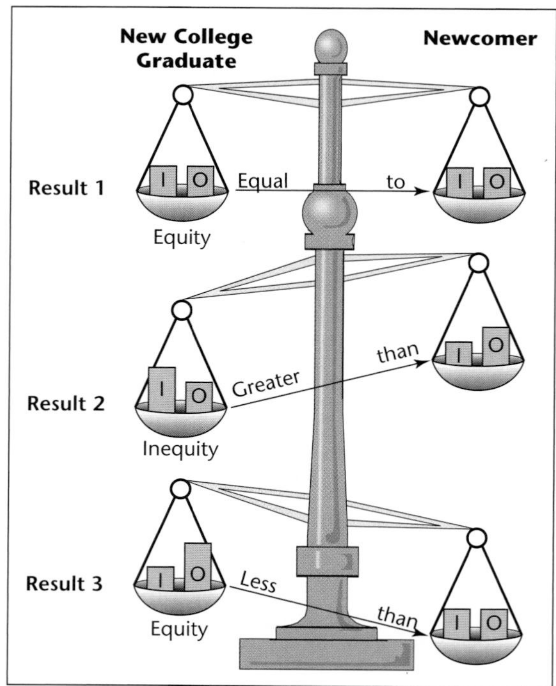

other new employee has an advanced degree and 10 years of experience. After first feeling inequity, the new employee may conclude that the person with whom he compared himself is actually contributing more to the organization. That employee is equitably entitled, therefore, to receive more in return (Result 3).

When people feel they are being inequitably treated, they may do various things to restore fairness. For example, they may ask for raises, reduce their efforts, work shorter hours, or just complain to their bosses. They may also rationalize ("Management succumbed to pressure to promote a woman/Asian American"), find different people with whom to compare themselves, or leave their jobs.

Virtually perfect examples of equity theory at work can be found in professional sports. Each year, for example, rookies, sometimes fresh out of college, are often signed to lucrative contracts. No sooner than the ink is dry do veteran players start grumbling about raises or revised contracts.

STRATEGIES FOR ENHANCING JOB SATISFACTION AND MORALE

Why do today's managers prefer positive reinforcement techniques over the disciplinary techniques of the past?

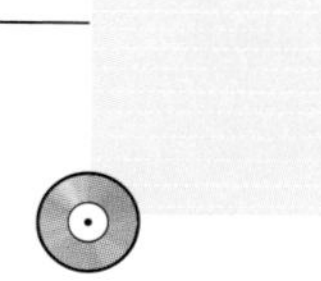

Deciding what provides job satisfaction and motivates workers is only one part of human resource management. The other part is applying that knowledge. Experts have suggested—and many companies have implemented—a range of programs designed to make jobs more interesting and rewarding and to make the work environment more pleasant.

Reinforcement/Behavior Modification Theory

Many companies try to control, and even alter or modify, workers' behavior through systematic rewards and punishments for specific behaviors. In other words, they first try to define the specific behaviors that they want their employees to exhibit (working hard, being courteous to customers, stressing quality) and the specific behaviors they want to

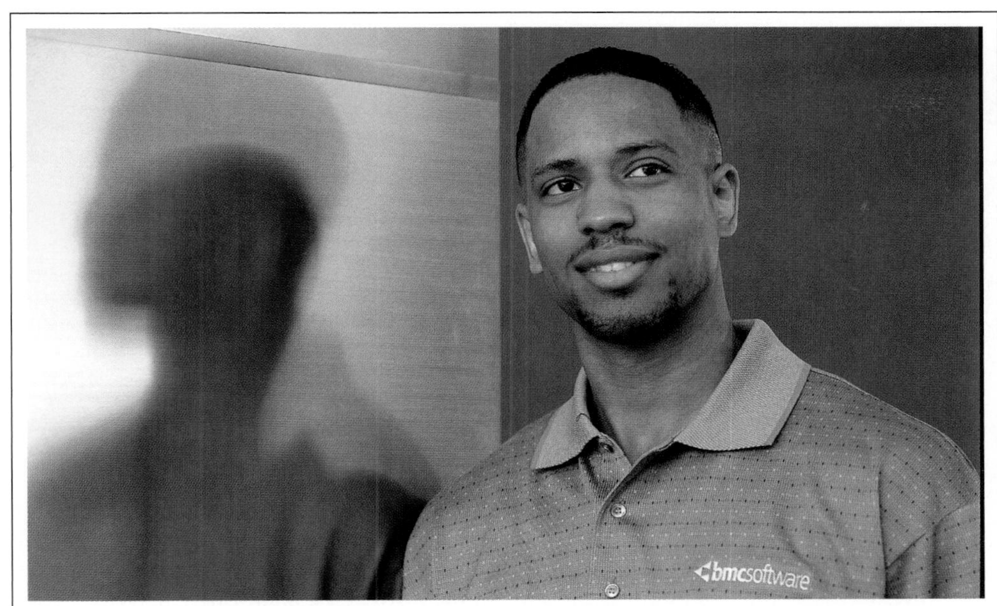

Brian Stevens started out at BMC Software, Inc. as a temporary worker in a non-tech job but took advantage of company-sponsored free software training. After some hard work, he was rewarded with positive reinforcement: He was promoted to a permanent position in quality assurance. Regarded as one of America's 100 Best Companies to work for, Houston-based BMC <www.bmc.com> *also offers top salaries, good benefits, and attractive on-site amenities (such as a full-service gym, two restaurants, and a car wash).*

eliminate (wasting time, being rude to customers, ignoring quality). Then they try to shape employee behavior by linking reinforcement with desired behaviors and punishment with undesired behaviors.

reinforcement
Theory that behavior can be encouraged or discouraged by means of rewards or punishments

Reinforcement is used when a company pays *piecework* rewards—when workers are paid for each piece or product completed. In reinforcement strategies, rewards refer to all the positive things that people get for working (pay, praise, promotions, job security, and so forth). When rewards are tied directly to performance, they serve as *positive reinforcement.* For example, paying large cash bonuses to salespeople who exceed quotas prompts them to work even harder during the next selling period. John Deere <www.deere.com> has recently adopted a new reward system based on positive reinforcement. The firm now gives pay increases when its workers complete college courses and demonstrate mastery of new job skills.

Punishment is designed to change behavior by presenting people with unpleasant consequences if they fail to change in desirable ways. Employees who are repeatedly late to work, for example, may be suspended or have their pay docked. Similarly, when the National Football League or Major League Baseball fines or suspends players found guilty of substance abuse, the organization is seeking to change players' behavior.

Extensive rewards work best when people are learning new behavior, new skills, or new jobs. As workers become more adept, rewards can be used less frequently. Because such actions contribute to positive employer–employee relationships, managers generally prefer giving rewards and placing positive value on performance. Conversely, most managers dislike doling out punishment, partly because workers may respond with anger, resentment, hostility, or even retaliation. To reduce this risk, many managers couple punishment with rewards for good behavior.

Management by Objectives

management by objectives (MBO)
Set of procedures involving both managers and subordinates in setting goals and evaluating progress

Management by objectives (MBO) is a system of collaborative goal setting that extends from the top of an organization to the bottom. As a technique for managing the planning process, MBO is concerned mainly with helping managers implement and carry out their plans. As you can see from Figure 9.7, MBO involves managers and subordinates in setting goals and evaluating progress. Once the program is set up, the first step is establishing

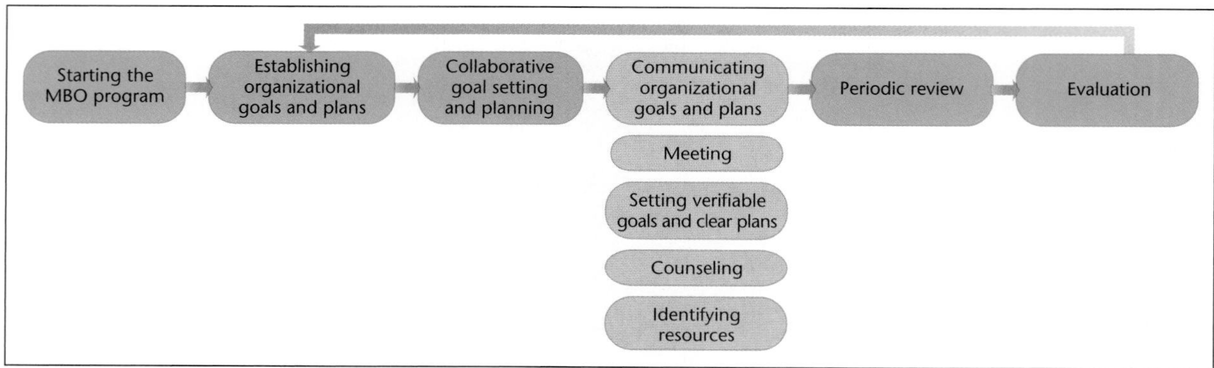

Figure 9.7
Management by Objectives

overall organizational goals. It is also these goals that will ultimately be evaluated to determine the success of the program. At the same time, however, collaborative activity—communicating, meeting, controlling, and so forth—is the key to MBO. Therefore, it can also serve as a program for improving satisfaction and motivation. (Note, too, that MBO represents an effort to apply throughout an entire organization the goal-setting theory of motivation that we discussed earlier.)

According to many experts, motivational impact is the biggest advantage of MBO. When employees sit down with managers to set upcoming goals, they learn more about companywide objectives, come to feel that they are an important part of a team, and see how they can improve companywide performance by reaching their own goals. If an MBO system is used properly, employees should leave meetings not only with an understanding of the value of their contributions, but also with fair rewards for their performances. They should also accept and be committed to the moderately difficult and specific goals they have helped set for themselves.

Participative Management and Empowerment

participative management and empowerment
Method of increasing job satisfaction by giving employees a voice in the management of their jobs and the company

In **participative management and empowerment,** employees are given a voice in how they do their jobs and how the company is managed—they become *empowered* to take greater responsibility for their own performance. Not surprisingly, participation and empowerment make employees feel more committed to organizational goals they have helped to shape.

Participation and empowerment can be used in large firms or small firms, both with managers and operating employees. For example, managers at General Electric <www.ge.com> who once needed higher-level approval for any expenditure over $5,000 have the autonomy to make their own expense decisions up to as much as $50,000. At Adam Hat Company, a small firm that makes men's dress, military, and cowboy hats, workers who previously had to report all product defects to supervisors now have the freedom to correct problems themselves or even return products to the workers who are responsible for them.

Team Management At one level, employees may be given decision-making responsibility for certain narrow activities, such as when to take lunch breaks or how to divide assignments with coworkers. On a broader level, employees are also being consulted on such decisions as production scheduling, work procedures and schedules, and the hiring of new employees. Among the many organizations actively using teams today are Texas Instruments <www.ti.com>, Lucent Technologies <www.lucent.com>, Ford Motor Co. <www.ford.com>, and Shell Oil <www.countonshell.com>.

Fastenal <www.fastenal.com> *sells nuts and bolts to North America. Over the past five years, profits have skyrocketed 38.1% annually. At 39.3% annually, total return to Fastenal stockholders has outstripped even Coca-Cola. How? The company will tell you that Fastenal empowers its employees. Even people in entry-level positions make decisions. As a result of quick decision making, Fastenal customers can count on getting what they need on time, and they're willing to pay a higher price for that service.*

Although some employees thrive in participative programs, such programs are not for everyone. Many people will be frustrated by responsibilities they are not equipped to handle. Moreover, participative programs may actually result in dissatisfied employees if workers see the invitation to participate as more symbolic than substantive. One key, say most experts, is to invite participation only to the extent that employees want to have input and only if participation will have real value for an organization.

Managers, therefore, should remember that teams are not for everyone. Levi Strauss <www.levi.com>, for example, has encountered major problems in its efforts to use teams. Previously, individual workers performed repetitive, highly specialized tasks, such as sewing zippers into jeans, and were paid according to the number of jobs they completed each day. In an attempt to boost productivity, company management reorganized everyone into teams of 10 to 35 workers and assigned tasks to the entire group. Each team member's pay was determined by the team's level of productivity. In practice, however, faster workers became resentful of slower workers because they reduced the group's total output. Slower workers, meanwhile, resented the pressure put on them by faster-working coworkers. As a result, motivation, satisfaction, and morale all dropped, and Levi's eventually abandoned the teamwork plan altogether.[6]

By and large, however, participation and empowerment in general, and team management in particular, continue to be widely used as enhancers of employee motivation and company performance. Although teams are not often less effective in traditional and rigidly structured bureaucratic organizations, they often help smaller, more flexible organizations make decisions more quickly and effectively, enhance companywide communication, and encourage organizational members to feel more like a part of an organization. In turn, these attitudes usually lead to higher levels of both employee motivation and job satisfaction.[7]

Job Enrichment and Job Redesign

While MBO programs and empowerment can work in a variety of settings, *job enrichment* and *job redesign* programs are generally used to increase satisfaction in jobs significantly lacking in motivating factors.[8]

job enrichment
Method of increasing job satisfaction by adding one or more motivating factors to job activities

Job Enrichment Programs **Job enrichment** is designed to add one or more motivating factors to job activities. For example, *job rotation programs* expand growth opportunities

job redesign
Method of increasing job satisfaction by designing a more satisfactory fit between workers and their jobs

by rotating employees through various positions in the same firm. Workers thus gain not only new skills but also broader overviews of their work and their organization. Other programs focus on increasing responsibility or recognition. At Continental Airlines <www.continental.com>, for example, flight attendants now have more control over their own scheduling. The jobs of flight service managers were enriched when they were given more responsibility and authority for assigning tasks to flight crew members.

Job Redesign Programs Job redesign acknowledges that different people want different things from their jobs. By restructuring work to achieve a more satisfactory fit between workers and their jobs, **job redesign** can motivate individuals with strong needs for career growth or achievement. Job redesign is usually implemented in one of three ways: through *combining tasks, forming natural work groups,* or *establishing client relationships.*

Combining Tasks The job of combining tasks involves enlarging jobs and increasing their variety to make employees feel that their work is more meaningful. In turn, employees become more motivated. For example, the job done by a programmer who maintains computer systems might be redesigned to include some system design and system development work. While developing additional skills, then, the programmer also gets involved in the overall system package.

Forming Natural Work Groups People who do different jobs on the same projects are candidates for natural work groups. These groups are formed to help employees see the place and importance of their jobs in the total structure of the firm. They are valuable to management because the people working on a project are usually the most knowledgeable about it, and thus the most capable problem solvers.

Establishing Client Relationships Establishing client relationships means letting employees interact with customers. This approach increases job variety. It gives workers both a greater sense of control and more feedback about performance than they get when their jobs are not highly interactive.

For example, software writers at Microsoft <www.microsoft.com> watch test users work with programs and discuss problems with them directly rather than receive feedback from third-party researchers. In Fargo, North Dakota, Great Plains Software <www.greatplains.com> has employee turnover of less than 7 percent, compared with an industry average of 15 to 20 percent. The company recruits and rewards in large part according to candidates' customer service skills and their experience with customer needs and complaints.

Modified Work Schedules

As another way of increasing job satisfaction, many companies are experimenting with *modified work schedules*—different approaches to working hours and the workweek. The two most common forms of modified scheduling are *work-share programs* and *flextime programs,* including *alternative workplace strategies.*[9]

"Work sharing brought sanity back to our lives."

—Employee at Steelcase

Work-Share Programs At Steelcase Inc. <www.steelcase.com>, the country's largest maker of office furnishings, two very talented women in the marketing division both wanted to work only part-time. The solution: They now share a single full-time job. With each working 2.5 days a week, both got their wish and the job gets done—and done well. In another situation, one person might work mornings and the other afternoons. The practice, known as **work sharing** (or **job sharing**), has "brought sanity back to our lives," according to at least one Steelcase employee.

work sharing (or **job sharing)**
Method of increasing job satisfaction by allowing two or more people to share a single full-time job

Job sharing usually benefits both employees and employers. Employees, for instance, tend to appreciate the organization's attention to their personal needs. At the same time, the company can reduce turnover and save on the cost of benefits. On the negative side, job-share employees generally receive fewer benefits than their full-time counterparts and may be the first to be laid off when cutbacks are necessary.

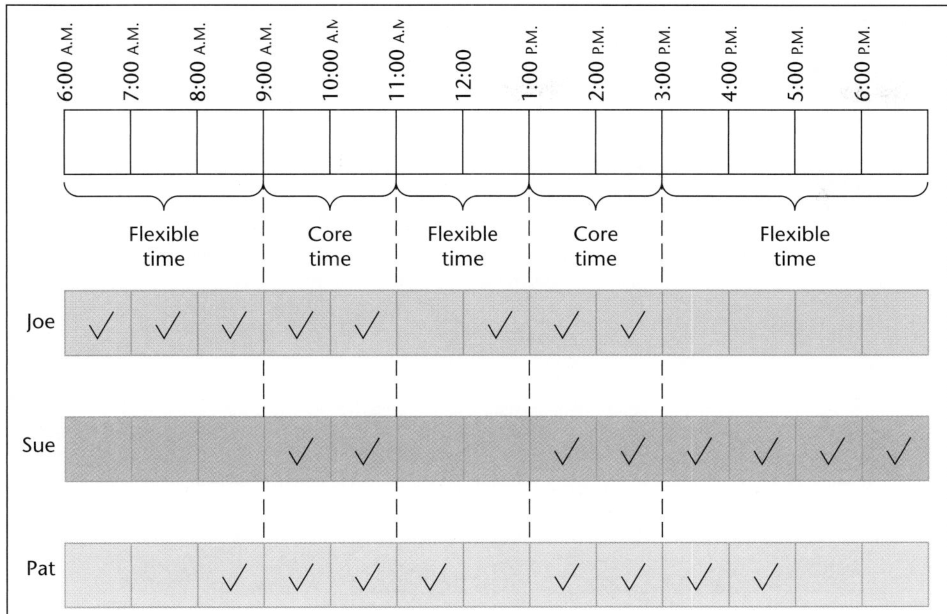

Figure 9.8
Sample Flextime Schedule

Flextime Programs and Alternative Workplace Strategies **Flextime programs** allow people to choose their working hours by adjusting a standard work schedule on a daily or weekly basis. There are, of course, limits. The Steelcase program, for instance, requires all employees to work certain core hours. This practice allows everyone to reach coworkers at a specified time of day. Employees can then decide whether to make up the rest of the standard 8-hour day by coming in and leaving early (by working 6:00 A.M. to 2:00 P.M. or 7:00 A.M. to 3:00 P.M.) or late (9:00 A.M. to 5:00 P.M. or 10:00 A.M. to 6:00 P.M.).

flextime programs
Method of increasing job satisfaction by allowing workers to adjust work schedules on a daily or weekly basis

Figure 9.8 shows a hypothetical flextime system that could be used by three different people. The office is open from 6:00 A.M. until 7:00 P.M. *Core time* is 9:00 A.M. to 11:00 A.M. and 1:00 P.M. to 3:00 P.M. Joe, an early riser, comes in at 6:00, takes an hour for lunch between 11:00 and noon, and finishes his day by 3:00. Sue, a working mother, prefers a later day. She comes in at 9:00, takes a long lunch from 11:00 to 1:00, and then works until 7:00. Pat works a more traditional 8-to-5 schedule.

In a world of increasing competition and costs, how can a small company attract desirable employees? Paying decent salaries and any kind of benefits eats up any profits. What else can be done to convince a high-quality employee to come aboard?

In one variation, companies may also allow employees to choose 4, 5, or 6 days on which to work each week. Some, for instance, may choose Monday through Thursday, others Tuesday through Friday. Still others may work Monday–Tuesday and

www.ams.com

Ninety percent of the employees of American Management Systems, a Virginia-based technology-consulting firm, use flextime; thirty percent telecommute. Other benefits and programs aimed at "balancing work and personal life" include free child care, elder care, and adoption counseling services. To learn more about the company's approach to employee motivation, log on to its Web site.

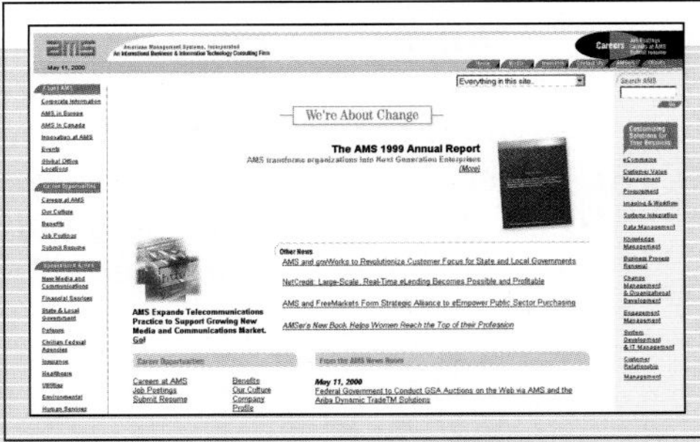

Alcoa Aluminum <www.alcoa.com> chairman Paul H. O'Neill had an office just like those of everyone else in the company's new Pittsburgh headquarters: 9 feet by 9 feet and no more than 45 feet from a window. O'Neill (who later became Secretary of the Treasury under President George W. Bush) ordered the building constructed so that people were encouraged to interact. There are no hallways or private offices; there are escalators instead of elevators, and meeting rooms are walled in glass. And everyone has a parking space.

Thursday–Friday and take Wednesday off. By working 10 hours over four workdays, employees still complete 40-hour weeks.

Telecommuting and Virtual Offices Kelly Ramsey-Dolson is an accountant employed by Ernst & Young <www.ey.com>. Because she has a young son, she does not want to be away from home more than she absolutely must. Ramsey-Dolson and the company have worked out an arrangement whereby she works at home two or three days a week and comes into the office the other days. Her home office is outfitted with a PC, modem, and fax machine, and she uses this technology to keep abreast of everything going on at the office.

telecommuting
Form of flextime that allows people to perform some or all of a job away from standard office settings

Ramsey-Dolson is one of a rapidly growing number of U.S. workers who do a significant portion of their work by a relatively new version of flextime known as **telecommuting**—performing some or all of a job away from standard office settings. Among salaried employees, the telecommuter workforce grew by 21.5 percent in 1994, to 7.6 million; the number of telecommuters now exceeds 25 million employees.

The key to telecommuting is technology. The availability of networked computers, fax machines, cellular telephones, and overnight-delivery services makes it possible for many professionals to work at home or while traveling. Cisco Systems <www.cisco.com>, the Internet networking giant, is at the forefront of telecommuting arrangements for its workers. The firm estimates that by allowing employees to do some of their work at home, it has boosted productivity by 25 percent, lowered overhead costs by $1 million, and achieved a higher retention rate among key knowledge workers who might have otherwise left for more flexibility elsewhere.[10]

"The work environment was designed around the concept that one's best thinking isn't necessarily done at a desk or in an office. Sometimes it's done in a conference room with other people. Other times it's done on a ski slope or driving to a client's office."

—Adelaide Horton, Director of Operations, Chiat Day Mojo advertising firm

Other companies have experimented with so-called virtual offices. They have redesigned conventional office space to accommodate jobs and schedules that are far less dependent on assigned spaces and personal apparatus. At the advertising firm of Chiat Day Mojo <www.chiatday.com> in Venice, California, only about one-third of the salaried workforce is in the office on any given day. The office building features informal work carrels or nooks and open areas available to every employee. "The work environment," explains Director of Operations Adelaide Horton, "was designed around the concept that one's best thinking

One of the most conspicuous features of the "new company town" is the presence of workplace amenities. At the Kansas City architectural firm of Gould Evans Goodman Associates <www.geaf.com>, pooped employees can escape to one of three "spent tents"—retreats with sleeping bags, pillows, alarm clocks, and soothing music. The principle is to ease overwork by making the workplace—or certain alternative areas of it—as comfortable as home. In theory, such amenities renew the body and spirit so that an employee is more productive during the time he or she spends at a workstation.

isn't necessarily done at a desk or in an office. Sometimes it's done in a conference room with other people. Other times it's done on a ski slope or driving to a client's office."

Advantages and Disadvantages of Modified Schedules and Alternative Workplaces Flextime gives employees more freedom in their professional and personal lives. It allows workers to plan around the work schedules of spouses and the school schedules of young children. Studies show that the increased sense of freedom and control reduces stress and thus improves individual productivity.

Companies also benefit in other ways. In urban areas, for example, such programs can reduce traffic congestion and similar problems that contribute to stress and lost work time. Furthermore, employers benefit from higher levels of commitment and job satisfaction. John Hancock Insurance <www.jhancock.com>, Atlantic Richfield <www.arco.com>, and Metropolitan Life <www.metlife.com> are among the major American corporations that have successfully adopted some form of flextime.

Conversely, flextime sometimes complicates coordination because people are working different schedules. In the schedules shown in Figure 9.8, for instance, Sue may need some important information from Joe at 4:30 P.M., but because Joe is working an earlier schedule, he leaves for the day at 3:00. In addition, if workers are paid by the hour, flextime may make it difficult for employers to keep accurate records of when employees are actually working.

As for telecommuting and virtual offices, although they may be the wave of the future, they may not be for everyone. For example, consultant Gil Gordon points out that telecommuters are attracted to the ideas of "not having to shave and put on makeup or go through traffic, and sitting in their blue jeans all day." However, he suggests that would-be telecommuters ask themselves several other questions: "Can I manage deadlines? What will it be like to be away from the social context of the office five days a week? Can I renegotiate the rules of the family, so my spouse doesn't come home every night expecting me to have a four-course meal on the table?" One study has shown that even though telecommuters may be producing results, those with strong advancement ambitions may miss networking and rubbing elbows with management on a day-to-day basis.

"Can I manage deadlines? What will it be like to be away from the social context of the office five days a week? Can I renegotiate the rules of the family, so my spouse doesn't come home every night expecting me to have a four-course meal on the table?"

—Consultant Gil Gordon, self-test for the would-be telecommuter

Another obstacle to establishing a telecommuting program is convincing management that it can be beneficial for all involved. Telecommuters may have

"Good grief, Bradbury! How long have you been working at home?"

to fight the perception, from both bosses and coworkers, that if they are not being supervised, they are not working. Managers, admits one experienced consultant, "usually have to be dragged kicking and screaming into this. They always ask, 'How can I tell if someone is working when I can't see them?' " By the same token, he adds, "that's based on the erroneous assumption that if you can see them they are working." Most experts agree that reeducation and constant communication are requirements of a successful telecommuting arrangement. Both managers and employees must determine expectations in advance.

MANAGERIAL STYLES AND LEADERSHIP

leadership
Process of motivating others to work to meet specific objectives

In trying to enhance morale, job satisfaction, and motivation, managers can use many different styles of leadership. **Leadership** is the process of motivating others to work to meet specific objectives. Leading is also one of the key aspects of a manager's job and an important component of the directing function.

Joe Liemandt, for example, dropped out of Stanford in 1990 to start a software company in Austin, Texas. As part of his strategy, he was determined to develop and maintain a workforce of creative people who worked well in teams, adapted to rapid change, and felt comfortable taking risks. A decade later, people with these qualities—now numbering nearly 1,000—have helped build Liemandt's company, Trilogy Software, Inc. <www.trilogy.com>, into a rapidly growing maker of industry-leading software for managing product pricing, sales plans, and commissions.

When Trilogy hires a new group of employees, Liemandt himself oversees their training. He sees himself as the firm's leader and believes that, as such, it is his responsibility to ensure that every employee shares his vision and understands his way of doing business. Training takes several weeks, starting with a series of classes devoted to the technical aspects of Trilogy's products and methods of software development. Then recruits move into areas in which Liemandt truly believes they make a real difference—developing risk-taking skills and the ability to recognize new opportunities.

"Managers always ask, 'How can I tell if someone is working when I can't see them?' That's based on the erroneous assumption that if you can see them they are working."

—HR consultant on managerial qualms about telecommuting

Recruits are formed into teams, and each team is given three weeks to complete various projects, ranging from the creating of new products to the developing of marketing campaigns for existing products. Teams actually compete with one another and are scored on such criteria as risk and innovation, goal setting, and goal accomplishment. Evaluations are completed by Liemandt, other Trilogy managers, and some of the firm's venture capital backers. Winners get free trips to Las Vegas. Losers go straight to work.

Liemandt's leadership doesn't stop there, even for those who go to Las Vegas, where Liemandt challenges everyone to place a $2,000 bet at the roulette wheel. He argues that $2,000 is a meaningful sum, and one that can cause real pain, but not so much that it will cause financial disaster for anyone. Actually, Liemandt puts up the money, which losers pay back through payroll deductions of $400 over 5 months. Not everyone, of course, decides to take the chance, but enough do to make the message clear: Liemandt aims to succeed by taking chances, and he expects employees to share the risks. Those who do, stand to earn bigger returns on more intrepid investments.[11]

In this section, we begin by describing some of the basic features of and differences in managerial styles and then focus on an approach to managing and leading that, like Joe Liemandt's, understands those jobs as responses to a variety of complex situations.

Managerial Styles

Early theories of leadership tried to identify specific traits associated with strong leaders. For example, physical appearance, intelligence, and public speaking skills were once thought to be "leadership traits." Indeed, it was once believed that taller people made better leaders than shorter people. The trait approach, however, proved to be a poor predictor of leadership potential. Ultimately, attention shifted from managers' traits to their behaviors, or **managerial styles**—patterns of behavior that a manager exhibits in dealing with subordinates. Managerial styles run the gamut from autocratic to democratic to free rein. Naturally, most managers do not clearly conform to any one style, but these three major types of styles involve very different kinds of responses to human relations problems. Under different circumstances, any given style or combination of styles may prove appropriate.

managerial style
Pattern of behavior that a manager exhibits in dealing with subordinates

- Managers who adopt an **autocratic style** generally issue orders and expect them to be obeyed without question. The military commander prefers and usually needs the autocratic style on the battlefield. Because no one else is consulted, the autocratic style allows for rapid decision making. It may, therefore, be useful in situations testing a firm's effectiveness as a time-based competitor.
- Managers who adopt a **democratic style** generally ask for input from subordinates before making decisions but retain final decision-making power. For example, the manager of a technical group may ask other group members to interview and offer opinions about job applicants. The manager, however, will ultimately make the hiring decision.
- Managers who adopt a **free-rein style** typically serve as advisers to subordinates who are allowed to make decisions. The chairperson of a volunteer committee to raise funds for a new library may find a free-rein style most effective.

autocratic style
Managerial style in which managers generally issue orders and expect them to be obeyed without question

democratic style
Managerial style in which managers generally ask for input from subordinates but retain final decision-making power

free-rein style
Managerial style in which managers typically serve as advisers to subordinates who are allowed to make decisions

According to many observers, the free-rein style of leadership is currently giving rise to an approach that emphasizes broad-based employee input into decision making and the fostering of workplace environments in which employees increasingly determine what needs to be done and how.

Regardless of theories about the ways in which leaders ought to lead, the relative effectiveness of any leadership style depends largely on the desire of subordinates to share input or to exercise creativity. Whereas some people, for example, are frustrated, others prefer autocratic managers because they do not want a voice in making decisions. The democratic approach, meanwhile, can be disconcerting both to people who want decision-making responsibility and to those who do not. A free-rein style lends itself to employee creativity, and thus to creative solutions to pressing problems. This style also appeals to employees who like to plan their own work. Not all subordinates, however, have the necessary background or skills to make creative decisions. Others are not sufficiently self-motivated to work without supervision.

The Contingency Approach to Leadership

Because each managerial style has both strengths and weaknesses, most managers vary their responses to different situations. Flexibility, however, has not always characterized managerial style or responsiveness. For most of the twentieth century, in fact, managers tended to believe that all problems yielded to preconceived, pretested solutions. If raising pay reduced turnover in one plant, for example, it followed that the same tactic would work equally well in another.

contingency approach Approach to managerial style holding that the appropriate behavior in any situation is dependent (contingent) on the unique elements of that situation

More recently, however, managers have begun to adopt a **contingency approach** to managerial style. They have started to view appropriate managerial behavior in any situation as dependent, or contingent, on the elements unique to that situation. This change in outlook has resulted largely from an increasing appreciation of the complexity of managerial problems and solutions. For example, pay raises may reduce turnover when workers have been badly underpaid. The contingency approach, however, recognizes that raises will have little effect when workers feel adequately paid but ill-treated by management. This approach also recommends that training managers in human relations skills may be crucial to solving the problem in the second case.[12]

The contingency approach also acknowledges that people in different cultures behave differently and expect different things from their managers. A certain managerial style, therefore, is more likely to be successful in some countries than in others. Japanese workers, for example, generally expect managers to be highly participative and to give them input in decision making. In contrast, many South American workers actually balk at participation and want take-charge leaders. The basic idea, then, is that managers will be more effective when they adapt their styles to the contingencies of the situations they face.[13]

Motivation and Leadership in the Twenty-First Century

Motivation and leadership remain critically important areas of organizational behavior. As times change, however, so do the ways managers motivate and lead their employees.

Changing Patterns of Motivation From the motivational side, today's employees want rewards that are often quite different from those valued by earlier generations. Money, for example, is no longer the prime motivator for most people. In addition, because businesses today cannot offer the degree of job security that many workers want, motivating employees to strive toward higher levels of performance requires skillful attention from managers.

One recent survey asked workers to identify those things they most wanted at work. Among the things noted were flexible working hours (67%), casual dress (56%), unlim-

WebConnection

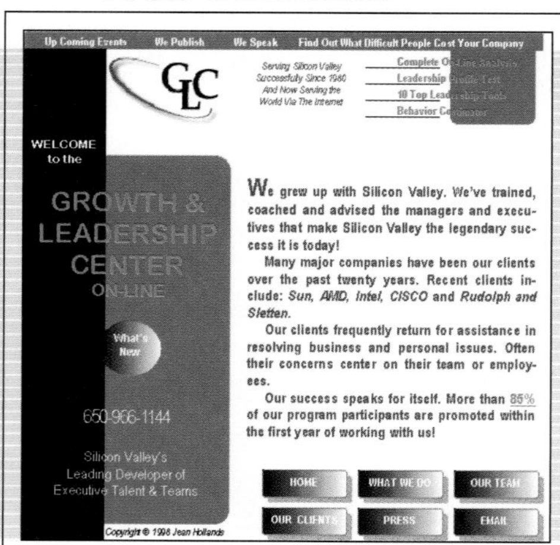

www.glcweb.com

Located in Mountain View, California, the Growth & Leadership Center offers professional and psychological assistance to Silicon Valley executives who are feeling the pressures of increasing workloads and stress levels. Using a variety of techniques, the company helps managers from such companies as Lucent Technologies, Sun Microsystems, Netscape, and Intel develop the patterns of behavior and communication that make them more valuable to their employers as leaders.

ited Internet access (51%), opportunities to telecommute (43%), nap time (28%), massages (25%), day care (24%), espresso machines (23%), and the opportunity to bring a pet to work (11%).[14] In another study focusing on fathers, many men also said they wanted more flexible working hours in order to spend more time with their families.[15] Managers, then, must recognize the fact that today's workers have a complex set of needs and must be motivated in increasingly complicated ways.

Finally, as we saw in Chapter 8, the diversity inherent in today's workforce also makes motivating behavior more complex. The reasons why people work reflect more varying goals than ever before, and the varying lifestyles of diverse workers mean that managers must first pay closer attention to what their employees expect to get for their efforts and then try to link rewards with job performance.

Changing Patterns of Leadership Leadership, too, is taking different directions as we head into the twenty-first century. For one thing, today's leaders are finding it necessary to change their own behavior. As organizations become flatter and workers more empowered, managers naturally find it less acceptable to use the autocratic approach to leadership. Instead, many are becoming more democratic—functioning more as "coaches" than as "bosses." Just as an athletic coach teaches athletes how to play and then steps back to let them take the field, many leaders now try to provide workers with the skills and resources to perform at their best before backing off to let them do their work with less supervision.

Diversity, too, is also affecting leadership processes. In earlier times, most leaders were white males who were somewhat older than the people they supervised—people who were themselves relatively similar to one another. But as organizations become more and more diverse, leaders are also becoming increasingly diverse—women, African Americans, and Hispanics, are entering the managerial ranks in ever greater numbers. They are also increasingly likely to be younger than some of the people they are leading. Leaders, therefore, must have greater sensitivity to the values, needs, and motives of a diverse group of people as they examine their own behavior in its relations to other people.

Finally, leaders must also adopt more of a "network" mentality rather than a "hierarchical" one. As long as people worked in the same place at the same time, the organizational hierarchy had a clear vertical chain of command and lines of communication. But now people work in different places and at different times. New forms of organization design may call for one person to be the leader on one project and a team member on another. Thus, people need to get comfortable with leadership based more on expertise than on organizational position and with interaction patterns not tied to specific places or times. The leader of tomorrow, then, will need a different set of skills and a different point of view than did the leader of yesterday.

Continued from page 239

What Did You Expect?

So, how does a hard-charging business that pushes its employees to the limit come to be known as one of the best places to work? At BMC Software, as at many other businesses today, it's mostly a matter of the "new deal" that has been forged between businesses and employees. Gone is the lifetime employment security once offered by businesses. Gone, too, is the steadfast employee loyalty that once kept a worker with a single employer for an entire career. In their places are new bargaining positions for both employer and employee that are fundamental to the new employment contract.

Employees now offer a new set of contributions and have different expectations. They are generally willing to work long, hard hours and put their jobs at or near the top of their priorities. Often they also have cutting-edge skills and a solid understanding of how businesses, markets, and technology fit together. In return, they expect employers to provide an increasingly diverse set of benefits and perks and want to share in the organization's successes.

Business has also learned to expect and offer different things than in the past. They often meet the challenges of a tight labor market by offering lavish signing bonuses for the very best talent, high salaries, stock options, and benefits only dreamed of a few years ago. But they offer little or no job security. Instead, they offer ample opportunity for employees to keep current in their fields and to learn more advanced skills. Thus, while they don't promise job security, they do offer "employability," giving workers the tools to find jobs elsewhere if their current employers can't keep them. In return, they expect—explicitly or implicitly—that employees will devote a large proportion of their waking hours to the company's success.

Questions for Discussion

1. Which sounds better to you personally—the "old deal" or the "new deal"?
2. In what industries, markets, and kinds of businesses is the new deal most likely to exist? In what industries, markets, and kinds of businesses is the old deal most likely to still remain in place?
3. Aside from the factors noted in the case, what other changes may have contributed to this new employment relationship?
4. Under what circumstances might employment relationships change again? Would this change more likely be a reversion to the old relationship or to a new one altogether?
5. What are the most fundamental risks that a business takes in adopting the new employment relationship?
6. What are the most fundamental risks an individual employee takes in adopting the new employment relationship?

SUMMARY OF LEARNING OBJECTIVES

1 **Describe the nature and importance of *psychological contracts* in the workplace.** A *psychological contract* is the set of expectations held by employees concerning what they will contribute to an organization (referred to as *contributions*) and what the organization will in return provide to the employees (referred to as *inducements*). Until the last decade or so, businesses generally offered their employees high levels of job security and employees were very loyal to their employers. More recently, however, new psychological contracts have been created in many sectors. Now, organizations offer less security but more benefits. In turn, employees are often willing to work longer hours but also more willing to leave an employer a better opportunity elsewhere.

2 **Discuss the importance of *job satisfaction* and *employee morale* and summarize their roles in human relations in the workplace.** Good *human relations*—the interactions between employers and employees and their attitudes toward one another—are important to business because they lead to high levels of *job satisfaction* (the degree of enjoyment that workers derive from their jobs) and *morale* (workers' overall attitudes toward their workplaces). Satisfied employees generally exhibit lower levels of absenteeism and turnover. They also have fewer grievances and engage in fewer negative behaviors.

3 **Identify and summarize the most important *theories of employee motivation.*** Views of employee motivation have changed dramatically over the years. The *classical theory* holds that people are motivated solely by money. *Scientific management* tried to analyze jobs and increase production by finding better ways to perform tasks. The *Hawthorne studies* were the first to demonstrate the importance of making workers feel that their needs were being considered. The *human resources model* identifies two kinds of managers—*Theory X managers,* who believe that people are inherently uncooperative and must be constantly punished or rewarded, and *Theory Y managers,* who believe that people are naturally responsible and self-motivated to be productive.

Maslow's *hierarchy of needs model* proposes that people have several different needs (ranging from physiological to self-actualization), which they attempt to satisfy in their work. People must fulfill lower-level needs before seeking to fulfill higher-level needs. *Two-factor theory* suggests that if basic hygiene factors are not met, workers will be dissatisfied. Only by increasing more complex motivation factors can companies increase employees' performance.

Expectancy theory holds that people will work hard if they believe that their efforts will lead to desired rewards. *Equity theory* says that motivation depends on the way employees evaluate their treatment by an organization relative to its treatment of other workers.

4 **Describe some of the strategies used by organizations to improve *job satisfaction* and *employee motivation.*** Managers can use several strategies to increase employee satisfaction and motivation. The principle of *reinforcement,* or *behavior modification theory,* holds that reward and punishment can control behavior. *Rewards,* for example, are positive reinforcement when they are tied directly to desired or improved performance. *Punishment* (using unpleasant consequences to change undesirable behavior) is generally less effective.

Management by objectives (a system of collaborative goal setting) and *participative management and empowerment* (techniques for giving employees a voice in management decisions) can improve human relations by making an employee feel like part of a team. *Job enrichment, job redesign,* and *modified work schedules* (including *work-share programs, flextime,* and *alternative workplace strategies*) can enhance job satisfaction by adding motivation factors to jobs in which they are normally lacking.

5 **Discuss different managerial styles of *leadership* and their impact on human relations in the workplace.** Effective *leadership*—the process of motivating others to meet specific objectives—is an important determinant of employee satisfaction and motivation. Generally speaking, managers practice one of three basic managerial styles. *Autocratic managers* generally issue orders that they expect to be obeyed. *Democratic managers* generally seek subordinates' input into decisions. *Free-rein managers* are more likely to advise than to make decisions. The *contingency approach to leadership* views appropriate managerial behavior in any situation as dependent on the elements of that situation. Managers thus need to assess situations carefully, especially to determine the desire of subordinates to share input or exercise creativity. They must also be aware of the changing nature of both motivation and leadership as we move into the twenty-first century.

QUESTIONS AND EXERCISES

Questions for Review

1. Describe the psychological contract you currently have or have had in the past with an employer. If you have never worked, describe the psychological contract that you have with the instructor in this class.
2. Do you think that most people are relatively satisfied or dissatisfied with their work? Why are they mainly satisfied or dissatisfied?
3. Compare and contrast Maslow's hierarchy of needs with the two-factor theory of motivation.
4. How can participative management programs enhance employee satisfaction and motivation?

Questions for Analysis

5. Some evidence suggests that recent college graduates show high levels of job satisfaction. Levels then drop dramatically as they reach their late twenties, only to increase gradually once they get older. What might account for this pattern?
6. As a manager, under what sort of circumstances might you apply each of the theories of motivation discussed in this chapter? Which would be easiest to use? Which would be hardest? Why?
7. Suppose you realize one day that you are dissatisfied with your job. Short of quitting, what might you do to improve your situation?
8. List five U.S. managers who you think would also qualify as great leaders.

Application Exercises

9. At the library, research the manager or owner of a company in the early twentieth century and the manager or owner of a company in the 1990s. Compare and contrast the two in terms of their times, leadership styles, and views of employee motivation.
10. Interview the manager of a local manufacturing company. Identify as many different strategies for enhancing job satisfaction at that company as you can.

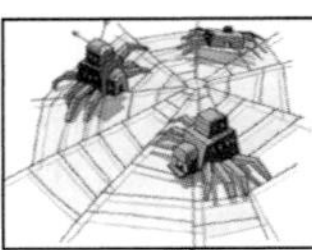

EXPLORING THE WEB

A SATISFACTION SURVEY

This chapter stresses the fact that employee satisfaction and morale are important to any organization. However, it is also quite difficult for managers to know for sure just how satisfied and motivated their employees actually are. In most cases, managers interested in assessing satisfaction and morale do so with surveys. Employees are asked to respond to various questions about how they feel about their work, and their responses are scored to provide an indication of their satisfaction and morale. To examine such a survey, visit the Web site at:

www.quicken.com/small_business/cch/tools/?article=satsrv_m

After you have examined the satisfaction questionnaire at this site, consider the following questions:

1. For whose use is this questionnaire geared? Can you identify two or three key principles of instruments like this one?
2. At face value, how valid does this survey instrument seem to be?
3. Fill out the survey and then analyze your responses. (Total the number of positive, negative, and neutral responses you've given, for instance.)
4. What appear to be the biggest strengths and weaknesses of this particular survey? Assuming this questionnaire to be typical, what would you judge to be the strengths and weaknesses of job satisfaction surveys in general?
5. Try writing a survey yourself. Focus it on job satisfaction in your present job, in a previous job, or in this class. What information do you most want to elicit? What aspect of this information is hardest to elicit? Why?

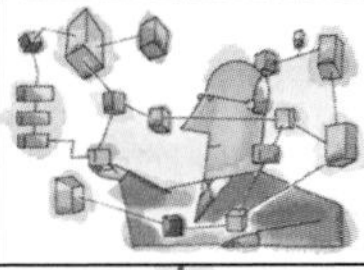

BUILDING YOUR BUSINESS SKILLS

TOO MUCH OF A GOOD THING

This exercise enhances the following SCANS workplace competencies: demonstrating basic skills, demonstrating thinking skills, exhibiting interpersonal skills, working with information, and applying systems knowledge.

GOAL

To encourage students to apply different motivational theories to a workplace problem involving poor productivity.

BACKGROUND

For years, working for the George Uhe Co., a small chemicals broker in Paramus, New Jersey, made employees feel as if they were members of a big family. Unfortunately, this family was going broke because too few members were working hard enough to make money for it. They were happy, comfortable, complacent—and lazy.

With sales dropping in the pharmaceutical and specialty-chemicals division, Uhe brought in management consultants to analyze the situation and make recommendations. The outsiders quickly identified a motivational problem affecting the sales force: Reps were paid a handsome salary and received automatic, year-end bonuses regardless of performance. They were also treated to bagels every Friday and regular group birthday lunches that cost as much as $200. Employees felt satisfied, but had little incentive to work very hard.

Eager to return to profitability, Uhe's owners waited to hear the consultants' recommendations.

METHOD

Step 1

In groups of four, step into the role of Uhe's management consultants. Start by analyzing your client's workforce-motivation problems from the following perspectives (our questions focus on key motivational issues):

- *Job satisfaction and morale.* As part of a 77-year-old family-owned business, Uhe employees were happy and loyal, in part, because they were treated so well. Can high morale have a downside? How can it breed stagnation, and what can managers do to prevent stagnation from taking hold?

- *Theory X versus Theory Y.* Although the behavior of these workers seems to make a case for Theory X, why is it difficult to draw this conclusion about a company that focuses more on satisfaction than on sales and profits?
- *Two-factor theory.* Analyze the various ways in which improving such motivational factors as recognition, added responsibility, advancement, and growth might reduce the importance of hygiene factors, including pay and security.
- *Expectancy theory.* Analyze the effect on productivity of redesigning the company's sales force compensation structure: namely, by paying lower base salaries while offering greater earnings potential through a sales-based incentive system. Why would linking performance with increased pay that is achievable through hard work motivate employees? Why would the threat of a job loss also motivate greater effort?

Step 2

Writing a short report based on your analysis, make recommendations to Uhe's owners. The goal of your report is to change the working environment in ways that will motivate greater effort and generate greater productivity.

FOLLOW-UP QUESTIONS

1. What is your group's most important recommendation? Why do you think it is likely to succeed?
2. Changing the corporate culture to make it less paternalistic may reduce employees' sense of belonging to a family. If you were an employee, would you consider a greater focus on profits to be an improvement or a problem? How would it affect your motivation and productivity?
3. What steps would you take to improve the attitude and productivity of longtime employees who resist change?

CRAFTING YOUR BUSINESS PLAN

MAKING RESERVATIONS AND OTHER PLANS

THE PURPOSE OF THE ASSIGNMENT

1. To acquaint you with the process of navigating the *Business PlanPro* (*BPP*) software package (Version 4.0).
2. To familiarize students with the ways in which employee considerations (morale, motivation, and job satisfaction) enter into the development of a business plan.
3. To stimulate students' thinking about the application of textbook information on employee morale, motivation, job satisfaction, and leadership to the preparation of a BPP business plan.

Assignment

After reading Chapter 9 in the textbook, open the BPP *software* and look around for information about the plans being made by a sample firm:* Puddle Jumpers Airline. *Familiarize yourself with this firm by clicking on* ***1.0 Executive Summary.*** *Then respond to the following questions:*

1. Consider Puddle Jumpers' plans to lower costs by using its flight crews more effectively than its competition does. If implemented, how might these plans affect employee morale? Job satisfaction? [Sites to see in *BPP* (for this assignment): In the Plan Outline screen, click on each of the following: **1.2 Mission** and **1.3 Keys to Success.** After returning to the Plan Outline screen, click on **3.2 Competitive Comparison.** Finally, return to the Plan Outline screen and explore any listed categories in which you would expect to find information about employee motivation and job satisfaction.]
2. Consider both Puddle Jumpers' plans for dealing with the high turnover among airline reservationists and its plans for training reservationists. Do you think the planned redesign will enrich the reservationist's job? Will it affect job satisfaction? [Sites to see in *BPP:* In the Plan Outline screen, click on each of the following: **3.2 Competitive Comparison** and **3.5 Technology.** After returning to the Plan

Outline screen, click on **5.0 Stratgey and Implementation Summary.**]

3. Consider the qualifications of Judy Land, director of reservations. Based on her background, would you say that she is qualified to lead and motivate employees under the new reservations system? [Sites to see in *BPP:* In the Plan Outline screen, click on **6.2 Management Team.**]
4. How will employees be affected by Puddle Jumpers' plans to acquire additional aircraft and offer expanded routes? What kinds of motivational considerations would you anticipate when Puddle Jumpers implements its expansion plans? [Sites to see in *BPP:* In the Plan Outline screen, click on **1.0 Executive Summary.**]

FOR YOUR OWN BUSINESS PLAN

5. Implementation of your business plan depends on leadership. Identify those individuals in your organization who will provide leadership in implementing each of your organization's activity areas. Describe specific leadership activities that you expect to rely upon at various times from each of the key personnel in your organization.

*GENERAL TIPS FOR NAVIGATING IN *BPP*

1. Open the *BPP* program, examine the Welcome screen, and click on **Open a Sample Plan.**
2. From the **Open a Sample Plan** dialogue box, click on a sample company name; then click on **Open.**
3. On the Plan Manager screen, click on **Your Plan Outline**; then click on any line (for example, **6.0 Management Summary**).
4. You can always return to the Plan Outline screen by going to the bottom of the screen and clicking on the **Plan Outline** icon.
5. After finishing with one sample company, you can get to the next one by going to the top of the screen and clicking on **File** (on the menu bar). Then beneath that, select **Open Sample Plan.** This will exit you from the current company file and take you to the **Open Sample Plan** dialogue box, where you can select your next sample company.
6. When you are finished, you can close the program by going to the top of the screen and clicking on **File** (on the bar menu). Then beneath that, select **Exit.**

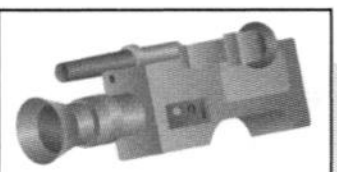

VIDEO EXERCISE

SETTING THE GOLD STANDARD: RITZ-CARLTON

Learning Objectives

The purpose of this video exercise is to help you

1. Appreciate the concept of motivation in a service business.
2. Understand the role of empowerment in motivating employees.
3. Understand why hiring the right people contributes to greater job satisfaction.

BACKGROUND INFORMATION

The 35 Ritz-Carlton hotels <www.ritzcarlton.com> in North America, Australia, Europe, Asia, and the Middle East are renowned for luxury, sumptuous surroundings, and legendary service. The company's service philosophy is expressed in a set of core values called "The Gold Standards," which consists of the "Credo," the "Three Steps of Service," the "Motto," and the "Twenty Basics." All 14,000 employees, who each receive 120 hours of training a year, carry these guidelines on a pocket-sized laminated card.

THE VIDEO

This segment explains the standards and illustrates the training procedures that guide Ritz-Carlton employees—whom the company refers to as "ladies and gentlemen"—in offering top-quality service to guests. Selective hiring and rigorous training ensure that employees treat guests and each other with the utmost care. Hotel employees are encouraged to tell management what they need in order to be successful and are given wide latitude in on-the-job problem solving.

DISCUSSION QUESTIONS

1. Why do you think Ritz-Carlton is able to achieve such a high level of service while turning day-to-day decision making over to employees?
2. Why do you think management at Ritz-Carlton is concerned about the way employees treat one another?
3. Many firms issue employees cards bearing the company's mission statement or set of core values. Do you think that this is an effective motivational tool? Would it encourage you to perform at your best? Why or why not?

FOLLOW-UP ASSIGNMENT

Compare the use of empowerment at Ritz-Carlton with empowerment at a manufacturing company. How might selection and training differ? What different types of authority might manufacturing employees be given, and how and when would they use it? (*Hint:* Who are really their customers?)

FOR FURTHER EXPLORATION

Explore the "About Us" and "Employment" sections of the Ritz-Carlton Web site and compare them to similar information on the sites of other luxury hotels (such as <www.sonesta.com> and <www.hyatt.com>. What can you deduce about employee motivation at each firm? Consider such factors as training, career development, empowerment, and responsibility. Which program seems to offer the kind of reward or support that would motivate you?

MASTERING BUSINESS ESSENTIALS

Go to the "Work Motivation" episode on the Mastering Business Essentials CD-ROM for an interactive, video-enhanced exercise on the efforts of managers at CanGo, an e-business start-up, to motivate young employees to take on a challenging task.

The episode titled "Leadership" explores the problem of leading two quite different groups of workers: senior managers and young employees. A third episode, "Groups and Teams," examines the problems of getting a team of employees to work effectively.

Chapter 10

Understanding Labor and Management Relations

After reading this chapter, you should be able to:

1. ***Explain*** why workers unionize.
2. ***Trace*** the evolution and discuss trends in *unionism* in the United States.
3. ***Describe*** the *major laws governing labor–management relations.*
4. ***Describe*** the union *certification* and *decertification processes.*
5. ***Identify*** the steps in the *collective bargaining process.*

Labor Rolls the Dice in Las Vegas

They work hard all day as hotel waiters and waitresses, cooks, and housekeepers, but when they get to the union hall, they're filled with energy. "Unions, yes," they chant as they listen to stories of recruiting successes at the MGM Grand <**www.mgmgrand.com/lv**>, the world's largest hotel, and New York New York <**www.nynyhotelcasino.com**>, one of the area's newest hotels. All told, local union membership has doubled in the past decade to 40,000 members. At the Grand alone, Local 226 of the Hotel Employees & Restaurant Employees Union <**www.hereunion.org**> signed up 2,700 new members.

Where is this hotbed of union activism? Not in any traditional labor stronghold, such as Detroit or Chicago, but in Las Vegas, which, along with its casinos, is fast becoming a proving ground for organized labor. "Las Vegas," reports one labor historian, "is where the future of the union movement is being hammered out."

The AFL-CIO, the umbrella organization for the union movement, chose to test its recruiting power in Las Vegas for a good reason: It's a boomtown with a burgeoning population and an abundance of jobs. When labor leaders look at all the casinos, hotels, and houses under construction, they see opportunity to nourish the movement and add to the ranks. The Venetian

<**www.venetian.com**> is just one example of the fertile field that labor is tilling in Vegas. With its gaming palaces, 6,000 hotel rooms, and "authentic" Italian touches (including canals), building costs topped $2 billion and during its peak period the project employed thousands of construction and service workers.

In targeting these workers in its latest membership push, the AFL-CIO is promising improved wages and benefits. This message may be traditional, but the approach is not. Sidestepping union elections administered by the National Labor Relations Board (NLRB), organizers are instead showing employers rosters of recruited workers and petitioning for voluntary union recognition. "Card signing," as this tactic is known, has worked in casinos, and it increased membership in the building-trades and hotel-workers unions by 20 percent in a year.

"I spend a day a week volunteering for the union because otherwise we would earn $7.50 an hour and no benefits."

—Edelisa Wolf, MGM Grand waitress

Union organizers are workers themselves—people like Edelisa Wolf, an $11.25-an-hour waitress at the MGM Grand who signs up recruits as they walk out of the New York New York hiring office. "I spend a day a week volunteering for the union," says Wolf, "because otherwise we would earn $7.50 an hour and no benefits." Charley Phillips, a construction worker with years of experience in Las Vegas, takes jobs in nonunion companies for the sole purpose of recruiting new members. When he was fired by one company for his pro-union activities, he was quickly rehired on the order of the NLRB. He stayed on that job for six more weeks and, his union work done, headed for another company.

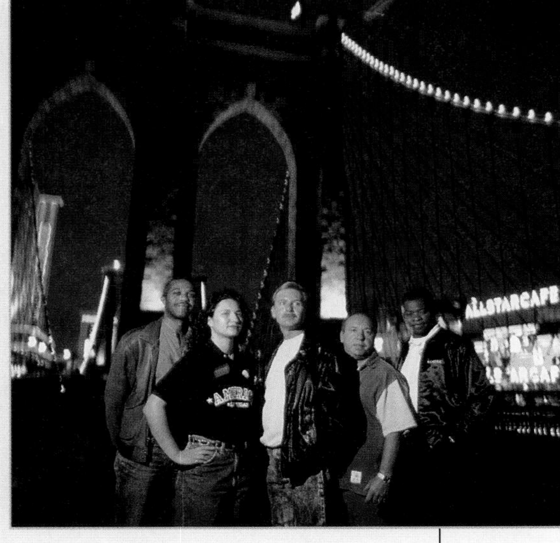

Las Vegas is so important to the union movement because it represents a challenge in nonmanufacturing industries. With fewer and fewer factory jobs being created in the United States, organized labor can ensure its own survival only by convincing service and construction workers to embrace the movement. Obviously, the job won't be an easy one. New York New York has already thwarted unionization attempts by hiring nonunion catering companies to run its restaurants. It's a first for Las Vegas and a new move for unions to contemplate.

Our opening story continues on page 288

Many of the dynamics at work in Las Vegas illustrate the challenges and opportunities that underlie contemporary labor–management relations. By focusing on the learning objectives of this chapter, you will better understand how and why workers organize into labor unions, how unions and businesses relate to each other, and how the collective bargaining process works.

WHY DO WORKERS UNIONIZE?

labor union
A group of individuals working together to achieve shared job-related goals, such as higher pay, shorter working hours, more job security, greater benefits, or better working conditions

labor relations
Process of dealing with employees who are represented by a union

collective bargaining
Process by which labor and management negotiate conditions of employment for union-represented workers

A **labor union** is a group of individuals working together to achieve shared job-related goals, such as higher pay, shorter working hours, more job security, greater benefits, or better working conditions.[1] **Labor relations** describes the process of dealing with employees who are represented by a union.

Labor unions grew in popularity in the United States in the nineteenth and early twentieth centuries. The labor movement was born with the Industrial Revolution, which also gave birth to a factory-based production system that carried with it enormous economic benefits. Job specialization and mass production allowed businesses to create ever greater quantities of goods at ever lower costs.

But there was also a dark side to this era. Workers became more dependent on their factory jobs. Eager for greater profits, some owners treated their workers like other raw materials: resources to be deployed with little or no regard for the individual worker's well-being. Many businesses forced employees to work long hours—60-hour weeks were common, and some workers were routinely forced to work 12 to 16 hours a day. With no minimum-wage laws or other controls, pay was also minimal and safety standards virtually nonexistent. Workers enjoyed no job security and received few benefits. Many companies, especially textile mills, employed large numbers of children at poverty wages. If people complained, nothing prevented employers from firing and replacing them at will.

Unions appeared and ultimately prospered because they constituted a solution to the worker's most serious problem: They forced management to listen to the complaints of all their workers rather than to just the few who were brave (or foolish) enough to speak out. The power of unions, then, comes from collective action. **Collective bargaining** (which we discuss more fully later in this chapter) is the process by which union leaders and managers negotiate common terms and conditions of employment for the workers represented by unions. Although collective bargaining does not often occur in small businesses, many midsize and larger businesses must engage in the process.

THE EVOLUTION OF UNIONISM IN THE UNITED STATES

As we discuss the growth—and more recent decline—of unionism in this section, it is important to remember that the influence of labor unions goes far beyond their membership. For example, many nonunion members have benefited from the improved working conditions won by unions. Union gains often set standards for entire industries, and some organizations make workplace improvements just to keep unions out.

Early Unions

Labor unions grew up with the United States. Indeed, the earliest formal organizations of U.S. workers appeared during the Revolutionary War. These early organizations were craft unions: Each limited itself to representing workers whose common interest was a specific skilled job, and each sought to promote the economic welfare of the skilled craftspeople who made up its membership.

For example, the Federal Society of Journeymen Cordwainers, formed in Philadelphia in 1794, worked to better the pay and working conditions of shoemakers. The Cordwainers was also one of the first unions to encounter legal roadblocks to collective action. When the union struck for higher wages in 1806, the court ruled in favor of employers, who claimed that unions were illegal "combinations" conspiring to restrain trade. The court's ruling applied the *common law conspiracy doctrine:* the principle that the public interest was harmed when two or more people conspired to do something jointly. Unions continued to organize, but for the next four decades they found it extremely difficult to take action in the face of the conspiracy doctrine.

The Knights of Labor A milestone in the history of U.S. labor occurred with the formation of the Knights of Labor in 1869. Like earlier unions, the Knights began as a craft union. Soon, however, the organization set larger goals for itself: In a drive to organize any workers who were interested in its representation, the Knights expanded to encompass workers in numerous fields (noteworthy exceptions were lawyers, bankers, and bartenders). The Knights was also the first union that actively sought women and blacks as members, and one of the few unions that has ever focused on political lobbying rather than collective bargaining as a means of reaching its goals.

The Knights championed such traditional union issues as better working conditions, campaigning especially for the eight-hour day and the abolition of child labor. At the same time, the union also hoped to achieve a broad range of social goals. Chief among these were such liberal, or reformist, objectives as worker ownership of factories and free public land for those who wished to farm.

These same goals also attracted to the labor movement a variety of radicals and other political reformers, many of whom came in the waves of European immigrants who had begun arriving a few decades earlier. Their activities were directed against what they saw as the oppressive nature of the industrial capitalist system, and their tactics did not necessarily reflect the typical strategies of the labor unions. Spurred by a severe depression in 1873, for example, a series of violent labor actions characterized labor–management relations from the mid-to-late 1870s. Demonstrators and locked-out strikers blockaded factories, battled strikebreakers in the streets of major cities, and exchanged fire with municipal police, state militia, and armed private agents. Assassinations and bombings led to the trial and execution of anarchists and labor agitators.

In 1886, the McCormick Harvester Co. in Chicago locked out 1,400 unionized workers and hired strikebreakers. Fired on by police, workers retreated to the area known as the Haymarket to conduct a protest meeting. At first, the meeting was peaceful. Then, however, 70 policemen were injured when a bomb exploded, and the notorious Haymarket riot erupted. Ultimately, "labor agitators" were blamed for the violence, and four anarchists were hanged for conspiring to commit murder. In reality, the role of radicals was exaggerated by unsympathetic newspapers and employer propaganda.

However, much of the violence in this period came in direct response to the extraordinary pressures of the depression. Most American laborers were conservative by nature and sought the stability of organizations such as the Knights of Labor. Under the leadership of Terence V. Powderly, the Knights grew to include roughly 700,000 members by the mid-1880s. The union was never successful, however, at increasing the number of skilled workers among its members. In addition, it was weakened by internal disagreements about social goals and outside charges of union violence. By the turn of the century, the Knights had disbanded.

The Emergence of the Major Unions

With its focus on the social welfare of unskilled workers, the Knights of Labor tended to forget that its economic strength lay with its skilled craft workers. As a result, many of these workers soon began to look for organizations that would better represent their interests: namely, unions whose primary concern was to improve wages, hours, and working conditions.

American Federation of Labor (AFL)
Group of craft unions formed in 1866 to stress collective bargaining, economic action, and a pragmatic approach to union-management relations

The AFL Many workers disenchanted with the social agenda of the Knights of Labor found a home in the **American Federation of Labor (AFL).** Made up of craft unions, the AFL was formed in 1886 by Samuel Gompers and other veteran organizers. Unlike the Knights of Labor, the AFL stressed no broad, idealistic legislative or political program. Gompers himself saw the labor union as an integral component, not the inherent enemy, of the capitalist system: "As we get a 25-cents-a-day wage increase," he argued, the process "brings us nearer the time when a greater degree of social justice and fair dealing will obtain among men." The enduring importance of the AFL lies in the fact that it established a solid organizational basis for collective bargaining, economic action, and a pragmatic approach to union–management relations.

The AFL grew rapidly in the early decades of the twentieth century, and by the end of World War I, membership had reached more than 5 million. The 1920s proved difficult for the AFL, as increased employer resistance to unions contributed to a steady decline in membership. By 1929, membership had dropped to 3.4 million.

The Great Depression of the 1930s witnessed further decline. By 1933, membership stood at just 2.9 million. In the same year, however, newly elected President Franklin D. Roosevelt introduced the nation to the New Deal, a far-reaching program aimed at stimulating the U.S. economy and creating jobs. The New Deal inspired an era of recovery for organized labor. Moreover, as we will see later in this chapter, the New Deal Congress passed a series of laws that made it easier for workers to organize.

industrial unionism
Organizing of workers by industry rather than by skill or occupation

Congress of Industrial Organizations (CIO)
Group of industrial unions formed in 1938 that rapidly organized the auto, steel, mining, meatpacking, paper, textile, and electrical industries

The CIO By the mid-1930s, the advent of mass production had significantly increased the demand for semiskilled workers in the automobile, steel, and mining industries. The AFL, while continuing to grow throughout the 1930s, remained open only to skilled craftspeople. In fact, most AFL leaders opposed **industrial unionism**—the organizing of employees by industry rather than by skill or occupation. When a 1935 convention of AFL unions confirmed this stance, dissident leaders, including John L. Lewis of the United Mine Workers, objected bitterly. Ultimately, the AFL expelled 32 national unions, which in 1938 banded together to form the **Congress of Industrial Organizations (CIO).**

Soon, the CIO had organized the auto, steel, mining, meatpacking, paper, textile, and electrical industries. By the early 1940s, CIO unions claimed close to 5 million of the slightly more than 10 million unionized U.S. workers. Not surprisingly, the AFL soon abandoned rigid craft unionism and began to charter industrial unions.

The AFL-CIO Union membership continued to increase during World War II, reaching more than 14 million by the end of the war. However, a series of postwar strikes led Congress to curtail the power of unions. Partly in response to this change, and partly in response to growing conflicts within their ranks, leaders of the AFL and the CIO began

WebConnection

www.aflcio.org

The AFL-CIO Web site is an information center for all things labor related. In addition to news pages devoted to "News for Working Families" and the "Working Families Agenda," it includes special features on such topics as "Your Paycheck," "Reaching a New Generation," and "Civil Rights/Workers' Rights." To find out more about union affiliations with the AFL-CIO and its various programs, log on to the organization's Web site.

merger negotiations. These meetings culminated in the 1955 formation of the AFL-CIO, with a total membership of 15 million. At the same time, organized labor reached its membership zenith, claiming almost 35 percent of the nonfarm workforce.

Today, in addition to lobbying for pro-union issues, the AFL-CIO <www.aflcio.org> settles jurisdictional disputes between unions. Remember, however, that the AFL-CIO is not a union itself. Rather, it is a federation of 86 individual unions with about 13 million individual members who belong to various trade or industrial departments (such as building trades, maritime trades, and public employees). The United Food and Commercial Workers <www.ufcw.org> is a union, as are the International Brotherhood of Teamsters <www.teamster.org> and the National Education Association <www.nea.org>.

UNIONISM TODAY

While understanding the historical context of labor unions is important, so too is appreciating the role of unionism today, especially trends in union membership, union–management relations, and bargaining perspectives. We discuss these topics in the sections that follow.

Are labor unions a necessity among workers in our economy today?

Trends in Union Membership

Since the mid-1950s, U.S. labor unions have experienced increasing difficulties in attracting new members. As a result, although millions of workers still belong to labor unions, union membership *as a percentage of the total workforce* has continued to decline at a very steady rate. In 1977, for example, over 26 percent of U.S. wage and salary employees belonged to labor unions. Today, that figure is about 14 percent. Figure 10.1(a) traces the decades-long decline in union membership. Moreover, if public employees are excluded from consideration, then only around 11 percent of all private industry wage and salary employees currently belong to labor unions. Figure 10.1(b) illustrates the different trends in membership for public employees versus private nonfarm employees.

Furthermore, just as union membership has continued to decline, so has the percentage of successful union-organizing campaigns. In the years immediately following World War II and continuing through the mid-1960s, most unions routinely won certification elections. In recent years, however, labor unions have been winning certification fewer than 50 percent of the time in which workers are called upon to vote. By the same token,

Figure 10.1
Trends in Union Membership

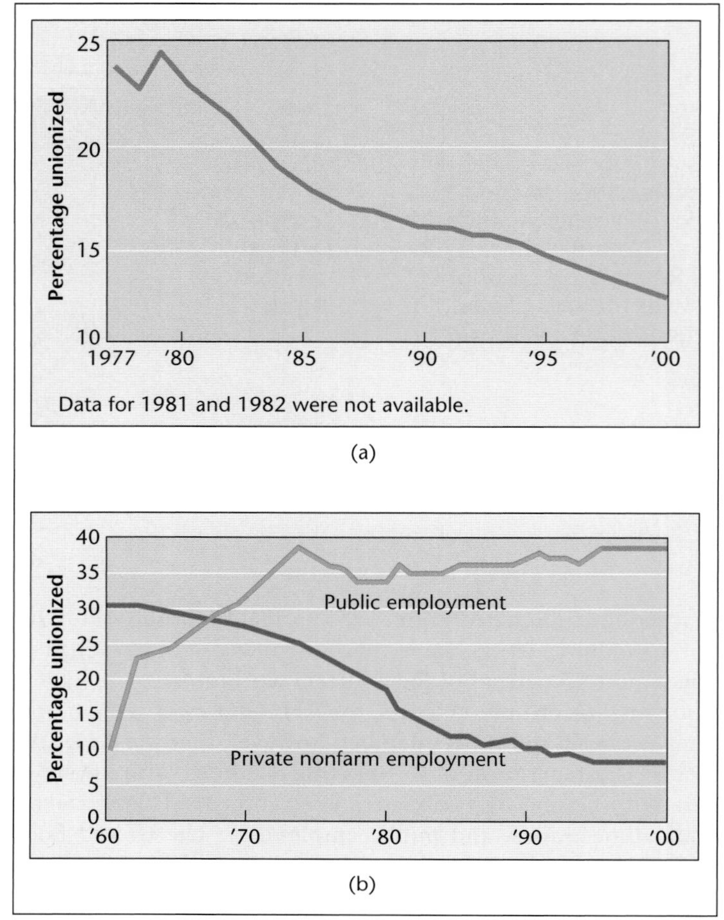

of course, unions still do win. Meat cutters at a Florida Wal-Mart store recently voted to unionize—the first-ever successful organizing campaign against the retailing giant. "You'll see a lot more attention to Wal-Mart now," exulted one AFL-CIO official. "It's not like Wal-Mart stands out as some unattainable goal."[2]

"You'll see a lot more attention to Wal-Mart now. It's not like Wal-Mart stands out as some unattainable goal."

—AFL-CIO official on the unionization of Wal-Mart meat cutters in Florida

From most indications, then, the power and significance of U.S. labor unions, while still quite formidable, are also measurably lower than they were just a few decades ago. A number of factors help to explain the decline in union membership.

Composition of the Workforce Traditionally, union members have been predominantly white males in blue-collar jobs. But as most of us know, today's workforce is increasingly composed of women and ethnic minorities. Because these groups have much weaker traditions of union affiliation, their members are less likely to join unions when they enter the workforce. In a related trend, much of the workforce has shifted toward geographic areas in the South and toward occupations in the service sector that have traditionally been less heavily unionized.

Anti-Unionization Activities A second reason is more aggressive anti-unionization activity on the part of employers. Although the National Labor Relations Act and other laws specify strict management practices with regard to labor unions, companies are still free to pursue certain strategies intended to eliminate or minimize unionization. Both Motorola and Procter & Gamble, for example, now offer no layoff guarantees for most

Life Cycle of an e-Business

The Common Grounds of Labor Relations

Because employees at Garden.com were not unionized, the firm did not really need to worry too much about organized labor, right? Well, not exactly. In fact, organized labor was relevant to Garden.com on at least two levels, one general and one specific.

First of all, Jamie O'Neill acknowledges that the work environment at Garden.com, had it not been managed properly, could actually have been conducive to unionization. There was, for example, a fairly broad spectrum of income levels, skills, and so forth across the Garden.com workforce. Moreover, many people worked long hours. Thus, there was at least the potential that some people could perceive inequities or unfair treatment. If such perceptions had become widespread—and if people had felt sufficiently unhappy about them—union organizing might well have been considered as a solution.

As a result, says O'Neill, the organization had to make sure that people were treated fairly—even if they were not necessarily treated the same—so that everyone recognized that they were all working together toward the same goals. The goal, therefore, was to maintain a cohesive, positive work environment so that employees would not be predisposed to think that a union would be of value to them.

On a much more specific level, unions were also relevant to Garden.com because of the firm's high level of interdependence with its various business partners. The firm depended quite heavily on both its network of suppliers and on Federal Express <www.fedex.com> as its primary distributor. Just a few years ago, a labor strike shut down United Parcel Service (UPS) <www.ups.com> for several days. Had Garden.com been partnered with UPS, it too would have been forced to reduce its operations during the strike. Similarly, some workers in the nurseries and other suppliers on whom Garden.com relied are unionized. A strike or a serious labor problem at one or more of these suppliers could have had serious repercussions for Garden.com as well. What, then, is the moral? If your business partners have union problems, you have union problems.

of their employees and have created a formal grievance system for all workers. These arrangements were once available only through unions. But because these and other firms offer them independent of any union contract, employees have two fewer reasons for unionizing. The "Life Cycle of an e-Business" box in this chapter explains how managers at Garden.com followed a similar approach.

Some companies have also worked to create much more employee-friendly work environments and to treat all employees with respect and dignity. One goal of this approach is to minimize the attractiveness of labor unions for employees. Many Japanese manufacturers who have set up shop in the United States have successfully avoided unionization efforts by the United Auto Workers (UAW) <www.uaw.org> by providing job security, higher wages, and a work environment in which employees are allowed to participate and be actively involved in plant management.

Trends in Union–Management Relations

The gradual decline in unionization in the United States has been accompanied by some significant trends in union–management relations. In some sectors of the economy, perhaps most notably the automobile and steel industries, labor unions still remain quite strong. In these areas, unions have large memberships and considerable power in negotiating with management. The UAW, for example, is still one of the strongest unions in the United States.

In most sectors, however, unions are clearly in a weakened position, and as a result, many have taken much more conciliatory stances in their relations with management. This situation contrasts sharply with the more adversarial relationship that once dominated labor relations in this country. Increasingly, for instance, unions recognize that they

"Actually, Tommy, we're just about full-blooded management, except for your grandfather on your mom's side, who was one-quarter labor."

don't have as much power as they once held and that it is in their own best interests, as well as in those of the workers that they represent, to work with management instead of working against it. Ironically, then, union–management relations are in many ways better today than they have been in many years. Admittedly, the improvement is attributable in large part to the weakened power of unions. Even so, however, most experts agree that improved union–management relations have benefited both sides.

Trends in Bargaining Perspectives

Given the trends described in the two previous sections, we should not be surprised to find changes in bargaining perspectives as well. In the past, most union–management bargaining situations were characterized by union demands for dramatic increases in wages and salaries. A secondary issue was usually increased benefits for members. Now, however, unions often bargain for different benefits, such as job security. Of particular interest in this area is the trend toward relocating jobs to take advantage of lower labor costs in other countries. Unions, of course, want to restrict job movement, whereas companies want to save money by moving facilities—and jobs—to other countries.

As a result of organizational downsizing and several years of relatively low inflation in this country, many unions today find themselves, rather than striving for wage increases, fighting against wage cuts. Similarly, as organizations are more likely to seek lower health care and other benefits, a common goal of union strategy is preserving what's already been won. Unions also place greater emphasis on improved job security. A trend that has become especially important in recent years is toward improved pension programs for employees.

Unions have also begun increasingly to set their sights on preserving jobs for workers in the United States in the face of business efforts to relocate production in some sectors to countries where labor costs are lower. For example, the AFL-CIO has been an outspoken opponent of efforts to normalize trade relations with China, fearing that more businesses might be tempted to move jobs there. General Electric <www.ge.com> has been targeted for union protests recently because of its strategy to move many of its own jobs—and those of key suppliers—to Mexico.[3]

The Future of Unions

Despite declining membership and some loss of power, labor unions remain a major factor in the U.S. business world. The 86 labor organizations in the AFL-CIO, as well as

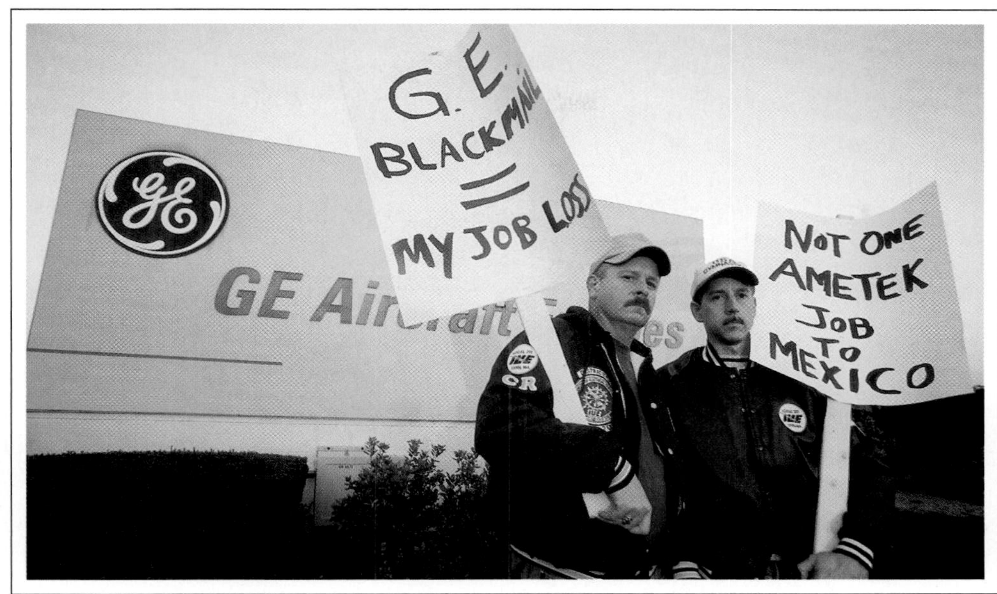

As part of a massive cost-cutting drive, General Electric <www.ge.com> *has begun urging its suppliers to move to Mexico, where the labor is cheaper. The company even sponsors "supplier migration" conferences to help companies work out the logistics of moving. At Ametek, Inc.* <www.ametek.com>*, a supplier of parts to GE's jet engine plant in Lynn, Massachusetts, members of the International Union of Electronic Workers protest the export of U.S. jobs across the border. Since 1986, GE's domestic workforce has decreased by 50 percent while foreign employment has nearly doubled.*

independent major unions such as the Teamsters and the National Education Association, still play a major role in U.S. business. Moreover, some unions still wield considerable power, especially in the traditional strongholds of goods-producing industries. Labor and management in some industries, notably airlines and steel, are beginning to favor contracts that establish formal mechanisms for greater worker input into management decisions. Inland Steel <www.inland.com>, for instance, recently granted its major union the right to name a member to the board of directors. Union officers can also attend executive meetings.

A View to the Future The big question still remains: Will unions dwindle in power and perhaps disappear, or can they evolve, survive to face new challenges, and play a new role in U.S. business? They will probably evolve to take on new roles and responsibilities. More and more unions are asking for—and often getting—voices in management. In 1980, for example, as a part of the Chrysler bailout, UAW president Douglas Fraser became the first labor official appointed to the board of directors of a major corporation. Several other companies have since followed suit. F. C. Dubinsky, president of United Airlines' pilots union <ual.alpa.org>, sits on the firm's board of directors.[4] He has also taken a strong stance on issues facing the board, especially as an advocate of pay increases for pilots.

By the same token, unions are increasingly aware that they must cooperate with employers if both are to survive. Critics of unions contend that excessive wage rates won through years of strikes and hard-nosed negotiation are partly to blame for the demise of large employers such as Eastern Airlines. Others argue that excessively tight work rules limit the productivity of businesses in many industries. More often, however, unions are working with organizations to create effective partnerships in which managers and workers share the same goals: profitability, growth, and effectiveness with equitable rewards for everyone.

Contemporary Union Structure

Just as each organization has its own unique structure, each union creates a structure that best serves its own needs. As Figure 10.2 shows, a general structure characterizes most national and international unions. A major function of unions is to provide service and support to both members and local affiliates. Most of these services are carried out by the

Figure 10.2
Organization of a Large National Union

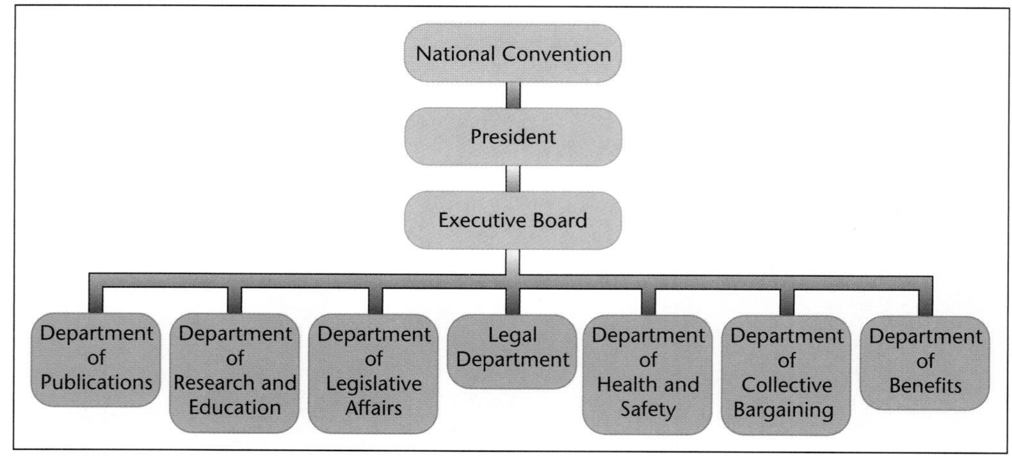

types of specialized departments shown in Figure 10.2. In other unions, departments serve specific employment groups. The Machinists' Union—the International Association of Machinists and Aerospace Workers <www.iamaw.org>—has departments for automotive, railroad, and airline workers.

local union (local)
Union organized at the level of a single company, plant, or small geographic region

Locals At the same time, most national unions are composed of **local unions (locals)**, which are organized at the level of a single company, plant, or small geographic region. The functions of these locals vary, depending not only on governance arrangements but also on bargaining patterns in particular industries. Some local unions bargain directly with management regarding wages, hours, and other terms of employment. Many local unions are also active in disciplining members for violations of contract standards and in pressing management to consider worker complaints. Local unions also serve as grassroots bases for union political activities, registering voters and getting them out to vote on election day.

shop steward
Union employee who acts as liaison between union members and supervisors

business agent (or business representative)
Full-time official who acts as liaison between members of a large union and their supervisors

Officers and Functions Each department or unit represented at the local level elects a **shop steward:** a regular employee who acts as a liaison between union members and supervisors. For example, if workers have a grievance, they take it to the steward, who tries to resolve the problem with the supervisor. If the local is very large, the union might hire a full-time **business agent** (or **business representative**) to play the same role.

Within a given union, the main governing bodies are the national union (or international union when members come from more than one country) and its officers. Among their other duties, national and international unions charter local affiliates and establish general standards of conduct and procedures for local operations. For example, they set dues assessments, arrange for the election of local officers, sanction strikes, and provide guidance in the collective bargaining process. Many national unions also engage in a variety of political activities, such as lobbying. They may also help coordinate organizing efforts and establish education programs.

Given the magnitude of their efforts, it is little wonder that unions often take on many of the same characteristics as the companies for which their members work. For example, almost all large unions have full-time administrators, formal organizational structures (see Figure 10.2), goals and strategic plans, and so forth. James P. Hoffa, current president of the International Brotherhood of Teamsters <www.teamster.org>, earns an annual salary of $225,000 and oversees a large full-time staff.[5] Because of their size, power, and importance, Congress has passed numerous laws to govern union activities. It is to these laws that we now turn our attention.

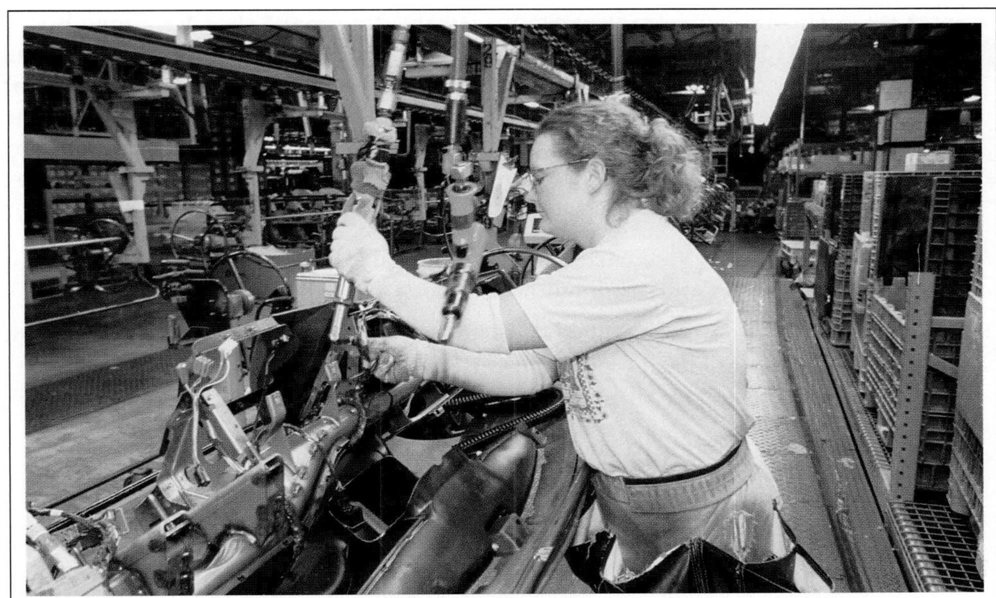

Teri Jones installs instrument panels at Ford's Taurus factory in Atlanta, which was recently designated the most efficient automotive plant in North America. Productivity increases at the plant have resulted largely from improved management and organization and, especially, strong labor-management relations. Absenteeism (AWOLs) had gone down to two percent by mid-2000, but when the rate rose to three percent later in the year, the local unit of the United Automobile Workers <www.uaw.org> *reminded employees that "If AWOLs go down, job security goes up."*

LAWS GOVERNING LABOR–MANAGEMENT RELATIONS

Like almost every other aspect of labor–management relations today, the process of unionizing workers is governed by numerous laws, administrative interpretations, and judicial decisions. In fact, the growth and decline of unionism in the United States can be traced by following the history of labor laws.

For the first 150 years of U.S. independence, workers were judged to have little legal right to organize. Indeed, interpretation of the 1890 Sherman Antitrust Act classified labor unions as monopolies, thus making them illegal. During the first 30 years of the twentieth century, however, social activism and turmoil in the labor force changed the landscape of U.S. labor relations.

The Major Labor Laws

Five major federal laws, all enacted between 1932 and 1959, laid the groundwork for all the rules, regulations, and judicial decisions governing union activity in the United States. A number of more recent laws have dealt with specific groups and specific issues.

Norris-LaGuardia Act
Federal law (1932) limiting the ability of courts to issue injunctions prohibiting certain union activities

yellow-dog contract
Illegal contract clause requiring workers to begin and continue employment without union affiliation

National Labor Relations Act (Wagner Act)
Federal law (1935) protecting the rights of workers to form unions, bargain collectively, and engage in strikes to achieve their goals

Norris-LaGuardia Act During the 1930s, labor leaders finally persuaded lawmakers that the legal environment discriminated against the collective efforts of workers to improve working conditions. Legislators responded with the **Norris-LaGuardia Act** in 1932. This act imposed severe limitations on the ability of the courts to issue injunctions prohibiting certain union activities, including strikes. Norris-LaGuardia also outlawed **yellow-dog contracts:** requirements that workers state that they did not belong to and would not join a union.

National Labor Relations (Wagner) Act In 1935 Congress passed the **National Labor Relations Act** (also called the **Wagner Act**), which is the cornerstone of contemporary labor relations law. This act put labor unions on a more equal footing with management in terms of the rights of employees to organize and bargain:

- It gave most workers the right to form unions, bargain collectively, and engage in group activities (such as strikes) to reach their goals.
- It forced employers to bargain with duly elected union leaders and prohibited employer practices that unjustly restrict employees' rights (for example, discriminating against union members in hiring, promoting, and firing).

Why is the National Labor Relations Act important to people in business, including labor unions?

The Wagner Act also established the **National Labor Relations Board (NLRB)** to administer its provisions. Today, the NLRB administers virtually all labor law in this country. For example, it determines the appropriate unit for conducting bargaining at any workplace. The NLRB also oversees most of the elections held by employees to determine whether they will be represented by particular unions. It decides who is eligible to vote and who will be covered by bargaining agreements once they have been reached.

National Labor Relations Board (NLRB)
Federal agency established by the National Labor Relations Act to enforce its provisions

Fair Labor Standards Act
Federal law (1938) setting minimum wage and maximum number of hours in the workweek

Labor-Management Relations Act (Taft-Hartley Act)
Federal law (1947) defining certain union practices as unfair and illegal

closed shop
Workplace in which an employer may hire only workers already belonging to a union

right-to-work laws
Statutes making it illegal to require union membership as a condition of employment

union shop
Workplace in which workers must join a union within a specified period after being hired

Fair Labor Standards Act

Enacted in 1938, the **Fair Labor Standards Act** addressed issues of minimum wages and maximum work hours:

- It set a minimum wage (originally $.25 an hour) to be paid to workers. The minimum wage has been increased many times since 1938 and now stands at $5.15 per hour.
- It set a maximum number of hours for the workweek, initially 44 hours per week, later 40 hours.
- It mandated time-and-a-half pay for those who worked beyond the legally stipulated number of hours.
- It outlawed child labor.

Taft-Hartley Act

Supported by the Norris-LaGuardia, Wagner, and Fair Labor Standards Acts, organized labor eventually grew into a powerful political and economic force. But a series of disruptive strikes in the immediate post–World War II years turned public opinion against unions. Inconvenienced by strikes and the resulting shortages of goods and services, the public became openly critical of unions and pressured the government to take action. Congress responded by passing the **Labor-Management Relations Act** (more commonly known as the **Taft-Hartley Act**) in 1947.

Unfair and Illegal Union Practices The Taft-Hartley Act defined certain union practices as unfair and illegal. For example, it prohibited such practices as featherbedding (requiring extra workers solely in order to provide more jobs) and refusing to bargain in good faith. It also generally forbade the **closed shop:** a workplace in which only workers already belonging to a union may be hired by an employer. Instead, Taft-Hartley promoted open shops by allowing states to enact **right-to-work laws.** Such laws prohibit both union shops and agency shops, thus making it illegal to require union membership as a condition of employment. A **union shop** requires employees to join a union within a specified period after being hired. An **agency shop** requires employees to pay union fees even if they choose not to join. To date, 21 states have enacted right-to-work laws. As you can see from Figure 10.3, most of those states are in the South and West.

Injunctions and Cooling-Off Periods Passed in the wake of crippling strikes in the steel industry, the Taft-Hartley Act also established procedures for resolving any strike deemed to pose a national emergency. Initially, the concept of national emergency was broadly interpreted. For example, virtually any large company could claim that a strike was doing

WebConnection

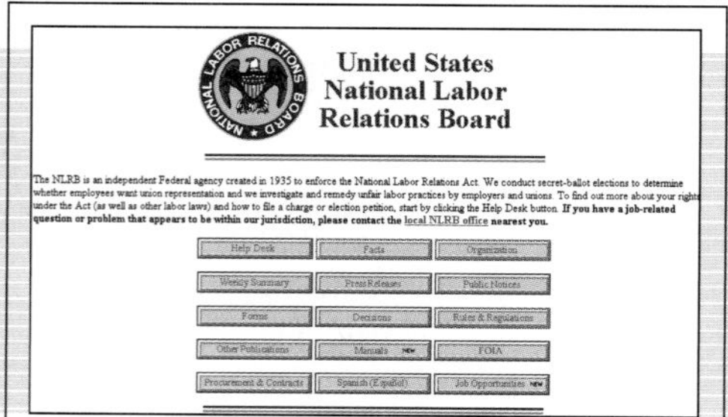

www.nlrb.gov

Created in 1935, the National Labor Relations Board administers and enforces the National Labor Relations Act by conducting secret ballots to determine union representation and investigating and repairing unfair labor practices. To get a better idea of how the NLRB pursues this mandate, visit the organization's Web site.

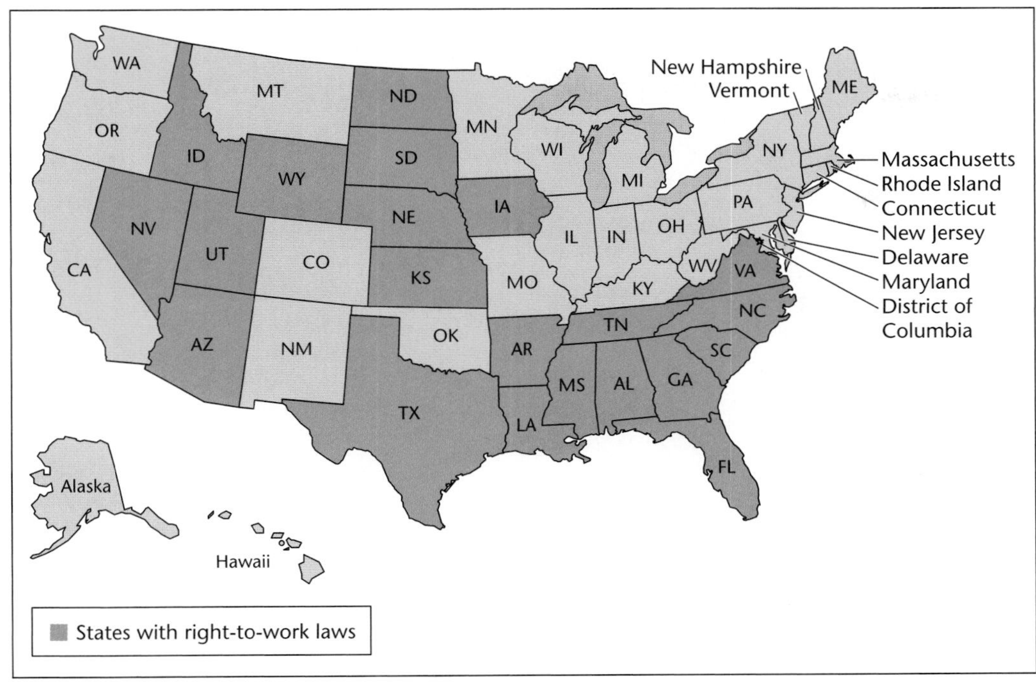

Figure 10.3
Right-to-Work States

irreparable harm to its financial base and that the nation's economy would be harmed if workers were not forced back to their jobs.

Today, however, the courts use a more precise definition of national emergency. For example, a strike must affect a whole industry or most of it. Similarly, the use of Taft-Hartley is more restrictive. Now the president may request an injunction requiring that workers restrain from striking for 60 days. During this cooling-off period, labor and management must try to resolve their differences.

agency shop
Workplace in which workers must pay union dues even if they do not join

Enforced Resolution If differences are not resolved during the cooling-off period, the injunction may be extended for another 20 days. During this period, employees must vote, in a secret ballot election, on whether to accept or reject the employer's latest offer. If they accept the offer, the threat of strike is ended and the contract signed. If they do not accept the offer, the president reports to Congress and the workers may either be forced back to work under threat of criminal action or fired and replaced by nonunion employees. Presidential intervention has been invoked only 35 times since Taft-Hartley was passed.

Landrum-Griffin Act The National Labor Relations Act was further amended by the **Landrum-Griffin Act** in 1959. Officially titled the **Labor-Management Reporting and Disclosure Act,** this law resulted from congressional hearings that revealed unethical, illegal, and undemocratic union practices. The act thus imposed regulations on internal union procedures:

- It required the election of national union leaders at least once every five years.
- It gave union members the right to participate in various union affairs.
- It required unions to file annual financial disclosure statements with the Department of Labor.

Labor-Management Reporting and Disclosure Act (Landrum-Griffin Act)
Federal law (1959) imposing regulations on internal union procedures, including elections of national leaders and filing of financial disclosure statements

HOW UNIONS ARE ORGANIZED AND CERTIFIED

Many of the laws described previously address the issue of union certification. Figure 10.4 illustrates a simplified version of this process. First, there must be some interest among workers in having a union. Sometimes this interest comes from dissatisfied employees; sometimes it is stirred by professional organizers sent by unions themselves.

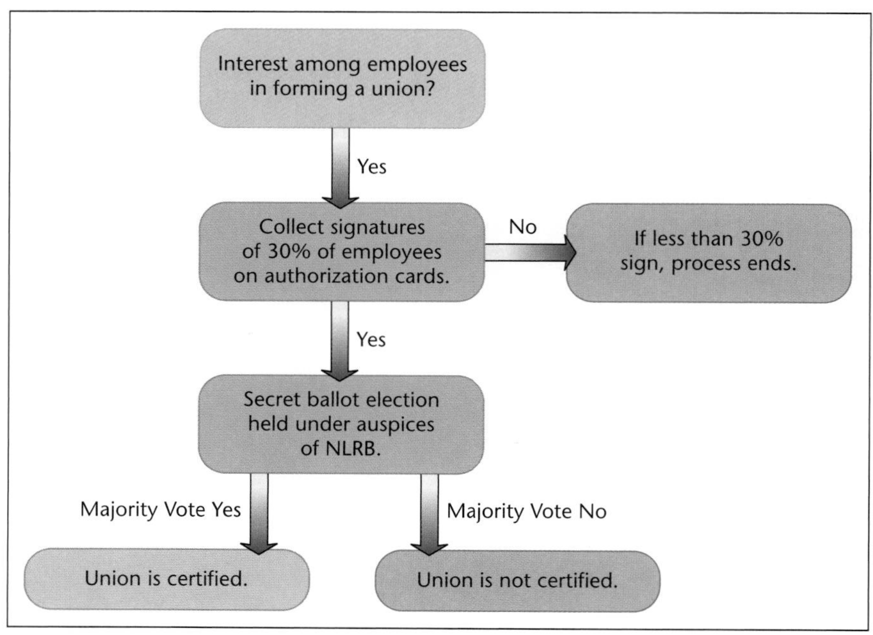

Figure 10.4
Certifying a Labor Union

For example, the United Auto Workers has for years dispatched organizers to promote interest among workers at the Honda plant in Marysville, Ohio. To date, they have had no success in Marysville or in Smyrna, Tennessee, where Nissan built its major American plant. The process unfolds as follows:

bargaining unit
Designated group of employees who will be represented by a union

1. *Defining the bargaining unit.* Interested organizers start by asking the NLRB to define the **bargaining unit:** the group of employees who will be represented by the union. For instance, a bargaining unit might be all nonmanagement employees in an organization or all electrical workers at a certain plant.
2. *Gaining authorization.* Organizers must then get 30 percent of the eligible workers within the bargaining unit to sign authorization cards requesting a certification election. If less than 30 percent of the workers want an election, the process ends.
3. *Conducting an election.* If the required number of signatures is obtained, the organizers petition the NLRB to conduct the election. The NLRB then holds a secret ballot election. If a simple majority of those voting approves the certification, the union becomes the official bargaining agent of eligible employees. If a majority fails to approve certification, the process ends and an election cannot be called again for at least one year.

Decertification Unions are not necessarily permanent fixtures in a workplace, and if conditions warrant, a union may be *decertified*. For example, workers may become disenchanted with a union and may even feel that they are being hurt by its presence. They may believe that management is trying to be cooperative while the union is refusing to negotiate in good faith.

Decertification requires two conditions:

1. The union must have served the unit as its official bargaining agent for at least one year.
2. There must be no labor contract currently in effect.

If these conditions are met, employees or their representatives can solicit signatures on decertification cards. If 30 percent of the employees in the unit sign, the NLRB conducts a decertification election. If a majority of those voting favor decertification, the union is removed as the unit's official bargaining agent. Following decertification, a new election cannot be requested for at least one year. The "Wired World" box in this chapter

It's a WiredWorld

• *The Web as a Bargaining Tool*

It's no secret, of course, that the Internet now plays a key role in the plans and operations of many businesses. A bit less obvious, though certainly no less important, is the approach that organized labor is taking to the Internet. There are at least three different areas in which labor is taking advantage of the Internet to promote various agendas.

First, just like many if not most businesses, many unions have Web sites. Some of these sites are posted by national and international unions, others by local unions. Sites provide information for members, promote the union's current agenda, and contain links to other relevant sites. Some of the more aggressive union Web sites go so far as to provide warnings and directives to management as to what it can and cannot do during ongoing organizing or collective bargaining periods—even pointing out that the Web site itself is a union organizing location and thus off-limits to managers.

The Internet is also important to unions as a source of information and site for research. A critical part of effective collective bargaining—for both sides—is having the right information. Both sides, for example, need to know such statistics as employment rates, cost-of-living changes and projections, and so forth. They also need to know what contract terms have been negotiated in similar industries and settings. The Internet makes this information more accessible.

The Internet also makes it easier for a union to learn more about a company, especially when it is a privately held corporation. A longtime union practice has been to obtain employment for what is called a "salt"—essentially, an employee planted for espionage purposes. These individuals try to find out whatever they can about the lifestyles and wealth of business owners. Learning, for instance, that a business owner has expensive hobbies, travels in lavish style, and maintains a fleet of expensive cars makes it easier for the union to argue for higher wages. The Internet makes it easier to locate this same kind of information more quickly and more easily.

Finally, the Internet is used more and more frequently as a recruiting tool during organizing campaigns. Whereas organizers once had little choice but to hang out in company parking lots or neighborhood bars to strike up conversations with a business's employees, they can now do most of their work electronically. Today, for example, they can put up Web sites at the start of a campaign. All they have to do is recruit a few people and then wait for the recruits to pass along the Web address to coworkers. Interested parties can visit the site, review what the union says it can and will do, and post e-mails with questions and comments. One day soon, certification elections may even be conducted online.

explains some of the uses to which unions can put the Internet not only during the certification process, but for a variety of other activities.

COLLECTIVE BARGAINING

When a union has been legally certified, it assumes the role of official bargaining agent for the workers whom it represents. Collective bargaining is an ongoing process involving both the drafting and the administering of the terms of a labor contract.

Reaching Agreement on Contract Terms

The collective bargaining process begins when the union is recognized as the exclusive negotiator for its members. The bargaining cycle itself begins when union leaders meet with management representatives to agree on a contract. By law, both parties must sit down at the bargaining table and negotiate in good faith.

When each side has presented its demands, sessions focus on identifying the *bargaining zone*. The process is shown in Figure 10.5. For example, although an employer may initially offer no pay raise, it may expect to grant a raise of up to 6 percent. Likewise, the union may initially *demand* a 10-percent pay raise while *expecting* to accept a raise as low as 4 percent. The bargaining zone, then, is a raise between 4 and 6 percent. Ideally, some compromise is reached between these levels and the new agreement submitted for a ratification vote by union membership.

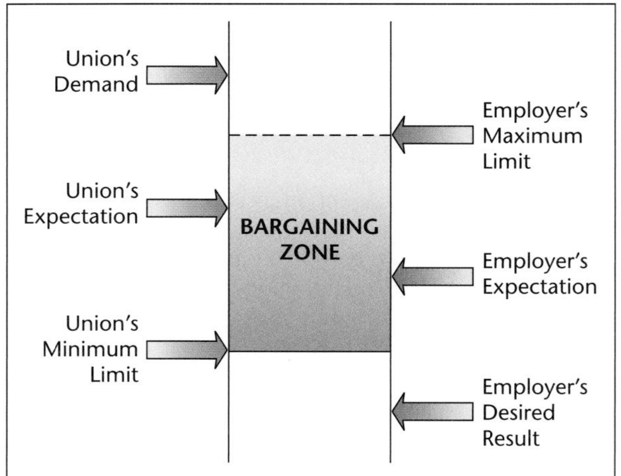

Figure 10.5
The Bargaining Zone

Sometimes, this process goes quite smoothly. At other times, however, the two sides cannot—or will not—agree. The speed and ease with which such an impasse is resolved depend in part on the nature of the contract issues, the willingness of each side to use certain tactics, and the prospects for mediation or arbitration.

Contract Issues

The labor contract itself can address an array of different issues. Most of these concern demands that unions make on behalf of their members. In this section we will survey the categories of issues that are typically most important to union negotiators: *compensation, benefits,* and *job security.* Although few issues covered in a labor contract are company sponsored, we will also describe the kinds of management rights that are negotiated in most bargaining agreements.

First, note that bargaining items generally fall into two categories:

- *Mandatory items* are matters over which both parties must negotiate if either wants to. This category includes wages, working hours, and benefits.
- *Permissive items* may be negotiated if both parties agree. A union demand for veto power over the promotion of managerial personnel would be a permissive bargaining item.

Illegal items may not be brought to the table by either party. A management demand for a nonstrike clause would be an illegal item.

Compensation The most common issue is compensation. One aspect of compensation is current wages. Obviously, unions generally want their employees to earn higher wages and try to convince management to raise hourly wages for all or some employees.

cost-of-living adjustment (COLA)
Labor contract clause tying future raises to changes in consumer purchasing power

wage reopener clause
Clause allowing wage rates to be renegotiated during the life of a labor contract

Of equal concern to unions is future compensation: wage rates to be paid during subsequent years of the contract. One common tool for securing wage increases is a **cost-of-living adjustment (COLA).** Most COLA clauses tie future raises to the *consumer price index,* a government statistic that reflects changes in consumer purchasing power. The premise is that as the CPI increases by a specified amount during a given period of time, wages will automatically be increased. Almost half of all labor contracts today include COLA clauses.

Wage reopener clauses are now included in almost 10 percent of all labor contracts. Such a clause allows wage rates to be renegotiated at preset times during the life of the contract. For example, a union might be uncomfortable with a long-term contract based solely on COLA wage increases. A long-term agreement might be more acceptable, however, if management agrees to renegotiate wages every two years.

WebConnection

violet.berkeley.edu/~iir/workfam/home.html

Founded in 1992, the Labor Project for Working Families works with unions to develop family-oriented policies—including family leave, flexible hours, dependent care, and domestic partner benefits—at the workplace. The organization then helps unions negotiate contracts that reflect the needs of working families.

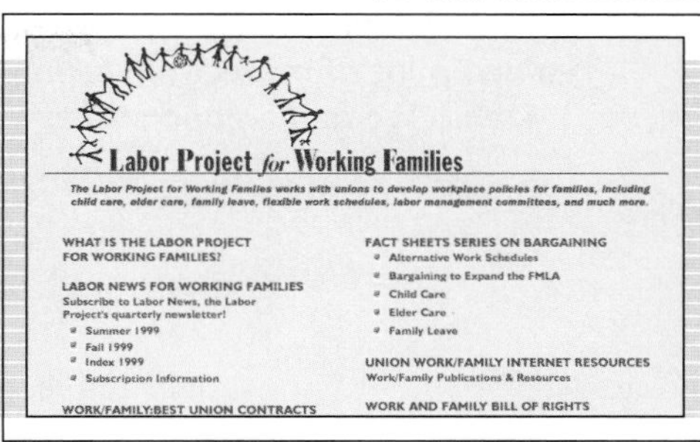

Benefits Employee benefits are also an important component in most labor contracts. Unions typically want employers to pay all or most of the costs of insurance for employees. Other benefits commonly addressed during negotiations include retirement benefits, paid holidays, and working conditions.

Job Security Nevertheless, the UAW's top priority in its most recent negotiations with U.S. automakers has been job security, an increasingly important agenda item in many bargaining sessions today. In some cases, demands for job security entail the promise that a company not move to another location. In others, the contract may dictate that if the workforce is reduced, seniority will be used to determine which employees lose their jobs.

Other Union Issues Other possible issues might include such things as working hours, overtime policies, rest period arrangements, differential pay plans for shift employees, the use of temporary workers, grievance procedures, and allowable union activities (dues collection, union bulletin boards, and so forth).

Management Rights Management wants as much control as possible over hiring policies, work assignments, and so forth. Unions, meanwhile, often try to limit management rights by specifying hiring, assignment, and other policies. At a DaimlerChrysler plant in Detroit, for example, the contract stipulates that three workers are needed to change fuses in robots: a machinist to open the robot, an electrician to change the fuse, and a supervisor to oversee the process. As in this case, contracts often bar workers in one job category from performing work that falls in the domain of another. Unions try to secure jobs by defining as many different categories as possible (the DaimlerChrysler plant has over 100). Of course, management resists the practice, which limits flexibility and makes it difficult to reassign workers.

When Bargaining Fails

An impasse occurs when, after a series of bargaining sessions, management and labor have failed to agree on a new contract or a contract to replace an agreement that is about to expire. Although it is generally agreed that both parties suffer when an impasse is reached and action is taken, each side can use several tactics to support its cause until the impasse is resolved.

Union Tactics When their demands are not met, unions may bring a variety of tactics to the bargaining table. Chief among these is the *strike,* which may be supported by *pickets, boycotts,* or *both.*

The Strike A **strike** occurs when employees temporarily walk off the job and refuse to work. Most strikes in the United States are **economic strikes,** triggered by stalemates over mandatory bargaining items, including such noneconomic issues as working hours. For

strike
Labor action in which employees temporarily walk off the job and refuse to work

economic strike
Strike usually triggered by stalemate over one or more mandatory bargaining items

example, the Teamsters union struck United Parcel Service (UPS) a few years ago over several noneconomic issues. Specifically, the union wanted the firm to transform many of its temporary and part-time jobs into permanent and full-time jobs. Strikers returned to work only when UPS agreed to create 10,000 new jobs. More recently, the same union struck Union Pacific Corp. <www.up.com> in January 2000 over wages and new jobs. In April 2000, machinists at a Lockheed-Martin <www.lmco.com> plant in Fort Worth, Texas, staged a two-week strike. Reflected the president of the union local: "I think our people gained a lot of respect for taking a stand. We had a good strike."

> ***"I think our people gained a lot of respect for taking a stand. We had a good strike."***
>
> *—President of Machinists Local 776, reflecting on a strike at Lockheed-Martin*

Still, there are far fewer strikes today than there were in previous years. For example, there were 222 strikes in the United States in 1960 involving a total of 896,000 workers. In 1970, 2,468,000 workers took part in 381 strikes. But in 1990 there were only 44 strikes involving 185,000 workers. Since 1990, the annual number of strikes has ranged from a high of 45 (in 1994) to a low of 29 (in 1997).[6]

Not all strikes are legal. **Sympathy strikes** (also called **secondary strikes**), which occur when one union strikes in sympathy with action initiated by another, may violate the sympathetic union's contract. **Wildcat strikes**—strikes unauthorized by the union that occur during the life of a contract—deprive strikers of their status as employees and thus of the protection of national labor law.

sympathy strike (or **secondary strike**)
Strike in which one union strikes to support action initiated by another

wildcat strike
Strike that is unauthorized by the strikers' union

Other Labor Actions To support a strike, a union faced with an impasse has recourse to additional legal activities:

- In **picketing,** workers march at the entrance to the employer's facility with signs explaining their reasons for striking.
- A **boycott** occurs when union members agree not to buy the products of a targeted employer. Workers may also urge consumers to boycott the firm's products.
- Another alternative to striking is a work **slowdown.** Instead of striking, workers perform their jobs at a much slower pace than normal. A variation is the sickout, during which large numbers of workers call in sick. Pilots at American Airlines engaged in a massive "sickout" in early 1999, causing the airline to cancel thousands of flights before a judge ordered them back into the cockpit.[7]

picketing
Labor action in which workers publicize their grievances at the entrance to an employer's facility

boycott
Labor action in which workers refuse to buy the products of a targeted employer

slowdown
Labor action in which workers perform jobs at a slower than normal pace

Management Tactics Like workers, management can respond forcefully to an impasse:

- **Lockouts** occur when employers deny employees access to the workplace. Lockouts are illegal if they are used as offensive weapons to give management a bargaining advantage. However, they are legal if management has a legitimate business need (for instance, avoiding a buildup of perishable inventory). Although rare today, ABC <www.abc.go.com> locked out its off-camera employees in 1998 because they staged an unannounced one-day strike during a critical broadcasting period.[8] Likewise, almost half of the 1998–99 NBA season was lost when team owners <www.nba.com> locked out their players over contract issues.[9]
- A firm can also hire temporary or permanent replacements called **strikebreakers.** However, the law forbids the *permanent* replacement of workers who strike because of unfair practices. In some cases, an employer can also obtain legal injunctions that either prohibit workers from striking or prohibit a union from interfering with its efforts to use replacement workers.

lockout
Management tactic whereby workers are denied access to the employer's workplace

strikebreaker
Worker hired as permanent or temporary replacement for a striking employee

Mediation and Arbitration Rather than wield these often unpleasant weapons against one another, labor and management can agree to call in a third party to help resolve the dispute:

- In **mediation,** the neutral third party (the mediator) can advise, but cannot impose a settlement on the other parties.
- In **voluntary arbitration,** the neutral third party (the arbitrator) dictates a settlement between the two sides, who have agreed to submit to outside judgment.

mediation
Method of resolving a labor dispute in which a third party suggests, but does not impose, a settlement

The tactic is called CHAOS—Creating Havoc Around Our System. It isn't typically union-ordered, but it's often effective because, at least in the airline business, it hits employers where it hurts the most—in passenger service. CHAOS consists of a series of service disruptions, which in the airline industry means intermittent strikes against individual flights. In 2000, when U.S. Airways <www.usair.com> *demanded a 5-percent cut in pay and benefits, members of the Association of Flight Attendants* <www.flightattendants-afa.org> *resorted to CHAOS and won an 11-percent pay hike.*

- In some cases, arbitration is legally required to settle bargaining disputes. **Compulsory arbitration** is used to settle disputes between the government and public employees such as firefighters and police officers.

voluntary arbitration
Method of resolving a labor dispute in which both parties agree to submit to the judgment of a neutral party

Administering a Labor Agreement

Once a labor agreement has been reached, its details are written into the form of a contract legally enforceable in the courts. Labor contracts almost always have precise agreements as to how the agreement will be enforced. In some cases, of course, enforcement is quite clear. If the two sides agree that the company will increase wages by 2 percent per year over the next three years according to a prescribed schedule, then there is little opportunity for disagreement: Wage increases can be mathematically calculated and union members will see the effects in their paychecks. But other provisions may be much more prone to misinterpretation and different perceptions.

compulsory arbitration
Method of resolving a labor dispute in which both parties are legally required to accept the judgment of a neutral party

Suppose, for example, that a labor contract specifies the process for allocating overtime assignments. Such strategies are often complex, and the employer may have to take into account a variety of factors, such as seniority, previous overtime allocations, the hours or days in which the overtime work is needed, and so forth. Now suppose that a

WebConnection

www.adr.org

If selection of an arbitrator by mutual agreement fails, most union and management negotiators turn to one of two sources: the Federal Mediation and Conciliation Service (FMCS) or the American Arbitration Service (AAA). Founded in 1926, the AAA is a private, not-for-profit organization that arbitrates a wide variety of disputes. Typically, the AAA offers a list of potential arbitrators from which the two parties will make a mutually acceptable choice. To learn more about the AAA, its principles, and its services, go to its Web site.

factory supervisor is trying to follow the labor contract and offers overtime to a certain employee. This employee, however, indicates that before accepting, it may be necessary to check with the individual's spouse or partner to learn more about other obligations and commitments. The supervisor, however, may feel the pressure of a deadline and award the overtime opportunity to someone else. If the first employee objects to this course of action, the individual may file a complaint with the union.

When such differences of opinions arise, the union member takes the complaint to the shop steward. The shop steward may advise the employee that the supervisor handled things properly, but there are other appeal mechanisms, and the employee, even if refuted by the shop steward, still has channels for appeal.

Of course, if the shop steward agrees with the employee, the shop steward may follow prescribed methods for pursuing the complaint. The prescribed methods might include talking with the supervisor to get the other side of the story and then provide for lines of appeal on up the hierarchy of both the union and the company. In some cases, mediation or arbitration may be called into play, as may other efforts to resolve the dispute. The overtime, for example, may be reassigned to the employee to whom it was first offered. Or the overtime may remain with the second employee while the first employee is also paid.

Let's return for a moment to the agreement reached by the Teamsters and United Parcel Service that we described earlier. In early 2000, the union became concerned that UPS was not moving quickly enough to create the new jobs to which it had agreed two years earlier. The union submitted its complaint to arbitration and won. UPS was given a specific timetable for adding the new jobs as agreed.[10]

Continued from page 269

Membership Is Job #1

To AFL-CIO President John J. Sweeney, every union win in Las Vegas is a win for the union movement throughout the country. With Las Vegas as a model, Sweeney has focused union activities on recruiting new members instead of defending the jobs, pay, and benefits of current members. His chief targets are the women and minorities who comprise the majority of the country's low-wage service workers.

With the union movement still hemorrhaging members (AFL-CIO membership dropped by 100,000 in 1996 alone), how will Sweeney turn things around? He'll start by increasing the money spent on recruitment, which has languished for decades at a mere 3 percent of unions' annual budgets. The strategy seems promising: In a period during which the United Farm Workers **<www.ufw.org>** earmarked 40 percent of its resources for recruiting, it won 13 straight certification elections. Likewise, once the Teamsters had begun to recruit more aggressively, they were able to unionize such long-elusive targets as the Overnite Transportation Company **<www.overnite.com>**. With the annual income of unions estimated to be about $5 billion, unions could dramatically shift the employer–employee power relationship by spending approximately one-third of that sum—$1.65 billion—on recruitment. Currently, they spend only about $200 million a year on membership drives.

To free resources for organizing, union leaders are also cleaning house. Like big business, they are restructuring and insisting on layoffs, when necessary, and performance standards for staff workers. "We have a product to deliver," says Douglas J. McCarron, president of the United Brotherhood of Carpenters <www.necarpenters.org/UBC.htm>, "and we have to do it more efficiently. Who says you're entitled to a lifetime job just because you work at a union?" At UNITE, the needle-trades union, 25 percent of the staff was let go as 20 percent more money was channeled into recruitment. Receiving the first pink slips were those with no recruiting skills.

"We have a product to deliver, and we have to do it more efficiently. Who says you're entitled to a lifetime job just because you work at a union?"

—Douglas J. McCarron, President of the United Brotherhood of Carpenters

Questions for Discussion

1. Why is Las Vegas such an important battleground for the union movement?
2. Why do low-paid service workers provide a promising opportunity for the expansion of the movement?
3. How has the change in leadership at the top of the AFL-CIO refocused the union movement? Do you agree with John J. Sweeney that it is smarter to focus the union movement on recruiting new members than on defending the jobs, pay, and benefits of current members?
4. In what ways might a shift from a nonunion to a union company affect staffing, promotion, training, compensation, and benefits decisions?
5. Why do you think that "card signing" has been more successful in unionizing companies than NLRB elections?
6. In what ways are unions like any other business organization in terms of human resources and labor relations?

SUMMARY OF LEARNING OBJECTIVES

1 **Explain why workers unionize.** The Industrial Revolution and the emergence of a factory-based production system made many workers dependent on continuing factory employment. The treatment of labor as a raw material led to such abuses as minimal pay, long workdays and weeks, unsafe working conditions, and even child labor. Individuals had little recourse in rectifying problems. By organizing into labor unions, however, workers are able to act collectively to improve work conditions. Most importantly, acting as a group, they can engage in *collective bargaining* for higher wages, greater benefits, or better working conditions.

2 **Trace the evolution and discuss recent trends in *unionism* in the United States.** The earliest unions in the United States were local *craft unions* of specialized workers. Important early national unions included the *National Trades Union*, the *Knights of Labor*, the *American Federation of Labor (AFL)*, and the *Congress of Industrial Organizations (CIO)*, the first U.S. *industrial union*. The last two merged in 1955 to form the *AFL-CIO*. Although their membership has slipped in recent years, unions remain an important force in U.S. business and political life and have gained better pay and working conditions for all workers, unionized and nonunionized.

Since the mid-1950s, labor unions in the United States have experienced increasing difficulties in attracting new members. Indeed, while millions of U.S. workers still belong to labor unions, union membership as a percentage of the total workforce has continued to decline at a very steady rate. Increasingly, unions recognize that they don't have as much power as they once held and that it is in their own best interests, as well as the best interests of the workers that they represent, to work with management instead of against it. Bargaining perspectives have also altered in recent years.

3 **Describe the *major laws governing labor-management relations*.** Several significant laws affect labor-management relations. The *Norris-LaGuardia Act* and the *National Labor Relations (Wagner) Act* limited the ability of employers to keep unions out of the workplace. The *Fair Labor Standards*

Act established a minimum wage and outlawed child labor. But the *Taft-Hartley Act* and the *Landrum-Griffin Act* limited the power of unions and provided for the settlement of strikes in key industries. Other important laws include the Postal Reorganization Act of 1970, the Federal Service Labor-Management Relations Statute, the Civil Rights Act of 1964, and the Plant-Closing Notification Act.

4 **Describe the union *certification* and *decertification processes.*** Successful unionization requires first of all an interest among workers in forming a union. Those interested in forming the union begin by defining the *bargaining unit.* Organizers must then get 30 percent of the eligible workers in the bargaining unit to sign authorization cards requesting a *union certification election.* The *National Labor Relations Board* then sends representatives to the organization and holds a secret ballot election. If a majority of those voting approve the union certification, the union becomes the official bargaining agent of eligible employees. To decertify a union, 30 percent of eligible employees must sign decertification authorization cards. The NLRB will then conduct a *decertification election.* For the union to be decertified, a majority of those voting must favor the decertification.

5 **Identify the steps in the *collective bargaining process.*** Once certified, the union engages in collective bargaining with the organization. The initial step in collective bargaining is reaching agreement on a *labor contract.* Contract demands usually involve wages, job security, or management rights.

Both labor and management have several tactics that can be used against the other if negotiations break down. Unions may attempt a *strike* or a *boycott* of the firm or may engage in a *slowdown.* Companies may hire replacement workers (*strikebreakers*) or *lock out* all workers. In extreme cases, mediation or arbitration may be used to settle disputes. Once a contract has been agreed on, union and management representatives continue to interact to settle worker *grievances* and interpret the contract.

QUESTIONS AND EXERCISES

Questions for Review

1. Why do workers in some companies unionize whereas workers in others do not?
2. Why did the AFL succeed whereas the Knights of Labor failed?
3. Compare the effects of the Norris-LaGuardia and Wagner Acts with the effects of the Taft-Hartley and Landrum-Griffin Acts. What circumstances of the times led to the passage of such different laws?
4. What steps must be taken to certify a union?
5. What circumstances might cause union membership to rise again in the future?

Questions for Analysis

6. Workers at Ford, GM, and Chrysler are represented by the United Auto Workers (UAW). However, the UAW has been unsuccessful in its attempts to unionize U.S. workers employed at Toyota, Nissan, and Honda plants in the United States. Why do you think this is so?
7. Suppose you are a manager in a nonunionized company. You have just found out that some of your workers are talking about forming a union. What would you do?
8. Do you think unions serve a useful purpose today? Under what circumstances would you be willing to join a union?

Application Exercises

9. Interview the managers of two local companies, one unionized and one nonunionized. Compare the wage and salary levels, benefits, and working conditions of employees at the two firms.
10. With your instructor playing the role of a manager and a student playing the role of a union organizer, role-play the processes involved in attempting to form a union.

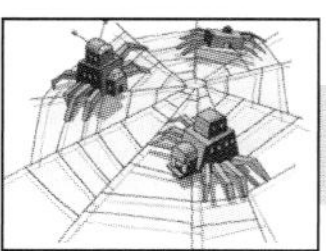

EXPLORING THE WEB

WORK SITES

Both the AFL-CIO and the NLRB maintain Web sites to help explain what they do, how, and why. Visit these Web sites at the following addresses and then consider the questions below:

www.aflcio.org
www.nlrb.gov

1. What specific information can you find on each site that might be of benefit to you as a manager?
2. What specific information can you find on each site that might be of benefit to you as an individual worker interested in forming a union?
3. What improvements might you suggest to make each Web site more effective in communicating to its intended audience?

BUILDING YOUR BUSINESS SKILLS

A LITTLE COLLECTIVE BRAINSTORMING

This exercise enhances the following SCANS workplace competencies: demonstrating basic skills, demonstrating thinking skills, exhibiting interpersonal skills, and working with information.

GOAL

To encourage students to understand why some companies unionize and others do not.

SITUATION

You've been working for the same nonunion company for five years. Although there are problems in the company, you like your job and have confidence in your ability to get ahead. Recently, you've heard rumblings that a large group of workers want to call for a union election. You're not sure how you feel about this because none of your friends or family are union members.

METHOD

Step 1

Come together with three other "coworkers" who have the same questions as you do. Each person should target four companies to learn their union status. Avoid small businesses—choose large corporations such as General Motors, Intel, and Sears. As you investigate, answer the following questions:

- Is the company unionized?
- Is every worker in the company unionized or just selected groups of workers? Describe the groups.
- If a company is unionized, what is the union's history in that company?
- If a company is unionized, what are the main labor–management issues?
- If a company is unionized, how would you describe the current status of labor–management relations? For example, is it cordial or strained?
- If a company is not unionized, what factors are responsible for its nonunion status?

To learn the answers to these questions, contact the company, read corporate annual reports, search the company's Web site, contact union representatives, or do research on a computerized database.

Step 2

Go to the Web site of the AFL-CIO <www.aflcio.org/> to learn more about the current status of the union movement. Then, with your coworkers, write a short report about the advantages of union membership.

Step 3

Research the disadvantages of unionization. A key issue to address is whether unions make it harder for companies to compete in the global marketplace.

FOLLOW-UP QUESTIONS

1. Based on everything you learned, are you sympathetic to the union movement? Would you want to be a union member?
2. Are the union members you spoke with satisfied or dissatisfied with their union's efforts to achieve better working conditions, higher wages, and improved benefits?
3. What is the union's role when layoffs occur?
4. Based on what you learned, do you think the union movement will stumble or thrive in the years ahead?

CRAFTING YOUR BUSINESS PLAN

TAKING THE OCCASION TO DEAL WITH LABOR

THE PURPOSE OF THE ASSIGNMENT

1. To acquaint you with the process of navigating the *Business PlanPro* (*BPP*) software package (Version 4.0).
2. To familiarize students with the labor and management relations issues faced by a start-up as it develops its business plan.
3. To stimulate students' thinking about the application of textbook information on labor and management relations to the preparation of a *BPP* business plan.

ASSIGNMENT

After reading Chapter 10 in the textbook, open the BPP *software* and look around for information about labor and management relations as it applies to a sample firm:* Occasions *(Occasions, The Events Planning Specialists). Then respond to the following questions:*

1. Explore the business plan for this company, paying special attention to its product line and the types of clients that will be buying its products. Do you suspect that there will be union members among the employees of some Occasions customers? [Sites to see in *BPP* (for this assignment): In the Plan Outline screen, click on each of **1.0 Executive Summary, 1.1 Objectives,** and **1.2 Mission.** After returning to the Plan Outline screen, examine each of the following: **Table: Startup** (located beneath **2.2 Startup Summary**), **3.3 Sourcing, 3.4 Future Products, 6.2 Management Team,** and **6.5 Other Management Considerations.**]
2. Considering Occasions's growth projections, do you foresee increasing likelihood for unionization of its employees? Why or why not? What should Occasions do to accommodate clients' unions? [Sites to see in *BPP:* In the Plan Outline screen, click on **1.1 Objectives.** Also look at each of **2.0 Company Summary** and **6.1 Organization Structure.**]
3. Explain why some experience with labor laws and management–union contract issues would be valuable for Occasions's salespeople in their dealings with clients. [Sites to see in *BPP:* In the Plan Outline screen, click on each of **1.0 Executive Summary, 3.0 Products,** and **3.3 Sourcing.** After returning to the Plan Outline screen, click on each of **4.2 Industry Analysis** and **4.2.1 Industry Participants.** After returning once again to the Plan Outline screen, click on **1.3 Keys to Success.** Finally, look at each of **4.1 Market Segmentation** and **4.3 Industry Analysis.**]
4. Judging from their business plan, what effect do you anticipate the planned geographic dispersion will have on management–labor relations in Occasions? [Sites to see in *BPP:* In the Plan Outline screen, click on **1.1 Objectives.** Also look at each of **2.0 Company Summary** and **6.1 Organization Structure.**]

FOR YOUR OWN BUSINESS PLAN

5. Analyzing your own plan, identify your thoughts regarding management–labor relations. What specific goals do you visualize? Do you want your employees to unionize? Identify the main elements in your plans and indicate where to present them in your planning document.

*GENERAL TIPS FOR NAVIGATING IN *BPP*

1. Open the *BPP* program, examine the Welcome screen, and click on **Open a Sample Plan.**
2. From the **Open a Sample Plan** dialogue box, click on a sample company name; then click on **Open.**
3. On the Plan Manager screen, click on **Your Plan Outline**; then click on any of the lines (for example, **6.0 Management Summary**).
4. You can always return to the Plan Outline screen by going to the bottom of the screen and clicking on the **Plan Outline** icon.
5. After finishing with one sample company, you can get to the next one by going to the top of the screen and clicking on **File** (on the menu bar). Then beneath that, select **Open Sample Plan.** This will exit you from the current company file and take you to the **Open Sample Plan** dialogue box, where you can select your next sample company.
6. When you are finished, you can close the program by going to the top of the screen and clicking on **File** (on the bar menu). Then beneath that, select Exit.

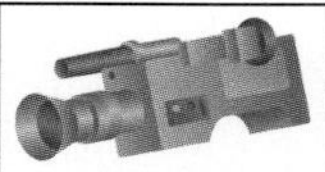

VIDEO EXERCISE

WORKING OUT A PACKAGE: UPS AND THE TEAMSTERS

Learning Objectives

The purpose of this video exercise is to help you

1. Recognize the kinds of issues that can divide management and labor.
2. Understand the trade-offs a labor strike demands from both labor and management.
3. Assess the future of the labor movement.

BACKGROUND INFORMATION

United Parcel Service (UPS), the largest package carrier in the world, is now over 90 years old. Headquartered in Atlanta, Georgia, the company earned revenues over $27 billion in 1999 and delivers over 15 million packages a day to 200 countries around the world. It employs 344,000 people, of whom 308,000 work in the United States.

In 1997, its U.S. workers went on strike, seeking to upgrade many of the company's part-time jobs to full-time status. (At that time, 60 percent of UPS workers were considered part time.) Despite the resulting interruption of delivery service, public opinion sided with the strikers. The settlement brought higher wages and several thousand new full-time jobs, raising speculation that the U.S. labor movement, in decline for several years, might witness a nationwide renewal.

In 1999, UPS sold 10 percent of its stock on the New York Stock Exchange, the second-largest initial public offering (IPO) in U.S. history.

THE VIDEO

This segment is a news analysis conducted during the final days of the strike, when a settlement was anticipated at any moment. Some of the issues behind the strike are discussed, and the demands of both management and labor are identified.

DISCUSSION QUESTIONS

1. What were the main issues that divided management and labor in the UPS strike? How are they typical of labor–management conflicts?
2. One of the striking workers comments that the small percentage of colleagues who crossed picket lines during the strike had destroyed the unity of the strikers. How important do you think worker unity is to labor leaders? What does it mean to management?
3. Do you think this kind of settlement, in which labor appears to have won most of what it wanted, can help bring unions back to their former level of influence? Why or why not? How much influence do you think unions should have in management decisions?

FOLLOW-UP ASSIGNMENT

Investigate another recent strike and assess the demands of both parties, the steps taken to avert (or provoke) a strike, and the eventual or probable result for both sides. Do you think this strike lends credence to the idea that the UPS settlement helped swing the balance of labor–management power in labor's direction? Why or why not?

FOR FURTHER EXPLORATION

Visit the UPS Web site at <www.ups.com> and look at the "Workforce/Labor Issues" page in the UPS Facts section. How does the company present the current state of its labor–management relations?

C h a p t e r

11

Understanding Marketing Processes and Consumer Behavior

After reading this chapter, you should be able to:

1. **Define** *marketing.*

2. **Describe** the five forces that constitute the *external marketing environment.*

3. **Explain** market *segmentation* and show how it is used in *target marketing.*

4. **Explain** the purpose and value of *marketing research.*

5. **Describe** the key factors that influence the *consumer buying process.*

6. **Discuss** the three categories of *organizational markets* and explain how *organizational buying behavior* differs from consumer buying behavior.

Baggy Brands and Deep Pockets

Adults don't know how to pronounce "JNCO" jeans, and, more importantly, they have no idea why teenagers like to wear them. With billowing 40-inch bottoms and cavernous 17-inch-deep pockets, JNCO has made wide legs fashionable, albeit no easier to wear. Ever try climbing stairs with pants that wide? And what about the dirt and chewing gum that collect at the cuff? Most adults won't even think about walking in the rain.

Nevertheless, JNCO was recently rated the sixth "coolest brand" by boys aged 12 to 15, right behind Tommy Hilfiger and Adidas. Strength in this market translates into millions of consumer dollars. According to *Tactical Retail Monitor,* a New York–based market report, the market for wide-leg jeans has recently grown five times as fast as the entire men's-jean category. That's why Revatex, the Los Angeles firm that manufactures JNCO <www.jnco.com>, pays serious attention to marketing research that tells them what teenagers want and how they are likely to spend their consumer dollars.

Conscious of the independent, rebellious spirit of their target audience, Revatex marketers take a stealth approach to cultivating JNCO's cool image. No billboards or GAP-type ads in popular magazines. Instead, Revatex supplies free clothes to trendsetting DJs and band members who play the all-night techno-dance parties known as "raves." They advertise in such magazines as *Electric Ink* and *Thrasher,* which target skateboarders and extreme rollerbladers. Recording artist J-Smooth will be wearing JNCO brand clothes in targeted ads in *Spin, Vibe, Blaze,* and *Urb.*

With wholesale revenues somewhere between $100 million and $200 million, Revatex is hitting Levi Strauss and other mainstream less-than-cool jeans makers where it hurts—in the wallet. Nicholas Lynch, who owns 11 pairs of JNCOs, says you'll never find a pair of Levi's in his closet: "Levi's came out with wide jeans," he admits, "but it just isn't the same because of who wears them." Translation: Baby boomers (also known as losers) wear Levi's, but those on the cutting edge wear JNCOs.

Finding and defining the cutting edge in teen taste is the work of marketing researchers who specialize in the teen market. Companies pay a high price for this research to attract a share of the roughly $4 billion that teens spend every year on clothes, cosmetics, CDs, and other personal and fashion items. According to Teen-Age Research Unlimited <www.teenresearch.com>, one of the most respected marketing research firms in the segment, figuring out teen buying behavior means identifying and targeting the teen decision makers known as "influencers." A dream-come-true category for marketers, influencers spend money on fashion trends before they are popular and then influence "conformers" to follow suit. Conformers, explains one researcher, "make up the bulk of the teenage population. They're looking for brands and badges to . . . get them to the next level."

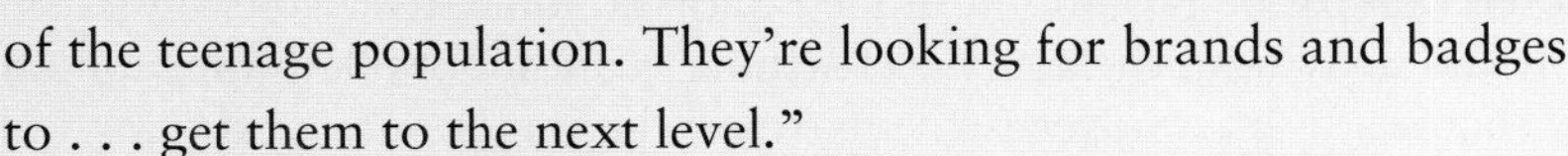

With 30 million teenagers currently living in the United States and 35 million projected in 2010, the importance of the teen market is self-evident. What may not be so obvious is the fact that this group has more money in its pocket and more control over spending than any teen generation before it. With both parents working and their spending habits learned at the knees of self-gratifying baby-boomer parents, teens are worth studying.

"Levi's came out with wide jeans, but it just isn't the same because of who wears them."

—Nicholas Lynch, JNCO wearer

Our opening story continues on page 318

Identifying a market segment and targeting messages to its members are among the crucial marketing activities that you will learn about in this chapter. As you will see, business success depends on these activities in what has increasingly become a market-oriented environment. By focusing on the learning objectives of this chapter, you will gain a better understanding of marketing activities and the ways in which marketing influences consumer purchases.

WHAT IS MARKETING?

What comes to mind when you think of *marketing?* Most people usually think of advertising for products such as detergent or soft drinks, but marketing encompasses a much wider range of activities. The American Marketing Association <www.ama.org> has formally defined **marketing** as "the process of planning and executing the conception, pricing, promotion, and distribution of ideas, goods, and services to create exchanges that satisfy individual and organizational goals."[1] In this section, we discuss the multifaceted activity of marketing by exploring this definition. We then explore the marketing environment and the development of marketing strategy. We focus on the four activities—developing, pricing, promoting, and placing products—that comprise the *marketing mix.*

marketing
The process of planning and executing the conception, pricing, promotion, and distribution of ideas, goods, and services to create exchanges that satisfy individual and organizational objectives

Marketing: Goods, Services, and Ideas

The marketing of tangible goods is obvious in everyday life. You walk into a department store and a woman with a clipboard asks if you would like to try a new cologne. A pharmaceutical company proclaims the virtues of its new cold medicine. Your local auto dealer offers an economy car at an economy price. These products—the cologne, the cold medicine, and the car—are all **consumer goods:** products that you, the consumer, may buy for personal use. Firms that sell products to consumers for personal consumption are engaged in *consumer marketing.*

consumer goods
Products purchased by consumers for personal use

Marketing also applies to **industrial goods:** products used by companies to produce other products. Conveyors, surgical instruments, and earthmovers are industrial goods, as are components and raw materials such as transistors, integrated circuits, coal, steel, and unformed plastic. Firms that sell their products to other manufacturers are engaged in *industrial marketing.*

industrial goods
Products purchased by companies to produce other products

Marketing techniques can also be applied to **services:** intangible products such as time, expertise, or an activity that can be purchased. *Service marketing* has become a major area of growth in the United States. Insurance companies, airlines, investment counselors, health clinics, and public accountants all engage in service marketing, either to individuals or to other companies.

services
Intangible products, such as time, expertise, or an activity, that can be purchased

Marketing is relevant to the promotion of ideas. For example, television advertising and other promotional activities proclaim that teaching is an honorable profession and that teachers are "heroes." Other advertisements stress the importance of driving only when sober and the advantages of not smoking.

Relationship Marketing Although marketing often focuses on single transactions for products, services, or ideas, a longer-term perspective has become equally important for successful marketing. Rather than emphasizing a single transaction, **relationship marketing** emphasizes lasting relationships with customers and suppliers. Stronger relationships—including stronger economic and social ties—can result in greater long-term satisfaction and retention of customers.[2]

relationship marketing
Marketing strategy that emphasizes lasting relationships with customers and suppliers

Commercial banks, for example, feature "loyalty banking" programs that offer *economic* incentives to encourage longer-lasting relationships. Customers who purchase more of the bank's products (for example, checking accounts, savings accounts, and loans) accumulate credits toward free or reduced-price services, such as free travelers checks or lower interest rates. Harley-Davidson <www.harley-davidson.com> offers social incentives

WebConnection

www.harleydavidsonofdallas.com

The 500,000-member Harley Owners Group (H.O.G.) is a club of Harley-Davidson motorcycle enthusiasts. You can examine the latest Harley models and related merchandise, check out upcoming motorcycle events, and, of course, join H.O.G. at the consumer group's Web site.

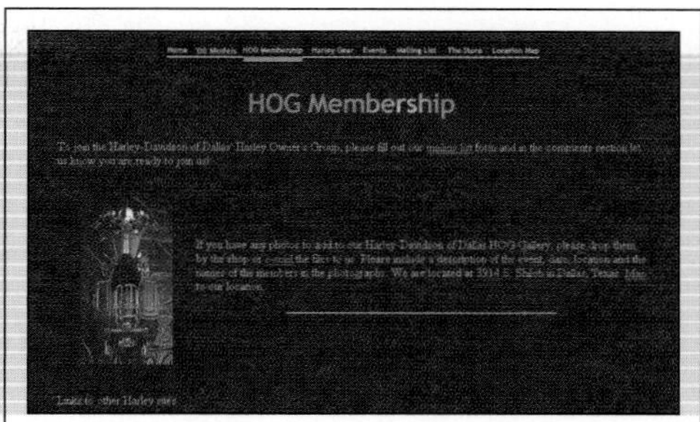

through the Harley Owners Group (H.O.G.)—the largest motorcycle club in the world, with 500,000 members and approximately 900 dealer-sponsored chapters worldwide. H.O.G., explain Harley marketers, "is dedicated to building customers for life. H.O.G. fosters long-term commitments to the sport of motorcycling by providing opportunities for our customers to bond with other riders and develop long-term friendships."

The Marketing Environment

Marketing plans, decisions, and strategies are not determined unilaterally by any business, not even by marketers as experienced and influential as Coca-Cola <www.coke.com> and Procter & Gamble <www.pg.com>. Rather, they are strongly influenced by powerful outside forces. As you can see in Figure 11.1, any marketing program must recognize the outside factors that comprise a company's **external environment.** In this section, we describe five of these environmental factors: the *political-legal, social-cultural, technological, economic,* and *competitive environments.*

external environment Outside factors that influence marketing programs by posing opportunities or threats

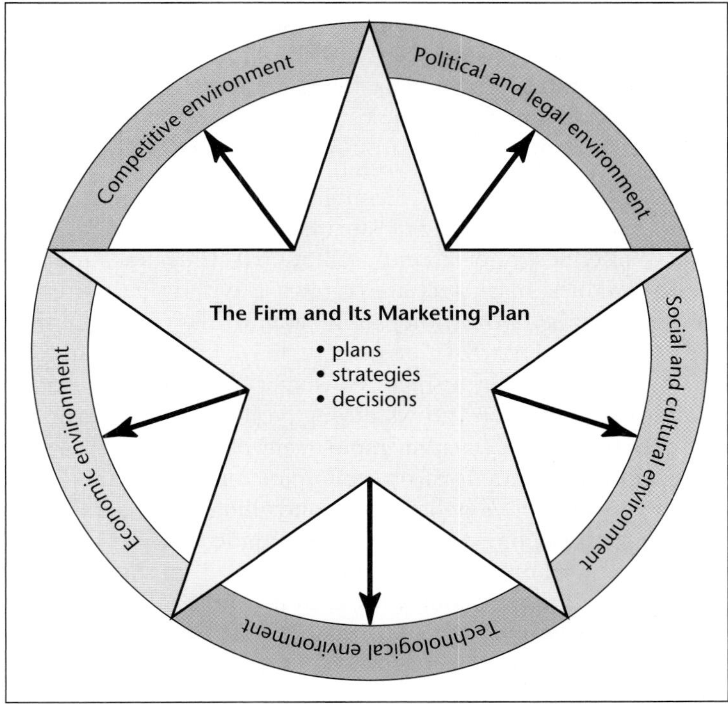

Figure 11.1 The External Marketing Environment

Political and Legal Environment Political activities, both foreign and domestic, have profound effects on business. For example, congressional hearings on tobacco, budgetary decisions on national defense expenditures, and enactment of the Clean Air Act have substantially determined the destinies of entire industries. e-commerce activities are changing because of expected increases of federal and state taxes for sales on the Internet.

To help shape their companies' futures, marketing managers try to maintain favorable political-legal environments in several ways. For example, to gain public support for their products and activities, marketing uses advertising campaigns for public awareness on issues of local, regional, or national import. They also contribute to political candidates (although there are legal restrictions on how much they can contribute). Frequently, they support the activities of political action committees (PACs) maintained by their respective industries. Such activities sometimes result in favorable laws and regulations and may even open up new international business opportunities.

Social and Cultural Environment More people are working in home offices, the number of single-parent families is increasing, food preferences and physical activities reflect the growing concern for healthful lifestyles, violent crimes are on the decrease, and the growing recognition of cultural diversity continues. These and other issues reflect the values, beliefs, and ideas that form the fabric of U.S. society today.

The need to recognize social values stimulates marketers to take fresh looks at the ways they conduct their business, by developing and promoting new products for both consumers and industrial customers. For example, there are now more than 8 million female golfers spending nearly $250 million on equipment, most of which, in earlier years, had been modeled after men's gear. Responding to the growth in the number of female golfers, Spalding <www.spalding.com> has introduced a line of golf gear designed specifically for women. Marketing such equipment has entailed new methods for advertising, promoting, and distributing products to meet the emerging preferences of women golfers.

Technological Environment New technologies affect marketing in several ways. They create new goods (the satellite dish) and services (home television shopping). New products make some existing products obsolete (compact discs are replacing audiotapes), and many of them change our values and lifestyles. In turn, they often stimulate new goods and services not directly related to the new technology itself. Cellular phones, for example, not only facilitate business communication but free up time for recreation and leisure. New communications technologies, which we discuss in Chapter 17, have blazed entirely new paths for marketers to travel. Internet accessibility, for example, provides a new medium for selling, buying, and even distributing products from your own home to customers around the world.

How will information technology change the marketing environment in the future?

Economic Environment Economic conditions determine spending patterns by consumers, businesses, and governments. They thus influence every marketer's plans for product offerings, pricing, and promotional strategies. Among the more significant economic variables, marketers are concerned with inflation, interest rates, recession, and recovery. In other words, they must monitor the general business cycle, which typically features a pattern of transition from periods of prosperity to recession to recovery (return to prosperity). Not surprisingly, consumer spending increases as "consumer confidence" in economic conditions grows during periods of prosperity. Spending decreases during low-growth periods, when unemployment rises and purchasing power declines.

Traditionally, analysis of economic conditions focused on the national economy and the government's policies for controlling or moderating it. Increasingly, however, as nations form more and more economic connections, the "global economy" is becoming more prominent in the thinking of marketers everywhere.[3] At Wal-Mart <www.walmartstores.com>, for example, about 11 percent of sales revenues come from its international division. At the same time, however, although overall international sales were up 51 percent for 1999, sales in Latin America stalled. Why? Because economic conditions in such markets as Argentina, Brazil, and Mexico are entirely dif-

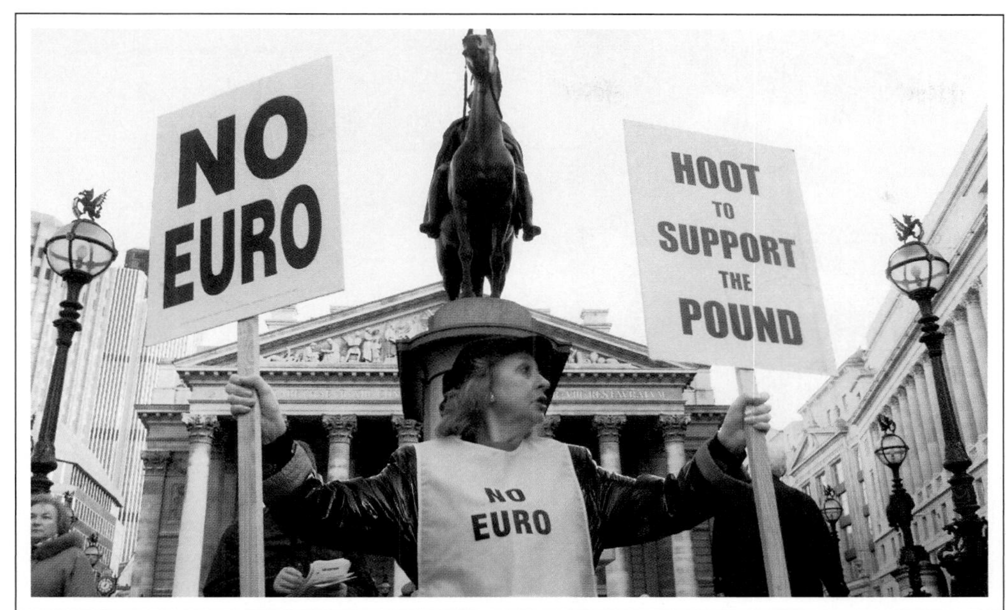

The euro, *the common currency of the European Union, has certain advantages for member-nation companies doing international business. It eliminates* exchange-rate risk—*the risk that changes in exchange rates might adversely affect a firm conducting international transactions. The exchange rate is an economic variable. Thus multinationals and banks in England—a non-euro nation—want to adopt the euro. Protestors like this one fear that in order to keep the British economy in line with those of other members, the government would have to enact labor and other regulations like those that are common in other EU countries.*

ferent than in European and Asian countries. Certainly, marketers must now consider a variety of unpredictable economic variables in developing both domestic and foreign marketing strategies.[4]

Competitive Environment In a competitive environment, marketers must convince buyers that they should purchase their products rather than those of some other seller. Because both consumers and commercial buyers have limited resources, every dollar spent on one product is no longer available for other purchases. Each marketing program, therefore, seeks to make its product the most attractive. Theoretically, a failed program loses the buyer's dollar forever (or at least until it is time for the next purchase decision).

By studying the competition, marketers determine how best to position their own products for three specific types of competition:

- **Substitute products** are dissimilar from those of competitors but can fulfill the same need. For example, your cholesterol level may be controlled with either a physical fitness program or a drug regimen. The fitness program and the drugs compete as substitute products.
- **Brand competition** occurs between similar products, such as the auditing services provided by the large accounting firms of Ernst & Young <www.ey.com> and KPMG Peat Marwick <www.kpmg.com>. The competition is based on buyers' perceptions of the benefits of products offered by particular companies.
- **International competition** matches the products of domestic marketers against those of foreign competitors—a flight on Swissair <www.swissair.com> versus Delta Airlines <www.delta-air.com>. The intensity of international competition has of course been heightened by the formation of alliances such as the European Community and NAFTA.

substitute product
Product that is dissimilar to those of competitors but that can fulfill the same need

brand competition
Competitive marketing that appeals to consumer perceptions of similar products

international competition
Competitive marketing of domestic products against foreign products

Planning and Executing Marketing Strategy

As a business activity, marketing requires management. Although many individuals contribute to the marketing of a product, a company's **marketing managers** are typically responsible for planning and implementing all the marketing activities that result in the transfer of goods or services to its customers. These activities culminate in the **marketing plan:** a detailed and focused strategy for gearing the marketing efforts to meet consumer

marketing manager
Manager who plans and implements the marketing activities that result in the transfer of products from producer to consumer

marketing plan
Detailed and focused strategy for gearing marketing efforts to meet consumer needs and wants

Mobile phone penetration in Finland is 60 percent, compared with only 28 percent in the United States. Why the big difference? For one thing, Finland is home to Nokia, marketer of the world's most successful brand of cellular phone, with a 27-percent global market share. Nokia <www.nokiausa.com> *created Europe's first digital phone network in 1982 and is now focusing on the technology to provide cell phones with affordable Web content. Internet penetration in Finland is also greater than in the United States—24.5 percent to 20.3 percent.*

needs and wants. Therefore, marketing actually begins when a company identifies a consumer need and develops a product to meet it. One way of identifying those needs—market research—is explored later in this chapter. Here, however, we will begin by noting two important aspects of the larger marketing process: developing the marketing plan and setting marketing goals.

First, marketing managers must realize that planning takes time. Indeed, the planning process may begin years before a product becomes available for sale. Next, marketing managers must set goals and then establish ways to evaluate performance. In 1994, for instance, Barnes & Noble (B&N) <www.barnesandnoble.com>, the world's largest bookseller, had 112 superstores and planned to open a stream of additional outlets. By 1999 it had grown to 520 superstores displaying up to 175,000 titles in an atmosphere especially conducive to browsing. It takes about four years for a new superstore to become as productive as older stores, and the performance of individual store managers is evaluated against sales goals set on a store-by-store basis. At the same time, B&N was planning to expand into a new distribution channel: online book retailing with a global reach. Finally, in 1997 B&N not only launched its own online business but also became the exclusive bookseller in America Online's (AOL) Marketplace. B&N's planning efforts are paying off: The company can now display, sell, and distribute more than 750,000 titles, and as of March 2000, more than 2.9 million customers in 215 countries had purchased books and music from B&N's online store.[5]

The Marketing Mix

In planning and implementing strategies, marketing managers rely on four basic components. These elements, often called the "Four P's" of marketing, constitute the **marketing mix.** In this section, we describe each of the following activities:

marketing mix
The combination of product, pricing, promotion, and distribution strategies used to market products

- Product
- Pricing
- Promotion
- Place

product
Good, service, or idea that is marketed to fill consumer needs and wants

Product Marketing begins with a **product**—a good, a service, or an idea designed to fill a consumer need. Conceiving and developing new products is a constant challenge for marketers, who must always consider the factor of change. Marketers, for example, must consider changing technology, changing consumer wants and needs, and changing economic conditions.

Meeting consumer needs, then, often means changing existing products. Consider the current debate about the wisdom of replacing current PCs with an entirely new product. Advocates of the existing PC include "establishment" PC firms such as Intel Corp. <www.intel.com>, Microsoft <www.microsoft.com>, and, of course, PC makers. Working toward a different concept for PCs is Sun Microsystems, Inc. <www.sun.com>, which proposes a simpler, less expensive desktop unit more intimately connected to the Internet. With Sun's unit, computer users would not buy expensive operating systems and other software; nor would your computer need the powerful computing capacity that it needs today. Instead, when it needs software or added capacity, the unit would "borrow" them instantaneously from powerful networked servers accessed over the Internet.[6]

product differentiation Creation of a product or product image that differs enough from existing products to attract consumers

Product Differentiation Often producers promote particular features or characteristics of their products for the sake of distinguishing them on the marketplace. **Product differentiation** is the creation of a product feature or product image that differs enough from competing products to attract consumers. For example, Volvo automobiles <www.volvo.com> provide newer, better safety features to set them apart from competitors. Services can also be differentiated. Customers of E*Trade™, <www.etrade.com> the online investment service, gain value from after-hours trading that is unavailable from conventional investment-service firms. People differentiation, too, can provide value to customers: Southwest Airlines <www.southwest.com> employees are known for their sense of humor, friendliness, and company spirit. Says CEO Herb Kelleher, who often touts the importance of Southwest's people: "We like mavericks—people who have a sense of humor. We've always done it differently."[7]

> ***"We like mavericks—people who have a sense of humor. We've always done it differently."***
>
> *—Herb Kelleher, CEO, Southwest Airlines*

Combinations of physical goods and services can also be sources of differentiation. For example, Weyerhaeuser Co. <www.weyerhaeuser.com> developed a computer system that allows customers at retail home centers and lumberyards to custom-design decks and shelving. As a result, the company has differentiated its commodity two-by-fours by turning them into premium products.

Pricing

Pricing a product—selecting the most appropriate price at which to sell it—is often a balancing act. On the one hand, prices must support a variety of costs—the organization's operating, administrative, and research costs as well as marketing costs such as advertising and sales salaries. On the other hand, prices cannot be so high that consumers turn to competitors. Successful pricing means finding a profitable middle ground between these two requirements. An appliance retailer, for instance, sells refrigerators and washing machines at prices that are both profitable and attractive to customers. The same products, however, are priced lower when customers buy sets of kitchen or laundry appliances to furnish new homes. The retailers' lower transaction costs enable them to reduce their selling prices.

Whereas some firms succeed by offering lower prices than competitors, others price successfully on the high side. Both low- and high-price strategies can be effective in different situations. Low prices, for example, generally lead to larger sales volumes. High prices usually limit market size but increase profits per unit. High prices may also attract customers by implying that a product is of especially high quality. We discuss pricing in more detail in Chapter 12.

Promotion

The most highly visible component of the marketing mix is no doubt promotion, which refers to techniques for communicating information about products. We describe promotional activities more fully in Chapter 13. Here we briefly describe the most important promotional tools.

Advertising Advertising is any form of paid nonpersonal communication used by an identified sponsor to persuade or inform potential buyers about a product. For example, The

MonyGroup <www.mony.com>, a financial adviser that provides investment and securities products, reaches its customer audience by advertising its services in *Fortune* magazine.

Personal Selling Many products (for example, insurance, clothing, and real estate) are best promoted through personal selling, or person-to-person sales. Industrial goods receive the bulk of personal selling. When companies buy from other companies, purchasing agents and others who need technical and detailed information are usually referred to the selling company's sales representatives.

Sales Promotions Relatively inexpensive items are often marketed through sales promotions, which involve one-time direct inducements to buyers. Premiums (usually free gifts), coupons, and package inserts are all sales promotions meant to tempt consumers to buy products.

Public Relations Public relations includes all communication efforts directed at building goodwill. It seeks to build favorable attitudes toward the organization and its products. Ronald McDonald Houses <www.rmhc.com> are a famous example of public relations. *Publicity* also refers to a firm's efforts to communicate to the public, usually through mass media. Publicity, however, is not paid for by the firm, nor does the firm control its content. Publicity, therefore, can sometimes hurt a business. In 1999, for example, the outbreak of illness associated with Coca-Cola in Europe was widely publicized and contributed to the company's falling stock price.

distribution
Part of the marketing mix concerned with getting products from producers to consumers

Place (Distribution) In the marketing mix, *place* refers to **distribution.** Placing a product in the proper outlet—say, a retail store—requires decisions about several distribution activities, all of which are concerned with getting the product from the producer to the consumer. For example, transportation options include railroad, truck, air freight, and pipelines. Decisions about warehousing and inventory control are also distribution decisions.

Firms must also make decisions about the *channels* through which they distribute their products. Many manufacturers, for instance, sell to other companies that, in turn, distribute the goods to retailers. Del Monte Foods <www.delmonte.com>, for example, produces canned foods that it sells to Nash Finch Co. <www.nashfinch.com> and other distributors, who then sell the food to grocery stores. Other companies sell directly to major retailers such as Sears, Wal-Mart, Kmart, and Safeway. Still others sell directly to final consumers. We explain distribution decisions further in Chapter 14.

TARGET MARKETING AND MARKET SEGMENTATION

target market
Group of people that has similar wants and needs and that can be expected to show interest in the same products

market segmentation
Process of dividing a market into categories of customer types

Marketers recognized long ago that products and services cannot be "all things to all people." Buyers have different tastes, interests, goals, lifestyles, and so on. Among other things, the emergence of the marketing concept and the recognition of consumer needs and wants led marketers to think in terms of *target marketing.* **Target markets** are groups of people with similar wants and needs. For most companies, selecting target markets is the first step in the marketing strategy.

Target marketing clearly requires **market segmentation**—dividing a market into categories of customer types or "segments." Once they have identified market segments, companies may adopt a variety of strategies. Some firms try to market products to more than one segment of the population. For example, General Motors <www.gm.com> offers compact cars, vans, trucks, luxury cars, and sports cars with various features and at various price levels. GM's strategy is to provide an automobile for nearly every segment of the market.

In contrast, some businesses appeal to the optimal number of market segments by offering fewer products, each aimed toward a specific market segment. Note that segmentation is a strategy for analyzing consumers, not products. In marketing, the process of fixing, adapting, and communicating the nature of the product itself is called *positioning.*

Identifying Market Segments

By definition, the members of a *market segment* must share some common traits that will affect their purchasing decisions. In identifying market segments, researchers look at several different influences on consumer behavior. Four of the most important are *geographic, demographic, psychographic,* and *product use variables.*[8]

Geographic Variables In many cases, buying decisions are affected by the places that people call home. The heavy rainfall in Washington State, for instance, means that inhabitants purchase more umbrellas than people living in the Sun Belt. Urban residents have little need for four-wheel-drive vehicles, and sailboats sell better along the coasts than in the Great Plains. **Geographic variables** are the geographical units, from countries to neighborhoods, that may be considered in developing a segmentation strategy.

geographic variables Geographical units that may be considered in developing a segmentation strategy

These patterns affect decisions about the marketing mix for a huge range of products. For example, consider a project to market down-filled parkas in rural Minnesota. Demand will be high and price competition intense. Local newspaper advertising may be very effective, and the best retail location may be one that is easily reached from several small towns. Marketing the same parkas in downtown Honolulu would be considerably more challenging.

Although the marketability of some products is geographically sensitive, others benefit from nearly universal acceptance. Coca-Cola, for example, derives more than 70 percent of its cola sales from international markets. Coke is the market leader in Great Britain, China, Germany, Japan, Brazil, and Spain. Pepsi's international sales equal only about 15 percent of Coke's. In fact, Coke's chief competitor in most countries is some local soft drink, not Pepsi, which earns 78 percent of its income at home.[9]

Demographic Variables The **demographic variables** describe populations by identifying such traits as age, income, gender, ethnic background, marital status, race, religion, and social class. Table 11.1 lists some possible demographic breakdowns. Depending on the marketer's purpose, a segment could be a single classification (*aged 20–34*) or a combination of categories (*aged 20–34, married with children, earning $25,000–$34,999*). Foreign competitors, for example, are gaining market share in U.S. auto sales by appealing to young buyers. Germany, Japan, and Korea are attracting the young buyers (under age 30) with limited incomes (under $30,000). While companies such as Hyundai <www.hyundai.net>, Kia <www.kia.com>, and Daewoo <www.daewoous.com> are winning entry-level customers with high quality and generous warranties, Volkswagen <www.vw.com> has succeeded in targeting under-35 buyers with its entertainment-styled VW Jetta.[10]

demographic variables Characteristics of populations that may be considered in developing a segmentation strategy

Table 11.1

Demographic Variables

Age	Under 5, 5–11, 12–19, 20–34, 35–49, 50–64, 65+
Education	Grade school or less, some high school, graduated high school, some college, college degree, advanced degree
Family life cycle	Young single, young married without children, young married with children, older married with children under 18, older married without children under 18, older single, other
Family size	1, 2–3, 4–5, 6+
Income	Under $9,000, $9,000–14,999, $15,000–24,999, $25,000–34,999, $35,000–45,000, over $45,000
Nationality	Including African, American, Asian, British, Eastern European, French, German, Irish, Italian, Latin American, Middle Eastern, and Scandinavian
Race	Including American Indian, Asian, Black, and White
Religion	Including Buddhist, Catholic, Hindu, Jewish, Muslim, and Protestant
Sex	Male, female

Figure 11.2
Changes in the U.S. Population

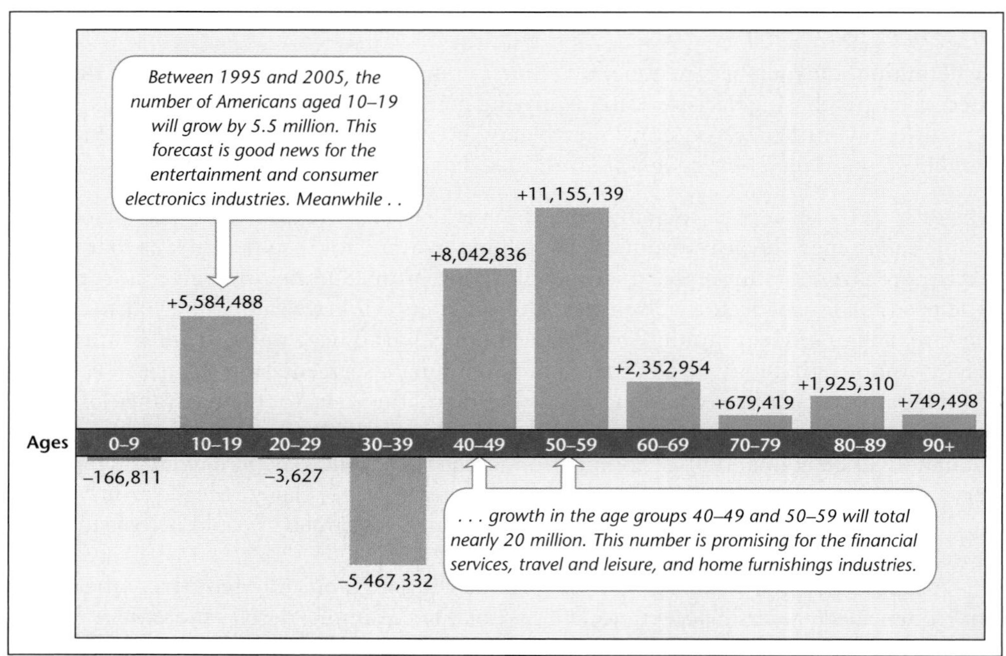

Naturally, demographics affect marketing decisions. For example, several general consumption characteristics can be attributed to certain age groups (*18–25, 26–35, 36–45,* and so on). Marketers can thus divide markets into age groups as they develop specific marketing plans.

In addition, marketers can use demographics to identify trends that might shape future spending patterns. Nursing care and funeral service companies, for example, are expanding offerings in response to projected changes in the U.S. population in the years 1995 to 2005. Those changes are shown in Figure 11.2. As you can see, the number of people between ages 60 and 89—and even the number of those in their 90s—is expected to rise. So-called death care companies, such as Stewart Enterprises and Service Corporation International <www.sci-corp.com>, are preparing for the upturn by acquiring additional cemetery and funeral homes that give customers one-stop shopping.

The "Wired World" box in this chapter shows the computerized collection of demographic data is being used to cut costs in the health care industry.

psychographic variables Consumer characteristics, such as lifestyles, opinions, interests, and attitudes, that may be considered in developing a segmentation strategy

Psychographic Variables Members of a market can also be segmented according to such **psychographic variables** as lifestyles, opinions, interests, and attitudes. One company that is using psychographic variables to revive its brand is Burberry, whose plaid-lined gabardine raincoats have been a symbol of British tradition since 1856. With a recent downturn in sales, Burberry is repositioning itself as a global luxury brand, like Gucci <www.gucci.com> and Louis Vuitton <www.vuitton.com>. The strategy calls for luring a different type of customer—the top-of-the-line fashion conscious—who shop at such stores as Neiman Marcus and Bergdorf Goodman. Burberry <net2.netacc./~burberry/index.html> pictures today's luxury-product shopper as a world traveler who identifies with prestige fashion brands and watches social and fashion trends in *Harper's Bazaar.*[11]

Psychographics are particularly important to marketers because, unlike demographics and geographics, they can sometimes be changed by marketing efforts. For example, many companies in Poland have succeeded in overcoming consumer resistance by promoting the safety and desirability of using credit rather than depending solely on cash for

It's a WiredWorld

• Better Health through Cyberspace Demographics

As we have seen, demographic, geographic, and lifestyle variables are useful in identifying market segments for effective target marketing. In an era of heightened concern for costly health care, many insurers are converting demographic and lifestyle information into personal health assessments for employees of their client companies. One way to gather personal information is by paper and pencil, but with online access, the process is fast, convenient, and secure for confidentiality. The approach was developed by Network Health Systems™ (NHS). First, the employee fills out a personal questionnaire with items on physical characteristics, lifestyle practices, dietary patterns, work environment, emotional feelings, medical status, and health history. This information forms the individual's personal demographics package. Online subscribers at Network's Web site <www.nhsinfo.com> can conveniently access the questionnaire, answer the questions, receive instantaneous feedback in the form of a personal report, and pay for the service.

The NHS system evaluates the individual's data using statistical models that determine the chances for experiencing various diseases or ailments. A personalized report is created instantaneously. Based on the individual's response demographics and lifestyle practices, it shows which of some 52 possible conditions and diseases—such as nerve disorders, benign tumors, pregnancy complications, and suicide—are expected. The report offers comments and suggestions about the individual's future health, including recommendations for specific lifestyle changes that can be taken for improvement.

The assessment system is based on a vast database of mortality and hospitalization data for 52 diseases and 24 age, sex, and race categories. Data are updated using medical research and national statistics from such sources as the Centers for Disease Control and the National Center for Health Statistics. The database also incorporates information from a panel of health professionals whose clinical judgments indicate correlations among demographics and various health problems. When an individual's demographics and lifestyle items are entered online, they are assessed against the database by the statistical model. Results are presented instantaneously. Processing reports via the Internet saves time and money for NHS, and it is faster in getting the results to clients.

In addition to individuals, business marketers for various health products benefit from the NHS system. Suppose, for example, a marketer for an insulin product wants to target specific geographic areas with high sales potential. Using demographic data, NHS will search its database to locate concentrations of population, by zip code, that are predisposed to diabetes. Perhaps results will show that while 40 percent of the population is predisposed in one region, just 10 percent is predisposed in another. NHS can report this information to health care providers—hospitals, physicians, HMOs—who can, in turn, use it to deliver services to areas most in need of it.

The French cosmetics giant L'Oréal <www.lorealparisusa.com> is working to reposition the 96-year-old Helena Rubenstein brand by appealing to a new psychographic segment. Through trendy spas like this one in New York (L'Oréal's first-ever retailing venture), the parent company is targeting the skin care and cosmetic brand at 20- to 30-year-old women in such urban centers as New York, Paris, London, and Tokyo.

family purchases. One product of such changing attitudes is a booming economy and the emergence of a growing and robust middle class. The increasing number of Polish households owning televisions, appliances, automobiles, and houses is fueling the status of Poland's middle class as the most stable in the former Soviet bloc.[12]

product use variables Consumer characteristics based on the ways in which a product is used, the brand loyalty it enjoys, and the reasons for which it is purchased

Product Use Variables The term **product use variables** includes the ways in which consumers use a product, their brand loyalty to it, and their reasons for purchasing it. A women's shoemaker, for example, might identify three segments—wearers of athletic, casual, and dress shoes. Each market segment is looking for different benefits in a shoe. A woman buying an athletic shoe, for instance, may not care much about its appearance but cares a great deal about arch support, sturdiness, and traction in the sole. A woman buying a casual shoe, however, will want it to look good and feel comfortable. A woman buying a dress shoe may require a specific color or style and may even accept some discomfort.

MARKETING RESEARCH

marketing research The study of consumer needs and wants and the ways in which sellers can best meet them

Decisions for marketing are seldom perfect, and in today's competitive world, the consequences of a firm's choice of marketing mix and market-segmentation strategy can be long-lasting. Effectiveness depends on avoiding misguided directions and making decisions that are customer focused and based on timely, valid information about trends in the marketplace. A powerful tool for effectiveness is **marketing research:** the study of what customers need and how best to meet those needs.[13]

The relationship of marketing research in the overall marketing process is shown in Figure 11.3. Ultimately, its role is to increase the firm's competitiveness by understanding the relationship among the firm's stakeholders (including consumers), its marketing variables, environmental considerations, and its marketing decisions. Marketing researchers use a variety of methods to obtain, interpret, and use information about customers. They determine the kinds of information that are needed for decisions on marketing strategy, goal setting, and target-market selection. In doing so, they may conduct studies on how customers will respond to proposed changes in the current marketing mix. One researcher, for example, might study consumer response to an experimental paint formula (new product). Another might explore the response to a price reduction (new price) on calculators. Still a third might check response to a proposed advertising campaign (new promotion). Marketers can also try to learn whether customers are more likely to purchase a given product in a specialty shop or on the Internet (new place).

Moreover, the importance of selling products in today's international markets is expanding the role of marketing research into new areas. For example, when companies decide to sell goods or services in other countries, they must decide whether to standardize products or to specialize them by offering different versions for each new market.

The Research Process

Market research can occur at almost any point in a product's existence. Most commonly, however, it is used when developing new or altered products. These are the five basic steps in performing market research:

1. *Study the current situation.* What is the need and what is currently being done to meet it? Such a study should note how well a firm is currently meeting the need that has been identified.
2. *Select a research method.* Marketers have a wide range of methods available. In choosing one, they must bear in mind the effectiveness and costs of different methods.
3. *Collect data.* There are two types of research data. **Secondary data** are already available as a result of previous research. For example, the *Statistical Abstract of the United States* <www.census.gov/statab.www> offers data on geographic and demo-

secondary data Data readily available as a result of previous research

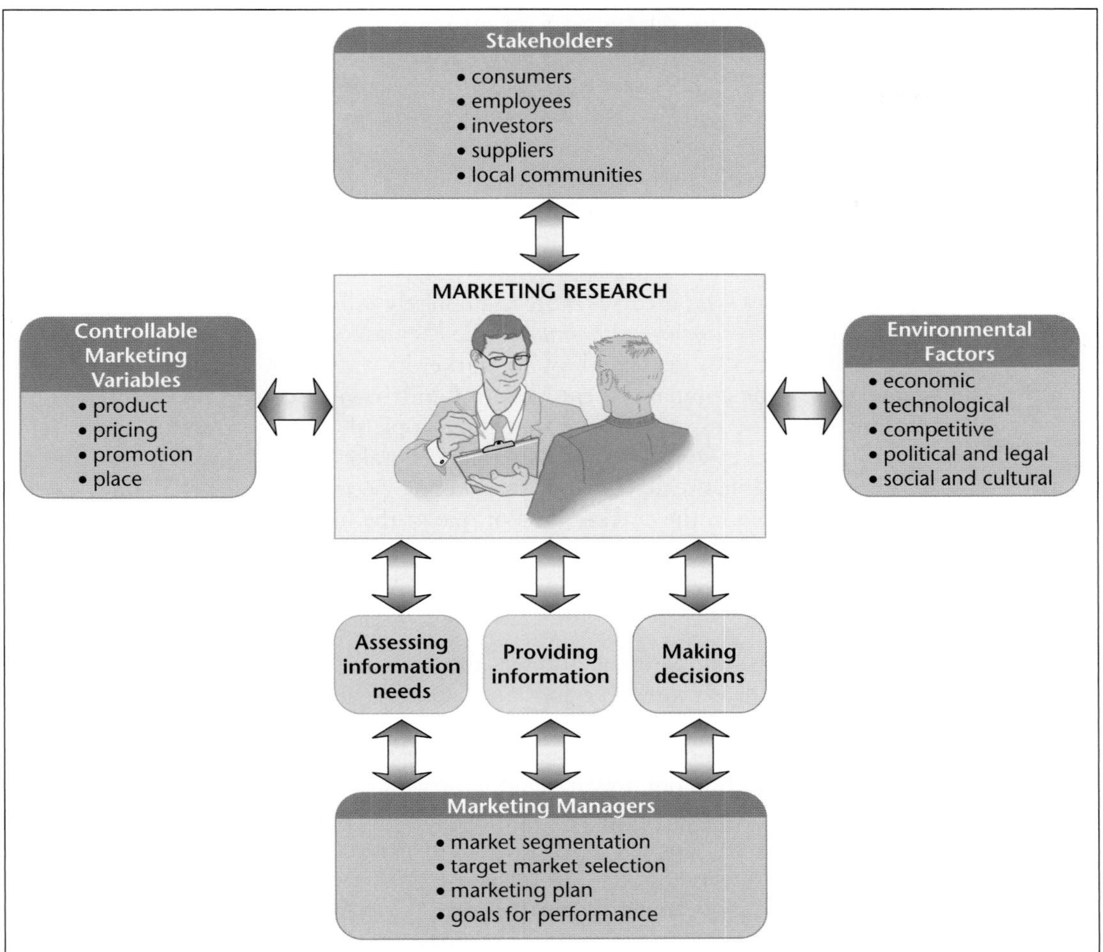

Figure 11.3
Market Research and the Marketing Process

graphic variables. Using secondary data can save time, effort, and money. When secondary data are unavailable or inadequate, however, **primary data**—new data from research performed by a firm or its agents—must be obtained.

4. *Analyze the data.* Data are of no use until they have been organized into information.
5. *Prepare a report.* This report should include a summation of the study's methodology and findings. It should also identify alternative solutions and (where appropriate) make recommendations for the best course of action.

primary data
Data developed through new research

What is the best research method in determining the needs of the consumer?

Research Methods

The success of a marketing research study often depends on the appropriateness of the method used. The four basic methods of market research are *observation, surveys, focus groups,* and *experimentation.*

observation
Market research technique that involves simply watching and recording consumer behavior

Observation Probably the oldest form of market research is simple **observation.** Perhaps the owner of a toy store notices that customers are buying red wagons instead of green ones. When the retailer reorders more red wagons, the manufacturer's records show high sales of red wagons, and marketing concludes that customers want red wagons. Today, computerized systems allow marketers to observe consumer preferences rapidly and with incredible accuracy. For example, electronic supermarket scanners allow managers to see what is and is not selling without having to check shelves. Observation is also inexpensive, often drawing on data that must be collected for some other reason, such as reordering.

Observation, however, involves more than merely tallying sales electronically. It also means watching *how consumers behave* while they are shopping. For example, when Galilee Splendor, Inc. was deciding how to market its wafer-thin Bible Bread crackers in the United States, the company spent time in family-owned convenience stores, supermarkets, and other food stores quietly watching people shop in the cracker section. They discovered that cracker customers in supermarkets take about 10 seconds to find the cracker they want. Bible Bread, concluded marketing vice president Peter Shamir, "would clearly not get noticed in the cracker aisle of one of the big markets." But Galilee knew that it had a good cracker and so chose instead to sell it in specialty, health-food, and gourmet stores. Annual sales for this start-up company have since surpassed $1 million and the crackers are sold in more than 30 states.[14]

survey
Market research technique using a questionnaire that is either mailed to individuals or used as the basis of interviews

Surveys Sometimes, however, marketers must go a step further and ask questions about marketing ideas or product performance. One way to get answers is by conducting **surveys.** The heart of any survey is a questionnaire that is either mailed to individuals or used as the basis of telephone or personal interviews. For example, United Parcel Service surveyed customers to find out how it could improve service. Surprisingly, clients wanted more interaction with drivers because they can offer practical advice on shipping. UPS thus added extra drivers, freeing up some time for drivers to get out of their trucks and spend time with customers. Surveys, however, can be expensive and may vary widely in accuracy. In addition, because no firm can afford to survey everyone, marketers must be careful to contact representative groups of respondents. To address specific issues being researched, questions must be constructed carefully.

focus group
Market research technique in which a group of people is gathered, presented with an issue, and asked to discuss it in depth

Focus Groups In a **focus group,** 6 to 15 people are gathered in one place, where they are presented with an issue and asked to discuss it. The researcher takes notes but provides only a minimal amount of structure. At its best, this technique allows researchers to explore issues too complex for questionnaires and it can produce creative solutions. But because a focus group is small, its responses may not represent the feelings or opinions of

"Geez, you're the worst focus group I've ever seen."

the larger market. Thus focus groups are most often used as a first step to some other form of research.

Experimentation **Experimentation** also tries to get answers to questions that surveys cannot address. As in scientific research, experimentation in marketing research tries to compare the responses of the same or similar people under different circumstances. For example, a firm trying to decide whether to include walnuts in a new candy bar probably would not learn much by asking people what they thought of the idea. But if it made up some bars with nuts and some without and then asked people to try both, the responses could be quite helpful. Unfortunately, however, experimentation is very expensive. Thus, in deciding whether to use it (or any other research method, for that matter) marketers must carefully weigh costs against possible benefits.

experimentation
Market research technique that attempts to compare the responses of the same or similar people under different circumstances

UNDERSTANDING CONSUMER BEHAVIOR

Although marketing managers can tell us what qualities people want in a new VCR, they cannot tell us *why* people buy a particular VCR. What desire are they fulfilling? Is there a psychological or sociological explanation for why consumers purchase one product and not another? These questions and many others are addressed in the area of marketing known as **consumer behavior**—the study of the decision process by which customers come to purchase and consume products.

consumer behavior
Various facets of the decision process by which customers come to purchase and consume products

Influences on Consumer Behavior

According to the title of one classic study, we are "social animals." To understand consumer behavior, marketers draw heavily on the fields of psychology and sociology. The result is a focus on four major influences on consumer behavior: *psychological, personal, social,* and *cultural.* By identifying the four influences that are most active, marketers try to explain consumer choices and predict future purchasing behavior:

1. *Psychological influences* include an individual's motivations, perceptions, ability to learn, and attitudes.
2. *Personal influences* include lifestyle, personality, and economic status.
3. *Social influences* include family, opinion leaders (people whose opinions are sought by others), and such reference groups as friends, coworkers, and professional associates.
4. *Cultural influences* include culture (the "way of living" that distinguishes one large group from another), subculture (smaller groups, such as ethnic groups, with shared values), and social class (the cultural ranking of groups according to such criteria as background, occupation, and income).

Although these factors can have a strong impact on consumers' choices, their impact on the actual purchase of some products is either very weak or negligible. Some consumers, for example, exhibit high **brand loyalty,** which means they regularly purchase products because they are satisfied with their performance. Such people (for example, users of Maytag appliances) are generally less subject to typical influences and stick with preferred brands. Closer to home, however, the clothes you wear and the food you eat often reflect social and psychological influences on your consuming behavior.

brand loyalty
Pattern of regular consumer purchasing based on satisfaction with a product

The "Life Cycle of an e-Business" box in this chapter shows how Garden.com used a strategy called "narrowcasting" to determine the interests that influenced the needs and wants of its customers.

The Consumer Buying Process

Students of consumer behavior have constructed various models to help marketers understand how consumers come to purchase products. Figure 11.4 presents one such model. At the core of this and similar models is an awareness of the psychosocial influences that lead to consumption. Ultimately, marketers use this information to develop marketing plans.

Figure 11.4
The Consumer Buying Process

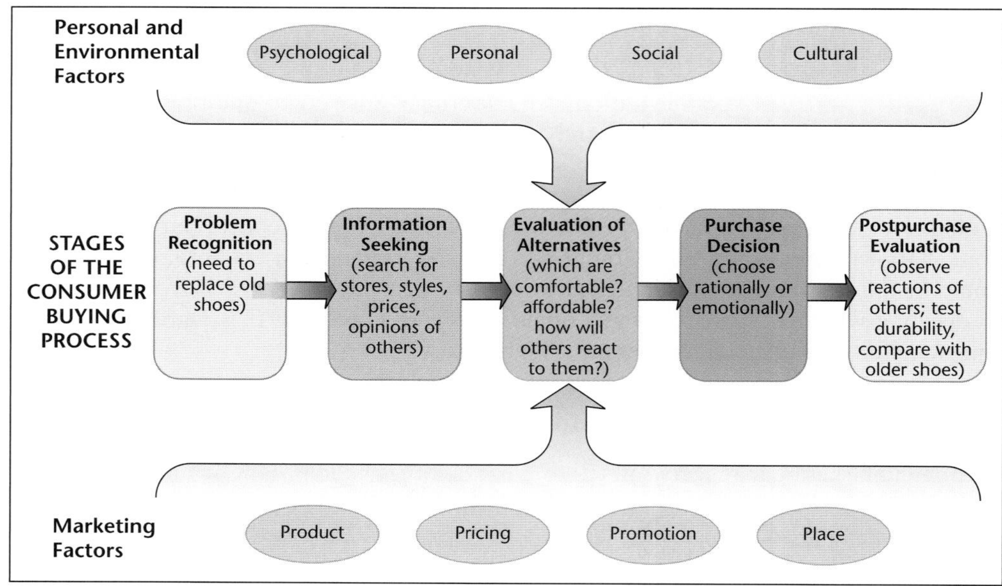

Problem/Need Recognition The buying process begins when the consumer recognizes a problem or need. After strenuous exercise, for example, you may realize that you are thirsty. After the birth of twins, you may find your one-bedroom apartment too small for comfort.

Need recognition also occurs when you have a chance to change your purchasing habits. For example, when you obtain your first job after graduation, your new income may let you purchase items that were once too expensive for you. You may also discover a need for professional clothing, apartment furnishings, and a car. American Express and Sears recognize this shift in typical needs when they market credit cards to college seniors.

Information Seeking Once they have recognized a need, consumers often seek information. This search is not always extensive. If you are thirsty, for instance, you may simply ask someone to point you to a soft drink machine. At other times, you may simply rely on your memory for information.

Before making major purchases, however, most people seek information from personal sources, marketing sources, public sources, and experience. For example, if you move to a new town, you will want to identify the best dentist, physician, hair stylist, butcher, or pizza maker in your area. To get this information, you may check with personal sources, such as acquaintances, coworkers, and relatives. Before buying an exercise bike, you may go to the library and read the relevant issue of *Consumer Reports* <www.consumerreports.org>. You may also question market sources such as salesclerks or rely on direct experience by test-riding several bikes before you buy.

Evaluation of Alternatives If you are in the market for a set of skis, you probably have some idea of who makes skis and how they differ. You may have accumulated some of this knowledge during the information-seeking stage and combined it with what you knew previously. By analyzing the product attributes that apply to a given product (color, taste, price, prestige, quality, service record) you will consider your choices and decide which product best meets your needs.

rational motives
Reasons for purchasing a product that are based on a logical evaluation of product attributes

emotional motives
Reasons for purchasing a product that are based on nonobjective factors

Purchase Decision Ultimately, consumers must make purchase decisions. They may decide to defer a purchase until a later time or they may decide to buy now. "Buy" decisions are based on rational motives, emotional motives, or both.[15] **Rational motives** involve the logical evaluation of product attributes: cost, quality, and usefulness. **Emotional motives** involve nonobjective factors and lead to irrational decisions. Although not all irrational decisions are sudden, many spur-of-the-moment decisions are

Life Cycle of an e-Business

"Narrowcasting" to the Enthusiast

Although Garden.com eventually boasted some 1.5 million members and customers, this figure represents just a tiny portion of a $70-billion-a-year-industry. The target market, of course, was gardeners—the gardening community—which is geographically fragmented, graying, and affluent. Garden.com's strategy hinged on some further assumptions about its customer base. With busy lifestyles, for instance, gardeners have little time for going store to store to find what they need. They have four hours for gardening on Saturday, and, not surprisingly, they want to spend that time in their gardens. They need to know that their plants and gardening supplies will be on hand. Even more importantly, gardeners are interested in the art and design that go into their hobby. They thrive on creativity and harbor a passion for gardening that they want to share with others who feel the same way. Demographically, this group includes college-educated women in all age groups, but especially ages 30-55. How accurate are these assumptions? To the extent that they are accurate, the typical brick-and-mortar garden store, though carrying large inventories of plants, fertilizers, and hardware, falls short of addressing the gardener's real needs.

Starting with the profile that we just sketched in above, Lisa Sharples, Jamie O'Neill, and Cliff Sharples gave a great deal of thought to what hobbyists do not get from traditional sources and what, in contrast, would be possible with an e-business concept. Materials and supplies are only part of the gardener's needs, but it was an obvious place to start. The founders of Garden.com realized that a consumer-oriented, one-stop Internet shopping site had an advantage in being able to ensure reliable deliveries for everything—flowers, plants, seeds, and equipment. Reliability would replace the guesswork of on-shelf availability and reduce shopping time. "A really well-executed, one-stop Internet shop," said Jamie O'Neill, "is an extremely powerful tool from the customer's standpoint."

Relationship building began with what Lisa Sharples called "narrowcasting": using Garden.com's proprietary software technology to personalize the Web page according to each customer's demographics and interactions with the site. Members provided information indicating their interests (say, vegetable gardening, shade gardening, water ponds, etc.), and a private history of each individual's consumer behavior was filed away at Garden.com. Then the company's online message content was tailored especially for each customer. It might notify one member, for example, of a special promotion that, based on past purchases or inquiries, Garden.com expected to be of particular interest to that member. A notice might remind members that it was time to plant tulip bulbs or apply fertilizer treatments in their regions.

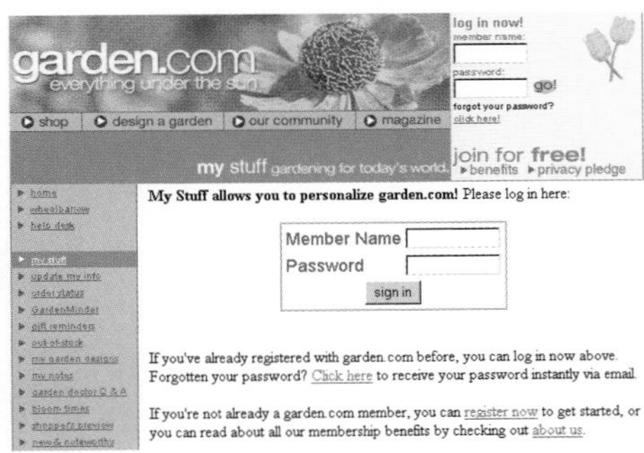

Although Garden.com's combination of merchandise, information, and community interaction, all available from a single site, was a true source of practical and spiritual nourishment for gardeners, market growth continued to lag behind the firm's growing expenses. What was the problem? One e-consumer expert at Forrester Research <www.forrester.com> suggests that some of Garden.com's assumptions about its customer base were flawed: Garden products, he argues, "tend to be something that *people want to go to the store to buy*." At bottom, this reading of the market questions the wisdom of a solely online marketing strategy. Which view is valid? Do gardeners prefer in-store shopping, or would they prefer to use the Internet?

The Forrester analyst also contends that because most gardening products don't command much brand loyalty, retailers have a tough time competing for repeat sales. Would Garden.com have been better prepared had it conducted more market research on the consumer-behavior patterns of gardeners? More reliable consumer information might have made a difference five years earlier, when the company was a start-up, but by November 2000, it was too late for Garden.com to question its original assumptions.

emotionally driven. Emotional motives include sociability, imitation of others, and aesthetics—motives that are common. For example, you might buy the same brand of jeans as your friends to feel comfortable among that group, not because your friends happen to have the good sense to prefer durable, comfortably priced jeans.

Irrational, therefore, does not mean wrong. It merely refers to a decision based on nonobjective factors. Such decisions can be either satisfying or, largely because they were not based on objective criteria, ill considered. We have all purchased items, taken them home, and then wondered, "Why in the world did I spend good money on this thing?"

Postpurchase Evaluations Marketing does not stop with the sale of a product. It includes the process of consumption. What happens *after* the sale is important. Marketers want consumers to be happy after the consumption of products so that they are more likely to buy them again. Because consumers do not want to go through a complex decision process for every purchase, they often repurchase products they have used and liked.

Not all consumers are satisfied with their purchases, of course. Dissatisfied consumers may complain to sellers, criticize products publicly, or even file lawsuits. Dissatisfied consumers are not likely to purchase the same products again. Moreover, dissatisfied customers are much more likely to broadcast their experiences than are satisfied customers.

ORGANIZATIONAL MARKETING AND BUYING BEHAVIOR

Buying behavior is observable daily in the consumer market, where marketing activities, including buying and selling transactions, are visible to the public. Equally important, however, but far less visible, are *organizational* (or *commercial*) *markets*. Some 23 million organizations in the United States buy goods and services to be used in creating and delivering consumer products. As we will see in the following sections, marketing to these buyers must deal with different kinds of organizational markets and with buying behaviors that are different from those found in consumer markets.

Organizational Markets

Organizational or commercial markets fall into three categories—*industrial, reseller,* and *government/institutional markets*. Taken together, these three markets in the United States do about $8 *trillion* in business annually, approximately three times the business done in the consumer market.

industrial market
Organizational market consisting of firms that buy goods that are either converted into products or used during production

Industrial Market The **industrial market** includes businesses that buy goods to be converted into other products and goods that are used up during production. This market includes farmers, manufacturers, and some retailers. For example, Seth Thomas

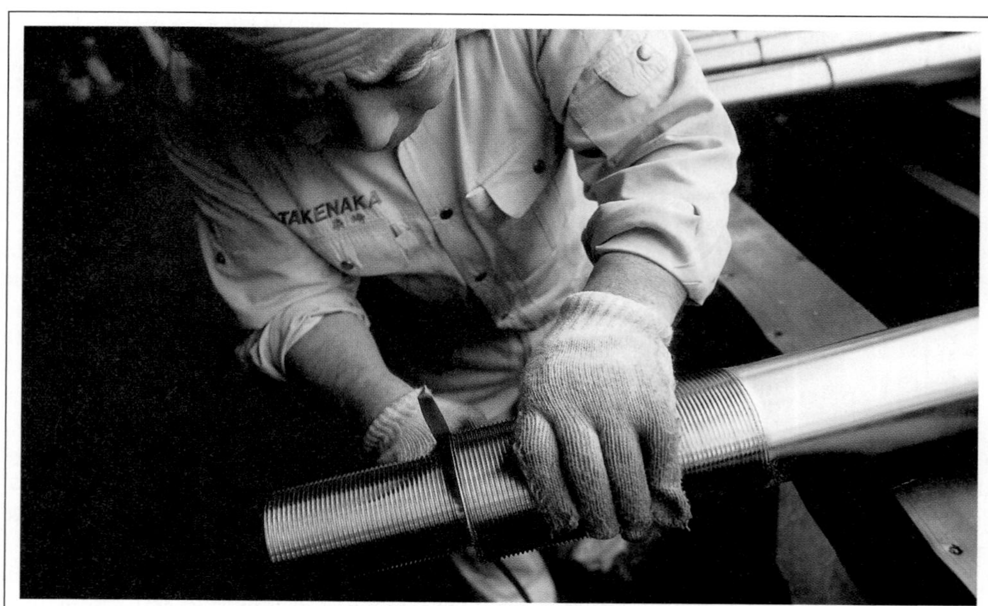

Located outside Osaka, the Takenaka Seisakusho Co. is one of 6,000 nut-and-bolt makers in Japan. Founded in 1935, it still has the same motto: "Totally devoted to screws." R&D is not typically an important part of small-company operations in this industrial market, but Takenaka took a gamble and spent five years developing a better stress-resistant bolt. The company is now on Exxon's "master vendor list," and while most of its competitors have annual sales of under $1 million, Takenaka now does $25 million.

<www.seththomas.com> purchases electronics, metal components, and glass to make clocks for the consumer market. The company also buys office supplies, tools, and factory equipment—items never seen by clock buyers—to be used during production. Baskin-Robbins <www.baskinrobbins.com> buys not only ingredients for ice cream but also paper bags and wrappers to package products for customers and freezer cabinets for storage.

Reseller Market Before products reach consumers, they pass through a **reseller market** consisting of intermediaries, including wholesalers and retailers, who buy the finished goods and resell them (wholesalers and retailers are discussed in detail in Chapter 14). The Coast Distribution System, for example, is a leading distributor of parts and accessories for the pleasure boat market. It buys items such as lights, steering wheels, and propellers and resells them to marinas and boat repair shops. On the products resold to their customers, 750,000 U.S. wholesalers have annual sales of $2.4 trillion. Some 2.5 million U.S. retailers purchase merchandise which, when resold to consumers, is valued at $2.6 trillion per year. Retailers also buy such services as maintenance, housekeeping, and communications.[16]

reseller market
Organizational market consisting of intermediaries who buy and resell finished goods

Government and Institutional Market In addition to federal and state governments, more than 87,000 local governments (municipalities, counties, townships, and school districts) are in the United States. State and local governments alone make annual purchases of $1.3 trillion for durable goods, nondurables, purchased services, and construction. Note that, after a 10-year reduction, spending for military procurement is down 46 percent—from $82 billion to $44 billion—since 1989.[17]

The **institutional market** consists of nongovernment organizations, such as hospitals, churches, museums, and charitable organizations, that also comprise a substantial market for goods and services. Like organizations in other commercial markets, these institutions use supplies and equipment, as well as legal, accounting, and transportation services.

institutional market
Organizational market consisting of such nongovernmental buyers of goods and services as hospitals, churches, museums, and charitable organizations

Organizational Buying Behavior

In many respects, organizational buying behavior bears little resemblance to consumer buying practices. Industrial product demand is stimulated by demand for consumer products and is less sensitive to price changes. Other differences include the buyers' purchasing skills and buyer–seller relationships.

Differences in Demand Recall our definition of *demand* in Chapter 1—the willingness and ability of buyers to purchase a good or service. The two major differences in demand between consumer and industrial products are *derived demand* and *inelasticity of demand.*

Derived Demand The term **derived demand** refers to the fact that demand for industrial products often results from demand for related consumer products (that is, industrial demand is frequently *derived from* consumer demand).[18]

derived demand
Demand for industrial products that results from demand for consumer products

Consider the chain of industrial demand that was ignited when AMC Entertainment, Inc. <www.amctheatres.com> realized how many moviegoers demanded the new plus-system concept in movie theaters that the theater chain launched during the 1990s. To open its 24-screen megaplex in Mesa, Arizona, in 1999, AMC required an array of services—property sales, architecture, financial—and such materials as structural steel, windows, bathroom fixtures, heating apparatus, concrete, display cases, and carpeting. In turn, these needs stimulated demand back through the supply chain. For example, to make materials for the theater's construction, the steel supplier had to buy more scrap steel, carbon, and other raw materials from its suppliers. Also needed for the theater were wall-to-wall/ceiling-to-floor movie screens, full sound systems, and 4,600 plush high-backed seats, in addition to the everyday consumables such as paper products and concession items—hot foods, treats, drinks—and the equipment to prepare them.

Inelasticity of Demand We use the term **inelastic demand** when a price change for a product does not have much effect on demand. Take, for instance, the demand for cardboard

inelastic demand
Demand for industrial products that is not largely affected by price changes

used to package products such as file cabinets. Because cardboard packaging is such a small part of the manufacturer's overall cabinet cost, an increase in cardboard prices will not lessen the demand for cardboard. In turn, because cabinet buyers will see little price increase, demand for filing cabinets and their accompanying cardboard packaging will remain at about the same level.[19]

Differences in Buyers Unlike most consumers, organizational buyers are professional, specialized, and expert (or at least well informed):

1. As *professionals,* organizational buyers are trained in arranging buyer–seller relationships and in methods for negotiating purchase terms. Once buyer–seller agreements have been reached, industrial buyers also arrange for formal contracts.
2. As a rule, industrial buyers are company *specialists* in a line of items. As one of several buyers for a large bakery, for example, you may specialize in food ingredients such as flour, yeast, butter, and so on. Another buyer may specialize in baking equipment (industrial ovens and mixers), whereas a third may purchase office equipment and supplies.
3. Industrial buyers are often *experts* about the products they are buying. On a regular basis, organizational buyers learn about competing products and alternative suppliers by attending trade shows, reading trade magazines, and conducting technical discussions with sellers' representatives.

Differences in Decision Making

Recall that we illustrated the five stages in the consumer buying process in Figure 11.4. As you can see in Figure 11.5, the organizational buyer's decision process differs in three important respects: *developing product specifications, evaluating alternatives,* and *making postpurchase evaluations.*

Developing Product Specifications Following problem recognition, the first stage of the buying process, industrial buying takes an additional step, developing product specifications: A document is drawn up to describe the detailed product characteristics that are needed by the buyer and must be met by the supplier. These specifications are then used in the information-seeking stage, when buyers search for products and suppliers capable of meeting their specific needs.

Evaluating Alternatives In evaluating alternatives, buyers carefully measure prospective suppliers against the product specifications developed earlier. Only suppliers that can meet those requirements are considered further. Then prospective vendors are evaluated according to other factors, such as price, reliability, and service reputation.

Making Postpurchase Evaluations The final stage, postpurchase evaluation, is more systematic in organizational buying than in consumer buying. The buyer's organization examines the product and compares it, feature-by-feature, for conformance to product specifications. Buyers retain records on product and service quality received from suppliers as the basis for evaluating their performance. These performance ratings become important considerations for selecting future suppliers.

Figure 11.5

The Industrial Buying Process

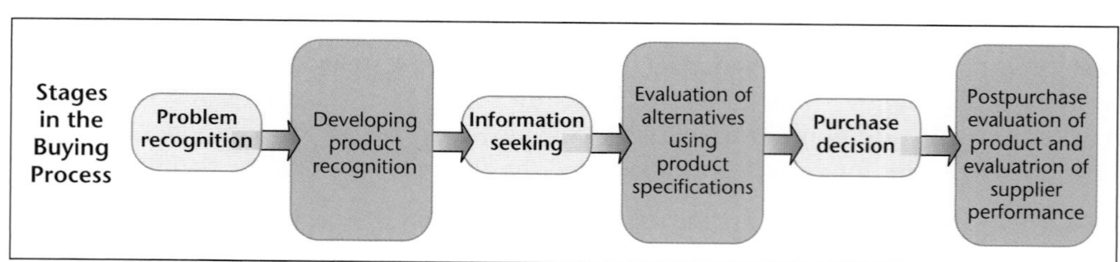

Differences in the Buyer–Seller Relationship Consumer–seller relationships are often impersonal and fleeting; they are often short-lived, one-time interactions. In contrast, industrial situations often involve frequent, enduring buyer–seller relationships. The development of a long-term relationship is beneficial to both parties. It provides each with access to the technical strengths of the other as well as the security that comes from knowing what future business each can expect. Thus a buyer and supplier may jointly form a design team to create products that will benefit both parties. Accordingly, industrial sellers emphasize personal selling by trained representatives who can better understand the needs of each customer.

THE INTERNATIONAL MARKETING MIX

Marketing products internationally means mounting a strategy to support global business operations, which is no easy task. Foreign customers, for example, differ from domestic buyers in language, customs, business practices, and consumer behavior. When they decide to go global, marketers must thus reconsider each element of the marketing mix—product, pricing, promotion, and place.

International Products Some products can be sold abroad with virtually no changes. Budweiser, Coca-Cola, and Marlboros are exactly the same in Peoria and Paris. In other cases, U.S. firms have been obliged to create products with built-in flexibility, for instance, electric shavers that adapt to either 115- or 230-volt outlets.

As noted earlier, sometimes only a redesigned or completely different product will meet the needs of foreign buyers. To sell the Macintosh in Japan, for example, Apple had to develop a Japanese-language operating system. Nevertheless, more companies are designing products for universal application. Whether designed for unique or universal markets, the branding and labeling of products are especially important for communicating global messages about them. For example, KFC (formerly Kentucky Fried Chicken) boxes and Pepsi-Cola cans display universal logos that are instantly recognizable in many nations.

International Pricing When pricing for international markets, marketers must handle all the considerations of domestic pricing while also considering the higher costs of transporting and selling products abroad. Bass Pro Shops <www.basspro.com>, for example, sells outdoor sports equipment to customers in Europe at higher prices that

This Range Rover in Paris represents an upsurge in the sales of American-made sports utility vehicles (SUVs) throughout Europe. The product, however, has required some modification. Because European roads are smaller, the European SUV is essentially a miniature version of the American SUV (some models are nearly 30 inches shorter than American counterparts). Likewise, since gas prices are higher, many European SUVs come with diesel engines, and most feature four-cylinder rather than V6 or V8 engines.

cover the added costs of delivery. In contrast, major products such as jet airplanes are priced the same worldwide because delivery costs are incidental—huge development and production costs are the major considerations regardless of customer location. Meanwhile, because of the higher costs of buildings, rent, equipment, and imported meat, a McDonald's Big Mac that sells for $2.43 in the United States has a price tag of $3.58 in Denmark.

International Promotion Occasionally, a good advertising campaign here is a good advertising campaign just about everywhere else—it can be transported to another country virtually intact. Quite often, however, standard U.S. promotional devices do not succeed in other countries. In fact, many Europeans believe that a product must be inherently shoddy if a company resorts to any advertising, particularly the American hard-sell variety.

International marketers must also be aware that cultural differences can cause negative reactions to products that are advertised improperly. Some Europeans, for example, are offended by television commercials that show weapons or violence. Advertising practices are regulated accordingly. Consequently, Dutch commercials for toys do not feature the guns and combat scenes that are commonplace on Saturday morning U.S. television. Meanwhile, liquor and cigarette commercials that are banned from U.S. television are thriving in many Asian and European markets. Product promotions must be carefully matched to the customs and cultural values of each country.

International Distribution International distribution presents several problems. In some industries, delays in starting new distribution networks can be costly. Therefore, companies with existing distribution systems often enjoy an advantage over new businesses. Similarly, several companies have gained advantages in time-based competition by buying existing businesses. Procter & Gamble, for example, saved three years of start-up time by buying Revlon's Max Factor and Betrix cosmetics, both of which are well established in foreign markets. P&G can thus immediately use these companies' distribution and marketing networks for selling its own U.S. brands in the United Kingdom, Germany, and Japan.

Why is it important to have a clear understanding of international marketing techniques?

Given the need to adjust the marketing mix, success in international markets is hard won. Even experienced firms can err in marketing to other countries. International success requires flexibility and a willingness to adapt to the nuances of other cultures. Whether a firm markets in domestic or international markets, however, the basic principles of marketing still apply. It is only the implementation of those principles that changes.

SMALL BUSINESS AND THE MARKETING MIX

As noted in Chapter 7, far more small businesses fail than succeed. Yet many of today's largest firms were yesterday's small businesses. McDonald's began with one restaurant, a concept, and one individual (Ray Kroc) who had foresight. Behind the success of many small firms lies a skillful application of the marketing concept and careful consideration of each element in the marketing mix.[20]

Small-Business Products Some new products and firms are doomed at the start simply because few consumers want or need what they have to offer. Too often, enthusiastic entrepreneurs introduce products that they and their friends like but fail to estimate realistic market potential. Other small businesses offer new products before they have clear pictures of their target segments and how to reach them. They try to be everything to everyone, and they end up serving no one well.

In contrast, a thorough understanding of what customers want has paid off for many small firms. A Rhode Island retailer, for example, has observed that consumers are more affected by merchandise that is displayed in wider space. Thus when he opened a new store, he created a dramatic display experience by suspending displays from 14-feet high ceilings. A small Boston brewery learned from experience that customers use two key decision points in stores that sell beer: at the cooler in the back of the store and at the front register. Now, this brewer prefers to display its beer in the aisle closest to the register and in a space just outside the nearby cooler. Little Earth Productions, Inc. <www.littlearth.com>, a company that makes fashion accessories, found a new consideration in designing its handbags: Formerly, the company merely considered how the consumer would use the handbag. But after examining customers' shopping habits, Little Earth decided to redesign for better store display: Because stores can give handbags better visibility by hanging them instead of placing them on the floor or on low countertops, Little Earth added little handles designed specifically for that purpose.[21]

Small-Business Pricing Haphazard pricing that is often little more than guesswork can sink even a firm with a good product. Most often, small-business pricing errors result from a failure to project operating expenses accurately. Owners of failing businesses have often been heard to say, "I didn't realize how much it costs to run the business!" and "If I price the product high enough to cover my expenses, no one will buy it!" But when small businesses set prices by carefully assessing costs, many earn very satisfactory profits—sometimes enough to expand or diversify.

Small-Business Promotion Many small businesses are also ignorant when it comes to the methods and costs of promotion. To save expenses, for example, they may avoid advertising and rely instead on personal selling. As a result, too many potential customers remain unaware of their products.

Successful small businesses plan for promotional expenses as part of start-up costs. Some hold down costs by taking advantage of less-expensive promotional methods. Local newspapers, for example, are sources of publicity when they publish articles about new or unique businesses. Other small businesses have succeeded by identifying themselves and their products with associated groups, organizations, and events. Thus, a custom crafts gallery might join with a local art league and local artists to organize public showings of their combined products.

Small-Business Distribution Problems in arranging distribution can also make or break small businesses. Perhaps the most critical aspect of distribution is facility location, especially for new service businesses. The ability of many small businesses (retailers, veterinary clinics, and gourmet coffee shops) to attract and retain customers depends partly on the choice of location.

In distribution, as in other aspects of the marketing mix, smaller companies may have advantages over larger competitors, even in highly complex industries. They may be quicker in applying service technologies. Everex Systems, Inc. of Fremont,

www.everex.com

Everex designs, manufactures, and services a complete line of computer products. To examine its online distribution outlet for products and services, including technical support systems and downloadable software to remedy problems with servers, workstations, and PCs, contact the company on its Web site.

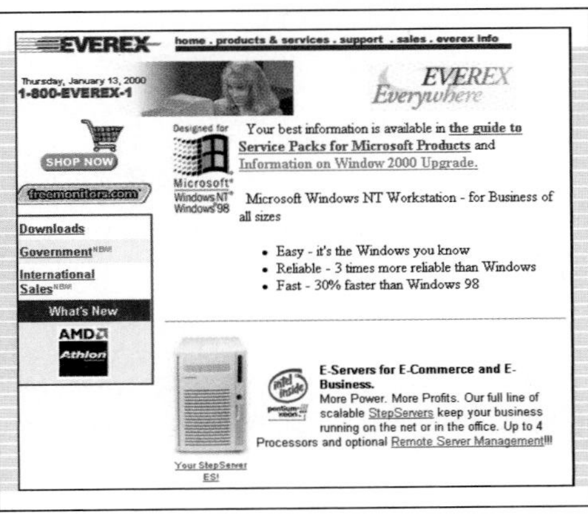

California <www.everex.com>, sells personal computers to wholesalers and dealers through a system the company calls zero response time: Because the company is small and flexible, phone orders can be reviewed every two hours and factory assembly adjusted to match demand.

Continued from page 295

Between the Barbie Doll and the Driver's License

Remember the days when teenagers had all the discretionary cash and 4- to 12-year-olds only had change for a pack of gum? To the delight of marketers, those days are long gone, as is the distinction between what young kids and teenagers want to buy. Today's 4- to 12-year-olds now spend more than $24 billion a year (of their parents' money) on food and drink, clothes, movies, games, and toys—an amount that tripled in the 1990s.

Both this surge in children's spending power and their maturing tastes are linked to the ways in which dual-career parents raise their kids. "The style of child rearing today," suggests one child psychologist, "is to empower very young children and give them choices about everything. When you give small children power, they act like adolescents."

With newfound maturity and anchored buying decisions, children are now viewed as a prime marketing target. It's no coincidence that retail stores for sophisticated tikes are opening in malls throughout the country. The Limited Too, Abercrombie & Fitch **<www.abercrombie.com>**, Gap Kids **<www.gap.com/onlinestore/gapkids>**, and Gymboree **<www.gymboree.com>** are stocking clothes and gear for 6- to 12-year-olds and doing land-office business.

Even when parents make the final buying decision, marketers now realize the influence exerted by kids. That's why Ford's Lincoln Mercury division launched its new Mercury Villager minivan with the 1998 premier of the *Rugrats* movie. That's why Liberty Financial Companies **<www.lib.com>** is pitching a mutual fund to children. The fund controls $725 million in assets from investors whose average age is 9 years.

"We're losing them sooner."

—Mattel President Bruce Stein on 7- and 8-year-old consumers

While some marketers are thriving because of the maturity shift, others are being forced to rethink longstanding strategies. Mattel Inc., manufacturer of the Barbie Doll **<www.mattel.com/branded/barbie>**, can no longer count on 7- to 8-year-old buyers. "We're losing them sooner," laments Mattel president Bruce Stein, whose core Barbie market has been trimmed to 2- to 6-year-olds. "They're in sensory overload. . . . There are too many things competing for their interests."

Other marketers have decided to cater to the special needs of the youngest sophisticates. When the Limited Too **<www.limitedtoo.com>** opened in 1991, it targeted girls aged 2 to 16. Six years later, it narrowed its focus to 6- to 14-year-olds, because it recognized preteens as a special market segment. The preteen girl, explains the chain's VP of marketing, is "moving out of the fantasy play world. She's kind of caught between Barbie and a driver's license."

Questions for Discussion

1. What social and cultural factors have influenced the growth of the teen and preteen markets?
2. How would you define the teenage target market? Why is it growing in importance?
3. What characteristics would you include in a psychographic profile of teenagers and preteenagers?
4. Do you agree or disagree with Revatex's stealth marketing tactics to reach teenage influencers? How do influencers affect consumer buying behavior?
5. If you worked in the marketing department of Mattel, what would you do to reattract 7- to 8-year-old buyers? Can you think of any spin-off Barbie products that might interest this market segment?

SUMMARY OF LEARNING OBJECTIVES

1 **Define *marketing*.** According to the American Marketing Association, *marketing* is the process of planning and executing the conception, pricing, promotion, and distribution of ideas, goods, and services to create exchanges that satisfy individual and organizational objectives.

2 **Describe the five forces that constitute the *external marketing environment*.** The *external environment* consists of the outside forces that influence marketing strategy and decision making. The *political/legal environment* includes laws and regulations, both domestic and foreign, that may define or constrain business activities. The *social/cultural environment* is the context within which people's values, beliefs, and ideas affect marketing decisions. The *technological environment* includes the technological developments that affect existing and new products. The *economic environment* consists of the conditions, such as inflation, recession, and interest rates, that influence both consumer and organizational spending patterns. Finally, the *competitive environment* is the environment in which marketers must persuade buyers to purchase their products rather than their competitors'.

3 **Explain *market segmentation* and show how it is used in *target marketing*.** *Market segmentation* is the process of dividing markets into categories of customers. Businesses have learned that marketing is more successful when it is aimed toward specific *target markets:* groups of consumers with similar wants and needs. Markets may be segmented by *geographic, demographic, psychographic,* or *product use variables.*

4 **Explain the purpose and value of *market research*.** *Market research* is the study of what buyers need and of the best ways to meet those needs. This process entails studying the firm's customers, evaluating possible changes in the marketing mix, and helping marketing managers make better decisions about marketing programs. *The marketing research process* involves the selection of a research method, the collection of data, the analysis of data, and the preparation of a report that may include recommendations for action. The four most common research methods are *observation, surveys, focus groups,* and *experimentation.*

5 **Describe the key factors that influence the *consumer buying process*.** A number of personal and psychological considerations, along with various social and cultural influences, affect consumer behavior. When making buying decisions, consumers first determine or respond to a problem or need and then collect as much information as they think necessary before making a purchase. *Postpurchase evaluations* are also important to marketers because they influence future buying patterns.

6 **Discuss the three categories of *organizational markets* and explain how *organizational buying behavior* differs from consumer buying behavior.** The *industrial market* includes firms that buy goods falling into one of two categories: goods to be converted into other products and goods that are used up during production. Farmers and manufacturers are members of the industrial market. Members of the *reseller market* (mostly wholesalers) are intermediaries who buy and resell finished goods. Besides governments and agencies at all levels, the *government and institutional market* includes such nongovernment organizations as hospitals, museums, and charities.

There are four main differences between consumer and organizational buying behavior. First, the nature of *demand* is different in organizational markets; it is often *derived* (resulting from related consumer demand) or *inelastic* (largely unaffected by price changes). Second, organizational buyers are typically professionals, specialists, or experts. Third, organizational buyers develop product specifications, evaluate alternatives more thoroughly, and make more systematic postpurchase evaluations. Finally, they often develop enduring buyer–seller relationships.

QUESTIONS AND EXERCISES

Questions for Review

1. What are the key similarities and differences between consumer buying behavior and organizational buying behavior?
2. Why and how is market segmentation used in target marketing?
3. What elements of the marketing mix may need to be adjusted to market a product internationally? Why?
4. How do the needs of organizations differ according to the different organizational markets of which they are members?

Questions for Analysis

5. Using examples of everyday products, explain why marketing plans must consider both the external marketing environment and the marketing mix.
6. Select an everyday product (books, CDs, skateboards, dog food, or shoes, for example). Show how different versions of your chosen product are aimed toward different market segments. Explain how the marketing mix differs for each segment.
7. Select a second everyday product and describe the consumer buying process that typically goes into its purchase.
8. If you were starting your own small business (say, marketing a consumer good that you already know something about), which of the forces in the external marketing environment would you believe to have the greatest potential impact on your success?

Application Exercises

9. Interview the marketing manager of a local business. Identify the degree to which this person's job is oriented toward each element in the marketing mix.
10. Select a product made by a foreign company and sold in the United States. Compare it with a similar domestically made product in terms of product features, price, promotion, and distribution. Which of the two products do you believe is more successful with U.S. buyers? Why?

Extra Exercise

11. Break the class into small groups and assign each group a specific industry. Have each group discuss the marketing strategies that they believe important to the effective marketing of products in that industry.

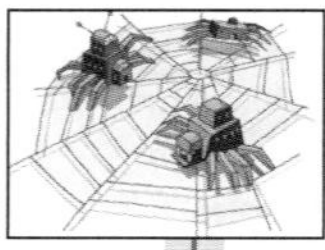

EXPLORING THE WEB

DEALING IN SEGMENTS AND VARIABLES (I)

To find out about some of the marketing methods used by a world-class company, log on to the Marriott Hotels Web site at:

www.marriott.com

In the left column of the Marriott home page, click on **Marriott Hotels, Resorts & Suites.** Next, return to the **home page.** From here, explore the Web site and read the general description of the company's lodging business. Finally, return to the home page and go to the category **Our Hotels.** One at a time, look into each of Marriott's various hotel brands. Consider the following issues, all of which pertain to the company's marketing processes:

1. Identify a Marriott product that seems oriented toward the consumer market and one that is directed more at the commercial market. What are some specific services that you found that are different for the two product markets?
2. Consider the way in which Marriott has identified market segments for five brands:
   - Marriott Hotels, Resorts, and Suites
   - Courtyard by Marriott
   - Residence Inn
   - Fairfield Inn
   - Renaissance Hotels and Resorts.

   Can you find an example of segmentation by geographic variables? By demographic variables? By psychographic variables? By product use variables?
3. Cite examples of incentives that Marriott uses and services that it offers to build relationships with its clients.

BUILDING YOUR BUSINESS SKILLS

DEALING IN SEGMENTS AND VARIABLES (II)

This exercise enhances the following SCANS workplace competencies: demonstrating basic skills, demonstrating thinking skills, exhibiting interpersonal skills, and working with information.

GOAL

To encourage students to analyze the ways in which various market segmentation variables affect business success.

SITUATION

You and four partners are thinking of purchasing a heating and air conditioning (H/AC) dealership that specializes in residential applications priced between $2,000 and $40,000. You are now in the process of deciding where that dealership should be. You are considering four locations: Miami, Florida; Westport, Connecticut; Dallas, Texas; and Spokane, Washington.

METHOD

Step 1

Working with four classmates (your partnership group), do library research to learn how H/AC makers market their residential products. Check for articles in the *Wall Street Journal*, *Business Week*, *Fortune*, and other business publications.

Step 2

Continue your research. This time, focus on the specific marketing variables that define each prospective location. Check Census Bureau and Department of Labor data at your library and on the Internet and contact local chambers of commerce (by phone and via the Internet) to learn about the following factors for each location:

1. Geography
2. Demography (especially age, income, gender, family status, and social class)
3. Psychographic factors (lifestyles, interests, and attitudes)

Step 3

Come together with group members to analyze which location holds the greatest promise as a dealership site. Base your decision on your analysis of market segment variables and their effects on H/AC sales.

FOLLOW-UP QUESTIONS

1. Which location did you choose? Describe the market segmentation factors that influenced your decision.
2. Identify the two most important variables that you believe will have the greatest impact on the dealership's success. Why are these factors so important?
3. Which factors were least important in your decision? Why?
4. When equipment manufacturers advertise residential H/AC products, they often show them in different climate situations (in winter, summer, or high-humidity conditions). Which market segments are these ads targeting? Describe these segments in terms of demographic and psychographic characteristics.

CRAFTING YOUR BUSINESS PLAN

PICKING AND PACKAGING THE RIGHT PRODUCTS

THE PURPOSE OF THE ASSIGNMENT

1. To acquaint students with the process of navigating the *Business PlanPro* (*BPP*) software package (Version 4.0).
2. To familiarize students with various marketing issues that a sample firm faces in developing its business plan.
3. To demonstrate how four chapter topics—the definition of marketing, relationship

marketing, market segmentation, and product differentiation—can be integrated as components in the *BPP* planning environment.

ASSIGNMENT

After reading Chapter 11 in the textbook, open the BPP *software* and look around for information about the marketing plans for a sample firm:* Elsewhere Products *(Elsewhere Promotional Products & Packaging). Then respond to the following items:*

1. Is Elsewhere involved in *consumer marketing* or *organizational marketing?* [Sites to see in *BPP* (for this assignment): In the Plan Outline screen, click on **1.0 Executive Summary.** Then click on and read each of **1.1 Objectives, 1.2 Mission,** and **1.3 Keys to Success.**]
2. Identify Elsewhere's strategy and methods for *building relationships with its customers.* [Sites to see in *BPP:* In the Plan Outline screen, click on **5.0 Strategy and Implementation.** Also visit: **5.1.4 Service and Support.** Then read: **1.0 Executive Summary** and **1.3 Keys to Success.**]
3. What basis—demographic, psychographic, geographic, or product use—does Elsewhere plan to use for its *market segmentation* strategy? [Sites to see in *BPP:* In the Plan Outline screen, click on **4.0 Market Analysis Summary;** then click on **4.1 Market Segmentation.**]
4. Describe Elsewhere's plans for *differentiating* its product. Do you believe that the plan is clear enough on this matter? Why or why not? [Sites to see in *BPP:* In the Plan Outline screen, click on **4.0 Market Analysis Summary.** Also visit: **4.2 Industry Analysis** and explore throughout that section.]

FOR YOUR OWN BUSINESS PLAN

5. Consider market segmentation—demographic, geographic, or product use—as it relates to the business plan that you are developing. Where in the *BPP* framework is (are) the most appropriate location(s) for your presentation on segmentation? How do you intend to explain the segmentation choices in your plan?

*GENERAL TIPS FOR NAVIGATING IN *BPP*

1. Open the *BPP* program, examine the Welcome screen, and click on **Open a Sample Plan.**
2. From the **Open a Sample Plan** dialogue box, click on a sample company name; then click on **Open.**
3. On the Plan Manager screen, click on **Your Plan Outline;** then click on any of the lines (for example, **1.0 Executive Summary**).
4. You can always return to the Plan Outline screen by going to the bottom of the screen and clicking on the **Plan Outline** icon.
5. After finishing with one sample company, you can get to the next one by going to the top of the screen and clicking on **File** (on the menu bar). Then beneath that, select **Open Sample Plan.** This will exit you from the current company file and take you to the **Open Sample Plan** dialogue box, where you can select your next sample company.
6. When you are finished, you can close the program by going to the top of the screen and clicking on **File** (on the bar menu). Then beneath that, select **Exit.**

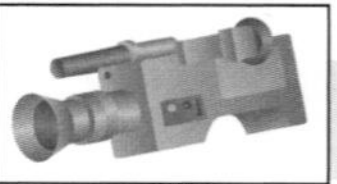

VIDEO EXERCISE

NICHE NOSHING: TERRA CHIPS

Learning Objectives

The purpose of this video exercise is to help you

1. Understand marketing research methods.
2. Understand how a niche market can be identified.
3. Appreciate the importance of appropriate pricing, packaging, and distribution in creating a successful new product.

BACKGROUND INFORMATION

In the early 1990s, Dana Sinkler and Alex Dzieduszycki gave up a successful New York catering business to start a new venture called Terra Chips. The company's product was a new kind of snack. Terra Chips are made not from potatoes but from root and vegetable chips: taro, ruby taro, sweet potato, batata, parsnip, yucca, lotus root, blue potato, celeriac root, and Jerusalem artichokes.

By 1993, production was up to 150 cases a day, and orders were pouring in from over 20 states. Dedicated to expanding its presence from gourmet markets to natural food stores, specialty food shops, and supermarkets, Terra Chips adopted distinctive silver and black packaging and widened its distribution. The strategy worked. Today the firm, now a division of the Hain Food Group <www.albafoods.com>, continues to focus on new-product development and market growth.

THE VIDEO

Dana Sinkler discusses Terra Chips' early days, beginning with the owners' recognition of a market niche they could fill, and explains how some of their initial marketing decisions were made. He recalls their focus on a high-quality, affordable luxury item and explains how the packaging and distribution of the product were carefully chosen to match that image—and to assure buyers that the product was worth its premium price. Photos of newspaper and magazine articles about the new chips indicate some of the early publicity that the company was able to garner.

DISCUSSION QUESTIONS

1. Of the research methods discussed in the chapter, which describes best Sinkler and Dzieduszycki's original approach? Which method do you think is most appropriate to the business now, as it seeks to expand its product line and market?
2. Terra Chips has considered going international, although the ingredients of its chip products are not as unusual abroad as they are in the United States. How much do you think novelty contributes to the success of the product, and how well do you think it would fare abroad? What elements of the marketing mix might need to be adjusted for international consumers?
3. How well do you think Terra Chips could succeed if, instead of marketing abroad, it decided to increase market share in the United States by selling to ordinary grocery stores, convenience stores, or cafeterias and vending outlets? What kind of challenges would it face in doing so?

FOLLOW-UP ASSIGNMENT

Find out as much as you can about the range of products made by national snack brands such as Frito-Lay <www.fritolay.com>, Nabisco <www.nabisco.com>, and Newman's Own <www.newmansown.com>. Do you think the product-line breadth of these firms boosts the sales of their individual products? Why or why not? What does a small firm have to do in order to compete with these giant firms?

FOR FURTHER EXPLORATION

Visit Terra Chips' Web site at <www.terrachips.com> and examine the New Products page. How well do you think its current new products fit the company's original marketing mix? Do you think the possibilities for new products are limited for this firm? What other new products do you think Terra Chips could research, such as flavored popcorns or whole-wheat pretzels? How should the company go about investigating the market potential for such products?

MASTERING BUSINESS ESSENTIALS

Go to the "Marketing Concept/Strategy" episode on the Mastering Business Essentials CD-ROM for an interactive, video-enhanced exercise on the efforts of managers at CanGo, an e-business start-up, to define the company's competitive position and to develop an appropriate marketing strategy.

In addition, the episode entitled "Understanding Consumer Behavior" follows marketing managers as they use a program for analyzing consumer preferences to evaluate their company's Web site.

Chapter 12

Developing and Pricing Products

After reading this chapter, you should be able to:

1. ***Identify*** a *product* and distinguish between *consumer* and *industrial products*.
2. ***Trace*** the stages of the *product life cycle*.
3. ***Explain*** the importance of *branding, packaging,* and *labeling*.
4. ***Identify*** the various *pricing objectives* that govern *pricing decisions* and describe the *price-setting tools* used in making these decisions.
5. ***Discuss*** *pricing strategies* and *tactics* for both existing and new products.

Everybody Has a Price

In issuing U.S. patent number 5,794,207 to Walker Digital, a Connecticut-based intellectual property laboratory **<www.walkerdigital.com>**, the U.S. Patent and Trademark Office (PTO) acknowledged that unique approaches to Internet retailing are inventions in their own right. The acknowledgment was good news for Walker, which had invested millions of dollars and years of effort to develop, fine-tune, and implement priceline.com—the world's first buyer-driven electronic commerce system.

Led by founder and vice chairman Jay Walker, the company observed an unfilled "open" consumer demand for such "perishable" products as airline tickets at prices below retail. "That demand creates a 'catch-22' for sellers," explains a Walker spokesperson. "On the one hand, sellers want the increased sales revenue. However, if they publicly discount their retail prices, or sell their products through a liquidator, sellers risk harming their retail channels and profitability." In other words, otherwise unsold tickets could be sold at discount prices, but sellers needed a channel that did not disrupt those through which they did the great majority of their business at regular retail prices.

Walker's answer was Priceline.com, a brand-name system that allows individual consumers to submit their own prices for products or services to various sellers via the World Wide Web or toll-free telephone numbers. Every electronic offer is privately presented to sellers, who then decide if it is worth accepting. The transaction is confidential—no other retail customer knows about any offer or deal—and costs nothing unless the seller accepts the buyer's offer in writing.

In 1998, Priceline.com launched its "name your own price" service in the leisure airline ticket market. Fifteen major domestic and international carriers signed up in an effort to fill some of the 500,000 seats that fly empty each day. This is how the system works: Customers submit the prices that they are willing to pay, guaranteeing offers with credit cards. Priceline.com then finds an airline that is interested in each potential deal and informs all buyers, within one hour for domestic flights and 24 hours for international flights, that they have purchased a nonrefundable ticket. Buyers with Internet access are notified electronically. Others call a toll-free number to find out if their offers have been accepted. "Priceline.com," says Walker, "lets consumers communicate the price they want with potential sellers in a quick and powerful way."

"A buyer-driven commerce model will be very attractive to consumers who want more control over their purchases and to sellers as they continue to look for alternative means to sell their inventory."

—Nicole Vanderbilt, Director of digital commerce, Jupiter Communications

The idea of buyer-driven commerce caught on quickly, thanks to an aggressive advertising campaign featuring former *Star Trek* captain William Shatner that turned Priceline.com into a national brand. By early 2000, the company was selling more than 30,000 tickets weekly and had emerged as one of the Internet's leading sellers of leisure airline tickets. According to Nicole Vanderbilt, director of digital commerce at New York–based Jupiter Communications, the success of Priceline.com resides in the pricing advantages that it gives both buyers and sellers. "A buyer-driven commerce model," says Vanderbilt, "will be very attractive to consumers who want more control over their purchases and to sellers as they continue to look for alternative means to sell their inventory."

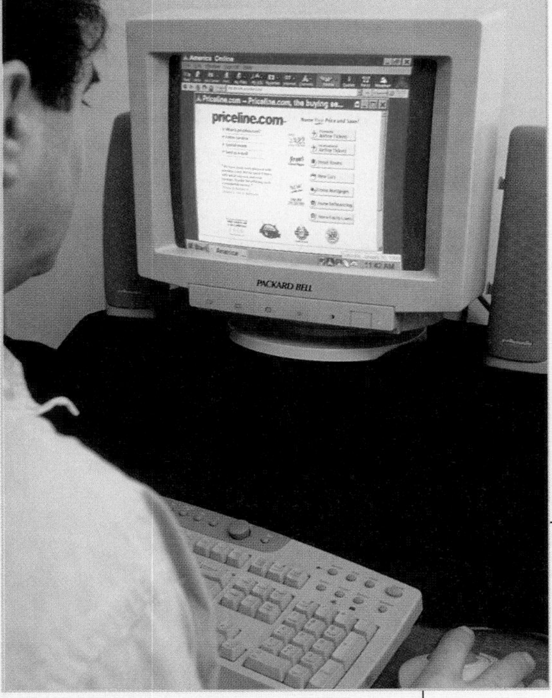

Our opening story continues on page 344

The story of Priceline.com demonstrates the willingness of companies to explore different pricing alternatives as they open new marketing channels in electronic commerce. It also illustrates the process by which an idea is developed and branded at the start of the product life cycle. As you will see in this chapter, it is the challenge of all marketers to meet their strategic goals by making the right development and pricing choices. By focusing on the learning objectives of this chapter, you will better understand how product development and pricing fit into the marketing mix.

In Chapter 11, we introduced the four components of the marketing mix: product, price, promotion, and place (distribution). In this chapter, we will look more closely at the first two of these components. Specifically, we will examine the complex nature of products. Managers must keep these complexities in mind when developing, naming, packaging, labeling, and pricing both new and existing products.

Let's begin by looking at the way in which one well-known company responded to competitive threats in its marketing environment. Porsche AG <www.porsche.com>, the renowned German sports-car maker, has learned that playing catch-up is not easy for a late entrant in the cutthroat sport utility vehicle (SUV) market. Porsche plans to make 20,000 SUVs a year, both to gain a share in the U.S. market and to protect against wild fluctuations in the volatile sports-car market. But the cost of entering the new market is high: Porsche is investing $500 million in product development over three years, spending an additional $50 million to build a new SUV factory, and plans to start production in 2002. The development cost, of course, will have an impact on the final product price. To save costs in product development and production, Porsche will share the vehicle "platform" (frame) with Volkswagen <www.vw.com>. Porsche, however, must protect its brand image by taking great pains to differentiate the two versions of the final product.[1]

In making the decisions that it ultimately did, Porsche faced a basic fact of business reality: It is virtually impossible to focus on one element of the marketing mix (product design) without encountering other marketing variables (product price and brand image). In this chapter, we will look more closely at the complex nature of perhaps the most important component in the marketing mix: the product. In particular, we will show why managers must keep in mind their wide variety when developing, naming, packaging, labeling, and pricing products.

WHAT IS A PRODUCT?

In developing the marketing mix for any products, whether ideas, goods, or services, marketers must consider what consumers really buy when they purchase products. Only then can they plan their strategies effectively. We begin this section where product strategy begins: with an understanding of product *features* and *benefits*. Next, we describe the major *classifications of products*, both consumer and industrial. Finally, we discuss the most important component in the offerings of any business: its *product mix*.

Features and Benefits

feature
Tangible and intangible qualities that a company builds into a product

Customers do not buy products simply because they like the products themselves: They buy products because they like what the products can do for them, either physically or emotionally. To succeed a product must include the right features and offer the right benefits. Product **features** are the qualities, tangible and intangible, that a company builds into its products, such as a 12-horsepower motor on a lawn mower. To be sellable, a product's features also must provide *benefits:* The mower must provide an attractive lawn.

Features and benefits play extremely important roles in the pricing of products. If you look carefully at the Diners Club ad in Figure 12.1, you will realize that products are much more than visible features and benefits. In buying a product, customers are also

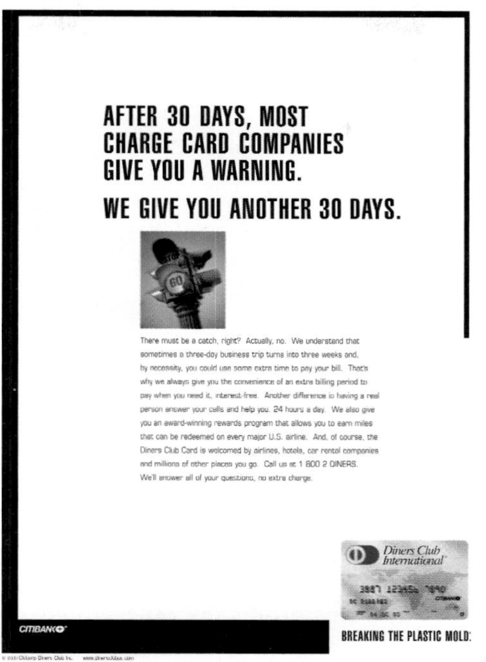

Figure 12.1
The Product: Features and Benefits

buying an image and a reputation. The marketers of the charge card advertised here <www.dinersclub.com> are well aware that brand name, labeling, and after-purchase satisfaction are indispensable facets of their product. The ad is designed to remind customers—especially business customers—that such features as extended billing periods, hands-on service, bonus air miles, and widespread acceptance go hand in hand with the familiar plastic card.

Classifying Goods and Services

One way to classify a product is according to expected buyers. Buyers fall into two groups: buyers of *consumer* products and buyers of *industrial* products.[2] As we saw in Chapter 11, the consumer and industrial buying processes differ significantly. Not surprisingly, marketing products to consumers is vastly different from marketing them to other companies.

Classifying Consumer Products Consumer products are commonly divided into three categories that reflect buyer behavior:

- **Convenience goods** (such as milk and newspapers) and **convenience services** (such as those offered by fast-food restaurants) are consumed rapidly and regularly. They are inexpensive and are purchased often and with little expenditure of time and effort.
- **Shopping goods** (such as stereos and tires) and **shopping services** (such as insurance) are more expensive and are purchased less often than convenience products. Consumers often compare brands, sometimes in different stores. They may also evaluate alternatives in terms of style, performance, color, price, and other criteria.
- **Specialty goods** (such as wedding gowns) and **specialty services** (such as catering for wedding receptions) are extremely important and expensive purchases. Consumers usually decide on precisely what they want and will accept no substitutes. They will often go from store to store, sometimes spending a great deal of money and time to get a specific product.

convenience good/service Inexpensive product purchased and consumed rapidly and regularly

shopping good/service Moderately expensive, infrequently purchased product

specialty good/service Expensive, rarely purchased product

Classifying Industrial Products Depending on how much they cost and how they will be used, industrial products can be divided into two categories: *expense* and *capital items*.

"And notice, gentlemen, this year's model has twenty percent more trunk space."

expense item
Industrial product purchased and consumed rapidly and regularly for daily operations

Expense Items **Expense items** are any materials and services that are consumed within a year by firms producing other goods or supplying other services. The most obvious expense items are industrial goods used directly in the production process (for example, bulkloads of tea processed into tea bags).

In addition, support materials help to keep a business running without directly entering the production process. Oil, for instance, keeps the tea-bagging machines running but is not used in tea bags. Similarly, supplies (pencils, brooms, gloves, paint) are consumed quickly and regularly by every business. Services such as window cleaning, equipment installation, and temporary office help are essential to daily operations. Because these items are used frequently, purchases are often automatic or require little decision making.

capital item
Expensive, long-lasting, infrequently purchased industrial product such as a building

Capital Items **Capital items** are permanent (expensive and long-lasting) goods and services. All these items have expected lives of more than a year and typically up to several years. Expensive buildings (offices, factories), fixed equipment (water towers, baking ovens), and accessory equipment (computers, airplanes) are *capital goods. Capital services* are those for which long-term commitments are made. These may include purchases for employee food services, building and equipment maintenance, or legal services. Because capital items are expensive and purchased infrequently, they often involve decisions by high-level managers.

The Product Mix

product mix
Group of products that a firm makes available for sale

The group of products that a company makes available for sale, whether consumer, industrial, or both, is its **product mix.**[3] Black & Decker <www.blackanddecker.com>, for example, makes toasters, vacuum cleaners, electric drills, and a variety of other appliances and tools. 3M Corp. <www.3m.com> makes everything from Post-It notes to laser optics.

product line
Group of similar products intended for a similar group of buyers who will use them in similar ways

Product Lines Many companies begin with a single product. Over time they find that their initial products fail to suit all the consumers shopping for the product type. To meet market demand, they often introduce similar products designed to reach other consumers. ServiceMaster <www.servicemaster.com> was among the first successful home services, offering mothproofing and carpet cleaning. Then the company expanded into lawn care (TruGreen, ChemLawn), pest control (Terminix), cleaning (Merry Maids), and home warranty services (American Home Shield) for various residential services applications. A group of similar products intended for similar but not identical buyers who will use them in similar ways is a **product line.**

Companies may extend their horizons and identify opportunities outside existing product lines. The result—*multiple* (or *diversified*) *product lines*—is evident at firms such as ServiceMaster. After years of serving residential customers, ServiceMaster has added Business and Industry Services (landscaping and janitorial), Education Services (management of schools and institutions, including physical facilities and financial and personnel resources), and Healthcare Services (management of support services—plant operations, asset management, laundry/linen, clinical equipment maintenance—for long-term care facilities). Multiple product lines allow a company to grow rapidly and can help to offset the consequences of slow sales in any one product line.

DEVELOPING NEW PRODUCTS

To expand or diversify product lines—just to survive—firms must develop and successfully introduce streams of new products. Faced with competition and shifting consumer preferences, no firm can count on a single successful product to carry it forever. Even basic products that have been widely purchased for decades require constant renewal. Consider one of America's most popular brands—Levi's <www.levistrauss.com>. Its riveted denim styles were once market leaders, but ultimately, the company failed to keep pace with changing tastes, falling behind new products from competitors and losing market share among 14-to-19-year-old males during the 1990s. By 1999, at least one industry analyst was forced to report that Levi's "hasn't had a successful new product in years."[4]

In this section, we focus on the process by which companies develop the new goods and services that allow them to survive. We will also briefly discuss the special issues that arise when firms develop products for international markets.

The New Product Development Process

The demand for food and beverage ingredients has grown more than 6 percent per year, and will reach $5 billion in the year 2000. Flavors and flavor enhancers will be the biggest part of that growth, especially artificial sweeteners. However, companies that develop and sell these products face a big problem: It costs between $30 million and $50 million and can take as long as 8 to 10 years to get a new product through the approval process at the Food and Drug Administration <www.fda.gov>. Testing, both for FDA approval and for marketing, can be the most time-consuming stage of development. For example, acesulfame K beverage sweetener, which is made by Hoechst Celanese Corp. <www.hoechst.com>, has been through more than 90 safety studies and 1,000 technical studies to see how it performs in various kinds of beverages. After testing, additional stages include advertising and demonstration to food producers at the right time (when they are ready to reformulate their products with new ingredients). Cashing in on the growth of the food- and beverage-ingredients market requires an immense amount of time, patience, and money.[5]

Like Hoechst Celanese, many firms maintain research and development departments or divisions for exploring new product possibilities. Why do they devote so many resources to thinking about products and exploring their possibilities, rejecting many seemingly good ideas along the way? How do they conduct these early explorations into new product possibilities?

We address these questions in this section. We see that the high mortality rate for new ideas means that only a few new products eventually reach the market. For many companies, speed to market with a product is often as important as care in developing it. Product development is a long, complex, and expensive process. Companies do not dream up new products one day and ship them to retailers the next. In fact, new products usually involve carefully planned and sometimes risky commitments of time and resources.

Product Mortality Rates It is estimated that it takes 50 new product ideas to generate one product that finally reaches the market. Even then, only a few of those survivors

WebConnection

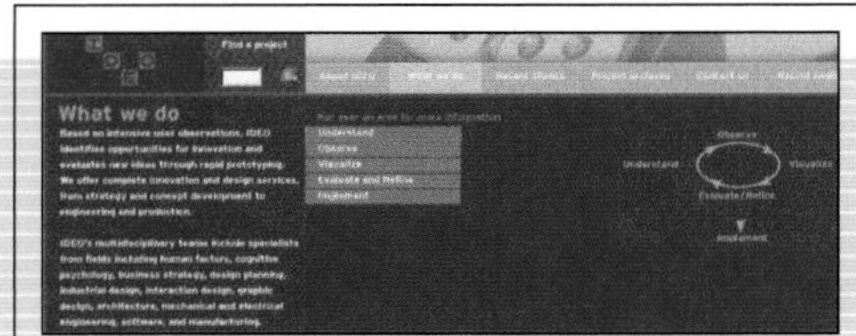

www.ideo.com

IDEO is a design consulting firm. To find out what sort of products the company has designed and engineered—and to get an idea of how its designers go about the process of prompting and realizing commercial inspirations—log on to IDEO's Web site.

become successful products. Many seemingly great ideas have failed as products. Indeed, creating a successful new product has become increasingly more difficult, even for the most experienced marketers. The number of new products hitting the market each year has increased dramatically. More than 25,000 new household, grocery, and drugstore items are introduced annually. Each year, the beverage industry alone launches up to 3,400 new products. At any given time, however, the average supermarket carries a total of only 20,000 to 25,000 different items. Because of lack of space and customer demand, about 9 out of 10 new products will fail. Products with the best chances for success are the ones that are innovative and deliver unique benefits.

Speed to Market The more rapidly a product moves from the laboratory to the marketplace, the more likely it is to survive. By introducing new products ahead of competitors, companies quickly establish market leadership. They become entrenched in the market before being challenged by late-arriving competitors. How important is **speed to market**—that is, a firm's success in responding to customer demand or market changes? One study has estimated that any product that is only three months late to market (three months behind the leader) sacrifices 12 percent of its lifetime profit potential. A product that is six months late will lose 33 percent.[6]

speed to market
Strategy of introducing new products to respond quickly to customer or market changes

The Seven-Step Development Process

To increase their chances of developing a successful new product, many firms adopt some variation on a basic seven-step process. This process is not entirely the same for goods producers and service producers.[7]

1. *Product ideas* Product development begins with a search for ideas for new products. Product ideas can come from consumers, the sales force, research and development people, or engineering personnel.
2. *Screening* The second stage is an attempt to eliminate all product ideas that do not mesh with the firm's abilities, expertise, or objectives. Representatives from marketing, engineering, and production must have input at this stage.
3. *Concept testing* Once ideas have been screened, companies use market research to get consumers' input about product benefits and price.
4. *Business analysis* After consumers have given their opinions, marketers must compare manufacturing costs and benefits to see whether the product meets minimum profitability goals.
5. *Prototype development* Once the firm has determined the potential profitability of a product, engineering or research and development produce a preliminary version. Prototypes can be extremely expensive, often requiring extensive handcrafting, tooling, and development of components.
6. *Product testing and test marketing* Using what it has learned from the prototype, the company goes into limited production. It then tests the product to see whether it meets performance requirements. If it does, it is made available for sale in limited areas. Because promotional campaigns and distribution channels must be established for test markets, this stage is quite costly.

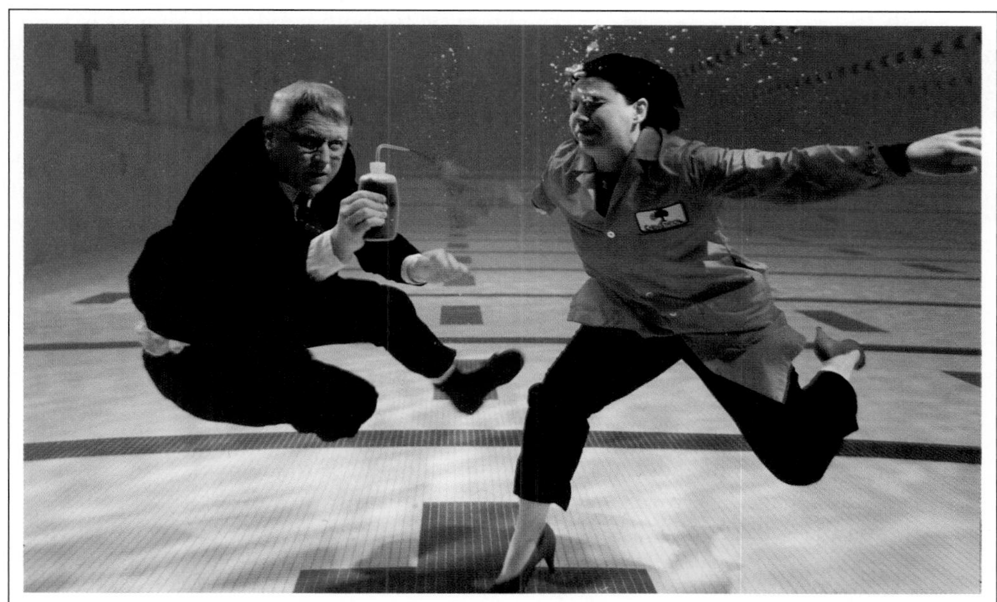

At ChemStation <www.chemstation.com>, a small industrial-detergent maker based in Dayton, Ohio, the computer database is called the Tank Management System (TMS) because it controls a network of vats for mixing formulas customized to fit the cleaning needs of client firms. Pictured here, however, is not the TMS: This is a real tank, in which chemist Kathy Hansen and CEO George Homan are developing a new product.

7. *Commercialization* If test-marketing results are positive, the company will begin full-scale production and marketing. Gradual commercialization, with the firm providing the product to more and more areas over time, prevents undue strain on initial production capabilities. On the other hand, delays in commercialization may give competitors a chance to bring out their own versions of the product.

Variations in the Process for Services

The development of services involves many of the same stages as goods development.[8] Basically, steps 2, 3, 4, 6, and 7 are the same. There are, however, some important differences in steps 1 and 5:

service package
Tangible and intangible features that characterize a service product

service process design
Three aspects (process selection, worker requirements, and facilities requirements) of developing a service product

1. *Service ideas* The search for service ideas includes a task called definition of the **service package:** identification of the tangible and intangible features that characterize the service (see Chapter 15) and service specifications.[9] For example, a firm that wants to offer year-end cleaning services to office buildings might commit itself to the following specifications: The building interior will be cleaned by midnight, January 5, including floor polishing of all aisles, carpets swept free of all dust and debris, and washbowls and lavatory equipment polished, with no interruption or interference to the customer.
2. *Service process design* Instead of prototype development, services require a three-part **service process design.** Process selection identifies each step in the service, including the sequence and the timing. Worker requirements specify employee behaviors, skills, capabilities, and interactions with customers during the service encounter. Facility requirements designate all the equipment that supports delivery of the service.[10]

product life cycle (PLC)
Series of stages in a product's profit-producing life

If a company is introducing a new product to the market, and if there is no prior demand for this product because the company is the first to produce it, how does the company decide how much of it to produce?

The Product Life Cycle

A product that reaches the market enters the **product life cycle (PLC):** a series of stages through which it passes during its profit-producing life. Depending on the product's ability to attract and keep customers over time, its PLC may be a matter of months, years, or decades. Strong, mature products (Clorox bleach, Maxwell House coffee, H&R Block tax preparation) have had long, productive lives.

Stages in the Product Life Cycle The life cycle for both goods and services is a natural process in which products are born, grow in stature, mature, and finally decline and die.[11] Look at the two graphics in Figure 12.2. In Figure 12.2(a), the four phases of the PLC are applied to several products with which you are familiar:

1. *Introduction* The introduction stage begins when the product reaches the marketplace. During this stage, marketers focus on making potential consumers aware of the product and its benefits. Because of extensive promotional and development costs, profits are nonexistent.
2. *Growth* If the new product attracts and satisfies enough consumers, sales begin to climb rapidly. During this stage, the product begins to show a profit. Other firms in the industry move rapidly to introduce their own versions.
3. *Maturity* Sales growth begins to slow. Although the product earns its highest profit level early in this stage, increased competition eventually leads to price cutting and lower profits. Toward the end of the stage, sales start to fall.
4. *Decline* During this final stage, sales and profits continue to fall. New products in the introduction stage take away sales. Companies remove or reduce promotional support (ads and salespeople) but may let the product linger to provide some profits.

Figure 12.2(b) plots the relationship of the PLC to a product's typical sales, costs, and profits. As you can see, although the early stages of the PLC often result in negative

Figure 12.2

Products in Life Cycle: Stages, Sales, Cost, and Profit

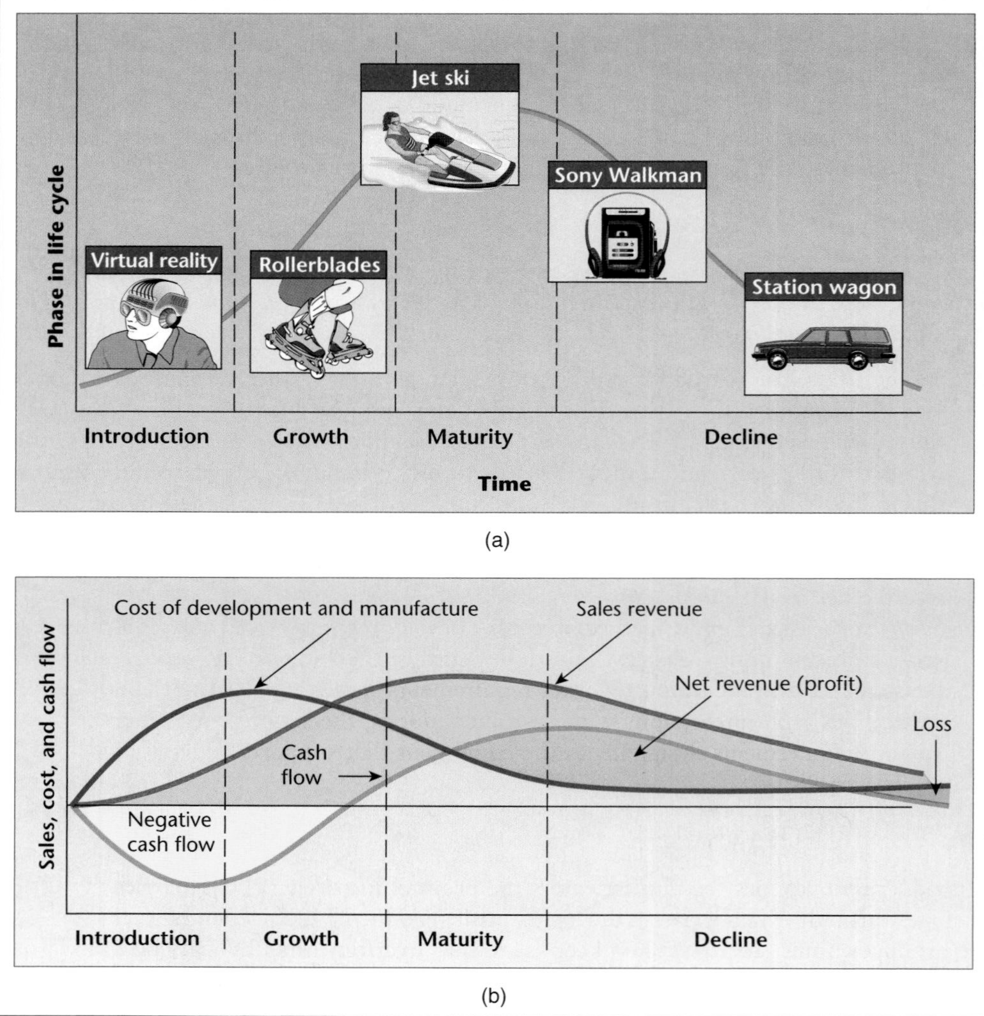

Table 12.1

Marketing Strategy over the Life Cycle

	Introduction	Growth	Maturity	Decline
Marketing strategy emphasis	Market development	Increase market share	Defend market share	Maintain efficiency in exploiting product
Pricing strategy	High price, unique product/cover introduction costs	Lower price with passage of time	Price at or below competitors'	Set price to stay profitable or decrease to liquidate
Promotion strategy	Mount sales promotion for product awareness	Appeal to mass market; emphasize features, brand	Emphasize brand differences, benefits, loyalty	Reinforce loyal customers; reduce promotion expenditures
Place strategy	Distribute through selective outlets	Build intensive network of outlets	Enlarge distribution network	Be selective in distribution; trim away unprofitable outlets

cash flows, successful products will usually recover those losses and, in fact, will continue to generate profits until they enter the decline stage. Remember that, for most products, profitable life spans are short—thus the importance placed by so many firms on the constant replenishment of their product lines.

Adjusting Marketing Strategy during the Life Cycle As a product passes from stage to stage, marketing strategy changes, too. Each aspect of the marketing mix—product, price, promotion, place (distribution)—is reexamined for each stage of the life cycle. Changes in strategy for all four life cycle stages are summarized in Table 12.1.

Extending Product Life: An Alternative to New Products Not surprisingly, companies wish that they could maintain a product's position in the maturity stage for longer periods of time. Sales of television sets, for example, have been revitalized time and time again by introducing changes such as color, portability, miniaturization, and stereo capability. In fact, many companies have extended product life through a variety of creative means. Foreign markets, for example, offer three approaches to longer life cycles:

1. In **product extension,** an existing product is marketed globally, instead of just domestically. Coca-Cola and Levi's 501 jeans are prime examples of successful international product extensions.
2. With **product adaptation,** the basic product is modified to give it greater appeal in different countries. In Germany the McDonald's meal includes beer, and Ford puts the steering wheel on the right side for exports to Japan. Because it involves product changes, this approach is usually more costly than product extension.
3. **Reintroduction** means reviving, for new markets, products that are becoming obsolete in older ones. NCR has reintroduced manually operated cash registers in Latin America.

product extension
Existing, unmodified product that is marketed globally

product adaptation
Product modified to have greater appeal in foreign markets

reintroduction
Process of reviving for new markets products that are obsolete in older ones

These examples show that the beginning of a sales downturn in the maturity stage is not necessarily the time to start abandoning a product; rather, it is often a time to realize that the old approach is starting to fade and to search for a new approach.

IDENTIFYING PRODUCTS

As we noted earlier, developing a product's features is only part of a marketer's job. Marketers must also encourage consumers to identify products. Three important tools for accomplishing this task are *branding, packaging,* and *labeling.*

Branding Products

Coca-Cola <www.coca-cola.com> is the best-known brand in the world. The *name* is so valuable that its executives like to say that if all of the company's other assets were obliterated, they could walk over to the bank and borrow $100 billion for rebuilding, just on the strength of the brand name. Brand names such as Coca-Cola and McDonald's are symbols for characterizing products and distinguishing them from one another. They were originally introduced to simplify the process when consumers are faced with a wealth of purchase decisions. **Branding** is a process of using symbols to communicate the qualities of a particular product made by a particular producer. Brands are designed to signal uniform quality: Customers who try and like a product can return to it by remembering its name.

branding
Process of using symbols to communicate the qualities of a product made by a particular producer

E-Business Branding It takes a long time to establish national or global brand recognition. The expensive, sometimes fierce struggle for brand recognition is perhaps nowhere more evident than in the current branding battles among the dot.com firms. Paying up to $1.3 million for 30-second ads, dot.com companies, dominated the advertising spots for Super Bowl XXXIV in January 2000. Why so much expensive promotional activity? Says Priceline.com vice chairman Jay S. Walker: "A lot of companies are saying, 'We have to make it big, fast, or we're not going to make it at all.' " Collectively, the top Internet brands—America Online, Yahoo!, and Amazon.com—spent more than $2 billion in 2000 even though they are just beginning to crack the ranks of the top-60 global brands. Even so, advertising alone is not enough: If a dot-com brand identity is going to emerge, it will be through an accumulation of customer contacts and experiences with products and brands. As the cost of building brand identity increases, it seems increasingly likely that many would-be e-businesses will not make it.[12]

"A lot of companies are saying, 'We have to make it big, fast, or we're not going to make it at all.' "

—Jay S. Walker,
Vice Chairman, Priceline.com

Types of Brand Names Virtually every product has a brand name. Generally, the different types of brand names—*national, licensed,* and *private brands*—increase buyers' awareness of the nature and quality of products that must compete with any number of

Although domestic growth has been sluggish, McDonald's <www.mcdonalds.com> *has taken advantage of its worldwide name recognition to pursue a long-term strategy of international expansion. In a variety of far-flung markets, McDonald's has also succeeded in finding local sources for the ingredients that go into products that, as necessary, it redesigns to appeal to local palates. Thus, the McOz Burger (Australia), the Chicken Tatsuta (Japan), and the Maharajah Mac (India).*

WebConnection

www.interbrand.com

An international brand consulting firm, Interbrand Group offers such services as corporate branding, brand research, and brand valuation. To find out what these services consist of and how they can be delivered to corporate clients, visit the Interbrand Web site.

other products. When the consumer is satisfied with the quality of a recognizable product, marketers work to achieve brand loyalty among the largest possible segment of repeat buyers.

National Brands **National brands** are produced by, widely distributed by, and carry the name of the manufacturer. These brands (for example, Scotch tape or Scope mouthwash) are often widely recognized by consumers because of national advertising campaigns. The costs of developing a positive image for a national brand are high. Some companies, therefore, use a national brand on several related products. Procter & Gamble <www.pg.com> now markets Ivory shampoo, capitalizing on the widely recognized name of its bar soap and dishwashing liquid.

national brand
Brand-name product produced by, widely distributed by, and carrying the name of a manufacturer

Many national brand names are valuable assets that signal product recognition. Millions of dollars have been spent developing names such as Noxzema, Prudential, and Minute Maid. Millions more have been spent in getting consumers to attach meaning to these names. As a rule, they rarely change. At the same time, however, the product associated with the brand may change. The Smith Corona (SC) <www.smithcorona.com> brand has been associated with typewriters since 1886. Although the typewriter business, thanks to word processors, is all but dead, the SC brand is alive and well in the office-supplies business—on cordless phones and fax machines. The SC brand remains a valuable asset because 90 percent of Americans know it.[13]

Licensed Brands It has become increasingly common for nationally recognized companies (and even personalities) to sell the rights to place their names on products. These **licensed brands** are very big business today. Ferrari <www.ferrari.com> found that selling its name can be more profitable than selling its famous cars. According to Michele Scannavini, manager of sales and marketing, "Ferrari is as much style as substance . . . as much a legend as it is a car company." Marketers reconceived the company name as a brand to extend and exploit it. The famous stallion logo now appears on luxury goods, sportswear, toys, and school supplies. Brands like Dilbert <www.dilbert.com>, the NFL <www.nfl.com>, and *South Park* <www.southpark.com> will all make millions on licensed-product sales this year. The free advertising that accompanies some licensing—such as T-shirts and other clothing—is an added bonus.[14]

licensed brand
Use of an established brand name by purchasing the right from the organization or individual who owns it

Private Brands When a wholesaler or retailer develops a brand name and has the manufacturer place that name on the product, the resulting product name is a **private brand** (or **private label**). One of the best-known sellers of private brands is Sears, which carries such lines as Craftsman tools <www.craftsman.com>, Canyon River Blues denim clothing, and Kenmore appliances <www.kenmore.com>.

private brand (or **private label**)
Brand-name product that a wholesaler or retailer has commissioned from a manufacturer

Packaging Products

packaging
Physical container in which a product is sold, advertised, or protected

How does packaging influence the success of a product?

With a few exceptions (fresh fruits and vegetables, structural steel), products need some form of **packaging** in which to be sold. A package also serves as an in-store advertisement that makes the product attractive, displays the brand name, and identifies features and benefits. It also reduces the risk of damage, breakage, or spoilage and increases the difficulty of stealing small products. Recent advances in product usage and the materials available for packaging have created additional roles for packaging. A paper-based material that can be used as a cooking container has made Budget Gourmet <www.budgetgourmet.com> dinners a low-cost entry in the dinner-entree market. No-drip-spout bottles have enhanced sales and brand loyalty for Clorox bleach <www.clorox.com>.

Labeling Products

label
Part of product packaging that identifies its name, manufacturer, and contents

Every product has a **label** on its package. Like packaging, labeling can help market the product. Campbell Soup Co. <www.campbellsoups.com> recently replaced its classic red-and-white label with a new design that has time-pressed shoppers in mind. Five colored banners have been added to the new labels (such as "fat free") so that shoppers can choose soups easily.

In addition to convenience, labels on some products must address issues of consumer safety. Thus information on many labels is regulated by the federal government. Labels for foods, drugs, and health and beauty products come under the authority of the Food, Drug and Cosmetic Act of 1938, which empowers the Food and Drug Administration to check the accuracy of product ingredients as reported on labels. The Fair Packaging and Labeling Act of 1966 also requires labels to include the product name, the name and address of the manufacturer or distributor, and the net quantity of product contained in the package. In effect since January 1, 1995, the Child Safety Protection Act requires labels to identify toys that are choking hazards. It also stipulates criteria for clarity and placement (for instance, labels must be visible when packages are displayed on shelves).

DETERMINING PRICES

pricing
Process of determining what a company will receive in exchange for its products

In product development, managers decide what products the company will offer to customers. In **pricing,** the second major component of the marketing mix, managers decide what the company will receive in exchange for its products. In this section we first discuss the objectives that influence a firm's pricing decisions. Then we describe the major tools companies use to meet those objectives.

Pricing to Meet Business Objectives

pricing objectives
Goals that producers hope to attain in pricing products for sale

Companies often price products to maximize profits, but sellers hope to attain other **pricing objectives,** or goals, in selling products. Some firms are more interested in dominating the market or securing high market share than in making the highest possible profits. Pricing decisions are also influenced by the need to survive in competitive marketplaces, by social and ethical concerns, and even by corporate image.

Profit-Maximizing Objectives Pricing to maximize profits is tricky. If prices are set too low, the company will probably sell many units of its product but may miss the opportunity to make additional profit on each unit (and may even lose money on each exchange). If prices are set too high, the company will make a large profit on each item but will sell fewer units. Again, the firm loses money. In addition, it may be left with excess inventory and may have to reduce or even close production operations. To avoid these problems, companies try to set prices to sell the number of units that will generate the highest possible total profits.

In calculating profits, managers weigh receipts against costs for materials and labor. However, they also consider the capital resources (plant and equipment) that the company must tie up to generate that level of profit. The costs of marketing (such as maintaining a large sales staff) can also be substantial. Concern over the efficient use of these resources has led many firms to set prices so as to achieve a targeted level of return on sales or capital investment.

Pricing for e-Business Objectives Marketers pricing for sales on the Internet must consider different kinds of costs and different forms of consumer awareness than those pricing products to be sold conventionally. Many e-businesses are lowering both costs and prices because of the Web's unique marketing capabilities. Because the Web typically provides a more direct link between producer and ultimate consumer, buyers avoid the costs entailed by wholesalers and retailers. Another factor in lower Internet prices is the ease of comparison shopping: Obviously, point-and-click shopping is much more efficient than driving from store to store in search of the best price. In addition, both consumers and businesses can force lower prices by joining together in the interest of greater purchasing power. Numerous small businesses are joining forces on the Web to negotiate lower prices on the health care services offered by employee benefits plans.[15]

Market Share Objectives In the long run, a business must make a profit to survive. Nevertheless, many companies initially set low prices for new products. They are willing to accept minimal profits, even losses, to get buyers to try products. They use pricing to establish **market share**—a company's percentage of the total market sales for a specific product type. Even with established products, market share may outweigh profits as a pricing objective. For a product such as Philadelphia Brand Cream Cheese, dominating a market means that consumers are more likely to buy it because they are familiar with a well-known, highly visible product. Market domination means the continuous sales of more units and thus higher profits even at a lower unit price.

market share
Company's percentage of total market sales for a specific product

Other Pricing Objectives In some instances, neither profit maximizing nor market share is the best objective. During difficult economic times loss containment and survival may become a company's main objectives. In the mid-1980s, John Deere priced agricultural equipment low enough to ensure the company's survival in a severely depressed farm economy.

A still different objective might be to provide a benefit to customers. To introduce its services to industrial clients, International Graffiti Control offered a set-fee pricing system (typically charging $60 a month per building) to owners who needed graffiti removed from building walls. This method shifted the risk from the customer to IGC. It appeals to customers who never know from day to day how much new graffiti will appear but who do know that removal is covered by a fixed fee.

Price-Setting Tools

Whatever a company's objectives, managers must measure the potential impact before deciding on final prices. Two basic tools are often used for this purpose: *cost-oriented pricing* and *breakeven analysis*. These tools are combined to identify prices that will allow the company to reach its objectives.

Cost-Oriented Pricing Cost-oriented pricing considers the firm's desire to make a profit and takes into account the need to cover production costs. A music store manager would begin to price CDs by calculating the cost of making them available to shoppers. Included in this figure would be store rent, employee wages, utilities, product displays, insurance, and, of course, the cost of buying CDs from the manufacturer.

Let's assume that the cost from the manufacturer is $8 per CD. If the store sells CDs for this price, it will not make any profit. Nor will it make a profit if it sells CDs for

markup
Amount added to an item's cost to sell it at a profit

$8.50 each or even $10 or $11. The manager must account for product and other costs and stipulate a figure for profit. Together, these figures constitute **markup.** In this case, a reasonable markup of $7 over costs would result in a $15 selling price. Markup is usually stated as a percentage of selling price. Markup percentage is thus calculated as follows:

$$\text{Markup percentage} = \frac{\text{Markup}}{\text{Sales price}}$$

In the case of our CD retailer, the markup percentage is 46.7:

$$\text{Markup percentage} = \frac{\$7}{\$15} = 46.7\%$$

Out of every dollar taken in, $.467 cents will be gross profit for the store. From this profit the store must still pay rent, utilities, insurance, and all other costs. Markup can also be expressed as a percentage of cost: The $7 markup is 87.5 percent of the $8 cost of a CD ($7/$8).

variable cost
Cost that changes with the quantity of a product produced or sold

fixed cost
Cost unaffected by the quantity of a product produced or sold

breakeven analysis
Assessment of the quantity of a product that must be sold before the seller makes a profit

breakeven point
Quantity of a product that is sold such that the seller's revenues equal all variable and fixed costs

Breakeven Analysis: Cost-Volume-Profit Relationships Using cost-oriented pricing, a firm will cover its **variable costs:** costs that change with the number of goods or services produced or sold. It will also make some money toward paying its **fixed costs:** costs that are unaffected by the number of goods or services produced or sold. But how many units must the company sell before all its fixed costs are covered and it begins to make a profit? To determine this figure, it needs a **breakeven analysis.**[16]

To continue our music store example, suppose that the variable cost for each CD (in this case, the cost of buying the CD from the producer) is $8. This means that the store's annual variable costs depend on how many CDs are sold—the number of CDs sold times $8 cost for each CD. Say that fixed costs for keeping the store open for one year are $100,000. These costs are unaffected by the number of CDs sold; costs for lighting, rent, insurance, and salaries are steady whether the store sells any CDs. Therefore, how many CDs must be sold to cover both fixed and variable costs and to generate some profit? The answer is the **breakeven point,** which is 14,286 CDs. We arrive at this number through the following equation:

$$\text{Breakeven point (in units)} = \frac{\text{Total fixed costs}}{\text{Price} - \text{Variable cost}}$$

$$= \frac{\$100{,}000}{\$15 - \$8} = 14{,}286 \text{ CDs}$$

Figure 12.3 shows the breakeven point graphically. If the store sells fewer than 14,286 CDs, it loses money for the year. If sales exceed 14,286 CDs, profits grow by $7 for each CD sold. If the store sells exactly 14,286 CDs, it will cover all its costs but will earn zero profit.

Zero profitability at the breakeven point can also be seen by using the profit equation:

$$\begin{aligned}\text{Profit} &= \text{total revenue} - (\text{Total fixed cost} + \text{Total variable cost})\\ &= (14{,}286 \text{ CDs} \times \$15) - (\$100{,}000 \text{ Fixed cost} + [14{,}286 \text{ CDs} \times \$8 \text{ Variable cost}])\\ \$0 &= (\$214{,}290) - (\$100{,}000 + \$114{,}288) \text{ (rounded to the nearest whole CD)}\end{aligned}$$

The store owner would certainly like to hit the breakeven point as early as possible; after all, that is when profits will start rolling in. Why not charge $20.00 per CD, therefore, and break even earlier? Because at $20.00 per CD, unit sales would drop. In setting a price, the manager must thus consider how much buyers will pay for a CD and what the store's local competitors charge.

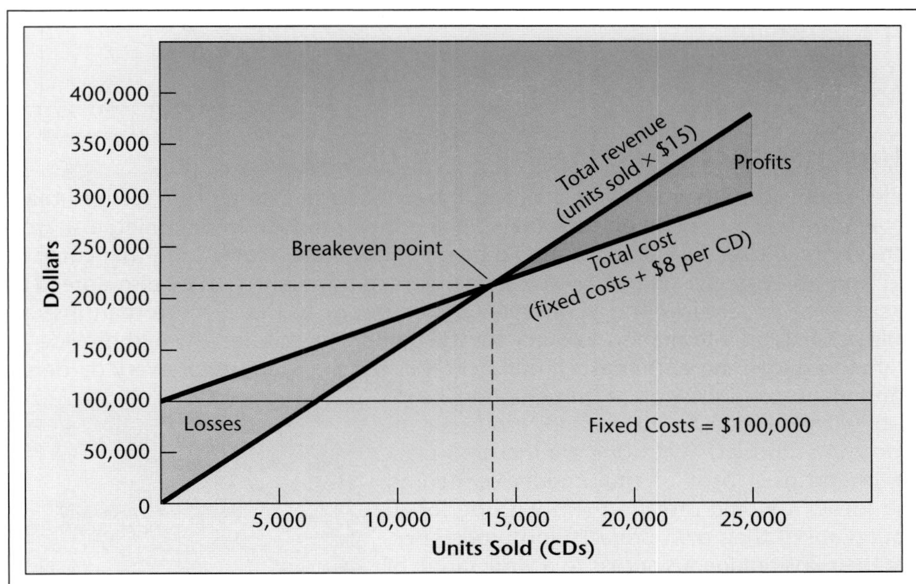

Figure 12.3
Breakeven Analysis

PRICING STRATEGIES AND TACTICS

The pricing tools discussed in the previous section are valuable in helping managers set prices on specific goods; however, they do not help in setting pricing philosophies. In this section, we discuss pricing strategy—pricing as a planning activity. We then describe some basic *pricing tactics:* ways in which managers implement a firm's pricing strategies. We conclude this section by examining some of the common problems and solutions in pricing for international markets.

Pricing Strategies

We begin this section by addressing two questions. First, can a manager really identify a single best price for a product? Probably not. A study of prices for popular nonaspirin pain relievers (such as Tylenol and Advil) found variations of 100 percent. In this market, some products sold for twice the price of other products with similar properties. Such differences may reflect some differences in product costs, however, the issue is more complex. Such wide price differences reflect differing brand images that attract different types of customers. In turn, these images reflect vastly different pricing philosophies and strategies.

This brings us to our second question, which is how important is pricing as an element in the marketing mix? Because pricing has a direct and visible impact on revenues, it is extremely important to overall marketing plans. Moreover, it is a very flexible tool: It is certainly easier to change prices than to change products or distribution channels. In this section, we focus on the ways in which pricing strategies for both new and existing products can result in widely differing prices for very similar products. The "Life Cycle of an e-Business" box in this chapter shows how the founders of Garden.com defined and designed their product.

Pricing Existing Products A firm has three options for pricing existing products:

- Pricing above prevailing market prices for similar products
- Pricing below market prices
- Pricing at or near market prices

Pricing above the market plays on the common assumption that higher price means higher quality. Curtis Mathes <www.curtismathes.com>, which manufactures consumer

Life Cycle of an e-Business

Cultivating Products and Winnowing Prices

In the early development of their business concept, the founders of Garden.com realized that the success of their venture would depend on how they defined their product. In designing a strategy for an e-business, they agreed that their product should be entirely unique—something that could be clearly distinguished from the product offered by traditional gardening retailers. They also agreed that their product—the sum of its features and benefits—would amount to much more than just a physical good. It would serve as an information resource for the gardening culture. It would provide a sense of community among gardening enthusiasts and function as a clearinghouse for every gardening need, from seeds and plants to fertilizing tips and emotional support. The product would be an interactive resource connecting gardening enthusiasts with one another and placing at their fingertips a host of multimedia gardening products and ideas. It would provide them with personalized information about their own projects and procedures. It would give them instantaneous access to a wide range of gardening products that save time, enhance creativity, and enrich the gardening experience. "Our customers," explained Cliff Sharples, "are short on time, yet hungry for knowledge about how to do things in an artful way." This definition of product set the tone for all of Garden.com's marketing and operations activities.

The pricing of the product, however, was a continuing issue, especially as marketing costs alone surpassed revenues each year from 1997 to 1999. In 1999, for instance, marketing and sales costs ran to $13.3 million, compared to product revenues of just $4.9 million. What role did pricing play in this shortfall? Lisa Sharples noted that the company's pricing strategy was designed to build trust and a sense of community. Because Garden.com added high value to its product in the form of information, interaction, gardening expertise, and a wide range of high-quality merchandise, customers were willing to pay a quality price. The firm's pricing approach, then, began by providing added value and then pricing up rather than competing as a "low-price" provider.

Each merchandise product had a fixed national price, but Lisa Sharples indicated that variable pricing for seasonal and geographic variations was a possibility. Pricing to cover the costs of shipping was tricky because it had to be simple and understandable. Some shipments, however, originated from several rather than just one supplier, thus driving up shipping costs. After studying shipment patterns, Garden.com settled on a straight percentage of subtotal (of purchases), regardless of the number of suppliers involved.

The question facing Garden.com was whether this overall pricing strategy would withstand the test of time and enable the company to become profitable. While Garden.com's pricing was attracting new customers (up to 1.5 million gardeners by 2000), its revenues did not cover costs of shipping, sales, computer technology, and marketing. As further losses accumulated, top managers faced a troubling dilemma: If they abandoned costly marketing plans to reduce costs, they would both attract fewer new customers and lose some loyal customers. In short, lower marketing costs would curtail any growth of revenues. Unfortunately, decisions about cost cutting would soon become unavoidable.

electronics, including Internet-enabled televisions, promotes itself as the most expensive television set in the United States—but worth it. The prestige and quality images of such products as the Metropolitan Opera <www.metopera.org> Godiva Chocolates <www.godiva.com>, and Patek Phillipe watches <www.patek.com> have also enabled them to succeed with this pricing philosophy.

In contrast, both Budget <www.budget.com> and Dollar <www.dollar.com> car rental companies promote themselves as low-priced alternatives to Hertz <www.hertz.com> and Avis <www.avis.com>. Similarly, ads for Suave hair-care products <www.suave.com> argue that Suave does what theirs does for a lot less. Pricing below prevailing market price can succeed if a firm can offer a product of acceptable quality while keeping costs below those of higher-priced competitors.

Finally, in some industries, a dominant firm called the **price leader** establishes product prices that other companies follow. This approach is called *market pricing,* and when it prevails, there are fewer price wars in an industry. Follower companies avoid the trouble of determining prices that consumers are willing to pay—the price leader has already done that. (Do not confuse this approach with *price fixing,* which occurs when producers illegally agree on prices among themselves.) Companies often resort to market pricing when products differ little in quality from one firm to another (for example, structural steel, gasoline, and many processed foods). These companies generally compete through promotion, personal selling, and service, not through price.

price leader
Dominant firm that establishes product prices that other companies follow

Pricing New Products Companies introducing new products must often choose between two pricing policy options, selecting either very high prices or very low ones. The first option is called *price skimming.* The second is called *penetration pricing.*[17]

Price Skimming **Price skimming** may allow a firm to earn a large profit on each item sold. The cash income is often needed to cover development and introduction costs. Skimming works only if marketers can convince consumers that a product is truly different from those already on the market. Today's expensive high-definition television (HDTV) is an example. The initial high profits will eventually attract competition. Like HDTVs, microwave ovens, calculators, video games, and video cameras were all introduced at high skim prices. Naturally, prices fell as soon as new companies entered the market. The same is true of cellular phones.

price skimming
Setting an initial high price to cover new product costs and generate a profit

Fixed Versus Dynamic Pricing for e-Business The electronic marketplace has introduced a highly variable pricing system as an alternative to more conventional—and more stable—pricing structures for both consumer and business-to-business products. So-called dynamic pricing is feasible because the flow of information on the Web notifies millions of buyers around the world of instantaneous changes in product availability. In order to attract sales that might be lost under traditional fixed-price structures, sellers can alter prices privately, on a one-to-one, customer-to-customer basis.[18] At present, *fixed pricing* remains the most widely available option for cybershoppers. e-tail giant Amazon.com has maintained the practice as the pricing strategy for its 16 million retail items. That situation, however, is beginning to change as dynamic-price challengers, such as eBay—the online person-to-person auction Web site—and Priceline.com—the online clearinghouse for person-to-business price negotiation—grow in popularity.

In questioning which way to go—fixed versus dynamic pricing—the answer among e-retailers and other experts is mixed. Although eBay epitomizes dynamic pricing, many recently polled eBay members said that they wanted to see some fixed-price sales. Amazon.com is starting to supplement fixed prices with auctions, thus competing head-to-head with eBay. Currently, there is a clear trend: Dynamic pricing now garners 15 percent of all consumer e-business spending. Why? For one thing, close interaction between buyers and sellers at eBay seems to foster a sense of community that results in customer loyalty and more time at the Web site.

An even more novel approach is taken by NexTag.com, Inc., whose dynamic-price strategy differs from both online auctions and the Priceline.com model. Instead of requiring buyers to bid up prices against each other, NexTag asks prospective customers to state the price that they are willing to pay for a product—merchants then compete for the sale. Unlike Priceline customers, NexTag customers do not commit in advance to sale prices; they also know in advance which companies they will be dealing with. NexTag gathers the offers and dispenses them to merchants, each of whom decides how low to price a product. NexTag even supplies merchants with software that keeps track of inventory and costs so that they can calculate instantly to see if a given sales margin is worth the effort to bid. According to Patti Maes of the Massachusetts Institute of Technology's

Media Lab, NexTag's dynamic pricing moves a step further from fixed pricing and may indicate the trend of the future. "Fixed prices," she points out, "are only a 100-year-old phenomenon. I think they will disappear online, simply because it is possible—cheap and easy—to vary prices online."[19]

The "Wired World" box in this chapter discusses in detail the methods of online pricing used by FreeMarkets, an Internet auction firm.

penetration pricing
Setting an initial low price to establish a new product in the market

Penetration Pricing In contrast to price skimming, **penetration pricing** seeks to generate consumer interest and stimulate trial purchase of new products. New food products (convenience foods, cookies, and snacks) are often promoted at special low prices to stimulate early sales. Penetration pricing provides for minimal (if any) profit. It can succeed only if sellers can raise prices as consumer acceptance grows. Increases must be managed carefully to avoid alienating customers.

Pricing Tactics

Regardless of its pricing strategy, a company may adopt one or more pricing tactics, such as *price lining* or *psychological pricing.* Managers must also decide whether to use *discounting* tactics.

price lining
Setting a limited number of prices for certain categories of products

Price Lining Companies selling multiple items in a product category often use **price lining,** offering all items in certain categories at a limited number of prices. A department store carries thousands of products. Setting separate prices for each brand and style of suit, glassware, or couch would take far too much time. With price lining, a store predetermines three or four *price points* at which a particular product will be sold. For men's suits, the price points might be $175, $250, and $400; all men's suits in the store will be priced at one of these three points. The store's buyers, therefore, must select suits that can be purchased and sold profitably at one of these three prices.

psychological pricing
Pricing tactic that takes advantage of the fact that consumers do not always respond rationally to stated prices

Psychological Pricing Customers are not completely rational when making buying decisions, and **psychological pricing** takes advantage of this fact. One type of psycholog-

Since the end of the compact-disk boom in about 1994, the ranks of U.S. record store chains have been decimated by a long-running price war. It was started by Best Buy <www.bestbuy.com>*—which is an electronics store, not a record store. In the early 1990s, Best Buy tried to attract electronics customers by selling compact disks at discount prices—$2 to $3 less than what record store chains were charging. Circuit City* <www.circuitcity.com>*—another electronics retailer—followed suit, and soon both chains were featuring discount-CD sections boasting 60,000 titles. Record stores could not match the selection or prices, and in 1995–1996, many—including the nation's largest chains—were forced to declare bankruptcy.*

It's a WiredWorld

• The World of Cyberprice Bidding

Sometimes a company getting into e-business is better off outsourcing some e-activities rather than doing them all itself. Consider the experience of United Technologies Corp. (UTC) <www.utc.com>. The Connecticut-based conglomerate needed to renew contracts for printed circuit boards it was buying from eight suppliers to be used in UTC elevators, air conditioners, and other products. What prices would various suppliers charge? Before accepting estimates from suppliers, UTC hoped to reduce overall prices by four percent and, based on the going rate, expected to pay out $74 million. At that point UTC decided to outsource the entire bidding process to FreeMarkets, Inc. <www.freemarkets.com>, an Internet auction company. The results were stunning. FreeMarkets received bids from 29 circuit-board companies in the United States, Europe, and Asia. The winning suppliers signed contracts for $42 million—some 43 percent below UTC's projections.

The Net has created an auction marketplace for industrial goods that makes price setting an art and a gamble for industrial buyers and sellers, just as it did earlier with auction sites for consumer items (such as CyberBuyer.com). The existence of such a marketplace changes the entire method for price setting by firms selling to industrial customers. The conventional price-setting method generally follows established patterns:

- Incumbent suppliers have the inside edge for the new contracts.
- Closed bids prohibit suppliers from knowing competitors' prices.
- Only a few suppliers are invited to submit bids.
- If a firm's bid is not accepted, it has no opportunity to revise it.

FreeMarkets is changing all of that, and in so doing, it saves client companies an average of 15 percent on the costs of their purchases. The savings potential in the $5 trillion industrial-parts market is obvious. That's why FreeMarkets is attracting customers such as Raytheon, Quaker Oats, Emerson Electric, and Owens Corning.

To get suppliers to participate, FreeMarkets does not charge them fees for bidding. Instead, industrial buyers (large companies) pay fixed subscription fees of up to $4 million a year. The auction infrastructure includes not just the software and computer technology necessary to conduct the bidding, but the standardizing of relevant technical requirements: delivery quantities and schedules, inventory quantities, and quality standards are all clarified before bidding starts. In a recent auction for a parts contract, the client set the most recent price, $745,000, as the starting point. The 25 suppliers at remote locations instantly saw each bid as it was received and posted at FreeMarkets' communications headquarters. With an official 20-minute total time deadline for submitting a better price, the low bid dropped to $612,000 after 10 minutes and then to $585,000 with 30 seconds left. When a bid is received in the last minute of regulation time, the auction kicks into a 60-second overtime period. After 13 minutes of overtime bidding, the final price landed at $518,000—which was 31 percent below the client's expectations. In this environment, the fixed-price approach to selling industrial goods is quickly becoming a thing of the past.

ical pricing, **odd-even pricing,** is based on the theory that customers prefer prices that are not stated in even dollar amounts. Thus, customers see prices of $1,000, $100, $50, and $10 as significantly higher than $999.95, $99.95, $49.95, and $9.95, respectively.

odd-even pricing
Psychological pricing tactic based on the premise that customers prefer prices not stated in even dollar amounts

Discounting Of course, the price that is eventually set for a product is not always the price at which it is sold. Often a seller must offer price reductions—**discounts**—to stimulate sales. Hyatt Hotels <www.hyatt.com> offer discount room prices to stimulate demand during off-peak seasons. Hyatt also offers commercial room discounts for frequent business users and for large-scale events—conventions, trade shows, and special events—whose high attendance fills guest rooms to capacity. For other products, such as business-to-business sales of raw materials and equipment, discounts are frequently negotiated when large quantities are purchased.[20]

discount
Price reduction offered as an incentive to purchase

International Pricing

Would a business benefit from using discounts and specials when starting up in order to gain more customers?

When Procter & Gamble (P&G) reviewed the possibilities for marketing products in new overseas markets, it encountered an unsettling fact: Because it typically priced products to cover hefty R&D costs, profitably priced items were out of reach for too many foreign consumers. The solution was, in effect, to reverse the process: Now P&G conducts research to find out what foreign buyers can afford and then develops products that they can buy. The strategy is to penetrate markets with lower-priced items and encourage customers to trade up as they become acquainted with and can afford higher-quality P&G products.

As P&G's experience shows, pricing products for sale in other countries is complicated because additional factors are involved. Income and spending trends must be analyzed. In addition, the number of intermediaries varies from country to country, as does their effect on a product's cost. Exchange rates change daily, shipping costs may occur, import tariffs must be considered (Chapter 3), and different types of pricing agreements are permitted.

An alternative strategy calls for increasing foreign market share by pricing products below cost. As a result, a given product would be priced lower in a foreign market than in its domestic market. As we saw in Chapter 3, this practice is called *dumping*, which is illegal. In recent years, the U.S. International Trade Commission <www.usitc.gov> has agreed that motorcycles made by Honda and Kawasaki were being dumped on the U.S. market, as were computer memory chips. As a result, special U.S. tariffs were imposed on these products.

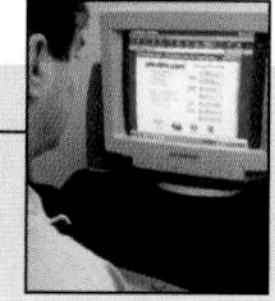

Continued from page 325

The Joy of Take-It-or-Leave-It Shopping

Within months of introducing its buyer-driven service for airline tickets, Priceline.com began offering hotel rooms, rental cars, and new cars and trucks on a name-your-own-price basis. Like airline tickets, hotel rooms and rental cars constitute time-sensitive services and are subject to so-called perishability losses: If they are not sold before a given date, the hotel cannot recover any portion of the room price or any profit for the date. To reduce such losses, hotels in 26 cities agreed to consider offers via the Priceline.com network.

New cars and trucks are the first nonperishable products in the Priceline.com system. Launched first in New York, New Jersey, and Connecticut, the service permits Internet consumers to buy new vehicles without ever talking to salespeople—and without haggling. Although there are other car-buying services on the Internet, including Auto-by-Tel **<www.autobytel.com>** and Microsoft CarPoint **<www.carpoint.msn.com>**, they operate in a more traditional marketplace than Priceline.com: They pay for the right to contact prospective customers and try to sell them vehicles. According to Gary Arlen, president of Arlen Communications, a research firm specializing in electronic media, "Priceline turns the car-buying process upside down. It takes advantage of the Web's capabilities by letting the buyer name the price and inviting dealers to take it or leave it."

How does Priceline.com earn money? It charges customers $25 and dealers $75 once a sale is complete. To discourage browsing, consumers face a $200 penalty if they walk away after a dealer accepts an offer. Buyers who cannot break the haggling habit can use Priceline.com to purchase vehicles and then argue with dealers about financing and trade-ins.

Questions for Discussion

1. Priceline.com plans to expand its buyer-driven electronic commerce system into the rental car and home mortgage markets. How will the introduction of these new products be affected by the public's recognition of other Priceline.com brands?
2. Why was an aggressive promotional campaign especially important during the introduction of Priceline.com? What marketing advantages—and burdens—do innovative products face?
3. Why is Priceline.com described as a "buyer-driven" electronic commerce system? Can you think of any other buyer-driven pricing systems?
4. Why is it important for sellers to keep Priceline.com deals private?
5. Why would an airline reject any offer from a Priceline.com customer on the day of a flight if the seat is likely to remain empty? Isn't selling inventory a primary pricing goal?
6. Why would a Priceline.com customer be more likely to strike a deal for a car near the end of the model year rather than near the beginning of the year?

www.priceline.com

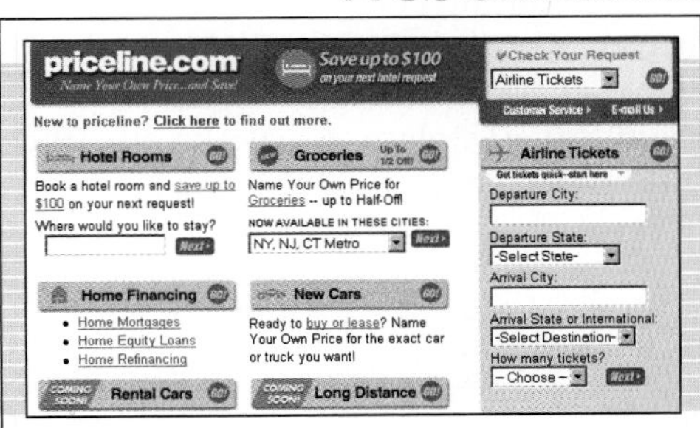

As a pioneer in buyer-driven commerce, Priceline.com permits consumers to submit their own prices to the sellers of various products and prices. Presently, the company does most of its business in the travel industry, but you can get an idea of the steps that it's taking to diversify by logging on to its Web site.

SUMMARY OF LEARNING OBJECTIVES

1 **Identify a *product* and distinguish between *consumer* and *industrial products*.** Products are a firm's reason for being. Product *features*—the tangible and intangible qualities that a company builds into its products—offer benefits to buyers, whose purchases are the main source of most companies' profits. In developing products, firms must decide whether to produce *consumer goods* for direct sale to individual consumers or *industrial goods* for sale to other firms. Marketers must recognize that buyers will pay less for common, rapidly consumed *convenience goods* than for less frequently purchased *shopping* and *specialty goods*. In industrial markets, *expense items* are generally less expensive and more rapidly consumed than such *capital items* as buildings and equipment.

2 **Trace the stages of the *product life cycle*.** New products have a life cycle that corresponds to the following stages: *introduction* (the product reaches the marketplace and receives extensive promotion); *growth* (if it attracts and satisfies enough customers, it shows a profit); *maturity* (although it begins to earn its highest profits, the product's sales begin to slow); and *decline* (profits fall as sales are lost to new products in the introduction stage).

The fact that 9 out of 10 new products will fail reflects the current *product mortality rate*. Among the strategies for increasing the likelihood of product success is *speed to market*—introducing new products to respond quickly to customer or market changes. In foreign markets, there are also three strategies for lengthening a product's life cycle: *product extension* (marketing an existing product globally instead of just domestically); *product adaptation* (modifying a product to give it greater appeal in other countries); and *reintroduction* (reviving for new markets a product that is becoming obsolete in old ones).

3 **Explain the importance of *branding, packaging,* and *labeling*.** Each product is given an identity by its brand and the way it is packaged and labeled. The goal in developing

brands—symbols to distinguish products and signal their uniform quality—is to increase *brand loyalty* (the preference that consumers have for a product with a particular brand name). *National brands* are products that are produced and widely distributed by the same manufacturer. *Licensed brands* are items for whose names sellers have bought the rights from organizations or individuals. *Private brands* (or *private labels*) are developed by wholesalers or retailers and commissioned from manufacturers.

Packaging provides an attractive container and advertises a product's features and benefits. It also reduces the risk of damage, spoilage, or theft. *Labeling* is the part of a product's packaging that usually identifies the producer's name, the manufacturer, and the contents. Labeling information is often heavily regulated.

4 **Identify the various *pricing objectives* that govern *pricing decisions* and describe the *price-setting tools* used in making these decisions.** A firm's *pricing decisions* reflect the *pricing objectives* set by its management. Although these objectives vary, they all reflect the goals that a seller hopes to reach in selling a product. They include *profit maximizing* (pricing to sell the number of units that will generate the highest possible total profits) and *meeting market share goals* (ensuring continuous sales by maintaining a strong percentage of the total sales for a specific product type). Other considerations include the need to survive in a competitive marketplace, social and ethical concerns, and even a firm's image.

Price-setting tools are chosen to meet a seller's pricing objectives. *Cost-oriented pricing* recognizes the need to cover the variable costs of producing a product (costs that change with the number of units produced or sold). In determining the price level at which profits will be generated, *breakeven analysis* also considers *fixed costs* (costs, such as facilities and salaries, that are unaffected by the number of items produced or sold).

5 **Discuss *pricing strategies* and *tactics* for both existing and new products.** Either a *price-skimming strategy* (pricing very high) or a *penetration-pricing strategy* (pricing very low) may be effective for new products. Depending on the other elements in the marketing mix, existing products may be priced at, above, or below prevailing prices for similar products. Guided by a firm's pricing strategies, managers set prices using tactics such as *price lining* (offering items in certain categories at a set number of prices), *psychological pricing* (appealing to buyers' perceptions of relative prices), and *discounting* (reducing prices to stimulate sales).

The electronic marketplace has introduced two competing pricing systems—dynamic versus fixed. *Dynamic pricing* is feasible because the flow of information on the Net notifies millions of buyers around the world of instantaneous changes in product availability. Sellers can also alter prices privately, on a customer-to-customer basis, to attract sales that might be lost under traditional fixed-price structures.

QUESTIONS AND EXERCISES

Questions for Review

1. What are the various classifications of consumer and industrial products? Give an example of a good and a service for each category other than those discussed in the text.
2. List the four stages in the product life cycle and discuss some of the ways in which a company can extend product life cycles.
3. Explain how brand names and packaging can be used to foster brand loyalty.
4. How do cost-oriented pricing and breakeven analysis help managers measure the potential impact of prices?
5. What is the overall goal of price skimming? Of penetration pricing?

Questions for Analysis

6. How would you expect the branding, packaging, and labeling of convenience, shopping, and specialty goods to differ? Why? Give examples to illustrate your answers.
7. Suppose that a small publisher selling to book distributors has fixed operating costs of $600,000 each year and variable costs of $3.00 per book. How many books must the firm sell to break even if the selling price is $6.00? If the company expects to sell 50,000 books next year and decides on a 40-percent markup, what will the selling price be?
8. Suppose your company produces industrial products for other firms. How would you go about determining the prices of your products? Describe the method you would use to arrive at a pricing decision.

Application Exercises

9. Interview the manager of a local manufacturing firm. Identify the company's different products according to their positions in the product life cycle.
10. Select a product with which you are familiar and analyze various possible pricing objectives for it. What information would you want to have if you were to adopt a profit-maximizing objective? A market share objective? An image objective?

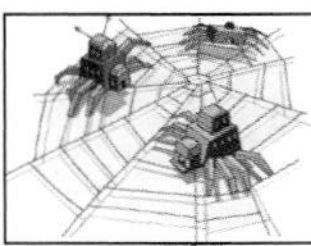

EXPLORING THE WEB

THE WEB SITE AS PRODUCT

Each e-commerce Web site is itself a product that competes in the marketplace. Some are new entrants while others are more established and known. Each site offers a product line, a get-acquainted tour, and pricing information for the products that it sells. To consider these variables and compare them in greater detail, visit each of the following sites:

www.ebay.com
www.priceline.com
www.nextag.com
www.amazon.com

Look first at the contents of the homepage for an overview of each site. Click on some of the browse categories (e.g., *Products, How to Enter the Store, How to Buy*). Then consider the following questions:

1. Compare the product offerings across the sites. Among the products offered, what percentage of them are consumer products? How many are industrial products?
2. What percentage of advertised products are convenience items? Shopping items? How many are specialty items? Explain the similarities and differences among the sites in terms of product offerings.
3. On each site, how many product lines can you identify? What distinguishes any given product line from the others?
4. Compare the pricing methods of Priceline.com versus the way prices are determined at NexTag.com. Explain the similarities and differences.
5. Explore the Amazon.com and eBay.com sites, noting the ranges of products and pricing choices that are available. Describe the ways in which they are similar and the ways that they differ from one another.
6. Recall the price-setting objectives and tools described in this chapter. Which of them are most important to each of the four Web sites? Explain.

BUILDING YOUR BUSINESS SKILLS

WHAT'S BRAND NEWS?

This exercise enhances the following SCANS workplace competencies: demonstrating basic skills, demonstrating thinking skills, exhibiting interpersonal skills, and working with information.

GOAL

To encourage students to evaluate the ways in which branding affects their personal awareness of products available in the marketplace.

METHOD

Step 1

Working individually, examine a recent Sunday newspaper from a nearby large city. Focusing on paid advertisements, list the brands of various products that you see. For example, you may see food store ads, a Saturn ad, or an ad for an HMO health care system, and so on. Draw up a selective list of the various brands that are featured in the ads—include only those that attract your attention for one reason or another. Then, divide the items on your list into two columns—national brands and private brands.

Step 2

Join with three or four classmates to compare your lists. Analyze the extent to which private brands versus national brands are more prominent in that newspaper. Which brands are more familiar to you? Less familiar? Discuss the reasons for your familiarity or nonfamiliarity with specific brands.

FOLLOW-UP QUESTIONS

1. What do you think motivated the national brands (companies) on your list to advertise in this newspaper rather than elsewhere? For those brands, are you influenced by brand reputation or advertising?
2. Can you say what attracted you to select the private brands that you put on your list?

Were you influenced mainly by price? Visual appeal? Were other factors involved?

3. Find a national brand that appears on the list of just one group member. Given the fact that only one group member listed a certain national brand that other group members ignored, what factors were responsible for the different choices?
4. Based on this exercise, are you likely to change the way you look at brands? Will you be attracted more to national brands or to private brands? Explain your answer.

CRAFTING YOUR BUSINESS PLAN

SPICING UP THE PRODUCT DEVELOPMENT PROCESS

THE PURPOSE OF THE ASSIGNMENT

1. To acquaint students with the process of navigating the *Business PlanPro* (*BPP*) software package (Version 4.0).
2. To familiarize students with certain product development and product pricing issues that a sample firm faces in developing its business plan.
3. To demonstrate how four chapter topics—product line, product pricing, breakeven analysis, and packaging—affect the *BPP* planning environment.

ASSIGNMENT

After reading Chapter 12 in the textbook, open the BPP *software* and look around for information about product line, product pricing, packaging, and breakeven analysis as they apply to a sample firm:* Salvadore's Sauces Food Dis. *(Salvadore's, Inc.). Then respond to the following items:*

1. Is Salvadore's Sauces planning to offer consumer products or industrial products? Explain. [Sites to see in *BPP* (for this assignment): In the Plan Outline screen, click on **4.0 Marketing Analysis Summary.** Then click on **4.1 Market Segmentation.** After returning to the Plan Outline screen, click on each of the following: **5.1 Marketing Strategy, 5.2 Sales Strategy,** and **5.3 Strategic Alliances.**]
2. How would you describe the pricing strategy that Salvadore's Sauces plans to use? [Sites to see in *BPP:* In the Plan Outline screen, click on **5.2.1 Sales Forecast.** After returning to the Plan Outline screen, click on **5.1.1 Pricing Strategy.**]
3. Suppose you want to help Salvadore's Sauces set prices on the basis of cost-oriented pricing. Does the Salvadore's plan contain enough data to allow this method of pricing? Explain why or why not. [Sites to see in *BPP:* In the Plan Outline screen, click on **7.4 Projected Profit or Loss.** After returning to the Plan Outline screen, go beneath **7.4 Projected Profit or Loss** and click on **Table: Profit and Loss.**]
4. What role does packaging play in Salvadore's plan? [Sites to see in *BPP* (for this assignment): In the Plan Outline screen, click on **4.3 Industry Analysis.** Then click on **4.3.1 Industry Participants.** After returning to the Plan Outline screen, click on each of the following: **3.0 Products and Services** and **3.2 Competitive Comparison.**]
5. Explain how product pricing relates to breakeven analysis in the Salvadore's plan. [Sites to see in *BPP:* In the Plan Outline screen, click on **7.3 Breakeven Analysis.** After returning to the Plan Outline screen, go beneath **7.3 Breakeven Analysis** and click on **Table: Breakeven Analysis.** Also go beneath **7.3 Breakeven Analysis** and examine **Chart: Breakeven Analysis.**]

FOR YOUR OWN BUSINESS PLAN

6. Many bankers and investors are interested in seeing evidence that a prospective business will be on solid (profitable) financial footing. Accordingly, your business plan will be stronger if you can project profits based on forecasts of sales, pricing, and breakeven analysis. Describe your pricing strategy and make sales forecasts. In which sections of the

BPP document will you present this sort of information?

*GENERAL TIPS FOR NAVIGATING IN *BPP*

1. Open the *BPP* program, examine the Welcome screen, and click on **Open a Sample Plan.**
2. From the Open a Sample Plan dialogue box, click on a sample company name; then click on **Open.**
3. On the Plan Manager screen, click on Your Plan Outline; then click on any of the lines (for example, **5.1.1 Pricing Strategy**).
4. You can always return to the Plan Outline screen by going to the bottom of the screen and clicking on the Plan Outline icon.
5. After finishing with one sample company, you can get to the next one by going to the top of the screen and clicking on **File** (on the menu bar). Then beneath that, select **Open Sample Plan.** This will exit you from the current company file and take you to the Open Sample Plan dialogue box, where you can select your next sample company.
6. When you are finished, you can close the program by going to the top of the screen and clicking on **File** (on the bar menu). Then beneath that, select **Exit.**

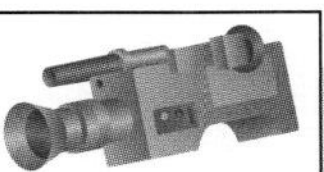

VIDEO EXERCISE

KEEPING THE BRAND HEALTHY: DOC MARTENS

Learning Objectives

The purpose of this video exercise is to help you:

1. Appreciate the way brands are developed.
2. Understand the marketing value of a brand and its image.
3. Recognize the challenges in extending the life of a successful brand.

BACKGROUND INFORMATION

British shoe manufacturer Doc Martens employs 3,000 people, mostly in England, and has been in business for 40 years. Although the shoe-manufacturing industry is on the decline in England (as in other developed countries), the firm takes pride in the fact that its products are still made in England and attributes a large part of its success to the cutting-edge image of its popular brand, whose 70,000 different styles are now exported to over 80 countries around the world.

THE VIDEO

Director of Corporate Affairs Andrew Borge talks about the Doc Martens brand, its image, its past, and its future. He discusses the ways in which the firm protects the Doc Martens brand and some of its plans for extending its life without altering its identity.

DISCUSSION QUESTIONS

1. In the past, Doc Martens had a negative experience with licensing its brand. What do you think a product company like this needs to do in order to maintain control of its brand in a licensing agreement?
2. With 70,000 different styles, how does Doc Martens retain integrity as a brand?
3. Where would you place Doc Martens in the product life cycle? What do you think is the probable future of the brand?

FOLLOW-UP ASSIGNMENT

What brand extensions might make sense for Doc Martens? Consider non-apparel products as well as accessories, such as luggage or leather goods. Draft a proposal for a brand extension that includes a product description, profile of the target market, and reasons why the product fits or enhances the Doc Martens brand.

FOR FURTHER EXPLORATION

Check the Web sites of several other popular footwear and clothing manufacturers, such as Adidas <www.adidas.com>, Nike <www.nike.com>, and FUBU <www.fubu.com>. What sort of brand image do they project on the Internet? Is it consistent with the image they project in their advertising? In retail outlets? Why or why not? What effect do you think this consistency (or lack of it) has on customers' perception of the brand?

Chapter

13

Promoting Products

After reading this chapter, you should be able to:

1. ***Identify*** the important objectives of *promotion* and discuss the considerations entailed in selecting a *promotional mix.*
2. ***Discuss*** the most important *advertising strategies* and describe the key *advertising media.*
3. ***Outline*** the tasks involved in *personal selling* and list the steps in the *personal selling process.*
4. ***Describe*** the various types of *sales promotions.*
5. ***Describe*** the development of *international promotional strategies.*
6. ***Show*** how small businesses use promotional activities.

Log On and Get Rational

Please forgive us for using a phrase that most students love to hate, but it's the best way we know to describe the way in which traditional product-promotion strategies are changing in the era of the Internet: There has been a *paradigm shift*—the emergence of a new world view—in the way companies promote products in the virtual world. It is a shift that combines traditional promotional methods with new approaches geared to the interactivity of the Web.

Advertisers have discovered (often the hard way) that tried-and-true promotional tactics don't work online. For example, an emotion-filled vignette may be just right for television, but it has no impact in cyberspace where online customers won't take the time to get involved. "You're not allowed to say or market anything online unless the customer wants to hear it," explains Chan Suh, CEO of Agency.com Ltd. <www.agency.com>, an interactive consulting company. "In [cyberspace] marketing, the customer is in charge."

According to research, the best way to reach online customers is through something called *rational marketing*—product promotions that provide concrete, interactive services. Consider a recent theme promoted on the MasterCard International Web site. "Shop Smart" <www.mastercard.com/shoponline/shopsmart/shopsmartdetails.html> is a program that guides online shoppers to retail sites with state-of-the-art credit card security systems. In contrast, the company's traditional marketing message for television uses the emotional tag line "Priceless" and shows Mark McGwire hitting his 62nd home run. Debra Coughlin, a member of MasterCard's Internet marketing team, explains the thinking behind the different approaches: "The TV user is looking for entertainment. The Internet user is online for more practical reasons. Our brand efforts reflect that end-user goal."

Marketers at General Motors' Saturn division use television and other traditional media to introduce consumers to the help they'll receive online. The Saturn Web site <**www.saturn.com**> includes a lease-price calculator, a purchase-payment calculator, an interactive method for choosing options and seeing how they look on different cars, a dealer locator, and an online order form. The Web site is featured on a humorous television commercial that shows a college student ordering a Saturn from his dorm room as easily as he might order a pizza. The synergy created through the television and virtual promotions has tripled the number of annual visitors to the Saturn Web site.

Not all products are equally promotable on the Web, as packaged-goods manufacturers have learned. Although marketers for Tide laundry detergent <**www.tide.com**>, Ragú sauces <**www.ragu.com**>, and Clairol haircare products <**www.clairol.com**> have filled their sites with practical interactive help, they still use traditional channels for the bulk of their promotions. Fast-food companies are also taking a cautious promotional approach. Although McDonald's does some marketing on the Web, marketing executives are waiting for the technology that allows full-motion video and audio programming before they make a greater commitment. As a promotional medium, explains David G. Green, McDonald's senior vice president for international marketing, the Internet "is more difficult for those of us who do not have a good or service that is transferable to a virtual experience."

"You're not allowed to say or market anything online unless the customer wants to hear it. In cyberspace marketing, the customer is in charge."

—Chan Suh, CEO, Agency.com Ltd.

Our opening story continues on page 371

Most marketers believe that, sooner rather than later, online marketing will be a critical element in their promotional strategies. In fact, as the online market grows, mastering the art of reaching online consumers through rational marketing and other methods may be necessary for corporate survival. As you will see in this chapter, it is the challenge of marketers to meet their strategic goals by making the right promotional choices on all media. By focusing on the learning objectives of this chapter, you will become acquainted with the different approaches to promotional strategy and better understand when and why companies choose particular strategies and tools.

THE IMPORTANCE OF PROMOTION

promotion
Aspect of the marketing mix concerned with the most effective techniques for selling a product

As we noted in Chapter 11, **promotion** is any technique designed to sell a product. It is part of the communication mix: the total message any company sends to consumers about its product. Promotional techniques, especially advertising, must communicate the uses, features, and benefits of products. Sales promotions also include various programs that add value beyond the benefits inherent in the product. For example, it is nice to get a high-quality product at a reasonable price but even better when the seller offers a rebate or a bonus pack with "20 percent more free." In promoting products, then, marketers have an array of tools at their disposal.

In this chapter, we will look at the different objectives of and approaches to promotion. We will show when and why companies use particular strategies and tools and then describe the special promotional problems faced by both international and small businesses. First, however, we will explain the two general values to be gained from any promotional activity, regardless of the particular strategy or tools involved: *communicating information* and *creating more satisfying exchanges*.

Information and Exchange Values

In free-market systems, a business uses promotional methods to communicate information about itself and its products to consumers and industrial buyers. The purpose is to influence purchase decisions. From an information standpoint, promotions seek to accomplish four things with potential customers:

- Make them aware of products.
- Make them knowledgeable about products.
- Persuade them to like products.
- Persuade them to purchase products.

In terms of the exchange relationship, the firm hopes that marketing promotions will make its product more attractive. The buyer gains more from the exchange (a more attractive product), as does the seller (more unit sales or higher prices).

Successful promotions therefore provide communication about the product and create exchanges that satisfy both the customer's and the organization's objectives. However, because promotions are expensive, choosing the best promotional mix becomes critical. The promotional program . . . whether at the introduction stage (promoting for new product awareness) or maturity stage (promoting brand benefits and customer loyalty), can determine the success or failure of any business or product.

Promotional Objectives

The ultimate objective of any promotion is to increase sales. In addition, marketers may use promotion to *communicate information, position products, add value,* and *control sales volume.*

Communicating Information Promotion is effective in communicating information from one person or organization to another. Consumers cannot buy products unless they have been informed about them. Information may thus advise customers that a product exists or educate them about its features. If you are trying to connect your business to the Internet economy, for example, a KPMG Consulting <www.kpmg.com> advertisement in the *Wall Street Journal* not only announces the availability of KPMG's experienced consultants but also informs readers about the need to integrate e-strategy, e-branding, and e-services. Information may be communicated in writing (in newspapers and magazines), verbally (in person or over the telephone), or visually (on television, matchbook covers, or billboards). Today, the communication of information about a company's goods or services is so important that marketers try to place it everywhere consumers can be found: Experts estimate that the average consumer comes into contact with approximately 1,500 bits of promotional information each day.

Positioning Products As we saw in Chapter 11, **positioning** is the process of establishing an easily identifiable product image in the minds of consumers. Positioning a product is difficult because a company is trying to appeal to a specific segment of the market rather than to the market as a whole. First, it must identify which segments are likely to purchase its product and who are its competitors. Only then can it focus its strategy on differentiating its product from the competition's while still appealing to its target audience.

positioning
Process of establishing an identifiable product image in the minds of consumers

The St. Louis Bread Co. <www.stlouisbread.com>, for example, has used positioning to differentiate its restaurants from competitors' throughout the Midwest. It offers a limited menu of light, healthful foods—for both eat-in and takeout—for morning, noon, and early evening service. The "light and healthy" theme of the menu—fresh, wholesome baked goods, soups, salads, sandwiches, and flavored coffees—is complemented by quiet surroundings, fresh flowers on dining tables, light classical music, and cleanliness. Within any metropolitan area, sites are chosen to ensure that each St. Louis Bread outlet is not far away for upper-middle-class professionals looking for quick, wholesome, reasonably priced meals in a pleasant atmosphere.[1]

Adding Value Today's value-conscious customers gain benefits when the promotional mix is shifted so that it communicates value-added benefits in its products. Burger King <www.burgerking.com> shifted its promotional mix by cutting back on advertising dollars and using those funds for customer discounts: Receiving the same food at a lower price is "value-added" for BK's customers. Similarly, in upstate New York, Lawless Container Corp., whose customers are other companies that buy cardboard boxes and packaging materials, has shifted its emphasis to certain unique services such as special credit terms, storage, and delivery times that are valued by individual customers. Like BK's discounts, Lawless's new services add greater value for the dollar.

In addition to adding value promotion is the main means of establishing a product's perceived value. It means creating communications and directing them to value-conscious customers. Customers must be given information about the value-adding characteristics—warranties, repair contracts, and after-purchase service—by which a product provides greater value than its competitors.

Controlling Sales Volume Many companies, such as Hallmark Cards <www.hallmark.com>, experience seasonal sales patterns. By increasing promotional activities in slow periods, these firms can achieve more stable sales volume throughout the year. They can keep production and distribution systems running evenly. Promotions can even turn slow seasons into peak sales periods. Greeting card companies and florists together have done much to create Grandparents' Day. The result has been increased consumer demand for cards and flowers in the middle of what was once a slow season for both industries.

Promotional Strategies

Once its larger marketing objectives are clear, a firm must develop a promotional strategy to achieve them. Two fundamentally different strategies are often used:[2]

pull strategy
Promotional strategy designed to appeal directly to consumers who will demand a product from retailers

push strategy
Promotional strategy designed to encourage wholesalers or retailers to market products to consumers

- A **pull strategy** is designed to appeal directly to consumers who will demand the product from retailers. In turn, retailers will demand the product from wholesalers. When publishing a Stephen King novel, for example, Doubleday directs its promotions at horror story fans. If a bookstore does not stock the book, requests from readers will prompt it to order copies from Doubleday.
- Using a **push strategy,** a firm aggressively markets its product to wholesalers and retailers who then persuade consumers to buy it. Brunswick Corp., for instance, uses a push strategy to promote Bayliner boats, directing its promotions at dealers and persuading them to order more inventory. Dealers are then responsible for stimulating demand among boaters in their respective districts.

Many large firms use combination pull and push strategies. For example, General Foods uses advertising to create consumer demand (pull) for its cereals. At the same time, it pushes wholesalers and retailers to stock them.

The Promotional Mix

promotional mix
Combination of tools used to promote a product

As we noted in Chapter 12, there are four types of promotional tools: *advertising, personal selling, sales promotions,* and *publicity and public relations.* The best combination of these tools—that is, the best **promotional mix**—depends on many factors. The company's product, the characteristics of the target audience, and budget considerations are all important.

The Product Obviously, the nature of the product being promoted affects the promotional mix greatly. Advertising can reach a large number of widely dispersed consumers. It is the promotional tool used for products that are widely purchased, such as sunglasses, radios, snack foods, and thousands of others. Companies introducing new products also favor advertising because it reaches a large number of people very quickly and can repeat a message many times. Personal selling, on the other hand, is important when the product appeals to a very specific audience, such as an industrial company that needs highly specialized equipment. (We will discuss personal selling in more detail later in this chapter.)

The Target Audience: Promotion and the Buyer Decision Process Another consideration in establishing the promotional mix is matching the promotional tool with the relevant stage in the buyer decision process. As we noted in Chapter 11, this process can be broken down into five steps:

1. Buyers must first recognize the need to make a purchase. At this stage, marketers must make sure the buyer is aware that their products exist. Advertising and publicity, which can reach a large number of people very quickly, are very important.
2. Buyers also want to learn more about available products. Advertising and personal selling are important in this stage because both can be used to educate the customer.
3. Buyers evaluate and compare competing products. Personal selling can be vital at this point: Sales representatives can demonstrate their product's quality and performance in direct relation to competitors' products.
4. Buyers decide on specific products and purchase them. Sales promotion is effective at this stage because it can give consumers an incentive to buy. Personal selling can also help by bringing products to convenient purchase locations.
5. Buyers evaluate products after purchasing them. Advertising, or even personal selling, is sometimes used after the sale to remind consumers that they made a prudent purchase.

Figure 13.1 summarizes the effective promotional tools for each stage of the consumer buying process.

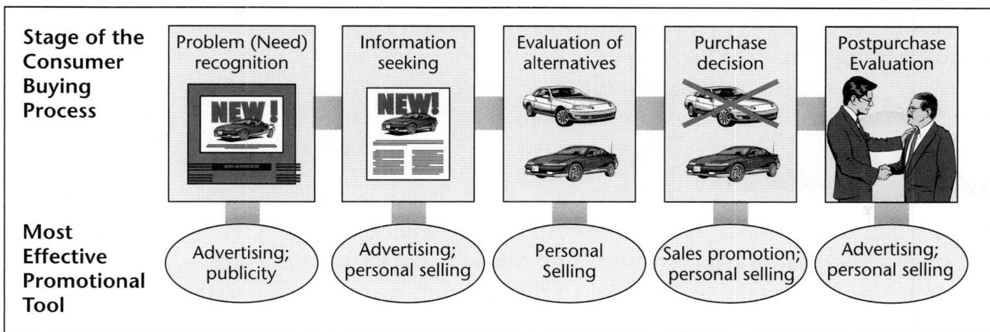

Figure 13.1
The Consumer Buying Process and the Promotional Mix

The Promotional Mix Budget Choosing the promotional mix begins by determining the promotional budget—one of the marketing manager's most difficult decisions. The budget specifies how much of the firm's total resources will be spent on promotions. The combined costs of personal selling, advertising, sales promotion, and public relations must fall within the budgeted amount. The elements of the mix must be balanced if they are to have the desired effects on attitudes and purchasing decisions.

ADVERTISING PROMOTIONS

Advertising is paid, nonpersonal communication used by an identified sponsor to inform an audience about a product. In 1998, U.S. firms spent more than $202 billion on advertising, with $65 billion of this amount being spent by just 100 companies.[3]

In this section, we will begin by describing some key elements in advertising strategy. Then we will describe each of the different types of advertising media, noting both advantages and limitations of each. We will also identify three main types of advertising according to product type and purpose. Finally, we will describe the advertising campaign and the role of the advertising agency in designing it.

Advertising Strategies

The advertising strategies used for a product most often depend on which stage of the product life cycle (see Chapter 12) the product is in. During the introduction stage, for example, informative advertising can help develop an awareness of the company and its product among buyers and help establish a demand for the product.[4] Thus, when a new textbook is published, instructors receive direct-mail informative advertisements notifying them of the book's contents and availability.

As products become established and competition increases, advertising strategies must change. During a product's growth and maturity stages, marketers may choose one of three common approaches:

- **Persuasive advertising** seeks to influence consumers to buy the company's products rather than those of its rivals. This approach usually emphasizes the quality of the firm's goods or services.[5] Goodyear advertises its Eagle #1 NASCAR street tires <www.goodyear.com/us/tires/tirecatalog/EAG_1NAS.html> for year-round traction, long wear, and responsive cornering. They also have the same gold color lettering as the Goodyear racing Eagles in the 2000 Daytona 500.
- Another useful strategy during the maturity stage is **comparative advertising,** in which two or more products are compared directly. The goal is to steal sales from the competition.[6] An example is a recently run television ad for Pepsi One: Ferry passengers sitting side by side are reading and working while their Coca-Cola and Pepsi One cans slide from person-to-person as the boat sways on its journey. The message suggests that inasmuch as passengers can't taste any difference between the two brands, why not switch to Pepsi One?

persuasive advertising Advertising strategy that tries to influence consumers to buy one company's products instead of those of its rivals

comparative advertising Advertising strategy that directly compares two or more products

reminder advertising Advertising strategy that tries to keep a product's name in the consumer's mind

- During the late part of the maturity stage and throughout the decline stage, **reminder advertising** can help to keep the product's name in the consumer's mind. Atari <www.atari.org> continues to advertise home video games even though market attention has shifted to newer competitors such as Nintendo, Sega, and Genesis.

Advertising Media

advertising media Variety of communication devices for carrying a seller's message to potential customers

Bombarded with thousands of advertisements, consumers tend to ignore the bulk of the ads they see or hear. Marketers must find out who their customers are, which media they attend to, what message will appeal to them, and how to get their attention. Marketers thus use several different **advertising media**—that is, specific communication devices for carrying a seller's message to potential customers. IBM <www.ibm.com> uses television ads to keep its name fresh in consumers' minds. It uses newspaper and magazine ads, however, to educate consumers on product features and trade publications to introduce new software. The following are the most common advertising media. Each medium has its own advantages and disadvantages.

Newspapers Newspapers are the most widely used medium, accounting for about 25 percent of all advertising expenditures. Because each local market has at least one daily newspaper, newspapers provide excellent coverage. Each day they reach more than 113 million U.S. adults.

The main advantage of newspaper advertising is flexible, rapid coverage: Ads can easily be changed from day to day. However, newspapers are generally thrown out after one day, are usually not printed in color, and have poor reproduction quality. Because their readership is so broad, newspapers do not usually allow advertisers to target audiences very well.

Television Television accounts for about 22 percent of all advertising outlays. Figure 13.2 shows network TV advertising expenditures for some U.S. firms.[7] In addition to the

Figure 13.2
Top 10 Network TV Advertisers

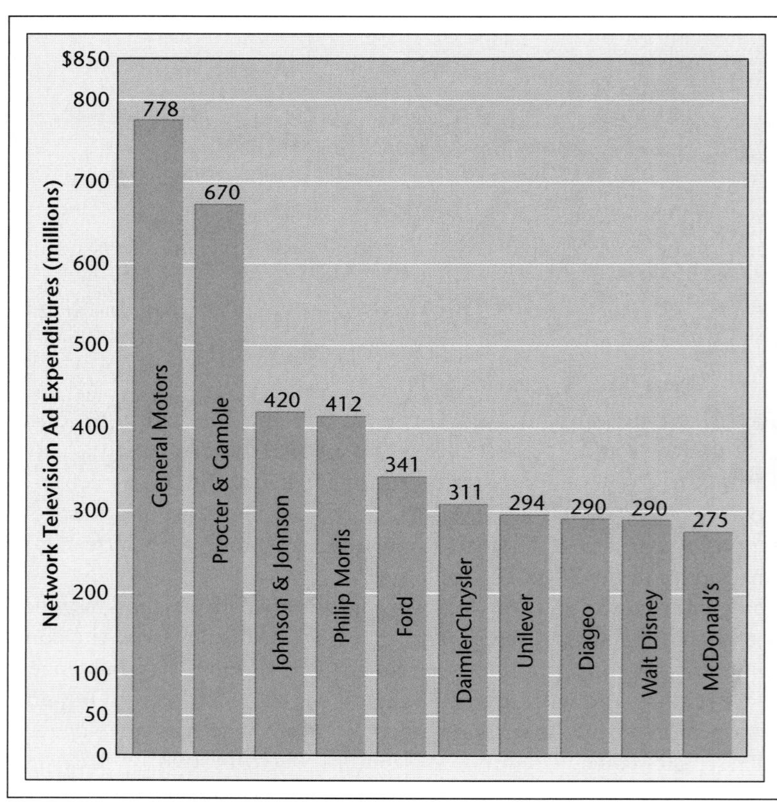

major networks, cable television has become an important advertising medium. Cable network ad revenues increased from $3.4 billion in 1995 to more than $10 billion in 1999.[8]

Combining sight, sound, and motion, television appeals to a full complement of the viewer's senses. In addition, information on viewer demographics for a particular program allows advertisers to aim at target audiences. Finally, television reaches more people than any other medium. Super Bowl XXXIV attracted over 45 million households and nearly 130 million viewers. The fact that there are so many commercials on TV often causes viewers to confuse products. Most people cannot recall whether a tire commercial advertised the virtues of Firestone, Goodyear, or B. F. Goodrich. In addition, the brevity of TV ads makes television a poor medium in which to educate viewers about complex products. Finally, television is also the most expensive medium in which to advertise. Companies such as Federal Express, Pepsi, Anheuser-Busch, and the now defunct Pets.com, along with 16 other dot.com companies paid an average of $2.2 million for 30-second commercials during Super Bowl XXXIV. Many of the dot.coms were unknowns trying to build brand impact with major one-shot ad expenditures. Unfortunately, their messages didn't register well with consumers, who rated several of the dot.com ads as least popular. "If any dot.coms are still under the illusion that advertising was the simple solution to building brands, then the Super Bowl will have put an end to that," says Simon Williams, chairman of Sterling Group <www.sterlinggroup.com>, a brand consulting company.[9]

"If any dot-coms are still under the illusion that advertising was the simple solution to building brands, then the Super Bowl will have put an end to that."

—Simon Williams, Chairman of the Sterling Group consulting company

Direct Mail **Direct mail** advertisements account for 18 percent of all advertising outlays. Direct mail involves fliers or other types of printed advertisements mailed directly to consumers' homes or places of business. It allows the company to select its audience and personalize its message. Although many people discard junk mail, advertisers can predict in advance how many recipients will take a mailing seriously. These people have a stronger-than-average interest in the product advertised and are more likely than most to buy the promoted product. Although direct mail involves the largest advance costs of any advertising technique, it does appear to have the highest cost-effectiveness. It is credited with generating $421 million in U.S. sales for 1998.[10]

direct mail
Advertising medium in which messages are mailed directly to consumers' homes or places of business

Radio About seven percent of all advertising outlays are for radio advertising. Over 180 million people in the United States listen to the radio each day, and radio ads are quite inexpensive. A small business in a Midwestern town of 100,000 people pays only about $20 for a 30-second local radio spot. (A television spot in the same area costs over $250.) In addition, stations are usually segmented into categories such as rock and roll, country and western, jazz, talk shows, news, and religious programming; their audiences are largely segmented. Unfortunately, radio ads, like television ads, are over quickly. Furthermore, they provide only audio presentations, and people tend to use the radio as background while doing other things.

Magazines Magazine ads account for roughly 5 percent of all advertising. The huge variety of magazines provides a high level of ready market segmentation. Magazines also allow advertisers plenty of space for detailed product information. They allow for excellent reproduction of photographs and artwork. Because magazines have long lives and tend to be passed from person to person, ads constantly get increased exposure. Ads must be submitted well in advance, however, and there is often no guarantee of where an ad will appear within a magazine. Magazines are so effective for reaching some targeted audiences that advertisers—including Philip Morris, Mercedes-Benz, and Sears & Roebuck—have sponsored their own magazines.[11]

Outdoor Advertising Outdoor advertising—billboards, signs, and advertisements on buses, street furniture, taxis, stadiums, and subways—makes up about one percent of all advertising. These ads are inexpensive, face little competition for customers' attention, and are subject to high repeat exposure. Once regarded as visually inferior to more

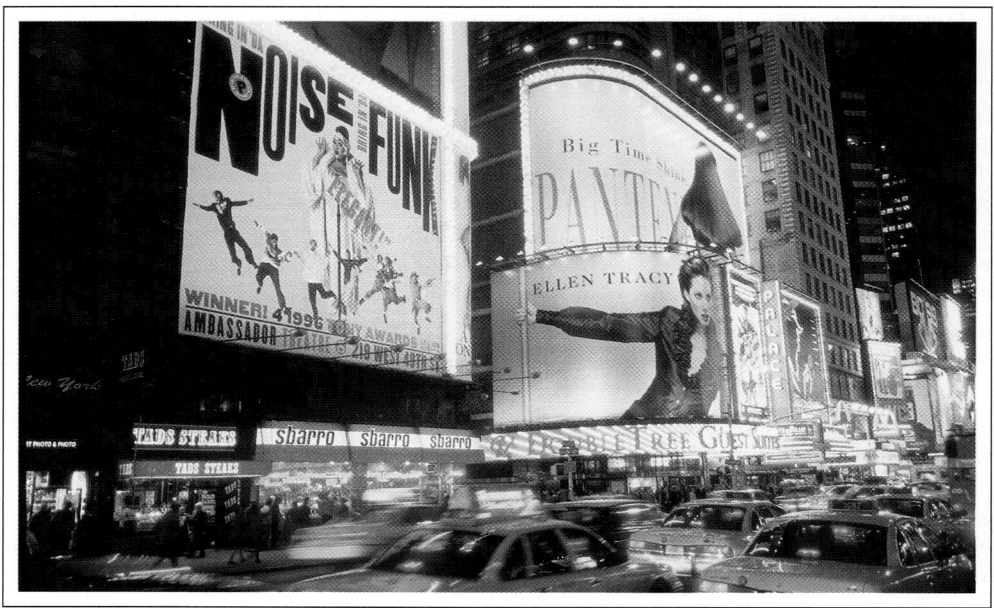

Speed and creativity have given billboards like these in New York's Times Square a new prominence in the world of advertising media. Instead of relying on highly skilled human artists, outdoor ad sellers can now commission digital creations that not only turn heads but still cost less than most other media. Whereas it used to take a month to launch a billboard-based campaign, it now takes just days.

glamorous media, new technology has made outdoor advertising more creative and is leading the revival in spending on outdoor advertising: At 10 percent per year, it's growing faster than newspapers, magazines, and television. Many of the 400,000 billboards in the United States display attractive realistic images, while others experiment with animation and changing images. In New York, fake fir trees appeared to grow out of a Poland Spring billboard. Dayton Hudson Corp. had a board that emitted a mint scent to remind pedestrians about Valentine's Day candy in downtown Minneapolis. Today, billboard messages are cheaper because they can be digitally color-printed from computers in large quantities. However, outdoor ads can present only limited amounts of information, and sellers have little control over audiences.[12]

The Internet The most recent advertising medium is the Internet, where such well-known names as 3M Corp., Burlington Coat Factory, Miller Genuine Draft, MCI Communications, Reebok, and thousands of lesser-known firms have all placed ads. Although Internet advertising is still in its infancy and offers high potential, many marketers recognize that it also has limitations: Consumers don't want to wade through electronic pages looking at details about hundreds of products. One expert offers the disap-

pointing opinion that most of the commercial advertisements on the Internet may never be read by anyone.

Targeted advertising, however, is meeting with success because, unlike print or television ad buyers, Internet advertisers can measure the success of each ad they place: They get a count of how many people see each ad and they can track the number of "click-throughs" by users looking for more information from the advertiser's own Web page. Electronic tracking devices are available for market analysis that relate to e-businesses such information as which ads generate more purchases, the sales margins resulting from each sale, and which ads attract the most attention from each target audience. DoubleClick <www.doubleclick.net> was one of the first companies to help other advertisers take advantage of the Web's unique opportunities for linking up with users, tracking their behavior online, and tailoring ad messages to them.

DoubleClick, Inc. is a global internet advertising solutions company that makes advertising work for web marketers and publishers. Using DART (Dynamic Advertising Reporting and Targeting) ad serving technology, DoubleClick provides sites and advertisers with high level targeting and extensive feedback on the performance of their ad campaigns.

DoubleClick sells ad space that allows advertisers to reach as many as 80 million monthly unique users worldwide on thousands of Web sites, such as Nasdaq.com, Zagat.com, TravelWeb, Macromedia, and Hollywood.com.

Ultimately, the potential payoff for the advertiser is greater sales revenues for each ad dollar spent. Ease of access to users has led U.S. Internet expenditures to rise from $301 million in 1996 to $4 billion in 1999. They are projected to surpass $23 billion by 2002.[13] The "Wired World" box in this chapter tells the story of one company that called on an e-marketing marketing specialist to help it devise and implement an overall Internet strategy.

Virtual Advertising An even newer method, called *virtual advertising,* uses digital implants of brands or products onto live or taped programming, giving the illusion that the product is part of the show. With this technique, an advertiser's product can appear as part of the television show, when viewers are paying more attention, instead of during commercial breaks. In a televised basketball game, the digital image of a brand—the round face of a Rolex watch or an Acura hubcap—can be electronically enlarged and superimposed on center court without physically changing the playing floor. It will be seen for the duration of the whole game. For taped movies, digital images can be inserted easily: A Kmart shopping bag can be digitally added to the table in a kitchen scene, a Philips Flat TV can be superimposed on the wall for display during a dramatic scene in the den, and your favorite stars can be digitally redressed to display Polo and other brands on their shirts and sweaters. In addition to television applications, virtual advertising shows promise for use in radio and outdoor media as well.[14]

www.doubleclick.net

DoubleClick, Inc. is a global internet advertising-solutions company that makes advertising work for Web marketers and publishers. Using DART (Dynamic Advertising Reporting and Targeting) ad serving technology, DoubleClick provides sites and advertisers with high-level targeting and extensive feedback on the performance of their ad campaigns. DoubleClick has global headquarters in New York City and maintains over 40 offices around the world.

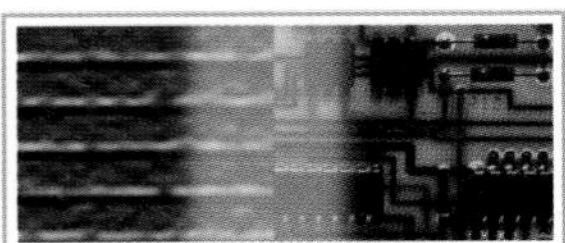

It's a WiredWorld

• The Sound Approach to Internet Marketing

You may not recognize the name Altec Lansing Technologies, Inc., but you've probably heard its products. Altec designs, manufactures, and markets high-quality sound systems for personal computers and home entertainment. Its customers are mostly other companies—Compaq, Dell Computers, IBM, Gateway—that use Altec's products in making consumer products. Its marketing strength helped in building strategic partnerships with such leading companies as Intel Corp., Dolby® Labs, and Texas Instruments. But getting into Internet marketing, Altec managers decided, was a venture for which they could use some outside help. They selected Agency.Com Ltd., experts in e-business marketing, to determine how they could best promote Altec for competitive advantage on the Net.

The first step was to decide on an overall Internet strategy: that is, to identify just what the firm's purpose in Net marketing should be and then to come up with a way to implement that strategy. The overall strategy had to recognize that Altec intends to maintain long-lasting relationships with its business customers. Another consideration was changing industry trends: At the time, there was a convergence in the markets for home computing, office computing, and home entertainment, and the technology was changing from analog to digital audio. With these considerations in mind Altec and Agency.Com proposed a strategy featuring five elements:

1. Online commerce would be implemented and would emphasize relationship marketing to ensure ongoing relationships with customers.
2. Altec Lansing products would be positioned on quality—as providing the best audio experience possible.
3. Current customers would be secured and encouraged for further sales.
4. New customers would be captured.
5. Greater brand recognition would be built.

Implementation called for a Web site <www.altecmm.com> as the focal point for all online activity. The Altec site is a commerce center that offers information pages and, along with e-mail, provides an online communication channel for building and maintaining customer relationships. Altec's online media strategy includes space purchased on third-party sites, content sponsorships and alliances, and comarketing to bring new customers to the site. Customers can access a listing of products, evaluate system requirements and performance specifications, download speaker-system software, be direct-linked to Altec's distributors, or make online purchases. Finally, the site includes sections devoted to customer support and System Builders, which provides special services to companies who purchase Altec audio systems for use in building computers and sound systems.

Other Advertising Channels A combination of many additional media, including catalogs, sidewalk handouts, yellow pages, skywriting, telephone calls, special events, and door-to-door communication, make up the remaining 22 percent of all U.S. advertising.

media mix
Combination of advertising media chosen to carry message about a product

The Media Mix The combination of media that a company chooses to advertise its products is called its **media mix.** As Table 13.1 suggests, different industries use very different mixes, and most depend on a variety of different media, rather than using just one, for reaching their target audiences.

WebConnection

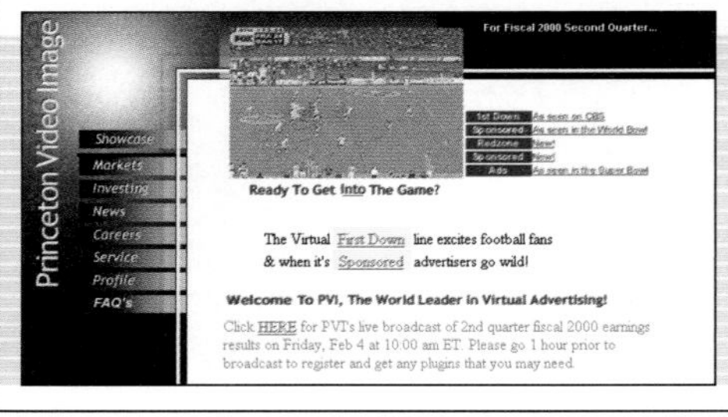

www.pvi-inc.com

If you want to know more about "Virtual Signage" and "Virtual Product Placement" and see examples of the "Virtual First Down" and "Virtual Strike Zone," including QuickTime video demos, use the Web to visit Princeton Video Image, Inc., a leader in video insertion services.

Table 13.1
Media Mix by Industry

Industry*	Magazine	Newspaper	Outdoor	Television	Radio
Retail stores	5.6%	50.3%	1.8%	37.6%	4.9%
Communications	7.6	23.6	1.8	58.3	8.6
Insurance and real estate	11.6	39.0	4.3	39.7	5.3
Food	20.7	0.8	1.1	74.1	3.2
Apparel	59.8	1.1	2.0	36.4	0.7

*Comparative Internet figures not available.

Types of Advertising

Regardless of the medium used, advertisements fall into one of these three categories:

- **Brand advertising** promotes a specific brand, such as *People* magazine, Amtrak rail service, and Ricoh copiers. (A variation on brand advertising, product advertising promotes a general good or service, such as milk or dental services.)
- **Advocacy advertising** promotes a particular cause, viewpoint, or candidate. The Sierra Club <www.sierraclub.org.> actively promotes a policy of population stabilization for the United States and internationally because they believe that population growth is a major cause of degradation in the environment. Financial institutions, such as credit unions and banks, advertise the idea that private home ownership leads to happiness, pride, and a more fulfilling life. Others focus on even more specialized concepts: the Aruba Gastronomic Association <www.arubadining.com> promotes Aruba's reputation as an island for culinary excellence.
- **Institutional advertising** promotes a firm's long-term image. Hoechst <www2.aventis.com> runs a continuing series of ads to acquaint the public with its name, its industries, and its long-term vision: "Creating Value Through Technology." Their colorful ads cleverly capitalize on the firm's unusual name (pronounced "Herkst") and announce its leadership in diverse life sciences and other industries, such as crop protection, vaccines for animal health, drugs for allergies and cancer, and industrial gases and gas supply systems.

brand advertising
Advertising promoting a specific brand

advocacy advertising
Advertising promoting a cause, viewpoint, or candidate

institutional advertising
Advertising promoting a firm's long-term image

Advertising to Specific Markets

Advertisements differ in their direction. The types of advertisements used by a company depend on its target market. In consumer markets, local stores usually concentrate retail advertising geographically to encourage local consumers to patronize the store. Larger retailers, such as Sears and JC Penney, use retail advertising to reach more geographically dispersed consumers on both the local and national levels.

Ads are also designed to reach specific audiences in terms of demographics, such as gender, age, income level, or ethnicity. Naturally, decisions about the tone of an ad, the type of medium (magazine versus television), and the specific vehicle (*People* versus *Cosmopolitan magazine*) are made with target groups in mind.

Target markets for advertising industrial products are often easier to identify than those for consumer goods. The existence of professional buyers, well-defined industrial groupings, and trade associations are, in effect, the demographics for defining the target audience. To reach the professional purchasing agents and managers at firms that buy raw materials or components, companies use industrial advertising. American Standard <www.amstd-comfort.com>, which makes toilets and other plumbing fixtures, advertises in *Hardware Retailer* to persuade large hardware stores to carry its products. Similarly, Chaparral Steel <www.txi.com/steel> reaches its target audience of steel fabricators and distributors by advertising through trade shows, trade magazines, and direct mail. Geographic location is simplified in industrial marketing because the professional target market has a limited number of buyers whose locations are well known within the industry.

Data Mining The Internet allows efficient targeting because volumes of data can be gathered electronically from Internet users. User behavior patterns can be traced by analyzing files of information, gathered over time, from millions of users. Called *data mining,* this efficient searching, sifting, and reorganizing of vast pools of data on user purchase behavior reveals who has bought which products, how many, when, over what Web site, how they paid, and so on. By analyzing what customers actually do, the e-marketer can determine what subsequent purchases they are likely to make and then send them tailor-made ads. "All we're doing," says Howard Draft, chairman of Draft Worldwide in Chicago <www.draftworldwide.com>, "is using information we have on our customers, with overlays of demographic or psychographic information, to enhance our knowledge of them and market back to them." Instead of using one advertisement to blanket all consumers, data mining makes it feasible to use niche advertising that is targeted one-on-one to individual consumers.[15]

"All we're doing is using information we have on our customers to enhance our knowledge of them and market back to them."

—Howard Draft, Draft Worldwide Marketing Agency

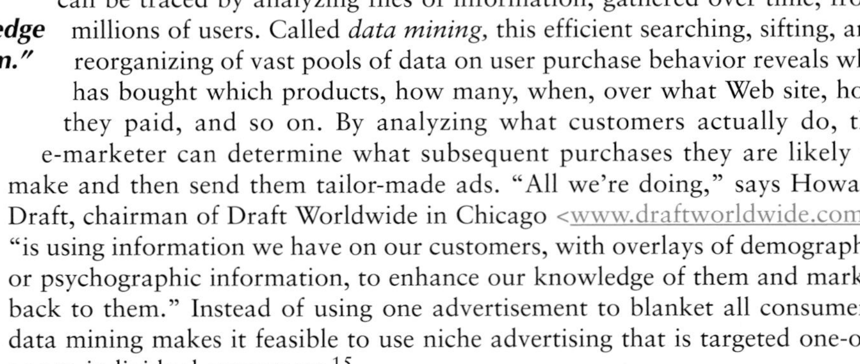

Do you feel that in today's business environment, the college graduate who has taken computer courses has an advantage over businesspeople who have been doing the same job the same way for years?

Preparing the Campaign with an Advertising Agency

advertising campaign
Arrangement of ads in selected media to reach targeted audiences

An **advertising campaign** is the arrangement of ads in selected media to reach target audiences. It includes several activities that, taken together, constitute a program for meeting a marketing objective, such as introducing a new product or changing a company's image in the public mind. A campaign typically includes six steps:

1. Identify the target audience.
2. Establish the advertising budget.
3. Define the objectives of the advertising messages.
4. Create the advertising messages.
5. Select the appropriate media.
6. Evaluate advertising effectiveness.

advertising agency
Independent company that provides some or all of a client firm's advertising needs

Advertising agencies assist in the development of advertising campaigns by providing specialized services. They are independent companies that provide some or all of their clients' advertising needs. The agency works together with the client company to determine the campaign's central message, create detailed message content, identify ad media, and negotiate media purchases.[16]

The advantage offered by agencies includes expertise in developing ad themes, message content, and artwork, as well as in coordinating ad production and advising on relevant legal matters. Today, even more specialized agencies have emerged to cater to clients with very specific goals in specific industries or market segments. Some agencies specialize in the marketing of pharmaceuticals. Burrell Communications Group <www.thestandard.com/companies> is the largest African American advertising agency.

As payment for its services, the agency usually receives a percentage, traditionally 15 percent of the media purchase cost. If an agency purchases a $1 million television commitment for a client's campaign, it would receive $150,000 for its services.

PERSONAL SELLING

personal selling
Promotional tool in which a salesperson communicates one-to-one with potential customers

In **personal selling,** a salesperson communicates one-to-one with potential customers to identify their needs and to line them up with the seller's products. The oldest form of selling, it provides the personal link between seller and buyer and adds to a firm's credibility because it allows buyers to interact with and ask questions of the seller. This professional intimacy is especially effective for relationship marketing: It places the seller closer to the buyer, it provides a clearer exposure of the customer's business, and the salesperson can then assist the buying company in creating value-adding services for the buyer's target customers.[17]

Because it involves personal interaction, personal selling requires a certain level of trust between buyer and seller—a relationship that must often be established over time.

Moreover, because presentations are generally made to only one or two individuals at a time, personal selling is the most expensive form of promotion per contact. Expenses may include salespeople's compensation and their overhead, usually travel, food, and lodging. Indeed, the average cost of a single industrial sales call has been estimated at approximately $300.

Such high costs have prompted many companies to turn to telemarketing: using telephone solicitations to perform the personal selling process. Telemarketing can be used to handle any stage of the personal selling process or to set up appointments for outside salespeople. For example, it saves the cost of personal sales visits to industrial customers. Each industrial buyer requires an average of nearly four visits to complete a sale; thus some companies have realized savings in sales visits of $1,000 or more. Such savings are stimulating the remarkable growth of telemarketing, which sold over $460 billion in goods and services in 1998, from some 30 billion phone calls in the United States. The Direct Marketing Association <www.the-dma.org> estimates that telemarketing sales could grow to $600 billion, with as many as 5 million more people to be employed in the year 2000.[18]

Sales Force Management

Sales force management means setting goals at top levels of the organization, setting practical objectives for salespeople, organizing a sales force that can meet those objectives, and implementing and evaluating the success of the overall sales plan. Obviously, then, sales management is an important factor in meeting the marketing objectives of any large company.

Personal Selling Situations

Managers of both telemarketers and traditional salespeople must always consider the ways in which personal sales are affected by the differences between consumer and industrial products:

- **Retail selling** is selling a consumer product for the buyer's own personal or household use.
- **Industrial selling** is selling products to other businesses, either for the purpose of manufacturing other products or for resale.

retail selling
Personal selling situation in which products are sold for buyers' personal or household use

industrial selling
Personal selling situation in which products are sold to businesses, either for manufacturing other products or for resale

Ha-Lo Industries <www.halo.com> sells things that have logos on them—desk clocks, sweatshirts, basketball goals. According to CEO Lou Weisbach, a one-time Ha-Lo salesman, the key to the company's success is a hard-driving, well-trained sales force. Ha-Lo's top salesperson will take home about $3 million per year, and Weisbach delayed entering the lucrative New York market until he had completed a $4 million upgrade on the order-processing system on which his sales reps depend.

Levi's <www.levi.com> sells jeans to the retail clothing operation The Gap <www.gap.com> (industrial selling). In turn, consumers purchase Levi's jeans at one of The Gap's stores (retail selling).

Each of these situations has distinct characteristics. In retail selling, the buyer usually comes to the seller. In contrast, the industrial salesperson almost always goes to the prospect's place of business. The industrial decision process also may take longer than a retail decision because more money, decision makers, and weighing of alternatives are involved. As we saw in Chapter 11, industrial buyers are professional purchasing agents accustomed to dealing with salespeople. Consumers in retail stores, on the other hand, may actually be intimidated by salespeople.

With the ease of shopping online, what can the average business do to entice customers to actually make the trip to the store?

Personal Selling Tasks

One important aspect of sales force management is overseeing salespeople as they perform the three basic tasks generally associated with personal selling: order processing, creative selling, and missionary selling. Depending on the product and company, sales jobs usually require individuals to perform all three tasks to some degree.

order processing
Personal selling task in which salespeople receive orders and see to their handling and delivery

Order Processing In **order processing,** a salesperson receives an order and sees to its handling and delivery. Route salespeople, who call on regular customers to check their supplies, are often order processors: With the customer's consent, they may determine the sizes of reorders, fill them directly from their trucks, and even stock the customer's shelves.

creative selling
Personal selling task in which salespeople try to persuade buyers to purchase products by providing information about their benefits

Creative Selling When the benefits of a product are not entirely clear, **creative selling** can help to persuade buyers. Most industrial products involve creative selling, especially when a buyer is unfamiliar with a product or the features and uses of a specific brand. Personal selling is also crucial for high-priced consumer products, such as homes and cars, for which buyers comparison shop. Any new product can benefit from creative selling that works to differentiate it from competitors.

missionary selling
Personal selling tasks in which salespeople promote their firms and products rather than try to close sales

Missionary Selling A company may also use **missionary selling** when its purpose is to promote itself and its products rather than simply to close a sale. Drug company representatives promote drugs to doctors who, in turn, prescribe them to patients. The sale, then, is actually made at the drugstore. In this case, the goal of missionary selling may be to promote the company's long-term image as much as any given product. Another form of missionary selling is the after-sale technical assistance that companies offer for complex products. IBM uses after-sale missionary selling both to ensure that customers know how to use IBM equipment and to promote good will.

The Personal Selling Process

Although all three sales tasks are important to an organization that uses personal selling, perhaps the most complicated is creative selling. The creative salesperson is responsible for undertaking and following through on most of the steps in the personal selling process.

prospecting
Step in the personal selling process in which salespeople identify potential customers

qualifying
Step in the personal selling process in which salespeople determine whether prospects have the authority and ability to pay

1. *Prospecting and qualifying.* In order to sell, a salesperson must first have a potential customer, or prospect. **Prospecting** is the process of identifying potential customers. Salespeople find prospects through past company records, customers, friends, relatives, company personnel, and business associates. Prospects must then be **qualified** to determine whether they have the authority to buy and the ability to pay.
2. *Approaching.* The first few minutes of a salesperson's contact with a qualified prospect make up the approach. Because it affects the salesperson's credibility, the success of later stages in the process depends on the prospect's first impression of the salesperson. For this reason, a salesperson must present a neat, professional appearance and greet prospects in a strong, confident manner.

3. *Presenting and demonstrating.* After the approach, the salesperson must present the promotional message to the prospect. A presentation is a full explanation of the product, its features, and its uses. Most important, it links the product's benefits to the prospect's needs. A presentation may or may not include a demonstration of the product. However, because many people have trouble fully appreciating what they have been told verbally about a product's performance, experienced salespeople try to demonstrate products whenever possible.
4. *Handling objections.* No matter what the product, prospects will have some objections. At the very least, they will angle for a discount by objecting to price. Objections not only show the salesperson that the buyer is interested but also pinpoint the parts of the presentation with which the buyer has a problem. Obviously, the salesperson must then work to overcome these objections.
5. *Closing.* The most critical part of the selling process is the **closing,** in which the salesperson asks the prospective customer to buy the product. Successful salespeople recognize the signs that a customer is ready to buy. Prospects who start to figure out monthly payments for the product are clearly indicating a readiness to buy. The salesperson should then attempt to close the sale. Salespeople can either ask directly for the sale or imply a close indirectly. Questions such as "Could you take delivery Tuesday?" and "Why don't we start you off with an initial order of 10 cases?" are implied closes. The experienced salesperson knows that indirect closes place the burden of rejecting the sale on the prospect, who may find it a little harder to say no.
6. *Following up.* Follow-up is a key activity, especially for relationship marketing. For lasting relationships with buyers, the sales process does not end with the close of the sale. Sellers want this sale to be so successful that the customer wants to buy from this seller again in the future. Therefore, sellers supply additional services that customers want: after-sale support that provides convenience and added value. They require sales follow-ups that include quick processing of the customer's orders, on-time delivery, and speedy repair service. Training the customer in the proper care and use of the purchase may also be part of the follow-up that stimulates repeated future sales.

closing
Step in the personal selling process in which salespeople ask prospective customers to buy products

SALES PROMOTIONS

Sales promotions are short-term promotional activities designed to stimulate consumer buying or cooperation from distributors, sales agents, or other members of the trade. They are important because they increase the likelihood that buyers will try products. They also enhance product recognition and can increase purchase size and amount. Soap is sometimes bound in packages of four with the promotion "Buy three and get one free."

To be successful, sales promotions must be convenient and accessible when the decision to purchase occurs. If Harley-Davidson has a 1-week motorcycle promotion and you have no local dealer, the promotion is neither convenient nor accessible to you, and you will not buy. On the other hand, if Folgers offers a $1-off coupon that you can save for use later, the promotion is both convenient and accessible.

sales promotion
Short-term promotional activity designed to stimulate consumer buying or cooperation from distributors and sales agents

Types of Sales Promotions

The best-known forms of promotions are coupons, point-of-purchase displays, various purchasing incentives (especially free samples and premiums), trade shows, and contests and sweepstakes.

- A certificate that entitles the bearer to a stated savings off a regular price is a **coupon.** Coupons may be used to encourage customers to try new products, to attract customers away from competitors, or to induce current customers to buy more of a product. They appear in newspapers and magazines, are included with other products, and are often sent through direct mail.
- To grab customers' attention as they walk through stores, some companies use **point-of-purchase (POP) displays.** Located at the ends of aisles or near checkout counters,

coupon
Sales promotion technique in which a certificate is issued entitling the buyer to a reduced price

point-of-purchase (POP) display
Sales promotion technique in which product displays are located in certain areas to stimulate purchase

POP displays make it easier for customers to find products and easier for sellers to eliminate competitors from consideration.

- Free samples and premiums are *purchasing incentives*. Free samples allow customers to try products without risk. They may be given out at local retail outlets or sent by manufacturers to consumers by direct mail. **Premiums** are gifts, such as pens, pencils, calendars, and coffee mugs, that are given away to consumers in return for buying a specified product. Retailers and wholesalers also receive premiums for carrying some products.
- Periodically, industries sponsor **trade shows** for members and customers. Trade shows allow companies to rent booths to display and demonstrate products to customers who have a special interest in them or who are ready to buy. Trade shows are inexpensive and, because the buyer comes to the seller already interested in a given type of product, are quite effective.
- Customers, distributors, and sales representatives may all be persuaded to increase sales by means of *contests*. For example, consumers may be asked to enter their cats in the Purina Cat Chow calendar contest by submitting entry blanks from the backs of cat food packages.

premium
Sales promotion technique in which offers of free or reduced-price items are used to stimulate purchases

trade show
Sales promotion technique in which various members of an industry gather to display, demonstrate, and sell products

PUBLICITY AND PUBLIC RELATIONS

publicity
Promotional tool in which information about a company or product is created and transmitted by general mass media

Much to the delight of marketing managers with tight budgets, **publicity** is free. Because it is presented in a news format, consumers often see publicity as objective and highly believable. It is a very important part of the promotional mix.[19] However, marketers often have little control over publicity.

As an example of adverse publicity, consider the case of Tyco International Ltd. <www.tyco.com>, a diversified conglomerate in electronics, security systems, medical supplies, commercial cable, and other interests. Tyco received a jolt in 1999 when the Securities and Exchange Commission launched an informal investigation into the company's accounting practices. When word of the inquiry was released, Tyco's stock fell 23 percent, losing $14 billion in market value, and was the most actively traded stock on the New York Stock Exchange that day.[20]

Organizers of such events as the New Orleans Jazz and Heritage Festival <www.nojazzfest.com> rely increasingly on money from corporate sponsors such as Ray-Ban <www.rayban.com> to pay for entertainment, keep ticket prices down, and finance promotional appeals to broader audiences. Sponsors are trying to foster good public relations, and in the last 15 years, the number of events with corporate sponsors has risen from 25 percent to 85 percent. Corporations now spend nearly $700 million a year on festivals, fairs, and other events.

Public relations is company-influenced publicity that seeks to build good relations with the public and to deal with the effects of unfavorable events. It attempts to establish goodwill with customers (and potential customers) by performing and publicizing a company's public service activities. Anheuser-Busch's *1998 Annual Report* proudly announced the company's role in alcohol-awareness efforts to encourage responsible consumption of beer. During the recent 17-year period, Anheuser-Busch <www.anheuser-busch.com> invested more than $250 million in efforts to curb alcohol abuse, fight drunk driving, and discourage underage drinking at both the high school and college levels. Anheuser-Busch further announced its commitment to provide continuing programs and activities that will address these issues in the future.[21]

public relations
Company-influenced publicity directed at building good will between an organization and potential customers

The "Life Cycle of an e-Business" box in this chapter shows how Garden.com combined publicity and public relations with other promotional tools in its brand-building strategy.

INTERNATIONAL PROMOTIONAL STRATEGIES

As we saw in Chapter 3, recent decades have witnessed a profound shift from home-country marketing to multicountry and now to global marketing. Nowhere is this rapidly growing global orientation more evident than in marketing promotions, especially advertising.

Emergence of the Global Perspective

Every company that markets its products in several countries faces a basic choice: use a decentralized approach with separate marketing management for each country or adopt a global perspective with a coordinated marketing program directed at one worldwide audience. The **global perspective,** therefore, is a company philosophy that directs marketing toward a worldwide rather than a local or regional market. American companies such as IBM, PepsiCo, and the accounting firm Arthur Andersen are in the forefront of global orientation in advertising. The movement is in the global direction, but one world market remains a concept more than a reality.

global perspective
Company's approach to directing its marketing toward worldwide rather than local or regional markets

Movement Toward Global Advertising The truly global perspective means designing products for multinational appeal—that is, genuinely global products.[22] A few brands, such as Coca-Cola, McDonald's, Mercedes, Rolex, and Xerox, enjoy global recognition in a variety of countries and cultures, and thus have become truly global brands. Not surprisingly, globalization is affecting many firms' promotional activities. In effect, they have already posed the question "Is it possible to develop global advertising?"

Certainly one universal advertising program would be more efficient and cost-effective than developing different programs for each of many countries. For several reasons, global advertising is not feasible for many companies. Here, we will touch on four factors that make global advertising a challenging proposition: *product variations, language differences, cultural receptiveness,* and *image differences.*

Product Variations Even if a basic product has universal appeal, at least modest product variations, or slightly different products, are usually preferred in different cultures. In the magazine business, Hearst Corp. <www.hearst.com> has expanded to 33 editions of *Cosmopolitan* magazine, including one for Central America, English and Spanish editions for the United States, and local editions for Italy, Turkey, Russia, Hong Kong, and Japan. *Reader's Digest* <www.readersdigest.com> has 48 editions in 19 languages.

Language Differences The most obvious barrier to the global ad is language. Compared with those in other languages, ads in English require less print space and airtime because English is an efficient language with greater precision of meaning than most. Translations from one language to another are often inexact and lead to confusion and misunderstanding. When Coca-Cola first went to China the translation of its name read "Bite the wax tadpole." For these reasons, acquisitions and mergers of advertising

Life Cycle of an e-Business

How to Make the Brand Flower

As with any new business, brand building was a high priority at Garden.com. But founders Jamie O'Neill, Lisa Sharples, and Cliff Sharples took the process to fairly rare heights: Garden.com was satisfied with nothing less than being a national "megabrand"—*the* brand that dominates an industry. Their branding strategy used a variety of media and methods to position Garden.com as a superbrand or so-called "category killer." Advertising, sales promotions, relationship building, public relations, and publicity were all deployed in creating brand visibility, image, and public awareness. Although marketing activities are expensive, as recently as 1999 investors were eagerly pumping funds into the branding campaigns of e-commerce firms without expecting quick returns. By mid-2000, however, investor attitudes had changed: Investors wanted better and faster results. Declared one e-commerce observer: "The insane levels of spending on marketing and branding will simply no longer be tolerated. The emphasis will now be on companies that are profitable." For how long could Garden.com justify the increasing drain on its cash entailed by its branding efforts? How long would it take for revenues to catch up with expenses and enable the company to show a profit?

Even as pressure for profitability mounted, Garden.com's branding activities continued on several fronts. In the company's promotional mix, both a print magazine, *Garden Escape,* and an online magazine, *Garden.com,* were used to position and brand the Garden.com name and its products. In contrast, the prime objective of the *Garden.com Catalog* was to get the customer to make a first purchase and then go to the Internet for some e-shopping.

Special promotions were always in blossom on the Garden.com Web site. The main objective was brand building by means of increasing awareness and encouraging interest among prospective customers. But off-site promotions also added exposure in diverse regions. Consider the 2000 Grassroots Tour. In this eight-week journey across the United States, the firm's employees met gardeners face-to-face and urged people to "Get Back to Their Roots" through gardening. Led by a fleet of 1950s pickup trucks, the tour visited six cities—San Francisco, Atlanta, Chicago, Boston, New York, and Washington, DC—in search of great gardening stories. In addition to presenting workshops and demonstrations, Garden.com planted trees at the schools of the winners of the "Historic Trees Essay Contest," conducted Web site demonstrations, and gave away a trip to the 2001 Chelsea (England) Flower Show. The campaign promoted gardening in general as well as the Garden.com brand.

Publicity, both in the printed media and on the Internet, played a role in positioning and brand awareness. Some publicity pieces went beyond technical and business formalities to reveal the personalities inside the company. *Inc.,* the popular magazine for start-up companies, carried a background story on Cliff, Jamie, and Lisa in a featured article, "The Perfect Internet Business." The publicized accounts of the founders' visions, hopes, and dedication constituted public testimony to Garden.com's dedication to gardening culture. Other publicity focused on business activities, such as a *Fortune* magazine article that rated Garden.com tops in performance among 45 e-commerce stores that were tested in depth by an independent shopping research firm. A technical article on Garden.com's Web developer in *Inc.Online* featured background information on the development of Garden.com's latest Internet technology. Additional publicity stemmed from publicly announced industry awards, such as the "1999 Best in Retail Internet Award," in which the presenting association, the Retail Systems Alert Group, noted that "Garden.com is arguably the best retail site on the Web." Such publicity, both on the technical side of the firm's operations and on the personalities behind it, gave widespread exposure to brand visibility, image, and products.

But despite the upbeat publicity, marketing costs continued to outpace sales revenues. By June 2000, market analysts were predicting that Garden.com would be among the online companies that failed to survive the year. In September, the firm wavered from its earlier all-out branding practices by announcing it was cutting costs for advertising and customer acquisition. "We have cut back on a number of programs," announced Cliff Sharples, "and have focused on programs that deliver consumers at the most efficient and lowest price." The time for delivering bottom-line results was fast approaching.

agencies have resulted in the growth of worldwide agency networks that can coordinate an ad campaign's central theme and yet allow regional variations.

Cultural Receptiveness Another variable is cultural receptiveness to alien ideas, products, and methods of marketing. There is considerable difference across nations regarding the acceptability of mass advertising for sensitive products or those that cause social discomfort (such as underwear, birth control products, personal hygiene products), not to mention those for which advertising may be legally restricted (pharmaceuticals, alcohol, cigarettes). Generally speaking, the European Union (EU) countries have more liberal advertising environments than countries in North America, Asia, the Middle East, and Latin America. But each country still has its own limits of acceptability: An American tourist in Paris may be surprised to see nudity in advertisements on billboards and even more surprised to discover that France is the only EU country that doesn't allow wine to be advertised or sold on the Internet.

Marketing methods, too, must be carefully selected. In the EU and much of Asia, comparative advertising is considered distasteful or even illegal. Media ads cannot proclaim that one brand of car outperforms another. Because some countries do not allow free samples, sampling promotions are not feasible. In some societies, coupons for price reductions are acceptable to attract sales, but it is unacceptable to return to the regular price when the promotion ends.

Image Differences Each company's overall image can vary from nation to nation, regardless of any advertising appeals for universal recognition and acceptance. A study comparing well-known global brands in the United States and the United Kingdom found that American Express, IBM, and Nestlé had higher-ranking images in the United States than in the United Kingdom. In contrast, Heinz, Coca-Cola, and Ford had higher-ranking images in the United Kingdom.

Universal Messages and Regional Advertising Skills In recognizing national differences, many global marketers try to build on a universal advertising theme that nevertheless allows for variations. In doing so, they rely on help from different advertising agencies in various geographic regions. KFC Corp. <www.kfc.com> with more than

The Coca-Cola Co. <www.coca-cola.com> earns no less than 80 percent of its profits from markets outside North America. The company's marketing strategy is essentially the same everywhere: Coke (which is really little more than flavored, carbonated, sweetened water) is positioned as unique. Something better than the next soft drink. "The real thing." The product itself, however, is not necessarily uniform. Its taste, for example, is often altered to suit local preferences.

How do language barriers affect the global market of advertising?

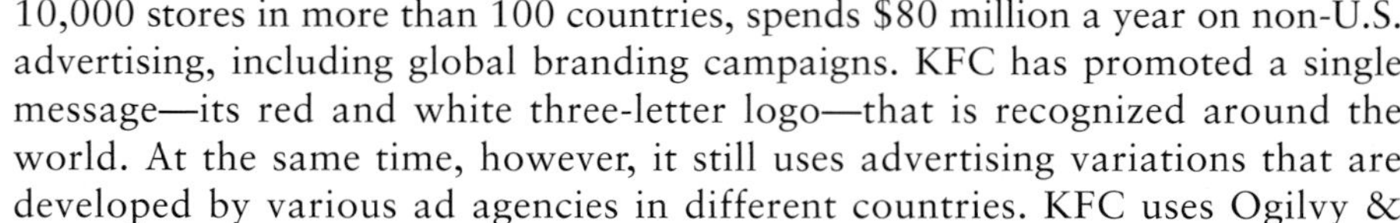

10,000 stores in more than 100 countries, spends $80 million a year on non-U.S. advertising, including global branding campaigns. KFC has promoted a single message—its red and white three-letter logo—that is recognized around the world. At the same time, however, it still uses advertising variations that are developed by various ad agencies in different countries. KFC uses Ogilvy & Mather Worldwide <www.ogilvy.com> (Europe, Canada, Mexico, Singapore, China, Ireland) as its international agency, John Singleton Advertising <www.singo.com.au> for its Australian and New Zealand activities, and Young & Rubicam in the United States, Latin America, Hong Kong, and Thailand.

PROMOTIONAL PRACTICES IN SMALL BUSINESS

From our discussion so far, you may think that only large companies can afford to promote their products. Although small businesses generally have fewer resources, cost-effective promotions can improve sales and allow small firms to compete with much larger firms.

Small-Business Advertising

Perhaps no other development in modern history has provided advertising opportunities on the scale made possible by the Internet, especially for small businesses. Cheaper access to computing equipment, to online services, and to expertise for developing Web sites places cyberspace within the grasp of nearly every firm. Still, owners must decide which audiences to target and what messages to use. And even though distant customers can be reached instantaneously on the Web, the other methods available for small-business advertising depend on the market that the firm is trying to reach: local, national, or international.

Local Markets Advertising in non-prime-time slots on local television or cable TV offers great impact at a cost that many small firms can afford. More often, however, small businesses with local markets use newspaper, radio, and, increasingly, direct mail. Although billboards are beyond the means of many small businesses, outdoor store signs can draw strong responses from passers-by.

The timing of advertising can be as critical for small businesses as the medium. For year-round advertising, the yellow pages are popular for advertising both industrial and consumer products in local markets. However, many small businesses, especially those selling to consumer markets, rely more on seasonal advertising. Retail stores advertise for the holidays, and ads for lawn care and home maintenance services appear in the early spring.

National Markets Many businesses have grown from small to large by using direct mail, particularly catalogs. Sears & Roebuck was once a small mail-order house, as was L.L. Bean. By purchasing mailing lists of other companies' customers, a small firm can reduce costs by targeting its mailings.

The ability to target an audience also makes specialized magazines attractive to small businesses. For example, Turnquist Lumber Co. of Foster, Rhode Island, advertises its specialty, the exporting of quality red oak, in *Southern Lumberman,* a trade magazine for the lumber industry. Similarly, Georgetown Galleries of Bethesda, Maryland, and Omaha Steaks of Omaha, Nebraska, reach for upscale nationwide audiences by advertising in *Smithsonian* magazine.

International Markets Television, radio, and newspapers are seldom viable promotional options for small businesses to use in reaching international markets. For one thing, they are too expensive for many small firms. The market research used by large companies to determine the best message and style for reaching the target audience is expensive. Additional costs are incurred in developing broadcast and newsprint advertisements with the necessary variations in language and cultural appeal. Instead, most small firms find direct mail and carefully targeted magazine advertising the most effective tools.

The Role of Personal Selling in Small Business

As with advertising, the personal selling strategies used by small businesses depend on their intended markets. Some small firms maintain sales forces to promote and sell their products, especially in local markets, where clients can be quickly visited. Others prefer not to do their own selling, but contract with sales agencies: companies that handle the products of several clients to act on their behalf.

For national markets, the costs of operating a national sales force are high, so sales agencies and other methods such as telemarketing are used. By combining telemarketing with catalogs or other product literature, small businesses can sometimes compete against much larger companies on a national scale. Syncsort Inc. <www.syncsort.com> combined a telemarketing staff with eight national sales representatives to become the number-one developer of computer software for sorting data into convenient formats. Number two is IBM.

Small-Business Promotions

Small companies use the same sales promotion incentives as larger companies. However, larger firms tend to use more coupons, POP displays, and sales contests. Because these tools are expensive and difficult to manage, smaller firms rely on premiums and special sales.[23] An automobile dealership might offer you a fishing reel at a bargain price if you just come on down and road-test a new four-wheel-drive vehicle. Gas stations use premiums when they offer free car washes with fill-ups. Special sale prices are commonly offered by service companies ranging from martial arts centers to remodelers and dry cleaners.

Continued from page 351

The Rationale of Alienating Traditional Partners

Even though the Internet may be the most effective sales tool since the telephone, it also has the potential to throw a monkey wrench into traditional sales and distribution channels. Naturally, this prospect worries marketers who are aware that traditional methods, which rely on armies of sales representatives and retail partners, still account for at least 90 percent of most companies' orders.

Online selling eliminates paperwork and sales commissions and can potentially reduce costs by as much as 15 percent. These savings, however, come out of the pockets of sales reps and distributors, many of whom wonder if they will survive the cybernetic future. As a result, companies wanting to maintain their current sales and distribution networks while simultaneously venturing onto the Web find themselves walking on egg shells. "In some cases," reports one business journalist, companies are "launching Web commerce sites with no publicity or limited merchandise offerings. In other cases, [they are] keeping online prices high, so traditional vendors can lead the way in offering discounts. Some manufacturers are even trying to placate dealers and salespeople with a cut of each Internet sale, regardless of whether they played a role in generating it."

Software maker Intuit Inc. <**www.intuit.com**>, wary of alienating its traditional distribution network by discounting Quicken, TurboTax, and other software programs on the Web, is leaving discounting to the retailers who are responsible for most of its sales. "We could decide to market aggressively on the Web," explains CEO William Harris, "but we don't do that in deference to our third-party resellers." Marketers at 3M Corporation <**www.3m.com**> also see the danger of Web-based selling and use the Web for promotion only, not for sales. Although the company's Web site lists hundreds of 3M products, it posts no order form—a policy that suits the traditional distribution network just fine. "We are very concerned about our distribution-channel structure," says a 3M Internet specialist. "We take care not to damage those relationships." In any case, most online orders would be relatively small by comparison with those brought in through current distributors (whereas a consumer might order a box of 10 floppy disks, a retailer like Staples will order in bulk). 3M is also acting in its own economic best interest.

Meanwhile, other companies are moving rapidly into online discounting, despite the impact on traditional channels. When Compaq <**www.compaq.com**> began selling computers at discounted prices on the Web, dealers saw a dramatic sales drop. "It's taking a chunk out of our business," admits Richard Wong, head of San Francisco–based Sefco Computers, Inc. <**www.sefco.com**>. "We still have people ask us for bids on small business installations, but we don't win the orders anymore." The reason, says Wong, is pricing: Compaq's online site sells each machine for about $50 less than companies like Sefco can afford to sell them.

As the Internet becomes more sophisticated and its use more widespread, companies that are now resisting online sales and distribution may be forced to find ways of keeping traditional network members happy as they move onto the Web. "We'll learn as we go," says James Cyrier, head of medical sales and marketing for Hewlett-Packard <**www.hp.com**>. His hospital customers want the convenience of online shopping, but what does Cyrier do with the 500 HP sales reps and distributors who bring in more than $1 billion a year worldwide? There are no easy answers.

Questions for Discussion

1. What do you think of rational marketing as an approach to reaching Internet consumers?
2. Why is it necessary for marketers to introduce Internet sites on television and other media? Can marketers plan promotional strategies for one medium without considering others?
3. Why are sales representatives so concerned about Web-based marketing? Do you agree or disagree with their concerns? Explain.
4. Do you envision a changing role for direct mail in this era of online marketing? How do you think direct mail will be used in this new environment?
5. Argue for or against this statement: Marketers will always look to traditional sales and distribution channels for the bulk of their orders.
6. How do you think the Web will change the sale and distribution of consumer products? Of industrial products?

SUMMARY OF LEARNING OBJECTIVES

1 **Identify the important objectives of *promotion* and discuss the considerations entailed in selecting a *promotional mix*.** Although the ultimate goal of a *promotion* is to increase sales, other goals include *communicating information, positioning a product, adding value,* and *controlling sales volume.* In deciding on the appropriate *promotional mix,* marketers must consider the good or service being offered, characteristics of the target audience and the buyer's decision process, and the promotional mix budget.

2 **Discuss the most important *advertising strategies* and describe the key *advertising media*.** *Advertising strategies* often depend on the *product life cycle stage.* In the introductory stage, *informative advertising* helps to build aware-

ness. As a product passes through the growth and maturity stages, *persuasive advertising, comparative advertising,* and *reminder advertising* are often used. *Advertising media* include the Internet, newspapers, television, direct mail, radio, magazines, and outdoor advertising, as well as other channels such as *Yellow Pages,* special events, and door-to-door selling. The combination of media that a company chooses is called its *media mix.*

3 **Outline the tasks involved in *personal selling* and list the steps in the *personal selling process.*** *Personal selling* tasks include *order processing, creative selling* (activities that help persuade buyers), and *missionary selling* (activities that *promote firms and products rather than simply close sales).* The personal selling process consists of six steps: *prospecting and qualifying* (identifying potential customers with the authority to buy), *approaching* (the first moments of contact), *presenting and demonstrating* (presenting the promotional message that explains the product), *handling objections, closing* (asking for the sale), and *following up* (processing the order and ensuring after-sale service).

4 **Describe the various types of *sales promotions.*** *Coupons* provide savings off the regular price of a product. *Point-of-purchase (POP) displays* are intended to grab attention and help customers find products in stores. Purchasing incentives include *samples* (which let customers try products without buying them) and *premiums* (rewards for buying products). At *trade shows,* sellers rent booths to display products to customers who already have an interest in buying. *Contests* are intended to increase sales by stimulating buyers' interest in products.

5 **Describe the development of *international promotional strategies.*** Many firms began exploring the possibilities of international sales when domestic sales flattened out in the mid-twentieth century. Because advertising is the best tool for stimulating product awareness on a country-by-country basis, it has played a key role in the growth of international marketing. Whereas some firms prefer a *decentralized approach* (separate marketing management for different countries), others have adopted a *global perspective* (coordinating marketing programs directed at one worldwide audience). Because the global perspective requires products designed for multinational markets, companies such as Coca-Cola, McDonald's, and many others have developed *global brands.* In promoting these products, global advertising must overcome such challenges as product variations, language differences, cultural receptiveness, and image differences.

6 **Show how small businesses use promotional activities.** Small business can advertise effectively and economically on the Internet. They can also engage in personal selling activities in local, national, and international markets. Because coupons and contests are more expensive and harder to manage, small business owners are likely to rely more heavily on premiums and special sales.

QUESTIONS AND EXERCISES

Review Questions

1. What are the differences between push and pull strategies? Why would a firm choose one over the other?
2. Compare the advantages and disadvantages of different advertising media.
3. What are the advantages of personal selling over other promotional tools?
4. Which promotional tools have proven most useful in mounting global advertising campaigns? Why?
5. Is publicity more or less available to small firms than to larger firms? Why?

Questions for Analysis

6. Take a look at some of the advertising conducted by locally based businesses in your area. Choose two campaigns: one that you think effective and one that you think ineffective. What differences in the campaigns make one better than the other?
7. Select a good or a service that you have purchased recently. Try to retrace the relevant steps in the buyer decision process as you experienced it. Which steps were most important to you? Least important?
8. Find some examples of publicity about some business, either a local firm or a national firm. Did the publicity have, or is it likely to have, positive or negative consequences for the business involved? Why?

Application Exercises

9. Select a product that is sold nationally. Identify as many media used in its promotion as you can. Which medium is used most? On the whole, do you think the campaign is effective? Why or why not?
10. Interview the owner of a local small business. Identify the company's promotional objectives and strategies and the elements in its promotional mix. What (if any) changes would you suggest? Why?

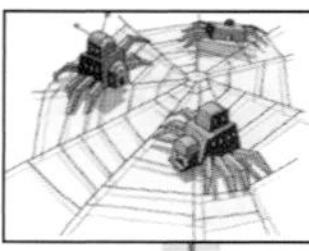

EXPLORING THE WEB

NEED HELP FOR E-MAIL MARKETING?

To find out about the kinds of expertise available to help companies that want to do e-mail marketing, log on to the following Web site:

www.digitalimpact.com

Read through the posted material, including the following pages: "About Digital Impact" (Partner Programs), "Client List," and "Services for Marketers"(including "Campaigns That Work"). Then respond to the following questions:

1. What line of business is Digital Impact in? What does the company sell and to whom?
2. Who are some of Digital's Internet clients? List some of the client companies that are familiar to you. Were you previously aware that they were involved in e-marketing?
3. Digital Impact refers to "measurable results" that it generates for its clients. What measurements does Digital use to indicate "results"? Can you suggest potentially better measurements?
4. Look at the Web category titled "Campaigns That Work." After reading the information, identify a specific promotional service that Digital Impact provided. Which kind of promotional method was involved? How do you suppose Digital and its client measured the success of this method?
5. Examine the Web category titled "Press Center" and read any of the recent articles about Digital's success in helping a client company with marketing efforts. List the types of promotional methods that Digital used and the media, if any, that it chose. Explain why those methods and media were selected for the target audience.
6. Why do you suppose companies hire Digital Impact rather than conducting their own marketing promotions? Can you find anything in the Web site that indicates why a company would choose Digital rather than conducting its own e-mail promotions?

BUILDING YOUR BUSINESS SKILLS

GREETING START-UP DECISIONS

This exercise enhances the following SCANS workplace competencies: demonstrating basic skills, demonstrating thinking skills, exhibiting interpersonal skills, and working with information.

GOAL

To encourage students to analyze the potential usefulness of two promotional methods—personal selling and direct mail—for a start-up greeting card company.

SITUATION

You are the marketing adviser for a local start-up company that makes and sells specialty greeting cards in a city with 400,000 residents. Last year's sales totaled some 14,000 cards, including personalized holiday cards, birthday cards, and special-events cards for individuals. Although revenues increased last year, you see a way of boosting sales even more by expanding into card shops, grocery stores, and gift shops. You see two alternatives for entering these outlets:

1. Use direct mail to reach more individual customers for specialty cards, or
2. Use personal selling to gain display space in retail stores.

Your challenge is to convince the owner of the start-up company which alternative is the more financially sound decision.

METHOD

Step 1

Get together with four or five classmates to research the two kinds of product segments: *personalized cards* and *retail store cards*. Find out which of the two kinds of marketing promotions will be more effective for each of the two segments. What will be the reaction to each method of customers, retailers, and card company owners?

Step 2

Draft a proposal to the card company owner. Leaving budget and production factors to other outside advisers, list as many reasons as possible for adopting direct mail. For adopting personal selling. Then defend each reason. Among the reasons to consider in your argument are the following:

- *Competitive environment:* Analyze the impact of other card suppliers that offer personalized cards and cards for sale in retail stores.
- *Expectations of target markets:* Who buys personalized cards and who buys ready-made cards from retail stores?
- *Overall cost of the promotional effort:* Which method, direct mail or personal selling, will be more costly?
- *Marketing effectiveness:* Which of the promotional methods will result in the greater consumer response?

FOLLOW-UP QUESTIONS

1. Why do you think some buyers want personalized cards? Why do some consumers want ready-made cards from retail stores?
2. Today's computer operating systems provide easy access to software for making cards that users design on personal computers at home. How does the availability of this product affect your recommendation?
3. What was your most convincing argument for using direct mail? For using personal selling?
4. Can a start-up company compete in retail stores against industry giants such as Hallmark and American Greetings?

CRAFTING YOUR BUSINESS PLAN

HITTING THE SAUCE CUSTOMER

THE PURPOSE OF THE ASSIGNMENT

1. To acquaint students with the process of navigating the *Business PlanPro* (*BPP*) software package (Version 4.0).
2. To familiarize students with promotion-related issues that a sample firm must address in developing its business plan.
3. To demonstrate how four chapter topics—promotional strategy, product positioning, personal selling, and advertising—can be integrated as components of the *BPP* planning environment.

ASSIGNMENT

After reading Chapter 13 in the textbook, open the BPP *software* and look around for information on plans for promotion as it applies to a sample firm: Salvadore's Sauces Food Dis. (Salvadore's, Inc.). Then respond to the following items:*

1. As we saw in Chapter 13, product positioning is an important promotional objective. What are Salvadore's Sauces' plans for positioning its products? [Sites to see in *BPP* (for this assignment): In the Plan Outline screen, click on **4.1 Market Segmentation.** After returning to the Plan Outline screen, click on each of the following in turn: **4.3.1 Industry Participants, 4.3.2 Distribution Services, 4.3.3 Competition and Buying Patterns,** and **4.3.4 Main Competitors.**]
2. Describe Salvadore's Sauces' promotional strategy. [Sites to see in *BPP:* In the Plan Outline screen, click on **5.1.2 Promotion Strategy.** After returning to the Plan Outline screen, click on **5.1.1 Pricing Strategy.**]
3. Suppose you want to help Salvadore's Sauces set prices on the basis of cost-oriented pricing. Does the Salvadore's plan contain enough data to allow this method of pricing? Explain why or why not. [Sites to see in *BPP:* In the Plan Outline screen, click on each of the following in turn: **4.3.2 Distribution Patterns** and **4.3.3 Competition and Buying Patterns.**]
4. What kinds of advertising does Salvadore's Sauces plan to use? Do you agree or disagree with their advertising plans? Explain. [Sites to see in *BPP:* In the Plan Outline screen, click on each of the following in turn: **4.0 Market Analysis** and **5.0 Strategy and Implementation.**]
5. What role does personal selling play in the promotional plans at Salvadore's? Who will do the

personal selling? Are these individuals qualified for the role? [Sites to see in *BPP* (for this assignment): In the Plan Outline screen, click on **5.2 Sales Strategy** and **5.2.2 Sales Programs.** After returning to the Plan Outline screen, click on each of the following: **6.0 Management Summary** and **6.2 Management Team.**]

FOR YOUR OWN BUSINESS PLAN

6. Consider the various promotional approaches that could be used by the company for which your business plan is being developed. Explain how your choices on product positioning, promotional strategy, personal selling, and advertising might be presented in the various *BPP* Plan Outline sections. In which sections of the document will you present your plans for each of those elements?

*GENERAL TIPS FOR NAVIGATING IN *BPP*

1. Open the *BPP* program, examine the Welcome screen, and click on **Open a Sample Plan.**
2. From the Open a Sample Plan dialogue box, click on a sample company name; then click on **Open.**
3. On the Plan Manager screen, click on Your Plan Outline; then click on any of the lines (for example, **5.1.1 Pricing Strategy**).
4. You can always return to the Plan Outline screen by going to the bottom of the screen and clicking on the **Plan Outline** icon.
5. After finishing with one sample company, you can get to the next one by going to the top of the screen and clicking on **File** (on the menu bar). Then beneath that, select **Open Sample Plan.** This will exit you from the current company file and take you to the Open Sample Plan dialogue box, where you can select your next sample company.
6. When you are finished, you can close the program by going to the top of the screen and clicking on **File** (on the bar menu). Then beneath that, select **Exit.**

VIDEO EXERCISE

PROMOTING WHITE MOUSTACHES: THE "GOT MILK?" CAMPAIGN

Learning Objectives

The purpose of this video exercise is to help you

1. Understand the purpose of promotional objectives.
2. Identify different ways in which commodities can be promoted.
3. Recognize the link between advertising and promotion.

BACKGROUND INFORMATION

Everyone knows that milk is good for you. Just about everyone keeps milk in the refrigerator. Yet per capita sales of milk were slipping in the mid-1990s, from 29 gallons in 1980 to 23 gallons by 1993. The California Milk Processor Board decided to do something to spark milk consumption—hence, the "Got Milk?" campaign.

THE VIDEO

The segment introduces Jeff Manning, executive director of the California Milk Processor Board <www.gotmilk.com>, and the two ad executives who created the Got Milk? campaign, Jeffrey Goodby and Jon Steel. Each contributes his perspective on the problem of milk's reputation, the research and brainstorming that went into addressing it, and the advertisers' solution, which began with an innovative (and award-winning) series of television ads and continues today with the famous milk-moustache campaign.

DISCUSSION QUESTIONS

1. What are some of the difficulties that marketers face in promoting a commodity like milk? What other commodities can you think of that would present similar challenges?
2. Why do you think the Got Milk? campaign was first launched on television instead of in another medium?
3. Why do you think it was important for the milk campaign to be somewhat irreverent?

FOLLOW-UP ASSIGNMENT

What brand of bottled water do you prefer? Why? How did the marketer of your brand convince you that this particular water, which is a commodity like milk, is better than others? Make a list of the attributes that your brand's advertising claims for its product. Do you think they are really unique? If so, why?

FOR FURTHER EXPLORATION

Check out the latest entries in the milk moustache campaign and other promotional activities at <www.whymilk.com>. How successfully do you think the campaign is continuing in these other avenues? Now that "Got Milk?" has become a familiar phrase, do you think the promotion should be revitalized with something different? If so, what would you suggest?

Chapter 14

Distributing Products

After reading this chapter, you should be able to:

1. ***Identify*** the different *channels of distribution* and explain different *distribution strategies.*
2. ***Explain*** the differences between *merchant wholesalers* and agents/brokers.
3. ***Identify*** the different types of *retailing* and *retail stores.*
4. ***Describe*** the major activities in the *physical distribution process.*
5. ***Compare*** the five basic forms of *transportation.*

Strike Up the Bandwidth

How about that latest Jennifer Lopez album? Prefer the Metabolics? What about Violent Femmes or maybe Elvis Costello? How about for free? The Internet is changing the way we get our musical entertainment—everything from when we buy, to whom we get it from, to what we pay, to how it gets from sellers to consumers. Consider some of the latest trends. Just five years ago, the record shop was the standard site for finding CDs and tapes in malls, shopping centers, and discount stores. You could save some money by going store to store and comparing prices. In fact, browsing display stands for artists and labels was a way of life for many music buyers.

Then came Internet stores, many of them with discount prices. For example, you can go to a Web site like <**www.cdhitlist.com**>, which offers more than 55,000 titles among CDs, cassettes, and VHS/DVD movies. You can search every list, place orders electronically or over the phone, and then get your music or movie by mail. You can still browse, of course—electronically, at home—and compare prices without burning gasoline or wearing out shoe leather going from store to store. Web sites such as <**www.evenbetter.com**> will even do your comparison shopping for you, listing prices from low to high for any product offered by as many as 50 different e-stores. Now—at least for the time being—there's the online music service called Napster. When you register at <**www.napster.com**>, you get access to "the world's largest online music community." What do you do once you're in? Basically, you can exchange music by sending your albums to others on the Internet and receiving albums from them. For free. Napster is accessible 24 hours a day, and there's no waiting for the mail because albums are transmitted digitally and downloaded onto your computer in just a few minutes.

A 19-year-old music lover named Shawn Fanning invented the software that got Napster rolling in 1999. By February 2000, officials at Indiana University had noticed that 60 percent of the institution's Internet bandwidth (system capacity) was consumed by students using Napster to trade online music. The university's servers were so clogged that filters had to be installed to block Napster. The same thing happened on other campuses. By March 2000—just six months after its launch—more than 5 million people had downloaded Napster software and the user base was growing at a rate between 5 to 25 percent daily. "I love Napster," says one 15-year- old fan. "I'm never buying a CD again."

The music itself is not actually traded on Napster's Web site. Instead, you go to the Web site to get the Napster software, which you can download for free onto your computer. The software finds albums that you've stored on your hard disk and publishes that information in the list on Napster's Web site, along with lists of millions of other users. Then, using an MP3 format (digital file), you can start trading with anyone else who's live on the Net at the same time. You get what you want from their hard drives and they get what they want from yours. "Napster," boasts the company's site, "is music at Internet speed." You can enjoy music from your computer speakers or copy it onto an MP3 player, such as the Compressor Personal Jukebox, and listen to as much as 80 hours of stored music while you work, jog, or even sit in your favorite classroom.

"The music business as we know it today is hosed. If I were a music-biz exec, I'd be singing the blues."

—Journalist and venture capitalist Stewart Alsop

What does all this mean for the music industry—for album producers, distributors, and retail stores? According to Stewart Alsop, a partner with the venture capital firm New Enterprise Associates, it means that "the music business as we know it today is hosed. . . . If I were a music-biz exec . . . I'd be singing the blues."

Our opening story continues on page 402

Although online shopping has enormous potential, it is only one way of getting products to customers. As the fourth element in the marketing mix (place), distribution takes many forms. By focusing on the learning objectives of this chapter, you will better understand the importance of distribution in the marketing process.

THE DISTRIBUTION MIX

distribution mix
Combination of distribution channels by which a firm gets its products to end users

We have already seen that a company needs an appropriate product mix. But the success of any product also depends on its **distribution mix:** the combination of distribution channels that a firm selects to get a product to end users. In this section, we will consider some of the many factors that enter into the distribution mix. First, we will look at the role of the target audience and explain the need for intermediaries. We will then discuss the basic distribution strategies. Finally, we will consider some special issues in channel relationships—namely, conflict and leadership.

Intermediaries and Distribution Channels

intermediary
Individual or firm that helps to distribute a product

wholesaler
Intermediary who sells products to other businesses for resale to final consumers

retailer
Intermediary who sells products directly to consumers

Once called *middlemen,* **intermediaries** are the individuals and firms who help to distribute a producer's goods by either moving the goods or by providing information that stimulates the movement of goods to customers. They are generally classified as wholesalers or retailers. **Wholesalers** sell products to other businesses, who resell them to final consumers. **Retailers** sell products directly to consumers. Some firms rely on independent intermediaries, and others employ their own distribution networks and sales forces. The decision normally hinges on three factors:

1. The company's target markets
2. The nature of its products
3. The costs of maintaining distribution and sales networks

In this section, we will examine these factors closely by describing some of the distribution decisions that go into the marketing of consumer products.

distribution channel
Network of interdependent companies through which a product passes from producer to end user

Distribution of Consumer Products A **distribution channel** is the path that a product follows from producer to end user. Figure 14.1 shows how the eight primary distribution channels can be identified according to the kinds of channel members who participate in getting products to their ultimate destinations. As we move through this discussion, note first that all channels begin with a producer and end either with a consumer or an industrial (business) user. Channels 1 through 4 are most often used for the distribution of consumer goods and services.

direct channel
Distribution channel in which a product travels from producer to consumer without intermediaries

Channel 1: Direct Distribution of Consumer Products In a **direct channel,** the product travels from the producer to the consumer without intermediaries. Using their own sales forces, companies such as Avon, Fuller Brush, and Tupperware use this channel.

This direct channel is also prominent on the Internet for thousands of products ranging from books and automobiles to insurance and vacation packages sold directly by producers to consumers. A leader in direct sales of computer products, for example, the Gateway 2000 Internet storefront <www.gateway.com> generates annual sales of $9 billion in computers and related products for PC users at home and at the workplace. Likewise, you can purchase airline reservations directly from such Internet sites as TWA <www.twa.com>, Southwest <www.southwestairlines.com>, and Delta <www.deltaairlines.com>.

Channel 2: Retail Distribution of Consumer Products In Channel 2, producers distribute products through retailers. Goodyear, for example, maintains its own system of retail outlets. Levi's has its own outlets but also produces jeans for other retailers such as The Gap. Many retailers offer Internet sales. Grocery shoppers, for example, can browse the electronic aisles of the Kroger Co. <www.kroger.com>, one of America's largest grocery

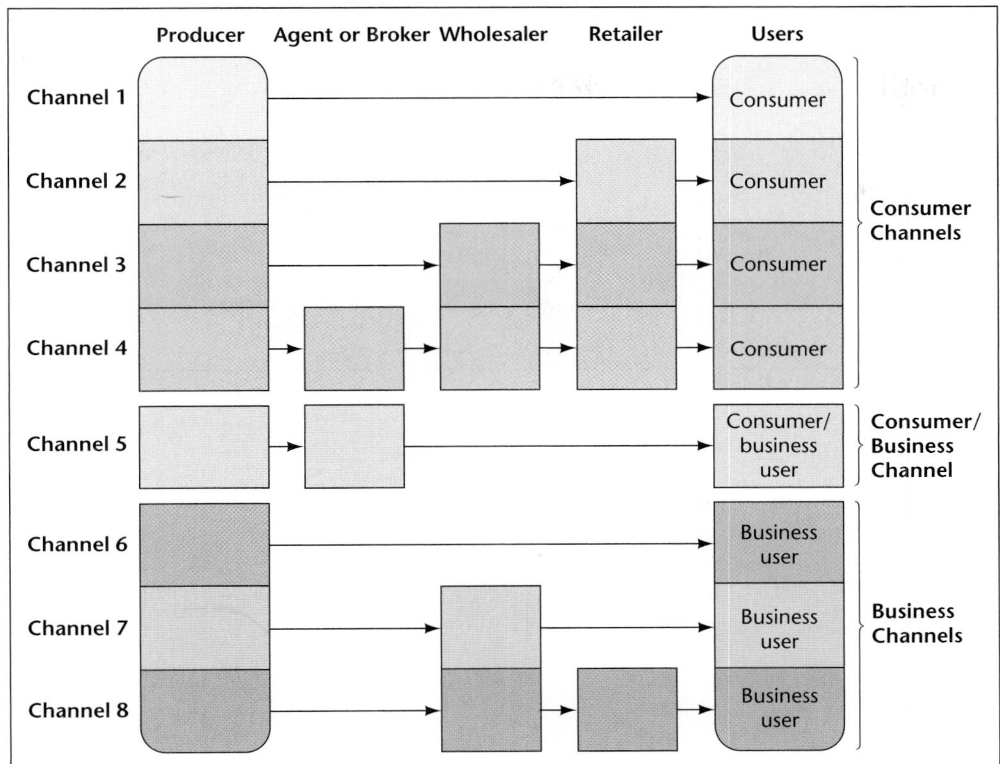

Figure 14.1
Channels of Distribution

retailers. Kroger's grocery list is actually compiled and delivered under agreements with specialty service providers such as PeaPod.com that partner with the grocery chain in getting goods delivered to the consumer.

Channel 3: Wholesale Distribution of Consumer Products Until the mid-1960s, Channel 2 was the most widely used method of nondirect distribution. It requires a large amount of floor space, however, both for storing merchandise and for displaying it in retail stores. Faced with the rising cost of retail space, many retailers found that they could not afford both retail and storage space. Thus, wholesalers entered the distribution network to take over more and more of the storage service. An example of Channel 3 is combination convenience stores/gas stations. Approximately 90 percent of the space in these stores is used for merchandise displays while only about 10 percent is left for storage and office facilities. Merchandise in the store is stocked frequently by wholesalers.

Wholesalers are prominent in e-commerce because Internet stores can provide customers with access to information and product displays 24 hours a day. They also make it possible to place orders electronically and confirm delivery commitments almost instantaneously. In the diamond industry, retail companies can access wholesalers such as Diasqua Group <www.gemkey.com/diasqua>, visually examine diamonds for grade and quality, place orders, and receive delivery dates.

Channel 4: Distribution through Sales Agents or Brokers Channel 4 uses **sales agents,** or **brokers,** who represent producers and sell to wholesalers, retailers, or both. They receive commissions based on the price of goods they sell. Lafferty and Co. Food Brokers, Inc. <www.laffertyandco.com> represents several prominent food manufacturers—Pillsbury, Old El Paso, Sunkist—in the Midwest. By relieving manufacturers of their own sales activities, Lafferty's salespeople efficiently arrange sales of the products to other companies, allowing manufacturers to concentrate on what they do best—process food products—rather than diverting resources to sales and distribution.

sales agent/broker
Independent intermediary who usually represents many manufacturers and sells to wholesalers or retailers

Figure 14.2
The Value-Adding Intermediary

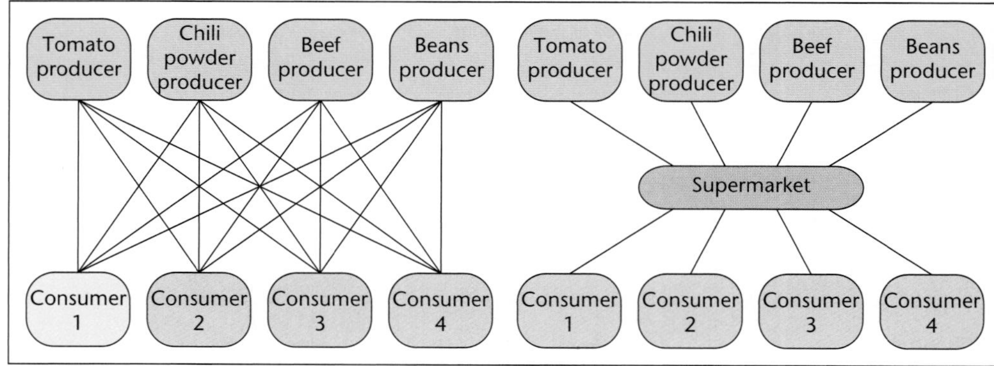

Agents generally deal in the related product lines of a few producers, serving as their sales representatives on a long-term basis. For example, travel agents represent airlines, car rental companies, and hotels. In contrast, brokers are hired to assist in buying and selling temporarily, matching sellers and buyers as needed. This channel is often used in the food and clothing industries. The real estate industry also relies on brokers for matching buyers and sellers of property.

The Pros and Cons of Nondirect Distribution Ultimately, each link in the distribution chain makes a profit by charging a markup or commission. Nondirect distribution channels mean higher prices for end users: The more members in the channel—the more intermediaries—the higher the final price. Calculated as a percentage of cost, markups are applied each time a product is sold. Markups may range from 10 to 40 percent for manufacturers, from 2 to 25 percent for wholesalers, and from 5 to 100 percent for retailers. So-called *e-intermediaries*—wholesalers and agents who operate through Internet distribution channels—also charge markups for their services, as we will see later in this chapter. In general, markup depends on traditional practices in the particular industry and competitive conditions.

A can of Coca-Cola Classic selling for about 76 cents in U.S. vending machines sells in Japan (where it is labeled simply "Coca-Cola") for about $1.14. The wholesale price for a Coke made in the United States is $.23 a can, versus $.83 cents wholesale for a Japanese-made Coke. Actually, the product can be made in America and then shipped, taxed, and delivered to Japan for a wholesale price of $.48—which is still well below the Japanese-made wholesale price.[1]

At the same time, however, intermediaries can save consumers both time and money. In doing so they provide *added value* for customers. Moreover, this value-adding activity continues and accumulates at each stage of the supply chain. Intermediaries add value by providing time-saving information and by making the right quantities of products available where and when you need them. Consider Figure 14.2, which illustrates the problem of making chili without benefit of a common intermediary—the supermarket. You would obviously spend a lot more time, money, and energy if you tried to gather all the ingredients yourself. Moreover, if we eliminated intermediaries, we would not eliminate either their functions or the costs entailed by what they do. Intermediaries exist because they perform necessary functions in cost-efficient ways.

Distribution by Agents to Consumers and Businesses *Channel 5* differs from the previous channels in two ways: (1) it includes an agent as the sole intermediary and (2) it distributes to both consumers and business customers. Consider Vancouver-based Uniglobe Travel International, a travel agent that represents airlines, car rental companies, and hotels. Uniglobe books flight reservations and provides arrangements for complete packages of recreational travel services for consumers. They also provide services to companies whose employees need lodging and transportation for businesses travel.

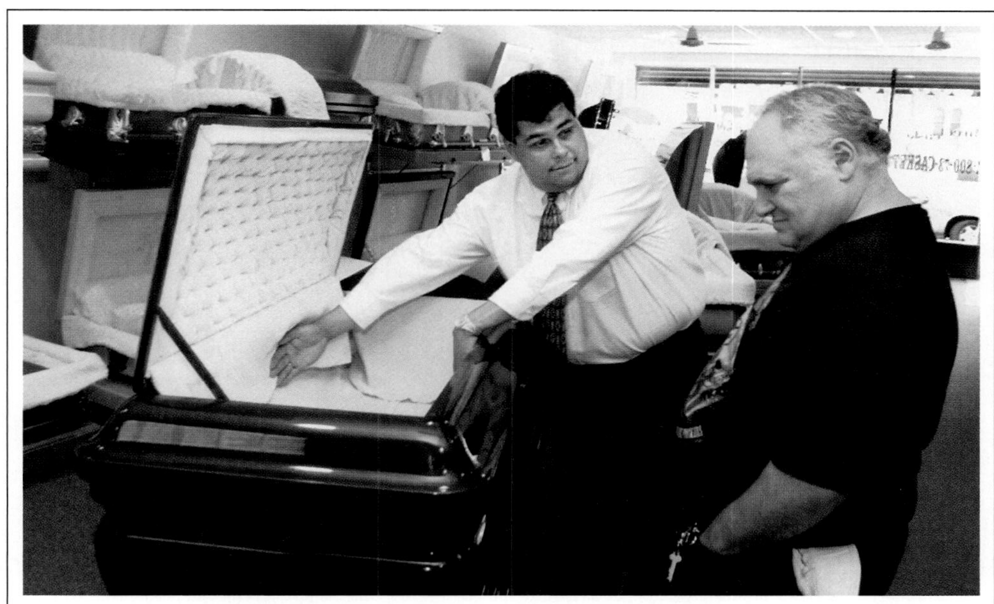

At Direct Casket <www.directcasket.com>, shoppers in Brooklyn can take advantage of retail coffin sales. The company is now one of about 50 firms nationwide that buy from manufacturers and sell directly to the public through showrooms, catalogs, and even the Internet. Markups are typically 100 percent—compared to about 350 percent at funeral homes. Funeral homes, of course, offer convenience and services that storefront retailers do not, but as Direct Casket president Ray Silvas puts it, "Smart shoppers don't want to spend thousands of dollars that aren't necessary."

Expansion into e-commerce is well suited to this distribution channel because it allows more people to find out directly about products. Uniglobe expanded its traditional services by implementing a new online strategy. Its online subsidiary <www.uniglobe.com> combines a high-tech Web site with an old-fashioned human touch in a specialty market—booking cruises. Customers can scan for destinations, cruise lines, restaurants, deck plans, and cabin locations on any of the 70 ships that the firm represents. Moreover, with Uniglobe's online chat function, you can simply open a window to chat in real time with any of the 75 cruise specialists. The strategy has paid off: Uniglobe.com is the market leader in online cruise bookings.[2]

Distribution of Business Products

Industrial channels are important because every company is itself a customer that buys other companies' products. The Kellogg Co. <www.kelloggs.com> buys grain to make breakfast cereals, and Humana Inc. <www.humana.com>, a nationwide chain of for-profit hospitals, buys medicines and other supplies to provide medical services. **Industrial** (business) **distribution,** therefore, is the network of channel members involved in the flow of manufactured goods to business customers. Unlike consumer products, business products are traditionally distributed through Channels 6, 7, and 8 as shown in Figure 14.1.

industrial distribution
Network of channel members involved in the flow of manufactured goods to industrial customers

Channel 6: Direct Distribution of Business Products Most business goods are sold directly by the manufacturer to the industrial buyer. Lawless Container Corporation, for instance, produces packaging containers that are sold directly to such customers as Fisher-Price (toys), Dirt Devil (vacuum cleaners), Peak antifreeze, and Mr. Coffee (coffeemakers). As contact points with their customers, manufacturers maintain **sales offices.** These offices provide all services for the company's customers and serve as headquarters for its salespeople.

sales office
Office maintained by a manufacturer as a contact point with its customers

E-commerce technologies have intensified the use of Channel 6. Dell Computer Corp. <www.dell.com>, a pioneer in direct Internet sales, now gets about two-thirds of its $25 billion in sales from other businesses, governments, and schools. Armed with the ever-expanding reach of the Internet, Dell is trying to establish a foothold in the massive Chinese market, where it faces entrenched local market leaders, such as Legend, who, to make matters worse, have no compunctions about copying Dell's direct producer-to-buyer model.[3]

Dell Computer Corp., one of the world's most successful direct distributors of business products, faces competition in China from such entrenched local firms as Legend. Legend and other domestic manufacturers dominate two key markets: retail buyers and state-owned enterprises. The former market accounts for only 10 percent of Dell's China sales, but by relying on speed, convenience, and service, Dell Asia-Pacific <www.dell.com/ap> *has managed to get a foot in the door at many of the country's massive state-owned companies.*

Other products distributed through Channel 6 include steel, transistors, and conveyors. Intermediaries are often unnecessary because such goods are usually purchased in large quantities. In some cases, however, brokers or agents may enter the distribution chain between manufacturers and buyers.

Channel 7: Wholesale Distribution of Industrial Products Wholesalers function as intermediaries between manufacturers and end users in a very small percentage of industrial channels. Brokers and agents are even rarer. Channel 7 is most often used for accessory equipment (computers, fax machines, and other office equipment) and supplies (floppy disks, pencils, copier paper). Whereas manufacturers produce these items in large quantities, companies buy them in small quantities. For example, few companies order truckloads of paper clips. As with consumer goods, then, intermediaries help end users by representing manufacturers or by breaking down large quantities into smaller sales units. The traditional office supply store, then, is a wholesaler that sells a variety of goods to other businesses.

Channel 8: Wholesale Distribution to Business Retailers For some industries, the roles of channel members are changing. In the office products industry, Channel 7 is being displaced by the emergence of a newer channel that looks very much like Channel 3 for consumer products: Instead of buying office supplies from wholesalers (Channel 7), many buyers are now shopping at office discount stores such as Staples, Office Depot, and Office Max. Before selling to large companies, these warehouse-like superstores originally targeted retail consumers and small and midsize businesses that bought supplies at retail stores (and retail prices). Today, however, small business buyers stroll down the aisles of discount stores for industrial users, selecting from 7,000 items at prices 20 to 75 percent lower than manufacturers' suggested retail.

E-commerce is fueling the rapid growth in the office superstore industry. In the United States, for example, Staples Inc., the office superstore pioneer, relies on e-business for continued rapid growth. In Japan, customers of the largest office supplier, Askul <club.askul.co.jp>, can use the Internet to shop in real time and get orders delivered within 24 hours. Low prices are possible because Askul's high-tech distribution warehouses can be located on cheap land and because electronic transactions eliminate the workforce needed to conduct face-to-face selling.

Distribution Strategies

Selecting an appropriate distribution network is a strategic decision that determines not only the amount of market exposure that a product receives but also the cost of getting it.

Generally, distribution strategy depends on the product class and the degree of market exposure that is most effective in getting a product to the greatest number of customers. The goal is to make a product accessible in just enough locations to satisfy customers' needs. Whereas milk can be purchased in numerous retail outlets, there is only one Rolls-Royce distributor in any city, region, or even state. Different degrees of market exposure are available through strategies of intensive, exclusive, and selective distribution.

Intensive Distribution **Intensive distribution** entails distributing a product through as many channels and channel members as possible (both wholesalers and retailers). It is normally used for low-cost consumer goods with widespread appeal, such as candy and magazines. M&M's candies enter the market through all suitable retail outlets—supermarkets, candy machines, drugstores, and so forth. Various retailers are supplied by many different wholesalers.

intensive distribution
Strategy by which a product is distributed through as many channels as possible

Exclusive Distribution With **exclusive distribution,** a manufacturer grants the exclusive right to distribute or sell a product to a limited number of wholesalers or retailers, usually in a given geographic area. Such agreements are most common for high-cost prestige products. Rolex watches are sold only in selected jewelry stores. Jaguar automobiles are sold by a limited number of dealers serving large metropolitan areas, regions, or states.

exclusive distribution
Strategy by which a manufacturer grants exclusive rights to distribute or sell a product to a limited number of wholesalers or retailers in a given geographic area

Selective Distribution **Selective distribution** falls between intensive and exclusive distribution. Using this strategy, a producer selects only wholesalers and retailers who will give a product special attention in sales effort, display advantage, and so forth. Selective distribution policies are used most often for consumer products such as furniture and appliances. A company such as General Electric <www.ge.com> uses selective distribution for appliances because it can form good relationships with selected wholesalers who will emphasize GE rather than other brands. By dealing with a few devoted channel members, GE keeps distribution costs lower while giving its products good market coverage.

selective distribution
Strategy by which a company uses only wholesalers and retailers who give special attention to specific products

Channel Conflict and Channel Leadership

Manufacturers can choose to distribute through more than one channel or wholesaler. They can also choose to make new uses of existing channels. Similarly, many retailers (for example, RiteAid drugstores) are free to strike agreements with as many producers (the makers of Tylenol, Advil, and Bayer) as capacity permits. In such cases, channel conflict may arise. Conflicts are resolved when members' efforts are better coordinated. A key factor in coordinating the activities of independent organizations is *channel leadership.*

Channel Conflict **Channel conflict** occurs when members of the channel disagree over the roles they should play or the rewards they should receive. For example, John Deere would object if its dealers began distributing Russian and Japanese tractors. Similarly, when a manufacturer-owned factory outlet store discounts the company's apparel or housewares, it runs the risk of alienating the manufacturer's retail accounts. Channel conflict may also arise if one member has more power than the others or is viewed as receiving preferential treatment. Needless to say, such conflicts defeat the purpose of the system by disrupting the flow of goods to their destinations.

channel conflict
Conflict arising when the members of a distribution channel disagree over the roles they should play or the rewards they should receive

Channel Leadership Usually, one channel member is most powerful in determining the roles and rewards of other members. That member is the **channel captain.** Often, the channel captain is a manufacturer. The jewelry made by New Orleans artisan Thomas Mann is so unusual and treasured that wholesalers and retailers wait years for the chance

channel captain
Channel member who is most powerful in determining the roles and rewards of other members

to distribute it. Mann <www.thomasmann.com> selects channel members, sets prices, and determines product availability. In other industries, an influential wholesaler or a large retailer such as Wal-Mart or Sears may emerge as channel captain because of large sales volume.

WHOLESALING

Now that you know something about distribution channels, we can consider the role played by intermediaries in more detail. Wholesalers provide a variety of services to customers who are buying products for resale or business use. In addition to storing and providing an assortment of products, wholesalers offer delivery, credit, and product information. Of course, not all wholesalers perform all these functions. Services offered depend on the type of intermediary involved: merchant wholesalers or agents/brokers.

Merchant Wholesalers

merchant wholesaler
Independent wholesaler who takes legal possession of goods produced by a variety of manufacturers and then resells them to other businesses

full-service merchant wholesaler
Merchant wholesaler who provides credit, marketing, and merchandising services in addition to traditional buying and selling services

Do consumers save money when buying wholesale?

limited-function merchant wholesaler
Merchant wholesaler who provides a limited range of services

drop shipper
Limited-function merchant wholesaler who receives customer orders, negotiates with producers, takes title to goods, and arranges for shipment to customers

rack jobber
Limited-function merchant wholesaler who sets up and maintains display racks in retail stores

Most wholesalers are independent operations that sell various consumer or business goods produced by a variety of manufacturers. **Merchant wholesalers,** the largest single group of wholesalers, play dual roles, buying products from manufacturers and selling them to other businesses. Merchant wholesalers purchase and own the goods that they resell. Usually, they also provide storage and delivery. In the United States, the merchant wholesaling industry employs 6 million people with a total yearly payroll of $210 billion.

A full-service merchant wholesaler also provides credit, marketing, and merchandising services. Approximately 80 percent of all merchant wholesalers are **full-service merchant wholesalers. Limited-function merchant wholesalers** provide only a few services, sometimes merely storage. Their customers are normally small operations that pay cash and pick up their own goods. One such wholesaler, the **drop shipper,** does not even carry inventory or handle the product. Drop shippers receive orders from customers, negotiate with producers to supply goods, take title to them, and arrange for shipment to customers. The drop shipper bears the risks of the transaction until the customer takes title to the goods.

Other limited-function wholesalers, known as **rack jobbers,** market consumer goods (mostly nonfood items) directly to retail stores. Procter & Gamble <www.pg.com>, for example, uses rack jobbers to distribute products such as Pampers diapers. After marking prices, setting up display racks, and displaying diapers in one store, the rack jobber moves on to another outlet to check inventories and shelve products.

Agents and Brokers

Agents and brokers, including e-agents on the Internet, serve as sales forces for various producers. They are independent representatives of many companies' products. They work on commissions, usually about four to five percent of net sales. Unlike merchant wholesalers, they do not take title to (they do not own) the merchandise they sell. Rather, they serve as sales and merchandising arms of producers who do not have their own sales forces.

Consider the role of On Air Digital Audio as an *e-agent* (or *shopping agent*). Corporate clients need the right kind of voices for radio ads; likewise, voice talents are looking for jobs. As the intermediary between clients and artists, On Air Digital <www.mediadog.net/Portfolio/small4index.html> transmits ad scripts and artists' readings electronically and, in doing so, saves clients' time. Samples from On Air's voice bank are transmitted digitally to clients who scan and select the best voices. On Air then arranges for the artist to record the message, receives it electronically, and sends it electronically to the client, avoiding the cost entailed by mailing CDs and tapes back and forth.[4]

The value of agents and brokers lies primarily in their knowledge of markets and their merchandising expertise. They also provide a wide range of services, including shelf and display merchandising and advertising layout. They maintain product salability by removing open, torn, or dirty packages, arranging products neatly, and generally keeping them attractively displayed. Many supermarket products are handled through brokers.

The Advent of the e-Intermediary

The ability of e-commerce to bring together millions of widely dispersed consumers and businesses continues to change the types and roles of intermediaries in distribution channels. **E-intermediaries** are Internet-based distribution channel members who perform one or both of two functions: (1) they collect information about sellers and present it in convenient form to consumers or (2) they help deliver Internet products to consumers. Two Internet intermediaries, America Online and Amazon.com, account for sales to some 31 million consumers who otherwise might be walking to traditional retail outlets instead of shopping online. MSNBC <www.msnbc.com> and CNNFn <www.cnnfn.com> are among many online news distributors who compete with traditional print and media news distributors.[5]

e-intermediary
Internet distribution channel member who assists in moving products through to customers or who collects information about various sellers to be presented in convenient format for Internet customers

In addition to such prominent examples, certain other major intermediaries are emerging for both consumers and business customers. We will examine three types of emerging e-intermediaries: *syndicated sellers, shopping agents,* and *business-to-business brokers.*

Syndicated Sellers The early years of the Internet spawned widely held expectations that traditional intermediaries would be eliminated by producers selling directly to consumers. The resulting shorter supply chains would lower costs and consumers would benefit from lower prices. Although this has happened in some cases, some new and unexpected cyber-intermediaries also have emerged. One of these new marketing developments, called **syndicated selling,** occurs when a Web site offers other Web sites a commission for referring customers. One such company is Expedia.com, which, with 7.5 million users, was the most-visited Web site for travel services in 1999. Expedia has given Uniglobe.com, the travel agent that we described earlier, a special cruise section on its Web page. Here's how it works. When Expedia customers click on the Uniglobe banner ad, they are transferred from the Expedia to the Uniglobe Web site. Uniglobe pays a fee to Expedia for each booking that comes through this channel. Although the new intermediary increases the cost of Uniglobe's supply chain, it adds value for customers: Travelers avoid endless searches in cyberspace and are efficiently guided to experts specializing in recreational cruises.[6]

syndicated selling
E-commerce practice whereby a Web site offers other Web sites commissions for referring customers

Shopping Agents Another new intermediary is the **shopping agent** (or **e-agent**). Shopping agents help Internet consumers by gathering and sorting information they need for making purchases. They do not take possession of any products. The e-agent knows which Web sites and stores to visit, shows accurate comparison prices, identifies product features, and helps consumers complete transactions by pulling information from worldwide sites, sorting it, and presenting it in a usable format, in a matter of seconds. PriceScan <www.pricescan.com> is a well-known shopping agent for computer products. For CDs and tapes, evenbetter.com will search for vendors, do price comparisons (including shipping costs), list the prices from low to high, and then transfer you to the Web sites of up to 50 different e-stores.[7]

shopping agent (or **e-agent**)
E-intermediary (middleman) in the Internet distribution channel who assists users in finding products and prices but who does not take possession of products

Business-to-Business Brokers E-commerce intermediaries have also emerged for business customers. Consider the start-up Internet company Efdex (which stands for *electronic food and drink exchange*). The concept is a massive food exchange to buy and sell foodstuffs among food manufacturers, restaurants, grocers, and farmers. Established first in the United Kingdom in early 2000, Efdex plans to be operating soon in the United States and Europe. Like a stock exchange, the Web site <www.efdex.com> provides

WebConnection

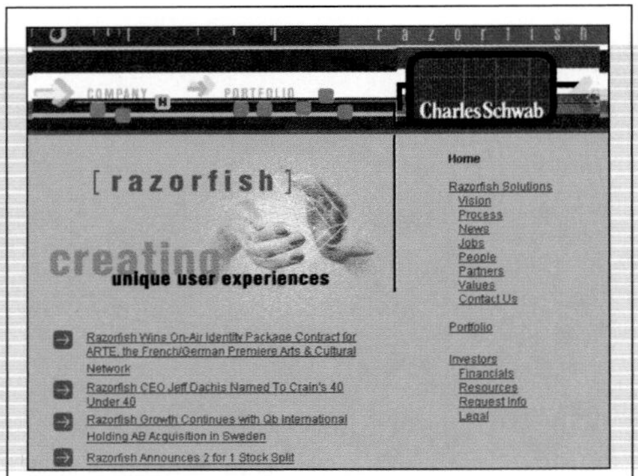

www.razorfish.com

Boasting a client list that includes Time Warner, Charles Schwab, and the Smithsonian, Razorfish is a consulting firm for companies that conduct or want to conduct e-commerce. To find out how the company promotes digital technology in the building of new business models, including new channels and new value chains, log on to its Web site.

up-to-date market information and price and product data from both suppliers and buyers—all listed by type and size of business. Efdex enables businesses to buy and sell from one another and confirm transactions electronically. As a broker, Efdex does not take possession of products. Rather, it functions to bring together timely information and business-to-business exchange linkages.[8]

All of the these new e-intermediaries have emerged because of new Internet technology. They are start-up leaders who envisioned innovative methods to provide value-adding services for customers and for product suppliers in the e-distribution channel.

RETAILING

There are more than 1.6 million retail establishments in the United States. Most of them are small operations, often consisting of owners and part-time help. Indeed, over one-half of the nation's retailers account for less than 10 percent of all retail sales. Retailers also include huge operations such as Wal-Mart, the largest employer in the United States, and Sears. Although there are large retailers in many other countries—Kaufhof <www.kaufhof.de> in Germany, Carrefour in France <www.carrefour.com>, and Daiei in Japan <www.cybercitykobe.com/daiei/index.htm>—more of the world's largest retailers are based in the United States than in any other country.

In this section, we will begin by describing in some depth the different types of outlets, both store and nonstore, that dot the U.S. retailing landscape. We will then look at the growth of at-home shopping, including *electronic retailing*. Finally, we will briefly review the history of retailing and discuss the growth in retailing options for the at-home shopper.

Types of Retail Outlets

U.S. retail operations vary as widely by type as they do by size. They can be classified in various ways: by pricing strategies, location, range of services, or range of product lines. Choosing the right types of retail outlets is a crucial aspect of every seller's distribution strategy. Consider the experience of the Sara Lee Corp. <www.saralee.com>, whose name usually conjures visions of cheesecake and chocolate brownies. The Sara Lee of the 2000s, however, has as much to do with pantyhose as it does with pies. To achieve broad distribution on its pantyhose line, Sara Lee had to design product lines that appealed to a variety of retailers. To appeal to food retailers, Sara Lee developed two inexpensive hosiery lines: L'Eggs <www.leggs.com> and Just My Size <jms.buy-here.com>. In this section, we describe U.S. retail stores by using two classifications: *product line retailers* and *bargain retailers*.

Product Line Retailers Retailers that feature broad product lines include *department stores, supermarkets,* and *hypermarkets; specialty stores* are typified by narrow product lines.

Department Stores As the name implies, **department stores** are organized into specialized departments: shoes, furniture, women's petite sizes, and so on. Department stores are usually large and handle a wide range of goods. In addition, they usually offer a variety of services, such as generous return policies, credit plans, and delivery.

department store
Large product line retailer characterized by organization into specialized departments

In the past, department stores differentiated themselves by what they sold and the prices they charged. Today, consumers report that ambiance and service levels differ more than merchandise and thus drive buyer preferences among stores. Lord & Taylor <www.mayco.com/lt>, with stores in 8 of the top 10 U.S. metro areas, is associated with tradition and security. Belk Stores <www.belk.com>, the largest privately held U.S. department store, is known for its broad line of fashion apparel and designer brands. Bergdorf Goodman <nmdirect.com/E/bergdorf.html>, on New York's Fifth Avenue, is known for sophistication.

Supermarkets Like department stores, **supermarkets** are divided into departments of related products: food products, household products, and so forth. The emphasis is on low prices, self-service, and wide selection. The largest supermarkets are chain stores such as Safeway <www.safeway.com>, Kroger <www.kroger.com>, Publix <www.publix.com>, Winn-Dixie <www.winn-dixie.com>, Marsh <www.marsh.net>, and Albertson's <www.albertsons.com>.

supermarket
Large product line retailer offering a variety of food and food-related items in specialized departments

Online supermarkets are in the infancy stage, with grocery sales of just $63 million in 1997. Growth to $3.5 billion is projected for 2002, but still that will be less than 1 percent of total industry sales for groceries. Granted, many shoppers like the convenience of e-shopping: logging onto a Web site <www.streamline.com> or <www.shoplink.com>, browsing electronic "aisles," choosing grocery categories—soups, snacks, baby foods—filling a grocery cart, paying, and receiving delivery at home. But most shoppers still prefer the brick-and-mortar store that is more familiar and easier to navigate. They want to test firsthand the freshness, color, and texture before selecting food products.[9]

hypermarket
Very large product line retailer carrying a wide variety of unrelated products

scrambled merchandising
Retail practice of carrying any product that is expected to sell well regardless of a store's original product offering

Hypermarkets A phenomenon begun in the late 1970s, **hypermarkets** are much larger than supermarkets (up to 200,000 square feet) and sell a much wider variety of products. They also practice **scrambled merchandising:** carrying any product, whether similar or

Although supermarkets are beginning to feel pressure from such Internet retailers as WebVan Group <www.webvan.com> and Priceline.com, they are responding with technology-oriented conveniences of their own. At this Stop & Shop supermarket in Massachusetts, a customer uses a handheld price scanner to speed her trip through the checkout line; when she gets to the cashier, she will simply hand over the scanner and a credit card. Stop & Shop is owned by a Dutch firm called Royal Ahold <www.ahold.nl>, which is the fourth-largest food retailer in the United States.

dissimilar to the store's original product offering, that promises to sell. In Dallas, Hypermart U.S.A. sells a wide range of food and grocery items, including specialty foods and fresh bakery goods. It also offers television sets, auto accessories, and dry-cleaning services.

specialty store
Small retail store carrying one product line or category of related products

Specialty Stores **Specialty stores** are small stores that carry one line of related products. They serve clearly defined market segments by offering full product lines in narrow product fields and often feature knowledgeable sales personnel. Sunglass Hut International <www.sunglasshut.com> has 1,600 outlets carrying a deep selection of sunglasses at competitive prices. In the United States, Canada, Europe, and Australia its stores are located in malls, airports, and anywhere else that is convenient for quick, one-stop shopping. "People's time," contends CEO Jack Chadsey, "is so limited, they don't want to walk through a maze of categories. If they're looking for electronics, they're going to go to an electronics specialty store. Sunglasses are no different."

"People's time is limited. If they're looking for electronics, they're going to go to an electronics specialty store. Sunglasses are no different."

—Jack B. Chadsey, CEO of Sunglass Hut International

Bargain Retailers **Bargain retailers** carry wide ranges of products and come in many forms. Included in this category are *discount houses, off-price stores, catalog showrooms, factory outlets, warehouse clubs,* and *convenience stores.*

bargain retailer
Retailer carrying a wide range of products at bargain prices

discount house
Bargain retailer that generates large sales volume by offering goods at substantial price reductions

Discount Houses After World War II, some U.S. retailers began offering discounts to certain customers. These first **discount houses** sold large numbers of items such as televisions and other appliances by featuring substantial price reductions. As name-brand items became more plentiful in the early 1950s, discounters offered even better product assortments while still embracing a philosophy of cash-only sales conducted in low-rent facilities. As they became firmly entrenched, they began moving to better locations, improving decor, and selling better-quality merchandise at higher prices. They also began offering a few department store services, such as credit plans and noncash sales.

off-price store
Bargain retailer that buys excess inventories from high-quality manufacturers and sells them at discounted prices

Off-Price Stores The 1980s witnessed the growth of the discount house variation commonly called the **off-price store.** Off-price stores buy the excess inventories of well-recognized high-quality manufacturers and sell them at prices up to 60 percent off regular department store prices. They are often prohibited from using manufacturers' names in their advertising because producers fear that a product's marketplace value and prestige will be compromised. One of the more successful off-price chains is Marshall's <www.marshallsonline.com>, which reduces prices on brand-name apparel for men, women, and children in its more than 475 stores.

catalog showroom
Bargain retailer in which customers place orders for catalog items to be picked up at on-premises warehouses

Catalog Showrooms Another form of bargain store that has grown dramatically in recent years is the **catalog showroom.** These firms mail out catalogs with color pictures, product descriptions, and prices to attract customers into their showrooms. Once there, customers view display samples, place orders, and wait briefly while clerks retrieve orders from attached warehouses. Service Merchandise <www.servicemerchandise.com>, Best Products, and LaBelle's are major catalog showroom retailers.

factory outlet
Bargain retailer owned by the manufacturer whose products it sells

Factory Outlets **Factory outlets** are manufacturer-owned stores that avoid wholesalers and retailers by selling merchandise directly from the factory to consumers. The first factory outlets featured apparel, linens, food, and furniture. Because they were usually located in warehouse-like facilities next to the factories, distribution costs were quite low. Lower costs were passed on to customers as lower prices.

warehouse club (or **wholesale club)**
Bargain retailer offering large discounts on brand-name merchandise to customers who have paid annual membership fees

Warehouse Clubs The **warehouse club** (or **wholesale club**) offers large discounts on brand-name clothing, groceries, appliances, automotive supplies, and other merchandise. Unlike customers at discount houses and factory outlets, club customers pay annual membership fees. The first warehouse club, Price Club, opened in 1976. It merged with rival Costco in 1993, and today the sales of the combined company, called Costco, total $24 billion each year—tops among the nation's warehouse clubs. Selling everything from salmon to diamonds, Costco isn't complacent with its current success. It has expanded

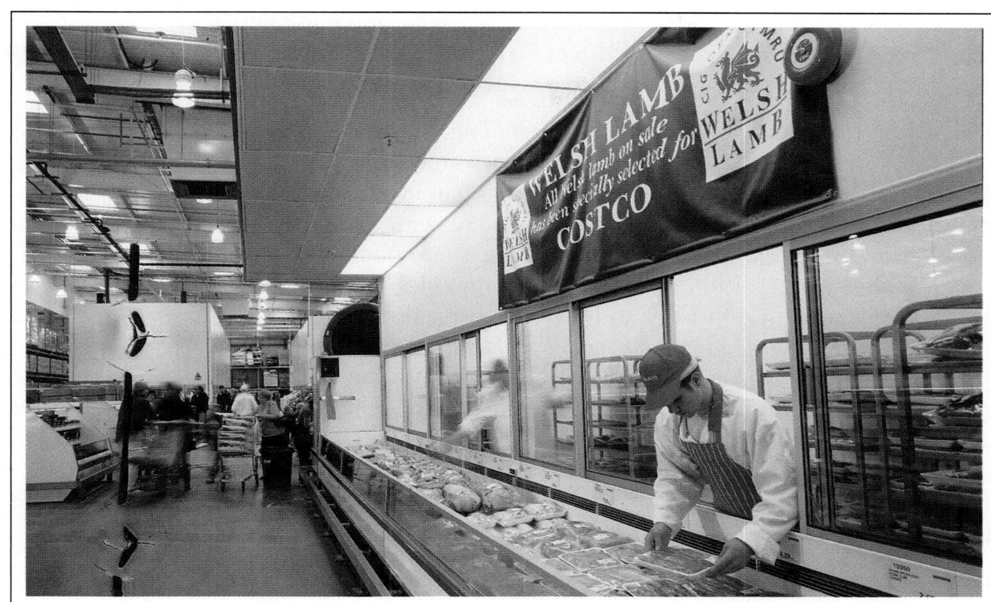

In 1993, top management at Costco warehouse clubs <www.costco.com> *began to worry that their American market had become saturated. That particular concern turned out to be unwarranted, but it prompted Costco to expand into other countries. The company now operates 20 warehouse stores in Great Britain, Taiwan, South Korea, and Japan. The Costco concept—low prices on high-quality merchandise available to members only—travels well: This store in the London suburb of Watford, England, is one of the chain's most successful outlets anywhere.*

into e-retailing with CostcoOnline <www.costco.com>, where you can take out a club membership, chat with other members, and shop electronically. Expanding beyond the United States, Costco buys in bulk for its 20 warehouse stores in South Korea, Japan, Taiwan, and Britain. When its Watford, England, store opened, the Costco concept surprised local customers: "At first people said, 'Huh? You don't buy rubber boats where you buy baked beans,' " recalls Jim Murphy, manager of seven stores in the U.K. locations.[10]

"At first people said, 'Huh? You don't buy rubber boats where you buy baked beans.' "

—Jim Murphy, Costco manager in the United Kingdom

Convenience Stores Neighborhood food retailers such as 7-Eleven and Circle K stores are successful convenience store chains. As the name suggests, **convenience stores** offer ease of purchase: They stress easily accessible locations with parking, extended store hours (in many cases 24 hours), and speedy service. They differ from most bargain retailers in that they do not feature low prices. Like bargain retailers they control prices by keeping in-store service levels to a minimum.

convenience store
Retail store offering easy accessibility, extended hours, and fast service

Nonstore and Electronic Retailing

Not all goods and services are sold in stores. Some of the nation's largest retailers sell all or most of their products without brick-and-mortar stores. Certain types of consumer goods—soft drinks, candy, and cigarettes—lend themselves to distribution in vending machines. Even at $107 billion per year, vending machine sales still represent less than 4 percent of all U.S. retail sales. And in e-retailing, sales are projected to reach $36 billion by 2002, as some 30 million households with personal computers continue online shopping.[11]

Major Types of Nonstore Retailing In this section, we will survey a few of the more important forms of nonstore retailing. In particular, we will examine **direct-response retailing,** in which firms make direct contact with customers both to inform them about products and to receive sales orders. This type of retailing includes *mail-order (catalog) marketing, telemarketing, direct selling,* and *electronic marketing* (including *video shopping*). Another important form of nonstore retailing is *mail marketing.*

direct-response retailing
Nonstore retailing by direct interaction with customers to inform them of products and to receive sales orders

Mail Marketing Direct mail marketing results in billions of sales dollars annually in both retail and industrial sales. Direct mail is effective because it targets audiences that have been identified from research lists as likely to be interested in specific products. The single mailings sent by insurance companies, magazine and book publishers, and clothing and furniture stores are expensive direct mail promotions. These various pamphlets, letters, brochures, and convenient order forms result in high-response sales rates.

Mail Order (or Catalog Marketing) In retailing, the world's largest mail-order business is run by Otto Versand, <www.otto.de>, a privately held company based in Hamburg, Germany. Company founder Werner Versand began in mail order back in 1950 by pasting pictures of shoes in hand-bound catalogs. Today, with annual sales topping $13 billion, Otto Versand has used mail order to build itself into one of the world's biggest multinational retailers. In addition to mail-order companies in Hungary, Japan, Italy, France, Britain, and Germany, Otto Versand owns 90 percent of Spiegel <www.spiegel.com> and its Eddie Bauer <www.eddiebauer.com> subsidiary in the United States.

mail order (or **catalog marketing**)
Form of nonstore retailing in which customers place orders for catalog merchandise received through the mail

Firms which, like Versand, sell by **mail order** (or **catalog marketing**) typically send out splashy color catalogs describing a variety of merchandise. Currently, they garner sales of $143 billion in the United States each year. L. L. Bean alone ships more than 10 million packages to mail-order customers annually. As a whole, the world of interactive commerce is an incredibly busy place: Each year, for example, AT&T's 800-line unit generates 13 billion calls, and competitors carry another 9 billion.[12]

telemarketing
Nonstore retailing in which the telephone is used to sell directly to consumers

Telemarketing **Telemarketing** is the use of the telephone to sell directly to consumers. WATS (wide area telephone service) lines can be used to receive toll-free calls from consumers responding to television and radio ads. Using live or automated dialing, message delivery, and order taking, telemarketers can also use WATS lines to call consumers to promote products and services. Telemarketing is used not only for consumer goods but also for industrial goods and insurance and accounting services. Currently, telemarketing is experiencing exceptional growth in the United States, Canada, and Great Britain. Sales topped $460 billion in 1998 and $600 billion for the year 2000.[13]

direct selling
Form of nonstore retailing typified by door-to-door sales

Direct Selling Possibly the oldest form of retailing, **direct selling** is still used by more than 600 U.S. companies that sell door-to-door or through home-selling parties. For example, some of us have attended Tupperware parties at friends' houses. Avon Products has 465,000 independent U.S. sales representatives.[14]

Office-to-office direct selling is also common in the wholesaling of such industrial goods as commercial copying equipment. Although direct selling is convenient and gives

"Mr. Watson, have you ever thought what would happen to your loved ones if you died tomorrow?"

customers one-on-one attention, prices are usually driven up by labor costs (salespeople often receive commissions of 40 to 50 cents on every sales dollar). Even so, there are about 3.5 million direct salespeople in the United States, 80 percent of whom are women. Worldwide, 9 million direct salespeople now generate annual retail sales of $35 billion. In Japan alone, 1.2 million distributors have made Amway Corp. second only to Coca-Cola as the most profitable foreign retailer.

The Boom in Electronic Retailing **Electronic retailing** is made possible by communications networks that allow sellers to connect to consumers' computers with digital information about products. With over 1.5 million subscribers, Prodigy Communications Corp. <www.prodigy.com>, which was formed as a joint venture of IBM and Sears, is among the largest home networks. As an *Internet service provider (ISP),* Prodigy employs an access network covering more than 750 U.S. cities that can be accessed by 90 percent of the population with a local telephone call. Prodigy provides members with access to the Internet and displays of available products ranging from travel packages to financial services to consumer goods. The viewer can examine detailed descriptions, compare brands, send for free information, or purchase by credit card from home. As an industry leader in Internet shopping transactions, Prodigy operates outside the United States with networks throughout the world.[15]

electronic retailing
Nonstore retailing in which information about the seller's products and services is connected to consumers' computers, allowing consumers to receive the information and purchase the products in the home

Internet-Based Stores Use of the Internet to interact with customers—to inform them, to sell to them, and to distribute to them—is booming. Internet usage by small businesses in the United States doubled in 1998, nearly doubled again in 1999, and added another 2.1 million Web sites during 2000. Figure 14.3 tells the story of this growth by showing the percentages of small businesses with Web sites (Figure 14.3[a]), those planning to post Web sites (Figure 14.3[b]), and the marketing functions that small businesses expect Web sites to perform for them (Figure 14.3[c]).[16]

The rampant growth of e-commerce is undoubtedly just the beginning. Business-to-business e-commerce is a $131 billion industry that is expected to reach $1.5 trillion by 2002. In addition, while e-retail sales were 13 times higher in 2000 than they were in 1997, at $36 billion they were still less than 4 percent of total retail sales. There is a lot

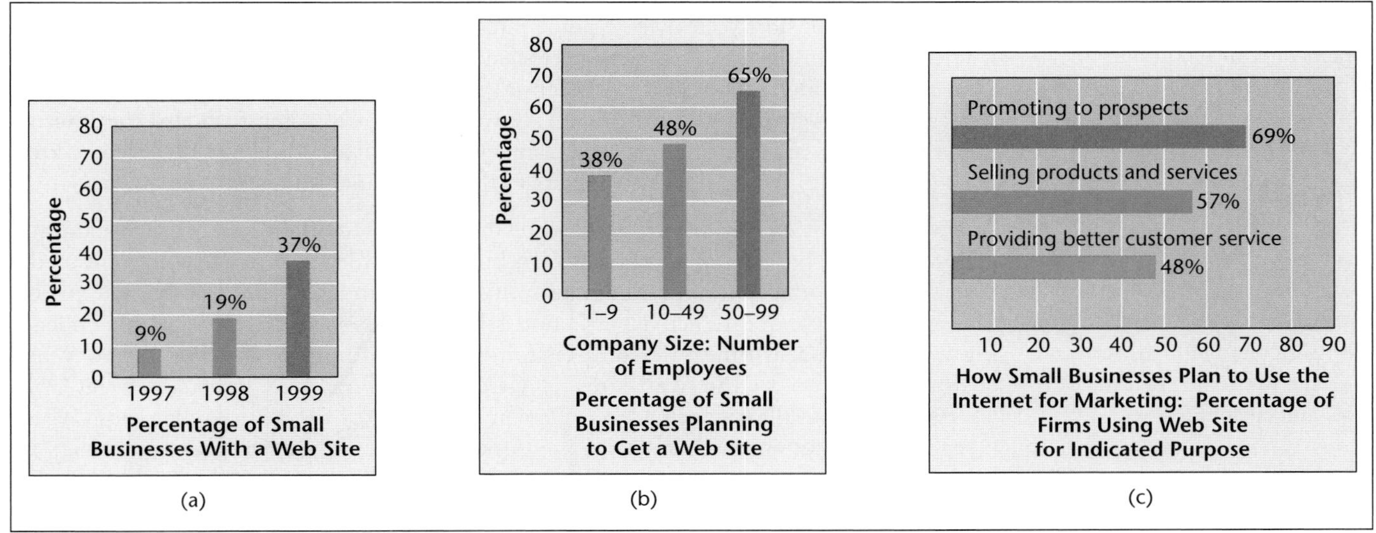

Figure 14.3
Small Business and the Web

of room for growth, and huge growth prospects are fueling the scramble among firms to position themselves in the e-business industry.[17]

e-catalog
Nonstore retailing in which the Internet is used to display products

Electronic Catalogs **E-catalogs** use the Internet to display products and services for both retail shoppers and business customers. By sending an electronic version (instead of traditional mail catalogs), firms give millions of users instant access to pages of products. Naturally, the seller avoids mail distribution and printing costs. Once the online catalog is in place, there is little cost in maintaining and accessing it. Recognizing these advantages, about 85 percent of all catalogers are now on the Internet, with sales via Web sites accounting for 10 percent of all catalog sales. The top 10 consumer e-catalogs include such names as JC Penney (#1), Fingerhut (#3), L. L. Bean (#7), and Victoria's Secret (#8). Top business-to-business e-catalogs include Dell Computer (#1) and Office Depot (#5).[18]

electronic storefront
Commercial Web site in which customers gather information about products, buying opportunities, placing orders, and paying for purchases

cybermall
Collection of virtual storefronts (business Web sites) representing a variety of products and product lines on the Internet

Electronic Storefronts and Cybermalls Pioneer Internet shoppers of just five years ago can readily appreciate the friendly browsing offered by today's e-storefronts. A seller's Web site is an **electronic storefront** in which consumers collect information about products and buying opportunities, place sales orders, and pay for their purchases. Sites are also called *virtual storefronts* because digital imaging gives them the appearance of a store that may not exist in real brick and mortar. Producers of large product lines, such as Dell Computer <www.dell.com>, have storefronts dedicated to their own product lines. Other sites, such as CDNOW <www.cdnow.com>, which offers CDs and audio and video tapes, are category sellers whose storefronts feature products from many manufacturers. Search engines like Yahoo! <www.yahoo.com> serve as **cybermalls:** collections of virtual storefronts representing diverse products. After entering a cybermall, shoppers can navigate easily by choosing from a list of stores (Eddie Bauer or Macy's), product listings (Pokémon or MP3 players), or departments (apparel or bath/beauty). When your virtual shopping cart is full, you check out and pay your bill. The value-added properties of cybermalls are fairly obvious: speed, convenience, 24-hour access, and, most importantly, an efficient search that avoids the "click-'til-you-drop" syndrome—the endless wandering through cyberspace experienced by early Internet users.

multilevel marketing
Distribution channel consisting of self-employed distributors who receive commissions for selling products to customers and for recruiting new distributors

From Door-to-Door to e-Sales? Not surprisingly, cyberspace is encroaching on door-to-door distribution channels. Amway is famous for its **multilevel marketing** channel in which self-employed distributors are paid commissions for recruiting new customers and new Amway representatives. Now Amway is expanding its system of multilevel marketing onto the Internet with a spin-off called Quixstar <www.quixstar.com>. With assistance from Quixstar, you can start your own at-home Internet business. You will be paid for directing new customers to the Quixstar site and for encouraging others to become Quixstar reps. The Internet's huge at-home sales potential is also luring other famous door-to-door names—Tupperware, Avon, and Mary Kay. Such firms are racing to board the Internet even though they are courting potential channel conflict: In all probability, millions of loyal door-to-door sales reps will lose customers to their companies' Internet outlets.[19]

interactive marketing
Nonstore retailing that uses a Web site to provide real-time sales and customer service

Interactive and Video Marketing E-stores no longer provide just numerical data and pictures. Today, both retail and business-to-business customers interact with multimedia Web sites using voice, graphics, animation, film clips, and access to live human advice. One good example of **interactive marketing** is LivePerson <www.liveperson.com>, a leading provider of real-time sales and customer service for over 450 Web sites. When customers log on to the Web sites of e-Loan, Playboy, CBS Sportsline's IgoGolf, USABancShares—all of which are LivePerson clients—they enter a live chat room where a service operator initiates a secure one-on-one text chat. Questions and answers go back-and-forth to give customers user-friendly personal service during the crucial moments when they have specific questions that must be answered before they decide on a product. Another form of interaction is the so-called banner ad that changes as the user's mouse moves about on the Web page, revealing new drop-down boxes, check boxes, and search boxes.[20]

It's a WiredWorld

• How Far Is It to Detroit.com?

Ford Motor Co. jolted the advertising world in 1999 by announcing that up to $90 million of its advertising will be shifted from magazines and newsprint to Internet ads on sites such as <www.carpoint.msn.com>. Following this trend are General Motors, American Honda Motor Co., and Toyota Motor Sales USA. The automakers are going to where customers are looking. As of 2000, some 40 percent of buyers were shopping the Internet for their next vehicle. In one month alone in 1999, the top 10 automotive Web sites tallied more than 7 million visits from potential buyers. The question that arises, then, is how far will Detroit go with its Internet sales initiative? Will automakers reduce the distribution channel by selling directly to new car buyers, eliminating the retail automobile dealership as we currently know it? Not likely, at least not in the near future.

At present, about 30 states in the United States have laws prohibiting automakers from owning dealerships. In addition, laws in most states do not allow manufacturers to sell vehicles directly to consumers. The Internet, however, has introduced some new tests of the old regulations. So sensitive is this issue that in 1999, Ford had to shut down a Web site that sold off-lease vehicles (not new vehicles) after a ruling by a Texas regulatory commission. The closing was ordered even though Houston-area dealers participated in the transactions. The ruling indicates how sensitive regulators are to automakers' experiments in adapting the Internet to their distribution channels.

Aside from legal regulations, it isn't likely that automakers would make effective retailers. Nor do they necessarily want to get away from what they do best—make cars—by diverting their resources into retailing and customer service. Instead, the Net's role on the marketing side of the business involves cultivating closer relationships with customers. If you log on to automakers' Web sites—<www.saturn.com>, <www.ford.com>, <www.toyota.com>, <www.gm.com>—you will see that they assist shoppers with information about new products, service, and pricing. Their main value is in helping buyers to select personalized packages of features on the cars they want. Ford CEO Jacques Nasser expects that the percentage of customers using the Internet to get prepurchase information will rise to 80 percent in the year 2000.

Meanwhile, Web site visitors are referred to dealerships so that the retailing is left to those who know best how to do it. This is the area in which Internet new car sales are growing—namely, the use of the Web as a sales tool among dealers: Toyota reports that some dealers are selling up to 25 to 30 percent of their entire volume on the Net.

Video marketing, a long-established form of interactive marketing, lets viewers shop at home from television screens. Most cable systems offer video marketing through home-shopping channels that display and demonstrate products—jewelry, dinnerware, home-accessory items, and even real estate—and allow viewers to phone in or e-mail orders. One home-shopping network, QVC <www.qvc.com>, operates internationally in the United Kingdom, Germany, Mexico, and South America. More recently the company launched iQVC, its interactive Web site.

video marketing
Nonstore retailing to consumers via standard and cable television

A Century of Change in Retailing

Near the end of the nineteenth century, America's rural landscape was dotted with local general stores that often served isolated communities. From these beginnings, retail companies have continued to expand their "reach" to more customers by locating more stores in bigger population centers, by changing lines of merchandise, and by grouping different kinds of stores in single locations. Today's global retail giants have thousands of stores with millions of employees serving consumers in nearly every country on Earth. The widening "reach" of retailers is shown in Figure 14.4. Why does this reach continue to widen? With the passage of time, retailers adopt a variety of distribution methods that, collectively, enable them to reach more and more customers.

Figure 14.4

Retail "Reach": Growth in Retailing Customer Base

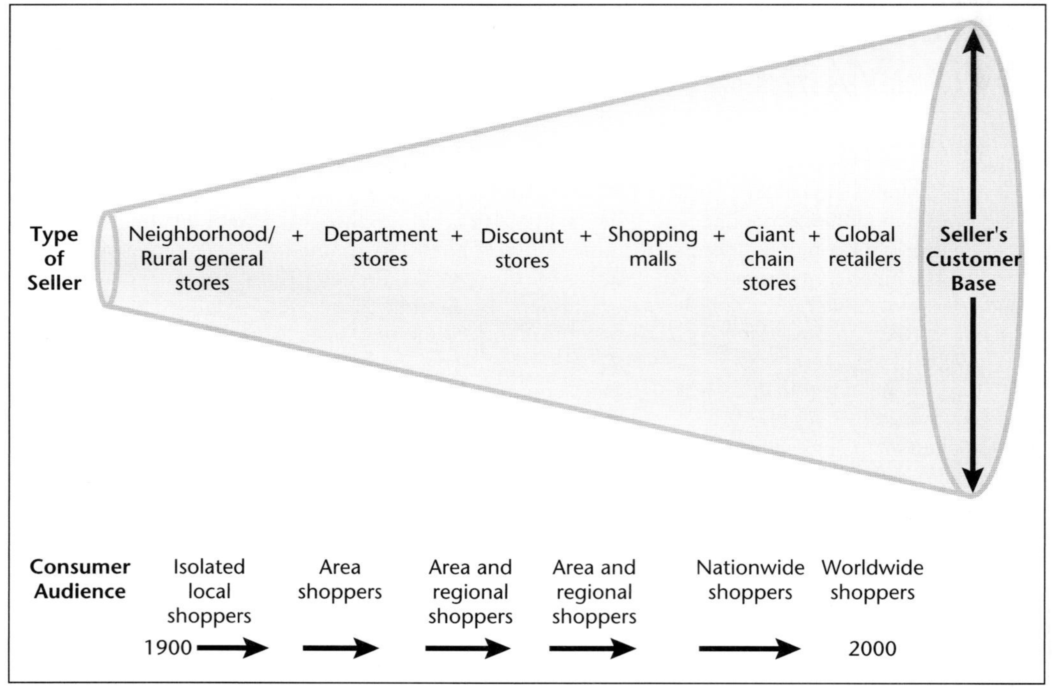

Retailing to the At-Home Shopper At-home shopping in the nineteenth century was provided by traveling salesmen who peddled household wares from door-to-door. By 1895, an up-and-coming firm called Sears, Roebuck and Co. was mailing a 532-page catalog offering cut-rate prices for mail-order sales to rural customers throughout the United States. As you can see in Figure 14.5, retailers were quick to develop additional methods that, collectively, have stimulated ever-expanding opportunities for at-home shopping. In particular, electronic technologies have fueled explosive growth by offering ever-increasing added value—convenience, lower prices, accessibility, speed—that attracts consumers and spurs even further growth.

The "Life Cycle of an e-Business" box in this chapter shows how Garden.com stocked its electronic storefront through a distribution network of specialty suppliers.

PHYSICAL DISTRIBUTION

physical distribution
Activities needed to move a product efficiently from manufacturer to consumer

Physical distribution refers to the activities needed to move products efficiently from manufacturer to consumer. The goals of physical distribution are to make goods available when and where consumers want them, to keep costs low, and to provide services that keep customers satisfied. Thus physical distribution includes *warehousing* and *transportation operations,* as well as *distribution for e-customers.*

Warehousing Operations

warehousing
Physical distribution operation concerned with the storage of goods

Storing, or **warehousing,** is a major part of distribution management. In selecting a strategy, managers must keep in mind both the different characteristics and costs of warehousing operations.

Types of Warehouses There are two basic types of warehouses: private and public. Facilities can be further divided according to their use as *storage warehouses* or *distribution centers.*

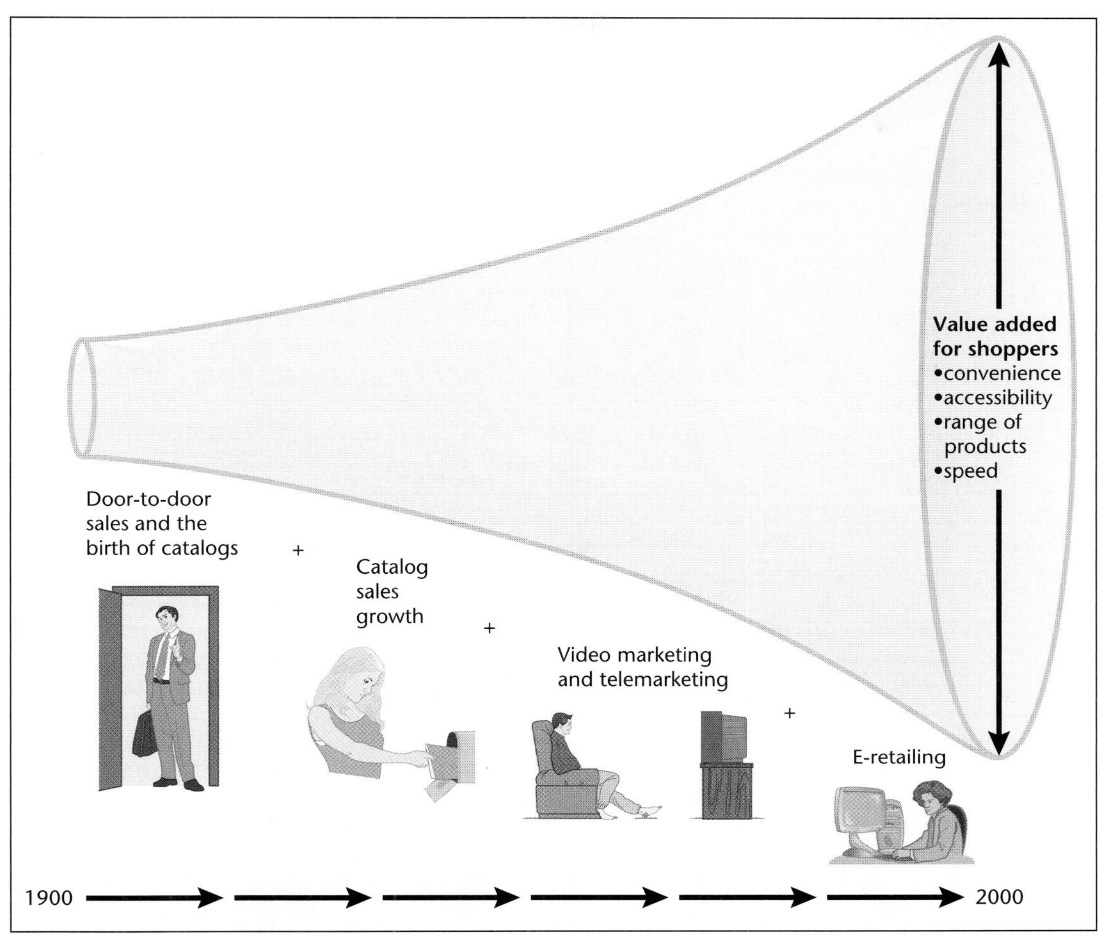

Figure 14.5

A Century of Evolution in At-Home Retailing

Public and Private Warehouses **Private warehouses** are owned and used by a single manufacturer, wholesaler, or retailer. Most are operated by large firms that deal in mass quantities and need storage on a regular basis. JC Penney eases the movement of products to retail stores by maintaining its own warehouses.

Public warehouses are independently owned and operated. Companies rent only the space they need. Public warehouses are popular with firms that need storage only during peak periods. They are also used by manufacturers needing multiple storage locations to get products to numerous markets.

Storage Warehouses and Distribution Centers **Storage warehouses** provide storage for extended periods of time. Producers of seasonal items, such as agricultural crops, use this type of warehouse. **Distribution centers** store products whose market demand is both constant and high. They are used by retail chains, wholesalers, and manufacturers that need to break down large quantities of merchandise into the smaller quantities that stores or customers demand.

Distribution centers are common in the grocery and food industry. Kellogg, for example, stores virtually no products at its plants. Instead, it ships cereals from factories directly to regional distribution centers. As wholesalers place orders for combinations of products, warehouses fill and ship them. Because warehouses are regional, wholesalers receive orders quickly.

private warehouse
Warehouse owned by and providing storage for a single company

public warehouse
Independently owned and operated warehouse that stores goods for many firms

storage warehouse
Warehouse providing storage for extended periods of time

distribution center
Warehouse providing short-term storage of goods for which demand is both constant and high

Life Cycle of an e-Business

How to Farm Out the Supply Function

As an e-business, Garden.com was an electronic retailer, an e-agent, and a "virtual" store—all located on the Internet at <www.garden.com>. But the core of the company's strategy was its channel of distribution. The *marketing channel* concept begins with the development of the product, then builds the distribution chain to meet customers' needs, and, finally, determines how buyers will receive the product. First, the Garden.com distribution system recognized that each gardener wants access to a wide range of specialty items for his or her tastes and needs. *Customer fulfillment* meant speedy order filling, timely delivery, and real-time access in tracking the progress of shipments. From anywhere in Garden.com's customer market (which was quite fragmented, geographically) you could visit a one-stop location for both information about gardening and shopping. The firm's line of specialty products was stocked by a distribution network of the best suppliers in each of eight product categories. These 83 suppliers were chosen to provide rapid response using priority Fed Ex shipping services.

Visitors to the electronic storefront were shown a wide array of services and a gardener's dream list of merchandise, all on one Web site. In reality, however, only about 10 percent of all merchandise moved through Garden.com's own Austin facility. The other 90 percent was shipped around the country from the firm's suppliers. Suppliers were linked by a so-called *extranet*—a private, restricted-access electronic information system—that used Garden.com's TRELLIS technology. TRELLIS tied all its niche growers into Garden.com's one-stop virtual store. Thus the supply chain for a fruit tree and some cut flowers extends from a tree grower in one part of the country and a flower grower in another to the customer in a third. All customer transactions, however, were made at the one-stop location that displayed products, accepted payment, answered questions, and let customers keep track of delivery status. Unfortunately, although it was among the best supply-chain technologies in the industry, TRELLIS was expensive to develop. In the quarter ended September 30, 2000 alone, costs for TRELLIS and Web site development were $1.9 million, against product revenues of just $2.2 million. The system was thus contributing to the firm's growing cash deficits.

Garden.com's distribution expert, Jamie O'Neill, had worked at W. W. Granger, a large distributor of industrial products, where he had helped assemble a network that tied together suppliers and distributors of millions of industrial products. He knew from experience that the new venture would have to establish and maintain special relationships with specialty suppliers. At Garden.com, supplier selection was stringent, and two-way loyalty was essential. Garden.com selected the best-quality specialty suppliers, such as Papa Geno's Herb Farm <www.papagenos.com> in Nebraska, and acted as the agent for Geno's products by funneling its many herb customers exclusively to Geno. In return, suppliers were dedicated to building the capacity necessary for keeping up with growing sales and for giving fast turnaround and accurate order fulfillment to Garden.com customers. So effective were their suppliers that, at the eventual shutdown of Garden.com's retail operations, Cliff Sharpless thanked "our suppliers for their strong support [and] commitment to quality. The . . . support we received from our . . . suppliers has been instrumental in fueling our passion for this business over the past five years."

Warehousing Costs Typical warehouse costs include such obvious expenses as storage space rental or mortgage payments (usually computed on a square-foot basis), insurance, and wages. They also include the costs of *inventory control* and *materials handling.*

inventory control
Warehouse operation that tracks inventory on hand and ensures that an adequate supply is in stock at all times

Inventory Control **Inventory control** goes beyond keeping track of what is on hand at any time. It often involves the very tricky balancing act of ensuring that although an adequate supply of a product is in stock at all times, excessive supplies are avoided.

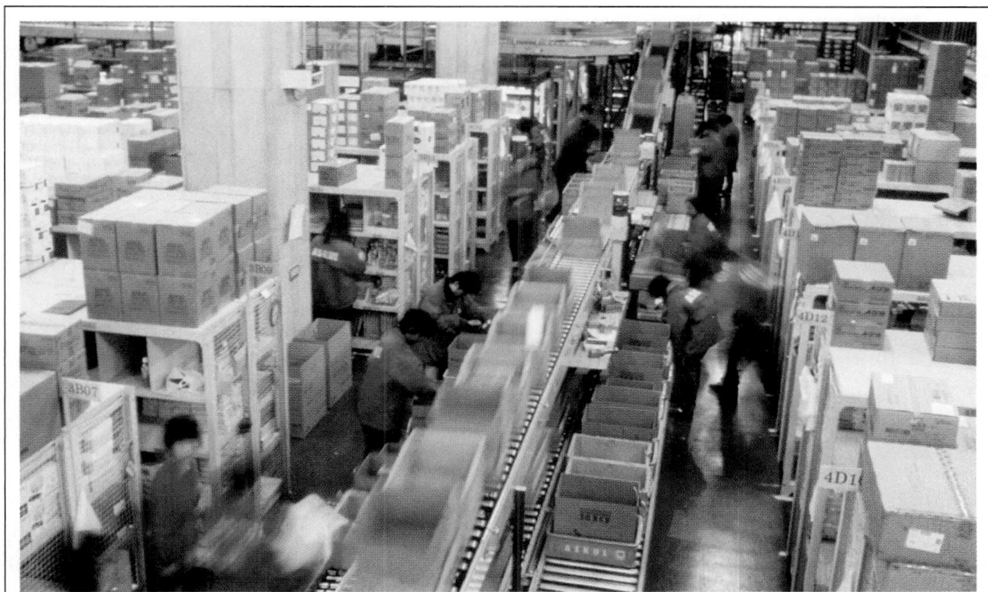

Askul <www.askul.co.jp>, *Japan's biggest office-products supplier, built this high-tech distribution center on cheap land near Tokyo Bay. The facility takes advantage of the Internet to offer real-time ordering and 24-hour delivery. The productivity gains have been impressive: a doubling of sales with no increase in the size of the workforce. Even so, Japanese business and government leaders worry that the country as a whole does not spend enough on information technology: Japan devotes about 20 percent of total business investment to technologies like those used by Askul, compared to 34 percent in the United States.*

Material Handling Most warehouse personnel are involved in **material handling:** the transportation, arrangement, and orderly retrieval of inventoried goods. Holding down material-handling costs means developing a product storage strategy that takes into account product locations within the warehouse. Other considerations include packaging decisions, such as whether to store a product as individual units, in multiple packages, or in sealed containers.

material handling
Warehouse operation involving the transportation, arrangement, and orderly retrieval of goods in inventory

One strategy for managing materials is *unitization,* which makes storage and handling more systematic by standardizing the weight and form of materials. General Electric's Louisville, Kentucky, warehouse receives apartment-size refrigerators from Europe in containers holding 56 refrigerators. Using the huge containers rather than individual boxes not only makes handling easier but also reduces theft and damage. It also optimizes shipping space and allows for easier restocking.

Transportation Operations

The highest cost faced by many companies is the cost of physically moving a product. Thus, cost is a major factor in choosing a transportation method. But firms must also consider several other factors: the nature of the product, the distance it must travel, the speed with which it must be received, and customer wants and needs.

Transportation Modes The major transportation modes include trucks, railroads, planes, water carriers, and pipelines. Differences in cost are most directly related to delivery speed.

Trucks The advantages of trucks include flexibility, fast service, and dependability. Nearly all areas of the United States can be reached by truck. Because less breakage occurs than with railroad transport, trucked goods need less packing—a major cost savings. Trucks are a particularly good choice for short-distance distribution and for expensive products. They carry more freight than any other form of transport except rail carriers.

Railroads Railroads have been the backbone of the U.S. transportation system since the late 1800s. Until the 1960s, when trucking firms attracted many of their customers with lower rates, railroads were also fairly profitable. They are now used primarily to transport heavy, bulky items such as cars, steel, and coal. To regain market share, railroads have expanded services to include faster delivery times and piggyback service, in which truck trailers are placed on railcars. This service alone can save shippers up to one-half the cost of shipping by truck.

Planes Air is the fastest available mode of transportation. Other advantages include much lower costs in handling and packing and unpacking compared with other modes. Inventory carrying costs can also be reduced. Shipments of fresh fish can be picked up by restaurants each day, avoiding the risk of spoilage from packaging and storing. However, air freight is the most expensive form of transportation.

Water Carriers Of all transport modes, water is the least expensive. Modern networks of internal waterways, locks, rivers, and lakes allow water carriers to reach many areas in the United States and throughout the world. Unfortunately, water transport is also the slowest mode. Thus, boats and barges are used mostly for heavy, bulky materials and products (such as sand, gravel, oil, and grain), for which delivery speed is unimportant. Today, companies use water carriers because many ships are now specially constructed to hold large standardized containers.

Pipelines Like water transportation, pipelines are slow. Used to transport liquids and gases, pipelines are also inflexible. But pipelines do provide a constant flow of products and are unaffected by weather conditions. The Trans-Alaska Pipeline transports oil through Alaska on its route to the lower 48 states. Lack of adaptability to other products makes pipelines an unimportant transportation method for most industries.

Changes in Transportation Operations For many years, U.S. transport companies specialized in one mode or another. Since deregulation in 1980, however, this pattern has changed. New developments in cost-efficiency and competitiveness include intermodal transportation, containerization, and information technology.

intermodal transportation
Combined use of several different modes of transportation

Intermodal Transportation **Intermodal transportation**—the combined use of different modes of transportation—has come into widespread use. For example, shipping by a combination of air and rail or truck is sometimes called *birdyback* transport. Large railroad companies, such as Burlington Northern and Union Pacific, have merged with trucking, air, and shipping lines. The goal is to offer simplified source-to-destination delivery by any necessary combination of methods.

containerization
Transportation method in which goods are sealed in containers at shipping sources and opened when they reach final destinations

Containerization To make intermodal transport more efficient, **containerization** uses standardized heavy-duty containers in which many items are sealed at points of shipment and opened only at final destinations. On the trip, containers may be loaded onto ships for ocean transit, transferred onto trucks, loaded onto railcars (piggyback service), and delivered to final destinations by other trucks. Sealed containers are then unloaded and returned for future use.

Physical Distribution and e-Customer Satisfaction New e-commerce companies often focus on Internet sales, only to discover that after-sale distribution delays cause customer dissatisfaction and discourage repeat sales. Any delay in physical distribution, is a breakdown in fulfillment and an obstacle to growth. **Order fulfillment** begins when the sale is made: It involves getting the product, in good condition and on time, to the customer for each sales transaction. Bear in mind that the volume of transactions can be huge—Web retailers shipped more than 230 million packages in 1999. Fulfillment performance has been disappointing for some e-businesses, especially during busy holiday seasons.

What role does order processing play in overall customer service operations?

order fulfillment
All activities involved in completing a sales transaction, beginning with making the sale and ending with on-time delivery to the customer

To improve on-time deliveries, many businesses, such as Amazon.com, maintain their own distribution centers and ship themselves from their own warehouses near major shipping hubs. Other e-tailers, however, entrust their order-filling services to distribution specialists such as Fingerhut Business Services, Inc. <www.fingerhut.com> and Keystone Fulfillment, Inc. <www.kfulfillment.com>. Fingerhut, whose clients include Wal-Mart Stores, Levi Strauss, and Etoys, boasts a 1.2-million-square-foot, high-tech distribution center that employs up to 1,200 workers during the holiday peak. Fingerhut processes customer orders, ships items, provides information about product availability, informs customers about the real-time status of orders, and handles returns for their clients. For Fingerhut to do all this, the client e-tailer's computer system must be integrated with the distributor's. In deciding whether to build their own distribution centers or to use a third-party distributor, e-tailers must keep in mind the fixed costs as well as the shipping expertise they will need. The capital investment required for a 1-million-square-foot distribution center is $60 to $80 million; only a high-volume business can afford it. The alternative is to pay a third-party distributor about 10 percent of each sale to fulfill orders, but only after ensuring that they will make reliable on-time deliveries.[21]

Distribution as a Marketing Strategy

Distribution is an increasingly important way of competing for sales. Instead of just offering advantages in product features and quality, price, and promotion, many firms have turned to distribution as a cornerstone of their business strategies. This approach means assessing and improving the entire stream of activities (wholesaling, warehousing, and transportation) involved in getting products to customers. Its importance is illustrated at Molex <www.molex.com>, a large manufacturer of electronic connectors and switches. The firm's 100,000 products are used by manufacturers of cars, computers, and consumer products who not only want fast, just-in-time delivery but who are becoming more and more globalized. To meet its customers' needs, Molex became the first connector manufacturer to sign distribution agreements on a global basis. Its relationships with Arrow Electronics <www.arrow.com> and Avnet <www.avnet.com>, the world's largest distributors of electronic components, allow Molex to better service customers who want a single worldwide source for their products.

The Use of Hubs One approach to streamlining is the use of **hubs:** central distribution outlets that control all or most of a firm's distribution activities. Two contrasting strategies have emerged from this approach: *supply-side and prestaging hubs* on one hand and *distribution-side hubs* on the other.

hub
Central distribution outlet that controls all or most of a firm's distribution activities

Supply-Side and Prestaging Hubs *Supply-side hubs* make the most sense when large shipments of supplies flow regularly to a single industrial user, such as a large manufacturer. They are used by automobile factories, where thousands of incoming supplies can arrive by train, truck, and air. Incoming shipments can create a nightmare of traffic jams, loading-dock congestion, paperwork logjams, and huge storage space requirements.

To clear this congestion, some firms operate *prestaging hubs.* Saturn maintains such a facility—managed by Ryder System <www.ryder.com>—located two miles from its factory. All incoming transportation schedules and supplies are managed by Ryder to satisfy one requirement: meeting Saturn's production schedules. The long-haul tractors at the hub are disconnected from trailers and sent on their return trips to any of 339 suppliers located in 39 states. Responding to Saturn's up-to-the-minute needs, hub headquarters arranges the transport of presorted and preinspected materials to the factory by loading them onto specially designed shuttle tractors.

The chief job of the hub, then, is to coordinate the customer's materials needs with supply chain transportation. If the hub is successful, the factory's inventories are virtually eliminated, storage space requirements are reduced, and long-haul trucks keep moving, instead of lining up at the customer's unloading dock. By outsourcing distribution activities to its hub, Saturn can focus on what it does best: manufacturing. Meanwhile, Ryder, the nation's largest logistics management firm, is paid for its specialty: handling transportation flows.

Distribution-Side Hubs Whereas supply-side hubs are located near industrial customers, *distribution-side hubs* may be located much farther away, especially if customers are geographically dispersed. National Semiconductor <www.national.com>, one of the world's largest chip makers, is an example. National's finished products, silicon microchips, are produced in plants throughout the world and shipped to customers such as IBM, Toshiba, Siemens, Ford, and Compaq at factory locations around the globe. On the journey from producer to customer, chips originally sat waiting at one location after another—on factory floors, at customs, in distributors' facilities, and in customers' warehouses. Typically, they traveled 20,000 different routes on as many as 12 airlines and spent time in 10 warehouses before reaching their customers. National has streamlined its delivery system by shutting down six warehouses around the world. Now it airfreights microchips worldwide from a single distribution center in Singapore. All of its activities—storage, sorting, shipping—are run by Federal Express <www.fedex.com>. As a result, distribution costs have fallen, delivery times have been reduced by half, and sales have increased.

Continued from page 379

Why RIAA Is Riled

The Napster phenomenon underscores three features of contemporary commerce which, when taken together, go a long way toward explaining why battle lines are forming in the music industry:

1. As long as they can be converted into digital format, products can be transmitted on the Internet rather than by mail. Now, this in itself is nothing new. JAVA has been delivering software products for years on the Internet.
2. At present, Napster users get the service for free. The availability of such a large menu of free products is in fact revolutionary.
3. The enormous number of participants is significant. Little wonder, then, that music-industry businesses—members of the traditional distribution channel—are up in arms.

Entertainment artists, of course, earn their livings from royalties on the sales of their albums. Revenues from those royalties are denied them each time a Napster user gets a free album instead of buying it from a legitimate vendor, such as a record store. Without revenues, how can the costs of production be recovered? And at a market price of $0 for an album, how can record stores hope to stay in business when, obviously, they cannot lower their costs to zero? It comes as no surprise, therefore, that an industry trade organization, the Recording Industry Association of America (RIAA) **<www.riaa.org>**, has filed suit claiming that Napster's main function is to violate copyright regulations. Napster, claims the RIAA, is "operating a haven for music piracy on an unprecedented scale." Napster proclaims its innocence, arguing that it does nothing more than supply software. It neither takes possession of albums nor does it buy or sell them. The trading of albums occurs solely among individuals on the open market.

While the battle heats up, some companies are getting ready to sell albums via MP3 (though not for free, of course). They see the Internet as a new distribution alternative. Meanwhile, Napster CEO Eileen Richardson thinks that record companies would be better off joining her firm instead of fighting it. She proposes that Napster would be a terrific asset for selling concert tickets and promoting artists and albums. RIAA attorney Cary Sherman replies that working with Napster would be basically wrong. Performers and recording companies would be forfeiting their rights to make money.

As the battle continues, both the legal and financial stakes grow higher. The RIAA claims the industry has lost more than $300 million in sales. In July 2000, a U.S. District Court judge in San Francisco, noting that 70 million people would be using Napster by year's end, ordered a halt to music swapping on the site. The next day 20 million users got a reprieve when the 9th Circuit Court allowed Napster to continue operating while appealing the lower court ruling.

By the end of the year, however, the battle was not going well for Napster: The worldwide media industry was suing the 18-month-old company for massive copyright infringement. Then in November, one of the companies allied against Napster offered an attractive if-you-can't-beat-'em-join-'em deal. The German conglomerate Bertelsmann **<www.bertelsmann.com>** loaned Napster $50 million for the express purpose of developing technology and services designed to get users to *buy music instead of stealing it*. In turn, Bertelsmann will drop its lawsuit and lobby other media companies to do the same. The Bertelsmann plan has far-reaching ramifications: The German firm not only wants to turn Napster into a legitimate generator of royalties for properties copyrighted by companies like itself, but to build a model for downloading a whole spectrum of media products—such as Bertelsmann's own books, magazines, newspapers, music recordings, television programming, and Internet products. As of this writing, the matter wasn't settled, and there remained a significant catch: If rival media companies don't buy in, the courts may eventually put Napster out of business.

Questions for Discussion

1. What do you think of Napster as an approach for distributing music?
2. Consider the more traditional channels of distribution for music albums. Which channel elements are most affected by the presence of Napster-like services? Explain how those elements are affected.
3. What other products, besides music albums, are the most likely candidates for distribution on the Internet, now and in the future?
4. Why is the music industry so concerned about Internet distribution? In addition to threats, do you see any opportunities for the industry in Internet distribution?
5. Identify the major legal issues that the music industry faces from Napster's presence. Develop a legal argument against Napster. Then take the reverse position and develop an argument in Napster's defense.
6. Aside from legal arguments, does Napster's emergence raise any ethical issues or social responsibility concerns?

SUMMARY OF LEARNING OBJECTIVES

1 **Identify the different *channels of distribution* and explain different *distribution strategies*.** In selecting a *distribution mix,* a firm may use all or any of eight *distribution channels*. The first four are aimed at getting products to consumers, the fifth is for consumers or business customers, and the last three are aimed at getting products to business customers. Channel 1 involves direct sales to consumers. Channel 2 includes a *retailer.* Channel 3 involves both a retailer and a *wholesaler,* and Channel 4 includes an *agent* or *broker* who enters the system before the wholesaler and retailer. Channel 5 includes only an agent between the producer and the customer. Channel 6, which is used extensively for e-commerce, involves a direct sale to an industrial user. Channel 7, which is used infrequently, entails selling to business users through wholesalers. Channel 8 includes retail superstores that get products from producers or wholesalers (or both) for reselling to business customers. *Distribution strategies* include *intensive, exclusive,* and *selective distribution,* which differ in the number of products and channel members involved and in the amount of service performed in the channel.

2 **Explain the differences between *merchant wholesalers* and *agents/brokers*.** *Wholesalers* act as distribution *intermediaries.* They may extend credit as well as store, repackage, and deliver products to other members of the channel. *Full-service* and *limited-function merchant wholesalers* differ in the number and types of distribution functions they offer. Unlike

wholesalers, *agents* and *brokers* never take legal possession of products. Rather, they function as sales and merchandising arms of manufacturers who do not have their own sales forces. They may also provide such services as advertising and display merchandising. In e-commerce, *e-agents* assist Internet users in finding products and best prices.

3 **Identify the different types of *retailing* and *retail stores*.** *Retailers* can be described according to two classifications: *product line retailers* and *bargain retailers*. Product line retailers include *department stores, supermarkets, hypermarkets,* and *specialty stores*. Bargain retailers include *discount houses, off-price stores, catalog showrooms, factory outlets, warehouse clubs,* and *convenience stores*. These retailers differ in terms of size, goods and services offered, and pricing. Some retailing also takes place without stores.

Nonstore retailing may use *direct mail catalogs, vending machines, video marketing, telemarketing, electronic retailing,* and *direct selling*. Internet retail shopping includes *electronic storefronts* where customers can examine a store's products, receive information about sellers and their products, place orders, and make payments electronically. Customers can also visit *cybermalls*—collection of virtual storefronts representing a variety of product lines on the Internet.

4 **Describe the major activities in the *physical distribution process*.** *Physical distribution* includes all the activities needed to move products from manufacturers to consumers, including *customer service, warehousing,* and *transportation* of products. Warehouses may be *public* or *private* and may function either as long-term *storage warehouses* or as *distribution centers*. In addition to storage, insurance, and wage-related costs, the cost of warehousing goods also includes *inventory control* (maintaining adequate but not excessive supplies) and *material handling* (transporting, arranging, and retrieving supplies).

5 **Compare the five basic forms of *transportation*.** Trucks, railroads, planes, water carriers (boats and barges), and pipelines are the major *transportation modes* used in the distribution process. They differ in cost, availability, reliability, speed, and number of points served. Air is the fastest but most expensive mode; water carriers are the slowest but least expensive. Since transport companies were deregulated in 1980, they have become more cost-efficient and competitive by developing such innovations as *intermodal transportation* and *containerization*.

QUESTIONS AND EXERCISES

Questions for Review

1. From the manufacturer's point of view, what are the advantages and disadvantages of using intermediaries to distribute products? From the end user's point of view?
2. Identify the eight channels of distribution. In what key ways do the four channels used only for consumer products differ from the channels used only for industrial products?
3. Identify and explain the differences between the three distribution strategies.
4. Explain the different roles played by merchant wholesalers and agents/brokers.
5. Explain how the activities of e-agents (Internet shopping agents) or brokers differ from those of traditional agents/brokers.
6. Identify the five modes of transportation used in product distribution. What factors lead companies to choose one over the others to deliver products to end users?

Questions for Analysis

7. Give three examples (other than those in the chapter) of products that use intensive distribution. Do the same for products that use exclusive distribution and selective distribution. For which category was it easiest to find examples? Why?
8. Consider the various kinds of nonstore retailing. Give examples of two products that typify the products sold to at-home shoppers through each form of nonstore retailing. Explain why different products are best suited to each form of nonstore retailing.
9. If you could own a firm that transports products, would you prefer to operate an intermodal transportation business or one that specializes in a single mode of transportation (say, truck or air)? Explain your choice.

Application Exercises

10. Interview the manager of a local manufacturing firm. Identify the firm's distribution strategy and the channels of distribution that it uses. Where applicable, describe the types of wholesalers or retail stores used to distribute the firm's products.
11. Choose any consumer item at your local supermarket and trace the chain of physical distribution activities that brought it to the store shelf.

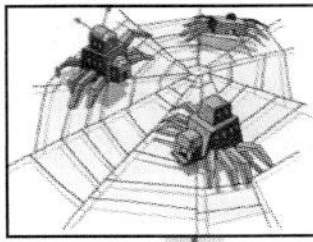

EXPLORING THE WEB

PLACING THE SERVICE KEYSTONE

To find out what a real-world company can do to assist e-commerce retailers, log on to the Web site of Keystone Internet Services, Inc. at:

www.keystonefulfillment.com/tele.html

After you have browsed Keystone's homepage and visited the supporting pages, respond to the following items:

1. Consider Keystone's description of "Product Fulfillment" services. List all the activities and services that Keystone identifies for product fulfillment. How does Keystone's description of product fulfillment compare with the definition given in this textbook?
2. Look at the page entitled "E-Commerce." Describe the services that Keystone provides to its clients. Describe the resources that Keystone employs to create customer satisfaction.
3. In its page for "Customized Services," describe the types of services Keystone offers. Are these services solely for online businesses, or might they also be used by non-e-businesses?
4. Examine Keystone's "Telemarketing" services. What kinds of telemarketing services does the firm provide? What resources are available at Keystone for delivering these services?

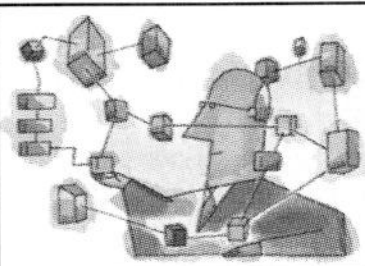

BUILDING YOUR BUSINESS SKILLS

ARE YOU SOLD ON THE NET?

This exercise enhances the following SCANS workplace competencies: demonstrating basic skills, demonstrating thinking skills, exhibiting interpersonal skills, and working with information.

GOAL

To encourage students to consider the value of online retailing as an element in a company's distribution system.

SITUATION

As the distribution manager of a privately owned clothing manufacturer, specializing in camping gear and outdoor clothing, you are convinced that your product line is perfect for online distribution. But the owner of the company is reluctant to expand distribution from a successful network of retail stores and a catalog operation. Your challenge is to convince the boss that retailing via the Internet can boost sales.

METHOD

Step 1

Join together with four or five classmates to research the advantages and disadvantages of an online distribution system for your company. Among the factors to consider are the following:

- The likelihood that target consumers are Internet shoppers. Camping gear is generally purchased by young, affluent consumers who are comfortable with the Web.
- The industry trend to online distribution. Are similar companies doing it? Have they been successful?
- The opportunity to expand inventory without increasing the cost of retail space or catalog production and mailing charges.
- The opportunity to have a store that never closes.
- The lack of trust many people have about doing business on the Web. Many consumers are reluctant to provide credit card data on the Web.
- The difficulty that electronic shoppers have in finding a Web site when they do not know the store's name.
- The frustration and waiting time involved in Web searches.
- The certainty that the site will not reach consumers who do not use computers or who are uncomfortable with the Web.

Step 2

Based on your findings, write a persuasive memo to the company's owner stating your position about expanding to an online distribution system. Include information that will counter expected objections.

FOLLOW-UP QUESTIONS

1. What place does online distribution have in the distribution network of this company?
2. In your view, is online distribution the wave of the future? Is it likely to increase in importance as a distribution system for apparel companies? Why or why not?

CRAFTING YOUR BUSINESS PLAN

GETTING THE CAFFEINE INTO YOUR CUP

THE PURPOSE OF THE ASSIGNMENT

1. To acquaint students with the process of navigating the *Business PlanPro* (*BPP*) software package (Version 4.0).
2. To familiarize students with product distribution issues that a sample firm must address in developing its business plan.
3. To demonstrate how channels of distribution, supply chains, and warehousing can be integrated as components of the *BPP* planning environment.

ASSIGNMENT

After reading Chapter 14 in the textbook, open the BPP *software* and look around for information about plans for supply chains and channels of distribution as they apply to a sample firm:* Silvera & Sons *(Silvera & Sons Ltd.). Then respond to the following items:*

1. Describe Silvera's products and customers. Then identify the steps in the supply chain beginning from raw materials through to the final consumer. [Sites to see in *BPP* (for this assignment): In the Plan Outline screen, click on **1.0 Executive Summary.** Then click on each of the following in turn: **1.1 Objectives, 2.0 Company Summary, 2.2 Company History,** and **3.0 Products.**]
2. Where is Silvera's main warehouse located? What are its activities? [Sites to see in *BPP:* In the Plan Outline screen, click on **2.3 Company Locations and Facilities.** After returning to the Plan Outline screen, click on **3.0 Products.**]
3. Describe the equipment that Silvera uses and the operations that it performs in the warehouse in order to prepare coffee beans for shipment. [Sites to see in *BPP:* From the Plan Outline screen, click on each of the following in turn: **3.1 Competitive Comparison** and **3.4 Technology.**]
4. Where are Silvera's raw materials located? [Sites to see in *BPP:* In the Plan Outline screen, click on **3.5 Future Products.**]
5. What steps are involved in getting the product from Silvera's plant in Ouro Fino to Miami? Who is responsible for paying the distribution charges? [Sites to see in *BPP:* In the Plan Outline screen, click on **4.2.2 Distribution Patterns.** After returning to the Plan Outline screen, click on **5.3.4 Distribution Strategy.**]

FOR YOUR OWN BUSINESS PLAN

6. Consider the supply chains and channels of distribution that could be used by the company for which your business plan is being developed. Explain how your choices of distribution channels and supply chains might be presented in the various *BPP* Plan Outline sections. In which sections of the document will you present your plans for each of those elements?

*GENERAL TIPS FOR NAVIGATING IN *BPP*

1. Open the *BPP* program, examine the Welcome screen, and click on **Open a Sample Plan.**
2. From the Open a Sample Plan dialogue box, click on a sample company name; then click on **Open.**
3. On the Plan Manager screen, click on Your Plan Outline; then click on any of the lines (for example, **5.1.1 Pricing Strategy**).

4. You can always return to the Plan Outline screen by going to the bottom of the screen and clicking on the **Plan Outline** icon.
5. After finishing with one sample company, you can get to the next one by going to the top of the screen and clicking on **File** (on the menu bar). Then beneath that, select **Open Sample Plan.** This will exit you from the current company file and take you to the Open Sample Plan dialogue box, where you can select your next sample company.
6. When you are finished, you can close the program by going to the top of the screen and clicking on **File** (on the bar menu). Then beneath that, select **Exit.**

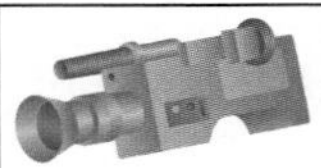

VIDEO EXERCISE

SUPPLYING THE BASIC FOOD GROUPS: HAIN FOODS

Learning Objectives

The purpose of this video exercise is to help you

1. Understand the use of intermediaries and distribution channels.
2. Recognize the variety of retail outlets.
3. Understand the link between marketing strategy and distribution.

BACKGROUND INFORMATION

The Hain Food Group, Inc. <www.thehainfoodgroup.com> markets, distributes, and sells branded natural, organic, and specialty food products primarily to specialty and natural-food distributors. The primary retail markets for Hain products are supermarkets, natural food stores, warehouse clubs, vending machines, and other outlets such as military PX's. The firm considers the acquisition of other food companies and product lines to be an integral part of its business strategy and integrates all of its brands under one management team and a uniform marketing, sales, and distribution program.

THE VIDEO

Several executives of the Hain Food Group introduce us to the firm's wide range of products and identify the various channels, such as food brokers and wholesale distributors, through which it reaches approximately 20,000 retail outlets nationwide. Ellen Deutsch, senior vice president of global marketing, discusses the way in which distribution strategy is affected by demographics, such as the fact that West Coast consumers use a higher percentage of natural products than their counterparts elsewhere in the United States.

DISCUSSION QUESTIONS

1. What is the role of the Hain Food Group's sales force?
2. Hain currently supplies retail outlets like vending machines and military PX's and is considering supplying the prison market. What other unusual outlets might Hain, or any food marketer, consider reaching?
3. Other than the "place value" defined by the marketing mix, what do Hain's distribution partners contribute to its success?

FOLLOW-UP ASSIGNMENT

Compare distribution through wholesalers with direct distribution (distribution of a product or service such as a restaurant meal or a haircut), and then compare each to the unique form of distribution that occurs over the Internet (of products and services such as news, information, Webcasts, and book and music downloads). What advantages and disadvantages does each distribution method offer? (Consider the question of copyright when you examine the Internet as a distribution channel.)

FOR FURTHER EXPLORATION

Visit the Hain Food Group's website at <www.thehainfoodgroup.com> and become familiar with its range of products. Do you recognize any? Look in your supermarket or health-food store to see how many of Hain's products you can find. Does the company seem to be distributing many of its products in your area? Why or why not? Consider demographics and geography in your answer.

Chapter 15

Producing Goods and Services

After reading this chapter, you should be able to:

1. ***Explain*** the meaning of the term *production* or *operations* and describe the four kinds of *utility* it provides.

2. ***Describe*** and explain the two classifications of *operations processes.*

3. ***Identify*** the characteristics that distinguish *service operations* from *goods production* and explain the main differences in the *service focus.*

4. ***Describe*** the factors involved in *operations planning.*

5. ***Explain*** some of the activities involved in *operations control,* including *materials management* and the use of certain *operations control tools.*

Getting the Big Bird to Fly Right

The "big bird"—Boeing—is America's biggest exporter, having delivered more than 60 percent of all commercial planes sold from 1995 to 1999. In January 2000, Boeing **<www.boeing.com>** Chairman Phil Condit announced that profits for the 1999 year had doubled to $2.3 billion. The announcement came just one year after Condit had warned senior management that if they didn't get their production problems ironed out, they faced competitors that would do it for them—by taking away Boeing's market. Heeding the warning, Boeing boosted production efficiencies, and as a result, operating revenues also rose even though Asian demand was weak and Boeing's European rival, Airbus Industrie **<www.airbus.com>**, made inroads with more new customer orders. With optimistic forecasts of even larger revenues for 2000, Boeing's market share value rose by 25 percent in 1999.

For Boeing, 1997 and 1998 had been production nightmares. Factories bogged down, fell behind delivery schedules, and ran in the red with excessive production costs. At one point, the company had to resort to a month-long shutdown of two production lines, including the 747 assembly line, to sort out inefficiencies and figure out how to get stalled production lines rolling again. Getting out of the rut was expensive: Boeing employees worked 23 percent overtime. The time required to assemble an aircraft was bloated, and production write-offs totaling $4 billion gave the firm a loss for 1998.

By 1999, however, overtime had been reduced to 9 percent, and 25,000 jobs had been cut (21 percent of total production jobs). The time needed to assemble an aircraft had been reduced by four-fifths from its previous peak, and the commercial aircraft division delivered 10 percent more planes than in the previous year. Projections call for even better earnings through 2003. How has Boeing managed this turnaround? "Pure and simple," says Condit. "The biggest part of [increasing profits] will be [cutting] the number of hours it takes to build each aircraft." Besides eliminating unprofitable models, including the MD-80 and MD-90, Boeing also changed its management structure and focused more closely on cost controls and production schedules. Workers report increasingly rigorous production standards. For example, when parts are missing or assembly-line workers can't figure out engineering specifications, the problem has to be solved on the spot rather than put off until later. Whenever a deviation from projected costs or scheduling arises, it is dealt with immediately, even if it means working into the night.

"Pure and simple, the biggest part of increasing profits will be cutting the number of hours it takes to build each aircraft."

—Boeing CEO Phil Condit on Boeing's plan to increase productivity

Perhaps most importantly, Boeing's new $1 billion automation system is being fully activated: It cuts 10 percent off the time to build each aircraft. On one product, for example—the 737 jet—the company's 30-year-old equipment required workers to align parts manually and required five days' assembly time on each jet. New laser-alignment technology gets the job done in two days. Ironically, getting new production systems up and running was partly to blame for the 1997 stoppages; Boeing was trying to get rid of old equipment and modernize production at the very time that it launched a market-share war with Airbus. Losses mounted as production snarls clogged up factories, and plane orders stacked up when production couldn't keep up with customer demand.

Our opening story continues on page 430

It took two years for Boeing to straighten out its production problems, and as you will see in this chapter, solving operations problems on such a scale can be an expensive, time-consuming process. By focusing on the learning objectives of this chapter, you will better understand how complex such reorganization can be for producers of both goods and services.

service operations
Produces tangible and intangible services, such as entertainment, transportation, and education

goods production
Produces tangible products, such as radios, newspapers, buses, and textbooks

Everywhere you go today, you encounter business activities that provide goods and services to their customers. You wake up in the morning to the sound of your favorite radio station. You stop at the corner newsstand for a newspaper on your way to the bus stop, where you catch the bus to work or school. Your instructors, the bus driver, the clerk at the 7-Eleven store, and the morning radio announcer are all examples of people who work in **service operations.** They provide you with tangible and intangible service products, such as entertainment, transportation, education, and food preparation. Firms that make tangible products—radios, newspapers, buses, textbooks—are engaged in **goods production.**

WHAT DOES PRODUCTION MEAN TODAY?

Although the term *production* has historically referred to companies engaged in goods production, the concept as we now use it means services as well as goods. An abundance of necessities and conveniences on which we rely, from fire protection and health care to mail delivery and fast food, are all produced by service operations. Traditionally, service sector managers have focused less on such manufacturing-centered goals as equipment and technology. Rather, they have stressed the human element in their activities. Why? Because success or failure depends on contact with the customer during service delivery. The provider's employees—their human resources—who deal directly with their customers affect the customer's feelings about the service. As we will see throughout this chapter, one of the main differences between production and service operations is the customer's involvement in the latter.

"Our biggest pitfall is that we go offline and make plans. The customer is online, and he doesn't care about your plan. He wants what he wants now and is always one click away from your competitor."

—Gerhard Schulmeyer, CEO of U.S. operations for Siemens Corporation

Today, customers are increasingly involved in both goods and services production because electronic communications and the Internet are vital components in the effort to win and keep customers in a huge range of competitive industries. Customers place orders faster, production schedules are accelerated, and delivery times are shrinking. Internet consumers can be linked electronically to the production floor itself, where their orders for products ranging from cell phones and audio music to automobiles are launched into production in real time. Business-to-business customers also expect real-time responses and online fast delivery, rather than by traditional offline methods. "Our biggest pitfall," says Gerhard Schulmeyer, CEO of U.S. operations for the German electronics engineering firm Siemens Corp. <www.siemens.de>, "is that we go offline and make plans. The customer is online, and he doesn't care about your plan. He wants what he wants now and is always one click away from your competitor."[1]

The Growth of Global Operations

Many countries have joined in the global competition that has reshaped production into a faster-paced, more complex business activity. Although the factory remains the centerpiece for manufacturing, it is virtually unrecognizable when compared with its counterpart of even just a decade ago. The smoke, grease, and danger have been replaced in many companies by glistening high-tech machines, computers, and "clean rooms" that are contaminant-free and carefully controlled for temperature.

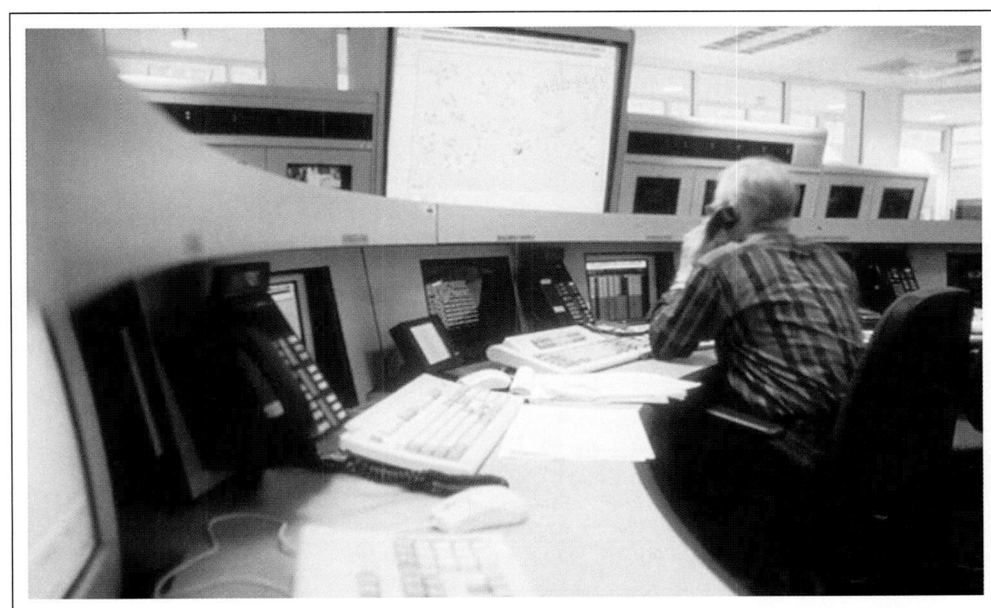

VF Corp. <www.vfc.com> sells more jeans—Lee, Wrangler, and other brands—than anybody else in the world. In 1995, the company began developing its Data Services Control Center in Greensboro, North Carolina. The idea was to aggregate key data—demographics, point-of-sale information on sizes and colors—so that managers could pinpoint the precise mix of products that was likely to sell at a particular retail location. Today, VF's corporate-level system also runs software to handle all financial operations as well as order-management and materials-management functions.

Instead of the need to maintain continuous mass production, firms today face constant change. New technologies are allowing machines to run cleaner, faster, and safer and to operate on a global scale. For online manufacturing, industrial machines can log on to the Internet, adjust their own settings, and make minor decisions without human help. They can communicate both with other machines in the company (via an intranet) and with other companies' machines (via the Internet). So-called smart equipment stores performance data that becomes available at desktops around the world, where designers can click on machine data, simulate machine action, and evaluate performance before the machines themselves ever swing into action. With the Internet, producers of both services and goods are integrating their production activities with those of far-off suppliers and customers. IBM's growing Internet activities, for example, include designs for new services, outsourcing, research, and even running Web businesses for other firms.[2]

How can the government play a positive role in the production of goods and services?

www.lantronix.com

Located in Irvine, California, Lantronix markets so-called universal thin servers that permit industrial machines to log on to the Internet or an intranet to get the information needed for making decisions without human help. To find out more about "network enabling technology," contact Lantronix on its Web site.

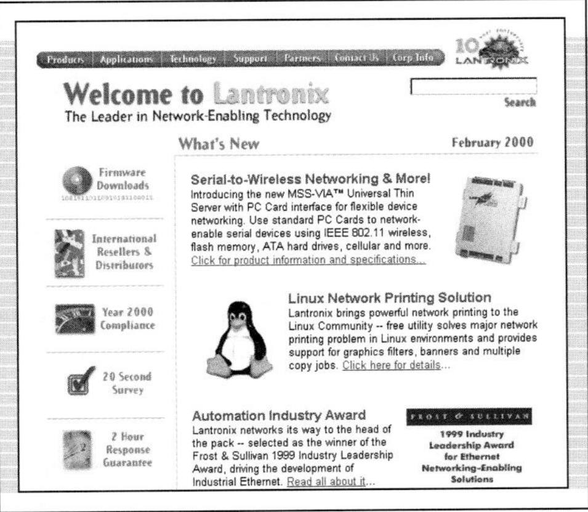

Figure 15.1
Employment in Goods and Service Sectors

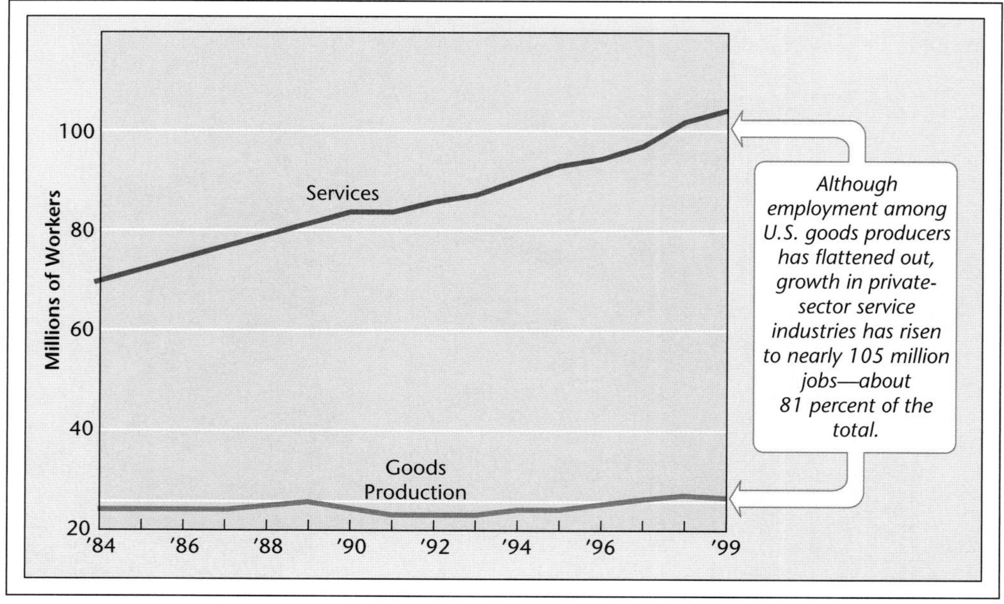
100
80
60
40
20
Millions of Workers
Services
Goods
Production
'84
'86
'88
'90
'92
'94
'96
'99
Although employment among U.S. goods producers has flattened out, growth in private-sector service industries has risen to nearly 105 million jobs—about 81 percent of the total.

Growth in the Service and Goods Sectors

Manufacturing industries still account for about 25 percent of all private sector jobs in the United States—just as they have for the past four decades. Nevertheless, the economic significance of manufacturing activity is rising. For example, real income from manufacturing has been rising steadily, increasing by over 30 percent in the past 10 years. So effective are new manufacturing methods, and so committed are U.S. manufacturers to using them, that in 1999 the United States remained ahead of Germany and Japan in manufactured exports, retaining the number-one spot for the sixth consecutive year.

Naturally, both goods and service industries are important to the economy. As you can see from Figures 15.1 and 15.2, services have grown far more rapidly since 1984. For one thing, employment has risen significantly in the service sector while remaining stagnant in goods production (Figure 15.1). In fact, by 1999 employment in service industries accounted for 81 percent of the total U.S. workforce: nearly 105 million jobs. Much of this growth comes from new e-commerce jobs and from the business services, social services, health care, amusement and recreation, and educational industries. Employment projections indicate that services will remain the faster-growing employment source in the immediate future.[3] With this growth, the gap in average wages between the two sectors has closed to just $19 per week more for goods-producing workers. More importantly, the distribution of high-paying and low-paying jobs in each sector is now equal.

By 1999, the service sector also provided nearly 60 percent of national income, as opposed to just over 50 percent in 1947. As Figure 15.2 shows, the service sector's share of the U.S. gross domestic product (GDP)—the value of all the goods and services produced by the economy, excluding foreign income—has climbed since 1984 until it is now nearly 50 percent greater than that of the goods-producing sector. At the same time, the 20 percent of the U.S. workforce in manufacturing produces about 40 percent of the nation's GDP.[4] In China, by contrast, manufacturing employs 70 percent of the urban labor force but produces only 30 percent of the country's national income.[5]

Remember that although companies are typically classified as either goods producers or service providers, the distinction is often blurred. For one thing, all businesses are service operations to some extent. Consider General Electric <www.ge.com>, which popularly conjures up thoughts of appliances for laundry and kitchen (and jet engines). But

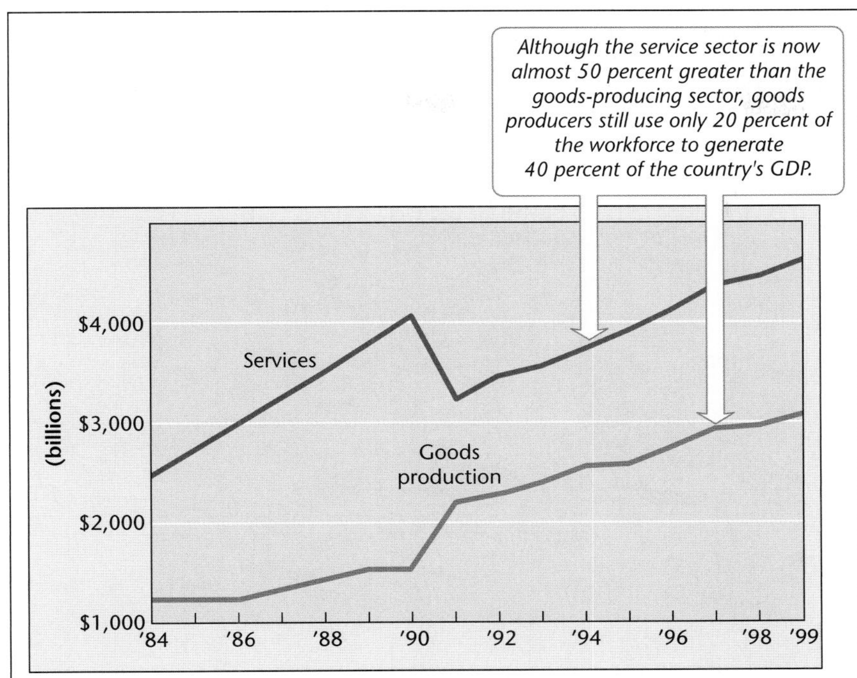
Although the service sector is now almost 50 percent greater than the goods-producing sector, goods producers still use only 20 percent of the workforce to generate 40 percent of the country's GDP.
$4,000
$3,000
$2,000
$1,000
(billions)
Services
Goods production
'84
'86
'88
'90
'92
'94
'96
'98
'99

Figure 15.2
GDP from Goods and Services

GE is not just a goods producer. According to its own annual report, "The General Electric Company is the world's largest diversified services company as well as a provider of high-quality, high-technology industrial and consumer products."[6] GE's many service operations include broadcasting (NBC), commercial and consumer finance, reinsurance of primary insurers, equity investing, real estate, and aviation services.

CREATING VALUE THROUGH PRODUCTION

To understand the production processes of a firm we need to know how to measure the value of services and goods. Products provide businesses with economic results: profits, wages, and goods purchased from other companies. At the same time, they provide consumers with **utility**—the ability of a product to satisfy a human want.

utility
A product's ability to satisfy a human want

There are four basic kinds of production-based utility:

- When a company turns out ornaments in time for Christmas, it creates *time utility;* that is, it makes products available when consumers want them.
- When a department store opens its annual Trim-a-Tree department, it creates *place utility:* It makes products available where they are convenient for consumers.
- By making a product available for consumers to own and use, production creates *ownership* or *possession utility,* which customers enjoy when they buy boxes of ornaments and decorate their trees.
- Production makes products available in the first place: By turning raw materials into finished goods, production creates *form utility,* as when an ornament maker combines glass, plastic, and other materials to create tree decorations.

Because the term *production* was historically associated just with manufacturing, writers have recently replaced it with *operations,* a term that reflects both service and goods production. **Operations** (or **production**) **management** is the systematic direction and control of the processes that transform resources into finished services and goods.

operations (or production) management
Systematic direction and control of the processes that transform resources into finished products

Figure 15.3
Resource Transformation Process

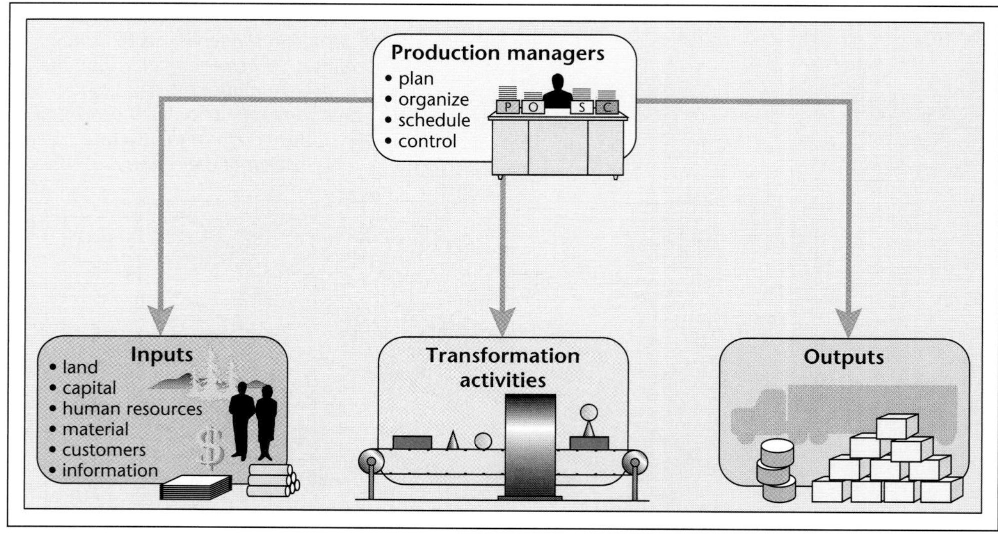

operations (or production) managers
Managers responsible for production, inventory, and quality control of goods and services

Thus, **operations** (or **production**) **managers** are ultimately responsible for creating utility for customers.

As Figure 15.3 shows, operations managers must draw up plans to transform resources into products. First, they must bring together basic resources: knowledge, physical materials, equipment, and labor. Naturally, they must put those resources to effective use in the production facility. As demand for a product increases, managers must schedule and control work to produce the required amounts of products. Finally, they must also control costs, quality levels, inventory, and facilities and equipment.

Farmers are also operations managers. They create utility by transforming soil, seeds, fuel, and other inputs into soybeans, milk, and other outputs. As production managers, they may employ crews of workers to plant and harvest. Or they may opt for automated machinery or some combination of workers and machinery. These decisions affect costs, the role of buildings and equipment in their operations, and the quality and quantity of goods that they produce.

Operations Processes

operations process
Set of methods used in the production of a good or service

An **operations process** is a set of methods and technologies used in the production of a good or a service. We classify various types of production according to differences in their operations processes. We can describe goods according to whether their operations process combines resources or breaks them into component parts. We can describe services according to the *extent of customer contact* required.

analytic process
Production process in which resources are broken down into components to create finished products

synthetic process
Production process in which resources are combined to create finished products

Goods-Manufacturing Processes: Analytic versus Synthetic Processes All goods-manufacturing processes can be classified by the *analytic or synthetic nature of the transformation process*. An **analytic process** breaks down resources into components. Tyson reduces incoming whole chickens to the packaged parts we find at the meat counter. The reverse approach, a **synthetic process,** combines raw materials to produce a finished product. General Electric uses this approach in manufacturing refrigerators. It forms and shapes steel to produce the basic refrigerator, then it adds motors, lightbulbs, trays, and shelves. Finally, it packages the refrigerator in a shipping carton and delivers it to an appliance store.

Service Processes: Extent of Customer Contact One way of classifying services is to ask whether a given service can be provided without the customer's being part of the production system. In answering this question, we classify services according to the extent of *customer contact.*

High-Contact Processes Think for a moment about your local public transit system. The service provided is transportation, and when you purchase transportation, you must board a bus or train. The Bay Area Rapid Transit System (BART) <www.bart.gov> connects San Francisco with many of its outlying suburbs. Like all public transportation systems, BART is a **high-contact system:** To receive the service, the customer must be a part of the system. For this reason, BART managers must worry about the cleanliness of the trains and the appearance of the stations. This is usually not the case in low-contact systems, where large industrial concerns that ship coal in freight trains, for example, are generally not concerned with the appearance inside those trains.

high-contact system
Level of customer contact in which the customer is part of the system during service delivery

Low-Contact Processes Now consider the check-processing operations at your bank. Workers sort the checks that have been cashed that day and dispatch them to the banks on which they were drawn. This operation is a **low-contact system:** Customers are not in contact with the bank while the service is performed. They receive the service—their funds are transferred to cover their checks—without ever setting foot in the check-processing center. Gas and electric utilities, auto repair shops, and lawn care services are also low-contact systems.

Do consumers prefer personal or professional relationships with businesses?

low-contact system
Level of customer contact in which the customer need not be a part of the system to receive the service

Differences Between Service and Manufacturing Operations

Service and manufacturing operations share several important features. For example, both transform raw materials into finished products. In service production, the raw materials, or inputs, are not glass or steel. Rather, they are people who choose among sellers because they have either unsatisfied needs or possessions for which they need some form of care or alteration. In service operations, then, "finished products" or "outputs" are people with needs met and possessions serviced.

Focus on Performance Thus, at least one very obvious difference exists between service and manufacturing operations: Whereas goods are produced, services are performed. Therefore, customer-oriented performance is a key factor in measuring the effectiveness of a service company.

Wal-Mart <www.walmart.com> sells to millions of people from California to China to Argentina out of nearly 4,000 stores. Its superstar status stems from an obsession with speedy product delivery that it measures not in days or even hours, but in minutes and seconds. Wal-Mart's keen customer focus emphasizes avoiding unnecessary inventories, getting fast responses from suppliers, streamlining transactions processes, and knowing accurately the sales and restocking requirements for keeping the right merchandise moving from warehouses to store shelves. To implement this strategy, Wal-Mart has made technology—namely, its vaunted computer and telecommunications system—a core competency.[7]

In many ways, the focus of service operations is more complex than that of goods production. First, service operations feature a unique link between production and consumption—between process and outcome. Second, services are more intangible and more customized and less storable than most products. Finally, quality considerations must be defined, and managed, differently in the service sector than in manufacturing operations.

Focus on Process and Outcome As we saw earlier, manufacturing operations focus on the outcome of the production process. The products offered by most service operations, however, are actually combinations of goods and services. Services, therefore, must focus on both the transformation *process* and its outcome—both on making a pizza and on delivering it to the buyer. Service operations thus require different skills from manufacturing operations. Local gas company employees may need the interpersonal skills necessary to calm and reassure frightened customers who have reported gas leaks. The job, therefore, can mean more than just repairing defective pipes. Factory workers who install gas pipes while assembling mobile homes are far less likely to need such skills.

Focus on Service Characteristics Service companies' transactions always reflect the fact that service products are characterized by three key qualities: *intangibility, customization,* and *unstorability.*

Intangibility Often services cannot be touched, tasted, smelled, or seen. An important value, therefore, is the *intangible* value that the customer experiences in the form of pleasure, satisfaction, or a feeling of safety. When you hire an attorney to resolve a problem, you purchase not only the intangible quality of legal expertise but also the equally intangible reassurance that help is at hand. Although all services have some degree of intangibility, some provide tangible elements as well. Your attorney can draw up the living will that you want to keep in your safe deposit box.

Customization When you visit a physician, you expect to be examined for your symptoms. Likewise, when you purchase insurance, get your pet groomed, or have your hair cut, you expect these services to be designed for your needs. Therefore, services are *customized.*

Unstorability Services such as rubbish collection, transportation, child care, and house cleaning cannot be produced ahead of time and then stored. If a service is not used when available, it is usually wasted. Services, then, are typically characterized by a high degree of *unstorability.*

Focus on the Customer-Service Link Because they transform customers or their possessions, service operations often acknowledge the customer as part of the operations process itself. For example, to purchase a haircut you must usually go to the barbershop or beauty salon.

As physical participants in the operations process, service consumers have a unique ability to affect that process. In other words, as the customer, you expect the salon to be conveniently located, to be open for business at convenient times, to offer needed services at reasonable prices, and to extend prompt service. Accordingly, the manager adopts hours of operation, available services, and an appropriate number of employees to meet the requirements of the customer.

E-Commerce: The "Virtual Presence" of the Customer The growth of e-commerce has introduced a "virtual presence," as opposed to a physical presence, of customers in the service system. Consumers interact electronically, in real time, with sellers, collecting information about product features, delivery availability, and after-sales service. They get around-the-clock access to information via automated call centers, and those who want human interaction can talk with live respondents or log in to chat rooms. Many companies have invited "the virtual customer" into their service systems by building customer-communications relationships. The online travel agency Expedia.com responds to your personalized profile with a welcome e-mail letter, presents you with a tailor-made Web page the next time you sign on, offers chat rooms in which you can compare notes with other customers, and notifies you of upcoming special travel opportunities.

WebConnection

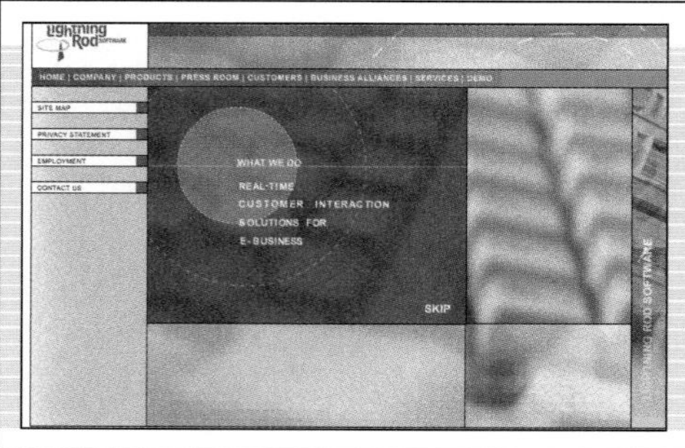

www.lightrodsoft.com

If your company's Web site uses Lightning Rod Software, a customer can click on a "callback" button. A form will appear asking the prospective buyer to type in a name and telephone number. Your server then sends the information to your next available sales rep, who calls it up and phones the customer. To find out more about Lightning Rod Software, access the company at its Web site.

Internet technology also enables firms to build relationships with industrial customers. Electronic Data Systems (EDS) <www.eds.com>, for example, helps client firms develop networks among their many desktop computers. In managing more than 700,000 desktops for clients throughout the world, EDS has created a special service called Renasence <www.eds.com/geographic_sites/new_zealand/offerings/nz_renascence> that links clients, suppliers, and employees in a private 500,000-computer electronic marketplace. Some 2,000 software products can be viewed, purchased, tracked, and delivered if you are a member of the network.[8]

Focus on Service Quality Considerations Consumers use different criteria to judge services and goods. Service managers must understand that quality of work and quality of service are not necessarily synonymous. For example, although your car may have been flawlessly repaired, you might feel dissatisfied with the service if you were forced to pick it up a day later than promised. The "Life Cycle of an e-Business" box in this chapter focuses on the role of order processing and other factors in customer service at Garden.com.

OPERATIONS PLANNING

Now that we've contrasted goods and services we can return to a more general consideration of production encompassing both goods and services. Like all good managers, we start with planning. Managers from many departments contribute to the firm's decisions about operations management. As Figure 15.4 shows, however, no matter how many decision makers are involved, the process can be described as a series of logical steps. The success of any firm depends on the final result of this logical sequence of decisions.

The overall business plan and forecasts developed by a company's top executives guide operations planning. The business plan outlines the firm's goals and objectives, including the specific goods and services that it will offer in the upcoming years. In addition to the business plan, managers develop the firm's long-range production plan through **forecasts** of future demand for both new and existing products. The long-range plan covers a two- to five-year period. It specifically details the number of plants or service facilities, as well as the labor, equipment, and transportation and storage facilities, that will be needed to meet demand. It also specifies how resources will be obtained.

forecast
Facet of a long-range production plan that predicts future demand

In this section we survey the development of the main parts of operations planning. We discuss the key planning activities that fall into one of five major categories: capacity, location, layout, quality, and methods planning.

Capacity Planning

The amount of a product that a company can produce under normal working conditions is its **capacity.** The capacity of a goods or service firm depends on how many people it employs and the number and size of its facilities. Long-range planning must take into account both current and future capacity.

capacity
Amount of a product that a company can produce under normal working conditions

Capacity Planning for Producing Goods Capacity planning for goods means ensuring that a manufacturing firm's capacity slightly exceeds the normal demand for its product. To see why this policy is best, consider the alternatives. If capacity is too small to meet demand, the company must turn away customers—a situation that not only cuts into profits but also alienates both customers and salespeople. If capacity greatly exceeds demand, then the firm is wasting money by maintaining a plant that is too large, by keeping excess machinery on-line, or by employing too many workers.

The stakes are high in the company's capacity decisions: While expanding fast enough to meet future demand and to protect market share from competitors, they must also weigh the increased costs of expanding. One reason that Intel Corp. <www.intel.com> enjoys more than 70-percent market share in the worldwide semiconductor business is the $11 billion it invested in capacity expansion between 1991 and 1995 (including $1.8 billion for its

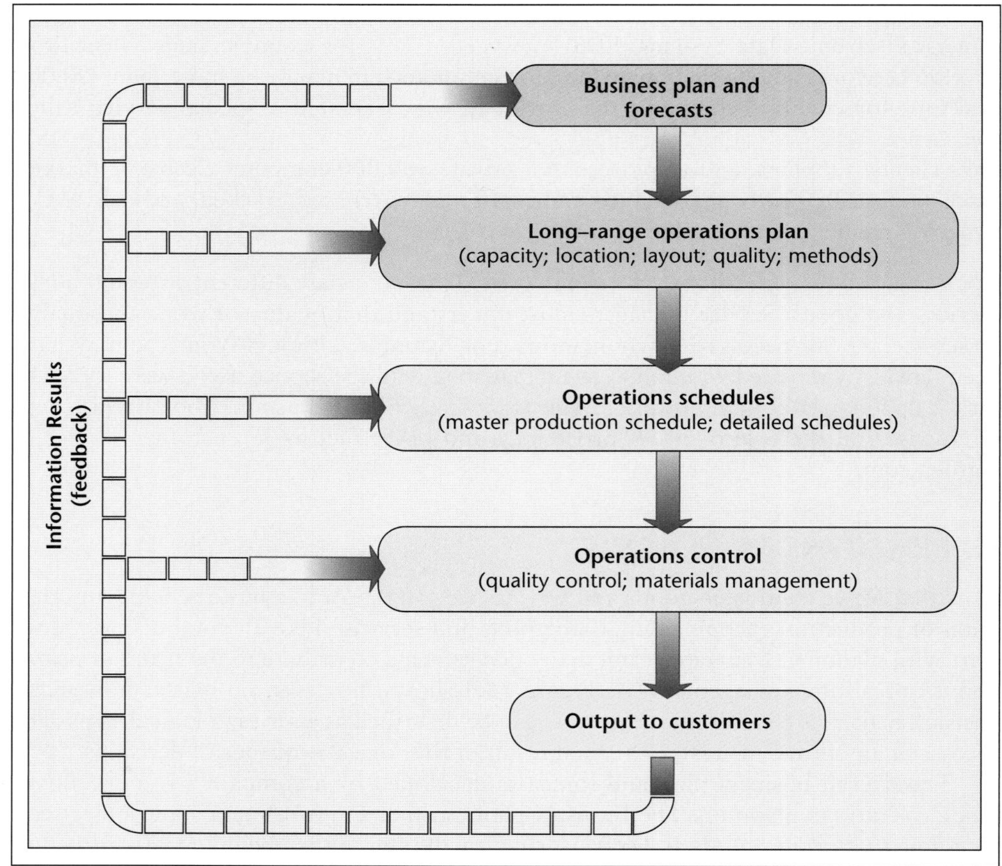

Figure 15.4
Operations Planning and Control

plant in Rio Rancho, New Mexico) and the additional $625 million to buy Digital Equipment's Hudson, Massachusetts, semiconductor plant in 1998. Will demand for semiconductors continue to grow even further? With so much invested thus far, Intel must decide whether the risks of additional capacity are worth the potential gains.[9]

Capacity Planning for Producing Services In low-contact processes, maintaining inventory lets managers set capacity at the level of *average demand.* The JC Penney <www.jcpenney.com> catalog sales warehouse may hire enough order fillers to handle 1,000 orders each day. When daily orders exceed this average demand, some orders are placed in inventory—set aside in a "to be done" file—to be processed on a day when fewer than 1,000 orders are received.

In high-contact processes, managers must plan capacity to meet *peak demand.* A supermarket, for instance, has far more cash registers than it needs on an average day; but on a Saturday morning or during the three days before Thanksgiving, all registers will be running full speed.

Location Planning

Because the location of a factory, office, or store affects its production costs and flexibility, sound location planning is crucial. Depending on the site of its facility, a company may be capable of producing a low-cost product or may find itself at an extreme cost disadvantage relative to its competitors.

Location Planning for Producing Goods Managers in goods-producing operations must consider many factors in location planning. Their location decisions are influenced by proximity to raw materials and markets, availability of labor, energy and transportation costs, local and state regulations and taxes, and community living conditions.

Life Cycle of an *e-Business*

"The Assembly Line of This Business Is Processing Orders"

In sizing up Garden.com's production orientation, Jamie O'Neill noted that "the assembly line of this business is processing orders." But Garden.com processed much more than sales transactions for seeds and plants: The company also processed information requests and orders for customer assistance. Service operations constituted 90 percent of what went on inside the company's 24,000-square-foot building in Austin.

"We put our production dollars into getting customers comfortable with the Web," said O'Neill. Instead of relying on person-to-person selling and transaction processing, the system at Garden.com used "automated production" and self-service to transact 90 percent of its sales. First, however, customers usually got presales information from the Web. This core production activity, therefore, meant maintaining the most user-friendly Web site in the industry. Doing so, however, proved very expensive and contributed heavily to the company's ever-growing financial losses.

In addition, the Austin facility housed Garden.com's "call center," a service that provided customer assistance from 80 people who were skilled at handling customer inquiries. Some 20 horticulturists gave live, first-person assistance on technical matters regarding plant growth, soil, and weather conditions under diverse growing conditions from region to region. Other members of the Solutions Team helped customers complete orders. In other words, the "call center" handled all incoming inquiries—including 15,000 e-mails each month and sometimes up to 1,500 a day. Moreover, keeping close to the customer was more than an 8-to-5 job: Garden.com was equipped to respond 7 days a week from 7 A.M. to midnight, both over the telephone and online. With the benefit of flexible work schedules, it was not unusual to find employees, either at the office or from home, actively engaged with customers at any hour of the day or night. Once again, however, the costs of the operation proved to be prohibitive. In September 2000, Garden.com announced that it was cutting costs by laying off 93 employees.

Only about 10 percent of Garden.com's product shipments flowed through the Austin facility. The other 90 percent shipped directly to customers from suppliers around the country. Not surprisingly, then, only a relatively small portion of the Austin building was devoted to warehousing, packing, and shipping. Employees came and went as needed at any of five workstations placed side by side in a packaging area located between the product warehouse and the shipping area. When an order came in, the requested products were picked off the warehouse shelves, gathered together, matched with shipping tags, and delivered to a workstation where they were packed in protective boxes. Employees carried completed packages just a few feet away to waiting FedEx trucks that make pickups at prescheduled intervals.

Because the company was designed from the outset as an Internet-based business, Garden.com was able to design its operations knowing that in-house product flows would be minimal. Thus the firm avoided the expensive facility changeovers that other firms face in redesigning facilities for the transition from traditional brick-and-mortar to e-business operations.

In 1998, General Motors <www.gm.com> announced plans for new plants in North America to increase productivity and competitiveness. These agile, highly efficient assembly plants will rely on outside producers to supply large components such as fully assembled dashboards, stamped hoods, and other body parts. GM intends for production efficiencies to arise from a system in which each supplier specializes in making just one major component. To resupply GM assembly plants quickly and to reduce transportation costs, suppliers will locate factories nearby.[10]

Location Planning for Producing Services In planning low-contact services, companies have some options: Services can be located near resource supplies, labor, or transportation outlets. The typical Wal-Mart distribution center is located near the hundreds of Wal-Mart stores it supplies, not the companies that supply the distribution center. Distribution managers regard Wal-Mart stores as their customers. To better serve them, distribution centers are located so that truckloads of merchandise flow quickly to the stores.

On the other hand, high-contact services are more restricted. They must locate near the customers who are a part of the system. Accordingly, fast-food restaurants such as Taco Bell, McDonald's, and Burger King have begun moving into nontraditional locations with high traffic—dormitories, hospital cafeterias, and shopping malls. They can also be found in Wal-Mart outlets and Meijer Supermarkets that draw large crowds. Similarly, some McDonald's are located on interstate highway rest stops, and Domino's Pizza and KFC restaurants can be found on military bases.

Layout Planning

Once a site has been selected, managers must decide on plant layout. Layout of machinery, equipment, and supplies determines whether a company can respond quickly and efficiently to customer requests for more and different products or finds itself unable to match competitors' production speed or convenience of service.

Layout Planning for Producing Goods In facilities that produce goods, layout must be planned for three different types of space:

- *Productive facilities:* workstations and equipment for transforming raw materials, for example
- *Nonproductive facilities:* storage and maintenance areas
- *Support facilities:* offices, restrooms, parking lots, cafeterias, and so forth

In this section, we focus on productive facilities. Alternatives include *process, cellular,* and *product layouts.*

process layout
Spatial arrangement of production activities that groups equipment and people according to function

Process Layouts In a **process layout,** which is well suited to job shops specializing in custom work, equipment and people are grouped according to function. In a woodworking shop, for instance, machines cut the wood in an area devoted to sawing, sanding occurs in a dedicated area, and jobs that need painting are taken to a dust-free area where all the painting equipment is located. The various tasks are each performed in specialized locations.

The job shop produces many one-of-a-kind products, and each product, as you can see from Figure 15.5(a), requires different kinds of work. Whereas Product X needs only three production steps prior to packaging, Product Y needs four. When there is a large variety of products, there will be many flow paths through the shop and potentially much congestion. Machine shops, custom bakeries, and dry-cleaning shops often feature process layouts.

cellular layout
Spatial arrangement of production facilities designed to move families of products through similar flow paths

Cellular Layouts Another workplace arrangement for some applications is called the **cellular layout.** Cellular layouts are used when a family of products (a group of similar products) follow a fixed flow path. A clothing manufacturer may establish a cell, or designated area, dedicated to making a family of pockets—pockets for shirts, coats, blouses, trousers, and slacks. Although each type of pocket is unique in shape, size, and style, all go through the same production steps. Within the cell, various types of equipment (for cutting, trimming, and sewing) are arranged close together in the appropriate sequence. All pockets pass stage by stage through the cell from beginning to end, in a nearly continuous flow.

In plants that produce a variety of products, there may be one or two high-volume products that justify separate manufacturing cells. Figure 15.5(b) shows two production

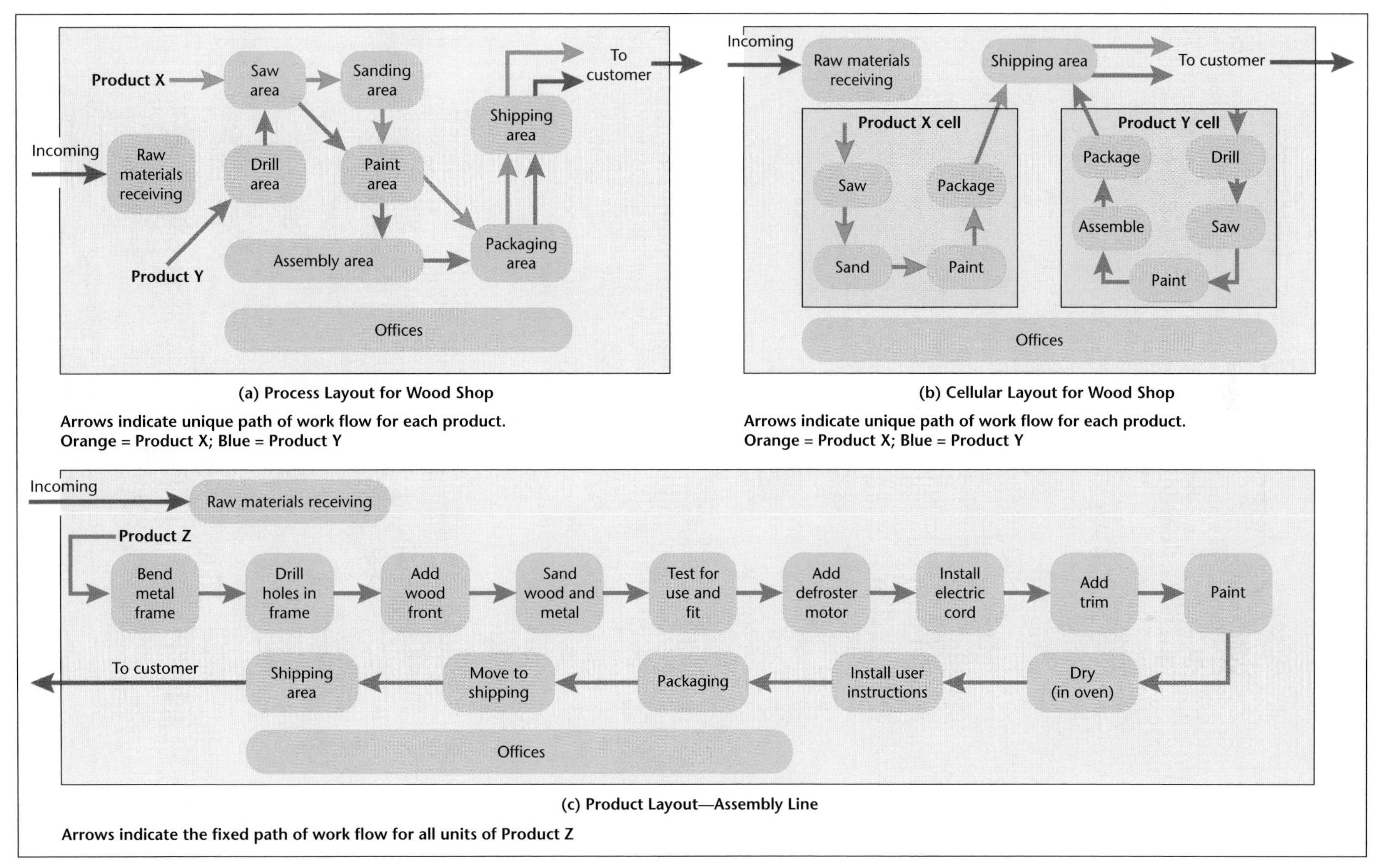

Figure 15.5
Layouts for Producing Goods

cells, one each for Products X and Y, while all other smaller-volume products are produced elsewhere in the plant.

Cellular layouts have several advantages. Because similar products require less machine adjustment, equipment setup time in the cell is reduced, as compared with setup times in process layouts. Because flow distances are usually shorter, there is less material handling and transit time. Finally, inventories of goods in progress are lower and paperwork is simpler because material flows are more orderly. A disadvantage of cells is the duplication of equipment. Note, for example, in Figure 15.5(b) that two saws are needed (one in each cell) as well as two paint areas, but only one of each is needed in the process layout (Figure 15.5[a]).

product layout
Spatial arrangement of production activities designed to move resources through a smooth, fixed sequence of steps

assembly line
Product layout in which a product moves step by step through a plant on conveyor belts or other equipment until it is completed

Product Layouts In a **product layout,** equipment and people are set up to produce one type of product in a fixed sequence of steps and are arranged according to its production requirements. Product layouts are efficient for producing large volumes of product quickly and often use **assembly lines:** A partially finished product moves step-by-step through the plant on conveyor belts or other equipment, often in a straight line, until the product is completed. Figure 15.5(c) shows the sequence of production steps performed identically, from start to finish, on all units of Product Z as they move through the line. Automobile, food-processing, and television-assembly plants use product layouts.

Product layouts are efficient because the work skill is built into the equipment—simplified work tasks can then use unskilled labor. They tend to be inflexible because, traditionally, they have required a heavy investment in specialized equipment that is hard to rearrange for new applications. In addition, workers are subject to boredom, and when someone is absent or overworked, those farther down the line cannot help out.

Layout Planning for Producing Services Service firms use some of the same layouts as goods-producing firms. In a low-contact system, for instance, the facility should be arranged to enhance the production of the service. A mail-processing facility at UPS or Federal Express, therefore, looks very much like a product layout in a factory: Machines and people are arranged in the order in which they are used in the mass processing of mail. In contrast, Kinko's Copy Centers <www.kinkos.com> use process layouts for different custom jobs: Specific functions such as photocopying, computing, binding, photography, and laminating are performed in specialized areas of the store.

McDonald's <www.mcdonalds.com> claims that a new wrinkle in layout planning ranks with indoor seating and drive-through windows among the most important innovations in the company's first half century. The change is in the kitchen, where such nonmeat ingredients as bread, onions, and lettuce are now spared the wilting heat of holding bins and the microwave. Now only the meat is kept warm, and everything else is added after microwaving. McDonald's expects to save $100 million per year in food costs.

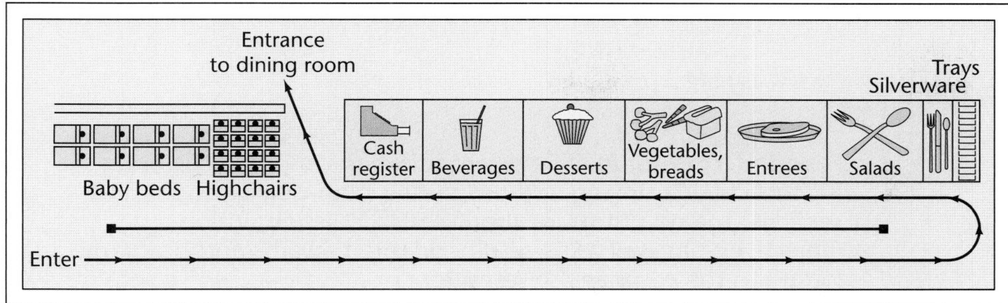

Figure 15.6

Layout of a Typical Piccadilly Cafeteria

High-contact systems should be arranged to meet customer needs and expectations. Piccadilly Cafeterias <www.piccadilly.com> focuses both layout and services on the groups that constitute its primary market: families and elderly people. As you can see in Figure 15.6, families enter to find an array of highchairs and rolling baby beds that make it convenient to wheel children through the line. Servers are willing to carry trays for elderly people and for those pushing strollers. Note that customers must pass by the whole serving line before making selections. Not only does this layout help them make up their minds; it also tempts them to select more.

Quality Planning

In planning production systems and facilities, managers must keep in mind the firm's quality goals. Thus, any complete operations plan must ensure that products are produced to meet the firm's standards of quality. The American Society for Quality Control defines *quality* as "the totality of features and characteristics of a product or service that bear on its ability to satisfy stated or implied needs."

Such features may include a product's reasonable price and its consistent performance in delivering the benefit it promises. Perrigo <www.perrigo.com>, the largest U.S. manufacturer of over-the-counter pharmaceuticals and personal-care products, treats quality planning as a central part of its competitive strategy. Quality is enhanced through the continuous improvement of manufacturing methods, the careful control of every step in production and packaging, and a quality improvement program that empowers employees to reduce waste and increase production capabilities.[11]

Methods Planning

In designing operations systems, managers must clearly identify every production step and the specific methods for performing them. They can then work to reduce waste, inefficiency, and poor performance by examining procedures on a step-by-step basis—an approach sometimes called *methods improvement.*

Methods Improvement in Goods Improvement of production for goods begins when a manager documents the current method. A detailed description, often using a diagram called the *process flow chart,* is usually helpful for organizing and recording all information. The process flow chart identifies the sequence of production activities, movements of materials, and work performed at each stage as the product flows through production. The flow can then be analyzed to identify wasteful activities, sources of delay in production flows, and other inefficiencies. The final step is implementing improvements.

Mercury Marine <www.mercurymarine.com> used methods improvement to streamline the production of stern-drive units for power boats. Examination of the process flow from raw materials to assembly (the final production step) revealed numerous wastes and inefficiencies. Each product passed through 122 steps, traveled nearly 21,000 feet (almost four miles) in the factory, and was handled by 106 people. Analysis revealed that only 27 steps actually added value to the product (for example, drilling, painting). Work methods were revised to eliminate nonproductive activities. Mercury ultimately identified

WebConnection

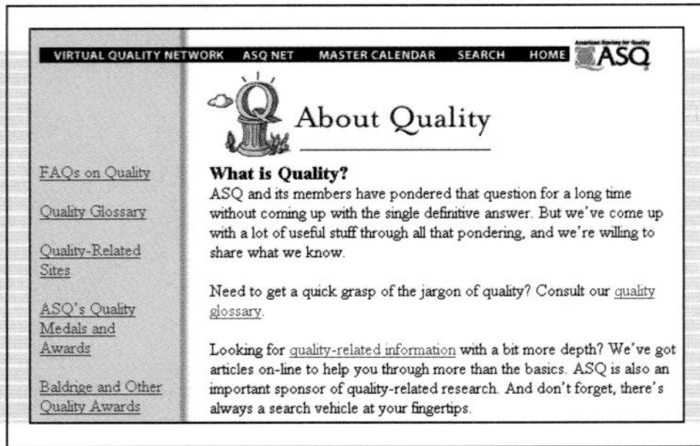

www.asq.org

Founded in 1946, ASQ helps organizations improve customer satisfaction by identifying and promoting high-quality goods and services. To find out more about ASQ's "Mission, Vision, Objectives," as well as its quality-oriented awards and programs, log on to the company's Web site.

potential savings in labor, inventory, paperwork, and space requirements. Because production lead time was also reduced, customer orders were filled faster.

Methods Improvement in Services In a low-contact process, managers can use methods improvements to speed services ranging from mowing lawns to filling prescriptions and drawing up legal documents. Dell Computer <www.dell.com>, for example, sells its computers online and over the phone, mostly to medium and large companies. Methods analysis eliminates unnecessary steps so that orders can be processed quickly for production and delivery. Dell's emphasis on efficient selling by means of electronic technology speeds its response time to provide customers with a specific value—extremely fast delivery service.

Why is high quality in the service sector difficult to achieve?

service flow analysis Method for analyzing a service by showing the flow of processes that constitute it

Service Flow Analysis By showing the flow of processes that make up a given service, **service flow analysis** helps managers decide whether all those processes are necessary. Moreover, because each process is a potential contributor to good or bad service, analysis also helps identify and isolate potential problems (known as *fail points*). In Figure 15.7, for instance, the manager of a photofinishing shop has determined that the standard execution time for developing a roll of film is 48.5 minutes. The manager has also found that the "develop film" stage is the one most likely to delay service because it is the most complex. Thus, the manager has marked it as a potential fail point, as a reminder to give special attention to this stage of operations.

Designing to Control Employee Discretion in Services So far, we have stressed the importance of the human factor in service activities—that is, the direct contact of server

"I preferred their 'Take a number' system."

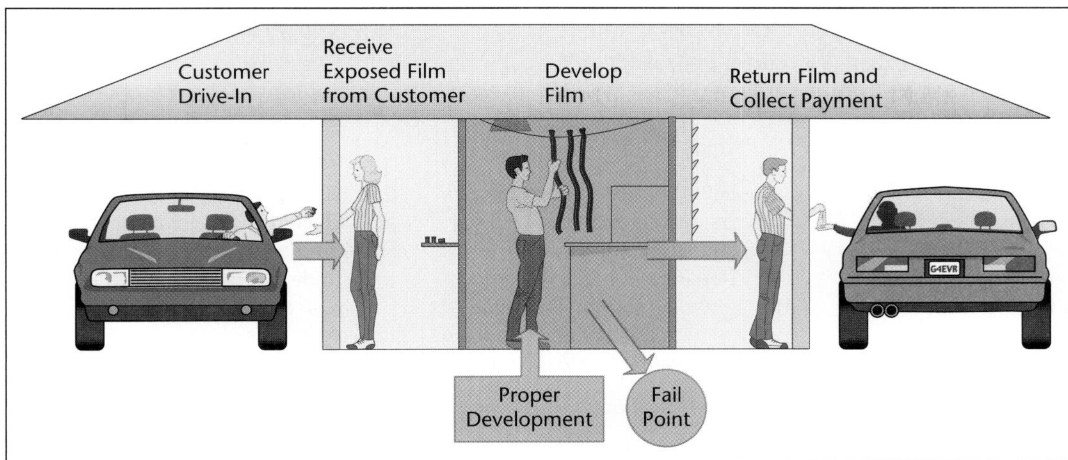

Figure 15.7
Service Flow Analysis

and customer. In some cases, however, the purpose of service design is to limit the range of activities of both employees and customers. By careful planning—and sometimes even by automating to control human discretion—managers can make services more customer-oriented because they can ensure product consistency.

McDonald's <www.mcdonalds.com> has done an outstanding job of designing the fast-food business as a mass production system. By automating processes that would otherwise rely on judgment, McDonald's has been able to provide consistent service from a staff with little specialized training. At a central supply house, for instance, hamburger patties are automatically measured and packed. Specially designed scoops measure the same amount of French fries and other items into standard-size containers. In addition, all drawers, shelves, and bins are designed to hold the ingredients for McDonald's standard product mixes only.

Design for Customer Contact in Services In a high-contact service, the demands on system designs are somewhat different. Here, managers must develop procedures that clearly spell out the ways in which workers interact with customers. These procedures must cover such activities as exchanging information or money, delivering and receiving materials, and even making physical contact. The next time you visit your dentist's office, for instance, notice the way dental hygienists scrub up and wear disposable gloves. They also scrub after patient contact, even if they intend to work on equipment or do paperwork, and they rescrub before working on the next patient. The high-contact system in a dental office consists of very strict procedures designed to avoid contact that can transmit disease.

The "Wired World" box in this chapter tells how the failure to prepare employees for a new information technology system disrupted customer contact and service at Hershey Foods.

OPERATIONS SCHEDULING

Once plans identify needed resources and how they will be used to reach a firm's goals, managers must develop timetables for acquiring resources for production. This aspect of operations is called *scheduling*.

Scheduling Goods Operations

Scheduling of goods production occurs on different levels within the firm. First, a top-level or **master production schedule** shows which products will be produced, when production will occur, and what resources will be used during specified time periods.

master production schedule Schedule showing which products will be produced, when production will take place, and what resources will be used

It's a WiredWorld

• *Hershey Kisses Off Profits*

By 1999, Hershey Foods Corp. <www.hersheys.com>—manufacturers of such well-known candies as Hershey Kisses, Reese's Peanut Butter Cups, and Hershey chocolate bars—had spent three years and $112 million to implement a new information technology (IT) system called Enterprise 12 with which to enter the e-commerce arena. The core of the new technology is SAP, a complex software system that electronically links all of a firm's main business functions, including manufacturing, materials flows, inventories, materials purchasing, production scheduling, warehousing, order entry, billing, and accounting. By integrating all of these activities, SAP's unified database offers powerful up-to-the-minute information sharing throughout the firm and generates efficient flows of incoming raw materials into production and on through to deliveries to customers. A fine-tuned SAP application can reduce inventories, shorten cycle times, and lower costs. To get up and running, however, Hershey had a lot to do. For one thing, 5,000 outdated desktop computers had to be upgraded and standardized. For another, employees in every department had to be trained to use the new system. During the installation, a flock of expert consultants roamed the company, and, after 30 months, Hershey's SAP began running in July, 1999.

In the same month, retailers began ordering candy for the back-to-school and Halloween seasons. Unfortunately, the new system required big changes in the way Hershey employees did their jobs, and they weren't ready for peak demand: By mid-September, the company was already having trouble pushing orders through the new system. Shipments were delayed, and it wasn't long before management realized Hershey couldn't deliver enough candy for the October Halloween season. For Hershey, that's sort of like asking a rival to take your place at your own wedding. By missing one of its prime shipping seasons, Hershey was hit with a 19-percent drop in third-quarter profits. Although no one announced the exact cause of the failure, it seemed to revolve around the way that information flowed—or didn't flow—from department to department through the IT system. In particular, there was a breakdown in order processing. Analysts attributed the problem to the effort to implement an intricate system at one fell swoop. It should have been tested gradually, they concluded, in order to confirm that each piece was working properly.

Meanwhile, as Hershey's six plants kept producing its well-known products, chocolate continued piling up in warehouses instead of getting to retail shelves. As retailers were saddled with partial deliveries, customer relations naturally became strained. Typical delivery times escalated from 5 days to 12, inventory costs increased 29 percent, and sales for the fourth quarter dropped another 12 percent. While Hershey employees continued to master their new system, inefficient order processing took another bite out of Hershey's sales during the 1999 Christmas season.

Consider the case of Logan Aluminum, Inc. Logan produces coils of aluminum that its main customers, Atlantic Richfield and Alcan Aluminum, use to produce aluminum cans. Logan's master schedule extends out to 60 weeks and shows how many coils will be made each week. For various types of coils, the master schedule specifies how many of each will be produced. "We need this planning and scheduling system," says material manager Candy McKenzie, "to determine how much of what product we can produce each and every month."

This information is not complete. Manufacturing personnel must also know the location of all coils on the plant floor and their various stages of production. Start-up and stop times must be assigned, and employees must be given scheduled work assignments. Short-term detailed schedules fill in these blanks on a daily basis. These schedules use incoming customer orders and information about current machine conditions to update the sizes and variety of coils to make each day.

Scheduling Service Operations

Service scheduling may involve both work and workers. In a low-contact service, work scheduling may be based either on desired completion dates or on the time of order arrivals. For example, several cars may be scheduled for repairs at a local garage. If your car is not scheduled for work until 3:30, it may sit idle for several hours even if it was the first to be dropped off. In such businesses, reservations and appointments systems can help smooth ups and downs in demand.

In contrast, if a hospital emergency room is overloaded, patients cannot be asked to make appointments and come back later. As we have seen, in high-contact services, the customer is part of the system and must be accommodated. Thus, precise scheduling of services may not be possible in high-contact systems.

In scheduling workers, managers must also consider efficiency and costs. McDonald's, for example, guarantees workers that they will be scheduled for at least four hours at a time. To accomplish this goal without having workers idle, McDonald's uses overlapping shifts—the ending hours for some employees overlap the beginning hours for others. The overlap provides maximum coverage during peak periods. McDonald's also trains employees to put off minor tasks, such as refilling napkin dispensers, until slow periods.

OPERATIONS CONTROL

Once long-range plans have been put into action and schedules have been drawn up, **operations control** requires production managers to monitor production performance by comparing results with detailed plans and schedules. If schedules or quality standards are not met, these managers must take corrective action. **Follow-up**—checking to ensure that production decisions are being implemented—is an essential and ongoing facet of operations control.

operations control
Process of monitoring production performance by comparing results with plans

follow-up
Production control activity for ensuring that production decisions are being implemented

Operations control features *materials management* and *production process control.* Both activities ensure that schedules are met and that production goals are fulfilled, both in quantity and in quality. In this section, we consider the nature of materials management and look at some important methods of process control.

Materials Management

Both goods-producing and service companies use materials. For many manufacturing firms, material costs account for 50 to 75 percent of total product costs. For goods whose production uses little labor, such as petroleum refining, this percentage is even higher. Thus, companies have good reasons to emphasize materials management.

The process of **materials management** not only controls but also plans and organizes the flow of materials. Even before production starts, materials management focuses on product design by emphasizing materials **standardization**—the use of standard and uniform components rather than new or different components. Law firms maintain standardized forms and data files for estate wills, living wills, trust agreements, and various contracts that can be adjusted easily to meet your individual needs. In manufacturing, Ford's engine plant in Romeo, Michigan, uses common parts for several different kinds of engines rather than unique parts for each. Once components were standardized, the total number of different parts was reduced by 25 percent. Standardization also simplifies paperwork, reduces storage requirements, and eliminates unnecessary material flows.

materials management
Planning, organizing, and controlling the flow of materials from design through distribution of finished goods

standardization
Use of standard and uniform components in the production process

Once the product has been designed, materials managers purchase the necessary materials and monitor the production process through the distribution of finished goods. There are five major areas in materials management:

- *Transportation* includes the means of transporting resources to the company and finished goods to buyers.
- *Warehousing* is the storage of both incoming materials for production and finished goods for physical distribution to customers.
- **Purchasing** is the acquisition of all the raw materials and services that a company needs to produce its products; most large firms have purchasing departments to buy proper materials in the amounts needed.
- **Supplier selection** means finding and choosing suppliers of services and materials to buy from. It includes evaluating potential suppliers, negotiating terms of service, and maintaining positive buyer-seller relationships.

purchasing
Acquisition of the raw materials and services that a firm needs to produce its products

supplier selection
Process of finding and selecting suppliers from whom to buy

inventory control
In materials management, receiving, storing, handling, and counting of all raw materials, partly finished goods, and finished goods

- **Inventory control** includes the receiving, storing, handling, and counting of all raw materials, partly finished goods, and finished goods. It ensures that enough materials inventories are available to meet production schedules.

Managers in each area of materials management are constantly on the lookout for cost savings. Consider the cost-cutting possibilities in just one area—purchasing. Industrial buyers are banding together on the Internet. By forming online buying groups, they can purchase equipment and supplies in huge quantities for big discounts. PurchasingCenter.com is a brokerage site that brings together buyers and sellers into a single Internet marketplace, where it is easier for companies to contact and negotiate with each other on prices.[12]

Tools for Operations Process Control

Numerous tools assist managers in controlling operations. Chief among these are *worker training, just-in-time production systems, material requirements planning,* and *quality control.*

Worker Training Customer satisfaction is closely linked to the employees who provide the service. Says Kip Tindell, chief operating officer at the Container Store <www.containerstore.com>, a Dallas-based retailer of storage products: "We are just wild-eyed fanatics when it comes to human resources and training." Naturally, effective customer relationships do not come about by accident: Service workers can be trained and motivated in customer-oriented attitudes and behavior. In service-product design, it is important to remember that most services are delivered by people: That is, service system employees are both the producers of the product and the salespeople. Human relations skills are vital in anyone who has contact with the public. Tindell, who attributes the Container Store's high profits to effective employees, contends that human resources and training are "the most difficult and the most joyous part of the retail business." Like Tindell, more and more human resource experts now realize that without employees' trained relationship skills for pleasing their clients, businesses such as airlines, employment agencies, and hotels can lose customers to better-prepared competitors.

"Human resources and training are the most difficult and the most joyous part of the retail business."

—Kip Tindell,
Chief operating officer of the Container Store

just-in-time (JIT) production
Production method that brings together all materials and parts needed at each production stage at the precise moment they are required

material requirements planning (MRP)
Production method in which a bill of materials is used to ensure that the right amounts of materials are delivered to the right place at the right time

bill of materials
Production control tool that specifies the necessary ingredients of a product, the order in which they should be combined, and how many of each are needed to make one batch

Just-in-Time Production Systems To minimize manufacturing inventory costs, some managers use **just-in-time (JIT) production** systems. JIT brings together all the needed materials and parts at the precise moment they are required for each production stage, not before. All resources are continuously flowing, from their arrival as raw materials to subassembly, final completion, and shipment of finished products. JIT reduces to practically nothing the number of goods in process (that is, goods not yet finished) and saves money by replacing stop-and-go production with smooth movement. Once smooth movements become the norm, disruptions become more visible and thus get resolved more quickly. Finding and eliminating disruptions by continuous improvement of production is a major objective of JIT.

By implementing JIT, Harley-Davidson <www.harley-davidson.com> reduced its inventories by over 40 percent, improved production work flows, and reduced its costs of warranty work, rework, and scrap by 60 percent. In addition, Harley motorcycles have retained their coveted quality reputation: The annual number of shipments more than doubled from 1988 to 1996. With the help of JIT, the company's Plan 2003 calls for another doubling of production for Harley's 100th anniversary in 2003.[13]

Material Requirements Planning Like JIT, **material requirements planning (MRP)** seeks to deliver the right amounts of materials at the right place and the right time for goods production. MRP uses a **bill of materials** that is basically a recipe for the finished

When American manufacturers turned to leaner operations to counter foreign competition in the 1990s, they shifted to just-in-time inventory methods and cut workforces—and capacity. Today, economic good times mean accelerated demand and hard-pressed, understaffed assembly lines at many firms. At General Electric's locomotive plant in Erie, Pennsylvania <www.ge.com/transportation>, *managers have tried to head off problems by relying on certified parts supplied on time and in full quantities only by carefully monitored subcontractors.*

product. It specifies the necessary ingredients (raw materials and components), the order in which they should be combined, and the quantity of each ingredient needed to make one batch of the product (for example, 2,000 finished telephones). The recipe is fed into a computer that controls inventory and schedules each stage of production. The result is fewer early arrivals, less frequent stock shortages, and lower storage costs. MRP is most popular among companies whose products require complicated assembly and fabrication activities, such as automobile manufacturers, appliance makers, and furniture companies.

Manufacturing resource planning (MRP II) is an advanced version of MRP that ties all parts of the organization into the company's production activities. For example, MRP II inventory and production schedules are translated into cost requirements for the financial management department and into personnel requirements for the human resource department; information about available capacity for new orders goes to the marketing department.

manufacturing resource planning (MRP II)
Advanced version of MRP that ties together all parts of an organization into its production activities

Quality Control Another operation control tool is **quality control**—the management of the production process in order to manufacture goods or supply services that meet specific quality standards. United Parcel Service, Inc. (UPS) <www.ups.com> delivers 13 million packages every day, and all of them are promised to arrive on strict delivery schedules, mostly for business clients. Quality control is essential because delivery reliability—namely, avoiding late deliveries—is critical for customer satisfaction. UPS tracks the locations, time schedules, and on-time performance for some 500 aircraft and 150,000 vehicles as they carry packages through the delivery system. Its record in quality control is one reason why *Fortune* magazine rates UPS as America's Most Admired company in the mail, package, and freight-delivery category. It's also why *Forbes* magazine declared UPS 1999 Company of the Year.[14] Our discussion of quality control is continued in Chapter 16.

quality control
Management of the production process designed to manufacture goods or supply services that meet specific quality standards

Special Production Control Problems in Service Operations

The unique characteristics of services—customization, unstorability, and the presence of customers within the production process—create special challenges. In this final section, we will consider some techniques for meeting these challenges.

Customization The customized nature of services often makes scheduling difficult or impossible. This difficulty is one reason why you often have to wait at your doctor's office even though you have an appointment. Because the patients ahead of you also purchased customized services, the receptionist who schedules appointments can never know exactly when service will be completed.

Because scheduling is harder in high-contact services, it can often be improved by reducing customer contact. Routine transactions, such as approval for small loans, for example, can be handled by telephone or mail; only exceptions need be handled on a face-to-face basis. Locating drop-off points away from main facilities also reduces the level of customer contact. Consider the success of automatic teller machines: Not only are they more convenient for customers, but they free bank tellers from processing routine deposits and withdrawals.

Scheduling can also be improved by separating information gathering from provision of the service itself. For example, a well-run medical office will give you a medical history form to fill out while you wait. This system frees all office personnel, including the doctor, for other duties.

Unstorability As we noted earlier, the unstorability of services creates a potential for waste. Many hotels therefore accept more reservations than they can accommodate on a given night: If some customers fail to keep reservations, the hotel's ability to provide rooms has not been wasted (although it does risk offending customers who must be turned away if everyone shows up). Likewise, airlines overbook flights because they can usually count on no-shows.

Customer Involvement We have already seen that service production is complicated when customers are part of the process. However, some businesses have found a way to turn customer presence into an advantage: They actually get the customer more involved in the process. Consider the process of making a direct-dial long-distance telephone call. Back in 1970, over half of all long-distance calls were still being placed with the assistance of operators. Then in 1971, AT&T <www.att.com> introduced special switching systems. It also introduced a major marketing program that explained the change, promised benefits to customers (reduced cost and faster connections), and requested customer cooperation. By the end of 1971, 75 percent of all long-distance calls were direct-dialed. Today, the figure is well over 90 percent. What AT&T had done was shift some productive effort to the customer.

Continued from page 409

The Art and Science of Disciplinary Finance

In addition to direct production costs, late deliveries add a further cost burden: Contractually, late-delivery clauses can lead to penalties for Boeing. Scandinavian Airline Systems (SAS) **<www.flysas.com>**, for example, has reportedly sought late-delivery payments of up to $10 million for two 737 aircraft that Boeing failed to deliver on time. "We slipped on some deliveries in terms of schedule," admits Boeing executive Fernando Vivanco. "We are working with airline customers to set appropriate compensations, which we are contractually obliged to do." With plans to deliver 20,150 new airplanes over the next 20 years, Boeing is well aware of the fact that it must avoid future late-delivery penalties by better coordinating production with market demand.

To control the direct costs of production Boeing must first isolate and identify them. Surprisingly, however, before the arrival of Deborah Hopkins, who has been Chief Financial Officer since 1998, Boeing didn't keep accurate records of the costs of making airplanes. It was hard to know which costs were out of control and by how much. Today, however, each plane is scrutinized in every stage of production to keep costs down to $4 million per plane (on average). "My goal," says Hopkins, "is to drive [the discipline] of finance as a force in this company."

Her approach is numbers oriented. "If you can measure it," she says, "you can improve it." Hopkins wants to measure how fast each production line goes through its inventory and how many man-hours it takes to build each plane. She wants the goal of improving efficiency to be adopted by everyone, including the rank and file on the production lines. The hunt is on for every possible cost savings: Designing parts digitally reduces costs. Better work methods help, too: By speeding up the insertion of 1.4 million pins and rivets, Boeing cut assembly costs by nearly one percent. To save inventory and materials-logistics costs, Boeing also plans to cut its huge supplier base from 31,000 down to 18,000 by 2003.

Using the measurements that her team has developed, Hopkins has put together a "value scorecard" that allows departments and work groups to understand their production problems and to compare their performances against others. According to Hopkins, cutting back excessive inventories will free up billions of dollars for future expansion. With employee cutbacks currently running at 3,000 jobs a month, her message was clear: The only way to ensure job security at Boeing is to fashion a financially healthy operation that makes high-quality airplanes.

"If you can measure it, you can improve it."

—Deborah Hopkins, CFO of Boeing

Questions for Discussion

1. It can be argued that production scheduling at Boeing is complicated by having too many suppliers providing components and systems. Explain how the number of suppliers might affect Boeing's production schedules.
2. How is it possible that Boeing's new assembly line technology could actually slow down production rather than speed it up? Explain the factors that might cause such a slowdown.
3. Why do you think customers want a "late-delivery clause" in their contracts with Boeing? Suppose you are a customer: What considerations would determine the size of the late-delivery penalty you would build into your contract?
4. List the methods that Boeing has used to reduce production costs and give a brief example to demonstrate how and why each method helps to control costs.
5. What do you think of Deborah Hopkins's approach to better production efficiency? What are the key elements in this approach?
6. Looking ahead to Boeing's ambitious plans for the future, what are some possible events that might once again cause production costs to spiral out of control and thus lead to financial losses?

SUMMARY OF LEARNING OBJECTIVES

1 **Explain the meaning of the term *production* or *operations* and describe the four kinds of *utility* it provides.** *Production* (or *operations*) refers to the processes and activities for transforming resources into finished services and goods for customers. Resources include knowledge, physical materials, equipment, and labor that are systematically combined in a production facility to create four kinds of *utility* for customers: *time utility* (which makes products available when customers want them), *place utility* (which makes products available where they are convenient for customers), possession or *ownership utility* (by which customers benefit from possessing and using the product), and *form utility* (which results from the creation of the product).

2 **Describe and explain the two classifications of *operations processes*.** Operations managers in manufacturing describe operations processes according to whether products are submitted to *analytic or synthetic processes* (that is, whether the process breaks down resources into components or combines raw materials into finished products). Service operations are classified according to the *extent of customer contact,* as either high-contact systems (the customer is part of the system) or low-contact (customers are not in contact while the service is provided).

3 **Identify the characteristics that distinguish *service operations* from *goods production* and explain the main differences in the *service focus*.** Although the creation of both goods and services involves resources, transformations, and finished products, service operations differ from goods manufacturing in several important ways. In service production, the raw materials are not, say, glass or steel, but rather people who choose among sellers because they have unsatisfied needs or possessions in need of care or alteration. Therefore, whereas services are typically performed, goods are physically produced. In addition, services are largely *intangible,* more likely than physical goods to be *customized* to meet the purchaser's needs, and more *unstorable* than most products. Service businesses therefore focus explicitly on these characteristics of their products. Because services are intangible, for instance, providers work to ensure that customers receive value in the form of pleasure, satisfaction, or a feeling of safety. Often, they also focus on both the transformation process and the final product (say, making the loan interview a pleasant experience as well as providing the loan itself). Finally, service providers typically focus on the *customer-service link,* often acknowledging the customer as part of the operations process.

4 **Describe the factors involved in *operations planning*.** *Operations planning* involves the analysis of six key factors. *Forecasts* of future demand for both new and existing products provide information for developing production plans. In *capacity planning,* the firm analyzes how much of a product it must be able to produce. In high-contact services, managers must plan capacity to meet peak demand. Capacity planning for goods means ensuring that manufacturing capacity slightly exceeds the normal demand for its product. *Location planning* for goods and for low-contact services involves analyzing proposed facility sites in terms of proximity to raw materials and markets, availability of labor, and energy and transportation costs. Location planning for high-contact services, in contrast, involves locating the service near customers, who are part of the system. *Layout planning* involves designing a facility so that customer needs are supplied for high-contact services and so as to enhance production efficiency. Layout alternatives include product, process, and cellular configurations. In *quality planning,* systems are developed to ensure that products meet a firm's quality standards. Finally, in *methods planning,* specific production steps and methods for performing them are identified. *Service flow analysis* and *process flow charts* are helpful for identifying all operations activities and eliminating wasteful steps from production.

5 **Explain some of the activities involved in *operations control*, including *materials management* and the use of certain *operations control tools*.** *Operations control* requires production managers to monitor production performance, by comparing results with detailed plans and schedules, and then to take corrective action as needed. *Materials management* is the planning, organizing, and controlling of the flow of materials. It focuses on the control of *transportation* (transporting resources to the manufacturer and products to customers), *warehousing* (storing both incoming raw materials and finished goods), *purchasing* (acquiring the raw materials and services that a manufacturer needs), *supplier selection,* and *inventory control.* To control operations processes, managers use various methods. For example, *worker training* programs can assist in quality control, the management of the operations process so as to ensure that services and goods meet specific quality standards. *Just-in-time (JIT) production* systems bring together all materials and parts needed at each production stage at the precise moment they are required. JIT reduces manufacturing inventory costs and reveals production problems that need improvement. *Material requirements planning (MRP)* is another method for ensuring that the right amounts of materials are delivered to the right place at the right time for manufacturing. It uses computer-controlled schedules for moving inventories through each stage of production.

QUESTIONS AND EXERCISES

Review Questions

1. What are the four different kinds of production-based utility?
2. What are the major differences between goods production operations and service operations?
3. What are the major differences between high-contact and low-contact service systems?
4. What are the six major categories of operations planning?

Questions for Analysis

5. What are the resources and finished products in the following services?
   Real estate firm
   Child care facility
   Bank
   City water and electric department
   Hotel
6. Analyze the location of a local firm where you do business (perhaps a restaurant, a supermarket, or a manufacturing firm). What problems do you see with this location? What recommendations would you make to management?
7. Find good examples of a synthetic production process and an analytic process. Explain your choices.
8. Develop a service flow analysis for some service that you use frequently, such as buying lunch at a cafeteria, having your hair cut, or riding a bus. Identify areas of potential quality or productivity failures in the process.

Application Exercises

9. Interview the manager of a local service business, such as a laundry or dry-cleaning shop. Identify the major decisions that were involved in planning its service operations. Prepare a class report suggesting areas for improvement.
10. Select a high-contact industry. Write an advertisement seeking workers for this business. Draw up a plan for motivating workers to produce high-quality services for the firm.

EXPLORING THE WEB

COPYING A FORMULA FOR EFFICIENT SERVICE

Today, nearly everyone needs documents for communications in both their personal and professional lives. Various documents can sometimes be created in routine formats but, at other times, special formats are more appropriate. Moreover, we typically want to get our documents quickly and conveniently. A number of companies are available to help meet these needs. Perhaps the best-known is Kinko's. To learn more about the company's operations, log on to the Kinko's Web site at

www.kinkos.com

First, browse the homepage. Then explore the page entitled *Find Products and Services*. For each product/service category, examine descriptions for various offerings and think about each from the perspective of the operations involved in creating and delivering it. Look also at the page entitled *Kinkos.com*. Again, think about the company's production operations. Finally, consider the following items:

1. Who are Kinko's customers? Are they mostly consumers or other businesses? Explain.
2. Is Kinko's product line primarily goods or services? Explain using examples.
3. Think about location planning for Kinko's facilities. Identify the main factors that must be considered in location planning for Kinko's.
4. From the page entitled *Find Products and Services*, choose any three Kinko's services and for each identify its input resources, describe the steps in its transformation process, and describe the outputs from the transformation.
5. From the page entitled *Find Products and Services*, choose three contrasting products and identify the amount of customer contact in the production system. Is it high contact or low contact? In answering, explain the customer's role in production. How will the amount of customer contact affect the in-store operations?
6. After looking at the page entitled *Kinkos.com*, describe the product(s) it offers. Identify the elements in the conversion process of each product. What

role does the customer play in the production system? Is this a high- or low-contact conversion process?

7. Identify the materials requirements for each of three Kinko's services. In what quantities does Kinko's probably purchase those materials? Describe the flow paths of materials through the facility for the three services.
8. Is production scheduling involved in Kinko's operations? Explain.
9. For on-site services, identify key operations items that will determine product quality. In other words, what production activities are most critical for determining quality?

BUILDING YOUR BUSINESS SKILLS

THE ONE-ON-ONE ENTREPRENEUR

This exercise enhances the following SCANS workplace competencies: demonstrating basic skills, demonstrating thinking skills, exhibiting interpersonal skills, and working with information.

GOAL

To encourage students to apply the concept of customization to an entrepreneurial idea.

SITUATION

Imagine that you are an entrepreneur with the desire to start your own service business. You are intrigued with the idea of creating some kind of customized one-on-one service that would appeal to baby boomers, who traditionally have been pampered, and working women, who have little time to get things done.

METHOD

Step 1

Get together with three or four other students to brainstorm business ideas that would appeal to harried working people. Among the ideas to consider are the following:

- A concierge service in office buildings that would handle such personal and business services as arranging children's birthday parties and booking guest speakers for business luncheons.
- A personal image consultation service aimed at helping clients improve their appearance, personal etiquette, and presentation style.
- A mobile pet care network in which veterinarians and personal groomers make house calls.

Step 2

Choose an idea from these or others you might think of. Then write a memo explaining why you think your idea will succeed. Research may be necessary as you target any of the following:

- A specific demographic group or groups. (Who are your customers and why would they buy your service?)
- The features that make your service attractive to this group.
- The social factors in your local community that would lead to success.

FOLLOW-UP QUESTIONS

1. Why is the customization of and easy access to personal services so attractive in the twenty-first century?
2. As services are personalized, do you think quality will become more or less important? Why?
3. Why does the trend to personalized, one-on-one service present unique opportunities for entrepreneurs?
4. In a personal one-on-one business, how important are the human relations skills of those delivering the service? Can you make an argument that they are more important than the service itself?

CRAFTING YOUR BUSINESS PLAN

GETTING ON A PAR WITH CUSTOMERS

THE PURPOSE OF THE ASSIGNMENT

1. To acquaint students with the process of navigating the *Business PlanPro* (*BPP*) software package (Version 4.0).
2. To familiarize students with the ways in which operations considerations enter into the business planning framework in *BPP.*
3. To stimulate students' thinking about applying the textbook's information on operations management to the preparation of their business plan in *BPP.*

ASSIGNMENT

After reading Chapter 15 in the textbook, open the BPP *software* and look around for information about the plans for managing operations as they apply to a sample firm:* Golf Pro Shop *(Golf Master Pro Shops, Inc.). Then respond to the following items:*

1. What type of product—physical good or service—is Golf Master Pro Shops creating in its production process? Explain. [Sites to see in *BPP* (for this assignment): In the Plan Outline screen, click on **1.0 Executive Summary.** Then click on each of the following in turn: **1.1 Objectives, 1.2 Mission, 3.2 Competitive Comparison,** and **5.1 Marketing Strategy.**]
2. Describe the characteristics of the transformation (operations) process that produces this company's products. [Sites to see in *BPP:* In the Plan Outline screen, click on **2.0 Company Summary** and **2.2 Start-Up Summary.** After returning to the Plan Outline screen, click on each of the following in turn: **3.2 Competitive Comparison** and **6.1 Organization Structure.**]
3. How many Golf Master stores are planned for the future? What steps can be taken to ensure that the same consistent services are given to all customers regardless of store location? [Sites to see in *BPP:* In the Plan Outline screen, click on **1.0 Executive Summary.** Then click on each of the following in turn: **1.1 Objectives, 3.1 Product and Service Description, 3.2 Competitive Comparison,** and **6.3 Management Team Gaps.**]
4. Identify and describe some issues and problems that Golf Master might face in developing a layout for its facilities. [Sites to see in *BPP:* In the Plan Outline screen, click on each of the following in turn: **1.0 Executive Summary, 6.1 Organizational Structure, 3.1 Product and Services, 3.6 Future Products and Services,** and **6.3 Management Team Gaps.**]

FOR YOUR OWN BUSINESS PLAN

5. Consider the planning that would be appropriate for the following three aspects of production: (1) the steps involved in producing your company's product, (2) the types of equipment and facilities that will be used, and (3) the steps that will be taken to predict demand and schedule production. Among these three aspects, which is most important to emphasize for your business plan? Which is least important? In how much detail will you cover each of these aspects in the write-up of your plan?

*GENERAL TIPS FOR NAVIGATING IN *BPP*

1. Open the *BPP* program, examine the Welcome screen, and click on **Open a Sample Plan.**
2. From the Open a Sample Plan dialogue box, click on a sample company name; then click on **Open.**
3. On the Plan Manager screen, click on **Your Plan Outline;** then click on any of the lines (for example, **5.1.1 Pricing Strategy**).
4. You can always return to the Plan Outline screen by going to the bottom of the screen and clicking on the **Plan Outline** icon.
5. After finishing with one sample company, you can get to the next one by going to the top of the screen and clicking on **File** (on the

menu bar). Then beneath that, select **Open Sample Plan.** This will exit you from the current company file and take you to the Open Sample Plan dialogue box, where you can select your next sample company.

6. When you are finished, you can close the program by going to the top of the screen and clicking on **File** (on the bar menu). Then beneath that, select **Exit.**

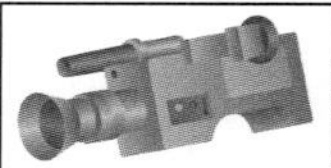

VIDEO EXERCISE

TUMBLING SOME PROCESSES: WHIRLPOOL

Learning Objectives

The purpose of this video exercise is to help you

1. Understand the impact of market forces on production planning
2. Recognize the different kinds of contributions that manufacturing workers can make
3. Appreciate the importance of quality planning in production

BACKGROUND INFORMATION

Occupying 2 million square feet of space, Whirlpool's <www.whirlpool.com> manufacturing plant in Clyde, Ohio, is the largest maker of automatic washers in the world, producing 14,000 washers every day, about 20 percent of them for export. The plant's 3,000 employees make five brands of machines, including Whirlpool, Kenmore, and Kitchen-Aid. Recent changes have taken the plant from a functional organization to organization by business unit and have given employees more input in the strategic planning process.

THE VIDEO

This segment illustrates the operations on the factory floor and introduces several top executives of Whirlpool and of the Clyde facility. They discuss the recent consolidation of manufacturers in the industry, the maturity of the industry in the United States, and the need for the plant to adopt new quality standards in order to become competitive abroad. We also hear about employee input to the strategic planning process, from the viewpoints of both an employee and a manager.

DISCUSSION QUESTIONS

1. What type of transformation process is used in the Clyde manufacturing facility?
2. The Clyde plant has its own vision statement, separate from that of the rest of the Whirlpool organization. Why do you think a manufacturing facility needs a vision statement?
3. Workers at the Clyde plant have input to the strategic planning process and the opportunity to make improvements in the assembly process. To what other types of operations planning do you think workers in general can contribute? Do you think that there are any drawbacks to worker participation in planning?

FOLLOW-UP ASSIGNMENT

Visit a local service business such as a restaurant, hair stylist, bank, or copy center. Is it a high-contact or low-contact operation? How does the layout and general appearance of the store indicate to customers the areas where they are permitted to go and those reserved for employees? Does the layout facilitate or hinder the delivery of the firm's services? From the customer's point of view, what improvements do you think could be made? What improvements could be made from the employee's point of view?

FOR FURTHER EXPLORATION

Internet service providers (ISPs) are service businesses with which customers usually have no physical contact. Evaluate your own ISP, whether it is a national company like AOL or a local provider like Mindspring. What characteristics does it share with other service firms, such as customization, unstorability, customer-service link, and employee-customer interaction? What characteristics of Internet service in general are unique, and how do you think an ISP controls the quality of these characteristics?

MASTERING BUSINESS ESSENTIALS

Go to the "Putting Operations under the Microscope" episode on the Mastering Business Essentials CD-ROM for an interactive, video-enhanced exercise on the efforts of management at CanGo, an e-business start-up, to compare annual performance data and to analyze the causes of and solutions to some problems in the firm's processes.

Chapter

16

Managing for Quality and Productivity

After reading this chapter, you should be able to:

1. ***Describe*** the connection between *productivity* and *quality*.

2. ***Explain*** the decline and recovery in U.S. productivity that has occurred in the last 25 or 30 years.

3. ***Identify*** the activities involved in *total quality management* and describe six tools that companies can use to achieve it.

4. ***Identify*** two trends in productivity and quality management and discuss three ways in which companies can compete by improving productivity and quality.

"Speed Is Everything"

Dell Computer Corp. has never done business in quite the same way that other computer makers have. One of the country's fastest-growing high-tech firms, Dell sells computers directly to customers, and it is making a big splash on the Internet, writing up $40 million worth of orders a day from its Web site <www.dell.com>. It is now the number-one PC retailer on the Web, with sales continuing to grow at an astounding rate of 54 percent per year for the last 10 years. "We've become the poster boy for the Internet," says company founder Michael Dell. In fact, Dell's company has led the way to a whole new world of selling: In the last quarter of its 2000 fiscal year, direct sales accounted for nearly half of Dell's $6.8 billion in new PC sales.

What's the secret of Dell's success? Michael Dell, chairman and CEO, has stressed a few key production principles that sustain productivity and keep costs and inventories low. For one thing, information is replacing inventory: By keeping up-to-the-minute information on supplies, customer orders, and production status, Dell keeps 10 times less inventory than its competitors and passes the savings along to customers. By redesigning its products—in particular, simplifying them with fewer parts—Dell has made production faster and, of course, has to purchase fewer parts.

Perhaps the most important principle at Dell is speed. Just-in-time manufacturing has always been a key tenet at the firm, and Dell has recently extended it to suppliers. Dell now requires its supply chain to warehouse most computer components within 15 minutes of Dell's factories in Texas, Ireland, and Malaysia, and it has dropped suppliers who can't comply. Dell doesn't even buy components until it's received an order for at least one unit of a computer, thus realizing big savings on parts whose prices can drop almost overnight. When it gets a customer order, Dell quickly relays the information to its suppliers, who are committed to quick delivery. Despite the squeeze on suppliers, the firm can still book a custom order and ship a finished machine within 48 hours.

Dell also collects on sales faster than the competition, averaging 24 hours from order to cash. That's days sooner than rivals Gateway <**www.gateway.com**> and Compaq <**www.compaq.com**>. "Speed is everything in this business," says CEO Dell. "We're setting the pace for the industry." With the firm's stock price continuing to climb, it seems that investors as well as customers must agree that Dell has figured out how to achieve an enviable mix of productivity and quality.

"Speed is everything in this business. We're setting the pace for the industry."

—Michael Dell,
CEO of Dell Computer

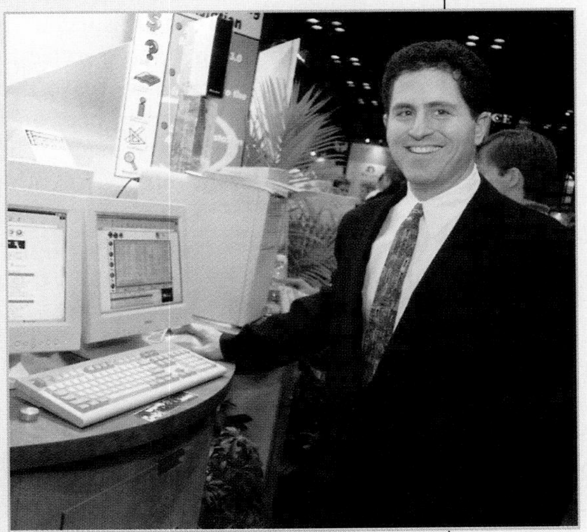

Our opening story continues on page 461

It is no secret that productivity and quality are the watchwords in today's business competition. Companies are not only measuring productivity and insisting on improvements, but also insisting that quality means bringing to market products that satisfy customers, improve sales, and boost profits. By focusing on the learning objectives of this chapter, you will better understand the increasingly important concepts of productivity and quality.

THE PRODUCTIVITY-QUALITY CONNECTION

Productivity is a measure of economic performance: As we saw in Chapter 1, it compares how much we produce with the resources we use to produce it. The formula is fairly simple: The more we can produce while using fewer resources, the more productivity grows and the more everyone—the economy, businesses, and workers—benefits.

However, productivity also refers to the *quantity* and *quality* of what we produce. When resources are used more efficiently, the quantity of output is certainly greater. But experience has shown marketers of goods and services that unless the resulting products are of satisfactory quality, consumers will reject them. Producing **quality,** then, means creating fitness for use plus offering features that consumers want.

quality
A product's fitness for use plus its success in offering features that consumers want

The importance of quality cannot be overstated. Poor quality has created some long-standing competitive problems for U.S. firms that have focused too narrowly on efficiency and quantity. In 1970, for instance, the United States enjoyed the highest levels of productivity in the industrialized world. Through the 1980s, however, productivity and quality grew faster in several other industrialized nations, and the United States lost ground to global competitors.

By the beginning of the twenty-first century, many U.S. firms had reversed this trend by focusing on the need for greater quantity and improved quality. United Parcel Service <www.ups.com> regularly surveys customers to identify and correct problems in its pickup and delivery services. General Electric Co. <www.ge.com> is using six-sigma quality to increase productivity. Cisco Systems <www.cisco.com>, the worldwide leader in networking for the Internet, is providing technologies for more efficient exchanges of information which, in turn, will lead to higher productivity and quality for other companies. Reflecting the quality–productivity connection, the former American Productivity Center in Houston has been renamed the American Productivity and Quality Center <www.apqc.org>. The center offers seminars, conferences, data exchanges, and other resources to assist companies in improving productivity and quality.

Is it important for decision-makers to take into account the relationship between productivity and quality?

WebConnection

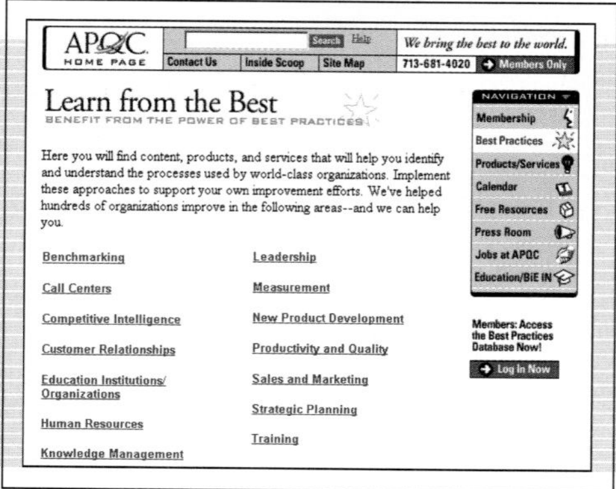

www.apqc.org

APQC offers a broad range of services designed to assist businesses in improving the quality and productivity of both their products and their organizations and operations. For a survey of the Center's programs, log on to its Web site.

RESPONDING TO THE PRODUCTIVITY CHALLENGE

Productivity has both international and domestic ramifications. When one country is more productive than another, it will accumulate more wealth. Similarly, a nation whose productivity fails to increase as rapidly as that of competitor nations will see its standard of living fall.

A Reality Check for International Business Survival

For decades, U.S. products dominated world markets because U.S. businesses were so successful in producing goods and distributing them in both domestic and foreign markets. The 1960s found U.S. manufacturers unchallenged as the world's industrial leaders. U.S. industry, it seemed, could make anything, and because U.S. products were the best, Americans could sell whatever they made, both at home and abroad. In the 1970s, however, U.S. productivity began a dramatic downslide that continued into the 1980s. Then, a remarkable turnaround in productivity occurred in the years leading up to 1994, when American businesses regained significant market shares in several large industries including industrial machinery (Caterpillar), automobiles (Ford), and electronic equipment (IBM and Motorola). By 1999, U.S. companies remained the world's leading exporters in several major industries, including airplanes, computers, construction equipment, and transistors. Today, more and more Asian and European firms are once again concerned with catching U.S. businesses in a world of intense global competition.

How did this change in fortunes come about? For one thing, U.S. businesses that once focused on and complained about the foreign competition's advantage in lower labor rates began looking elsewhere for competitive advantage. They studied ways to revitalize sagging sales. First, they concentrated on understanding the true meaning of *productivity* and devised means of measuring it. Soon learning that *quality* must be defined in terms of value to the customer, they redesigned their organizations and marketing efforts so that the focus was more customer oriented. As quality-improvement practices were gradually implemented, more and more firms began to realize payoffs from these efforts. These successes highlighted the interdependence of four key ingredients: customers, quality, productivity, and profits.

TSMC, which makes silicon chips, is the first step in the production of the ASICs (application specific integrated circuits) manufactured by a company called Adaptec. Adaptec <www.adaptec.com> is located in Singapore, TSMC <www.tsmc.com.tw/> in Taiwan, and other members of the supply chain are located in Hong Kong and South Korea. With half of its $692 million in annual revenues coming from the United States, Adaptec is truly an international company, and in order to compete, the company's productivity standards must meet those of firms located around the world.

Figure 16.1

International Productivity Comparisons

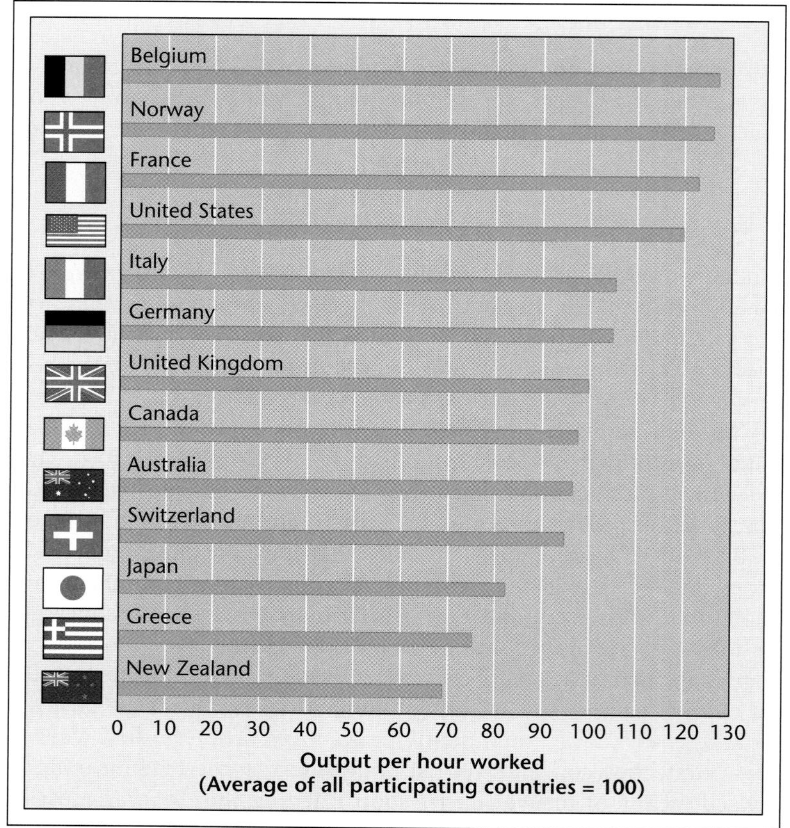

Productivity Among Global Competitors A report on the Organization for Economic Cooperation and Development (OECD) <www.oecdwash.org> reveals productivity levels in 23 participating countries. Figure 16.1 shows productivity comparisons among several OECD countries including the leader, Belgium, whose economic output per hour worked is 28 percent higher than the average output for all OECD countries. Canada's output is 3 percent below the average, while New Zealand's, at 31 percent below the average, is lowest among the nations listed in Figure 16.1.

Why such differences from nation to nation? The answer lies in many factors: technologies, human skills, economic policies, natural resources, and even in traditions. Consider just one industrial sector—food production (see <www.foodservice.com>). In Japan, the food-production industry employs more workers than the automotive, computer, consumer-electronics, and machine-tool industries combined. It is a fragmented, highly protected industry and, compared with U.S. food production, an extremely inefficient one. The average U.S. worker produces 3.5 times as much food as his or her Japanese counterpart. What about overall productivity, with all industries taken together? In the time that it takes a U.S. worker to produce $100 worth of goods, Japanese workers produce about $68 worth. Belgian workers produce $107 worth.[1]

Domestic Productivity

Nations must care about domestic productivity regardless of their global standing. A country that improves its ability to make something out of its existing resources can increase the wealth of all its inhabitants. Conversely, a decline in productivity shrinks a nation's total wealth. Therefore, an increase in one person's wealth comes only at the expense of others with whom the individual shares a social economic system.

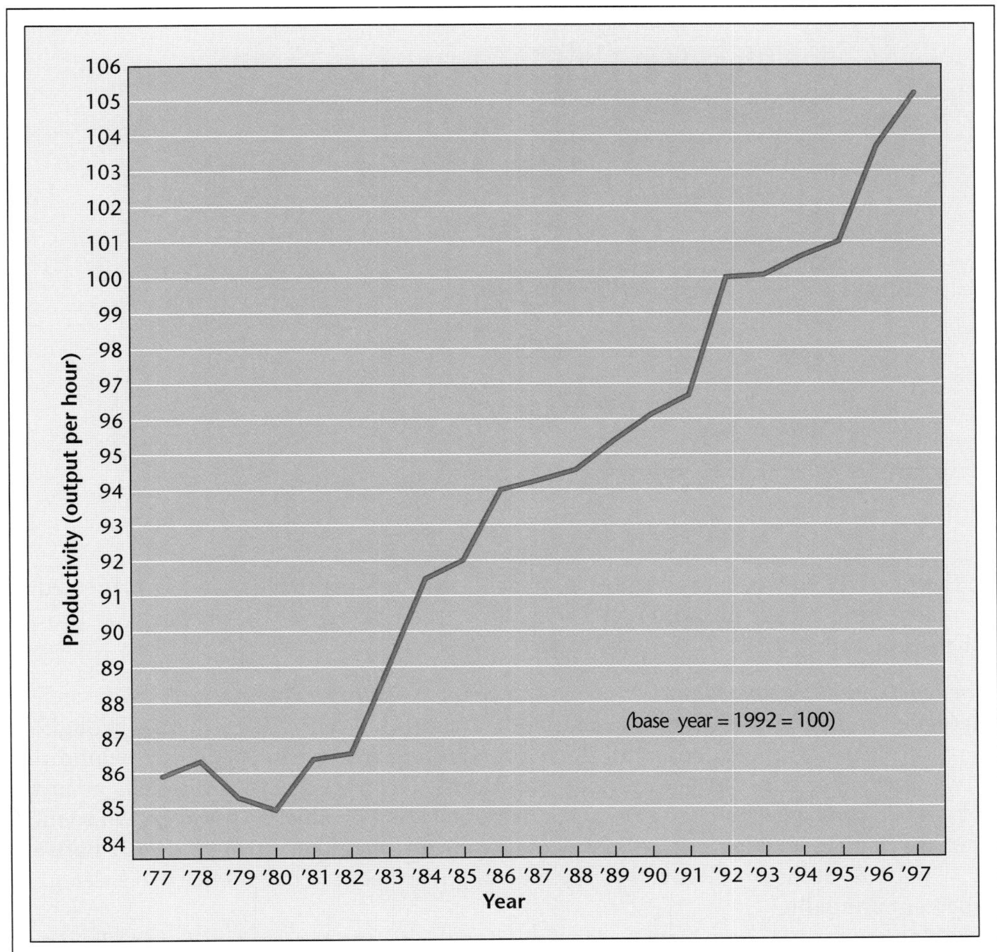

Figure 16.2
Increasing U.S. Productivity

For example, additional wealth from higher productivity can be shared among workers (as higher wages), investors (as higher profits), and customers (as stable prices). When productivity drops, however, wages can be increased only by reducing profits (penalizing investors) or by increasing prices (penalizing customers). It is understandable that investors, suppliers, managers, and workers are all concerned about the productivity of specific industries, companies, departments, and even individuals. Next we survey recent trends in U.S. productivity on various levels: national, industrywide, companywide, and departmental and individual.

National Productivity Trends The United States remains one of the most productive nations in the world. In 1997, for instance, the value of goods and services produced by each U.S. worker was $65,400. This **level of productivity** is higher than that of any other country. In second place, Norwegian workers produced $62,300 per worker, followed by Swiss workers at $56,700. Canadian workers produced $51,100.[2] As Figure 16.2 shows, the output per hour worked also rose steadily in the United States throughout most of the 1980s and 1990s.

level of productivity
Dollar value of goods and services relative to the resources used to produce them

Growth Rates for U.S. Productivity Many observers consider the trends in productivity to be an indicator of a nation's economic health. In the 1980s the United States experienced slowdown in its **growth rate of productivity**—the annual increase in a nation's output over the previous year. In short, U.S. productivity was not increasing as fast as it had

growth rate of productivity
Annual increase in a nation's output over the previous year

Figure 16.3

U.S. Productivity Growth, 1978–2008

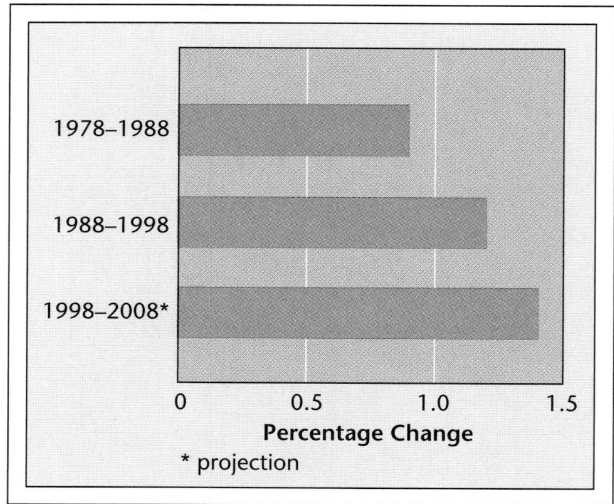

in the past. Then, recovery began, continued through the 1990s, and is projected to increase in the decade ahead. Figure 16.3 shows the pattern of U.S. productivity growth for three decades.

Uneven Growth in the Manufacturing and Service Sectors A close look at the manufacturing and service sectors reveals important productivity differences. Throughout most of the 1970s, productivity in the manufacturing sector trailed slightly behind that of the service sector. But U.S. service productivity averaged zero improvement in the years 1978 through 1990. By 1993, U.S. manufacturing productivity had grown to more than double the productivity of services, a margin sustained through 1999. Between 1977 and 1998, the productivity of the federal government, a key service producer, grew 1 percent annually.[3]

Manufacturing is primarily responsible for the recent increases in overall U.S. productivity. In 1998 the value of goods produced by each U.S. manufacturing worker was $116,000, compared with $47,800 for each service worker.[4] As we saw in Chapter 15, however, services are growing faster than goods production as a proportion of all U.S. business and now account for about 60 percent of national income. In the years ahead, productivity must increase more rapidly in the service sector if the United States is to maintain its competitive edge in world markets.

Productivity Within Industries and Firms In addition to the nation's overall performance, productivity can be analyzed in greater detail by focusing on specific industries. In this section, we will see why a variety of parties, such as governments, investors, and labor unions, are interested in the productivity not only of different industries but also of specific companies.

Industrywide Productivity Various industries differ vastly in terms of productivity. During the 1990s the productivity of electric utilities (see <www.eei.org>) increased by 40 percent and that of commercial banks by 27 percent. In contrast, grocery store productivity (see <www.progressivegrocer.com>) declined by 5 percent. Manufacturers also differ considerably: Producers of cigarettes (see <www.tobaccoindustry.com>), increased productivity by more than 40 percent while plywood manufacturing productivity (see <www.hpva.org>) fell by nearly 6 percent. Figure 16.4 shows contrasting productivity levels for several selected services and manufacturing industries. The contrasts reveal that consumer-electronics stores are nearly three times as productive as newspaper manufacturing.[5]

The productivity of specific industries concerns different people for different reasons. Because highly productive industries can better afford raises than less productive industries, labor unions must consider productivity when negotiating contracts. Investors and

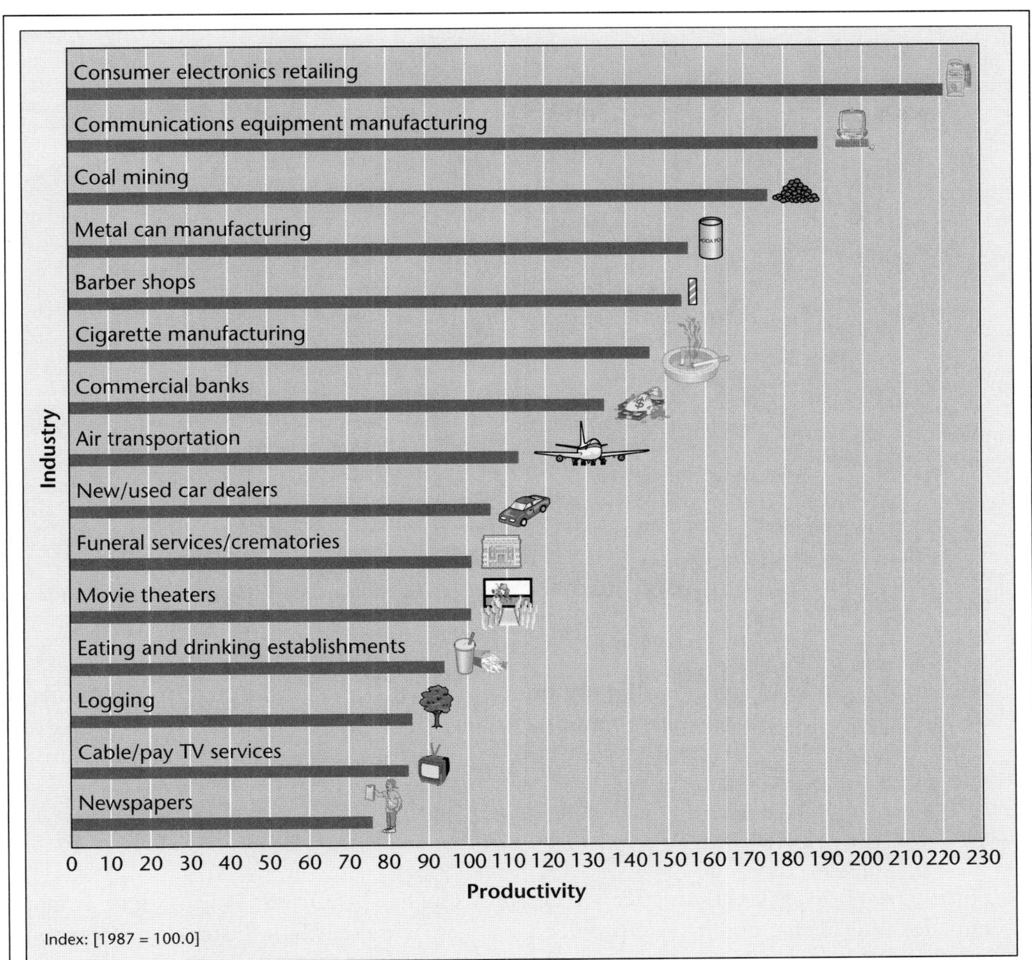

Figure 16.4
Productivity in Selected U.S. Industries

suppliers consider industry productivity when making loans, buying securities, and planning production. Government bodies use productivity as a means of authorizing programs and projecting tax revenues.

Companywide Productivity High productivity gives a company a competitive edge because its costs are lower than those of other companies. A firm can thus choose to offer products at lower prices or to make a greater profit on each unit sold. Increased productivity also allows firms to pay higher wages without raising prices. Job security, too, is bolstered by higher productivity. Consider a production line at Westinghouse Air Brake's <www.wabco-rail.com> Chicago factory: It produced 10 times more output in 1999 than in 1991. By boosting productivity on that line, Westinghouse was able to keep other, less productive jobs at the plant. Otherwise, the work may have gone overseas.[6]

For all these reasons, the productivity of individual companies is important to investors, workers, and managers. Comparing the productivity of several companies in the same industry guides investors in buying and selling stocks. In addition, employee profit-sharing plans are often based on employers' annual productivity growth. Managers use information about productivity trends to plan for new products, factories, and funds.

Departmental and Individual Productivity Within companies, managers are concerned with the productivity of various divisions, departments, workstations, and individuals. Improved productivity in any of these areas can improve a firm's overall productivity.

Recent statistics show that average real wages in the so-called "New Economy"—industries whose main product is information—have risen by 11 percent since 1994. In contrast, real wages in the rest of the economy are up by only 3 percent. People in many "Old Economy" industries are understandably concerned, but there has been some positive spillover from New Economy to Old. The demand for truckers is up because of the surge in online retailing: While the Internet specializes in getting information from buyers to e-tailers, products still have to be moved physically from suppliers to buyers.

However, an overemphasis on the performance of individuals and departments tends to discourage working together, as teams, for overall company improvement. For this reason, many companies are cautious about using departmental and individual productivity measures.

TOTAL QUALITY MANAGEMENT

For the past 50 years, the American Society for Quality (ASQ) <www.asq.org> has maintained standards for quality and provided services to assist U.S. industry's quality efforts. The "quality revolution" that continues today ranks among the most profound business developments in the history of modern commerce. In the first years after World War II, U.S. business consultant W. Edwards Deming tried to persuade domestic firms that they needed to improve quality at least as much as quantity. Like many prophets, however, Deming was more honored abroad than at home: His arguments appealed to the Japanese, who named their national quality award the Deming Prize. Fortunately, many U.S. companies have also embraced Deming's message in more recent years. Deming's ideas on quality encouraged U.S. companies to adopt a whole new quality orientation—a corporate-cultural revolution—if they were to stay competitive. By and large, Deming has been proved right: U.S. companies today are increasingly customer-driven; all employees, rather than just managers, participate in quality efforts; and more measurements are used to document progress objectively and to identify areas for improvement. Quality improvement has become a continuous way of life, rather than an occasional activity.

Managing for Quality

total quality management (TQM) (or **quality assurance**) The sum of all activities involved in getting high-quality products into the marketplace

Total quality management (TQM) (sometimes called **quality assurance**) includes all of the activities necessary for getting high-quality goods and services into the marketplace. It must consider all parts of the business, including customers, suppliers, and employees. The strategic approach for TQM in any company begins with leadership and the desire for TQM. This approach involves getting people's attention, getting them to think in an entirely new way about what they do, then getting them to improve things. Sometimes managers have to confront thoroughly entrenched mind-sets before quality orientation can begin. On his first day in office, one new CEO gave a less than subtle hint that a new quality orientation was underway when he took a pile of airsickness bags from his briefcase and placed them at each seat around the conference table. Holding up a bag, he opened the meeting by saying, "The quality of our products makes me want to puke." Under the leadership of CEO Mike Ruetters, EMC <www.emc.com> has since gone on to become one of the top-performing information-technology firms in the world.[7]

Customer focus is the starting spot; it includes using methods for determining what customers want, and then causing all the company's activities and people to be directed onto fulfillment of those needs to gain greater customer satisfaction. Total participation, as Deming noted years ago, is mandatory; if all employees are not working toward improved quality, then the firm is wasting potential contributions from its human resources, and it's missing a chance to become a stronger competitor in the marketplace. TQM in today's competitive markets is more than part-time; it demands unending and continuous improvement of products, after-sales services, and improvement in all of the company's internal processes, such as accounting, delivery, billing, and information flows.

Says John Kay, director of Oxford University's School of Management: "You can't run a successful company if you don't care about customers and employees, or if you are systematically unpleasant to suppliers."[8] To bring the interests of all these stakeholders together, TQM involves planning, organizing, directing, and controlling.

"You can't run a successful company if you don't care about customers and employees or if you are systematically unpleasant to suppliers."

—John Kay, Director, Oxford University School of Management

Planning for Quality Planning for quality begins *before* products are designed or redesigned. To ensure that their needs are not overlooked, customers may be invited to participate in the planning process. In the predesign stage, managers must set goals for both performance quality and quality reliability. **Performance quality** refers to the *performance features* of a product. Maytag <www.maytagcorp.com> gets premium prices for its appliances because they are perceived as offering more advanced features and a longer life than competing brands. Through its advertising, the firm has made sure that consumers recognize the Maytag repairman as the world's loneliest service professional.

performance quality The performance features offered by a product

Performance quality may be related to a product's **quality reliability**—the *consistency* of product quality from unit to unit. Toyotas, for example, enjoy high quality reliability—the firm <www.toyota.com> has a reputation for producing very few "lemons." For both goods and services, consistency is achieved by controlling the quality of raw materials, encouraging conscientious work, and keeping equipment in good working order.

quality reliability Consistency of a product's quality from unit to unit

Some products offer both high quality reliability and high performance quality. Kellogg's <www.kelloggs.com> has a reputation for consistently producing cereals made of high-quality ingredients. To achieve any form of high quality, managers must plan for production processes (equipment, methods, worker skills, and materials) that will result in high-quality products.

Organizing for Quality Perhaps most important to the quality concept is the belief that producing high-quality goods and services requires an effort from all parts of the organization. Having a separate "quality control" department is no longer enough. Everyone from the chairperson of the board to the part-time clerk—purchasers, engineers, janitors, marketers, machinists, and other personnel—must work to ensure quality. At Merrill Lynch Credit Corp. <www.ml.com> all employees are responsible for taking initiative and responsibility in responding to customers' credit needs. They are also encouraged to be flexible in helping customers and in the development of their own employee skills. The overall goal is to reduce problems to a minimum by providing credit selectively and skillfully right from the beginning. As a result, the number of loans and market share are increasing while loan delinquencies are decreasing.

Although everyone in a company contributes to product quality, responsibility for specific aspects of total quality management is often assigned to specific departments and jobs. In fact, many companies have quality assurance or quality control departments staffed by quality experts. These people may be called in to help solve quality-related problems in any of the firm's other departments. They keep other departments informed of the latest developments in equipment and methods for maintaining quality. In addition, they monitor all quality control activities to identify areas for improvement.

Directing for Quality Too often, firms fail to take the initiative in making quality happen. Directing for quality means that managers must motivate employees throughout the company to achieve quality goals. Managers companywide must help employees see how they affect quality and how quality affects both their jobs and the company. General Electric chairman John F. Welch has led the changeover to such a quality program by committing more than $1 billion and 3 years of effort to converting all of GE's divisions <www.ge.com>. The new program, says Welch, "has galvanized our company with an intensity the likes of which I have never seen in my 40 years at GE."[9] Welch's willingness to take drastic action to ensure the program's success was a visible display of a quality emphasis that had the added value of raising the quality consciousness of all GE's employees.

Like Welch, leaders must continually find ways to foster a quality orientation by training employees, encouraging involvement, and tying compensation to work quality. Ideally, if managers succeed, employees will ultimately accept **quality ownership:** the idea that quality belongs to each person who creates it while performing a job.

quality ownership
Principle of total quality management that holds that quality belongs to each person who creates it while performing a job

Controlling for Quality By monitoring its products and services, a company can detect mistakes and make corrections. First, however, managers must establish specific quality standards and measurements. For example, the control system for a bank's teller services might use the following procedure. Supervisors periodically observe the tellers' work and evaluate it according to a checklist. Specific aspects of each teller's work—appearance, courtesy, efficiency—are recorded. The results are reviewed with employees and either confirm proper performance or indicate changes needed to bring performance up to standards.

TOOLS FOR TOTAL QUALITY MANAGEMENT

Many companies rely on proven tools to manage quality. Often, ideas for improving both the product and the production process come from **competitive product analysis.** Toshiba might take apart a Xerox copier and test each component. Test results will then help managers decide which Toshiba product features are satisfactory, which features should be upgraded, and which operations processes need improvement.

competitive product analysis
Process by which a company analyzes a competitor's products to identify desirable improvements in its own

In this section, we will survey six of the most commonly used tools for total quality management: *value-added analysis, statistical process control, quality/cost studies, quality improvement teams, benchmarking,* and *getting closer to the customer.*

Value-Added Analysis One effective method of improving quality and productivity is **value-added analysis:** the evaluation of all work activities, material flows, and paperwork to determine the value that they add for customers. Value-added analysis often reveals wasteful or unnecessary activities that can be eliminated without harm to (and may even improve) customer service. When Hewlett-Packard <www.hewlett-packard.com> simplified its contracts and reduced them from 20 pages to as few as two pages for all customers, computer sales rose by more than 18 percent.

value-added analysis
Process of evaluating all work activities, materials flows, and paperwork to determine the value they add for customers

Statistical Process Control Although every company would like complete uniformity in its output, the goal is unattainable: Every business experiences unit-to-unit variations in products and services. Firms can better control product quality by understanding sources of variation. **Statistical process control (SPC)** refers to methods by which employees can gather data and analyze variations in production activities to determine when adjustments are needed. The Glidden Co. <www.icidecorative-paints.com> uses SPC to control paint-making processes more effectively. Litton Precision Gear uses SPC to ensure the quality of transmission gears installed in

statistical process control (SPC)
Methods for gathering data to analyze variations in production activities to see when adjustments are needed

Describe the role played by statistical analysis in keeping operations at an optimum performance level.

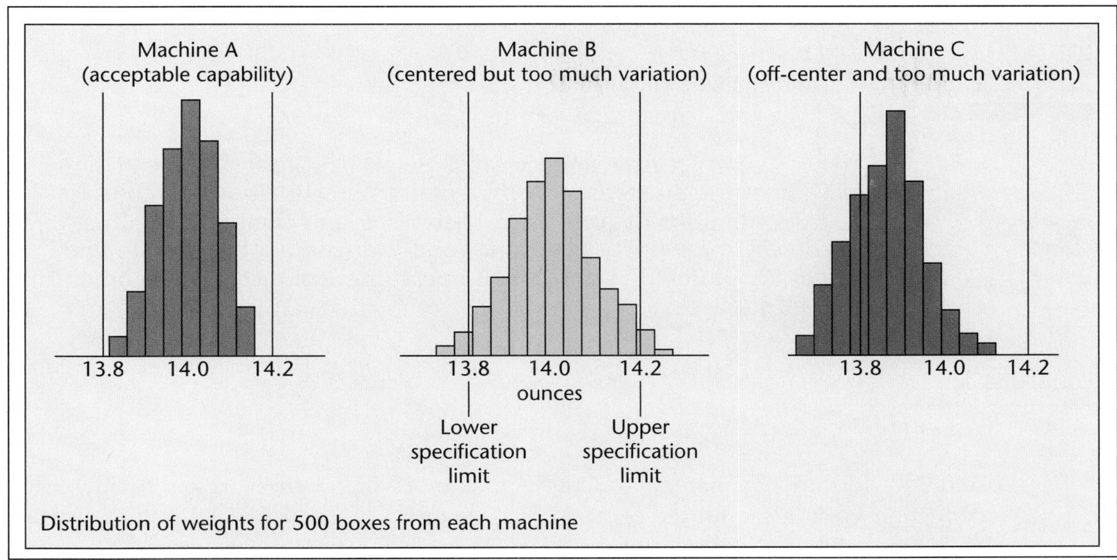

Figure 16.5
Process Variation Study at Honey Nuggets Cereal

military helicopters. At Farbex, a plastics manufacturer, SPC analysts spot-check numerous standards such as the weight of samples of plastic pellets at several different points in the production process. Forty percent of all North American pulp and paper mills use SPC to reduce waste and increase productivity during production. Two of the most common SPC methods are *process variation studies* and *control charts.*

Process Variations Variations in a firm's products arise from the inputs used in the production process. As employees, materials, work methods, and equipment change, so do production outputs (that is, the company's products). These variations are called **process variations.** Although some amount of process variation is inevitable, too much can result in poor quality and excessive operating costs.

process variation
Variation in products arising from changes in production inputs

Consider the box-filling operation for Honey Nuggets, a hypothetical cereal. Each automated machine fills two 14-ounce boxes per second. Even under proper conditions, slight variations in cereal weight from box to box are normal. However, company managers want to know how much variation is occurring. How much is acceptable? Information about variation in a process can be obtained from a process capability study. At the Honey Nuggets factory, boxes are taken from the filling machines and weighed. The results are plotted, as in Figure 16.5, and compared for weight against upper and lower specification limits, which serve as acceptable quality limits. Boxes with over 14.2 ounces are considered wasteful giveaways of the company's product. Boxes with less than 13.8 ounces are also costly, not only because they will anger a lot of buyers but because they are unlawful.

Analyzing the results of the Honey Nuggets capability study, we see that the output from Machine A is acceptable; none of its boxes violates quality limits. Machine A, then, is fully capable of meeting company quality standards. Machines B and C, however, have problems. Neither machine reliably meets Honey Nuggets standards: They are not capable. Our process capability study reveals that unless Machines B and C are renovated, the company will continue to be plagued by substandard production quality.

Electricity provides an example of process variation that causes problems around us every day. Computers and other infotech equipment are vulnerable to both electrical surges and the opposite problem, voltage sags. Although we can't see it, the typical sag is a momentary decrease of voltage that can damage electrical equipment. These and other distortions of electrical flow cause big problems in U.S. offices and factories. One estimate puts the damage as high as $12 billion a year. Power variations (called "soiled" electricity) knocked out the electric furnace in a Tennessee metalworking plant, reducing

WebConnection

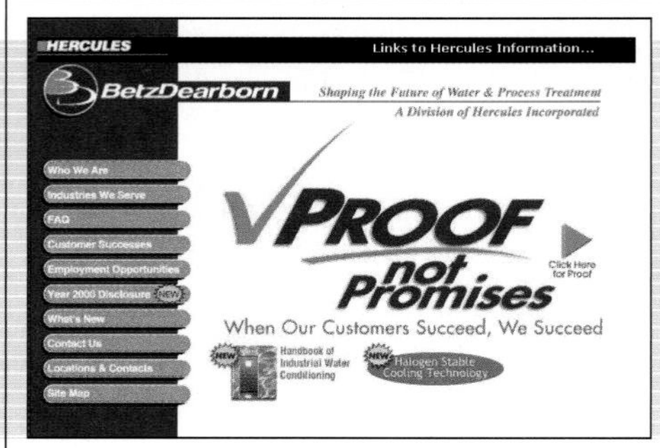

www.betzdearborn.com

Located in Trevose, Pennsylvania, BetzDearborn tests water. Using state-of-the-art statistical process control technology, the company monitors the quality of wastewater and chemicals for customers in the utility, steel, and food-processing industries. To find out about BetzDearborn's B2B operations, contact the firm on its Web site.

$500,000 worth of raw material to scrap. A maker of windows for cars had to shut down production when a sag hit the control panel, resulting in a loss of $2.5 million in windows. One solution is detecting electrical variations before they cause damage. New electronic devices display electric waveforms on easy-to-read screens and warn plant technicians instantaneously when "soiled" electricity flows through. Using detection equipment made by a firm called Cutler-Hammer <www.cutler-hammer.com>, DaimlerChrysler's engine transmission plant <www.daimlerchrysler.com> now displays power quality right along with production data on the PCs that control the production system.[10]

control chart
Process control method that plots test sampling results on a diagram to determine when a process is beginning to depart from normal operating conditions

Control Charts Knowing that a process is capable of meeting quality standards is not enough. Managers must still monitor the production process to prevent it from going astray. To detect the beginning of departures from normal conditions, employees can check production periodically and plot the results on a **control chart.** Three or four times a day a machine operator at Honey Nuggets might weigh several boxes of cereal together to determine the average weight. That average is then plotted on the control chart.

Figure 16.6 shows the control chart for Machine A at the Honey Nuggets plant. As you can see, the first five points are randomly scattered around the center line, indicating that the machine was operating well from 8 A.M. until noon. However, the points for sam-

Figure 16.6
Process Control Chart at Honey Nuggets

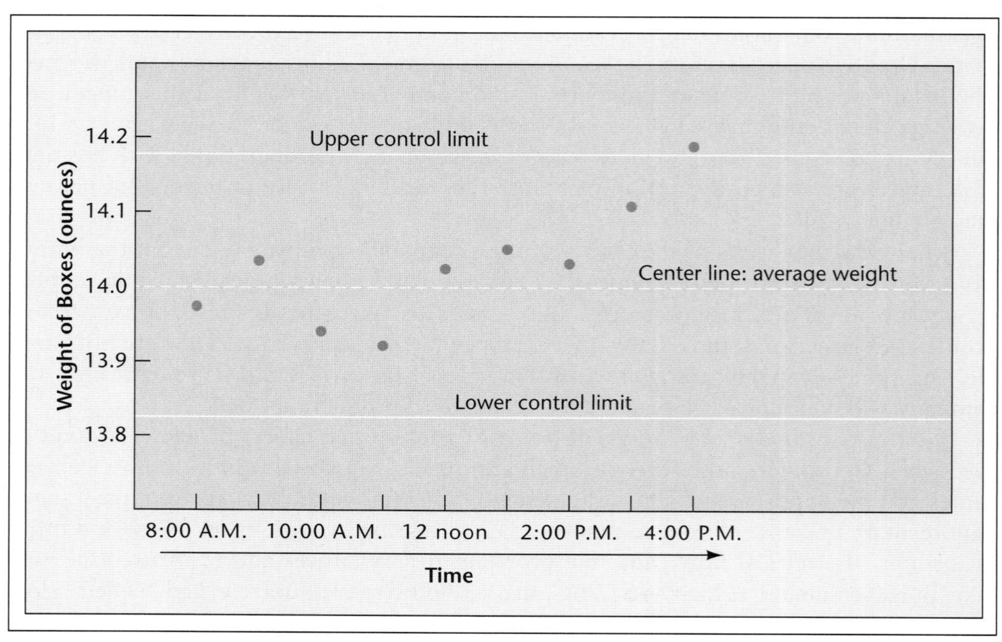

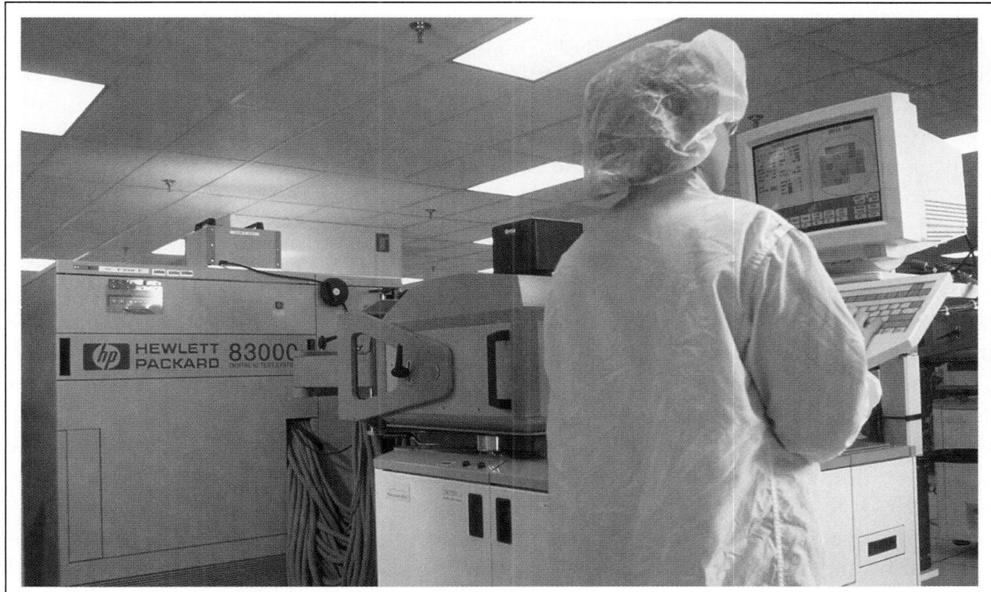

At Hewlett-Packard <www.hp.com>, testing machines use miniscule probes to ensure that the electronic characteristics of every semiconductor are correct. Such systems are designed to check primarily for so-called "class defects"—problems that can affect a whole parade of products on the assembly line. One bad wafer at the end of the line can represent a waste of $10,000 in costs, and its commercial value is $0.00.

ples 5 through 9 are all above the center line, indicating that something caused boxes to overfill. The last point falls outside the upper *control limit,* confirming that the process is out of control. At this point, the machine must be shut down so that an operator can investigate the cause of the problem, be it equipment, people, materials, or work methods. Control is completed when the problem is corrected and the process is restored to normal.

Quality/Cost Studies Statistical process controls help keep operations up to existing capabilities. But in today's competitive environment, firms must consistently raise quality capabilities. However, any improvement in products or production processes means additional costs, whether for new facilities, equipment, training, or other changes. Managers thus face the challenge of identifying the improvements that offer the greatest promise. **Quality/cost studies** are useful because they not only identify a firm's current costs but also reveal areas with the largest cost-savings potential.

quality/cost study
Method of improving quality by identifying current costs and areas with the greatest cost-saving potential

Quality costs are associated with making, finding, repairing, or preventing defective goods and services. All of these costs should be analyzed in a quality/cost study. For example, Honey Nuggets must determine its costs for **internal failures.** These are expenses including the costs of overfilling boxes and the costs of sorting out bad boxes incurred during production and before bad products leave the plant. Studies indicate that many U.S. manufacturers incur costs for internal failures up to 50 percent of total costs.

internal failures
Reducible costs incurred during production and before bad products leave a plant

Despite quality control procedures, however, some bad boxes may get out of the factory, reach the customer, and generate complaints from grocers and consumers. These **external failures** are discovered outside the factory. The costs of correcting them (refunds to customers, transportation costs to return bad boxes to the factory, possible lawsuits, and factory recalls) should also be tabulated in the quality/cost study.

external failures
Reducible costs incurred after defective products have left a plant

The percentage of costs in the different categories varies widely from company to company. Thus, every firm must conduct systematic quality/cost studies to identify the most costly and often the most vital areas of its operations. These areas should be targets for improvement. Too often, however, firms substitute hunches and guesswork for data and analysis.

Quality Improvement Teams In their quest for quality, many U.S. businesses have adopted **quality improvement (QI) teams** (patterned after the Japanese concept of *quality circles*): groups of employees from various work areas who meet regularly to define,

quality improvement (QI) team
TQM tool in which groups of employees work together to improve quality

analyze, and solve common production problems. Their goal is to improve both their own work methods and the products they make.

Many QI teams organize their own efforts, select leaders, and attack problems in the workplace. Motorola <www.motorola.com> sponsors companywide team competitions to emphasize the value of the team approach, to recognize outstanding team performance, and to reaffirm the team's role in the company's continuous-improvement culture. Some 5,000 teams—with names like Irish Risky, Document Doctors, and Green Tray Packers—are evaluated on overall performance, including project selection: The team gets higher marks for selecting projects that are tied closely to Motorola's key initiatives. As to results, one team found ways to increase cellular phone production by 50 percent. Another, with an 85-percent reduction in electronic-circuit defects, saved $1.8 million in one year. The winning team's project saved over $6 million in one year.[11]

One of the greatest benefits of QI teams, in addition to direct cost savings, is their effect on employees' attitudes. Instead of viewing themselves as passive production resources, employees develop a sense of self-worth and quality ownership. In short, the talents and job knowledge of team members, rather than being dormant, are put to use. Although QI teams can improve job satisfaction, they also involve risks. Not all employees want to participate. Moreover, management cannot always adopt group recommendations, no matter how much careful thought, hard work, and enthusiasm went into them. The challenge for management, then, is to make wise decisions about when and how to use quality improvement teams.

benchmarking
Process by which a company implements the best practices from its own past performance and those of other companies to improve its own products

Benchmarking A powerful TQM tool that has been effective for some firms is called **benchmarking:** To improve its own products or its business procedures, a company compares its current performance against its own past performance, or one company finds and implements the best practices of others. With *internal benchmarking,* a firm tracks its own performance over time to evaluate its progress and to set goals for further improvement. As an example, the percentage of customer phone calls with more than two minutes of response time may be 15 percent this month. Compared with past months, the 15 percent may be high or low. In short, past performance is the benchmark for evaluating recent results.

External benchmarking begins with a critical review of competitors (or even companies in other lines of business) to determine which goods or services perform the best; these activities and products are called best practices. Why is one good or service better? Which specific features do customers like? Critical comparisons of the company's own products and procedures with selected benchmarks reveal specific areas where improvement is likely to result in greater competitiveness. L.L. Bean <www.llbean.com>, regularly attracts observers who want to see its world-class methods for processing customer orders so efficiently.

Getting Closer to the Customer As one advocate of quality improvement has put it, "Customers are an economic asset. They're not on the balance sheet, but they should be." One of the themes of this chapter has been that struggling companies have often lost sight of customers as the driving force for all business activity. Perhaps they waste resources designing products that customers do not want. Sometimes they ignore customer reactions to existing products or fail to keep up with changing consumer tastes. By contrast, the most successful businesses keep close to their customers and know what they want in the products they consume.

"Customers are an economic asset. They're not on the balance sheet, but they should be."

—Claess Fornell, Quality improvement advocate

MBNA <www.mbnainternational.com>, a Wilmington, Delaware, credit-card company, has learned that speed of service is vital for serving 4,300 groups with custom Visas and MasterCards, including such groups as the National Education Association and Ringling Brothers. These premium customers want good service and they want it now. MBNA was one of the first in the industry to make service representatives available 24 hours a day. MBNA continually monitors

WebConnection

www.fedex.com/us/careers/working.html

FedEx refers to its policy for satisfying both customers and employees as "PSP," for "People—Service—Profit." The idea is that the customers of a service company deal directly with its employees and that satisfied employees will be more committed to its customers. For other firms, the FedEx PSP is a benchmark in workplace culture. To find out more about PSP, access the FedEx Web site.

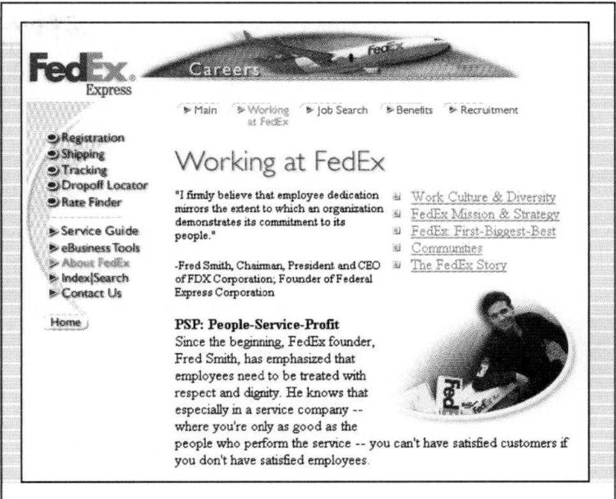

its own performance using 15 measures, many of them relating to speed of service. The phone must be picked up within two rings, incoming calls at the switchboard must be transferred within 21 seconds to the correct party, and customer address changes must be processed in one day. The companywide goal on the 15 standards is 98.5 percent. That means that responses to credit line inquiries will be answered in half an hour 98.5 percent of the time and the phone will be answered within two rings 98.5 percent of the time. Results are posted daily on 60 scoreboards throughout the company. By placing the customer at the head of its organizational culture, MBNA is able to retain a remarkable 98 percent of its profitable customers and its common stock price has increased 600 percent in five years.

TRENDS IN PRODUCTIVITY AND QUALITY MANAGEMENT

Intensified competition has stimulated some new considerations for quality management. Among these are the emergence of international quality standards and the radical redesign of business processes to improve products. A third approach emphasizes the need for quality improvement programs to show monetary benefits.

ISO 9000

Consider the following case in quality control diagnosis and correction. The Du Pont Co.'s <www.dupont.com> Emigsville, Pennsylvania, plant had a problem: A molding press used to make plastic connectors for computers had a 30-percent defect rate. Efforts to solve the problem went nowhere until, as part of a plantwide quality program, press operators were asked to submit detailed written reports describing how they did their jobs. After comparing notes, operators realized that they were incorrectly measuring the temperature of the molding press; as a result, temperature adjustments were often wrong. With the mystery solved, the defect rate dropped to 8 percent.

The quality program that led to this solution is called *ISO 9000*—a certification program attesting to the fact that a factory, a laboratory, or an office has met the rigorous quality management requirements set by the International Organization for Standardization <www.iso.ch>. ISO 9000 (pronounced *ICE-o nine thousand*) originated in Europe as an attempt to standardize materials received from suppliers in such high-technology industries as electronics, chemicals, and aviation. Today, more than 90 countries have adopted ISO 9000 as a national standard. It is being adopted by U.S.–based multinationals such as General Electric, Eastman Kodak, Motorola, and Xerox. In turn, these companies are requiring certification from their own suppliers, including employment agencies. Some 340 suppliers working with GE's plastics division have been told to meet ISO 9000 standards if they want to continue doing business with the company.

Life Cycle of an e-Business

Tapping Into Customer Input

Customer focus was the key to Garden.com's position as one of the country's most promising e-businesses. Naturally, most of the company's 290 employees—including the Development Team (the software developers who kept the Web site operating properly), the Data Team (those who created content for the Web site and ensured that it was accurate and up to date), the technical support staff, and the shipping department—did not interact directly with customers. Even so, their work affected customer quality and satisfaction. At Garden.com, one tool for keeping everyone tuned in to the customer's experience was the "Customer Solutions (CS) Listen-In": Receiving various questions from customers—what products were available, when to plant, how best to use a shady corner of a garden—the CS Team gave expert advice on every aspect of gardening and was accessible to Web site visitors at <www.garden.com>.

The CS team consisted of 80 people, including 20 horticulturists, who were skilled at handling customer inquiries on topics ranging from plant growth to new plant varieties to problematical weather conditions. Interestingly, customer callers were often a rich source of information on the subjects that concerned them. Their responses to Garden.com products and services were also useful, and they could be a fount of information even for employees who thought they were far removed from the world of direct customer interaction. From time to time, therefore, Garden.com held a Listen-In at which employees were encouraged to listen as customers talked with the Solutions Team. A packaging employee was probably surprised to learn that the shelf life of cut flowers could be extended by wrapping the stems with Garden.com's own reusable packaging material. The employee learned not only that customers were concerned about cut-flower shelf life and that certain packaging materials could extend shelf life, but that it was time to update the Web site to spread the news—and thus provide better customer service.

JUST IN TIME FOR SPRING 2000
THURSDAY APRIL 13TH &
THURSDAY APRIL 20TH

guaranteed to inform !

CUSTOMER SOLUTIONS LISTEN-IN

Three times to choose from:

10–11am

2–3pm

4–5pm

Join the Customer Solutions Team for an hour to see how and why we are consistently rated tops in e-commerce customer service.

How do the decisions that you make affect our customers? Your coworkers in CS? This is an excellent opportunity to find the answer to these questions.

get in touch with our customers!

The best reason to join us for the Listen-In? Sometimes it is easy to lose sight of where our customers are coming from. Spend a little time in CS–you may be surprised at what you find!

Our commitment to providing exceptional customer service will continue to set us apart from our competitors, and take us to the top of our industry.

Questions? wendy.clark@garden.com

SPACE IS LIMITED! RESERVE YOUR SEAT TODAY!
SIGN UP AT THE ENTRANCE TO CS!

The Listen-In, therefore, let employees hear firsthand how their activities at the Austin facility could lead to increased customer satisfaction (or dissatisfaction). By listening to customers, employees in all activity areas were better motivated to do their jobs with a view toward customer satisfaction. They got a better idea of what was important to customers, and they got customer-motivated ideas for new services and products. The poster above, which announces an upcoming Listen-In, was posted throughout the Austin facility in early April 2000.

ISO 9000 standards allow firms to demonstrate that they follow documented procedures for testing products, training workers, keeping records, and fixing product defects. To become certified, companies must document the procedures that workers follow during every stage of production. The purpose of ISO 9000, explains the International Division of the U.S. Chamber of Commerce <www.uschamber.com>, is to ensure that a manufacturer's product is exactly the same today as it was yesterday and as it will be tomorrow. The goal of standardization is to guarantee that goods will be produced at the same level of quality even if all the employees were replaced by a new set of workers.

Companies seeking ISO 9000 certification are audited by an elite group of quality system registrars. Not surprisingly, the certification process is time-consuming and costly: It can take up to 18 months for a manufacturing plant employing 300 workers and cost up to $200,000.

Why do companies put themselves through this ordeal? For one thing, an ISO 9000 certificate has become the passkey to doing business in Western Europe. Explains Richard Thompson, general manager of Caterpillar's <www.cat.com> engine division, whose Mossville, Illinois, plant was one of the first U.S. diesel engine factories to win certification: "Today, having ISO 9000 is a competitive advantage. Tomorrow, it will be the ante to the global poker game." Today, more and more U.S. companies are jumping on the ISO 9000 bandwagon. Currently, about 10,000 ISO 9000 certificates have been issued in the United States, compared with 53,000 in Great Britain. In total, some 128,000 certificates have been issued in 99 countries.

"Today, having ISO 9000 is a competitive advantage. Tomorrow, it will be the ante to the global poker game."

—Richard Thompson, General manager of Caterpillar's engine division

Process Reengineering

Every business consists of processes—activities that it performs regularly and routinely in conducting business. Examples abound: receiving and storing materials from suppliers, billing patients for medical treatment, processing insurance claims for auto accidents, inspecting property for termite infestation, opening checking accounts for new customers, filling customer orders from Internet sales. In each instance, any business process can add value and customer satisfaction if performed well. By the same token, it can disappoint customers and irritate business partners if done improperly.

Business process reengineering focuses on improving both the productivity and quality of business processes—rethinking each step of an organization's operations by starting from scratch. *Reengineering* can be defined as the fundamental rethinking and radical redesign of business processes to achieve dramatic improvements in measures of performance, such as cost, quality, service, and speed. The calling-services company GTE <www.gte.com> found that its over-the-phone service was not very user friendly for customers who wanted to make different kinds of transactions, such as getting a service problem corrected or getting a billing question answered. To give customers fast, accurate "one-stop" service, GTE reengineered its call-in–service process by improving equipment, retraining employees, and connecting software into corporate databases that were formerly inaccessible.

business process reengineering
Quality improvement process that entails rethinking an organization's approach to productivity and quality

The Reengineering Process Figure 16.7 shows the six steps involved in the reengineering process. The process starts with a statement justifying the proposed reengineering based on benefits envisioned for customers and the company. The company's vision statement is a key resource for step one; it provides guidance, as does management's awareness of the competition's capabilities. The process then flows logically through the next five steps:

- Identify the business activity that will be changed.
- Evaluate information and human resources to see if they can meet the requirements for change.
- Diagnose the current process to identify its strengths and weaknesses.
- Create the new process design.
- Implement the new design.

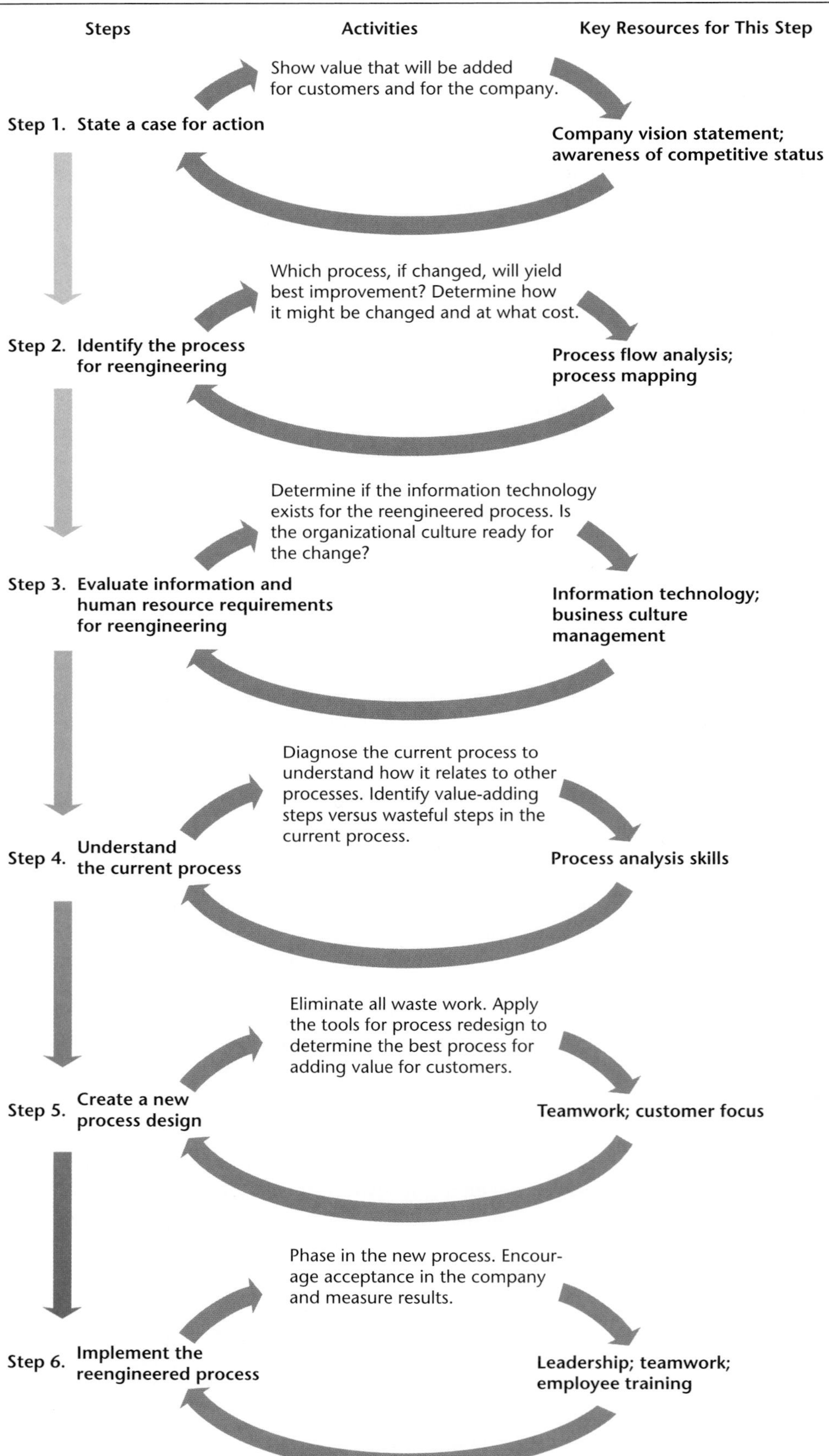

Steps
Activities
Key Resources for This Step
Step 1. State a case for action
Show value that will be added for customers and for the company.
Company vision statement; awareness of competitive status
Step 2. Identify the process for reengineering
Which process, if changed, will yield best improvement? Determine how it might be changed and at what cost.
Process flow analysis; process mapping
Step 3. Evaluate information and human resource requirements for reengineering
Determine if the information technology exists for the reengineered process. Is the organizational culture ready for the change?
Information technology; business culture management
Step 4. Understand the current process
Diagnose the current process to understand how it relates to other processes. Identify value-adding steps versus wasteful steps in the current process.
Process analysis skills
Step 5. Create a new process design
Eliminate all waste work. Apply the tools for process redesign to determine the best process for adding value for customers.
Teamwork; customer focus
Step 6. Implement the reengineered process
Phase in the new process. Encourage acceptance in the company and measure results.
Leadership; teamwork; employee training

Figure 16.7
Steps in Reengineering Process

Key resources in each step are essential for performing the activities required by that stage. Reengineering is a broad undertaking that requires know-how in technical matters, depends on leadership and management skills, and must be based on knowledge about what customers want and how well their needs are being met by the company and its competition.

The bottom line in every reengineering process is redesigning systems to better serve the needs of customers and to adopt a customer-first value system throughout the company. Redesign is dominated by a desire to improve operations so that goods and services are produced at the lowest possible cost and at the highest value for the customer.

PRODUCTIVITY AND QUALITY AS COMPETITIVE TOOLS

A company's ability to compete by improving productivity and quality depends on participation by all parts of the firm. Total firm involvement stems from having company-wide strategies that we consider in this section: the company's willingness to invest in innovation, its long-run perspective on its goals, its concern for the quality of work life, and the streamlining of its service operations.

Investing in Innovation and Technology

Many U.S. firms that have continued to invest in innovative technology have enjoyed rising productivity and rising incomes. For example, while Steinway & Sons piano factory <www.steinway.com> is just as concerned as ever about maintaining the highest quality

It's a WiredWorld

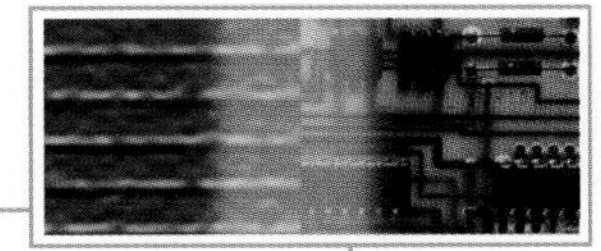

• *Selling the Idea of Culture Shift*

When a firm decides to trade in its traditional operations for high-tech processes, there's more involved than just financial and technical considerations. Consider a company with successful sales procedures established long before today's electronic-sales processes were available. What problems does it face in moving from its established (and highly personalized) sales process into the realm of Internet sales?

That's the issue at Mercury Marine <www.mercurymarine.com>, the market leader in recreational boat engines. With various choices of engine types, horsepower ratings, and "salt water" versus "blue water" options, Mercury sells about 400 different outboard engines and enjoys a 40-percent share of the U.S. market. Sales are even better for inboard engines and stern drives, where Mercury's market share is over 70 percent. Mercury's $1.4 billion annual sales are vital to its parent company, Brunswick Corp. <www.brunswickcorp.com>.

Mercury's markets consist of two kinds of customers:

1. Outboard motors are sold mainly to distributors and boat dealers, who resell them.
2. Inboard engines and stern drives are sold to boatbuilders.

In addition to its current person-to-person selling process, Mercury wants to sell motors to outboard dealers and boatbuilders over the Internet. Mercury wants to use technology as a competitive weapon by making it easier for customers to do business with Mercury. Internet access can increase sales productivity and promote better service quality for customers. So what's the problem? Resistance from the sales department. With person-to-person sales, Mercury's salespeople get to know the customers, and *up-selling* and *cross-selling* are important sales tools that would be threatened by the changeover. Currently, salespeople can explain to customers the advantages of upgrading to a more expensive motor (up-selling), thus increasing Mercury's sales revenues. They can also talk customers into buying some of Mercury's complementary products (cross-selling), such as propellers, inflatable boats, and other accessories, all of which increase sales revenues. Admits Geof Storm, Mercury's chief information officer: "There are a lot of culture changes involved when tightening the supply chain." Although the sales department still prefers the more personal touch, some of its resistance is being overcome—Mercury has decided to proceed with Internet sales of inboard engines to boatbuilders. But until the climate changes further, the decision to sell outboards on the Internet is likely to remain on hold.

"That's settled, then. We'll lower our standards to meet the competition."

in their products, they're using newer technology to help the woodworkers do their jobs more efficiently and precisely. "It still takes us a year to craft one of these things," says Steinway president Bruce Stevens, "but technology is assisting us in making more precise parts that our people can assemble. It's helping us create a better instrument."[12]

Increasingly, the Internet and information technology investments are rising, with new applications in every major industry, including transportation, retailing, insurance, banking, health care, and manufacturing. GE expects its turbine engine productivity to rise because the company's technology allows customers to use the Internet to compare the performance of its various turbine models before they buy. Sana Bank Corp. expects operational productivity to increase 20 percent in one year because it now uses data-mining to direct the best customer service to its most profitable clients. At the Weyerhauser Co. door factory in Marshfield, Wisconsin, Internet technology was used to increase financial performance. The system was used to cut out the plant's least-valuable customers, thus reducing the customer roster in half, but it also permitted the firm to double the order volumes for efficient delivery to remaining customers.[13]

Similarly, innovative product technologies are creating changes in electricity distribution services. For example, in most big cities the major cost of delivering electricity, one-third to one-half of your bill, is in the distribution lines that bring the electricity to your house. The cost of delivering by underground wires is eight times higher than sending it on wires and poles above ground. One way to avoid expensive distribution charges is with a microturbine: a refrigerator-size generator that businesses can install to make their own electricity. A generator offered by AlliedSignal <www.honeywell.com>, the jet engine and auto parts company, can provide enough electricity for a small business and pay for itself ($15,000) in two years. These lower energy costs result in higher energy productivity for office buildings, apartments, restaurants, and other businesses that adopt the new electricity-generating technology.

continuous improvement An ongoing commitment to improving products and processes in the pursuit of ever-increasing customer satisfaction

Adopting a Long-Run Perspective

Many quality-oriented firms are committed to long-term efforts at **continuous improvement:** the ongoing commitment to improving products and processes, step by step, in pursuit of ever-increasing customer satisfaction. Motorola is a good example of a company that emphasizes continuous, long-run improvement. Its Six-Sigma program called

Steinway & Sons <www.steinway.com> *of New York City still builds the same number of pianos that it did 100 years ago. Basically, the manufacturing process also remains the same. Now, however, technicians use programmable logical controllers (PLCs) to control the kilns that dry raw lumber (85 percent of a Steinway is wood), condition hand-formed rims, and replace manually operated machines. PLCs also perform some design functions and even aid in the stringing of pianos.*

for the unheard-of target of having only three defects per million parts; for all practical purposes this would be zero defects. In 1981, Motorola started by adopting a five-year goal of a 90-percent reduction of errors. In 1986, it extended that goal to 99 percent by 1992. During just five years, the defect rate dropped from 6,000 defects per million to just 40 by 1992. When, by 1996, Six Sigma quality had been achieved, Motorola began planning for errors per *billion* rather than errors per million quality levels. As of 1999, the company had reduced errors to an unimaginable two defects per billion parts.[14]

Emphasizing Quality of Work Life

The products and services of businesses represent such a large part of total national output that the well-being and participation of their workers is central to improving national productivity. How can firms make their employees' jobs more challenging and interesting? Many companies are enhancing workers' physical and mental health through recreational facilities, counseling services, and other programs. In addition, more firms have started programs to empower and train employees.

Is it better for a company to promote competition among workers to increase productivity, or does teamwork seem to generate better results?

Employee Empowerment Many firms are replacing the environments of yesterday, based on the principle of management-directed mass production, with worker-oriented environments that foster loyalty, teamwork, and commitment. Trident Precision Manufacturing <www.tridentprecision.com> has a program for full employee involvement. Over 95 percent of employee recommendations for process improvements have been accepted since the program started. As a result, employee turnover has fallen from 41 percent to less than 5 percent. Sales per employee more than doubled.

Firms using this approach have found success in the concept of **employee empowerment:** the principle that all employees are valuable contributors to a business and should be entrusted with certain decisions regarding their work. The Hampton Inns motel chain <www.hampton-inn.com> initiated a program of refunds to customers who were dissatisfied with their stays for any reason. Managers were pleased, and the refund policy created far more additional business than it cost. A surprise bonus was the increased morale when employees—everyone from front-desk personnel to maids—were empowered to

employee empowerment
Concept that all employees are valuable contributors to a firm's business and should be entrusted with decisions regarding their work

grant refunds. With greater participation and job satisfaction, employee turnover was reduced to less than one-half its previous level. Such confidence in employee involvement contrasts sharply with the traditional belief that managers are the primary source of decision making and problem solving.

Employee Training For employee involvement to be effective, it must be implemented with preparation and intelligence. Training is one of the proven methods for avoiding judgments and actions that can lead to impaired performance. In a recent survey, for example, insufficient training is the most common barrier reported by work teams. The study reconfirms the belief that training is a key to implementing a successful quality management program. At Heath Tecna Aerospace Co. <www.wilbur.com/aeros> team members are taught how to work in groups, as well as trained in job skills, work flow planning, and basic knowledge about the company's markets and operations. With increased training and experience, the rate of material waste has diminished and product quality has increased.

Improving the Service Sector

As important as employee attitude is to goods production, it is even more crucial to service production, where employees often are the service. Although the U.S. service sector has grown rapidly (far more rapidly than the service sectors of other nations), this growth has often been accompanied by high levels of inefficiency. Many newly created service jobs have not been streamlined. Whereas some companies, such as UPS and Federal Express, operate effectively, many others are so inefficient that they drag down overall U.S. productivity. As new companies enter these markets, increased competition is giving service providers a better understanding of how to operate more productively by emphasizing service quality.

In trying to offer more satisfactory services, many companies have discovered five criteria that customers use to judge service quality:[15]

- *Reliability* Perform the service as promised, both accurately and on time.
- *Responsiveness* Be willing to help customers promptly.
- *Assurance* Maintain knowledgeable and courteous employees who will earn the trust and confidence of customers.
- *Empathy* Provide caring, individualized attention.
- *Tangibles* Maintain a pleasing appearance among personnel and in materials and facilities.

Among the 1,600 customers surveyed in one recent study, reliability was mentioned most often as the essence of good service. In the performance of many services, however, these criteria are difficult to separate. Consider two seemingly different service products: window designs from Andersen Windows and swimsuit designs offered by Software Sportswear. What they share in common is designs that are created by customers using interactive computers at the retailer's showroom. Using this tool, the salesperson at Andersen <www.andersencorp.com> helps customers choose the features and shapes that please them. After the computer checks the window design for structural soundness, it gives a price quote. Then the computer transmits the order to the factory for production.

Software Sportswear makes custom swimsuits with the aid of a computerized video camera. With the customer's profile displayed on a computer screen, a variety of styles are superimposed on the monitor. The digital display shows the customer's image clothed in each of hundreds of individually tailored designs. The patterns can then be stored for future use with new designs for each customer. These services certainly provide empathy (individualized attention and care). Moreover, by using the customer's recipe for a custom product, both companies are prepared to provide both reliability and responsiveness in future transactions with each customer.

Continued from page 439

Got a Problem with Your Peripheral? Ask Dudley

Dell's success stems in no small way from its strong customer orientation: Knowing what customers want and helping them feel comfortable while visiting a Web site that has been designed to provide customers with services they really need increases customer loyalty. Originally, the Dell site was intended to be a reference for technical information. But by the beginning of 2000, the 7-year-old site had emerged as a multifaceted source of customer assistance. Whether individual consumers or large firms with thousands of computers, customers can ask questions, exchange messages with technicians, and chat online with each other. Each Dell product, for example, has a unique service code. When a customer calls in for help, a customer rep accesses Dell's database for a specific code number. With that number, the rep can look at every detail of the customer's system and provide tailor-made advice.

Another feature is an information database called "Ask Dudley," which customers can search when they have technical questions. "Ask Dudley" was developed after a series of focus-group studies on the ways customers actually search the Dell site. Dell found that customers don't mind spending several minutes searching the site—as long as they can ask a few questions. They do not, however, like to spend hours searching for something. Dudley allows users to ask natural-language questions, searches through mounds of technical content supplied by experienced Dell technicians (and based, in turn, on questions received by the technicians in past years). Finally, Dudley sends a response. Currently, Dudley handles about 150,000 questions a week.

Yet another feature to be found at <www.dell.com> is "Dell Talk"—a chat room in which more than 200,000 registered customers can post messages. Postings are not just social messages. Several Dell owners have banded together as a problem-solving group to help other Dell owners. For customer-to-technician assistance, the site receives more than 25,000 messages each week, to which it sends professional responses via e-mail.

In addition to quality, Dell also wants high productivity in providing customer assistance. Responses for the customer-to-technician service are now answered within 24 hours. The current goal is to get the staff up to the point at which responses are issued within 12 hours. As technology continues to improve, self-help and automated services, such as Ask Dudley, will further reduce the need for human assistance on tech-support phone calls. Technicians will then be able to spend their time solving the most complex customer problems.

Questions for Discussion

1. Why do you suppose lower inventory levels can cause productivity to increase?
2. Explain how product redesign and product simplification can improve productivity. How might they improve quality at Dell?
3. How do its relationships with suppliers affect Dell's quality?
4. Explain how Dell's service productivity would be affected if "Ask Dudley" were replaced by live customer-response personnel.
5. List some of the methods that Dell uses to "keep close" to its customers.

SUMMARY OF LEARNING OBJECTIVES

1 **Describe the connection between *productivity* and *quality*.** *Productivity* is a measure of economic performance: It compares how much is produced with the resources used to produce it. *Quality* is a product's fitness for use. However, an emphasis solely on productivity or solely on quality is not enough. Profitable competition in today's business world demands high levels of both productivity and quality.

2 **Explain the decline and recovery in U.S. productivity that has occurred over the last 25 or 30 years.** Although the United States is the most productive country in the world, by the early 1970s other nations had begun catching up with U.S. productivity. In particular, the U.S. *growth rate of productivity* slowed from about 1979 into the early 1990s. Moreover, even though U.S. manufacturing productivity is increasing, the service sector is bringing down overall productivity growth. Because services now account for 60 percent of national income, productivity in this area must improve. Finally, certain industries and companies remain less productive than others.

On the other hand, in the years just before 1994, U.S. firms began regaining significant market share in such industries as airplanes, computers, construction equipment, and transistors. Abandoning a long-standing focus on lower wage rates in other countries, U.S. companies focused instead on revitalizing productivity by becoming more customer oriented. In addition, quality improvement practices were widely implemented. Recovery has resulted from a recognition of the connection among customers, quality, productivity, and profits.

3 **Identify the activities involved in *total quality management* and describe six tools that companies can use to achieve it.** *Total quality management (TQM)* is the planning, organizing, directing, and controlling of all the activities needed to get high-quality goods and services into the marketplace. Managers must set goals for and implement the processes needed to achieve high quality and reliability levels. *Value-added analysis* evaluates all work activities, materials flows, and paperwork to determine what value they add for customers. *Statistical process control methods,* such as *process variation studies* and *control charts,* can help keep quality consistently high. *Quality/cost studies,* which identify potential savings, can help firms improve quality. *Quality improvement teams* also can improve operations by more fully involving employees in decision making. *Benchmarking*—studying the firm's own performance and the best practices of other companies to gather information for improving a company's own goods and services—has become an increasingly common TQM tool. Finally, *getting closer to the customer* provides a better understanding of what customers want so that firms can satisfy them more effectively.

4 **Identify two trends in productivity and quality management and discuss three ways in which companies can compete by improving productivity and quality.** Recent trends include *ISO 9000,* a certification program (originating in Europe) attesting that an organization has met certain international quality management standards. *Business process reengineering* involves the fundamental redesign of business operations in the interest of gaining improvements in quality, cost, and service. The reengineering process consists of six steps, starting with the company's vision statement and ending with the implementation of the reengineered process.

Productivity and quality can be competitive tools only if firms attend to all aspects of their operations. To increase quality and productivity, businesses must invest in innovation and technology. They must also adopt a long-run perspective for continuous improvement. In addition, they should realize that placing greater emphasis on the quality of work life can also help firms compete. Satisfied, motivated employees are especially important in increasing productivity in the fast-growing service sector.

QUESTIONS AND EXERCISES

Questions for Review

1. What is the relationship between productivity and quality?
2. Why do labor unions care about the productivity of an industry?
3. What activities are involved in total quality management?
4. What is the purpose of ISO 9000?
5. What are the essential steps in process reengineering?

Questions for Analysis

6. How would you suggest that benchmarking be used to increase productivity in the service sector?
7. Why is employee empowerment essential to successful quality improvement teams?
8. Why is high productivity in the service sector so difficult to achieve?

Application Exercises

9. Using a local company as an example, show how you would conduct a quality/cost study. Identify the cost categories and give some examples of the costs in each category. Which categories do you expect to have the highest and lowest costs? Why?
10. Select a company of interest to you and consider the suggestions for competing that are detailed in this chapter. Which of these suggestions apply to this company? What additional suggestions would you make to help this company improve its overall quality and productivity?

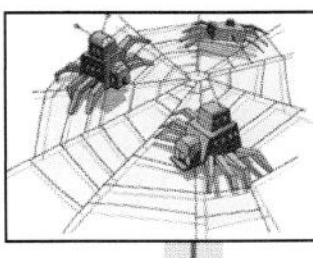

EXPLORING THE WEB

BECOMING ACCULTURATED TO QUALITY

At a time when rigorous competition has driven many U.S. companies out of the electronics products business, Motorola has maintained its position as one of the industry's most successful firms. To learn more about Motorola's leadership in quality and the role played by quality assurance in a world-class company, log on to the Motorola Web site at

www.motorola.com

First browse the homepage. Then click on "About Motorola" (at the top of the page). Next, click on Motorola University and explore the items on that page to gain a perspective on the scope of Motorola's offerings. Finally, consider the following questions:

1. Describe the types of quality-related services offered by Motorola University. Which of the quality topics at Motorola University are also topics that are discussed here in Chapter 16 of the textbook?
2. On the **Motorola University** page, select "Site Navigator" (at top of page). Then go to "Keyword Search" and enter the word *quality* in the search engine. The result is a listing of "Briefings," "Courses," and "Books"; examine the contents in each listing and describe the kinds of quality issues that are covered.
3. This company is famous for its "six-sigma" quality program. To find out more about six sigma, start at **Motorola University** page, then in the left column menu click on "Six Sigma Black Belt." Describe Motorola's results from using six sigma. How do they measure those results?
4. For further information on six-sigma services, start again on the **Motorola University** page. Go to "Keyword Search" and enter the words *six sigma* in the search engine. The result is a listing of "Courses," including CIC 501: Motorola Vision and Application. Examine the contents of this course and describe the various topics in it. Are any of those topics included in Chapter 16 of this textbook? How important is quality at Motorola?
5. Continuing in the list of courses for six-sigma quality, select three or more courses and examine their content. Do you think that some of these courses (topics) are more essential to a good foundation for quality than others? Explain why or why not. Which course(s) sound most interesting to you? Why?
6. While exploring the **Motorola University** page be sure to examine the "Frequently Asked Questions (FAQ)" selection, then respond to the following question: Why do you suppose Motorola qualifies as an expert on quality?

BUILDING YOUR BUSINESS SKILLS

MAKING YOUR BENCHMARK IN THE BUSINESS WORLD

This exercise enhances the following SCANS workplace competencies: demonstrating basic skills, demonstrating thinking skills, exhibiting interpersonal skills, and working with information.

GOAL

To encourage students to understand ways in which benchmarking can improve quality and productivity.

SITUATION

As the director of maintenance for a regional airline, you are disturbed to learn that the cost of maintaining your 100-plane fleet is skyrocketing. A major factor is repair time: When maintenance or repairs are required, work often proceeds slowly. As a result, additional aircraft are required to meet the schedule. To address the problem, you decide to use a powerful total quality management tool called benchmarking: You will approach your problem by studying ways in which other companies have successfully managed similar problems. Your goal is to apply the best practices to your own maintenance and repair operation.

METHOD

Step 1

Working with three or four other students, choose your benchmarking target from among the following choices:

- The maintenance and repair operations of a competing airline
- The pit crew operations of an Indianapolis 500 race car team
- The maintenance and repair operations of a nationwide trucking company

Write a memo explaining the reasons for your choice.

Step 2

Write a list of benchmarking questions that will help you learn the best practices of your targeted company. Your goal is to ask questions that will help you improve your own operation. These questions will be asked during on-site visits.

Step 3

As part of a benchmarking project, you will be dealing with your counterparts in other companies. You have a responsibility to prepare for these encounters, and you must remember that what you learn during the exchange process is privileged information. Given these requirements, describe the steps that you would take before your first on-site visit and outline your benchmarking code of ethics.

FOLLOW-UP QUESTIONS

1. Why is benchmarking an important method for improving quality?
2. Why did you make your benchmarking choice? Explain why the company you selected holds more promise than other companies in helping you solve your internal maintenance problems.
3. What kind of information would help you improve the efficiency of your operations? Are you interested in management information, technical information, or both?
4. In an age of heightened competition, why do you think companies are willing to benchmark with each other?

CRAFTING YOUR BUSINESS PLAN

ENSURING STRUCTURAL INTEGRITY

THE PURPOSE OF THE ASSIGNMENT

1. To acquaint students with the process of navigating the *Business PlanPro* (*BPP*) software package (Version 4.0).
2. To familiarize students with the ways in which quality considerations enter into the business planning framework in *BPP.*
3. To stimulate students' thinking about applying the textbook's information on quality improvement and quality management to the preparation of their business plan in *BPP.*

ASSIGNMENT

After reading Chapter 16 in the textbook, open the BPP *software* and look around for information about managing and implementing quality at a sample firm:* StructurAll *(StructurAll Ltd.). Then respond to the following questions:*

1. Who are StructurAll's customers? What do you suppose these customers expect regarding quality of the services they receive from StructurAll? What aspects of quality are important to them? [Sites to see in *BPP* (for this assignment): In the Plan Outline screen, click on **1.0 Executive Summary.** Then, click on each of the following in turn: **1.2 Mission, 1.3 Keys to Success, 3.1 Service Description, 3.2 Competitive Comparison, 4.0 Market Analysis Summary, 4.1 Market segmentation,** and **5.1 Marketing Strategy.**]
2. What role does quality play in StructurAll's business strategy? [Sites to see in *BPP:* In the Plan Outline screen, click on each of the following in turn: **1.2 Mission** and **1.3 Keys to Success.** After returning to the Plan Outline screen, click on **3.2 Competitive Comparison.**]
3. What are some specific dimensions of quality in the services offered by StructurAll? [Sites to see in *BPP:* In the Plan Outline screen, click on **1.0 Executive Summary.** Then, click on each of the following in turn: **3.1 Service Description** and **3.2 Competitive Comparison.**]
4. What are some procedures, methods, and policies StructurAll uses to ensure quality? [In the Plan Outline screen, click on each of the following, in turn: **3.1 Service Description, 3.4 Fulfillment, 3.5 Technology, 3.6 Future Services,** and **5.1 Competitive Edge.**]
5. Can you find any evidence that StructurAll's management has experience in managing for quality? [Sites to see in *BPP:* In the Plan Outline screen, click on each of **6.1 Management Team** and **6.3 Management Team Gaps.**]

FOR YOUR OWN BUSINESS PLAN

6. Consider the planning for quality that would be appropriate in the company for which you are developing the business plan. How are you determining the specific performance items that your customers consider most important in the goods and services that you will be delivering to them? For each performance item, what measurements will you use in your quality evaluations? How do you plan to set quality goals to include in your company's business plan? In how much detail will you cover each of these aspects in the write-up of your plan?

*GENERAL TIPS FOR NAVIGATING IN *BPP*

1. Open the *BPP* program, examine the Welcome screen, and click on **Open a Sample Plan.**
2. From the **Open a Sample Plan** dialogue box, click on a sample company name; then click on **Open.**
3. On the Plan Manager screen, click on **Your Plan Outline**; then click on any of the lines (for example, **5.1.1 Pricing Strategy**).

4. You can always return to the Plan Outline screen by going to the bottom of the screen and clicking on the **Plan Outline** icon.
5. After finishing with one sample company, you can get to the next one by going to the top of the screen and clicking on **File** (on the menu bar). Then beneath that, select **Open Sample Plan.** This will exit you from the current company file and take you to the **Open Sample Plan** dialogue box, where you can select your next sample company.
6. When you are finished, you can close the program by going to the top of the screen and clicking on **File** (on the bar menu). Then beneath that, select **Exit.**

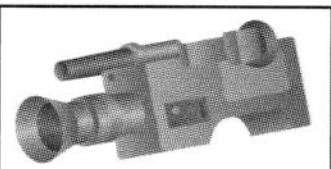

VIDEO EXERCISE

MAKING ROOM FOR QUALITY: MARRIOTT

Learning Objectives

The purpose of this video exercise is to help you

1. Understand the quality issues faced by a firm in a service industry.
2. Understand the connection between quality and productivity.
3. Recognize the different ways in which customers define *quality.*

BACKGROUND INFORMATION

In 1927, 26-year-old J. Willard Marriott and his new bride Allie opened a nine-seat root beer stand in Washington, D.C. With the addition and acquisition over the years of food-service management, airline catering, and restaurant and hotel businesses, Marriott's company grew to its present size. Today Marriott International, Inc. is a leading worldwide hospitality company with over 2,000 operating units in the United States and 57 other countries and territories. Marriott Lodging operates and franchises hotels under the Marriott, Renaissance, Residence Inn, Courtyard, TownePlace Suites, Fairfield Inn, SpringHill Suites, and Ramada International brand names and also operates the Ritz-Carlton Hotel Company, LLC. The company is headquartered in Washington, D.C., and has approximately 145,000 employees.

THE VIDEO

This segment illustrates several of the ways in which Marriott managers pursue world-class quality in the hospitality business. We learn how the company stresses training and benchmarking to establish quality criteria, and we also see how an unusual partnership with office furniture maker Steelcase, Inc. has helped Marriott achieve a new level of quality by adapting to customers' changing needs.

DISCUSSION QUESTIONS

1. How do you think the concept that "everyone in the organization works for the customer" has made a difference in service quality at Marriott?
2. Checkout time has been reduced at Marriott by allowing front-desk personnel to work with customers without the distraction of the telephone. Do you think this approach to productivity has any drawbacks?
3. How does Marriott's partnership with Steelcase represent an improvement in quality? What particular aspects of The Room That Works seem particularly representative of Marriott's concept of quality?

FOLLOW-UP ASSIGNMENT

Guests can now request The Room That Works at dozens of Marriott facilities at no extra charge. How do you think the corporation has absorbed the cost of adding this improvement in services?

What returns might Marriott expect from its latest quality innovation?

FOR FURTHER EXPLORATION

See a complete description of The Room That Works on the Marriott Web page at <marriotthotels.com/roomthatworks/>. What other kinds of customized rooms do you think a hotel chain could consider offering? Choose a customer group with specific demographic characteristics (handicapped travelers, families with very small children, travelers with pets, those with allergies or special dietary requirements, etc.) and draw up a plan for specialized hotel accommodations for this market. Consider every aspect of the travel experience that could serve as a quality criteria for the customer and account for each aspect in your plan.

Chapter 17

Managing Information Systems and Communication Technology

After reading this chapter, you should be able to:

1. ***Explain*** why businesses must manage *information* and show how computer systems and communication technologies have revolutionized *information management.*
2. ***Identify*** and briefly describe three elements of *data communication networks*—the Internet, the World Wide Web, and intranets.
3. ***Describe*** five *new options for organizational design* that have emerged from the rapid growth of information technologies.
4. ***Discuss*** different information-system *applications programs* that are available for users at various organizational levels.
5. ***Identify*** and briefly describe the *main elements of an information system.*

"Life, the Universe, and Everything"

Why does a boss want information on such varied topics as the anatomy of dragonflies, juvenile crime, and Japanese irises instead of just standard reports on department budgets and sales figures? And if gathering these eclectic tidbits is high on the agenda, how does a firm use its "knowledge workers" to build a networked information system for getting it? Consider the information system at Highsmith, Inc. of Fort Atkinson, Wisconsin. With more than 25,000 products, Highsmith is the country's largest mail-order supplier of equipment (book displays, audio-visual equipment), furniture, and supplies (educational software) for libraries and schools. Because its mission focuses on libraries and learning, it may come as no surprise that a central resource in Highsmith's information system is its corporate library.

President and CEO Duncan Highsmith believes that external events—even some that seem remote and unrelated to the business—can create threats and opportunities for companies. He believes that if employees are focused only on internal operations, they won't see the bigger picture, so he encourages a more eclectic approach of information gathering from a broad range of sources. New cultural trends and political forces eventually change the way a society thinks and lives, and Highsmith doesn't want to get caught short when they do: He wants to foresee changes that can reshape the social environment, and he wants to be prepared in advance rather than forced to react after the fact. Clues might emerge from unexpected and seemingly unrelated sources ranging from *Popular Mechanics* to *South Park* to a UN health report. The job of his company's library is to fuel information brainstorming.

Highsmith is also convinced that if the right data is assembled in the right way, information gleaned from a variety of sources—from seemingly eclectic sources—is the only way to get a clear picture of things to come. He believes that, with access to the right information, his people can not only anticipate changes but can turn them to the company's advantage. However, he does not believe that focusing on the future comes naturally to most people. "We tend to behave as though the future will be like the present," he says. "Only bigger and faster." That approach, he contends, doesn't work when you need to make strategic-level decisions.

"We tend to behave as though the future will be like the present. Only bigger."

—CEO Duncan Highsmith of Highsmith Inc.

To promote greater linkages with events in the external world, Highsmith launched an information–stimulation program called "Life, the Universe, and Everything"—a weekly closed-door, free-association session in which he and company librarian Lisa Guedea Carreño scan every available information source, from radio to software to newspapers to the Web. They're looking for trends. They search the world for clues to events that might reshape the world around them. Why Guedea Carreño? "The right information," says Highsmith, "can help create strategic choices for a business." An information system, therefore, has to provide more than just sales reports, internally generated cost-control documents, and spreadsheets. For external information gathering, Guedea Carreño is a premier knowledge worker with a knack for gleaning nonquantitative information and collating it with seemingly unrelated resources in different formats. Somehow, she can detect the trends and relationships that emerge as she collates seemingly unrelated information.

As for Guedea Carreño, she believes that being in a small company is an advantage for a professional information provider: She can be more effective in providing value for coworkers if she knows their needs, what they do, and the kinds of problems they deal with. Highsmith sees enormous value in his information–stimulation project, but he also believes that it should go beyond the top-management level. He wants to broaden participation to include other employees. He wants to generate an interest in the long-term development of the business instead of merely its routine operations.

Our opening story continues on page 494

As the Highsmith experience illustrates, information systems and communication networks can have a dramatic effect on the firm's culture and its performance. As an asset that managers rely on for decision making and problem solving, the information system requires a commitment of resources to establish, maintain, and upgrade as new technologies emerge. In addition to human resources, including knowledge workers such as librarian Lisa Guedea Carreño, information networks rely on electronic technologies for retrieving and assimilating information from sources inside the company and from external sources around the world. Computer systems, electronic devices, supporting software, and access to the Internet are all integrated in networked information systems.

INFORMATION MANAGEMENT: AN OVERVIEW

Today's businesses rely on information management in ways that we could not foresee as recently as just a decade ago. Managers now turn to digital technology as an integral part of organizational resources and as a means of conducting everyday business. Every major firm's business activities—designing services, ensuring product delivery and cash flow, evaluating personnel, and creating advertising—are linked to information systems. Thus the management of information systems is a core business activity that can no longer be delegated to technical personnel.

information managers
Managers responsible for designing and implementing systems to gather, organize, and distribute information

information management
Internal operations for arranging a firm's information resources to support business performance and outcomes

In addition, most businesses regard their information as a private resource—an asset that they plan, develop, and protect. It is not surprising that companies have **information managers,** just as they have production, marketing, and finance managers. **Information management** is an internal operation that arranges the firm's information resources to support business performance and outcomes. Consider, for example, Chaparral Steel <www.chaparralsteel.com>—a high-performance steel mill that produces structural products from recycled steel. Chaparral's performance—customer service, delivery times, sales, profits, and customer loyalty—has been boosted by an information system that gives customers electronic access to the steel products that are currently available in Chaparral's inventories. The technology that allows customers to shop electronically through its storage yards gives Chaparral greater agility, and because it can respond more rapidly than its competitors, it gets more sales. Modern communications permit businesses to receive up-to-the-minute information from remote plants, branches, and sales offices.

To find the information that they need to make critical decisions, managers must often sift through a virtual avalanche of reports, memos, magazines, and phone calls. Thus the question that faces so many businesses today: How can they get useful information to the right people at the right time? In this section, we will explore the ways in which companies manage information with computers and related information technologies. First, however, in order to understand information management, you must understand what information is and what it is not. Only then can you appreciate what computers do and how they do it.

Data versus Information

data
Raw facts and figures

information
Meaningful, useful interpretation of data

Although businesspeople often complain that they get too much information, what they usually mean is that they get too many data. **Data** are raw facts and figures. **Information** is the useful interpretation of data.

For example, consider the following data:

- Last year, casino gambling was available in 37 states in the United States.
- Eighty-five percent of Americans live within a three-hour drive of a casino.
- In the past five years, visitor growth, especially among wealthy Asian gamblers, has been flat.

- In the last four years, Las Vegas has added $10 billion to its gaming capacity.
- Since Congress passed the 1988 Indian Gaming Regulation Act, some 24 states offer some form of Native American casino gambling.

If all these data were put together in a meaningful way, they might produce information about what sells gaming and, in particular, whether entertainment companies should construct new hotels and casinos to meet increasing demand. The challenge for businesses, then, is to turn a flood of data into manageable information.

Information Systems

One response to this challenge has been the growth of the **information system (IS):** a system for transforming data into information and transmitting it for use in decision making. Those charged with running a company's IS must first determine what information will be needed. Then they must gather the data and provide the technology to convert data into desired information. They must also control the flow of information so that it goes only to people who need it.

information system (IS) System for transforming raw data into information that can be used in decision making

Information supplied to employees and managers varies according to such factors as the functional areas in which they work (for example, accounting or marketing) and the levels of management they occupy. The quality of the information transmitted to all levels depends increasingly on an organization's technological resources and on the people who manage it. In this section, we discuss the evolution of the technology that processes information and then describe the information requirements in today's organization.

NEW BUSINESS TECHNOLOGIES IN THE INFORMATION AGE

Employees at every level in the organization, ranging from operational specialists to the top executive, use information systems to improve performance. Information systems assist in scheduling day-to-day vehicle trips, evaluating prospective employees, and formulating the firm's business strategy. The widening role of IS results from rapid developments in electronic technologies that allow faster and broader flows of information and communications. As we shall see, however, the networked enterprise is more than a firm equipped with the latest technology. Technology has inspired new organizational designs, innovative relationships with other organizations, and new management processes for improved competitiveness.

The Expanding Scope of Information Systems

The relationship between information systems and organizations is among the fastest-changing aspects of business today. At one time, IS applications were narrow in scope and technically focused—processing payroll data, simulating new engineering designs, compiling advertising expenditures. But as you can see in Figure 17.1, managers soon began using IS systems not merely to solve technical problems, but to analyze management problems, especially for control purposes—applying quality-control standards to production, comparing costs against budgeted amounts, keeping records on employee absences and turnover.

How is the implementation of information technology changing your business environment?

Today, information systems are also crucial in planning. Managers routinely use the IS to decide on a firm's products and markets for the next 5 to 10 years. The same database that helps marketing analyze demographics for millions of customers is also used for such higher-level applications as financial planning, managing materials flows, and setting up electronic funds transfers with suppliers and customers around the globe.

Another basic change in organizations is an increased interdependence between a company's business strategy and its IS. Today, the choice of a business strategy—to be the low-cost provider or the most flexible provider or the high-quality provider—requires an

Figure 17.1
Evolution of IS Scope

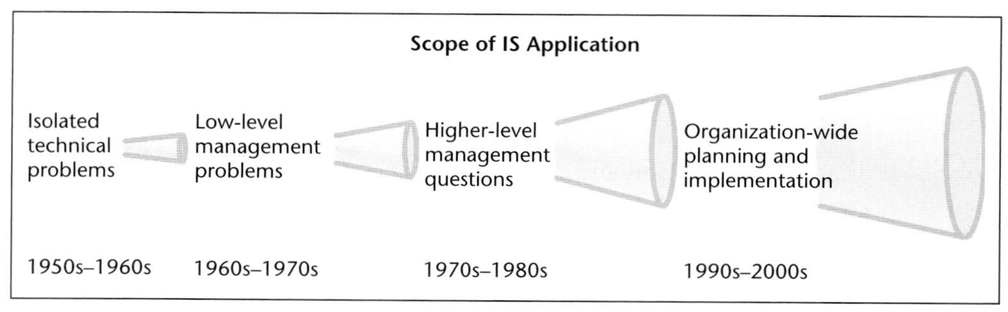

information system that can support that strategy. As Figure 17.2 shows, a given strategy will fail if a system's software, hardware, and other components are not integrated to support it. Consider a strategy that calls for the rapid receipt of customer orders and fast order fulfillment. Unless the system's components are specifically designed to handle these tasks, the best-laid plans are probably doomed to failure.

Electronic Business and Communications Technologies

The pressures to maintain better communications and information systems are increasing as competition intensifies and as organizations expand into global and e-business operations. Firms like Ralston Purina Co. <www.ralston.com> need instantaneous communications among managers in those countries in which they either sell products or buy raw materials, including China, Colombia, Canada, and Brazil. The needs of such companies are being met by new electronic information technologies and more advanced data communication networks.

electronic information technologies (EIT)
Information-systems applications, based on telecommunications technologies, that use networks of appliances or devices to communicate information by electronic means

Electronic Information Technologies **Electronic information technologies (EIT)** are IS applications based on telecommunications technologies. EITs use networks of appliances or devices (such as cell phones and computers) to communicate information by electronic means. EITs enhance the performance and productivity of general business activities by performing two functions:

1. Providing coordination and communication within the firm
2. Speeding up transactions with other firms

In this section, we will survey six of the most widely used innovations in today's digital business systems: *fax machines, voice mail, e-mail, electronic conferencing, groupware,* and *digital information services.*

fax machine
Machine that can transmit copies of documents (text and graphics) over telephone lines

Fax Machines The **fax machine** (short for *facsimile machine*) can transmit and receive digitized images of text documents, drawings, and photographs over telephone lines in a matter of seconds, thus permitting written communication over long distances. Fax machines are popular with both large and small firms because of speed and low cost.

Figure 17.2
Aligning Business Strategy and the IS

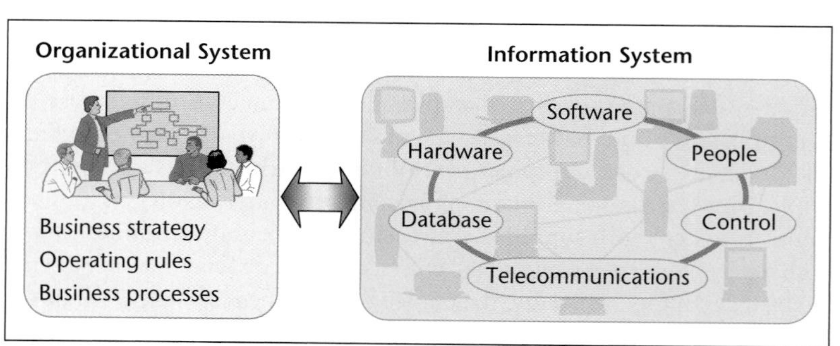

Voice Mail **Voice mail** refers to a computer-based system for receiving and delivering incoming telephone calls. Incoming calls are never missed because a voice responds to the caller, invites a message, and stores it for later retrieval. A company with voice mail networks each employee's phone for receiving, storing, and forwarding calls.

voice mail
Computer-based system for receiving and delivering incoming telephone calls

E-Mail An **electronic mail** (or **e-mail**) system electronically transmits letters, reports, and other information between computers, whether in the same building or in another country. It is also used for voice transmission and for sending graphics and videos from one computer to another. E-mail thus substitutes for the flood of paper and telephone calls that threatens to engulf many offices.

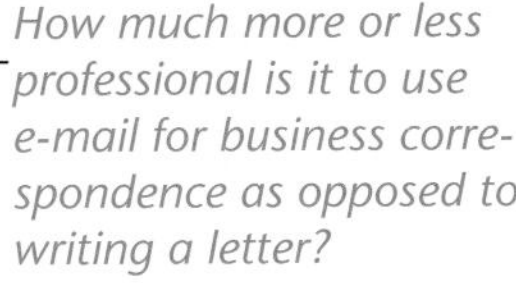

How much more or less professional is it to use e-mail for business correspondence as opposed to writing a letter?

electronic mail (e-mail)
Computer system that electronically transmits letters, reports, and other information between computers

Electronic Conferencing **Electronic conferencing** is becoming increasingly popular because it eliminates travel and thus saves money. Teleconferencing allows groups of people to communicate simultaneously from various locations via electronic mail or via telephone. One form of electronic conferencing, *dataconferencing,* allows people in remote locations to work simultaneously on the same document. Working as a team, they can modify part of a database, revise a marketing plan, or draft a press release. Another form of electronic conferencing, *videoconferencing,* allows participants to see one another on a video screen while the teleconference is in progress.

electronic conferencing
Computer-based system that allows people to communicate simultaneously from different locations via software or telephone

Groupware Collaborative work by teams and other groups is facilitated by **groupware:** software that connects members of the group for e-mail distribution, electronic meetings, message-storing, appointments and schedules, and group writing. Linked by groupware, they can work together on their own desktop computers even if they are remotely located. Groupware is especially useful when members work together regularly and rely on intensive information sharing. Groupware products include Lotus Development Corp.'s Lotus Notes <www.lotus.com/home.nsf/welcome/lotusnotes>, and Netscape Communicator <home.netscape.com/communicator/v4.5/index.html>.

groupware
Software that connects members of a group for shared e-mail distribution, electronic meetings, appointments, and group writing

Digital Information Services Information from outside a company can be linked to its electronic network and the information made available at every workstation. Commercial electronic information services provide online information for both special-purpose and general topics. Lexis <www.lexis-nexis.com> is specifically a source for legal-research information. In contrast, America Online <www.aol.com> offers a variety of business information as well as general-interest information.

Data Communication Networks

Popular on both home and business information systems are public and private **data communication networks:** global networks that carry streams of digital data (electronic messages, documents, and other forms of video and sound) back and forth quickly and economically on telecommunication systems. The most prominent network, the Internet, and its companion system, the World Wide Web, have emerged as powerful communication technologies. Let's look a little more closely at each of these networks.

data communication network
Global network (such as the Internet) that permits users to send electronic messages and information quickly and economically

The Internet The **Internet** (or "the Net," for short)—the largest public data communications network—is a gigantic system of networks serving millions of computers offering information on business, science, and government and providing communication flows among more than 170,000 separate networks around the world. Originally commissioned by the Pentagon <www.defenselink.mil> as a communication tool for use during war, the Internet allows personal computers in virtually any location to be linked together. Because it can transmit information fast and at low cost—lower than long-distance phone service, postal delivery, and overnight delivery—the Net has also become the most important e-mail system in the world. For thousands of businesses, therefore, the Net has joined—and is even replacing—the telephone, fax machine, and express mail as a standard means of communication.

Internet
Global data communication network serving millions of computers with information on a wide array of topics and providing communication flows among certain private networks

Although individuals cannot connect directly to the Internet, for small monthly usage fees they can subscribe to the Net via an **Internet service provider (ISP)**, such as

Internet service provider (ISP)
Commercial firm that maintains a permanent connection to the Net and sells temporary connections to subscribers

Prodigy <www.prodigy.com>, America Online, or Earthlink <www.earthlink.com>. An ISP is a commercial firm that maintains a permanent connection to the Net and sells temporary connections to subscribers.[1]

In 2000, more than 302 million Net users were active on links connecting more than 180 countries. In the United States, alone, more than 50 million users were on the Net every day. Its power to change the way business is conducted has been amply demonstrated in both large and small firms. Digital Equipment Corp. <www.compaq.com/enterprise> is a heavy Internet user: With more than 31,000 computers connected to the network, DEC's monthly e-mail volume has passed the one-million message mark. DEC also linked its Alpha AXP high-speed business computer to the Internet so that potential buyers and software developers could spend time using and evaluating it. Almost instantly, 2,500 computer users in 27 countries used the Net to explore the Alpha AXP.

World Wide Web
Subsystem of computers providing access to the Internet and offering multimedia and linking capabilities

The World Wide Web Thanks to the **World Wide Web** (WWW, or simply "the Web"), the Internet is easy to use and allows users around the world to communicate electronically with little effort. The World Wide Web is a system with universally accepted standards for storing, retrieving, formatting, and displaying information.[2] It provides the "common language" that enables us to "surf" the Net and makes the Internet available to a general audience, rather than merely to technical users, such as computer programmers. To access a Web site, for example, the user must specify the *Uniform Resource Locator (URL)* that points to the resource's unique address on the Web. Thus TWA's URL is <www.twa.com>—a designation that specifies the storage location of TWA's Web pages.

Web server
Dedicated workstation customized for managing, maintaining, and supporting Web sites

browser
Software supporting the graphics and linking capabilities necessary to navigate the World Wide Web

Servers and Browsers Each Web site opens with a *homepage*—a screen display that welcomes the visitor with a greeting that may include graphics, sound, and visual enhancements introducing the user to the site. Additional *pages* give details on the sponsor's products and explain how to contact help in using the site. Often, they furnish URLs for related Web sites that the user can link into by simply pointing and clicking. The person who is responsible for maintaining an organization's Web site is usually called a *Webmaster.* Large Web sites use dedicated workstations—large computers—known as **Web servers** that are customized for managing, maintaining, and supporting Web sites.

With hundreds of thousands of new Web pages appearing each day, cyberspace is now serving up billions of pages of publicly accessible information. Sorting through this maze would be frustrating and inefficient without access to a Web **browser**—the software that enables the user to access information on the Web. A browser runs on the user's PC and supports the graphics and linking capabilities needed to navigate the Web. Netscape Navigator <home.netscape.com/browsers/index.html> has enjoyed as much as an 80-percent market share, although its dominance is now being challenged by other browsers, including its own Netscape Communicator and Microsoft Corp.'s Internet Explorer <www.microsoft.com/windows/ie>.

WebConnection

www.candycommerce.com

The name pretty much tells the story: CandyCommerce.com is the B2B marketplace of the confection industry. Among other pages, the Web site includes an "Auction House" at which sellers can list products for sale and a "Product Showcase" that allows members to shop the organization's listing of online confectionery-supplier catalogs. You can visit the National Confectioners Association Web site for more information.

Directories and Search Engines The Web browser offers additional tools—Web site directories and search engines—for navigating on the Web. Among the most successful cyberspace enterprises are companies, such as Yahoo! <www.yahoo.com>, that maintain free-to-use *directories* of Web content. When Yahoo! is notified about new Web sites, it classifies them in its directory. The user enters one or two key words (for example, "compact disk") and the directory responds by retrieving from the directory a list of Web sites with titles containing those words.

In contrast to a directory, a **search engine** will search cyberspace's millions of Web pages without preclassifying them into a directory. It searches for Web pages that contain the same words as the user's search terms. Then it displays addresses for those that come closest to matching, then the next-closest, and so on. A search engine, such as AltaVista <www.altavista.com> or Lycos <www.lycos.com>, may respond to more than 10 million inquiries per day. It is thus no surprise that both directories and search engines are packed with paid ads.[3]

search engine
Tool that searches Web pages containing the user's search terms and then displays that match in certain degrees

Intranets The success of the Internet has led some companies to extend the Net's technology internally, for browsing internal Web sites containing information throughout the firm. These private networks, or **intranets,** are accessible only to employees via entry through electronic **firewalls**—hardware and software security systems that are not accessible to outsiders.[4] At Compaq Computer Corp. <www.compaq.com>, the intranet allows employees to shuffle their retirement savings among various investment funds. The Ford Motor Co. <www.ford.com> intranet connects 120,000 workstations in Asia, Europe, and the United States to thousands of Ford Web sites containing private information on Ford activities in production, engineering, distribution, and marketing. Sharing such information has helped reduce the lead time for getting models into production from 36 to 24 months. The savings to Ford will be billions of dollars in inventory and fixed costs.[5]

intranet
Private network of internal Web sites and other sources of information available to a company's employees

firewall
Software and hardware system that prevents outsiders from accessing a company's internal network

Extranets Sometimes firms allow outsiders access to their intranets. These so-called **extranets** allow outsiders limited access to a firm's internal information system. The most common application allows buyers to enter the seller's system to see which products are available for sale and delivery, thus providing product-availability information quickly to outside buyers. Industrial suppliers, too, are often linked into their customers' intranets so that they can see planned production schedules and ready supplies as needed for customers' upcoming operations.

extranet
Intranet allowing outsiders access to a firm's internal information system

New Options for Organizational Design: The Networked Enterprise

The rapid growth of information technologies has changed the very structure of business organizations. We begin this section with a discussion of changes wrought by technology in the workforce and organizational structures of many organizations. We then examine ways in which electronic networks are contributing to greater flexibility in dealing with customers. After discussing the growing importance of collaboration in the workplace, we look at the ways in which information networks can help make the workplace independent of a company's physical location. Finally, we describe new management processes inspired by the availability of electronic networks.

Leaner Organizations Information networks are leading to leaner companies with fewer employees and simpler organizational structures. Because today's networked firm can maintain information linkages among both employees and customers, more work can be accomplished with fewer people. As a bank customer, for example, you can dial into a 24-hour information system and find out your current balance from a digital voice. You no longer need tellers or phone operators. In the industrial sector, assembly workers at an IBM plant used to receive instructions from supervisors or special staff. Now instructions are delivered electronically to their workstations.

Widespread reductions in middle-management positions and the shrinkage of layers in organizational structure are possible because information networks now provide direct

Figure 17.3
Networking for Mass-Customization

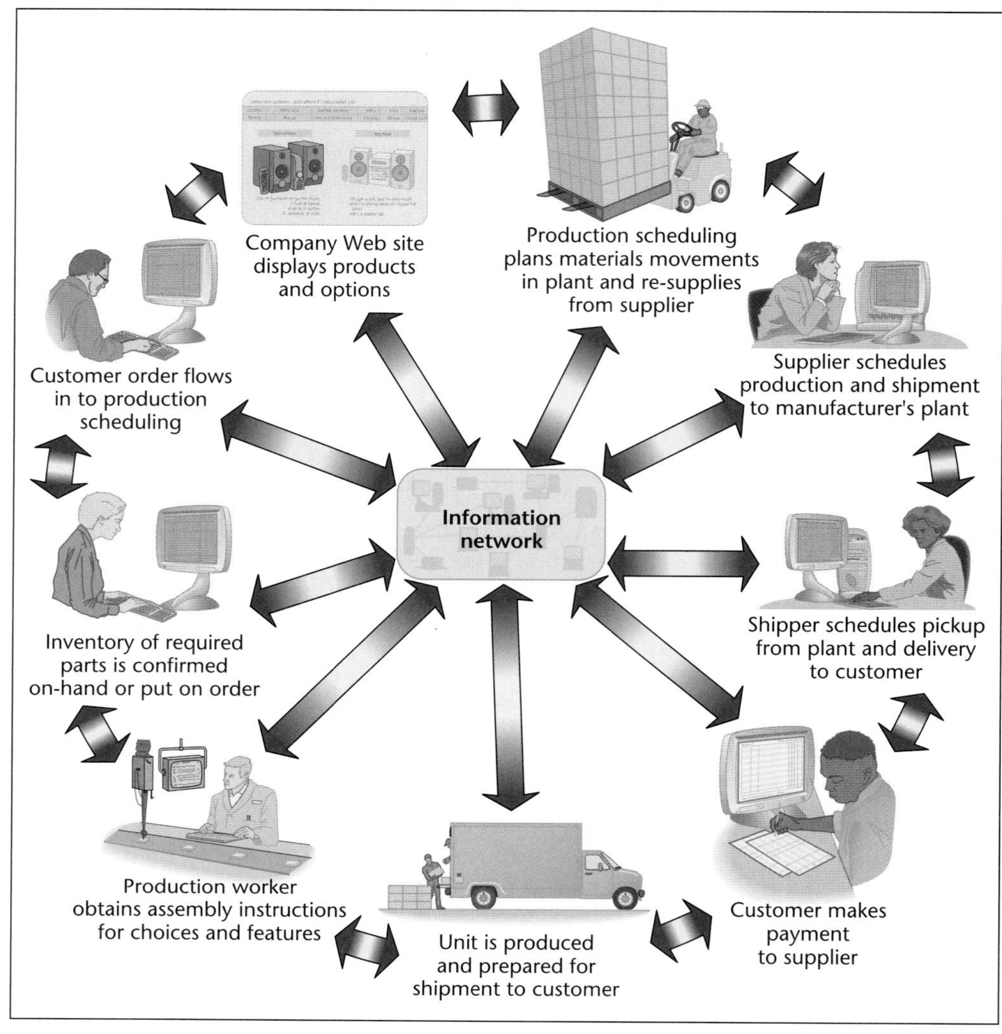
Company Web site displays products and options
Production scheduling plans materials movements in plant and re-supplies from supplier
Customer order flows in to production scheduling
Supplier schedules production and shipment to manufacturer's plant
Information network
Inventory of required parts is confirmed on-hand or put on order
Shipper schedules pickup from plant and delivery to customer
Production worker obtains assembly instructions for choices and features
Unit is produced and prepared for shipment to customer
Customer makes payment to supplier

communications between the top managers and workers at lower levels. The operating managers who formerly communicated company policies, procedures, or work instructions to lower-level employees are being replaced by electronic information networks.

More Flexible Operations Electronic networks allow businesses to offer customers greater variety and faster delivery cycles. Recovery after heart surgery is expedited by custom-tailored rehabilitation programs designed with integrated information systems: Each personalized program integrates the patient's history with information from physicians and rehabilitation specialists and then matches the patient with an electronically monitored exercise regimen. Products such as cellular phones, PCs, and audio systems can be custom-ordered, too, with your choice of features and options and next-day delivery. The principle is called **mass-customization:** Although companies produce in large volumes, each unit features the unique variations and options that the customer prefers. As you can see in Figure 17.3, flexible production and fast delivery depend on an integrated network to coordinate all the transactions, activities, and process flows necessary to make quick adjustments in the production process. The ability to organize and store massive volumes of information is crucial, as are the electronic linkages between customers, manufacturer, materials suppliers, and shippers.

mass-customization
Flexible production process that generates customized products in high volumes at low cost

Increased Collaboration Collaboration, not only among internal units but with outside firms as well, is on the rise because networked systems make it cheaper and easier to

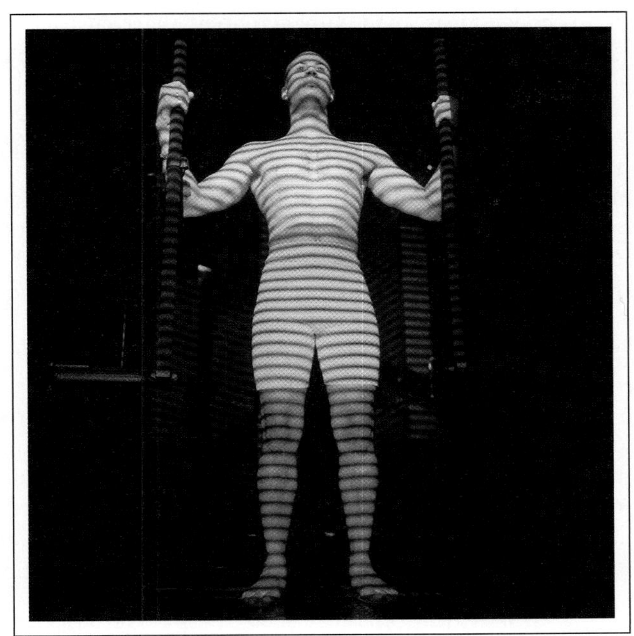

Thanks to networking technology, customers can give manufacturers information that manufacturers can feed into production systems at relatively little cost. The result is so-called mass customization. *At Levi Strauss & Co.* <www.levistrauss.com>, *new technologies can take an apparel buyer's body measurements and transfer the information, via the Web, to a manufacturing plant. There, the data is fed into equally advanced machines designed to handle one-of-a-kind items on an assembly line.*

contact everyone, whether other employees or outside organizations. Aided by intranets, more companies are learning that complex problems can be solved better by means of collaboration, either in formal teams or through spontaneous interaction. In the new networked organization, decisions that were once the domain of individuals are now shared among people and departments. The design of new products, for example, was once an engineering responsibility. Now, in contrast, it can be a shared responsibility because so much information is accessible for evaluation from various perspectives: Marketing, finance, production, engineering, and purchasing can share their different stores of information and determine a best overall design.

Networked systems are also helpful in furthering collaboration between companies: the so-called *virtual company* has become possible through networking. As we saw in Chapter 6, a virtual company can be a temporary team assembled by a single organization. But a virtual company can also be created when several firms join forces. Each contributes different skills and resources that, collectively, result in a competitive business that would not be feasible for any of the collaborators acting alone. A company with marketing and promotional skills, for example, may team up with firms that are experts in warehousing and distribution, engineering, and production. Networking allows collaborators

WebConnection

www.acumins.com

Because "a one-size-fits-all vitamin can't supply you with optimal nutrition," Acumins will customize the precise blend of vitamins, minerals, and herbs that each customer wants. To find out how the process works—and how the Net is essential to businesses in the world of mass-customization—log on to the Acumins Web site.

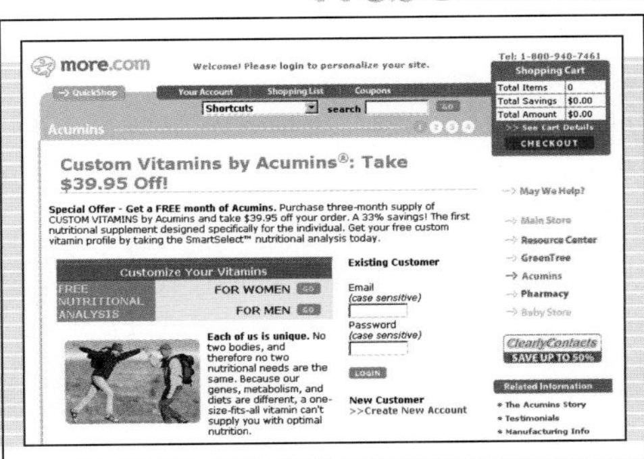

to exchange ideas, plan daily activities, share customer information, and otherwise coordinate their efforts, even if their respective facilities are far apart.

Greater Independence of Company and Workplace Geographic separation of the workplace from the company headquarters is more common than ever because of networked organizations. Employees no longer work only at the office or the factory, nor are all of a company's operations performed at one location. The sales manager for an advertising agency may visit the company office in New York only once every two weeks, preferring instead to work over the firm's electronic network from a home office in Florida. A medical researcher for the Cleveland Clinic may work at a home office networked into the clinic's system.

A company's activities may also be geographically scattered but highly coordinated thanks to a networked system. Many e-businesses, for example, conduct no activities at one centralized location. When you order products from an Internet storefront—say, a chair, a sofa, a table, and two lamps—the chair may come from a cooperating warehouse in Philadelphia and the lamps from a manufacturer in California, while the sofa and table may be direct-shipped from two manufacturers in North Carolina. All these activities are launched instantaneously by the customer's order and coordinated through the network, just as if all of them were being processed at one location.

Improved Management Processes Networked systems have changed the very nature of the management process. The activities, methods, and procedures of today's manager differ significantly from those that were common just a few years ago. At one time, upper-level managers did not concern themselves with all the detailed information that filtered upward in the workplace. Why? Because it was expensive to gather and slow in coming and quickly became out of date. Workplace management was delegated to middle and first-line managers.

With networked systems, however, instantaneous information is accessible in a convenient usable format. Consequently, more upper managers use it routinely for planning, leading, directing, and controlling operations. Today, a top manager can find out the current status of any customer order, inspect productivity statistics for each workstation, and analyze the delivery performance of any driver and vehicle. More importantly, managers can better coordinate companywide performance. They can identify departments that are working well together and those that are creating bottlenecks. The networked system at Hershey <www.hersheys.com> includes SAP—an enterprise-resource-planning model—that identifies the current status of any order and traces its progress from order entry on through customer delivery and receipt of payment. Progress and delays at intermediate stages—materials ordering, inventory availability, production scheduling, packaging, warehousing, distribution—can be checked continuously to determine which operations should be more closely coordinated with others to improve overall performance.

TYPES OF INFORMATION SYSTEMS

In a sense, the phrase "information system" may be a misnomer: It suggests that there is one system when, in fact, a firm's employees will have different interests, job responsibilities, and decision-making requirements. One information system cannot accommodate such a variety of information requirements. Instead, "the information system" is a complex of several information systems that share information while serving different levels of the organization, different departments, or different operations.

User Groups and System Requirements

knowledge workers Employees who use information and knowledge as raw materials and who rely on information technology to design new products or business systems

Four user groups, each with different system requirements, are identified in Figure 17.4, which also indicates the kinds of systems best suited to each user level. Among users we include the **knowledge worker**—the employee whose job involves the use of information and knowledge as the raw materials of their work. Knowledge workers are specialists,

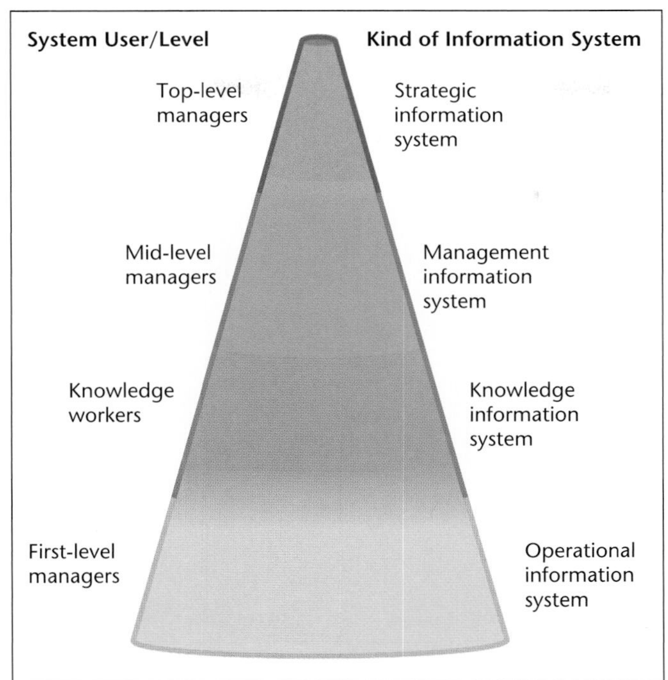

Figure 17.4
Matching Information Users and Systems

usually professionally trained and certified—engineers, scientists, information technology specialists, psychologists—who rely on information technology to design new products or create new business processes.

Managers at Different Levels Because they work on different kinds of problems, top managers, middle managers, knowledge workers, and first-line managers have different information needs. First-line (or operational) managers need information to oversee the day-to-day details of their departments or projects. Knowledge workers need special information for conducting technical projects. Meanwhile, middle managers need summaries and analyses for setting intermediate and long-range goals for the departments or projects under their supervision. Finally, top management analyzes broader trends in the economy, the business environment, and overall company performance in order to conduct long-range planning for the entire organization.

Consider the various information needs for a flooring manufacturer. Sales managers (first-level managers) supervise salespeople, assign territories to the sales force, and handle customer service and delivery problems. They need current information on the sales and delivery of products: lists of incoming customer orders and daily delivery schedules to customers in their territories. Regional managers (middle managers) set sales quotas for each sales manager, prepare budgets, and plan staffing needs for the upcoming year. They need information on monthly sales by product and region. Knowledge workers developing new flooring materials need information on the chemical properties of adhesives and compression strengths for floor structures. Finally, top managers need both external and internal information. Internally, they use sales data summarized by product, customer type, and geographic region, along with comparisons to previous years. Equally important is external information on consumer behavior patterns, the competition's performance, and economic forecasts.

Functional Areas and Business Processes Each business *function*—marketing, human resources, accounting, production, finance—has its own information requirements. In addition, as we saw in Chapter 7, many businesses are organized according to various business processes, and these process groups also need special information. Each of these user groups and departments is represented by an information system. When we

Figure 17.5

Matching User Levels with Functional Areas and Business Processes

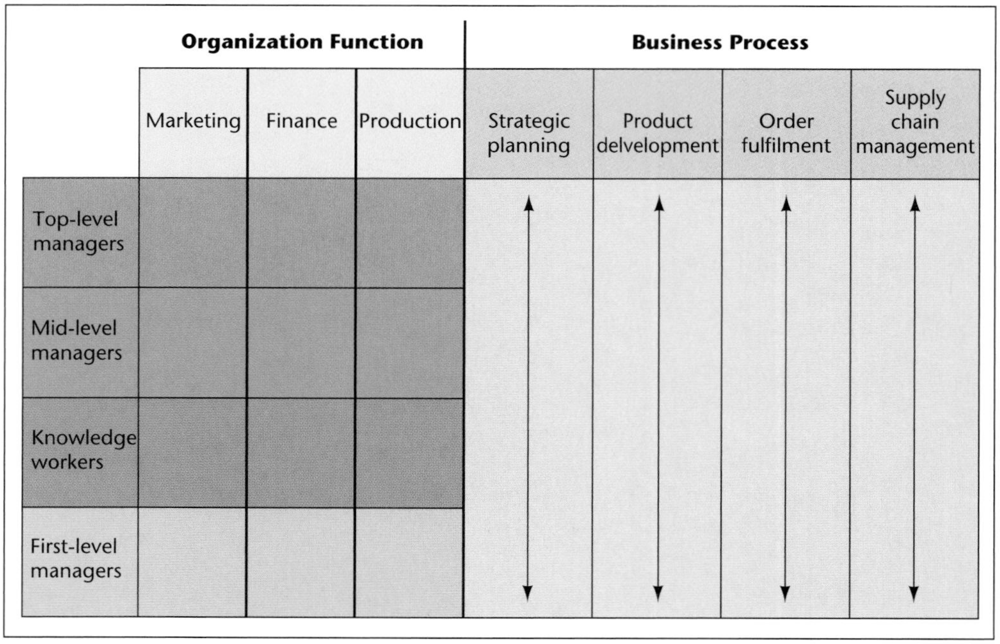

	Organization Function			Business Process			
	Marketing	Finance	Production	Strategic planning	Product delvelopment	Order fulfilment	Supply chain management
Top-level managers				↕	↕	↕	↕
Mid-level managers							
Knowledge workers							
First-level managers							

add to these systems the four systems needed by the four levels of users that we just discussed, we see that the total number of information systems and applications increases significantly.

Each cell in Figure 17.5 describes a potential information system associated with a particular user group. Top-level finance managers, for example, are concerned with long-range planning for capital expenditures for future facilities and equipment and with determining sources of capital funds. In contrast, the arrows on the right side of Figure 17.5 indicate that a business-process group will include users, both managers and employees, drawn from all organizational levels. The supply-chain management group, for instance, may be in the process of trimming down the number of suppliers. The information system supporting this project would contain information ranging across different organization functions and management levels: The group will need information and expert knowledge on marketing, warehousing and distribution, production, communications technology, purchasing, suppliers, and finance. It will also need different perspectives on operational, technical, and managerial issues: determining technical requirements for new suppliers, specifying task responsibilities for participating firms, and determining future financial requirements.

Major Systems by Level

In this section, we discuss different kinds of systems that provide applications at some organizational levels but not at others. For any routine, repetitive, highly structured decision, a specialized application will suffice. System requirements for knowledge workers will probably vary because knowledge workers often face a variety of specialized problems. Applications of information systems for middle- or top-level management decisions must also be flexible, though for different reasons: In particular, they will use a broader range of information collected from a variety of sources, both external and internal.

transaction processing systems (TPS)
Information-processing applications for routine, day-to-day business activities involving well-defined processing steps

Transaction Processing Systems **Transaction processing systems (TPS)** are applications of information processing for basic day-to-day business transactions. Customer order taking by online retailers, approval of claims at insurance companies, receiving and confirming reservations by airlines, payroll processing and bill payment at almost every company—all are routine business processes. Typically, the TPS for first-level (opera-

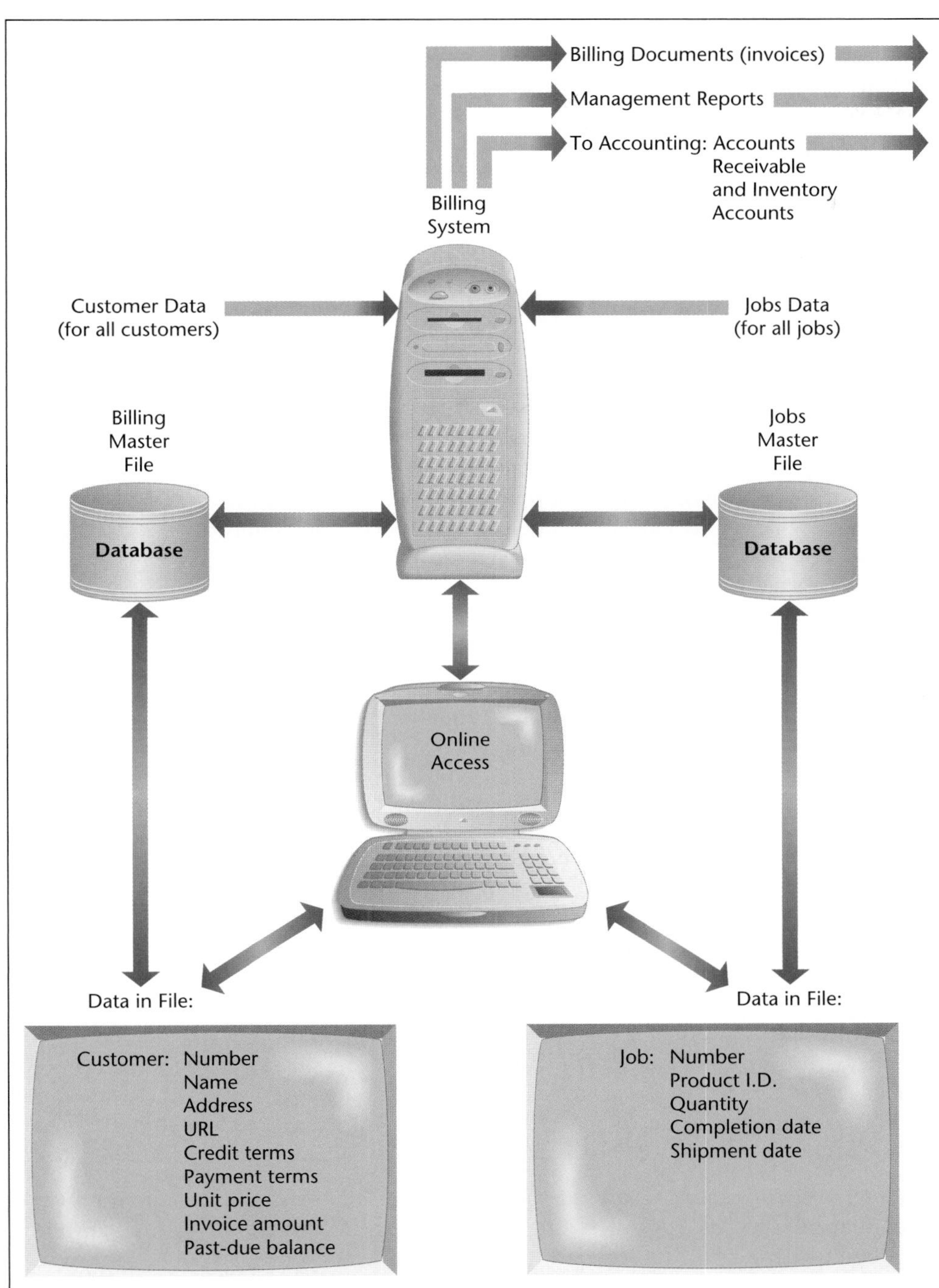

Figure 17.6

Flow Diagram for Customer-Billing TPS

tional) activities is well defined, with predetermined data requirements, and follows the same steps to complete all transactions in the system.

A diagram representing the TPS for a customer-billing process is shown in Figure 17.6. The process begins when finished products for a customer's order are packed and ready for shipment. Using data stored in the company's master files, billing staffers match the customer's identification number (from the billing master file) with code numbers for products (from the jobs master file). The system instantly tallies the payment amount due (including the bill of the current shipment plus any past-due payments), creates the billing document (invoice), and provides status reports to first-level managers and other system users with online access. Information from the billing and jobs master files flows electronically to the accounting system for updating accounts receivables and inventory accounts.

Systems for Knowledge Workers and Office Applications Systems for knowledge workers and office applications support the activities of both knowledge workers and employees in clerical positions. They provide assistance for data processing and other office activities, including the creation of communications documents. Like other departments, the IS department includes both knowledge workers and data workers.

IS Knowledge Workers IS knowledge workers include both systems analysts and application or systems programmers:

- *Systems analysts* deal with the entire computer system. They represent the IS group in working with users to learn users' requirements and to design systems that meet them. Generally, they decide on the types and sizes of computers and on how to set up linkages among computers to form a network of users.
- Using various language programs, *programmers* write the software instructions that tell computers what to do. Application programmers, for example, write instructions to address particular problems. Systems programmers ensure that a system can handle the requests made by various application programs.

system operations personnel Information-systems employees who run a company's computer equipment

Operations Personnel (Data Workers) People who run the company's computer equipment are called **system operations personnel.** They make sure that the right programs are run in the correct sequence and monitor equipment to ensure that it is operating properly. Many organizations also have personnel for entering data into the system for processing.

Knowledge-Level and Office Systems The explosion of new support systems—word processing, document imaging, desktop publishing, computer-aided design, simulation modeling—has increased the productivity of both office and knowledge workers. We will discuss word processing—systems for formatting, editing, and storing documents—later in this chapter. Desktop publishing, also discussed later, combines graphics and word-processing text to publish professional-quality print and Web documents. Document imaging systems can scan paper documents and images, convert them into digital form for storage on disks, retrieve them, and transmit them electronically to workstations throughout the network.

World-class firms such as Harley-Davidson <www.harley-davidson.com>, John Deere <www.deere.com>, and GE <www.ge.com> are using system applications for knowledge workers to reduce product-design times, reduce production-cycle times, and make faster deliveries to customers. Knowledge-level systems include *computer-aided design (CAD), computer-aided manufacturing (CAM),* and *computer operation control.*

computer-aided design (CAD) Computer-based electronic technology that assists in designing products by simulating a real product and displaying it in three-dimensional graphics

Computer-Aided Design **Computer-aided design** (CAD) assists in designing products by simulating the real product and displaying it in three-dimensional graphics. Immersion's MicroScribe-3D software <www.immerse.com.> uses a penlike tool to scan the surface of any three-dimensional object, such as a football helmet, and electronically transforms it into a 3D graphic. The helmet designer can then try different shapes and surfaces in the computer and analyze the new designs on a video monitor.[6] Products ranging from cell phones to auto parts are created using CAD because it creates faster designs at lower cost than manual modeling methods. The older method—making handcrafted prototypes (trial models) from wood, plastic, or clay—is replaced with *rapid prototyping (RP):* The CAD system electronically transfers instructions to a computer-controlled machine that automatically builds the prototype.[7]

computer-aided manufacturing (CAM) Computer system used to design and control equipment needed in the manufacturing process

Computer-Aided Manufacturing **Computer-aided manufacturing** (CAM) is used to design the manufacturing equipment, facilities, and plant layouts for better product flows and productivity. *Computer operations control* refers to any system for managing the day-to-day production activities for either goods or service production. Hospitals use computer-based scheduling for preparing patients' meals, just as manufacturers do for making cars, clocks, and paper products.

Management Information Systems **Management information systems (MIS)** support an organization's managers by providing daily reports, schedules, plans, and budgets. Each manager's information activities vary according to the individual's functional area (for example, accounting or marketing) and management level. Whereas midlevel managers focus mostly on internal activities and information, higher-level managers are also engaged in external activities. Middle managers, the largest MIS user group, need networked information to plan such upcoming activities as personnel training, materials movements, and cash flows. They also need to know the current status of the jobs and projects being carried out in their departments: What stage is it at now? When will it be finished? Is there an opening so we can start the next job? Many of a firm's management information systems—cash flow, sales, production scheduling, shipping—are indispensable for helping managers find answers to such questions.

management information system (MIS)
System used for transforming data into information for use in decision making

Decision Support Systems Middle- and top-level managers receive decision-making assistance from a **decision support system (DSS):** an interactive system that locates and presents information needed to support the decision-making process. Whereas some DSSs are devoted to specific problems, others serve more general purposes, allowing managers to analyze different types of problems. Thus a firm that often faces decisions on plant capacity, for example, may have a *capacity DSS:* The manager inputs data on anticipated levels of sales, working capital, and customer-delivery requirements. Then the DSS's built-in transaction processors manipulate the data and make recommendations on the best levels of plant capacity for each future time period.

decision support system (DSS)
Interactive computer-based system that locates and presents information needed to support decision making

In contrast, a general-purpose system, such as a marketing DSS, might respond to a variety of marketing-related problems. It may be programmed to handle "what-if" questions, such as "When is the best time to introduce a new product if my main competitor introduces one in three months, our new product has an 18-month expected life, demand is seasonal with a peak in the autumn, and my goal is to gain the largest possible market share?" The DSS can assist in decisions for which predetermined solutions are unknown by using sophisticated modeling tools and data analysis.

Executive Support Systems An **executive support systems (ESS)** is a quick-reference, easy-access application of information systems specially designed for instant access by upper-level managers. ESSs are designed to assist with executive-level decisions and problems, ranging from "What lines of business should we be in five years from now?" to "Based on forecasted developments in electronic technologies, to what extent should our firm be globalized in five years? In 10 years?" The ESS also uses a wide range of both internal information and external sources, such as industry reports, global economic forecasts, and reports on competitors' capabilities.

executive support system (ESS)
Quick-reference information-system application designed specially for instant access by upper-level managers

Because senior-level managers do not usually possess advanced computer skills, they prefer systems that are easily accessible and adaptable. Accordingly, ESSs are not designed to address only specific, predetermined problems. Instead, they allow the user some flexibility in attacking a variety of problem situations. They are easily accessible by means of simple keyboard strokes or even voice commands.

Artificial Intelligence and Expert Systems **Artificial intelligence (AI)** can be defined as the construction of computer systems, both hardware and software, to imitate human behavior—in other words, systems that perform physical tasks, use thought processes, and learn. In developing AI systems, knowledge workers—business specialists, modelers, information-technology experts—try to design computer-based systems capable of reasoning so that computers, instead of people, can perform certain business activities.

artificial intelligence (AI)
Computer-system application that imitates human behavior by performing physical tasks, using thought processes, sensing, and learning

One example is a credit-evaluation system that decides which loan applicants are creditworthy and which ones risky and then composes acceptance and rejection letters accordingly. Another example is an applicant-selection system that receives interviewees' job applications, screens them, then decides which applicants are best matched for each of several job openings.

robotics
Combination of computers and industrial robots for use in manufacturing operations

Robotics—the combination of computers with industrial robots—is a category of AI. With certain "reasoning" capabilities, robots can "learn" repetitive tasks such as painting, assembling components, and inserting screws. They also avoid repeating mistakes by "remembering" the causes of past mistakes and, when those causes reappear, adjusting or stopping until adjustments are made.

There are also designed AI systems that possess sensory capabilities, such as lasers that "see," "hear," and "feel." In addition, as machines become more sophisticated in processing natural languages, humans can give instructions and ask questions merely by speaking to a computer.

expert system
Form of artificial intelligence that attempts to imitate the behavior of human experts in a particular field

Expert Systems A special form of AI program, the **expert system,** is designed to imitate the thought processes of human experts in a particular field.[8] Expert systems incorporate the rules that an expert applies to specific types of problems, such as the judgments that a physician makes for diagnosing illnesses. In effect, expert systems supply everyday users with "instant expertise."

General Electric's Socrates Quick Quote imitates the decisions of a real estate expert and then places a package of recommendations about real estate transactions at the fingertips of real estate dealers on GE's private computer network. A system called *MOCA* (for *Maintenance Operations Center Advisor*), by imitating the thought processes of a maintenance manager, schedules routine maintenance for American Airlines' entire fleet.

ELEMENTS OF THE INFORMATION SYSTEM

computer network
All the computer and information technology devices which, by working together, drive the flow of digital information throughout a system

We now know that an *information system* is a group of interconnected devices at several different locations that can exchange information. We also know that *networking*—connecting these devices—allows otherwise decentralized computers to exchange data quickly and easily. A key component of the information system is its **computer network:** all the computer and information technology devices which, working together, drive the flow of digital information throughout the system.

Although the computer is a powerful machine, it is only one part of the information system. Every system has six components:

- Hardware
- Software
- Control
- Database
- People
- Telecommunications

In this section, we will describe each of the first four components in detail. We have already described the fifth element, the people at various levels who use and prepare the system. We will reserve our discussion of telecommunications for the next section. Remember that all six of these components must be present and properly coordinated for a networked information system to function effectively.

Hardware

hardware
Physical components of a computer system

Figure 17.7 shows the various systems and components that make up IS **hardware:** the physical components of a computer system. The functioning of a computer's hardware is not as complicated as it looks. To get a bird's-eye view of how the system works, suppose that you are a very simple piece of data (say, the number *3*).

input device
Part of the computer system that enters data into it

Inputting To get into the computer, data must be entered by an **input device.** Optical scanners, voice pickups, CD drives, and computer mice are all input devices, but let's

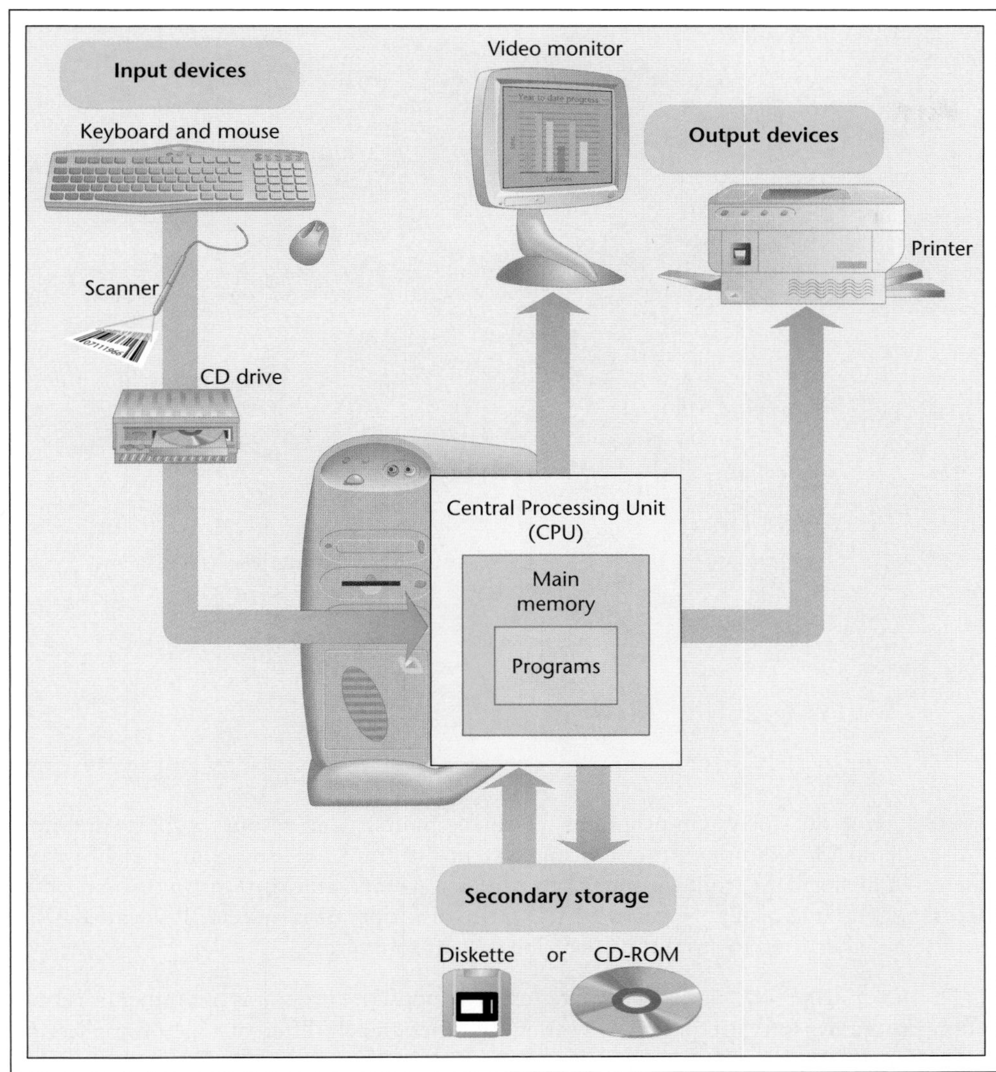

Figure 17.7
Hardware Components of an IS

assume that you are entered by a friend using the most common input device, a keyboard. When your friend presses the number *3* on the keyboard, an electronic signal is sent to the computer's **central processing unit (CPU)**, where the actual processing of data takes place.

Main Memory You are now inside the CPU in a form that the computer can handle. Now what happens? As a piece of data, you must go first to **main memory**—the part of the computer's CPU that stores those programs that it needs in order to operate.

Programs At this point, the CPU searches through its memory for instructions—**programs**—on what to do with you. Using the appropriate instructions, it then performs the calculations (addition, subtraction, multiplication, and division) and comparisons as directed by the program. Then, the CPU sends the results into one or more **output devices:** a video monitor, a printer, or a voice output.

central processing unit (CPU)
Part of the computer system where data processing takes place

main memory
Part of the computer CPU that houses the memory of programs it needs to operate

program
Set of instructions used by a computer to perform specified activities

output device
Part of a computer system that presents results, either visually or in printed form

Software

Although hardware is a vital component of a computer system, it is useless without the other components. As we have just seen, hardware needs programs—**software**—to function. There are basically two types of software programs: system and application.

software
Programs that instruct a computer in what to do

"Smaller, more powerful chips allow me to have a smaller head."

system program
Software that tells the computer what resources to use and how to use them

application program
Software (such as Lotus 1-2-3) that processes data according to a user's special needs

System Programs **System programs** tell the computer what resources to use and how to use them. For example, an operating system program tells the computer how and when to transfer data from secondary to primary storage and to return information to the user. You have probably heard of DOS, the disk operating system. It is called DOS because a disk is used to store the operating system software.

Application Programs Most computer users do not write programs but rather use **application programs:** software packages written by others. Each different type of application (such as financial analysis, word processing, or Web browsing) uses a program that meets

WebConnection

www.sgi.com

Most university and government research sites have computers manufactured by Minnesota-based Cray Research. To find out what a supercomputer product line looks like or what supercomputers do at such facilities as NASA and the Los Alamos National Lab, access Cray's Web site.

that need. Thus, a computer system usually has many application programs available, such as Lotus 1-2-3, Quicken, and WordPerfect. We review some of these later in this chapter.

Graphical User Interface One of the most helpful software developments is the **graphical user interface (GUI):** the user-friendly visual display that helps users select from among the many possible applications on the computer. Typically, the screen displays numerous **icons** (small images) representing such choices as word processing, graphics, DOS, fax, printing, CD, or games. The user tells the computer what to do by moving a pointing device (usually an arrow) around the screen to activate the desired icon. Printed text presents simple instructions for using activated features. Today, Microsoft Windows is the most popular GUI because it simplifies computer use while actually making it fun.

graphical user interface (GUI)
Software that provides a visual display to help users select applications

icon
Small image in a GUI that enables users to select applications or functions

Control

Control ensures that the system is operating according to specific procedures and within specific guidelines. These procedures include guidelines for operating the system, the responsibilities of the personnel involved with it, and plans for dealing with system failure. For example, a key aspect of information management is controlling two groups of people: those who have access to input or change the system's data and those who receive output from it. Thus most firms limit access to salary information.

Problems of Privacy and Security "Breaking and entering" no longer refers merely to physical intrusions into one's home or business. Today, it applies to IS intrusions as well. In this section, we will describe one of the most common forms of intrusion: *privacy invasion.* We will also discuss some of the methods that companies use to provide *security* for their information systems.[9]

Privacy Invasion With information systems, privacy invasion occurs when intruders (hackers) gain unauthorized access, either to steal information, money, or property or to tamper with data. We have all read about computer enthusiasts who have gained access to school systems to change grades. A 16-year-old British hacker made 150 intrusions into the Air Force's top command-and-control facility. He then used those entries to get access to the computers of several defense contractors and the South Korean Atomic Research Institute.

Security Security measures for protection against intrusion are a constant challenge. To gain entry into most systems, IS users have protected passwords that guard against unauthorized access, but many firms rely on additional protective software for safeguards. To protect against intrusions by unauthorized outsiders, companies use such security devices as firewalls in their systems.

Security for electronic communications is an additional concern. Electronic transmissions can be intercepted, altered, and read by intruders. To prevent unauthorized access, many firms rely on encryption: Use of a secret numerical code to scramble the characters in the message, so the message is not understandable during transmission. Only personnel with the deciphering codes can read them.

Finally, the most important security factor is the people in the system. At most firms, personnel are trained in the responsibilities of computer use and warned of the penalties for violating system security. For example, each time the computer boots up, a notice displays the warning that software and data are protected and spells out penalties for unauthorized use.

Databases and Application Programs

As we have noted, all computer processing is the processing of data. This processing is carried out by programs—instructions that tell the system to perform specified functions. In this section we begin by briefly describing the nature of computer data and databases. We then discuss a few of the specialized applications programs designed for business use.

Data and Databases Computers convert data into information by organizing the data in some meaningful manner. Within a computer system, chunks of data—numbers, words, and sentences—are stored in a series of related collections called *fields, records,* and *files.* Taken together, all these data files constitute a **database:** a centralized, organized collection of related data.

database
Centralized, organized collection of related data

Application Programs Programs are available for a huge variety of business-related tasks. Some of these programs address such common, long-standing needs as accounting, payroll, and inventory control. Others have been developed for application to an endless variety of specialized needs. Most business application programs fall into one of four categories—*word processing, spreadsheets, database management,* and *graphics.*[10] Of all PC software applications, 70 percent are designed for the first three types of programs.

Word Processing Popular **word-processing programs,** such as Microsoft Word for Windows <www.microsoft.com/windows>, Corel WordPerfect <www.corel.com/products/wordperfect>, and Lotus Development Corporation's Word Pro for Windows <www.lotus.com/home/nsf/welcome/smartsuite>, allow computer users to store, edit, display, and print documents. Sentences or paragraphs can be added or deleted without retyping or restructuring an entire document, and mistakes are easily corrected.

word-processing program
Applications program that allows computers to store, edit, and print letters and numbers for documents created by users

Spreadsheets **Electronic spreadsheets** spread data across and down the page in rows and columns. Users enter data, including formulas, at row and column intersections, and the computer automatically performs the necessary calculations. Payroll records, sales projections, and a host of other financial reports can be prepared in this manner.

Spreadsheets are useful planning tools because they allow managers to see how making a change in one item will affect related items. For example, a manager can insert various operating cost percentages, tax rates, or sales revenues into the spreadsheet. The computer will automatically recalculate all the other figures and determine net profit. Three popular spreadsheet packages are Lotus 1-2-3, Quattro Pro <www.corel/products/wordperfect/cqp>, and Microsoft Excel for Windows.

electronic spreadsheet
Applications program with a row-and-column format that allows users to store, manipulate, and compare numeric data

Database Management In addition to word processing and spreadsheets, another popular type of personal productivity software is a **database management program.** Such programs as Microsoft Access for Windows, and, from Borland <www.borland.com>, Paradox for Windows and dBase are popular for desktop applications. Oracle8i <www.oracle.com/ip/deploy/ias> is a popular database for internet computing. These systems can store, sort, and search through data and integrate a single piece of data into several different files.

database management program
Applications program for creating, storing, searching, and manipulating an organized collection of data

Graphics **Computer graphics programs** convert numeric and character data into pictorial information such as charts, graphs, and cartoon characters. These programs make computerized information easier to use and understand in two ways. First, graphs and charts summarize data and allow managers to detect problems, opportunities, and relationships more easily. Second, graphics are valuable in creating clearer and more persuasive reports and presentations.

computer graphics program
Applications program that converts numeric and character data into pictorial information such as graphs and charts

Presentation graphics software, such as CorelDraw, Microsoft PowerPoint for Windows, Corel Presentations, and Micosoft Visio 2000 offer choices for assembling graphics for visual displays, slides, video, and even sound splices for professional presentations. The ability to vary color and size, and to use pictures and charts with three-dimensional effects, shadows, and shading with animation and sound is more visually interesting than static presentations.

presentation graphics software
Applications that enable users to create visual presentations that can include animation and sound

Should a new employee invest in high-tech equipment to enhance his or her abilities to communicate and accomplish business-related tasks (software, cellular phones, pagers, etc.)?

Computer graphics capabilities extend beyond mere data presentation. They also include stand-alone programs for artists, designers, and special effects designers. Everything from simple drawings to fine art, television commercials, and motion picture special effects are now created by computer graphics software. The realism of the sinking ship in *Titanic* and the physical appearance of the space creatures in the latest *Star Wars*

Star Wars: Episode I: The Phantom Menace *was recorded on traditional film. Then, nearly all of the film's 2,200 separate shots were digitally scanned into a computer for editing. At director George Lucas's film effects company, Industrial Light and Magic* <www.ilm.com>, *plans for a* Star Wars II *call for shooting the entire film with a digital-videotape system developed in partnership by Sony* <www.sony. com> *and Panavision* <www.panavision. com>. *Videotaped images will be transferred to the hard drives of special computers for editing and special effects. Newly developed laser printers will then expose the footage onto photographic paper.*

movie, *Episode One: The Phantom Menace,* and *Terminator 2* are examples of special effects created with computer graphics.

Some software allows firms to publish their own sales brochures, in-house magazines, or annual reports. The latest of these **desktop publishing** packages combines word-processing and graphics capability to produce typeset-quality text with stimulating visual effects from personal computers. QuarkXpress <www.quark.com> is able to manipulate text, tables of numbers, graphics, and full-color photographs. Desktop publishing eliminates costly printing services for reports and proposals, and Quark is also used by ad agencies such as J. Walter Thompson, whose computer-generated designs offer greater control over color and format. Other desktop publishing packages include Microsoft Publisher and Adobe Systems PageMaker Plus <www.adobe.com/products/pagemaker/ main.html>.

desktop publishing
Process of combining word-processing and graphics capability to produce virtually typeset-quality text from personal computers

TELECOMMUNICATIONS AND NETWORKS

Although communications systems are constantly evolving, some of the fundamental elements are well established: computers, communications devices, and networking. The most powerful vehicle for using these elements to their full potential is the marriage of computers and communication technologies.

A network is a means of organizing telecommunications components into an effective system. When a company decides how to organize its equipment and facilities, it also determines how its information resources will be shared, controlled, and applied by users in its network. In this section, we will first discuss *multimedia communications technologies* and the devices found in today's systems. We will then describe different ways for organizing information resources into effective systems.

Multimedia Communication Systems

Today's information systems include not only computers but also **multimedia communication systems.** These systems are connected networks of communication appliances such as faxes, televisions, sound equipment, cell phones, printers, and photocopiers that may also be linked by satellite with other remote networks. Not surprisingly, the integration

multimedia communication system
Connected network of communication appliances (such as faxes or TVs) that may be linked to forms of mass media (such as print publications or TV programming)

of these elements is changing the way we live our lives and manage our businesses. A good example is the modern grocery store. The checkout scanner reads the bar code on the product you buy. Data are then transmitted to the store's inventory-control system, which updates the number of available units. If inventory falls below a given level, more product is ordered electronically. Meanwhile, the correct price is added to your bill, checkout coupons are printed automatically according to the specific product you bought. Your debit card transfers funds, sales reports are generated for the store's management, and all the while, satellite transmissions are dispatching a remote truck to begin loading replacement supplies for the store.

Communication Devices The explosion in personal communications devices now permits people to conduct business across large distances and from territories where communications were not before available. *Global-positioning-systems (GPSs),* for example, use satellite transmissions to track and identify the geographic location of a target, such as a boat or even a person. When you're linked into a GPS network, your firm can know your whereabouts at all times. *Personal digital assistants (PDAs)* are tiny handheld computers with wireless telecommunications capabilities. Several of these palm-size devices are capable of accessing the Internet, including receiving and sending e-mail messages from the most primitive locations. *Paging systems* and *cellular telephones* provide instant fingertip connections within one or more communications networks.

Communication Channels Communication channels are the media that make all these transmissions possible. These include wired and wireless transmission. Microwave systems, for example, transmit straight-line radio (wireless) signals through the air between transmission stations. Another system—satellite communications—has also gained popularity in the growing demand for wireless transmission. GE's Technical Response Center, for example, demonstrates the value of satellites for improving aircraft engine maintenance and safety. Relying on wireless systems instead of underground cables, laser beams and radio waves transmit signals from satellite to satellite.

Accessible through satellite networks under development by McCaw <www.mccaw.com>, Hughes <www.hns.com>, Motorola <www.gi.com>, AT&T <www.attws.com>, and Loral <www.loral.com>, the Net is available in remote areas where underground cable is not feasible. All the world is within the instant reach of the Internet. Most of us use communication channels when we use some type of telephone system. Even

Demonstrating how computers have changed communications, these engineers at GE's corporate research and development center <www.ge.com> *can monitor engines in flight from the ground via satellite. The new system can diagnose potential engine problems, plan for maintenance or overhaul, and resolve problems more quickly than ever.*

Life Cycle of an e-Business

The Seeds of Netpreneurial Success

While Garden.com's financial losses continued to mount throughout 2000, the firm's technology continued to enjoy its long-standing reputation as the industry's best. In presenting the 1999 Global Information Infrastructure (GII) Awards <www.gii.com/awards>, GII Awards general manager Melanie McMullen said, "Garden.com is a visionary company that exemplifies best practices and an innovative model in a new era of knowledge and communication." The company's technological success was no accident: From the very beginning, information systems and communication technology had been at the very heart of Garden.com's business strategy. In accepting the award as GII's Netpreneur of the Year, Garden.com CEO and cofounder Cliff Sharples remarked: "We have worked hard to build a company that is at the forefront of the e-commerce industry, and we plan to continue to innovate in the Internet space—pushing the envelope in our application of technology and innovative business models to produce lasting customer solutions."

Establishing a system that provided consumers with a centrally located, easy-to-use online environment for gardening required an extensive investment in information technology, networking, and infrastructure. After finalizing plans for their Internet business in 1995, the company's cofounders acquired the Garden.com URL. They went live on the Internet on March 20, 1996. Interaction with customers became a reality via several internally developed Web sites (<www.garden.com>, <www.virtualgarden.com>, and <www.hortmag.com>), while coordination with suppliers was conducted via a sophisticated extranet called Trellis <www.trellis-systems.com>. A proprietary system, Trellis not only provided information and submitted orders to suppliers but allowed customers to track their orders. Overall, it allowed the streamlined distribution of some 23,000 products from 83 key suppliers to customers nationwide.

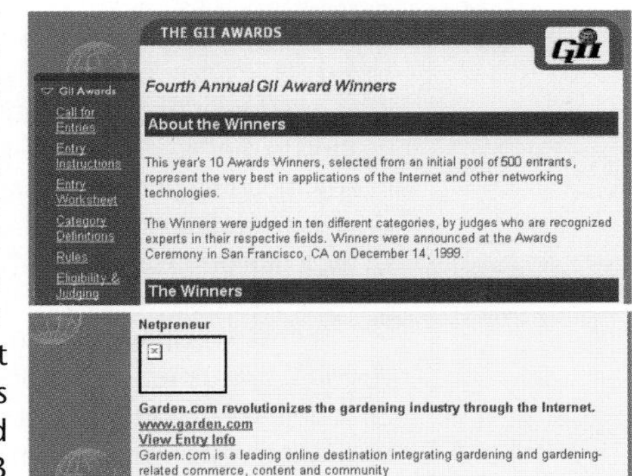

Setting up a communications network was just the beginning: It needed continual development and improvement if it was going to attract new customers and guarantee repeat business. Not surprisingly, this flow of quality Web site content meant that content development was a major area of capital expenditure at Garden.com. Equally expensive was the continuous upgrading of systems architecture and systems for processing customer orders and payments. While technology expenses totaled $1.9 million in just one fiscal quarter in 2000, product revenues were $2.2 million.

During the quarter ended June 30, 1999, Garden.com counted some 4.4 million visitors to its Web sites. But Garden.com naturally wanted to continue to set the pace in e-commerce. Thus, further development and upgrading were planned to prepare the company's system for an increase in the number of Internet users to an estimated 502 million by 2003 (up from 142 million in 1998). Those plans ended, however, with the following announcement on the Garden.com Web site on November 21, 2000: "This is not only the best sale of the season, it's our last sale. The doors of our cyber garden center are closing December 1."

Although Garden.com's retail business was closing, the company's founders continued to evaluate new possibilities for the firm's internally developed technology assets. Other companies, for example, could make use of Trellis, Garden.com's virtual supply chain technology. In December 2000, the firm announced agreement to license Trellis for use by Lowe's Companies <www.lowes.com>, the world's second-largest home improvement retailer, to help streamline Lowe's supply-chain operations, thus raising prospects for new revenue flows into the otherwise dormant Garden.com.

---

today, however, the bulk of telephone transmissions are data, not conversations. Fax data account for 90 percent of all telephone signals between the United States and Japan.

system architecture
Location of a computer system's elements (data-entry and data-processing operations, database, data output, and computer staff)

System Architecture

There are several ways to organize the components in computer and communications networks. As we see in the next section, one way to classify networks is according to *geographic scope*.

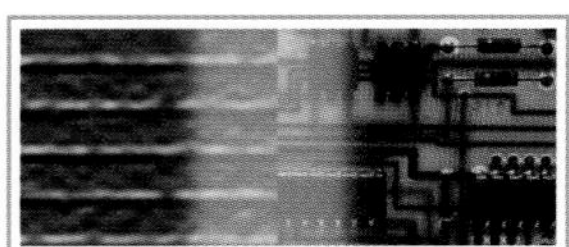

It's a WiredWorld

• "These Two Companies Are a Natural Fit"

Even a high-tech giant can't be an expert in every new development in the digital world. Consider, for example, America Online <www.aol.com> (including its CompuServ service <www.compuserve.com>—America's largest online Internet service provider (ISP), with 22 million subscribers. AOL's customers have Internet access through traditional phone lines. But AOL is thinking about ways to give them even faster Internet service by means of high-speed cable lines. Traditional phone lines are slower than cables in connecting to the Net. They're also slower in downloading information and slower in reading graphics files.

AOL already knows that if it's going to stay competitive in the home Internet market, it will need to offer customers faster Internet connections. On one level, the problem is fairly simple: How do you get from phone lines to cables? One approach—replacing all those phone lines with cables—is more than prohibitively expensive: It simply can't be done. Because AOL doesn't own the lines it uses (the phone company does), it can't replace them. A more feasible approach involves cable-service providers. They already have the capability, but they haven't yet exploited their cable technology in the Internet market.

Now consider the situation at Time Warner Inc. <www.timewarner.com/corp>—a cable-service provider that also happens to be the world's top media and entertainment company. Time Warner Inc. wants to harness the power of the Internet, which it sees as the future avenue for distributing its entertainment products. Unfortunately, Time Warner can't deliver magazines like Time, People, and Sports Illustrated without Internet technology. Nor can Time Warner deliver movies and music for downloading. Time Warner's problem, then, was how to get digital when it wasn't skilled at the technology? Ultimately, doing things internally turned out to be too costly: When Time Warner tried to reinvent its own Internet capabilities, it spent some $500 million (in 1999 alone) in a less than successful effort to rework its online approach.

In early 2000, AOL and Time Warner announced a permanent partnering conceived to give each company a much needed lift in overcoming its respective problem: Internet giant AOL is joining with media behemoth Time Warner in a corporate merger valued at $166 billion—the largest ever. The new firm, AOL Time Warner Inc., gains the advantages of each partner's technological expertise and resources. AOL, of course, has Internet expertise. It also has 22 million customers who can purchase and download Time Warner's entertainment products from the Internet. Meanwhile, Time Warner brings not only 13 million cable TV subscribers to the merger, but also expertise in the high-speed cable lines that AOL needs for faster Internet services. This large base of cable-ready households will be a big boost for AOL because only 6 percent of Web users currently have the high-speed (cable-modem) access that can be up to 100 times faster than modems on traditional phone lines (which are used by some 94 percent of Web users). Thus two giants, each wanting to grow but hindered by technology shortcomings, believe that, as one firm, they'll grow much faster than each could have grown separately. "These two companies," says Time Warner chairman Gerald Levin, "are a natural fit."

Local and Wide Area Networks Networked systems classified according to geographic scope may be either local or wide area networks. Computers may be linked statewide or even nationwide through telephone lines, microwave, or satellite communications, as in a **wide area network (WAN).** Firms can lease lines from communications vendors or maintain private WANs. Wal-Mart, for example, depends heavily on a private satellite network that links more than 2,000 retail stores to its Bentonville, Arkansas, headquarters.

wide area network (WAN) Network of computers and workstations located far from one another and linked by telephone wires or by satellite

Internal networks covering limited distances may link all of a firm's nearby computers, as in a **local area network (LAN).** Computers within a building, for example, can be linked by cabling (fiber optic, coaxial, or twisted-wire) or by wireless technology. Internally networked computers share processing duties, software, storage areas, and data. On cable TV's *Home Shopping Network* <www.hsn.com>, hundreds of operators seated at monitors in a large room are united by a LAN for entering call-in orders from customers. This arrangement allows the use of a single computer system with one database and software system.

local area network (LAN) Network of computers and workstations, usually within a company, that are linked together by cable

Connecting the Hardware Combination systems using local and wide area networks are also possible. Separate plants or offices might handle orders locally while electronically transmitting sales summaries to a corporate office. Using a personal computer with a **modem**—a computer-to-computer link over telephone wires—users can conduct searches in a remote database and exchange messages.

modem
Device that provides a computer-to-computer link over telephone wires

The materials used for making local and wide area networks are changing rapidly. **Fiber optic cable** is made from thousands of strands of ultrathin glass fibers that not only carry data faster, but are lighter and less expensive than older copper media, such as *coaxial cable* (as used in cable television) and *twisted-wire cable* (as in telephone wires). Whereas copper wire cables carry data as electrical signals, fiber optic cable carries data as laser-generated light beams.[11] Wire cables throughout the world are being replaced daily with fiber optic cable, but the change will require many years. Tele Danmark <www.teledanmark.dk/english>, Denmark's leading telecom company, is leading the way. In 1996, it installed the 250-mile BALTICA submarine cable between Poland, Denmark, and Sweden and a 450-mile underwater cable in Brazil.

fiber optic cable
Glass-fiber cables that carry data in the form of light pulses

Client Server Systems An obvious advantage of networks is the sharing of resources—and thus the avoidance of costly and unnecessary duplication. In a **client-server network,** *clients* are the users of services. They are the points of entry, usually laptop computers, workstations, or desktop computers. The *server* provides the services shared by network users. The powerful minicomputer at the network hub, for example, which is larger and more sophisticated than your PC, or microcomputer, may be the server for the surrounding client PCs in an office network.

client-server network
Information-technology system consisting of clients (users) that are electronically linked to share network resources provided by a server, such as a host computer

More specifically, the server may act as a file server, a print server, and a fax server. As a *file server,* the mini has a large-capacity disk for storing the programs and data shared by all the PCs in the network. It contains customer files plus the database, word-processing, graphics, and spreadsheet programs that may be used by clients. As a *print server,* the mini controls the printer, stores printing requests from client PCs, and routes jobs to the printer as it becomes available. As the *fax server,* it receives, sends, and otherwise controls the system's fax activities. Only one disk drive, one printer, and one fax, therefore, are needed for an entire system of users. Internet computing uses the client-server arrangement.

Continued from page 469

Researching with a Purpose

On Duncan Highsmith's organizational chart, the library is listed on the same level as the firm's other important functions, including marketing, human resources, and accounting. As part of the information system, it adds the power of the Internet to human judgment. It also directs information toward the people who can use it and get results with it, and it's readily available and affordable.

The strength of the system is its knowledge-management tool: Lisa Guedea Carreño. Although Guedea Carreño relies on the Internet, she also realizes that as an information source it isn't necessarily all that it's cracked up to be. It's full of hype and promises, and it's unfamiliar territory to new users. Web-search services—Internet search directories, Web browsers, and search engines—often provide spotty information, ranging from full-disclosure sites to sites that offer the truth but not the whole truth. Some Web services report information only for sites that pay to be listed and ignore others. Even among those that report on a huge number of companies, some may give preferential treatment—that is, more favorable reports—to business partners.

To help internal Highsmith users, Guedea Carreño has thus devised her own rules of thumb for navigating the Net efficiently, sorting through Web sites to discard the bad and retain the useful. Through experience, she's compiled a checklist and some questions. Here's a sample:

- *Quality control* A quick rule is watch for typos. If it's typed sloppily, the site's content is also probably of questionable quality.
- *Timeliness* Is the information current? Does the site tell you when it was updated? If not, chances are it's old information (and thus not information at all).
- *Purpose* What's the site's purpose? If it's ambiguous or not readily apparent, you, too, will probably end up wandering around without purpose.
- *Linkages* Does the site contain links to other sites? Are the others relevant, accessible, and current? If it links you to unreliable sites, you will be misdirected and lose precious time.
- *Scope of information* Is the range of information sufficiently rich to meet all your needs at this one site? Obviously, information-rich sites save time and help you get results.
- *Site ownership* Who owns the site? Who is the author, and what is the agenda? If you know the sponsor or owner, you can get a better idea of what the site's content is likely to be.
- *Bias* Bias can be good or bad, but it helps if the bias is apparent because it saves time and tells you in advance that you're likely to get just one side of a story.

Questions for Discussion

1. If you were designing a company's information system, how would you go about determining the kinds of external information to include?
2. Discuss the problems that might be encountered in selecting qualitative information consisting of subjective, nonquantifiable content for a communication network. How can such information be organized in electronic files for the database?
3. Do you think that every Highsmith employee would benefit from participating in "Life, the Universe, and Everything"? Identify the advantages and drawbacks to full employee participation.
4. What kind of training would you propose for a new employee who wants to develop the type of knowledge-worker skills that Guedea Carreño has?
5. Draw a diagram to display the components in Highsmith's information system. Describe how each element effects the company's performance.
6. Do you think that an expert system could be developed to capture Guedea Carreño's method for sorting out good and mediocre Web sites? Explain why or why not.

SUMMARY OF LEARNING OBJECTIVES

1 **Explain why businesses must manage *information* and show how computer systems and communication technologies have revolutionized *information management*.** Because businesses are faced with an overwhelming amount of *data* and *information* about customers, competitors, and their own operations, the ability to manage this input can mean the difference between success and failure. The management of its information system is a core activity because all of a firm's business activities are linked to it. New digital technologies have taken an integral place among an organization's resources for conducting everyday business.

2 **Identify and briefly describe three elements of *data communication networks*—the Internet, the World Wide Web, and intranets.** *Data communication networks,* both public and private, carry streams of digital data (electronic messages) back and forth quickly and economically via *telecommunication systems.* The largest public communications network, the *Internet,* is a gigantic system of networks linking millions of computers offering information on business around the world. The Net is the most important e-mail system in the world. Individuals can subscribe to the Net via an *Internet service provider (ISP).* The *World Wide Web* is a system with universally accepted standards for storing, formatting, retrieving, and displaying information. It provides the common language that enables users around the world to "surf" the Net using a common format. *Intranets* are private networks that any company can develop to extend Net technology internally—that is, for transmitting information throughout the firm. Intranets are accessible only to employees, with access to outsiders prevented by hardware and software security systems called *firewalls.*

3 **Describe five *new options for organizational design* that have emerged from the rapid growth of information technologies.** Information networks are leading to *leaner* organizations—businesses with fewer employees and simpler organizational structures—because networked firms can maintain electronic, rather than human, information linkages among employees and customers. Operations are *more flexible* because electronic networks allow businesses to offer greater product variety and faster delivery cycles. Aided by intranets and the Internet, *greater collaboration* is possible, both among internal units and with outside firms. *Geographic separation* of the workplace and company headquarters is more common because electronic linkages are replacing the need for physical proximity between the company and its workstations. *Improved management processes* are feasible because managers have rapid access to more information about the current status of company activities and easier access to electronic tools for planning and decision making.

4 **Discuss different information-system *applications programs* that are available for users at various organizational levels.** *Transaction processing systems (TPS)* are applications for basic day-to-day business transactions. They are useful for routine transactions, such as taking reservations and meeting payrolls, that follow predetermined steps. Systems for *knowledge workers and office applications* include personal productivity tools such as *word processing, document imaging, desktop publishing, computer-aided design,* and *simulation modeling. Management information systems (MISs)* support an organization's managers by providing daily reports, schedules, plans, and budgets. Middle managers, the largest MIS user group, need networked information to plan upcoming activities and to track current activities. *Decision support systems (DSSs)* are interactive applications that assist the decision-making processes of middle- and top-level managers. *Executive support systems (ESSs)* are quick-reference, easy-access programs to assist upper-level managers. *Artificial intelligence (AI)* and *expert systems* are designed to imitate human behavior and provide computer-based assistance in performing certain business activities.

5 **Identify and briefly describe the *main elements of an information system.*** *Hardware* is the physical devices and components, including the computer, in the *information system (IS).* It consists of an *input device* (such as a keyboard), a *central processing unit (CPU),* a *main memory,* disks for data storage, and *output devices* (such as video monitors and printers). *Software* includes the computer's operating system, *application programs* (such as *word processing, spreadsheets,* and Web *browsers*), and a *graphical user interface (GUI)* that helps users select among the computer's many possible applications.

Control is important to ensure not only that the system operates correctly but also that data and information are transmitted through secure channels to people who really need them. Control is aided by the use of electronic security measures, such as firewalls, that bar entry to the system by unauthorized outsiders. The *database* is the organized collection of all the data files in the system. *People* are also part of the information system. IS *knowledge workers* include systems analysts who design the systems and programmers who write software instructions that tell computers what to do. System users, too, are integral to the system. *Telecommunication* components include multimedia technology that incorporates sound, animation, video, and photography along with ordinary graphics and text. Electronic discussion groups, videoconferencing, and other forms of interactive dialog are possible with communication devices (such as global positioning systems and personal digital assistants) and communication channels (such as satellite communications).

QUESTIONS AND EXERCISES

Questions for Review

1. Why does a business need to manage information as a resource?
2. How can an e-mail system increase office productivity and efficiency?
3. Why do the four levels of user groups in an organization need different kinds of information from the information system?
4. In what ways are local area networks (LANs) different from or similar to wide area networks (WANs)?
5. What are the main types of electronic information technologies being applied in business information systems?

Questions for Analysis

6. Give two examples (other than those in this chapter) for each of the major types of applications programs used in business.
7. Describe three or four activities in which you regularly engage that might be made easier by multimedia technology.
8. Give three examples (other than those in this chapter) of how a company can become leaner by adopting a networked information system.

Application Exercises

9. Describe the information system at your college or university. Identify its components and architecture. Identify the features that either promote or inhibit collaboration among system users.
10. Visit a small business in your community to investigate the ways it is using communication technologies and the ways it plans to use them in the future. Prepare a report for presentation in class.
11. Identify two businesses, one locally in your community and one located elsewhere (perhaps one that you have read about or seen on television), that you think might be able to combine their efforts effectively in a new business venture. Describe what each company would contribute (in terms of services, skills, and business processes), then explain how they can use the Internet and World Wide Web to coordinate their activities.

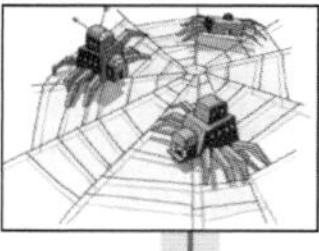

EXPLORING THE WEB

ON THE CUTTING EDGE WITH EXPERTS

Most firms rely on expert assistance to get started on network development and buy the technology they need for their Internet systems. Cisco Systems Inc. is the worldwide leader in Internet networking, providing most of the systems that make the Internet work. By looking at Cisco's products, including hardware, software, and services, we can get an idea about both the needs of Internet users and some of the leading-edge solutions that are available. To learn about Cisco, its products, and its customers, visit its Web site at:

www.cisco.com/

Spend some time navigating through the homepage. To get an idea of the variety of Cisco's products and services, enter each of the subject gates (point the mouse to the title and click) located up, down, and across the page. Scroll down the page and select "Services" and "Solutions" titles that seem interesting to you. Be sure to note the different kinds of customers at whom each product is directed. After getting acquainted with the site, consider the following items:

1. Under "Solutions for Your Network," look at Cisco's "Internet Communications Software." From the description, identify the company's software products, the purpose of those products, the ways they work, and the benefits from using them.
2. For Cisco's "Internet Business Solutions," look at the company's approach to "E-Commerce" and its approach to "Business-to-Business E-Commerce." Explain how these approaches differ from one another. Describe the purpose of "E-Commerce" and contrast it with "Business-to-Business E-Commerce."
3. Look at "Employee Productivity" for small-to-medium-size businesses. What Internet tools does Cisco offer? Explain the ways in which those tools could improve productivity and identify the kinds of organizational conditions under which they would be most appropriate.
4. Suppose you have questions about which products are best suited for your firm's Internet requirements and how certain products would apply to your situation. Where, in the Cisco Web site, would you turn for help?

BUILDING YOUR BUSINESS SKILLS

THE ART AND SCIENCE OF POINT-AND-CLICK RESEARCH

This exercise enhances the following SCANS workplace competencies: demonstrating basic skills, demonstrating thinking skills, exhibiting interpersonal skills, working with information, applying system knowledge, and using technology.

GOAL

To introduce students to World Wide Web search sites.

BACKGROUND

In a recent survey of nearly 2,000 Web users, two-thirds stated that they used the Web to obtain work-related information. With an estimated 320 million pages of information on the Web, the challenge for business users is fairly obvious: how to find what they're looking for.

METHOD

You'll need a computer and access to the World Wide Web to complete this exercise.

Step 1

Get together with three other classmates and decide on a business-related research topic. Choose a topic that interests you, for example, "Business Implications of the Year 2000 Census," "Labor Disputes in Professional Sports," or "Marketing Music Lessons and Instruments to Parents of Young Children."

Step 2

Search the following sites for information on your topic. Divide the sites among group members to speed the process:

- Yahoo! <www.yahoo.com>
- Hotbot <www.hotbot.com>
- Alta Vista <www.altavista.net>
- Excite <www.excite.com>
- Infoseek <www.infoseek.com>
- Lycos <www.lycos.com>
- Metacrawler <www.metacrawler.com>
- Dogpile <www.dogpile.com>
- Ask Jeeves <www.askjeeves.com>
- Northern Light <www.nlsearch.com>
- Internet Sleuth <www.isleuth.com>

Take notes as you search so that you can explain your findings to other group members.

Step 3

Working as a group, answer the following questions about your collective search:

1. Which sites were the easiest to use?
2. Which sites offered the most helpful results? What specific factors made these sites better than the others?
3. Which sites offered the least helpful results? What were the problems?
4. Why is it important to learn the special code words or symbols, called operators, that target a search? (Operators are words like AND, OR, and NOT that narrow search queries. For example, using AND in a search tells the system that all words must appear in the results—American AND Management AND Association.)

FOLLOW-UP QUESTIONS

1. Research the differences between search *engines* and search *directories*. Then place the sites listed in step 2 in the appropriate category. Did you find search engines or directories more helpful in this exercise?
2. Why is it important to learn to use the search-site "Help" function?
3. Based on your personal career goals, how do you think that mastering Web research techniques might help you in the future?
4. How has the World Wide Web changed the nature of business research?

CRAFTING YOUR BUSINESS PLAN

GETTING WIRED INTO BETTER INFORMATION

THE PURPOSE OF THE ASSIGNMENT

1. To acquaint students with the process of navigating the *Business PlanPro (BPP)* software package (Version 4.0).
2. To familiarize students with issues involving information systems that a sample firm faces in developing its business plan.
3. To demonstrate how communications technologies, the Internet, and database considerations can be integrated as components in the *BPP* planning environment.

ASSIGNMENT

After reading Chapter 17 in the textbook, open the BPP *software* and look around for information about plans for computer and communications technologies as they apply to a sample firm:* Travel Agency *(Adventure Travel International). Begin first by looking at ATI's Plan Outline, 1.0 Executive Summary, to get acquainted with the firm. Then respond to the following questions:*

1. How have the Internet and related communications technologies changed the travel agency industry? [Sites to see in *BPP* (for this assignment): In the *Plan Outline* screen, click in turn on each of the following: **3.2 Competitive Comparison** and **4.3.1 Industry Participants.**]
2. How might databases be used to advantage at ATI? [Sites to see in *BPP:* In the *Plan Outline* screen, click in turn on each of the following: **3.3 Sales Literature, 3.5 Technology, 4.1 Market Segmentation, 5.0 Strategy and Implementation Summary,** and **5.3.5 Marketing Programs.**]
3. What are the advantages in ATI's Computerized Reservation System? [Sites to see in *BPP:* From the *Plan Outline* screen, click in turn on each of the following: **3.5 Technology** and **4.3.2 Distribution Patterns.**]
4. How can ATI's distribution system benefit from using the World Wide Web? After exploring in ATI's Plan Outline, what suggestions would you give them about using the Web? [Sites to see in *BPP:* In the *Plan Outline* screen, click on **5.3.4 Distribution Strategy** and **5.5 Strategic Alliances.**]
5. How might ATI use its information systems and communications technologies to better advantage? [Sites to see in *BPP:* In the *Plan Outline* screen, click in turn on each of the following: **5.3.3 Promotion Strategy** and **5.3.4 Distribution Strategy.**]

FOR YOUR OWN BUSINESS PLAN

6. Consider the communications technologies for the business plan that you are developing. Explain your choices on computer systems, planned usage of the World Wide Web, and Internet communications for interacting with customers and suppliers. To what extent will your firm's success depend on such technologies? What are your plans for obtaining the necessary knowledge resources to implement those technologies?

*GENERAL TIPS FOR NAVIGATING IN *BPP*

1. Open the *BPP* program, examine the Welcome screen, and click on **Open a Sample Plan.**
2. From the **Open a Sample Plan** dialogue box, click on a sample company name; then click on **Open.**
3. On the Plan Manager screen, click on **Your Plan Outline;** then click on any of the lines (for example, **5.1.1 Pricing Strategy**).
4. You can always return to the Plan Outline screen by going to the bottom of the screen and clicking on the **Plan Outline** icon.
5. After finishing with one sample company, you can get to the next one by going to the top of the screen and clicking on **File** (on the menu bar). Then beneath that, select **Open Sample Plan.** This will exit you from the current company file and take you to the **Open Sample Plan** dialogue box, where you can select your next sample company.
6. When you are finished, you can close the program by going to the top of the screen and clicking on **File** (on the bar menu). Then beneath that, select **Exit.**

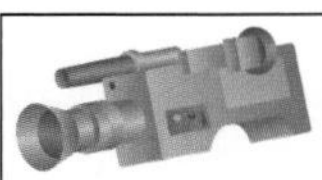

VIDEO EXERCISE

WHATEVER TIES US MUST CONVERGE

Learning Objectives

The purpose of this video exercise is to help you

1. Understand the concept of *convergence* in technology.
2. Describe the technological and human impact of converging technologies.
3. Appreciate the rapid progress being made in communications technology.

BACKGROUND INFORMATION

Communication is only one of the many functions of computer technology, but it is perhaps the one with which most of us are most familiar. In business, the convergence of telephone, cable-airwaves-satellite, and computer capabilities—the integration of communications and computer technologies—has wrought a revolution whose effects will continue to be felt as the pace of change increases. Issues of privacy and other ethical concerns will also be debated in the months and years to come.

THE VIDEO

Experts discuss the pros, cons, and logistics of converging communications technologies. We hear from Derrick de Kerchkovo, director of the McLuhan Program <www.mcluhan.utoronto.ca> Steve Warne of the Vivid Group <www.vividgroup.com>; Mike Walsh of Sun Microsystems of Canada <www.sun.ca>; and Heather Menzies, writer. Each offers a unique perspective on the impact of technology on our professional lives.

DISCUSSION QUESTIONS

1. How do you think convergence will affect personal communications?
2. What do you think are some of the benefits of converging communications technologies?
3. What do you think of the potential downside of an increasing reliance on technology in the workplace? Do you agree with the charge that employees will become mere extensions of a corporate personality?

FOLLOW-UP ASSIGNMENT

The American Management Association <www.amanet.org> surveyed human resource managers in more than 2,100 corporations of varying sizes and found that at least 54 percent monitor employees' Internet connections, and 38 percent store and review employees' e-mail. That percentage has been increasing every year as the necessary technology becomes more efficient and more widely available. Why do you think firms are adopting these new surveillance methods? What are they gaining? Are they losing anything? Do you think the practice is ethical? Why or why not?

FOR FURTHER EXPLORATION

Shareware, or downloadable software, ranges from games to top-notch office applications. Compare the offerings at the following Web sites and determine which would be most useful to you at home and on the job: <www.cnet.com>, <www.tucows.com>, <www.hotfiles.com>.

Chapter

18

Understanding Principles of Accounting

After reading this chapter, you should be able to:

1. ***Explain*** the role of accountants and distinguish between the kinds of work done by *public* and *private accountants.*
2. ***Discuss*** the *CPA Vision Project* and explain how the CPA profession is changing.
3. ***Explain*** how the following concepts are used in *accounting:* the *accounting equation* and *double-entry accounting.*
4. ***Describe*** the three basic *financial statements* and show how they reflect the activity and financial condition of a business.
5. ***Explain*** how computing key *financial ratios* can help in analyzing the financial strengths of a business.
6. ***Explain*** some of the special issues facing accountants at firms that do international business.

How Cooking the Books Left One Accountant with a Bad Taste

Let's say that you are the head of a corporation that is committing systematic fraud against the federal government worth hundreds of millions of dollars. Who's the last person you'd want on your team? Probably an ethical accountant, especially if that person is also determined and detail oriented. It would certainly be a mistake to ask this accountant to create two sets of accounting ledgers and thereby involve him directly in the fraud. That's the mistake that Columbia/HCA Healthcare Corp. <www.columbia-hca.com> and the Quorum Health Group <www.quorumhealth.com> made when they told hospital finance officer James F. Alderson to "cook the books." Alderson refused. He was fired but ultimately blew the whistle on his old employer to signal a federal lawsuit that has shaken the entire health care industry.

Alderson worked for years at North Valley Hospital in Whitefish, a ski town in northwest Montana. When the hospital's top administrator left in 1990, the board turned to Quorum Health Group to run the hospital. Quorum, a management company once affiliated with Columbia/HCA, got the account largely because of its promise to obtain maximum reimbursements for Medicare-related expenses.

Thus becoming a Quorum employee, Alderson was working on Medicare cost reports when he was told by his Quorum superiors to prepare two sets of books. The "official" set would aggressively claim expenses that never occurred. A second "unofficial" set, for internal use only, would be legitimate. This second set estimated the amount in claims made on the first set that Medicare <**www.medicare.gov**> might reject as bogus. A corresponding amount of money was placed in reserve. If there was no audit for two years, accountants would then credit these reserves as revenues.

Alderson advised his new employer that he "never did two tax returns for anyone" when he was a public accountant and "wasn't going to do two cost reports" now that he was a private accountant working for Quorum. Alderson suspected that the scheme in which he had been ordered to participate was standard practice not only at Quorum, but also at its former parent, Columbia/HCA. Both companies, he believed, were submitting false Medicare reports that were costing the taxpayers millions.

A few days later, Alderson was dismissed. Understandably outraged, he filed a wrongful termination suit against Quorum and began gathering evidence of the suspected fraud. At about this time, a friend told him about the federal whistle-blower law, which allows private citizens to file fraud-related lawsuits on behalf of the federal government and to receive a percentage of the money that the government ultimately recovers. By filing such a suit, Alderson instigated a government investigation during the course of which the Justice Department <**www.usdoj.gov**> subpoenaed years' worth of Quorum cost and reserve reports. "I couldn't believe what I was seeing," said former Medicare auditor (and Alderson advisor) Nicholas L. Bordeau. "It was an organized system to take advantage of the Medicare system."

Years after he had initiated his original case, Alderson filed a new complaint in Florida, a state with millions of Medicare-aged residents and a history of fraud offenses involving Columbia/HCA. By 1997, the Federal Bureau of Investigation had indicted three Columbia executives in Florida, and a year later, on October 5, 1998, the federal government officially joined Alderson's case against Quorum and Columbia. At that point, his lawyer, Stephen Meagher, attempted to put eight years of legal struggles into perspective: "A discovery made by one man at a small rural hospital ultimately unraveled a nationwide, systemwide scheme. One person can truly make a difference."

"A discovery made by one man ultimately unraveled a nationwide, systematic scheme. One person can truly make a difference."

—Whistle-blower attorney Stephen Meagher

Our opening story continues on page 522

This chapter will introduce you to the work performed by accountants and to the basic financial reports of economic activity that are the primary reason for accounting. As you will see in this chapter, accounting goes hand in hand with information management. In today's complex business environment, the need to manage information efficiently and quickly is crucial. Information can take many forms—information about expenses and assets, information about customers' locations and order patterns, information about supplies and finished goods on hand, information about workers' pay and productivity, information about products in development, and information about competitors and customers.

WHAT IS ACCOUNTING AND WHO USES ACCOUNTING INFORMATION?

accounting
Comprehensive system for collecting, analyzing, and communicating financial information

Accounting is a comprehensive system for collecting, analyzing, and communicating financial information. It is a system for measuring business performance and translating those measures into information for management decisions. Accounting also uses performance measures to prepare performance reports for owners, the public, and regulatory agencies. To meet these objectives, accountants keep records of such transactions as taxes paid, income received, and expenses incurred. They also analyze the effects of these transactions on particular business activities. By sorting, analyzing, and recording thousands of transactions, accountants can determine how well a business is being managed and how financially strong it is.[1]

bookkeeping
Recording of accounting transactions

Bookkeeping, which is sometimes confused with accounting, is just one phase of accounting—the recording of accounting transactions. Accounting is much more comprehensive than bookkeeping because accounting involves more than just the recording of information.

accounting system
Organized means by which financial information is identified, measured, recorded, and retained for use in accounting statements and management reports

Because businesses engage in many thousands of transactions, ensuring consistent, dependable financial information is mandatory. This is the job of the **accounting system:** an organized procedure for identifying, measuring, recording, and retaining financial information so that it can be used in accounting statements and management reports. The system includes all the people, reports, computers, procedures, and resources for compiling financial transactions.[2]

There are numerous users of accounting information:

- *Business managers* use accounting information to set goals, develop plans, set budgets, and evaluate future prospects.
- *Employees and unions* use accounting information to get paid and to plan for and receive such benefits as health care, insurance, vacation time, and retirement pay.
- *Investors and creditors* use accounting information to estimate returns to stockholders, determine a company's growth prospects, and determine whether it is a good credit risk before investing or lending.
- *Tax authorities* use accounting information to plan for tax inflows, determine the tax liabilities of individuals and businesses, and ensure that correct amounts are paid on time.
- *Government regulatory agencies* rely on accounting information to fulfill their duties. The Toronto Stock Exchange in Canada and the Securities and Exchange Commission in the United States require firms to file financial disclosures so that potential investors have valid information about a company's financial status.

WHO ARE ACCOUNTANTS AND WHAT DO THEY DO?

controller
Person who manages all of a firm's accounting activities (chief accounting officer)

At the head of the accounting system is the **controller,** who manages all the firm's accounting activities. As chief accounting officer, the controller ensures that the accounting system provides the reports and statements needed for planning, controlling, and

The Broadway musical Ragtime *was a hit—but not* that *big a hit. It seems that Toronto-based Livent Inc., the show's producer, used some creative accounting tactics to bolster the success of various projects. According to analysts, one "irregular" technique permitted Livent to buy advertising, scenery, and costumes without deducting them from the bottom line. Merely resorting to looser Canadian accounting standards enabled Livent head Garth Drabinsky to reduce one year's loss from $38 million to $29 million. It did not, however, prevent Wall Street from reckoning the firm's debt at $130 million and total value at $120 million. Within a few months, Livent was in bankruptcy.*

decision-making activities. This broad range of activities requires different types of accounting specialists. In this section, we begin by distinguishing between the two main fields of accounting: *financial* and *managerial*. Then we discuss the different functions and activities of *certified public accountants* and *private accountants*.

Financial Versus Managerial Accounting

In any company, two fields of accounting (financial and managerial) can be distinguished by the different users they serve. As we have just seen, it is both convenient and accurate to classify users of accounting information as users outside the company and users inside the company. This same distinction allows us to categorize accounting systems as either *financial* or *managerial*.[3]

Which accountant has more influence over business decisions: financial or managerial?

Financial Accounting A firm's **financial accounting system** is concerned with external users of information: consumer groups, unions, stockholders, and government agencies. It prepares and publishes income statements and balance sheets at regular intervals, as well as other financial reports that are published for shareholders and the general public. All of these documents focus on the activities of the company as a whole, rather than on individual departments or divisions.

financial accounting system
Field of accounting concerned with external users of a company's financial information

Managerial Accounting In contrast, **managerial** (or **management**) **accounting** serves internal users. Managers at all levels need information to make decisions for their departments, to monitor current projects, and to plan for future activities. Other employees also need accounting information. Engineers, for instance, want to know the costs for materials and production so that they can make product or operations improvements. To set performance goals, salespeople need data on past sales by geographic region. Purchasing agents use information on materials costs to negotiate terms with suppliers.

managerial (or **management**) **accounting system**
Field of accounting that serves internal users of a company's financial information

Certified Public Accountants

Certified public accountants (**CPAs**) offer accounting services to the public. CPAs are licensed at the state level after passing a three-day written exam prepared by the American Institute of Certified Public Accountants (AICPA), which is the national professional organization of CPAs. The AICPA <www.aicpa.org> also provides technical support to members and discipline in matters of professional ethics.

certified public accountant (CPA)
Accountant licensed by the state and offering services to the public

"It's the old story. I was in the middle of a successful acting career when I was bitten by the accounting bug."

Professional Practice and the Big 5 Whereas some CPAs work as individual practitioners, many join with other CPAs in partnerships or professional corporations. More than 40,000 CPA firms practice in the United States. However, nearly one-half of accounting's total revenues in the United States are received by the so-called Big 5 accounting firms: Arthur Andersen <www.arthurandersen.com>, Deloitte & Touche <www.deloitte.com>, Ernst & Young <www.ey.com>, KPMG LLP <www.kpmg.com>, and Price Waterhouse Coopers <www.pwcglobal.com>. In addition to their prominence in the United States, international growth into worldwide accounting operations is a major expansion area for Big 5 firms.

CPA Services Virtually all CPA firms, whether consisting of 10,000 employees in 100 nationwide offices or just one person in a small private facility, provide auditing, tax, and management services. Larger firms earn up to 60 percent of their revenue from auditing services. Consulting services constitute a growth area for larger firms. Smaller firms typically earn most of their income from tax and management services.

audit
Systematic examination of a company's accounting system to determine whether its financial reports fairly represent its operations

Auditing An **audit** examines a company's accounting system to determine whether its financial reports fairly present its operations. Companies must normally provide audit reports when applying for loans or selling stock. In 1999, for example, the accounting firm of Pricewaterhouse Coopers denied stock market rumors that the Big 5 firm was going to resign as auditors of Tyco International <www.tycoint.com>, a diversified service and manufacturing company. The rumors stemmed from controversy over Tyco's accounting methods, including accusations by market analysts that Tyco's financial reports were inflating its growth picture. Tyco's executives denied the accusations, but public reaction was swift: Tyco's stock price plummeted 23 percent in just one week.[4]

WebConnection

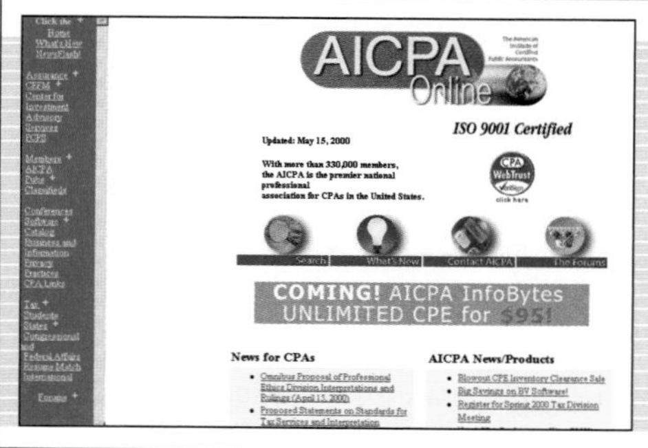

www.aicpa.org

The AICPA is a national professional association for CPAs with 330,000 members. The organization issues the *AICPA Code of Professional Conduct,* which sets down standards in such areas as "Responsibilities to Clients" and "Independence, Integrity, and Objectivity."

The auditor must also ensure that the client's accounting system follows **generally accepted accounting principles (GAAP)**: rules and procedures governing the content and form of financial reports. GAAPs are formulated by the Financial Accounting Standards Board (FASB) of the AICPA.[5] By using GAAP, the audit should determine whether a firm has controls to prevent errors and fraud. Ultimately, the auditor will certify whether the client's financial reports comply with GAAP.

generally accepted accounting principles (GAAP) Accepted rules and procedures governing the content and form of financial reports

Tax Services Tax laws are immensely complex. Tax services thus include assistance not only with tax return preparation but also with tax planning. A CPA's advice can help a business structure (or restructure) operations and investments and perhaps save millions of dollars in taxes. In order to best serve their clients, accountants must stay abreast of changes in tax laws. This is no simple matter: Legislators made more than 70 pages of technical corrections to the 1986 Tax Reform Act before it even became law.

Management Advisory Services When hired as consultants, accounting firms provide **management advisory services** ranging from personal financial planning to planning corporate mergers. Other services include plant layout and design, production scheduling,

management advisory services Specialized accounting services to help managers resolve a variety of business problems

It's a WiredWorld

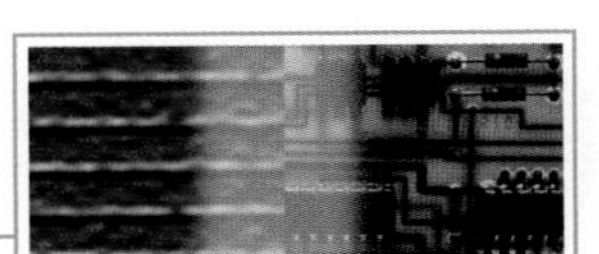

• A Roundabout Look at Conflicting Interests

With all the new dot.com companies popping up, things are looking up for accounting firms. Because all those e-businesses need accounting services—setting up accounting systems, preparing taxes and financial reports, conducting audits—prospects are good for an upsurge of new clients. Or are they? Two factors are getting in the way, one having to do with the lean purses of the dot.coms, and the other with the structure of today's large accounting firms. As a result, accounting firms are running into roadblocks in trying to pursue dot.com clients.

Many dot.coms are short on cash, most of them operating in the red even though prospects may be bright for future earnings. Some of today's financially strapped dot.coms will prosper and become tomorrow's e-commerce giants. Naturally, public accounting firms would like them to become giant clients in need of accounting services for years to come. Price Waterhouse Coopers expects that about half of its consulting revenues will eventually come from e-businesses. Unfortunately, would-be e-giants need accounting services now, including management advisory services to help formulate focused strategies, target desirable markets, and improve operations now, while they're getting started, not later. But they can't pay now.

The answer? Increasingly, accounting firms are accepting equity positions instead of cash payment: In return for its services, the accounting firm becomes part-owner of the dot.com. Generally speaking, it's a good arrangement: While the accounting firm gets a new client (and stands to gain future revenues from its ownership position), the dot.com gets timely professional management help without laying out badly needed cash.

But there's a problem: What the accounting firm gains in a present consulting client it may lose in a future auditing client. Public accounting firms are not allowed to make the kind of ownership–investment arrangement described above and also provide auditing (or some other financial accounting) services for the same client company. Both the accounting profession and federal regulations frown on the potential conflict of interest. Rules require that auditors have no investment stake in companies they audit. And in fact, it stands to reason that allowing a CPA firm to audit a company in which it has an ownership is an invitation to financial mischief. It would be like asking a bank to audit itself rather than hiring an independent auditor.

Nor do the problems stop here. As part-owner, a CPA firm must also steer away from other part-owners in the company. Let's say, for example, that a number of other firms, such as a shipping company, an investment firm, a wholesaler, and a computer supplier, also have ownership interests in the same dot.com. The accounting firm must also decline to audit those firms. Again, there is conflict of interest: The accounting firm could make the dot.com's financial position look good in order to burnish its fellow part-owners' financial positions.

Therefore, it looks as if the dot.com explosion that seems like such a terrific opportunity for CPA firms may turn out to be much more limited. Currently, the accountant is forced to make a choice: To take on the dot.com as a client for auditing services or as a client for management advisory services? Accountants can't have it both ways. And whatever choice it makes, the accounting firm also has to make sure that its auditors and management consultants know what the others are doing.

computer feasibility studies, and accounting system design. Some CPA firms even assist in executive recruitment. On staff at the largest firms are engineers, architects, mathematicians, and psychologists.

Noncertified Public Accountants Many accountants choose not to take the CPA exam; others work in the field while preparing to take it or while fulfilling requirements for state certification. Many small businesses, individuals, and even larger firms rely on these noncertified public accountants for income tax preparation, payroll accounting, and financial planning services.

Private Accountants

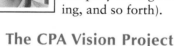

To ensure integrity in reporting, CPAs are always independent of the firms they audit. As employees of accounting firms, they provide services for many clients. However, many businesses also hire their own salaried employees—**private accountants**—to carry out day-to-day activities.

private accountant
Salaried accountant hired by a business to carry out its day-to-day financial activities

Private accountants perform a variety of jobs. An internal auditor at Phillips Petroleum might fly to the North Sea to confirm the accuracy of oil flow meters on offshore drilling platforms. Meanwhile, a supervisor responsible for $2 billion in monthly accounts payable to vendors and employees may travel no farther than the executive suite. Large businesses employ specialized accountants in such areas as budgets, financial planning, internal auditing, payroll, and taxation. In small businesses, a single person may handle all accounting tasks. Most private accountants are management accountants who provide services to support company managers in a variety of activities (marketing, production, engineering, and so forth).

Is it important for every business to have an independent private accountant?

The CPA Vision Project

The CPA Vision Project <www.cpavision.org> is an ambitious, professionwide assessment to see what the future of the accounting profession will be like.[6] A prime reason for the project is a disturbing decline in the number of young people who entered the profession during the 1990s. The growing shortage of talent has forced the profession to rethink its culture and lifestyle.[7] With grassroots participation from practicing CPAs, educators, and industry leaders, the AICPA has undertaken this comprehensive multiyear project to define the role of the accountant in the world economy of the twenty-first century. In recognizing the rapidly changing business world, the project focuses on certain desired results for the profession and identifies the changes that will be needed to accomplish those long-term goals.

Identifying Issues for the Future To begin, the Vision Project has identified key forces, both domestic and global, affecting the profession. Why are fewer students choosing to become CPAs? Technology is replacing many traditional CPA skills, the new borderless business world requires that accountants (like just about everybody else) expand to offer new skills and services, and the perceived value of some traditional accounting services, including auditing, tax preparation, and accounting itself, is declining. In addition, an increasing number of non-CPA competitors are not bound by the accounting profession's code of standards. In considering these forces, the Vision Project has identified the following as the most important issues in the profession's future:

- CPA success will depend on public perceptions of the CPA's abilities and roles
- CPAs must respond to market needs rather than relying on regulation to keep them in business
- The market demands more high-value consulting and fewer auditing and accounting services
- Specialization will be vital
- CPAs must be conversant in global strategies and global business practices

Global Forces as Drivers of Change The Vision Project explains how the six categories of global forces shown in Figure 18.1 are driving the profession's reorientation. The wide range of these forces touches on nearly all aspects of the CPA's life—everything from working hours to knowledge requirements to cultural relationships to lifestyle requirements.

Recommendations for Change According to surveys identifying the pertinent issues and forces for change, what needs to be done? The Vision Project indicates that CPAs working in the industry, accounting educators, and accounting professionals must make changes in the ways in which the profession functions. Among the top recommendations for change are the following:

- The profession will be enhanced by adopting a broader focus beyond "numbers" that includes "strategic thinking."
- The profession will provide more value to society by expanding knowledge, education, and experience.
- CPA education must be revitalized to meet the demands of the future.
- To attract qualified members, the professional culture must increase opportunities for advancement, rewards, and lifestyle preferences.

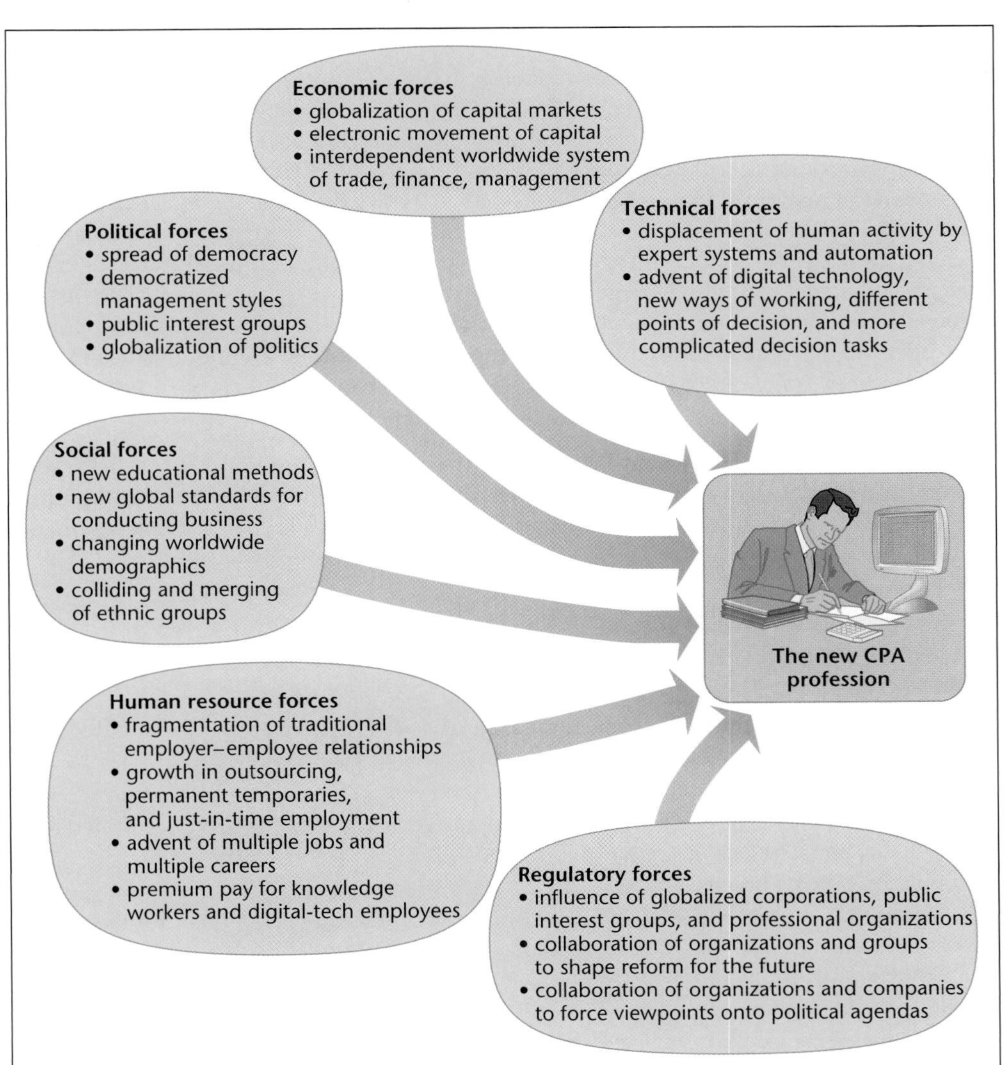

Figure 18.1 Global Forces in the Changing CPA Profession

WebConnection

www.deloitte.com

With 700 offices in more than 130 nations, Deloitte Touche Tohmatsu is one of the Big 5 companies that dominate the world of U.S. and international accounting. You can find out more about the nature and range of services that size and international presence permits the firm to offer by visiting its Web site.

A New Direction Responses from the many participants in the Vision Project reveal the profession's views of its own future. They are summarized in two categories—*Core Services* and *Core Competencies*—that are designed to shape and guide the CPA profession in the twenty-first century.

Core Services *Core services* refer to the work that the CPA performs. The Vision Project reports a stark departure from the traditional range of accounting activities and strongly recommends a broader perspective that moves into areas that have traditionally remained outside the accounting realm. As you can see in Table 18.1, CPAs will seek to expand their activities with new skills in a variety of business activities that must be integrated for better business performance. Financial planning arguably falls in the realm of financial management and beyond accounting's traditional role of reporting on historical financial performance. The distinction has largely been one of perspective—that is, futuristic outlook (financial planning) versus the historical (financial performance reporting). Most companies, however, agree that they could get a clearer picture of their competitive health if the two areas were integrated. The accounting profession's movement in this direction will require major commitments of personal and organizational time and resources.

Core Competencies The Vision Project identifies a unique combination of skills, technology, and knowledge—called *core competencies*—that will be necessary for the future CPA. As Table 18.2 shows, those skills go far beyond the ability to "crunch numbers."

Table 18.1

Core Services in Accounting

- *Assurance and Information Integrity*

A variety of services that improve and assure the quality of information for business activities.

- *Technology*

Services that utilize technology—new business applications in knowledge management, system security, and new-business practices—to improve business activities.

- *Management Consulting and Performance Management*

Broad business knowledge and judgment to supply advice on an organization's strategic, operational, and financial performance.

- *Financial Planning*

Various services—in tax planning, financial transactions, investment portfolio structuring, financial statement analysis—that help clients better understand, interpret, and utilize the full range of financial information.

- *International Business*

Services that enhance performance in global operations and facilitate global commerce.

Table 18.2

Core Competencies in Accounting

- *Strategic and Critical Thinking Skills*
The accountant can provide competent advice for strategic action by combining data, knowledge, and insight.
- *Communications and Leadership Skills*
The accountant can exchange information meaningfully in a variety of business situations with effective delivery and interpersonal skills.
- *Focus on the Customer, Client, and Market*
The accountant can meet the changing needs of clients, customers, and employers better than the competition and can anticipate those needs better than competitors.
- *Skills in Interpreting Converging Information*
The accountant can interpret new meaning by combining financial and nonfinancial information into a broader understanding that adds more business value.
- *Technology Skills*
The accountant can use technology to add value to activities performed for employers, customers, and clients.

Rather, they include certain behavioral skills, along with skills in critical thinking and leadership. Indeed, the Vision Project foresees CPAs who combine specialty skills with a broad-based orientation that permit them to communicate more effectively with people in a broad range of business activities.

TOOLS OF THE ACCOUNTING TRADE

All accountants rely on record keeping, either manual or electronic, to enter and track business transactions. Underlying all record-keeping procedures are the two key concepts of accounting: the *accounting equation* and *double-entry accounting.*

The Accounting Equation

At various points in the year, accountants use the following equation to balance the data pertaining to financial transactions:

$$\text{Assets} = \text{Liabilities} + \text{Owners' equity}$$

To understand the importance of this equation, we must first understand the terms *assets, liabilities,* and *owners' equity.*[8]

Assets and Liabilities Charm and intelligence are often said to be assets, and a nonswimmer is no doubt a liability on a canoeing trip. Accountants apply these same terms to items with quantifiable value. Thus, an **asset** is any economic resource that is expected to benefit a firm or an individual who owns it. Assets include land, buildings, equipment, inventory, and payments due the company (accounts receivable). A **liability** is a debt that the firm owes to an outside organization or individual.

asset
Any economic resource expected to benefit a firm or an individual who owns it

liability
Debt owed by a firm to an outside organization or individual

Owners' Equity You may also have heard of the "equity" that a homeowner has in a home—that is, the amount of money that could be made by selling the house and paying off the mortgage. Similarly, **owners' equity** is the amount of money that owners would receive if they sold all of a company's assets and paid all of its liabilities. We can rewrite the accounting equation to show this definition:

$$\text{Assets} - \text{Liabilities} = \text{Owners' equity}$$

owners' equity
Amount of money that owners would receive if they sold all of a firm's assets and paid all of its liabilities

If a company's assets exceed its liabilities, owners' equity is *positive:* If the company goes out of business, the owners will receive some cash (a gain) after selling assets and paying off liabilities. If liabilities outweigh assets, however, owners' equity is *negative:* Assets are insufficient to pay off all debts. If the company goes out of business, the owners will get no cash and some creditors will not be paid. Owners' equity is a meaningful number to both investors and lenders. For example, before lending money to owners, lenders want to know the amount of owners' equity existing in a business. Owners' equity consists of two sources of capital:

1. The amount that the owners originally invested
2. Profits earned by and reinvested in the company

When a company operates profitably, its assets increase faster than its liabilities. Owners' equity, therefore, will increase if profits are retained in the business instead of paid out as dividends to stockholders. Owners' equity can also increase if owners invest more of their own money to increase assets. However, owners' equity can shrink if the company operates at a loss or if the owners withdraw assets.

Double-Entry Accounting

If your business purchases inventory with cash, you decrease your cash and increase your inventory. Similarly, if you purchase supplies on credit, you increase your supplies and increase your accounts payable. If you invest more money in your business, you increase the company's cash and increase your owners' equity. In other words, *every transaction affects two accounts.* Accountants thus use a **double-entry accounting system** to record the dual effects of financial transactions.

double-entry accounting system
Bookkeeping system that balances the accounting equation by recording the dual effects of every financial transaction

Recording dual effects ensures that the accounting equation always balances. As the term implies, the double-entry system requires at least two bookkeeping entries for each transaction. This practice keeps the accounting equation in balance.

FINANCIAL STATEMENTS

As we noted earlier, the primary purposes of accounting are to summarize the results of a firm's transactions and to issue reports to help managers make informed decisions. Among the most important reports are **financial statements,** which fall into three broad categories—*balance sheets, income statements,* and *statements of cash flows.*[9] We will discuss these three types of financial statements, as well as the function of the *budget* as an internal financial statement. We will conclude by explaining the most important reporting practices and standards that guide accountants in drawing up financial statements.

financial statement
Any of several types of reports summarizing a company's financial status to aid in managerial decision making

Balance Sheets

Balance sheets supply detailed information about the accounting equation factors: assets, liabilities, and owners' equity. Because they also show a firm's financial condition at one point in time, balance sheets are sometimes called *statements of financial position.* Figure 18.2 shows the balance sheet for a hypothetical wholesaler called Perfect Posters.

balance sheet
Financial statement detailing a firm's assets, liabilities, and owners' equity

Assets

As we have seen, an asset is any economic resource that a company owns and from which it can expect to derive some future benefit. From an accounting standpoint, most companies have three types of assets: *current, fixed,* and *intangible.*

Current Assets The **current assets** include cash and assets that can be converted into cash within the following year. They are normally listed in order of **liquidity:** the ease with which they can be converted into cash. Business debts, for example, can usually be satisfied only through payments of cash. A company that needs but cannot generate cash—in other words, a company that is not liquid—may thus be forced to sell assets at sacrifice prices or even go out of business.

current asset
Asset that can or will be converted into cash within the following year

liquidity
Ease with which an asset can be converted into cash

By definition, cash is completely liquid. *Marketable securities* purchased as short-term investments are slightly less liquid but can be sold quickly if necessary. Marketable securities include stocks or bonds of other companies, government securities, and money market certificates. There are three other important nonliquid assets held by many companies: *accounts receivable, merchandise inventory,* and *prepaid expenses.*

Figure 18.2

Perfect Posters' Balance Sheet

Perfect Posters, INC.
555 RIVERVIEW, CHICAGO, IL 60606

Perfect Posters, Inc.
Balance Sheet
As of December 31, 2000

Assets		
Current Assets:		
Cash		$7,050
Marketable securities		2,300
Accounts receivable	$26,210	
Less: Allowance for doubtful accounts	(650)	25,560
Merchandise inventory		21,250
Prepaid expenses		1,050
Total current assets		**$ 57,210**
Fixed assets:		
Land		18,000
Building	65,000	
Less: Accumulated depreciation	(22,500)	42,500
Equipment	72,195	
Less: Accumulated depreciation	(24,815)	47,380
Total fixed assets		**107,880**
Intangible assets:		
Patents	7,100	
Trademarks	900	
Total intangible assets		**8,000**
Total assets		**$173,090**

Liabilities and Owners' Equity		
Current liabilities:		
Accounts payable	$16,315	
Wages payable	3,700	
Taxes payable	1,920	
Total current liabilities		**$ 21,935**
Long-term liabilities:		
Notes payable, 8% due 2001	10,000	
Bonds payable, 9% due 2003	30,000	
Total long-term liabilities		**40,000**
Total liabilities		**$ 61,935**
Owners' Equity:		
Common stock, $5 par	40,000	
Additional paid-in capital	15,000	
Retained earnings	56,155	
Total owners' equity		**111,155**
Total liabilities and owners' equity		**$173,090**

Perfect Posters' balance sheet as of December 31, 2000. Perfect Posters' balance sheet shows clearly that the firm's total assets equal its total liabilities and owners' equity.

Accounts Receivable The **accounts receivable** are amounts due from customers who have purchased goods on credit. Most businesses expect to receive payment within 30 days of a sale. In our hypothetical example, the entry labeled *Less: Allowance for doubtful accounts* in Figure 18.2 indicates $650 in receivables that Perfect Posters does not expect to collect. Total accounts receivable assets are decreased accordingly.

account receivable
Amount due from a customer who has purchased goods on credit

Merchandise Inventory Following accounts receivable on the Perfect Posters' balance sheet is **merchandise inventory**—the cost of merchandise that has been acquired for sale to customers and is still on hand. Accounting for the value of inventories on the balance sheet is difficult because inventories are flowing in and out throughout the year. Therefore, assumptions must be made about which ones were sold and which ones remain in storage.

merchandise inventory
Cost of merchandise that has been acquired for sale to customers and is still on hand

Prepaid Expenses The **prepaid expenses** include supplies on hand and rent paid for the period to come. They are assets because they have been paid for and are available to the company. In all, Perfect Posters' current assets as of December 31, 2000, totaled $57,210.

prepaid expense
Expense, such as prepaid rent, that is paid before the upcoming period in which it is due

Fixed Assets The next major classification on the balance sheet is usually **fixed assets.** Items in this category have long-term use or value (for example, land, buildings, and equipment). As buildings and equipment wear out or become obsolete, their value decreases. To reflect decreasing value, accountants use **depreciation** to spread the cost of an asset over the years of its useful life. Depreciation means calculating an asset's useful life in years, dividing its worth by that many years, and subtracting the resulting amount each year. Each year, therefore, the asset's remaining value decreases on the books. In Figure 18.2, Perfect Posters shows fixed assets of $107,880 after depreciation.

fixed asset
Asset with long-term use or value, such as land, buildings, and equipment

depreciation
Process of distributing the cost of an asset over its life

Intangible Assets Although their worth is hard to set, intangible assets have monetary value. **Intangible assets** usually include the cost of obtaining rights or privileges such as patents, trademarks, copyrights, and franchise fees. **Goodwill** is the amount paid for an

intangible asset
Nonphysical asset, such as a patent or trademark, that has economic value in the form of expected benefit

goodwill
Amount paid for an existing business above the value of its other assets

current liability
Debt that must be paid within the year

accounts payable
Current liabilities consisting of bills owed to suppliers, plus wages and taxes due within the upcoming year

long-term liability
Debt that is not due for more than one year

paid-in capital
Additional money, above proceeds from stock sale, paid directly to a firm by its owners

retained earnings
Earnings retained by a firm for its use rather than paid as dividends

income statement (or **profit-and-loss statement)**
Financial statement listing a firm's annual revenues and expenses so that a bottom line shows annual profit or loss

revenues
Funds that flow into a business from the sale of goods or services

cost of goods sold
Total cost of obtaining materials for making the products sold by a firm during the year

gross profit (or **gross margin)**
Revenues obtained from goods sold minus cost of goods sold

existing business beyond the value of its other assets. A purchased firm, for example, may have a particular good reputation or location.

Perfect Posters has no goodwill assets; however, it does own trademarks and patents for specialized storage equipment. These are intangible assets worth $8,000. Larger companies, of course, have intangible assets that are worth much more.

Liabilities Like assets, liabilities are often separated into different categories. **Current liabilities** are debts that must be paid within one year. These include **accounts payable:** unpaid bills to suppliers for materials as well as wages and taxes that must be paid in the coming year. Perfect Posters has current liabilities of $21,935.

Long-term liabilities are debts that are not due for at least a year. These normally represent borrowed funds on which the company must pay interest. Perfect Posters' long-term liabilities are $40,000.

Owners' Equity The final section of the balance sheet in Figure 18.2 shows owners' equity broken down into *common stock, paid-in capital,* and *retained earnings.* When Perfect Posters was formed, the declared legal value of its common stock was $5 per share. By law, this $40,000 ($5 × 8,000 shares) cannot be distributed as dividends. **Paid-in capital** is additional money invested in the firm by its owners. Perfect Posters has $15,000 in paid-in capital.

Retained earnings are net profits minus dividend payments to stockholders. Retained earnings accumulate when profits, which could have been distributed to stockholders, are kept instead for use by the company. At the close of 2000, Perfect Posters had retained earnings of $56,155.

Income Statements

The **income statement** is sometimes called a **profit-and-loss statement,** because its description of revenues and expenses results in a figure showing the firm's annual profit or loss. In other words,

Revenues − Expenses = Profit (or Loss)

Popularly known as "the bottom line," profit or loss is probably the most important figure in any business enterprise. Figure 18.3 shows the 2000 income statement for Perfect Posters, whose bottom line that year was $12,585. Like the balance sheet, the income statement is divided into three major categories: *revenues, cost of goods sold,* and *operating expenses.*

Revenues When a law firm receives $250 for preparing a will or when a supermarket collects $65 from a customer buying groceries, both are receiving **revenues:** the funds that flow into a business from the sale of goods or services. In 2000, Perfect Posters reported revenues of $256,425 from the sale of art prints and other posters.

Cost of Goods Sold In Perfect Posters' income statement, the **cost of goods sold** category shows the costs of obtaining materials to make the products sold during the year. Perfect Posters began 2000 with posters valued at $22,380. Over the year, it spent another $103,635 to purchase posters. During 2000, then, the company had $126,015 worth of merchandise available to sell. By the end of the year, it had sold all but $21,250 of those posters, which remained as merchandise inventory. The cost of obtaining the goods sold by the firm was thus $104,765.

Gross Profit (or Gross Margin) To calculate **gross profit** (or **gross margin**), subtract cost of goods sold from revenues. Perfect Posters' gross profit in 2000 was $151,660 ($256,425 − $104,765). Expressed as a percentage of sales, gross profit is 59.1 percent ($151,660 / $256,425).

Gross profit percentages vary widely across industries. In retailing, Home Depot <www.homedepot.com> reports a gross profit percentage of 30 percent. In manufactur-

Figure 18.3

Perfect Posters' Income Statement

Perfect Posters, INC.
555 RIVERVIEW, CHICAGO, IL 60606

Perfect Posters, Inc.
Income Statement
Year Ended December 31, 2000

Revenues (gross sales)			**$256,425**
Cost of goods sold:			
Merchandise inventory, January 1, 2000	$22,380		
Merchandise purchases during year	103,635		
Goods available for sale		$126,015	
Less: Merchandise inventory December 31, 2000	21, 250		
Cost of goods sold			**104,765**
Gross profit			**151,660**
Operating expenses:			
Selling and repackaging expenses:			
Salaries and wages	49,750		
Advertising	6,380		
Depreciation—warehouse and repackaging equipment	3,350		
Total selling and repackaging expenses		59, 480	
Administrative expenses:			
Salaries and wages	55,100		
Supplies	4,150		
Utilities	3,800		
Depreciation—office equipment	3,420		
Interest expense	2,900		
Miscellaneous expenses	1,835		
Total administrative expenses		71,205	
Total operating expenses			**130,685**
Operating income (income before taxes)			20,975
Income taxes			8,390
Net income			**$12,585**

Perfect Posters' income statement for year ended December 31, 2000. The final entry on the income statement, the bottom line, reports the firm's profit or loss.

ing, Harley-Davidson <www.harley-davidson.com> reports 34 percent, and in the pharmaceutical industry, American Home Products <www.ahp.com> reports 73 percent. For companies with low gross margins, product costs are a big expense. If a company has a high gross margin, it probably has low cost of goods sold but high selling and administrative expenses.

Operating Expenses In addition to costs directly related to acquiring goods, every company has general expenses ranging from erasers to the president's salary. Like cost of goods sold, **operating expenses** are resources that must flow out of a company for it to earn revenues. As you can see from Figure 18.3, Perfect Posters had 2000 operating expenses of $130,685. This figure consists of $59,480 in selling and repackaging expenses and $71,205 in administrative expenses.

Selling expenses result from activities related to selling the firm's goods or services. These may include salaries for the sales force, delivery costs, and advertising expenses. General and administrative expenses, such as management salaries, insurance expenses, and maintenance costs, are expenses related to the general management of the company.

operating expenses
Costs, other than the cost of goods sold, incurred in producing a good or service

operating income
Gross profit minus operating expenses

Operating and Net Income Sometimes managers must determine **operating income,** which compares the gross profit from business operations against operating expenses. This calculation for Perfect Posters ($151,660 − $130,685) reveals an operating income, or *income before taxes,* of $20,975. Subtracting income taxes from operating income ($20,975 − $8,390) reveals **net income** (also called **net profit** or **net earnings**). In 2000, Perfect Posters' net income was $12,585.

net income (or **net profit** or **net earnings)**
Gross profit minus operating expenses and income taxes

Statements of Cash Flows

statement of cash flows
Financial statement describing a firm's yearly cash receipts and cash payments

Some companies prepare only balance sheets and income statements. However, the Securities and Exchange Commission <www.sec.gov> also requires all firms whose stock is publicly traded to issue a third report: a **statement of cash flows.** This statement describes a company's yearly cash receipts and cash payments. It shows the effects on cash of three business activities:

- *Cash flows from operations.* This part of the statement is concerned with the firm's main operating activities: the cash transactions involved in buying and selling goods and services. It reveals how much of the year's profits result from the firm's main line of business (for example, Jaguar's sales of automobiles) rather than from secondary activities (for example, licensing fees a clothing firm paid to Jaguar for using the Jaguar logo on shirts).
- *Cash flows from investing* This section reports net cash used in or provided by investing. It includes cash receipts and payments from buying and selling stocks, bonds, property, equipment, and other productive assets.
- *Cash flows from financing* The final section reports net cash from all financing activities. It includes cash inflows from borrowing or issuing stock as well as outflows for payment of dividends and repayment of borrowed money.

The overall change in cash from these three sources provides information to lenders and investors. When creditors and stockholders know how firms obtained and used their funds during the course of a year, it is easier for them to interpret the year-to-year changes in the firm's balance sheet and income statement.

The Budget: An Internal Financial Statement

budget
Detailed statement of estimated receipts and expenditures for a period of time in the future

In addition to financial statements, managers need other types of accounting information to aid in internal planning, controlling, and decision making. Probably the most crucial internal financial statement is the budget. A **budget** is a detailed statement of estimated receipts and expenditures for a period of time in the future. Although that period is usually one year, some companies also prepare budgets for three- or five-year periods, especially when considering major capital expenditures.

Budgets are also useful for keeping track of weekly or monthly performance. Procter & Gamble evaluates all of its business units monthly by comparing actual financial results with monthly budgeted amounts. Discrepancies in actual versus budget totals signal potential problems and initiate action to get financial performance back on track.

Although the accounting staff coordinates the budget process, it requires input from many people in the company regarding proposed activities, needed resources, and input sources. Figure 18.4 is a sample sales budget. In preparing such a budget, the accounting department must obtain from the sales group both its projections for units to be sold and expected expenses for each quarter of the coming year. Accountants then draw up the final budget, and throughout the year, the accounting department compares the budget to actual expenditures and revenues in the sales group.

Reporting Standards and Practices

Accountants follow numerous standard reporting practices and principles when they prepare external reports, including financial statements. The common language dictated by standard practices is designed to give external users confidence in the accuracy and meaning of the information in any financial statement. Spelled out in great detail in GAAP, these principles cover a wide range of issues, such as when to recognize revenues from operations, the so-called *matching* of revenues and expenses, and full public disclosure of financial information to the public. Without agreed-upon practices in these and many other accounting categories, users of financial statements would be unable to compare financial information from different companies and thus misunderstand—or be led to misconstrue—a given company's true financial status.

Figure 18.4

Perfect Posters' Sales Budget

□□□□□□□□□□□□□ **Perfect Posters**, INC.
555 RIVERVIEW, CHICAGO, IL 60606

Perfect Posters, Inc.
Sales Budget
First Quarter, 2001

	January	February	March	Quarter
Budgeted sales (units)	7,500	6,000	6,500	20,000
Budgeted selling price per unit	$3.50	$3.50	$3.50	$3.50
Budgeted sales revenue	$ 26,250	$ 21,000	$ 22,750	$ 70,000
Expected cash receipts:				
From December sales	$26,210[a]			$26,210
From January sales	17,500[b]	$8,750		26,250
From February sales		14,000	$7,000	21,000
From March sales			15,200	15,200
Total cash receipts:	$ 43,710	$ 22,750	$ 22,200	$ 88,660

[a]This cash from December sales represents a collection of the accounts receivable appearing on the December 31, 2000, balance sheet.
[b]The company estimates that two-thirds of each month's sales revenues will result in cash receipts during the same month. The remaining one-third is collected during the following month.

Revenue Recognition As we noted earlier, revenues are funds that flow into a business as a result of its operating activities during the accounting period. *Revenue recognition* is the formal recording and reporting of revenues in the financial statements. Although any firm earns revenues continuously as it makes sales, earnings are not reported until the earnings cycle is completed. This cycle is complete under two conditions:

1. The sale is complete and the product has been delivered.
2. The sale price to the customer has been collected or is collectable (accounts receivable).

The completion of the earning cycle determines the timing for revenue recognition in the firm's financial statements. Revenues are recorded for the accounting period in which sales are completed and collectable (or collected). This practice assures the reader that the statement gives a fair comparison of what was gained for the resources that were given up.

Matching Net income is calculated by subtracting expenses from revenues. The matching principle states that expenses will be matched with revenues to determine net income for an accounting period.[10] Why is this principle important? It permits the user of the statement to see how much net gain resulted from the assets that had to be given up in order to generate revenues during the period covered in the statement. Consequently, when we match revenue recognition with expense recognition, we get net income for the period.

Consider the hypothetical case of Little Red Wagon Co. Let's see what happens when the books are kept in two different ways:

1. Revenue recognition is matched with expense recognition to determine net income when the earnings cycle is *completed* (the correct method).
2. Revenue recognition occurs *before* the earnings cycle is completed (an incorrect method).

Suppose that 500 red wagons are produced and delivered to customers at a sales price of $20 each during the year 2000. In the next year, 600 red wagons are produced and delivered. In part (A) of Table 18.3, the correct matching method has been used: Revenues are recorded for the accounting period in which sales are completed and collectable from customers, as are the expenses of producing and delivering them. The revenues from sales are matched against the expenses of completing them. By using the matching principle, we see clearly how much better off the company is at the end of each accounting period as a result of that period's operations: It earned $2,000 net income for the first year and did even better in 2001.

In part (B) of the table, revenue recognition and the matching principle have been violated. Certain activities of the two accounting periods are disguised and mixed together rather than being separated for each period. The result is a distorted performance report that incorrectly shows that 2000 was a better year than 2001. Here's what Red Wagon's accountants did wrong: The sales department sold 200 red wagons (with revenues of $4,000) to a customer late in year 2000. Those *revenues* are included in the $14,000 for year 2000. But because the 200 wagons were produced and delivered to the customer in year 2001, the *expenses* are recorded, as in (A), for year 2001. The result is a distorted picture of operations: It looks as if expenses for 2001 are out of line for such a low sales level, and it looks as if expenses (as compared to revenues) were kept under better control during 2000. The firm's accountants violated the matching principle by ignoring *the period during which the earnings cycle was completed.* Although $4,000 in sales of wagons occurred in 2000, the earnings cycle for those wagons is not completed until they were produced and delivered, which occurred in 2001. Accordingly, both the revenues and expenses for those 200 wagons should have been reported in the same period—namely, in 2001, as was reported in part (A). There, we can see clearly what was gained and what was lost on activities that were completed *in an accounting period.* By requiring this practice, the matching principle provides consistency in reporting and avoids financial distortions.

Full Disclosure Full disclosure means that financial statements should include not just numbers, but also interpretations and explanations by management so that external users can better understand information contained in the statements. Because they know more about inside events than outsiders, management prepares additional useful information that explains certain events or transactions or discloses the circumstances underlying certain financial results.

Table 18.3

Revenue Recognition and the Matching Principle

(A) THE CORRECT METHOD REVEALS EACH ACCOUNTING PERIOD'S ACTIVITIES AND RESULTS

	Year Ended December 31, 2000	Year Ended December 31, 2001
Revenues	$10,000	$12,000
Expenses	8,000	9,000
Net income	2,000	3,000

(B) THE INCORRECT METHOD DISGUISES EACH ACCOUNTING PERIOD'S ACTIVITIES AND RESULTS

	Year Ended December 31, 2000	Year Ended December 31, 2001
Revenues	$14,000	$8,000
Expenses	8,000	9,000
Net income	6,000	(1,000)

ANALYZING FINANCIAL STATEMENTS

Financial statements present a great deal of information, but what does it all mean? How, for example, can statements help investors decide what stock to buy or help managers decide whether to extend credit? Statements provide data, which can in turn be applied to various ratios (comparative numbers). These ratios can then be used to analyze the financial health of one or more companies. They can also be used to check a firm's progress by comparing current with past statements.

Ratios are normally grouped into three major classifications:

- **Solvency ratios,** both short- and long-term, estimate risk.
- **Profitability ratios** measure potential earnings.
- **Activity ratios** reflect management's use of assets.

Depending on the decisions to be made, a user may apply none, some, or all the ratios in a particular classification.

solvency ratio
Financial ratio, either short- or long-term, for estimating the risk in investing in a firm

profitability ratio
Financial ratio for measuring a firm's potential earnings

activity ratio
Financial ratio for evaluating management's use of a firm's assets

Short-Term Solvency Ratios

In the short run, a company's survival depends on its ability to pay its immediate debts. Such payments require cash. Short-term solvency ratios measure a company's relative liquidity and thus its ability to pay immediate debts. The higher a firm's **liquidity ratios,** then, the lower the risk involved for investors. The most commonly used liquidity ratio is the *current ratio.*

liquidity ratio
Solvency ratio measuring a firm's ability to pay its immediate debts

Current Ratio The most commonly used liquidity ratio is the current ratio, which has been called the "banker's ratio" because it concerns a firm's creditworthiness. The **current ratio** measures a company's ability to meet current obligations out of current assets. It thus reflects a firm's ability to generate cash to meet obligations through the normal, orderly process of selling inventories and collecting accounts receivable. It is calculated by dividing current assets by current liabilities.

current ratio
Solvency ratio that determines a firm's creditworthiness by measuring its ability to pay current liabilities

As a rule, a current ratio is satisfactory if it is 2:1 or higher—that is, if current assets more than double current liabilities. A smaller ratio may indicate that a company will have difficulty paying its bills. Note, however, that a larger ratio may imply that assets are not being used productively and should be invested elsewhere.

How does Perfect Posters measure up? Look again at the balance sheet in Figure 18.2. Judging from its current assets and current liabilities at the end of 2000, we see that

$$\frac{\text{Current assets}}{\text{Current liabilities}} = \frac{\$57,210}{\$21,935} = 2.61$$

How does Perfect Posters' ratio compare with those of other companies? Not bad: It's lower than O'Reilly Automotive <www.oreillyauto.com> (3.17) and higher than those of Gillette <www.gillette.com> (1.56), Cisco Systems <www.cisco.com> (1.54), and Starwood Hotels & Resorts Worldwide <www.sheraton.com> (0.23). Although Perfect Posters may be holding too much uninvested cash, it looks like a good credit risk.

Working Capital A related measure is **working capital:** the difference between the firm's current assets and its current liabilities. Working capital indicates the firm's ability to pay off short-term debts (liabilities) that it owes to outsiders. At the end of 2000, Perfect Posters' working capital was \$35,275 (that is, \$57,210 − \$21,935). Because current liabilities must be paid off within one year, current assets are more than enough to meet current obligations.

working capital
Difference between a firm's current assets and current liabilities

Long-Term Solvency Ratios

To survive in the long run, a company must be able to meet both its short-term (current) debts and its long-term liabilities. These latter debts usually involve interest payments.

A firm that cannot meet them is in danger of collapse or takeover—a risk that makes creditors and investors quite cautious. The 1998 Asian financial crisis was fueled by a loss of confidence by investors in large firms in Japan and Korea that could not meet their long-term cash obligations.

debt ratio
Solvency ratio measuring a firm's ability to meet its long-term debts

debt-to-owners' equity ratio (or debt-to-equity ratio)
Solvency ratio describing the extent to which a firm is financed through borrowing

debt
A firm's total liabilities

Debt-to-Owners' Equity Ratio To measure the risk that a company may encounter this problem, we use the long-term solvency ratios called **debt ratios.** The most commonly used debt ratio is the **debt-to-owners' equity ratio** (or **debt-to-equity ratio**), which describes the extent to which a firm is financed through borrowed money. It is calculated by dividing **debt**—total liabilities—by owners' equity.

This ratio is commonly used to compare a given company's status with industry averages. For example, companies with debt-to-equity ratios above 1 are probably relying too much on debt. Such firms may find themselves owing so much debt that they lack the income needed to meet interest payments or to repay borrowed money.

In the case of Perfect Posters, we can see from the balance sheet in Figure 18.2 that the debt-to-equity ratio works out as follows:

$$\frac{\text{Debt}}{\text{Owners' equity}} = \frac{\$61{,}935}{\$111{,}155} = 0.56$$

leverage
Ability to finance an investment through borrowed funds

Leverage Note that a fairly high debt-to-equity ratio may sometimes be not only acceptable but also desirable. Borrowing funds provides **leverage:** the ability to make otherwise unaffordable purchases. In *leveraged buyouts (LBOs),* firms have willingly taken on sometimes huge debt in order to buy out other companies. When the purchased company allows the buying company to earn profits above the cost of the borrowed funds, leveraging makes sound financial sense, even if it raises the buyer's debt-to-equity ratio. Unfortunately, many buyouts have fallen into financial trouble when actual profits dropped short of anticipated levels or when rising rates increased interest payments on the debt acquired by the buyer.

Profitability Ratios

Although it is important to know that a company is solvent in both the long and the short term, safety or risk alone is not an adequate basis for investment decisions. Investors also want some measure of the returns they can expect. *Return on equity* and *earnings per share* are two commonly used profitability ratios.

return on equity
Profitability ratio measuring income earned for each dollar invested

Return on Equity Owners are interested in the net income earned by a business for each dollar invested. **Return on equity** measures this performance by dividing net income (recorded in the income statement, Figure 18.3) by total owners' equity (recorded in the balance sheet, Figure 18.2).[11] For Perfect Posters, the return-on-equity ratio in 2000 can be calculated as follows:

$$\frac{\text{Net income}}{\text{Total owners' equity}} = \frac{\$12{,}585}{\$111{,}155} = 11.3\%$$

Is this figure good or bad? There is no set answer. If Perfect Posters' ratio for 2000 is higher than in previous years, owners and investors should be encouraged. But if 11.3 percent is lower than the ratios of other companies in the same industry, they should be concerned.

earnings per share
Profitability ratio measuring the size of the dividend that a firm can pay shareholders

Earnings per Share Defined as net income divided by the number of shares of common stock outstanding, **earnings per share** determines the size of the dividend that a company can pay its shareholders. Investors use this ratio to decide whether to buy or sell a company's stock. As the ratio gets higher, the stock value increases, because investors know that the firm can better afford to pay dividends. Naturally, stock will lose market value if the latest financial statements report a decline in earnings per share. For Perfect Posters, we can use the net income total from the income statement in Figure 18.3 to calculate earnings per share as follows:

$$\frac{\text{Net income}}{\text{Number of common shares outstanding}} = \frac{\$12{,}585}{8{,}000} = \$1.57 \text{ per share}$$

As a baseline for comparison, note that Gucci's recent earnings were $3.48 per share. The Walt Disney Co. <www.disney.go.com> earned $0.62.

Activity Ratios

The efficiency with which a firm uses resources is linked to profitability. As a potential investor, then, you want to know which company gets more mileage from its resources. Activity ratios measure this efficiency. For example, say that two firms use the same amount of resources or assets. If Firm A generates greater profits or sales, it is more efficient and thus has a better activity ratio.

What key accounting principles do failing business overlook?

inventory turnover ratio Activity ratio measuring the average number of times that inventory is sold and restocked during the year

Inventory Turnover Ratio Certain specific measures can be used to explain how one firm earns greater profits than another. One of the most important is the **inventory turnover ratio,** which measures the average number of times that inventory is sold and restocked during the year—that is, how quickly it is produced and sold.[12] First, you need to know your *average inventory:* the typical amount of inventory on hand during the year. You can calculate average inventory by adding end-of-year inventory to beginning-of-year inventory and dividing by 2. You can now find your inventory turnover ratio, which is expressed as the cost of goods sold divided by average inventory:

$$\frac{\text{Cost of goods sold}}{\text{Average inventory}} = \frac{\text{Cost of goods sold}}{(\text{Beginning inventory} + \text{Ending inventory})/2}$$

A high inventory turnover ratio means efficient operations: Because a smaller amount of investment is tied up in inventory, the company's funds can be put to work elsewhere to earn greater returns. However, inventory turnover must be compared with both prior years and industry averages. An inventory turnover rate of 5, for example, might be

As a retailer of both toys and childcare products, Toys "R" Us <www.amazon.com> experiences a wide range of turnover rates. For example, seasonal toys turn over less than three times per year. On the other hand, baby formula and diapers turn over more than 12 times annually. The average for an entire store is about three times per year. The benefits of high turnover include fewer markdowns and less depreciation, lower inventory expenses, and a higher rate of return on inventory investment.

excellent for an auto supply store, but it would be disastrous for a supermarket, where a rate of about 15 is common. Rates can also vary within a company that markets a variety of products. To calculate Perfect Posters' inventory turnover ratio for 2000, we take the merchandise inventory figures for the income statement in Figure 18.3. The ratio can be expressed as follows:

$$\frac{\$104{,}765}{(\$22{,}380 + \$21{,}250)/2} = 4.8 \text{ times}$$

In other words, new merchandise replaces old merchandise every 76 days (365 days/4.8). The 4.8 ratio is below the average of 7.0 for comparable wholesaling operations, indicating that the business is slightly inefficient.

International Accounting

More U.S. companies are buying and selling goods and services in other countries. Coca-Cola and Boeing receive large portions of their operating revenues from sales in many countries around the globe. Conversely, firms such as Toastmaster Inc. buy components for electric appliances from suppliers in Asia. Retailers such as Sears and Kmart buy merchandise from other countries for merchandising in the United States. In addition, more and more companies own subsidiaries in other countries. Obviously, accounting for foreign transactions involves some special procedures. One of the most basic is translating the values of the currencies of different countries.

Foreign Currency Exchange A unique consideration in international accounting is the value of currencies and their exchange rates. As we saw in Chapter 3, the value of any country's currency is subject to occasional change. Political and economic conditions, for instance, affect the stability of a nation's currency and its value relative to the currencies of other countries. Whereas the Swiss franc has a long history of stability, the Brazilian real has a history of instability.

foreign currency exchange rate
Value of a nation's currency as determined by market forces

As it is traded each day around the world, any currency's value is determined by market forces: what buyers are willing to pay for it. The resulting values are called **foreign currency exchange rates.** How volatile are such rates? Table 18.4 shows the changes in exchange rates for some foreign currencies during a one-year period. Each table entry shows the U.S. dollar value of a unit of that nation's currency. For example, one French franc was worth 0.173 U.S. dollars in January 2000. When a nation's currency becomes unstable—that is, when its value changes frequently—it is regarded as a *weak* currency. The value of the Brazilian real fluctuated between 0.55 and 0.93—a variation range of 70 percent in U.S. dollars—during the period from 1997 to 1999. On the other hand, the Swiss franc is said to be a strong currency because its value historically rises or holds steady in comparison to the U.S. dollar. As exchange rate changes occur, they must be considered by accountants when recording a firm's international transactions. They will have an impact, perhaps profound, on the amount that a firm pays for foreign purchases and the amount it gains from sales to foreign buyers.

Table 18.4
Foreign Currency Exchange Rates

Country	Monetary Unit	Dollar Value January 31, 1999	Dollar Value January 31, 2000	% Change in Value
Canada	dollar	0.6900	0.6600	−4.3
China	yuan	0.1200	0.1200	0.0
France	franc	0.1480	0.1730	+16.9
Japan	yen	0.0093	0.0086	−7.5
Switzerland	franc	0.6000	0.7100	+18.3

Life Cycle of an e-Business

How to Account for Growth

Of particular significance for any analysis of Garden.com's financial status was the company's unique position as both a start-up and an e-business. For such a company, traditional benchmarks for ratio analysis may not necessarily be meaningful. In fact, Garden.com's current ratio of 16:1 for the quarter ending in September 1999 was far above the traditional 2:1 benchmark. Furthermore, it is not surprising to see a start-up firm's financial ratios changing rapidly. Again, in the subsequent six-month period ending March 2000, Garden.com's current ratio had moved to about 7:1. When a company's financial history dates back no further than 1995, only limited historical period-to-period comparisons are possible. While ratios alone did not foretell its future, the company's first Annual Report became available in October 2000. The most glaring numbers for fiscal 2000 were a net income of –$38.7 million, along with earnings per share of –$2.74. When added to deficits from earlier years, these losses reflected a shaky financial position that could be overcome only by a gigantic upsurge in sales or an infusion of cash by investors.

Garden.com's unusual situation, then, attached exceptional importance to management's interpretations of the firm's financial position. Accordingly, Garden.com's *1999 Prospectus* contained a prophetic insight into the firm's precarious financial position in 2000. In part, a section entitled "Management's Discussion and Analysis of Financial Condition and Results of Operations" read as follows:

> *The following discussion and analysis of our financial condition and results of operations should be read in conjunction with the Financial Statements and the related notes. This discussion contains forward-looking statements based upon current expectations that involve risks and uncertainties, such as our plans, objectives, expectations and intentions. Our actual results and the timing of certain events could differ materially from those anticipated in these forward-looking statements. . . .*
>
> *. . . Since inception, we have incurred significant losses and, as of June 30, 1999, had incurred cumulative net losses of $26.8 million. We expect to experience operating losses and negative cash flow for the foreseeable future. We anticipate our losses will increase significantly from current levels. As a result, we will need to generate significant revenues to achieve and maintain profitability. . . .*
>
> *. . . We have a limited operating history on which to base an evaluation of our business and prospects. You must consider our prospects in light of the risks, expenses and difficulties frequently encountered by companies in their early stage of development, particularly companies in new and rapidly evolving markets such as online commerce. . . . We cannot assure you that we will be successful in addressing these risks, and our failure to do so could have a negative impact on our business, operating results and financial condition.*

The document also contained a "Report of the Independent Auditors," Ernst & Young LLP, which, again in part, stated the following:

> *We conducted our audits in accordance with generally accepted auditing standards. Those standards require that we plan and perform the audit to obtain reasonable assurance about whether the financial statements are free of material misstatement. . . . We believe that our audits provide a reasonable basis for our opinion.*
>
> *. . . In our opinion, the financial statements referred to above present fairly, in all material respects, the financial position of Garden.com, Inc. at June 30, 1998 and 1999 and the results of its operations and its cash flows for each of the three years in the period ended June 30, 1999, in conformity with generally accepted accounting principles. . . .*

Unfortunately, the financial and competitive problems expressed in the forgoing document continued to fester during the last half of 1999 and into 2000. The firm's financial losses did indeed continue to accumulate, eventually reaching more than $75 million. The financial picture became so dire that in September 2000, Garden.com's chief financial officer announced that there was not enough cash on-hand to get through the holiday season. In October, the firm's independent auditor, citing Garden.com's recurring operating losses and negative cash flows from operations, raised substantial doubt about the company's ability to continue as a viable concern.

International Transactions International purchases, sales on credit, and accounting for foreign subsidiaries all involve accounting transactions that include currency exchange rates. When a U.S. company called Village Wine and Cheese Shops imports Bordeau wine from a French company called Pierre Bourgeois, its accountant must be sure that Village's books reflect its true costs. The amount owed to Pierre Bourgeois changes daily along with the exchange rate between francs and dollars. Thus our accountant must identify the actual rate on the day that payment in francs is made so that the correct U.S. dollar cost of the purchased wine is recorded.

International Accounting Standards Professional accounting groups of about 80 countries are members of the International Accounting Standards Committee (IASC) <www.iasc.org.uk>, which is trying to eliminate differences in financial reporting across countries.[13] Bankers, investors, and managers would like to see financial reporting that is comparable from country to country and across all firms regardless of home nation. Standardization is occurring in some areas but is far from universal. The financial statements required by the IASC, for example, include an income statement, a balance sheet, and statement of cash flows similar to those issued by U.S. accountants. International standards, however, do not require a uniform format, and variety abounds.

WebConnection

www.iasc.org.uk

The IASC was founded in 1973, and its current membership consists of more than 140 professional accounting organizations from over 100 nations. Its Web site publishes its body of standards and interpretations, as well as a wealth of information about accounting on an international scale. To find out why the IASC has undertaken its various projects, log on to its Web site.

Continued from page 501

The Shrill Sound of Financial Repercussions

Just how serious can the consequences of misrepresentation be? Unfortunately for Columbia/HCA, Quorum Health Group, and their owners, the effects of the probe initiated by James Alderson's allegations linger even today. Litigation continues and more executives come under fire. Two Quorum executives—the chief financial officer and the executive vice president—departed in mid-1999 while the company's federal whistle-blower lawsuit was still pending. By September 1999, four Columbia/HCA executives had faced criminal trials. Two were convicted of fraud, and each faced sentences of up to 30 years in prison and fines of \$1.5 million. One defendant, facing charges of conspiracy to commit Medicare fraud, entered a plea agreement to cooperate, pay restitution, and perform community service. The fourth defendant was acquitted.

Investors have also made known their uncertainty about the financial prospects of the two companies. By October 1998, after the federal government had joined the case, Columbia/HCA's stock, which had been selling at a high near $38 per share in mid-1997, had fallen by more than half, to about $17. In February 2000, stockholders were still hurting as HCA's stock had recovered only slightly, hovering near $20. Quorum's market performance has been even more unsettling, falling from near $29 to around $10 in the two-year period ending in February 2000. In announcing the firm's declining earnings for the fourth quarter ending in June 1999, CEO James Dalton declared that the allegations of Medicare fraud were false and that Quorum would fight. The fourth-quarter income statement included a $1.5 million charge for litigation costs that contributed to a sharp decline in earnings per share.

Perhaps the seriousness of the concern for the public's perceptions and apprehensions is best reflected in a recent action by one of the two firms: Columbia/HCA Healthcare Corporation recently renamed itself: It is now HCA—The Healthcare Company. Perhaps a new image will take shape. The lesson, however, seems clear: The costly grappling with accusations of fraud can be avoided by applying strict accounting standards. Companies who disregard those standards can expect untold grief.

Questions for Discussion

1. What's wrong with keeping two sets of accounting books?
2. What do you believe is the role of a firm's accounting staff when accountants detect improper practices?
3. Suppose your company asks you to set up a program for internal accountants to follow in order to ensure that proper accounting standards are used throughout the firm. Outline a program that accountants should follow when any discrepancy is first noticed. If that first step fails to correct the discrepancy, identify the next steps that should be taken.
4. Considering the two-to-three-year time span covered by the Healthcare–Quorum episode, think about how such a series of events can affect a firm's balance sheets and income statements. How do you suppose the situation has affected Quorum's and HCA's financial statements.
5. Suppose that you, as a certified accountant, were in a situation similar to that of James F. Alderson. As a CPA, you have agreed to adhere to a professional code of ethics that obligates you to take action when you notice violations of accounting standards. Is it proper for you, as a whistle-blower and an accountant, to accept as payment a percentage of the money that the government eventually recovers from the violators? Why or why not?

SUMMARY OF LEARNING OBJECTIVES

1 **Explain the role of accountants and distinguish between the kinds of work done by *public* and *private accountants*.** By collecting, analyzing, and communicating financial information, accountants provide business managers and investors with an accurate picture of the firm's financial health. *Certified public accountants (CPAs)* are licensed professionals who provide auditing, tax, and management advisory services for other firms and individuals. *Public accountants* who have not yet been certified perform similar tasks. *Private accountants* provide diverse specialized services for the specific firms that employ them.

2 **Discuss the *CPA Vision Project* and explain how the CPA profession is changing.** The Vision Project is a professionwide assessment to see what the future of the accounting profession will be like. It was initiated because of the

declining number of students entering the accounting profession and because of rapid changes in the business world. Practicing CPAs and other industry leaders have participated in identifying key forces that are affecting the profession. Then they developed recommendations for change, including a set of *core services* that the profession should offer clients and a set of *core competencies* that CPAs should possess. Overall, the new vision reflects changes in the CPA's culture and professional lifestyle.

3 **Explain how the following two concepts are used in *recordkeeping:* the *accounting equation* and *double-entry accounting*.** The *accounting equation* (assets = liabilities + owners' equity) is used to balance the data in accounting documents. *Double-entry accounting* acknowledges the dual effects of financial transactions and ensures that the accounting equation always balances. These tools enable accountants not only to enter but to track transactions. They also serve as double checks for accounting errors.

4 **Describe the three basic *financial statements* and show how they reflect the activity and financial condition of a business.** The *balance sheet* summarizes a company's assets, liabilities, and owners' equity at a given point in time. The *income statement* details revenues and expenses for a given period of time and identifies any profit or loss. The *statement of cash flows* reports cash receipts and payments from operating, investing, and financing activities.

5 **Explain how computing *key financial ratios* can help in analyzing the financial strengths of a business.** Drawing on data from financial statements, ratios can help creditors, investors, and managers assess a firm's finances. The *liquidity ratios—current* and *debt-to-equity—*measure *solvency* (a firm's ability to pay its debt) in both the short and the long run. *Return on equity* and *earnings per share* measure *profitability. Inventory turnover ratios* show how efficiently a firm is using its funds.

6 **Explain some of the special issues facing accountants at firms that do international business.** Accounting for foreign transactions involves some special procedures. First, accountants must consider the fact that the *exchange rates* of national currencies change. Accordingly, the value of a foreign currency at any given time, its foreign currency exchange rate, is what buyers are willing to pay for it.

Exchange rates affect the amount of money that a firm pays for foreign purchases and the amount that it gains from foreign sales. U.S. accountants, therefore, must always translate foreign currencies into the value of the U.S. dollar. Then, in recording a firm's transactions, they must make adjustments to reflect shifting exchange rates over time. Shifting rates may result in either foreign currency transaction gains (a debt, for example, may be paid with fewer dollars) or foreign currency transaction losses.

QUESTIONS AND EXERCISES

Questions for Review

1. Identify the three types of services performed by CPAs.
2. How does the double-entry system reduce the chances of mistakes or fraud in accounting?
3. What are the three basic financial statements and what major information does each contain?
4. Identify the three major classifications of financial statement ratios and give an example of one ratio in each category.
5. Explain how financial ratios allow managers to monitor their own efficiency and effectiveness.

Questions for Analysis

6. If you were planning to invest in a company, which of the three types of financial statements would you most want to see? Why?
7. Dasar Co. reports the following data in its September 30, 2000, financial statements:
   - Gross sales $225,000
   - Current assets 40,000
   - Long-term assets 100,000
   - Current liabilities 16,000
   - Long-term liabilities 44,000
   - Owners' equity 80,000
   - Net income 7,200

   Compute the following ratios: current ratio, debt-to-equity ratio, and return on owners' equity.

Application Exercises

8. Interview an accountant at a local manufacturing firm. Trace the process by which budgets are developed in that company. How does the firm use budgets? How does budgeting help managers plan business activities? How does budgeting help them control business activities? Give examples.
9. Interview the manager of a local retail or wholesale business about taking inventory. What is the firm's primary purpose in taking inventory? How often is it done?

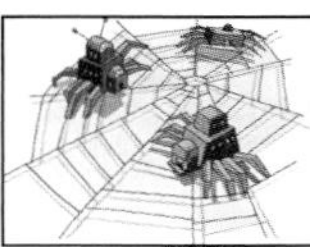

EXPLORING THE WEB

A FIELD TRIP TO THE AICPA

Most business practitioners belong to professional associations that provide services for members. The American Institute of Certified Public Accountants (AICPA) is one of accounting's best-known associations. To learn about the purpose of the AICPA and the activities that it offers, visit its Web site at:

www.aicpa.org/

Spend some time navigating through the homepage. To get an idea of the variety of topics covered and services offered for AICPA members, enter each of the subject gates (point the mouse to the title and click) ranged up and down the page. Next, scroll down the page into the Site Directory and select, for example, **AICPA Conferences.** After reviewing the area that you selected, consider the following questions:

1. Examine the list of AICPA conferences sorted by date. Notice the variety of conference topics and locations throughout the year. Are any of the topics or locations of interest to you? Do you think that anyone other than accountants might get some value from attending a conference? Explain.
2. Look at the AICPA Software offerings (in the Site Directory). Why does the AICPA offer this software to its members? As you scan down the AICPA Software screen, click on *Product Highlights* and examine the various product offerings. Identify at least three different kinds of software and explain what they do for the user.
3. After returning to the Site Directory, scan down the page and click on *Students*. Explore the Career section. From a career standpoint, which of the items (the aspects of accounting life) are appealing to you and which are not? Return to the Students page and scan down to *About Becoming a CPA*. Now go to *FAQs (Frequently Asked Questions) on Accounting Careers*. What is your opinion about the "150-hour education program"? What are its pros and cons?

BUILDING YOUR BUSINESS SKILLS

PUTTING THE BUZZ IN BILLING

This exercise enhances the following SCANS workplace competencies: demonstrating basic skills, demonstrating thinking skills, exhibiting interpersonal skills, working with information, and applying system knowledge.

GOAL

To encourage students to think about the advantages and disadvantages of using an electronic system for handling accounts receivable and accounts payable.

METHOD

Step 1

Study Figure 18.5 on the following page. The outside circle depicts the seven steps involved in the issuing of paper bills to customers, the payment of these bills by customers, and the handling by banks of debits and credits for the two accounts. The inside circle shows the same bill issuance and payment process handled electronically.

Step 2

As the chief financial officer of a Midwestern utility company, you are analyzing the feasibility of switching from a paper to an electronic system of billing and bill payment. You decide to discuss the ramifications of the choice with three business associates (choose three classmates to take on these roles). Your discussion requires that you research electronic payment systems now being developed. Specifically, using online and library research, you must find out as much as you can about the electronic bill-paying systems being developed by Visa International, Intuit, IBM, and the Checkfree Corp. After you have researched this information, brainstorm the advantages and disadvantages of using an electronic bill-paying system in your company.

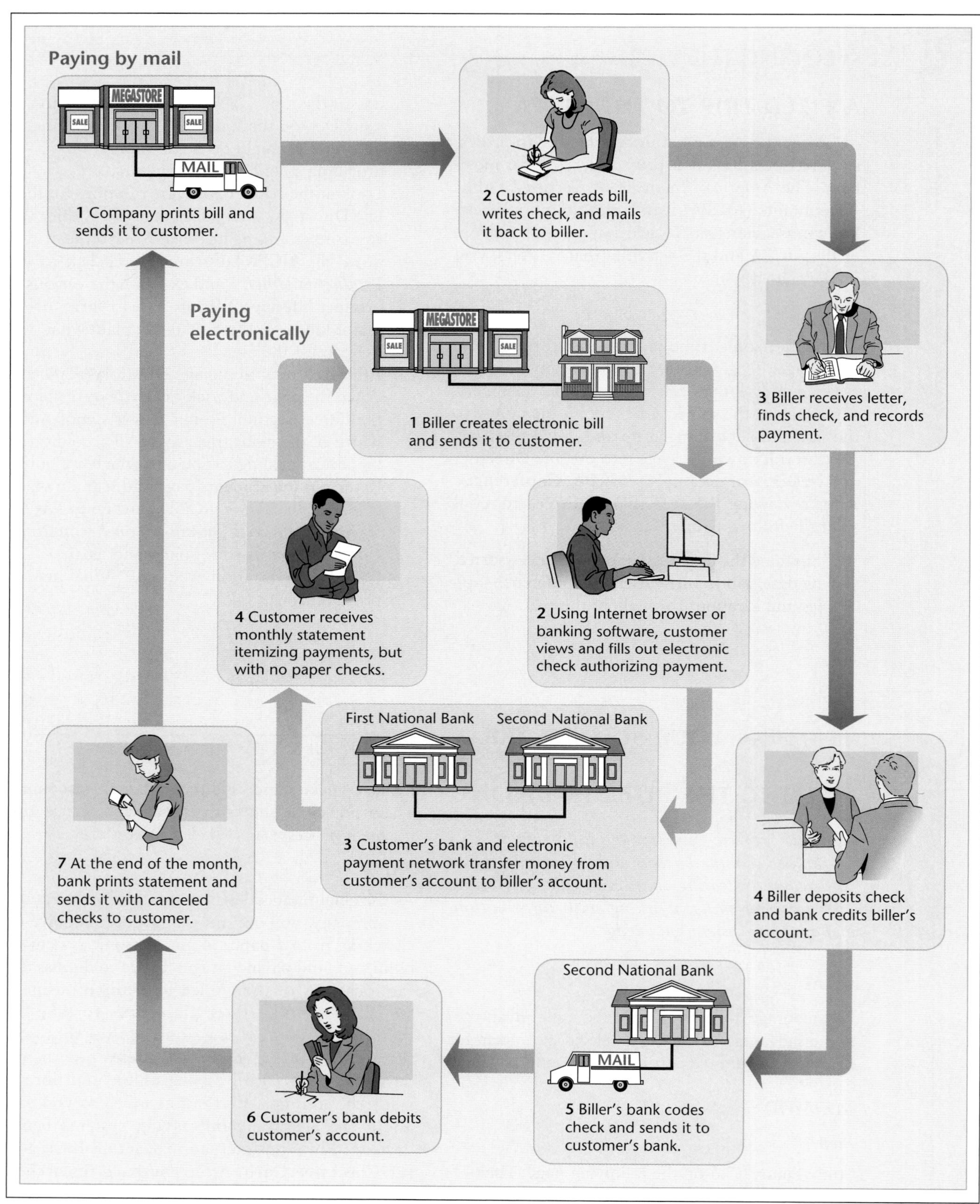
Paying by mail
MEGASTORE
SALE
SALE
MAIL
1 Company prints bill and sends it to customer.
2 Customer reads bill, writes check, and mails it back to biller.
3 Biller receives letter, finds check, and records payment.
4 Biller deposits check and bank credits biller's account.
Second National Bank
MAIL
5 Biller's bank codes check and sends it to customer's bank.
6 Customer's bank debits customer's account.
7 At the end of the month, bank prints statement and sends it with canceled checks to customer.
Paying electronically
MEGASTORE
SALE
SALE
1 Biller creates electronic bill and sends it to customer.
2 Using Internet browser or banking software, customer views and fills out electronic check authorizing payment.
First National Bank
Second National Bank
3 Customer's bank and electronic payment network transfer money from customer's account to biller's account.
4 Customer receives monthly statement itemizing payments, but with no paper checks.

Figure 18.5

Managing Operations and Information

FOLLOW-UP QUESTIONS

1. What cost savings are inherent in the electronic system for both your company and its customers? In your answer, consider such costs as handling, postage, and paper.
2. What consequences would your decision to adopt an electronic system have on others with whom you do business, including manufacturers of check-sorting equipment, the U.S. Postal Service, and banks?
3. Switching to an electronic bill-paying system would require a large capital expenditure for new computers and computer software. How could analyzing the company's income statement help you justify this expenditure?
4. How are consumers likely to respond to paying bills electronically? Are you likely to get a different response from individuals than you get from business customers?

CRAFTING YOUR BUSINESS PLAN

THE PROFITABILITY OF PLANNING

THE PURPOSE OF THE ASSIGNMENT

1. To acquaint students with the process of navigating the *Business PlanPro* (*BPP*) software package (Version 4.0).
2. To familiarize students with issues involving accounting that a sample firm faces in developing its business plan.
3. To demonstrate how four chapter topics—accounting skills, financial data reports, financial ratios, and the profit-and-loss statement—can be integrated as components in the *BPP* planning environment.

ASSIGNMENT

After reading Chapter 18 in the textbook, open the BPP *software* and search for information about plans for accounting as it applies to a sample firm:* AMT Computer Store *(American Management Technology). Then respond to the following items:*

1. What is your assessment of the accounting skills in AMT's management team? What do you recommend? [Sites to see in *BPP* (for this assignment): In the Plan Outline screen, click on each of the following, in turn: **6.1 Organizational Structure, 6.2 Management Team,** and **6.3 Management Team Gaps.**]
2. Use BPP's computer graphics to explore AMT's financial data reports. Describe the kinds of accounting information you find in the charts. [Sites to see in *BPP:* Begin by clicking on **Chart: Benchmarks** (located beneath **7.2 Key Financial Indicators**). Then, in the bottom tool bar, click on **Next** (to advance to the next chart) and continue through the various charts until you return again to **Benchmarks.**
3. At the time of this plan, AMT Computer Store was expecting large changes in annual net profits in the coming 3 years. Based on the company's planned profit-and-loss statement, identify the key factors–changes in the revenues and expenses categories–that account for changes in planned net profits from year to year. [Sites to see in *BPP:* From the Plan Outline screen, click on **Table: Profit and Loss** (located beneath **7.4 Projected Profit and Loss**).]
4. What do the financial ratios in its business plan tell you about the financial activities and conditions that AMT Computer Store expects over the next three years? Specifically, explain the information that is revealed by three of these ratios: inventory turnover, current, and return on equity. Next, choose any three other ratios and explain how they are calculated. [Sites to see in *BPP:* In the Plan Outline screen, click on **Table: Ratios** (located beneath **7.7 Business Ratios**). Notice that in the dialogue box above the tables you can read the ratio's definition and see how to calculate it.]

FOR YOUR OWN BUSINESS PLAN

5. Make an initial assessment of revenues versus expenses by preparing a trial income (profit-and-loss) statement for your business plan. You can prepare this *pro forma* (projected)

document for at least the first year (month by month) using *BPP*'s **Profit and Loss** spreadsheet.

GENERAL TIPS FOR NAVIGATING IN *BPP*

1. Open the *BPP* program, examine the Welcome screen, and click on **Open a Sample Plan.**
2. From the **Open a Sample Plan** dialogue box, click on a sample company name; then click on **Open.**
3. On the Plan Manager screen, click on **Your Plan Outline**; then click on any of the lines (for example, **5.1.1 Pricing Strategy**).
4. You can always return to the Plan Outline screen by going to the bottom of the screen and clicking on the **Plan Outline** icon.
5. After finishing with one sample company, you can get to the next one by going to the top of the screen and clicking on **File** (on the menu bar). Then beneath that, select **Open Sample Plan.** This will exit you from the current company file and take you to the **Open Sample Plan** dialogue box, where you can select your next sample company.
6. When you are finished, you can close the program by going to the top of the screen and clicking on **File** (on the bar menu). Then beneath that, select **Exit.**

VIDEO EXERCISE

ACCOUNTING FOR A FEW BILLION SOLD: MCDONALD'S

Learning Objectives

The purpose of this video exercise is to help you

1. Understand the value of generally accepted accounting principles (GAAP).
2. Recognize some of the accounting challenges facing multinational firms.
3. Appreciate the impact of foreign exchange rates on the accounting process for multinational firms.

BACKGROUND INFORMATION

From modest beginnings as a simple Illinois hamburger chain in 1954, McDonald's has grown to 25,000 restaurants around the world. Almost 1,800 new stores were added in 1999, about 90 percent of them outside the United States. The company has already opened its 1,000th restaurants in both Germany and the United Kingdom and its 3,000th in Japan. McDonald's not only accounts for nearly half of all globally branded fast-food restaurants outside the United States but achieves about two-thirds of total fast-food sales outside this country. Management attributes this huge market share to the power of the McDonald's brand.

There are only occasional clouds in the company's bright profit picture. Revenues in Latin America were adversely affected by the recent currency devaluation in Brazil and by difficult economic conditions in several markets whose severity McDonald's had underestimated.

THE VIDEO

Vice President and Assistant Corporate Controller Dave Pojman discusses the evolution of McDonald's financial reporting methods from an original highly manual process of collating worldwide data to the current, largely computerized method of capturing and analyzing data that is entered to a special Web site, automatically sorted, and transformed into a wide variety of reports in both English and other languages. Information about monthly sales is aggregated from individual store, to country, to country grouping, and finally to international headquarters, where it is incorporated into annual reports and required SEC filings.

DISCUSSION QUESTIONS

1. What are the special accounting problems faced by an international firm like McDonald's when it operates abroad?
2. How does McDonald's deal with some of these accounting challenges?
3. How does a company like McDonald's benefit from having operations in so many different parts of the world?

FOLLOW-UP ASSIGNMENT

Select a country in which McDonald's does business and research some of that country's business practices and social and religious customs. Make a list of as many specific factors as you can find that can affect McDonald's ability to operate in that country, its change of success there, and its ability to gather accurate financial information.

FOR FURTHER EXPLORATION

Visit the Investor Relations pages on the Web sites of some other multinationals, such as Coca- Cola <www.coca-cola.com>, Colgate-Palmolive <www.colgate.com>, and the Disney Co. <www.disney.go.com> to find out what proportion of the company's earnings is created overseas. What challenges do you think each of these firms faces in reporting earnings accurately?

MASTERING BUSINESS ESSENTIALS

Go to the "Managerial Accounting and Cost Analysis" episode on the Mastering Business Essentials CD-ROM for an interactive, video-enhanced exercise on the efforts of managers at CanGo, an e-business start-up, to revise the company's financial reporting system in preparation for an IPO.

Chapter 19

Understanding Money and Banking

After reading this chapter, you should be able to:

1. ***Define*** *money* and identify the different forms that it takes in the nation's money supply.
2. ***Describe*** the different kinds of *financial institutions* that comprise the U.S. financial system and explain the services they offer.
3. ***Explain*** how banks create money and describe the means by which they are regulated.
4. ***Discuss*** the functions of the *Federal Reserve System* and describe the tools that it uses to control the money supply.
5. ***Identify*** three important ways in which the financial industry is changing.
6. ***Understand*** some of the key activities in *international banking and finance*.

A Popular Bank in a Big Niche

The American Dream is to rise from poverty to wealth—or at least comfort—through hard work, determination, business savvy, and other virtues given meaning by opportunity. It is the dream not only of people who can trace their roots back to the *Mayflower* but also of new Hispanic immigrants to America who speak English as a second language. For many, the dream has long been possible because the American banking system loaned money to buy homes and build and expand businesses. For others, however, particularly minorities, loans were often hard to get, and insufficient financial help doomed plans for both families and businesses.

Reflecting on the state of the American Dream, at least one bank recognized opportunity in this situation. Instead of classifying low- to moderate-income Hispanics as credit risks to be avoided at all costs, Puerto Rico–based Banco Popular <**www.bancopopular.es**> saw them as an untapped market for personal and business banking services. When he looks at the multiethnic New York City neighborhoods that many mainstream banks are reluctant to enter, Jose Antonio Torres, Banco Popular's New York/New Jersey general manager, sees "strong retail areas with good, growing neighborhoods and housing stock. They are the kind of communities where we have done well before."

Indeed, Banco Popular's historical mission has been to serve the banking needs of Hispanic Americans. The bank entered the New York market in 1961 and through growth and acquisitions now boasts 32 metropolitan-area branches. In addition to New

York, Banco Popular has always focused on the five states with the largest Hispanic populations: California, Florida, Illinois, New Jersey, and Texas. The bank ended the year 1999 with 91 branches in those six states. In its growth strategy, every acquisition that the bank makes keeps the Hispanic market in mind. For example, Banco Popular acquired Houston-based Citizens National Bank in 1997 because its customer base was predominantly Hispanic. Citizens National Bank, explains Mike Cart, president at the time of the acquisition, had already "become lenders to ethnic minorities in low- to moderate-income areas all over Houston in the single-family mortgage finance business. We already served the market that satisfied Banco Popular's strategic plans."

In the New York area, which is home to 3.4 million Hispanics and 70,000 Hispanic-owned businesses, the bank found a niche in lending to small and midsize companies and is the metropolitan region's top provider of Small Business Administration–backed loans. With similar success in Florida and the Chicago area, the bank continues to be a national leader in SBA lending in terms of dollar volume ($99 million in 1999). One of the bank's new financing programs is aimed at second-generation, family-owned Hispanic groceries. It centers around loans to adult children who want to expand existing businesses run by their parents.

"Multiethnic New York City districts are strong retail areas with good, growing neighborhoods and housing stock. They are the kind of communities where we have done well before."

—Jose Antonio Torres, Banco Popular, New York/New Jersey General Manager

Having witnessed Banco Popular's success in New York's Hispanic communities, mainstream banks such as Chase Manhattan and Citibank are also moving aggressively into the Hispanic market. Chase <**www.chase.com**>, recently opened a small-business development center in the Bronx, equipped with a multilingual business library and a staff offering management help. Chase also took part in a two-year SBA pilot program to speed and simplify the lending process to minority businesses.

With a larger presence and more marketing money to spend than Banco Popular, will banks such as Chase and Citibank ultimately dominate New York's minority banking market? Although the answer to that question remains unclear, it is clear that many Hispanics prefer a bank with ethnic roots. Roberto Reyes, owner of Jeselvi Travel in the Bronx, may be typical. When he opened his agency, he had a choice of banking with Chase or Banco Popular. He chose Banco Popular because he wanted to do business with Hispanics.

Our opening story continues on page 551

Whether it caters to the minority communities of Los Angeles, Houston, Jersey City, or Miami or to nonminority communities across the United States, a complex system of financial institutions, especially banks, is needed to meet the money requirements of individuals and businesses. By focusing on the learning objectives of this chapter, you will better understand the environment for banking in the United States and the different kinds of institutions that conduct business in it.

WHAT IS MONEY?

When someone asks you how much money you have, do you count the dollar bills and coins in your pockets? Do you include your checking and savings accounts? What about stocks and bonds? Do you count your car? Taken together, the value of all these things is your "personal wealth." Not all of it, however, is "money." In this section, we consider more precisely what *money* is and does.

The Characteristics of Money

money
Any object that is portable, divisible, durable, and stable and serves as a medium of exchange, a store of value, and a unit of account

Modern money often takes the form of stamped metal or printed paper—U.S. dollars, British pounds, French francs, Japanese yen—issued by governments. Theoretically, however, just about any object can serve as **money** if it is *portable, divisible, durable,* and *stable.* To appreciate these qualities, imagine using something that lacks them—say, a 70-pound salmon:

- *Portability.* Try lugging 70 pounds of fish from shop to shop. In contrast, modern currency is light and easy to handle.
- *Divisibility.* Suppose that you want to buy a hat, a book, and some milk from three different stores. How would you divide your fish-money? Is a pound of its head worth as much as, say, two gills? Modern currency is easily divisible into smaller parts, each with a fixed value. A dollar, for example, can be exchanged for four quarters. More important, units of money can be easily matched with the value of all goods.
- *Durability.* Regardless of whether you "spend" it, your salmon will lose value every day (in fact, it will eventually be too smelly to be worth anything). Modern currency, however, neither dies nor spoils, and if it wears out, it can be replaced. It is also hard to counterfeit—certainly harder than catching more salmon.
- *Stability.* If salmon were in short supply, you might be able to make quite a deal for yourself. In the middle of a salmon run, however, the market would be flooded with fish. Sellers of goods would soon have enough fish and would refuse to produce anything for which they could get only salmon. Goods would become scarcer, but the salmon would continue (or cease) running, regardless of the plenitude or scarcity of buyable goods. The value of our paper money also fluctuates, but it is considerably more stable than salmon. Its value is related to what we can buy with it.

The Functions of Money

Imagine a successful fisherman who needs a new sail for his boat. In a barter economy—one in which goods are exchanged directly for one another—he would have to find someone who not only needs fish but who is also willing to exchange a sail for it. If no sailmaker wants fish, the fisherman must find someone else—say, a shoemaker—who wants fish. Then the fisherman must hope that the sailmaker will trade for his new shoes. Clearly, barter is inefficient in comparison with money. In a money economy, the fisherman would sell his catch, receive money, and exchange the money for such goods as a new sail.

Money serves three functions:[1]

- *Medium of exchange.* Like the fisherman "trading" money for a new sail, we use money as a way of buying and selling things. Without money, we would be bogged down in a system of barter.

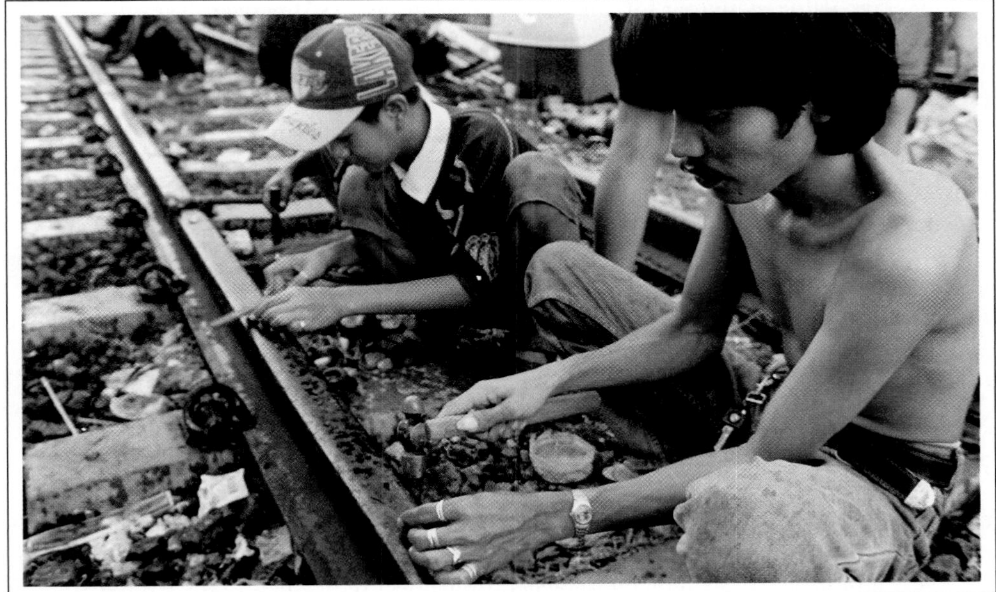

Of all the Asian nations struck by the financial crisis of 1997–1998, perhaps Indonesia was hardest hit. In an 8-month period, the value of the Indonesian currency, the rupiah, fell from 3,000 to the dollar to 15,000. As usual, the hardest hit among the hard hit were the poor, who found the local money worth more when it was pounded into jewelry than when it was held as a medium of exchange.

- *Store of value.* Pity the fisherman who catches a fish on Monday and wants to buy a few bars of candy on, say, the following Saturday, by which time the fish would have spoiled and lost its value. In the form of currency, however, money can be used for future purchases and so "stores" value.
- *Unit of account.* Money lets us measure the relative values of goods and services. It acts as a unit of account because all products can be valued and accounted for in terms of money. For example, the concepts of "$1,000 worth of clothes" or "$500 in labor costs" have universal meaning because everyone deals with money every day.

The Spendable Money Supply: M-1

For money to serve its basic functions, both buyers and sellers must agree on its value. That value depends in part on its *supply*—on how much money is in circulation. When the money supply is high, the value of money drops. When it is low, that value increases.

Unfortunately, it is not easy to measure the supply of money. One of the most commonly used measures, known widely as **M-1,** counts only the most liquid, or spendable, forms of money: currency, demand deposits, and other checkable deposits. These are all noninterest-bearing or low-interest-bearing forms of money.

Paper money and metal coins are **currency** issued by the government. Currency is widely used for small exchanges, and the law requires creditors to accept it in payment of debts. As of February 2000, currency in circulation in the United States amounted to $518 billion, or about 47 percent of M-1.

A **check** is essentially an order instructing a bank to pay a given sum to a "payee." Although not all sellers accept them as payment, many do. Checks are usually acceptable in place of cash because they are valuable only to specified payees and can be exchanged for cash. Checking accounts, which are known as **demand deposits,** are counted in M-1 because funds may be withdrawn at any time—"on demand."

M-1
Measure of the money supply that includes only the most liquid (spendable) forms of money

currency
Government-issued paper money and metal coins

check
Demand deposit order instructing a bank to pay a given sum to a specified payee

demand deposit
Bank account funds that may be withdrawn at any time

M-1 Plus the Convertible Money Supply: M-2

M-2 includes everything in M-1 plus items that cannot be spent directly but are easily converted to spendable forms. The major components of M-2 are M-1, *time deposits, money market mutual funds,* and *savings deposits.* Totaling over $4.6 trillion in February 2000, M-2 accounts for nearly all of the nation's money supply. It thus measures the store

M-2
Measure of the money supply that includes all the components of M-1 plus the forms of money that can be easily converted into spendable form

of monetary value available for financial transactions. As this overall level of money increases, more is available for consumer purchases and business investment. When the supply is tightened, less money is available, and financial transactions, spending, and business activity thus slow down.

time deposit
Bank funds that cannot be withdrawn without notice or transferred by check

Unlike demand deposits, **time deposits,** such as certificates of deposit (CDs) and savings certificates, require prior notice of withdrawal and cannot be transferred by check. However, time deposits pay higher interest rates. Time deposits in M-2 include only accounts of less than $100,000 that can be redeemed on demand with small penalties.

money market mutual fund
Fund of short-term, low-risk financial securities purchased with the assets of investor-owners pooled by a nonbank institution

Operated by investment companies that bring together pools of assets from many investors, **money market mutual funds** buy a collection of short-term, low-risk financial securities. Ownership of and profits (or losses) from the sale of these securities are shared among the fund's investors. In the wake of new, more attractive investments, traditional savings deposits, such as passbook savings accounts, have declined in popularity. Savings deposits represented 40 percent of M-2 in 1971 but only 37 percent by 2000.

Credit Cards

Citicorp <www.citicorp.com> is the world's largest credit card issuer, with more than 49 million accounts worldwide. It is estimated that more than 157 million U.S. cardholders carry 1.5 billion cards. Spending with general-purpose credit cards in the United States is estimated at $1.4 trillion—almost half of all transactions—for the year 2000.[2] Indeed, the use of cards such as Visa <www.visa.com>, MasterCard <www.mastercard.com>, American Express <www.americanexpress.com>, Discover <www.discover.com>, and Diners Club <www.dinersclub.com> has become so widespread that many people refer to them as "plastic money."

Credit cards are big business for two basic reasons. First, they are convenient. Second, they are extremely profitable for issuing companies. Profits derive from two sources:

1. Some cards charge annual fees to holders. All charge interest on unpaid balances. Depending on the issuer, and on certain state regulations, cardholders pay interest rates ranging from 11 to 20 percent.
2. Merchants who accept credit cards pay fees to card issuers. Depending on the merchant's agreement with the issuer, 2 to 5 percent of total credit sales dollars goes to card issuers.

THE U.S. FINANCIAL SYSTEM

Many forms of money, especially demand deposits and time deposits, depend on the existence of financial institutions to provide a broad spectrum of services to both individuals and businesses. Just how important are reliable financial institutions to both businesses and individuals? Try asking financial consumers in a country in which commercial banking can be an adventure.

In Russia there is almost no banking regulation and no way to distinguish qualified from unscrupulous bankers in the thousands of different financial institutions, large and small, that exist. Businesses need stable financial institutions to underwrite modernization and expansion, and individuals need them to handle currency. The Moscow City Bank <www.mcbank.ru> has no deposit insurance, and only recently added a customer service desk, loan officers, and a cash machine. Imagine, then, just before these new steps at modernization, the disappointment of Vladimir Shcherbakov, who needed to withdraw $500 from his account to buy a car but was turned away by a sign announcing that no withdrawals would be allowed for 10 days. "I'm resigned to losing my money," sighed Shcherbakov. "But if I do get it back, I'll change my rubles into dollars and hold on to it myself."

In the sections that follow, we describe the major types of financial institutions, explain how they work when they work as they are supposed to, and survey some of the special services that they offer. We also explain their role as creators of money and discuss the regulation of the U.S. banking system.

Financial Institutions

The main function of financial institutions is to ease the flow of money from sectors with surpluses to those with deficits. They do this by issuing claims against themselves and using the proceeds to buy the assets of—and thus invest in—other organizations. A bank, for instance, can issue financial claims against itself by making available funds for checking and savings accounts. In turn, its assets will be mostly loans invested in individuals and businesses and perhaps government securities. In this section, we discuss each of the major types of financial institutions: *commercial banks, savings and loan associations, mutual savings banks, credit unions,* and various organizations known as *nondeposit institutions.*

Commercial Banks

The United States today boasts nearly 10,000 **commercial banks**—companies that accept deposits that they use to make loans and earn profits. Commercial banks range from the very largest institutions in New York, such as Bank of America and Chase Manhattan, to tiny banks dotting the rural landscape. Bank liabilities include checking accounts and savings accounts. Assets consist of a wide variety of loans to individuals, businesses, and governments.

commercial bank
Federal- or state-chartered financial institution accepting deposits that it uses to make loans and earn profits

Diversification and Mergers Many observers today believe that traditional banking has become a "mature" industry, one whose basic operations have expanded as broadly as they can. For instance, 1993 marked the first year in which the money invested in mutual funds—almost $2 trillion—equaled the amount deposited in U.S. banks. Thus, financial industry competitors in areas such as mutual funds are growing, sometimes rapidly.

> ***"The only way banks can compete is to transform themselves into successful retailers of financial services, which involves dramatic, not incremental change."***
>
> *—Banking analyst Thomas Brown*

As consumers continue to look for alternatives to traditional banking services, commercial banks and savings and loan associations find themselves with a dwindling share of market. The investment bank Merrill Lynch <www.ml.com> has originated billions of dollars in commercial loans, formerly the province of commercial banks. Savers, too, have been putting their savings into the money market funds, stocks, and bonds offered by companies such as Charles Schwab <www.schwab.com> instead of into the traditional savings accounts offered by banks. Many observers contend that to compete, banks, too, must diversify their offerings. The only way that they can compete, says banking analyst Thomas Brown, "is to transform themselves into successful retailers of financial services, which involves dramatic, not incremental change."

A related option seems to be to get bigger. In efforts to regain competitiveness, banks were merging at a record-setting pace in the 1990s. When commercial banks merge with investment banks, the resulting companies hold larger shares of the financial market, and the lines become blurred between traditional banking and nonbank financial institutions. Citigroup Inc. <www.citigroup.com>, the result of a 1998 merger between Citicorp (a commercial bank) and Travelers Group (which includes investment bank Salomon Smith Barney <www.smithbarney.com>) is the world's second-largest bank with nearly $700 billion in

www.cob.ohio-state.edu/dept/fin/overview.htm

Do you want to know the top five minority- and women-owned financial institutions in the country? Try the Financial Data Finder. Do you need a quick definition of *financial leverage?* Try the International Financial Encyclopaedia. Looking for job opportunities in finance? Try the "Finance Student Information" page. Information such as this can be found on the OSU Virtual Finance Library maintained by the Ohio State University Department of Finance.

assets in 1999. Citigroup offers one-stop shopping on a global scale for both consumers and businesses, including private banking, credit card services, mortgages, mutual funds, stock brokerage services, insurance, and loans.

Mergers are the trend, and fewer but larger banks are offering a wide range of financial products. The strategy streamlines operations to reduce costs and focuses on providing products that will win back customers from nonbank competitors.

Commercial Interest Rates Every bank receives a major portion of its income from interest paid on loans by borrowers. As long as terms and conditions are clearly revealed to borrowers, banks are allowed to set their own interest rates. Traditionally, the lowest rates were made available to the bank's most creditworthy commercial customers. That rate is called the **prime rate.** Most commercial loans are set at markups over prime. However, the prime rate is no longer a strong force in setting loan rates. Borrowers can now get funds less expensively from other sources, including foreign banks that set lower interest rates. To remain competitive U.S. banks now offer some commercial loans at rates below prime.

prime rate
Interest rate available to a bank's most creditworthy customers

Savings and Loan Associations Like commercial banks, **savings and loan associations (S&Ls)** accept deposits and make loans. They lend money primarily for home mortgages. Most S&Ls were created to provide financing for homes. Many of them, however, have ventured into other investments, with varying degrees of success. S&Ls in the United States now hold $1.1 trillion in assets and deposits of $705 billion.[3]

savings and loan association (S&L)
Financial institution accepting deposits and making loans primarily for home mortgages

Mutual Savings Banks and Credit Unions In **mutual savings banks,** all depositors are considered owners of the bank. All profits, therefore, are divided proportionately among depositors, who receive dividends. Like S&Ls, mutual savings banks attract most of their funds in the form of savings deposits, and funds are loaned out in the form of mortgages.

mutual savings bank
Financial institution whose depositors are owners sharing in its profits

In **credit unions,** deposits are accepted only from members who meet specific qualifications, usually working for a particular employer. Most universities run credit unions, as do the U.S. Navy <www.navy.mil> and the Pentagon <www.defenselink.mil>. Credit unions make loans for automobiles and home mortgages, as well as other types of personal loans.

credit union
Financial institution that accepts deposits from, and makes loans to, only its members, usually employees of a particular organization

Nondeposit Institutions A variety of other organizations take in money, provide interest or other services, and make loans. Four of the most important are *pension funds, insurance companies, finance companies,* and *securities dealers.*

A **pension fund** is essentially a pool of funds managed to provide retirement income for its members. *Public pension funds* include Social Security <www.ssa.gov> and $1 trillion in retirement programs for state and local government employees. *Private pension funds,* operated by employers, unions, and other private groups, cover about 80 million people and have total assets of $5.4 trillion.

pension fund
Nondeposit pool of funds managed to provide retirement income for its members

Insurance companies collect large pools of funds from the premiums charged for coverage. Funds are invested in stocks, real estate, and other assets. Earnings pay for insured losses, such as death benefits, automobile damage, and health care expenses.

insurance company
Nondeposit institution that invests funds collected as premiums charged for insurance coverage

Finance companies specialize in making loans to businesses and individuals. Commercial finance companies lend to businesses needing capital or long-term funds. They may, for instance, lend to a manufacturer that needs new assembly-line equipment. *Consumer finance companies* devote most of their resources to small noncommercial loans to individuals.

finance company
Nondeposit institution that specializes in making loans to businesses and consumers

Securities investment dealers (brokers), such as Merrill Lynch and A.G. Edwards & Sons <www.agedwards.com>, buy and sell stocks and bonds on the New York and other stock exchanges for client investors. They also invest in securities—they buy stocks and bonds for their own accounts in hopes of reselling them later at a profit. These companies hold large sums of money for transfer between buyers and sellers. (We discuss the activities of brokers and investment bankers more fully in Chapter 20.)

securities investment dealer (broker)
Nondeposit institution that buys and sells stocks and bonds both for investors and for its own accounts

Life Cycle of an e-Business

Bank Services Help a Young Company Grow

Like most entrepreneurs, Garden.com's founders depended on the commercial banking system as a source of funds, a depository for cash, and a place to go for a variety of financial services. Various kinds of banking services were needed for various stages in the company's life. During the start-up years, it sometimes needed funds on short notice, particularly for buying equipment, materials, and supplies, for marketing promotions, or for other working-capital requirements. Obviously, establishing a banking relationship before you need funds or something else from your banker is a real plus. To get started, Garden.com began working with a bank in Austin, Texas, to obtain a line of credit for short-term loans. "We use the line of credit," explained COO Jamie O'Neill, "to build a banking relationship more than for any other reasons. With our first line of credit, we got $250,000 for computer equipment that secured the loan at prime plus 1 percent." As of June 30, 1999, $148,000 was outstanding on the $400,000 line of credit, which was still used mostly for buying computer equipment.

With the accelerated retail growth of the late 1990s, Garden.com also needed banking services for depositing cash from sales: Cash revenues, including electronic cash flows, had to be moved into Garden.com bank accounts. With product revenues growing rapidly (nearly 300 percent for 1999), reliable transaction services were essential for maintaining the high-quality, convenient online experience that Garden.com offered its customers. For just the six months ending December 31, 1999, product sales of $4.48 million were paid at Garden.com's Web site by credit card or offline by phone, by fax, or by check. Flows from these different sources were distributed unevenly, corresponding to the seasonal nature of the gardening industry and, consequently, of product shipments.

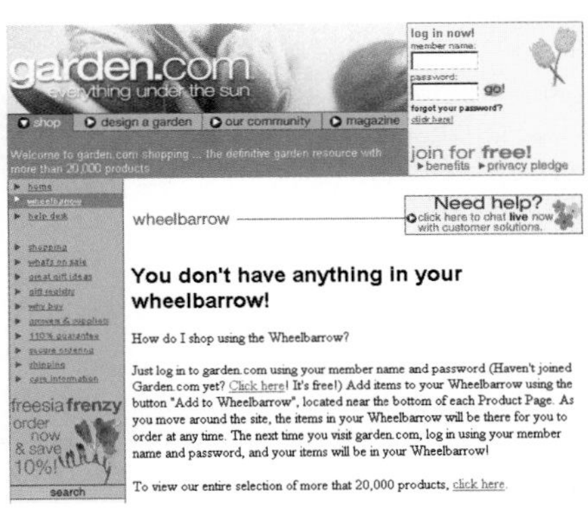

To handle such flows of cash, a firm's funds-flow system must function efficiently even during its busiest seasons. Garden.com developed transaction-processing systems that used electronic technology to process both orders and payments. Visitors to the Web site loaded up their "wheelbarrows" with the products they wanted and, when they were ready to buy, clicked the "Submit" button in the checkout process. The appropriate credit card was charged for the amount of the order. The online payments-clearing process was totally automated and flowed as follows:

- The customer submitted a credit card at the Garden.com Web site
- Electronic authorization was given at the point of sale
- The transaction was cleared electronically at the bank

Two days later, the funds were in Garden.com's bank account.

At first, because it was a start-up company, the bank required Garden.com to establish a line of credit to protect the bank against the possibility of "charge backs" from transaction failures. But, as Jamie O'Neill reported, "The impossible happened—there were no charge backs!" Why not? For one thing, there was the apparent integrity of Garden.com's user community in paying for purchases. For another, there was the reliability of the firm's electronic technology in securely processing payments transactions from the Web site to the bank.

Special Financial Services

The finance business today is a highly competitive industry. No longer is it enough for commercial banks to accept deposits and make loans. Most, for example, now offer bank-issued credit cards and safe-deposit boxes. In addition, many offer pension, trust, international, and brokerage services and financial advice. Most offer ATMs and electronic money transfer.

This Manhattan outlet looks like a branch bank, but there are no ATMs at Chase Checks-To-Cash Clubs. At this location, tellers simply exchange cash for payroll checks (for a fee, of course). Institutions such as Chase <www.chase.com> *have entered the check-cashing business, which now processes $60 billion worth of payroll and government checks every year. In industry lingo, customers are ALICs: people who are "asset limited, income constrained."*

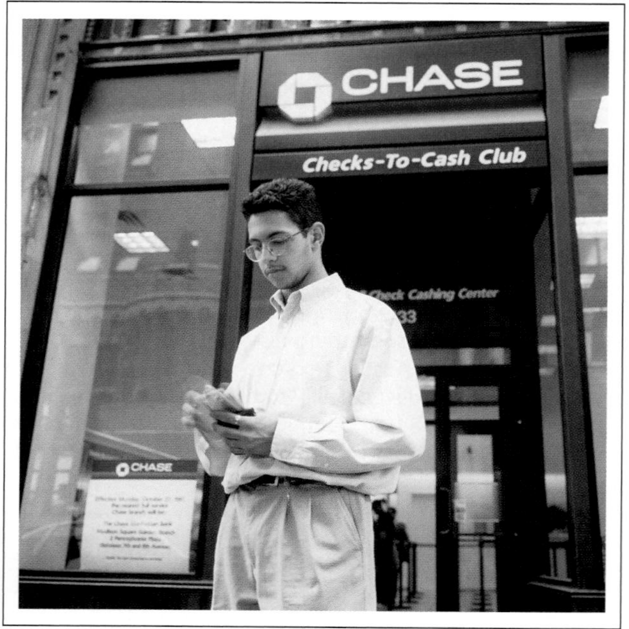

individual retirement account (IRA)
Tax-deferred pension fund with which wage earners supplement other retirement funds

trust services
Bank management of an individual's investments, payments, or estate

letter of credit
Bank promise, issued for a buyer, to pay a designated firm a certain amount of money if specified conditions are met

banker's acceptance
Bank promise, issued for a buyer, to pay a designated firm a specified amount at a future date

Pension and Trust Services Most banks help customers establish savings plans for retirement. **Individual retirement accounts (IRAs)** are pension funds that wage earners and their spouses can set up to supplement other retirement funds. All wage earners can invest up to $2,000 of earned income annually in an IRA. They offer a significant tax benefit: Under many circumstances, taxes on principal and earnings are deferred until funds are withdrawn upon retirement. Under the 1997 tax changes, some IRAs are entirely tax-free. Banks serve as financial intermediaries by receiving funds and investing them as directed by customers. They also provide customers with information on investment vehicles available for IRAs (deposit accounts, mutual funds, stocks, and so forth).

Many commercial banks offer **trust services**—the management of funds left "in the bank's trust." In return for a fee, the trust department will perform such tasks as making your monthly bill payments and managing your investment portfolio. Trust departments also manage the estates of deceased persons.

International Services The three main international services offered by banks are *currency exchange, letters of credit,* and *banker's acceptances.* Suppose a U.S. company wants to buy a product from a French supplier. For a fee, it can use one or more of three services offered by its bank:

1. It can exchange U.S. dollars for French francs at a U.S. bank and then pay the French supplier in francs.
2. It can pay its bank to issue a **letter of credit**—a promise by the bank to pay the French firm a certain amount if specified conditions are met.
3. It can pay its bank to draw up a **banker's acceptance,** which promises that the bank will pay some specified amount at a future date.

A banker's acceptance requires payment by a particular date. Letters of credit are payable only after certain conditions are met. The French supplier, for example, may not be paid until shipping documents prove that the merchandise has been shipped from France.

Financial Advice and Brokerage Services Many banks, both large and small, help their customers manage their money. Depending on the customer's situation, the bank may recommend different investment opportunities. The recommended mix might include CDs, mutual funds, stocks, and bonds. Many banks also serve as securities inter-

It's a WiredWorld

• To e-Bank or Not to e-Bank

Is banking ready for e-business? It depends on whom you talk to, but based on results to date, bankers have a long way to go before they're completely wired. This centuries-old industry isn't yet set up for Internet retail-customer transactions. Commenting on the relatively poor success of Internet banks, one Dutch banker notes: "We underestimate the value of the trust we have built up. It is one of the highest barriers to entry to our business." In other words, consumers are skeptical about trusting personal financial matters to impersonal Internet acquaintances. They're accustomed to dealing with a particular bank, usually at a local facility. Think of the typical services you use—checking, loans, trusts, investments. Think about face-to-face transactions in a familiar environment. Now contrast that image with an image of Internet transactions with your bank. What if it's a remote bank? What if your contact with your bank is a cyberspace third party?

E-banking raises a basic question that bankers have not encountered before: Should the bank be the party to whom the customer entrusts all of the customer's financial activities? Or, from a strictly financial point of view, would a third party be a better choice? This choice has emerged because the Internet, though introducing a third party into the relationship, offers global access to financial products and services beyond the reach of any single bank. As a nonbank third party, OnMoney.com <www.onmoney.com> allows you to see and manage all your accounts at one Web location. Banks can't match this service. You can receive and pay bills, prepare and file taxes, check out financial news, and get good deals on financial products from leading vendors (some tailored to your particular needs), all by storing your financial data with—and putting your trust in—a single Web destination. The third party also provides interactive financial management and access to services but does not sell financial products, such as car or mortgage loans or stocks and bonds. As a traditional banker, you may like the idea that your customers are linked to a third party that can provide them with a better range of consolidated services. Unfortunately, your customer also gains access to better deals from competing banks and financial services providers.

The alternative is to sell customers on the idea of a centralized bank, but that approach can make customers worry about a bank's objectivity in promoting its own financial products. The customer is likely to ask: If I buy all my products from this bank, how good a deal am I getting on any one of them? The strategic question for the bank, therefore, is how to position itself to win the customer relationship. Bankers disagree on the best approach. The e-Citi unit of Citigroup is hedging its Web strategy by offering a mixture of both Citibank and non-Citibank products for both kinds of customers—those who want one bank to supply all their needs and those who may prefer more diverse offerings. Meanwhile, other banks, especially smaller ones, are leaning toward the option of serving as an advisor who puts customers in touch with outside (third-party) experts for financial advice. Its choice in this matter will undoubtedly have a huge impact on a bank's Web services and customer relationships for the future.

Many bankers are convinced that banks are still dependent on traditional financial products with bank customers who want access to branch locations and human interaction via phone, video, or e-mail. The first generation of Web banks still needs human support and must furnish access to a physical infrastructure (bricks and mortar). Many industry analysts fear that too much technology may push customers into the hands of competitors who still offer face-to-face service.

mediaries, using their own stockbrokers to buy and sell securities and their own facilities to hold them. Bank advertisements often stress the role of banks as financial advisers.

automated teller machine (ATM) Electronic machine that allows customers to conduct account-related activities 24 hours a day, 7 days a week

Automated Teller Machines Electronic **automated teller machines (ATMs)** allow customers to withdraw money and make deposits 24 hours a day, 7 days a week. They also allow transfers of funds between accounts and provide information on account status. Some banks offer cards that can be used in affiliated nationwide systems. About 227,000 machines are now located at bank buildings, grocery stores, airports, shopping malls, and other locations. Bank of America, with 14,000 units, is this country's leading owner of ATMs. U.S. bank customers conduct more than 12 billion ATM transactions a year, withdrawing an average of $60 per transaction.[4]

Increasingly, ATMs are also becoming global fixtures. In fact, among the world's 708,000 ATMs, 68 percent are located outside the United States. Asia, with 32 percent of the world's total is the leading region for ATMs, followed by North America (31 percent),

Citibank <www.citibank.com/hungary> *now has consumer banking outlets in 41 countries, where it strives to make its once specialized products universal. At this ATM machine in Budapest, Hungary, for example, Americans can access their U.S. accounts in English. Then, says Victor Meneszes, head of Citibank's U.S./Europe consumer banking operations, "they can withdraw cash and go across the street to McDonald's. They feel completely at home."*

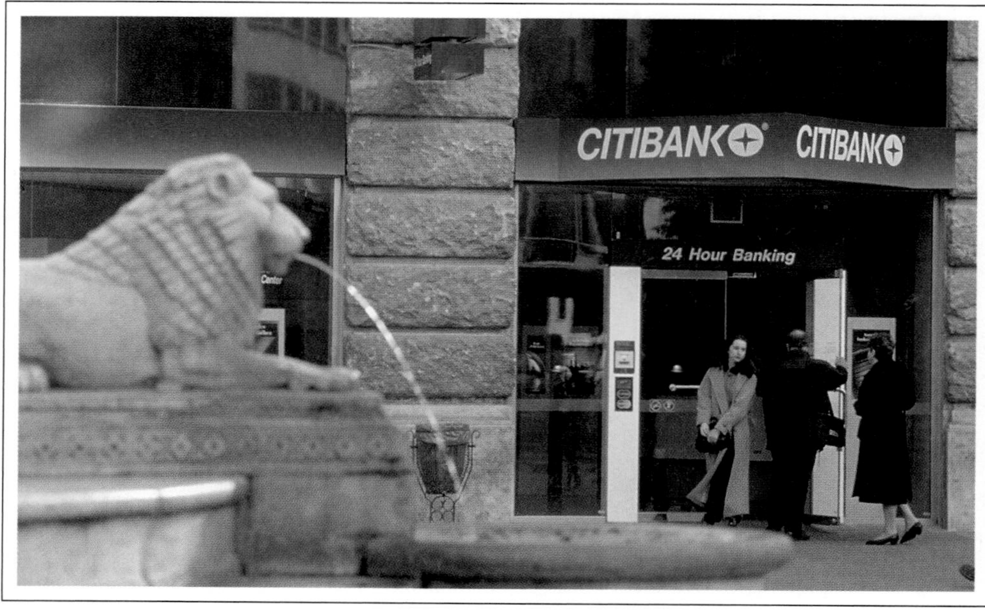

Western Europe (25 percent), and Latin America (8 percent). Many U.S. banks now offer international ATM services. Citicorp installed Shanghai's first 24-hour ATM and is the first foreign bank to receive approval from the People's Bank of China to issue local currency through ATMs. Elsewhere, Citibank machines feature touch screens that take instructions in any of 10 languages.

electronic funds transfer (EFT) Communication of fund-transfer information over wire, cable, or microwave

Electronic Funds Transfer ATMs are the most popular form of **electronic funds transfer (EFT).** These systems transfer many kinds of financial information via electrical impulses over wire, cable, or microwave. In addition to ATMs, EFT systems include automatic payroll deposit, bill payment, and automatic funds transfer. Such systems can help a businessperson close an important business deal by transferring money from San Francisco to Miami within a few hours.

Banks as Creators of Money

In the course of their activities, financial institutions provide a special service to the economy—they create money. This is not to say that they mint bills and coins. Rather, by taking in deposits and making loans, they *expand the money supply.*

As Figure 19.1 shows, the money supply expands because banks are allowed to loan out most (although not all) of the money they take in from deposits. Suppose that you deposit \$100 in your bank. If banks are allowed to loan out 90 percent of all their deposits, then your bank will hold \$10 in reserve and loan \$90 of your money to borrowers. (You, of course, still have \$100 on deposit.) Meanwhile, borrowers—or the people they pay—will deposit the \$90 loan in their own banks. Together, the borrowers' banks will then have \$81 (90 percent of \$90) available for new loans. Banks, therefore, have turned your original \$100 into \$271 (\$100 + \$90 + \$81). The chain continues, with borrowings from one bank becoming deposits in the next.

Regulation of Commercial Banking

Because commercial banks are critical to the creation of money, the government regulates them to ensure a sound and competitive financial system. Later in this chapter, we will see how the Federal Reserve System regulates many aspects of U.S. banking. Other federal and state agencies also regulate banks to ensure that the failure of some banks as a result of competition will not cause the public to lose faith in the banking system itself.

Deposit	Money Held in Reserve by Bank	Money to Lend	Total Supply
$100.00	$10.00	$90.00	$190.00
90.00	9.00	81.00	271.00
81.00	8.10	72.90	343.90
72.90	7.29	65.61	409.51
65.61	6.56	59.05	468.56

Figure 19.1
How Banks Create Money

Federal Deposit Insurance Corporation The **Federal Deposit Insurance Corporation (FDIC)** insures deposits in member banks. More than 99 percent of the nation's commercial banks pay fees for membership in the FDIC <www.fdic.gov>. In return, the FDIC guarantees, through its Bank Insurance Fund (BIF), the safety of all deposits up to the current maximum of $100,000. If a bank collapses, the FDIC promises to pay its depositors—through the BIF—for losses up to $100,000 per person. (A handful of the nation's 10,000 commercial banks are insured by states rather than by the BIF.)

Federal Deposit Insurance Corporation (FDIC)
Federal agency that guarantees the safety of all deposits up to $100,000 in the financial institutions that it insures

To insure against multiple bank failures, the FDIC maintains the right to examine the activities and accounts of all member banks. Such regulation was effective from 1941 through 1980, when fewer than 10 banks failed per year. At the beginning of the 1980s, however, banks were deregulated, and between 1981 and 1990, losses from nearly 1,100 bank failures depleted the FDIC's reserve fund. In recent years, the FDIC has thus raised the premiums charged to member banks to keep up with losses incurred by failed banks.

THE FEDERAL RESERVE SYSTEM

Perched atop the U.S. financial system and regulating many aspects of its operation is the Federal Reserve System. Established by Congress in 1913, the **Federal Reserve System** (or **the Fed**) <www.federalreserve.gov> is the nation's central bank. In this section, we describe the structure of the Fed, its functions, and the tools that it uses to control the nation's money supply.

Federal Reserve System (the Fed)
Central bank of the United States, which acts as the government's bank, serves member commercial banks, and controls the nation's money supply

The Structure of the Fed

The Federal Reserve System consists of a board of governors, a group of reserve banks, and member banks. As originally established by the Federal Reserve Act of 1913, the system consisted of 12 relatively autonomous banks and a seven-member committee whose powers were limited to coordinating their activities. By the 1930s, however, both the structure and function of the Fed had changed dramatically.

The Board of Governors The Fed's board of governors consists of seven members appointed by the president for overlapping terms of 14 years. The chair of the board serves on major economic advisory committees and works actively with the administration to formulate economic policy. The board plays a large role in controlling the money supply. It alone determines the reserve requirements, within statutory limits, for depository institutions. It also works with other members of the Federal Reserve System to set discount rates and handle the Fed's sale and purchase of government securities.

Reserve Banks The Federal Reserve System consists of 12 administrative areas and 12 banks. Each Federal Reserve bank holds reserve deposits from and sets the discount rate

WebConnection

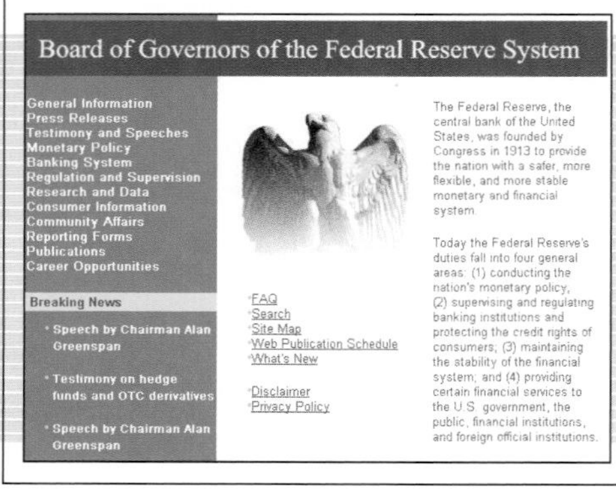

www.bog.frb.fed.us

Besides explaining the functions and operations of the Fed, the official site includes such pages as "Monetary Performance" (where you can access semiannual reports on monetary policy and economic performance) and "Research and Data" (which publishes staff studies on a wide range of economic and financial subjects).

for commercial banks in its region. Reserve banks also play a major role in the nation's check-clearing process.

Member Banks All nationally chartered commercial banks are members of the Federal Reserve System, as are some state-chartered banks. The accounts of all member bank depositors are automatically covered by the FDIC/BIF. Although many state-chartered banks do not belong to the Federal Reserve System, most pay deposit insurance premiums and are covered by the FDIC.

The Functions of the Fed

In addition to chartering national banks, the Fed serves as the federal government's bank and the "bankers' bank," regulating a number of banking activities. Most importantly, it controls the money supply. In this section, we describe these functions in some detail.

The Government's Bank Two of the Fed's activities are producing the nation's paper currency and lending money to the government. The Fed decides how many bills to produce and how many to destroy. To lend funds to the government, the Fed buys bonds issued by the Treasury Department <www.ustreas.gov>. The borrowed money is then used to help finance the national deficit.

The Bankers' Bank Individual banks that need money can borrow from the Federal Reserve and pay interest on the loans. In addition, the Fed provides storage for commercial banks, which are required to keep funds on reserve at a Federal Reserve bank.

Check Clearing The Fed also *clears checks,* some 65 billion of them each year, for commercial banks. To understand the check-clearing process, imagine that you are a photographer living in New Orleans. To participate in a workshop in Detroit, you must send a check for $50 to the Detroit studio. Figure 19.2 traces your check through the clearing process:

1. You send your check to the Detroit studio, which deposits it in its Detroit bank.
2. The Detroit bank deposits the check in its own account at the Federal Reserve Bank of Chicago.
3. The check is sent from Chicago to the Atlanta Federal Reserve Bank for collection because you, the check writer, live in the Atlanta district.
4. Your New Orleans bank receives the check from Atlanta and deducts the $50 from your personal account.
5. Your bank then has $50 deducted from its deposit account at the Atlanta Federal Reserve Bank.
6. The $50 is shifted from Atlanta to the Chicago Federal Reserve Bank. The studio's Detroit bank gets credited, whereupon the studio's account is then credited $50. Your bank mails the canceled check back to you.

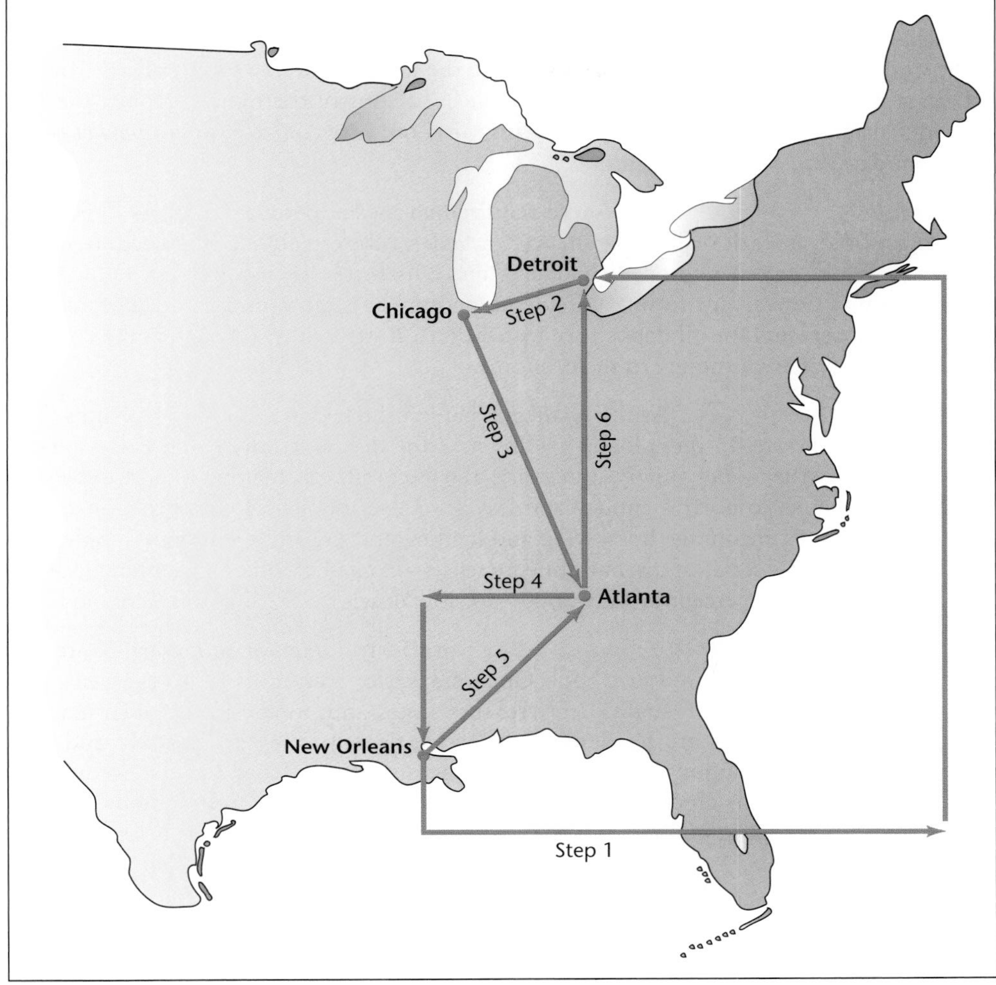

Figure 19.2
Clearing a Check

Depending on the number of banks and the distances between them, a check will clear in two to six days. Until the process is completed, the studio's Detroit bank cannot spend the $50 deposited there. Meanwhile, your bank's records will continue to show $50 in your account. Each day, approximately $1 billion in checks is processed by the system. The term **float** refers to all the checks in the process at any one time.

float
Total amount of checks written but not yet cleared through the Federal Reserve

Controlling the Money Supply The Federal Reserve System is responsible for the conduct of U.S. **monetary policy**—the management of the nation's economic growth by managing money supply and interest rates. By controlling these two factors, the Fed influences the ability and willingness of banks throughout the country to loan money.

monetary policy
Policies by which the Federal Reserve manages the nation's money supply and interest rates

Inflation Management As we defined it in Chapter 1, *inflation* is a period of widespread price increases throughout an economic system. It occurs if the money supply grows too large. Demand for goods and services increases, and the prices of everything rise. (In contrast, too little money means that an economy will lack the funds to maintain high levels of employment.) Because commercial banks are the main creators of money, much of the Fed's management of the money supply takes the form of regulating the supply of money through commercial banks.

The Tools of the Fed

According to the Fed's original charter, its primary duties were to supervise banking and to manage both the currency and commercial paper. The duties of the Fed evolved, however, along with a predominant philosophy of monetary policy. That policy includes an emphasis on the broad economic goals as discussed in Chapter 1—stability, full employment, and growth. The Fed's role in controlling the nation's money supply stems from its role in setting policies to help reach these goals. To control the money supply, the Fed uses four primary tools: *reserve requirements, discount rate controls, open-market operations,* and *selective credit controls.*

reserve requirement
Percentage of its deposits that a bank must hold in cash or on deposit with the Federal Reserve

Reserve Requirements The **reserve requirement** is the percentage of its deposits a bank must hold, in cash or on deposit, with a Federal Reserve bank. High requirements mean that banks have less money to lend. Thus, a high reserve requirement reduces the money supply. Conversely, low requirements permit the supply to expand. Because the Fed sets requirements for all depository institutions, it can adjust them to make changes in the overall supply of money to the economy.

How does the Federal Reserve System affect smaller businesses versus larger ones?

Discount Rate Controls As the "bankers' bank," the Fed loans money to banks. The interest rate on these loans is known as the **discount rate.** If the Fed wants to reduce the money supply, it increases the discount rate, making it more expensive for banks to borrow money and less attractive for them to loan it. Conversely, low rates encourage borrowing and lending and expand the money supply. The Fed used a series of discount rate increases—from 4.5 percent beginning in April 1999 to 6.0 percent in May 2000—to slow down the sizzling U.S. economy.

discount rate
Interest rate at which member banks can borrow money from the Federal Reserve

Open-Market Operations The third instrument for monetary control is probably the Fed's most important tool. **Open-market operations** refer to the Fed's sale and purchase of securities (usually U.S. Treasury notes and bonds) in the open market. Open-market operations are particularly effective because they act quickly and predictably on the money supply. How so? The Fed buys securities from dealers. Because the dealer's bank account is credited for the transaction, its bank has more money to lend, and so expands the money supply. The opposite happens when the Fed sells securities.

open-market operations
The Federal Reserve's sales and purchases of securities in the open market

selective credit controls
Federal Reserve authority to set both margin requirements for consumer stock purchases and credit rules for other consumer purchases

Selective Credit Controls The Federal Reserve can exert considerable influence on business activity by exercising **selective credit controls.** The Fed may set special requirements for consumer stock purchases and credit rules for other consumer purchases.

As we will see in Chapter 20, investors can set up credit accounts with stockbrokers to buy stocks and bonds. A margin requirement set by the Fed stipulates the amount of credit that the broker can extend to the customer. For example, a 60 percent margin rate means that approved customers can purchase stocks having $100,000 market value with $60,000 in cash (60 percent of $100,000) and $40,000 in loans from the dealer. If the Fed wants to increase securities transactions, it can lower the margin requirement. Customers can then borrow greater percentages of their purchase costs from dealers, thus increasing their purchasing power and the amount of securities that they can buy.

Within stipulated limits, the Fed is also permitted to specify the conditions of certain credit purchases. This authority extends to such conditions as allowable down payment percentages for appliance purchases and repayment periods on automobile loans. The Fed has chosen to not use these powers in recent years.

THE CHANGING MONEY AND BANKING SYSTEM

The U.S. money and banking systems have changed in recent years and continue to change today. Deregulation and interstate banking, for example, have increased competition not only among banks but also between banks and other financial institutions. Electronic technologies affect how you obtain money and how much interest you pay for it.

Deregulation

The Depository Institutions Deregulation and Monetary Control Act (DIDMCA) of 1980 brought many changes to the banking industry. Before its passage, there were clear distinctions between the types of services offered by different institutions. Although all institutions could offer savings accounts, only commercial banks could offer checking accounts, and S&Ls and mutual savings banks generally could not make consumer loans. The DIDMCA and subsequent laws sought to promote competition by eliminating many such restrictions.

Under deregulation, many banks were unable to survive in the new competitive environment. In the 1980s, more than 1,000 banks—1 more than 7 percent of the total—failed, as did 835 savings and loans. Many economists, however, regard some bank closings as a beneficial weeding out of inefficient competitors.

Interstate Banking

Although interstate banking is commonplace, it is a relatively new development. The Interstate Banking Efficiency Act was passed into law in September 1994, thus allowing banks to enter (gradually) into interstate banking—the operation of banks or branches across state lines. It also mandates regulation by government agencies to ensure proper operation and competition. The key provisions in this act include the following:

- Limited nationwide banking is permitted, beginning in 1995. Bank holding companies can acquire subsidiaries in any state.
- The ultimate *size* of any company is limited. No one company can control more than 10 percent of nationwide insured deposits. No bank can control more than 30 percent of a state's deposits (each state is empowered to set its own limit).
- Beginning in 1995, banks can provide limited transactions for affiliated banks in other states. They can thus accept deposits, close loans, and accept loan payments on behalf of other affiliated banks. (They cannot, however, originate loans or open deposit accounts for affiliates.)
- Beginning in June 1997, banks can convert affiliates into full-fledged interstate branches.

Interstate banking offers certain efficiencies. For example, it allows banks to consolidate services and eliminate duplicated activities. Opponents, however, remain concerned that some banks will gain undue influence, dominate other banks, and hinder competition.

The Impact of Electronic Technologies

Like so many other businesses, banks are increasingly investing in technology as a way to improve efficiency and customer service levels. Many banks offer ATMs and EFT systems. Some offer TV banking, in which customers use television sets and terminals—or home computers—to make transactions. The age of electronic money has arrived. Digital money is replacing cash in stores, taxi cabs, subway systems, and vending machines. Each business day, more than $2 trillion exists in and among banks and other financial institutions in purely electronic form. Each year, the Fed transfers electronically more than $250 trillion in transactions.

Debit Cards One of the electronic offerings from the financial industry that has gained popularity is the debit card. Unlike credit cards, **debit cards** allow only the transfer of money between accounts. They do not increase the funds at an individual's disposal. They can, however, be used to make retail purchases. The number of cards in use doubled from 173 million in 1990 to 353 million in 2000, with $368 billion in transactions.

debit card
Plastic card that allows an individual to transfer money between accounts

In stores with **point-of-sale (POS) terminals,** customers insert cards that transmit to terminals information relevant to their purchases. The terminal relays the information directly to the bank's computer system. The bank automatically transfers funds from the customer's account to the store's account.

point-of-sale (POS) terminal
Electronic device that allows customers to pay for retail purchases with debit cards

Smart Cards The so-called **smart card** is a credit-card-size computer that can be programmed with "electronic money." Also known as "electronic purses" or "stored-value cards," smart cards have existed for more than a decade. Phone callers and shoppers in Europe and Asia are the most avid users, holding the majority of the nearly 1.5 billion cards in circulation in 1999. Analysts expect 4 billion cards to be in use by the year 2002.[5]

smart card
Credit-card-size computer programmed with electronic money

"What customers want is convenience, and if you look at cash, it's really quite inconvenient."

—Donald J. Gleason, President, Smart Card Enterprise Division, Electronic Payment Services

Why are smart cards increasing in popularity today? For one thing, the cost of producing them has fallen dramatically, from as much as $10 to as little as $1. Convenience is equally important, notes Donald J. Gleason, president of Smart Card Enterprise, a division of Electronic Payment Services <www.eps.com.hk>. "What consumers want," Gleason contends, "is convenience, and if you look at cash, it's really quite inconvenient."

Smart cards can be loaded with money at ATM machines or, with special telephone hookups, even at home. After using your card to purchase an item, you can then check an electronic display to see how much money your card has left. Analysts predict that in the near future, smart cards will function as much more than electronic purses. For example, travel industry experts predict that people will soon book travel plans at home on personal computers and then transfer their reservations onto their smart cards. The cards will then serve as airline tickets and boarding passes. As an added benefit, they will allow travelers to avoid waiting in lines at car rental agencies and hotel front desks.

e-cash
Electronic money that moves among consumers and businesses via digital electronic transmissions

e-Cash A new, revolutionary world of electronic money has begun to emerge with the rapid growth of the Internet. Electronic money, known as **e-cash,** is money that moves along multiple channels of consumers and businesses via digital electronic transmissions. E-cash moves outside the established network of banks, checks, and paper currency overseen by the Federal Reserve. Companies as varied as new start-up Mondex <www.mondex.com> and giant Citicorp are developing their own forms of electronic money that allow consumers and businesses to spend money more conveniently, quickly, and cheaply than they can through the banking system. In fact, some observers predict that by the year 2005, as much as 20 percent of all household expenditures will take place on the Internet. "Banking," comments one investment banker, "is essential to the modern economy, but banks are not."

How is electronic money ultimately going to affect the economy?

How does e-cash work? Traditional currency is used to buy electronic funds, which are downloaded over phone lines into a PC or a portable "electronic wallet" that can store and transmit e-cash. e-cash is purchased from any company that issues (sells) it, including companies such as Mondex, Citicorp, and banks. When shopping online—for example, to purchase jewelry—a shopper sends digital money to the merchant instead of using traditional cash, checks, or credit cards. Businesses can purchase supplies and services electronically from any merchant that accepts e-cash. It flows from the buyer's into the seller's e-cash funds, which are instanta-

Commuters in metropolitan New York are getting accustomed to paying bridge and tunnel tolls with the E-Z Pass <www.drpa.org/ezintro>, a debit device that the driver attaches to the front windshield. A scanner electronically records trips through participating bridge and tunnel toll booths and debits an account established with the customer's credit card.

WebConnection

www.mondexinternational.com

Mondex International (MXI) is a leading provider of smart card-based solutions. With three core products—Mondex, MULTOS, and Interactive Loyalty—MXI can provide solutions for e-, t- and m-commerce needs. MXI can offer support in such areas as technology, risk management and commercial development.

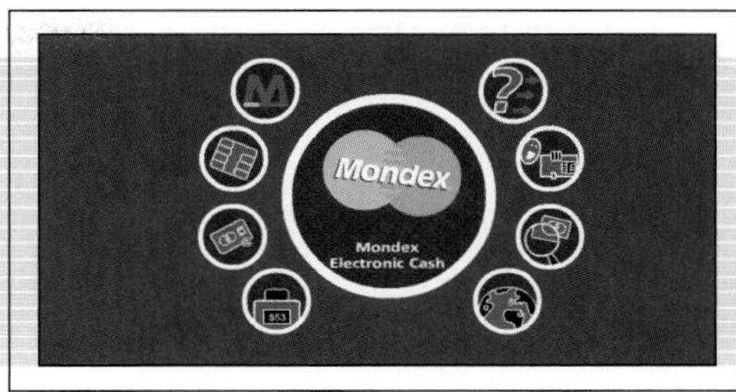

neously updated and stored on a microchip. One system, operated by CyberCash <www.cybercash.com>, tallies all e-cash transactions in the customer's account and, at the end of the day, converts the e-cash balance back into dollars in the customer's conventional banking account.

Although e-cash transactions are cheaper than handling checks and the paper records involved with conventional money, there are some potential problems. Hackers, for example, may break into e-cash systems and drain them instantaneously. Moreover, if the issuer's computer system crashes, it is conceivable that money "banked" in memory may be lost forever. Finally, regulation and control of e-cash systems remain largely nonexistent; there is virtually none of the protection that covers government-controlled money systems.

INTERNATIONAL BANKING AND FINANCE

Along with international banking networks, electronic technologies now permit nearly instantaneous financial transactions around the globe. The economic importance of international finance is evident from both the presence of foreign banks in the U.S. market and the sizes of certain banks around the world. In addition, each nation tries to influence its currency exchange rates for economic advantage in international trade. The subsequent country-to-country transactions result in an *international payments* process that moves money among buyers and sellers on different continents.

International Banking at U.S. Banks

The United States is heavily involved in international transactions that often entail exchanges between U.S. banks and other banks around the world. In 1999, these transactions amounted to some $2.2 trillion. Such sums have obviously attracted foreign banks to the U.S. market, where many now maintain a significant presence. In their U.S. branches and agencies, these banks hold $903 billion in assets and $324 billion in loans, mostly in New York, California, and Illinois. Meanwhile, foreign branches of U.S. banks, most notably in the United Kingdom, the Bahamas, and the Cayman Islands, hold $720 billion in assets.[6]

Exchange Rates and International Trade

As we saw in Chapter 18, every country's currency exchange rate affects its ability to buy and sell on the global market. The value of a given currency (say, the Canadian dollar) reflects the overall supply and demand for Canadian dollars both at home and abroad. This value changes with economic conditions. Worldwide, therefore, firms will watch those trends, and decisions about doing business in Canada will be affected by more or less favorable exchange rates. In 1999 the Canadian dollar was valued at $.68 (U.S.) whereas in the 1960s U.S. and Canadian dollars were about equal. Thus, with the Canadian dollar trading near historic lows, American companies have been buying Canadian companies at a record pace and at bargain prices. In the first nine months of 1999, U.S. companies bought 181 Canadian firms for $24 billion

"Canada has a 'for sale' sign on the lawn, courtesy of a very cheap exchange rate."

—David Rosenberg, senior economist, Nesbitt Burns, Toronto

"His mood is pegged to the dollar."

(U.S.)—twice the amount for the same period in 1998. Canada, admits one economist at the Toronto securities firm Nesbitt Burns <www.bmonesbittburns.com>, "has a 'for sale' sign on the lawn, courtesy of a very cheap exchange rate."[7]

The Law of One Price How do firms determine when exchange rates are favorable? When a country's currency becomes overvalued, its exchange rate is higher than warranted by its economic conditions. Its high costs make it less competitive: Because its products are too expensive to make and buy, fewer are purchased by other countries. The likely result is a trade deficit (see Chapter 3). In contrast, an undervalued currency means low costs and low prices: It attracts purchases by other countries, usually leading to a trade surplus.

How do we know whether a currency is overvalued or undervalued? One method involves a simple concept called the **law of one price:** the principle that identical products should sell for the same price in all countries. In other words, if the different prices of a Rolex watch in different countries were converted into a common currency, the common denominator price should be the same everywhere.

law of one price
Principle holding that identical products should sell for the same price in all countries

But what if prices are not equal? In theory, the pursuit of profits should equalize them: Sellers in high-priced countries will have to reduce prices if they are to compete successfully and make profits. As prices adjust, so should the exchange rates between different currencies until the Rolex can be purchased for the same price everywhere.

Big MacCurrencies A simple example that illustrates over- and undervalued currencies is the Big MacCurrencies, an index published annually in the British magazine *The Economist* <www.economist.com>. The identical product here is always McDonald's Big Mac, which is made locally in many countries. The first two columns in Table 19.1 list several countries and Big Mac prices in terms of local currencies. Each country's price is then converted into dollars (based on recent exchange rates). As you can see, Israel (14.50 shekels) is the most expensive, and China is the cheapest.

According to the Big Mac index, then, the Israel shekel is the most overvalued currency (against the dollar), and the Chinese yuan is the most undervalued. In theory, this means that you could buy Big Macs in China (using yuan) and resell them in Israel (for Israel shekels) at a handsome profit. In China, therefore, the demand for burgers would increase, driving the price up toward the higher prices in the other countries. In other words, the law of one price would set in. The index also indicates that the exchange rate of Argentina is neither over- nor undervalued, and France's franc is barely overvalued against the dollar. Governments and businesses use far more sophisticated methods to measure the purchasing power of different currencies in making much more complex transactions.

Government Influences on Exchange Rates What happens in reality when a currency becomes overvalued or undervalued? A nation's economic authorities may take action to correct its balance-of-payments conditions. Typically, they will devalue or

Table 19.1

Big Mac Currency Index

Country	Big Mac Prices in Local Currency	Big Mac Prices in Equivalent U.S. Dollars	Local Currency Overvaluation (+) or Undervaluation (−)
United States	$2.51	$2.51	—
Israel	14.50 shekels	3.58	+43%
Switzerland	5.90 S. francs	3.48	+39
Denmark	24.75 krone	3.08	+23
Britain	1.90 pounds	3.00	+20
Japan	294 yen	2.78	+11
S. Korea	3,000 won	2.71	+8
France	18.50 F. francs	2.62	+4
Argentina	2.50 A. pesos	2.50	0
Mexico	20.90 M. pesos	2.22	−11
New Zealand	$3.40 NZ	1.69	−33
Russia	39.50 rubles	1.39	−45
China	9.90 yuan	1.20	−52

revalue the nation's currency. The purpose of devaluing is to cause a decrease in the home country's exchange value. It will then be less expensive for other countries to buy the home country's products. As more of its products are purchased, the home country's payment deficit goes down. The purpose of revaluation, of course, is the reverse: to increase the exchange value and reduce the home country's payment surplus.

At the beginning of December 1994 the exchange rate was 3.5 Mexican pesos per U.S. dollar. Three weeks later, Mexican officials announced a devaluation, and the rate quickly changed to 4.65 pesos per dollar. By May 2000, the rate had gone to 9.53 on the world market. Mexican officials seek the more favorable exchange rate to encourage other countries to buy more Mexican products, thereby reducing Mexico's payments deficit.

The International Payment Process

Now we know why a nation tries to control its balance of payments and what it can do about an unfavorable balance. When transactions are made among buyers and sellers in different countries, exactly how are payments made? Payments are simplified through the services provided by their banks. For example, payments from buyers flow through a local bank that converts them from the local currency into the foreign currency of the seller. The local bank receives and converts incoming money from the banks of foreign buyers. The payment process is shown in Figure 19.3.

- *Step 1.* A U.S. olive importer withdraws $1,000 from its checking account to buy olives from a Greek exporter. The local U.S. bank converts those dollars into Greek drachmas at the current exchange rate (230 drachmas per dollar).
- *Step 2.* The U.S. bank sends a check for 230,000 drachmas (230 × 1,000) to the exporter in Greece.
- *Steps 3 and 4.* The exporter sends olives to its U.S. customer and deposits the check in its local Greek bank. The exporter now has drachmas that can be spent in Greece, and the importer has olives to sell in the United States.

At the same time, a separate transaction is being made between a U.S. machine exporter and a Greek olive oil producer. This time, importer/exporter roles are reversed between the two countries: The Greek firm needs to import a $1,000 olive oil press from the United States.

- *Steps 5 and 6.* Drachmas (230,000) withdrawn from a local Greek bank account are converted into $1,000 U.S. dollars and sent via check to the U.S. exporter.

Figure 19.3

International Payments Process

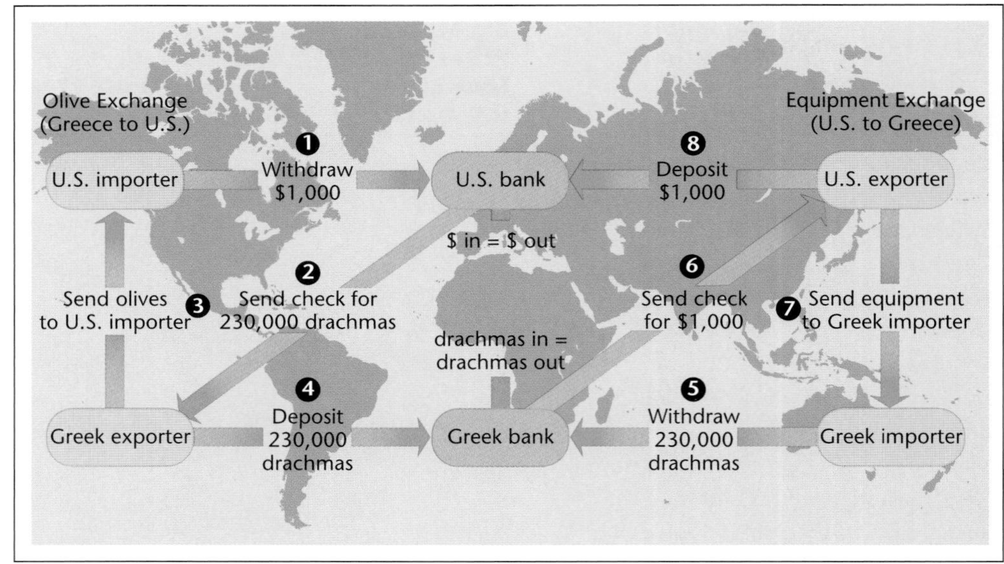

- *Steps 7 and 8*. The olive oil press is sent to the Greek importer, and the importer's check is deposited in the U.S. exporter's local bank account.

In this example, trade between the two countries is in balance. Money inflows and outflows are equal for both countries. When such a balance occurs, *money does not actually have to flow between the two countries.* Within each bank, the dollars spent by local importers offset the dollars received by local exporters. In effect, therefore, the dollars have simply flowed from U.S. importers to U.S. exporters. Similarly, the drachmas have moved from Greek exporters to Greek importers.

International Bank Structure

There is no worldwide banking system that is comparable, in terms of policy making and regulatory power, to the system of any industrialized nation. Rather, worldwide banking stability relies on a loose structure of agreements among individual countries or groups of countries.

World Bank
United Nations agency that provides a limited scope of financial services, such as funding national improvements in undeveloped countries

International Monetary Fund (IMF)
United Nations agency consisting of about 150 nations that have combined resources to promote stable exchange rates, provide temporary short-term loans, and serve other purposes

The World Bank and the IMF Two United Nations agencies, the World Bank and the International Monetary Fund, help to finance international trade. Unlike true banks, the **World Bank** (technically the International Bank for Reconstruction and Development) <www.worldbank.org> provides only a very limited scope of services. For instance, it funds national improvements by making loans to build roads, schools, power plants, and hospitals. The resulting improvements eventually enable borrowing countries to increase productive capacity and international trade.

The **International Monetary Fund (IMF)** <www.imf.org> is a group of some 150 nations that have combined resources for the following purposes:

- To promote the stability of exchange rates
- To provide temporary, short-term loans to member countries
- To encourage members to cooperate on international monetary issues
- To encourage development of a system for international payments

The IMF makes loans to nations suffering from temporary negative trade balances. By making it possible for these countries to continue buying products from other countries, the IMF facilitates international trade. However, some nations have declined IMF funds rather than accept the economic changes that the IMF demands. For example, some developing countries reject the IMF's requirement that they cut back social programs and spending in order to bring inflation under control.

Continued from page 531

Extending Credit Where Credit Is Due

Banco Popular, the largest issuer of credit cards in Puerto Rico, is expanding its card operation to the 50 states. It's a natural step for the bank, which is continuing to expand personal and business banking services to Hispanic clients at the same time that it enters the credit card market. "We have an understanding of the language and culture," explains Donald R. Simanoff, president of Banco Popular's U.S. card division, "and targeting the Hispanic consumer is what we do for a living."

> ***"We have an understanding of the language and culture, and targeting the Hispanic consumer is what we do for a living."***
>
> *—Donald R. Simanoff, President, Banco Popular's U.S. card division*

Since 1997, when Banco Popular officially entered the market, it has opened nearly 150,000 credit card accounts, 25 percent of which are secured accounts with credit lines backed by customer bank deposits. Thus, three-fourths of the bank's credit card portfolio is unsecured because the customers are considered good credit risks.

One of the main challenges facing Banco Popular is convincing the nearly half of all Hispanic consumers who have no access to credit through cards or other banking services that credit can be a good thing. To attract customers, Banco Popular offers card-related discounts on products popular in the Hispanic community, including Western Union money orders and purchases at Kmart pharmacies. It is also negotiating a discounted long-distance calling plan. A strong marketing campaign in 1999 included customer contests, employee incentives, and an expanded Hispanic affinity program to promote the acceptance of credit cards as a tool for personal finance.

With a keen understanding of the cultural needs of the Hispanic market, and with a clear strategic plan, Banco Popular is optimistic about future success in its primary New York, New Jersey, Texas, California, Florida, and Illinois markets. At the same time, however, managers realize that they are learning new things about the market every day. Recently, for example, the bank discovered that 4 of 10 people who call the bank choose to speak English instead of Spanish. Many Hispanic customers read English better than they do Spanish. This information convinced Banco Popular to issue credit card solicitations and statements in both English and Spanish and to make sure that every customer service representative is proficient in both languages.

Questions for Discussion

1. What are the demographic reasons underlying the growing importance of the Hispanic market to all U.S. banks?
2. Why have many mainstream U.S. banks thus far minimized their exposure in minority markets? What do you think of this business decision, and why do you think that many banks are now seeking a greater presence in these communities?
3. Why do you think a "cultural fit" is so important to many individual and small-business customers?
4. What do you think of Banco Popular's strategy to focus on the six states with the largest Hispanic populations instead of moving into all states?
5. Why is it smart for Banco Popular to issue secured credit cards to people who would otherwise be ineligible for credit?

SUMMARY OF LEARNING OBJECTIVES

1 **Define *money* and identify the different forms it takes in the nation's money supply.** Any item that is portable, divisible, durable, and stable satisfies the four basic characteristics of *money.* Money also serves three functions: It is a medium of exchange, a store of value, and a unit of account. The nation's money supply is often determined by two measures. *M-1* includes liquid (or spendable) forms of money: currency (bills and coins), demand deposits, and other checkable deposits (such as ATM account balances and NOW accounts). *M-2* includes M-1 plus items that cannot be directly spent but can be converted easily to spendable forms: time deposits, money market funds, and savings deposits. *Credit* must also be considered as a factor in the money supply.

2 **Describe the different kinds of *financial institutions* that make up the U.S. financial system and explain the services they offer.** The U.S. financial system includes federal- and state-chartered *commercial banks, savings and loan associations, mutual savings banks, credit unions,* and *nondeposit institutions* such as pension funds and insurance companies. These institutions offer a variety of services, including pension, trust, and international services, financial advice and brokerage services, and electronic funds transfer (EFT), including automated teller machines.

3 **Explain how banks create money and describe the means by which they are regulated.** By taking in deposits and making loans, banks create money or, more accurately, *expand the money supply.* The overall supply of money is governed by several federal agencies. The Comptroller of the Currency and the Federal Deposit Insurance Corporation (FDIC) are the primary agencies responsible for ensuring a sound, competitive financial system.

4 **Discuss the functions of the *Federal Reserve System* and describe the tools it uses to control the money supply.** The *Federal Reserve System* (or *the Fed*) is the nation's central bank. As the government's bank, the Fed produces currency and lends money to the government. As the bankers' bank, it lends money (at interest) to member banks, stores required *reserve funds* for banks, and clears checks for them. The Fed is empowered to audit member banks and sets U.S. *monetary policy* by controlling the country's money supply. To control the money supply, the Fed specifies *reserve requirements* (the percentage of its deposits that a bank must hold with the Fed). It sets the *discount rate* at which it lends money to banks and conducts *open-market operations* to buy and sell securities. It also exerts influence through *selective credit controls* (such as margin requirements governing the credit granted to buyers by securities brokers).

5 **Identify three important ways in which the financial industry is changing.** Many changes have affected the financial system in recent years. *Deregulation,* especially of interest rates, and the rise of *interstate banking* have increased competition. *Electronic technologies* offer a variety of new financial conveniences to customers. *Debit cards* are plastic cards that permit users to transfer money between bank accounts. *Smart cards* are credit-card-size computers that can be loaded with electronic money at ATMs or over special telephone hookups. *E-cash* is money that can be moved among consumers and businesses via digital electronic transmissions.

6 **Understand some of the key activities in *international banking and finance.*** Electronic technologies now permit speedy global financial transactions to support the growing importance of international finance. Country-to-country transactions are conducted according to an *international payment process* that moves money among buyers and sellers in different nations. Each nation tries to influence its *currency exchange* rates to gain advantage in international trade. For example, if its currency is *overvalued,* a higher exchange rate usually results in a *trade deficit.* Conversely, *undervalued* currencies can attract buyers and create *trade surpluses.* Governments may act to influence exchange rates by *devaluing* or *revaluing* their national currencies (that is, by decreasing or increasing them). Devalued currencies make it less expensive for other countries to buy the home country's products.

QUESTIONS AND EXERCISES

Questions for Review

1. What are the components of M-1? Of M-2?
2. Explain the roles of commercial banks, savings and loan associations, and nondeposit institutions in the U.S. financial system.
3. Explain the types of pension services that commercial banks provide for their customers.
4. Describe the structure of the Federal Reserve System.
5. Show how the Fed uses the discount rate to manage inflation in the U.S. economy.

Questions for Analysis

6. Do you think credit cards should be counted in the money supply? Why or why not? Support your argument by using the definition of money.

7. Should commercial banks be regulated, or should market forces be allowed to determine the money supply? Why?
8. Identify a purchase made by you or a family member in which payment was made by check. Draw a diagram to trace the steps in the clearing process followed by that check.

Application Exercises

9. Start with a $1,000 deposit and assume a reserve requirement of 15 percent. Now trace the amount of money created by the banking system after five lending cycles.
10. Interview the manager of a local commercial bank. Identify several ways in which the Fed either helps the bank or restricts its operations.

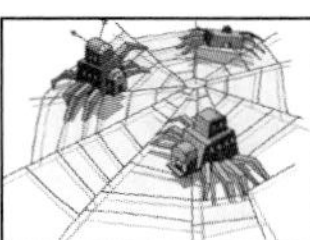

EXPLORING THE WEB

BANKING ON THE FED

The Federal Reserve Board, as the central controlling figure in the U.S. banking system, actively rules on a variety of banking issues. To find out about some of the Fed's recent activities, log on to its Web site at:

www.federalreserve.gov

Working from the left column of the homepage, you are asked to explore two areas—"Domestic and Foreign Banking Cases" and "Enforcement Actions"—as described here.

- Scroll down to Press Releases; then click on **Domestic and Foreign Banking Cases.** Scan the summaries of the 20 most recent cases and then consider the following questions:

1. Describe the various *types of actions* taken by the Fed.
2. How many of the cases involve *bank mergers?*
3. How many involve *international activities?*
4. Select a case that interests you, click on the date, and read the detailed press release. Then prepare a brief report for class that identifies the main banking issue, the business firms involved, the action taken by the Fed, and the economic significance of the case.

- Scroll down to Press Releases; then click on **Enforcement Actions.** Scan the summaries of any 10 recent cases. Describe the types of actions taken by the Fed in these cases.
- Next, select a case that interests you, click on the date, and read the detailed press release. Then prepare a report on the following:

5. Describe the *banking issue* involved in the case.
6. Who are the *contestants* in the case?
7. Explain the *enforcement actions* taken by the Federal Reserve Board in this case.

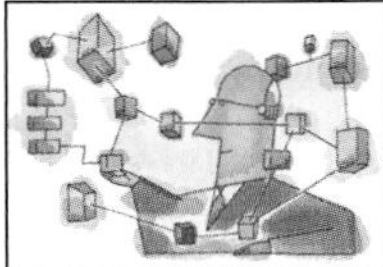

BUILDING YOUR BUSINESS SKILLS

FOUR ECONOMISTS IN A ROOM

This exercise enhances the following SCANS workplace competencies: demonstrating basic skills, demonstrating thinking skills, exhibiting interpersonal skills, working with information, and applying system knowledge.

GOAL

To encourage students to understand the economic factors considered by the Federal Reserve Board in determining current interest rates.

BACKGROUND

One of the Federal Reserve's most important tools in setting monetary policy is the adjustment of the interest rates it charges member banks to borrow money. To determine interest rate policy, the Fed analyzes current economic conditions from its 12 districts. Its findings are published eight times a year in a report commonly known as the *Beige Book.*

METHOD

Step 1

Working with three other students, access the Federal Reserve Web site at <www.bog.frb.fed.us/>. Look for the heading "Monetary Policy" and then look for "Federal Open Market Committee." Next, click on the subheading **Beige Book.** When you reach that page, click on **Summary** of the **Current Report.**

Step 2

Working with group members, study each of the major summary sections:

- Consumer spending
- Manufacturing
- Construction and real estate
- Banking and finance
- Nonfinancial services
- Labor market, wages, and pricing
- Agriculture and natural resources

Working with team members, discuss ways in which you think that key information contained in the summary might affect the Fed's decision to raise, lower, or maintain interest rates.

Step 3

At your library find back issues of *Barron's* <www.barrons.com>, the highly respected weekly financial publication. Look for the issue published immediately following the appearance of the most recent Beige Book. Search for articles analyzing the report. Discuss with group members what the articles say about current economic conditions and interest rates.

Step 4

Based on your research and analysis, what factors do you think the Fed will take into account to control inflation? Working with group members, explain your answer in writing.

Step 5

Working with group members, research what the Federal Reserve chairperson says next about interest rates. Do the chairperson's reasons for raising, lowering, or maintaining rates agree with your group's analysis?

FOLLOW-UP QUESTIONS

1. What are the most important factors in the Fed's interest rate decision?
2. Consider the old joke about economists that goes like this: *When there are four economists in a room analyzing current economic conditions, there are at least eight different opinions.* Based on your research and analysis, why do you think economists have such varying opinions?

CRAFTING YOUR BUSINESS PLAN

HOW TO BANK ON YOUR MONEY

THE PURPOSE OF THE ASSIGNMENT

1. To acquaint students with the process of navigating the *Business PlanPro* (*BPP*) software package (Version 4.0).
2. To familiarize students with banking issues that a sample firm faces in developing its business plan.
3. To demonstrate how two chapter topics—bank services and interest rates—can be integrated as components in the *BPP* planning environment.

ASSIGNMENT

After reading Chapter 19 in the textbook, open the BPP software and search for information about the financial plans of a sample firm: Flower Importer (Fantastic Florals, Inc.). Then respond to the following items:*

1. Consider interest rates that are assumed in the business plan. Are the short-term and long-term rates reasonable in today's economy? Explain. [Sites to see in *BPP* (for this assignment): In the Plan Outline screen, click on **Table: General Assumptions** (located beneath **7.1 Important Assumptions**). Also, read the Instructions section near the top of the screen.]
2. Identify some international banking services that would benefit FFI in its daily operations. [Sites to see in *BPP:* In the Plan Outline screen, click on **1.0 Executive Summary.** Return to the Plan Outline screen and click, in turn, on each of **3.4 Sourcing** and **3.6 Future Products.**]
3. From FFI's financial plan, can you see any need for bank credit? When, during the planning horizon, might the firm need a line of credit and how much? To meet what financial needs? [Sites to see in *BPP:* From the Plan Outline screen, click on each of **7.0 Financial Plan** and **Table: Cash Flow** (located beneath **7.5 Projected Cash Flow**).]
4. Does FFI plan to have excess cash from sales that can be deposited in the bank to earn interest? When, during the planning horizon,

might the firm accumulate excess cash and how much? [Sites to see in *BPP:* In the Plan Outline screen, click on **Table: Sales Forecast** (located beneath **5.2.1 Sales Forecast**). Return to the Plan Outline screen, then click on **Table: Cash Flow** (located beneath **7.5 Projected Cash Flow**). Observe the cash balance at the bottom of the table.]

FOR YOUR OWN BUSINESS PLAN

5. Planning for cash is an important part of your financial plan. To get started, go to the Business Plan Outline screen and click on its **Task Manager** option (at top). Scroll down to the section entitled "Cash is King"; then explore each of the cash-flow tools and tables. After filling in projected cash inflows and outflows for your company, select the cash-flow document that you think will best demonstrate your planned cash position.

*GENERAL TIPS FOR NAVIGATION IN *BPP*

1. Open the *BPP* program, examine the Welcome screen, and click on **Open a Sample Plan.**
2. From the **Open a Sample Plan** dialogue box, click on a sample company name; then click on **Open.**
3. On the Plan Manager screen, click on **Your Plan Outline;** then click on any of the lines (for example, **5.1.1 Pricing Strategy**).
4. You can always return to the Plan Outline screen by going to the bottom of the screen and clicking on the **Plan Outline** icon.
5. After finishing with one sample company, you can get to the next one by going to the top of the screen and clicking on **File** (on the menu bar). Then beneath that, select **Open Sample Plan.** This will exit you from the current company file and take you to the **Open Sample Plan** dialogue box, where you can select your next sample company.
6. When you are finished, you can close the program by going to the top of the screen and clicking on **File** (on the bar menu). Then beneath that, select **Exit.**

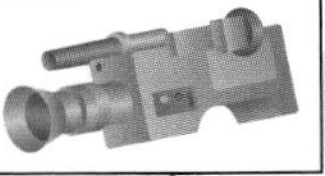

VIDEO EXERCISE

THE WORLD'S LENDERS: THE WORLD BANK AND THE IMF

Learning Objectives

The purpose of this video exercise is to help you

1. Understand the role of the World Bank.
2. Understand the role of the International Monetary Fund.

BACKGROUND INFORMATION

The World Bank <www.worldbank.org> is an international agency established in 1944, the same year as the International Monetary Fund (IMF) <www.imf.org>. It provides loans for development to countries in need and, together with the IMF, is a major player in today's international monetary system.

THE VIDEO

This segment discusses the roles and purposes of the World Bank and International Monetary Fund and describes their origin in the Bretton Woods agreement.

DISCUSSION QUESTIONS

1. What is the role of the World Bank in global financial markets?
2. What was the significance of the 1944 Bretton Woods Agreement?
3. What is the role of the IMF in the contemporary world economy?

FOLLOW-UP ASSIGNMENT

Research some recent articles about the World Bank and the IMF. What are some of the criticisms of the actions being taken by these two organizations around the world? What are some of the positive effects being reported? Do you think the World Bank and the IMF are positive or negative forces in developing nations? Explain your answer and give examples.

FOR FURTHER EXPLORATION

Explore the World Bank's Web site at <www.worldbank.com> and look specifically at the "About Us" page. What are the five different units that make up the World Bank? What is the function of each?

Chapter 20

Understanding Securities and Investments

After reading this chapter, you should be able to:

1. ***Explain*** the difference between *primary* and *secondary securities markets.*
2. ***Discuss*** the value to shareholders of *common* and *preferred stock,* and describe the secondary market for each type of security.
3. ***Distinguish*** among various types of *bonds* in terms of their issuers, safety, and retirement.
4. ***Describe*** the investment opportunities offered by *mutual funds* and *commodities.*
5. ***Explain*** the process by which securities are bought and sold.
6. ***Explain*** how securities markets are regulated.

Is Volatility Here to Stay?

Like the space-age roller coaster rides at Disney World and Coney Island, today's stock market promises a little nerve-shattering volatility for everyone with the guts to hop a ride. The best advice for the timid—or those prone to motion sickness—is stay away, especially if the swings that characterized the market in recent years are here to stay.

Why are today's market swings so violent? Why did traders sell off $74 billion in stocks in just one day—55 percent more than in the previous day and 43 percent more than the next trading day—on the New York Stock Exchange in April 2000? Why did the Dow Jones Industrial Average <**averages.dowjones.com**> surge upward 17 percent between October 1999 and January 2000, only to lose those gains during the next two months while U.S. unemployment remained at record-low levels? Similarly, the Dow shot up nearly 300 points in a single half hour in October 1998 after the Federal Reserve Board <**www.federalreserve.gov**> announced that it would cut interest rates by a quarter of a percentage point. Only a month earlier, the Dow had surged nearly 400 points on a single day, only to give it all back on the following two days. Market volatility can be traced to several factors, including new Internet stocks, large pools of available cash, new technologies to speed up trading, and global financial interrelationships.

Technology stocks have also added to the market volatility. An abundance of cash-starved e-businesses and high-tech stocks are capturing investor interest and attracting investment dollars as never before, even though many of these firms have yet to turn a profit. High-risk investors, looking beyond today's red ink, are betting on future performance. Thus it's no surprise when economic conditions, political events, or just plain fright stimulate wild ups and downs in the stock market. The technology-heavy Nasdaq Composite Index, sitting at 2,500 in August 1999, suddenly shot up to a record-setting 5,100 in March 2000—a gain of more than 100 percent in just seven months—for no clear reason. Then, in a stark turnaround, it fell to 3,100 for a near 40-percent loss during the next two months, as the Fed raised interest rates to slow the economy.

On Black Monday—the day in 1987 when the stock market dropped 554 points—684 million shares were traded on the New York Stock Exchange. Thirteen years later, that volume is nothing special. In fact, during 1999 there were 20 days with trading volumes higher than 1 billion shares. For the first five months of 2000, there were 62 days with 1 billion shares traded, with a record-setting 1.5 billion traded on April 4. On a busy day in 2000, the Nasdaq market volume of 2.9 billion shares is nearly five times the 0.6 billion traded on the exchange's busiest day just five years earlier. The New York Stock Exchange, which is now preparing to handle 5 billion trades a day, traded a daily average of 1 billion shares in the first five months of 2000. "The speed of transactions," says Mike Holland, chairman of Holland & Company, a private investment company, "is increasing geometrically as information and technology allow it. That volatility is here to stay," he adds, especially with the proliferation of online brokers.

"The speed of transactions is increasing geometrically as information and technology allow it. That volatility is here to stay."

—Mike Holland,
Chairman, Holland & Co.

James B. Lee, vice chairman of Chase Manhattan Bank, agrees: "Today," he notes, "everything happens at a faster rate than it did 10 years ago. What took a year to happen in 1990 . . . occurred [in Fall 1998] in 90 days. It may be the speed and breadth of information was that much slower, that much narrower, then, so it took a year to filter through the system. Now it takes less time." Meanwhile, the ups and downs of stock prices—as much as 5 percent a day—remain a fact of life.

Our opening story continues on page 580

Stock market volatility, then, may be just another expression of the fast pace of modern life. It's a pace that American investors seem willing to tolerate, perhaps because of their fundamental faith in the U.S. economy or perhaps because they have few investment alternatives. As you will see in this chapter, investing in U.S. and international companies through the purchase of stocks and bonds is now an integral part of many Americans' plans for acquiring and building wealth. By focusing on the learning objectives of this chapter, you will better understand the importance of the marketplaces in which securities are traded and the nature of such investment vehicles as stocks and bonds, mutual funds, and commodities.

SECURITIES MARKETS

securities
Stocks and bonds representing secured, or asset-based, claims by investors against issuers

Stocks and bonds are known as **securities** because they represent *secured,* or *asset-based,* claims on the part of investors. In other words, holders of stocks and bonds have a stake in the business that issued them. As we saw in Chapter 2, stockholders have claims on some of a corporation's assets (and a say in how the company is run) because each share of stock represents part ownership.

In contrast, *bonds* represent strictly financial claims for money owed to holders by a company. Companies sell bonds to raise long-term funds. The markets in which stocks and bonds are sold are called *securities markets.*

Primary and Secondary Securities Markets

primary securities market
Market in which new stocks and bonds are bought and sold

In **primary securities markets,** new stocks and bonds are bought and sold by firms and governments.[1] Sometimes new securities are sold to single buyers or small groups of buyers. These so-called private placements are desirable because they allow issuers to keep their plans confidential.

Each year, more than $100 billion in new private placements are purchased in the United States by large pension funds and other institutions that privately negotiate prices with sellers.[2] Because private placements cannot be resold in the open market, buyers generally demand higher returns from the issuers.

Securities and Exchange Commission (SEC)
Federal agency that administers U.S. securities laws to protect the investing public and maintain smoothly functioning markets

investment bank
Financial institution engaged in issuing and reselling new securities

Investment Banking Most new stocks and some bonds are sold on the wider public market. To bring a new security to market, the issuing firm must get approval from the **Securities and Exchange Commission (SEC)** <www.sec.gov>—the government agency that regulates securities markets. It also needs the services of an **investment bank**—a financial institution that specializes in issuing and reselling new securities. Such investment banking firms as Merrill Lynch <www.ml.com> and Morgan Stanley <www.msdw.com> provide three important services:

WebConnection

www.sec.gov

The SEC administers laws regulating the issuance of securities in the United States. Principally, it supplies the information that investors need to make fair decisions about securities, and it also monitors the activities of insiders—directors, officers, major stockholders—that concern the securities of their own firms. To get a much closer look at how the SEC performs such duties, check out its EDGAR (Electronic Data Gathering, Analysis, and Retrieval) Database by logging on to the agency's Web site.

1. They advise companies on the timing and financial terms of new issues.
2. By *underwriting*—that is, buying—new securities, they bear some of the risks of issuing them.
3. They create the distribution networks for moving new securities through groups of other banks and brokers into the hands of individual investors.

In 1999, U.S. investment bankers brought to the market $131 billion in new corporate stocks and $941 billion in new corporate bonds.[3] New securities, however, represent only a minute portion of traded securities. Existing stocks and bonds are sold in the **secondary securities market,** which is handled by such familiar bodies as the New York Stock Exchange. We consider the activities of these markets later in this chapter.

secondary securities market
Market in which stocks and bonds are traded

STOCKS

Each year, financial managers, with millions of individual investors, buy and sell the stocks of thousands of companies. This widespread ownership has become possible because of the availability of different types of stocks and because markets have been established for conveniently buying and selling them. In this section, we focus on the value of *common* and *preferred stock* as securities. We also describe the *stock exchanges* on which they are bought and sold.[4]

Common Stocks

Individuals and other companies purchase a firm's common stock in the hope that it will increase in value, provide dividend income, or both. But how is the value of a common stock determined? Stock values are expressed in three different ways—as par, market, and book value.

I would like to know how long it is appropriate to keep stock options and how much I should let the price increase before exercising them.

- The face value of a share of stock at the time it is originally issued is the **par value.** To receive their corporate charters, all companies must declare par values for their stocks. Each company must preserve the par value money in its retained earnings, and it cannot be distributed as dividends.
- A stock's real value is its **market value**—the current price of a share in the stock market. Market value reflects buyers' willingness to invest in a company.
- Recall from Chapter 18 our definition of *stockholders' equity*—the sum of a company's common stock par value, retained earnings, and additional paid-in capital. The **book value** of common stock represents *stockholders' equity* (see Chapter 18) divided by the number of shares. Book value is used as a comparison indicator because, for successful companies, the market value is usually greater than its book value. Thus, when market price falls to near book value, some investors buy the stock on the principle that it is underpriced and will increase in the future.

par value
Face value of a share of stock, set by the issuing company's board of directors

market value
Current price of a share of stock in the stock market

book value
Value of a common stock expressed as total shareholders' equity divided by the number of shares of stock

Investment Traits of Common Stock Common stocks are among the riskiest of all securities. Uncertainties about the stock market itself, for instance, can quickly change a given stock's value. Furthermore, when companies have unprofitable years, they often cannot pay dividends. Shareholder income, therefore—and perhaps share price—drops. At the same time, however, common stocks offer high growth potential. Naturally the prospects for growth in various industries change from time to time, but the **blue-chip stocks** of well-established, financially sound firms such as Ralston Purina <www.ralston.com> and Exxon <www.exxon.com> have historically provided investors steady income through consistent dividend payouts.

blue-chip stock
Common stock issued by a well-established company with a sound financial history and a stable pattern of dividend payouts

The "Old" Economy versus the "New": What's a "Blue Chip" Now? Because the very nature of the stock market is continually changing, the future performance of any stock is often unpredictable. With the proliferation of Internet and start-up dot.coms, experts are beginning to realize that many of the old rules for judging the market prospects of stocks are changing. Conventional methods don't seem to apply to the surprising surges

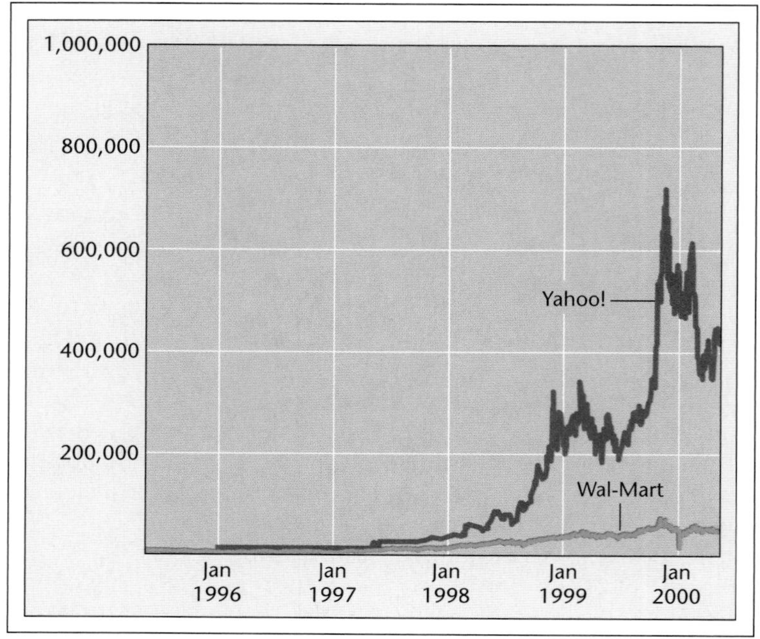

Figure 20.1
Market Value Growth: Wal-Mart versus Yahoo!

in "new economy" stock prices. Old performance yardsticks—a company's history of dividend payouts, steady growth in earnings per share, and a low price-earnings ratio (current stock price divided by annual earnings per share)—do not seem to measure the value of "new economy" stocks. In some cases, market prices are soaring for start-ups that have yet to earn a profit.

While some of the newcomers—America Online, Amazon, eBay, Yahoo!—are regarded by many on Wall Street as "Internet Blue Chips," their financial performance is quite different from that of traditional blue-chip stocks.[5] Let's compare Yahoo! and Wal-Mart. If you had invested $10,000 in Wal-Mart stock in June 1995, the market value of this blue chip would have increased to more than $40,000 in just five years (see Figure 20.1) The same investment in Yahoo! would have grown to $500,000.

Could this gigantic difference be predicted from indicators traditionally used by market experts? Hardly. The initial public offering (IPO) of Yahoo! stock in 1996 was priced at $13 per share. It quickly jumped to $43, then settled down to close the day at $33 even though the company had not yet turned a profit. Because Yahoo! was the leading Internet portal brand name, investors were betting that it would become a profitable business in the future—a bet that many traditionalists would view as extremely risky.

Consider the fact that Wal-mart's book value is more than double that of Yahoo!. Even more glaring is the fact that Wal-Mart's recent net income is nearly 100 times higher than Yahoo's!. Moreover, Wal-Mart's net earnings have grown steadily during the previous 10 years. The comparison is similar for dividends: Whereas Wal-Mart has a steady history of payouts to stockholders, Yahoo! has never paid a cash dividend. Overall, then, the traditional performance yardsticks favor Wal-Mart heavily. Nevertheless, investors are betting the future on Yahoo!: In June 2000, the original $10,000 investment had accumulated in five years to a market value more than 12 times that of the same investment in Wal-Mart.

Preferred Stock

Preferred stock is usually issued with a stated par value, and dividends are typically expressed as a percentage of par value. If a preferred stock with a $100 par value pays a 6 percent dividend, holders will receive an annual dividend of $6 per share.

Some preferred stock is *callable.* The issuing firm can call in shares by requiring preferred stockholders to surrender them in exchange for cash payments. The amount of this payment—the *call price*—is specified in the purchase agreement between the firm and its preferred stockholders.

Investment Traits of Preferred Stock Because preferred stock has first rights to dividends, income is less risky than income from the same firm's common stock. Most preferred stock is **cumulative preferred stock,** which means that any missed dividend payments must be paid as soon as the firm is able to do so. In addition, the firm cannot pay any dividends to common stockholders until it has made up all late payments to preferred stockholders. Let's take the example of a firm with preferred stock having a $100 par value and paying a 6 percent dividend. If the firm fails to pay that dividend for two years, it must make up arrears of $12 per share to preferred stockholders before it can pay dividends to common stockholders.

cumulative preferred stock
Preferred stock on which dividends not paid in the past must be paid to stockholders before dividends can be paid to common stockholders

Stock Exchanges

Most of the secondary market for stocks is handled by organized stock exchanges. In addition, a dealer or the over-the-counter market handles the exchange of some stocks. A **stock exchange** is an organization of individuals formed to provide an institutional setting in which stock can be bought and sold. The exchange enforces certain rules to govern its members' trading activities. Most exchanges are nonprofit corporations established to serve their members.

stock exchange
Organization of individuals formed to provide an institutional setting in which stock can be traded

To become a member, an individual must purchase one of a limited number of memberships, called *seats,* on the exchange. Only members (or their representatives) are allowed to trade on the exchange. In this sense, because all orders to buy or sell must flow through members, members of the exchange have a legal monopoly. Memberships can be bought and sold like other assets.

The Trading Floor Each exchange regulates the places and times at which trading may occur. Trading is allowed only at an actual physical location called the trading floor. The floor is equipped with a vast array of electronic communications equipment for conveying buy-and-sell orders or confirming completed trades. A variety of news services furnish

These servers are operated by Island ECN <www.islandecn.com> *one block away from the New York Stock Exchange. To some people, however, they are a world away: They represent the forces—technology and entrepreneurship—that are pulling the securities industry off of the traditional trading floor and into the electronic marketplace.* ECNs—electronic communications networks—*make fast electronic connections between buyers and specific orders. ECNs started by catering to day-traders and now handle about 20 percent of all shares traded on Nasdaq.*

up-to-the-minute information about world events and business developments. Any change in these factors, then, may be swiftly reflected in share prices.

broker
Individual or organization who receives and executes buy-and-sell orders on behalf of other people in return for commissions

Brokers Some of the people on the trading floor are employed by the exchange. Others are trading stocks for themselves. Many, however, are **brokers,** who receive and execute buy-and-sell orders from nonexchange members. Although they match buyers with sellers, brokers do not own the securities. They earn commissions from the individuals and organizations for whom they place orders.

Discount Brokers Like many products, brokerage assistance can be purchased at either discount or at full-service prices. Buying 200 shares of a $20 stock in 1999 cost the investor $8 at Ameritrade <www.ameritrade.com>, $14.95 at E*Trade <www.etrade.com>, $29.95 at Charles Schwab <www.schwab.com>, and $116 at a full-service brokerage firm. Price differences are obvious even among the discount brokers—Ameritrade, E*Trade, and Schwab—but the highest discount price is well below the price of the full-service broker.[6]

Discount brokers offer well-informed individual investors a fast, low-cost way to participate in the market. Charles Schwab's customers are "do-it-yourself" investors: They know what they want to buy or sell, and they usually make trades by using personal computers or Schwab's automated telephone order system without talking with a broker. Why are discount brokerage services low cost? For one thing, sales personnel receive fees or salaries, not commissions. Unlike many full-service brokers, they do not offer investment advice or person-to-person sales consultations. They do, however, offer automated online services, such as stock research, industry analysis, and screening for specific types of stocks.

Online Trading The popularity of online trading stems from convenient access to the Internet, fast no-nonsense transactions, and the opportunity for self-directed investors to manage their own portfolios while paying low fees for trading. Although only 14 percent of all equity trades were executed online in 1998, that number is growing rapidly. So popular is online investing that it has become the Internet's second most popular activity, topped only by surfing pornography. The Internet, says Gideon Sasson, head of Schwab's electronic brokerage unit, "is fundamentally changing the story of investing."[7] As you can see in Figure 20.2, the volume of online trading is increasing as competition among brokers drives prices further downward.

"The Internet is fundamentally changing the story of investing."

—Gideon Sasson,
Head of electronic brokerage,
Charles Schwab & Company

Figure 20.2
Growth of Online Trading

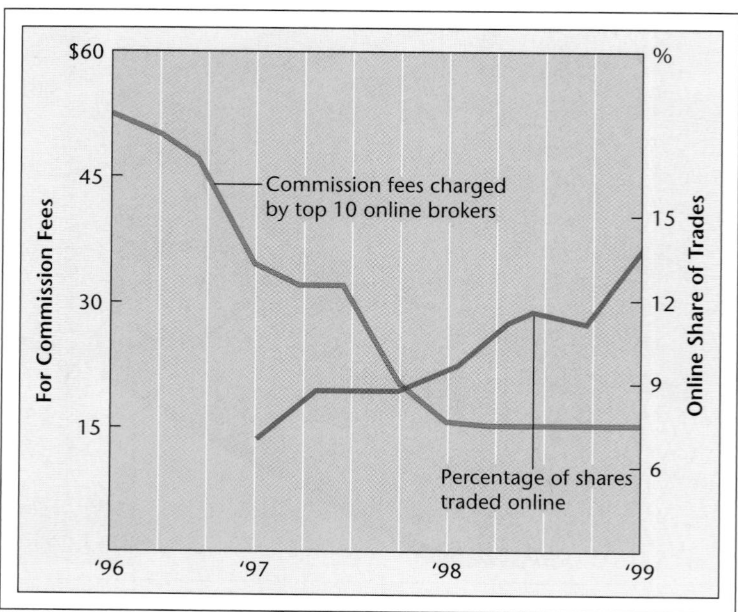

Full-Service Brokers Despite the growth in online investing, there remains an important market for full-service brokerages, both for new, uninformed investors and for experienced investors who don't have time to keep up with all the latest developments. When you deal with busy people who want to invest successfully, says Joseph Grano of PaineWebber <www.painewebber.com>, "you can't do it through a telephone response system. In a world that's growing more and more complicated, the advice and counsel of a broker will be more important, not less important."

With full lines of financial services, firms such as Merrill Lynch can offer clients consulting advice in personal financial planning, estate planning, and tax strategies, along with a wider range of investment products. Initial public offerings (IPOs) of stock, for example are generally not available to the public through online retail brokers. Rather, a full-service broker—who is also the investment banker that sells the IPO shares—can sell IPO shares to their clients. Financial advisors also do more than deliver information: They offer interpretations of and suggestions on investments that clients might overlook when trying to sift through an avalanche of online financial data.[8]

The Major Exchanges and the OTC Market The two major stock exchanges that operate on trading floors in the United States are the New York and American Stock Exchanges. The New York Stock Exchange, for many years the largest exchange in the United States, has recently begun to face stiff competition from both the electronic market in the United States and large foreign exchanges, especially in London and Tokyo.

The most important differences between exchanges and the electronic market are (1) the activity of *dealers* and (2) the geographic location of the market. On the trading floor of an exchange, one dealer, called a *specialist,* is appointed by the exchange to control trading for each stock. The specialist not only buys and sells that stock for his or her own inventory but acts as exclusive auctioneer for it.[9] The electronic market, on the other hand, conducts trades electronically among thousands of dealers in remote locations around the world.

The New York Stock Exchange For many people, "the stock market" means the New York Stock Exchange (NYSE) <www.nyse.com>. Founded in 1792 and located at the corner of Wall and Broad Streets in New York City, the largest of all U.S. exchanges is the model for exchanges worldwide. An average of 809 million shares valued at $36 billion change hands each day. About 40 percent of all shares traded on U.S. exchanges are traded here. Only firms meeting certain minimum requirements—earning power, total value of outstanding stock, and number of shareholders—are eligible for listing on the NYSE.

The American Stock Exchange The second-largest floor-based U.S. exchange, the American Stock Exchange (AMEX) <www.amex.com>, is also located in New York. It accounts for about 3 percent of all shares traded on U.S. exchanges and, like the NYSE, has minimum requirements for listings. They are, however, less stringent. The minimum number of publicly held shares, for example, is 500,000 versus 1.1 million for the NYSE.

Regional Stock Exchanges Established long before the advent of modern communications, the seven regional stock exchanges were organized to serve investors in places other than New York. The largest regional exchanges are the Chicago (formerly the Midwest) Stock Exchange and the Pacific Stock Exchange in Los Angeles and San Francisco. Other exchanges are located in Philadelphia, Boston, Cincinnati, and Spokane. Many corporations list their stocks both regionally and on either the NYSE or the AMEX.

Foreign Stock Exchanges As recently as 1980, the U.S. market accounted for more than half the value of the world market in traded stocks. Indeed, as late as 1975, the equity of IBM alone <www.ibm.com> was greater than the national market equities of all but four countries. Market activities, however, have shifted as the value of shares listed on foreign exchanges continues to grow. The annual dollar value of trades on exchanges in London, Tokyo, and other cities is in the trillions. In fact, the London exchange exceeds even the NYSE in number of stocks listed. In market value, however, transactions on U.S.

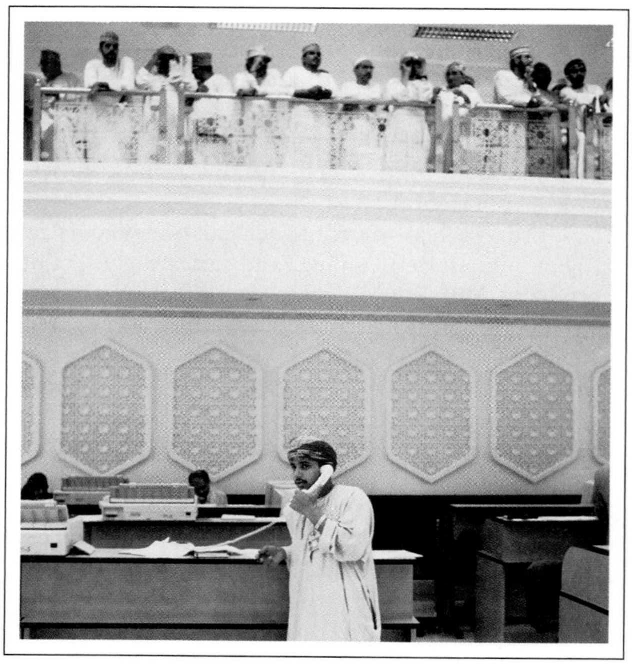

In Muscat, the capital of Oman, a tiny sultanate on the Arabian peninsula, the tax laws have been changed to encourage more foreign investment. One immediate result has been a 62-percent increase in activity on the Muscat Securities Market, where "high-tech" accoutrements still consist of telephones and (for interested local parties stationed in the gallery) binoculars. There is, of course, a Web site: <www.msm-oman.com>.

exchanges remain larger than those on exchanges in other countries. Relatively new exchanges are also flourishing in cities from Shanghai to Warsaw.

over-the-counter (OTC) market
Organization of securities dealers formed to trade stock outside the formal institutional setting of the organized stock exchanges

Over-the-Counter Market The **over-the-counter (OTC) market** is so called because its original traders were somewhat like retailers. They kept supplies of shares on hand and, as opportunities arose, sold them over the office counter to interested buyers. Even today, the OTC market has no trading floor. Rather, it consists of many people in different locations who hold an inventory of securities that are not listed on any of the national U.S. securities exchanges. The OTC consists of independent dealers who own the securities that they buy and sell at their own risk. Although OTC activities are of interest from an historical perspective, trading volume is small in comparison to other markets.

National Association of Securities Dealers Automated Quotation (Nasdaq) system
Organization of over-the-counter dealers who own, buy, and sell their own securities over a network of electronic communications

Nasdaq and NASD In the 1960s, an SEC study reported that the OTC, on which the shares of thousands of companies were traded, was unduly fragmented. One proposal recommended automation of the OTC, calling for a new system be to implemented by the National Association of Securities Dealers Inc. (NASD). The resulting automated OTC system, launched in 1971, is known as the **National Association of Securities Dealers Automated Quotation—or Nasdaq—system,** the world's first electronic stock market.[10]

With more than 5,500 member firms, NASD <www.nasd.com> is the largest securities-regulation organization in the United States. Every broker/dealer in the United States who conducts securities business with the public is required by law to be a member of the NASD.[11] NASD includes dealers (not just brokers) who must pass qualification exams and meet certain standards for financial soundness. The privilege of trading in the market is granted by federal regulators and by NASD. The organization's telecommunications system includes the Nasdaq system, which operates the Nasdaq Stock Market by broadcasting trading information on an intranet to over 350,000 terminals worldwide. Whereas orders at the NYSE are paired on the trading floor, Nasdaq orders are paired and executed on a computer network. Currently, the NASD is working with officials in an increasing number of countries who want to replace the trading floors of traditional exchanges with electronic networks like Nasdaq.

The stocks of some 4,800 companies are traded by Nasdaq. Newer firms are often listed here when their stocks first become available in the secondary market. Current list-

WebConnection

www.nasd.com

The National Association of Securities Dealers (NASD) is authorized by the Securities and Exchange Commission to set standards of conduct for about 500,000 brokers and dealers who issue and sell securities to the public. In this capacity, the NASD monitors the trading of shares in the thousands of companies in the over-the-counter market. To find out more about the Nasdaq Stock Market or the NASD's merger with the American Stock Exchange, log on to the organization's Web site.

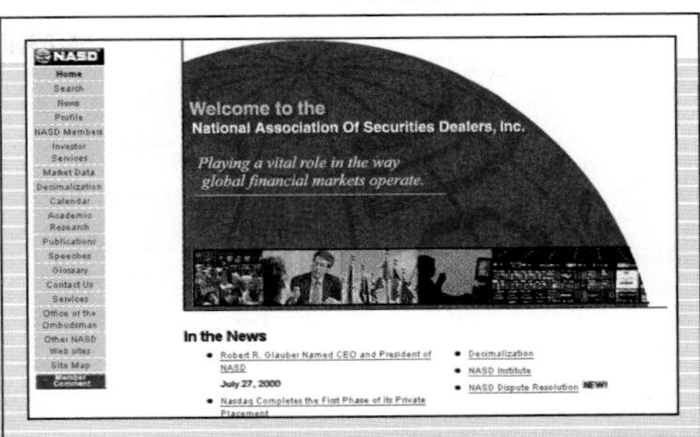

ings include such well-known technology stocks as Intel <www.intel.com>, Dell Computer <www.dell.com>, Oracle Technology <www.oracle.com>, and Microsoft <www.microsoft.com>.

In early 2000, Nasdaq, the fastest-growing U.S. stock market, set a record volume of over 2 billion shares traded in one day. Its 1999 volume of 270 billion shares traded was the industry leader, and it is the leading U.S. market for non-U.S. listings, with a total of 429 non-U.S. companies. Although the volume of shares traded surpasses that of the New York Stock Exchange, the total market value of Nasdaq's U.S. stocks is only about one-half of that of the NYSE.

The Steps to a Global Stock Market With its electronic telecommunication system, Nasdaq possesses an infrastructure that could eventually lead to a truly global stock market—one that would allow buyers and sellers to interact from any point in the world. Currently, Nasdaq provides equal access to both the market and market information via simultaneous broadcasts of quotes from more than 1,000 participating firms. Nasdaq communication networks enter customer orders and then display new quotes reflecting those orders.

In the battle for premier companies, both the New York Stock Exchange <www.nyse.com> and Nasdaq <www.nasd.com> have taken to marketing themselves much more aggressively. Each, for example, has expanded operations at its broadcast center and permitted more and more TV stations to air real-time stock prices. A virtual high-tech market site, the Nasdaq center features 100 video monitors and provides a showplace to impress new or prospective companies.

Life Cycle of an e-Business

A Prospectus for Growth

With the initial public offering (IPO) of 4.1 million shares of Garden.com common stock in 1999, the management team of the Internet start-up had more in mind than just raising additional capital. The *Prospectus* for the sale reveals that they also wanted to create a public market for their common stock and to facilitate future access to public markets. The new securities were brought to market by a group of investment bankers headed by Hambrecht & Quist LLC <www.hambrecht.com>, BancBoston Robertson Stephens, Inc. <www.rsco.com>, and Thomas Weisel Partners LLC <www.e-weisel.com>. An electronic prospectus was available to potential investors on the Web site of Charles Schwab & Co., Inc., another of the 20 participating investment bankers.

At the time of the issue, Garden.com stock had a par value of $.01. It was offered at $12 per share, and the *Prospectus* listed the pro-forma book value per share—that is, anticipated value per share after the IPO—at $3.93. After commissions and expenses, Garden.com expected proceeds of $44.5 million. These funds were targeted for several uses: nearly 57 percent for marketing and sales, about 18 percent for product development and Web site content development, and the rest—25 percent—for upgrading computer-systems architecture.

Following the IPO, the stock (symbol GDEN) was being traded publicly on the Nasdaq market, and its day-to-day price displayed the rather sizable variations that often characterize the performance of newly listed firms. Between mid-September 1999 and early July 2000, the market (or closing) price ranged between a high of $20.813 and a low of $2.375. By December, the stock had bottomed out at $0.03 per share. As you can see from the graph below, overall market performance showed a general downward trend in per-share value in the period after the IPO and through June 30, 2000. During the same period, key market indexes remained relatively level.

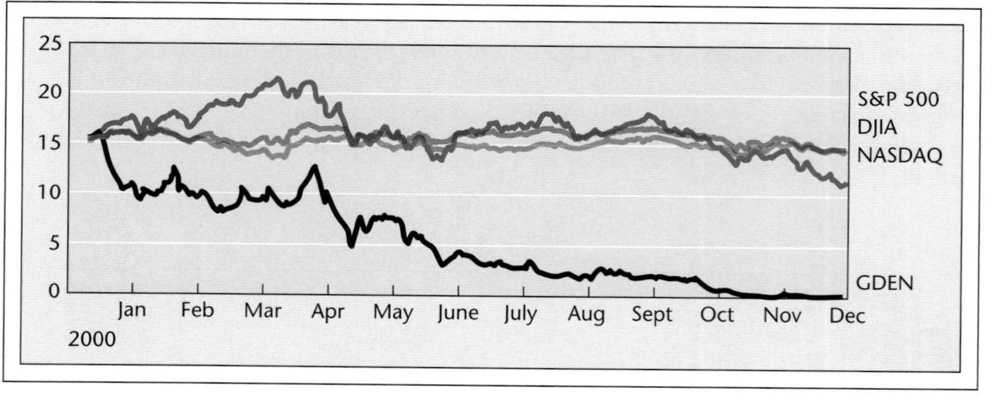

Combined with common shares issued privately before the IPO, the 4.1 million-share IPO resulted in a total of more than 17.5 million shares outstanding. At the closing price for June 30, the total market value of Garden.com's common shares was $42.8 million, indicating a sizable decrease in overall common value since the September IPO. The market's unkindness was to continue until December, when, as you can see from the graph, the combined market value for all stock had tumbled to a lowly $0.5 million.

In laying the groundwork for a system that would connect listed companies and investors for worldwide 24-hour-a-day trading, Nasdaq is taking the following steps:

- The Nasdaq Japan Market was launched in 2000, in partnership with the Osaka Securities Exchange <www.ose.or.jp/e>. This electronic securities market uses a technology that can eventually link Europe and the United States as well.

It's a WiredWorld

• Opening the Portals to Cross-Border Trading

In addition to being prominent European cities, what do London, Amsterdam, Frankfurt, Paris, and Stockholm have in common? In the world of business and investments, they are among the many cities with their own stock markets. Some, like Frankfurt, are just one of several stock exchanges in a given country, where trading on any one market is independent of the others. Lately, Europe's traditional exchanges have gotten bogged down; they're too cumbersome for today's business world. There are so many stock exchanges that the system isn't user-friendly for European investors who want a system that makes trades across national boundaries easier and cheaper.

As often happens in the business world, some upstart companies have recognized the gap and are responding to customers' needs: Internet-based newcomers are opening their portals all over Europe. Nasdaq-Europe, for example, was launched in November 1999 and targets traders who want to deal in the stocks of technology and start-up firms. Similarly, Jiway, which plans to open in autumn 2000, is luring retail brokers who want to trade across European borders. Two new Internet-based exchanges—Tradepoint <www.tradepoint.co.uk> and EASDAQ <www.easdaq.be>—are just getting started by connecting brokers to a system built for cross-border trading. Easdaq allows transactions in euros, pounds sterling, or U.S. dollars. Two other Web sites, Posit <www.itginc.com> and E-Crossnet <www.escrossnet.com>, bypass stock exchanges altogether and match up buyers and sellers directly, allowing them to complete their trades independently.

In addition to technology's influence, some organizational changes are also forcing European exchanges to rethink their traditional roles. In March 2000, three exchanges—the French, Dutch, and Belgian—announced that they were merging into a new exchange called Euronext, thus putting additional pressure on competitors to become more Pan-European. As a result, merger negotiations are underway between two of Europe's giant exchanges—London and Frankfurt. For years the London Stock Exchange (LSE) <www.londonstockexchange.com> has held the premier spot among Europe's equities markets, the value of shares listed there being double that of any other European exchange. The Frankfurt exchange <www.exchange.de> has not only worked its way up to the number-two position among Europe's financial centers but is also twice as profitable as the LSE. Now, as the LSE and Frankfurt negotiate a merger, they watch while newer competitors, especially Internet exchanges, encroach on their traditional markets. Just how long negotiations will continue is anybody's guess. Meanwhile, however, reports indicate that other European exchanges—Milan, Madrid, Ireland, Austria—have approached Frankfurt with a view to joining the newly merged exchange.

- Plans are underway for expanding Nasdaq-Europe, an Internet-accessible stock market patterned after Nasdaq. It would offer European traders access to the stocks of listed U.S. and Asian companies.
- It has agreed to a deal with the government of Quebec to launch Nasdaq Canada.
- An agreement with the Hong Kong Stock Exchange allows some of Nasdaq's shares to trade in Hong Kong, and some of Hong Kong's shares to trade in the United States.
- News reports indicate that Nasdaq has established relationships with Sydney, Australia's stock market and that negotiations are underway with South Korea's stock market.[12]

Although these initiatives are promising, it will take several years to resolve differences in market regulation and trading practices that currently separate various countries.

BONDS

A **bond** is an IOU—a promise by the issuer to pay the buyer a certain amount of money by a specified future date, usually with interest paid at regular intervals. The U.S. bond market is supplied by three major sources—the U.S. government, municipalities, and corporations. Bonds differ in terms of maturity dates, tax status, and level of risk versus potential yield.

bond
Security through which an issuer promises to pay the buyer a certain amount of money by a specified future date

To aid bond investors in making purchase decisions, several services rate the quality of bonds. Table 20.1, for example, shows the systems of two well-known services,

Table 20.1
Bond Rating Systems

	High Grades	Medium Grades (Investment Grades)	Speculative	Poor Grades
Moody's	Aaa, Aa	A, Baa	Ba, B	Caa to C
Standards & Poor's	AAA, AA	A, BBB	BB, B	CCC to D

Moody's <www.moodys.com> and Standard & Poor's <www.standardpoor.com>. Ratings measure default risk—the chance that one or more promised payments will be deferred or missed altogether. The highest grades are *AAA* and *Aaa,* the lowest *C* and *D*. Low-grade bonds are usually called *junk bonds.*

U.S. Government Bonds

The U.S. government is the world's largest debtor. New federal borrowing from the public actually decreased by $72 billion in 1999. In other words, the federal government's repayments of loans exceeded the funds it raised in new loans. Nevertheless, the total U.S. debt reached $5.8 trillion.[13] To finance its debt, the federal government issues a variety of government bonds. The U.S. Treasury issues Treasury bills (T-bills), Treasury notes, and Treasury bonds (including U.S. savings bonds). Many government agencies (for example, the Federal Housing Administration) also issue bonds.

government bond
Bond issued by the federal government

Government bonds are among the safest investments available. Securities with longer maturities are somewhat riskier than short-term issues because their longer lives expose them to more political, social, and economic changes. All federal bonds, however, are backed by the U.S. government. Government securities are sold in large blocks to institutional investors who buy them to ensure desired levels of safety in their portfolios. As investors' needs change, they may buy or sell government securities to other investors.

Municipal Bonds

municipal bond
Bond issued by a state or local government

State and local governments issue **municipal bonds** to finance school and transportation systems and a variety of other projects. In 1997, new municipal bonds were issued at a value of more than $215 billion.

Some bonds, called *obligation bonds,* are backed by the issuer's taxing power. A local school district, for example, may issue $50 million in obligation bonds to fund new elementary and high schools. The issuer intends to retire the bonds from future tax revenues. In contrast, revenue bonds are backed only by the revenue generated by a specific project.

The most attractive feature of municipal bonds is the fact that investors do not pay taxes on interest received. Commercial banks invest in bonds nearing maturity because they are relatively safe, liquid investments. Pension funds, insurance companies, and even private citizens also make longer-term investments in municipals.

Corporate Bonds

corporate bond
Bond issued by a company as a source of long-term funding

Although the U.S. government and municipalities are heavy borrowers, corporate long-term borrowing is even greater. **Corporate bonds** issued by U.S. companies are a large source of financing, involving more money than government and municipal bonds combined. U.S. companies raised nearly $941 billion from new bond issues in 1999. Bonds have traditionally been issued with maturities ranging from 20 to 30 years. In the 1980s, 10-year maturities came into wider use.

Like municipal bonds, longer-term corporate bonds are somewhat riskier than shorter-term bonds. To help investors evaluate risk, Standard & Poor's and Moody's rate both new and proposed issues on a weekly basis. Remember, however, that negative ratings do not necessarily keep issues from being successful. Rather, they raise the interest rates that issuers must offer. Corporate bonds may be categorized in terms of the method of interest payment or in terms of whether they are *secured* or *unsecured.*

Interest Payment: Registered and Bearer Bonds **Registered bonds** register the names of holders with the company, which simply mails out checks. Certificates are of value only to registered holders. **Bearer** (or **coupon**) **bonds** require bondholders to clip coupons from certificates and send them to the issuer to receive payment. Coupons can be redeemed by anyone, regardless of ownership.

registered bond
Bond bearing the name of the holder and registered with the issuing company

bearer (or **coupon) bond**
Bond requiring the holder to clip and submit a coupon to receive an interest payment

Secured Bonds With **secured bonds,** issuers can reduce the risk to holders by pledging assets in case of default. Bonds can be backed by first mortgages, other mortgages, or other specific assets. In 1994, Union Pacific Railroad Co. <www.uprr.com> issued $76 million in bonds to finance the purchase and renovation of equipment. Rated *Aaa* (prime) by Moody's and maturing in 2012, the bonds are secured by the newly purchased and rehabilitated equipment itself—80 diesel locomotives, 1,300 hopper cars, and 450 auto-rack cars.

secured bond
Bond backed by pledges of assets to the bondholders

Debentures Unsecured bonds are called **debentures.** No specific property is pledged as security. Rather, holders generally have claims against property not otherwise pledged in the company's other bonds. Thus, debentures are said to have "inferior claims" on a corporation's assets. Financially strong firms often use debentures. An example is the $175 million debenture issued by Boeing <www.boeing.com> in 1993, with maturity on April 15, 2043. Similar issues by weaker companies often receive low ratings and may have trouble attracting investors.

debenture
Unsecured bond for which no specific property is pledged as security

The Retirement of Bonds

Maturity dates on bonds of all kinds may be very long. Of course, all bonds must be paid off, or retired, at some point. With regard to maturity dates, there are three types of bonds: callable, serial, and convertible.

Callable Bonds The issuer of **callable bonds** may call them in and pay them off at a price stipulated in the indenture, or contract. Usually, the issuer cannot call the bond for a certain period of time after issue. For example, most Treasury bonds cannot be called within the first five years.

callable bond
Bond that may be called in and paid for by the issuer before its maturity date

Issuers usually call in existing bonds when prevailing interest rates are lower than the rate being paid on the bond. The issuer must still pay a call price in order to call in the bond. The call price usually gives a premium to the bondholder. The premium is merely the difference between the face value and call price. For example, a bond offered by the Wisconsin Power Co. <www.wpl.com> bears a $100 face value and can be called by the firm for $108.67 any time during the first year after issue. The call price and the premium decrease annually as bonds approach maturity.

Sinking Funds Callable bonds are often retired by the use of **sinking fund provisions.** The issuing company is required annually to put a certain amount of money into a special bank account. At the end of a certain number of years, the money (including interest) will be sufficient to redeem the bonds. Failure to meet the sinking fund provision places the issue in default. Obviously, such bonds are generally regarded as safer investments than many other bonds.

sinking fund provision
Method for retiring bonds whereby the issuer puts enough money into a banking account to redeem the bonds at maturity

Serial and Convertible Bonds Some corporations issue serial or convertible bonds. With a **serial bond,** the firm retires portions of the bond issue in a series of different preset dates. For example, a company with a $100 million issue maturing in 20 years may retire $5 million each year. Serial bonds are most popular among local and state governments.

serial bond
Bond retired when the issuer redeems portions of the issue at different preset dates

Only corporations, however, can issue **convertible bonds.** These bonds can be converted into the common stock of the issuing company. At the option of the holder, payment is made in stock instead of in cash. When holders are given such flexibility and the potential benefits of converting bonds into stock, firms can offer lower interest rates when the bonds are issued. However, because holders cannot be forced to accept stock instead of cash, conversion works only when the bond buyer also regards the issuing corporation as a good investment.

convertible bond
Bond that can be retired by converting it to common stock

Secondary Markets for Bonds Nearly all secondary trading in bonds occurs in the OTC market rather than on organized exchanges. Thus, precise statistics about annual trading volumes are not recorded. As with stocks, however, market values and prices change daily. The direction of bond prices moves *opposite* to interest rate changes. As interest rates move up, bond prices tend to go down. The prices of riskier bonds fluctuate more widely than those of higher-grade bonds.

OTHER INVESTMENTS

Stocks and bonds are not the only marketable securities available to businesses. Financial managers are also concerned with financial opportunities in *mutual funds* and *commodities*.

Mutual Funds

mutual fund
Company that pools investments from individuals and organizations to purchase a portfolio of stocks, bonds, and short-term securities

no-load fund
Mutual fund in which investors pay no sales commissions when they buy in or sell out

load fund
Mutual fund in which investors are charged sales commissions when they buy in or sell out

futures contract
Agreement to purchase specified amounts of a commodity at a given price on a set future date

commodities market
Market in which futures contracts are traded

Companies called **mutual funds** pool investments from individuals and organizations to purchase a portfolio of stocks, bonds, and other securities. Investors are thus part-owners of the portfolio. If you invest $1,000 in a mutual fund with a portfolio worth $100,000, you own one percent of that portfolio. Investors in **no-load funds** are not charged sales commissions when they buy into or sell out of funds. Investors in **load funds** generally pay commissions of two to eight percent.

Reasons for Investing The total assets invested in U.S. mutual funds has grown significantly every year since 1991, to a total of $6.8 trillion in more than 10,300 different funds in 1999.[14] Why do investors find them so attractive? Remember first of all that mutual funds vary in their investment goals. Naturally, different funds are designed to appeal to the different motives and goals of investors. Funds stressing safety often include money market mutual funds and other safe issues offering immediate income. Investors seeking higher current income must generally sacrifice some safety. Typically, these people look to long-term municipal bond, corporate bond, and income mutual funds that invest in common stocks with good dividend-paying records.

Mutual funds that stress growth include *balanced mutual funds*—portfolios of bonds and preferred and common stocks, especially the common stocks of established firms. Aggressive growth funds seek maximum capital appreciation. They sacrifice current income and safety and invest in stocks of new (and even troubled) companies and other high-risk securities.

Commodities

Individuals and businesses can buy and sell commodities as investments. **Futures contracts**—agreements to purchase specified amounts of commodities at given prices on set dates—can be bought and sold in the **commodities market.** These contracts are available not only for stocks but also for commodities ranging from coffee beans and hogs to propane and platinum. Because selling prices reflect traders' estimates of future events and values, futures prices are quite volatile and trading is risky.

WebConnection

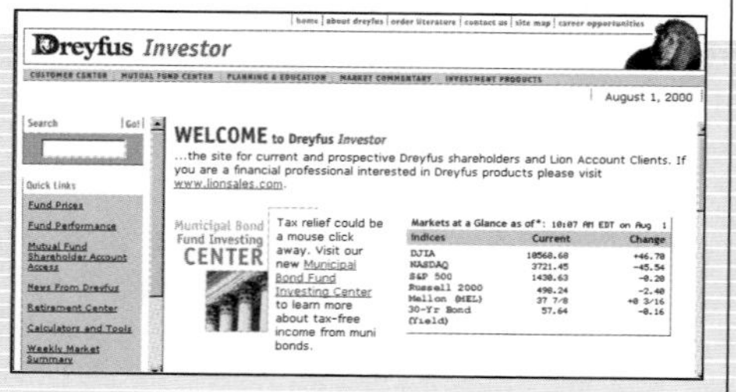

www.dreyfus.com

A subsidiary of Mellon Bank, Dreyfus manages $120 billion in 150 mutual fund portfolios. You can find out more about Dreyfus' various funds, such as the Dreyfus S&P 500 Index Fund, as well as the rationale for arranging them on a spectrum running from "aggressive" to "conservative" to meet the differing needs of individual investors, by logging on to the company's Mutual Fund Center.

To clarify the workings of the commodities market, let us look at an example. On October 5, 1999, the price of gold on the open market was $312 per ounce. Futures contracts for June 2000 gold were selling for $320 per ounce. This price reflected investors' judgment that gold prices would be higher the following June. Now suppose that you purchased a 100-ounce gold futures contract in October for $32,000 ($320 × 100). If in December 1999 the June gold futures sold for $345, you could sell your contract for $34,500. Your profit after the two months would be $2,500.

Margins Usually, buyers of futures contracts need not put up the full purchase amount. Rather, the buyer posts a smaller amount—the **margin**—that may be as little as $3,000 for contracts up to $100,000. Let us look again at our gold futures example. As we saw, if you had posted a $3,000 margin for your June gold contract, you would have earned a $2,500 profit on that investment of $3,000 in only two months.

margin
Percentage of the total sales price that a buyer must put up to place an order for stock or futures contracts

However, you also took a big risk involving two big *ifs:* If you had held onto your contract until June, and if gold had dropped, say to $283 (as it really did by June 2000), you would have lost $3,700 ($32,000 − 28,300). If you had posted a $3,000 margin to buy the contract, you would have lost all of that margin and would owe an additional $700. In fact, between 75 and 90 percent of all small-time investors lose money in the futures market. For one thing, the action is fast and furious, with small investors trying to keep up with professionals ensconced in seats on the major exchanges. Although the profit potential is exciting, experts recommend that most novices retreat to safer stock markets. Of course, as one veteran financial planner puts it, commodities are tempting. "After trading commodities," he reports, "trading stocks is like watching the grass grow."

"After trading commodities, trading stocks is like watching the grass grow."

—Veteran financial planner

BUYING AND SELLING SECURITIES

The process of buying and selling securities is complex. First, you need to find out about possible investments and match them to your investment objectives. Then you must select a broker and open an account. Only then can you place orders and make different types of transactions.

Financial Information Services

Have you ever looked at the financial section of your daily newspaper and wondered what all those tables and numbers mean? It is a good idea to know how to read stock, bond, and mutual fund quotations if you want to invest in issues. Fortunately, this skill is easily mastered.

Stock Quotations Daily transactions for NYSE securities are reported in most city newspapers. Figure 20.3 shows part of a listing from the *Wall Street Journal,* with columns numbered 1 through 12. Let us analyze the listing for the company at the top, The Gap Inc. <www.gap.com>:

- The first two columns ("High" and "Low") show the highest and lowest prices paid for one share of The Gap stock *during the past year.* Note that stock prices throughout are expressed in dollars per share, with the smallest fraction of a dollar being 1/16 or 6¼ cents. In the past year, then, The Gap's stock ranged in value from $53.75 to $30.81 per share. This range reveals a fairly volatile stock price.
- The third column ("Stock") is the abbreviated company name. (Sometimes the notation "pf" appears after the company's name to show that the stock is *preferred,* not common. The listing reveals that Healthcare Property Investors [HCP] offers a common stock in addition to two different preferred stocks, pfA and pfB.)
- The NYSE *symbol* for the stock is listed in column 4 ("Sym").
- The fifth column ("Div") indicates that The Gap pays an annual *cash dividend* of $0.09 per share. This amount can be compared with payouts by other companies.

Figure 20.3

Reading a Stock Quotation

	1	2	3	4	5	6	7	8	9	10	11	12
	52 Weeks											
	High	Low	Stock	Sym	Div	Yld %	PE	Vol 100s	High	Low	Close	Net Chg
s	53¾	30 13/16	Gap Inc	GPS	.09	.2	28	23751	37 3/16	36	36⅝	+⅜
	21¾	11	GardnrDenvr	GDI		...	15	81	18¼	18	18 1/16	−⅛
	24 15/16	9 9/16	GartnerGp	IT	1.19e	9.7	25	5812	12¾	12⅛	12 5/16	−1/16
n	26	9⅜	GartnerGp B	ITB		...	...	1181	9 15/16	9½	9⅛	+5/16
s	84	23⅜	Gateway	GTW		...	37	11898	53 11/16	51⅝	52½	−½
▼	9⅛	2¾	GenesisWrld	GWO	.15j	...	dd	391	2¾	2 5/16	2 5/16	−½
	31½	21 11/16	HlthCrProp	HCP	2.88f	10.5	12	436	27⅝	27¼	27⅜	+3/16
	24¼	13½	HlthCrProp pfA		1.97	11.9	...	54	16 11/16	16 7/16	16 9/16	+⅛
	25 1/16	14	HlthCrProp pfB		2.18	12.0	...	55	18 3/16	18⅛	18⅛	+1/16
	61 7/16	37¾	Hershey	HSY	1.04	2.0	24	2807	51 15/16	50½	51⅜	−3/16
	62 1/16	26⅝	Hertz	HRZ	.20	.6	10	934	33 11/16	32	32⅜	−1 3/16

- Column 6 ("Yld %") is the *dividend yield* expressed as a percentage of the stock's current price (shown in column 11). The Gap's dividend yield is .2 percent (0.09/36.625, rounded). Potential buyers can compare this yield with returns they might get from alternative investments.
- Column 7 ("PE") shows the **price-earnings ratio**—the current price of the stock divided by the firm's current annual earnings per share. On this day, The Gap's PE is 28, meaning that investors are willing to pay $28 for each dollar of reported profits to own The Gap stock. This figure can be compared with PE ratios of other stocks to decide which is the best investment.

price-earnings ratio Current price of a stock divided by the firm's current annual earnings per share

- The last five columns detail the day's trading. Column 8 ("Vol 100s") shows the *number of shares* (in hundreds) that were traded—in this case 23,751. Some investors interpret increases in trading volume as an indicator of forthcoming price changes in a stock.
- Column 9 ("High") shows the highest price paid *that day*—$37.187. Column 10 ("Low") shows the lowest price paid *that day*, $36.00.
- Column 11 ("Close") shows that The Gap's *last sale of the day* was for $36.625.
- The final column ("Net Chg") shows the *difference between the previous day's close and the close on the day being reported*. The closing price of The Gap stock is ⅜ higher than it was on the previous business day. Day-to-day changes are indicators of recent price stability or volatility.

Finally, look back at the far-left column, which has no heading. This column reports unusual conditions of importance to investors. Note, the *s* to the left of the "52 Weeks High" column for The Gap. This symbol indicates either a *stock split* (a division of stock that gives stockholders a greater number of shares but that does not change each individual's proportionate share of ownership) or an *extra stock dividend* paid by the company during the past 52 weeks. The *n* accompanying the Gartner Group B (ITB) indicates that this stock was *newly issued* during the past 52 weeks. The downward-pointing symbol (†)indicates a new 52-week low in the price of Genesis Worldwide Inc. (GWO) stock.

Bond Quotations Daily quotations on corporate bonds from the NYSE are also widely published. As you can see in Figure 20.4, bond quotations contain essentially the same type of information as stock quotations. One difference is that the year in which it is going to mature is listed beside each bond. Again, let's focus on the first bond listed, ATT.

1		2	3	4	5
Bonds		Cur Yld	Vol	Close	Net Chg
ATT	8⅝ 31	8.7	163	99¼	+⅛
BPAmer	7⅞ 02	7.9	50	100	−½
Bellso	6⅜ 28	8.1	35	78½	−¾
BellsoT	6¼ 03	6.5	5	96⅜	...
BellsoT	7s05	7.2	4	97¾	−⅛
Caterplnc	9s06	8.5	7	105¼	+1⅞
CentrTrst	7½ 01	cv	41	95¾	− 3/16
ChaseM	6½ 05	6.9	10	94¼	+1
ChaseM	6¼ 06	6.8	15	92⅝	+⅝
Dole	7s03	7.5	153	92⅞	+1⅛

Figure 20.4
Reading a Bond Quotation

- Column 1 ("Bonds") is the *bond identifier:* the abbreviation for both the company and a specific bond issue. Here, we see that the ATT bond bears an annual interest payment of 8⅝ percent of the bond's face value. The digits *31* mean that the bond matures in the year 2031. (The *s* that sometimes appears between the rate and maturity year is meaningless; it simply keeps numbers from running together.)
- Column 2 shows the *current yield:* the annual dollar coupon amount divided by the current market price. Holders can turn in bonds each year. For every $100 worth of bonds they own, they will receive $8⅝ ($8.70) in cash. If we jump ahead momentarily to column 4 ("Close"), we see that the same bond (and remaining coupons) can now be purchased for $99¼. This means that the bond currently yields an annual return of 8.70 percent (8⅝ divided by 99¼, rounded off). (The designation CV in column 2 means that the bond is *convertible.*)
- Columns 3, 4, and 5 refer to the *current day's activities.* Under "Vol," for example, we see that 163 ATT bonds were traded.

"The market closed down forty-three points, Mr. Murray, but the wind chill factor makes it feel like a hundred points."

"Close" is the particular bond's *closing price.* Note that this price, 99¼, is expressed as a percentage of the bond's par value. Let's say that ATT had set a par value of $1,000. Today's closing price means that the actual price to a buyer would be 99.25 percent of par value: that is, $992.50 instead of $1,000.

"Net Chg" refers to the *difference between today's closing price and yesterday's.* This bond is currently up ⅛ of a dollar, or $0.125.

Mutual Funds Quotations Selling prices for mutual funds are reported daily in most city newspapers. Additional investor information is also available in the financial press. Figure 20.5 shows how to read a typical weekly mutual funds quotation.

- Column 1 is the *net asset value* (NAV), or the value of a single share as calculated by the fund.
- Column 2 shows the *net asset value change,* the gain or loss based on the previous day's NAV.
- Column 3 lists the *fund family* at the top and the individual fund names beneath the family name.
- Column 4 reports *each fund's objective.* The "IB" code stands for an intermediate-term bond fund; "GR" indicates a growth stock fund. This allows readers to compare the performance of funds with similar objectives.

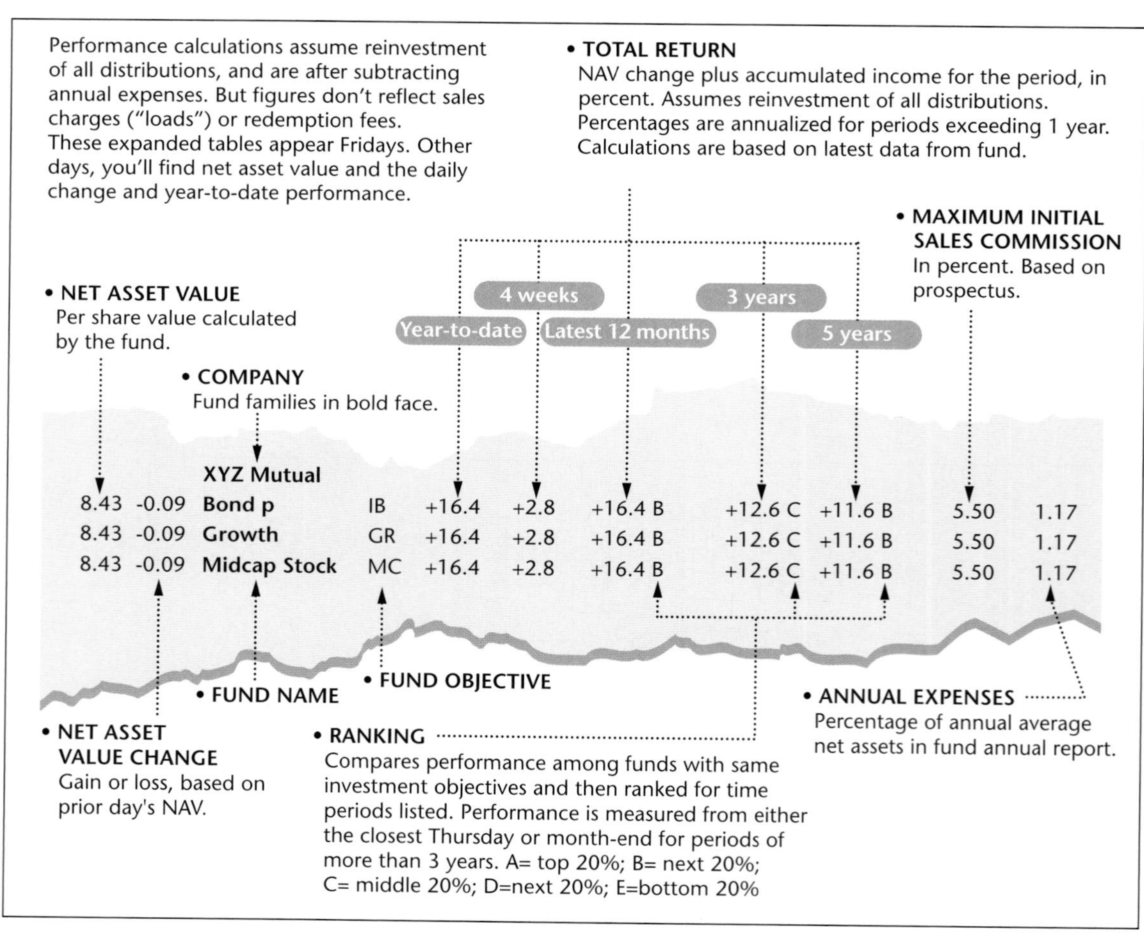

Figure 20.5

Reading Mutual Fund Quotations

- The next five columns report *each fund's recent and long-term performance,* and rank the funds within each investment objective. These numbers reflect the percentage change in NAV plus accumulated income for each period, assuming that all distributions are reinvested in the fund. These five columns show the return of the fund for the year to date, the last 4 weeks, 12 months, 3 years, and 5 years. The numbers for periods exceeding a year show an average annual return for the period, and are followed by letters indicating the fund's performance relative to other funds with the same objective. "A" means the fund was among the top 20 percent of funds in that category, "B" indicates the second 20 percent, and so on.
- The next column reports the *maximum initial sales commission,* expressed in percent, which the investor would have to pay to purchase shares in the fund.
- The last column shows the *fund's average annual expenses,* as a percentage of the fund's assets, paid annually by investors in the fund.

market index
Summary of price trends in a specific industry and/or the stock market as a whole

bull market
Period of rising stock prices

bear market
Period of falling stock prices

Market Indexes Although they do not indicate the status of particular securities, **market indexes** provide useful summaries of trends, both in specific industries and in the stock market as a whole. Market indexes, for example, reveal bull and bear market trends. **Bull markets** are periods of rising stock prices. Periods of falling stock prices are called **bear markets.**

As Figure 20.6 shows, the years 1981 to 2000 boasted a strong bull market, the longest in history. Inflation was under control as business flourished in a healthy economy. In contrast, the period 1972 to 1974 was characterized by a bear market. The Mideast oil embargo caused a business slowdown, and inflation was beginning to dampen economic growth. As you can see, the data that characterize such periods are drawn from three leading market indexes—the Dow Jones, Standard & Poor's, and the Nasdaq Composite.

How does Dow Jones performance reflect attitudes toward the economy?

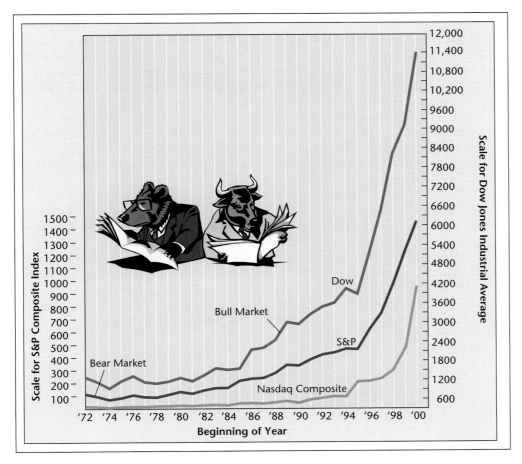

Figure 20.6
Bull and Bear Markets, 1972–2000

Dow Jones Industrial Average (DJIA)
Market index based on the prices of 30 of the largest industrial firms listed on the NYSE

The Dow The **Dow Jones Industrial Average (DJIA)** is the most widely cited American index. The "Dow" measures the performance of U.S. financial markets by focusing on 30 blue-chip companies as reflectors of economic health. The Dow is an average of the stock prices for these 30 large firms and, by tradition, traders and investors use it as a barometer of the market's overall movement. Since it includes only 30 of the thousands of companies on the market, the Dow is only an approximation of the overall market's price movements.

Over the decades, the Dow has been revised and updated to reflect the changing composition of U.S. companies and industries. The most recent modification occurred in November 1999, when four companies were added—Home Depot <www.homedepot.com>, Intel, Microsoft, and SBC Communications <www.sbc.com>—replacing Chevron <www.chevron.com>, Goodyear <www.goodyear.com>, Sears <www.sears.com>, and Union Carbide <www.unioncarbide.com>. These changes not only reflect the increasing importance of technology stocks, but also include for the first time two stocks from the Nasdaq market rather than including only companies listed on the NYSE.

What is the significance of the Dow Jones Industrial Average to the stock market?

The Dow average is computed as the sum of the current prices of the 30 stocks divided not by 30 (as might be expected) but rather by a number that compensates for stock splits and each stock's available number of shares. On November 1, 1999, the value of that divisor was 0.2044. Each day, the divisor's value is printed in the *Wall Street Journal,* as is the DJIA.

Standard & Poor's Composite Index
Market index based on the performance of 400 industrial firms, 40 utilities, 40 financial institutions, and 20 transportation companies

The S&P 500 Because it considers very few firms, the Dow is a limited gauge of the overall U.S. stock market. **Standard & Poor's Composite Index** is a broader report. It consists of 500 stocks, including 400 industrial firms, 40 utilities, 40 financial institutions, and 20 transportation companies. Because the index average is weighted according to the total market values of each stock, the more highly valued companies exercise a greater influence on the index.

Nasdaq Composite Index
Value-weighted market index that includes all Nasdaq-listed companies, both domestic and foreign

The Nasdaq Composite For several reasons, some Wall Street observers regard the **Nasdaq Composite Index** as the most important of all market indexes. First, unlike the Dow and the S&P 500, it includes not only domestic stocks, but non-U.S.–based common stocks listed on the Nasdaq market. In addition, all Nasdaq-listed companies, not just a selected few, are included in the index, for a total of over 5,000 firms (both U.S. and non-U.S.)—more than most other indexes. Like the S&P, the Nasdaq Composite is market-value–weighted (more highly valued companies have a greater impact). Finally, it includes many new and small companies which, along with technology stocks, have been driving the stock market in recent years. The index experienced rapid growth near the end of the 1990s.

The popularity of the Nasdaq Index goes hand in hand with investors' growing interest in technology and small-company stocks. Compared with other markets, the Nasdaq market has enjoyed a remarkable level of activity. By 1995, so many shares were being traded on Nasdaq that its share-of-market surpassed that of the NYSE. Figure 20.7 shows steady growth in the dollar volume of Nasdaq trades, which continue to capture market share. In a further display of Nasdaq's emerging role in the stock market, it has also overtaken the NYSE in terms of investor awareness. NYSE's historical dominance as the market's flagship brand is being challenged by the newer Nasdaq, which, according to one study, even enjoys greater name recognition among U.S. investors.

Placing Orders

After doing your own research and getting recommendations from your broker, you can choose to place several different types of orders:

market order
Order to buy or sell a security at the market price prevailing at the time the order is placed

- A **market order** requests that a broker buy or sell a certain security at the prevailing market price at the time of the order. For example, look again at Figure 20.3. On that

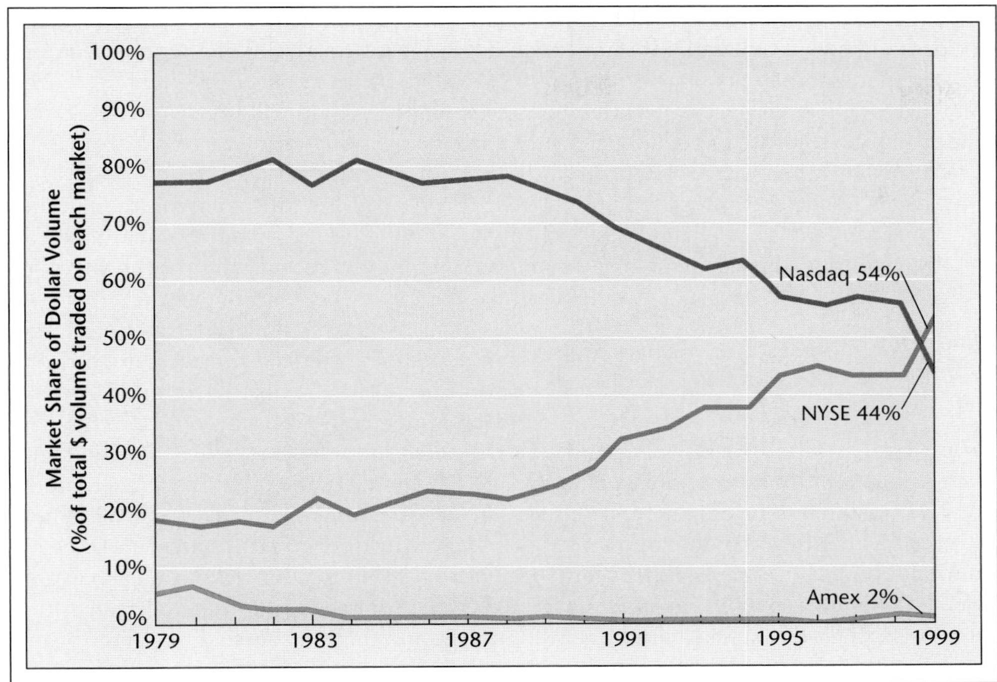

Figure 20.7
The Stock Markets: Comparative Dollar Volume of Trades

day, your broker would have sold your Gap, Inc. stock for between $36.00 and $37.188 per share.

Note that when you gave your order to sell, you did not know exactly what the market price would be. This situation can be avoided with limit and stop orders, which allow for buying and selling only if certain price conditions are met.

- A **limit order** authorizes the purchase of a stock only if its price is less than or equal to a specified limit. For example, an order to buy at $30 a share means that the broker is to buy if and only if the stock becomes available for a price of $30 or less. A **stop order** instructs the broker to sell if a stock price falls to a certain level. For example, an order of $25 on a particular stock means that the broker is to sell that stock if and only if its price falls to $25 or below.
- Orders also differ by size. An order for a **round lot** requests 100 shares of a particular stock or some multiple thereof. Fractions of round lots are called **odd lots.** Because an intermediary—an *odd-lot broker*—is often involved, odd-lot trading is usually more expensive than round-lot trading.

limit order
Order authorizing the purchase of a stock only if its price is equal to or less than a specified amount

stop order
Order authorizing the sale of a stock if its price falls to or below a specified level

round lot
Purchase or sale of stock in units of 100 shares

odd lot
Purchase or sale of stock in fractions of round lots

Financing Purchases

When you place a buy order of any kind, you must tell your broker how you will pay for the purchase. For example, you might maintain a cash account with your broker. Then, as you buy and sell stocks, your broker adds proceeds to your account while deducting commissions and purchase costs. Like almost every product in today's economy, securities can also be purchased on credit.

Margin Trading Like futures contracts, stocks can be bought on *margin*—that is, the buyer can put down a portion of the stock's price. The rest is borrowed from the buyer's broker, who secures special-rate bank loans with stock. Controlled by the Federal Reserve Board, the margin requirement has remained fixed at 50 percent since 1974.

Margin trading offers several advantages. Suppose you purchased $100,000 worth of stock in Intel Corp. Let's also say that you paid $50,000 of your own money and borrowed the other $50,000 from your broker at 10 percent interest. Valued at its market price, your stock serves as your collateral. If shares have risen in value to $115,000 after one year, you can sell them and pay your broker $55,000 ($50,000 principal plus $5,000 interest). You will have $60,000 left over. Your original investment of $50,000 will have earned a 20 percent profit of $10,000. If you had paid the entire price out of your own pocket, you would have earned only a 15 percent return.

Although investors often recognize possible profits to be made in margin trading, they sometimes fail to consider that losses, too, can be amplified. The rising use of margin credit by investors has become a growing concern during the recent bull market. Investors seem focused on the upside benefits with confidence that the market trend will continue upward, and they're less sensitive to the downside risks of margin trading. Especially at online brokerages, inexperienced traders are borrowing at an alarming rate, and some are using the borrowed funds for risky and speculative day trading. Day traders visit Web sites online to buy and sell a stock in the same day (so-called intraday trades), seeking quick in-and-out fractional gains on large volumes (many shares) of each stock. While some day traders are successful, most end up financial losers. With more investors buying on debt, more of them are headed for a serious accelerated crash. Bradley Skolnick, president of the North American Securities Administrators Association, voices the opinion held by many investment experts: "A lot of people are purchasing rather speculative, high-risk stocks with borrowed money, and that's a source of concern for me. In a volatile market, trading on margin can find you in a whole lot of hurt very quickly."[15]

"In a volatile market, trading on margin can find you in a whole lot of hurt very quickly."

—Bradley Skolnick, President, North American Securities Administrators Association

short sale
Stock sale in which an investor borrows securities from a broker to be sold and then replaced at a specified future date

Short Sales In addition to lending money, brokerages also lend securities. A **short sale** begins when you borrow a security from your broker and sell it (one of the few times that it is legal to sell something that you do not own). At a given point in the future, you must restore an equal number of shares of that issue to the brokerage, along with a fee.

We now return to our Gap example. Suppose that in January you believe the price of Gap stock will soon fall. You therefore order your broker to "sell short" 100 shares at the market price of $30.125 per share. Your broker will make the sale and credit $3,012.50 to your account. If The Gap's price falls to $25 per share in July, you can buy 100 shares for $2,500 and use them to repay your broker. You will have made a $512.50 profit (before commissions). Your risk, of course, is that The Gap's price will not fall. If it holds steady or rises, you will take a loss.

SECURITIES MARKET REGULATION

In addition to regulation by government agencies, both the NASD and the NYSE exercise self-regulation to maintain the public trust and to assure professionalism in the financial industry. A visible example is the NYSE's actions in establishing so-called circuit breakers—trading rules for reducing excessive market volatility and promoting investor confidence—that suspend trading for a preset length of time. Adopted first in October 1988, with approval of the SEC, the rules suspend trading on the NYSE whenever the market begins spiraling out of control during a single day. The 1988 rules stipulated that trading would halt for one hour on any day when the Dow Jones Industrial Average dropped 250 points and would close for two hours with any 400 point decline. The interruption provides a "cooling off" period that slows trading activity and allows investors to reconsider their trading positions, and allows computer programs to be revised or shut down.

Because circuit-breaker thresholds are updated periodically to keep up with the Dow's growth, effective April 2000 the following single-day declines will halt trading market wide:

- A 1,050-point drop in the DJIA before 2 P.M. halts trading for one hour.
- A 2,100-point drop before 1 P.M. halts trading for two hours.
- A 3,150-point drop at any time halts trading for the day.

Although circuit-breaker rules were initiated in response to severe market plunges in October 1987 and October 1988, they have been triggered only once, on October 27, 1997, when the DJIA fell 350 points at 2:35 P.M. and 550 points at 3:30 P.M., for an overall 7 percent plunge that shut down trading for the day.

One oft-cited cause of sudden market fluctuations is **program trading**—the portfolio trading strategy involving the sale or purchase of a group of stocks valued at $1 million or more, often triggered by computerized trading programs that can be launched without human supervision or control. It works in the following way. As market values change and economic events transpire during the course of a day, computer programs are busy recalculating the future values of stocks. Once a calculated value reaches a critical point, the program automatically signals a buy or sell order. Because electronic trading could cause the market to spiral out of control, it has contributed to the setting up of circuit breakers.

program trading
Large purchase or sale of a group of stocks, often triggered by computerized trading programs that can be launched without human supervision or control

The Securities and Exchange Commission

To protect the investing public and to maintain smoothly functioning markets, the Securities and Exchange Commission (SEC) <www.sec.gov> oversees many phases in the process through which securities are issued. The SEC regulates the public offering of new securities by requiring that all companies file prospectuses before proposed offerings commence. To protect investors from fraudulent issues, a **prospectus** contains pertinent information about both the offered security and the issuing company. False statements are subject to criminal penalties.

prospectus
Registration statement filed with the SEC before the issuance of a new security

Insider Trading The SEC also enforces laws against **insider trading**—the use of special knowledge about a firm for profit or gain. In June 2000, for example, the SEC filed suit in U.S. District Court for Northern California against 12 people on charges of using insider information and tips to gain at least $680,000 in illegal profits. The suit alleges that in 1995, one of the defendants, while working for Bay Networks Inc. <www.baynetworks.com>, learned of Bay's agreement to buy Xylogics Inc. <www.nortelnetworks.com>, before any public announcement. The defendant then allegedly purchased 6,215 shares of Xylogics during the two trading days before the public announcement. He subsequently made $105,000 in profits from the trades. He also contacted several friends who, in turn, contacted others who also grabbed up Xylogics stock and allegedly profited from trading in violation of the Securities Exchange Act of 1934.[16]

insider trading
Illegal practice of using special knowledge about a firm for profit or gain

The SEC also offers a bounty to any person who provides information leading to a civil penalty for illegal insider trading. The courts can render such a penalty of up to three times the illegal profit that was gained, and the bounty can, at most, be 10 percent of that penalty.

Along with the SEC's enforcement efforts, the stock exchanges cooperate in detecting and stopping insider action. In any given year, NASD may refer more than 100 cases to the SEC for charges of possible insider trading. In addition, NASD's self-regulation results in actions ranging from fining member firms and officers to barring or suspending them. In 1998, Hampton Capital Management Corp. was suspended from membership and fined and its principal officer fined and barred from any association with any NASD member in any capacity: The firm had refused to allow NASD staff to enter and examine the firm's books and records.

Blue-Sky Laws State governments also regulate the sale of securities. For example, commenting that some promoters would sell stock "to the blue sky itself," one legislator's speech led to the phrase **blue-sky laws** and the passage of statutes requiring securities to be registered with state officials. In addition, securities dealers must be registered and licensed by the states in which they do business. Finally, states may prosecute the sale of fraudulent securities.

blue-sky laws
Laws requiring securities dealers to be licensed and registered with the states in which they do business

Continued from page 557

The Stuff That Rumors and Inflated Expectations Are Made Of

Never before have investors had such immediate access to financial market information and analysis. From such sources as Reuters financial news services **<www.reuters.com>**, we can access our home PCs for real-time securities quotes and financial news from any market in the world. We can plug into hundreds of Internet-based online brokers for both analysis and full-color graphic explanations. We can watch CNBC's 24-hour cable operation **<www.cnbc.com>** or listen to the Bloomberg financial radio network **<www.bloomberg.com/wbbr>** for news and trends. We can get a copy of Fed chairman Alan Greenspan's latest speech by clicking on the Fed's Web site. The media give us not only instant information, but an instant "feedback loop" through which our reactions to facts, expectations, and rumors have the power to influence market swings.

Media analysts who feel compelled to give their spin on market changes also affect volatility. Without analysis, the business report would be little more than a recitation of numbers that would sell very few newspapers or hold the attention of very few viewers. "It's impossible to know why the stock market rose or fell," admits Associated Press **<www.ap.org>** business editor Rick Gladstone, "when there's no . . . obvious news. It may have nothing to do with the news or with anything. But reporters are obliged to say what might've been at work." This penchant for public speculation is the stuff that rumors, inflated expectations, and volatility are made of.

Immediate media access has turned many avid investors into 24-hour-a-day tradaholics. Securities are traded among investors in New York, Tokyo, London, and Buenos Aires any time day or night. When investors wake up in the morning, they can check the latest dollar–yen relationship or Standard & Poor's futures prices. The pace is exhausting and so is the volatility.

Questions for Discussion

1. How do you think stock market volatility will affect today's investors in both the short term and in the long term?
2. What is the relationship between the growth of privately managed retirement accounts, in the form of Individual Retirement Accounts, Roth IRAs, and 401(K) pension plans, and stock market volatility?
3. In a volatile stock market, why is it important for investors to assess their reaction to financial risk and to put together short-term and long-term financial plans?
4. Is increasingly more sophisticated computer technology necessarily a good thing for the market? Explain your answer.
5. Computer programs now use mathematical formulas to make buy-and-sell decisions for large institutions without benefit of human intervention. Is this progress? Explain your answer.
6. What do you think about the media's role in stock market volatility?

SUMMARY OF LEARNING OBJECTIVES

1 **Explain the difference between *primary* and *secondary securities markets*.** *Primary securities markets* involve the buying and selling of new securities, either in public offerings or through private placements (sales to single buyers or small groups of buyers). *Investment bankers* specialize in issuing securities in primary markets. *Secondary markets* involve the trading of stocks and bonds through such familiar bodies as the New York and American Stock Exchanges.

2 **Discuss the value to shareholders of *common* and *preferred stock*, and describe the secondary market for each type of security.** *Common stock* affords investors the prospect of capital gains and/or dividend income. Common stock values are expressed in three ways: as *par value* (the face value of a share when it is issued), *market value* (the current market price of a share), and *book value* (the value of shareholders' equity divided by the number of shares). Market value is most important to investors. *Preferred stock* is less risky. Cumulative preferred stock entitles holders to missed dividends as soon as the company is financially capable of paying. It also offers the prospect of steadier income. Shareholders of preferred stock must be paid dividends before shareholders of common stock.

Both common and preferred stock are traded on *stock exchanges* (institutions formed to conduct the trading of existing securities) including floor-based exchanges, electronic markets, and in *over-the-counter (OTC) markets* (dealer organizations formed to trade securities outside stock exchange settings). "Members" who hold seats on exchanges act as brokers—agents who execute buy-and-sell orders—for nonmembers. Floor-based exchanges include the New York, American, and regional and foreign exchanges. Nasdaq is a leading electronic market.

3 **Distinguish among various types of *bonds* in terms of their issuers, safety, and retirement.** The issuer of a *bond* promises to pay the buyer a certain amount of money by a specified future date, usually with interest paid at regular intervals. U.S. *government bonds* are backed by government institutions and agencies such as the Treasury Department or the Federal Housing Administration. *Municipal bonds,* which are offered by state and local governments to finance a variety of projects, are also usually safe, and the interest is ordinarily tax exempt. *Corporate bonds* are issued by companies to gain long-term funding. They may be secured (backed by pledges of the issuer's assets) or unsecured, and offer varying degrees of safety. The safety of bonds issued by various borrowers is rated by Moody's and Standard & Poor's.

4 **Describe the investment opportunities offered by *mutual funds* and *commodities*.** Like stocks and bonds, *mutual funds*—companies that pool investments to purchase portfolios of financial instruments—offer investors different levels of risk and growth potential. *Load funds* require investors to pay commissions of 2 to 8 percent. *No-load funds* do not charge commissions when investors buy in or out. *Futures contracts*—agreements to buy specified amounts of commodities at given prices on preset dates—are traded in the *commodities market*. Commodities traders often buy on *margins*—percentages of total sales prices that must be put up to order futures contracts.

5 **Explain the process by which securities are bought and sold.** Investors generally use such *financial information services* as newspaper and online stock, bond, and OTC quotations to learn about possible investments. *Market indexes* such as the Dow Jones Industrial Average, the Standard & Poor's Composite Index, and the Nasdaq Composite provide useful summaries of trends, both in specific industries and in the market as a whole. Investors can then place different types of orders. *Market orders* are orders to buy or sell at current prevailing prices. Because investors do not know exactly what prices will be when market orders are executed, they may issue *limit* or *stop orders* that are to be executed only if prices rise to or fall below specified levels. *Round lots* are purchased in multiples of 100 shares. *Odd lots* are purchased in fractions of round lots. Securities can be bought on margin or as part of *short sales*—sales in which investors sell securities that are borrowed from brokers and returned at a later date.

6 **Explain how securities markets are regulated.** To protect investors, the *Securities and Exchange Commission (SEC)* regulates the public offering of new securities and enforces laws against such practices as *insider trading* (using special knowledge about a firm for profit or gain). To guard against fraudulent stock issues, the SEC lays down guidelines for *prospectuses*—statements of information about stocks and their issuers. Many state governments also prosecute the sale of fraudulent securities as well as enforce *blue-sky laws,* which require dealers to be licensed and registered where they conduct business. The securities industry also regulates itself through the National Association of Securities Dealers (NASD), which sets standards for membership and oversees enforcement of NASD rules.

QUESTIONS AND EXERCISES

Questions for Review

1. What are the purposes of the primary and secondary markets for securities?
2. Which of the three measures of common stock value is most important? Why?
3. How do government, municipal, and corporate bonds differ from one another?
4. How might an investor lose money in a commodities trade?
5. How does the Securities and Exchange Commission regulate securities markets?
6. Which U.S. stock market has the largest volume of trade?

Questions for Analysis

7. Suppose you decide to invest in common stocks as a personal investment. Which kind of broker—full service or online discount—would you use for buying and selling? Why?
8. Which type of mutual fund would be most appropriate for your investment purposes at this time? Why?
9. Using a newspaper, select an example of a recent day's transactions for each of the following: a stock on the NYSE, a stock on the AMEX, a Nasdaq stock, a bond on the NYSE, and a mutual fund. Explain the meaning of each element in the listing.

Application Exercises

10. Interview the financial manager of a local business or your school. What are the investment goals of this person's organization? What securities does it use? What advantages and disadvantages do you see in its portfolio?
11. Either in person or through a toll-free number, contact a broker and request information about setting up a personal account for trading securities. Prepare a report on the broker's policies regarding the following: buy/sell orders, credit terms, cash account requirements, services available to investors, and commissions/fees schedules.

EXPLORING THE WEB

WHAT TO DO DURING TRADING HOURS

Because stock market action can be fast and furious, up-to-date information is a must for most investors. Current regulations allow information about sales to become publicly available only minutes after transactions have been made on the stock markets. To get an idea of the types of information available on the Internet, access the Web site maintained by Nasdaq at:

www.nasdaq.com

To observe the process and results of trading activity, both current and past, explore the diverse information that this Web site provides to potential investors. Accessing it during actual daytime trading hours enables you to see minute-to-minute changes. On the initial Nasdaq–AMEX screen, for example, examine "Site Map and Tour" for an overview of the Nasdaq system. Explore the **Symbol Look-Up** option as well as **Quotes for Nasdaq, AMEX & NYSE.** The **Reference** option accesses foreign stock exchanges throughout the world. Now consider the following questions:

1. What is the Nasdaq Composite Index? How many and what types of companies are included in it? Compare it with the Dow Jones Industrial Average Index. Which of the indexes is more representative of overall market activity? Why?
2. Select any two stocks (from the newspaper or other source). Using the **Symbol Look-Up** option on the initial screen, examine the volatility of the stocks' values during the past six months. Which stock was most volatile? What was the percentage change (from high to low) during the six months? [To get there, first look up the stock's symbol, enter it, and click on **Get InfoQuotes.** Then click on **Charting,** set the selector on **6 month,** then click on **Get Chart.**]
3. Select any two mutual funds (from the newspaper or other source). Using the **Symbol Look-Up** option on the initial screen, examine the volatility of the funds' values during the past six months. Which of the funds was most volatile? What was the percentage change (from high to low) during the six months?
4. Compare and contrast the operations of any major U.S. stock exchange (NYSE, AMEX, Nasdaq) with other exchanges by accessing the **Reference** option on the initial screen. In addition to the U.S. Regional group, how many

groups of foreign exchanges are available for examination? Select any two exchanges from different groups and examine their operations as described in their Web sites. In what ways are they similar to and in what ways do they differ from the U.S. stock exchanges?

5. Select the **News** option and explore some current news releases. How recently were these news items published? Why do you think Nasdaq displays these news releases at its Web site?
6. Using the **News** option, can you find a news release that might influence investors to buy or sell the stock of a particular company? An item that might influence investors to trade the stocks of companies in a particular industry?

BUILDING YOUR BUSINESS SKILLS

MARKET UPS AND DOWNS

This exercise enhances the following SCANS workplace competencies: demonstrating basic skills, demonstrating thinking skills, exhibiting interpersonal skills, and working with information.

GOAL

To encourage students to understand the forces that affect fluctuations in stock price.

BACKGROUND

Investing in stocks requires an understanding of the various factors that affect stock price. These factors may be intrinsic to the company itself or part of the external environment.

- Internal factors relate to the company itself, such as an announcement of poor or favorable earnings, earnings that are more or less than expected, major layoffs, labor problems, management issues, and mergers.
- External factors relate to world or national events, such as a threatened war in the Persian Gulf, the Asian currency crisis, weather conditions that affect sales, the Federal Reserve Board's adjustment of interest rates, and employment figures that were higher or lower than expected.

By analyzing these factors, you will often learn a lot about why a stock did well or why it did poorly. Being aware of these influences will help you anticipate future stock movements.

METHOD

Step 1

Working alone, choose a common stock that has experienced considerable price fluctuations in the past few years. Here are several examples, but there are many others: IBM, J.P. Morgan, AT&T, Amazon.com, Oxford Health Care, and Apple Computer. Find the symbol for the stock (for example, J.P. Morgan is JPM) and the exchange on which it is traded (JPM is traded on the New York Stock Exchange).

Step 2

At your library, find the *Daily Stock Price Record*, a publication that provides a historical picture of daily stock closings. There are separate copies for the New York Stock Exchange, the American Stock Exchange, and the OTC markets. Find your stock and study its trading pattern.

Step 3

Find four or five days over a period of several months or even a year when there have been major price fluctuations in the stock. (A two- or three-point price change from one day to the next is considered major.) Then research what happened on that day that might have contributed to the fluctuation. The best place to begin is with the *Wall Street Journal* or on the business pages of a national newspaper, such as the *New York Times* or the *Washington Post*.

Step 4

Write a short analysis that links changes in stock price to internal and external factors. As you analyze the data, be aware that sometimes it is difficult to know why a stock price fluctuates.

Step 5

Get together with three other students who studied different stocks. As a group, discuss your findings, looking for fluctuation patterns.

FOLLOW-UP QUESTIONS

1. Do you see any similarities in the movement of the various stocks during the same period? For example, did the stocks move up or

down at about the same time? If so, do you think the stocks were affected by the same factors? Explain your thinking.

2. Based on your analysis, did internal or external factors have the greatest impact on stock price? Which factors had the most long-lasting effect? Which factors had the shortest effect?
3. Why do you think it is so hard to predict changes in stock price on a day-to-day basis?

CRAFTING YOUR BUSINESS PLAN

A CAPITAL IDEA

PURPOSE OF THE ASSIGNMENT

1. To acquaint students with the process of navigating the *Business PlanPro* (*BPP*) software package (Version 4.0).
2. To familiarize students with securities and investments issues that a sample firm may face in developing its business plan.
3. To demonstrate how three chapter topics—issuing stock, issuing bonds, and making securities-market transactions—can be integrated as components in the *BPP* planning environment.

ASSIGNMENT

After reading Chapter 20 in the textbook, open the BPP *software* and search for information about financial plans, equity financing (stocks), and debt financing via bonds as they apply to a sample firm:* Sample Software Company *(Sample Software, Inc.). Then respond to the following questions:*

1. Evaluate Sample Software's use of bonds and stocks to finance its operations. Does the company have any outstanding stock? Does it plan to issue stock in the future? Does it use bonds as a source of debt financing? Explain the basis for your answers. [Sites to see in *BPP* (for this assignment): In the Plan Outline screen, click on **7.0 Financial Plan.**]
2. Evaluate the soundness of Sample Software's plans for using bonds versus stocks to raise capital. How much financing will be needed according to this plan, and at what points in time? What equity (stock) sources are available for meeting the firm's financial needs? What debt sources are available? [Sites to see in *BPP:* In the Plan Outline screen, click on **1.0 Executive Summary.** Return to the Plan Outline screen and click, in turn, on each of **2.1 Company Ownership, 2.2 Company History, 7.1 Important Assumptions,** and then **Table: General Assumptions.**]
3. Based on the company's "net profit" projections, at what points in time will Sample Software be able to pay dividends or repay its debt obligations? [Sites to see in *BPP:* From the Plan Outline screen, click on each of **7.4 Projected Profit and Loss** and **Table: Profit and Loss.**]
4. According to the company's plans, will Sample Software qualify for listing on a stock exchange? If so, which exchange is best suited for it? If it will not qualify, explain why. [Sites to see in *BPP:* In the Plan Outline screen, click on **7.0 Financial Plan.**]

FOR YOUR OWN BUSINESS PLAN

5. What type of financing—bonds (debt) or stocks (equity)—are you going to propose in the business plan that you are developing? What are the advantages and drawbacks of the types of financing you are choosing? What reasons will you give to explain your choices? In what section(s) of the *BPP* planning document will you present your plans for financing your business?

*GENERAL TIPS FOR NAVIGATING IN *BPP*

1. Open the *BPP* program, examine the Welcome screen, and click on **Open a Sample Plan.**
2. From the **Open a Sample Plan** dialogue box, click on a sample company name; then click on **Open.**
3. On the Plan Manager screen, click on **Your Plan Outline**; then click on any of the lines (for example, **5.1.1 Pricing Strategy**).
4. You can always return to the Plan Outline screen by going to the bottom of the screen and clicking on the **Plan Outline** icon.

5. After finishing with one sample company, you can get to the next one by going to the top of the screen and clicking on **File** (on the menu bar). Then beneath that, select **Open Sample Plan.** This will exit you from the current company file and take you to the **Open Sample Plan** dialogue box, where you can select your next sample company.
6. When you are finished, you can close the program by going to the top of the screen and clicking on **File** (on the bar menu). Then beneath that, select Exit.

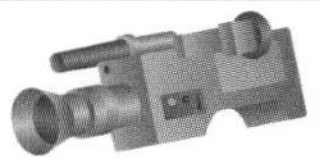

VIDEO EXERCISE

INFORMATION PAYS OFF: ANATOMY OF A STOCK TRADE

Learning Objectives

The purpose of this video exercise is to help you

1. Identify the basic characteristics of stocks and bonds.
2. Understand the nature of other marketable securities, such as mutual funds.
3. Describe the process by which securities are bought and sold.

BACKGROUND INFORMATION

Today's news is sprinkled liberally with stories of instant millionaires whose shares of Internet start-up companies appear to have mushroomed into enormous fortunes overnight. In reality, investing in the stock market—or any other market for securities—is a complex process that entails a certain amount of risk. Investors should be prepared to research the firms in which they are interested, but even before taking this step, they should know what kinds of securities are available and what regulations govern their sale. They should also have a very good idea of what constitutes an acceptable risk for them.

THE VIDEO

Experts in the fields of finance and investing answer questions about the types of securities and the differences between them, the kinds of securities markets in which they are traded, and the regulations that govern them. They also present an anatomy of an actual stock trade.

DISCUSSION QUESTIONS

1. What are securities and why do they exist?
2. What role do you think the Internet may play in the future of securities trading? What kind of regulation do you think will be necessary?
3. What are some reliable sources of information about securities?

FOLLOW-UP ASSIGNMENT

Select a publicly traded company in which you have some personal interest; perhaps you use its products, would like to work there, or know someone who works there. Follow the firm's stock price for a week or 10 days until you see a change in price, whether positive or negative. What is your best guess as to the reason for the change? Did the company take some important action or make a major announcement? Or is its stock price simply following a general market trend (all prices are rising or falling)? If the latter, what do you think is the reason for the general trend?

FOR FURTHER EXPLORATION

Mutual funds that seek out environmentally and socially conscious firms in which to invest are becoming more popular, offering investors a way to earn returns that don't offend their principles. Investigate two or three of the following and find out what types of firms they avoid and what type they invest in:

- <www.socialinvest.org>
- <www.coopamerica.org>
- <socialfunds.com>
- <goodmoney.com>
- <greenmoney.com>

If you were to invest in a mutual fund, would you choose one of these? Why or why not?

Chapter

21

Understanding Financial and Risk Management

After reading this chapter, you should be able to:

1. ***Describe*** the responsibilities of a *financial manager.*
2. ***Identify*** four sources of *short-term financing* for businesses.
3. ***Distinguish*** among the various sources of *long-term financing* and explain the risks entailed by each type.
4. ***Explain*** how *risk* affects business operations and identify the five steps in the *risk management process.*
5. ***Explain*** the distinction between *insurable* and *uninsurable risks.*
6. ***Distinguish*** among the different *types of insurance* purchased by businesses.

From Cluelessness to a Juicy Future

Most people have heard the story of how Apple Computer was founded by two young men who put together a prototype in a California garage. The story is unusual but not unique: Two young men in Nantucket, Massachusetts, began a juice drink company with little more than an original recipe once concocted for a cooking contest, and a collection of recycled wine bottles to sell it in.

Now bringing in $60 million a year and rapidly growing in a market dominated by such giants as Coca-Cola and Tropicana, Nantucket Allserve, Inc. <www.juiceguys.com> was started by Tom First and Tom Scott, who recall their beginning as "a combination of passion and naivete." In their early days in business, the two Toms, now known as the "Juice Guys," did indeed manage to steer a course to success that ran along the cliff edge of disaster. Some of their drink flavors were bizarre, their salesmanship was as inept as their skill at distribution, and their employees stole more than $100,000 in merchandise from their new Boston warehouse without being detected. Even their radio ads were homemade. "We were just clueless," says Tom First.

But Michael Egan, a business executive who had made millions on the sale of his Alamo car-rental company, saw some potential in the two Toms' "new age" product and attitude. So in 1993, he gave them $500,000 for a half share in their company. "These guys," explains Egan, "were just personally attractive, very hard working, dedicated, and visionary. Really, when you invest in a business, especially a start-up business, you invest in the people."

Egan's investment has proven to be a smart risk. With a new outsourced distribution system, 100 employees, and 50 "nectar" flavors, Nantucket Allserve has enjoyed a 2,800 percent increase in revenues during the last five years and plans to expand its reach across the country. From a few bottles sold off the back of a boat in Nantucket harbor to an empire that sells its products in 35 states and as far away as Latin America, South Korea, and Europe, the "Juice Guys" have made the most of their opportunities.

"When you invest in a business, especially a start-up business, you invest in the people."

—Michael Egan, Investor in Nantucket Allserve

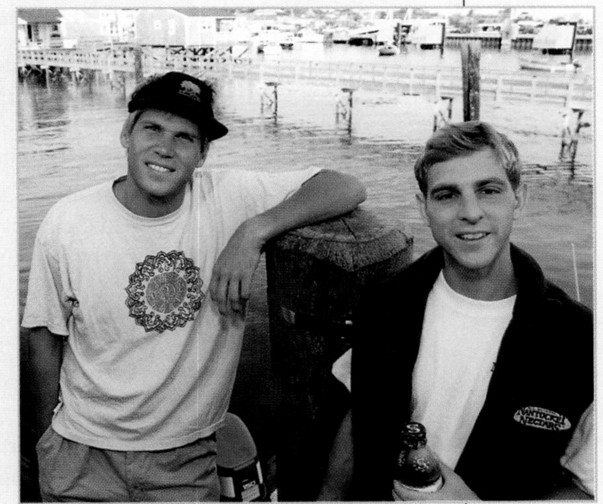

Our opening story continues on page 608

Tom First and Tom Scott's experience reflects one of the most basic lessons in business: The difference between a firm's life and death can hinge on the handling of its finances. This fundamental truth applies equally to established firms and start-ups. Nantucket Allserve needed start-up capital, revenue from sales, and internal financial controls. In this chapter we will examine the role of financial managers and show why businesses need financial management. By focusing on this chapter's learning objectives, you will see how risks arise when companies deploy their funds and how management works to protect firms from unnecessary financial loss.

THE ROLE OF THE FINANCIAL MANAGER

finance (or **corporate finance**)
Activities concerned with determining a firm's long-term investments, obtaining the funds to pay for them, conducting the firm's everyday financial activities, and managing the firm's risks

financial manager
Manager responsible for planning and controlling the acquisition and dispersal of a firm's financial resources

The business activity known as **finance** (or **corporate finance**) typically entails four responsibilities:

- Determining a firm's long-term investments
- Obtaining funds to pay for those investments
- Conducting the firm's everyday financial activities
- Helping to manage the risks that the firm takes

As we saw in Chapter 15, production managers plan and control the output of goods and services. In Chapter 11, we saw that marketing managers plan and control the development and marketing of products. Similarly, **financial managers** plan and control the acquisition and dispersal of a firm's financial resources. In this section, we will see in some detail how those activities are channeled into specific plans for protecting—and enhancing—a firm's financial well-being.

Responsibilities of the Financial Manager

Financial managers collect funds, pay debts, establish trade credit, obtain loans, control cash balances, and plan for future financial needs. But a financial manager's overall objective is to increase a firm's value—and thus stockholders' wealth. Whereas accountants create data to reflect a firm's financial status, financial managers make decisions for improving that status. Financial managers, then, must ensure that a company's earnings exceed its costs—in other words, that it earns a profit. In sole proprietorships and partnerships, profits translate directly into increases in owners' wealth. In corporations, profits translate into an increase in the value of common stock.

The various responsibilities of the financial manager in increasing a firm's wealth fall into three general categories: *cash-flow management, financial control,* and *financial planning.*

cash-flow management
Management of cash inflows and outflows to ensure adequate funds for purchases and the productive use of excess funds

Cash-Flow Management To increase a firm's value, financial managers must ensure that it always has enough funds on hand to purchase the materials and human resources that it needs to produce goods and services. At the same time, there may be funds that are not needed immediately. These must be invested to earn more money for the firm. This activity—**cash-flow management**—requires careful planning. If excess cash balances are allowed to sit idle instead of being invested, a firm loses the cash returns that it could have earned.

How important to a business is the management of its idle cash? One study has revealed that companies averaging $2 million in annual sales typically hold $40,000 in noninterest-bearing accounts. Larger companies hold even larger sums. More and more companies, however, are learning to put idle funds to work. In 1999, General Electric Company <www.ge.com> earned $101 million in interest income during the year by investing otherwise idle incoming cash that was not needed immediately to meet other

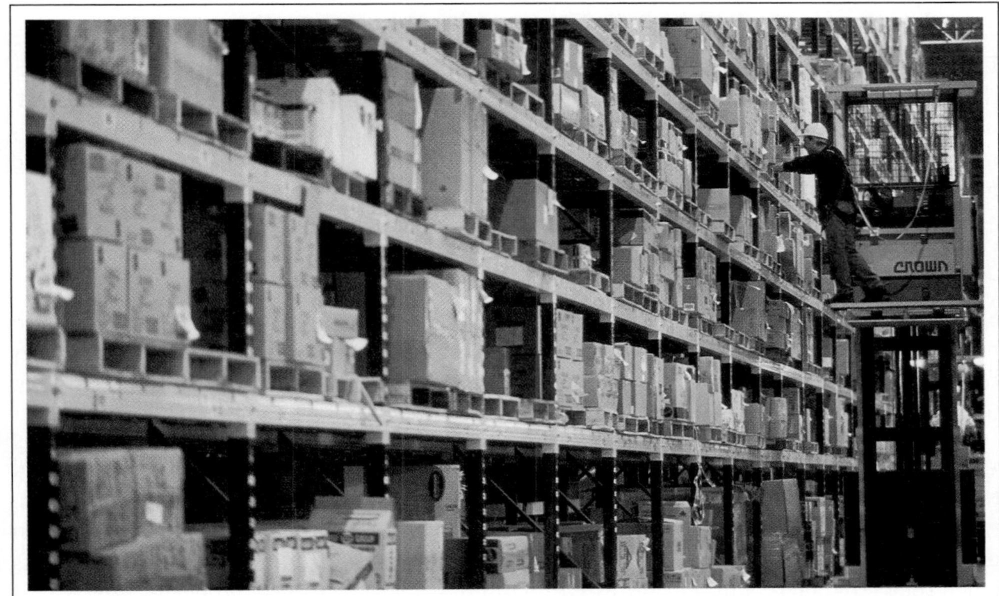

To some analysts, this immense distribution center in Atlanta represents not the promise of e-tailing, but rather some serious problems underlying the business model on which Amazon.com is built. These critics say that retail success means generating positive cash flow by estimating the proper amounts of inventories needed to meet demand—without overstocking. Amazon, however, has built a huge network of warehouses in which to store vast inventories of merchandise, and so far, it has depended on money supplied by investors and lenders, not on cash furnished by operations—that is, profit generated by the efficient selling of retail merchandise.

obligations.[1] By locating idle cash and putting it to work, firms not only gain additional income, but also can avoid having to borrow from outside sources. The savings on interest payments can be substantial.

Financial Control Because things rarely go exactly as planned, financial managers must make adjustments for actual financial changes that occur each day. **Financial control** is the process of checking actual performance against plans to ensure that desired financial results occur. For example, planned revenues based on forecasts usually turn out to be higher or lower than actual revenues because sales are largely unpredictable. Control involves monitoring revenue inflows and making appropriate financial adjustments. Excessively high revenues may be deposited in short-term interest-bearing accounts. Or they may be used to pay off short-term debt. In contrast, lower-than-expected revenues may necessitate short-term borrowing to meet current debt obligations.

financial control
Process of checking actual performance against plans to ensure that desired financial results occur

Budgets (as we saw in Chapter 18) are often the backbone of financial control. The budget provides the measuring stick against which performance is evaluated. The cash flows, debts, and assets not only of the whole company but also of each department are compared at regular intervals against budgeted amounts. Discrepancies indicate the need for financial adjustments so that resources are used to the best advantage.

Financial Planning The cornerstone of effective financial management is the development of a financial plan. A **financial plan** describes a firm's strategies for reaching some future financial position. In constructing the plan, a financial manager must ask several questions:

financial plan
A firm's strategies for reaching some future financial position

- What amount of funds does the company need to meet immediate needs?
- When will it need more funds?
- Where can it get the funds to meet both its short- and long-term needs?

To answer these questions, a financial manager must develop a clear picture of why a firm needs funds. Managers must also assess the relative costs and benefits of potential funding sources. In the sections that follow, we will examine the main reasons for which companies generate funds and describe the main sources of business funding, both for the short term and the long term.

WHY DO BUSINESSES NEED FUNDS?

Every company must spend money to survive: According to the simplest formula, funds that are spent on materials, wages, and buildings eventually lead to the creation of products, revenues, and profits. In planning for funding requirements, financial managers must distinguish between two different kinds of expenditures: *short-term (operating)* and *long-term (capital) expenditures.*

Short-Term (Operating) Expenditures

Short-term expenditures are incurred regularly in a firm's everyday business activities. To manage these outlays, managers must pay special attention to *accounts payable, accounts receivable,* and *inventories.* We will also describe the measures used by some firms in managing the funds known as *working capital.*

Accounts Payable In Chapter 18, we defined *accounts payable* as unpaid bills owed to suppliers plus wages and taxes due within the upcoming year. For most companies, this is the largest single category of short-term debt. To plan for funding flows, financial managers want to know *in advance* the amounts of new accounts payable as well as when they must be repaid. For information about such obligations and needs—for example, the quantity of supplies required by a certain department in an upcoming period—financial managers must rely on other managers.

Accounts Receivable As we also saw in Chapter 18, *accounts receivable* consist of funds due from customers who have bought on credit.[2] A sound financial plan requires financial managers to project accurately both how much and when buyers will make payments on these accounts. Managers at Kraft Foods must know how many dollars' worth of cheddar cheese Kroger's supermarkets will order each month; they must also know Kroger's payment schedule. Because they represent an investment in products for which a firm has not yet received payment, accounts receivable temporarily tie up its funds. Clearly, the seller wants to receive payment as quickly as possible.

credit policy
Rules governing a firm's extension of credit to customers

Credit Policies Predicting payment schedules is a function of **credit policy:** the rules governing a firm's extension of credit to customers. This policy sets standards as to which buyers are eligible for what type of credit. Typically, credit is extended to customers who have the ability to pay and who honor their obligations. Credit is denied to firms with poor payment histories. Information about such histories is available from many sources, including the Credit Interchange developed by the National Association of Credit Management.

Credit policy also sets payment terms. For example, credit terms of 2/10, net 30 mean that the selling company offers a 2 percent discount if the customer pays within 10 days. The customer has 30 days to pay the regular price. Under these terms, the buyer would have to pay only $980 on a $1,000 invoice on days 1 to 10, but all $1,000 on days 11 to 30. The higher the discount, the more incentive buyers have to pay early. Sellers can thus adjust credit terms to influence when customers pay their bills.

inventory
Materials and goods that are held by a company but will be sold within the year

Inventories Between the time a firm buys raw materials and the time it sells finished products, it ties up funds in **inventory**—materials and goods that it will sell within the year. There are three basic types of inventories:

- The supplies that a firm purchases for use in production are its raw *materials inventory.* Raw materials inventory at Lee Apparel Co. includes huge rolls of denim.
- *Work-in-process inventory* consists of goods that have moved partway through the production process. Thus, jeans that have been cut out but not yet sewn are work-in-process inventory at Lee.
- *Finished-goods inventory* consists of items ready for sale. Completed blue jeans ready for shipment to dealers are part of Lee's finished-goods inventory.

Dell Computer <www.dell.com> can not only make a computer within 24 hours of receiving an order—it can also deliver it. Dell attributes this level of efficiency to what it calls the "direct model," which means more than just eliminating middlemen and selling PCs directly to consumers. It also means streamlining every process so that capital does not get tied up in unnecessary activities or materials. By requiring suppliers to do the same thing, Dell is able to maintain the low level of inventory that translates into a high rate of return on invested capital.

Failure to manage inventory can have grave financial consequences. Too little inventory of any kind can cost a firm sales. Too much inventory means tied-up funds that cannot be used elsewhere. In extreme cases, a company may have to sell excess inventory at low profits simply to raise cash.

Working Capital Basically, **working capital** consists of a firm's current assets on hand.[3] It is a liquid asset out of which current debts can be paid. A company calculates its working capital by adding up the following:

working capital
Liquid current assets out of which a firm can pay current debts

- Inventories—that is, raw materials, work-in-process, and finished goods on hand
- Accounts receivable (minus accounts payable)

How much money is tied up in working capital? Fortune 500 companies typically devote 20 cents of every sales dollar—about $1.2 trillion total—to working capital. What are the benefits of reducing these sums? There are two very important pluses:

1. Every dollar that is not tied up in working capital becomes a dollar of more useful cash flow.
2. Reduction of working capital raises earnings permanently.

The second advantage results from the fact that money costs money (in interest payments and the like). Reducing working capital, therefore, means saving money.

Long-Term (Capital) Expenditures

In addition to needing funds for operating expenditures, companies need funds to cover long-term expenditures on fixed assets. As we saw in Chapter 18, *fixed assets* are items with long-term use or value, such as land, buildings, and machinery.

Long-term expenditures are usually more carefully planned than short-term outlays because they pose special problems. They differ from short-term outlays in the following ways, all of which influence the ways that long-term outlays are funded:

- Unlike inventories and other short-term assets, they are not normally sold or converted into cash.
- Their acquisition requires a very large investment.
- They represent a binding commitment of company funds that continues long into the future.

SOURCES OF SHORT-TERM FUNDS

Firms can call on many sources for the funds they need to finance day-to-day operations and to implement short-term plans. These sources include *trade credit, secured* and *unsecured loans,* and *factoring accounts receivable.*

Trade Credit

Accounts payable are not merely expenditures. They also constitute a source of funds for the buying company. Until it pays its bill, the buyer has the use of both the purchased product and the price of the product. This situation results when the seller grants **trade credit,** which is effectively a short-term loan from one firm to another. Trade credit can take several forms:

trade credit
Granting of credit by one firm to another

open-book credit
Form of trade credit in which sellers ship merchandise on faith that payment will be forthcoming

promissory note
Form of trade credit in which buyers sign promise-to-pay agreements before merchandise is shipped

trade draft
Form of trade credit in which buyers must sign statements of payment terms attached to merchandise by sellers

trade acceptance
Trade draft that has been signed by the buyer

- The most common form, **open-book credit,** is essentially a good faith agreement. Buyers receive merchandise along with invoices stating credit terms. Sellers ship products on faith that payment will be forthcoming.
- When sellers want more reassurance, they may insist that buyers sign legally binding **promissory notes** before merchandise is shipped. The agreement states when and how much money will be paid to the seller.
- The **trade draft** is attached to the merchandise shipment by the seller and states the promised date and amount of payment due. To take possession of the merchandise, the buyer must sign the draft. Once signed by the buyer, the document becomes a **trade acceptance.** Trade drafts and trade acceptances are useful forms of credit in international transactions.

Secured Short-Term Loans

collateral
Borrower-pledged legal asset that may be seized by lenders in case of nonpayment

secured loan
Loan for which the borrower must provide collateral

For most firms, bank loans are a very important source of short-term funding. Such loans almost always involve promissory notes in which the borrower promises to repay the loan plus interest. In secured loans, banks also require **collateral:** a legal interest in certain assets that can be seized if payments are not made as promised.

Secured loans allow borrowers to get funds when they might not qualify for unsecured credit. Moreover, they generally carry lower interest rates than unsecured loans. Collateral may be in the form of inventories or accounts receivable, and most businesses have other types of assets that can be pledged. Some, for instance, own marketable securities, such as stocks or bonds of other companies (see Chapter 20). Many more own fixed assets, such as land, buildings, or equipment. Fixed assets, however, are generally used to secure long-term rather than short-term loans. Most short-term business borrowing is secured by inventories and accounts receivable.

Inventory Loans When a loan is made with inventory as a collateral asset, the lender lends the borrower some portion of the stated value of the inventory. Inventory is more attractive as collateral when it provides the lender with real security for the loan amount. For example, if the inventory can be readily converted into cash, it is more valuable as collateral. Other inventory (for example, boxes full of expensive, partially completed lenses for eyeglasses) is of little value on the open market. Meanwhile, a thousand crates of boxed, safely stored canned tomatoes might well be convertible into cash.[4]

pledging accounts receivable
Using accounts receivable as loan collateral

Accounts Receivable When accounts receivable are used as collateral, the process is called **pledging accounts receivable.** In the event of nonpayment, the lender may seize the receivables. If these assets are not enough to cover the loan, the borrower must make up the difference. Loans on receivables are granted only when lenders are confident that they can recover funds from the borrower's debtors. Receivables are especially important to service companies such as accounting firms and law offices because they do not maintain inventories of physical products; accounts receivable are their main source of collateral. Typically, lenders who will accept accounts receivable as collateral are financial institutions with credit departments capable of evaluating the quality of the receivables.[5]

Unsecured Short-Term Loans

With an **unsecured loan,** the borrower does not have to put up collateral. In many cases, however, the bank requires the borrower to maintain a compensating balance: the borrower must keep a portion of the loan amount on deposit with the bank in a noninterest-bearing account.

unsecured loan
Loan for which collateral is not required

The terms of the loan—amount, duration, interest rate, and payment schedule—are negotiated between the bank and the borrower. To receive an unsecured loan, then, a firm must ordinarily have a good banking relationship with the lender. Once an agreement is made, a promissory note will be executed and the funds transferred to the borrower. Although some unsecured loans are one-time-only arrangements, many take the form of *lines of credit, revolving credit agreements,* or *commercial paper.*

Line of Credit A **line of credit** is a standing agreement between a bank and a business in which the bank promises to lend the firm a maximum amount of funds on request. Suppose that First National Bank gives Sunshine Tanning, Inc. a $100,000 line of credit for the coming year. Under this arrangement, Sunshine's borrowings can total up to $100,000 at any time, and Sunshine benefits by knowing in advance that the bank regards it as creditworthy and will lend funds on short notice.

line of credit
Standing arrangement in which a lender agrees to make available a specified amount of funds upon the borrower's request

Revolving Credit Agreement **Revolving credit agreements** are similar to consumer bank cards. A lender agrees to make some amount of funds available on a continuing basis. The lending institution guarantees that these funds will be available when sought by the borrower. In return for this guarantee, the bank charges the borrower a commitment fee for holding the line of credit open. This fee is payable even if the customer does not borrow any funds. It is often expressed as a percentage of the loan amount (usually .5 to 1 percent of the committed amount).

revolving credit agreement
Arrangement in which a lender agrees to make funds available on demand and on a continuing basis

Say that First National agrees to lend Sunshine Tanning up to $100,000 under a revolving credit agreement. If Sunshine borrows $80,000, it still has access to $20,000. If it pays off $50,000 and reduces its debt to $30,000, it then has $70,000 available. Sunshine pays interest on the borrowed funds, plus a fee on the unused funds in its line of credit.

Commercial Paper Some firms can raise short-term funds by issuing **commercial paper:** short-term securities, or notes, containing the borrower's promise to pay.[6] Because it is backed solely by the issuing firm's promise to pay, commercial paper is an option for only the largest and most creditworthy firms.

commercial paper
Short-term securities, or notes, containing a borrower's promise to pay

How does commercial paper work? Corporations issue commercial paper with a certain face value. Buying companies pay less than that value. At the end of a specified period (usually 30 to 90 days, but legally up to 270 days), the issuing company buys back the paper at face value. The difference between the price paid and the face value is the buyer's profit. For the issuing company, the cost is usually lower than prevailing interest rates on short-term loans.

If Consolidated Edison <www.coned.com> needs to borrow $10 million for 90 days, it might issue commercial paper with a face value of $10.2 million. Who will buy the paper? Among other investors, insurance companies with $10 million in available cash may buy it. After 90 days, Consolidated Edison will pay a total of $10.2 million to the insurance companies who invested.

Factoring Accounts Receivable

A firm can raise funds rapidly by *factoring:* selling the firm's accounts receivable. In this process, the purchaser of the receivables, usually a financial institution, is known as the factor. The factor pays some percentage of the full amount of receivables due to the selling firm. The seller gets this money immediately.[7]

For example, a factor might buy $40,000 worth of receivables for 60 percent of that sum ($24,000). The factor profits to the extent that the money it eventually collects exceeds the amount it paid. This profit depends on the quality of the receivables, the cost of collecting them, and interest rates.

SOURCES OF LONG-TERM FUNDS

Firms need long-term funding to finance expenditures on fixed assets: the buildings and equipment necessary for conducting their business. They may seek long-term funds through *debt financing* (that is, from outside the firm) or through *equity financing* (by drawing on internal sources). We will discuss both options in this section, as well as a middle ground called *hybrid financing.* We will also analyze some of the options that enter into decisions about long-term financing, as well as the role of the *risk-return relationship* in attracting investors to a firm.

Debt Financing

debt financing
Long-term borrowing from sources outside a company

Long-term borrowing from sources outside the company—**debt financing**—is a major component of many firms' long-term financial planning.[8] Long-term debts are obligations that are payable more than one year after they were originally issued. The two primary sources of such funding are *long-term loans* and the sale of *corporate bonds.*

Long-Term Loans Most corporations get long-term loans from commercial banks, usually those with which they have developed longstanding relationships. Credit companies (such as Household Finance Corp. <www.hfc.com>), insurance companies, and pension funds also grant long-term business loans.

Long-term loans are attractive to borrowers for several reasons:

- Because the number of parties involved is limited, loans can often be arranged very quickly.
- The firm need not make public disclosure of its business plans or the purpose for which it is acquiring the loan. (In contrast, the issuance of corporate bonds requires such disclosure.)
- The duration of the loan can easily be matched to the borrower's needs.
- If the firm's needs change, loans usually contain clauses making it possible to change terms.

Long-term loans also have some disadvantages. Borrowers, for instance, may have trouble finding lenders to supply large sums. Long-term borrowers may also face restrictions as conditions of the loan. For example, they may have to pledge long-term assets as collateral or agree to take on no more debt until the loan is paid.

Interest Rates Interest rates are negotiated between borrower and lender. Although some bank loans have fixed rates, others have floating rates tied to the prime rate that the bank charges its most creditworthy customers (see Chapter 19). A loan at one percent above prime, then, is payable at one percentage point higher than the prime rate. This rate may fluctuate, or float, because the prime rate itself goes up and down as market conditions change.

Corporate Bonds As we saw in Chapter 20, a *corporate bond,* like commercial paper, is a contract—a promise by the issuer to pay the holder a certain amount of money on a specified date. Unlike issuers of commercial paper, however, bond issuers do not pay off quickly. In many cases, bonds may not be redeemable for 30 years. Also, unlike commercial paper, most bonds pay bondholders a stipulated sum of annual or semiannual interest. If the company fails to make a bond payment, it is said to be *in default.*

Bonds are the major source of long-term debt financing for most corporations.[9] They are attractive when firms need large amounts for long periods of time. The issuing company also gains access to large numbers of lenders through nationwide bond markets and stock exchanges. On the other hand, bonds entail high administrative and selling costs. They may also require stiff interest payments, especially if the issuing company has a poor credit rating.

Bond Indentures The terms of a bond, including the amount to be paid, the interest rate, and the maturity date (the date when the principal is to be paid) differ from com-

WebConnection

www.moodys.com

Founded when John Moody began rating bonds in 1909, Moody's is one of the country's leading rating companies of both corporate and municipal bonds. To find out more about Moody's "Rating Methodologies" and "Rating Approach"—and its "Track Record"—log on to the company's Web site.

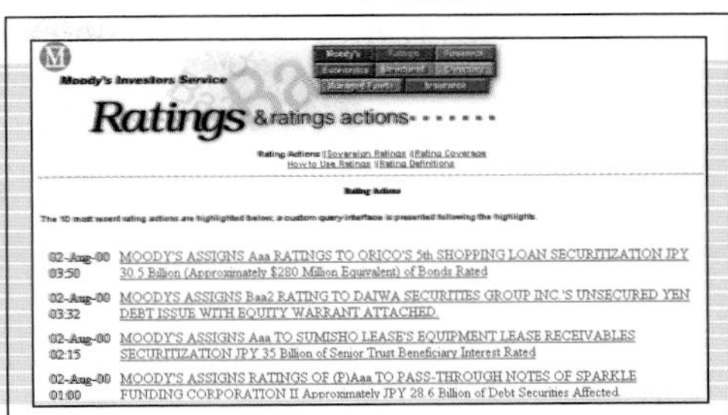

pany to company and issue to issue. They are spelled out in the bond contract, or **bond indenture.** The indenture also identifies which of the firm's assets, if any, are pledged as collateral for the bonds.

bond indenture
Statement of the terms of a corporate bond

PPG Industries <www.ppg.com>, a leading manufacturer of fiberglass, industrial chemicals, and medical supplies, has a $150 million debt issue that matures on May 1, 2021. Until the maturity date, the bondholders, including those who purchased the initial offering in 1991, will be paid 9.12 percent interest each year. In addition, they will receive a total of $150 million, the principal amount owed by PPG, when the bonds mature and are retired. The bond indenture contains no specific pledge of particular assets for security.

Equity Financing

Although debt financing often has strong appeal, looking inside the company for long-term funding is sometimes preferable. In small companies, founders may increase personal investments in their own firms. In most cases, **equity financing** means issuing common stock or retaining the firm's earnings. Both options involve putting the owners' capital to work.

equity financing
Use of common stock and/or retained earnings to raise long-term funding

Common Stock People who purchase common stock seek profits in two forms—dividends and appreciation. Overall, shareholders hope for an increase in the market value of their stock (appreciation) because the firm has profited and grown. By issuing shares of stock, the company gets the funds it needs for buying land, buildings, and equipment.

Suppose that Sunshine Tanning's founders invested $10,000 by buying the original 500 shares of common stock (at $20 per share) in 1994. The company used these funds to buy equipment, and it succeeded financially. By 2000, it needed funds for expansion. A pattern of profitable operations and regularly paid dividends now allows Sunshine to raise $50,000 by selling 500 new shares of stock at $100 per share. This $50,000 would constitute *paid-in capital*—additional money, above the par value of its original stock sale, paid directly to a firm by its owners (see Chapter 18). As Table 21.1 shows, this additional paid-in capital would increase total stockholders' equity to $60,000.

As we learned in Chapter 2, the first public offering of its common stock by a company is called an *initial public offering (IPO)*. In 1999, the IPO for Garden.com in Austin, Texas, made a spectacular debut when its stock price rose from $12 to $20 in its first few days on the market.

We should note that the use of equity financing by means of common stock can be expensive because paying dividends is more expensive than paying bond interest. Why? Because interest paid to bondholders is a business expense and, therefore, a tax deduction for the firm. Stock dividends are not tax-deductible.

Retained Earnings Recall our discussion in Chapter 18 where we defined retained earnings as profits retained for the firm's use rather than paid out in dividends. If a company uses retained earnings as capital, it will not have to borrow money and pay interest. If a firm has a history of reaping profits by reinvesting retained earnings, it may be very

Table 21.1

Stockholders' Equity for Sunshine Tanning

Common Stockholders' Equity, 1994	
Initial common stock (500 shares issued @ $20 per share, 1994)	$10,000
Total stockholders' equity	$10,000
Common Stockholders' Equity, 2000	
Initial common stock (500 shares issued @ $20 per share, 1994)	$10,000
Additional paid-in capital (500 shares issued @ $100 per share, 2000)	50,000
Total stockholders' equity	$60,000

attractive to some investors. Retained earnings, however, mean smaller dividends for shareholders. In this sense, then, the practice may decrease the demand for—and thus the price of—the company's stock.

If Sunshine Tanning had net earnings of $50,000 in 2000, it could pay a $50-per-share dividend on its 1,000 shares of common stock. Let's say, however, that Sunshine plans to remodel at a cost of $30,000, intending to retain $30,000 in earnings to finance the project. Only $20,000—$20 per share—will be available for shareholders.

Financial Burden on the Firm As we have already noted, a firm cannot deduct paid-out dividends as business expenses, but it can deduct the interest that it pays on bonds. If equity funding can be so expensive, why do firms not rely entirely on debt financing? Loans and bonds carry fixed interest rates and represent fixed promises to pay, regardless of changes in economic conditions. If a firm defaults on its obligations, it may lose assets and may even go bankrupt. Indeed, a classic example was the widespread defaulting on loans made in the 1980s that brought about the U.S. savings and loan catastrophe. S&Ls had granted loans to farmers, foreign businesses, and U.S. businesses that were unable to repay debts during the economic downturn. As a result, many S&Ls suffered bankruptcy because they could not recover funds they had loaned to their customers.

What is the difference between filing bankruptcy under Chapter 7, Chapter 11, and Chapter 13? Under which of the aforementioned sections of the Bankruptcy Code do most individuals and businesses file?

Likewise, during the 1997 Asian financial crisis, Korean banks suffered when borrowers (large companies) could not repay outstanding debt. Borrower companies went bankrupt, frightened foreign investors pulled their money out of the country, and borrowing costs soared as global lenders demanded higher returns for the increased risks of loaning funds to Korean firms. As more and more borrowers teetered on the verge of default, the Korean economy weakened. Hyundai Motor Co. <www.hyundai.com>, for example, was forced to halt car production because of lack of parts from Mando Machinery, which had to file for court protection from creditors. With so much investor pessimism, firms were unable to raise badly needed funds to pay their debts. Thus the Korean government had to issue bonds with guaranteed payment to lenders. But even with government assistance, investor confidence dwindled and, without access to additional loans for business expansion, the Korean economy remained dormant until initial signs of recovery began emerging in late 1999.

Because of the risk of default, debt financing appeals most strongly to companies in industries that have predictable profits and cash flow patterns. For example, demand for electric power is quite steady from year to year and predictable from month to month. Thus, electric utility companies enjoy steady streams of income and can carry substantial amounts of debt. Detroit Edison <www.detroitedison.com>, a major privately owned utility, is a representative example. About 63 percent of its long-term funding is in the form of debt. Equity from common stock provides only 32 percent. The remaining 5 percent of Edison's long-term capital is equity from preferred stock, a topic discussed in the next section.

Hybrid Financing: Preferred Stock

A middle ground between debt financing and equity financing is the use of preferred stock (see Chapter 20). Preferred stock is a "hybrid" because it has some of the features of both corporate bonds and common stocks. As with bonds, for instance, payments on preferred stock are fixed amounts such as $6 per share per year. Unlike bonds, preferred stock never matures; like common stock, it can be held indefinitely. In addition, preferred stocks have first rights (over common stock) to dividends.

A major advantage to the issuer is the flexibility of preferred stock. Because preferred stockholders have no voting rights, the stock secures funds for the firm without jeopardizing corporate control of its management. Furthermore, corporations are not obligated to repay the principal and can withhold payment of dividends in lean times.

Choosing between Debt and Equity Financing

An aspect of financial planning is striking a balance between debt and equity financing. Because a firm relies on a mix of debt and equity to raise the cash needed for capital outlays, that mix is called its **capital structure.**[10] Financial plans thus contain targets for capital structure; an example would be 40 percent debt and 60 percent equity. But choosing a target is not easy. A wide range of mixes is possible, and strategies range from conservative to risky.

capital structure
Relative mix of a firm's debt and equity financing

The most conservative strategy is all-equity financing and no debt: a company has no formal obligations to make financial payouts. As we have seen, however, equity is an expensive source of capital. The riskiest strategy is all-debt financing. Although less expensive than equity funding, indebtedness increases the risk that a firm will be unable to meet its obligations (and even go bankrupt). Somewhere between the two extremes, financial planners try to find mixes that will increase stockholders' wealth with a reasonable exposure to risk.

Indexes of Financial Risk To help understand and measure the amount of financial risk they face, financial managers often rely on published indexes for various investments. *Financial World* publishes independent appraisals of mutual funds (see Chapter 20), using risk-reward ratings of A (very good) to E (poor) to indicate each fund's riskiness in comparison to its anticipated financial returns. An A-rated fund is judged to offer very good returns relative to the amount of risk involved. An E-rated fund carries the greatest risk with smaller returns. Similarly, Standard & Poor's <www.standardpoor.com> publishes various indexes for numerous funds and for stocks that are available for purchase by financial managers.

By using such indexes, financial managers can determine how a particular investment compares to other opportunities in terms of its stability. A bond is considered investment grade if it qualifies for one of the top four ratings by either S&P or Moody's <www.moodys.com>. Bonds below investment grade are called junk bonds because they have unusually high default rates. Nonetheless, junk bonds appeal to many investors because they promise uncommonly high yields.

www.rims.org

Risk and Insurance Management Society, Inc. (RIMS) is a not-for-profit organization dedicated to advancing the practice of risk management, a professional discipline that protects physical, financial and human resources. The RIMS Web site includes the only search engine in the world dedicated to risk and insurance management. To find out more about the specific objectives of RIMS and about the range of services that it offers members, visit the organization's Web site.

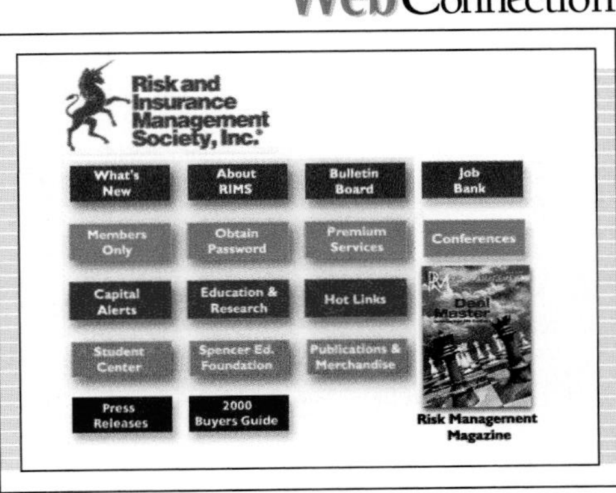

The Risk–Return Relationship

While developing plans for raising capital, financial managers must be aware of the different motivations of individual investors. Why do some individuals and firms invest in stocks while others invest only in bonds? Investor motivations determine who is willing to buy a given company's stocks or bonds. Investors give money to firms and, in return, anticipate receiving future cash flows. Thus everyone who invests money is expressing a personal preference for safety versus risk.

Some cash flows are more certain than others. Investors generally expect to receive higher payments for higher uncertainty. They do not generally expect large returns for secure investments like government-insured bonds. Each type of investment, then, has a **risk–return relationship** reflecting the principle that whereas safer investments tend to offer lower returns, riskier investments tend to offer higher returns. Figure 21.1 shows the general risk–return relationship for various financial instruments, along with the types of investors they attract. Thus conservative investors, who have a low tolerance for risk, will opt for high-grade corporate bonds that rate low in terms of risk on future returns but also low on the size of expected returns. The reverse is true of aggressive investors who prefer the higher risks and potential returns from junk bonds and common stocks.

risk–return relationship Principle that, whereas safer investments tend to offer lower returns, riskier investments tend to offer higher returns

Risk–return differences are recognized by financial planners, who try to gain access to the greatest funding at the lowest possible cost. By gauging investors' perceptions of their riskiness, a firm's managers can estimate how much they must pay to attract funds to their offerings. Over time, a company can reposition itself on the risk continuum by improving its record on dividends, interest payments, and debt repayment.

Figure 21.1
The Risk–Return Relationship

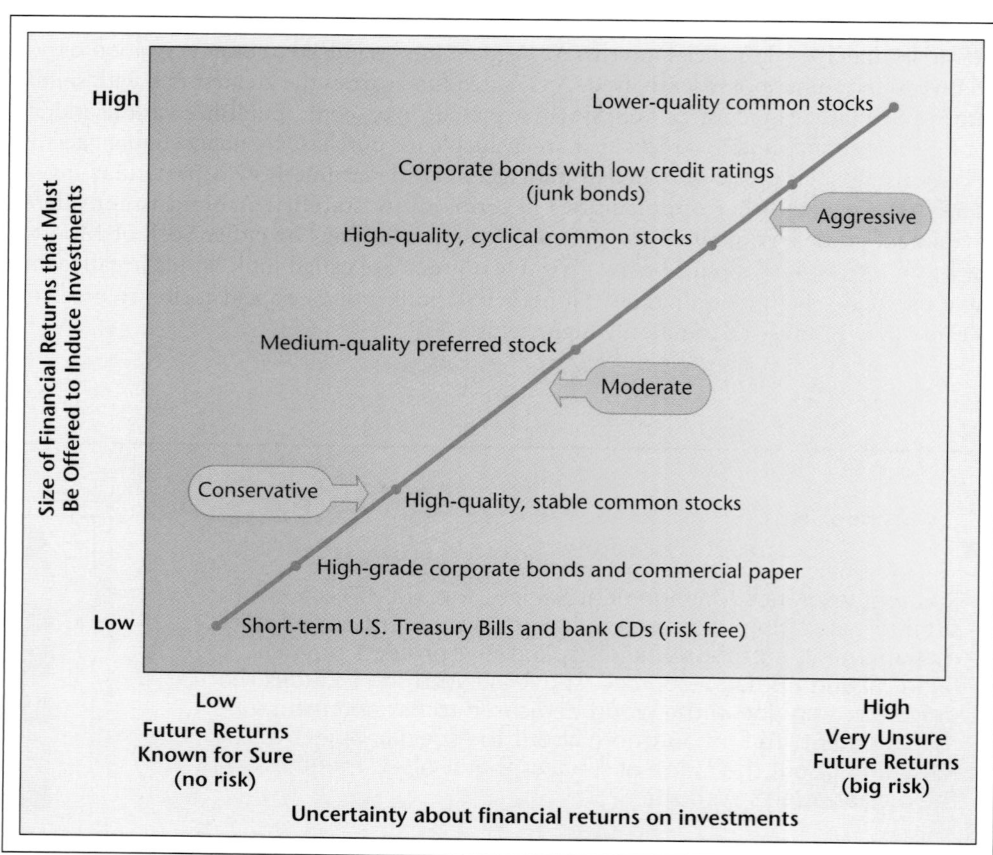

FINANCIAL MANAGEMENT FOR SMALL BUSINESS

As we saw in Chapter 7, new business success and failure are often closely related to adequate or inadequate funding. One study of nearly 3,000 new companies revealed a survival rate of 84 percent for new businesses with initial investments of at least $50,000. Unfortunately, those with less funding have a much lower survival rate. Why are so many start-ups underfunded? Entrepreneurs often underestimate the value of establishing *bank credit* as a source of funds and use trade credit ineffectively. In addition, they often fail to consider *venture capital* as a source of funding, and they are notorious for not planning *cash-flow needs* properly.

Establishing Bank and Trade Credit

Some banks have liberal credit policies and offer financial analysis, cash-flow planning, and suggestions based on experiences with other local firms. Some provide loans to small businesses in bad times and work to keep them going. Some, do not. Obtaining credit begins with finding a bank that can—and will—support a small firm's financial needs. Once a line of credit is obtained, the small business can seek more liberal credit policies from other businesses. Sometimes, suppliers give customers longer credit periods—45 or 60 days rather than 30 days. Liberal trade credit terms with their suppliers let firms increase short-term funds and avoid additional borrowing from banks.

Long-Term Funding Obtaining long-term loans is more difficult for new businesses than for established companies. With unproven repayment ability, start-up firms can expect to pay higher interest rates than older firms. If a new enterprise displays evidence of sound financial planning, however, the Small Business Administration (see Chapter 7) may support a guaranteed loan.

The Business Plan as a Tool for Credit Start-up firms without proven financial success usually must present a business plan to demonstrate that the firm is a good credit risk.[11] The business plan is a document that tells potential lenders why the money is needed, the amount, how the money will be used to improve the company, and when it will be paid back.

Photographer David Cupp needed $50,000 funding for his new firm, Photos Online, Inc., in Columbus, Ohio, which displays and sells photos over the Internet. His business plan had to be rewritten many times until it became understandable, in financial terms, to potential lenders. The plan eventually reached 35 pages and contained information on the competition as well as cash-flow projections. After four failed attempts, the fifth bank approved a $26,000 term loan and granted a $24,000 line of credit, to be used for computers, software, and living expenses to get the business started.[12]

www.onlinewbc.org

The WBC's Finance Center is an excellent primer for small-business financial management. It offers extended coverage in such areas as borrowing and lending, sources of money, and financing the growing business. Though intended for women, the Center provides a wealth of information for anyone interested in small-business financing.

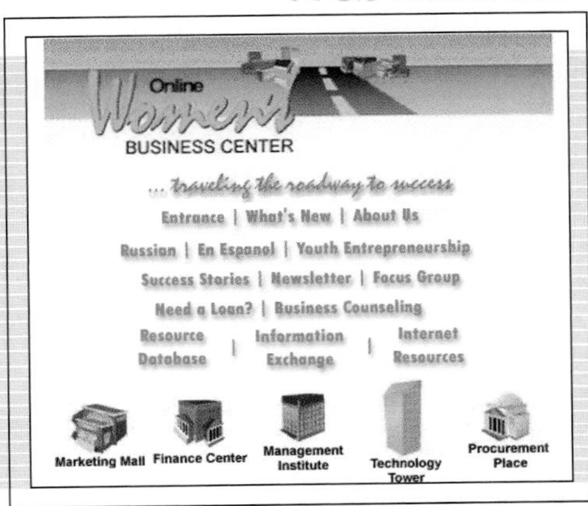

Figure 21.2

Projected Cash Flow for Slippery Fish Bait Supply Co.

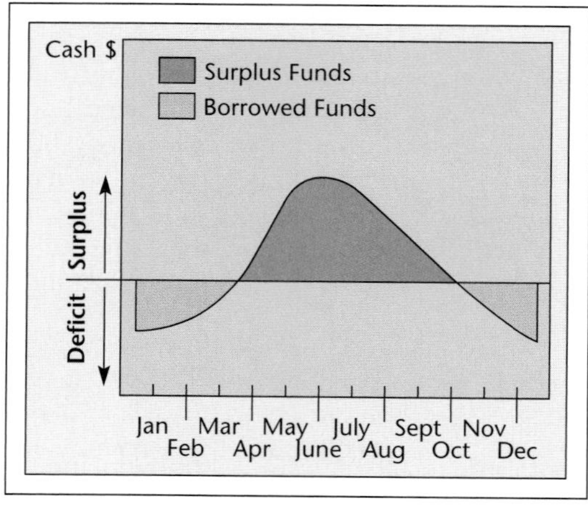

Venture Capital

venture capital
Outside equity financing provided in return for part ownership of the borrowing firm

risk
Uncertainty about future events and their desirable or negative outcomes

Many newer businesses—especially those undergoing rapid growth—cannot get the funds they need through borrowing alone. They may, therefore, turn to **venture capital:** outside equity funding provided in return for part ownership of the borrowing firm. As we saw in Chapter 7, venture capital firms actively seek chances to invest in new firms with rapid growth potential. Because failure rates are high, they typically demand high returns, which are now often 20 to 30 percent.

Planning for Cash-Flow Requirements

Although all businesses should plan for their cash flows, this planning is especially important for small businesses. Success or failure may hinge on anticipating those times when either cash will be short or excess cash can be expected.[13]

Figure 21.2 shows possible cash inflows, cash outflows, and net cash position (inflows minus outflows) month by month for Slippery Fish Bait Supply—a highly seasonal business. Bait stores buy heavily from Slippery during the spring and summer months. Revenues outpace expenses, leaving surplus funds that can be invested. During the fall and winter, however, expenses exceed revenues. Slippery must borrow funds to keep going until revenues pick up again in the spring. Comparing predicted cash inflows from sales with outflows for expenses shows the firm's expected monthly cash-flow position.

speculative risk
Risk involving the possibility of gain or loss

pure risk
Risk involving only the possibility of loss or no loss

Such knowledge can be invaluable for the small business manager. By anticipating shortfalls, for example, a financial manager can seek funds in advance and minimize their cost. By anticipating excess cash, a manager can plan to put the funds to work in short-term, interest-earning investments.

RISK MANAGEMENT

"We are all paid to take risks."

—Lawrence A. Bossidy, Chairman of Honeywell

"We are all paid to take risks," says Lawrence A. Bossidy, chairman of New Jersey–based Honeywell, a manufacturer of consumer and industrial products <www.honeywell.com>. Risk is a factor in every manager's job, and because nearly every managerial action involves risk—that is, the possibility of either desirable outcomes or negative results—risk management is essential.[14] Not surprisingly, then, firms devote considerable resources not only to recognizing potential risks, but to positioning themselves to make the most advantageous decisions.

Life Cycle of an e-Business

The Job of Pruning

Throughout its various stages of development, Garden.com faced risks for two broad reasons:

1. It was a newly formed and growing company, and
2. The market for national-brand gardening was newly evolving.

Why were these conditions sources of potential risk? In addition to the normal day-to-day risks faced by every company—threats of possible fire, natural disaster, job-related accidents—Garden.com also had to be concerned with strategic-level risks related to the problems of winning customers and gaining market share, managing cash flows, managing the firm's present and future financial condition, and managing its technology as a competitive weapon.

In its *1999 Prospectus,* the management of Garden.com had recognized several forms of potential business risk, including the following:

- Because substantial net losses and negative cash flow were expected for the foreseeable future, financial condition and stock price could suffer.
- If cash flows generated from operations did not cover operating costs, additional debt or equity financing might be necessary for company growth.
- If the Garden.com brand was not established quickly enough, the company might not capture enough market share to become profitable.
- If gardening consumers did not accept electronic shopping over traditional shopping methods, revenues would suffer.
- The firm's computers and communications systems were vulnerable to damage or interruption that might hinder their ability to deliver timely information or execute online transactions.
- To ensure both profitability and customer satisfaction, Garden.com relied on its ability to maintain relationships with outside suppliers.

By November 2000, it was obvious that the firm had handled some of these risks—in particular, the last two in the list above—quite well: Its information technology systems and supplier relations had become decided assets. Taken together, however, the other four risks could not ultimately be managed and eventually proved fatal. Burdened with cumulative net losses of $75.5 million and starved for cash to generate revenue from the promotion and sale of products, Garden.com watched its stock price fall to unattractive lows. Why did this happen? The possibility raised by management back in 1999—namely, the possibility that the company would be unable to establish its brand quickly enough—turned out to be prophetic. Apparently because gardeners were not ready to accept electronic shopping over traditional shopping methods, revenues suffered. With operating costs rising faster than revenues, additional debt or equity financing was vital for Garden.com's survival. At this point, unfortunately, skeptical investors perceived the risks as greater than the potential paybacks. They turned their backs on Garden.com in favor of less risky investments. Thus, while Garden.com's founders had always known the risks that would be involved, they were unable to overcome them and the company reached the final stage in its life cycle: By the end of 2000, their creative business concept had become history, along with dozens of other promising Internet start-ups.

Coping with Risk

Businesses constantly face two basic types of **risk**—that is, uncertainty about future events. **Speculative risks,** such as financial investments, involve the possibility of gain or loss. **Pure risks** involve only the possibility of loss or no loss. Designing and distributing a new product is a speculative risk. The product may fail, or it may succeed and earn high profits. In contrast, the chance of a warehouse fire is a pure risk.

For a company to survive and prosper, it must manage both types of risk in a cost-effective manner. We can define the process of **risk management** as "conserving the firm's earning power and assets by reducing the threat of losses due to uncontrollable events."[15]

risk management
Process of conserving the firm's earning power and assets by reducing the threat of losses due to uncontrollable events

In every company, each manager must be alert for risks to the firm and their impact on profits. The risk-management process usually entails five steps outlined in Figure 21.3.

What are the differences in the risk management approach between large and small businesses?

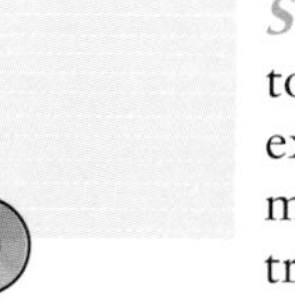

Step 1: Identify Risks and Potential Losses Managers analyze a firm's risks to identify potential losses. For example, a firm with a fleet of delivery trucks can expect that one of them will eventually be involved in an accident. The accident may cause bodily injury to the driver or others, may cause physical damage to the truck or other vehicles, or both.

Step 2: Measure the Frequency and Severity of Losses and Their Impact To measure the frequency and severity of losses, managers must consider both past history and current activities. How often can the firm expect the loss to occur? What is the likely size of the loss in dollars? For example, our firm with the fleet of delivery trucks may

Figure 21.3

The Risk-Management Process

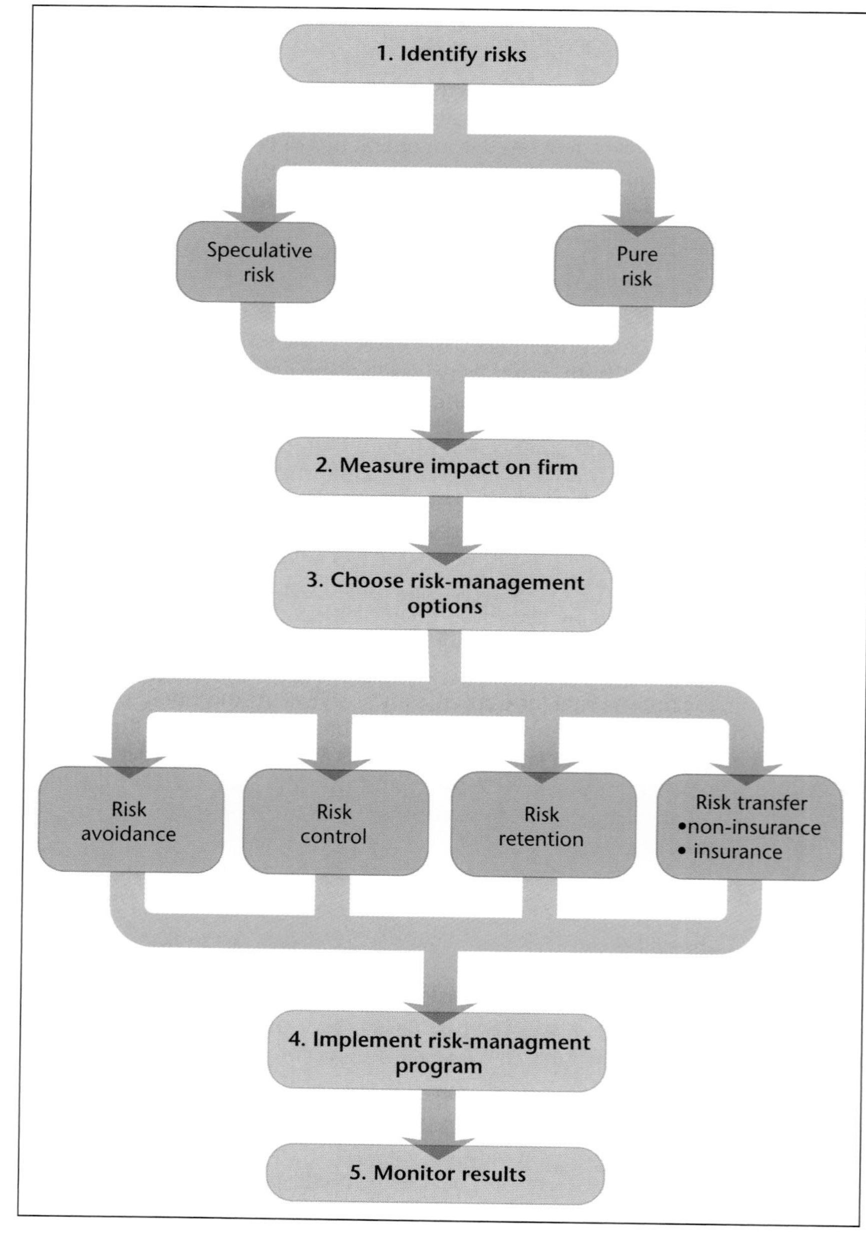

have had two accidents per year in the past. If it adds trucks, it may reasonably expect the frequency of accidents to increase.

Step 3: Evaluate Alternatives and Choose the Techniques That Will Best Handle the Losses Having identified and measured potential losses, managers are in a better position to decide how to handle them. With this third step, they generally have four choices: risk avoidance, control, retention, or transfer.

Risk Avoidance A firm opts for **risk avoidance** by declining to enter or by ceasing to participate in a risky activity. For example, the firm with the delivery trucks could avoid any risk of physical damage or bodily injury by closing down its delivery service. Similarly, a pharmaceutical maker may withdraw a new drug for fear of liability suits.

risk avoidance
Practice of avoiding risk by declining or ceasing to participate in an activity

Risk Control When avoidance is not practical or desirable, firms can practice **risk control**—say, the use of loss-prevention techniques to minimize the frequency of losses. A delivery service, for instance, can prevent losses by training its drivers in defensive-driving techniques, mapping out safe routes, and conscientiously maintaining its trucks.

risk control
Practice of minimizing the frequency or severity of losses from risky activities

Risk Retention When losses cannot be avoided or controlled, firms must cope with the consequences. When such losses are manageable and predictable, they may decide to cover them out of company funds. The firm is thus said to "assume" or "retain" the financial consequences of the loss: hence the practice known as **risk retention.** For example, our firm with the fleet of trucks may find that vehicles suffer vandalism totaling $100 to $500 per year. Depending on its coverage, the company may find it cheaper to pay for repairs out of pocket rather than to submit claims to its insurance company.

risk retention
Practice of covering a firm's losses with its own funds

risk transfer
Practice of transferring a firm's risk to another firm

Risk Transfer When the potential for large risks cannot be avoided or controlled, managers often opt for **risk transfer.** They transfer the risk to another firm—namely, an insurance company. In transferring risk to an insurance company, a firm pays a sum called a **premium.** In return, the insurance company issues an insurance policy—a formal agreement to pay the policyholder a specified amount in the event of certain losses. In some cases, the insured party must also pay a deductible—an agreed-upon amount of the loss that the insured must absorb prior to reimbursement. Thus, our hypothetical company may buy insurance to protect itself against theft, physical damage to trucks, and bodily injury to drivers and others involved in an accident.

premium
Fee paid by a policyholder for insurance coverage

Step 4: Implement the Risk-Management Program The means of implementing risk-management decisions depends on both the technique chosen and the activity being managed. For example, risk avoidance for certain activities can be implemented by purchasing those activities from outside providers—for example, hiring delivery services instead of operating delivery vehicles. Risk control might be implemented by training employees and designing new work methods and equipment for on-the-job safety. For situations in which risk retention is preferred, reserve funds can be set aside out of revenues. When risk transfer is needed, implementation means selecting an insurance company and buying the right policies.

Step 5: Monitor Results Because risk management is an ongoing activity, follow-up is always essential. New types of risks, for example, emerge with changes in customers, facilities, employees, and products. Insurance regulations change, and new types of insurance become available. Consequently, managers must continually monitor a company's risks, reevaluate the methods used for handling them, and revise them as necessary.

The Contemporary Risk Management Program

Virtually all business decisions involve risks having financial consequences. As a result, the company's chief financial officer, along with managers in other areas, has a major voice in applying the risk management process. In some industries, most notably insurance, the companies' main line of business revolves around risk taking and risk management for themselves and their clients.

Today, many firms are taking a systematic approach to risk management. The key to that approach is developing a program that is both comprehensive and companywide. In the past, risk management was often conducted by different departments or by narrowly focused financial officers. Now, however, more and more firms have not only created high-level risk-management positions, but also are stressing the need for middle managers to practice risk management on a daily basis. Advises one global risk-management expert: "The breadth of products offered, the complexity of those products, and the global nature of markets, all make top-down, centralized risk management a necessity."

Insurance as Risk Management

To deal with some risks, both businesses and individuals may choose to purchase one or more of the products offered by insurance companies. Buyers find insurance appealing for a very basic reason: in return for a relatively small sum of money, they are protected against certain losses, some of them potentially devastating. In this sense, buying insurance is a function of risk management. To define it as a management activity dealing with insurance, we can thus amplify our definition of *risk management* to say that it is the logical development and implementation of a plan to deal with chance losses.

With insurance, individuals and businesses share risks by contributing to a fund out of which those who suffer losses are paid. But why are insurance companies willing to accept these risks for other companies? Insurance companies make profits by taking in more premiums than they pay out to cover policyholders' losses. Quite simply, although many policyholders are paying for protection against the same type of loss, by no means will all of them suffer such a loss.

Insurable versus Uninsurable Risks Like every business, insurance companies must avoid certain risks. Insurers thus divide potential sources of loss into *insurable* and *uninsurable risks.*[16] Obviously, they issue policies only for insurable risks. Although there are some exceptions, an insurable risk must meet the four criteria described in the following sections.

Predictability The insurer must be able to use statistical tools to forecast the likelihood of a loss. For example, an auto insurer needs information about the number of car accidents in the past year to estimate the expected number of accidents for the following year. With this knowledge, the insurer can translate expected numbers and types of accidents into expected dollar losses. The same forecast also helps insurers determine premiums charged to policyholders.

Casualty A loss must result from an accident, not from an intentional act by the policyholder. Insurers do not have to cover damages if a policyholder deliberately sets fire to corporate headquarters. To avoid paying in cases of fraud, insurers may refuse to cover losses when they cannot determine whether policyholders' actions contributed to them.

Unconnectedness Potential losses must be random and must occur independently of other losses. No insurer can afford to write insurance when a large percentage of those who are exposed to a particular kind of loss are likely to suffer such a loss. One insurance company, for instance, would not want all the hurricane coverage in Miami or all the earthquake coverage in Los Angeles. By carefully choosing the risks that it will insure, an insurance company can reduce its chances of a large loss or even insolvency.

Verifiability Insured losses must be verifiable as to cause, time, place, and amount. Did an employee develop emphysema because of being exposed to a chemical or because of smoking 40 cigarettes a day for 30 years? Did the policyholder pay the renewal premium before the fire destroyed the policyholder's factory? Were the goods stolen from company offices or from the president's home? What was the insurable value of the destroyed inventory? When all these points have been verified, payment by the insurer goes more smoothly.

The Insurance Product Insurance companies are often distinguished by the types of insurance coverage they offer. Whereas some insurers offer only one area of coverage—life insurance, for example—others offer a broad range. In this section, we describe the four major categories of business insurance: *liability, property, life,* and *health.*

Liability Insurance As we will see in Appendix I, *liability* means responsibility for damages in case of accidental or deliberate harm to individuals or property. **Liability insurance** covers losses resulting from damage to people or property when the insured party is judged liable.

liability insurance
Insurance covering losses resulting from damage to people or property when the insured is judged responsible

Workers' Compensation A business is liable for any injury to an employee when the injury arises from activities related to occupation. When workers are permanently or temporarily disabled by job-related accidents or disease, employers are required by law to provide **workers' compensation coverage** for medical expenses, loss of wages, and rehabilitation services. U.S. employers now pay out approximately $60 billion in workers' compensation premiums each year, much of it to public insurers.

workers' compensation coverage
Coverage provided by a firm to employees for medical expenses, loss of wages, and rehabilitation costs resulting from job-related injuries or disease

Property Insurance Firms purchase **property insurance** to cover injuries to themselves resulting from physical damage to or loss of real estate or personal property. Property losses may result from fire, lightning, wind, hail, explosion, theft, vandalism, or other destructive forces. Losses from fire alone in the United States come to over $10 billion per year.

property insurance
Insurance covering losses resulting from physical damage to or loss of the insured's real estate or personal property

Business Interruption Insurance In some cases, loss to property is minimal in comparison to loss of income. A manufacturer, for example, may have to close down for an extended time while repairs to fire damage are being completed. During that time, of course, the company is not generating income. Even so, however, certain expenses—such as taxes, insurance premiums, and salaries for key personnel—may continue. To cover such losses, a firm may buy **business interruption insurance.**

business interruption insurance
Insurance covering income lost during times when a company is unable to conduct business

Life Insurance Insurance can also protect a company's human assets. As part of their benefits packages, many businesses purchase **life insurance** for employees. Life insurance companies accept premiums in return for the promise to pay beneficiaries after the death of insured parties. A portion of the premium is used to cover the insurer's own expenses. The remainder is invested in various types of financial instruments such as corporate bonds and stocks.

life insurance
Insurance paying benefits to the policyholder's survivors

Group Life Insurance Most companies buy **group life insurance,** which is underwritten for groups as a whole rather than for each individual member. The insurer's assessment of potential losses and its pricing of premiums are based on the characteristics of the whole group. Johnson & Johnson's benefit plan, for example, includes group life coverage with a standard program of protection and benefits—a master policy purchased by J & J <www.jj.com>—that applies equally to all employees.

group life insurance
Insurance underwritten for a group as a whole rather than for each individual in it

Health Insurance **Health insurance** covers losses resulting from medical and hospital expenses as well as income lost from injury or disease. It is no secret that the cost of health insurance has skyrocketed in recent years. In one recent year, for example, companies paid an average of $4,563 per employee on health insurance premiums to both commercial insurers like Prudential <www.prudential.com>, Metropolitan <www.metlife.com>, and Nationwide <www.nationwide.com> and special health insurance providers like Blue Cross/Blue Shield <www.bluecares.com> and other organizations called *health maintenance organizations* and *preferred provider organizations.*

health insurance
Insurance covering losses resulting from medical and hospital expenses as well as income lost from injury or disease

Disability Income Insurance **Disability income insurance** provides continuous income when disability keeps the insured from gainful employment. Many health insurance policies cover "short-term" disabilities, sometimes up to two years. Coverage for permanent disability furnishes some stated amount of weekly income—usually 50 to 70 percent of

disability income insurance
Insurance providing continuous income when disability keeps the insured from gainful employment

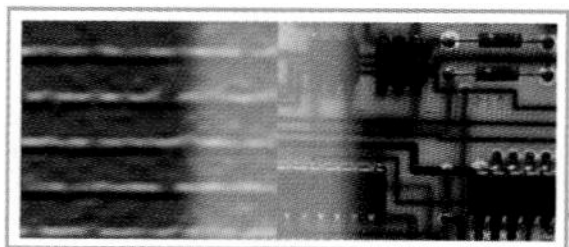

It's a WiredWorld

• *A Healthy Approach to Risk Response*

In Chapter 11, we explained how an Internet-based system for health assessment called Network Health Systems™ <www.nhsinfo.com> uses demographics and lifestyle data to evaluate the chances that any particular individual will experience various kinds of diseases or ailments. That same system also serves as an online resource for managing employee health programs: Many companies use it to assess the risk they run from poor employee health, the costs that they can expect to incur from those risks, and actions that they can take to counter those risks. Employee health is a pure risk for employers: Poor health results in the disruption of business and potentially high costs. Although risk transfer—usually in the form of health insurance for medical services—offsets part of the risk, there still remain health-related consequences (such as absenteeism) that insurance alone does not cover. To overcome these additional consequences, firms can turn to some form of risk control, usually an effective health-promotion program. Although such programs cannot guarantee against additional losses, they permit firms to minimize their harm by responding with planned actions.

Armed with health profiles for all client-company employees, the NHS system collates them into a summary profile—a kind of "company health profile." NHS provides two kinds of organizational reports that are useful in managing health risks:

- The *Organizational Assessment* uses personal data collected from employees' responses to an NHS Questionnaire to provide a breakdown of the specific risks from unhealthy behaviors. It also itemizes predicted costs of care in terms of hospitalization, medical care, lost time, and replacement of employees. The client company is given detailed reports on 44 separate risk factors (such as weight and age at first pregnancy) and their impact on a possible 52 different diseases or conditions (nerve disorders, suicide). Finally, it lists potential problem areas applicable to this specific group of employees. The demographic information then breaks down the group by work type, gender, and specific health risks. The reports also provide information on various resources that the client company can adopt—intervention programs, education materials, benefit plans, and incentive systems—to influence lifestyle changes that will improve employee health.
- The *Cost Analysis* evaluates the costs that the organization will incur over an upcoming 12-month period as a result of risk factors present and specifies the portion of those costs likely to be entailed by employee lifestyle. Further, it identifies which costs are nonreversible versus those that can be reversed through various wellness actions. It also cites the costs of implementing those actions. Using this data, the organization targets those areas of risk that offer savings; thus justifying the program expense. The report makes specific recommendations on those areas that are most likely to realize the greatest savings.

In essence, health-profile reports provide a cost/benefit analysis in the area of health promotion which, until now, has been either neglected or at best an area of subjective decision making. They thus form the basis for the planning of case management, employee-assistance programs, health promotion, and wellness programs, as well as structuring the company's benefit and insurance offerings.

the insured's weekly wages—with payments beginning after a six-month waiting period. Group policies account for over 70 percent of all disability coverage in the United States.

Special Health Care Providers Instead of reimbursement for a health professional's services, Blue Cross/Blue Shield, which is made up of not-for-profit health care membership groups, provides specific service benefits to its subscribers. Many other commercial insurers do the same. What is the advantage to the subscriber or policyholder? No matter what the service actually costs, the special health care provider will cover the cost. In contrast, when policies provide reimbursement for services received, the policyholder may pay for a portion of the expense if the policy limit is exceeded. Other important options include *HMOs*, *PPOs* and *POSs:*

"These tests are completely unnecessary. I just want to see how your insurance reacts."

- A **health maintenance organization (HMO)** is an organized health care system providing comprehensive medical care to its members for a fixed, prepaid fee. In an HMO, all members agree that, except in emergencies, they will receive their health care through the organization.
- A **preferred provider organization (PPO)** is an arrangement whereby selected hospitals and/or doctors agree to provide services at reduced rates and to accept thorough review of their recommendations for medical services. The objective of the PPO is to help control health care costs by encouraging the use of efficient providers' health care services.
- A **point-of-service (POS) plan** allows member patients to select a primary care doctor who provides medical services but may refer patients to other providers in the plan. In a POS plan, members can refer themselves outside the plan if they are willing to pay an additional fee for services. If a plan doctor makes a referral out of network, the plan pays all or most of the bill.

health maintenance organization (HMO) Organized health care system providing comprehensive care in return for fixed membership fees

preferred provider organization (PPO) Arrangement whereby selected professional providers offer services at reduced rates and permit thorough review of their service recommendations

point-of-service (POS) plan Healthcare plan allowing members to select primary-care doctors who may provide services or refer patients to other plan providers

Special Forms of Business Insurance Many forms of insurance are attractive to both businesses and individuals. Homeowners are as concerned about insuring property from fire and theft as are businesses. Businesses, however, have some special insurable concerns. In this section, we will discuss two forms of insurance that apply to the departure or death of key employees or owners.

Key Person Insurance Many businesses choose to protect themselves against loss of the talents and skills of key employees. If a salesperson who annually rings up $2.5 million dies or takes a new job, the firm will suffer loss. It will also incur recruitment costs to find a replacement and training expenses once a replacement is hired. **Key person insurance** is designed to offset both lost income and additional expenses.[17]

key-person insurance Special form of business insurance designed to offset expenses entailed by the loss of key employees

Business Continuation Agreements Who takes control of a business when a partner or associate dies? Surviving partners are often faced with the possibility of having to accept an inexperienced heir as a management partner. This contingency can be handled in **business continuation agreements,** whereby owners make plans to buy the ownership interest of a deceased associate from the associate's heirs. The value of the ownership interest is determined when the agreement is made. Special policies can also provide survivors with the funds needed to make the purchase.

business continuation agreement Special form of business insurance whereby owners arrange to buy the interests of deceased associates from their heirs

Continued from page 587

Getting Juiced for New Age Business

Super Nectars—nutritionally enhanced fruit juices with extra protein—and calcium-enriched Mama Calcium are among a stream of new products that are boosting sales in the premium juice industry. Nantucket Allserve, an industry leader, was number 71 on the *Inc.500* ranking of the fastest-growing private companies in America. However, creating a tasty new juice is no assurance of success. Although the "New Age" juice market has experienced phenomenal growth over the past five years, about three percent of the market dried up in 1999, and the overall market is shrinking even though being flooded with an outpouring of new flavors. The risk is high for new entrants.

Growth is desirable, but growth itself entails new risks for a company, including problems entailed by higher operating costs and challenges in distributing products to retailers. As a result, Nantucket and competitor firms such as Odwalla **<www.odwallazone.com>** and Fresh Samantha **<www.freshsamantha.com>** are finding that, even as sales are growing rapidly, it's easy to let costs get out of control. Profitability can be elusive. For small firms especially, hand labor can be costly, expensive automation isn't feasible. One challenge, therefore, is to counter high production and bottling costs. In addition, TV and radio advertising are expensive, and newcomers often find that advertising promotions don't always provide the sales boost they need to justify the costs. Thus advertising expenditures must also be kept in check. Even the shelf life of juice poses potential financial risks: For example, Nantucket's new brand—Original Nectars—has a 45-day shelf life versus competitor Fresh Samantha's 23 days. Nantucket, therefore, enjoys lower replacement and distribution costs. Smaller firms also have the higher distribution costs resulting from partial-load deliveries when demand doesn't justify dispatching fully loaded trucks.

To get better control over distribution, Nantucket's founders decided early on to take charge of the company's distribution activities. Unfortunately, as a result of this well-intentioned but ill-fated decision, they encountered another business risk: Getting into something you're not good at can be a costly experience. In 1994, Nantucket formed a distribution arm to distribute Nantucket Nectars in the Boston, Nantucket, and Washington, DC areas. They lost $2 million in the process. "We were young and we were scared," says Tom Scott. "But the bank told us that we had to turn a profit in three months and we did."

Wisely, the two young entrepreneurs sold their distribution business and focused on the process of making juice. "We got through it," says Scott. "It's the kind of thing they don't teach you: That you can fail to succeed." By shifting to outside distribution, Nantucket reduced the risk of getting sidetracked from its core business—making juice.

How did investor Michael Egan react after the firm had lost $2 million in its ill-fated distribution attempt? He invested another $1.5 million. Nantucket has since built a successful "outside" distribution network that includes relationships with more than 140 wholesalers distributing into some 35 states, Canada, and the Caribbean. "We could sell in 50 states," says one company executive, "but we haven't found the right distributors in some areas." They believe the safer approach for the long run is not to look for explosive growth right off the bat, but instead, first establish good relationships with a distributor who will believe in your brand and who will work with the producer to make the brand grow.

In 1998 Ocean Spray <www.oceanspray.com>, a cooperative of 1,000 cranberry growers, purchased half the company for an undisclosed sum. In the deal, financier Michael Egan transferred his stock in the company over to Ocean Spray. Although Nantucket Allserve was courted by several outside entities, First and Scott went with Ocean Spray in part because the cooperative agreed to their stipulation that Nantucket operate independently. This agreement avoids the risk that Nantucket might get swallowed up by a larger company that would give it second-class treatment and cause it to lose its market position.

> ***"We were young and we were scared. But the bank told us that we had to turn a profit in three months."***
>
> *—Tom Scott, Co-President, Nantucket Allserve*

Questions for Discussion

1. What are some additional risks, other than those discussed in the case, that its founders encountered in starting up Nantucket Allserve?
2. Why do you suppose Michael Egan was willing to withdraw his financial stake from Nantucket Allserve when it formed the partnership with Ocean Spray? What business risks did he avoid by transferring his stock to Ocean Spray? What new risks did he take on?
3. For a start-up company such as Nantucket Allserve, in what ways can growth cause costs to increase faster than sales revenues? What risks are involved when this situation occurs?
4. Why was Michael Egan willing to invest another $1.5 million just after Nantucket Allserve lost $2 million on its ill-fated distribution system? What risks did he face in deciding to invest instead of declining to invest the additional funds?
5. Why was it smart for Scott and First to insist that Nantucket's operations remain independent in its relationship with Ocean Spray? What risks are involved in retaining such independence? What risks are avoided?

SUMMARY OF LEARNING OBJECTIVES

1 **Describe the responsibilities of a financial manager.** The job of the *financial manager* is to increase the firm's value by planning and controlling the acquisition and dispersal of its financial assets. This task involves three key responsibilities: *cash-flow management* (making sure the firm has enough available money to purchase the materials it needs to produce goods and services), *financial control* (checking actual performance against plans to ensure that desired financial results occur), and *financial planning* (devising strategies for reaching future financial goals).

2 **Identify four sources of *short-term financing* for businesses.** To finance short-term expenditures, firms rely on *trade credit* (credit extended by suppliers) and loans. *Secured loans* require *collateral* (legal interest in assets that may include inventories or accounts receivable). *Unsecured loans* may be in the form of *lines of credit* or *revolving credit agreements*. Smaller firms may choose to *factor accounts receivable* (that is, sell them to financial institutions).

3 **Distinguish among the various sources of *long-term financing* and explain the risks entailed by each type.** Long-term sources of funds include *debt financing, equity financing,* and the use of preferred stock. Debt financing uses *long-term loans* and *corporate bonds* (promises to pay holders specified amounts by certain dates), both of which obligate the firm to pay regular interest. Equity financing involves the use of owners' capital, either from the sale of common stock or from retained earnings. Preferred stock is a hybrid source of funding that has some of the features of both common stock and corporate bonds. Financial planners must choose the proper mix of long-term funding. All-equity financing is the most conservative, least risky, and most expensive strategy. All-debt financing is the most speculative option.

4 **Explain how risk affects business operations and identify the five steps in the *risk management process*.** Businesses operate in an environment pervaded by risk. *Speculative risks* involve the prospect of gain or loss. *Pure risks* involve only the prospect of loss or no loss. Firms manage their risks by following some form of a five-step process: identifying risks, measuring possible losses, evaluating alternative techniques, implementing chosen techniques, and monitoring programs on an ongoing basis. Four general methods for dealing with risk are *risk avoidance, control, retention,* and *transfer.*

5 **Explain the distinction between *insurable* and *uninsurable risks*.** Insurance companies issue policies only for insurable risks—those that meet four criteria: First, the risk must be *predictable* in a statistical sense; the insurer must be able to use statistical tools to forecast the likelihood of a loss. A loss must also pass the test of *casualty,* which indicates the loss is accidental rather than intentional. Potential losses must also display *unconnectedness*—they must be random and occur independently of other losses. Finally, losses must be *verifiable* in terms of cause, time, place, and amount.

6 **Distinguish among the different *types of insurance* purchased by businesses.** ***Liability insurance*** covers losses resulting from damage to people or property when the insured is judged responsible. *Property insurance* covers losses to a firm's own buildings, equipment, and financial assets. *Life insurance* pays benefits to the survivors of a policyholder and has a cash value that can be claimed before the policyholder's death. *Health insurance* covers losses resulting from medical and hospital expenses.

QUESTIONS AND EXERCISES

Questions for Review

1. What are four short-term sources of funds for financing day-to-day business operations? Identify the advantages and disadvantages of each.
2. In what ways do the two sources of debt financing differ from each other? How do they differ from the two sources of equity financing?
3. Describe the relationship between investment risk and return. In what ways might the risk–return relationship affect a company's financial planning?
4. Give two examples of risks that are uninsurable. Why are they uninsurable?
5. Describe the risk-management process. What are the major roles of a company's risk manager?

Questions for Analysis

6. How would you decide on the best mix of debt, equity, and preferred stock for a company?
7. Why is liability insurance important to business firms?
8. As a risk manager of a large firm, what risks do you think your firm faces? For a small firm? What accounts for the most important differences?

Application Exercises

9. Interview the owner of a small local business. Identify the types of short-term and long-term funding that this firm typically uses. Why has the company made the financial management decisions that it has?
10. Interview the owner of a small local business. Ask this person to describe the company's risk-management process. What role, for example, is played by risk transfer? Why has the company made the risk-management decisions that it has?

EXPLORING THE WEB

TAKING RISKS THROUGH THE SBA

Because small-business entrepreneurs typically encounter several new problems in the early stages of start-up, up-to-date information and assistance can be helpful in recognizing financial risks and knowing the steps to take in avoiding unnecessary financial losses. The U.S. government's Small Business Administration provides a variety of services for just that purpose. To get an idea of the types of services and information available on the Internet from the SBA, access its Web site at:

www.sbaonline.gov

Starting on the homepage, review the list of options for various kinds of services that might be of interest to managers of a start-up company.

Choose three or four categories and briefly review their contents to help you become acquainted with the content and organization of the Web site. Then, perform each of the following activities:

1. On the homepage, select **Starting Your Business;** then select **Do Your Research.** How might the information here help you to better manage the risks encountered by a start-up business? Describe each kind of risk involved in the information presented at this Web site location.
2. Return again to **Starting Your Business.** Select **Success Series,** and then look at *Small Business Success Magazine.* Explore the contents in the *Magazine,* and then report on any two of its write-up items (such as "Finance for the Long Term"), describing how the information in those items can help reduce risks for a small business firm.
3. Return to **Starting Your Business** and select some additional categories to explore the variety of available resources. Among those you selected, which do you regard as especially useful for financial management in a small business? Which resources might be useful for risk management? Explain.
4. Starting again on the homepage, select **Financing;** then select **Loan Programs.** From the information available here, describe the kinds of loans small businesses can obtain through the SBA. Identify some financial risks that a small business firm takes in getting an SBA loan.
5. Return to **Financing** and select **Secondary Market.** Explain what is meant by "secondary market" and explain how it affects the financial risk of a firm that borrows money through the SBA.
6. Returning again to **Financing,** select **Surety Bond.** What risks of the borrower and the lender are affected by the "Surety Bond Program"? How might the "Surety Bond Program" affect financial management in the borrowing firm? Explain.

BUILDING YOUR BUSINESS SKILLS

MINIMIZING THE NEGATIVES

This exercise enhances the following SCANS workplace competencies: demonstrating basic skills, demonstrating thinking skills, exhibiting interpersonal skills, working with information, and applying system knowledge.

GOAL

To encourage students to better understand the major financial and risk management issues that face large companies.

BACKGROUND

In 1999 to 2000, all of the following companies reported financial problems relating to risk management:

- Levis Strauss & Company <www.levi.com>
- TWA <www.twa.com>
- Sony <www.sony.com>
- EarthLink Inc. <www.earthlink.com>
- Compaq Computer <www.compaq.com>

METHOD

Step 1

Working alone, research one of the companies just listed to learn more about the financial risks that were reported in the news.

Step 2

Write a short explanation of the financial and management issues that were faced by the firm that you researched.

Step 3

Join in teams with students who researched other companies and compare your findings.

FOLLOW-UP QUESTIONS

1. Were there common themes in the "big stories" in financial management?
2. What have the various companies done to minimize future risks and losses?

CRAFTING YOUR BUSINESS PLAN

PICKING UP SPEED ON THE FAST TRACK

THE PURPOSE OF THE ASSIGNMENT

1. To acquaint students with the process of navigating the *Business PlanPro* (*BPP*) software package (Version 4.0).
2. To familiarize students with financial and risk management issues that a sample firm may face in developing its business plan.
3. To demonstrate how three chapter topics—credit policies, risk management, and pure risks—can be integrated as components in the *BPP* planning environment.

ASSIGNMENT

After reading Chapter 21 in the textbook, open the BPP *software* and search for information about financial risks, credit worthiness, credit policies, and risk management as they apply to a sample firm:* Southeast Racing *(Southeast Racing Parts). Then respond to the following questions:*

1. Based on their business plan, would you loan Southeast Racing the $60,625 start-up capital? What are your reasons? What payback terms would you require? Explain. [Sites to see in *BPP* (for this assignment): In the Plan Outline screen, click on each of the following, in turn: **1.1 Objectives, 2.1 Company Ownership, 2.2 Startup Summary, 6.1 Management Team,** and **7.0 Financial Plan.**]
2. Consider Southeast Racing's facility needs, specifically, 3,000 square feet in the office building. If you were the building manager, are there any risks involved in leasing to Southeast Racing? If so, identify them. [Sites to see in *BPP:* In the Plan Outline screen, click on each of the following, in turn: **2.4 Company Facility** and **7.4 Projected Profit and Loss.**]
3. Chapter 21 discusses pure risks and ways to cope with them. Identify some pure risks and potential losses that Southeast Racing faces in their day-to-day operations. What techniques do you recommend for handling Southeast's potential losses? [Sites to see in *BPP:* From the Plan Outline screen, click on each of the following, in turn: **3.0 Products and Services, 3.1 Product and Service Description, 3.6 Future Products and Services, 4.2.2 Market Trends,** and **5.1.3 Distribution Strategy.**]
4. Tim and Molly plan to not sell anything on credit to their customers. What is your assessment of the risk associated with the "no-credit policy"? What do you recommend regarding customer-credit policy for Southeast Racing? [Sites to see in *BPP:* In the Plan Outline screen, click on each of the following, in turn: **6.1 Management Team, 7.1 Important Assumptions, Table: Breakeven Analysis** (beneath **7.5 Projected Cash Flow.**]

FOR YOUR OWN BUSINESS PLAN

5. Outline the credit policy you plan to apply to customers for the business plan you are developing. Identify the risks, advantages, and drawbacks associated with the policy you have chosen. Aside from customer credit, identify other day-to-day activities that have risks; explain how you intend to manage these risks. Where, in your business plan, will you present information on risks for your proposed business?

*GENERAL TIPS FOR NAVIGATION IN *BPP*

1. Open the *BPP* program, examine the Welcome screen, and click on **Open a Sample Plan.**
2. From the **Open a Sample Plan** dialogue box, click on a sample company name; then click on **Open.**
3. On the Plan Manager screen, click on **Your Plan Outline**; then click on any of the lines (for example, **5.1.1 Pricing Strategy**).
4. You can always return to the Plan Outline screen by going to the bottom of the screen and clicking on the **Plan Outline** icon.
5. After finishing with one sample company, you can get to the next one by going to the top of the screen and clicking on **File** (on the menu bar). Then beneath that, select **Open Sample Plan.** This will exit you from the current company file and take you to the **Open Sample Plan** dialogue box, where you can select your next sample company.
6. When you are finished, you can close the program by going to the top of the screen and clicking on **File** (on the bar menu). Then beneath that, select **Exit.**

VIDEO EXERCISE

HOW FINANCIAL OPTIONS STACK UP: IHOP

Learning Objectives

The purpose of this video exercise is to help you

1. Understand why firms need financing.
2. Understand how firms make financing decisions.
3. Identify some of the factors that affect the price of a firm's stock.

BACKGROUND INFORMATION

International House of Pancakes, or IHOP <www.ihop.com>, is a worldwide chain of over 700 franchisee-owned family restaurants. A leveraged buyout in 1987 left the firm with a large debt and high interest payments. Seeking funds to invest in the company, management had to choose between waiting for interest rates to go down or issuing shares of company stock to the public. IHOP went public in 1991.

THE VIDEO

We hear from CFO Frederick Silny and CEO Richard Herzer, who offer their perspectives on the stock offering and the relationship between the company and its shareholders. They discuss some of the factors that make the stock desirable and some that continue to affect its price.

DISCUSSION QUESTIONS

1. What is the relationship between stock price and earnings?
2. Why is it important for a firm like IHOP to respond to the needs of the marketplace? How does it do so?
3. IHOP's managers feel that name recognition helped contribute to the success of its stock offering. What do you think appeals to investors in Internet firms that are too new to have name recognition?

FOLLOW-UP ASSIGNMENT

How close are the relationships among customer satisfaction, earnings, and stock price? Investigate a firm that has recently been in the news because of environmental violations, a product recall, accounting irregularities, wide-scale layoffs, or some other negative actions. Compare its earnings and stock price for the period beginning six months before the incident with a period extending for an appreciable length of time afterwards. What sort of changes do you notice in your data? What do you think accounts for those changes?

FOR FURTHER EXPLORATION

Choose an idea for a small business that you might like to open if you could. Visit the Small Business Administration's business plan Web site <www.sbaonline.sba.gov/starting/businessplan.html> and use it as a guide for your own hypothetical business plan. Fill out as many details as you can and make your best estimates for the rest. What areas would you need to research if this were a real business?

MASTERING BUSINESS ESSENTIALS

Go to the "Raising Capital" episode on the Mastering Business Essentials CD-ROM for an interactive, video-enhanced exercise on the lessons learned by managers at CanGo, an e-business start-up, as they plan to meet with an investment banker to get an infusion of cash needed to expand the business.

Appendix 1

Understanding the Legal Context of Business

In this appendix, we describe the basic tenets of U.S. law and show how these principles work through the court system. We will also survey a few major areas of business-related law. By focusing on the learning objectives of this appendix, you will see that laws may create opportunities for business activity just as readily as they set limits on them.

THE U.S. LEGAL AND JUDICIAL SYSTEMS

If people could ignore contracts or drive down city streets at any speed, it would be unsafe to do business on Main Street—or even to set foot in public. Without law, people would be free to act "at will," and life and property would constantly be at risk. **Laws** are the codified rules of behavior enforced by a society. In the United States, laws fall into three broad categories according to their origins: *common, statutory,* and *regulatory.* After discussing each of these types of laws, we will briefly describe the three-tier system of courts through which the judicial system administers the law in the United States.

laws
Codified rules of behavior enforced by a society

Types of Law

Law in the United States originates primarily with English common law. Its sources include the U.S. Constitution, state constitutions, federal and state statutes, municipal ordinances, administrative agency rules and regulations, executive orders, and court decisions.

Common Law Court decisions follow *precedents,* or the decisions of earlier cases. Following precedent lends stability to the law by basing judicial decisions on cases anchored in similar facts. This principle is the keystone of **common law:** the body of decisions handed down by courts ruling on individual cases. Although some facets of common law predate the American Revolution (and even hearken back to medieval Europe), common law continues to evolve in the courts today.

common law
Body of decisions handed down by courts ruling on individual cases

Statutory Law Laws created by constitutions or by federal, state, or local legislative acts constitute **statutory law.** For example, Article I of the U.S. Constitution is a statutory law that empowers Congress to pass laws on corporate taxation, the zoning authority of municipalities, and the rights and privileges of business operating in the United States.

State legislatures and city councils also pass statutory laws. Some state laws, for example, prohibit the production or sale of detergents containing phosphates, which are believed to be pollutants. Nearly every town has ordinances specifying sites for certain types of industries or designating areas where cars cannot be parked during certain hours.

statutory law
Law created by constitutions or by federal, state, or local legislative acts

Regulatory Law Statutory and common law have long histories. Relatively new is **regulatory** (or **administrative**) **law:** law made by the authority of administrative agencies. By and large, the expansion of U.S. regulatory law has paralleled the nation's economic and technological development. Lacking the technical expertise to develop specialized legislation for specialized business activities, Congress established the first administrative agencies to create and administer the needed laws in the late 1800s. Before the early 1960s, most agencies concerned themselves with the *economic* regulation of specific areas of business—for example, transportation or securities. Since then many agencies have been established to pursue narrower *social* objectives. They focus on issues that cut across different sectors of the economy—clean air, for example, or product testing.

regulatory (or **administrative) law**
Law made by the authority of administrative agencies

Today a host of agencies, including the Equal Employment Opportunity Commission (EEOC), the Environmental Protection Agency (EPA), the Food and Drug Administration (FDA), the Federal Trade Commission (FTC), and the Occupational Safety and Health Administration (OSHA), regulate U.S. business practices.

In this section, we look briefly at the nature of regulatory agencies and describe some of the key legislation that makes up administrative law in this country. We also discuss an area of increasing importance in the relationship between government and business: regulation—or, more accurately, *deregulation.*

Agencies and Legislation Although Congress retains control over the scope of agency action, once passed, regulations have the force of statutory law. Government regulatory agencies act as a secondary judicial system, determining whether regulations have been violated and imposing penalties. A firm that violates OSHA rules, for example, may receive a citation, a hearing, and perhaps a heavy fine. Much agency activity consists of setting standards for safety or quality and monitoring the compliance of businesses. The FDA, for example, is responsible for ensuring that food, medicines, and even cosmetics are safe and effective.

Regulatory laws have been on the books for nearly a century. As early as 1906, for example, the Pure Food and Drug Act mandated minimum levels of cleanliness and sanitation for food and drug companies. More recently, the Children's Television Act of 1990 requires that broadcasters meet the educational and informational needs of younger viewers and limit the amount of advertising broadcast during children's programs. In 1996, a sweeping new law to increase competition in the communications industry required television makers to install a "V-chip," which allows parents to block undesirable programming. And Congress continues to debate the possibility of regulating the Internet.

Congress has created many new agencies in response to pressure to address social issues. In some cases, agencies were established in response to public concern about corporate behavior. The activities of these agencies have sometimes forced U.S. firms to consider the public interest almost as routinely as they consider their own financial performance.

The Move toward Deregulation Although government regulation has benefited U.S. business in many ways, it is not without its drawbacks. Businesspeople complain—with some justification—that government regulations require too much paperwork. To comply with just one OSHA regulation for a year, Goodyear once generated 345,000 pages of computer reports weighing 3,200 pounds. It now costs Goodyear $35.5 million each year to comply with the regulations of six government agencies, and it takes 36 employee-years annually (the equivalent of one employee working full time for 36 years) to fill out the required reports.

Not surprisingly, many people in both business and government support broader **deregulation:** the elimination of rules that restrict business activity. Advocates of both regulation and deregulation claim that each acts to control business expansion and prices, increase government efficiency, and right wrongs that the marketplace cannot or does not handle itself. Regulations such as those enforced by the EEOC, for example, are supposed to control undesirable business practices in the interest of social equity. In contrast, the court-ordered breakup of AT&T was prompted by a perceived need for greater market efficiency. For these and other reasons, the federal government began deregulating certain industries in the 1970s.

It is important to note that the United States is the only industrialized nation that has deregulated key industries—financial services, transportation, telecommunications, and a host of others. A 1996 law, for instance, allowed the seven "Baby Bells"—regional phone companies created when AT&T was broken up—to compete for long-distance business. It also allowed cable television and telephone companies to enter each other's markets by offering any combination of video, telephone, and high-speed data communications services. Many analysts contend that such deregulation is now, and will become, an even greater advantage in an era of global competition. Deregulation, they argue, is a primary incentive to innovation.

According to this view, deregulated industries are forced to innovate in order to survive in fiercely competitive industries. Those firms that are already conditioned to compete by being more creative will outperform firms that have been protected by regulatory climates in their home countries. "What's important," says one economist, "is that competition energizes new ways of doing things." The U.S. telecommunications industry, proponents of this view say, is twice as productive as its European counterparts because it is the only such industry forced to come out from under a protective regulatory umbrella.

The U.S. Judicial System

Laws are of little use unless they are enforced. Much of the responsibility for law enforcement falls to the courts. Although few people would claim that the courts are capable of resolving every dispute, there often seem to be more than enough lawyers to handle them all: Indeed, there are 140 lawyers for every 100,000 people in the United States. Litigation is a significant part of contemporary life, and we have given our courts a voice in a wide range of issues, some touching profoundly personal concerns, some ruling on matters of public policy that affect all our lives. In this section, we look at the operations of the U.S. judicial system.

The Court System There are three levels in the U.S. judicial system—*federal, state,* and *local.* These levels reflect the federalist structure of a system in which a central government shares power with state or local governments. Federal courts were created by the U.S. Constitution. They hear cases on questions of constitutional law, disputes relating to maritime laws, and violations of federal statutes. They also rule on regulatory actions and on such issues as bankruptcy, postal law, and copyright or patent violation. Both the federal and most state systems embody a three-tiered system of *trial, appellate,* and *supreme courts.*

Trial Courts At the lowest level of the federal court system are the **trial courts,** general courts that hear cases not specifically assigned to another court. A case involving contract violation would go before a trial court. Every state has at least one federal trial court, called a district court.

trial court
General court that hears cases not specifically assigned to another court

Trial courts also include special courts and administrative agencies. Special courts hear specific types of cases, such as cases involving tax evasion, fraud, international disputes, or claims against the U.S. government. Within their areas of jurisdiction, administrative agencies also make judgments much like those of courts.

Courts in each state system deal with the same issues as their federal counterparts. However, they may rule only in areas governed by state law. For example, a case involving state income tax laws would be heard by a state special court. Local courts in each state system also hear cases on municipal ordinances, local traffic violations, and similar issues.

Appellate Courts A losing party may disagree with a trial court ruling. If that party can show grounds for review, the case may go before a federal or state **appellate court.** These courts consider questions of law, such as possible errors of legal interpretation made by lower courts. They do not examine questions of fact. There are now 13 federal courts of appeal, each with 3 to 15 judges. Cases are normally heard by three-judge panels.

appellate court
Court that reviews case records of trials whose findings have been appealed

Supreme Courts Cases still not resolved at the appellate level can be appealed to the appropriate state supreme courts or to the U.S. Supreme Court. If it believes that an appeal is warranted or that the outcome will set an important precedent, the U.S. Supreme Court also hears cases appealed from state supreme courts. Each year, the U.S. Supreme Court receives about 5,000 appeals but typically agrees to hear fewer than 200.

BUSINESS LAW

Most legal issues confronted by businesses fall into one of six basic areas: *contract, tort, property, agency, commercial,* or *bankruptcy law.* These areas cover a wide range of business activity.

Contract Law

contract
Any agreement between two or more parties that is enforceable in court

A **contract** is any agreement between two or more parties that is enforceable in court. As such, it must meet six conditions. If all these conditions are met, one party can seek legal recourse from another if the other party breaches (that is, violates) the terms of the agreement.

1. *Agreement.* Agreement is the serious, definite, and communicated offer and acceptance of the same terms. Let us say that an auto parts supplier offers in writing to sell rebuilt engines to a repair shop for $500 each. If the repair shop accepts the offer, the two parties have reached an agreement.
2. *Consent.* A contract is not enforceable if any of the parties have been affected by an honest mistake, fraud, or pressure. For example, a restaurant manager orders a painted sign, but the sign company delivers a neon sign instead.
3. *Capacity.* To give real consent, both parties must demonstrate legal **capacity** (competence). A person under legal age (usually 18 or 21) cannot enter into a binding contract.
4. *Consideration.* An agreement is binding only if it exchanges **considerations,** that is, items of value. If your brother offers to paint your room for free, you cannot sue him if he changes his mind. Note that "items of value" do not necessarily entail money. For example, a tax accountant might agree to prepare a homebuilder's tax return in exchange for a new patio. Both services are items of value. Contracts need not be "rational," nor must they provide the "best" possible bargain for both sides. They need only include "legally sufficient" consideration. The terms are met if both parties receive what the contract details.
5. *Legality.* A contract must be for a lawful purpose and must comply with federal, state, and local laws and regulations. For example, an agreement between two competitors to engage in price fixing—that is, to set a mutually acceptable price—is not legal.
6. *Proper form.* A contract may be written, oral, or implied from conduct. It must be written, however, if it involves the sale of land or goods worth more than $500. It must be written if the agreement requires more than a year to fulfill—for example, a contract for employment as an engineer on a 14-month construction project. All changes to written contracts must also be in writing.

capacity
Competence required of individuals entering into a binding contract

consideration
Any item of value exchanged between parties to create a valid contract

Breach of Contract What can one party do if the other fails to live up to the terms of a valid contract? Contract law offers a variety of remedies designed to protect the reasonable expectations of the parties and, in some cases, to compensate them for actions taken to enforce the agreement.

As the injured party to a breached contract, any of the following actions might occur:

- You might cancel the contract and refuse to live up to your part of the bargain. For example, you might simply cancel a contract for carpet shampooing if the company fails to show up.
- You might sue for damages up to the amount that you lost as a result of the breach. Thus, you might sue the original caterer if you must hire a more expensive caterer for your wedding reception because the original company canceled at the last minute.
- If money cannot repay the damage you suffered, you might demand specific performance—that is, require the other party to fulfill the original contract. For example, you might demand that a dealer in classic cars sell you the antique Stutz Bearcat he agreed to sell you and not a classic Jaguar instead.

Tort Law

tort
Civil injury to people, property, or reputation for which compensation must be paid

Tort law applies to most business relationships *not governed by contracts.* A **tort** is a *civil*—that is, noncriminal—injury to people, property, or reputation for which compensation must be paid. For example, if a person violates zoning laws by opening a convenience store in a residential area, the person cannot be sent to jail as if the act were a criminal violation. But a variety of other legal measures can be pursued, such as fines or seizure of property. Trespass, fraud, defamation, invasion of privacy, and even assault can be torts, as can interference with contractual relations and wrongful use of trade secrets. In this section, we explain three classifications of torts: *intentional, negligence,* and *product liability.*

Intentional Torts **Intentional torts** result from the deliberate actions of another person or organization—for instance, a manufacturer knowingly fails to install a relatively inexpensive safety device on a product. Similarly, refusing to rectify a product design flaw, as in the case of the space shuttle *Challenger* disaster, can render a firm liable for an intentional tort. The actions of employees on the job may also constitute intentional torts—say, an overzealous security guard who wrongly accuses a customer of shoplifting. To remedy torts, courts will usually impose **compensatory damages:** payments intended to redress an injury actually suffered. They may also impose **punitive damages:** fines that exceed actual losses suffered by plaintiffs and that are intended to punish defendants.

intentional tort
Tort resulting from the deliberate actions of a party

compensatory damages
Monetary payments intended to redress injury actually suffered because of a tort

punitive damages
Fines imposed over and above any actual losses suffered by a plaintiff

In 1992, for example, a jury awarded $300,000 in compensatory damages plus $4 million in punitive damages to a couple who alleged that a two-way mirror in their penthouse suite had allowed strangers to spy on them at a local hotel. The compensatory damages were awarded because the jury agreed that the couple's privacy had been invaded. The large punitive award cited the plaintiff's emotional distress in the aftermath of the incident. (The case was later settled for $1 million in total damages.)

Negligence Torts Ninety percent of tort suits involve charges of **negligence,** conduct falling below legal standards for protecting others against unreasonable risk. If a company installs a pollution-control system that fails to protect a community's water supply, it may later be sued by an individual who gets sick from drinking the water.

negligence
Conduct falling below legal standards for protecting others against unreasonable risk

Negligence torts may also result from employee actions. For example, if the captain of a supertanker runs aground and spills 11 million gallons of crude oil into coastal fishing waters, the oil company may be liable for potentially astronomical damages. Thus in September 1994, a jury in Alaska ordered Exxon Corporation to pay $5 billion in punitive damages to 34,000 fishermen and other plaintiffs as a consequence of the *Exxon Valdez* disaster of 1989. (Plaintiffs had asked for $15 billion.) A month earlier, the jury had awarded plaintiffs $287 million in compensatory damages. In 1993, the firm responsible for pipeline operations at the Valdez, Alaska, terminal (which is partially owned by Exxon) agreed to pay plaintiffs in the same case $98 million in damages. In a separate case, Exxon paid $20 million in damages to villages whose food supply had been destroyed. Even before any awards was handed down, Exxon had spent $2.1 billion on the cleanup effort and paid $1.3 billion in civil and criminal penalties.

Product Liability Torts In cases of **product liability,** a company may be held responsible for injuries caused by its products. Product liability is an issue in each of the following situations:

product liability tort
Tort in which a company is responsible for injuries caused by its products

- In a raft of recent lawsuits, plaintiffs have charged that certain three-wheel all-terrain vehicles are unsafe; they contend that they are unstable and too easily overturned. They argue that manufacturers are liable for injuries suffered by drivers operating those vehicles.
- In 1997, several suits were filed against Mattel. During the preceding Christmas season, the toymaker had sold thousands of Cabbage Patch dolls with a brand-new feature: the dolls could "chew" play food. Unfortunately, they were also prone to gnaw on the hair of young children.

According to a special government panel on product liability, about 33 million people are injured and 28,000 killed by consumer products each year. Even so, U.S. courts seem to be taking a harder look at many product liability claims, especially when they are based on "soft" science:

- An appeals court overturned a $1 million award to a psychic who claimed that a CAT scan destroyed her special abilities.
- A federal judge barred as "unreliable" medical testimony linking carpal tunnel syndrome to a computer keyboard made by Unisys.
- Another federal judge dismissed a case claiming that cellular phone use caused a woman's brain tumor.

strict product liability
Principle that liability can result not from a producer's negligence but from a defect in the product itself

Strict Product Liability Since the early 1960s, businesses have faced a number of legal actions based on the relatively new principle of **strict product liability:** the principle that liability can result not from a producer's negligence but from a defect in the product itself. An injured party need show only that

1. The product was defective.
2. The defect was the cause of injury.
3. The defect caused the product to be unreasonably dangerous.

Many recent cases in strict product liability have focused on injuries or illnesses attributable to toxic wastes or other hazardous substances that were legally disposed of. Because plaintiffs need not demonstrate negligence or fault, these suits frequently succeed. Not surprisingly, the number of such suits promises to increase.

Property Law

property
Anything of value to which a person or business has sole right of ownership

As the name implies, *property law* concerns property rights. But what exactly is "property"? Is it the land under a house? The house itself? A car in the driveway? A dress in the closet? The answer in each case is yes: In the legal sense, **property** is anything of value to which a person or business has sole right of ownership. Indeed, property is technically those rights.

Within this broad general definition, we can divide property into four categories. In this section, we define these categories and then examine more fully the legal protection of a certain kind of property—intellectual property.

tangible real property
Land and anything attached to it

tangible personal property
Any movable item that can be owned, bought, sold, or leased

intangible personal property
Property that cannot be seen but that exists by virtue of written documentation

intellectual property
Property created through a person's creative activities

copyright
Exclusive ownership right belonging to the creator of a book, article, design, illustration, photo, film, or musical work

- **Tangible real property** is land and anything attached to it. A house and a factory are both tangible real property, as are built-in appliances or the machines inside the buildings.
- **Tangible personal property** is any movable item that can be owned, bought, sold, or leased. Examples are automobiles, clothing, stereos, and cameras.
- **Intangible personal property** cannot be seen but exists by virtue of written documentation. Examples are insurance policies, bank accounts, stocks and bonds, and trade secrets.

Intellectual property is created through a person's creative activities. Books, articles, songs, paintings, screenplays, and computer software are all intellectual property.

Protection of Intellectual Rights The U.S. Constitution grants protection to intellectual property by means of copyrights, trademarks, and patents. Copyrights and patents apply to the tangible expressions of an idea—not to the ideas themselves. Thus, you could not copyright the idea of cloning dinosaurs from fossil DNA. Michael Crichton could copyright his novel, *Jurassic Park,* which is a tangible result of that idea, and sell the film rights to producer-director Steven Spielberg. Both creators are entitled to the profits, if any, that may be generated by their tangible creative expressions.

Copyrights **Copyrights** give exclusive ownership rights to the creators of books, articles, designs, illustrations, photos, films, and music. Computer programs and even semiconductor chips are also protected. Copyrights extend to creators for their entire lives and to their estates for 50 years thereafter. All terms are automatically copyrighted from the moment of creation.

Trademarks Because the development of products is expensive, companies must prevent other firms from using their brand names. Often they must act to keep competitors from seducing consumers with similar or substitute products. A producer can apply to the U.S. government for a **trademark**—the exclusive legal right to use a brand name.

trademark
Exclusive legal right to use a brand name or symbol

Trademarks are granted for 20 years and may be renewed indefinitely if a firm continues to protect its brand name. If a firm allows the brand name to lapse into common usage, it may lose protection. Common usage takes effect when a company fails to use the ® symbol to indicate that its brand name is a registered trademark. It also takes effect if a company seeks no action against those who fail to acknowledge its trademark. Recently, for example, the popular brand-name sailboard Windsurfer lost its trademark. Like *trampoline, yo-yo,* and *thermos, windsurfer* has become the common term for the product and can now be used by any sailboard company. In contrast, Formica Corporation successfully spent the better part of a decade in court to protect the name *Formica* as a trademark. The Federal Trade Commission had contended that the word had entered the language as a generic name for any similar laminate material.

Patents **Patents** provide legal monopolies for the use and licensing of manufactured items, manufacturing processes, substances, and designs for objects. A patentable invention must be *novel, useful,* and *nonobvious.* Since June 1995, U.S. patent law has been in harmony with that of most developed nations. For example, patents are now valid for 20 years rather than 17 years. In addition, the term now runs from the date on which the application was *filed,* not the date on which the patent itself was *issued.*

patent
Exclusive legal right to use and license a manufactured item or substance, manufacturing process, or object design

Although the U.S. Patent Office issues about 1,200 patents a week, requirements are stringent, and U.S. patents actually tend to be issued at a slow pace. While Japan and most European countries have installed systems to speed up patent filing and research, the U.S. system can extend the process to years. Other observers argue that American firms trail their foreign counterparts in patents because of the sluggishness with which U.S. companies move products through their own research and development programs.

Restrictions on Property Rights Property rights are not always absolute. For example, rights may be compromised under any of the following circumstances:

- Owners of shorefront property may be required to permit anglers, clam diggers, and other interested parties to walk near the water.
- Utility companies typically have rights called easements, such as the right to run wire over private property or to lay cable or pipe under it.
- Under the principle of **eminent domain,** the government may, upon paying owners fair prices, claim private land to expand roads or erect public buildings.

eminent domain
Principle that the government may claim private land for public use by buying it at a fair price

Agency Law

The transfer of property—whether the deeding of real estate or the transfer of automobile title—often involves agents. An **agent** is a person who acts for, and in the name of, another party, called the **principal.** The most visible agents are those in real estate, sports, and entertainment. Many businesses, however, use agents to secure insurance coverage and handle investments. Every partner in a partnership and every officer and director in a corporation is an agent of that business. Courts have also ruled that both a firm's employees and its outside contractors may be regarded as its agents.

agent
Individual or organization acting for, and in the name of, another party

principal
Individual or organization authorizing an agent to act on its behalf

Authority of Agents Agents have the authority to bind principals to agreements. They receive that authority, however, from the principals themselves; they cannot create their own authority. An agent's authority to bind a principal can be express, implied, or apparent. The following illustration involves all three forms of agent authority:

> Ellen is a salesperson in Honest Sam's Used Car Lot. Her written employment contract gives her **express authority** to sell cars, to provide information to prospective buyers, and to approve trade-ins up to $2,000. Derived from the custom of used-car dealers,

express authority
Agent's authority, derived from written agreement, to bind a principal to a certain course of action

implied authority
Agent's authority, derived from business custom, to bind a principal to a certain course of action

apparent authority
Agent's authority, based on the principal's compliance, to bind a principal to a certain course of action

she also has **implied authority** to give reasonable discounts on prices and to make reasonable adjustments to written warranties. Furthermore, Ellen may—in the presence of Honest Sam—promise a customer that she will match the price offered by another local dealer. If Honest Sam assents—perhaps merely nods and smiles—Ellen may be construed to have the **apparent authority** to make this deal.

Responsibilities of Principals Principals have several responsibilities to their agents. They owe agents reasonable compensation, must reimburse them for related business expenses, and should inform them of risks associated with their business activities. Principals are liable for actions performed by agents *within the scope of their employment.* Thus, if agents make untrue claims about products or services, the principal is liable for making amends. Employers are similarly responsible for the actions of employees. In fact, firms are often liable in tort suits because the courts treat employees as agents.

Businesses are increasingly being held accountable for *criminal* acts by employees. Court findings, for example, have argued that firms are expected to be aware of workers' propensities for violence, to check on their employees' pasts, and to train and supervise employees properly. Suppose, for instance, that a delivery service hires a driver with a history of driving while intoxicated. If the driver has an accident with a company vehicle while under the influence of alcohol, the company may be liable for criminal actions.

Commercial Law

Managers must be well acquainted with the most general laws affecting commerce. Specifically, they need to be familiar with the provisions of the *Uniform Commercial Code,* which sets down rules regarding *warranties.*

Uniform Commercial Code (UCC)
Body of standardized laws governing the rights of buyers and sellers in transactions

The Uniform Commercial Code For many years, companies doing business in more than one state faced a special problem: Laws governing commerce varied, sometimes widely, from state to state. In 1952, however, the National Conference of Commissioners on Uniform State Laws and the American Law Institute drew up the **Uniform Commercial Code (UCC).** Subsequently accepted by every state except Louisiana, the UCC describes the rights of buyers and sellers in transactions.

For example, buyers who believe that they have been wronged in agreements with sellers have several options. They can cancel contracts, refuse deliveries, and demand the return of any deposits. In some cases, they can buy the same products elsewhere and sue the original contractors to recover any losses incurred. Sellers, too, have several options. They can cancel contracts, withhold deliveries, and sell goods to other buyers. If goods have already been delivered, sellers can repossess them or sue the buyers for purchase prices.

warranty
Seller's promise to stand by its products or services if a problem occurs after the sale

express warranty
Warranty whose terms are specifically stated by the seller

implied warranty
Warranty, dictated by law, based on the principle that products should fulfill advertised promises and serve the purposes for which they are manufactured and sold

Warranties A **warranty** is a seller's promise to stand by its products or services if a problem occurs after the sale. Warranties may be *express* or *implied.* The terms of an **express warranty** are specifically stated by the seller. For example, many stereo systems are expressly warranted for 90 days. If they malfunction within that period, they can be returned for full refunds.

An **implied warranty** is dictated by law. Implied warranties embody the principle that a product should (1) fulfill the promises made by advertisements and (2) serve the purpose for which it was manufactured and sold. If you buy an advertised frost-free refrigerator, the seller implies that the refrigerator will keep your food cold and that you will not have to defrost it. It is important to note, however, that warranties, unlike most contracts, are easily limited, waived, or disclaimed. Consequently, they are the source of more and more tort action, as dissatisfied customers seek redress from producers.

bankruptcy
Permission granted by the courts to individuals and organizations not to pay some or all of their debts

Bankruptcy Law

At one time, individuals who could not pay their debts were jailed. Today, however, both organizations and individuals can seek relief by filing for **bankruptcy**—the court-granted permission not to pay some or all debts.

Hundreds of thousands of individuals and tens of thousands of businesses file for bankruptcy each year, and their numbers continue to increase. Why do individuals and businesses file for bankruptcy? Cash-flow problems and drops in farm prices caused many farmers, banks, and small businesses to go bankrupt. In recent years, large enterprises such as Continental Airlines and R. H. Macy have sought the protection of bankruptcy laws as part of strategies to streamline operations, cut costs, and regain profitability.

Three main factors account for the increase in bankruptcy filings:

1. The increased availability of credit
2. The "fresh-start" provisions in current bankruptcy laws
3. The growing acceptance of bankruptcy as a financial tactic

In some cases, creditors force an individual or firm into **involuntary bankruptcy** and press the courts to award them payment of at least part of what they are owed. Far more often, however, a person or business chooses to file for court protection against creditors. In general, individuals and firms whose debts exceed total assets by at least $1,000 may file for **voluntary bankruptcy.**

involuntary bankruptcy
Bankruptcy proceedings initiated by the creditors of an indebted individual or organization

voluntary bankruptcy
Bankruptcy proceedings initiated by an indebted individual or organization

Business Bankruptcy A business bankruptcy may be resolved by one of three plans:

- Under a *liquidation plan,* the business ceases to exist. Its assets are sold and the proceeds used to pay creditors.
- Under a *repayment plan,* the bankrupt company simply works out a new payment schedule to meet its obligations. The time frame is usually extended, and payments are collected and distributed by a court-appointed trustee.
- *Reorganization* is the most complex form of business bankruptcy. The company must explain the sources of its financial difficulties and propose a new plan for remaining in business. Reorganization may include a new slate of managers and a new financial strategy. A judge may also reduce the firm's debts to ensure its survival. Although creditors naturally dislike debt reduction, they may agree to the proposal, since 50 percent of one's due is better than nothing at all.

New legislation passed in 1994 has made some major revisions in bankruptcy laws. For example, it is now easier for individuals with up to $1 million in debt to make payments under installment plans instead of liquidating assets immediately. In contrast, the new law restricts how long a company can protect itself in bankruptcy while continuing to do business. Critics have charged, for instance, that many firms have succeeded in operating for many months under bankruptcy protection. During that time, they were able to cut costs and prices, not only competing with an unfair advantage but dragging down overall industry profits. The new laws place time limits on various steps in the filing process. The intended effect is to speed the process and prevent assets from being lost to legal fees.

THE INTERNATIONAL FRAMEWORK OF BUSINESS LAW

Laws can vary dramatically from country to country, and many businesses today have international markets, suppliers, and competitors. It follows that managers need a basic understanding of the international framework of business law that affects the ways in which they can do business.

National laws are created and enforced by countries. The creation and enforcement of international law is more complicated. For example, if a company shipping merchandise between the United States and Mexico breaks an environmental protection law, to whom is that company accountable? The answer depends on several factors. Which country enacted the law in question? Where did the violation occur? In which country is the alleged violator incorporated?

Issues such as pollution across borders are matters of **international law:** the very general set of cooperative agreements and guidelines established by countries to govern the

international law
Set of cooperative agreements and guidelines established by countries to govern actions of individuals, businesses, and nations

actions of individuals, businesses, and nations themselves. In this section, we examine the various sources of international law. We then discuss some of the important ways in which international trade is regulated and place some key U.S. trade laws in the international context in which they are designed to work.

Sources of International Law

International law has several sources. One source is custom and tradition. Among countries that have been trading with each other for centuries, many customs and traditions governing exchanges have gradually evolved into practice. Although some trading practices still follow ancient unwritten agreements, there has been a clear trend in more recent times to approach international trade within a more formal legal framework. Key features of that framework include a variety of formal trade agreements.

Trade Agreements In addition to subscribing to international rules, virtually every nation has formal trade treaties with other nations. A *bilateral agreement* is one involving two countries; a *multilateral agreement* involves several nations.

General Agreement on Tariffs and Trade (GATT) International trade agreement to encourage the multilateral reduction or elimination of trade barriers

General Agreement on Tariffs and Trade The **General Agreement on Tariffs and Trade (GATT)** was first signed shortly after the end of World War II. Its purpose is to reduce or eliminate trade barriers, such as tariffs and quotas. It does so by encouraging nations to protect domestic industries within internationally agreed-upon limits and to engage in multilateral negotiations.

In December 1994, the U.S. Congress ratified a revision of GATT that had been worked out by 124 nations over a 12-year period. Still, many issues remain unresolved—for example, the opening of foreign markets to most financial services. Governments may still provide subsidies to manufacturers of civil aircraft, and no agreement was reached on limiting the distribution of American cultural exports—movies, music, and the like—in Europe. With those agreements that have been reached, however, one international economic group predicts that world commerce will have increased by $270 billion by 2002.

North Amercian Free Trade Agreement (NAFTA) Agreement to gradually eliminate tariffs and other trade barriers between the United States, Canada, and Mexico

North American Free Trade Agreement The **North American Free Trade Agreement (NAFTA)** was negotiated to remove tariffs and other trade barriers among the United States, Canada, and Mexico. NAFTA also included agreements to monitor environmental and labor abuses. It took effect on January 1, 1994, and immediately eliminated some tariffs; others will disappear after 5-, 10-, or 15-year intervals.

In the first year after its passage, observers agreed that, by and large, NAFTA achieved what it was supposed to: a much more active North American market. The following were among the results after one year:

- Direct foreign investment increased. U.S. and Canadian firms, for example, accounted for 55 percent of all foreign investment in Mexico, investing $2.4 billion. Companies from other nations—for instance, Toyota Motor Corporation—also made new investments, such as expanding production facilities, to take advantage of the freer movement of goods in the new market.
- U.S. exports to Mexico increased by about 20 percent. Proctor & Gamble, for example, enjoyed an increase of nearly 75 percent, and the giant agribusiness firm of Archer Daniels Midland reported a tripling of its exports to Mexico. Mexico passed Japan as the second-largest buyer of U.S. goods, and trade with Canada rose 10 percent (twice the gain in Europe and Asia).
- U.S. imports from Mexico and Canada rose even faster than rates in the opposite direction, setting records of $48 billion and $120 billion, respectively. In particular, electronics, computers, and communications products came into the United States twice as fast as they went out. "We pointed out," says one NAFTA opponent, "that there was a fairly sophisticated manufacturing base in Mexico that pays peanuts, and the numbers bear that out."

- NAFTA created fewer jobs than proponents had hoped. Although the U.S. economy added 1.7 million new jobs in 1994, the Labor Department estimates that only 100,000 jobs were NAFTA related. At the same time, however, the flood of U.S. jobs to Mexico predicted by Ross Perot and other NAFTA critics, especially by labor union officials, did not occur. In fact, the president of Ford Motor Company's Mexico operations has boasted that his activities "have created jobs here and in the U.S." His reasoning: Ford's exports of Mexican-made vehicles to the United States are up 30 percent, and 80 percent of all components in those cars are made in the United States. Ford also reports that its exports of American-made cars to Mexico rose from 1,200 to 30,000 in NAFTA's first year.

European Union Originally called the Common Market, the **European Union** (EU) includes the principal Western European nations. These countries have eliminated most quotas and have set uniform tariff levels on products imported and exported within their group. In 1992, virtually all internal trade barriers were eliminated, making the European Union the largest free marketplace in the world.

European Union (EU) Agreement among major Western European nations to eliminate or make uniform most trade barriers affecting group members

Glossary

absolute advantage The ability to produce something more efficiently than any other country can [72]

accommodative stance Approach to social responsibility by which a company, if specifically asked to do so, exceeds legal minimums in its commitments to groups and individuals in its social environment [113]

accountability Liability of subordinates for accomplishing tasks assigned by managers [157]

accounting Comprehensive system for collecting, analyzing, and communicating financial information [502]

accounting system Organized means by which financial information is identified, measured, recorded, and retained for use in accounting statements and management reports [502]

account receivable Amount due from a customer who has purchased goods on credit [511]

accounts payable Current liabilities consisting of bills owed to suppliers, plus wages and taxes due within the upcoming year [512]

acquisition The purchase of one company by another [56]

Active Corps of Executives (ACE) SBA program in which currently employed executives work with small businesses on a volunteer basis [198]

activity ratio Financial ratio for evaluating management's use of a firm's assets [517]

advertising agency Independent company that provides some or all of a client firm's advertising needs [362]

advertising campaign Arrangement of ads in selected media to reach targeted audiences [362]

advertising media Variety of communication devices for carrying a seller's message to potential customers [356]

advocacy advertising Advertising promoting a cause, viewpoint, or candidate [361]

affirmative action plan Practice of recruiting qualified employees belonging to racial, gender, or ethnic groups who are underrepresented in an organization [226]

Age Discrimination and Employment Act (ADEA) Federal law prohibiting discrimination against people over 40 on the basis of age [225]

agency shop Workplace in which workers must pay union dues even if they do not join [281]

agent Individual or organization acting for, and in the name of, another party [AP-7]

American Federation of Labor (AFL) Group of craft unions formed in 1866 to stress collective bargaining, economic action, and a pragmatic approach to union-management relations [272]

Americans with Disabilities Act of 1990 (ADA) Federal law prohibiting discrimination on the basis of disability and requiring employers to make reasonable accommodation for disabled applicants and employees [225]

analytic process Production process in which resources are broken down into components to create finished products [414]

apparent authority Agent's authority, based on the principal's compliance, to bind a principal to a certain course of action [AP-8]

appellate court Court that reviews case records of trials whose findings have been appealed [AP-3]

application program Software (such as Lotus 1-2-3) that processes data according to a user's special needs [486]

artificial intelligence (AI) Computer-system application that imitates human behavior by performing physical tasks, using thought processes, sensing, and learning [483]

assembly line Product layout in which a product moves step by step through a plant on conveyor belts or other equipment until it is completed [422]

asset Any economic resource expected to benefit a firm or an individual who owns it [509]

audit Systematic examination of a company's accounting system to determine whether its financial reports fairly represent its operations [504]

authority Power to make the decisions necessary to complete a task [156]

autocratic style Managerial style in which managers generally issue orders and expect them to be obeyed without question [259]

automated teller machine (ATM) Electronic machine that allows customers to conduct account-related activities 24 hours a day, 7 days a week [539]

balance of payments Flow of all money into or out of a country [74]

balance of trade Economic value of all products a country imports minus the economic value of all products it exports [74]

balance sheet Financial statement detailing a firm's assets, liabilities, and owners' equity [510]

banker's acceptance Bank promise, issued for a buyer, to pay a designated firm a specified amount at a future date [538]

bankruptcy Permission granted by the courts to individuals and organizations not to pay some or all of their debts [AP-8]

bargaining unit Designated group of employees who will be represented by a union [282]

bargain retailer Retailer carrying a wide range of products at bargain prices [390]

bearer (or **coupon**) **bond** Bond requiring the holder to clip and submit a coupon to receive an interest payment [569]

bear market Period of falling stock prices [575]

benchmarking Process by which a company implements the best practices from its own past performance and those of other companies to improve its own products [452]

benefits Compensation other than wages and salaries [221]

bill of materials Production control tool that specifies the necessary ingredients of a product, the order in which they should be combined, and how many of each are needed to make one batch [428]

blue-chip stock Common stock issued by a well-established company with a sound financial history and a stable pattern of dividend payouts [559]

blue-sky laws Laws requiring securities dealers to be licensed and registered with the states in which they do business [579]

board of directors Governing body of a corporation that reports to its shareholders and delegates power to run its day-to-day operations, but remains responsible for sustaining its assets [52]

bond Security through which an issuer promises to pay the buyer a certain amount of money by a specified future date [567]

bond indenture Statement of the terms of a corporate bond [595]

bookkeeping Recording of accounting transactions [502]

book value Value of a common stock expressed as total shareholders' equity divided by the number of shares of stock [559]

boycott Labor action in which workers refuse to buy the products of a targeted employer [286]

branch office Foreign office set up by an international or multinational firm [81]

brand advertising Advertising promoting a specific brand [361]

brand competition Competitive marketing that appeals to consumer perceptions of similar products [299]

branding Process of using symbols to communicate the qualities of a product made by a particular producer [334]

brand loyalty Pattern of regular consumer purchasing based on satisfaction with a product [309]

breakeven analysis Assessment of the quantity of a product that must be sold before the seller makes a profit [338]

breakeven point Quantity of a product that is sold such that the seller's revenues equal all variable and fixed costs [338]

broker Individual or organization who receives and executes buy-and-sell orders on behalf of other people in return for commissions [562]

browser Software supporting the graphics and linking capabilities necessary to navigate the World Wide Web [474]

budget Detailed statement of estimated receipts and expenditures for a period of time in the future [514]

budget deficit Situation in which a government body spends more money than it takes in [22]

bull market Period of rising stock prices [575]

business An organization that provides goods or services to earn profits [5]

business agent (or **business representative**) Full-time official who acts as liaison between members of a large union and their supervisors [278]

business continuation agreement Special form of business insurance whereby owners arrange to buy the interests of deceased associates from their heirs [607]

business ethics Ethical or unethical behaviors by a manager or employer of an organization [95]

business interruption insurance Insurance covering income lost during times when a company is unable to conduct business [605]

business plan Document that tells potential lenders why money is needed, how it will be used, and when it will be repaid [195]

business practice laws Laws or regulations governing business practices in given countries [85]

business process reengineering Quality improvement process that entails rethinking an organization's approach to productivity and quality [455]

cafeteria benefit plan Benefit plan that sets limits on benefits per employee, each of whom may choose from a variety of alternative benefits [223]

callable bond Bond that may be called in and paid for by the issuer before its maturity date [569]

capacity In operations management, amount of a product that a company can produce under normal working conditions [417] In law, competence required of individuals entering into a binding contract [AP-4]

capital The funds needed to create and operate a business enterprise [6]

capitalism Market economy that provides for private ownership of production and encourages entrepreneurship by offering profits as an incentive [9]

capital item Expensive, long-lasting, infrequently purchased industrial product such as a building [328]

capital structure Relative mix of a firm's debt and equity financing [597]

cartel Association of producers whose purpose is to control supply and prices [85]

cash-flow management Management of cash inflows and outflows to ensure adequate funds for purchases and the productive use of excess funds [588]

catalog showroom Bargain retailer in which customers place orders for catalog items to be picked up at on-premises warehouses [390]

cellular layout Spatial arrangement of production facilities designed to move families of products through similar flow paths [420]

centralized organization Organization in which most decision-making authority is held by upper-level management [158]

central processing unit (CPU) Part of the computer system where data processing takes place [485]

certified public accountant (CPA) Accountant licensed by the state and offering services to the public [503]

chain of command Reporting relationships within a company [152]

channel captain Channel member who is most powerful in determining the roles and rewards of other members [385]

channel conflict Conflict arising when the members of a distribution channel disagree over the roles they should play or the rewards they should receive [385]

check Demand deposit order instructing a bank to pay a given sum to a specified payee [533]

check kiting Illegal practice of writing checks against money that has not yet been credited at the bank on which the checks are drawn [111]

chief executive officer (CEO) Top manager hired by the board of directors to run a corporation [54]

Civil Rights Act of 1991 Amendment that extends Title VII of the Civil Rights Act of 1964 and provides for compensatory and punitive damages [225]

classical theory of motivation Theory holding that workers are motivated solely by money [245]

client-server network Information-technology system consisting of clients (users) that are electronically linked to share network resources provided by a server, such as a host computer [493]

closed shop Workplace in which an employer may hire only workers already belonging to a union [280]

closely held (or **private**) **corporation** Corporation whose stock is held by only a few people and is not available for sale to the general public [46]

closing Step in the personal selling process in which salespeople ask prospective customers to buy products [365]

collateral Borrower-pledged legal asset that may be seized by lenders in case of nonpayment [592]

collective bargaining Process by which labor and management negotiate conditions of employment for union-represented workers [270]

collusion Illegal agreement between two or more companies to commit a wrongful act [108]

commercial bank Federal- or state-chartered financial institution accepting deposits that it uses to make loans and earn profits [535]

commercial paper Short-term securities, or notes, containing a borrower's promise to pay [593]

committee and **team authority** Authority granted to committees or work teams involved in a firm's daily operations [161]

commodities market Market in which futures contracts are traded [570]

common law Body of decisions handed down by courts ruling on individual cases [AP-1]

common stock Stock that pays dividends and guarantees corporate voting rights, but offers last claims over assets [51]

comparable worth Principle that jobs which are worth the same should be compensated at the same level regardless of who performs them [225]

comparative advantage The ability to produce some products more efficiently than others [72]

comparative advertising Advertising strategy that directly compares two or more products [355]

compensation Set of rewards that organizations provide to individuals in return for their willingness to perform various jobs and tasks [218]

compensatory damages Monetary payments intended to redress injury actually suffered because of a tort [AP-5]

competition Vying among businesses for the same resources or customers [14]

competitive product analysis Process by which a company analyzes a competitor's products to identify desirable improvements in its own [448]

compulsory arbitration Method of resolving a labor dispute in which both parties are legally required to accept the judgment of a neutral party [287]

computer-aided design (CAD) Computer-based electronic technology that assists in designing products by simulating a real product and displaying it in three-dimensional graphics [482]

computer-aided manufacturing (CAM) Computer system used to design and control equipment needed in the manufacturing process [482]

computer-assisted instruction Instruction-based training in which knowledge and information are presented via computer [215]

computer graphics program Applications program that converts numeric and character data into pictorial information such as graphs and charts [488]

computer network All the computer and information technology devices which, by working together, drive the flow of digital information throughout a system [484]

conceptual skills Abilities to think in the abstract, diagnose and analyze different situations, and see beyond the present situation [137]

Congress of Industrial Organizations (CIO) Group of industrial unions formed in 1938 that rapidly organized the auto, steel, mining, meatpacking, paper, textile, and electrical industries [272]

considerations Any item of value exchanged between parties to create a valid contract [AP-4]

consumer behavior Various facets of the decision process by which customers come to purchase and consume products [309]

consumer goods Products purchased by consumers for personal use [296]

consumerism Form of social activism dedicated to protecting the rights of consumers in their dealings with businesses [107]

containerization Transportation method in which goods are sealed in containers at shipping sources and opened when they reach final destinations [400]

contingency approach Approach to managerial style holding that the appropriate behavior in any situation is dependent (contingent) on the unique elements of that situation [260]

contingency planning Identifying aspects of a business or its environment that might entail changes in strategy [130]

contingent worker Employee hired on something other than a full-time basis to supplement an organization's permanent workforce [231]

continuous improvement An ongoing commitment to improving products and processes in the pursuit of ever-increasing customer satisfaction [458]

contract An agreement between two or more parties enforceable in court [AP-4]

control chart Process control method that plots test sampling results on a diagram to determine when a process is beginning to depart from normal operating conditions [450]

controller Person who manages all of a firm's accounting activities (chief accounting officer) [502]

controlling Management process of monitoring an organization's performance to ensure that it is meeting its goals [133]

convenience good/service Inexpensive product purchased and consumed rapidly and regularly [327]

convenience store Retail store offering easy accessibility, extended hours, and fast service [391]

convertible bond Bond that can be retired by converting it to common stock [569]

cooperative Form of organization in which a group of sole proprietorships and/or partnerships agrees to work together for common benefits. [42]

copyright Exclusive ownership right belonging to the creator of a book, article, design, illustration, photo, film, or musical work [AP-6]

corporate bond Bond issued by a company as a source of long-term funding [568]

corporate culture The shared experiences, stories, beliefs, and norms that characterize an organization [140]

corporate governance Roles of shareholders, directors, and other managers in corporate decision making [50]

corporation Business that is legally considered an entity separate from its owners and is liable for its own debts; owners' liability extends to the limits of their investments [44]

cost of goods sold Total cost of obtaining materials for making the products sold by a firm during the year [512]

cost-of-living adjustment (COLA) Labor contract clause tying future raises to changes in consumer purchasing power [284]

coupon Sales promotion technique in which a certificate is issued entitling the buyer to a reduced price [365]

creative selling Personal selling task in which salespeople try to persuade buyers to purchase products by providing information about their benefits [364]

credit policy Rules governing a firm's extension of credit to customers [590]

credit union Financial institution that accepts deposits from, and makes loans to, only its members, usually employees of a particular organization [536]

crisis management An organization's methods for dealing with emergencies [130]

critical incident method Performance rating method based on stated examples that reflect especially good or poor performance [217]

cumulative preferred stock Preferred stock on which dividends not paid in the past must be paid to stockholders before dividends can be paid to common stockholders [561]

currency Government-issued paper money and metal coins [533]

current asset Asset that can or will be converted into cash within the following year [510]

current liability Debt that must be paid within the year [512]

current ratio Solvency ratio that determines a firm's creditworthiness by measuring its ability to pay current liabilities [517]

customer departmentalization Departmentalization according to types of customers likely to buy a given product [154]

cybermall Collection of virtual storefronts (business Web sites) representing a variety of products and product lines on the Internet [394]

data Raw facts and figures [470]

database Centralized, organized collection of related data [488]

database management program Applications program for creating, storing, searching, and manipulating an organized collection of data [488]

data communication network Global network (such as the Internet) that permits users to send electronic messages and information quickly and economically [473]

debenture Unsecured bond for which no specific property is pledged as security [569]

debit card Plastic card that allows an individual to transfer money between accounts [545]

debt A firm's total liabilities [518]

debt financing Long-term borrowing from sources outside a company [594]

debt ratio Solvency ratio measuring a firm's ability to meet its long-term debts [518]

debt-to-owners' equity ratio (or **debt-to-equity ratio**) Solvency ratio describing the extent to which a firm is financed through borrowing [518]

decentralized organization Organization in which a great deal of decision-making authority is delegated to levels of management at points below the top [158]

decision-making skills Skills in defining problems and selecting the best courses of action [137]

decision support system (DSS) Interactive computer-based system that locates and presents information needed to support decision making [483]

defensive stance Approach to social responsibility by which a company meets only minimum legal requirements in its commitments to groups and individuals in its social environment [112]

delegation Assignment of a task, responsibility, or authority by a manager to a subordinate [157]

demand The willingness and ability of buyers to purchase a good or service [11]

demand and supply schedule Assessment of the relationships between different levels of demand and supply at different price levels [12]

demand curve Graph showing how many units of a product will be demanded (bought) at different prices [12]

demand deposit Bank account funds that may be withdrawn at any time [533]

democratic style Managerial style in which managers generally ask for input from subordinates but retain final decision-making power [259]

demographic variables Characteristics of populations that may be considered in developing a segmentation strategy [303]

departmentalization Process of grouping jobs into logical units [154]

department store Large product line retailer characterized by organization into specialized departments [389]

depreciation Process of distributing the cost of an asset over its life [511]

depression Particularly severe and long-lasting recession [18]

deregulation The elimination of rules that restrict business activity [AP-2]

derived demand Demand for industrial products that results from demand for consumer products [313]

desktop publishing Process of combining word-processing and graphics capability to produce virtually typeset-quality text from personal computers [489]

direct channel Distribution channel in which a product travels from producer to consumer without intermediaries [380]

directing Management process of guiding and motivating employees to meet an organization's objectives [133]

direct mail Advertising medium in which messages are mailed directly to consumers' homes or places of business [357]

direct-response retailing Nonstore retailing by direct interaction with customers to inform them of products and to receive sales orders [391]

direct selling Form of nonstore retailing typified by door-to-door sales [392]

disability income insurance Insurance providing continuous income when disability keeps the insured from gainful employment [605]

discount Price reduction offered as an incentive to purchase [343]

discount house Bargain retailer that generates large sales volume by offering goods at substantial price reductions [390]

discount rate Interest rate at which member banks can borrow money from the Federal Reserve [544]

distribution Part of the marketing mix concerned with getting products from producers to consumers [302]

distribution center Warehouse providing short-term storage of goods for which demand is both constant and high [397]

distribution channel Network of interdependent companies through which a product passes from producer to end user [380]

distribution mix Combination of distribution channels by which a firm gets its products to end users [380]

divestiture Strategy whereby a firm sells one or more of its business units [57]

division Department that resembles a separate business in producing and marketing its own products [163]

divisional organization Organizational structure in which corporate divisions operate as autonomous businesses under the larger corporate umbrella [162]

double-entry accounting system Bookkeeping system that balances the accounting equation by recording the dual effects of every financial transaction [510]

double taxation Situation in which taxes may be payable both by a corporation on its profits and by shareholders on dividend incomes [46]

Dow Jones Industrial Average (DJIA) Market index based on the prices of 30 of the largest industrial firms listed on the NYSE [576]

drop shipper Limited-function merchant wholesaler who receives customer orders, negotiates with producers, takes title to goods, and arranges for shipment to customers [386]

dumping Practice of selling a product abroad for less than the cost of production [85]

earnings per share Profitability ratio measuring the size of the dividend that a firm can pay shareholders [518]

e-cash Electronic money that moves among consumers and businesses via digital electronic transmissions [546]

e-catalog Nonstore retailing in which the Internet is used to display products [394]

economic strike Strike usually triggered by stalemate over one or more mandatory bargaining items [285]

economic system A nation's system for allocating its resources among its citizens [5]

e-intermediary Internet distribution channel member who assists in moving products through to customers or who collects information about various sellers to be presented in convenient format for Internet customers. [387]

electronic conferencing Computer-based system that allows people to communicate simultaneously from different locations via software or telephone [473]

electronic funds transfer (EFT) Communication of fund-transfer information over wire, cable, or microwave [540]

electronic information technologies (EIT) Information-systems applications, based on telecommunications technologies, that use networks of appliances or devices to communicate information by electronic means [472]

electronic mail (e-mail) Computer system that electronically transmits letters, reports, and other information between computers [473]

electronic retailing Nonstore retailing in which information about the seller's products and services is connected to consumers' computers, allowing consumers to receive the information and purchase the products in the home [393]

electronic spreadsheet Applications program with a row-and-column format that allows users to store, manipulate, and compare numeric data [488]

electronic storefront Commercial Web site in which customers gather information about products, buying opportunities, placing orders, and paying for purchases [394]

embargo Government order banning exportation and/or importation of a particular product or all products from a particular country [83]

eminent domain Principle that the government may claim private land for public use by buying it at a fair price [AP-7]

emotional motives Reasons for purchasing a product that are based on nonobjective factors [310]

employee empowerment Concept that all employees are valuable contributors to a firm's business and should be entrusted with decisions regarding their work [459]

employee information system (or **skills inventory**) Computerized system containing information on each employee's education, skills, work experiences, and career aspirations [211]

Employee Retirement Income Security Act of 1974 (ERISA) Federal law regulating private pension plans [226]

employee stock ownership plan (ESOP) Arrangement in which a corporation holds its own stock in trust for its employees, who gradually receive ownership of the stock and control its voting rights [55]

employment-at-will Principle, increasingly modified by legislation and judicial decision, that organizations should be able to retain or dismiss employees at their discretion [228]

entrepreneur Businessperson who accepts both the risks and the opportunities involved in creating and operating a new business venture [183]

environmental analysis Process of scanning the business environment for threats and opportunities [128]

equal employment opportunity Legally mandated nondiscrimination in employment on the basis of race, creed, sex, or national origin [224]

Equal Employment Opportunity Commission (EEOC) Agency created by Title VII to enforce discrimination-related laws [226]

Equal Pay Act of 1963 Federal law requiring organizations to pay men and women the same pay for doing equal work [224]

equity financing Use of common stock and/or retained earnings to raise long-term funding [595]

equity theory Theory of motivation holding that people evaluate their treatment by employers relative to the treatment of others [248]

ethical behavior Behavior conforming to generally accepted social norms concerning beneficial and harmful actions [95]

ethics Beliefs about what is right and wrong or good and bad in actions that affect others [95]

European Union (EU) Agreement among major Western European nations to eliminate or make uniform most trade barriers affecting group members [AP-11]

exchange rate Rate at which the currency of one nation can be exchanged for the currency of another country [75]

exclusive distribution Strategy by which a manufacturer grants exclusive rights to distribute or sell a product to a limited number of wholesalers or retailers in a given geographic area [385]

executive support system (ESS) Quick-reference information-system application designed specially for instant access by upper-level managers [483]

expectancy theory Theory of motivation holding that people are motivated to work toward rewards that they want and that they believe they have a reasonable chance of obtaining [248]

expense item Industrial product purchased and consumed rapidly and regularly for daily operations [328]

experimentation Market research technique that attempts to compare the responses of the same or similar people under different circumstances [309]

expert system Form of artificial intelligence that attempts to imitate the behavior of human experts in a particular field [484]

export Product made or grown domestically but shipped and sold abroad [66]

exporter Firm that distributes and sells products to one or more foreign countries [79]

express authority Agent's authority, derived from written agreement, to bind a principal to a certain course of action [AP-7]

express warranty Warranty whose terms are specifically stated by the seller [AP-8]

external environment Outside factors that influence marketing programs by posing opportunities or threats [297]

external failures Reducible costs incurred after defective products have left a plant [451]

external recruiting Practice of attracting people outside an organization to apply for jobs [212]

extranet Intranet allowing outsiders access to a firm's internal information system [475]

factors of production Resources used in the production of goods and services—natural resources, labor, capital, and entrepreneurs [6]

factory outlet Bargain retailer owned by the manufacturer whose products it sells [390]

Fair Labor Standards Act Federal law (1938) setting minimum wage and maximum number of hours in the workweek [226, 280]

Family and Medical Leave Act of 1993 Federal law requiring employers to provide unpaid leave for specified family and medical reasons [226]

fax machine Machine that can transmit copies of documents (text and graphics) over telephone lines [472]

feature Tangible and intangible qualities that a company builds into a product [326]

Federal Deposit Insurance Corporation (FDIC) Federal agency that guarantees the safety of all deposits up to $100,000 in the financial institutions that it insures [541]

Federal Reserve System (the Fed) Central bank of the United States, which acts as the government's bank, serves member commercial banks, and controls the nation's money supply [541]

fiber optic cable Glass-fiber cables that carry data in the form of light pulses [493]

finance (or **corporate finance**) Activities concerned with determining a firm's long-term investments, obtaining the funds to pay for them, conducting the firm's everyday financial activities, and managing the firm's risks [588]

finance company Nondeposit institution that specializes in making loans to businesses and consumers [536]

financial accounting system Field of accounting concerned with external users of a company's financial information [503]

financial control Process of checking actual performance against plans to ensure that desired financial results occur [589]

financial manager Manager responsible for planning and controlling the acquisition and dispersal of a firm's financial resources [588]

financial plan A firm's strategies for reaching some future financial position [589]

financial statement Any of several types of reports summarizing a company's financial status to aid in managerial decision making [510]

firewall Software and hardware system that prevents outsiders from accessing a company's internal network [475]

first-line managers Managers responsible for supervising the work of employees [135]

fiscal policies Government economic policies that determine how the government collects and spends its revenues [22]

fixed asset Asset with long-term use or value, such as land, buildings, and equipment [511]

fixed cost Cost unaffected by the quantity of a product produced or sold [338]

flat organizational structure Characteristic of decentralized companies with relatively few layers of management and relatively wide spans of control [158]

flextime programs Method of increasing job satisfaction by allowing workers to adjust work schedules on a daily or weekly basis [255]

float Total amount of checks written but not yet cleared through the Federal Reserve [543]

focus group Market research technique in which a group of people is gathered, presented with an issue, and asked to discuss it in depth [308]

follow-up Production control activity for ensuring that production decisions are being implemented [427]

forced distribution method Performance appraisal method that classifies employees into different performance categories based on a predetermined distribution [217]

forecast Facet of a long-range production plan that predicts future demand [417]

foreign currency exchange rate Value of a nation's currency as determined by market forces [520]

foreign direct investment Arrangement in which a firm buys or establishes tangible assets in another country [81]

franchise Arrangement in which a buyer (franchisee) purchases the right to sell the good or service of the seller (franchiser) [199]

free-rein style Managerial style in which managers typically serve as advisers to subordinates who are allowed to make decisions [259]

full-service merchant wholesaler Merchant wholesaler who provides credit, marketing, and merchandising services in addition to traditional buying and selling services [386]

functional departmentalization Departmentalization according to groups' functions or activities [155]

functional organization Form of business organization in which authority is determined by the relationships between group functions and activities [161]

futures contract Agreement to purchase specified amounts of a commodity at a given price on a set future date [570]

gainsharing program Group-based incentive plan that gives rewards for productivity improvements [221]

general (or **active**) **partner** Partner who actively manages a firm and who has unlimited liability for its debts [42]

General Agreement on Tariffs and Trade (GATT) International trade agreement to encourage the multilateral reduction or elimination of trade barriers [AP-10]

general partnership Business with two or more owners who share in both the operation of the firm and in financial responsibility for its debts [39]

generally accepted accounting principles (GAAP) Accepted rules and procedures governing the content and form of financial reports [505]

geographic departmentalization Departmentalization according to areas served by a business [155]

geographic variables Geographical units that may be considered in developing a segmentation strategy [303]

globalization Process by which the world economy is becoming a single interdependent system [66]

global perspective Company's approach to directing its marketing toward worldwide rather than local or regional markets [367]

goal Objective that a business hopes and plans to achieve [125]

goods production Produces tangible products, such as radios, newspapers, buses, and textbooks [410]

goodwill Amount paid for an existing business above the value of its other assets [512]

government bond Bond issued by the federal government [568]

grapevine Informal communication network that runs through an organization [168]

graphical user interface (GUI) Software that provides a visual display to help users select applications [487]

graphic rating scale Performance rating method using a numerical scale to rate performance along a set of dimensions [217]

gross domestic product (GDP) The value of all goods and services produced in a year by a nation's economy through domestic factors of production [19]

gross national product (GNP) The value of all goods and services produced by an economic system in a year regardless of where the factors of production are located [19]

gross profit (or **gross margin**) Revenues obtained from goods sold minus cost of goods sold [512]

group life insurance Insurance underwritten for a group as a whole rather than for each individual in it [605]

groupware Software that connects members of a group for shared e-mail distribution, electronic meetings, appointments, and group writing [473]

growth Increase in the amount of goods and services produced by a nation's resources [18]

growth rate of productivity Annual increase in a nation's output over the previous year [443]

guaranteed loans program Program in which the SBA guarantees to repay 75 to 85 percent of small-business commercial loans up to $750,000 [196]

hardware Physical components of a computer system [484]

Hawthorne effect Tendency for productivity to increase when workers believe they are receiving special attention from management [245]

health insurance Insurance covering losses resulting from medical and hospital expenses as well as income lost from injury or disease [605]

health maintenance organization (HMO) Organized health care system providing comprehensive care in return for fixed membership fees [607]

hierarchy of human needs model Theory of motivation describing five levels of human needs and arguing that basic needs must be fulfilled before people work to satisfy higher-level needs [246]

high-contact system Level of customer contact in which the customer is part of the system during service delivery [415]

hostile work environment Form of sexual harassment, deriving from off-color jokes, lewd comments, and so forth, that makes the work environment uncomfortable for some employees [227]

hub Central distribution outlet that controls all or most of a firm's distribution activities [401]

human relations Interactions between employers and employees and their attitudes toward one another [240]

human relations skills Skills in understanding and getting along with people [137]

human resource management (HRM) Set of organizational activities directed at attracting, developing, and maintaining an effective workforce [209]

hypermarket Very large product line retailer carrying a wide variety of unrelated products [389]

icon Small image in a GUI that enables users to select applications or functions [487]

illegal discrimination Discrimination against protected classes that causes them to be unfairly differentiated from others [224]

immediate participation loans program Program in which small businesses are loaned funds put up jointly by banks and the SBA [196]

implied authority Agent's authority, derived from business custom, to bind a principal to a certain course of action [AP-8]

implied warranty Warranty, dictated by law, based on the principle that products should fulfill advertised promises and serve the purposes for which they are manufactured and sold [AP-8]

import Product made or grown abroad but sold domestically [66]

importer Firm that buys products in foreign markets and then imports them for resale in its home country [79]

income statement (or **profit-and-loss statement**) Financial statement listing a firm's annual revenues and expenses so that a bottom line shows annual profit or loss [512]

independent agent Foreign individual or organization that agrees to represent an exporter's interests [80]

individual incentive plan Incentive-based pay plan that rewards individual performance on a real-time basis [220]

individual retirement account (IRA) Tax-deferred pension fund with which wage earners supplement other retirement funds [538]

industrial distribution Network of channel members involved in the flow of manufactured goods to industrial customers [383]

industrial goods Products purchased by companies to produce other products [296]

industrial market Organizational market consisting of firms that buy goods that are either converted into products or used during production [312]

Industrial Revolution Major mid-eighteenth-century change in production characterized by a shift to the factory system, mass production, and the specialization of labor [34]

industrial selling Personal selling situation in which products are sold to businesses, either for manufacturing other products or for resale [363]

industrial unionism Organizing of workers by industry rather than skill or occupation [272]

inelastic demand Demand for industrial products that is not largely affected by price changes [313]

inflation Phenomenon of widespread price increases throughout an economic system [17]

informal organization Network, unrelated to the firm's formal authority structure, of everyday social interactions among company employees [168]

information Meaningful, useful interpretation of data [470]

information management Internal operations for arranging a firm's information resources to support business performance and outcomes [470]

information managers Managers responsible for designing and implementing systems to gather, organize, and distribute information [470]

information resources Data and other information used by business [6]

information system (IS) System for transforming raw data into information that can be used in decision making [471]

initial public offering (IPO) First offer of shares in a closely held corporation to outside investors [51]

input device Part of the computer system that enters data into it [484]

input market Market in which firms buy resources from supplier households [8]

insider trading Illegal practice of using special knowledge about a firm for profit or gain [579]

institutional advertising Advertising promoting a firm's long-term image [361]

institutional investors Large investors, such as mutual funds and pension funds, that purchase large blocks of corporate stock [56]

institutional market Organizational market consisting of such nongovernmental buyers of goods and services as hospitals, churches, museums, and charitable organizations [313]

instructional-based program Training designed to impart new knowledge and information [215]

insurance company Nondeposit institution that invests funds collected as premiums charged for insurance coverage [536]

intangible asset Nonphysical asset, such as a patent or trademark, that has economic value in the form of expected benefit [512]

intangible personal property Property that cannot be seen but that exists by virtue of written documentation [AP-6]

intellectual property Property created through a person's creative activities [AP-6]

intensive distribution Strategy by which a product is distributed through as many channels as possible [385]

intentional tort Tort resulting from the deliberate actions of a party [AP-5]

interactive marketing Nonstore retailing that uses a Web site to provide real-time sales and customer service [394]

intermediary Individual or firm that helps to distribute a product [380]

intermediate goals Goals set for a period of one to five years into the future [127]

intermodal transportation Combined use of several different modes of transportation [400]

internal failures Reducible costs incurred during production and before bad products leave a plant [451]

internal recruiting Practice of considering present employees as candidates for job openings [212]

international competition Competitive marketing of domestic products against foreign products [299]

international firm Firm that conducts a significant portion of its business in foreign countries [79]

international law Set of cooperative agreements and guidelines established by countries to govern actions of individuals, businesses, and nations [AP-9]

International Monetary Fund (IMF) United Nations agency consisting of about 150 nations that have combined resources to promote stable exchange rates, provide temporary short-term loans, and serve other purposes [550]

international organizational structures Approaches to organizational structure developed in response to the need to manufacture, purchase, and sell in global markets [164]

Internet Global data communication network serving millions of computers with information on a wide array of topics and providing communication flows among certain private networks [473]

Internet service provider (ISP) Commercial firm that maintains a permanent connection to the Net and sells temporary connections to subscribers [473]

intranet Private network of internal Web sites and other sources of information available to a company's employees [475]

intrapreneuring Process of creating and maintaining the innovation and flexibility of a small-business environment within the confines of a large organization [168]

inventory Materials and goods that are held by a company but will be sold within the year [590]

inventory control In distribution, warehouse operation that tracks inventory on hand and ensures that an adequate supply is in stock at all times [398] In materials management, receiving, storing, handling, and counting of all raw materials, partly finished goods, and finished goods [428]

inventory turnover ratio Activity ratio measuring the average number of times that inventory is sold and restocked during the year [519]

investment bank Financial institution engaged in issuing and reselling new securities [558]

involuntary bankruptcy Bankruptcy proceedings initiated by the creditors of an indebted individual or organization [AP-9]

job analysis Systematic analysis of jobs in an organization [209]

job description Systematic evaluation of the duties, working conditions, tools, materials, and equipment related to the performance of a job [209]

job enrichment Method of increasing job satisfaction by adding one or more motivating factors to job activities [253]

job evaluation Methods for determining the relative worth of jobs in order to set compensation levels [219]

job redesign Method of increasing job satisfaction by designing a more satisfactory fit between workers and their jobs [254]

job satisfaction Degree of enjoyment that people derive from performing their jobs [241]

job specialization The process of identifying the specific jobs that need to be done and designating the people who will perform them [153]

job specification Description of the skills, abilities, and other credentials required by a job [209]

joint venture Strategic alliance in which the collaboration involves joint ownership of new venture [55]

just-in-time (JIT) production Production method that brings together all materials and parts needed at each production stage at the precise moment they are required [428]

key-person insurance Special form of business insurance designed to offset expenses entailed by the loss of key employees [607]

knowledge workers Skilled employees in high-tech industries; employees who use information and knowledge as raw materials and who rely on information technology to design new products or business systems [18, 478] Employee who is of value because of the knowledge that the employee possesses [229]

label Part of product packaging that identifies its name, manufacturer, and contents [336]

labor (or human resources) The physical and mental capabilities of people as they contribute to economic production [6]

Labor-Management Relations Act (Taft-Hartley Act) Federal law (1947) defining certain union practices as unfair and illegal [280]

Labor-Management Reporting and **Disclosure Act (Landrum-Griffin Act)** Federal law (1959) imposing regulations on internal union procedures, including elections of national leaders and filing of financial disclosure statements [281]

labor relations Process of dealing with employees who are represented by a union [270]

labor union A group of individuals working together to achieve shared job-related goals, such as higher pay, shorter working hours, more job security, greater benefits, or better working conditions [270]

law of demand Principle that buyers will purchase (demand) more of a product as its price drops and less as its price increases [11]

law of one price Principle holding that identical products should sell for the same price in all countries [548]

law of supply Principle that producers will offer (supply) more of a product for sale as its price rises and less as its price drops [11]

laws Codified rules of behavior enforced by a society [AP-1]

leadership Process of motivating others to work to meet specific objectives [258]

lecture or **discussion approach** Instructional-based training in which knowledge and information are descriptively presented [215]

letter of credit Bank promise, issued for a buyer, to pay a designated firm a certain amount of money if specified conditions are met [538]

level of productivity Dollar value of goods and services relative to the resources used to produce them [443]

leverage Ability to finance an investment through borrowed funds [518]

liability Debt owed by a firm to an outside organization or individual [509]

liability insurance Insurance covering losses resulting from damage to people or property when the insured is judged responsible [605]

licensed brand Use of an established brand name by purchasing the right from the organization or individual who owns it [335]

licensing arrangement Arrangement in which firms choose foreign individuals or organizations to manufacture or market their products in another country [81]

life insurance Insurance paying benefits to the policyholder's survivors [605]

limit order Order authorizing the purchase of a stock only if its price is equal to or less than a specified amount [577]

limited liability Legal principle holding investors liable for a firm's debts only to the limits of their personal investments in it [44]

limited liability corporation, or **LLC** Hybrid of a publicly held corporation and a partnership in which owners are taxed as partners but enjoy the benefits of limited liability [47]

limited partner Partner who does not share in a firm's management and is liable for its debts only to the limit of the said partner's investment [42]

limited partnership Type of partnership consisting of limited partners and an active or managing partner [42]

limited-function merchant wholesaler Merchant wholesaler who provides a limited range of services [386]

line authority Organizational structure in which authority flows in a direct chain of command from the top of the company to the bottom [160]

line department Department directly linked to the production and sales of a specific product [160]

line of credit Standing arrangement in which a lender agrees to make available a specified amount of funds upon the borrower's request [593]

liquidity Ease with which an asset can be converted into cash [510]

liquidity ratio Solvency ratio measuring a firm's ability to pay its immediate debts [517]

load fund Mutual fund in which investors are charged sales commissions when they buy in or sell out [570]

local area network (LAN) Network of computers and workstations, usually within a company, that are linked together by cable [492]

local content law Law requiring that products sold in a particular country be at least partly made there [85]

local development companies (LDCs) program Program in which the SBA works with local for-profit or not-for-profit organizations seeking to boost a community's economy [196]

local union (local) Union organized at the level of a single company, plant, or small geographic region [278]

lockout Management tactic whereby workers are denied access to the employer's workplace [286]

long-term goals Goals set for an extended time, typically five years or more into the future [127]

long-term liability Debt that is not due for more than one year [512]

low-contact system Level of customer contact in which the customer need not be a part of the system to receive the service [415]

M-1 Measure of the money supply that includes only the most liquid (spendable) forms of money [533]

M-2 Measure of the money supply that includes all the components of M-1 plus the forms of money that can be easily converted into spendable form [533]

mail order (or **catalog marketing**) Form of nonstore retailing in which customers place orders for catalog merchandise received through the mail [392]

main memory Part of the computer CPU that houses the memory of programs it needs to operate [485]

management Process of planning, organizing, directing, and controlling an organization's resources to achieve its goals [132]

management advisory services Specialized accounting services to help managers resolve a variety of business problems [505]

management by objectives (MBO) Set of procedures involving both managers and subordinates in setting goals and evaluating progress [251]

management consultant Independent outside specialist hired to help managers solve business problems [198]

management information system (MIS) System used for transforming data into information for use in decision making [483]

managerial (or **management**) **accounting system** Field of accounting that serves internal users of a company's financial information [503]

managerial style Pattern of behavior that a manager exhibits in dealing with subordinates [259]

manufacturing resource planning (MRP II) Advanced version of MRP that ties together all parts of an organization into its production activities [429]

margin Percentage of the total sales price that a buyer must put up to place an order for stock or futures contracts [571]

market Mechanism for exchange between buyers and sellers of a particular good or service [8]

market economy Economy in which individuals control production and allocation decisions through supply and demand [8]

market index Summary of price trends in a specific industry and/or the stock market as a whole [575]

marketing The process of planning and executing the conception, pricing, promotion, and distribution of ideas, goods, and services to create exchanges that satisfy individual and organizational objectives [296]

marketing concept Idea that a business must focus on identifying and satisfying consumer wants in order to be profitable [36]

marketing manager Manager who plans and implements the marketing activities that result in the transfer of products from producer to consumer [299]

marketing mix The combination of product, pricing, promotion, and distribution strategies used to market products [300]

marketing plan Detailed and focused strategy for gearing marketing efforts to meet consumer needs and wants [299]

marketing research The study of consumer needs and wants and the ways in which sellers can best meet them [306]

market order Order to buy or sell a security at the market price prevailing at the time the order is placed [576]

market price (or **equilibrium price**) Profit-maximizing price at which the quantity of goods demanded and the quantity of goods supplied are equal [12]

market segmentation Process of dividing a market into categories of customer types [302]

market share Company's percentage of total market sales for a specific product [337]

market value Current price of a share of stock in the stock market [559]

markup Amount added to an item's cost to sell it at a profit [338]

mass-customization Flexible production process that generates customized products in high volumes at low cost [476]

master limited partnership (MLP) Form of organization that sells shares to investors who receive profits and pay taxes on individual income from profits [42]

master production schedule Schedule showing which products will be produced, when production will take place, and what resources will be used [425]

material handling Warehouse operation involving the transportation, arrangement, and orderly retrieval of goods in inventory [399]

material requirements planning (MRP) Production method in which a bill of materials is used to ensure that the right amounts of materials are delivered to the right place at the right time [428]

materials management Planning, organizing, and controlling the flow of materials from design through distribution of finished goods [427]

matrix structure Organizational structure in which teams are formed and team members report to two or more managers [163]

media mix Combination of advertising media chosen to carry a message about a product [360]

mediation Method of resolving a labor dispute in which a third party suggests, but does not impose, a settlement [286]

merchandise inventory Cost of merchandise that has been acquired for sale to customers and is still on hand [511]

merchant wholesaler Independent wholesaler who takes legal possession of goods produced by a variety of manufacturers and then resells them to other businesses [386]

merger The union of two corporations to form a new corporation [56]

merit pay plan Performance-based pay plan basing part of compensation on employee merit [220]

middle managers Managers responsible for implementing the strategies, policies, and decisions made by top managers [135]

minority enterprise small-business investment company (MESBIC) Federally sponsored company that specializes in financing businesses that are owned and operated by minorities [195]

missionary selling Personal selling tasks in which salespeople promote their firms and products rather than try to close sales [364]

mission statement Organization's statement of how it will achieve its purpose in the environment in which it conducts its business [126]

mixed market economy Economic system featuring characteristics of both planned and market economies [10]

modem Device that provides a computer-to-computer link over telephone wires [493]

monetary policy Government economic policies that determine the size of a nation's money supply; policies by which the Federal Reserve manages the nation's money supply and interest rates [23, 543]

money Any object that is portable, divisible, durable, and stable and serves as a medium of exchange, a store of value, and a unit of account [532]

money market mutual fund Fund of short-term, low-risk financial securities purchased with the assets of investor-owners pooled by a nonbank institution [534]

monopolistic competition Market or industry characterized by numerous buyers and relatively numerous sellers trying to differentiate their products from those of competitors [15]

monopoly Market or industry in which there is only one producer, which can therefore set the prices of its products [16]

morale Overall attitude that employees have toward their workplace [241]

motivation The set of forces that cause people to behave in certain ways [244]

multilevel marketing Distribution channel consisting of self-employed distributors who receive commissions for selling products to customers and for recruiting new distributors [394]

multimedia communication system Connected network of communication appliances (such as faxes or TVs) that may be linked to forms of mass media (such as print publications or TV programming) [489]

multinational firm Firm that designs, produces, and markets products in many nations [80]

multinational or **transnational corporation** Form of corporation spanning national boundaries [50]

municipal bond Bond issued by a state or local government [568]

mutual fund Company that pools investments from individuals and organizations to purchase a portfolio of stocks, bonds, and short-term securities [570]

mutual savings bank Financial institution whose depositors are owners sharing in its profits [536]

Nasdaq Composite Index Value-weighted market index that includes all Nasdaq-listed companies, both domestic and foreign [576]

National Association of Securities Dealers Automated Quotation (Nasdaq) system Organization of over-the-counter dealers who own, buy, and sell their own securities over a network of electronic communications [564]

national brand Brand-name product produced by, widely distributed by, and carrying the name of a manufacturer [335]

national competitive advantage International competitive advantage stemming from a combination of factor conditions, demand conditions, related and supporting industries, and firm strategies, structures, and rivalries [73]

national debt Total amount that a nation owes its creditors [22]

National Labor Relations Act (Wagner Act) Federal law (1935) protecting the rights of workers to form unions, bargain collectively, and engage in strikes to achieve their goals [279]

National Labor Relations Board (NLRB) Federal agency established by the National Labor Relations Act to enforce its provisions [280]

natural monopoly Industry in which one company can most efficiently supply all needed goods or services [16]

negligence Conduct falling below legal standards for protecting others against unreasonable risk

net income (or **net profit** or **net earnings**) Gross profit minus operating expenses and income taxes [513]

networking Interactions among businesspeople for the purpose of discussing mutual problems and opportunities and perhaps pooling resources [198]

no-load fund Mutual fund in which investors pay no sales commissions when they buy in or sell out [570]

North American Free Trade Agreement (NAFTA) Agreement to gradually eliminate tariffs and other trade barriers between the United States, Canada, and Mexico [AP-10]

Norris-LaGuardia Act Federal law (1932) limiting the ability of courts to issue injunctions prohibiting certain union activities [279]

observation Market research technique that involves simply watching and recording consumer behavior [308]

obstructionist stance Approach to social responsibility that involves doing as little as possible and may involve attempts to deny or cover up violations [112]

Occupational Safety and Health Act of 1970 (OSHA) Federal law setting and enforcing guidelines for protecting workers from unsafe conditions and potential health hazards in the workplace [227]

odd-even pricing Psychological pricing tactic based on the premise that customers prefer prices not stated in even dollar amounts [343]

odd lot Purchase or sale of stock in fractions of round lots [577]

off-price store Bargain retailer that buys excess inventories from high-quality manufacturers and sells them at discounted prices [390]

oligopoly Market or industry characterized by a handful of (generally large) sellers with the power to influence the prices of their products [15]

on-the-job training Work-based training, sometimes informal, conducted while an employee is in an actual work situation [214]

open-book credit Form of trade credit in which sellers ship merchandise on faith that payment will be forthcoming [592]

open-market operations The Federal Reserve's sales and purchases of securities in the open market [544]

operating expenses Costs, other than the cost of goods sold, incurred in producing a good or service [513]

operating income Gross profit minus operating expenses [513]

operational plans Plans setting short-term targets for daily, weekly, or monthly performance [130]

operations control Process of monitoring production performance by comparing results with plans [427]

operations (or **production**) **management** Systematic direction and control of the processes that transform resources into finished products [413]

operations (or **production**) **managers** Managers responsible for production, inventory, and quality control of goods and services [414]

operations process Set of methods used in the production of a good or service [414]

order fulfillment All activities involved in completing a sales transaction, beginning with making the sale and ending with on-time delivery to the customer [400]

order processing Personal selling task in which salespeople receive orders and see to their handling and delivery [364]

organization chart Diagram depicting a company's structure and showing employees where they fit into its operations [152]

organizational analysis Process of analyzing a firm's strengths and weaknesses [128]

organizational stakeholders Those groups, individuals, and organizations that are directly affected by the practices of an organization and, therefore, have a stake in its performance [101]

organizational structure Specification of the jobs to be done within an organization and the ways in which they relate to one another [151]

organizing Management process of determining how best to arrange an organization's resources and activities into a coherent structure [133]

orientation Process of introducing new employees to the organization so that they can more quickly become effective contributors [214]

output device Part of a computer system that presents results, either visually or in printed form [485]

output market Market in which firms supply goods and services in response to demand on the part of households [8]

over-the-counter (OTC) market Organization of securities dealers formed to trade stock outside the formal institutional setting of the organized stock exchanges [564]

owners' equity Amount of money that owners would receive if they sold all of a firm's assets and paid all of its liabilities [509]

packaging Physical container in which a product is sold, advertised, or protected [336]

paid-in capital Additional money, above proceeds from stock sale, paid directly to a firm by its owners [512]

par value Face value of a share of stock, set by the issuing company's board of directors [559]

participative management and **empowerment** Method of increasing job satisfaction by giving employees a voice in the management of their jobs and the company [252]

patent Exclusive legal right to use and license a manufactured item or substance, manufacturing process, or object design [AP-7]

pay survey Method used to obtain information about compensation paid to employees by other employers [219]

penetration pricing Setting an initial low price to establish a new product in the market [342]

pension fund Nondeposit pool of funds managed to provide retirement income for its members [536]

per capita income Average income per person in a country [67]

performance appraisal Formal evaluation of an employee's job performance in order to determine the degree to which the employee is performing effectively [216]

performance quality The performance features offered by a product [447]

personal selling Promotional tool in which a salesperson communicates one-to-one with potential customers [362]

persuasive advertising Advertising strategy that tries to influence consumers to buy one company's products instead of those of its rivals [355]

physical distribution Activities needed to move a product efficiently from manufacturer to consumer [396]

physical resources Tangible things organizations use in the conduct of their business [6]

picketing Labor action in which workers publicize their grievances at the entrance to an employer's facility [286]

piece-rate incentive plan Incentive-based pay plan that provides payment for each unit produced [220]

planned economy Economy that relies on a centralized government to control all or most factors of production and to make all or most production and allocation decisions [8]

planning Management process of determining what an organization needs to do and how best to get it done [132]

pledging accounts receivable Using accounts receivable as loan collateral [592]

point-of-purchase (POP) display Sales promotion technique in which product displays are located in certain areas to stimulate purchase [365]

point-of-sale (POS) terminal Electronic device that allows customers to pay for retail purchases with debit cards [545]

point-of-service (POS) plan Healthcare plan allowing members to select primary-care doctors who may provide services or refer patients to other plan providers [607]

positioning Process of establishing an identifiable product image in the minds of consumers [353]

preferred provider organization (PPO) Arrangement whereby selected professional providers offer services at reduced rates and permit thorough review of their service recommendations [607]

preferred stock Stock that guarantees its holders fixed dividends and priority claims over assets but no corporate voting rights [51]

Pregnancy Discrimination Act of 1979 Federal law forbidding discrimination against women who are pregnant [225]

premium In sales promotion, technique in which offers of free or reduced-price items are used to stimulate purchases [366] In risk management, fee paid by a policyholder for insurance coverage [603]

prepaid expense Expense, such as prepaid rent, that is paid before the upcoming period in which it is due [511]

presentation graphics software Applications that enable users to create visual presentations that can include animation and sound [488]

price-earnings ratio Current price of a stock divided by the firm's current annual earnings per share [572]

price leader Dominant firm that establishes product prices that other companies follow [341]

price lining Setting a limited number of prices for certain categories of products [342]

price skimming Setting an initial high price to cover new product costs and generate a profit [341]

pricing Process of determining what a company will receive in exchange for its products [336]

pricing objectives Goals that producers hope to attain in pricing products for sale [336]

primary data Data developed through new research [307]

primary securities market Market in which new stocks and bonds are bought and sold [558]

prime rate Interest rate available to a bank's most creditworthy customers [536]

principal Individual or organization authorizing an agent to act on its behalf [AP-7]

private accountant Salaried accountant hired by a business to carry out its day-to-day financial activities [506]

private brand (or **private label**) Brand-name product that a wholesaler or retailer has commissioned from a manufacturer [335]

private enterprise Economic system that allows individuals to pursue their own interests without undue governmental restriction [12]

private pension plan Prearranged company pensions provided to retired employees [223]

private property rights The right to buy, own, use, and sell almost any form of property [14]

private warehouse Warehouse owned by and providing storage for a single company [397]

privatization Process of converting government enterprises into privately owned companies [10]

proactive stance Approach to social responsibility by which a company actively seeks opportunities to contribute to the well-being of groups and individuals in its social environment [113]

process departmentalization Departmentalization according to production processes used to create a good or service [155]

process layout Spatial arrangement of production activities that groups equipment and people according to function [420]

process variation Variation in products arising from changes in production inputs [449]

product Good, service, or idea that is marketed to fill consumer needs and wants [300]

product adaptation Product modified to have greater appeal in foreign markets [333]

product departmentalization Departmentalization according to specific products being created [154]

product differentiation Creation of a product or product image that differs enough from existing products to attract consumers [301]

product extension Existing, unmodified product that is marketed globally [333]

production era Period during the early twentieth century in which U.S. business focused primarily on improving productivity and manufacturing efficiency [35]

productivity Measure of economic growth that compares how much a system produces with the resources needed to produce it [19]

product layout Spatial arrangement of production activities designed to move resources through a smooth, fixed sequence of steps [422]

product liability tort Tort in which a company is responsible for injuries caused by its products [AP-5]

product life cycle (PLC) Series of stages in a product's profit-producing life [331]

product line Group of similar products intended for a similar group of buyers who will use them in similar ways [328]

product mix Group of products that a firm makes available for sale [328]

product use variables Consumer characteristics based on the ways in which a product is used, the brand loyalty it enjoys, and the reasons for which it is purchased [306]

professional corporation Form of ownership allowing professionals to take advantage of corporate benefits while granting them limited business liability and unlimited professional liability [48]

profit center Separate company unit responsible for its own costs and profits [154]

profit sharing Group-based incentive plan in which employees are paid a share of company profits [221]

profitability ratio Financial ratio for measuring a firm's potential earnings [517]

profits The difference between a business's revenues and its expenses [5]

program Set of instructions used by a computer to perform specified activities [485]

program trading Large purchase or sale of a group of stocks, often triggered by computerized trading programs that can be launched without human supervision or control [579]

promissory note Form of trade credit in which buyers sign promise-to-pay agreements before merchandise is shipped [592]

promotion Aspect of the marketing mix concerned with the most effective techniques for selling a product [352]

promotional mix Combination of tools used to promote a product [354]

property Anything of value to which a person or business has sole right of ownership [AP-6]

property insurance Insurance covering losses resulting from physical damage to or loss of the insured's real estate or personal property [605]

prospecting Step in the personal selling process in which salespeople identify potential customers [364]

prospectus Registration statement filed with the SEC before the issuance of a new security [579]

protected class Set of individuals who by nature of one or more common characteristics are protected by law from discrimination on the basis of any of those characteristics [224]

protectionism Practice of protecting domestic business against foreign competition [84]

protection plan Mandated coverage protecting employees whose income is threatened or reduced by illness, disability, death, or retirement [222]

proxy Authorization granted by shareholders for someone else to vote their shares [52]

psychographic variables Consumer characteristics, such as lifestyles, opinions, interests, and attitudes, that may be considered in developing a segmentation strategy [304]

psychological contract Set of expectations held by employees concerning what they will contribute to an organization (referred to as *contributions*) and what the organization will in return provide the employees (referred to as *inducements*) [240]

psychological pricing Pricing tactic that takes advantage of the fact that consumers do not always respond rationally to stated prices [342]

public relations Company-influenced publicity directed at building good will between an organization and potential customers [367]

public warehouse Independently owned and operated warehouse that stores goods for many firms [397]

publicity Promotional tool in which information about a company or product is created and transmitted by general mass media [366]

publicly held (or **public**) **corporation** Corporation whose stock is widely held and available for sale to the general public [46]

pull strategy Promotional strategy designed to appeal directly to consumers who will demand a product from retailers [354]

punitive damages Fines imposed over and above any actual losses suffered by a plaintiff [AP-5]

purchasing Acquisition of the raw materials and services that a firm needs to produce its products [427]

pure competition Market or industry characterized by numerous small firms producing an identical product [14]

pure risk Risk involving only the possibility of loss or no loss [600]

push strategy Promotional strategy designed to encourage wholesalers or retailers to market products to consumers [354]

qualifying Step in the personal selling process in which salespeople determine whether prospects have the authority and ability to pay [364]

quality A product's fitness for use plus its success in offering features that consumers want [440]

quality control Management of the production process designed to manufacture goods or supply services that meet specific quality standards [429]

quality/cost study Method of improving quality by identifying current costs and areas with the greatest cost-saving potential [451]

quality improvement (QI) team TQM tool in which groups of employees work together to improve quality [451]

quality ownership Principle of total quality management that holds that quality belongs to each person who creates it while performing a job [448]

quality reliability Consistency of a product's quality from unit to unit [447]

quid pro quo harassment Form of sexual harassment in which sexual favors are requested in return for job-related benefits [227]

quota Restriction on the number of products of a certain type that can be imported into a country [83]

rack jobber Limited-function merchant wholesaler who sets up and maintains display racks in retail stores [386]

rational motives Reasons for purchasing a product that are based on a logical evaluation of product attributes [310]

real gross national product (real GNP) Gross national product adjusted for inflation and changes in the value of a country's currency [19]

recession Period characterized by decreases in employment, income, and production [18]

recruiting Process of attracting qualified persons to apply for open jobs [212]

registered bond Bond bearing the name of the holder and registered with the issuing company [569]

regulatory (or administrative) law Law made by the authority of administrative agencies [AP-1]

reinforcement Theory that behavior can be encouraged or discouraged by means of rewards or punishments [251]

reintroduction Process of reviving for new markets products that are obsolete in older ones [333]

relationship marketing Marketing strategy that emphasizes lasting relationships with customers and suppliers [296]

reminder advertising Advertising strategy that tries to keep a product's name in the consumer's mind [356]

replacement chart Listing of each managerial position, who occupies it, how long that person will likely stay in the job, and who is qualified as a replacement [210]

reseller market Organizational market consisting of intermediaries who buy and resell finished goods [313]

reserve requirement Percentage of its deposits that a bank must hold in cash or on deposit with the Federal Reserve [544]

responsibility Duty to perform an assigned task [156]

retailer Intermediary who sells products directly to consumers [380]

retail selling Personal selling situation in which products are sold for buyers' personal or household use [363]

retained earnings Earnings retained by a firm for its use rather than paid as dividends [512]

return on equity Profitability ratio measuring income earned for each dollar invested [518]

revenues Funds that flow into a business from the sale of goods or services [512]

reverse discrimination Practice of discriminating against well-represented groups by overhiring members of underrepresented groups [226]

revolving credit agreement Arrangement in which a lender agrees to make funds available on demand and on a continuing basis [593]

right-to-work laws Statutes making it illegal to require union membership as a condition of employment [280]

risk Uncertainty about future events and their desirable or negative outcomes [600]

risk avoidance Practice of avoiding risk by declining or ceasing to participate in an activity [603]

risk control Practice of minimizing the frequency or severity of losses from risky activities [603]

risk management Process of conserving the firm's earning power and assets by reducing the threat of losses due to uncontrollable events [601]

risk retention Practice of covering a firm's losses with its own funds [603]

risk–return relationship Principle that, whereas safer investments tend to offer lower returns, riskier investments tend to offer higher returns [598]

risk transfer Practice of transferring a firm's risk to another firm [603]

robotics Combination of computers and industrial robots for use in manufacturing operations [484]

round lot Purchase or sale of stock in units of 100 shares [577]

royalty Payment made to a license holder in return for the right to market the licenser's product [81]

salary Compensation in the form of money paid for discharging the responsibilities of a job [219]

sales agent/broker Independent intermediary who usually represents many manufacturers and sells to wholesalers or retailers [381]

sales commission Individual incentive plan rewarding employees with a percentage of sales volume that they generate [221]

sales office Office maintained by a manufacturer as a contact point with its customers [383]

sales promotion Short-term promotional activity designed to stimulate consumer buying or cooperation from distributors and sales agents [365]

savings and loan association (S&L) Financial institution accepting deposits and making loans primarily for home mortgages [536]

S corporation Hybrid of a closely held corporation and a partnership; organized and operated like a corporation but treated as a partnership for tax purposes [47]

scrambled merchandising Retail practice of carrying any product that is expected to sell well regardless of a store's original product offering [389]

search engine Tool that searches Web pages containing the user's search terms and then displays that match in certain degrees [475]

secondary data Data readily available as a result of previous research [306]

secondary securities market Market in which stocks and bonds are traded [559]

secured bond Bond backed by pledges of assets to the bondholders [569]

secured loan Loan for which the borrower must provide collateral [592]

securities Stocks and bonds representing secured, or asset-based, claims by investors against issuers [558]

Securities and Exchange Commission (SEC) Federal agency that administers U.S. securities laws to protect the investing public and maintain smoothly functioning markets [558]

securities investment dealer (broker) Nondeposit institution that buys and sells stocks and bonds both for investors and for its own accounts [536]

selective credit controls Federal Reserve authority to set both margin requirements for consumer stock purchases and credit rules for other consumer purchases [544]

selective distribution Strategy by which a company uses only wholesalers and retailers who give special attention to specific products [385]

serial bond Bond retired when the issuer redeems portions of the issue at different preset dates [569]

Service Corps of Retired Executives (SCORE) SBA program in which retired executives work with small businesses on a volunteer basis [198]

service flow analysis Method for analyzing a service by showing the flow of processes that constitute it [424]

service operations Produces tangible and intangible services, such as entertainment, transportation, and education [410]

service package Tangible and intangible features that characterize a service product [331]

service process design Three aspects (process selection, worker requirements, and facilities requirements) of developing a service product [331]

services Intangible products, such as time, expertise, or an activity, that can be purchased [296]

sexual harassment Practice or instance of making unwelcome sexual advances in the workplace [227]

shopping agent (or **e-agent**) E-intermediary (middleman) in the Internet distribution channel who assists users in finding products and prices but who does not take possession of products [387]

shopping good/service Moderately expensive, infrequently purchased product [327]

shop steward Union employee who acts as liaison between union members and supervisors [278]

shortage Situation in which quantity demanded exceeds quantity supplied [12]

short sale Stock sale in which an investor borrows securities from a broker to be sold and then replaced at a specified future date [578]

short-term goals Goals set for the very near future, typically less than one year [127]

simple ranking method Performance appraisal method that ranks employees from best to worst [217]

sinking fund provision Method for retiring bonds whereby the issuer puts enough money into a banking account to redeem the bonds at maturity [569]

skill-based or **knowledge-based pay** Performance-based pay plan rewarding employees for acquiring new skills or knowledge [220]

slowdown Labor action in which workers perform jobs at a slower than normal pace [286]

small business Independently owned and managed business that does not dominate its market [176]

Small Business Administration (SBA) Federal agency charged with assisting small businesses [176]

Small Business Development Center (SBDC) SBA program designed to consolidate information from various disciplines and make it available to small businesses [198]

Small Business Institute (SBI) SBA program in which college and university students and instructors work with small-business owners to help solve specific problems [198]

small-business investment company (SBIC) A government-regulated investment company that borrows money from the SBA to invest in or lend to a small business [195]

smart card Credit-card-size computer programmed with electronic money [545]

social audit Systematic analysis of a firm's success in using funds earmarked for meeting its social responsibility goals [114]

social responsibility The attempt of a business to balance its commitments to groups and individuals in its environment, including customers, other businesses, employees, and investors [101]

social security Mandated federal retirement program [222]

socialism Planned economic system in which the government owns and operates only selected major sources of production [11]

software Programs that instruct a computer in what to do [485]

sole proprietorship Business owned and usually operated by one person who is responsible for all of its debts [38]

solvency ratio Financial ratio, either short- or long-term, for estimating the risk in investing in a firm [517]

span of control Number of people supervised by one manager [159]

specialty good/service Expensive, rarely purchased product [327]

specialty store Small retail store carrying one product line or category of related products [390]

speculative risk Risk involving the possibility of gain or loss [600]

speed to market Strategy of introducing new products to respond quickly to customer or market changes [330]

spin-off Strategy of setting up one or more corporate units as new, independent corporations [57]

stability Condition in which the balance between the money available in an economy and the goods produced in it are growing at about the same rate [17]

staff authority Authority based on expertise that usually involves advising line managers [160]

staff members Advisors and counselors who aid line departments in making decisions but do not have the authority to make final decisions [160]

Standard & Poor's Composite Index Market index based on the performance of 400 industrial firms, 40 utilities, 40 financial institutions, and 20 transportation companies [576]

standardization Use of standard and uniform components in the production process [427]

statement of cash flows Financial statement describing a firm's yearly cash receipts and cash payments [514]

statistical process control (SPC) Methods for gathering data to analyze variations in production activities to see when adjustments are needed [448]

statutory law Law created by constitutions or by federal, state, or local legislative acts [AP-1]

stock Share of ownership in a corporation [51]

stock exchange Organization of individuals formed to provide an institutional setting in which stock can be traded [561]

stockholder (or shareholder) Owner of shares of stock in a corporation [50]

stop order Order authorizing the sale of a stock if its price falls to or below a specified level [577]

storage warehouse Warehouse providing storage for extended periods of time [397]

strategic alliance (or **joint venture**) Arrangement in which a company finds a foreign partner to contribute approximately half of the resources needed to establish and operate a new business in the partner's country [55, 81]

strategic goals Long-term goals derived directly from a firm's mission statement [127]

strategic plans Plans reflecting decisions about resource allocations, company priorities, and steps needed to meet strategic goals [129]

strategy formulation Creation of a broad program for defining and meeting an organization's goals [127]

strict product liability Principle that liability can result not from a producer's negligence but from a defect in the product itself [AP-6]

strike Labor action in which employees temporarily walk off the job and refuse to work [285]

strikebreaker Worker hired as permanent or temporary replacement for a striking employee [286]

subsidy Government payment to help a domestic business compete with foreign firms [84]

substitute product Product that is dissimilar to those of competitors but that can fulfill the same need [299]

supermarket Large product line retailer offering a variety of food and food-related items in specialized departments [389]

supplier selection Process of finding and selecting suppliers from whom to buy [427]

supply The willingness and ability of producers to offer a good or service for sale [11]

supply curve Graph showing how many units of a product will be supplied (offered for sale) at different prices [12]

surplus Situation in which quantity supplied exceeds quantity demanded [12]

survey Market research technique using a questionnaire that is either mailed to individuals or used as the basis of interviews [308]

sympathy strike (or **secondary strike**) Strike in which one union strikes to support action initiated by another [286]

syndicated selling e-commerce practice whereby a Web site offers other Web sites commissions for referring customers [387]

synthetic process Production process in which resources are combined to create finished products [414]

system architecture Location of a computer system's elements (data-entry and data-processing operations, database, data output, and computer staff) [491]

systematic job rotation and **transfer** Work-based training in which employees are systematically moved from one job to another so that they can learn a wider array of tasks and skills [215]

system operations personnel Information-systems employees who run a company's computer equipment [482]

system program Software that tells the computer what resources to use and how to use them [486]

tactical plans Generally short-range plans concerned with implementing specific aspects of a company's strategic plans [129]

tall organizational structure Characteristic of centralized companies with multiple layers of management and relatively narrow spans of control [158]

tangible personal property Any movable item that can be owned, bought, sold, or leased [AP-6]

tangible real property Land and anything attached to it [AP-6]

target market Group of people that has similar wants and needs and that can be expected to show interest in the same products [302]

tariff Tax levied on imported products [83]

technical skills Skills needed to perform specialized tasks [137]

telecommuting Form of flextime that allows people to perform some or all of a job away from standard office settings [256]

telemarketing Nonstore retailing in which the telephone is used to sell directly to consumers [392]

tender offer Offer to buy shares made by a prospective buyer directly to a target corporation's shareholders, who then make individual decisions about whether to sell [45]

Theory X Theory of motivation holding that people are naturally irresponsible and uncooperative [246]

Theory Y Theory of motivation holding that people are naturally responsible, growth oriented, self-motivated, and interested in being productive [246]

time deposit Bank funds that cannot be withdrawn without notice or transferred by check [534]

time management skills Skills associated with the productive use of time [139]

Title VII of the Civil Rights Act of 1964 Federal law forbidding employment discrimination on the basis of race, color, religious beliefs, sex, or national origin [224]

top managers Managers responsible to the board of directors and stockholders for a firm's overall performance and effectiveness [135]

tort Civil injury to people, property, or reputation for which compensation must be paid

total quality management (TQM) (or **quality assurance**) The sum of all activities involved in getting high-quality products into the marketplace [446]

trade acceptance Trade draft that has been signed by the buyer [592]

trade credit Granting of credit by one firm to another [592]

trade deficit Situation in which a country's imports exceed its exports, creating a negative balance of trade [74]

trade draft Form of trade credit in which buyers must sign statements of payment terms attached to merchandise by sellers [592]

trade show Sales promotion technique in which various members of an industry gather to display, demonstrate, and sell products [366]

trade surplus Situation in which a country's exports exceed its imports, creating a positive balance of trade [74]

trademark Exclusive legal right to use a brand name or symbol [AP-7]

transaction processing systems (TPS) Information-processing applications for routine, day-to-day business activities involving well-defined processing steps [480]

trial court General court that hears cases not specifically assigned to another court [AP-3]

trust services Bank management of an individual's investments, payments, or estate [538]

two-factor theory Theory of motivation holding that job satisfaction depends on two types of factors, hygiene and motivation [247]

unemployment Level of joblessness among people actively seeking work [18]

unemployment insurance Mandated coverage protecting employees who are laid off [222]

unethical behavior Behavior that does not conform to generally accepted social norms concerning beneficial and harmful actions [95]

Uniform Commercial Code (UCC) Body of standardized laws governing the rights of buyers and sellers in transactions [AP-8]

union shop Workplace in which workers must join a union within a specified period after being hired [280]

unlimited liability Legal principle holding owners responsible for paying off all debts of a business [39]

unsecured loan Loan for which collateral is not required [593]

utility A product's ability to satisfy a human want [413]

validation Process of determining the predictive value of information [213]

value-added analysis Process of evaluating all work activities, materials flows, and paperwork to determine the value they add for customers [448]

variable cost Cost that changes with the quantity of a product produced or sold [338]

venture capital Outside equity financing provided in return for part ownership of the borrowing firm [600]

venture capital company Group of small investors that invest money in companies with rapid growth potential [195]

vestibule training Worked-based training conducted in a simulated environment away from the work site [215]

video marketing Nonstore retailing to consumers via standard and cable television [395]

voice mail Computer-based system for receiving and delivering incoming telephone calls [473]

voluntary arbitration Method of resolving a labor dispute in which both parties agree to submit to the judgment of a neutral party [287]

voluntary bankruptcy Bankruptcy proceedings initiated by an indebted individual or organization [AP-9]

wage reopener clause Clause allowing wage rates to be renegotiated during the life of a labor contract [284]

wages Compensation in the form of money paid for time worked [218]

warehouse club (or **wholesale club**) Bargain retailer offering large discounts on brand-name merchandise to customers who have paid annual membership fees [390]

warehousing Physical distribution operation concerned with the storage of goods [396]

warranty Seller's promise to stand by its products or services if a problem occurs after the sale [AP-8]

Web server Dedicated workstation customized for managing, maintaining, and supporting Web sites [474]

wellness program Benefit in the form of programs designed to help employees from becoming sick [223]

whistle-blower Employee who detects and tries to put an end to a company's unethical, illegal, or socially irresponsible actions by publicizing them [110]

wholesaler Intermediary who sells products to other businesses for resale to final consumers [380]

wide area network (WAN) Network of computers and workstations located far from one another and linked by telephone wires or by satellite [492]

wildcat strike Strike that is unauthorized by the strikers' union [286]

word-processing program Applications program that allows computers to store, edit, and print letters and numbers for documents created by users [488]

work sharing (or **job sharing**) Method of increasing job satisfaction by allowing two or more people to share a single full-time job [254]

work-based program Training technique that ties training and development activities directly to task performance [214]

workers' compensation coverage Coverage provided by a firm to employees for medical expenses, loss of wages, and rehabilitation costs resulting from job-related injuries or disease [605]

workers' compensation insurance Legally required insurance covering workers who are injured or become ill on the job [223]

workforce diversity Range of workers' attitudes, values, and behaviors that differ by gender, race, and ethnicity [228]

working capital Difference between a firm's current assets and current liabilities; liquid current assets out of which a firm can pay current debts [517, 591]

World Bank United Nations agency that provides a limited scope of financial services, such as funding national improvements in undeveloped countries [550]

World Wide Web Subsystem of computers providing access to the Internet and offering multimedia and linking capabilities [474]

yellow-dog contract Illegal contract clause requiring workers to begin and continue employment without union affiliation

Notes, Sources, and Credits

Reference Notes

Chapter 1

[1]See Robert A. Collinge and Ronald M. Ayers, *Economics by Design: Principles and Issues,* 2nd ed. (Upper Saddle River, NJ: Prentice Hall, 2000) 41–42; Michael J. Mandel, "The New Economy," *Business Week,* January 31, 2000, 73–77.
[2]Go also to Rick Kuhn. "Marxism Page." <www.anu.edu.au/polsci/marx/>. (March 8, 2000).
[3]Also go to Oracle Corp. "Partner Solutions." <www.oracle.com/partners/content.html>. (March 8, 2000); Ford Motor Co. "Inside the Company Newsroom." <www.ford.com/default.asp?pageid=106&storyid=695>. (March 8, 2000).
[4]See Karl E. Case and Ray C. Fair, *Principles of Economics,* 5th ed. (Upper Saddle River, NJ: Prentice Hall, 1999) 69–74; Collinge and Ayers, *Economics by Design,* 51–52.
[5]Cait Murphy, "Will the Future Belong to Germany?" *Fortune,* August 2, 1999, 129–36. Also go to "Intershop: Creating the Digital Economy." <www.intershop.com>. (March 8, 2000).
[6]Deborah Orr, "The Post Office with a Ticker," *Forbes,* November 29, 1999, 77–78; Matthew L. Wald, "Canada's Private Control Towers," *New York Times,* October 23, 1999, C1. Go also to National Center for Policy Analysis. "Privatization." <www.public-policy.org/~ncpa/pd/private/privat.html>. (March 8, 2000).
[7]Peter Burrows, "Personal Computers: Are the Glory Days Over?" *Business Week,* February 14, 2000, 50.
[8]See Case and Fair, *Principles of Economics,* 70–90; Collinge and Ayers, *Economics by Design,* 74–77.
[9]Murphy, "Will the Future Belong to Germany?" 130.
[10]Norman M. Scarborough and Thomas W. Zimmerer, *Effective Small Business Management: An Entrepreneurial Approach,* 6th ed. (Upper Saddle River, NJ: Prentice Hall, 2000) 10.
[11]See Gabrielle Saveri, "This Is No Fashion Victim," *Business Week,* May 31, 1999, 89.
[12]Alex Taylor III, "Blue Skies for Airbus," *Fortune,* August 2, 1999, 102–04+; Laurence Zuckerman, "The Jet Wars of the Future," *New York Times,* July 9, 1999, C1, C5; "Let's Play Oligopoly!" *Wall Street Journal,* March 8, 1999, B1, B10.
[13]Stephanie Anderson Forest et al., "Inflation: The Storm Ahead?" *Business Week,* February 14, 2000, 42–43.
[14]See Robert Levering and Milton Moskowitz, "The 100 Best Companies to Work For," *Fortune,* January 10, 2000, 82–84+.
[15]Louis Uchitelle, "A Clearer View of the Economy," *New York Times,* October 29, 1999, C1, C6.
[16]See Collinge and Ayers, *Economics by Design,* 351–53.
[17]*New York Times Almanac 2000* (New York: Penguin Reference, 2000) 330–331.
[18]"Sears, Oracle Try B2B Venture," *USA Today,* February 28, 2000, 1B; Jennifer Reingold et al., "Why the Productivity Revolution Will Spread," *Business Week,* February 14, 2000, 112, 114+. Also go to TheStreet.com. <www.thestreet.com/_yahoo/brknews/retail/ 891328.html>. (March 8, 2000).
[19]Louis Uchitelle, "The $1.2 Trillion Spigot," *New York Times,* December 30, 1999, C1, C16.
[20]"The National Debt," *Business Week,* August 9, 1999, 32.
[21]"China to Prime Economic Pump with Mammoth Building Outlay," *New York Times,* March 6, 1998, A1, A6.
[22]"Economists Surveyed Forecast at Least Two Rate Hikes," *USA Today,* January 31, 2000, 1B.
[23]Michael J. Mandel et al., "The 21st Century Economy," *Business Week,* August 31, 1998, 58–67. See also David Fairlamb and Gail Edmondson, "Work in Progress—Signs Abound of a Nascent New Economy," *Business Week,* January 31, 2000, 80–87.
[24]See also Brian Bremner and Moon Ihlwan, "Edging toward the Information Age," *Business Week,* January 31, 2000, 90–91.
[25]Bremner and Ihlwan, "Edging toward the Information Age," 91.
[26]Rich Miller et al., "How Prosperity Is Reshaping the American Economy," *Business Week,* February 14, 2000, 100–04+.

Chapter 2

[1]See Nancy K. Kubasek, Bartley A. Brennan, and M. Neil Browne, *The Legal Environment of Business: A Critical Thinking Approach,* 2nd ed. (Upper Saddle River, NJ: Prentice Hall, 1999) Chapter 22.
[2]See Jerald Greenberg and Robert A. Baron, *Behavior in Organizations: Understanding and Managing the Human Side of Work,* 7th ed. (Upper Saddle River, NJ: Prentice Hall, 2000) 6–7.
[3]See Philip Kotler, *Marketing Management: The Millennium Edition* (Upper Saddle River, NJ: Prentice Hall, 2000) 19–25.
[4]See Norman M. Scarborough and Thomas W. Zimmerer, *Effective Small Business Management,* 6th ed. (Upper Saddle River, NJ: Prentice Hall, 2000) 73–76.
[5]U.S. Bureau of the Census, *Statistical Abstract of the United States: 1998* (Washington, DC: U.S. Government Printing Office, 1999).
[6]See Henry R. Cheeseman, *Essentials of Contemporary Business Law* (Upper Saddle River, NJ: Prentice Hall, 1999) Chapter 23; Scarborough and Zimmerer, *Effective Small Business Management,* 77–84.
[7]Emily Barker, "The Pentagram Papers," *Inc.,* September 1999, 58–61+.

[8]Jerry Useem, "Partners on the Edge," *Inc.,* August 1998, 52–54+.
[9]*Statistical Abstract of the United States: 1998.*
[10]Ocean Spray. "About the Company." <www.oceanspray.com/about.htm>. (March 14, 2000).
[11]*Statistical Abstract of the United States:* 1998.
[12]Christina Binkley, "MGM's Mirage Deal May Close a Chapter in Gambling Business," *Wall Street Journal,* March 7, 2000, A1, A12.
[13]See Ann Marsh et al., "500 Biggest Private Companies," *Forbes,* December 13, 1999, 167–70+.
[14]See Cheeseman, *Essentials of Contemporary Business Law,* 567–69.
[15]Also go to IPOs on the Net and TradingDay.com. <tradingday.com/ipos/> and <advocacy-net.com/ipomks.htm>. (March 17, 2000).
[16]David F. Scott Jr. et al., *Basic Financial Management,* 8th ed. (Upper Saddle River, NJ: Prentice Hall, 1999) 439.
[17]See Nelson D. Schwartz, "The Ugly Truth about IPOs," *Fortune,* November 23, 1998, 190–92+.
[18]Jennifer Reingold, "Dot.com Boards are Flouting the Rules," *Business Week,* December 20, 1999, 130–32+.
[19]Dana Canedy and Reed Abelson, "Can Kellogg Break Out of the Box?" *New York Times,* January 24, 1999, sec. 3, 1, 12.
[20]Debra Sparks, "Partners," *Business Week,* October 25, 1999, 106–30.
[21]Also go to The National Center for Employee Ownership. <www.nceo.org>. (March 17, 2000).
[22]Kenneth N. Gilpin, "Workers Ready to Cash In as U.P.S. Goes Public," *New York Times,* November 11, 1999, A1, C12.
[23]John A. Byrne, "The Teddy Roosevelts of Corporate Governance," *Business Week,* May 31, 1999, 75+. Also go to TIAA-CREF Web Center. <www.tiaa-cref.org/>. (March 17, 2000).
[24]James Cox, "Climate 'Incredible' for Mergers, Acquisitions," *USA Today,* January 17, 2000, 1B. See also Richard Siklos et al., "Welcome to the 21st Century," *Business Week,* January 24, 2000, 36–40+.
[25]Howard W. French, "With Daewoo, a Twilight of Korean Conglomerates," *New York Times,* September 3, 1999, C1, C4.

Chapter 3

[1]*Hoover's Handbook of World Business 2000* (Austin, TX: Hoover's Business Press, 2000).
[2]Ricky W. Griffin and Michael W. Pustay, *International Business: A Managerial Perspective,* 2nd ed. (Reading, MA: Addison-Wesley, 1999) 44–45. See also Warren J. Keegan, *Global Marketing Management,* 6th ed. (Upper Saddle River, NJ: Prentice Hall, 1999) 42–45.
[3]David Fairlamb and Gail Edmondson, "Work in Progress," *Business Week,* January 31, 2000, 80–81+.
[4]See Stephen Baker, "Invasion of the e-Vikings," *Business Week,* July 26, 1999, EB53–EB54+; Rob Norton, "The Luck of the Irish," *Fortune,* October 25, 1999, 194–96+.
[5]See Edmund L. Andrews, "The Metamorphosis of Germany Inc.," *New York Times,* March 12, 2000, sec. 3, 1, 12.
[6]See Mark Landler, "Mapping Out Silicon Valley East," *New York Times,* April 5, 1999, C1, C10; and Bruce Einhorn with Cathy Yang, "Portal Combat," *Business Week,* January 17, 2000, 96–97.
[7]See Griffin and Pustay, *International Business,* Chapter 3. See also Dominick Salvatore, *International Economics,* 6th ed. (Upper Saddle River, NJ: Prentice Hall, 1998) 27–33; and Karl E. Case and Ray C. Fair, *Principles of Economics,* 5th ed. (Upper Saddle River, NJ: Prentice Hall, 1999) 813–17.
[8]This section is based on Michael Porter, *The Competitive Advantage of Nations* (Boston: Harvard Business School Press, 1990), Chapters 3 and 4. See also Keegan, *Global Marketing Management,* 312–21, and John J. Wild, Kenneth L. Wild, and Jerry C.Y. Han, *International Business: An Integrated Approach* (Upper Saddle River, NJ: Prentice Hall, 2000) 175–78.
[9]*Hoover's Handbook of World Business 2000,* 56.
[10]See Case and Fair, *Principles of Economics,* 818–21.
[11]Robyn Meredith, "Dollar Makes Canada a Land of the Spree," *New York Times,* August 1, 1999, sec. 3, 1, 11.
[12]Jeremy Kahn, "Wal-Mart Goes Shopping in Europe," *Fortune,* June 7, 1999, 105–12; and Wendy Zellner, "Someday, Lee, This May All Be Yours," *Business Week,* November 15, 1999, 84, 88, 92; Michael McCarthy, "Wal-Mart Takes Slow Road in Germany," *USA Today,* May 10, 2000, 3B.
[13]John Tagliabue, "Now Playing Europe: The Invasion of the Multiplex," *New York Times,* January 27, 2000, C1, C23.
[14]*Hoover's Handbook of World Business 2000.*
[15]See Norman M. Scarborough and Thomas W. Zimmerer, *Effective Small Business Management: An Entrepreneurial Approach,* 6th ed. (Upper Saddle River, NJ: Prentice Hall, 2000) 374–98.
[16]Jeremy Kahn, "The Fortune Global 500—The World's Largest Corporations," *Fortune,* August 2, 1999, 144–46; F-1–F-22.
[17]See Wild, Wild, and Han, *International Business,* chapter 7; Griffin and Pustay, *International Business,* 436–39.
[18]See Robert L. Simison and Scott Miller, "Ford Grabs Big Prize as Steep Losses Force BMW to Sell Rover," *Wall Street Journal,* March 17, 2000, A1, A8; Shelly Branch and Ernest Beck, "For Unilever, It's Sweetness and Light," *Wall Street Journal,* April 13, 2000, B1, B4.
[19]Thomas G. Condon and Kurt Badenhausen, "Spending Spree," *Forbes,* July 26, 1999, 208–19.
[20]See Robert Frank, "In Paddies of Vietnam, Americans Once Again Land in Quagmire," *Wall Street Journal,* April 21, 2000, A1, A6.
[21]David E. Sanger, "Miffed at Europe, U.S. Raises Tariffs for Luxury Goods," *New York Times,* March 4, 1999, A1, A5.
[22]See Keegan, *Global Marketing Management,* 417–19.
[23]David E. Sanger, "U.S. Says Japan, Brazil Dumped Steel," *New York Times,* February 13, 1999, C1, C2.

Chapter 4

[1]This section follows the logic of Gerald F. Cavanaugh, *American Business Values with International Perspectives,* 4th ed. (Upper Saddle River, NJ: Prentice Hall, 1998), Chapter 3.
[2]See Patricia Sellers, "Crunch Time for Coke," *Fortune,* July 19, 1999, 72–74+.

[3]See Quentin Hardy, "All Carly All the Time," *Forbes,* December 13, 1999, 138–44; Peter Burrows with Peter Elstrom, "The Boss," *Business Week,* August 2, 1999, 76–80+.
[4]Jeffrey S. Harrison and R. Edward Freeman, "Stakeholders, Social Responsibility, and Performance: Empirical Evidence and Theoretical Perspectives," *Academy of Management Journal,* 1999, vol. 42, no. 5, 479–85. See also David P. Baron, *Business and Its Environment,* 3rd ed. (Upper Saddle River, NJ: Prentice Hall, 2000), Chapter 17.
[5]See Edward Iwata, "More Firms Falsify Revenue to Boost Stocks," *USA Today,* March 29, 2000, 1B.
[6]James R. Healey, "Ford to Reveal Plans for Think Brand," *USA Today,* January 10, 2000, 1B; Gwen Kinkead, "In the Future, People Like Me Will Go to Jail," *Fortune,* May 24, 1999, 190–200.
[7]Andrew C. Revkin, "Who Cares About a Few Degrees?" *New York Times,* December 12, 1997, F1, F4.
[8]See Baron, *Business and Its Environment,* Chapter 12.
[9]Marilyn Adams, "Careless Cargo," *USA Today,* January 26, 2000, 1B, 2B.
[10]Susan Warren, "Recycler's Nightmare: Beer in Plastic," *Wall Street Journal,* November 16, 1999, B1, B4.
[11]David Barboza, "Drug Maker Accepts a Fine over the Making of Test Kits," *New York Times,* November 3, 1999, C1, C8.
[12]David J. Morrow, "Fen-Phen Maker to Pay Billions in Settlement of Diet-Injury Cases," *Wall Street Journal,* October 8, 1999, C1, C6.
[13]Jayne O'Donnell, "U.S. Fines Drug Companies $725M for Price Fixing," *USA Today,* May 21, 1999, B1.
[14]Michael McCarthy and Lorrie Grant, "Sears Drops Benetton after Controversial Death Row Ads," *USA Today,* February 18, 2000, 2B.
[15]See Baron, *Business and Its Environment,* 704–06; Jerald Greenberg and Robert A. Baron, *Behavior in Organizations: Understanding and Managing the Human Side of Work,* 7th ed. (Upper Saddle River, NJ: Prentice Hall, 2000) 374–75.
[16]Rick Lyman, "A Tobacco Whistle-Blower's Life is Transformed," *New York Times,* October 15, 1999, A24.
[17]Andy Pasztor, "Whistle-Blower in Toshiba Case Stands to Gain," *Wall Street Journal,* November 9, 1999, B1, B4.
[18]Dan Seligman, "Blowing Whistles, Blowing Smoke," *Forbes,* September 6, 1999, 158–62.
[19]See Henry R. Cheesman, *Contemporary Business Law,* 3rd ed. (Upper Saddle River, NJ: Prentice Hall, 2000) 700–03.
[20]Tom Lowry, "Merger Mania Revives Insider Trading," *USA Today,* August 11, 1998, A1.
[21]Bruce Horovitz, "Employers Back Olympic Hopefuls," *USA Today,* February 7, 2000, 1B.
[22]See Michael E. Porter and Mark R. Kramer, "Philanthropy's New Agenda: Creating Value," *Harvard Business Review,* November–December 1999, 121–30.
[23]See Sandra Waddock and Neil Smith, "Corporate Responsibility Audits: Doing Well by Doing Good," *Sloan Management Review,* Winter 2000, 75–85.

Chapter 5

[1]Louise Lee, "A Savvy Captain for Old Navy," *Business Week,* November 8, 1999, 133–34; "Old Navy's Skipper," *Business Week,* January 10, 2000, 64.
[2]David Leonhardt, "The Sage of Lloyd Ward," *Business Week,* August 9, 1999, 59–70.
[3]Mark Gimein, "CEO in Motion Speed," *Fortune,* September 4, 2000, 244–50.
[4]Geoffrey Colvin, "The Ultimate Manager," *Fortune,* November 22, 1999, 185–87.
[5]Janet Guyon, "Getting the Bugs Out at VW," *Fortune,* March 29, 1999, 96–102.
[6]Melanie Wells, "Red Baron," *Forbes,* July 3, 2000, 150–60; Andrew Ross Sorkin, "Taking Virgin's Brand Into Internet Territory," *New York Times,* February 14, 2000, C1, C17.
[7]"Cruise-Ship Delays Leave Guests High and Dry," *Wall Street Journal,* October 24, 1997, B1, B10; *Hoover's Handbook of American Business 2000* (Austin, TX: Hoover's Business Press, 2000) 1512–13.
[8]John Markoff, "A Disruptive Virus Invades Computers around the World," *New York Times,* May 5, 2000, A1, C9; Markoff, "Law Officials Seek Origins of the Virus," *New York Times,* May 6, 2000, C1, C3; Kevin Maney, "Tainted Love," *USA Today,* May 5, 2000, 1B, 2B.
[9]Peter Burrows, "The Hottest Property in the Valley?" *Business Week,* August 30, 1999, 69–74.
[10]Brian O'Reilly, "The Mechanic Who Fixed Continental," *Fortune,* December 20, 1999, 176–86; David Field, "Fliers Give Continental Sky-High Marks," *USA Today,* May 10, 2000, 3B.
[11]Jennifer Reingold, "Executive Pay," *Business Week,* April 17, 2000, 101.
[12]"Rallying the Troops at P&G," *Wall Street Journal,* August 31, 2000, B1, B4.

Chapter 6

[1]Robert L. Simison, "Ford Rolls Out New Model of Corporate Culture," *Wall Street Journal,* January 13, 1999, B1, B4.
[2]See Jerald Greenberg and Robert A. Baron, *Behavior in Organizations: Understanding and Managing the Human Side of Work,* 7th ed. (Upper Saddle River, NJ: Prentice Hall, 2000) 519–24.
[3]"Lucent to Break Up into Four Divisions," Associated Press news story reported in *Houston Chronicle,* October 27, 1999, B2.
[4]Bruce Horovitz, "Restoring the Golden-Arch Shine," *USA Today,* June 16, 1999, 3B.
[5]Linda Formichelli, "Letting Go of the Details," *Nation's Business,* November 1997, 50+.
[6]Horovitz, "Restoring the Golden-Arch Shine," 3B.
[7]Donna Fenn, "Redesign Work," *Inc.,* June 1999, 75–83.
[8]Philip Siekman, "Where 'Build to Order' Works Best," *Fortune,* April 26, 1999, 160C–160V.
[9]Robert Berner and Kevin Helliker, "Heinz's Worry: 4,000 Products, Only One Star," *Wall Street Journal,* September 17, 1999, B1, B4.
[10]Diane Brady, "Martha Inc.," *Business Week,* January 17, 2000, 62–66+.
[11]Gail Edmondson, "Danone Hits Its Stride," *Business Week,* February 1, 1999, 52–53.
[12]Frank Rose, "Think Globally, Script Locally," *Fortune,* November 8, 1999, 156–60.

[13]Thomas A. Stewart, "See Jack. See Jack Run," *Fortune,* September 27, 1999, 124–27+.
[14]See Jerald Greenberg and Robert A. Baron, *Behavior in Organizations: Understanding and Managing the Human Side of Work,* 7th ed. (Upper Saddle River, NJ: Prentice Hall, 2000) 308–09.

Chapter 7

[1]U.S. Department of Commerce, *Statistical Abstract of the United States: 1999* (Washington, DC: Bureau of the Census, 1999).
[2]"Small Business 'Vital Statistics.'" <www. sba.gov/aboutsba/>. (May 24, 2000).
[3]"Small Business 'Vital Statistics.'" Online. Internet.
[4]"Small Business 'Vital Statistics.'" Online. Internet.
[5]Chuck Salter, "Insanity, Inc.," *Fast Company,* January 1999, 100–08.
[6]*Hoover's Handbook of American Business 2000* (Austin, TX: Hoover's Business Press, 2000) 1540–41; Wendy Zellner, "Peace, Love, and the Bottom Line," *Business Week,* December 7, 1998, 79–82.
[7]Debra Nussbaum, "Giving Birth to a Web Business," *New York Times,* October 15, 1998, G5.
[8]Nussbaum, "Giving Birth to a Web Business," G5.
[9]Nancy J. Lyons, "Moonlight over Indiana," *Inc.,* January 2000, 71–74.
[10]Jim McCraw, "Three Biker-Entrepreneurs Take on Mighty Harley," *New York Times,* August 20, 1999, F1.
[11]See also Paulette Thomas, "A New Generation Re-Writes the Rules," *Wall Street Journal,* May 22, 2000, R4.
[12]Nicholas Stein, "The Renaissance Man of e-Commerce," *Fortune,* February 7, 2000, 181–82.
[13]Brian O'Reilly, "What It Takes to Start a Startup," *Fortune,* June 7, 1999, 135–40.
[14]George Hager, "Internet Industry Surges 'Startling' 62%," *USA Today,* June 6, 2000, 1B.
[15]"Up-and-Comers," *Business Week,* May 15, 2000, EB70–EB72.
[16]Andy Serwer, "There's Something about Cisco," *Fortune,* May 15, 2000, 114–38.
[17]John Markoff, "High-Tech Advances Push C.I.A. into New Company," *New York Times,* September 29, 1999, A14.
[18]Dana Canedy, "The Courtship of Black Consumers," *New York Times,* August 16, 1998, D1, D5.
[19]See *Wall Street Journal Almanac 1999,* 179, 182.
[20]Noelle Knox, "Women Entrepreneurs Attract New Financing," *New York Times,* July 26, 1998, 10.
[21]Bill Meyers, "Women Increase Standing as Business Owners," *USA Today,* June 29, 1999, 1B.
[22]Michael Hopkins, "The Antihero's Guide to the New Economy," *Inc.,* January 1998, 36–48.
[23]Norman M. Scarborough and Thomas W. Zimmerer, *Effective Small Business Management: An Entrepreneurial Approach,* 6th ed. (Upper Saddle River, NJ: Prentice Hall, 2000) 412–13.
[24]Jim Hopkins, "Expert Entrepreneur Got Her Show on the Road at an Early Age," *USA Today,* May 24, 2000, 5B.
[25]Thea Singer, "Brandapalooza," *Inc. 500,* 1999, 69–72.
[26]Joanne Gordon, "Cheap Tricks," *Forbes,* February 21, 2000, 116.
[27]U.S. Department of Commerce, *Statistical Abstract of the United States: 1999* (Washington, DC: Bureau of the Census, 1999).
[28]Susan Greco, "get$$$now.com," *Inc.,* September 1999, 35–38.

Chapter 8

[1]See Angelo S. DeNisi and Ricky W. Griffin, *Human Resource Management* (Boston: Houghton Mifflin, 2001) for a complete overview.
[2]"U.S. Tells Airlines They Should Offer Peanut-Free Rows," *Wall Street Journal,* September 2, 1998, A1, A8.
[3]Abby Ellin, "Training Programs Often Miss the Point on the Job," *New York Times,* March 29, 2000, C12.
[4]Stephanie Armour, "Show Me the Money, More Workers Say," *USA Today,* June 6, 2000, 1B.
[5]Del Jones, "Coke Cooks up Some Perks to Refresh Workers," *USA Today,* May 4, 2000, 1B.
[6]"Biotech Firm Opens Largest Corporate Day Care Center," Associated Press news release published in *Bryan-College Station Eagle,* June 13, 2000, B7.
[7]"Recent Suits Make Pregnancy Issues Workplace Priorities," *Wall Street Journal,* January 14, 1998, B1.
[8]"Laws, Juries Shift Protection to Terminated Employees," *USA Today,* April 2, 1998, 1B, 2B.
[9]Max Boisot, *Knowledge Assets* (Oxford: Oxford University Press, 1998).
[10]Thomas Stewart, "In Search of Elusive Tech Workers," *Fortune,* February 16, 1998, 171–72.
[11]Matt Richtel, "Need for Computer Experts Is Making Recruiters Frantic," *New York Times,* December 18, 1999, C1.
[12]Aaron Bernstein, "When is a Temp Not a Temp?" *Business Week,* December 7, 1998, 90–92.

Chapter 9

[1]For a detailed treatment of this entire subject area, see Gregory Moorhead and Ricky W. Griffin, *Organizational Behavior,* 6th ed. (Boston: Houghton Mifflin, 2001).
[2]Jerry Useem, "Welcome to the New Company Town," *Fortune,* January 10, 2000, 62–70.
[3]Linda Grant, "Happy Workers, High Returns," *Fortune,* January 12, 1998, 81.
[4]"Perks That Work," *Time,* November 9, 1998.
[5]See Moorhead and Griffin, *Organizational Behavior,* Chapters 5 and 6.
[6]Ralph King, Jr., "Levi's Factory Workers Are Assigned to Teams, and Morale Takes a Hit," *Wall Street Journal,* May 20, 1998, A1, A6.
[7]Jon R. Katzenbach, *Teams at the Top* (Boston: Harvard Business School Press, 1998).
[8]See Moorhead and Griffin, *Organizational Behavior,* Chapter 7.
[9]See Moorhead and Griffin, *Organizational Behavior,* Chapter 7.
[10]Jack Dawson, "Making Stay-at-Homes Feel Welcome," *Business Week,* October 12, 1999, 155–56.
[11]"Insanity, Inc.," *Fast Company,* January 1999, 100–08.
[12]See Moorhead and Griffin, *Organizational Behavior,* Chapters 13 and 14.
[13]See Moorhead and Griffin, *Organizational Behavior,* Chapters 13 and 14.
[14]"A Better Workplace," *Time,* April 17, 2000, 87.
[15]Stephanie Armour, "More Dads Tap into Family Benefits at Work," *USA Today,* June 16, 2000, 1B.

Chapter 10

[1]David Lipsky and Clifford Donn, *Collective Bargaining in American Industry* (Lexington, MA: Lexington Books, 1981).
[2]David Koenig, "Labor Unions Say Recent Victories Signal a Comeback," Associated Press news release published in *The Bryan-College Station Eagle,* June 11, 2000, E1, E6.
[3]Aaron Bernstein, "Welch's March to the South," *Business Week,* December 6, 1999, 74, 78.
[4]David Field, "UAL 'Nice Guy' in Tough Spot," *USA Today,* June 16, 2000, 1B, 2B.
[5]Paula Dwyer, "Hoffa at Halftime," *Business Week,* June 26, 2000, 156–60.
[6]*New York Times Almanac 2000* (New York: Penguin Reference, 1999), 351.
[7]Stephanie Amour, "Will Fine Divide or Solidify Pilots?" *USA Today,* February 15, 1999, 1B.
[8]Stephanie Amour, "ABC Locks Out Striking Employees," *USA Today,* November 3, 1998, B1.
[9]Phil Taylor, "To the Victor Belongs the Spoils," *Sports Illustrated,* January 18, 1999, 48–52.
[10]Paula Dwyer, "Hoffa at Halftime," 156–60.

Chapter 11

[1]American Marketing Association, "Marketing Services Guide." <www.ama.org/about/ama/markdef.asp>. (March 1, 2000).
[2]See Philip Kotler, *Marketing Management,* Millennium ed. (Upper Saddle River, NJ: Prentice Hall, 2000) 50–54.
[3]See Warren J. Keegan, *Global Marketing Management,* 6th ed. (Upper Saddle River, NJ: Prentice Hall, 1999) 10–11.
[4]"Yankee Imperialist," *Forbes,* December 13, 1999, 56.
[5]"About barnesandnoble.com." <www.barnesandnoble.com>. (March 1, 2000); "Barnes & Noble, Inc. Announces Initiative to Launch World's Largest Bookseller Online," News Release, Barnes & Noble Inc. and Direct Report Corporation, January 28, 1997.
[6]Robert D. Hof, Steve Hamm, and Ira Sager, "Sunpower," *Business Week,* January 18, 1999, 64–68+.
[7]Herb Kelleher, "A Brief History of Southwest Airlines." ><www.southwest.com/about_swa>. (March 1, 2000).
[8]See Leon G. Schiffman and Leslie Lazar Kanuk, *Consumer Behavior,* 7th ed. (Upper Saddle River, NJ: Prentice Hall, 2000), Chapter 3; Kotler, *Marketing Management,* Chapter 9.
[9]*Pepsico, Inc. 1998 Annual Report; The Coca-Cola Company. 1998 Annual Report.*
[10]Alex Taylor III, "Detroit: Every Silver Lining Has a Cloud," *Fortune,* January 24, 2000, 92–93.
[11]Lauren Goldstein, "Dressing Up an Old Brand," *Fortune,* November 9, 1998, 54–56.
[12]Jane Perlez, "Joy of Debts: Eastern Europe on Credit Fling," *New York Times,* May 30, 1998, A3.
[13]See also Naresh K. Malhorta, *Marketing Research: An Applied Orientation,* 3rd. ed. (Upper Saddle River, NJ: Prentice Hall, 1999) 11–12; and American Marketing Association, "Marketing Services Guide." <www.ama.org/about/ama/markdef.asp>. (March 1, 2000).
[14]Joshua Macht, "The New Market Research," *Inc.,* July 1998, 86–90+.
[15]See Schiffman and Kanuk, *Consumer Behavior,* 69–70.
[16]U.S. Department of Commerce, *Statistical Abstract of the United States: 1998* (Washington, DC: Bureau of the Census, 1999) 305–09, 547, 768, 776.
[17]*Statistical Abstract of the United States: 1998,* 306, 358.
[18]See Edward G. Brierty, Robert W. Eckles, and Robert R. Reeder, *Business Marketing,* 3rd ed. (Upper Saddle River, NJ: Prentice Hall, 1998) 31–33.
[19]See Paul G. Keat and Philip K.Y. Young, *Managerial Economics: Economic Tools for Today's Decision Makers,* 3rd ed. (Upper Saddle River, NJ: Prentice Hall, 2000) 103–05.
[20]See Norman N. Scarborough and Thomas W. Zimmerer, *Effective Small Business Management: An Entrepreneurial Approach,* 6th ed. (Upper Saddle River, NJ: Prentice Hall, 2000), Chapter 6.
[21]Paco Underhill, "What Shoppers Want," *Inc.,* July 1999, 76, 80.

Chapter 12

[1]Scott Miller, "Porsche Profits May Leave the Fast Lane," *Wall Street Journal,* December 9, 1999, A21.
[2]See Philip Kotler, *Marketing Management: The Millennium Edition* (Upper Saddle River, NJ: Prentice Hall, 2000) 396–98.
[3]See Kotler, *Marketing Management,* 398–400.
[4]Nina Munk, "How Levi's Trashed a Great American Brand," *Fortune,* April 12, 1999, 83.
[5]"To Market, To Market," *Beverage Industry,* December 1996, 43–46.
[6]See James C. Anderson and James A. Narus, *Business Market Management: Understanding, Creating, and Delivering Value* (Upper Saddle River, NJ: Prentice Hall, 1999) 203–06.
[7]See Edward G. Brierty, Robert W. Eckles, and Robert R. Reeder, *Business Marketing,* 3rd ed. (Upper Saddle River, NJ: Prentice Hall, 1998) 297–304.
[8]See also Cengiz Haksever et al., *Service Management and Operations,* 2nd ed. (Upper Saddle River, NJ: Prentice Hall, 2000) 193–201.
[9]See William J. Stevenson, *Production Operations Management,* 6th ed. (Boston: Irwin McGraw-Hill, 1999) 166–70.
[10]See Roger W. Schmenner, *Service Operations Management* (Englewood Cliffs, NJ: Prentice Hall, 1995), Chapters 1–3.
[11]See Kotler, *Marketing Management,* 303–16.
[12]Paul C. Judge et al., "The Name's the Thing," *Business Week,* November 15, 1999, 36–39.
[13]Claudia Deutsch, "Using a Key That Still Works," *New York Times,* March 23, 1998, D1, D7.
[14]Monica Larner and Karen Miller, "The Man Who Saved Ferrari," *Business Week,* March 8, 1999, 74–75; Larner, "Those High-End Italians Are Revving Up Again," *Business Week,* October 19, 1998, 138.
[15]Robert D. Hof, "The Buyer Always Wins," *Business Week,* March 22, 1999, EB26, EB28.
[16]See Charles T. Horngren, Walter T. Harrison, and Linda Smith Bamber, *Accounting,* 4th ed. (Upper Saddle River, NJ: Prentice Hall, 1999) 957–64.
[17]See Brierty, Eckles, and Reeder, *Business Marketing,* 480–81.
[18]See Judy Strauss and Raymond Frost, *Marketing on the Internet: Principles of Online Marketing* (Upper Saddle

River, NJ: Prentice Hall, 1999) 139–44.

[19]Robert D. Hof and Linda Himelstein, "eBay vs. Amazon.com," *Business Week,* May 31, 1999, 128–32+; Hof, "The Buyer Always Wins," *Business Week,* EB 26, EB 28; Janet Rae-Dupree and Diane Brady, "Let the Buyer Be in Control," *Business Week,* November 8, 1999, 100.

[20]See Brierty, Eckles, and Reeder, *Business Marketing,* 483–85.

Chapter 13

[1]See "St. Louis Bread Co." <www.stlouisbread.com>. (April 25, 2000).

[2]See Philip Kotler, *Market Management: The Millennium Edition* (Upper Saddle River, NJ: Prentice Hall, 2000), 567.

[3]*Advertising Age,* September 27, 1999, s3.

[4]See William Wells, John Burnett, and Sandra Moriarty, *Advertising: Principles and Practice,* 5th ed. (Upper Saddle River, NJ: Prentice Hall, 2000), Chapter 7.

[5]See Wells, Burnett, and Moriarty, *Advertising,* 157–60.

[6]See Wells, Burnett, and Moriarty, *Advertising,* 46–47.

[7]*Advertising Age,* September 27, 1999, s34.

[8]R. Craig Endicott, "100 Leading National Advertisers," *Advertising Age,* September 27, 1999, s1, s3.

[9]Stuart Elliott, "Big Plays, Surprise Heroes, Shocking Defeats, and Other Super Bowl XXXIV Marketing Memories," *New York Times,* February 1, 2000, C10; Elliott, "Not X's, Not O's, It's the Dot-Coms That Matter," *New York Times,* January 28, 2000, C1, C9.

[10]Stuart Elliott, "You've Got Mail, Indeed," *New York Times,* October 25, 1999, C1, C23.

[11]Alex Kuczynski, "Making Hay with 'Custom' Magazines," *New York Times,* September 6, 1999, C6.

[12]Marc Gunther, "The Great Outdoors," *Fortune,* March 1, 1999, 150–57.

[13]J. William Gurley, "How the Web Will Warp Advertising," *Fortune,* November 9, 1998, 119–20; R. Craig Endicott, "Leaders Swell Spending," *Advertising Age,* September 28, 1998, s49–s50; "Internet Stock Reports with Steve Harmon." <www.internetnews.com/stocks/>. (February 23, 1999); Eryn Brown, "The Silicon Alley Heart of Internet Advertising," *Fortune,* December 6, 1999, 167–68; *Advertising Age,* December 20, 1999, 32.

[14]Stuart Elliott, "Real or Virtual? You Call It," *New York Times,* October 1, 1999, C1, C6.

[15]Elliott, "You've Got Mail, Indeed," C1, C23.

[16]See Wells, Burnett, and Moriarty, *Advertising,* 77–83.

[17]See Michael D. Hutt and Thomas W. Speh, *Business Marketing Management,* 6th ed. (New York: Dryden Press, 1998) 504–05.

[18]Mary Lou Roberts and Paul D. Berger, *Direct Marketing Management,* 2nd ed. (Upper Saddle River, NJ: Prentice Hall, 1999) 329; Gene Gray, "The Future of the Teleservices Industry: Are You Aware," *Telemarketing,* January 1999, 90–96. See also "DMA Interactive." <www.the-dma.org>. (April 25, 2000).

[19]See Scott M. Cutlip, Allen H. Center, and Glen M. Broom, *Effective Public Relations,* 8th ed. (Upper Saddle River, NJ: Prentice Hall, 2000) 9–10.

[20]Mark Maremont, "Probe of Tyco's Accounting Hits Its Stock," *Wall Street Journal,* December 10, 1999, A3, A11.

[21]*1998 Annual Report* (St. Louis: Anheuser-Busch Companies Inc., 1999) 6.

[22]See Warren J. Keegan, *Global Marketing Management,* 6th ed. (Upper Saddle River, NJ: Prentice Hall, 1999), Chapter 15; Wells, Burnett, and Moriarty, *Advertising,* Chapter 18.

[23]See Norman M. Scarborough and Thomas W. Zimmerer, *Effective Small Business Management: An Entrepreneurial Approach,* 6th ed. (Upper Saddle River, NJ: Prentice Hall, 2000), Chapter 11.

Chapter 14

[1]Constance L. Hays, "In Japan, What Price Coca-Cola?" *New York Times,* January 26, 2000, C1, C2.

[2]Ahmad Diba, "An Old-Line Agency Finds an Online Niche," *Fortune,* April 3, 2000, 258.

[3]Neel Chowdhury, "Dell Cracks China," *Fortune,* June 21, 1999, 120–24.

[4]Leigh Buchanan, "The Best of the Small Business Web," *Inc. Technology* No. 4 (1999): 67, 72.

[5]Christine Chen, "The Fortune-50," *Fortune,* December 6, 1999, 141, 146.

[6]"Expedia.com." <www.expedia.com>. (April 19, 2000).

[7]Judy Strauss and Raymond Frost, *Marketing On the Internet* (Upper Saddle River, NJ: Prentice Hall, 1999), 14, 153–55; Ahmad Diba, "An Old-Line Agency Finds an Online Niche," *Fortune,* April 3, 2000, 258.

[8]Diane Brady, "From Nabisco to Tropicana to . . . EFDEX?" *Business Week,* September 20, 1999, 100; "Efdex™." <www.efdex.com>. (April 19, 2000).

[9]Dana Canedy, "Need Asparagus? Just Click It," *New York Times,* September 10, 1999, C1, C18.

[10]Shelly Branch, "Inside the Cult of Cosco," *Fortune,* September 6, 2000, 184–86+.

[11]Patrick C. O'Connor, "Which Retail Properties Are Getting Market Share?" *Appraisal Journal* (January 1999): 37–40.

[12]"Catalog-News.com." <www.catalog-news.com>. (April 19, 2000).

[13]Gene Gray, "The Future of the Teleservices Industry—Are You Aware," *Telemarketing* (January 1999): 90–96.

[14]Dennis Berman, "Is the Bell Tolling for Door-to-Door Selling?" *Business Week,* November 1, 1999, EB58.

[15]"Prodigy.com™." <www.prodigy.com>. (April 19, 2000).

[16]"Small Biz Web Sites on the Rise, Yet Many Owners Slow to Embrace the Internet." Prodigy.com. <www.prodigy.com/pcom/business/business/content>. (April 19, 2000).

[17]"efdex Launches the First Global e-Market for the Food & Drink Industry." Press release from Connors Communications. <www.connors.com/press/efdex>. (April 19, 2000); Dana, "Need Asparagus? Just Click It," C1, C18.

[18]"Did You Know?" Catalog News.com. Maxwell Sroge Publishing. <www.catalog-news.com>. (April 19, 2000); Strauss and Frost, *Marketing On the Internet,* 140.

[19]Peter Elkind, "Shhhhh! Amway's on the Web," *Fortune,* March 6, 2000, 76; Berman, "Is the Bell Tolling for Door-to-Door Selling?" EB 58–EB 60.

[20]"LivePerson.com™." <www.liveperson.com>. (April 19, 2000).

[21]Saul Hansell, "As Sales Boom Online, Some Customers Boo,"

New York Times, December 17, 1999, C1, C10; Bob Tedeschi, "e-Commerce Report," *New York Times,* September 27, 1999, C4.

Chapter 15

[1]Thomas A. Stewart, "It's 10 p.m. Do You Know Where Your Business Is?" *Fortune,* April 3, 2000, 270.
[2]Ira Sager, "Inside IBM: Internet Business Machines," *Business Week,* December 13, 1999, EB 20+; Gene Bylinsky, "Hot New Technologies for America's Factories," *Fortune,* July 5, 1999, 169(N).
[3]Jennifer L. Martel and Laura A. Kelter, "The Job Market Remains Strong in 1999," *Monthly Labor Review* (February 2000): 3–23.
[4]Martel and Kelter, "The Job Market Remains Strong in 1999," 3–23.
[5]Richard Tomlinson, "China's Reform: Now Comes the Hard Part," *Fortune,* March 1, 1999, 159.
[6]*GE Annual Report: 1999* (Fairfield, CT: General Electric Co., 2000), 8.
[7]Eryn Brown, "America's Most Admired Companies," *Fortune,* March 1, 1999, 68, 70–73; Online. Internet <www.walmartstores.com>. (April 24, 2000).
[8]Judy Strauss and Raymond Frost, *Marketing on the Internet* (Upper Saddle River, NJ: Prentice Hall, 1999) 266–71.
[9]"Digital and Intel Complete Sale of Digital Semi-conductor Manufacturing Operations," *Intel Press Release* (Santa Clara, CA, and Maynard, MA), May 18, 1998.
[10]Keith Bradsher, "General Motors Plans to Build New, Efficient Assembly Plants," *New York Times,* August 6, 1998, A1, D3.
[11]*Perrigo: 1998 Annual Report* (Allegan, MI: Perrigo, 1998).
[12]Kevin Ferguson, "Purchasing in Packs," *Business,* November 1, 1999, EB 33.
[13]*The Art & Science of Harley-Davidson: 1998 Annual Report* (Milwaukee, WI: Harley-Davidson, Inc., 1998); Gina Imperato, "Harley Shifts Gears," *Fast Company* (June–July 1997): 104–05+.
[14]*United Parcel Service 1999 Annual Report* (Atlanta, GA: United Parcel Service, Inc., 2000).

Chapter 16

[1]Bart VanArk and Robert McGuckin, "International Comparisons of Labor Productivity and Per Capita Income," *Monthly Labor Review* (Washington, DC: U.S. Dept. of Labor, July 1999) 33–41.
[2]Estimated from VanArk and McGuckin, "International Comparisons of Labor Productivity and Per Capita Income," 33–41; and *Survey of Current Business* (Washington, DC: U.S. Dept. of Commerce, April 2000) 85.
[3]*Survey of Current Business* (Washington, DC: U.S. Dept. of Commerce, April 2000) 43, 85.
[4]Estimated from *Survey of Current Business,* April 2000, 41, 43, 85.
[5]*Monthly Labor Review* (Washington, DC: U.S. Dept. of Labor, January 2000) 92–93; *Monthly Labor Review,* February 2000, 100–01.
[6]Timothy Aeppel, "Rust-Belt Factory Lifts Productivity, and Staff Finds It's No Picnic," *Wall Street Journal,* May 18, 1999, A1, A10.
[7]To come?
[8]Paul C. Judge, "The Inside Story of How Mike Ruettgers Turned EMC into a High Flyer," *Business Week,* March 15, 1999, 72–76+.
[9]Joel Kurtzman, "Is Your Company Off Course? Now You Can Find Out Why," *Fortune,* February 17, 1997, 133.
[10]Claudia Deutsch, "Six Sigma Enlightenment," *New York Times,* December 7, 1998, C1, C7.
[11]Gene Bylinsky, "Hot New Technologies for America's Factories," *Fortune,* July 5, 1999, 168[A].
[12]James Evans and James Dean Jr., *Total Quality: Management, Organization, and Strategy,* 2nd ed. (Cincinnati, OH: South-Western, 2000) 230; Leigh Ann Klaus, "Motorola Brings Fairy Tales to Life," *Quality Progress* (June 1997): 25–28.
[13]Catherine Greenman, "An Old Craft Learns New Tricks," *New York Times,* June 10, 1999, G1, G7.
[14]Jennifer Reingold, Marcia Stepanek, and Diane Brady, "Why the Productivity Revolution Will Spread," *Business Week,* February 14, 2000, 112–18.
[15]"Motorola." <www.motorola.com>. (May 24, 2000).
[16]Leonard L. Berry, A. Parasuraman, and Valerie A. Zeithaml, "Improving Service Quality in America: Lessons Learned," *Academy of Management Executive* 8, no. 2 (1994): 32–45.

Chapter 17

[1]Kenneth C. Laudon and Jane P. Laudon, *Essentials of Management Information Systems,* 3rd ed. (Upper Saddle River, NJ: Prentice Hall, 1999) 267.
[2]Laudon and Laudon, *Essentials of Management Information Systems,* 270.
[3]David Kirkpatrick, "Why Have Investors Ignored Lycos for So Long?" *Fortune,* February 1, 1999, 150.
[4]Laudon and Laudon, *Essentials of Management Information Systems,* 273.
[5]Mary J. Cronin, "Ford's Intranet Success," *Fortune,* March 30, 1998, 158.
[6]Joshua Macht, "The Ultimate Head Trip," *Inc. Technology,* no. 3 (1997): 77.
[7]Gene Bylinsky, "Industry's Amazing Instant Prototypes," *Fortune,* January 12, 1998, 120(B–D).
[8]Laudon and Laudon, *Essentials of Management Information Systems,* 383–88. See also E. Wainwright Martin et al., *Managing Information Technology: What Managers Need to Know,* 3rd ed. (Upper Saddle River, NJ: Prentice Hall, 1999) 225–27.
[9]Heather Green et al., "It's Time for Rules in Wonderland," *Business Week,* February 21, 2000, 82–88+; Ira Sager et al., "Cyber Crime," *Business Week,* February 21, 2000, 36–42; Ira Sager, Neil Gross, and John Carey, "Locking Out the Hackers," *Business Week,* February 28, 2000, 32–34.
[10]See Martin et al., *Managing Information Technology,* 61–68.
[11]See Larry Long and Nancy Long, *Computers,* 6th ed. (Upper Saddle River, NJ: Prentice Hall, 1999) 165–69.

Chapter 18

[1]Charles T. Horngren, Walter T. Harrison Jr., and Linda Smith Bamber, *Accounting,* 4th ed. (Upper Saddle River, NJ: Prentice Hall, 1999) 6–7.
[2]See Kumen H. Jones et al., *Introduction to Accounting: A User Perspective* (Upper Saddle River, NJ: Prentice Hall, 2000) F-231.
[3]See Walter T. Harrison Jr. and Charles T. Horngren, *Financial Accounting,* 4th ed. (Upper Saddle River, NJ: Prentice Hall, 2000) 6.
[4]William C. Symonds et al., "Tyco: Aggressive or Out of Line?" *Business*

Week, November 1, 1999, 160–65; Jim McTague, "D.C. Current: As Tyco Stock Went Radioactive, Options Market Makers Went South," *Barron's,* October 18, 1999, 36; Jonathon R. Laing, "Tyco's Tumble," *Barron's,* December 13, 1999, 15.
[5]See Horngren, Harrison, and Bamber, *Accounting,* 10–12.
[6]This section is based on material from the following sources: AICPA, "CPA Vision Project." <www.aicpa.org>. (May 16, 2000); AICPA, "CPA Vision Project: 2011 and Beyond." <www.cpavision.org/final_report/>. (May 16, 2000).
[7]Nanette Byrnes, "Where Have All the Accountants Gone?" *Business Week,* March 27, 1999, 203–04.
[8]See Horngren, Harrison, and Bamber, *Accounting,* 12–14.
[9]See Harrison and Horngren, *Financial Accounting,* 13–19.
[10]Billie Cunningham, Loren Nikolai, and John Bazley, *Accounting: Information for Business Decisions* (Fort Worth: Dryden, 2000) 133–34.
[11]See Horngren, Harrison, and Bamber, *Accounting,* 562–63; Arthur J. Keown et al., *The Foundations of Finance: The Logic and Practice of Financial Management,* 2nd ed. (Upper Saddle River, NJ: Prentice Hall, 1998) 89–95.
[12]See Horngren, Harrison, and Bamber, *Accounting,* 201–02.
[13]See Loren Nikolai and John Bazley, *Intermediate Accounting,* 7th ed. (Cincinnati: South-Western, 1997) 16–17, 303, 899.

Chapter 19

[1]See Arthur O'Sullivan and Steven M. Sheffrin, *Economics: Principles and Tools,* 2nd ed. (Upper Saddle River, NJ: Prentice Hall, 2001) 566–68.
[2]Citigroup. <www.citigroup.com>. (June 16, 2000); *Statistical Abstract of the United States* (1999) 527.
[3]*Statistical Abstract of the United States* (1999) 516, 524.
[4]American Bankers Association. <www.aba.com/aba/PDF_Files/GR_ATM Factsheet.pdf>. (June 16, 2000).
[5]*Statistical Abstract of the United States* (1999) 528; Lisa Daigle, "Beyond Expectations," *Credit Card Management* (May 2000): 50–52; Rutrell Yasin, "U.S. Slow to Play Smart Card Hand," *Internetweek,* October 4, 1999, 33–34.
[6]*Survey of Current Business* (Washington, DC: U.S. Dept. of Commerce, April 2000) D-7; *Federal Reserve Bulletin* (May 2000) A64, A72.
[7]James Brooke, "Is the Dollar Leaving Canada Feeling Drained?" *New York Times,* November 13, 1999, C1, C4.

Chapter 20

[1]See Arthur J. Keown et al., *Foundations of Finance: The Logic and Practice of Financial Management* (Upper Saddle River, NJ: Prentice Hall, 1998) 40–42.
[2]*Federal Reserve Bulletin* (Washington, DC: Board of Governors of the Federal Reserve System, May 2000) A31.
[3]*Federal Reserve Bulletin* (May 2000) A31.
[4]See David F. Scott Jr., et al., *Basic Financial Management,* 8th ed. (Upper Saddle River, NJ: Prentice Hall, 1999) 291–92, 296–300.
[5]Joseph Nocera, "Do You Believe? How Yahoo Became a Bluechip," *Fortune,* June 7, 1999, 76–80+.
[6]Leah Nathans Spiro and Edward C. Baig, "Who Needs a Broker?" *Business Week,* February 22, 1999, 113–16+.
[7]Spiro and Baig, "Who Needs a Broker?", 113; Joseph Kahn, "Schwab Lands Feet First on Net," *New York Times,* February 10, 1999, C1, C5.
[8]Saul Hansell, "Low-Cost Trading is Planned By Merrill Lynch," *New York Times,* June 2, 1999, A1, C26.
[9]See Frank J. Fabozzi, Franco Modigliani, and Michael G. Ferri, *Foundations of Financial Markets and Institutions,* 2nd ed. (Upper Saddle River, NJ: Prentice Hall) 292–95, 347–48.
[10]Nasdaq. <www.nasdaq.com/about/timeline.stm>. (June 25, 2000).
[11]NASD. <www.nasd.com>. (June 25, 2000).
[12]"The World in Its Hands," *The Economist,* May 6, 2000, 77; "The Nasdaq Japan Market Launches First Day of Trading; First Step in Creating Nasdaq Global Platform is Achieved." <www.nasdaq.co.uk/reference>. (June 19, 2000); "Globalization and International Reach." *Nasdaq Initiatives.* <www.nasdaq.com>. (June 23, 2000).
[12]See Scott Jr., et al., *Basic Financial Management,* 266–70.
[13]*Federal Reserve Bulletin* (2000), A27, A28, A31, A37.
[14]*Wiesenberger Mutual Funds Update* (Rockville, MD: CDA Investment Technologies, January 31, 2000) v; *Investment Company Institute 1999 Annual Report* (Washington, DC: Investment Company Institute, 1999) 42.
[15]Gretchen Morgenson, "Buying on Margin Becomes a Habit," *New York Times,* March 24, 2000, C1, C7; David Barboza, "Wall Street after Dark," *New York Times,* February 13, 2000, BU1, BU14–BU15.
[16]U.S. Securities and Exchange Commission, *SEC Litigation Release* no. 16591 (June 15, 2000). <www.sec.gov>. (June 29, 2000).

Chapter21

[1]*GE Annual Report 1999* (Fairfield, CT: General Electric Co., 2000) 58.
[2]See Douglas Emery, John D. Finnerty, and John D. Stowe, *Principles of Financial Management* (Upper Saddle River, NJ: Prentice Hall, 1998), Chapter 17.
[3]See David F. Scott Jr., et al., *Basic Financial Management,* 8th ed. (Upper Saddle River, NJ: Prentice Hall, 1999) 612–13.
[4]See Scott et al., *Basic Financial Management,* 627.
[5]See Scott et al., *Basic Financial Management,* 625–26.
[6]See Scott et al., *Basic Financial Management,* 624–25.
[7]See Scott et al., *Basic Financial Management,* 626–27.
[8]See Zvi Bodie and Robert C. Merton, *Finance* (Upper Saddle River, NJ: Prentice Hall, 2000) 419–22.
[9]See Frank J. Fabozzi, *Bond Markets, Analysis and Strategies,* 4th ed. (Upper Saddle River, NJ: Prentice Hall, 2000), Chapter 7.
[10]See Bodie and Merton, *Finance,* Chapter 16.
[11]See Norman M. Scarborough and Thomas W. Zimmerer, *Effective Small Business Management: An Entrepreneurial Approach,* 6th ed. (Upper Saddle River, NJ: Prentice Hall, 2000) 298–300.
[12]Susan Hodges, "One Big Step toward a Loan," *Nation's Business* (August 1997): 34–36.

[13]See Scarborough and Zimmerer, *Effective Small Business Management,* Chapter 8.
[14]Richard S. Boulton, Barry D. Libert, and Steve M. Samek, "Managing Risk in an Uncertain World," *Upside* (June 2000): 268–78.
[15]See Mark S. Dorfman, *Introduction to Risk Management and Insurance,* 6th ed. (Upper Saddle River, NJ: Prentice Hall, 2000), Chapter 3.
[16]See Dorfman, *Risk Management and Insurance,* Chapter 1.
[17]See Dorfman, *Risk Management and Insurance,* 420–21.

Source Notes

Chapter 1

What's Hot on the Cyberspace Hit List/Sounding Out the Music Industry Oligopoly Robert La Franco, "Record Companies, Awake!" *Forbes,* November 15, 1999, 76–80; *Hoover's Handbook of American Business 2000* (Austin, TX: Hoover's Business Press, 2000), 116–117, 122–123; *Hoover's Handbook of Emerging Companies 2000* (Austin, TX: Hoover's Business Press, 2000), 57, 227. See also Artists Direct Network, "Downloads Direct," and Tunes.com, "Downloads." Online. Internet. Accessed 6 March 2000. Available World Wide Web: <content.ubl.com/downloadsdirect> and <www.tunes.com/dds/default.asp?from=>. **Table 1.1** La Franco, "Record Companies, Awake!" 78. Data from Media Metrix and company sources. **Growing An e-Business: *Sowing the Seeds of a Good Idea*** Edward O. Welles, "The Perfect Internet Business," *Inc.,* August 1999, 70–74+. **Figure 1.1** John J. Wild, Kenneth L. Wild, and Jerry C. Y. Han, *International Business: An Integrated Approach* (Upper Saddle River, NJ: Prentice Hall, 2000). **It's a Wired World: *Electronic B2B in the Auto Industry*** Keith Bradsher, "Carmakers to Buy Parts on Internet," *The New York Times,* February 26, 2000, A1, C14; "Three Carmakers Create Link," *USA Today,* February 28, 2000, 8B; "Big Three Car Makers Plan Net Exchange," *Wall Street Journal,* February 28, 2000, A3, A16. **Figure 1.1** Adapted from Karl E. Case and Ray C. Fair, *Principles of Economics,* 5th ed. (Upper Saddle River, NJ: Prentice Hall, 1999), 69. **Table 1.3** Adapted from "10 Reasons Driving the Economic Expansion," *USA Today,* January 31, 2000, 3B. **Figure 1.7** Michael J. Mandel, "The New Economy," *Business Week,* January 31, 2000, 75. Data from *Computer Industry Almanac.* **Figure 1.8** Mandel, "The New Economy," 77. Data from International Data Cor **Figure 1.9** Mandel, "The New Economy," 75. Data from Standard & Poor's DRI.

Chapter 2

Twin Pacts/Fiddling Around with Alliances Doreen D. Fitzpatrick, "Making Connections," *Crain's New York Business,* September 14, 1998, 251; Jon Kalish, "Woodworkers Profit by Becoming Joiners," *Crain's New York Business,* September 14, 1998, 28; Twin Computer Training Inc. Online. Internet. Accessed 14 March 2000. Available World Wide Web: <www.twincomputers.com>. **Figures 2.1 & 2.4** Based on Norman M. Scarborough and Thomas W. Zimmerer, *Effective Small Business Management: An Entrepreneurial Approach* (Prentice Hall: Upper Saddle River, NJ: 2000), 96, 97. **Figure 2.2** Data from U.S. Department of Commerce, *Statistical Abstract of the United States: 1998* (Washington, DC: U.S. Bureau of the Census, 1999). **Figure 2.3** Based on Henry R. Cheeseman, *The Legal and Regulatory Environment: Contemporary Perspectives in Business* (Upper Saddle River, NJ: Prentice Hall, 1997), 335. Reprinted by permission of Prentice Hall Inc., Upper Saddle River, NJ. **Figure 2.5** Based on Nancy A. Kubasek, Bartley A. Brennan, and M. Neil Browne, *The Legal Environment of Business,* 2nd ed. (Upper Saddle River, NJ: Prentice Hall, 1999), 346. Reprinted by permission of Prentice Hall Inc., Upper Saddle River, NJ. **It's a Wired World: *Profit Is No Object*** John A. Byrne, "The Fall of a Dot-Com," *Business Week,* May 1, 2000, 150–60; James R. Hagerty, "How a High-Flying e-Commerce Entrepreneur Fell Back to Earth," *Wall Street Journal,* January 7, 2000, B1, B4; Jeremy Kahn, "Presto Change! Sales Are Huge," *Fortune,* March 20, 2000, 90–96.

Chapter 3

The New ETO (European Theater of Operations/It's a Smallworld.com After All William Echikson, Carol Matlack, and David Vannier, "American e-Tailers Take Europe by Storm," *Business Week,* August 7, 2000, 54–55; Echikson, "Home Field Disadvantage," *Business Week,* December 13, 1999, EB72-EB74; George Anders, "First e-Shopping, Now e-Swapping," *Wall Street Journal,* January 17, 2000, B1, B4. **Figure 3.1** David Hale, "A Second Chance," *Fortune,* November 22, 1999), 190. **Table 3.1** *Hoover's Handbook of World Business 2000* (Austin, TX: Hoover's Business Press, 2000), 56. Data from Bureau of the Census, Foreign Trade Division. **It's a Wired World: *Nokia Puts the Finishing Touches on a Communications Giant*** *Hoover's Handbook of World Business 2000* (Austin, TX: Hoover's Business Press, 2000), 410–11; Justin Fox, "Nokia's Secret Code," *Fortune,* May 1, 2000, 160–74; "It Takes a Cell Phone," *Wall Street Journal,* June 25, 1999, B1, B4. **Table 3.2** Robyn Meredith, "Dollar Makes Canada a Land of the Spree," *New York Times,* August 1, 1999, C11. **Figure 3.5 & Figure 3.6** *Survey of Current Business,* July 2000 (Washington, DC: U.S. Department of Commerce), 88–89. **Web Connection** Used with permission of Shenyang Shawnee Cowboy Food Co., Ltd. **Building Your Business Skills: *"I Intend To Be a Global Company"*** Maria Atanasov, "Taking Her Business on the Road," Fortune, April 13, 1998, 158–60.

Chapter 4

A Tale of Two Companies/Some Ethical Rants and Raves *Hoover's Handbook of American Business 2000* (Austin, TX: Hoover's Business Press, 2000), 750–51; Roger Rosenblatt, "Reaching the Top by Doing the Right Thing," *Time,* October 18, 1999, 89–91; Elliott Blair Smith, "Stench Chokes Nebraska Meatpacking Towns," *USA Today,* February 14, 2000, 1B, 2B. **Figures 4.1 & 4.2** Based on Gerald S. Cavanaugh, *American*

Business Values: With International Perspectives, 4th ed. (Upper Saddle River, NJ: Prentice Hall, 1998), 71 and 84. **It's a Wired World: *When It Comes to Privacy, It's a Small World After All*** Michael Schrage, "If You Passed Notes in School, You'll Love This Idea," *Fortune,* May 1, 2000, 340; Michael J. McCarthy, "Your Manager's Policy on Employees' e-Mail May Have a Weak Spot," *Wall Street Journal,* April 25, 2000, A1, A10; "It's Time for Rules in Wonderland," *Time,* March 20, 2000, 83–96. **Figure 4.3** David Baron, *Business and Its Environment,* 3rd ed. (Upper Saddle River, NJ: Prentice Hall, 2000), 669. **Figure 4.5** Based on Andrew C. Revkin, "Who Cares about a Few Degrees?" *New York Times,* December 12, 1997, F1. **Table 4.1** The Foundation Center, "Fifty Largest Corporate Foundations by Total Giving." Online. Internet. Accessed 10 May 2000. Available World Wide Web: <fdncenter.org>.

Chapter 5

Grounds for the Defense/Down East Showdown Louise Lee, "Now, Starbucks Uses Its Bean," *Business Week,* February 14, 2000, 92–93; Vijay Vishwanath and David Harding, "The Starbucks Effect," *Harvard Business Review,* March–April 2000, 17–18; *Hoover's Handbook of American Business 2000* (Austin, TX: Hoover's Business Press, 2000), 1326–27; Joseph Rosenbloom, "Battle Grounds," *Inc.,* July 1999, 53–57; Joel Kotkin, "Helping the Little Guy Fight the Big Guy," *New York Times,* October 24, 1999, 7. **Figure 5.1** Based on Stephen Robbins and Mary Coulter, *Management,* 6th ed. (Upper Saddle River, NJ: Prentice Hall, 1999), 239. **It's a Wired World: *How to Spot the e-CEO*** Geoffrey Colvin, "How to Be a Great e-CEO," *Fortune,* May 24, 1999, 104–10; Patricia Sellers, "The Big Score," *Fortune,* February 7, 2000, 134–46; David Leonhardt, "At Graduate Schools, a Great Divide Over e-Business Studies," *New York Times,"* January 16, 2000, 7. **Table 5.1** Geoffrey Colvin, "How to Be a Great e-CEO," *Fortune,* May 24, 1999, 107. **Building Your Business Skills: *Skillful Talking*** Information from Justin Martin, "How You Speak Shows Where You Rank," *Fortune,* February 2, 1998, 156.

Chapter 6

Building e-Connections/Building on Cybersites Bob Tedeschi, "Construction Heads into the Internet Age," *The New York Times,* February 21, 2000, C1, C9; Melanie Warner, "Bidcom," *Fortune,* July 5, 1999, 100–04; Edward Iwata, "Despite the Hype, B2B Marketplaces Struggle," *USA Today,* May 10, 2000, 1B, 2B. **It's a Wired World: *Hot-Wiring Ford*** David Welch, "At Ford, e-Commerce Is Job 1," *Business Week,* February 28, 2000, 74–78; Eryn Brown, "Nine Ways to Win on the Web," *Fortune,* May 24, 1999, 112–25.

Chapter 7

Please Turn to Chapter 11/The Next Installment Patti Bond, "Chapter 11 on Musical Page with Onyx Deal," *Atlanta Journal Constitution,* March 27, 1998, H1; Bond "Retail Shapes Metro Atlanta's Horizon," *Atlanta Journal Constitution,* July 27, 1998, E7; Jeffrey A. Tannenbaum, "Small Bookseller Beats the Giants at Their Own Game," *Wall Street Journal,* November 4, 1997, B1. **Figures 7.1 & 7.4** U.S. Department of Commerce, *Statistical Abstract of the United States* (Washington, DC: Bureau of the Census, 1999). **Figure 7.2** *Hoover's Handbook of American Business 2000* (Austin, TX: Hoover's Business Press, 2000). **Figure 7.3** *Wall Street Journal,* May 5, 1999, R28. **Table 7.1** Marc J. Dollinger, *Entrepreneurship: Strategies and Resources,* 2nd ed. (Upper Saddle River, NJ: Prentice Hall, 1999), 9. Adapted from Tom Richman, "The Evolution of the Professional Entrepreneur," *Inc.'s The State of Small Business* (1997), 50–53. **Figure 7.5** *Wall Street Journal Almanac 2000* (New York: Ballantine Books, 2000). **Figure 7.6** Norman M. Scarborough and Thomas W. Zimmerer, *Effective Small Business Management: An Entrepreneurial Approach,* 6th ed. (Upper Saddle River, NJ: Prentice Hall, 2000), 15. Data from Forrester Research Inc. **Figure 7.7** *Wall Street Journal,* May 24, 1999, R12. Data from Catalyst; National Foundation for Women Business Owners. **Figure 7.8** Adapted from NFIB Foundation/VISA Business Card Primer (Washington, DC). **It's a Wired World: A Wealth of Investors for Picky Tech Start-Ups** Deborah Solomon, "A Wealth of Investors for Picky Tech Start-Ups," *USA Today,* February 8, 2000, 1B. **Figure 7.9** *Wall Street Journal,* May 24, 1999, R6. Data from National Federation of Independent Business.

Chapter 8

And All the M&Ms You Can Eat . . . / How Paternal Is Too Paternal? Charles Fishman, "Sanity Inc.," *Fast Company,* January 1999, 84–96; Robert Levering and Milton Moskowitz, "The 100 Best Companies to Work For," *Fortune,* January 10, 2000, 82–110; Michelle Conlin and Kathy Moore with Anne States, "Dr. Goodnight's Company Town," *Business Week,* June 19, 2000, 192–96+; *Hoover's Handbook of Private Companies 2000* (Austin: Hoover's Business Press, 2000), 434–35. **It's a Wired World: *Companies Put Web To Work as Recruiter*** Stephanie Arour, "Companies Put Web to Work as Recruiter," *USA Today,* January 25, 2000, 1B. **Figure 8.3** *Wall Street Journal Almanac 1999,* 226. Reprinted by Permission of Dow Jones Inc. via Copyright Clearance Center Inc. © 1999 Dow Jones and Co. Inc. All rights reserved.

Chapter 9

A New Deal in the Workplace/What Did You Expect? Jerry Useem, "Welcome to the New Company Town," *Fortune,* January 10, 2000, 62–70; Nicholas Stein, "Winning the War to Keep Top Talent," *Fortune,* May 29, 2000, 132–138; Robert Levering and Milton Moskowitz, "The 100 Best Companies to Work For," *Fortune,* January 10, 2000, 82–110; John J. Clancy, "Is Loyalty Really Dead?" *Across the Board,* June 1999, 15–19. **Figure 9.1** Linda Grant, "Happy Workers, High Returns," *Fortune,* January 12, 1998, 81. Reprinted from the January 12 issue of FORTUNE by special permission; copyright 1998, Time Inc. **Figure 9.2** "Corporations That Prize Skills and

Hands-On Experience Are Adapting at the Fringes," *Time,* November 9, 1998, 21. **Figure 9.3** A.H. Maslow, *Motivation and Personality,* 2d ed. (Upper Saddle River, NJ: Prentice Hall, 1970). Reprinted by permission of Prentice Hall, Inc. **It's a Wired World: *The Future of Compensation?*** "Hire Now, Pay Later?" *Forbes,* August 23, 1999, 62; "Net Start-Ups Pull Out of the Garage," *USA Today,* October 1, 1999, 1B, 2B.

Chapter 10

Labor Rolls the Dice in Las Vegas/Membership Is Job #1 Vivienne Walt, "Labor's Big Bet," *U.S. News & World Report,* February 9, 1998, 52–53; Franklin Foer, "Winners & Losers," *U.S. News & World Report,* November 16, 1998, 37; Steven Greenhouse, "Despite Defeat on China Bill, Labor Is on Rise," *The New York Times,* May 30, 2000, A1, A18; Aaron Bernstein, "Meet the Al Dunlap of the Union Hall," *Business Week,* February 17, 1997, 62; Bernstein, "Sweeney's Blitz," *Business Week,* February 17, 1997, 56–62. **Figure 10.1(a)** Adapted from David Whitford, "Labor's Lost Chance," *Fortune,* September 28, 1998, 180. **Figure 10.1(b)** Dan Seligman, "Driving the AFL-CIO Crazy," *Forbes,* November 1, 1999, 106. Data from Leo Troy and Neil Sheflin, *Union Sourcebook* (1985) and Barry T. Hirsch and David A. MacPherson, *Union Membership and Earnings Data Book* (1999). **It's a Wired World: *The Web as a Bargaining Tool*** L.M. Sixel, "Networking on the Web: Union Leaders Turn to Internet for Recruiting, Doing Research," *Houston Chronicle,* March 30, 2000, B1; Bill Leonard, "Disgruntled Employees Take Their Beefs to the World Wide Web," *HRMagazine,* November 1999, 89–94.

Chapter 11

Baggy Brands and Deep Pockets/Between the Barbie Doll and the Driver's License Julie McElwain, "JNCO Branches Out from Wide-Leg Jeans Roots," *Bobbin,* April 1999, 32–38; Becky Ebenkamp and T.L. Stanley, "Lee Takes the Niche Road in Jeans: Retail Eyes Destination Departments," *Brandweek,* September 6, 1999, 12; Lisa Bannon, "As Children Become More Sophisticated, Marketers Think Older," *Wall Street Journal,* October 13, 1998, A1; Nina Munk, "How Teens Buy," *Fortune,* April 13, 1998, 28–30; Jennifer Steinhauer, "Lulu and Her Friends Are, Therefore They Shop," *New York Times,* April 29, 1998, 6. JNCO Jeans USA. Online. Internet. Accessed 20 March 2000. Available World Wide Web: <www.jnco.com>. **Figure 11.1** Erick Schonfield, "Changes in the U.S. Population: Betting on the Boomers," *Fortune,* December 25, 1995, 78–80. Reprinted from the December 25, 1995 issue of FORTUNE by special permission; copyright 1995, Time Inc. **It's a Wired World: *Better Health through Cyberspace Demographics*** *Costpredict: Organizational Health Cost Analysis* (Columbia, MO: Network Health Systems®, 2000); © *Health & Lifestyle Assessment Handbook* (Columbia, MO: Network Health Systems®, 1999). **Figure 11.2** Adapted from Naresh K. Malhorta, *Marketing Research: An Applied Orientation,* 3rd ed. (Upper Saddle River, NJ: Prentice Hall, 1999), 10.

Chapter 12

Everybody Has a Price/The Joy of Take-It-or-Leave-It Shopping Katherine T. Beddingfield, "Airfare Roulette," *U.S. News & World Report,* April 27, 1998, 75; "For the First Time, Consumers Can Use the Power of the Internet to Name Their Own Price for Major Purchases," *Business Wire,* February 11, 1998, 2111120; "Priceline.com Expands 'Name Your Own Price' Service with an Entirely New Way to Buy a Car or Truck," *Business Wire,* July 6, 1998, 7061006; "Priceline.com Issued U.S. Patent No. 5,794,207 for the World's First Buyer-Driven e-Commerce System," *Business Wire,* August 11, 1998, 8110066; "Priceline.com Keeps Affordable Leisure Airline Tickets within Reach of Nation's Budget-Conscious Travelers," *Business Wire,* August 19, 1998, 8191346; Bob Wallace, "Pick a Car, Name Your Price," *Computerworld,* July 27, 1998, 45. **Figure 12.2** Jay Heizer and Barry Render, *Operations Management,* 5th ed. (Upper Saddle River, NJ: Prentice Hall, 1999), 197. **It's a Wired World: *The World of Cyberprice Bidding*** Shawn Tully, "The B2B Tool That Really Is Changing the World," *Fortune,* March 20, 2000, 132–34+.

Chapter 13

Log On and Get Rational/The Rationale of Alienating Traditional Partners George Anders, "Some Big Companies Long to Embrace Web but Settle for Flirtation," *The Wall Street Journal,* November 4, 1998, A1; Ellen Neuborne and Robert D. Hof, "Branding on the Net," *Business Week,* November 9, 1998, 76–86. Figure 12.2 R. Craig Endicott, "Leaders Swell Spending by 8.6% to $58 Billion," *Advertising Age,* September 28, 1998, s38. Table 12.1 Craig Endicott, "Top Marketers Invest $47.3 Billion in '95 Ads," Advertising Age, November 30, 1996, s54. **Figure 13.2** Data from *Advertising Age,* September 27, 1999, s34. **It's a Wired World: *The Sound Approach to Internet Marketing*** Matt Beer, "Eight Extraordinary Gizmos Stand Out at the Fall Show," *San Francisco Examiner,* November 21, 1999, B5; "Agency.Com" and "Altec Lansing." Online. Internet. Accessed 25 April 2000. Available World Wide Web: <www.agency.com> and <www.altecmm.com>; J.A. Hitchcock, "IBM Thinkpad," *Link-Up,* July/August 1999, 12–13. **Table 13.1** Data from *Advertising Age,* September 27, 1999, s3. **Growing an e-Business: *How to Make the Brand Flower*** Edward O. Welles, "The Perfect Internet Business," *Inc.,* August 1999, 71–78; "Click Here to Avoid the Mall," *Fortune,* November 8, 1999. **Table 13.2** Data from *Advertising Age,* November 8, 1999, s34.

Chapter 14

Strike Up the Bandwidth/Why RIAA Is Riled Amy Kover, "Who's Afraid of This Kid?" *Fortune,* March 20, 2000, 129–30; Kover, "The Hot Idea of the Year," *Fortune,* June 26, 2000, 128–30+; Stewart Alsop, "Bye-Bye Music Business," *Fortune,* March 20, 2000, 72; Napster. Online. Internet. Accessed 18 April 2000. Available World Wide Web: <www.napster.com>;

Napster, "A Message to the Napster Community from Hank Barry and Shawn Fanning." Online. Internet. Accessed 28 July 2000. Available World Wide Web: <www.napster.com/message-000728.html>; CNNAmerica, "Napster 20 Million Users." Online. Internet. Accessed 9 August 2000. Available World Wide Web: <cgi.cnnfn.com>; ABC News Internet Ventures. "Swan Song?: Judge Shuts Down Napster. Online. Internet. Accessed 27 July 2000. Available World Wide Web: <www.abcnews.go.com>. **Figure 14.3** Prodigy, "Small Biz Web Sites on the Rise, Yet Many Owners Slow to Embrace the Internet." Online. Internet. Accessed 13 April 2000. Available World Wide Web: <www.prodigy.com/pcom business/business content>.

Chapter 15

Getting the Big Bird to Fly Right/The Art and Science of Disciplinary Finance Kenneth Labich, "Boeing Finally Hatches a Plan," *Fortune,* March 1, 1999, 100–106; "Business: A New Kind of Boeing," *Economist,* January 22, 2000, 62–63; "FAA to Investigate Boeing's Recent Manufacturing Mishaps," *USA Today,* December 1, 1999, 5B; David Field, "FAA to Begin Special Audit of Boeing," *USA Today,* November 30, 1999, 1; "Boeing Faces Compensation Claims for Late Deliveries," *Airfinance Journal,* February 1999, 16; John Olienyk and Robert Carbaugh, "Competition in the World Jetliner Industry," *Challenge!* July/August 1999, 60–81; Perry Flint and Arthur Reed, "New Programs Take Back Seat to Orders," *Air Transport World,* July 1999, 42–43; Alex Taylor III, "Blue Skies for Air Bus," *Fortune,* August 2, 1999, 102–108; Paul Sharke, "Long Line in Long Beach," *Mechanical Engineering,* October 1999, 82–83; Janet Rae-Dupree, "Can Boeing Get Lean Enough?" *Business Week,* August 30, 1999, 182; Seanna Browder, "Getting Boeing to Fly Right," *Business Week,* September 27, 1999, 104, 108. **Figure 15.1** Jennifer L. Martel and Laura A. Kelter, "The Job Market Remains Strong in 1999," *Monthly Labor Review,* February 2000, 3–23; "Profile of the Economy," *U.S. Treasury Bulletin,* December 1999, 38; *Monthly Labor Review,* U.S. Dept. of Labor (October 1998), 52. **Figure 15.2** Martel and Kelter, "The Job Market Remains Strong in 1999," 3–23; "Profile of the Economy," *U.S. Treasury Bulletin,* December 1999, 38; *Survey of Current Business* (Washington, DC: U.S. Dept. of Commerce, January 1999), D-3. **It's a Wired World: *Hershey Kisses Off Profits*** Michael Dornheim, "No Kisses for SAP," *Aviation Week & Space Technology,* November 15, 1999, 21; Craig Stedman, "Failed ERP Gamble Haunts Hershey," *Computerworld,* November 1, 1999, 1, 89; Charles Waltner, "New Recipe for IT Implementation," *Informationweek,* September 27, 1999, 169–174; Peter Galuszka and Stephanie Forest-Anderson, "Just-in-Time Manufacturing Is Working Overtime," *Business Week,* November 8, 1999, 36, 37; Tim Minahan, "Enterprise Resource Planning: Strategies Not Included," *Purchasing,* July 16, 1998, 112–127.

Chapter 16

"Speed Is Everything"/Got a Problem with Your Peripheral? Ask Dudley John H. Sheridan, "Dell Courts Customers Online," *Industry Week,* April 3, 2000, 23; April Jacobs, "Dell Takes Aim at Internet with One-Stop Shopping," *Network World,* April 10, 2000, 8; Paul McDougall, "Dell Mounts Internet Push to Diversify Revenue," *Informationweek,* April 10, 2000, 32; Judi Patrizi, "Dell Dominates Direct Sales," *Industry Week,* April 17, 2000, 60; John H. Sheridan, "Now It's a Job for the CEO," *Industry Week,* March 20, 2000, 22–26; Barbara Schmitz, "Dell Computer Builds a Framework for Success," *CAE: Computer-Aided Engineering,* February 2000, 10; Michael Dell, "21st Century Commerce," *Executive Excellence,* December 1999, 3–4. **Figure 16.1** Bart Van Ark and Robert McGuckin, "International Comparisons of Labor Productivity and Per Capita Income," *Monthly Labor Review,* July 1999, 33–41. **Figure 16.2** Data from *Monthly Labor Review,* February 2000, 98. **Figure 16.3** Data from *Monthly Labor Review,* November 1999, 16. **Figure 16.4** Data from *Monthly Labor Review,* January 2000, 92–93, and February 2000, 100–01. **Figure 16.7** Adapted from Richard B. Chase, Nicholas J. Aquilano, and F. Robert Jacobs, *Production and Operations Management,* 8th ed. (Boston: Irwin McGraw Hill, 1998, 771. **It's a Wired World: *Selling the Idea of Culture Shift*** Philip Siekman, "Mercury Marine: Focusing on the Demand Side," *Fortune [Industrial Management & Technology],* November 8, 1999, 272[N]-272[O]; "Mercury: The Water Calls," Online. Internet. Accessed 22 May 2000. Available World Wide Web: <www.mercurymarine.com/mercury home/merchome.cfm>; Lynne M. Almvig, "Robotics Milling Department," *Robotics Today,* First Quarter 2000, 1–4.

Chapter 17

"Life, the Universe, and Everything"/Researching with a Purpose Leigh Buchanan, "The Smartest Little Company in America," *Inc.,* January 1999, 42–54; Edward C. Baig, "'Shopping Bots' Are Hot to Trot," *USA Today,* December 1, 1999, 8D; Mick O'Leary, "Dialog's New Tools for Web-Age Knowledge Workers," *Online,* May/June 2000, 91–92; Baig, "Online Buying Assistants Produce a Mixed Bag," *USA Today,* December 1, 1999, 8D; Rick Dove, "The Knowledge Worker," *Production,* June 1998, 26–28; "What's Ahead for 2000?" *Information Today,* January 2000, 1, 62+. **Figure 17.2** Adapted from Kenneth C. Laudon and Jane Laudon, *Essentials of Management Information Systems,* 3rd ed. (Upper Saddle River, NJ: Prentice Hall, 1999), 15. **17.4** Adapted from Laudon and Laudon, *Essentials of Management Information Systems,* 39. **17.6** Adapted from Laudon and Laudon, *Essentials of Management Information Systems,* 43. **It's a Wired World: *"These Two Companies Are a Natural Fit"*** Sally C. Pipes, "AOL's Access Saga," *Chief Executive,* March 2000, 18; Associated Press, "Media Deal Biggest Ever," *Columbia Daily Tribune,* January 10, 2000, B1; Associated Press, "Merger

Gives AOL Fast Track to Speedy Net," *Columbia Daily Tribune,* January 11, 2000, B6; Vicki Zunitch, "Principal Deal Makers Less Than Forthcoming," *Columbia Daily Tribune,* January 11, 2000, B6.

Chapter 18

How Cooking the Books Left One Accountant with a Bad Taste/The Shrill Sound of Financial Repercussions Barbara Kirchheimer, "Second Quorum Executive Heads for Exit," *Modern Healthcare,* May 31, 1999, 18; Mark Taylor, "Columbia Exec Enters Plea Agreement," *Modern Healthcare,* September 13, 1999, 10; Kirchheimer, "Quorum Profits Slide; No Progress on Suit," *Modern Healthcare,* August 23, 1999, 16; "HCA the Healthcare Company. New Name Unveiled," HCA—The Healthcare Company, Press Release (May 25, 2000). Online. Internet. Accessed 6 June 2000. Available World Wide Web: <www.hcahealthcare.com>; Kurt Eichenwald, "He Blew the Whistle, and Health Giant Quaked," *New York Times,* October 18, 1998, sec. 3, 1; Pamela Sherrid, "How to Really Make a Killing in Health Care," *U.S. News & World Report,* November 2, 1998, 48. **It's a Wired World: *A Roundabout Look at Conflicting Interests*** David LeonHardt, "Consultants Are Putting a New Price On Advice," *New York Times,* January 19, 2000, C1, C10; Floyd Norris, "Accounting Firm Is Said to Violate Rules Routinely," *New York Times,* January 7, 2000, A1, C6; Norris, "Rules That Only an Accountant Could Fail to Understand?" *New York Times,* January 8, 2000, C1, C14. **Figure 18.1** Adapted from "CPA Vision Project: 2011 and Beyond." Online. Internet. Accessed 19 July 2000. Available World Wide Web: <www.cpavision.org/final report> **Tables 18.1 & 18.2** Adapted from "CPA Vision Project: 2011 and Beyond." Online. Internet. Accessed 19 July 2000. Available World Wide Web: <www.cpavision.org/final report> **Growing an e-Business: *"See 'Forward-Looking Statements'"*** Online. Internet. Accessed 8 June 2000. Available World Wide Web: <199.230.26.96/cgi-bin/ir/gden/quarbalsheet.html>; *PROSPECTUS: Garden.com* (Austin, TX: Garden.com, September 15, 1999), 27, 28, F-2.

Chapter 19

A Popular Bank in a Big Niche/Extending Credit Where Credit Is Due Tami Luhby, "Bank Vies for Popularity with Minority Businesses," *Crain's New York Business,* November 16, 1998, 43–44; Lisa Fickenscher, "Banco Popular Targets U.S. Mainland Card Market," *American Banker,* October 19, 1998, 7; Monica Perin, "Puerto Rican Bank Gains Share of Hispanic Market," *Houston Business Journal,* September 26, 1997, 11. **It's a Wired World: *To e-Bank or not to e-Bank*** Bill Streeter, "Who's In Charge: The Dot-Coms vs. the Banks," *ABA Banking Journal,* February 2000, 43, 45, 46; "You and Your Bank on the Net: The Next Generation and the 'Nyet' Generation," *ABA Banking Journal,* February 2000, S13–S15; Bill Orr, "Easy Money," *ABA Banking Journal,* March 2000, 41, 42, 46, 47; Alex Sheshunoff, "Internet Banking—An Update from the Frontlines," *ABA Banking Journal,* January 2000, 51–55. **Table 19.1** *The Economist,* April 29, 2000, 75.

Chapter 20

Is Volatility Here to Stay?/The Stuff That Rumors and Inflated Expectations Are Made Of E. S. Browning, Greg Ip, and Leslie Scism, "With Dazzling Speed, Market Roars Back to Another New High," *Wall Street Journal,* November 24, 1998, A1; James M. Pethokoukis and Mind Charski, "Lessons Learned: The Volatile Market Is Trying to Tell Us Something," *U.S. News & World Report,* September 21, 1998, 651; Fred Vogelstein and William J. Holstein, "Fasten Your Seat Belts," *U.S. News & World Report,* October 26, 1998, 43–46; "Billion Share Days." Online. Internet. Accessed 25 July 2000. Available World Wide Web: <www.nyse.com/pdfs/billiondays.pdf>; "Dow Jones.com." Online. Internet. Accessed 25 July 2000. Available World Wide Web: <www.dowjones.com>. **Figure 20.1** Quicken.com. Online Internet. Accessed 24 June 2000. Available World Wide Web: <www.quicken.com/inv...&mavg>. **Figure 20.2** Leah Nathans Spiro and Edward C. Baig, "Who Needs a Broker?" *Business Week,* February 22, 1999, 113–16+. **Growing an e-Business: *A Prospectus for Growth*** Quicken.com. Online. Internet. Accessed 3 July 2000. Available World Wide Web: <www.quicken.com/investments/charts/?symbol=GDEN>; NASDAQ, "Infoquotes." Online. Internet. Accessed 3 July 2000. Available World Wide Web: <quotes.nasdaq.com>. **It's a Wired World: *Opening the Portals to Cross-Border Training*** "Grappling With Change," *The Economist,* April 29, 2000, 71–72; "The World at Its Hands," *The Economist,* May 6, 2000, 77. **Figure 20.6** Data from the *Wall Street Journal.* **Figure 20.7** Nasdaq, "Market Performance & Highlights: Section 3." Online. Internet. Accessed 23 June 2000. Available World Wide Web: <www.nasdaq.com/about/NBW2000Sec3.pdf>.

Chapter 21

From Cluelessness to a Juicy Future/Getting Juiced for New Age Business <www.oceanspray.com> accessed 10 July 2000; Gerry Khermouch, "Nantucket Set to Widen Fresh Line," *Brandweek,* November 22, 1999, 6; Kenneth Hein, "Squeezed Dry?" *Incentive,* August 1999, 39–44; Gerry Khermouch, "Nantucket Nectors Sets First National Promo," *Brandweek,* June 14, 1999, 7; Rachael Butler, "Looking for . . . a Few Good Distributors," *Beverage World,* May 15, 1999, 52–56; "Two Men and a Bottle," *Inc.,* May 19, 1998, 60–63; Julie Flaherty, "Sailing on a Rising Tide of Juice," *The New York Times,* September 11, 1997, D1, D5; Mike Hofman, "The Year of Dealing Dangerously," *Inc.,* October 20, 1998, 69–77; Ocean Spray, *Hoovers Online,* Nantucket Allserve, *Inc.com.* Online. Internet. Accessed 10 July 2000. Available World Wide Web: <www.oceanspray.com>, <www.hoovers.com/co/news> <www.juiceguys.com>,

<www.inc.com>. **Figure 21.1** Carl Beidleman, The Handbook of International Investing (Chicago: Probus, 1987), 133. **Growing an e-Business: *How to Prune Risk*** *Prospectus: Garden.com* (Austin, TX: Garden.com, September 15, 1999), 7–21. **It's a Wired World: *A Healthy Approach to Risk Response*** *Costpredict: Organizational Health Cost Analysis* (Columbia, MO: Network Health Systems®, 2000); © *Health & Lifestyle Assessment Handbook* (Columbia, MO: Network Health Systems®, 1999).

Cartoon, Photo, and Screen Credits

Chapter 1

Pages 2/26: Reuters/Fred Prouser/Archive Photos. page 5: © 2000 The New Yorker Collection from cartoonbank.com. All Rights Reserved. page 7: Bill Bastas/Pearson Education/PH College. page 9: Thomas Sandberg. page 16 (top): Used with permission of bebe stores, Inc. page 16 (bottom): Reuters/HO/Archive Photos. page 20: Ricardo Azoury/SABA Press Photos, Inc. page 21: Used with permission of Exodus Communications, Inc.

Chapter 2

Pages 33/58: Robin F. Siegel, President and CEO, and Mandi F. Bergenfeld, CFO, of Twin Computer Training, Inc. page 34: Used with permission of Twin Computer Training, Inc. page 35: Carnegie Library of Pittsburgh. page 36: Lewis W. Hine/Library of Congress. page 37: © Adrian Bradshaw/SABA. page 39: Rex Rystedt/Rex Rystedt Photography. page 40: Used with permission of Pentagram Design, Inc. page 44: Used with permission of Blue Diamond Growers. page 47: Bill Bastas/Pearson Education/PH College. page 50: Andy Johnstone/Impact Photos Ltd. page 52: Used with permission of SpencerStuart. page 55: © 2000 The New Yorker Collection from cartoonbank.com. All Rights Reserved. page 57: Peter Blakely/SABA Press Photos, Inc.

Chapter 3

Pages 65/86: Amazon.co.uk. page 67: Thomas J. Mueller. page 70 (top): Used with permission of LetsBuyit.com. page 70 (bottom): Heimo Aga. page 78: © AFP/Corbis. page 79: © 2000 The New Yorker Collection from cartoonbank.com. All Rights Reserved. page 80: Klaus D. Francke/Bilderberg/AURORA. page 82: Used with permission of CowboyCandy.com. page 84: Used with permission of Al Ahram Beverages Co. page 85: Claude Paris/AP/Wide World Photos.

Chapter 4

Pages 93/115: Jean-Marc Giboux/Liaison Agency, Inc. page 95: Used with permission of Patagonia, Inc. page 99 (top): Used with permission of Privada, Inc. page 99 (bottom): AP/Wide World Photos. page 102: © 2000 The New Yorker Collection from cartoonbank.com. All Rights Reserved. page 104: Bill Bastas/Pearson Education/PH College. page 106: Ch. Simonpietri/Corbis/Sygma. page 108: John G. Mabanglo/Agence France-Presse. page 109: Used with permission of ESOMAR. page 115: Ken Gabrielsen/Kenneth Gabrielsen Photography.

Chapter 5

Pages 123/142: Tim Gray/Furnald/Gray Photography. page 126: Used with permission of Jeremy's MicroBatch® Ice Creams. page 128: Bastienne Schmidt/Bastienne Schmidt. page 129: Used with permission of Virgin Group P.L.C. page 131: Bill Bastas/Pearson Education/PH College. page 133: © Kristine Larsen 2000. page 136: Courtesy Boeing Commercial Airplane Group, Boeing Image #K57866. page 139: Used with permission of At Home Corporation. page 141: © 2000 The New Yorker Collection from cartoonbank.com. All Rights Reserved. page 142: © Ted Rice 1999.

Chapter 6

Pages 149/169: Thor Swift/New York Times Pictures. page 155: Used with permission of IBM, Inc. page 158: Ritz Foods International, Inc. page 163: © 2000 The New Yorker Collection from cartoonbank.com. All Rights Reserved. page 166: Bill Cawley.

Chapter 7

Pages 175/200: Adam Taylor/Barbara Babbit Kaufman. page 181 (top): Norman Y. Lono/New York Times Pictures. page 181 (bottom): Used with permission of JustBalls.com, Inc. page 183: © Mark Langello Photography. page 187: Used with permission of Fúxito Worldwide, Inc. page 190: © 2000 The New Yorker Collection from cartoonbank.com. All Rights Reserved. page 191: Robert King/Corbis/Sygma. page 192: Bill Bastas/Pearson Education/PH College. page 194: © Kevin Fleming/Corbis. page 195: Used with permission of Garage.com. page 197: Used with permission of U.S. Small Business Administration. page 200: Used with permission of International Franchise Association.

Chapter 8

Pages 207/232: Ann States/SABA Press Photos, Inc. page 211: Ann Grillo/New York Times Pictures. page 212: Len Rubenstein Photography. page 214: Used with permission of ManagedOps.com. page 216: Used with permission of the American Society for Training and Development. page 220: Copyright 2000 Rick Friedman. page 222: Bill Bastas/Pearson Education/PH College. page 225: © 2000 The New Yorker Collection from cartoonbank.com. All Rights Reserved. page 230: John Madere/The Stock Market. page 231: Mark Richards.

Chapter 9

Pages 239/261: Robert Wright/Robert Wright Photography. page 241: Bill Bastas/Pearson Education/PH College. page 242: Todd Buchanan. page 243: Used with permission of The Container Store®. page 251: Greg Smith/SABA Press Photos, Inc. page 253: Layne Kennedy/Corbis. page 255: Used with permission of American Management Systems, Inc. page 256: Joseph Pluchino/Bill Charles. page 257: Robert Wright Photography. page 258: © 2000 The New Yorker Collection from cartoonbank.com. All Rights Reserved. page 260: Used with permission of Growth & Leadership Center.

Chapter 10

Pages 269/288: William Mercer McLeod. page 271: Stock Montage, Inc./Historical Pictures Collection. page 273: Used with permission of The American Federation of Labor and Congress of Industrial Organizations. page 276: © 2000 The New Yorker Collection from cartoonbank.com. All Rights Reserved. page 277: Porter Gifford/Liaison Agency, Inc. page 278: Robin Nelson. page 280: Used with permission of the National Labor Relations Board. page 285: Used with permission of the Institute of Industrial Relations. University of California, Berkeley. page 287 (top): AP/Wide World Photos. page 287 (bottom): Used with permission of the American Arbitration Association.

Chapter 11

Pages 295/318: David M. Barron/Oxygen Group Photography. page 297: Used with permission of Harley-Davidson of Dallas. page 299: AP/Wide World Photos. page 300: Decout/REA/SABA Press Photos, Inc. page 304: Nina Berman/SIPA Press. page 308: © 2000 The New Yorker Collection from cartoonbank.com. All Rights Reserved. page 311: Courtesy of Garden.com. page 312: Mamoru Tsukada/Aria Pictures. page 315: 1999 © Patrick ARTINIAN/CONTACT Press Images. page 317: Used with permission of Everex Systems, Inc.

Chapter 12

Pages 325/344: Churchill & Klehr Photography. page 328: © 2000 The New Yorker Collection from cartoonbank.com. All Rights Reserved. page 330: Used with permission of IDEO Product Development. page 331: Patrick Harbron. page 335 (top): Ali Kabas. page 335 (bottom): Used with permission of Interbrand Group. page 340: Courtesy of Garden.com. page 344: James Schnepf Photography, Inc. page 345: Used with permission of Priceline.com, Inc.

Chapter 13

Pages 351/371: Used with permission of Ragu.com. page 358 (top): Alon Reininger/Contact Press Images Inc. page 358 (bottom): © 2000 The New Yorker Collection from cartoonbank.com. All Rights Reserved. page 359: Used with permission of Doubleclick.net. page 360: Used with permission of Princeton Video Image, Inc. page 363: Michael L. Abramson Photography. page 366: Copyright 1999 Girard Mouton, III. All Rights Reserved. page 368: Courtesy of Garden.com. page 369: Jeffrey Aaronson/Network Aspen.

Chapter 14

Pages 379/402: Eric O'Connell Photography. page 383: Keith Meyers/New York Times Pictures. page 384: Greg Girard/Contact Press Images Inc. page 388: Used with permission of razorfish.com. page 389: Porter Gifford/Liaison Agency, Inc. page 391: David Gamble. page 392: © 2000 The New Yorker Collection from cartoonbank.com. All Rights Reserved. page 398: Bill Bastas/Pearson Education/PH College. page 399: Tom Wagner/SABA Press Photos, Inc.

Chapter 15

Pages 409/430: Louis Psihoyos/Matrix International, Inc. page 411 (top): Kenneth Chen/Kenneth Chen. page 411 (bottom): Used with permission of Lantronix. page 416: Used with permission of Lightning Rod Software. page 417: Courtesy of Garden.com. page 422: Nancy Siesel/NYT Pictures. page 424 (top): Used with permission of American Society of Quality. page 424 (bottom): © 2000 The New Yorker Collection from cartoonbank.com. All Rights Reserved. page 429: Joe Traver/Liaison Agency, Inc.

Chapter 16

Pages 439/461: Richard Drew/AP/Wide World Photos. page 440: Used with permission of American Productivity & Quality Center. page 441: KVO Public Relations. page 446: Randy Duchaine/The Stock Market. page 450: Used with permission of Hercules, Inc. page 452: Ray Ng Photography. page 453: Used with permission of Federal Express Corp. page 458: © 2000 The New Yorker Collection from cartoonbank.com. All Rights Reserved. page 459: Craig Wallace Dale/New York Times Pictures.

Chapter 17

Pages 469/494: Marc Hauser Photography. page 474: Used with permission of National Confectioners Association. page 477 (top): Robert Houser/Robert Houser Photography. page 477 (bottom): Used with permission of Acumins. page 486 (top): © 2000 The New Yorker Collection from cartoonbank.com. All Rights Reserved. page 486 (bottom): Used with permission of Silicon Graphics, Inc. page 489: Photofest. page 490: Brownie Harris/Brownie Harris. page 491: Courtesy of Garden.com.

Chapter 18

Pages 501/522: Porter Gifford/Liaison Agency, Inc. page 503: Sara Krulwich/NYT Pictures. page 504 (top): © 2000 The New Yorker Collection from cartoonbank.com. All Rights Reserved. page 504 (bottom): Used with permission of American Institute of Certified Public Accountants. page 508: Used with permission of Deloitte Touche Tohmatsu International. page 520: Toys "R" Us, Inc. page 521: Courtesy of Garden.com. page 522: Used with permission of International Accounting Standards Committee.

Chapter 19

Pages 531/551: Steinway/Banco Popular. page 533: Ed Wray/AP/Wide World Photos. page 535: Used with permission of Tim Opler. page 537: Courtesy of Garden.com. page 538: Greg Miller Photography. page 540: Peter Korniss. page 546: Richard B. Levine; Frances M. Roberts. page 547: Used with permission of Mondex International Ltd. page 548: © 2000 The New Yorker Collection from cartoonbank.com. All Rights Reserved.

Chapter 20

Pages 557/580: Jonathan Saunders/Jonathan Saunders. page 558: Used with permission of U.S. Securities and Exchange Commission. page 561: ©Raimund Koch. page 564: Dod Miller/Network/SABA Press Photos, Inc. page 565 (top): Used with permission of National Association of

Securities Dealers, Inc. page 565 (bottom): Richard B. Levine/Frances M. Roberts. page 570: Used with permission of Dreyfus Corp. page 573: © 2000 The New Yorker Collection from cartoonbank.com. All Rights Reserved.

Chapter 21

Pages 587/608: Bob Benchley/New York Times Pictures. page 589: David Burnett/Contact Press Images Inc. page 591: AP/Wide World Photos. page 595: Used with permission of Moody's Investors Service. page 597: Used with permission of Risk and Insurance Management Society, Inc. page 599: Used with permission of SBA's Office of Women's Business Ownership and SBA Women's Business Centers. page 607: © 2000 The New Yorker Collection from cartoonbank.com. All Rights Reserved.

Index

Name, Company, Product Index

Subject Index

Notes

Notes

Notes

Notes

Notes

Notes

Notes

Notes